Butterworths Handbook on Immigration Law

A comprehensive collection of annotated immigration and asylum materials selected from Butterworths Immigration Law Service

Editors

His Honour Judge Eugene Cotran, LLD
Circuit Judge; Visiting Professor of Law, School of Oriental and African Studies, University of London formerly; Law Commissioner, Kenya; Puisne Judge, Kenya

His Honour Judge David Pearl, PhD (Cantab)
Circuit Judge; Director of Studies, Judicial Studies Board for England and Wales; Life Fellow, Fitzwilliam College Cambridge; formerly President, Immigration Appeal Tribunal; Chief Adjudicator, Immigration Appeals

Julia Onslow-Cole, LLB (Hons)
Solicitor, Partner of CMS Cameron McKenna, London; former Chair, Immigration Committee, International Bar Association

Dr Hugo Storey, BA (Hons), BPhil (Oxon), PhD
Vice President, Immigration Appeal Tribunal; former Honorary Research Fellow, Department of Law, University of Leeds; former Human Rights Research Fellow, Council of Europe.

Rick Scannell, BA, LLM (Cantab)
Barrister, 2 Garden Court Chambers

Alison Harvey, BA (Oxon), MA
of the Inner Temple

Butterworths

London

2001

United Kingdom:
Butterworths a Division of Reed Elsevier (UK) Ltd, Halsbury House, 35 Chancery Lane, London WC2A 1EL, and 4 Hill Street, Edinburgh EH2 3JZ

Australia:
Butterworths, a Division of Reed International Books Australia Pty Ltd, *Chatswood*, New South Wales

Canada:
Butterworths Canada Ltd, *Markham*, Ontario

Hong Kong:
Butterworths Hong Kong, a Division of Reed Elsevier (Greater China) Ltd, *Hong Kong*

India:
Butterworths India, *New Delhi*

Ireland:
Butterworth (Ireland) Ltd, *Dublin*

Malaysia:
Malayan Law Journal Sdn Bhd, *Kuala Lumpur*

New Zealand:
Butterworths of New Zealand Ltd, *Wellington*

Singapore:
Butterworths Asia, *Singapore*

South Africa:
Butterworth Publishers (Pty) Ltd, *Durban*

United States of America:
Lexis Law Publishing, *Charlottesville*, Virginia

ISBN 0 406 981 299

Typeset by Kerrypress Ltd, Luton, Bedfordshire
Printed and bound in Great Britain by Hobbs the Printers Ltd, Totton, Hampshire

Visit Butterworths LEXIS *direct* at: http://www.butterworths.com

Preface

Butterworths Immigration Law Service developed from a need to have handy in one concise volume all the relevant statute law, statutory instruments, and case law on a subject which, at the end of the 1980s and early 1990s was fast becoming a confused jungle. The service is now 10 years old and 33 issues have been published. Of the original editors, Eugene Cotran and David Pearl remain, although they are both now Judges on the Circuit Bench. Hugo Storey, Julia Onslow-Cole, Rick Scannell and Alison Harvey have joined the original team. The service has long outgrown its one volume, and it is now straining to be contained within three volumes. The reason for this expansion is not hard to find. Asylum law, both domestic and international, has developed out of all recognition in the last ten years, and three major Statutes have been enacted at a rate of one every three years. Case law is reported in two series of specialist law reports and the Tribunal decisions are instantly available on the internet site (Electronic Immigration Network). The number of adjudicators has increased from 14 full time and 65 part time in the early nineties to over 75 full time and more than 360 part time. The Tribunal has similarly been given substantially new powers, new resources, and is now presided over by a High Court Judge.

All of these developments have persuaded us that this is the right time to publish a new single volume in the form of this Handbook.

In selecting materials fit for inclusion in a 2001 Handbook on Immigration Law we have taken account of a variety of factors: the changing legislative framework which now features separate grounds of appeal on human rights and race discrimination grounds; the increasing emphasis placed by the courts and the Immigration Appeal Tribunal on the need for decisions on asylum claims to be made by reference to international human rights materials; and the incremental extension of EU legislation. In order, however, to ensure adequate coverage of these materials, we have opted to exclude certain materials which only indirectly raise immigration and nationality issues. In respect of social welfare materials in particular, these plainly required more comprehensive treatment than was possible in this publication. We have therefore limited ourselves to including provisions that relate to the new asylum support system established by the 1999 Act. By furnishing annotated texts of the 1971 and 1999 Acts, we hope not only to help readers better understand the context of the new legislation but to save them having to make cross-references to commencement and transitional orders and the like.

We hope that the Handbook will be of value to practitioners, to adjudicators and Tribunal members, to Judges, and to all others who have an interest in immigration and asylum law and who will now be able to refer to all the relevant source material in one volume.

The law is stated where possible as at 2 April 2001 and those parts of the text without commencement notes were not in force at this time.

The Editors
2001

Contents

Note References in bold are to paragraph number

Preface   v

A   UK materials
A.1   Statutes

A.2 Immigration Rules

A.3 Procedure Rules

A.5   Support for Asylum Seekers

B   European Materials

B.1   Statutes and Treaties

Treaty Establishing the European Community (consolidated version as amended by the Treaty on European Union and the Treaty on Amsterdam)

B.2   Secondary legislation

C.2   UN Materials

Part A

UK Materials

A1 Statutes

IMMIGRATION ACT 1971
(1971 c 77)

Arrangement of Sections

References in bold are to paragraph numbers

PART IV
SUPPLEMENTARY

SCHEDULES

An Act to amend and replace the present immigration laws, to make certain related changes in the citizenship law and enable help to be given to those wishing to return abroad, and for purposes connected therewith
[28 October 1971]

PART I
REGULATION OF ENTRY INTO AND STAY IN UNITED KINGDOM

[A.1.1]
1 General principles
(1)   All those who are in this Act expressed to have the right of abode in the United Kingdom shall be free to live in, and to come and go into and from, the United Kingdom without let or hindrance except such as may be required under and in accordance with this Act to enable their right to be established or as may be otherwise lawfully imposed on any person.
(2)   Those not having that right may live, work and settle in the United Kingdom by permission and subject to such regulation and control of their entry into, stay in and departure from the United Kingdom as is imposed by this Act; and indefinite leave to enter or remain in the United Kingdom shall, by virtue of this provision, be treated as having been given under this Act to those in the United Kingdom at its coming into force, if they are then settled there (and not exempt under this Act from the provisions relating to leave to enter or remain).
(3)   Arrival in and departure from the United Kingdom on a local journey from or to any of the Islands (that is to say, the Channel Islands and Isle of Man) or the Republic of Ireland shall not be subject to control under this Act, nor shall a person require leave to enter the United Kingdom on so arriving, except in so far as any of those places is for any purpose excluded from this subsection under the powers conferred by this Act; and in this Act the United Kingdom and those places, or such of them as are not so excluded, are collectively referred to as 'the common travel area'.
(4)   The rules laid down by the Secretary of State as to the practice to be followed in the administration of this Act for regulating the entry into and stay in the United Kingdom of persons not having the right to abode shall include provision for admitting (in such cases and subject to such restrictions as may be provided by the rules, and subject or not to conditions as to length of stay or otherwise) persons coming for the purpose of taking employment, or for purposes of study, or as visitors, or as dependants of persons lawfully in or entering the United Kingdom.
(5)   . . .

Notes   Sub-s (5) repealed by the Immigration Act 1988, s 1, in accordance with the order noted to s12 of that Act.

Commencement   1 January 1973 (s 1 1972/1514).

[A.1.2]
[2 Statement of right of abode in United Kingdom
(1)   A person is under this Act to have the right of abode in the United Kingdom if:

(*a*) he is a British citizen; or
(*b*) he is a Commonwealth citizen who:
   (i)   immediately before the commencement of the British Nationality Act 1981 was a Commonwealth citizen having the right of abode in the United Kingdom by virtue of section 2(1)(*d*) or section 2(2) of this Act as then in force; and

(ii) has not ceased to be a Commonwealth citizen in the meanwhile.

(2) In relation to Commonwealth citizens who have the right of abode in the United Kingdom by virtue of subsection (1)(*b*) above, this Act, except this section and [section 5(2)], shall apply as if they were British citizens; and in this Act (except as aforesaid) 'British citizen' shall be construed accordingly.]

Notes Section substituted by the British Nationality Act 1981, s 39(2).
  Words in square brackets in sub-s(2) substituted by the Immigration Act 1988, s 3(3).

Commencement 1 January 1983 (SI 1982/933).

[A.1.3]
3 General provisions for regulation and control
(1) Except as otherwise provided by or under this Act, where a person is not [a British citizen]

(*a*) he shall not enter the United Kingdom unless given leave to do so in accordance [the provisions of, or made under,] with this Act;

(*b*) he may be given leave to enter the United Kingdom (or, when already there, leave to remain in the United Kingdom) either for a limited or for an indefinite period;

[(*c*) if he is given limited leave to enter or remain in the United Kingdom, it may be given subject to all or any of the following conditions, namely:

(i) a condition restricting his employment or occupation in the United Kingdom;

(ii) a condition requiring him to maintain and accommodate himself, and any dependants of his, without recourse to public funds; and

(iii) a condition requiring him to register with the police.]

(2) The Secretary of State shall from time to time (and as soon as may be) lay before Parliament statements of the rules, or of any changes in the rules, laid down by him as to the practice to be followed in the administration of this Act for regulating the entry into and stay in the United Kingdom of persons required by this Act to have leave to enter, including any rules as to the period for which level is to be given and the conditions to be attached in different circumstances; and section 1(4) above shall not be taken to require uniform provision to be made by the rules as regards admission of persons for a purpose or in a capacity specified in section 1(4) (and in particular, for this as well as other purposes of this Act, account may be taken of citizenship or nationality).

  If a statement laid before either House of Parliament under this subsection is disapproved by a resolution of that House passed within the period of forty days beginning with the date of laying (and exclusive of any period during which Parliament is dissolved or prorogued or during which both Houses are adjourned for more than four days), then the Secretary of State shall as soon as may be make such changes or further changes in the rules as appear to him to be required in the circumstances, so that the statement of those changes be laid before Parliament at latest by the end of the period of forty days beginning with the date of the resolution (but exclusive as aforesaid).

(3)   In the case of a limited leave to enter or remain in the United Kingdom:

(*a*) a person's leave may be varied, whether by restricting, enlarging or removing the limit on its duration, or by adding, varying or revoking conditions, but if the limit on its duration is removed, any conditions attached to the leave shall cease to apply; and

(*b*) the limitation on and any conditions attached to a person's leave [(whether imposed originally or on a variation) shall], if not superseded, apply also to any subsequent leave he may obtain after an absence from the United Kingdom within the period limited for the duration of the earlier leave.

(4)   A person's leave to enter or remain in the United Kingdom shall lapse on his going to a country or territory outside the common travel area (whether or not he lands there), unless within the period for which he had leave he returns to the United Kingdom in circumstances in which he is not required to obtain leave to enter; but, if he does so return, his previous leave (and any limitation on it or conditions attached to it) shall continue to apply.

[(5)   A person who is not a British citizen is liable to deportation from the United Kingdom if:

(*a*) the Secretary of State deems his deportation to be conducive to the public good; or

(*c*) if another person to whose family he belongs is or has been ordered to be deported.]

(6)   Without prejudice to the operation of subsection (5) above, a person who is not [a British citizen] shall also be liable to deportation from the United Kingdom if, after he has attained the age of seventeen, he is convicted of an offence for which he is punishable with imprisonment and on his conviction is recommended for deportation by a court empowered by this Act to do so.

(7)   Where it appears to Her Majesty proper so to do by reason of restrictions or conditions imposed on [British citizens, British Dependent Territories citizens or British Overseas citizens] when leaving or seeking to leave any country or the territory subject to the government of any country, Her Majesty may by Order in Council make provision for prohibiting persons who are nationals or citizens of that country and are not [British citizens] from embarking in the United Kingdom, or from doing so elsewhere than at a port of exit, or for imposing restrictions or conditions on them when embarking or about to embark in the United Kingdom; and Her Majesty may also make provision by Order in Council to enable those who are not [British citizens] to be, in such cases as may be prescribed by the Order, prohibited in the interests of safety from so embarking on a ship or aircraft specified or indicated in the prohibition.

Any Order in Council under this subsection shall be subject to annulment in pursuance of a resolution of either House of Parliament.

(8)   When any question arises under this Act whether or not a person is [a British citizen], or is entitled to any exemption under this Act, it shall lie on the person asserting it to prove that he is.

[(9)   A person seeking to enter the United Kingdom and claiming to have the right of abode there shall prove that he has that right by means of either:

(*a*) a United Kingdom passport describing him as a British citizen or as a citizen of the United Kingdom and Colonies having the right of abode in the United Kingdom; or (*b*) a certificate of entitlement issued by or on behalf of the Government of the United Kingdom certifying that he has such a right of abode.]

Notes Words in square brackets in sub-ss (1), (5)–(8) substituted by the British Nationality Act 1981, s 39(6), Sch 4, paras 2, 4; for a saving see s 39(8) of that Act.

The words in square brackets in sub-s (1)(*a*) were inserted by the Immigration and Asylum Act 1999, s 169(1), Sch 14, paras 43, 44(1).

Sub-s (1)(*c*) substituted, and sub-s (5)(*aa*) inserted, by the Asylum and Immigration Act 1996, Sch 2, para 1(1)(2).

The words in square brackets in sub-s (3) were substituted by the Immigration Act 1988, s 10, Schedule, para 1, Immigration and Asylum Act 1999, s 169(1), Sch 14, para 44(1).

Sub-s (5) substituted by Immigration and Asylum Act 1999, s 169(1), Sch 14, para 44(2).

Sub-s (9) substituted (for sub-ss (9), (9A)) by the Immigration Act 1988, s 3(1) of that Act.

Commencement 1 January 1973 (SI 1972/1514).

Definitions For 'aircraft', 'certificate of entitlement', 'immigration rules', 'limited leave', 'port' (defined with 'aircraft') 'ship' and 'United Kingdom passport', see s 33(1); for 'common travel area', see s 1(3); for 'convicted', see s 6(3); for 'embarking', see s 11(2); and for 'port of exit', see s 33(3). As to when a person is deemed to enter the United Kingdom, see s 11(1), and note also s 10(1).

[A.1.4]
[3A Further provision as to leave to enter
(1)   The Secretary of State may by order make further provision with respect to the giving, refusing or varying of leave to enter the United Kingdom.

(2)   An order under subsection (1) may, in particular, provide for:

(a) leave to be given or refused before the person concerned arrives in the United Kingdom;

(b) the form or manner in which leave may be given, refused or varied;

(c) the imposition of conditions;

(d) a person's leave to enter not to lapse on his leaving the common travel area.

(3)   The Secretary of State may by order provide that, in such circumstances as may be prescribed:

(a) an entry visa, or

(b) such other form of entry clearance as may be prescribed,

is to have effect as leave to enter the United Kingdom.

(4)   An order under subsection (3) may, in particular:

(a) provide for a clearance to have effect as leave to enter:

(i) on a prescribed number of occasions during the period for which the clearance has effect;

(ii) on an unlimited number of occasions during that period;

(iii) subject to prescribed conditions; and

(b) provide for a clearance which has the effect referred to in paragraph (a)(i) or (ii) to be varied by the Secretary of State or an immigration officer so that it ceases to have that effect.

(5)   Only conditions of a kind that could be imposed on leave to enter given under section 3 may be prescribed.

(6)   In subsections (3), (4) and (5) 'prescribed' means prescribed in an order made under subsection (3).

(7)   The Secretary of State may, in such circumstances as may be prescribed in an order made by him, give or refuse leave to enter the United Kingdom.

(8)   An order under subsection (7) may provide that, in such circumstances as may be prescribed by the order, paragraphs 2, 4, 6, 7, 8, 9 and 21 of Part I of Schedule 2 to this Act are to be read, in relation to the exercise by the Secretary of State of functions which he has as a result of the order, as if references to an immigration officer included references to the Secretary of State.

(9)   Subsection (8) is not to be read as affecting any power conferred by subsection (10).

(10)   An order under this section may:

(a)   contain such incidental, supplemental, consequential and transitional provision as the Secretary of State considers appropriate; and

(b)   make different provision for different cases.

(11)   This Act and any provision made under it has effect subject to any order made under this section.

(12)   An order under this section must be made by statutory instrument.

(13)   But no such order is to be made unless a draft of the order has been laid before Parliament and approved by a resolution of each House.]

Note   Inserted by Immigration and Asylum Act 1999, s 1.

Allows orders to be made that would obviate the need for leave to enter to be given in writing and would allow for the use of new technologies in this regard. Particular attention should be drawn to the new section 3A(2)(*a*) inserted into the Immigration Act 1971 under which orders can be made to allow the Secretary of State or an Entry Clearance Officer abroad to grant or refuse leave to enter before the person arrives in the UK. See Schedule 14, paragraph 57 for the powers immigration officers at the port will have to refuse entry to persons granted leave to enter prior to arrival and for the rights of appeal in the event of such a refusal.

The Immigration (Leave to Enter and Remain) Order 2000 (SI 2000/1161) was made on 19 April 2000. Commencement date for Articles 1 to 12, 14 and 15(1) of the Order, in accordance with Article 1(2) of the order, 30 July 2000. Commencement date for Articles 13 and 15(2) of the Order 30 July 2000.

Under Article 3 of the Order, a visa or other entry clearance may have effect as leave to enter the United Kingdom if it specifies the purpose for which the holder wishes to enter the United Kingdom (Article 3(2)) and is endorsed with the conditions to which it is subject (Article 3(3)(*a*)) and a statement that it is to have effect as indefinite leave to enter the United Kingdom (Article 3(3)(*b*)). Article 4 of the Order sets out the nature of the leave given.

Part IV of the Order makes provision for circumstances in which leave to enter or remain is not to lapse on travel outside the Common Travel Area.

The Order was debated in a Committee of the House of Commons on 11 April 2000. The Minister of State noted

'The entry clearance officer will still consider the application in exactly the same way as happens now...The Foreign Office is also introducing new format entry clearances that will bear the conditions of entry on the face of the entry clearance...The immigration officer will be able to verify whether the passport and entry clearance are genuine, whether they are presented by the rightful holder and whether the purpose for which it was issued remains the same. If satisfied, the immigration officer will allow the holder to proceed'

(See Hansard, HC Report, Second Standing Committee on Delegated Legislation, Tuesday 11 April 2000, col 2) The Order was debated in the House of Lords on 13 April 2000. Lord Bassam of Brighton, the Minister responsible, stated:

> '...the immigration officer will be able to check the validity of the passport and entry clearance and that the person presenting it is the rightful holder... If the immigration officer is satisfied that the entry clearance, as leave, may have been obtained by false information or a failure to disclose material facts or that there has been a change of circumstances which removes the basis of entry clearance or leave, he is able to suspend the leave to enter and conduct a full examination which may ultimately result in cancellation of leave to enter. Leave may also be cancelled in some circumstances on medical or public good grounds.'

(Hansard, HL Report, Vol 612, No 75, 13 April 2000, col 362)

The Statement of Changes to the Immigration Rules giving effect to the Order was laid before parliament on 28 July 2000. An explanatory note can be found on the Home Office website (www.homeoffice.gov.uk/ind/policy_law) under the heading 'Changes in the Immigration Rules'. In summary, entry clearances will act as leave to enter the UK. An immigration officer can grant or refuse leave to enter outside the UK and also has the power to vary leave, whether at port or outside the UK. Immigration officers at port retain the power to examine those with entry clearance, to check the validity of the passport and entry clearance and that the person is the rightful holder of these documents. If satisfied that leave may have been obtained by failure to disclose material facts, or by giving false information, or if satisfied that there has been a change of circumstances taking away the basis of entry clearance or leave they can suspend the leave to enter and conduct a full examination. Leave may also be cancelled on medical or 'public good' grounds. Normally visas as to leave to enter will be stamped on first arrival only. Leave to enter and remain, other than leave conferred by a visit visa, granted for more than 6 months, will not lapse on leaving the Common Travel Area. Those with a visit visa will be allowed multiple entries to the UK while the visa is valid. The conditions of leave to enter and remain, including the length of such leave, can be communicated other than in writing. Oral leave may only be given to visitors. Asylum seekers may be granted or refused leave to enter by post. The 'Passports and Visas Handbook' is being updated to reflect the changes.

Articles 4 and 6 of the Order were modified by The Channel Tunnel (International Arrangements) (Amendment No 2) Order 2000 (SI 2000/1775) so that entry clearances will have effect as leave to enter the UK in control zones as well as on entry to the UK.

See also Immigration (Control of Entry through the Republic of Ireland) (Amendment) Order 2000 (SI 2000/1776). This amendment is made pursuant to Article 7 of SI 2000/1161 which is the article providing that a person may be given leave to enter before arrival in the UK, and Article 13 of SI 2000/1161 which provides that a person's leave to enter or remain in the UK is not to lapse on their leaving the Common Travel Area. SI 2000/1776 amends the Immigration (Control of Entry through Republic of Ireland) Order 1972 (SI 1972/1610) so that it does not apply to a person arriving in the UK with leave to enter or remain given before arrival and still in force.

1(5) makes clear that the conditions which the order may prescribe can be imposed on leave to enter are limited to those conditions which may be imposed under section 3 of the 1971 Act as amended by paragraph 1(1) of Schedule 2 to the Asylum and Immigration Act 1996. These are restrictions on employment or occupation, requirements that there be no recourse to public funds and requirements that a person register with the police.

1(7) would allow the Secretary of State to grant or refuse leave to enter and orders made under this section could be used to allow papers to be issued directly from the Immigration and Nationality Department, rather than having to return the file to the port as is currently required.

1(11) and *1(12)* Any orders made under this section must be made by affirmative resolution.

[A.1.5]
[3B Further provision as to leave to remain
(1)   The Secretary of State may by order make provision as to further provision with respect to the giving, refusing or varying of leave to remain in the United Kingdom.
(2)   An order under subsection (1) may, in particular, provide for:

(a) the form or manner in which leave may be given, refused or varied;
(b) the imposition of conditions;
(c) a person's leave to remain in the United Kingdom not to lapse on his leaving the common travel area.

(3)   An order under this section may:

(a) contain such incidental, supplemental, consequential and transitional provision as the Secretary of State considers appropriate; and
(b) make different provision for different cases.

(4)   This Act and any provision made under it has effect subject to any order made under this section.
(5)   An order under this section must be made by statutory instrument.
(6) But no such order is to be made unless a draft of the order has been laid before Parliament and approved by a resolution of each House.]

Note   Inserted by Immigration and Asylum Act 1999, s 2.
   This mirrors the provisions of s 3A, but in respect of leave to remain. See SI 2000/1161 (Immigration (Leave to Enter and Remain) Order 2000) and the notes to s 3A above.

[A.1.6]
[3C Continuation of leave pending decision]
(1)   This section applies if:

(a) a person who has limited leave to enter or remain in the United Kingdom applies to the Secretary of State, before his leave expires, for it to be varied; and
(b) when it expires, no decision has been taken on the application.

(2)   His leave is to be treated as continuing until the end of the period allowed under rules made under paragraph 3 of Schedule 4 to the Immigration and Asylum Act 1999 for bringing an appeal against a decision on the application.
(3)   An application for variation of a person's leave to enter or remain in the United Kingdom may not be made while that leave is treated as continuing as a result of this section.
(4)   But subsection (3) does not prevent the variation of an application mentioned in subsection (1).]

Note   Inserted by the Immigration and Asylum Act 1999, s 3.
   See the note to paragraph 17(1) of Schedule 4 IAA 1999 on the effect of changes to the VOLO provisions. See also the note to section 61 IAA1999.
   See SI 2000/2444, the 6th Commencement Order, and the Immigration (Variation of Leave) (Amendment) Order 2000 (SI 2000/2445), in force 2 October 2000. This provides that where a person makes an in-time application for variation of leave, section 3 will only apply where the decision on that application is taken before 2 October 2000. Where the decision is taken before 2 October 2000, the Immigration (Variation of

Leave) Order 1976 (SI 1976/1572, as amended by SI 1989/1005 and SI 1999/1657) will apply to that person. See Schedule 2, paragraph 2 of SI 2000/2444.

SI 2000/2445 amends the 1976 Order to exclude from its provisions people who have made an application for leave to enter or remain where the decision on that application is not made before 2 October 2000. The new section 3C of the 1971 Act, as inserted by this section, applies to such people.

[A.1.7]
4 Administration of control
(1)   The power under this Act to give or refuse leave to enter the United Kingdom shall be exercised by immigration officers, and the power to give leave to remain in the United Kingdom, or to vary any leave under section 3(3)(*a*) (whether as regards duration or conditions), shall be exercised by the Secretary of State; and, unless otherwise [allowed by or under] this Act, those powers should be exercised by notice in writing given to the person affected, except that the powers under section 3(3)(*a*) may be exercised generally in respect of any class of persons by order made by statutory instrument.
(2)   The provisions of Schedule 2 to this Act shall have effect with respect to:

(*a*) the appointment and powers of immigration officers and medical inspectors for purposes of this Act;
(*b*) the examination of persons arriving in or leaving the United Kingdom by ship or aircraft [. . .], and the special powers exercisable in the case of those who arrive as, or with a view to becoming, members of the crews of ships and aircraft; and
(*c*) the exercise by immigration officers of their powers in relation to entry into the United Kingdom, and the removal from the United Kingdom of persons refused leave to enter or entering or remaining unlawfully; and
(*d*) the detention of persons pending examination or pending removal from the United Kingdom;

and for other purposes supplementary to the foregoing provisions of this Act.
(3)   The Secretary of State may by regulations made by statutory instrument, which shall be subject to annulment in pursuance of a resolution of either House of Parliament, make provision as to the effect of a condition under this Act requiring a person to register with the police; and the regulations may include provision:

(*a*) as to the officers of police by whom registers are to be maintained, and as to the form and content of the registers;
(*b*) as to the place and manner in which anyone is to register and as to the documents and information to be furnished by him, whether on registration or on any change of circumstances;
(*c*) as to the issue of certificates of registration and as to the payment of fees for certificates of registration;

and the regulations may require anyone who is for the time being subject to such a condition to produce a certificate of registration to such persons and in such circumstances as may be prescribed by the regulations.
(4)   The Secretary of State may by order made by statutory instrument, which shall be subject to annulment in pursuance of a resolution of either House of Parliament, make such provision as appears to him to be expedient in connection with this Act for records to be made and kept of persons staying at hotels

and other premises where lodging or sleeping accommodation is provided, and for persons (whether [British citizens] or not) who stay at any such premises to supply the necessary information.

Notes Words in square brackets in sub-s (1) substituted by the Immigration and Asylum Act 1999, s 169(1), Sch 14, paras 43, 45.

Words in square brackets in sub-s (4) substituted by the British Nationality Act 1981, s 39(6), Sch 4, para 2.

Words in square brackets in sub-s (2)(*b*) originally added by SI 1990/2227, Sch 1, were repealed by SI 1993/ 1813, art 9(1), Sch 6, Pt I.

Commencement 1 January 1973 (SI 1972/1514).

Definitions For 'aircraft', 'crew' and 'ship', see s 33(1); for 'arriving in the United Kingdom by ship' see s 11(3).

[A.1.8]
5 Procedure for, and further provisions as to, deportation
(1) Where a person is under section 3(5) or (6) above liable to deportation, then subject to the following provisions of this Act the Secretary of State may make a deportation order against him, that is to say an order requiring him to leave and prohibiting him from entering the United Kingdom; and a deportation order against a person shall invalidate any leave to enter or remain in the United Kingdom given him before the order is made or while it is in force.
(2) A deportation order against a person may at any time be revoked by a further order of the Secretary of State, and shall cease to have effect if he becomes [a British citizen].
(3) A deportation order shall not be made against a person as belonging to the family of another person if more than eight weeks have elapsed since the other person left the United Kingdom after the making of the deportation order against him; and a deportation order made against a person on that ground shall cease to have effect if he ceases to belong to the family of the other person, or if the deportation order made against the other person ceases to have effect.
(4) For purposes of deportation the following shall be those who are regarded as belonging to another person's family

(*a*) where that other person is a man, his wife and his children or her children under the age of eighteen; and
[(*b*) where that other person is a woman, her husband and her or his children under the age of eighteen;]

and for purposes of this subsection an adopted child, whether legally adopted or not, may be treated as the child of the adopter and, if legally adopted, shall be regarded as the child only of the adopter; and illegitimate child (subject to the foregoing rules as to adoptions) shall be regarded as the child of the mother; and 'wife' includes each of two or more wives.
(5) The provisions of Schedule 3 to this Act shall have effect with respect to the removal from the United Kingdom of persons against whom deportation orders are in force and with respect to the detention or control of persons in connection with deportation.
(6) Where a person is liable to deportation under section [3(5)] or (6) above but without a deportation order being made against him, leaves the United Kingdom to live permanently abroad, the Secretary of State may make pay-

ments of such amounts as he may determine to meet that person's expenses in so leaving the United Kingdom, including travelling expenses for members of his family or household.

Notes   Words in square brackets in sub-s (2) substituted by the British Nationality Act 1981, s 39(6), Sch 4, para 2.
  Sub-s (4)(*b*) substituted by the Asylum and Immigration Act 1996, Sch 2, para 2.
  Words in square brackets in sub-s (6) substituted by the Immigration Act 1988, s 10, Sch, para 2.

Commencement   1 January 1973 (SI 1972/1514).

[A.1.9]
6 Recommendations by court for deportation
(1)   Where under section 3(6) above a person convicted of an offence is liable to deportation on the recommendation of a court, he may be recommended for deportation by any court having power to sentence him for the offence unless the court commits him to be sentenced or further dealt with for that offence by another court:

Provided that in Scotland the power to recommend a person for deportation shall be exercisable only by the sheriff or by the High Court of Justiciary, and shall not be exercisable by the latter on appeal unless the appeal is against a conviction on indictment or against a sentence upon such a conviction.

(2)   A court shall not recommend a person for deportation unless he has been given not less than seven days notice in writing stating that a person is not liable to deportation if he is [a British citizen], describing the persons who are [British citizens] and stating (so far as material) the effect of section 3(8) above and section 7 below; but the powers of adjournment conferred by [section 10(3) of the Magistrates' Courts Act 1980], [section 179 or 380 of the Criminal Procedure (Scotland) Act 1975] or any corresponding enactment for the time being in force in Northern Ireland shall include power to adjourn, after convicting an offender, for the purpose of enabling a notice to be given to him under this subsection or, if a notice was so given to him less than seven days previously, for the purpose of enabling the necessary seven days to elapse.

(3)   For purposes of section 3(6) above:

(*a*) a person shall be deemed to have attained the age of seventeen at the time of his conviction if, on consideration of any available evidence, he appears to have done so to the court making or considering a recommendation for deportation; and

(*b*) the question whether an offence is one for which a person is punishable with imprisonment shall be determined without regard to any enactment restricting the imprisonment of young offenders or [persons who have not previously been sentenced to imprisonment];

and for purposes of deportation a person who on being charged with an offence is found to have committed it shall, notwithstanding any enactment to the contrary and notwithstanding that the court does not proceed to conviction, be regarded as a person convicted of the offence, and references to conviction shall be construed accordingly.

(4)   Notwithstanding any rule of practice restricting the matters which ought to be taken into account in dealing with an offender who is sentenced to

imprisonment, a recommendation for deportation may be made in respect of an offender who is sentenced to imprisonment for life.

(5) Where a court recommends or purports to recommend a person for deportation, the validity of the recommendation shall not be called in question except on an appeal against the recommendation or against the conviction on which it is made; but

(*a*) . . . the recommendation shall be treated as a sentence for the purpose of any enactment providing an appeal against sentence;

(*b*) . . .

(6) A deportation order shall not be made on the recommendation of a court so long as an appeal or further appeal is pending against the recommendation or against the conviction on which it was made; and for this purpose an appeal or further appeal shall be treated as pending (where one is competent but has not been brought) until the expiration of the time for bringing that appeal or, in Scotland, until the expiration of twenty-eight days from the date of the recommendation.

(7) For the purpose of giving effect to any of the provisions of this section in its application to Scotland, the High Court of Justiciary shall have power to make rules by act of adjournal.

Notes Proviso to sub-s (1) applies to Scotland only.

Words in first and second square brackets in sub-s (2) substituted by the British Nationality Act 1981, s 39(6), Sch 4, para 2; words in third square brackets in sub-s (2) substituted by the Magistrates' Courts Act 1980, s 154, Sch 7, para 105; words in fourth square brackets in sub-s (2) substituted by the Criminal Procedure (Scotland) Act 1975, s 461(1), Sch 9, para 47.

Words in square brackets in sub-s (3) substituted by the Criminal Justice Act 1972, s 64(1), Sch 5, and the Criminal Justice Act 1982, s 77, Sch 15.

Words omitted from sub-s (5) repealed by the Criminal Justice (Scotland) Act 1980, s 83(3), Sch 8, and by the Criminal Justice Act 1982, ss 77, 78, Sch 15, para 15, Sch 16.

Sub-section (7) applies to Scotland only.

Commencement 1 January 1973 (SI 1972/1514).

[A.1.10]
7 Exemption from deportation for certain existing residents

(1) Notwithstanding anything in section 3(5) or (6) above but subject to the provisions of this section, a Commonwealth citizen or citizen of the Republic of Ireland who was such a citizen at the coming into force of this Act and was then ordinarily resident in the United Kingdom:

(*a*) shall not be liable to deportation under section 3(5)(*b*) [3(5)(*a*)] if at the time of the Secretary of State's decision he had at all times since the coming into force of this Act been ordinarily resident in the United Kingdom and Islands; and

(*b*) shall not be liable to deportation under section 3(5)(*a*), (*b*) or (*c*) [or (*b*) or 10 of the Immigration and Asylum Act 1999] if at the time of the Secretary of State's decision he had for the last five years been ordinarily resident in the United Kingdom and Islands; and

(c) shall not on conviction of an offence be recommended for deportation under section 3(6) if at the time of the conviction he had for the last five years been ordinarily resident in the United Kingdom and Islands.

(2)   A person who has at any time become ordinarily resident in the United Kingdom or in any of the Islands shall not be treated for the purposes of this section as having ceased to be so by reason only of his having remained there in breach of the immigration laws.

(3)   The 'last five years' before the material time under subsection (1)(b) or (c) above is to be taken as a period amounting in total to five years exclusive of any time during which the person claiming exemption under this section was undergoing imprisonment or detention by virtue of a sentence passed for an offence on a conviction in the United Kingdom and Islands, and the period for which he was imprisoned or detained by virtue of the sentence amounted to six months or more.

(4)   For purposes of subsection (3) above:

(a) 'sentence' includes any order made on conviction of an offence; and

(b) two or more sentences for consecutive (or partly consecutive) terms shall be treated as a single sentence; and

(c) a person shall be deemed to be detained by virtue of a sentence:

   (i) at any time when he is liable to imprisonment or detention by virtue of the sentence, but is unlawfully at large; and

   (ii) (unless the sentence is passed after the material time) during any period of custody by which under any relevant enactment the term to be served under the sentence is reduced.

In paragraph (c)(ii) above 'relevant enactment' means *section 67 of the Criminal Justice Act 1967* [section 9 of the Crime (Sentences) Act 1997] (or, before that section operated, section 17(2) of the Criminal Justice Administration Act 1962) and any similar enactment which is for the time being or has (before or after the passing of this Act) been in force in any part of the United Kingdom and Islands.

(5)   Nothing in this section shall be taken to exclude the operation of section 3(8) above in relation to an exemption under this section.

Note   Sub-s (1)(a): words in italics repealed and subsequent words in square brackets substituted by the Immigration and Asylum Act 1999, s 169(1), Sch 14, paras 43, 46(a).

Sub-s (1)(b): words in italics repealed and subsequent words in square brackets substituted by the Immigration and Asylum Act 1999, s 169(1), Sch 14, paras 43, 46(b).

Sub-s (4): words in italics prospectively repealed and subsequent words in square brackets prospectively substituted by the Crime (Sentences) Act 1997, s 55, Sch 4, para 7, as from a day to be appointed.

Commencement   1 January 1973 (SI 1972/1514).

Definitions   For 'immigration laws' and 'the United Kingdom and Islands' (defined with 'the Islands'), see s 33(1). As to 'last five years', note sub-s (3) above, and as to 'sentence' (for purposes of sub-s (3)), note sub-s (4) above.

[A.1.11]
8 Exceptions for seamen, aircrews and other special cases
(1)   Where a person arrives at a place in the United Kingdom as a member of the crew of a ship or aircraft under an engagement requiring him to leave on that ship

as a member of the crew, or to leave within seven days on that or another aircraft as a member of its crew, then unless either:

(*a*) there is in force a deportation order made against him; or
(*b*) he has at any time been refused leave to enter the United Kingdom and has not since then been given leave to enter or remain in the United Kingdom; or
(*c*) an immigration officer requires him to submit to examination in accordance with Schedule 2 to this Act;

he may without leave enter the United Kingdom at that place and remain until the departure of the ship or aircraft on which he is required by his engagement to leave.

(2)   The Secretary of State may by order exempt any person or class of persons, either unconditionally or subject to such conditions as may be imposed by or under the order, from all or any of the provisions of this Act relating to those who are not [British citizens].

An order under this subsection, if made with respect to a class of persons, shall be made by statutory instrument, which shall be subject to annulment in pursuance of a resolution of either House of Parliament.

(3)   [Subject to subsection (3A) below,] The provisions of this Act relating to those who are not [British citizens] shall not apply to any person so long as he is a member of a mission (within the meaning of the Diplomatic Privileges Act 1964), a person who is a member of the family and forms part of the household of such a member, or a person otherwise entitled to the like immunity from jurisdiction as is conferred by that Act on a diplomatic agent.

[(3A)   In the case of a member of a mission other than a diplomatic agent (within the meaning of the said Act of 1964) subsection (3) above shall apply only if he enters or has entered the United Kingdom:

(*a*) as a member of that mission; or
(*b*) in order to take up a post as such a member which was offered to him before his arrival;

and references in that subsection to a member of a mission shall be construed accordingly.]

(4)   The provisions of this Act relating to those who are not [British citizens], other than the provisions relating to deportation, shall also not apply to any person so long as either:

(*a*) he is subject, as a member of the home forces, to service law; or
(*b*) being a member of a Commonwealth force or of a force raised under the law of any . . . colony, protectorate or protected state, is undergoing or about to undergo training in the United Kingdom with any body, contingent or detachment of the home forces; or
(*c*) he is serving or posted for service in the United Kingdom as a member of a visiting force or of any force raised as aforesaid or as a member of an international headquarters defence organisation designated for the time being by an Order in Council under section 1 of the International Headquarters and Defence Organisations Act 1964.

(5)   Where a person having a limited leave to enter or remain in the United Kingdom becomes entitled to an exemption under this section, that leave shall continue to apply after he ceases to be entitled to the exemption, unless it has by then expired; and a person is not to be regarded for purposes of this Act as having been [settled in the United Kingdom at any time when he was entitled under the

former immigration laws to any exemption corresponding to any of those afforded by subsection (3) or (4)(*b*) or (*c*) above or by any order under subsection (2) above].

[(5A)   An order under subsection (2) above may, as regards any person or class of persons to whom it applies, provide for that person or class to be in specified circumstances regarded (notwithstanding the order) as settled in the United Kingdom for the purposes of section 1(1) of the British Nationality Act 1981.]

(6)   In this section 'the home forces' means any of Her Majesty's forces other than a Commonwealth force or a force raised under the law of any associated state, colony, protectorate or protected state; 'Commonwealth force' means a force of any country to which provisions of the Visiting Forces Act 1952 apply without an Order in Council under section 1 of the Act; and 'visiting force' means a body, contingent or detachment of the forces of a country to which any of those provisions apply, being a body, contingent or detachment for the time being present in the United Kingdom on the invitation of Her Majesty's Government in the United Kingdom.

Notes   First words in square brackets in sub-s (3) inserted by the Immigration Act 1988, s 4; other words in square brackets in sub-ss (2), (3), (4), (5) substituted, and sub-s (5A) inserted, by the British Nationality Act 1981, s 39(4), (6), Sch 4, paras 2, 5. Sub-s (3A) substituted by the Immigration and Asylum Act 1999, s 6. In sub-s (4)(*b*) words omitted repealed by the Statute Law (Repeals) Act 1995.

Section 8(3A) replaces section 8(3A) of the 1971 Immigration Act as amended and is intended to deal with a lacuna in that section. The original section 8(3A) ensured that foreign nationals in the UK who then took up a post in a diplomatic mission remained subject to immigration control. However, if they left the UK and then returned while still in post, the original section 8(3A)(*a*) operated to free them from immigration control on their return. Under the new section 8(3A)(*a*) they remain subject to immigration control on their return. The new section 8(3A)(*b*) ensures that they do not remain subject to immigration control forever. A person who has held such a post in the past, but has subsequently left it and been appointed from abroad as a member of a diplomatic mission is to be treated like any other member of that mission appointed outside the country.

Commencement   1 January 1973 (SI 1972/1514)

Definitions   For 'aircraft', 'crew', 'immigration laws', 'the islands', 'limited leave', 'settled', 'ship' and 'the United Kingdom and Islands' (defined with 'the islands'), see s 33(1), (2A). Note as to 'the home forces', 'Commonwealth force' and 'visiting force', sub-s (6) above, As to when a person is deemed to enter the United Kingdom, see s 11(1). For 'members of the mission', see, by virtue of sub-s (3) above, the Diplomatic Privileges Act 1964, Sch 1, Art I(b); and for 'diplomatic agent', by virtue of sub-s (3A) above, see Sch 1, Art I(e) to the 1964 Act.

[A.1.12]
[8A Persons ceasing to be exempt
(1)   A person is exempt for the purposes of this section if he is exempt from provisions of this Act as a result of section 8(2) or (3).
(2)   If a person who is exempt:

(a)   ceases to be exempt, and
(b)   requires leave to enter or remain in the United Kingdom as a result,

he is to be treated as if he had been given leave to remain in the United Kingdom for a period of 90 days beginning on the day on which he ceased to be exempt.

(3)   If:

(a) a person who is exempt ceases to be exempt, and
(b) there is in force in respect of him leave for him to enter or remain in the United Kingdom which expires before the end of the period mentioned in subsection (2),

his leave is to be treated as expiring at the end of that period.]

Note   Inserted by Immigration and Asylum Act 1999, s 7.

This section is intended to deal with another lacuna in the 1971 Immigration Act. Those exempt from immigration control under section 8(2) of the 1971 Immigration Act are those personnel of international organisations set out in the Immigration (Exemption from Control) Order 1972, SI 1972/1613. Those exempt under section 8(3) of the 1971 Immigration Act include members of diplomatic missions (subject to the amendments effected by section 6 of this Act, supra) and certain members of their families. The new section 8A(2)(*a*) imposes a limit of 90 days on the period for which such people can remain in the UK after their exemption ceases. The new section 8A(2)(*b*) protects those who have leave to remain on some other basis who are to continue to enjoy that leave.

[A.1.13]
[8B Persons excluded from the United Kingdom under international obligations
(1)   An excluded person must be refused:

(a) leave to enter the United Kingdom;
(b) leave to remain in the United Kingdom.

(2)   A person's leave to enter or remain in the United Kingdom is cancelled on his becoming an excluded person.
(3)   A person's exemption from the provisions of this Act as a result of section 8(1), (2) or (3) ceases on his becoming an excluded person.
(4)   'Excluded person' means a person:

(a) named by or under, or
(b) of a description specified in,

a designated instrument.
(5)   The Secretary of State may by order designate an instrument if it is a resolution of the Security Council of the United Nations or an instrument made by the Council of the European Union and it:

(a) requires that a person is not to be admitted to the United Kingdom (however that requirement is expressed); or
(b) recommends that a person should not be admitted to the United Kingdom (however that recommendation is expressed).

(6)   Subsections (1) to (3) are subject to such exceptions (if any) as may specified in the order designating the instrument in question.
(7)   An order under this section must be made by statutory instrument.
(8)   Such a statutory instrument shall be laid before Parliament without delay.]

Note Inserted by Immigration and Asylum Act 1999, s 8.

New subsection 8B(4)(*b*) would allow the exclusion of persons who were nowhere named in the order. However, the Minister, Lord Bassam of Brighton, gave an undertaking that 'We shall make every effort to ensure that there are no secret lists' (Hansard vol 605, no 136, col 761).

New subsection 8B(6) The Explanatory Notes state 'This would allow, for example, entry to be given to an individual named on a list on asylum or human rights grounds'.

See now The Immigration (Designation of Travel Bans) Order 2000 SI (2000/2734), in force 10 October 2000 and the Immigration (Designation of Travel Bans) (Amendment) Order 2000 (SI 2000/3338), in force 21 December 2000. These instruments designate United Nations and European Union instruments for the purposes of section 8B of the Immigration Act 1971. For the working of the travel bans, see SI 2000/2734. Article 3 of SI 2000/2734 provides inter alia that sections 8(B)(1)(2) and (3) of the 1971 Act shall not apply where to apply these provisions would violation the UK's obligations under the European Convention on Human Rights (article 3(*b*)), or the 1951 Convention relating to the Status of Refugees and its Protocol (article 3(*c*)). For the up to date list of travel bans, see the Schedule to SI 2000/3338, which entirely supersedes the schedule to SI 2000/2734 and the list of travel bans contained therein.

[A.1.14]
9 Further provisions as to common travel area

(1)　Subject to subsection (5) below, the provisions of Schedule 4 to this Act shall have effect for the purpose of taking account in the United Kingdom of the operation in any of the Islands of the immigration laws there.

(2)　Persons who lawfully enter the United Kingdom on a local journey from a place in the common travel area after having either:

(*a*)　entered any of the Islands or the Republic of Ireland on coming from a place outside the common travel area; or

(*b*)　left the United Kingdom while having a limited leave to enter or remain which has since expired;

if they are not [British citizens] (and are not to be regarded under Schedule 4 to this Act as having leave to enter the United Kingdom), shall be subject in the United Kingdom to such restrictions on the period for which they may remain, and such conditions restricting their employment or occupation or requiring them to register with the police or both, as may be imposed by an order of the Secretary of State and may be applicable to them.

(3)　Any provision of this Act applying to a limited leave or to conditions attached to a limited leave shall, unless otherwise provided, have effect in relation to a person subject to any restriction or condition by virtue of an order under subsection (2) above as if the provisions of the order applicable to him were terms on which he had been given leave under this Act to enter the United Kingdom.

(4)　Section 1(3) above shall not be taken to affect the operation of a deportation order; and, subject to Schedule 4 to this Act, a person who is not [a British citizen] may not by virtue of section 1(3) enter the United Kingdom without leave on a local journey from a place in the common travel area if either:

(*a*)　he is on arrival in the United Kingdom given written notice by an immigration officer stating that, the Secretary of State having issued directions for him not to be given entry to the United Kingdom on the ground that his exclusion is conducive to the public good as being in the interests of national security, he is accordingly refused leave to enter the United Kingdom; or

(*b*) he has at any time been refused leave to enter the United Kingdom and has not since then been given leave to enter or remain in the United Kingdom.

(5)   If it appears to the Secretary of State necessary so to do by reason of differences between the immigration laws of the United Kingdom and any of the Islands, he may by order exclude that island from section 1(3) above for such purposes as may be specified in the order, and references in this Act to the Islands. . . shall apply to an island so excluded so far only as may be provided by order of the Secretary of State.

(6)   The Secretary of State shall also have power by order to exclude the Republic of Ireland from section 1(3) for such purposes as may be specified in the order.

(7)   An order of the Secretary of State under this section shall be made by statutory instrument, which shall be subject to annulment in pursuance of a resolution of either House of Parliament.

Notes   Words in square brackets in sub-ss (2), (4), substituted, and words omitted from sub-s (5) repealed, by the British Nationality Act 1981, ss 39(6), 52(8), Sch 4, para 2, Sch 9.

Commencement   1 January 1973 (SI 1972/1514).

Definitions   For 'common travel area', see (by virtue of s 11(4), s 1(3); for 'immigration laws', 'the Islands' and 'limited leave', see s 33(1); for 'local journey', see s 11(4). As to when a person is deemed to enter the United Kingdom, see s 11(1).

[A.1.15]
10 Entry otherwise than by sea or air

(1)   Her Majesty may by Order in Council direct that any of the provisions of this Act shall have effect in relation to persons entering or seeking to enter the United Kingdom on arrival otherwise than by ship or aircraft [. . .] as they have effect in the case of a person arriving by ship or aircraft [. . .]; [. . .].

[(1A)   Her Majesty may by Order in Council direct that paragraph 27B or 27C of Schedule 2 shall have effect in relation to trains or vehicles as it has effect in relation to ships or aircraft.

(1B)   Any Order in Council under this section may make:

(a) such adaptations or modifications of the provisions concerned, and

(b) such supplementary provisions,

as appear to Her Majesty to be necessary or expedient for the purposes of the Order.]

(2)   The provision made by an Order in Council under [subsection (1)] may include provision for excluding the Republic of Ireland from section 1(3) of this Act either generally or for any specified purposes.

(3)   No recommendation shall be made to Her Majesty to make an Order in Council under this section unless a draft of the Order has been laid before Parliament and approved by a resolution of each House of Parliament.

Notes   Words in square brackets in sub-s (1) originally added by SI 1990/2227, Sch 1, were repealed by SI 1993/1813, at 9(1), Sch 6, Pt I.

Other words omitted repealed by the Immigration and Asylum Act 1999, s 169(1), (3), Sch 14, paras 43, 47(1), (2), Sch 16.

Sub-ss (1A), (1B) inserted by the Immigration and Asylum Act 1999, s 169(1), Sch 14, paras 43, 47(1), (3).

Sub-s (2): words in square brackets substituted by the Immigration and Asylum Act 1999, s 169(1), Sch 14, paras 43, 47(1), (4).

Commencement   1 January 1973 (SI 1972/1514).

Definitions   For 'aircraft' and 'ship', see s 33(1).

[A.1.16]
11 Construction of references to entry, and other phrases relating to travel
(1)   A person arriving in the United Kingdom by ship or aircraft shall for purposes of this Act be deemed not to enter the United Kingdom unless and until he disembarks, and on disembarkation at a port shall further be deemed not to enter the United Kingdom so long as he remains in such area (if any) at the port as may be approved for this purpose by an immigration officer; and a person who has not otherwise entered the United Kingdom shall be deemed not to do so as long as he is detained, or temporally admitted or released while liable to detention, under the powers conferred by Schedule 2 to this Act [or by Part III of the Immigration and Asylum Act 1999].
[(1A)   ..]
(2)   In this Act 'disembark' means disembark from a ship or aircraft, and 'embark' means embark in a ship or aircraft; and, except in subsection (1) above:

(a)   references to disembarking in the United Kingdom do not apply to disembarking after a local journey from a place in the United Kingdom or elsewhere in the common travel area; and

(b)   references to embarking in the United Kingdom do not apply to embarking for a local journey to a place in the United Kingdom or elsewhere in the common travel area.

(3)   Except in so far as the context otherwise requires, references in this Act to arriving in the United Kingdom by ship shall extend to arrival by any floating structure, and 'disembark' shall be construed accordingly; but the provisions of this Act specially relating to members of the crew of a ship shall not be virtue of this provision apply in relation to any floating structure not being a ship.

(4)   For purposes of this Act 'common travel area' has the meaning given by section 1(3), and a journey is, in relation to the common travel area, a local journey if but only if it begins and ends in the common travel area and is not made by a ship or aircraft which:

(a)   in the case of a journey to a place in the United Kingdom, began its voyage from, or has during its voyage called at, a place not in the common travel area; or

(b)   in the case of a journey from a place in the United Kingdom, is due to end its voyage in, or call in the course of its voyage at, a place not in the common travel area.

(5)   A person who enters the United Kingdom lawfully by virtue of section 8(1) above, and seeks to remain beyond the time limited by section 8(1), shall be treated for purposes of this Act as seeking to enter the United Kingdom.

Notes   Words in square brackets in sub-s (1) inserted by the Immigration and Asylum Act 1999, s 169 (1) Sch 14, paras 43, 48.
   Sub-s (1A) originally added by SI 1990/2227, Sch 1, repealed by SI 1993/1813, art 9(1), Sch 6, Pt I.

Commencement   1 January 1973 (SI 1972/1514).

Definitions   For 'aircraft', 'port' (defined with 'aircraft') and 'ships', see s 33(1). As to 'disembark', note sub-ss (2), (3) above; as to 'embark', note sub-s (2) above; as arriving in the United Kingdom by ship', note sub-s (3) above; and as to 'common travel area' and 'local journey', note sub-s (4) above.

PART II
APPEALS

[A.1.17]

Notes   Part II omitted by Immigration and Asylum Act 1999, s 169(1), Sch 14, para 219. See Schedule 14, para 49 (note).

PART III
CRIMINAL PROCEEDINGS

[A.1.18]
24 Illegal entry and similar offences
(1)   A person who is not [a British citizen] shall be guilty of an offence punishable on summary conviction with a fine of not more than [[level 5] on the standard scale] or with imprisonment for not more than six months, or with both, in any of the following cases:

(*a*)   if contrary to this Act he knowingly enters the United Kingdom in breach of a deportation order or without leave;
. . .
(*b*)   if, having only a limited leave to enter or remain in the United Kingdom, he knowingly either —
   (i) remains beyond the time limited by the leave; or
   (ii) fails to observe a condition of the leave;
(*c*)   if, having lawfully entered the United Kingdom without leave by virtue of section 8(1) above, he remains without leave beyond the time allowed by section 8(1);
(*d*)   if, without reasonable excuse, he fails to comply with any requirement imposed on him under Schedule 2 to this Act to report to a medical officer of health, or to attend, or submit to a test or examination, as required by such an officer;

(*e*) if, without reasonable excuse, he fails to observe any restriction imposed on him under Schedule 2 or 3 to this Act as to residence[, as to his employment or occupation] or as to reporting to the police or to an immigration officer;

(*f*) if he disembarks in the United Kingdom from a ship or aircraft after being placed on board under Schedule 2 or 3 to this Act with a view to his removal from the United Kingdom;

(*g*) if he embarks in contravention of a restriction imposed by or under an Order in Council under section 3(7) of this Act.

[(1A) A person commits an offence under subsection (1)(*b*)(i) above on the day when he first knows that the time limited by his leave has expired and continues to commit it throughout any period during which he is in the United Kingdom thereafter; but a person shall not be prosecuted under that provision more than once in respect of the same limited leave.]

(2) . . .

(3) The extended time limit for prosecutions which is provided for by section 28 below shall apply to offences under [subsection (1)(*a*) and (*c*)] above.

(4) In proceedings for an offence against subsection (1)(*a*) above of entering the United Kingdom without leave, —

(*a*) any stamp purporting to have been imprinted on a passport or other travel document by an immigration officer on a particular date for the purpose of giving leave shall be presumed to have been duly so imprinted, unless the contrary is proved;

(*b*) proof that a person had leave to enter the United Kingdom shall lie on the defence if, but only if, he is shown to have entered within six months before the date when the proceedings were commenced.

Notes Words in first square brackets in sub-s (1) substituted by the British Nationality Act 1981, s 39(6), Sch 4, para 2; words in second square brackets in sub-s (l) substituted by virtue of the Criminal Justice Act 1982, ss 37, 38, 46 and amended by the Asylum and Immigration Act 1996, s 6; words in third square brackets in sub-s (1) substituted by the Immigration Act 1988, s 10, Sch, para 10(3), (4). Sub-s (1)(*aa*) inserted by the Asylum and Immigration Act 1996, s 4.

Sub-s (1A) inserted, and words in square brackets in sub-s (3) substituted, by the Immigration Act 1988, s 6, except in relation to persons whose leave had expired before 10 July 1988.

Sub-ss (1)(aa) and (2) omitted by Immigration and Asylum Act 1999, Sch 14, para 50.

Commencement 1 January 1973 (SI 1972/1514).

Definitions For Aircraft', 'limited leave' and 'ship', see s 33(1); for 'disembark' and 'embark', see s 11(2), (3). As to when a person is deemed to enter the United Kingdom, see s 11(1), and note also s 10(1).

[A.1.19]
[24A Deception
(1) A person who is not a British citizen is guilty of an offence if, by means which include deception by him:

(a) he obtains or seeks to obtain leave to enter or remain in the United Kingdom; or

(b) he secures or seeks to secure the avoidance, postponement or revocation of enforcement action against him.

(2)   'Enforcement action', in relation to a person, means:

(a)   the giving of directions for his removal from the United Kingdom ('directions') under Schedule 2 to this Act or section 10 of the Immigration and Asylum Act 1999;
(b)   the making of a deportation order against him under section 5 of this Act; or
(c)   his removal from the United Kingdom in consequence of directions or a deportation order.

(3)   A person guilty of an offence under this section is liable:

(a)   on summary conviction, to imprisonment for a term not exceeding six months or to a fine not exceeding the statutory maximum, or to both; or
(b)   on conviction on indictment, to imprisonment for a term not exceeding two years or to a fine, or to both.

(4)   The extended time limit for prosecutions which is provided for by section 28 applies to an offence under this section.]

Note   Inserted by Immigration and Asylum Act 1999, s 28.

This section replaces section 21(1)(aa) of the 1971 Immigration Act as amended by section 4 of the Asylum and Immigration Act 1996. It broadens the scope of the previous deception offence, in particular by the wording in the new sub-section 24A(1)(b).

The new sub-section 24(A)(3) increases the maximum penalty for offences of deception under this section. Under section 24(1) of the 1971 Immigration Act as amended the offence is punishable on summary conviction with a fine or a maximum of 6 months imprisonment, or both. Offences under the new subsection 24(A) are punishable as set out in subsection 3.

Note that section 128 of the IAA 1999 gives powers to immigration officers to arrest without a warrant in connection with offences under this section and see the note on that section.

[A.1.20]
25 Assisting illegal entry, and harbouring
(1)   Any person knowingly concerned in making or carrying out arrangements for securing or facilitating:

[(a) the entry into the United Kingdom of anyone whom he knows or has reasonable cause for believing to be an illegal entrant;
(b)   the entry into the United Kingdom of anyone whom he knows or has reasonable cause for believing to be an asylum claimant; or
(c)   the obtaining by anyone of leave to remain in the United Kingdom by means which he knows or has reasonable cause for believing to include deception,]

shall be guilty of an offence, punishable on summary conviction with a fine of not more than [the prescribed sum] or with imprisonment for not more than six months, or with both, or on conviction on indictment with a fine or with imprisonment for not more than [ten] years, or with both.

[(1A)   Nothing in subsection (1)(b) above shall apply to anything which is done:

(a)   by a person otherwise than for gain, or in the course of his employment by a bona fide organisation whose purpose it is to assist refugees; or

25

(*b*) in relation to a person who has been detained under paragraph 16 of Schedule 2 to this Act, or has been granted temporary admission under paragraph 21 of that Schedule;

and in that provision 'asylum claimant' means a person who intends to make a claim for asylum (within the meaning of the Asylum and Immigration Appeals Act 1993).]

(2)   Without prejudice to subsection (1) above a person knowingly harbouring anyone whom he knows or has reasonable cause for believing to be either an illegal entrant or a person who has committed an offence under section 24 (1)(*b*) or (*c*) above, shall be guilty of an offence, punishable on summary conviction with a fine of not more than [level 5 on the standard scale] or with imprisonment for not more than six months, or with both.
. . .
(4)   The extended time limit for prosecutions which is provided for by section 28 below shall apply to offences under this section.
(5)   [Paragraphs (*a*) and (*b*) of subsection (1)] above shall apply to things done outside as well as to things done in the United Kingdom where they are done:

[(*a*) by a British citizen, a British Dependent Territories citizen, or a British Overseas citizen;
(*b*) by a person who under the British Nationality Act 1981 is a British subject; or
(*c*) by a British protected person (within the meaning of that Act)].

(6)   Where a person convicted on indictment of an offence under subsection (1) [(*a*) or (*b*)] above is at the time of the offence:

(*a*) the owner or one of the owners of a ship, aircraft or vehicle used or intended to be used in carrying out the arrangements in respect of which the offence is committed; or
(*b*) a director or manager of a company which is the owner or one of the owners of any such ship, aircraft or vehicle; or
(*c*) captain of any such ship or aircraft; [or
(*d*) the driver of any such vehicle;]

then subject to subsections (7) and (8) below the court before which he is convicted may order the forfeiture of the ship, aircraft or vehicle.

In this subsection (but not in subsection (7) below) 'owner' in relation to a ship, aircraft or vehicle which is the subject of a hire-purchase agreement, includes the person in possession of it under that agreement and, in relation to a ship or aircraft, includes a charterer.

(7)   A court shall not order a ship or aircraft to be forfeited under subsection (6) above on a person's conviction, unless:

(*a*) in the case of a ship, it is of less than 500 tons of gross tonnage or, in the case of an aircraft (not being a hovercraft), it is of less than 5,700 kilogrammes operating weight; or
(*b*) the person convicted is at the time of the offence the owner or one of the owners, or a director or manager of a company which is the owner or one of the owners, of the ship or aircraft; or
(*c*) the ship or aircraft, under the arrangements in respect of which the offence is committed, has been used for bringing more than 20 persons at one time to the United Kingdom as illegal entrants, and the intention to use the ship

or aircraft in bringing persons to the United Kingdom as illegal entrants was known to, or could by the exercise of reasonable diligence, have been discovered by, some person on whose conviction the ship or aircraft would have been liable to forfeiture in accordance with paragraph (*b*) above.

In this subsection 'operating weight' means in relation to an aircraft the maximum total weight of the aircraft and its contents at which the aircraft may take off anywhere in the world, in the most favourable circumstances, in accordance with the certificate of airworthiness in force in respect of the aircraft.

(8)   A court shall not order a ship, aircraft or vehicle to be forfeited under subsection (6) above, where a person claiming to be the owner of the ship, aircraft or vehicle or otherwise interested in it applies to be heard by the court, unless an opportunity has been given to him to show cause why the order should not be made.

Notes   Words in second square brackets in sub-s (1) substituted by virtue of the Magistrates' Courts Act, 1980, s 32(2).

Words in third square brackets in sub-s (1) substituted by the Immigration and Asylum Act 1999, s 29(1), (2).

Words in square brackets in sub-s (2) substituted by virtue of the Criminal Justice Act 1982, ss 37, 38, 46.

Word in square brackets in sub-s (3) substituted by the Police and Criminal Evidence Act 1984, s 119(1), Sch 6, Pt I, para 20.

Words in first square brackets in sub-s (5) substituted by the Immigration and Asylum Act 1999, s 29(1), (4).

Words in second square brackets in sub-s (5) substituted by the British Nationality Act 1981, s 39(6), Sch 4, para 6.

Sub-ss 1(*a*)–(*c*) and (1A) inserted, and sub-s (6) amended to refer to inserted provisions, by the Asylum and Immigration Act 1996, s 5.

Sub-s (3) omitted by Immigration and Asylum Act 1999, Sch 14, para 51.

Words in second square brackets in sub-s (6) inserted by the Immigration and Asylum Act 1999, s 38(1), (3).

Commencement   Sub-s (1), (3)–(8) 28 November 1971 (s 35(2)); sub-s (2) 1 January 1973 (SI 1972/1514); sub-s (1A) 1 October 1996 (SI 1996/2053).

Definitions   For 'aircraft', 'captain', 'illegal entrant' (defined with 'entrant') and 'ship', see s 33(1).

General Note   The new s 25(1)(*a*) reflects the old offence contained in s 25(1) prior to amendment. Sub-section 1(*b*) is intended to target the activities of 'immigration racketeers' — although there was widespread concern about the breadth of the new offence and in particular its applicability to lawyers. The Government purported to deal with such concern by widening the defence so as to exclude anything done in relation to persons detained or granted temporary admission (sub-s (1A)(*b*) refers) — although there would appear still to be lacunae.

Sub-paragraph (1)(b)

In *R v Naillie and Kanesarajah* [1993] AC 674, [1993] Imm AR 462 the House of Lords held that a s 25(1) offence was not committed in respect of the assistance of persons who claimed asylum on arrival without seeking to rely on forged documentation: the act drew a distinction between arrival and entry; a person did not enter on disembarkation but only sought to enter on presentation to the immigration officer and if such person claims asylum at that point without any reliance on forged documentation s/he does not enter or seek to enter in breach of the immigration laws and is not an illegal entrant. The sub-para (1)(*b*) offence uses same word entry and it is difficult to see how the reasoning in *Naillie* would not apply mutatis mutandis. In the case of those who assist asylum seekers to arrive at the port of entry absent any reliance (or intended reliance) on false documentation (of the sort usually provided by 'racketeers') in an attempt to actually enter, the most that will have been assisted is the asylum claimant's arrival (which is insufficient). But those who convey them in a lorry through a port of entry may be potentially guilty of an offence.

Note that in at least one case of an alleged offence under s 25(1) an acquittal resulted where the defence of 'necessity' was left to the jury.

See also *Nadarajah Vilvarajah v Secretary of State for the Home Department* [1990] Imm AR 457 where Sir John Donaldson MR (albeit in a different context) distinguished between the use of forged documentation to leave a country of feared persecution and the attempt to enter in on such documentation.

Defences

The Government declined to specify a list of bona fide refugee organisations, but Baroness Blatch made mention of the Refugee Legal Centre, the Refugee Council, Asylum Aid, the Refugee Arrivals Project and the Immigration Advisory Service as examples of genuine bodies.

There was express acknowledgement by the government that the defences (under sub-para (1A)(*a*)) were incomplete 'in as much as they do not protect those people such as lawyers who have a legitimate and lawful interest in providing advice, assistance and representation to asylum seekers who have applied for asylum on arrival in the United Kingdom' (Baroness Blatch, Hansard HL, vol 573, col 567). But such observation is not acknowledgement of the extent of concerns — not least because of the reference only to those who have 'applied for asylum on arrival'.

The position remains that there is no available defence to 'lawyers legitimately and lawfully providing advice, assistance and representation'. The addition of the sub-para (1A)(*b*) defence is a curious attempt to fill the gap dealing not with the activities of the adviser but rather the status of the recipient of the advice. It is potentially inadequate and might not cover (for example) advice given to someone who is an illegal entrant (perhaps having entered clandestinely) but who has yet to claim asylum (although such person may already have entered — albeit obviously in breach of the immigration laws — cf Immigration Act 1971, s 11). Concern was also expressed during debate about the position of a lawyer abroad — although Baroness Blatch stated that such person would not be in danger 'because his activities would be too remote from the entry of an asylum seeker here' (Hansard HL, vol 573, col 571). Judicial review might be in respect of a decision to prosecute in such cases.

[A.1.21]
[25A   Detention of ships, aircraft and vehicles in connection with offences under section 25(1)]
[[(1)   If a person has been arrested for an offence under section 25(1)(*a*) or (*b*), a senior officer or a constable may detain a relevant ship, aircraft or vehicle:

(*a*) until a decision is taken as to whether or not to charge the arrested person with that offence; or
(*b*) if the arrested person has been charged:

  (i) until he is acquitted, the charge against him is dismissed or the proceedings are discontinued; or
  (ii) if he has been convicted, until the court decides whether or not to order forfeiture of the ship, aircraft or vehicle.

(2)   A ship, aircraft or vehicle is a relevant ship, aircraft or vehicle, in relation to an arrested person, if it is one which the officer or constable concerned has reasonable grounds for believing could, on conviction of the arrested per-

son for the offence for which he was arrested, be the subject of an order for forfeiture made under section 25(6).

(3)   A person (other than the arrested person) who claims to be the owner of a ship, aircraft or vehicle which has been detained under this section may apply to the court for its release.

(4)   The court to which an application is made under subsection (3) may, on such security or surety being tendered as it considers satisfactory, release the ship, aircraft or vehicle on condition that it is made available to the court if:]

(*a*) the arrested person is convicted; and

(*b*) an order for its forfeiture is made under section 25(6).

(5)   In the application to Scotland of subsection (1), for paragraphs (*a*) and (*b*) substitute:

'(*a*) until a decision is taken as to whether or not to institute criminal proceedings against the arrested person for that offence; or

(*b*) if criminal proceedings have been instituted against the arrested person:

(i) until he is acquitted or, under section 65 or 147 of the Criminal Procedure (Scotland) Act 1995, discharged or liberated or the trial diet is deserted simpliciter;

(ii) if he has been convicted, until the court decides whether or not to order forfeiture of the ship, aircraft or vehicle,

and for the purposes of this subsection, criminal proceedings are instituted against a person at whichever is the earliest of his first appearance before the sheriff on petition, or the service on him of an indictment or complaint.'

(6)   'Court' means:

(*a*) in England and Wales:

(i) if the arrested person has not been charged, the magistrates' court for the petty sessions area in which he was arrested;

(ii) if he has been charged but proceedings for the offence have not begun to be heard, the magistrates' court for the petty sessions area in which he was charged;

(iii) if he has been charged and proceedings for the offence are being heard, the court hearing the proceedings;

(*b*) in Scotland, the sheriff; and

(*c*) in Northern Ireland:

(i) if the arrested person has not been charged, the magistrates' court for the county court division in which he was arrested;

(ii) if he has been charged but proceedings for the offence have not begun to be heard, the magistrates' court for the county court division in which he was charged;

(iii) if he has been charged and proceedings for the offence are being heard, the court hearing the proceedings.

(7)   'Owner' has the same meaning as it has in section 25(6).

(8)   'Senior officer' means an immigration officer not below the rank of chief immigration officer.]

Note Inserted by the Immigration and Asylum Act 1999, s 38(2), (4).

Commencement 3 April 2000 (in relation to persons arrested for offences alleged to have been committed after that date) (SI 2000/464).

[A.1.22]
26 General offences in connection with administration of Act
(1) A person shall be guilty of an offence punishable on summary convictions with a fine of not more than [[level 5] on the standard scale] or with imprisonment for not more than six months, or with both, in any of the following cases:

(*a*) if, without reasonable excuse, he refuses or fails to submit to examination under Schedule 2 to this Act;
(*b*) if, without reasonable excuse, he refuses or fails to furnish or produce any information in his possession, or any documents in his possession or control, which he is on an examination under that Schedule required to furnish or produce;
(*c*) if on any such examination or otherwise he makes or causes to be made to an immigration officer or other person lawfully acting in the execution of [a relevant enactment] a return, statement or representation which he knows to be false or does not believe to be true;
(*d*) if, without lawful authority, he alters any [certificate of entitlement], entry clearance, work permit or other document issued or made under or for the purposes of this Act, or uses for the purposes of this Act, or has in his possession for such use, any passport, [certificate of entitlement], entry clearance, work permit or other document which he knows or has reasonable cause to believe to be false;
(*e*) if, without reasonable excuse, he fails to complete and produce a landing or embarkation card in accordance with any order under Schedule 2 to this Act;
(*f*) if, without reasonable excuse, he fails to comply with any requirement of regulations under section 4(3) or of an order under section 4(4) above;
(*g*) if, without reasonable excuse, he obstructs an immigration officer or other person lawfully acting in the execution of this Act.

(2) The extended time limit for prosecutions which is provided for by section 28 below shall apply to offences under subsection (1)(*c*) and (*d*) above.
[(3) 'Relevant enactment' means:

(a) this Act;
(b) the Immigration Act 1988;
(c) the Asylum and Immigration Appeals Act 1993 (apart from section 4 or 5); or
(d) the Immigration and Asylum Act 1999 (apart from Part VI).]

Notes Words in square brackets in sub-s (1) substituted by virtue of the Criminal Justice Act 1982, ss 37, 38, 46 and amended by the Asylum and Immigration Act 1996, s 6; words in second and third square brackets in sub-s (1) substituted by the British Nationality Act 1981, s 39(6), Sch 4, para 3(1).
Words in square brackets in sub-s (1)(*c*) inserted by the Immigration and Asylum Act 1999, s 30(1), (2).
Sub-s (3) inserted by the Immigration and Asylum Act 1999, s 30(1), (3).

Commencement   1 January 1973 (SI 1972/1514).

Definitions   For 'certificate of entitlement', 'entry clearance' and 'work permit', see s 33(1).

[A.1.23]
27 Offences by persons connected with ships or aircraft or with ports
A person shall be guilty of an offence punishable on summary conviction with a fine of not more than [[level 5] on the standard scale] or with imprisonment for not more than six months, or with both, in any of the following cases:
(*a*) if, being the captain of a ship or aircraft:
    (i) he knowingly permits a person to disembark in the United Kingdom when required under Schedule 2 or 3 to this Act to prevent it, or fails without reasonable excuse to take any steps he is required by or under Schedule 2 to take in connection with the disembarkation or examination of passengers or for furnishing a passenger list or particulars of members of the crew; or
    (ii) he fails, without reasonable excuse, to comply with any directions given him under Schedule 2 or 3 [or under the Immigration and Asylum Act 1999] with respect to the removal of a person from the United Kingdom;
(*b*) if, as owner or agent of a ship or aircraft:
    (i) he arranges or is knowingly concerned in any arrangements, for the ship or aircraft to call at a port other than a port of entry contrary to any provision of Schedule 2 to this Act; or
    (ii) he fails, without reasonable excuse, to take any steps required by an order under Schedule 2 for the supply to passengers of landing or embarkation cards; or
    (iii) he fails, without reasonable excuse, to make arrangements for [or in connection with] the removal of a person from the United Kingdom when required to do so by directions given under Schedule 2 or 3 to this Act [or under the Immigration and Asylum Act 1999; or;
    (iv) he fails, without reasonable excuse, to comply with the requirements of paragraph 27B or 27C of Schedule 2];
(*c*) if, as owner or agent of a ship or aircraft or as a person concerned in the management of a port, he fails, without reasonable excuse, to take any steps required by Schedule 2 in relation to the embarkation or disembarkation of passengers where a control area is designated.
[(*d*) . . .]

Notes   Words in first and second square brackets substituted by virtue of the Criminal Justice Act 1982, ss 37, 38, 46 and amended by the Asylum and Immigration Act 1996, s 6.
Words in square brackets para (*a*), sub-para (ii) inserted by the Immigration and Asylum Act 1999, s 169(1), Sch 14, paras 43, 52(1), (2).
Words 'or in connection with' in square brackets in para (b), sub-para (iii) inserted by the Immigration and Asylum Act 1999, s 169(1), Sch 14, paras 43, 52(1), (3)(*a*).
Words 'or under the Immigration and Asylum Act 1999; or' in square brackets in para (*b*), sub-para (iv) inserted by the Immigration and Asylum Act 1999, s 169(1), Sch 14, paras 43, 52(1), (3)(*b*).
Sub-s (*d*) originally added by SI 1990/2227, Sch 1, was repealed by SI 1993/1813, art 9(1), Sch 6, Pt I.
See notes to Sch 2. See also the Immigration (Passenger Information) Order 2000 (SI 2000/912). A carrier who fails, without reasonable excuse, to comply with the

requirements of para 27B of Sch 2, commits an offence. See also the Channel Tunnel (International Arrangements) (Amendment) Order 2000 (SI 2000/913).

Commencement 1 January 1973 (SI 1972/1514).

Definitions For 'aircraft', 'captain', 'crew', 'port' (defined with 'aircraft') and 'ship', see s 33(1); for 'disembark', see s 11(2), (3); for 'port of entry', see s 33(3).

[A.1.24]
28 Proceedings
(1)   Where the offence is one to which, under section 24, [24A], 25 or 26 above, an extended time limit for prosecutions is to apply, then —

(*a*) an information relating to the offence may in England and Wales be tried by a magistrates' court if it is laid within six months after the commission of the offence, or if it is laid within three years after the commission of the offence and not more than two months after the date certified by [an officer of police above the rank of chief superintendent] to be the date on which evidence sufficient to justify proceedings came to the notice of an officer of [the police force to which he belongs]; and

(*b*) summary proceedings for the offence may in Scotland be commenced within six months after the commission of the offence, or within three years after the commission of the offence and not more than two months after the date on which evidence sufficient in the opinion of the Lord Advocate to justify proceedings came to his knowledge; and

(*c*) a complaint charging the commission of the offence may in Northern Ireland be heard and determined by a magistrates' court if it is made within six months after the commission of the offence, or if it is made within three years after the commission of the offence and not more than two months after the date certified by an officer of police not below the rank of assistant chief constable to be the date on which evidence sufficient to justify the proceedings came to the notice of the police in Northern Ireland.

(2)   For purposes of subsection 1(*b*) above proceedings shall be deemed to be commenced on the date on which a warrant to apprehend or to cite the accused is granted, if such warrant is executed without undue delay; and a certificate of the Lord Advocate as to the date on which such evidence as is mentioned in subsection (1)(*b*) came to his knowledge shall be conclusive evidence.

(3)   For the purposes of the trial of a person for an offence under this Part of this Act, the offence shall be deemed to have been committed either at the place at which it actually was committed or at any place at which he may be.

(4)   Any powers exercisable under this Act in the case of any person may be exercised notwithstanding that proceedings for an offence under this Part of this Act have been taken against him.

Notes   Words in square brackets in sub-s (1)(*a*) substituted by the Immigration Act 1988, s 10, Schedule, para 4; para (*b*) applies to Scotland only; Sub-s (2) applies to Scotland only.

Sub-s (1) amended by Immigration and Asylum Act 1999, Sch 14, para 53.

Commencement   Sub-ss (1), (2) 28 October 1971 (so far as relating to Commonwealth Immigrants Act 1962, s 4A) (s 35(3) post); 28 November 1971 (So far as relating to s 25(1) ante) (s 35(2) post); 1 January 1973 (otherwise) (SI 1972/1514); sub-ss (3), (4) 1 January 1973 (SI 1972/1514).

[A.1.25]
[28A Arrest without warrant
(1)   A constable or immigration officer may arrest without warrant a person:

(*a*) who has committed or attempted to commit an offence under section 24 or 24A; or
(*b*) whom he has reasonable grounds for suspecting has committed or attempted to commit such an offence.

(2)   But subsection (1) does not apply in relation to an offence under section 24(1)(d).
(3)   An immigration officer may arrest without warrant a person:

(*a*) who has committed an offence under section 25(1); or
(*b*) whom he has reasonable grounds for suspecting has committed that offence.

(4)   An immigration officer may arrest without warrant a person:

(*a*) who has committed or attempted to commit an offence under section 25(2); or
(*b*) whom he has reasonable grounds for suspecting has committed or attempted to commit that offence.

(5)   An immigration officer may arrest without warrant a person ('the suspect') who, or whom he has reasonable grounds for suspecting:

(*a*) has committed or attempted to commit an offence under section 26(1)(g); or
(*b*) is committing or attempting to commit that offence.

(6)   The power conferred by subsection (5) is exercisable only if either the first or the second condition is satisfied.
(7)   The first condition is that it appears to the officer that service of a summons (or, in Scotland, a copy complaint) is impracticable or inappropriate because:

(*a*) he does not know, and cannot readily discover, the suspect's name;
(*b*) he has reasonable grounds for doubting whether a name given by the suspect as his name is his real name;
(*c*) the suspect has failed to give him a satisfactory address for service; or
(*d*) he has reasonable grounds for doubting whether an address given by the suspect is a satisfactory address for service.

(8)   The second condition is that the officer has reasonable grounds for believing that arrest is necessary to prevent the suspect:

(*a*) causing physical injury to himself or another person;
(*b*) suffering physical injury; or
(*c*) causing loss of or damage to property.

(9)   For the purposes of subsection (7), an address is a satisfactory address for service if it appears to the officer:

(*a*) that the suspect will be at that address for a sufficiently long period for it to be possible to serve him with a summons (or copy complaint); or
(*b*) that some other person specified by the suspect will accept service of a summons (or copy complaint) for the suspect at that address.

(10)   In relation to the exercise of the powers conferred by subsections (3)(b), (4)(b) and (5), it is immaterial that no offence has been committed.
(11)   In Scotland the powers conferred by subsections (3), (4) and (5) may also be exercised by a constable.]

Note   Added by Immigration and Asylum Act 1999, s 128.

Part VII of the IAA 1999, which is modelled on the Police and Criminal Evidence Act 1984 (PACE), provides immigration officers with powers to arrest and search which were previously the sole province of the police force. This is effected by numerous interrelating amendments to the 1971 Immigration Act which do not make for ease of reference.

Although not expressly stated in Part VII of the IAA 99, Ministers have indicated their intention to pilot the use of the powers using a limited number of immigration officers, to be trained and supervised by the police, in the first instance. There is thus at the very least an expectation that immigration officers outside the pilot will not be using these powers from 14 February 2001.

Immigration officers exercising powers under this section must, under the provisions of section 145 of the IAA 99, have regard to any code of practice as specified. See the Immigration (PACE Codes of Practice) Direction 2000. See also the Immigration (PACE Codes of Practice No 2 and Amendment) Direction made 19 November 2000 and in operation 20 November 2000. All references in this note are to the first Direction, unless otherwise stated. The Direction takes as its starting point the PACE Codes. Schedule 2 of the Direction is presented in the form of a series of instructions to an editor and modifies the provisions of PACE. Schedule 1 sets out which section of the new code as created by Schedule 2 are to apply to which provisions of the 1971 Act as amended by Part VII of the 1999 Act. The Direction is thus comprehensive, but incomprehensible in its present form and all those involved in the operation of the new powers anxiously await the publication of the full text of the modified codes.

To take an example from the amendments to the 1971 Act effected by section 128 of the 1999 Act:

The first amendment effected by section 128 is the insertion of a new section 28A into the 1971 Act. The Schedule 1 of the Draft Direction states that all provisions of Codes C, D, and E will apply to the code for England and Wales, and similarly for Northern Ireland. In respect of England and Wales Schedule 2 of the Draft Direction sets out 11 modifications to Code C (the Schedule then goes on to set out the amendments in respect of Northern Ireland). The majority of these are provisions so that references to the police in defined sections can be read as references to the Immigration Service, references to police stations can be read as references to 'immigration offices'. The other modifications include inserting into Annexe A the provision: 'An immigration officer has no power to conduct an intimate search as defined in this Annexe'. Schedule 2 does not modify Code D. It modifies Code C insofar as references to 'police officer' are also to be read as references to 'immigration officer'.

As the example above makes apparent, this is not a wholesale rewriting of the PACE codes to tailor them to the special circumstances in which immigration officers are exercising these powers. For the most part, immigration officers are subject to something very similar to the PACE codes. As set out in the example above, certain powers have been denied them, notably the power to conduct intimate searches (they have not been denied the power to conduct strip searches). However, other modifications subject them to a lower level of control than police officers. For example, Schedule 2 of the Direction modifies provision 2.4 of Code A so that unlike a police officer an immigration office is not bound to give his name when conducting a search to which provision 2.4 applies.

In considering the scope of the powers given by these sections reference should be made to section 146 of the 1999 Act which provides that 'an immigration officer exercising any power conferred on him by the 1971 Act or this Act may, if necessary, use reasonable force.' See the notes to section 146 of the 1999 Act **[A.1.379]**.

The powers in section 128 of the IAA 99 for immigration officers to arrest without a warrant are provided in respect of offences set out in provisions of sections 24, 24A, 25, and 26 of this Act, as described in that section. It is important to note that it does apply to the new offences set out in sections 28 and 29 of the Immigration and Asylum Act 1999, because it is section 28 that inserts the new section 24A into this Act and section 29 amends section 25 of this Act. Thus while the powers are not new, the scope of the circumstances in which they can be used has been broadened considerably. This is because, as set out in the notes on those sections, sections 28 and 29 of the 1999 Act considerably broaden the range of offences in respect of which the powers may be used.

See also the note to section 145 of the IAA 1999 [**A.1.378**].

[A.1.26]
[28B Search and arrest by warrant

(1)   Subsection (2) applies if a justice of the peace is, by written information on oath, satisfied that there are reasonable grounds for suspecting that a person ('the suspect') who is liable to be arrested for a relevant offence is to be found on any premises.

(2)   The justice may grant a warrant authorising any immigration officer or constable to enter, if need be by force, the premises named in the warrant for the purpose of searching for and arresting the suspect.

(3)   Subsection (4) applies if in Scotland the sheriff or a justice of the peace is by evidence on oath satisfied as mentioned in subsection (1).

(4)   The sheriff or justice may grant a warrant authorising any immigration officer or constable to enter, if need be by force, the premises named in the warrant for the purpose of searching for and arresting the suspect.

(5)   'Relevant offence' means an offence under section 24(1)(a), (b), (c), (d), (e) or (f), section 24A or section 25(2).]

Note   Added by Immigration and Asylum Act 1999, s 129. See note to s 28A. This section gives immigration officers new powers. They are empowered, subject to the restrictions set out in the section, to enter and search 'any' premises.

[A.1.27]
[28C Search and arrest without warrant

(1)   An immigration officer may enter and search any premises for the purpose of arresting a person for an offence under section 25(1).

(2)   The power may be exercised:

(*a*)   only to the extent that it is reasonably required for that purpose; and

(*b*)   only if the officer has reasonable grounds for believing that the person whom he is seeking is on the premises.

(3)   In relation to premises consisting of two or more separate dwellings, the power is limited to entering and searching:

(*a*)   any parts of the premises which the occupiers of any dwelling comprised in the premises use in common with the occupiers of any such other dwelling; and

(*b*)   any such dwelling in which the officer has reasonable grounds for believing that the person whom he is seeking may be.

(4)   The power may be exercised only if the officer produces identification showing that he is an immigration officer (whether or not he is asked to do so).]

Note   Added by Immigration and Asylum Act 1999, s 130. See note to s 28A. The powers are provided in respect of section 25(1) which is concerned with the offence of assisting illegal entrants.

[A.1.28]
[28D Entry and search of premises

(1)   If, on an application made by an immigration officer, a justice of the peace is satisfied that there are reasonable grounds for believing that:

(*a*) a relevant offence has been committed,

(*b*) there is material on premises specified in the application which is likely to be of substantial value (whether by itself or together with other material) to the investigation of the offence,

(*c*) the material is likely to be relevant evidence,

(*d*) the material does not consist of or include items subject to legal privilege, excluded material or special procedure material, and

(*e*) any of the conditions specified in subsection (2) applies,

he may issue a warrant authorising an immigration officer to enter and search the premises.

(2)   The conditions are that:

(*a*) it is not practicable to communicate with any person entitled to grant entry to the premises;

(*b*) it is practicable to communicate with a person entitled to grant entry to the premises but it is not practicable to communicate with any person entitled to grant access to the evidence;

(*c*) entry to the premises will not be granted unless a warrant is produced;

(*d*) the purpose of a search may be frustrated or seriously prejudiced unless an immigration officer arriving at the premises can secure immediate entry to them.

(3)   An immigration officer may seize and retain anything for which a search has been authorised under subsection (1).

(4)   'Relevant offence' means an offence under section 24(1)(a), (b), (c), (d), (e) or (f), section 24A or section 25.

(5)   In relation to England and Wales, expressions which are given a meaning by the Police and Criminal Evidence Act 1984 have the same meaning when used in this section.

(6)   In relation to Northern Ireland, expressions which are given a meaning by the Police and Criminal Evidence (Northern Ireland) Order 1989 have the same meaning when used in this section.

(7)   In the application of subsection (1) to Scotland:

(*a*) read the reference to a justice of the peace as a reference to the sheriff or a justice of the peace; and

(*b*) in paragraph (b), omit the reference to excluded material and special procedure material.]

Note   Added by Immigration and Asylum Act 1999, s 131. See notes to ss 28A and C above. The powers of entry and search thus extend to 'any' premises. There is no requirement that the premises be connected with the person who is believed to have committed the 'relevant offence' as defined in subsection (4).

[A.1.29]
[28E Entry and search of premises following arrest

(1)   This section applies if a person is arrested for an offence under this Part at a place other than a police station.

(2)   An immigration officer may enter and search any premises:

(*a*) in which the person was when arrested, or
(*b*) in which he was immediately before he was arrested,

for evidence relating to the offence for which the arrest was made ('relevant evidence').

(3)   The power may be exercised:

(*a*) only if the officer has reasonable grounds for believing that there is relevant evidence on the premises; and
(*b*) only to the extent that it is reasonably required for the purpose of discovering relevant evidence.

(4)   In relation to premises consisting of two or more separate dwellings, the power is limited to entering and searching:

(*a*) any dwelling in which the arrest took place or in which the arrested person was immediately before his arrest; and
(*b*) any parts of the premises which the occupier of any such dwelling uses in common with the occupiers of any other dwellings comprised in the premises.

(5)   An officer searching premises under subsection (2) may seize and retain anything he finds which he has reasonable grounds for believing is relevant evidence.

(6)   Subsection (5) does not apply to items which the officer has reasonable grounds for believing are items subject to legal privilege.]

Note   Added by Immigration and Asylum Act 1999, s 132. See notes on s 28A. In contrast to the powers to search 'any' premises in s 28D above, the powers in this section extend only to searches of premises in which the person was arrested or in which he was immediately before he was arrested.

[A.1.30]
[28F Entry and search of premises following arrest under section 25(1)
(1)   An immigration officer may enter and search any premises occupied or controlled by a person arrested for an offence under section 25(1).

(2)   The power may be exercised:

(*a*) only if the officer has reasonable grounds for suspecting that there is relevant evidence on the premises;
(*b*) only to the extent that it is reasonably required for the purpose of discovering relevant evidence; and
(*c*) subject to subsection (3), only if a senior officer has authorised it in writing.

(3)   The power may be exercised:

(*a*) before taking the arrested person to a place where he is to be detained; and
(*b*) without obtaining an authorisation under subsection (2)(c),

if the presence of that person at a place other than one where he is to be detained is necessary for the effective investigation of the offence.

(4)   An officer who has relied on subsection (3) must inform a senior officer as soon as is practicable.

(5)   The officer authorising a search, or who is informed of one under subsection (4), must make a record in writing of:

(*a*) the grounds for the search; and
(*b*) the nature of the evidence that was sought.

(6)   An officer searching premises under this section may seize and retain anything he finds which he has reasonable grounds for suspecting is relevant evidence.

(7)   'Relevant evidence' means evidence, other than items subject to legal privilege, that relates to the offence in question.

(8)   'Senior officer' means an immigration officer not below the rank of chief immigration officer.]

Note   Added by Immigration and Asylum Act 1999, s 133. See notes at s 28A above.

[A.1.31]
[28G Searching arrested persons
(1)   This section applies if a person is arrested for an offence under this Part at a place other than a police station.

(2)   An immigration officer may search the arrested person if he has reasonable grounds for believing that the arrested person may present a danger to himself or others.

(3)   The officer may search the arrested person for:

(*a*) anything which he might use to assist his escape from lawful custody; or

(*b*) anything which might be evidence relating to the offence for which he has been arrested.

(4)   The power conferred by subsection (3) may be exercised:

(*a*) only if the officer has reasonable grounds for believing that the arrested person may have concealed on him anything of a kind mentioned in that subsection; and

(*b*) only to the extent that it is reasonably required for the purpose of discovering any such thing.

(5)   A power conferred by this section to search a person is not to be read as authorising an officer to require a person to remove any of his clothing in public other than an outer coat, jacket or glove; but it does authorise the search of a person's mouth.

(6)   An officer searching a person under subsection (2) may seize and retain anything he finds, if he has reasonable grounds for believing that that person might use it to cause physical injury to himself or to another person.

(7)   An officer searching a person under subsection (3) may seize and retain anything he finds, if he has reasonable grounds for believing:

(*a*) that that person might use it to assist his escape from lawful custody; or

(*b*) that it is evidence which relates to the offence in question.

(8)   Subsection (7)(b) does not apply to an item subject to legal privilege.]

Note   Added by Immigration and Asylum Act 1999, s 134. See notes at s 28A above.

[A.1.32]
[28H Searching persons in police custody
(1)   This section applies if a person:

(*a*) has been arrested for an offence under this Part; and (*b*) is in custody at a police station or in police detention at a place other than a police station.

(2) An immigration officer may, at any time, search the arrested person in order to see whether he has with him anything:

(*a*) which he might use to:

    (i)   cause physical injury to himself or others;
    (ii) damage property;
    (iii) interfere with evidence; or
    (iv) assist his escape; or

(*b*) which the officer has reasonable grounds for believing is evidence relating to the offence in question.

(3) The power may be exercised only to the extent that the custody officer concerned considers it to be necessary for the purpose of discovering anything of a kind mentioned in subsection (2).

(4) An officer searching a person under this section may seize anything he finds, if he has reasonable grounds for believing that:

(*a*) that person might use it for one or more of the purposes mentioned in subsection (2)(a); or

(*b*) it is evidence relating to the offence in question.

(5) Anything seized under subsection (4)(a) may be retained by the police.

(6) Anything seized under subsection (4)(b) may be retained by an immigration officer.

(7) The person from whom something is seized must be told the reason for the seizure unless he is:

(*a*) violent or appears likely to become violent; or

(*b*) incapable of understanding what is said to him.

(8) An intimate search may not be conducted under this section.

(9) The person carrying out a search under this section must be of the same sex as the person searched.

(10) 'Custody officer':

(*a*) in relation to England and Wales, has the same meaning as in the Police and Criminal Evidence Act 1984;

(*b*) in relation to Scotland, means the officer in charge of a police station; and

(*c*) in relation to Northern Ireland, has the same meaning as in the Police and Criminal Evidence (Northern Ireland) Order 1989.

(11) 'Intimate search':

(*a*) in relation to England and Wales, has the meaning given by section 65 of the Act of 1984;

(*b*) in relation to Scotland, means a search which consists of the physical examination of a person's body orifices other than the mouth; and

(*c*) in relation to Northern Ireland, has the same meaning as in the 1989 Order.

(12) 'Police detention':

(*a*) in relation to England and Wales, has the meaning given by section 118(2) of the 1984 Act; and (*b*) in relation to Northern Ireland, has the meaning given by Article 2 of the 1989 Order.

(13)   In relation to Scotland, a person is in police detention if:

(*a*) he has been taken to a police station after being arrested for an offence; or
(*b*) he is arrested at a police station after attending voluntarily at the station, accompanying a constable to it or being detained under section 14 of the Criminal Procedure (Scotland) Act 1995,

and is detained there or is detained elsewhere in the charge of a constable, but is not in police detention if he is in court after being charged.]

Note   Added by Immigration and Asylum Act 1999, s 135. See notes on s 28A above. This section sets out the circumstances in which a person in police custody may be searched by an immigration officer. This in no way affects police powers to search that person. The Explanatory Notes state 'The intention is not to duplicate searches but to allow an immigration officer to carry out a search where he is the arresting officer.'

[A.1.33]
[28I Seized material: access and copying
(1)   If a person showing himself:

(*a*) to be the occupier of the premises on which seized material was seized, or
(*b*) to have had custody or control of the material immediately before it was seized,

asks the immigration officer who seized the material for a record of what he seized, the officer must provide the record to that person within a reasonable time.
(2)   If a relevant person asks an immigration officer for permission to be granted access to seized material, the officer must arrange for him to have access to the material under the supervision:

(*a*) in the case of seized material within subsection (8)(a), of an immigration officer;
(*b*) in the case of seized material within subsection (8)(b), of a constable.

(3)   An immigration officer may photograph or copy, or have photographed or copied, seized material.
(4)   If a relevant person asks an immigration officer for a photograph or copy of seized material, the officer must arrange for:

(*a*) that person to have access to the material for the purpose of photographing or copying it under the supervision:

    (i)   in the case of seized material within subsection (8)(a), of an immigration officer;
    (ii)   in the case of seized material within subsection (8)(b), of a constable; or
(*b*) the material to be photographed or copied.

(5)   A photograph or copy made under subsection (4)(b) must be supplied within a reasonable time.
(6)   There is no duty under this section to arrange for access to, or the supply

of a photograph or copy of, any material if there are reasonable grounds for believing that to do so would prejudice:

(*a*) the exercise of any functions in connection with which the material was seized; or

(*b*) an investigation which is being conducted under this Act, or any criminal proceedings which may be brought as a result.

(7)   'Relevant person' means:

(*a*) a person who had custody or control of seized material immediately before it was seized, or

(*b*) someone acting on behalf of such a person.

(8)   'Seized material' means anything:

(*a*) seized and retained by an immigration officer, or

(*b*) seized by an immigration officer and retained by the police,

under this Part.]

Note   Added by Immigration and Asylum Act 1999, s 136.

[A.1.34]
[28J Search warrants: safeguards

(1)   The entry or search of premises under a warrant is unlawful unless it complies with this section and section 28K.

(2)   If an immigration officer applies for a warrant, he must:

(*a*) state the ground on which he makes the application and the provision of this Act under which the warrant would be issued;

(*b*) specify the premises which it is desired to enter and search; and

(*c*) identify, so far as is practicable, the persons or articles to be sought.

(3)   In Northern Ireland, an application for a warrant is to be supported by a complaint in writing and substantiated on oath.

(4)   Otherwise, an application for a warrant is to be made ex parte and supported by an information in writing or, in Scotland, evidence on oath.

(5)   The officer must answer on oath any question that the justice of the peace or sheriff hearing the application asks him.

(6)   A warrant shall authorise an entry on one occasion only.

(7)   A warrant must specify:

(*a*) the name of the person applying for it;

(*b*) the date on which it is issued;

(*c*) the premises to be searched; and

(*d*) the provision of this Act under which it is issued.

(8)   A warrant must identify, so far as is practicable, the persons or articles to be sought.

(9)   Two copies of a warrant must be made.

(10)   The copies must be clearly certified as copies.

(11)   'Warrant' means a warrant to enter and search premises issued to an immigration officer under this Part or under paragraph 17(2) of Schedule 2.]

Note   Added by Immigration and Asylum Act 1999, s 137.

[A.1.35]
[28K Execution of warrants
(1)   A warrant may be executed by any immigration officer.
(2)   A warrant may authorise persons to accompany the officer executing it.
(3)   Entry and search under a warrant must be:

(*a*) within one month from the date of its issue; and
(*b*) at a reasonable hour, unless it appears to the officer executing it that the purpose of a search might be frustrated.

(4)   If the occupier of premises which are to be entered and searched is present at the time when an immigration officer seeks to execute a warrant, the officer must:

(*a*) identify himself to the occupier and produce identification showing that he is an immigration officer;
(*b*) show the occupier the warrant; and
(*c*) supply him with a copy of it.

(5)   If:

(*a*) the occupier is not present, but
(*b*) some other person who appears to the officer to be in charge of the premises is present,

subsection (4) has effect as if each reference to the occupier were a reference to that other person.
(6)   If there is no person present who appears to the officer to be in charge of the premises, the officer must leave a copy of the warrant in a prominent place on the premises.
(7)   A search under a warrant may only be a search to the extent required for the purpose for which the warrant was issued.
(8)   An officer executing a warrant must make an endorsement on it stating:

(*a*) whether the persons or articles sought were found; and
(*b*) whether any articles, other than articles which were sought, were seized.

(9)   A warrant which has been executed, or has not been executed within the time authorised for its execution, must be returned:

(*a*) if issued by a justice of the peace in England and Wales, to the justices' chief executive appointed by the magistrates' court committee whose area includes the petty sessions area for which the justice acts;
(*b*) if issued by a justice of the peace in Northern Ireland, to the clerk of petty sessions for the petty sessions district in which the premises are situated;
(*c*) if issued by a justice of the peace in Scotland, to the clerk of the district court for the commission area for which the justice of the peace was appointed;
(*d*) if issued by the sheriff, to the sheriff clerk.

(10)   A warrant returned under subsection (9)(a) must be retained for 12 months by the justices' chief executive.
(11)   A warrant issued under subsection (9)(b) or (c) must be retained for 12 months by the clerk.
(12)   A warrant returned under subsection (9)(d) must be retained for 12 months by the sheriff clerk.

(13)   If during that 12 month period the occupier of the premises to which it relates asks to inspect it, he must be allowed to do so.

(14)   'Warrant' means a warrant to enter and search premises issued to an immigration officer under this Part or under paragraph 17(2) of Schedule 2.]

Note   Added by Immigration and Asylum Act 1999, s 138.

[A.1.36]
[28L Interpretation of Part III
In this Part, 'premises' and 'items subject to legal privilege' have the same meaning:

(*a*)   in relation to England and Wales, as in the Police and Criminal Evidence Act 1984;

(*b*)   in relation to Northern Ireland, as in the Police and Criminal Evidence (Northern Ireland) Order 1989; and

(*c*)   in relation to Scotland, as in section 33 of the Criminal Law (Consolidation) (Scotland) Act 1995.]

Note   Added by Immigration and Asylum Act 1999, s 139.

PART IV
SUPPLEMENTARY

[A.1.37]
29 Contributions for expenses of persons returning abroad
(1)   The Secretary of State may, in such cases as he may with the approval of the Treasury determine, make payments of such amount as may be so determined to meet or provide for expenses of persons who are not [British citizens] in leaving the United Kingdom for a country or territory where they intend to reside permanently, including travelling expenses for members of their families or households.

(2)   The Secretary of State shall, so far as practicable, administer this section so as to secure that a person's expenses in leaving the United Kingdom are not met by or out of a payment made by the Secretary of State unless it is shown that it is in that person's interest to leave the United Kingdom and that he wishes to do so.

Notes   Words in square brackets in sub-s (1) substituted by the British Nationality Act 1981, s 39(6), Sch 4, para 2.

Commencement   28 October 1971 (Royal Assent).

[A.1.38]
30 *(Repealed by the British Nationality Act 1981, s 52(8), Sch 9, and the Mental Health (Scotland) Act 1984, s 127(2), Sch 5)*

[A.1.39]
31 Expenses
There shall be defrayed out of moneys provided by Parliament any expenses incurred [by the Lord Chancellor under Schedule 5 to this Act or] by a Secretary of State under or by virtue of this Act:

(*a*) by way of administrative expenses . . . ; or
(*b*) in connection with the removal of any person from the United Kingdom under Schedule 2 or 3 or this Act or the departure with him of his dependants, or his or their maintenance pending departure; or
(*c*) . . . ; or
(*d*) on the making of any grants or payments under section 23 or 29 above.

Notes Words in square brackets inserted and para (*c*) repealed by the Transfer of Functions (Immigration Appeals) Order 1987, SI 1987/465.
    Words omitted from para (*a*) repealed by the British Nationality Act 1981, s 52(8), Sch 9.

Commencement 28 October 1971 (Royal Assent).

[A.1.40]
[31A Procedural requirements as to applications]
[(1) If a form is prescribed for a particular kind of application under this Act, any application of that kind must be made in the prescribed form.
(2) If procedural or other steps are prescribed in relation to a particular kind of application under this Act, those steps must be taken in respect of any application of that kind.
(3) 'Prescribed' means prescribed in regulations made by the Secretary of State.
(4) The power to make regulations under this section is exercisable by statutory instrument.
(5) Any such statutory instrument shall be subject to annulment in pursuance of a resolution of either House of Parliament.]

Note Inserted by the Immigration and Asylum Act 1999, s 165.

Commencement 22 May 2000 (for the purpose of enabling subordinate legislation to be made) (SI 2000/1282).

[A.1.41]
32 General provisions as to Orders in Council, etc
(1) Any power conferred by Part I of this Act to make an Order in Council or order (other than a deportation order) or to give any directions includes power to revoke or vary the Order in Council, order or directions.
(2) Any document purporting to be an order, notice or direction made or given by the Secretary of State for the purposes of [the Immigration Acts] and to be signed by him or on his behalf, and any document purporting to be a certificate of the Secretary of State so given and to be signed by him [or on his behalf], shall be received in evidence, and shall, until the contrary is proved, be deemed to be made or issued by him.
(3) Prima facie evidence of any such order, notice, direction or certificate as aforesaid may, in any legal proceedings or [other proceedings under the

Immigration Acts], be given by the production of a document bearing a certificate purporting to be signed by or on behalf of the Secretary of State and stating that the document is a true copy of the order, notice, direction or certificate.

(4) Where an order under section 8(2) above applies to persons specified in a schedule to the order, or any directions of the Secretary of State given for the purposes of [the Immigration Acts] apply to persons specified in a schedule to the directions, prima facie evidence of the provisions of the order or directions other than the schedule or any entry contained in the schedule may, in any legal proceedings or [other proceedings under the Immigration Acts], be given by the production of a document purporting to be signed by or on behalf of the Secretary of State and stating that the document is a true copy of the said provisions and of the relevant entry.

[(5) 'Immigration Acts' has the same meaning as in the Immigration and Asylum Act 1999.]

Commencement   28 October 1971 (Royal Assent).

Note   Sub-ss (2), (3), (4) amended and (5) added by Immigration and Asylum Act 1999, Sch 14, para 54.

[A.1.42]
33 Interpretation
(1)   For purposes of this Act, except in so far as the context otherwise requires:

'aircraft' includes hovercraft, 'airport' includes hoverport and 'port' includes airport;

'captain' means master (of a ship) or commander (of an aircraft);

'certificate of [entitlement]' means such a certificate as is referred to in section 3(9) above;

[. . .]

'crew', in relation to a ship or aircraft, means all persons actually employed in the working or service of the ship or aircraft, including the capital, and 'member of the crew' shall be construed accordingly;

['entrant' means a person entering or seeking to enter the United Kingdom and 'illegal entrant' means a person:

(a) unlawfully entering or seeking to enter in breach of a deportation order or of the immigration laws; or

(b) entering or seeking to enter by means which include deception by another person,

and includes also a person who has entered as mentioned in paragraph (a) or (b) above;]

'entry clearance' means a visa, entry certificate or other document which, in accordance with the immigration rules, is to be taken as evidence [or the requisite evidence] of a person's eligibility, though not [a British citizen], for entry into the United Kingdom (but does not include a work permit);

'immigration laws' means this Act and any law for purposes similar to this Act which is for the time being or has (before or after the passing of this Act) been in force in any part of the United Kingdom and Islands;

'immigration rules' means the rules for the time being laid down as mentioned in section 3(2) above;

'the islands' means the Channel Islands and the Isle of Man, and 'the United
    Kingdom and Islands' means the United Kingdom and the Islands taken
    together;
'legally adopted' means adopted in pursuance of an order made by any court
    in the United Kingdom and Islands or by any adoption specified as an over-
    seas adoption by order of the Secretary of State under [section 72(2) of the
    Adoption Act 1976];
'limited leave' and 'indefinite leave' mean respectively leave under this Act to
    enter or remain in the United Kingdom which is, and one which is not, lim-
    ited as to duration;
'settled' shall be construed in accordance [with subsection (2A) below];
'ship' includes every description of vessel used in navigation;
[. . .]
['United Kingdom passport' means a current passport issued by the Government
    of the United Kingdom, or by the Lieutenant — Governor of any of the
    Islands or by the Government of any territory which is for the time being a
    dependent territory within the meaning of the British Nationality Act 1981;]
'work permit' means a permit indicating, in accordance with the immigration
    rules, that a person named in it is eligible, though not [a British citizen], for
    entry into the United Kingdom for the purpose of taking employment.

(2)   It is hereby declared that, except as otherwise provided in this Act, a
person is not to be treated for the purposes of any provision of this Act as ordinarily resident in the United Kingdom or in any of the Islands at a time when
he is there in breach of the immigration laws.
[(2A)   Subject to section 8(5) above, references to a person being settled in
the United Kingdom are references to his being ordinarily resident there without being subject under the immigration laws to any restriction on the period
for which he may remain.]
(3)   The ports of entry for purposes of this Act, and the ports of exit for purposes of any Order in Council under section 3(7) above, shall be such ports as
may from time to time be designated for the purpose by order of the Secretary
of State made by statutory instrument.
[(4)   For the purposes of this Act, the question of whether an appeal is pending shall be determined:

   (a) in relation to an appeal to the Special Immigration Appeals
        Commission, in accordance with section 7A of the Special
        Immigration Appeals Commission Act 1997;
   (b) in any other case, in accordance with section 58(5) to (10) of the
        Immigration and Asylum Act 1999.]

(5)   This Act shall not be taken to supersede or impair any power exercisable
by Her Majesty in relation to aliens by virtue of Her prerogative.

Notes   Words in square brackets in sub-s (1) in definitions 'certificate of entitlement',
'entry clearance' (second pair only), 'settled', 'work permit' substituted, definition
'United Kingdom passport' inserted, by the BNA 1981, s 39(6), Sch 4, paras 2, 3(2), 7.
    First words in square brackets in definition 'entry clearance' in sub-s (1) inserted by
the IA 1988, s 10, Sch, para 5. Definitions of 'entrant' and 'illegal entrant' substituted
in sub-s (1) and first words in square brackets in sub-s (4) inserted by the Asylum and
Immigration Act 1996, Sch 2, para 4.
    Sub-s (1) in definition 'legally adopted' words in square brackets substituted by the
Adoption Act 1976, s 73(2), Sch 6, para 17.

Sub-s (2A) inserted by the BNA 1981, s 39(6), Sch 4, para 7.

Definitions of 'concessionaires' and 'tunnel system' originally added by SI 1990/2227, Sch 1, repealed by SI 1993/1813, art 9(1), Sch 6, Pt I.

Sub-s (4) substituted by the Immigration and Asylum Act 1999, s 169(1), Sch 14, paras 43, 55.

Commencement   28 October 1971 (Royal Assent).

[A.1.43]
34 Repeal, transitional and temporary
(1)   Subject to the following provisions of this section, the enactments mentioned in Schedule 6 to this Act are hereby repealed, as from the coming into force of this Act, to the extent mentioned in column 3 of the Schedule; and:

(*a*) this Act, as from its coming into force, shall apply in relation to entrants or others arriving in the United Kingdom at whatever date before or after it comes into force; and

(*b*) after this Act comes into force anything done under or for the purposes of the former immigration laws shall have effect, in so far as any corresponding action could be taken under or for the purposes of this Act, as if done by way of action so taken, and in relation to anything so done this Act shall apply accordingly.

(2)   Without prejudice to the generality of subsection (1)(*a*) and (*b*) above, a person refused leave to land by virtue of the Aliens Restriction Act 1914 shall be treated as having been refused leave to enter under this Act, and a person given leave to land by virtue of that Act shall be treated as having been given leave to enter under this Act; and similarly with the Commonwealth Immigrants Acts 1962 and 1968.

(3)   A person treated in accordance with subsection (2) above as having leave to enter the United Kingdom:

(*a*) shall be treated as having an indefinite leave, if he is not at the coming into force of this Act subject to a condition limiting his stay in the United Kingdom; and

(*b*) shall be treated, if he is then subject to such a condition, as having a limited leave of such duration, and subject to such conditions (capable of being attached to leave under this Act), as correspond to the conditions to which he is then subject, but not to conditions not capable of being so attached.

This subsection shall have effect in relation to any restriction or requirement imposed by Order in Council under the Aliens Restriction Act 1914 as if it had been imposed by way of a landing condition.

(4)   Notwithstanding anything in the foregoing provisions of this Act, the former immigration laws shall continue to apply, and this Act shall not apply:

(*a*) in relation to the making of deportation orders and matters connected therewith in any case where a decision to make the order has been notified to the person concerned before the coming into force of this Act;

(*b*) in relation to removal from the United Kingdom and matters connected therewith (including detention pending removal or pending the giving of directions for removal) in any case where a person is to be removed in pursuance of a decision taken before the coming into force of this Act or in pursuance of a deportation order to the making of which paragraph (*a*) above applies;

(*c*) in relation to appeals against any decision taken or other thing done under the former immigration laws, whether taken or done before the coming into force of this Act or by virtue of this subsection.

(5)   Subsection (1) above shall not be taken as empowering a court on appeal to recommend for deportation a person whom the court below could not recommend for deportation, or as affecting any right of appeal in respect of a recommendation for deportation made before this Act comes into force, or as enabling a notice given before this Act comes into force and not complying with section 6(2) to take the place of the notice required by section 6(2) to be given before a person is recommended for deportation. (6). . .

Notes   Sub-s (6) repealed by the Statute Law (Repeals) Act 1993, s 1, Sch 1, Pt XVI.

Commencement   28 October 1971 (Royal Assent).

[A.1.44]
35 Commencement, and interim provisions
(1)   Except as otherwise provided by this Act, Parts I to III of this Act shall come into force on such day as the Secretary of State may appoint by order made by statutory instrument; and references to the coming into force of this Act shall be construed as references to the beginning of the day so appointed.
(2)   Section 25 above, except section 25(2), and section 28 in its application to offences under section 25(1) shall come into force at the end of one month beginning with the date this Act is passed.
(3)–(5)   . . .

Notes   Sub-ss (3)-(5) repealed by the SL(R) Act 1986.

Commencement   28 October 1971 (Royal Assent).

[A.1.45]
36 Power to extend to Islands
Her Majesty may by Order in Council direct that any of the provisions of this Act shall extend, with such exceptions, adaptations and modifications, if any, as may be specified in the Order, to any of the Islands; and any Order in Council under this subsection may be varied or revoked by a further Order in Council.

Commencement   28 October 1971 (Royal Assent).

Order made   SI 1997/275 amending SI 1991/2630.

[A.1.46]
37 Short title and extent
(1)   This Act may be cited as the Immigration Act 1971.
(2)   It is hereby declared that this Act extends to Northern Ireland, and (without prejudice to an provision of Schedule 1 to this Act as to the extent of that Schedule) where an enactment repealed by this Act extends outside the United Kingdom, the repeal shall be of like extent.

Commencement   28 October 1971 (Royal Assent).

Schedules

(Schedule 1 repealed by the British Nationality Act 1981, s 52(8), Sch 9.)

SCHEDULE 2   ADMINISTRATIVE PROVISIONS AS TO CONTROL ON
ENTRY ETC (SECTION 4)

PART I
GENERAL PROVISIONS

[A.1.47]

Immigration officers and medical inspectors

1—(1)   Immigration officers for the purposes of this Act shall be appointed
by the Secretary of State, and he may arrange with the Commissioners of
Customs and Excise for the employment of officers of customs and excise as
immigration officers under this Act.
(2)   Medical inspectors for the purposes of this Act may be appointed by the
Secretary of State or, in Northern Ireland, by the Minister of Health and
Social Services or other appropriate Minister of the Government of Northern
Ireland in pursuance of arrangements made between that Minister and the
Secretary of State, and shall be fully qualified medical practitioners.
(3)   In the exercise of their functions under this Act immigration officers shall
act in accordance with such instructions (not inconsistent with the immigration
rules) as may be given them by the Secretary of State, and medical inspectors
shall act in accordance with such instructions as may be given them by the
Secretary of State, or in Northern Ireland, as may be given in pursuance of the
arrangements mentioned in sub-paragraph (2) above by the Minister making
appointments of medical inspectors in Northern Ireland.
(4)   An immigration officer or medical inspector may board any ship, [or air-
craft] for the purpose of exercising his functions under this Act.
(5)   An immigration officer, for the purpose of satisfying himself whether
there are persons he may wish to examine under paragraph 2 below,
may search any ship [or aircraft] and anything on board it, or any vehicle taken
off a ship or aircraft in which it has been brought to the United Kingdom.

Examination by immigration officers, and medical examination

2—(1)   An immigration officer may examine any persons who have arrived
in the United Kingdom by ship [or aircraft] (including transit passengers,
members of the crew and others not seeking to enter the United Kingdom) for
the purpose of determining:

(*a*) whether any of them is or is not [a British citizen]; and
(*b*) whether, if he is not, he may or may not enter the United Kingdom without leave; and
[(*c*) whether, if he may not:
    (i)   he has been given leave which is still in force;
    (ii) he should be given leave and for what period or on what conditions
        (if any), or
    (iii) he should be refused leave.]

(2) Any such person, if he is seeking to enter the United Kingdom, may be examined also by a medical inspector or by any qualified person carrying out a test or examination required by a medical inspector.

(3) A person, on being examined under this paragraph by an immigration officer or medical inspector, may be required in writing by him to submit to further examination; but a requirement under this sub-paragraph shall not prevent a person who arrives as a transit passenger, or as a member of the crew of a ship or aircraft, or for the purpose of joining a ship or aircraft as a member of the crew, from leaving by his intended ship or aircraft.

[Examination of persons who arrive with continuing leave

2A—(1) This paragraph applies to a person who has arrived in the United Kingdom with leave to enter which is in force but which was given to him before his arrival.

(2) He may be examined by an immigration officer for the purpose of establishing:

(*a*) whether there has been such a change in the circumstances of his case, since that leave was given, that it should be cancelled;

(*b*) whether that leave was obtained as a result of false information given by him or his failure to disclose material facts; or

(*c*) whether there are medical grounds on which that leave should be cancelled.

(3) He may also be examined by an immigration officer for the purpose of determining whether it would be conducive to the public good for that leave to be cancelled.

(4) He may also be examined by a medical inspector or by any qualified person carrying out a test or examination required by a medical inspector.

(5) A person examined under this paragraph may be required by the officer or inspector to submit to further examination.

(6) A requirement under sub-paragraph (5) does not prevent a person who arrives:

(*a*) as a transit passenger,

(*b*) as a member of the crew of a ship or aircraft, or

(*c*) for the purpose of joining a ship or aircraft as a member of the crew,

from leaving by his intended ship or aircraft.

(7) An immigration officer examining a person under this paragraph may by notice suspend his leave to enter until the examination is completed.

(8) An immigration officer may, on the completion of any examination of a person under this paragraph, cancel his leave to enter.

(9) Cancellation of a person's leave under sub-paragraph (8) is to be treated for the purposes of this Act and Part IV of the Immigration and Asylum Act 1999 as if he had been refused leave to enter at a time when he had a current entry clearance.

(10) A requirement imposed under sub-paragraph (5) and a notice given under sub-paragraph (7) must be in writing.]

3—(1) An immigration officer may examine any person who is embarking or seeking to embark in the United Kingdom [. . .] for the purpose of determining whether he is [a British citizen] and, if he is not, for the purpose of establishing his identity.

(2)   So long as any Order in Council is in force under section 3(7) of this Act, an immigration officer may examine any person who is embarking or seeking to embark in the United Kingdom [. . .] for the purpose of determining:

(*a*) whether any of the provisions of the Order apply to him; and
(*b*) whether, if so, any power conferred by the Order should be exercised in relation to him and in what way.

Information and documents

4—(1)   It shall be the duty of any person examined under paragraph 2[, 2A] or 3 above to furnish to the person carrying out the examination all such information in his possession as that person may require for the purpose of his functions under that paragraph.
(2)   A person on his examination under paragraph 2[, 2A] or 3 above by an immigration officer shall, if so required by the immigration officer:

(*a*) produce either a valid passport with photograph or some other document satisfactorily establishing his identity and nationality or citizenship; and
(*b*) declare whether or not he is carrying or conveying [, or has carried or conveyed,] documents of any relevant description specified by the immigration officer, and produce any documents of that description which he is carrying or conveying.

   In paragraph (*b*), 'relevant description' means any description appearing to the immigration officer to be relevant for the purposes of the examination.
[(2A)   An immigration officer may detain any passport or other document produced pursuant to sub-paragraph (2)(*a*) above until the person concerned is given leave to enter the United Kingdom or is about to depart or be removed following refusal to leave.]
(3)   Where under sub-paragraph (2)(*b*) above a person has been required to declare whether or not he is carrying or conveying [, or has carried or conveyed,] documents of any description,

[(*a*) he and any baggage or vehicle belonging to him or under his control; and
(*b*) any ship, aircraft or vehicle in which he arrived in the United Kingdom,]

may be searched with a view to ascertaining whether he is doing [or, as the case may be, has done] so by the immigration officer or a person acting under the directions of that officer:
   Provided that no woman or girl shall be searched except by a woman.
(4)   An immigration officer may examine any documents produced pursuant to sub-paragraph (2)(*b*) above or found on a search under sub-paragraph (3), and may for that purpose detain them for any period not exceeding seven days; and if on examination of any document so produced or found the immigration officer is of the opinion that it may be needed in connection with proceedings on an appeal under this Act or for an offence, he may detain it until he is satisfied that it will not be so needed.
5—The Secretary of State may by order made by statutory instrument make provision for requiring passengers disembarking or embarking in the United Kingdom, or any class of such passengers, to produce to an immigration officer, if so required, landing or embarkation cards in such form as the Secretary of State may direct, and for requiring the owners or agents of ships and aircraft to supply such cards to those passengers.

Notice of leave to enter or of refusal to leave

6—(1)   Subject to sub-paragraph (3) below, where a person examined by an immigration officer under paragraph 2 above is to be given a limited leave to enter the United Kingdom or is to be refused leave, the notice giving or refusing leave shall be given not later than [twenty-four hours] after the conclusion of his examination (including any further examination) in pursuance of that paragraph; and if notice giving or refusing leave is not given him before the end of those [twenty-four hours], he shall (if not [a British citizen]) be deemed to have been given [leave to enter the United Kingdom for a period of six months subject to a condition prohibiting his taking employment] and the immigration officer shall as soon as may be give him written notice of that leave.

(2)   Where on a person's examination under paragraph 2 above he is given notice of leave to enter the United Kingdom, then at any time before the end of [twenty-four hours] from the conclusion of the examination he may be given a further notice in writing by an immigration officer cancelling the earlier notice and refusing him leave to enter.

(3)   Where in accordance with this paragraph a person is given notice refusing him leave to enter the United Kingdom, that notice may at any time be cancelled by notice in writing given him by an immigration officer; and where a person is given a notice of cancellation under this sub-paragraph, [and the immigration officer does not at the same time give him indefinite or limited leave to enter, he shall be deemed to have been given leave to enter for a period of six months subject to a condition prohibiting his taking employment and the immigration officer shall as soon as may be give him written notice of that leave.]

(4)   Where an entrant is a member of a party in charge of a person appearing to the immigration officer to be a responsible person, any notice to be given in relation to that entrant in accordance with this paragraph shall be duly given if delivered to the person in charge of the party.

[Power to require medical examination after entry

7—(1)   This paragraph applies if an immigration officer examining a person under paragraph 2 decides:

(*a*)   that he may be given leave to enter the United Kingdom; but
(*b*)   that a further medical test or examination may be required in the interests of public health.

(2)   This paragraph also applies if an immigration officer examining a person under paragraph 2A decides:

(*a*)   that his leave to enter the United Kingdom should not be cancelled; but
(*b*)   that a further medical test or examination may be required in the interests of public health.

(3)   The immigration officer may give the person concerned notice in writing requiring him:

(*a*)   to report his arrival to such medical officer of health as may be specified in the notice; and
(*b*)   to attend at such place and time and submit to such test or examination (if any), as that medical officer of health may require.

(4)   In reaching a decision under paragraph (b) of sub-paragraph (1) or (2), the immigration officer must act on the advice of:

(*a*) a medical inspector; or

(*b*) if no medical inspector is available, a fully qualified medical practitioner.]

Removal of persons refused leave to enter and illegal entrants

8—(1)   Where a person arriving in the United Kingdom is refused leave to enter, an immigration officer may, subject to sub-paragraph (2) below:

(*a*) give the captain of the ship or aircraft in which he arrives directions requiring the capital to remove him from the United Kingdom in that ship or aircraft; or

(*b*) give those owners or agents of that ship or aircraft directions requiring them to remove him from the United Kingdom in any ship or aircraft specified or indicated in the directions, being a ship or aircraft of which they are the owners or agents; or

(*c*) give the owners or agents [. . .] directions requiring them to make arrangements for his removal from the United Kingdom in any ship or aircraft specified or indicated in the direction to a country or territory so specified, being either:

   (i) a country of which he is a national or citizen; or

   (ii) a country or territory in which he has obtained a passport or other document of identity; or

   (iii) a country or territory in which he embarked for the United Kingdom; or

   (iv) a country or territory to which there is reason to believe that he will be admitted.

(2)   No directions shall be given under this paragraph in respect of anyone after the expiration of two months beginning with the date on which he was refused leave to enter the United Kingdom [except that directions may be given under sub-paragraph (1)(*b*) or (*c*) after the end of that period if the immigration officer has within that period given written notice to the owners or agents in question of his intention to give directions to them in respect of that person].

9—[(1)]   Where an illegal entrant is not given leave to enter or remain in the United Kingdom, an immigration officer may give any such directions in respect of his as in the case within paragraph 8 above are authorised by paragraph 8(1).

[(2)   Any leave to enter the United Kingdom which is obtained by deception shall be disregarded for the purposes of this paragraph.]

10—(1)   Where it appears to the Secretary of State either:

(*a*) that directions might be given in respect of a person under paragraph 8 or 9 above, but that it is not practicable for them to be given or that, if given, they would be ineffective; or

(*b*) that directions might have been given in respect of a person under paragraph 8 above [but that the requirements of paragraph 8(2) have not been complied with];

then the Secretary of State may give to the owners or agents of any ship or aircraft any such directions in respect of that person as are authorised by paragraph 8(1)(*c*).

(2)   Where the Secretary of State may give directions for a person's removal in accordance with sub-paragraph (1) above, he may instead give directions for his removal in accordance with arrangements to be made by the Secretary of State to any country or territory to which he could be removed under sub-paragraph (1).

(3)   The costs of complying with any directions given under this paragraph shall be defrayed by the Secretary of State.

11   A person in respect of whom directions are given under any of paragraphs 8 to 10 above may be placed, under the authority of an immigration officer, on board any ship or aircraft in which he is to be removed in accordance with the directions.

Seamen and aircrews

12—(1)   If, on a person's examination by an immigration officer under paragraph 2 above, the immigration officer is satisfied that he has come to the United Kingdom for the purpose of joining a ship or aircraft as a member of the crew, then the immigration officer may limit the duration of any leave he gives that person to enter the United Kingdom by requiring him to leave the United Kingdom in a ship or aircraft specified or indicated by the notice giving leave.

(2)   Where a person (not being [a British citizen] arrives in the United Kingdom for the purpose of joining a ship or aircraft as a member of the crew, and having been given leave to enter as mentioned in sub-paragraph (1) above, remains beyond the time limited by that leave, or is reasonably suspected by an immigration officer of intending to do so, an immigration officer may:

(*a*)   give the captain of that ship or aircraft directions requiring the captain to remove him from the United Kingdom in that ship or aircraft; or

(*b*)   give the owners or agents of that ship or aircraft directions requiring them to remove him from the United Kingdom in any ship or aircraft specified or indicated in the directions, being a ship or aircraft of which they are the owners or agents; or

(*c*)   give those owners or agents directions requiring them to make arrangements for his removal from the United Kingdom in any ship or aircraft specified or indicated in the directions to a country or territory so specified, being either:

(i) a country of which he is a national or citizen; or

(ii) a country or territory in which he has obtained a passport or other document of identity; or

(iii) a country or territory in which he embarked for the United Kingdom; or

(iv) a country or territory where he was engaged as a member of the crew of the ship or aircraft which he arrived in the United Kingdom to join; or

(v) a country of territory to which there is reason to believe that he will be admitted.

13—(1)   Where a person being a member of the crew of a ship or aircraft is examined by an immigration officer under paragraph 2 above, the immigration officer may limit the duration of any leave he gives that person to enter the United Kingdom:

(*a*) in the manner authorised by paragraph 12(1) above; or

(*b*) if that person is to be allowed to enter the United Kingdom in order to receive hospital treatment, by requiring him, on completion of that treatment, to leave the United Kingdom in accordance with arrangements to be made for his repatriation; or

(*c*) by requiring him to leave the United Kingdom within a specified period in accordance with arrangements to be made for his repatriation.

(2)   Where a person (not being [a British citizen]) arrives in the United Kingdom as a member of the crew of a ship or aircraft, and either:

(*a*) having lawfully entered the United Kingdom without leave by virtue of section 8(1) of this Act, he remains without leave beyond the time allowed by section 8(1), or is reasonably suspected by an immigration officer of intending to do so; or

(*b*) having been given leave limited as mentioned in sub-paragraph (1) above, he remains beyond the time limited by that leave, or is reasonably suspected by an immigration officer of intending to do so;

an immigration officer may:

(*a*) give the captain of the ship or aircraft in which he arrived directions requiring the captain to remove him from the United Kingdom in that ship or aircraft; or

(*b*) give the owners or agents of that ship or aircraft directions requiring them to remove him from the United Kingdom, being a ship or aircraft specified or indicated in the directions, being a ship or aircraft of which they are the owners or agents; or

(*c*) give those owners or agents directions requiring them to make arrangements for his removal from the United Kingdom in any ship or aircraft specified or indicated in the directions to a country or territory so specified, being either:

(i) a country of which he is a national or citizen; or

(ii) a country or territory in which he has obtained a passport or other document of identity; or

(iii) a country in which he embarked for the United Kingdom; or

(iv) a country or territory in which he was engaged as a member of the crew of the ship or aircraft in which he arrived in the United Kingdom; or

(v) a country or territory in which there is reason to believe that he will be admitted.

14—(1)   Where it appears to the Secretary of State that directions might be given in respect of a person under paragraph 12 or 13 above, but that it is not practicable for them to be given or that, if given, they would be ineffective, then the Secretary of State may give to the owners or agents of any ship or aircraft any such directions in respect of that person as are authorised by paragraph 12(2)(*c*) or 13(2)(*c*).

(2)   Where the Secretary of State may give directions for a person's removal in accordance with sub-paragraph (1) above, he may instead give directions for his removal in accordance with arrangements to be made by the Secretary of State to any country or territory to which he could be removed under sub-paragraph (1).

(3)   The costs of complying with any directions given under this paragraph shall be defrayed by the Secretary of State.

15   A person in respect of whom directions are given under any of paragraphs 12 to 14 above may be placed, under the authority of an immigration officer, on board any ship or aircraft in which he is to be removed in accordance with the directions.

Detention of persons liable to examination or removal

16—(1)   A person who may be required to submit to examination under paragraph 2 above may be detained under the authority of an immigration officer pending his examination and pending a decision to give or refuse him leave to enter.

[(1A)   A person whose leave to enter has been suspended under paragraph 2A may be detained under the authority of an immigration officer pending:

(*a*)   completion of his examination under that paragraph; and
(*b*)   a decision on whether to cancel his leave to enter.]

[(2)   If there are reasonable grounds for suspecting that a person is someone in respect of whom directions may be given under any of paragraphs 8 to 10 or 12 to 14, that person may be detained under the authority of an immigration officer pending:

(*a*)   a decision whether or not to give such directions;
(*b*)   his removal in pursuance of such directions.]

(3)   A person on board a ship or aircraft may, under the authority of an immigration office, be removed from the ship or aircraft for detention under this paragraph; but if an immigration officer so requires the capital of a ship or aircraft shall prevent from disembarking in the United Kingdom any person who has arrived in the United Kingdom in the ship or aircraft and been refused leave to enter, and the captain may for that purpose detain him in custody on board the ship or aircraft.

(4)   The capital of a ship or aircraft, if so required by an immigration officer, shall prevent form disembarking in the United Kingdom or before the directions for his removal have been fulfilled any person placed on board the ship or aircraft under paragraph 11 or 15 above, and the captain may for that purpose detain him in custody on board the ship or aircraft.

[(4A)   . . .]

17—(1)   A person liable to be detained under paragraph 16 above may be arrested without warrant by a constable or by an immigration officer.

(2)   If:

(*a*)   a justice of the peace is by written information on oath satisfied that there is reasonable ground for suspecting that a person liable to be arrested under this paragraph is to be found on any premises; or
(*b*)   (*applies to Scotland only*);

he may grant a warrant authorising any constable. . . or in Northern Ireland any constable, . . . to enter, if need be by force, the premises named in the warrant for the purposes of searching for and arresting that person.

18—(1)   Persons may be detained under paragraph 16 above in such places as the Secretary of State may direct (when not detained in accordance with paragraph 16 on board a ship or aircraft).

(2)   Where a person is detained under paragraph 16, any immigration officer,

constable or prison officer, or any other person authorised by the Secretary of State, may take all such steps as may be reasonably necessary for photographing, measuring or otherwise identifying him.

[(2A) The power conferred by sub-paragraph (2) includes power to take fingerprints.]

(3) Any person detained under paragraph 16 may be taken in the custody of a constable, or of any person acting under the authority of an immigration officer, to and from any place where his attendance is required for the purpose of ascertaining his citizenship or nationality or of making arrangements for his admission to a country or territory other than the United Kingdom, or where he is required to be for any other purpose connected with the operation of this Act.

(4) A person shall be deemed to be in legal custody at any time when he is detained under paragraph 16 or is being removed in pursuance of sub-paragraph (3) above.

19—(1) Where a person is refused leave to enter the United Kingdom and directions are given in respect of him under paragraph 8 or 10 above, then subject to the provisions of this paragraph the owners or agents of the ship or aircraft in which he arrived [. . .] shall be liable to pay the Secretary of State on demand any expenses incurred by the latter in respect of the custody, accommodation or maintenance of that person [for any period (not exceeding 14 days)] after his arrival while he was detained or liable to be detained under paragraph 16 above.

(2) Sub-paragraph (1) above shall not apply to expenses in respect of a person who, when he arrived in the United Kingdom, held a [certificate of entitlement] or a current entry clearance or was the person named in a current work permit; and for this purpose a document purporting to be a [certificate of entitlement], entry clearance or work permit is to be regarded as being one unless its falsity is reasonably apparent.

(3) If, before the directions for a person's removal under paragraph 8 or 10 above have been carried out, he is given leave to enter the United Kingdom, or if he is afterwards given that leave in consequence of the determination in his favour of an appeal under this Act (being an appeal against a refusal of leave to enter by virtue of which the directions were given), or it is determined on an appeal under this Act that he does not require leave to enter (being an appeal occasioned by such a refusal), no sum shall be demanded under subparagraph (1) above for expenses incurred in respect of that person and any sum already demanded and paid shall be refunded.

(4) Sub-paragraph (1) above shall not have effect in relation to directions which, in consequence of an appeal under this Act, have ceased to have effect or are for the time being of no effect; and the expenses to which that sub-paragraph applies include expenses in conveying the person in question to and from the place where he is detained or accommodated unless the journey is made for the purpose of attending an appeal by him under this Act.

20—(1) Subject to the provisions of this paragraph, in either of the following cases, that is to say:

(*a*) where directions are given in respect of an illegal entrant under paragraph 9 or 10 above; and

(*b*) where a person lawfully entered the United Kingdom without leave by virtue of section 8(1) of this Act, but directions are given in respect of him under paragraph 13(2)(A) above or, in a case within paragraph 13(2)(A), under paragraph 14;

the owners or agents of the ship or aircraft in which he arrived in the United Kingdom [. . .] shall be liable to pay the Secretary of State on demand any expenses incurred by the latter in respect of the custody, accommodation or maintenance of that person [for any period (not exceeding 14 days)] after his arrival while he was detained or liable to be detained under paragraph 16 above.

[(1A) Sub-paragraph (1) above shall not apply to expenses in respect of an illegal entrant if he obtained leave to enter by deception and the leave has not been cancelled under paragraph 6(2) above.]

(2) If, before the directions for a person's removal from the United Kingdom have been carried out, he is given leave to remain in the United Kingdom, no sum shall be demanded under sub-paragraph (1) above for expenses incurred in respect of that person and any sum already demanded and paid shall be refunded.

(3) Sub-paragraph (1) above shall not have effect in relation to directions which, in consequence of an appeal under this Act, are for the time being of no effect; and the expenses to which that sub-paragraph applies include expenses in conveying the person in question to and from the place where he is detained or accommodated unless the journey is made for the purpose of attending an appeal by him under this Act.

Temporary admission or release of persons liable to detention

21—(1) A person liable to detention or detained under paragraph 16 above may, under the written authority of an immigration officer, be temporarily admitted to the United Kingdom without being detained or be released from detention; but this shall not prejudice a later exercise of the power to detain him.

(2) So long as a person is at large in the United Kingdom by virtue of this paragraph, he shall be subject to such restrictions as to residence [, as to his employment or occupation] and as to reporting to the police or an immigration officer as may from time to time be notified to him in writing by an immigration officer.

[(2A) The provisions that may be included in restrictions as to residence imposed under sub-paragraph (2) include provisions of such a description as may be prescribed by regulations made by the Secretary of State.

(2B) The regulations may, among other things, provide for the inclusion of provisions:

(a) prohibiting residence in one or more particular areas;

(b) requiring the person concerned to reside in accommodation provided under section 4 of the Immigration and Asylum Act 1999 and prohibiting him from being absent from that accommodation except in accordance with the restrictions imposed on him.

(2C) The regulations may provide that a particular description of provision may be imposed only for prescribed purposes.

(2D) The power to make regulations conferred by this paragraph is exercisable by statutory instrument and includes a power to make different provision for different cases.

(2E) But no regulations under this paragraph are to be made unless a draft of the regulations has been laid before Parliament and approved by a resolution of each House.]

[(3) Sub-paragraph (4) below applies where a person who is at large in the United Kingdom by virtue of this paragraph is subject to a restriction as to reporting to an immigration officer with a view to the conclusion of his examination under paragraph 2 [or 2A] above.

(4) If the person fails at any time to comply with that restriction:

(a) an immigration officer may direct that the person's examination . . . shall be treated as concluded at that time; but

(b) nothing in paragraph 6 above shall require the notice giving or refusing him leave to enter the United Kingdom to be given within twenty-four hours after that time.]

22—[(1) The following, namely:

(a) a person detained under paragraph 16(1) above pending examination; and

[(aa) a person detained under paragraph 16(1A) above pending completion of his examination or a decision on whether to cancel his leave to enter;]

(b) a person detained under paragraph 16(2) above pending the giving of directions,

may be released on bail in accordance with this paragraph.

(1A) An immigration officer not below the rank of chief immigration officer or an adjudicator may release a person so detained on his entering into a recognizance or, in Scotland, bail bond conditioned for his appearance before an immigration officer at a time and place named in the recognizance or bail bond or at such other time and place as may in the meantime be notified to him in writing by an immigration officer.

(1B) Sub-paragraph (1)(a) above shall not apply unless seven days have elapsed since the date of the person's arrival in the United Kingdom.]

(2) The conditions of a recognizance or bail bond taken under this paragraph may include conditions appearing to the [immigration officer or adjudicator] to be likely to result in the appearance of the person bailed at the required time and place; and any recognizance shall be with or without sureties as the [officer or adjudicator] may determine.

(3) In any case in which an [immigration officer or adjudicator] has power under this paragraph to release a person on bail, the [officer or adjudicator] may, instead of taking the bail, fix the amount and conditions of the bail (including the amount in which any sureties are to be bound) with a view to its being taken subsequently by any such person as may be specified by the [officer or adjudicator]; and on the recognizance or bail bond being so taken the person to be bailed shall be released.

23—(1) Where a recognizance entered into under paragraph 22 above appears to be an adjudicator to be forfeited, the adjudicator may by order declare it to be forfeited and adjudge the persons bound thereby, whether as principal or sureties, or any of them, to pay the sum in which they are respectively bound or such part of it, if any, as the adjudicator thinks fit; and an order under this sub-paragraph shall specify a magistrates' court or, in Northern Ireland court of summary jurisdiction, and:

(a) the recognizance shall be treated for the purposes of collection, enforcement and remission of the sum forfeited as having been forfeited by the court so specified; and (*b*)   the adjudicator shall, as soon as practicable, give particulars of the recognizance to the clerk of that court.

(2)   (*Applies to Scotland only.*)

(3)   Any sum the payment of which is enforceable by a magistrates' court in England and Wales by virtue of this paragraph shall be treated for the purposes of the [Justices of the Peace Act 1979 and, in particular, section 61 thereof] as being due under a recognizance forfeited by such a court. . .

(4)   Any sum the payment of which is enforceable by virtue of this paragraph by a court of summary jurisdiction in Northern Ireland shall, for the purposes of section 20(5) of the Administration of Justice Act (Northern Ireland) 1954, be treated as a forfeited recognizance.

24—(1)   An immigration officer or constable may arrest without warrant a person who has been released by virtue of paragraph 22 above:

(*a*)   if he has reasonable grounds for believing that that person is likely to break the condition of his recognizance or bail bond that he will appear at the time and place required or to break any other condition of it, or has reasonable ground to suspect that that person is breaking or has broken any such other condition; or

(*b*)   if, a recognizance with sureties having been taken, he is notified in writing by any sureties of the survey's belief that that person is likely to break the first-mentioned condition, and of the surety's wish for that reason to be relieved of his obligation as a surety;

and paragraph 17(2) above shall apply for the arrest of a person under this paragraph as it applies for the arrest of a person under paragraph 17.

(2)   A person arrested under this paragraph:

(*a*)   if not required by a condition on which he was released to appear before an immigration officer within twenty-four hours after the time of his arrest, shall as soon as practicable be brought before an adjudicator or, if that is not practicable within those twenty-four hours, before a justice of the peace acting for the petty sessions area in which he is arrested or, in Scotland, the sheriff; and

(*b*)   if required by such a condition to appear within those twenty-four hours before an immigration officer, shall be brought before that officer.

(3)   An adjudicator, justice of the peace or sheriff before whom a person is brought by virtue of sub-paragraph (2)(*a*) above

(*a*)   if of the opinion that that person has broken or is likely to break any condition on which he was released, may either:
   (i)   direct that he be detained under the authority of the person by whom he was arrested; or
   (ii)   release him, on his original recognizance or on a new recognizance, with or without sureties, or, in Scotland, on his original bail or on new bail; and

(*b*)   if not of that opinion, shall release him on his original recognizance or bail.

25   The power to make rules of procedure conferred by section 22 of this Act shall include power to make rules with respect to applications to an adjudicator under paragraphs 22 to 24 above and matters arising out of such applications.

[Entry and search of premises

25A—(1)   This paragraph applies if:

(*a*)   a person is arrested under this Schedule; or
(*b*)   a person who was arrested by a constable (other than under this Schedule) is detained by an immigration officer under this Schedule.

(2)   An immigration officer may enter and search any premises:

(*a*)   occupied or controlled by the arrested person, or
(*b*)   in which that person was when he was arrested, or immediately before he was arrested,

for relevant documents.

(3)   The power may be exercised:

(*a*)   only if the officer has reasonable grounds for believing that there are relevant documents on the premises;
(*b*)   only to the extent that it is reasonably required for the purpose of discovering relevant documents; and
(*c*)   subject to sub-paragraph (4), only if a senior officer has authorised its exercise in writing.

(4)   An immigration officer may conduct a search under sub-paragraph (2):

(*a*)   before taking the arrested person to a place where he is to be detained; and
(*b*)   without obtaining an authorisation under sub-paragraph (3)(c),

if the presence of that person at a place other than one where he is to be detained is necessary to make an effective search for any relevant documents.
(5)   An officer who has conducted a search under sub-paragraph (4) must inform a senior officer as soon as is practicable.
(6)   The officer authorising a search, or who is informed of one under sub-paragraph (5), must make a record in writing of:

(*a*)   the grounds for the search; and
(*b*)   the nature of the documents that were sought.

(7)   An officer searching premises under sub-paragraph (2):

(*a*)   may seize and retain any documents he finds which he has reasonable grounds for believing are relevant documents; but
(*b*)   may not retain any such document for longer than is necessary in view of the purpose for which the person was arrested.

(8)   But sub-paragraph (7)(a) does not apply to documents which the officer has reasonable grounds for believing are items subject to legal privilege.
(9)   'Relevant documents' means any documents which might:

(*a*)   establish the arrested person's identity, nationality or citizenship; or
(*b*)   indicate the place from which he has travelled to the United Kingdom or to which he is proposing to go.

(10)   'Senior officer' means an immigration officer not below the rank of chief immigration officer.]

[Searching persons arrested by immigration officers

25B—(1)   This paragraph applies if a person is arrested under this Schedule.
(2)   An immigration officer may search the arrested person if he has reasonable grounds for believing that the arrested person may present a danger to himself or others.
(3)   The officer may search the arrested person for:

(*a*) anything which he might use to assist his escape from lawful custody; or
(*b*) any document which might:

> (i)   establish his identity, nationality or citizenship; or
> (ii) indicate the place from which he has travelled to the United Kingdom or to which he is proposing to go.

(4)   The power conferred by sub-paragraph (3) may be exercised:

(*a*) only if the officer has reasonable grounds for believing that the arrested person may have concealed on him anything of a kind mentioned in that sub-paragraph; and
(*b*) only to the extent that it is reasonably required for the purpose of discovering any such thing.

(5)   A power conferred by this paragraph to search a person is not to be read as authorising an officer to require a person to remove any of his clothing in public other than an outer coat, jacket or glove; but it does authorise the search of a person's mouth.
(6)   An officer searching a person under sub-paragraph (2) may seize and retain anything he finds, if he has reasonable grounds for believing that the person searched might use it to cause physical injury to himself or to another person.
(7)   An officer searching a person under sub-paragraph (3)(a) may seize and retain anything he finds, if he has reasonable grounds for believing that he might use it to assist his escape from lawful custody.
(8)   An officer searching a person under sub-paragraph (3)(b) may seize and retain anything he finds, other than an item subject to legal privilege, if he has reasonable grounds for believing that it might be a document falling within that sub-paragraph.
(9)   Nothing seized under sub-paragraph (6) or (7) may be retained when the person from whom it was seized:

(*a*) is no longer in custody, or
(*b*) is in the custody of a court but has been released on bail.]

[Searching persons in police custody

25C—(1)   This paragraph applies if a person:

(*a*) has been arrested under this Schedule; and
(*b*) is in custody at a police station.

(2)   An immigration officer may, at any time, search the arrested person in order to ascertain whether he has with him:

(*a*) anything which he might use to:
> (i)   cause physical injury to himself or others;
> (ii) damage property;

(iii) interfere with evidence; or

(iv) assist his escape; or

(b) any document which might:

(i) establish his identity, nationality or citizenship; or

(ii) indicate the place from which he has travelled to the United Kingdom or to which he is proposing to go.

(3)   The power may be exercised only to the extent that the officer considers it to be necessary for the purpose of discovering anything of a kind mentioned in sub-paragraph (2).

(4)   An officer searching a person under this paragraph may seize and retain anything he finds, if he has reasonable grounds for believing that:

(a) that person might use it for one or more of the purposes mentioned in sub-paragraph (2)(a); or

(b) it might be a document falling within sub-paragraph (2)(b).

(5)   But the officer may not retain anything seized under sub-paragraph (2)(a):

(a) for longer than is necessary in view of the purpose for which the search was carried out; or

(b) when the person from whom it was seized is no longer in custody or is in the custody of a court but has been released on bail.

(6)   The person from whom something is seized must be told the reason for the seizure unless he is:

(a) violent or appears likely to become violent; or

(b) incapable of understanding what is said to him.

(7)   An intimate search may not be conducted under this paragraph.

(8)   The person carrying out a search under this paragraph must be of the same sex as the person searched.

(9)   'Intimate search' has the same meaning as in section 28H(11).]

[Access and copying

25D—(1)   If a person showing himself:

(a) to be the occupier of the premises on which seized material was seized, or

(b) to have had custody or control of the material immediately before it was seized,

asks the immigration officer who seized the material for a record of what he seized, the officer must provide the record to that person within a reasonable time.

(2)   If a relevant person asks an immigration officer for permission to be granted access to seized material, the officer must arrange for that person to have access to the material under the supervision of an immigration officer.

(3)   An immigration officer may photograph or copy, or have photographed or copied, seized material.

(4)   If a relevant person asks an immigration officer for a photograph or copy of seized material, the officer must arrange for:

(a) that person to have access to the material under the supervision of an immigration officer for the purpose of photographing or copying it; or (*b*) the material to be photographed or copied.

(5)   A photograph or copy made under sub-paragraph (4)(b) must be supplied within a reasonable time.

(6)   There is no duty under this paragraph to arrange for access to, or the supply of a photograph or copy of, any material if there are reasonable grounds for believing that to do so would prejudice:

(*a*) the exercise of any functions in connection with which the material was seized; or

(*b*) an investigation which is being conducted under this Act, or any criminal proceedings which may be brought as a result.

(7)   'Relevant person' means:

(*a*) a person who had custody or control of seized material immediately before it was seized, or

(*b*) someone acting on behalf of such a person.

(8)   'Seized material' means anything which has been seized and retained under this Schedule.]

[**25E**   Section 28L applies for the purposes of this Schedule as it applies for the purposes of Part III.]

Supplementary duties of those connected with ships or aircraft or with ports

26—(1)   The owners or agents of a ship or aircraft employed to carry passengers for reward shall not, without the approval of the Secretary of State, arrange for the ship or aircraft to call at a port in the United Kingdom other than a port of entry for the purpose of disembarking passengers, if any of the passengers on board may not enter the United Kingdom without leave . . ., or for the purpose of embarking passengers unless the owners or agents have reasonable cause to believe all of them to be [British citizens].

[(1A)   Sub-paragraph (1) does not apply in such circumstances, if any, as the Secretary of State may by order prescribe.]

(2)   The Secretary of State may from time to time give written notice to the owners or agents of any ships or aircraft designating control areas for the embarkation or disembarkation of passengers in any port in the United Kingdom and specifying the conditions and restrictions (if any) to be observed in any control area; and where by notice given to any owners or agents a control area is for the time being designated for the embarkation or disembarkation of passengers at any port, the owners or agents shall take all reasonable steps to secure that, in the case of their ships or aircraft, passengers do not embark or disembark, as the case may be, at the port outside the control area and that any conditions or restrictions notified to them are observed.

(3)   The Secretary of State may also from time to time give to any persons concerned with the management of a port in the United Kingdom written notice designation control areas in the port and specifying conditions or restrictions to be observed in any control area; and any such person shall take all reasonable steps to secure that any conditions or restrictions as notified to him are observed.

[(3A)   The power conferred by sub-paragraph (1A) is exercisable by statutory instrument; and any such instrument shall be subject to annulment by a resolution of either House of Parliament.]

27—(1)   The captain of a ship or aircraft arriving in the United Kingdom:

(*a*) shall take such steps as may be necessary to secure that persons on board do not disembark there unless either they have been examined by an immigration officer, or they disembark in accordance with arrangements approved by an immigration officer, or they are members of the crew who may lawfully enter the United Kingdom without leave by virtue of section 8(1) of this Act; and

(*b*) where the examination of persons on board is to be carried out on the ship or aircraft, shall take such steps as may be necessary to secure that those to be examined are presented for the purpose in an orderly manner.

(2)   The Secretary of State may by order made by statutory instrument make provision for requiring captains of ships or aircraft arriving in the United Kingdom or of such of them as arrive from or by way of countries or place specified in the order, to furnish to immigration officers:

(*a*) a passenger list showing the names and nationality or citizenship of passengers arriving on board the ship or aircraft;

(*b*) particulars of members of the crew of the ship or aircraft;

and for enabling an immigration officer to dispense with the furnishing of any such list or particulars.

[27A . . .]

[Passenger information

27B—(1)   This paragraph applies to ships or aircraft:

(a) which have arrived, or are expected to arrive, in the United Kingdom; or

(b) which have left, or are expected to leave, the United Kingdom.

(2)   If an immigration officer asks the owner or agent ('the carrier') of a ship or aircraft for passenger information, the carrier must provide that information to the officer.

(3)   The officer may ask for passenger information relating to:

(a) a particular ship or particular aircraft of the carrier;

(b) particular ships or aircraft (however described) of the carrier; or

(c) all of the carrier's ships or aircraft.

(4)   The officer may ask for:

(a) all passenger information in relation to the ship or aircraft concerned; or

(b) particular passenger information in relation to that ship or aircraft.

(5)   A request under sub-paragraph (2):

(a) must be in writing;

(b) must state the date on which it ceases to have effect; and

(c) continues in force until that date, unless withdrawn earlier by written notice by an immigration officer.

(6)   The date may not be later than six months after the request is made.

(7)   The fact that a request under sub-paragraph (2) has ceased to have effect as a result of sub-paragraph (5) does not prevent the request from being renewed.
(8)   The information must be provided:

(a) in such form and manner as the Secretary of State may direct; and
(b) at such time as may be stated in the request.

(9)   'Passenger information' means such information relating to the passengers carried, or expected to be carried, by the ship or aircraft as may be specified.
(10)   'Specified' means specified in an order made by statutory instrument by the Secretary of State.
(11)   Such an instrument shall be subject to annulment in pursuance of a resolution of either House of Parliament.]

[*Notification of non-EEA arrivals*

27C—(1)   If a senior officer, or an immigration officer authorised by a senior officer, gives written notice to the owner or agent ('the carrier') of a ship or aircraft, the carrier must inform a relevant officer of the expected arrival in the United Kingdom of any ship or aircraft:

(a) of which he is the owner or agent; and
(b) which he expects to carry a person who is not an EEA national.

(2)   The notice may relate to:

(a) a particular ship or particular aircraft of the carrier;
(b) particular ships or aircraft (however described) of the carrier; or
(c) all of the carrier's ships or aircraft.

(3)   The notice:

(a) must state the date on which it ceases to have effect; and
(b) continues in force until that date, unless withdrawn earlier by written notice given by a senior officer.

(4)   The date may not be later than six months after the notice is given.
(5)   The fact that a notice under sub-paragraph (1) has ceased to have effect as a result of sub-paragraph (3) does not prevent the notice from being renewed.
(6)   The information must be provided:

(a) in such form and manner as the notice may require; and
(b) before the ship or aircraft concerned departs for the United Kingdom.

(7)   If a ship or aircraft travelling to the United Kingdom stops at one or more places before arriving in the United Kingdom, it is to be treated as departing for the United Kingdom when it leaves the last of those places.
(8)   'Senior officer' means an immigration officer not below the rank of chief immigration officer.
(9)   'Relevant officer' means:

(a) the officer who gave the notice under sub-paragraph (1); or
(b) any immigration officer at the port at which the ship or aircraft concerned is expected to arrive.

(10) 'EEA national' means a national of a State which is a Contracting Party to the Agreement on the European Economic Area signed at Oporto on 2nd May 1992 as it has effect for the time being.]

Notes Para 1: Sub-paras (4) and (5): words substituted by SI 1990/2227, Sch 1; further substituted by SI 1993/1813, art 8, Sch 5, Pt I, para 1(*a*).

Paras 2, 3: Words in square brackets substituted by the British Nationality Act 1981, s 39(6), Sch 4, para 2; and SI 1990/2227, Sch 1; further substituted by SI 1993/1813, art 9(1), Sch 6, Pt I.

Para 2: Sub-para 1(c) substituted by Immigration and Asylum Act 1999, Sch 14, para 56.

Para 2A: Inserted by Immigration and Asylum Act 1999, Sch 14, para 57.

Para 4: Sub-para (2A) inserted by the Immigration Act 1988, s 10, Schedule, para 6, as from 10 July 1988, except in relation to any person whose examination under paras 2, 3 began before that date. Words in square brackets in sub-paras (2)(*b*) and (3) inserted by the Asylum and Immigration Act 1996, Sch 2, para 5. Sub-paras (1) and (2) amended by Immigration and Asylum Act 1999, Sch 14, para 58.

Para 6: Third words in square brackets substituted by the British Nationality Act 1981, s 39(6), Sch 4, para 2; remaining substituted made by the Immigration Act 1988, s 10, Schedule, para 8, as from 10 July 1988, subject to transitional provisions.

Para 7: Substituted by Immigration and Asylum Act 1999, Sch 14, para 59.

Para 8: sub-para (1)(*c*): Words originally inserted by SI 1990/2227, Sch 1 omitted and repealed by SI 1993/1813, art 9(1), Sch 6, Pt I.

Paras 8, 10: Words in square brackets added and substituted by the Immigration Act 1988, s 10, Schedule, para 9(1), (2), (4).

Para 9: Re-numbered as para 9(1) and para 9(2) inserted by the Asylum and Immigration Act 1996, Sch 2, para 6.

Paras 12, 13: Words in square brackets substituted by the British Nationality Act 1981, s 39(6), Sch 4, para 2.

Para 16: Sub-para (2) substituted and (1A) added by Immigration and Asylum Act 1999, s 140(1) and Sch 14, para 60, respectively. Sub-para (4A): added by SI 1990/2227, Sch 1; repealed by SI 1993/1813, art 9(1), Sch 6, Pt I. The old subparagraph 16(2) of Schedule 2 stated that 'A person in respect of whom directions may be given under any of paragraphs 8 to 14 above may be detained under the authority of an immigration officer pending his examination and pending a decision to give or refuse him leave to enter.' Under the old subparagraph the legality of the detention turned on a matter of fact – whether or not directions could be given under paragraphs 8 to 14. Section 140 changes the test to make it one of suspicion on reasonable grounds. This is of particular interest in relation to habeas corpus applications where the person is purportedly detained pending removal, but the Secretary of State has suspended removals to the destination in question. Can it be said that directions 'may be given' in such circumstances or not? The wording of the new subparagraph 2(a) may be relevant in this regard. It would appear that as soon as it is established that no removals are being made to the destination in question, there can be no question of giving the directions and thus that the requirement of subparagraph 2(a) that a decision be pending cannot be satisfied.

Para 17: Words omitted from sub-para (2) repealed by the Police and Criminal Evidence Act 1984, s 119(2), Sch 7, Pt I.

Para 18: Sub-para (2A) inserted by the Immigration and Asylum Act 1999, s 169(1), Sch 14, paras 43, 61

Para 19: Words in square brackets in sub-para (2) substituted by the British Nationality Act 1981, s 39(6), Sch 4, para 3(1), and words in first square brackets in sub-para (1): added by SI 1990/2227, Sch 1; repealed by SI 1993/1813. Words in second square brackets in sub-para (1) substituted by the Asylum and Immigration Act 1996, Sch 2, para 8.

Para 20: Sub-para (1): words in first square brackets added by SI 1990/2227, Sch 1, Part I, para 12; repealed by SI 1993/1813. Words in second square brackets in sub-para (1) substituted, and sub-para (1A) inserted, by the Asylum and Immigration Act 1996, Sch 2, para 9.

Para 21: Words in square brackets in sub-para (2) inserted by the Immigration Act 1988, s 10, Schedule, para 10(1), (4), applying in relation to persons granted temporary admission or released from detention under para 21 before, as well as after, 10 July 1988. Para 21(3)(4) inserted by the Asylum and Immigration Act 1996, Sch 2, para 10. Sub-paras (2A) to (2E) inserted by Immigration and Asylum Act 1999, Sch 14, para 62. Subparagraph (2) increases the Secretary of State's powers to impose restrictions as to residence. The old paragraph 21 of the 1971 Act, as amended permitted the imposition of restrictions as to residence, employment or occupation and reporting to an immigration officer or the police. Ministers stated during the passage of the IAA 1999 that these were powers to prevent the individual from absconding and that the powers had to be extended if restrictions were to be imposed for other purposes. The purposes they identified were those relating to public order, although the amendment does not on its face impose any restrictions upon the purposes for which the Secretary of State may make regulations to impose new restrictions (see Hansard HL Report, Vol 606, no 147, cols 734 to 743). The Explanatory Notes refer to two purposes 'to prevent potential public order problems or to relieve extreme pressure on local services and facilities in a particular area'. They further identify the purpose of imposing a condition to residence in section 4 accommodation as 'to enable reception facilities to be developed to assist the full and rapid consideration of claims'. These purposes find echoes in the descriptions of the reasons for setting up the new support schemes under Part VI and at the heart of these provisions is likely to be their interrelationship with the support scheme. However, while the support scheme under Part VI will apply to all asylum seekers, these powers are restricted to those on temporary admission or bail.

The face of the IAA 1999 does not impose any restrictions on the purposes for which the powers are to be used. The new subparagraph 2C of the regulations says that the Secretary of State 'may', not must, provide that a particular description of restriction may only be imposed for prescribed purposes.

While the new paragraph 2B sets out types of conditions that could be imposed, prohibiting residence in particular areas; requiring the person to reside in accommodation provided under section 4 of this Act and prohibiting him/her from being absent from that accommodation save in accordance with the restrictions imposed, this is not an exhaustive list.

The House of Lords Select Committee on Delegated Powers and Deregulation characterised the proposed power to prevent the person being absent from the accommodation as 'amounting to a power to impose house arrest' (See their Twenty-Seventh Report, 27 October 1999, paragraph 42). Fears were expressed during the passage of the Act that to take powers to confine a person for public order reasons could lead to pandering to racists in an area and locking up the victims rather than the perpetrators of racist acts (see Hansard, HC Report vol 337, no 147, cols 1027 to 1030). In this regard, the Race Relations (Amendment) Bill 1999, which will bring the actions of public bodies within the scope of race relations legislation, may have implications for the final form of any regulations made under these powers. See also the notes on Section 4 of this Act. The confusion in the debates on this section described therein is one of the reasons that there is so little clarity about how and why these powers might be used in the future.

Para 22: Sub-para (1), (1A), (1B) substituted and sub-paras (2)(3) amended by the Asylum and Immigration Act 1996, Sch 2, para 11(1), (2) and (3). Sub-para 1(aa) inserted by Immigration and Asylum Act 1999, Sch 14, para 63.

Para 23: Words in square brackets in sub-para (3) substituted by the Justices of the Peace Act 1997, s 73(2), Sch 5, para 10; words omitted repealed by the Criminal Justice Act 1972, ss 64(2), 66(7), Sch 6, Pt II.

Para 25A–25E: Inserted by Immigration and Asylum Act 1999, s 132(2).

Para 26: Words in square brackets substituted by the British Nationality Act 1981, s 39(6), Sch 4, para 2. Sub-para (1) amended, (1A) and (3A) inserted by Immigration and Asylum Act 1999, Sch 14, para 64. The amendments made by the IAA 1999 are related to the new sections 1 and 2 of that Act and give the Secretary of State greater flexibility in the arrangements made with the owners of ships and aircraft and the circumstances in which they may disembark passengers.

Para 27A: added by SI 1990/2227; repealed by SI 1993/1813; art 9(1), Sch 6, Pt I.

Para 27B: Inserted by the Immigration and Asylum Act 1999, s 18.

See Immigration (Passenger Information) Order 2000 (SI 2000/912) made 29 March 2000, laid before parliament 6 April 2000 and coming into force 28 April 2000. See also The Channel Tunnel (International Arrangements) (Amendment) Order 2000 (SI 2000/913 made 29 March 2000, laid before parliament 6 April 2000 and coming into force 28 April 2000 and Channel Tunnel (International Arrangements) (Amendment No 2) Order 2000 (SI 2000/1775).

SI 2000/912 defines 'passenger information' for the purposes of paragraph 27B of Schedule 2 as inserted by s 18 of the IAA 1999. SI 2000/912 sets out that the carrier must provide information on the full name, gender, age, date of birth, and nationality of the passenger, as well as the type of travel document the passenger holds and its number, and the expiry date of any UK visa or other form of entry clearance (SI 2000/912, Schedule, Part I). The carrier must also provide the following information, but only to the extent that it is known to the carrier (SI 2000/912 paragraph 2(2)): the name as it appears on the passenger's reservation, of the passenger and all other passengers appearing on the passenger's reservation, the ticket number, date and place of issue, the identity of the person who made the passenger's reservation, the method of payment for the ticket, the travel itinerary, and if the passenger is travelling with a vehicle (and trailer if any), the registration number of the vehicle (and trailer, if different).

SI 2000/913 amends the Channel Tunnel (International Arrangements) Order 1993 (SI 1993/1813) and modifies paragraph 27B of Schedule 2 as inserted by s 18 of the IAA 1999 to extend it to trains and shuttle trains travelling through the Channel Tunnel.

See also s 27C and the note thereto.

Para 27C: Inserted by the Immigration and Asylum Act 1999, s 19.

See Channel Tunnel (International Arrangements) Order 2000 (SI 2000/913). This order modifies paragraph 27C, as inserted by s 19 of the IAA 1999 to extend it to trains travelling through the Channel Tunnel. See also s 27B above and the note thereto. See also The Channel Tunnel (International Arrangements) (Amendment No 2) Order 2000 (SI 2000/1775).

Commencement 1 January 1973 (SI 1972/1514).

Definitions For 'aircraft', 'captain', 'certificate of entitlement', 'crew', 'entrant', 'entry clearance', 'illegal entrant', 'indefinite leave', 'limited leave', 'port', 'ship' and 'work permit', see s 33(1); for 'port of entry', see s 33(3); as to 'embark' and 'disembark', see s 11(1)–(3).

PART II
EFFECT OF APPEALS

[A.1.48]

Stay on directions for removal

28 . . .

Grant of bail pending appeal

29—(1) Where a person (in the following provisions of this Schedule referred to as 'an appellant') has an appeal pending under section [59, 65, 66,

67, 69(1) or (5) or 71 of the Immigration and Asylum Act 1999] and is for the time being detained under Part I of this Schedule, he may be released on bail in accordance with this paragraph.

(2) An Immigration Officer not below the rank of chief immigration officer or a police officer not below the rank of inspector may release an appellant on his entering into a recognizance or, in Scotland, bail bond conditions for his appearance before an adjudicator or the Appeal Tribunal at a time and place named in the recognizance or bail bond.

(3) An adjudicator may release an appellant on his entering into a recognizance, or in Scotland, bail bond conditioned for his appearance before that or any other adjudicator, or the Appeal Tribunal at a time and place named in the recognizance or bail bond; and where an adjudicator dismisses an appeal but grants leave to the appellant to apeal to the Tribunal, or, in a case in which leave to appeal is not required, the appellent has duly given notice of appeal to the Tribunal, the adjudicator shall, if the appellant so requests, exercise his powers under this sub-paragraph.

(4) Where an appellant has duly applied for leave to appeal to the Appeal Tribunal, the Tribunal may release him on his entering into a recognizance or, in Scotland, bail bond conditioned for his appearance before the Tribunal at a time and place named in the recognizance or bail bond; and where:

(*a*) the Tribunal grants leave to an appellant to appeal to the Tribunal; or
(*b*) in a case in which leave to appeal is not required, the appellant has duly given notice of appeal to the Tribunal;

the Tribunal shall, if the appellant so requests, release him as aforesaid.

(5) The conditions of a recognizance or bail bond taken under this paragraph may include conditions appearing to the person fixing the bail to be likely to result in the appearance of the appellant at the time and place named; and any recognizance shall be with or without sureties as that person may determine.

(6) In any case in which an adjudicator or the Tribunal has power or is required by this paragraph to release an appellant on bail, the adjudicator or tribunal may, instead of taking the bail, fix the amount and conditions of the bail (including the amount in which any sureties are to be bound) with a view to its being taken subsequently by any such person as may be specified by the adjudicator or the Tribunal; and on the recognizance or bail bond so taken the appellant shall be released.

Restrictions on grant of bail

30—(1) An appellant shall not be released under paragraph 29 above without the consent of the Secretary of State if directions for the removal of the appellant from the United Kingdom are for the time being in force, or the power to give such directions is for the time being exercisable.

(2) Notwithstanding paragraph 29(3) of (4) above, an adjudicator and the Tribunal shall not be obliged to release an appellant unless the appellant enters into a proper recognizance, with sufficient and satisfactory sureties if required, or in Scotland sufficient and satisfactory bail is found if so required; and an adjudicator and the Tribunal shall not be obliged to release an appellant if it appears to the adjudicator or the Tribunal, as the case may be:

(*a*) that the appellant, having on any previous occasion been released on bail (whether under paragraph 24 or under any other provision), has gailed to comply with the conditions of any recognizance or bail bond entered into by him on that occasion;

(*b*) that the appellant is likely to commit an offence unless he is retained in detention;

(*c*) that the release of the appellant is likely to cause danger to public health;

(*d*) that the appellant is suffering from mental disorder and that his continued detention is necessary in his own interests or for the protection of any other person; or

(*e*) that the appellant is under the age of seventeen, that arrangements ought to be made for his care in the event of his release and that no satisfactory arrangements for that purpose have been made.

Forfeiture of recognizances

31—(1)   Where under paragraph 29 above (as it applies in England and Wales or in Northern Ireland) a recognizance is entered into conditioned for the appearance of an appellant before an adjudicator or the Tribunal, and it appears to the adjudicator or the Tribunal, as the case may be, to be forfeited, the adjudicator or Tribunal may by order declare it to be forfeited and adjudge the persons bound thereby, whether as principal or sureties, or any of them, to pay the sum in which they are respectively bound or such party of it, if any, as the adjudicator or Tribunal thinks fit,

(2)   An order under this paragraph shall, for the purposes of this sub-paragraph, specify a magistrates' court or, in Northern Ireland, court of summary jurisdiction; and the recognizance shall be treated for the purposes of collection, enforcement and remission of the sum forfeited as having been forfeited by the court so specified.

(3)   Where an adjudicator or the Tribunal makes an order under this paragraph the adjudicator or Tribunal shall, as soon as practicable, give particulars of the recognizance to the clerk of the court specified in the order in pursuance of sub-paragraph (2) above.

(4)   Any sum the payment of which is enforceable by a magistrates' court in England and Wales by virtue of this paragraph shall be treated for the purpose of the [Justices of the Peace Act 1979 and, in particular, section 61 thereof] as being due under a recognizance forfeited by such a court . . .

(5)   Any sum the payment of which is enforceable by virtue of this paragraph by a court of summary jurisdiction in Northern Ireland shall, for the purposes of section 20(5) of the Administration of Justice Act (Northern Ireland) 1954, be treated as a forfeited recognizance.

32   (*Applies to Scotland only*)

Arrest of appellants released on bail

33—(1)   An Immigration Officer or constable may arrest without warrant a person who has been released by virtue of this Part of this Schedule:

(*a*) if he has reasonable grounds for believing that that person is likely to break the condition of his recognizance or bail bond that he will appear at the time and place required or to break any other condition of it, or has reasonable ground to suspect that that person is breaking or has broken any such other condition; or

(*b*) if, a recognizance with sureties have been taken, he is notified in writing by any surety or the surety's belief that that person is likely to break the first-mentioned condition, and of the surety's wish for that reason to be relieved of his obligations as a surety;

and paragraph 17(2) above shall apply for the arrest of a person under this paragraph as it applies for the arrest of a person under paragraph 17.

(2)   A person arrested under this paragraph:

(*a*) if not required by a condition on which he was released to appear before an adjudicator or Tribunal within twenty-four hours after the time of his arrest, shall as soon as practicable be brought before an adjudicator or, if that is not practicable within those twenty-four hours, before a justice of the peace acting for the petty sessions area in which he is arrested or, in Scotland, the sheriff; and

(*b*) if required by such a condition to appear within those twenty-four hours before an adjudicator or before the Tribunal, shall be brought before that adjudicator or before the Tribunal, as the case may be.

(3)   An adjudicator, justice of the peace or sheriff before whom a person is brought by virtue of sub-paragraph (2)(*a*) above:

(*a*) if of the opinion that that person has broken or is likely to break any condition on which he was released, may either:
  (i)   direct that he be detained under the authority of the person by whom he was arrested, or
  (ii) release him on his original recognizance or on a new recognizance, with or without sureties, or, in Scotland, on his original bail or on new bail; and

(*b*) if not of that opinion, shall release him on his original recognizance or bail.

Grant of bail pending removal

[**34**—(1)   Paragraph 22 above shall apply in relation to a person:

(*a*) directions for whose removal from the United Kingdom are for the time being in force; and

(*b*) who is for the time being detained under Part I of this Schedule,

as it applies in relation to a person detained under paragraph 16(1) above pending examination [, detained under paragraph 16(1A) above pending completion of his examination or a decision on whether to cancel his leave to enter] or detained under paragraph 16(2) above pending the giving of directions.

(2)   Paragraphs 23 to 25 above shall apply as if any reference to paragraph 22 above included a reference to that paragraph as it applies by virtue of this paragraph.]

Notes   Para 28 repealed by the Immigration and Asylum Act 1999, s 169(1), (3), Sch 14, paras 43, 65, Sch 16.

Para 29 words in square brackets substituted by the Immigration and Asylum Act 1999, s 169(1), Sch 14, paras 43, 66.

Paras 30–33 extended by the Asylum and Immigration Appeals Act 1993, s 9A(5).

Words in square brackets in para 31(4) substituted by the Justices of the Peace Act 1997, s 73(2), Sch 5, para 10; and words omitted from that provision repealed by the Criminal Justice Act 1972, s 64(2), Sch 6, Pt II.

Para 34 inserted by the Asylum and Immigration Act 1996, Sch 2, para 12. Words added by Immigration and Asylum Act 1999, Sch 14, para 64.

Commencement 1 January 1973 (SI 1972/1514).

Definitions For 'aircraft' and 'ship', see s 33(1).

SCHEDULE 3   SUPPLEMENTARY PROVISIONS AS TO DEPORTATION (SECTION 5)

[A.1.49]

Removal of persons liable to deportation

1—(1)   Where a deportation order is in force against any person, the Secretary of State may give directions for his removal to a country or territory specified in the directions being either:

(*a*) a country of which he is a national or citizen; or

(*b*) a country or territory to which there is reason to believe that he will be admitted.

(2)   The directions under sub-paragraph (1) above may be either:

(*a*) directions given to the captain of a ship or aircraft about to leave the United Kingdom requiring him to remove the person in question in that ship or aircraft; or

b) directions given to the owners or agents of any ship or aircraft requiring them to make arrangements for his removal in a ship or aircraft specified or indicated in the directions; or

(*c*) directions for his removal in accordance with arrangements to be made by the Secretary of State.

(3)   In relation to directions given under this paragraph, paragraphs 11 and 16(4) of Schedule 2 to this Act shall apply, with the substitution of references to the Secretary of State for references to an immigration officer, as they apply in relation to directions for removal given under paragraph 8 of that Schedule.
(4)   The Secretary of State, if he thinks fit, may apply in or towards payment of the expenses of or incidental to the voyage from the United Kingdom of a person against whom a deportation order is in force, or the maintenance until departure of such a person and his dependents, if any, any money belonging to that person; and except so far as they are paid as aforesaid, those expenses shall be defrayed by the Secretary of State.

Detention or control pending deportation

2—(1)   Where a recommendation for deportation made by a court is in force in respect of any person, and that person is neither detained in pursuance of the sentence or order of any court not for the time being released on bail by any court having power so to release him, he shall, unless the court by which the recommendation is made otherwise directs, [or a direction is given under sub-paragraph (1A) below,] be detained pending the making of a deportation order in pursuance of the recommendation, unless the Secretary of State directs him to be released pending further consideration of his case.

[(1A) Where:

(a) a recommendation for deportation made by a court on a conviction of a person is in force in respect of him; and

(b) he appeals against his conviction or against that recommendation,

the powers that the court determining the appeal may exercise include power to direct him to be released without setting aside the recommendation.]

(2) Where notice has been given to a person in accordance with regulations under section 18 of this Act of a decision to make a deportation order against him, and he is neither detained in pursuance of the sentence or order of a court nor for the time being released on bail by a court having power so to release him, he may be detained under the authority of the Secretary of State pending the making of the deportation order.

(3) Where a deportation order is in force against any person, he may be detained under the authority of the Secretary of State pending his removal or departure from the United Kingdom (and if already detained by virtue of sub-paragraph (1) or (2) above when the order is made, shall continue to be detained unless the Secretary of State directs otherwise).

(4) In relation to detention under sub-paragraph (2) or (3) above, paragraphs 17[, 18 and 25A to 25E] of Schedule 2 to this Act shall apply as they apply in relation to detention under paragraph 16 of that Schedule.

[(5) A person to whom this sub-paragraph applies shall be subject to such restrictions as to residence[, as to his employment or occupation] and as to reporting to the police [or an immigration officer] as may from time to time be notified to him in writing by the Secretary of State.]

(6) The persons to whom sub-paragraph (5) above applies are:

(a) a person liable to be detained under sub-paragraph (1) above, while by virtue of a direction of the Secretary of State he is not so detained; and

(b) a person liable to be detained under sub-paragraph (2) or (3) above, while he is not so detained.]

Effect of appeals

3 Part II of Schedule 2 to this Act, so far as it relates to appeals under section [66 or 67 of the Immigration and Asylum Act 1999], shall apply for purposes of this Schedule as if the references . . . in paragraph 29(1) to Part I of that Schedule were references to this Schedule; and paragraphs 29 to 33 shall apply in like manner in relation to appeals under section [63(1)(a) or 69(4)(a) of the Immigration and Asylum Act 1999].

[Powers of courts pending deportation

4 Where the release of a person recommended for deportation is directed by a court, he shall be subject to such restrictions as to residence], as to his employment or occupation] and as to reporting to the police as the court may direct.

5—(1) On an application made:

(*a*) by or on behalf of a person recommended for deportation whose release was so directed; or

(*b*) by a constable; or

(*c*) by an Immigration Officer,

the appropriate court shall have the powers specified in sub-paragraph (2) below.

(2) The powers mentioned in sub-paragraph (1) above are:

(*a*) if the person to whom the application relates is not subject to any such restrictions imposed by a court as are mentioned in paragraph 4 above, to order that he shall be subject to any such restrictions as the court may direct; and

(*b*) if he is subject to restrictions imposed by a court by virtue of that paragraph or this paragraph:

(i) to direct that any of them shall be varied or shall cease to have effect; or

(ii) to give further directions as to his residence and reporting.

6—(1) In this Schedule 'the appropriate court', means except in a case to which sub-paragraph (2) below applies, the court which directed release.

(2) This sub-paragraph applies where the court which directed release was:

(*a*) the Crown Court;

(*b*) the Court of Appeal;

(*c*) (*applies to Scotland only*);

(*d*) the Crown Court in Northern Ireland; or

(*e*) the Court of Appeal in Northern Ireland.

(3) Where the Crown Court or the Crown Court in Northern Ireland directed release, the appropriate court is:

(*a*) the court that directed release; or

(*b*) a magistrates' court acting for the commission area or county court division where the person to whom the application relates resides.

(4) Where the Court of Appeal or the Court of Appeal in Northern Ireland gave the direction, the appropriate court is the Crown Court or the Crown Court in Northern Ireland, as the case may be.

(5) (*Applies to Scotland only.*)

7—(1) A constable or Immigration Officer may arrest without warrant any person who is subject to restrictions imposed by a court under this Schedule and who at the time of the arrest is in the relevant part of the United Kingdom:

(*a*) if he has reasonable grounds to suspect that that person is contravening or has contravened any of those restrictions ;or

(*b*) if he has reasonable grounds for believing that that person is likely to contravene any of them.

(2) In sub-paragraph (2) above 'the relevant part of the United Kingdom' means:

(*a*) England and Wales, in a case where a court with jurisdiction in England or Wales imposed the restrictions;

(*b*) (*applies to Scotland only*)

(*c*) Northern Ireland, in a case where a court in Northern Ireland imposed them.

8—(1) A person arrested in England or Wales or Northern Ireland in pursuance of paragraph 7 above shall be brought as soon as practicable and in any event within 24 hours after his arrest before a justice of the peace for the petty sessions area or district in which he was arrested.

(2) In reckoning for the purposes of this paragraph any period of 24 hours, no account shall be taken of Christmas Day, Good Friday or any Sunday.

9 (*Applies to Scotland only.*)

10 Any justice of the peace or court before whom a person is brought by virtue of paragraph 8 or 9 above:

(*a*) if of the opinion that that person is contravening, has contravened or is likely to contravene any restriction imposed on him by a court under this Schedule, may direct-

  (i) that he be detained; or

  (ii) that he be released subject to such restrictions as to his residence and reporting to the police as the court may direct; and

(*b*) if not of that opinion, shall release him without altering the restrictions as to his residence and his reporting to the police.]

Notes Words in square brackets in para 2(1) substituted, para 2(1A) inserted, para 2(5), (6) substituted (for original para 2(5)), and paras 4-10 added, by the Criminal Justice Act 1982, s 64, Sch 10, paras 1, 2.

  Words in square brackets in para 2(4) amended by Immigration and Asylum Act 1999, Sch 14, para 68.

  Words in square brackets in paras 2(5), 4, inserted by the Immigration Act 1988, s 10, Schedule, para 10(2), (4), applying in relation to persons becoming liable to detention under para 2(2), (3) or directed to be released, before, as well as after 10 July 1988.

  Words 'or an immigration officer' inserted in para 2(5) by the Asylum and Immigration Act 1996, Sch 2, para 13.

  Words in square brackets in para 3 substituted, and words in para 3 omitted, by the Immigration and Asylum Act 1999, s 169(1), Sch 14.

Commencement 1 January 1973 (SI 1972/1514).

Definitions For 'aircraft', 'captain' and 'ship', see s 33(1).

SCHEDULE 4 INTEGRATION WITH UNITED KINGDOM LAW OF IMMIGRATION LAW OF ISLANDS (SECTION 9)

[A.1.50]

Leave to enter

1—(1) Where under the immigration laws of any of the Islands a person is or has been given leave to enter or remain in the island, or is or has been refused leave, this Act shall have effect in relation to him, if he is not [a British citizen], as if the leave were leave (of like duration) given under this Act to enter or remain the United Kingdom, or, as the case may be, as if he had under this Act been refused leave to enter the United Kingdom.

(2) Where under the immigration laws of any of the Islands a person has a limited leave to enter or remain in the island subject to any such condtiions as are authorised in the United Kingdom by section 3(1) of this Act (being conditions imposed by notice given to him, whether the notice of leave or a subsequent notice), then on his coming to the United Kingdom this Act shall apply, if he is not [a British citizen], as if those conditions related to his stay in the United Kingdom and had been imposed by notice under this Act.

(3) Without prejudice to the generality of sub-paragraphs (1) and (2) above, anything having effect in the United Kingdom by virtue of either of those sub-paragraphs may in relation to the United Kingdom be varied or revoked under this Act in like manner, and subject to the like appeal (if any), as if it had originated under this Act as mentioned in that sub-paragraph.

(4) Where anything having effect in the United Kingdom by virtue of sub-paragraph (1) or (2) above ceases to have effect or is altered in effect as mentioned in sub-paragraph (3) or otherwise by anything done under this Act, sub-paragraph (1) or (2) shall not thereafter apply to it or, as the case may be, shall apply to it as so altered in effect.

(5) Nothing in this paragraph shall be taken as conferring on a person a right of appeal under this Act against any decision or action taken in any of the Islands.

2 Notwithstanding section 3(4) of this Act, leave given to a person under this Act to enter or remain in the United Kingdom shall not continue to apply on his return to the United Kingdom after an absence if he has during that absence entered any of the Islands in circumstances in which he is required under the immigration laws of that island to obtain leave to enter.

Deportation

[3—(1) This Act has effect in relation to a person who is subject to an Islands deportation order as if the order were a deportation order made against him under this Act.

(2) Sub-paragraph (1) does not apply if the person concerned is:

(*a*) a British citizen;

(*b*) an EEA national;

(*c*) a member of the family of an EEA national; or

(*d*) a member of the family of a British citizen who is neither such a citizen nor an EEA national.

(3) The Secretary of State does not, as a result of sub-paragraph (1), have power to revoke an Islands deportation order.

(4) In any particular case, the Secretary of State may direct that paragraph (*b*), (*c*) or (*d*) of sub-paragraph (2) is not to apply in relation to the Islands deportiation order.

(5) Nothing in this paragraph makes it unlawful for a person in respect of whom an Islands deportation order is in force in any of the Islands to enter the United Kingdom on his way from that island to a place outside the United Kingdom.

(6) 'Islands deportation order' means an order made under the immigration laws of any of the Islands under which a person is, or has been, ordered to leave the island and forbidden to return.

(7) Subsections (10) and (12) to (14) of section 80 of the Immigration and

Asylum Act 1999 apply for the purposes of this section as they apply for the purposes of that section.]

Illegal entrants

4 Notwithstanding anything in section 1(3) of this Act, it shall not be lawful for a person who is not [a British citizen] to enter the United Kingdom from any of the Islands where his presence was unlawful under the immigration laws of that island, unless he is given leave to enter.

Notes Words in square brackets substituted by the British Nationality Act 1981, s 39(6), Sch 4, para 2. Para 3 substituted by the Immigration and Asylum Act 1999, s 169(1), Sch 14, paras 43, 70.

Commencement 1 January 1973 (SI 1972/1514).

Definitions For 'immigration laws' and 'the islands', see s 33(1).

SCHEDULE 5   THE ADJUDICATORS AND THE TRIBUNAL (SECTION 12)

PART I
THE ADJUDICATORS

[A.1.51]

. . .

Notes Repealed by Immigration and Asylum Act 1999, Sch 16. See note to Sch 16.

SCHEDULE 6   REPEALS (SECTION 34)

[A.1.52]

Chapter	Short Title	Extent of Repeal
4 &5 Geo 5 c 12	The Aliens Restriction Act 1914	The whole Act.
9 & 10 Geo 5 c 92	The Aliens Restriction (Amendment) Act 1919	Section 1. Section 2(1). Section 13(3). Section 14(1).
11 & 12 Geo 6 c 56	The British Nationality Act 1948	Section 6 (1) In section 6(2), the words from 'and, if' to 'Act'. Section 8(1) from 'and as if' onwards.
6 & 7 Eliz 2 c 10	The British Nationality Act 1958	Section 3(2). In section 5(3) the words from 'including' to 'this Act'.
10 & 11 Eliz 2 c 21	The Commonwealth Immigrants Act 1962	The whole Act, except section 12(2) and (4) and section 20(1) and (3). In section 12(2) the words from the beginning to 'six, and'.
1964 c 81	The Diplomatic Privileges Act 1964	Section 5(1).
1965 c 34	The British Nationality Act 1965	Section 2(3)
1967 c 4	The West Indies Act 1967	In Schedule 3, paragraph 3.
1967 c 80	The Criminal Justice Act 1967	Section 58.
1968 c 9	The Commonwealth Immigrants Act 1968	The whole Act.
1968 c 19	The Criminal Appeal Act 1968	In section 5(1), the definition of 'recommendation for deportation'.
1968 c 59	The Hovercraft Act 1968	In paragraph 1 of the Schedule, sub-paragraph (*f*) and the words from 'and 1962' to '1968'.
1969 c 21	The Immigration Appeals Act 1969	The whole Act.
1970 c 58	The Expiring Laws Continuance Act 1970	The whole Act.

Commencement   28 October 1971 (s 34(1)).

RACE RELATIONS ACT 1976
(1976 c 74)

Arrangement of sections (Extracts)

PART I
DISCRIMINATION TO WHICH ACT APPLIES

[A.1.53]
1 Racial discrimination
(1)   A person discriminates against another in any circumstances relevant for the purposes of any provision of this Act if—

(a) on racial grounds he treats that other less favourably than he treats or would treat other persons; or
(b) he applies to that other a requirement or condition which he applies or would apply equally to persons not of the same racial group as that other but—
   (i)   which is such that the proportion of persons of the same racial group as that other who can comply with it is considerably smaller than the proportion of persons not of that racial group who can comply with it; and
   (ii) which he cannot show to be justifiable irrespective of the colour, race, nationality or ethnic or national origins of the person to whom it is applied; and
   (iii) which is to the detriment of that other because he cannot comply with it.

(2)   It is hereby declared that, for the purposes of this Act, segregating a person from other persons on racial grounds is treating him less favourably than they are treated.

[A.1.54]
2 Discrimination by way of victimisation
(1)   A person ('the discriminator') discriminates against another person ('the person victimised') in any circumstances relevant for the purposes of any provision of this Act if he treats the person victimised less favourably than in those circumstances he treats or would treat other persons, and does so by reason that the person victimised has—

(a) brought proceedings against the discriminator or any other person under this Act; or

(b) given evidence or information in connection with proceedings brought by any person against the discriminator or any other person under this Act; or

(c) otherwise done anything under or by reference to this Act in relation to the discriminator or any other person; or

(d) alleged that the discriminator or any other person has committed an act which (whether or not the allegation so states) would amount to a contravention of this Act,

or by reason that the discriminator knows that the person victimised intends to do any of those things, or suspects that the person victimised has done, or intends to do, any of them.

(2)   Subsection (1) does not apply to treatment of a person by reason of any allegation made by him if the allegation was false and not made in good faith.

[A.1.55]
3 Meaning of 'racial grounds', 'racial group' etc
(1)   In this Act, unless the context otherwise requires—

'racial grounds' means any of the following grounds, namely colour, race nationality or ethnic or national origins;

'racial group' means a group of persons defined by reference to colour, race, nationality or ethnic or national origins, and references to a person's racial group refer to any racial group into which he falls.

(2)   The fact that a racial group comprises two or more distinct racial groups does not prevent it from constituting a particular racial group for the purposes of this Act.

(3)   In this Act—

(a) references to discrimination refer to any discrimination falling within section 1 or 2; and

(b) references to racial discrimination refer to any discrimination falling within section 1,

and related expressions shall be construed accordingly.

(4)   A comparison of the case of a person of a particular racial group with that of a person not of that group under section 1(1) must be such that the relevant circumstances in the one case are the same, or not materially different, in the other.

PART III
DISCRIMINATION IN OTHER FIELDS

Education

[A.1.56]
[19B Discrimination by public authorities]
[(1)   It is unlawful for a public authority in carrying out any functions of the

authority to do any act which constitutes discrimination.

(2)   In this section 'public authority'—

(a) includes any person certain of whose functions are functions of a public nature; but

(b) does not include any person mentioned in subsection (3).

(3)   The persons mentioned in this subsection are—

(a) either House of Parliament;

(b) a person exercising functions in connection with proceedings in Parliament;

(c) the Security Service;

(d) the Secret Intelligence Service;

(e) the Government Communications Headquarters; and

(f) any unit or part of a unit of any of the naval, military or air forces of the Crown which is for the time being required by the Secretary of State to assist the Government Communications Headquarters in carrying out its functions.

(4)   In relation to a particular act, a person is not a public authority by virtue only of subsection (2)(a) if the nature of the act is private.

(5)   This section is subject to sections 19C to 19F.

(6)   Nothing in this section makes unlawful any act of discrimination which—

(a) is made unlawful by virtue of any other provision of this Act; or

(b) would be so made but for any provision made by or under this Act.]

Note   Inserted by the Race Relations (Amendment) Act 2000, s 1.

[A.1.57]
[19C Exceptions or further exceptions from section 19B for judicial and legislative acts etc]
[(1)   Section 19B does not apply to—

(a) any judicial act (whether done by a court, tribunal or other person); or

(b) any act done on the instructions, or on behalf, of a person acting in a judicial capacity.

(2)   Section 19B does not apply to any act of, or relating to, making, confirming or approving any enactment or Order in Council or any instrument made by a Minister of the Crown under an enactment.

(3)   Section 19B does not apply to any act of, or relating to, making or approving arrangements, or imposing requirements or conditions, of a kind falling within section 41.

(4)   Section 19B does not apply to any act of, or relating to, imposing a requirement, or giving an express authorisation, of a kind mentioned in section 19D(3) in relation to the carrying out of immigration and nationality functions.

(5)   In this section—
'immigration and nationality functions' has the meaning given in section 19D; and

'Minister of the Crown' includes the National Assembly for Wales and a member of the Scottish Executive.]

Note   Inserted by the Race Relations (Amendment) Act 2000, s 1.

[A.1.58]
[19D Exception from section 19B for certain acts in immigration and nationality cases]
[(1)   Section 19B does not make it unlawful for a relevant person to discriminate against another person on grounds of nationality or ethnic or national origins in carrying out immigration and nationality functions.
(2)   For the purposes of subsection (1), 'relevant person' means—

(a) a Minister of the Crown acting personally; or
(b) any other person acting in accordance with a relevant authorisation.

(3)   In subsection (2), 'relevant authorisation' means a requirement imposed or express authorisation given—

(a) with respect to a particular case or class of case, by a Minister of the Crown acting personally;
(b) with respect to a particular class of case—
    (i)   by any of the enactments mentioned in subsection (5); or
(ii) by any instrument made under or by virtue of any of those enactments.

(4)   For the purposes of subsection (1), 'immigration and nationality functions' means functions exercisable by virtue of any of the enactments mentioned in subsection (5).
(5)   Those enactments are—

(a) the Immigration Acts (within the meaning of the Immigration and Asylum Act 1999 but excluding sections 28A to 28K of the Immigration Act 1971 so far as they relate to offences under Part III of that Act);
(b) the British Nationality Act 1981;
(c) the British Nationality (Falkland Islands) Act 1983;
(d) the British Nationality (Hong Kong) Act 1990;
(e) the Hong Kong (War Wives and Widows) Act 1996;
(f) the British Nationality (Hong Kong) Act 1997; and
(g) the Special Immigration Appeals Commission Act 1997;

and include any provision made under section 2(2) of the European Communities Act 1972, or any provision of Community law, which relates to the subject-matter of any of the enactments mentioned above.]

Note   Inserted by the Race Relations (Amendment) Act 2000, s 1.

[A.1.59]
[19E Monitoring of exception in relation to immigration and nationality cases]
[(1)   The Secretary of State shall appoint a person who is not a member of his staff to act as a monitor.
(2)   Before appointing any such person, the Secretary of State shall consult the Commission.

(3)   The person so appointed shall monitor, in such manner as the Secretary of State may determine—

(a) the likely effect on the operation of the exception in section 19D of any relevant authorisation relating to the carrying out of immigration and nationality functions which has been given by a Minister of the Crown acting personally; and
(b) the operation of that exception in relation to acts which have been done by a person acting in accordance with such an authorisation.

(4)   The monitor shall make an annual report on the discharge of his functions to the Secretary of State.
(5)   The Secretary of State shall lay a copy of any report made to him under subsection (4) before each House of Parliament.
(6)   The Secretary of State shall pay to the monitor such fees and allowances (if any) as he may determine.
(7)   In this section 'immigration and nationality functions' and 'relevant authorisation' have the meanings given to them in section 19D.]

Note   Inserted by the Race Relations (Amendment) Act 2000, s 1.

Extent

[A.1.60]
27 Extent of Part III
(1)   Sections 17 to 19 [18D] do not apply to benefits, facilities or services outside Great Britain except—

(a) travel on a ship registered at a port of registry in Great Britain; and
(b) benefits, facilities or services provided on a ship so registered.

[(1A)   In its application in relation to granting entry clearance (within the meaning of the Immigration Act 1971) section 19B applies in relation to acts done outside the United Kingdom, as well as those done within Great Britain.]
(2)   Section 20(1)—

(a) does not apply to goods, facilities or services outside Great Britain except as provided in subsections (3) and (4); and
(b) does not apply to facilities by way of banking or insurance or for grants, loans, credit or finance, where the facilities are for a purpose to be carried out, or in connection with risks wholly or mainly arising, outside Great Britain.

(3)   Section 20(1) applies to the provision of facilities for travel outside Great Britain where the refusal or omission occurs in Great Britain or on a ship, aircraft or hovercraft within subsection (4).
(4)   Section 20(1) applies on and in relation to—

(a) any ship registered at a port of registry in Great Britain; and
(b) any aircraft or hovercraft registered in the United Kingdom and operated by a person who has his principal place of business, or is ordinarily resident, in Great Britain,

even if the ship, aircraft or hovercraft is outside Great Britain.

(5)   This section shall not render unlawful an act done in or over a country outside the United Kingdom, or in or over that country's territorial waters, for the purpose of complying with the laws of that country.

Commencement   SI 1977/840.

Notes   Sub-s (1): reference to '19' in italics repealed and subsequent reference to '18D' in square brackets substituted by the Race Relations (Amendment) Act 2000, s 9(1), Sch 2, para 2.

Sub-s (1A): inserted by the Race Relations (Amendment) Act 2000, s 9(1), Sch 2, para 3.

PART IV
OTHER UNLAWFUL ACTS

[A.1.61]
30 Instructions to discriminate
It is unlawful for a person—

(a) who has authority over another person; or
(b) in accordance with whose wishes that other person is accustomed to act,

to instruct him to do any act which is unlawful by virtue of Part II or III, or procure or attempt to procure the doing by him of any such act.

[A.1.62]
31 Pressure to discriminate
(1)   It is unlawful to induce, or attempt to induce, a person to do any act which contravenes Part II or III.
(2)   An attempted inducement is not prevented from falling within subsection (1) because it is not made directly to the person in question, if it is made in such a way that he is likely to hear of it.

[A.1.63]
32 Liability of employers and principals
(1)   Anything done by a person in the course of his employment shall be treated for the purposes of this Act (except as regards offences thereunder) as done by his employer as well as by him, whether or not it was done with the employer's knowledge or approval.
(2)   Anything done by a person as agent for another person with the authority (whether express or implied, and whether precedent or subsequent) of that other person shall be treated for the purposes of this Act (except as regards offences thereunder) as done by that other person as well as by him.
(3)   In proceedings brought under this Act against any person in respect of an act alleged to have been done by an employee of his it shall be a defence for that person to prove that he took such steps as were reasonably practicable to prevent the employee from doing that act, or from doing in the course of his employment acts of that description.

Modification   Modified, in its application to employment by the governing body of a school having a right to a delegated budget, by the Education (Modification of Enactments Relating to Employment) Order 1999, SI 1999/2256, art 3, Schedule.

[A.1.64]
33 Aiding unlawful acts

(1)   A person who knowingly aids another person to do an act made unlawful by this Act shall be treated for the purposes of this Act as himself doing an unlawful act of the like description.

(2)   For the purposes of subsection (1) an employee or agent for whose act the employer or principal is liable under section 32 (or would be so liable but for section 32(3)) shall be deemed to aid the doing of the act by the employer or principal.

(3)   A person does not under this section knowingly aid another to do an unlawful act if—

(a) he acts in reliance on a statement made to him by that other person that, by reason of any provision of this Act, the act which he aids would not be unlawful; and

(b) it is reasonable for him to rely on the statement.

(4)   A person who knowingly or recklessly makes a statement such as is mentioned in subsection (3)(a) which in a material respect is false or misleading commits an offence, and shall be liable on summary conviction to a fine not exceeding [level 5 on the standard scale].

Note   Sub-s (4): maximum fine increased and converted to a level on the standard scale by the Criminal Justice Act 1982, ss 37, 38, 46.

PART VI
GENERAL EXCEPTIONS FROM PARTS II TO IV

[A.1.65]
41 Acts done under statutory authority etc

(1)   Nothing in Parts II to IV shall render unlawful any act of discrimination done—

(a) in pursuance of any enactment or Order in Council; or

(b) in pursuance of any instrument made under any enactment by a Minister of the Crown; or

(c) in order to comply with any condition or requirement imposed by a Minister of the Crown (whether before or after the passing of this Act) by virtue of any enactment.

References in this subsection to an enactment, Order in Council or instrument include an enactment, Order in Council or instrument passed or made after the passing of this Act.

(2) Nothing in Parts II to IV shall render unlawful any act whereby a person discriminates against another on the basis of that other's nationality or place of ordinary residence or the length of time for which he has been present or resident in or outside the United Kingdom or an area within the United Kingdom, if that Act is done—

(a) in pursuance of any arrangements made (whether before or after the passing of this Act) by or with the approval of, or for the time being approved by, a Minister of the Crown; or

(b) in order to comply with any condition imposed (whether before or after the passing of this Act) by a Minister of the Crown.

Transfer of Functions See further in relation to the exercise of functions under this section by the National Asembly for Wales, by the National Assembly for Wales (Transfer of Functions) Order 1999, SI 1999/672, art 2, Sch 1.

[A.1.66]
42 Acts safeguarding national security
Nothing in Parts II to IV shall render unlawful an act done for the purpose of safeguarding national security [if the doing of the act was justified by that purpose].

Notes Words from 'if the doing' to 'by that purpose' in square brackets inserted by the Race Relations (Amendment) Act 2000, s 7(1).

PART VIII
ENFORCEMENT

GENERAL

[A.1.67]
53 Restriction of proceedings for breach of act
(1) Except as provided by this Act [or the Special Immigration Appeals Commission Act 1997 or Part IV of the Immigration and Asylum Act 1999] no proceedings, whether civil or criminal, shall lie against any person in respect of an act by reason that the act is unlawful by virtue of a provision of this Act.
(2) Subsection (1) does not preclude the making of an order of certiorari, mandamus or prohibition.
(3) . . .
[(4) Subsections (2) and (3) do not, except so far as provided by section 76, apply to any act which is unlawful by virtue of section 76(5) or (9) or by virtue of section 76(10)(b) and (11).]

Notes Sub-s (1): words 'or the Special Immigration Appeals Commission Act 1997 or Part IV of the Immigration and Asylum Act 1999' in square brackets inserted by the Race Relations (Amendment) Act 2000, s 9(1), Sch 2, para 4.
  Sub-s (3): applies to Scotland only.

Sub-s (4): inserted by the Race Relations (Amendment) Act 2000, s 9(1), Sch 2, para 5.

Enforcement of Part III

[A.1.68]
57 Claims under Part III
(1) A claim by any person ('the claimant') that another person ('the respondent')—

(a) has committed an act of discrimination against the claimant which is unlawful by virtue of Part III; or
(b) is by virtue of section 32 or 33 to be treated as having committed such an act of discrimination against the claimant, may be made the subject of civil proceedings in like manner as any other claim in tort or (in Scotland) in reparation for breach of statutory duty.

(2) Proceedings under subsection (1)—

(a) shall, in England and Wales, be brought only in a designated county court; and
(b) . . .

but all such remedies shall be obtainable in such proceedings as, apart from this subsection and section 53(1) would be obtainable in the High Court or the Court of Session, as the case may be.
(3) As respects an unlawful act of discrimination falling within section 1(1)(b), no award of damages shall be made if the respondent proves that the requirement or condition in question was not applied with the intention of treating the claimant unfavourably on racial grounds.
(4) For the avoidance of doubt it is hereby declared that damages in respect of an unlawful act of discrimination may include compensation for injury to feelings whether or not they include compensation under any other head.
[(4A) As respects an act which is done, or by virtue of section 32 or 33 is treated as done, by a person in carrying out public investigator functions or functions as a public prosecutor and which is unlawful by virtue of section 19B, no remedy other than—

(a) damages; or
(b) a declaration or, in Scotland, a declarator;

shall be obtainable unless the court is satisfied that the remedy concerned would not prejudice a criminal investigation, a decision to institute criminal proceedings or any criminal proceedings.
(4B) In this section—

'criminal investigation' means—

(a) any investigation which a person in carrying out functions to which section 19B applies has a duty to conduct with a view to it being ascertained whether a person should be charged with, or in Scotland prosecuted for, an offence, or whether a person charged with or prosecuted for an offence is guilty of it;
(b) any investigation which is conducted by a person in carrying out functions

to which section 19B applies and which in the circumstances may lead to a decision by that person to institute criminal proceedings which the person has power to conduct; or

(c) any investigation which is conducted by a person in carrying out functions to which section 19B applies and which in the circumstances may lead to a decision by that person to make a report to the procurator fiscal for the purpose of enabling him to determine whether criminal proceedings should be instituted; and

'public investigator functions' means functions of conducting criminal investigations or charging offenders;

and in this subsection 'offence' includes any offence under the Army Act 1955, the Air Force Act 1955 or the Naval Discipline Act 1957 (and 'offender' shall be construed accordingly).

(4C) Subsection (4D) applies where a party to proceedings under subsection (1) which have arisen by virtue of section 19B has applied for a stay or sist of those proceedings on the grounds of prejudice to—

(a) particular criminal proceedings;
(b) a criminal investigation; or
(c) a decision to institute criminal proceedings.

(4D) The court shall grant the stay or sist unless it is satisfied that the continuance of the proceedings under subsection (1) would not result in the prejudice alleged.]

(5) Civil proceedings in respect of a claim by any person that he has been discriminated against in contravention of section 17 or 18 by a body to which section 19(1) [subsection (5A)] applies shall not be instituted unless the claimant has given notice of the claim to the Secretary of State and either the Secretary of State has by notice informed the claimant that the Secretary of State does not require further time to consider the matter, or the period of two months has elapsed since the claimant gave notice to the Secretary of State; but nothing in this subsection applies to a counterclaim.

[(5A) This subsection applies to—

(a) local education authorities in England and Wales;
(b) education authorities in Scotland; and
(c) any body which is a responsible body in relation to an establishment falling within paragraph 3, 3B or 7B of the table in section 17.]

(6) . . .

[(7) This section has effect subject to section 57A.]

Notes Sub-s (2): para (b) applies to Scotland only.

Sub-ss (4A)–(4D): inserted by the Race Relations (Amendment) Act 2000, s 5(1).

Sub-s (5): words 'section 19(1)' in italics revoked and subsequent words in square brackets substituted by the Race Relations (Amendment) Act 2000, s 9(1), Sch 2, para 6(*a*).

Sub-s (5): words from 'and either the' to 'to a counterclaim' in italics repealed by the Race Relations (Amendment) Act 2000, s 9, Sch 2, para 6(b), Sch 3.

Sub-s (5A): inserted by the Race Relations (Amendment) Act 2000, s 9(1), Sch 2, para 7.

Sub-s (6): applies to Scotland only.

Sub-s (7): inserted by the Race Relations (Amendment) Act 2000, s 6(1).

Transfer of Functions Functions of the Secretary of State, so far as exercisable in relation to Wales, transferred to the National Assembly for Wales, by the National Assembly for Wales (Transfer of Functions) Order 1999, SI 1999/672, art 2, Sch 1.

Functions under this section: functions under sub-s (5) are transferred, in so far as they are exercisable in or as regards Scotland, to the Scottish Ministers, by the Scotland Act 1998 (Transfer of Functions to the Scottish Ministers etc) Order 1999, SI 1999/1750, art 2, Sch 1.

Subordinate Legislation Act of Sederunt (Summary Applications, Statutory Applications and Appeals etc Rules) (Amendment) 2000, SSI 2000/148 (made under sub-s (6)).

[A.1.69]
[57A Claims under section 19B in immigration cases]
[(1) No proceedings may be brought by a claimant under section 57(1) in respect of an immigration claim if—

(a) the act to which the claim relates was done in the taking by an immigration authority of a relevant decision and the question whether that act was unlawful by virtue of section 19B has been or could be raised in proceedings on an appeal which is pending, or could be brought, under the 1997 Act or Part IV of the 1999 Act; or

(b) it has been decided in relevant immigration proceedings that that act was not unlawful by virtue of that section.

(2) For the purposes of this section an immigration claim is a claim that a person—

(a) has committed a relevant act of discrimination against the claimant which is unlawful by virtue of section 19B; or

(b) is by virtue of section 32 or 33 to be treated as having committed such an act of discrimination against the claimant.

(3) Where it has been decided in relevant immigration proceedings that an act to which an immigration claim relates was unlawful by virtue of section 19B, any court hearing that claim under section 57 shall treat that act as an act which is unlawful by virtue of section 19B for the purposes of the proceedings before it.

(4) No relevant decision of an immigration authority involving an act to which an immigration claim relates and no relevant decision of an immigration appellate body in relation to such a decision shall be subject to challenge or otherwise affected by virtue of a decision of a court hearing the immigration claim under section 57.

(5) In this section—

'the Immigration Acts' has the same meaning as in the 1999 Act;

'immigration appellate body' means an adjudicator appointed for the purposes of the 1999 Act, the Immigration Appeal Tribunal, the Special Immigration Appeals Commission, the Court of Appeal, the Court of Session or the House of Lords;

'immigration authority' means an authority within the meaning of section 65 of the 1999 Act (human rights and racial discrimination cases);

'immigration claim' has the meaning given by subsection (2) above;

'pending' has the same meaning as in the 1997 Act or, as the case may be, Part IV of the 1999 Act;

'relevant act of discrimination' means an act of discrimination done by an immigration authority in taking any relevant decision;

'relevant decision' means—

(a) in relation to an immigration authority, any decision under the Immigration Acts relating to the entitlement of the claimant to enter or remain in the United Kingdom; and

(b) in relation to an immigration appellate body, any decision on an appeal under the 1997 Act or Part IV of the 1999 Act in relation to a decision falling within paragraph (a);

'relevant immigration proceedings' means proceedings on an appeal under the 1997 Act or Part IV of the 1999 Act;

'the 1997 Act' means the Special Immigration Appeals Commission Act 1997;

'the 1999 Act' means the Immigration and Asylum Act 1999;

and, for the purposes of subsection (1)(a), any power to grant leave to appeal out of time shall be disregarded.]

Note Inserted by the Race Relations (Amendment) Act 2000, s 6(2).

Other enforcement by Commission

[A.1.70]
62 Persistent discrimination
(1) If, during the period of five years beginning on the date on which any of the following became final in the case of any person, namely—

(a) a non-discrimination notice served on him; or

(b) a finding by a tribunal or court under section 54 or 57; that he has done an unlawful discriminatory act; or

[(ba) a finding under the Special Immigration Appeals Commission Act 1997 or Part IV of the Immigration and Asylum Act 1999 that he has done an act which was unlawful by virtue of section 19B; or]

(c) a finding by a court in proceedings under section 19 or 20 of the Race Relations Act 1968 that he has done an act which was unlawful by virtue of any provision of Part I of that Act,

it appears to the Commission that unless restrained he is likely to do one or more acts falling within paragraph (b), or contravening section 28, the Commission may apply to a designated county court for an injunction, or to a sheriff court for an order, restraining him from doing so; and the court, if satisfied that the application is well-founded, may grant the injunction or order in the terms applied for or in more limited terms.

(2) In proceedings under this section the Commission shall not allege that the person to whom the proceedings relate has done an act falling within subsection (1)(b) or contravening section 28 which is within the jurisdiction of an [employment tribunal] unless a finding by an [employment tribunal] that he did that act has become final.

Notes Sub-s (1): para (ba) inserted by the Race Relations (Amendment) Act 2000, s 9(1), Sch 2, para 9.

Sub-s (2): words 'employment tribunal' in square brackets in each place they occur substituted by the Employment Rights (Dispute Resolution) Act 1998, s 1(2)(*a*).

Date in force: 1 August 1998: See SI 1998/1658, art 2(1), Sch 1.

Help for persons suffering discrimination

[A.1.71]
65 Help for aggrieved persons in obtaining information etc
(1)   With a view to helping a person ('the person aggrieved') who considers he may have been discriminated against in contravention of this Act to decide whether to institute proceedings and, if he does so, to formulate and present his case in the most effective manner, the Secretary of State shall by order prescribe—

(a) forms by which the person aggrieved may question the respondent on his reasons for doing any relevant act, or on any other matter which is or may be relevant; and
(b) forms by which the respondent may if he so wishes reply to any questions.

(2)   Where the person aggrieved questions the respondent (whether in accordance with an order under subsection (1) or not)—

(a) the question, and any reply by the respondent (whether in accordance with such an order or not) shall, subject to the following provisions of this section, be admissible as evidence in the proceedings;
(b) if it appears to the court or tribunal that the respondent deliberately, and without reasonable excuse, omitted to reply within a reasonable period or that his reply is evasive or equivocal, the court or tribunal may draw any inference from that fact that it considers just and equitable to draw, including an inference that he committed an unlawful act.

(3)   The Secretary of State may by order—

(a) prescribe the period within which questions must be duly served in order to be admissible under subsection (2)(a); and
(b) prescribe the manner in which a question, and any reply by the respondent, may be duly served.

(4)   Rules may enable the court entertaining a claim under section 57 to determine, before the date fixed for the hearing of the claim, whether a question or reply is admissible under this section or not.
[(4A)   In section 19B proceedings, subsection (2)(b) does not apply in relation to a failure to reply, or a particular reply, if the conditions specified in subsection (4B) are satisfied.
(4B)   Those conditions are that—

(a) at the time of doing any relevant act, the respondent was carrying out public investigator functions or was a public prosecutor; and
(b) he reasonably believes that a reply or (as the case may be) a different reply would be likely to prejudice any criminal investigation, any decision to institute criminal proceedings or any criminal proceedings or would reveal the reasons behind a decision not to institute, or a decision not to continue, criminal proceedings.

(4C)   For the purposes of subsections (4A) and (4B)—

'public investigator functions' has the same meaning as in section 57;
'section 19B proceedings' means proceedings in respect of a claim under section 57 which has arisen by virtue of section 19B.]
(5)   This section is without prejudice to any other enactment or rule of law regulating interlocutory and preliminary matters in proceedings before a county court, sheriff court or [employment tribunal], and has effect subject to any enactment or rule of law regulating the admissibility of evidence in such proceedings.
(6)   In this section 'respondent' includes a prospective respondent and 'rules'—

(a) in relation to county court proceedings, means county court rules;
(b) . . .

[(7)   This section does not apply in relation to any proceedings under—

(a) the Special Immigration Appeals Commission Act 1997; or
(b) Part IV of the Immigration and Asylum Act 1999.]

Notes   Sub-ss (4A)–(4C): inserted by the Race Relations (Amendment) Act 2000, s 5(2).

Sub-s (5): words 'employment tribunal' in square brackets substituted by the Employment Rights (Dispute Resolution) Act 1998, s 1(2)(*a*).

Date in force: 1 August 1998: see SI 1998/1658, art 2(1), Sch 1.

Sub-s (6): para (*b*) applies to Scotland only.

Sub-s (7): inserted by the Race Relations (Amendment) Act 2000, s 9(1), Sch 2, para 10.

[A.1.72]
66 Assistance by Commission
[(8)   This section (except for subsection (4)) applies to proceedings or prospective proceedings under the Special Immigration Appeals Commission Act 1997 or Part IV of the Immigration and Asylum Act 1999 so far as they relate to acts which may be unlawful by virtue of section 19B as it applies to proceedings or prospective proceedings under this Act.
(9)   In this section as it applies by virtue of subsection (8) 'rules and regulations' means—

(a) in relation to proceedings under the Act of 1997, rules under section 5 or 8 of that Act;
(b) in relation to proceedings under Part IV of the Act of 1999, rules under paragraph 3 or 4 of Schedule 4 to that Act.]

Notes   Sub-ss (8), (9): inserted by the Race Relations (Amendment) Act 2000, s 9(1), Sch 2, para 11.

Sheriff courts and designated county courts

[A.1.73]
67 Sheriff courts and designated county courts
(3)   A designated county court or a sheriff court shall have jurisdiction to entertain proceedings under this Act with respect to an act done on a ship, air-craft or hovercraft outside its district, including such an act done outside Great Britain.

Period within which proceedings to be brought

[A.1.74]
68 Period within which proceedings to be brought
(2)   [Subject to subsection (2A)] a county court or a sheriff court shall not consider a claim under section 57 unless proceedings in respect of the claim are instituted before the end of—

(a) the period of six months beginning when the act complained of was done; or

(b) in a case to which section 57(5) applies, the period of eight months so beginning.

[(2A)   In relation to an immigration claim within the meaning of section 57A, the period of six months mentioned in subsection (2)(a) begins on the expiry of the period during which, by virtue of section 57A(1)(a), no proceed-ings may be brought under section 57(1) in respect of the claim.]

Notes   Sub-s (2): words 'Subject to subsection (2A)' in square brackets inserted by the Race Relations (Amendment) Act 2000, s 9(1), Sch 2, para 13.
    Sub-s (2): para (b) and the word 'or' immediately preceding it repealed by the Race Relations (Amendment) Act 2000, s 9(2), Sch 3.
    Sub-s (2A): inserted by the Race Relations (Amendment) Act 2000, s 9(1), Sch 2, para 14.

Evidence

[A.1.75]
69 Evidence
(1)   Any finding by a court under section 19 or 20 of the Race Relations Act 1968, or by a court or [employment tribunal] under this Act, in respect of any act shall, if it has become final, be treated as conclusive in any proceedings under this Act.
(2)   In any proceedings under this Act [or any enactment mentioned in section 19D(5)] a certificate signed by or on behalf of a Minister of the Crown and cer-tifying—

(a) that any arrangements or conditions specified in the certificate were made, approved or imposed by a Minister of the Crown and were in operation at a time or throughout a period so specified; or

(b) that an act specified in the certificate was done for the purpose of safeguarding national security,

shall be conclusive evidence of the matters certified.

[(2A) Subsection (2)(b) shall not have effect for the purposes of proceedings on a complaint under section 54.]

(3) A document purporting to be a certificate such as is mentioned in subsection (2) shall be received in evidence and, unless the contrary is proved, shall be deemed to be such a certificate.

Commencement SI 1977/840.

Notes Sub-s (1): words 'employment tribunal' in square brackets substituted by the Employment Rights (Dispute Resolution) Act 1998, s 1(2)(a).

Date in force: 1 August 1998: see SI 1998/1658, art 2(1), Sch 1.

Sub-s (2): words 'or any enactment mentioned in section 19D(5)' in square brackets inserted by the Race Relations (Amendment) Act 2000, s 9(1), Sch 2, para 15.

Sub-s (2): para (b) and the word 'or' immediately preceding it repealed by the Race Relations (Amendment) Act 2000, ss 7(2), 9(2), Sch 3 .

Sub-s (2A): inserted by the Employment Relations Act 1999, s 41, Sch 8, para 6.

Sub-s (2A): repealed by the Race Relations (Amendment) Act 2000, s 9(2), Sch 3.

Transfer of Functions See further in relation to the exercise of functions under this section by the National Assembly for Wales, by the National Assembly for Wales (Transfer of Functions) Order 1999, SI 1999/672, art 2, Sch 1.

PART X
SUPPLEMENTAL

[A.1.76]
[71 Specified authorities: general statutory duty]

[(1) Every body or other person specified in Schedule 1A or of a description falling within that Schedule shall, in carrying out its functions, have due regard to the need—

(a) to eliminate unlawful racial discrimination; and
(b) to promote equality of opportunity and good relations between persons of different racial groups.

(2) The Secretary of State may by order impose, on such persons falling within Schedule 1A as he considers appropriate, such duties as he considers appropriate for the purpose of ensuring the better performance by those persons of their duties under subsection (1).

(3) An order under subsection (2)—

(a) may be made in relation to a particular person falling within Schedule 1A, any description of persons falling within that Schedule or every person falling within that Schedule;
(b) may make different provision for different purposes.

(4) Before making an order under subsection (2), the Secretary of State shall consult the Commission.

(5) The Secretary of State may by order amend Schedule 1A; but no such order may extend the application of this section unless the Secretary of State

considers that the extension relates to a person who exercises functions of a public nature.

(6) An order under subsection (2) or (5) may contain such incidental, supplementary or consequential provision as the Secretary of State considers appropriate (including provision amending or repealing provision made by or under this Act or any other enactment).

(7) This section is subject to section 71A and 71B and is without prejudice to the obligation of any person to comply with any other provision of this Act.]

Commencement SI 1977/840.

Notes Substituted, by new ss 71–71E, by the Race Relations (Amendment) Act 2000, s 2(1).

[A.1.77]
[71A General statutory duty: special cases]
[(1) In relation to the carrying out of immigration and nationality functions (within the meaning of section 19D(1)), section 71(1)(b) has effect with the omission of the words 'equality of opportunity and'.

(2) Where an entry in Schedule 1A is limited to a person in a particular capacity, section 71(1) does not apply to that person in any other capacity.

(3) Where an entry in Schedule 1A is limited to particular functions of a person, section 71(1) does not apply to that person in relation to any other functions.]

Notes Substituted, together with new ss 71, 71B–E, for existing s 71, by the Race Relations (Amendment) Act 2000, s 2(1).

[A.1.78]
73 Power to amend certain provisions of Act
(1) The Secretary of State may by an order the draft of which has been approved by each House of Parliament—

(a) amend or repeal section 9 (including that section as amended by a previous order under this subsection);

(b) amend Part II, III or IV so as to render lawful an act which, apart from the amendment, would be unlawful by reason of section 4(1) or (2), [19B,] 20(1), 21, 24 or 25;

(c) amend section 10(1) or 25(1)(a) so as to alter the number of partners or members specified in that provision.

(2) The Secretary of State shall not lay before Parliament the draft of an order under subsection (1) unless he has consulted the Commission about the contents of the draft.

Notes Sub-s (1): in para (b) reference to '19B,' in square brackets inserted by the Race Relations (Amendment) Act 2000, s 9(1), Sch 2, para 16.

[A.1.79]
74 Orders and regulations
(1) Any power of a Minister of the Crown to make orders or regulations

under the provisions of this Act (except [section] 50(2)(a)) shall be exercisable by statutory instrument.

(2) An order made by a Minister of the Crown under the preceding provisions of this Act (except sections . . . 50(2)(a) and 73(1)), and any regulations made under section [56(5), (6) or] 75(5)(a) [or (9A)], shall be subject to annulment in pursuance of a resolution of either House of Parliament.

(3) An order under this Act may make different provision in relation to different cases or classes of case, may exclude certain cases or classes of case, and may contain transitional provisions and savings.

(4) Any power conferred by this Act to make orders includes power (exercisable in the like manner and subject to the like conditions) to vary or revoke any order so made.

(5) Any document purporting to be an order made by the Secretary of State under section . . . 50(2)(a) and to be signed by him or on his behalf shall be received in evidence, and shall, unless the contrary is proved, be deemed to be made by him.

Amendment Sub-s (1): word in square brackets substituted by the Employment Act 1989, s 29(3), Sch 6, para 16.

Sub-s (2): words omitted repealed by the Employment Act 1989, s 29(4), Sch 7, Part II; first words in square brackets inserted by the Race Relations (Remedies) Act 1994, s 2(2); final words in square brackets inserted by the Armed Forces Act 1996, s 23(5).

Sub-s (5): words omitted repealed by the Employment Act 1989, s 29(4), Sch 7, Part II.

[A.1.80]
75 Application to Crown etc
(1) This Act applies—

(a) to an act done by or for purposes of a Minister of the Crown or government department; or
(b) to an act done on behalf of the Crown by a statutory body, or a person holding a statutory office,

as it applies to an act done by a private person.
(2) Parts II and IV apply to—

(a) service for purposes of a Minister of the Crown or government department, other than service of a person holding a statutory office; or
(b) service on behalf of the Crown for purposes of a person holding a statutory office or purposes of a statutory body; or
(c) service in the armed forces,

as they apply to employment by a private person, and shall so apply as if references to a contract of employment included references to the terms of service.

[(2A) Subsections (1) and (2) do not apply in relation to the provisions mentioned in subsection (2B).

(2B) Sections 19B to 19F, sections 71 to 71E (including Schedule 1A) and section 76 bind the Crown; and the other provisions of this Act so far as they relate to those provisions shall be construed accordingly (including, in particular, references to employment in Part IV).]

(3) Subsections (1) and (2) [to (2B)] have effect subject to section 16 [sections 76A and 76B].

(4) Subsection (2) of section 8 and subsection (4) of section 27 shall have effect in relation to any ship, aircraft or hovercraft belonging to or possessed by Her Majesty in right of the Government of the United Kingdom as it has effect in relation to a ship, aircraft or hovercraft such as is mentioned in paragraph (a) or (b) of the subsection in question; and section 8(3) shall apply accordingly.

(5) Nothing in this Act shall—

(a) invalidate any rules (whether made before or after the passing of this Act) restricting employment in the service of the Crown or by any public body prescribed for the purposes of this subsection by regulations made by the Minister for the Civil Service to persons of particular birth, nationality, descent or residence; or

(b) render unlawful the publication, display or implementation of any such rules, or the publication of advertisements stating the gist of any such rules.

In this subsection 'employment' includes service of any kind, and 'public body' means a body of persons, whether corporate or unincorporate, carrying on a service or undertaking of a public nature.

(6) The provisions of Parts II to IV of the Crown Proceedings Act 1947 shall apply to proceedings against the Crown under this Act as they apply to proceedings in England and Wales which by virtue of section 23 of that Act are treated for the purposes of Part II of that Act as civil proceedings by or against the Crown, except that in their application to proceedings under this Act section 20 of that Act (removal of proceedings from county court to High Court) shall not apply.

(7) . . .

(8) This subsection applies to any complaint by a person ('the complainant') that another person—

(a) has committed an act of discrimination against the complainant which is unlawful by virtue of section 4; or

(b) is by virtue of section 32 or 33 to be treated as having committed such an act of discrimination against the complainant,

if at the time when the act complained of was done the complainant was serving in the armed forces and the discrimination in question relates to his service in those forces.

[(9) No complaint to which subsection (8) applies shall be presented to an [employment tribunal] under section 54 unless—

(a) the complainant has made a complaint to an officer under the service redress procedures applicable to him and has submitted that complaint to the Defence Council under those procedures; and

(b) the Defence Council have made a determination with respect to the complaint.

(9A) Regulations may make provision enabling a complaint to which subsection (8) applies to be presented to an [employment tribunal] under section 54 in such circumstances as may be specified by the regulations, notwithstanding that subsection (9) would otherwise preclude the presentation of the complaint to an [employment tribunal].

(9B) Where a complaint is presented to an [employment tribunal] under section 54 by virtue of regulations under subsection (9A), the service redress procedures may continue after the complaint is so presented.]

(10)   In this section—

(a) 'the armed forces' means any of the naval, military or air forces of the Crown . . .

[(aa)   'regulations' means regulations made by the Secretary of State;

(ab) 'the service redress procedures' means the procedures, excluding those which relate to the making of a report on a complaint to Her Majesty, referred to in section 180 of the Army Act 1955, section 180 of the Air Force Act 1955 and section 130 of the Naval Discipline Act 1957;]

(b) 'statutory body' means a body set up by or in pursuance of an enactment, and 'statutory office' means an office so set up; and

(c) service 'for purposes of' a Minister of the Crown or government department does not include service in any office in Schedule 2 (Ministerial offices) to the House of Commons Disqualification Act 1975 as for the time being in force.

Notes   Sub-ss (2A), (2B): inserted by the Race Relations (Amendment) Act 2000, s 9(1), Sch 2, para 17.

Sub-s (3): words 'and (2)' in italics repealed and subsequent words in square brackets substituted by the Race Relations (Amendment) Act 2000, s 9(1), Sch 2, para 18(*a*).

Sub-s (3): words 'section 16' in italics repealed and subsequent words in square brackets substituted by the Race Relations (Amendment) Act 2000, s 9(1), Sch 2, para 18(*b*).

Sub-s (7): applies to Scotland only.

Sub-ss (9)–(9B): substituted, for sub-s (9) as originally enacted, by the Armed Forces Act 1996, s 23(2).

Sub-s (9): words 'employment tribunal' in square brackets substituted by the Employment Rights (Dispute Resolution) Act 1998, s 1(2)(*a*).

Date in force: 1 August 1998: see SI 1998/1658, art 2(1), Sch 1.

Sub-s (9A): words 'employment tribunal' in square brackets in each place they occur substituted by the Employment Rights (Dispute Resolution) Act 1998, s 1(2)(*a*).

Date in force: 1 August 1998: see SI 1998/1658, art 2(1), Sch 1.

Sub-s (9B): words 'employment tribunal' in square brackets substituted by the Employment Rights (Dispute Resolution) Act 1998, s 1(2)(*a*).

Date in force: 1 August 1998: see SI 1998/1658, art 2(1), Sch 1.

Sub-s (10): in para (*a*) words omitted repealed by the Armed Forces Act 1981, s 28(2), Sch 5, Pt I.

Sub-s (10): paras (*aa*), (*ab*) inserted by the Armed Forces Act 1996, s 23(3).

[A.1.81]
78 General interpretation provisions

(1)   In this Act, unless the context otherwise requires—

'access' shall be construed in accordance with section 40;

'act' includes a deliberate omission;

'advertisement' includes every form of advertisement or notice, whether to the public or not, and whether in a newspaper or other publication, by television or radio, by display of notices, signs, labels, showcards or goods, by distribution of samples, circulars, catalogues, price lists or other material, by exhibition of pictures, models or films, or in any other way, and references to the publishing of advertisements shall be construed accordingly;

['board of management', in relation to a self-governing school, has the same meaning as in the Education (Scotland) Act 1980;]

['board of management' in relation to a college of further education within the meaning of Part I of the Further and Higher Education (Scotland) Act 1992, has the same meaning as in that Part;]

['body' includes an unincorporated association;]

'the Commission' means the Commission for Racial Equality;

'Commissioner' means a member of the Commission;

['criminal investigation' has the meaning given by section 57(4B);]

['criminal proceedings' includes—

(a) proceedings on dealing summarily with a charge under the Army Act 1955 or the Air Force Act 1955 or on summary trial under the Naval Discipline Act 1957;

(b) proceedings before a summary appeal court constituted under any of those Acts;

(c) proceedings before a court-martial constituted under any of those Acts or a disciplinary court constituted under section 52G of the Act of 1957;

(d) proceedings before the Courts-Martial Appeal Court; and

(e) proceedings before a Standing Civilian Court;]

'designated county court' has the meaning given by section 67(1);

'discrimination' and related terms shall be construed in accordance with section 3(3);

'dispose', in relation to premises, includes granting a right to occupy the premises, and any reference to acquiring premises shall be construed accordingly;

'education' includes any form of training or instruction;

['the Education Acts' has the meaning given by section 578 of the Education Act 1996;]

'education authority' and 'educational establishment' have for Scotland the same meaning as they have respectively in [section 135(1) of the Education (Scotland) Act 1980];

'employment' means employment under a contract of service or of apprenticeship or a contract personally to execute any work or labour, and related expressions shall be construed accordingly;

'employment agency' means a person who, for profit or not, provides services for the purpose of finding employment for workers or supplying employers with workers;

['enactment' includes an enactment comprised in, or in an instrument made under, an Act of the Scottish Parliament;]

'estate agent' means a person who, by way of profession or trade, provides services for the purpose of finding premises for persons seeking to acquire them or assisting in the disposal of premises;

'final' shall be construed in accordance with subsection (4);

'firm' has the meaning given by section 4 of the Partnership Act 1890;

'formal investigation' means an investigation under section 48;

'further education' has . . . and for Scotland the meaning given by [section 135(1) of the Education (Scotland) Act 1980];

'general notice', in relation to any person, means a notice published by him at a time and in a manner appearing to him suitable for securing that the notice is seen within a reasonable time by persons likely to be affected by it;

'genuine occupational qualification' shall be construed in accordance with section 5;

'Great Britain' includes such of the territorial waters of the United Kingdom as are adjacent to Great Britain;

'independent school' has for England and Wales the meaning given by [section 463 of the Education Act 1996], and for Scotland the meaning given by [section 135(1) of the Education (Scotland) Act 1980];

. . .

'managers' has for Scotland the same meaning as in [section 135(1) of the Education (Scotland) Act 1980];

'Minister of the Crown' includes the Treasury and the Defence Council;

'nationality' includes citizenship;

'near relative' shall be construed in accordance with subsection (5);

'non-discrimination notice' means a notice under section 58;

'notice' means a notice in writing;

'prescribed' means prescribed by regulations made by the Secretary of State;

'profession' includes any vocation or occupation;

'proprietor', in relation to a school, has for England and Wales the meaning given by [section 579 of the Education Act 1996], and for Scotland the meaning given by [section 135(1) of the Education (Scotland) Act 1980];

'pupil' in Scotland includes a student of any age;

'racial grounds' and 'racial group' have the meaning given by section 3(1);

'school' has for England and Wales the meaning given by [section 4 of the Education Act 1996], and for Scotland the meaning given by [section 135(1) of the Education (Scotland) Act 1980];

'school education' has the meaning given by [section 135(1) of the Education (Scotland) Act 1980];

['self-governing school' has the same meaning as in the Education (Scotland) Act 1980;]

'trade' includes any business;

'training' includes any form of education or instruction;

'university' includes a university college and the college, school or hall of a university;

. . .

(2)   It is hereby declared that in this Act 'premises', unless the context otherwise requires, includes land of any description.

(3)   Any power conferred by this Act to designate establishments or persons may be exercised either by naming them or by identifying them by reference to a class or other description.

(4)   For the purposes of this Act a non-discrimination notice or a finding by a court or tribunal becomes final when an appeal against the notice or finding is dismissed, withdrawn or abandoned or when the time for appealing expires without an appeal having been brought; and for this purpose an appeal against a non-discrimination notice shall be taken to be dismissed if, notwithstanding that a requirement of the notice is quashed on appeal, a direction is given in respect of it under section 59 (3).

(5)   For the purposes of this Act a person is a near relative of another if that person is the wife or husband, a parent or child, a grandparent or grandchild, or a brother or sister of the other (whether of full blood or half-blood or by affinity), and 'child' includes an illegitimate child and the wife or husband of an illegitimate child.

(6) Except so far as the context otherwise requires, any reference in this Act to an enactment shall be construed as a reference to that enactment as amended by or under any other enactment, including this Act.

(7) In this Act, except where otherwise indicated—

(a) a reference to a numbered Part, section or Schedule is a reference to the Part or section of, or the Schedule to, this Act so numbered; and

(b) a reference in a section to a numbered subsection is a reference to the subsection of that section so numbered; and

(c) a reference in a section, subsection or Schedule to a numbered paragraph is a reference to the paragraph of that section, subsection or Schedule so numbered; and

(d) a reference to any provision of an Act (including this Act) includes a Schedule incorporated in the Act by that provision.

Notes Sub-s (1): definition 'board of management', in relation to a self-governing school, inserted by the Self-Governing Schools etc (Scotland) Act 1989, s 82(1), Sch 10, para 6(4).

Sub-s (1): definition 'board of management', in relation to a self-governing school, repealed by the Standards in Scotland's Schools etc Act 2000, s 60(2), Sch 3.

Sub-s (1): definition 'board of management', in relation to a college of further education, inserted by the Further and Higher Education (Scotland) Act 1992, s 93, Sch 9, para 5(5).

Sub-s (1): definition 'body' inserted by the Race Relations (Amendment) Act 2000, s 9(1), Sch 2, para 19.

Sub-s (1): definition 'criminal investigation' inserted by the Race Relations (Amendment) Act 2000, s 9(1), Sch 2, para 19.

Sub-s (1): definition 'criminal proceedings' inserted by the Race Relations (Amendment) Act 2000, s 9(1), Sch 2, para 19.

Sub-s (1): definition 'the Education Acts' inserted by the Education Act 1996, s 582(1), Sch 37, para 43.

Sub-s (1): in definition 'education authority' and 'educational establishment' words 'section 135(1) of the Education (Scotland) Act 1980' in square brackets substituted by the Education (Scotland) Act 1980, s 136(2), Sch 4, para 15.

Sub-s (1): definition 'enactment' inserted by SI 2000/2040, art 2(1), Schedule, Pt I, para 9.

Date in force: 27 July 2000: see SI 2000/2040, art 1(1).

Sub-s (1): in definition 'further education' words omitted repealed by the Education Reform Act 1988, s 237, Sch 13, Pt II.

Sub-s (1): in definition 'further education' words 'section 135(1) of the Education (Scotland) Act 1980' in square brackets substituted by the Education (Scotland) Act 1980, s 136(2), Sch 4, para 15.Sub-s (1): in definition 'independent school' words 'section 463 of the Education Act 1996' in square brackets substituted by the Education Act 1996, s 582(1), Sch 37, para 43.

Sub-s (1): in definition 'independent school' words 'section 135(1) of the Education (Scotland) Act 1980' in square brackets substituted by the Education (Scotland) Act 1980, s 136(2), Sch 4, para 15.

Sub-s (1): definition 'industrial tribunal' (omitted) repealed by the Industrial Training Act 1982, s 20, Sch 3, para 7(b), Sch 4.

Sub-s (1): in definition 'managers' words 'section 135(1) of the Education (Scotland) Act 1980' in square brackets substituted by the Education (Scotland) Act 1980, s 136(2), Sch 4, para 15.

Sub-s (1): in definition 'proprietor' words 'section 579 of the Education Act 1996' in square brackets substituted by the Education Act 1996, s 582(1), Sch 37, para 43.

Sub-s (1): in definition 'proprietor' words 'section 135(1) of the Education (Scotland) Act 1980' in square brackets substituted by the Education (Scotland) Act 1980, s 136(2), Sch 4, para 15.

Sub-s (1): in definition 'school' words 'section 4 of the Education Act 1996' in square brackets substituted by the Education Act 1996, s 582(1), Sch 37, para 43.

Sub-s (1): in definition 'school' words 'section 135(1) of the Education (Scotland) Act 1980' in square brackets substituted by the Education (Scotland) Act 1980, s 136(2), Sch 4, para 15.

Sub-s (1): in definition 'school education' words 'section 135(1) of the Education (Scotland) Act 1980' in square brackets substituted by the Education (Scotland) Act 1980, s 136(2), Sch 4, para 15.

Sub-s (1): definition 'self-governing school' inserted by the Self-Governing Schools etc (Scotland) Act 1989, s 82(1), Sch 10, para 6(4).

Sub-s (1): definition 'self-governing school' repealed by the Standards in Scotland's Schools etc Act 2000, s 60(2), Sch 3.Date in force: to be appointed: see the Standards in Scotland's Schools etc Act 2000, s 61(2).

Sub-s (1): definition 'upper limit of compulsory school age' (omitted) repealed by the Education Act 1996, s 582(2), Sch 38, Pt II.

BRITISH NATIONALITY ACT 1981
(1981 c 61)

Arrangement of sections

References in bold are to paragraph numbers

PART I

BRITISH CITIZENSHIP

Acquisition after commencement

Acquisition after commencement: special cases

Acquisition at commencement

Renunciation and resumption

Supplementary

PART II
BRITISH DEPENDENT TERRITORIES CITIZENSHIP

PART III
BRITISH OVERSEAS CITIZENSHIP

PART IV
BRITISH SUBJECTS

An Act to make fresh provision about citizenship and nationality, and to amend the Immigration Act 1971 as regards the right of abode in the United Kingdom
[30 October 1981]

Commencement   Sections 1–52 and Schs 1–9 came into force on 1 January 1983 (SI 1982/933); s 53 came into force on 30 October 1981 (s 53(3)).

PART I
BRITISH CITIZENSHIP

Acquisition after commencement

[A.1.82]
1 Acquisition by birth or adoption
(1) A person born in the United Kingdom after commencement shall be a British citizen if at the time of the birth his father or mother is:

(*a*) a British citizen; or
(*b*) settled in the United Kingdom.

(2) A new-born infant who, after commencement, is found abandoned in the United Kingdom shall, unless the contrary is shown, by deemed for the purposes of subsection (1):

(*a*) to have been born in the United Kingdom after commencement; and
(*b*) to have been born to a parent who at the time of the birth was a British citizen or settled in the United Kingdom.

(3) A person born in the United Kingdom after commencement who is not a British citizen by virtue of subsection (1) or (2) shall be entitled to be registered as a British citizen if, while he is a minor:

(*a*) his father or mother becomes a British citizen or becomes settled in the United Kingdom; and
(*b*) an application is made for his registration as a British citizen.

(4) A person born in the United Kingdom after commencement who is not a British citizen by virtue of subsection (1) or (2) shall be entitled, on an application for his registration as a British citizen made at any time after he has attained the age of ten years, to be registered as such a citizen if, as regards each of the first ten years of that person's life, the number of days on which he was absent from the United Kingdom in that year does not exceed 90.
(5) Where after commencement an order authorising the adoption of a minor who is not a British citizen is made by any court in the United Kingdom, he shall be a British citizen as from the date on which the order is made if the adopter or, in the case of a joint adoption, one of the adopters is a British citizen on that date.
(6) Where an order in consequence of which any person became a British citizen by virtue of subsection (5) ceases to have effect, whether on annulment or otherwise, the cesser shall not affect the statues of that person as a British citizen.
(7) If in the special circumstances of any particular case the Secretary of State thinks fit, he may for the purposes of subsection (4) treat the person to whom the application relates as fulfilling the requirement specified in that subsection although, as regards any one or more of the first ten years of that person's life, the number of days on which he was absent from the United Kingdom in that year or each of the years in question exceeds 90.
(8) In this section and elsewhere in this Act 'settled' has the meaning given by section 50.

Definitions For 'commencement', 'minor' and 'the United Kingdom', see s 50(1) (and see also, as to 'commencement', s 53(2); as to 'father', 'mother', and 'parent', see s 50(9) (but see s 47); as to 'settled', see s 50(2)–(4) (see also the Immigration Act 1971, s 8(5A)).

[A.1.83]
2 Acquisition by descent
(1)   A person born outside the United Kingdom after commencement shall be a British citizen if at the time of the birth his father or mother:

(*a*) is a British citizen otherwise than by descent; or
(*b*) is a British citizen and is serving outside the United Kingdom in service to which this paragraph applies, his or her recruitment for that service having taken place in the United Kingdom; or
(*c*) is a British citizen and is serving outside the United Kingdom in service under a Community institution, his or her recruitment for that service having taken place in a country which at the time of the recruitment was a member of the Communities.

(2)   Paragraph (*b*) of subsection (1) applies to:

(*a*) Crown service under the government of the United Kingdom; and
(*b*) service of any description for the time being designated under subsection (3).

(3)   For the purposes of this section the Secretary of State may by order made by statutory instrument designate any description of service which he considers to be closely associated with the activities outside the United Kingdom of Her Majesty's government in the United Kingdom.
(4)   Any order made under subsection (3) shall be subject to annulment in pursuance of a resolution of either House of Parliament.

Definitions   For 'British citizen by descent', see s 14; for 'commencement', 'Crown service', 'Crown service under the government of the United Kingdom' and 'the United Kingdom', see s 50(1) (and see also, as to 'commencement', s 53(2)); as to 'father' and 'mother', see s 50(9) (but see s 47).

[A.1.84]
3 Acquisition by registration: minors
(1)   If while a person is a minor an application is made for his registration as a British citizen, the Secretary of State may, if he thinks fit, cause him to be registered as such a citizen.
(2)   A person born outside the United Kingdom shall be entitled, on an application for his registration as a British citizen made within the period of twelve months from the date of birth, to be registered as such a citizen if the requirements specified in subsection (3) or, in the case of a person born stateless, the requirements specified in paragraphs (*a*) and (*b*) of that subsection, are fulfilled in the case of either that person's father or his mother ('the parent in question').
(3)   The requirements referred to in subsection (2) are:

(*a*)   that the parent in question was a British citizen by descent at the time of the birth; and

(*b*)   that the father or mother of the parent in question:

   (i)   was a British citizen otherwise than by descent at the time of the birth of the parent in question; or

   (ii)   became a British citizen otherwise than by descent at commencement, or would have become such a citizen otherwise than by descent at commencement but for his or her death; and

(*c*)   that, as regards some period of three years ending with a date not later than the date of the birth:

   (i)   the parent in question was in the United Kingdom at the beginning of that period; and

   (ii)   the number of days on which the parent in question was absent from the United Kingdom in that period does not exceed 270.

(4)   If in the special circumstances of any particular case the Secretary of State thinks fit, he may treat subsection (2) as if the reference to twelve months were a reference to six years.

(5)   A person born outside the United Kingdom shall be entitled, on an application for his registration as a British citizen made while he is a minor, to be registered as such a citizen if the following requirements are satisfied, namely:

(*a*)   that at the time of that person's birth his father or mother was a British citizen by descent; and

(*b*)   subject to subsection (6), that that person and his father and mother were in the United Kingdom at the beginning of the period of three years ending with the date of the application and that, in the case of each of them, the number of days on which the person in question was absent from the United Kingdom in that period does not exceed 270; and

(*c*)   subject to subsection (6), that the consent of his father and mother to the registration has been signified in the prescribed manner.

(6)   In the case of an application under subsection (5) of the registration of a person as a British citizen:

(*a*)   if his father or mother died, or their marriage was terminated, on or before the date of the application, or his father and mother were legally separated on that date, the references to his father and mother in paragraph (*b*) of that subsection shall be read either as references to his father or as references to his mother;

(*b*)   if his father or mother died on or before that date, the reference to his father and mother in paragraph (*c*) of that subsection shall be read as a reference to either of them; and

(*c*)   if he was born illegitimate, all those references shall be read as references to his mother.

Definitions   For 'British citizen by descent', see s 14; for 'commencement', 'minor', 'prescribed' and 'the United Kingdom', see s 50(1) (and see also, as to commencement', s 53(2); as to 'date of the application', see s 50(8); as 'from' a date, see s 50(10)(*a*); as to 'father', 'mother' and 'parent, see s 50(9) (but see s 47). Note as to 'the parent in question', sub-s (2) above.

[A.1.85]
4 Acquisition by registration: British Dependent Territories citizens etc
(1) This section applies to any person who is a British Dependent Territories citizen, [a British National (Overseas),] a British Overseas citizen, a British subject under this Act or a British protected person.
(2) A person to whom this section applies shall be entitled, on an application for his registration as a British citizen, to be registered as such a citizen if the following requirements are satisfied in the case of that person, namely:

(a) subject to subsection (3), that he was in the United Kingdom at the beginning of the period of five years ending with the date of the application and that the number of days on which he was absent from the United Kingdom in that period does not exceed 450; and
(b) that the number of days on which he was absent from the United Kingdom in the period of twelve months so ending does not exceed 90; and
(c) that he was not at any time in the period of twelve months so ending subject under the immigration laws to any restriction on the period for which he might remain in the United Kingdom; and
(d) that he was not any time in the period of five years so ending in the United Kingdom in breach of the immigration laws.

(3) So much of subsection (2)(a) as requires the person in question to have been in the United Kingdom at the beginning of the period there mentioned shall not apply in relation to a person who was settled in the United Kingdom immediately before commencement.
(4) If in the special circumstances of any particular case the Secretary of State thinks fit, he may for the purposes of subsection (2) do all or any of the following things, namely:

(a) treat the person to whom the application relates as fulfilling the requirement specified in subsection (2)(a) or subsection (2)(b), or both, although the number of days on which he was absent from the United Kingdom in the period there mentioned exceeds the number there mentioned;
(b) disregard any such restriction as is mentioned in subsection (2)(c), not being a restriction to which that person was subject on the date of the application;
(c) treat that person as fulfilling the requirement specified in subsection (2)(d) although he was in the United Kingdom in breach of the immigration laws in the period there mentioned.

(5) If, on an application for registration as a British citizen made by a person to whom this section applies, the Secretary of State is satisfied that the applicant has at any time served in service to which this subsection applies, he may, if he thinks fit in the special circumstances of the applicant's case, cause him to be registered as such a citizen.
(6) Subsection (5) applies to:

(a) Crown service under the government of a dependent territory; and
(b) paid or unpaid service (not falling within paragraph (a)) as a member of any body established by law in a dependent territory members of which are appointed by or on behalf of the Crown.

Notes Words in square brackets in sub-s (1) inserted by the Hong Kong (British Nationality) Order 1986, SI 1986/948, as from 1 July 1987.

Definitions For 'British National (Overseas)', 'British Overseas citizen', 'British protected person', 'commencement', 'Crown service', 'dependent territory', 'immigration laws' and 'United Kingdom', see s 50(1) (and see also, as to 'commencement', s 53(2); as to 'date of the application', see s 50(8); and as to 'settled', see s 1(8), and s 50(2), (3).

[A.1.86]
5 Acquisition by registration: nationals for purposes of the Community treaties

A British Dependent Territories citizen who falls to be treated as a national of the United Kingdom for the purposes of the Community Treaties shall be entitled to be registered as a British citizen if an application is made for his registration as such a citizen.

[A.1.87]
6 Acquisition by naturalisation

(1)   If, on an application for naturalisation as a British citizen made by a person of full age and capacity, the Secretary of State is satisfied that the applicant fulfils the requirements of Schedule 1 for naturalisation as such a citizen under this subsection, he may, if he thinks fit, grant to him a certificate of naturalisation as such a citizen.

(2)   If, on an application for naturalisation as a British citizen made by a person of full age and capacity who on the date of the application is married to a British citizen, the Secretary of State is satisfied that the applicant fulfils the requirements of Schedule 1 for naturalisation as such a citizen under this subsection, he may, if he thinks fit, grant to him a certificate of naturalisation as such a citizen.

Definitions As to 'date of the application', see s 50(8); as to 'full age' and 'full capacity', see s 50(11)(*a*).

Acquisition after commencement: special cases

[A.1.88]
7 Right to registration by virtue of residence in UK or relevant employment

(1)   A person shall be entitled, on an application for his registration as a British citizen made (subject to subsections (6) and (7)) within five years after commencement, to be registered as such a citizen if either of the following requirements is satisfied in his case, namely:

(*a*)   that, if paragraphs 2 and 3 (but not paragraph 4 or 5) of Schedule 1 to the Immigration Act 1971 had remained in force, he would (had he applied for it) have been, on the date of the application under this subsection, entitled under the said paragraph 2 to be registered in the United Kingdom as a citizen of the United Kingdom and Colonies; or (*b*) that, if section 5A of the 1948 Act (and section 2 of the Immigration Act 1971 as in force immediately before commencement) had remained in force, he would (had he applied for it) have been, both at commencement and on the date of the application under this subsection, entitled under section 5A(1) of the 1948 Act to be registered as a citizen of the United Kingdom and Colonies.

(2)　A person shall be entitled, on an application for his registration as a British citizen made (subject to subsection (8)) within six years after commencement, to be registered as such a citizen if he:

(*a*) was ordinarily resident in the United Kingdom throughout a period ending at commencement but not amounting to five years; and

(*b*) throughout the period from commencement to the date of the application:

(i)　remained ordinarily resident in the United Kingdom; and

(ii)　had the right of abode in the United Kingdom under the Immigration Act 1971; and

(*c*) had on the date of the application been ordinarily resident in the United Kingdom for the last five years or more.

(3)　Subject to subsection (5) if, in the case of an application for the registration of a person under subsection (2) as a British citizen, that person has been engaged in relevant service throughout any period (of whatever length), that period shall for the purposes of subsection (2) be treated as a period throughout which he was ordinarily resident in the United Kingdom.

(4)　For the purposes of subsection (3) 'relevant service' means:

(*a*) Crown service under the government of the United Kingdom; or

(*b*) service under any international organisation of which the United Kingdom or Her Majesty's government therein is a member; or

(*c*) service in the employment of any company or association established in the United Kingdom.

(5)　A person shall not be registered under subsection (2) wholly or partly by reason of service within subsection (4)(*b*) or (*c*) unless it seems to the Secretary of State fitting that he should be so registered by reason of his close connection with the United Kingdom.

(6)　If in the special circumstances of any particular case the Secretary of State thinks fit, he may treat subsection (1) as if:

(*a*) the reference to five years after commencement were a reference to eight years after commencement; or

(*b*) where subsection (7) applies, as if the reference to five years from the date on which the person to whom the application relates attains full age were a reference to eight years from that date,

but shall not do so in the case of an application based on paragraph (*b*) of subsection (1) unless the person to whom the application relates would have been entitled to be registered under that subsection on an application so based made immediately before the end of the five years after commencement.

(7)　In the case of any person who is a minor at commencement, the reference to five years after commencement in subsection (1) above shall be treated as a reference to five years from the date on which he attains full age.

(8) If in the special circumstances of any particular case the Secretary of State thinks fit, he may treat subsection (2) as if the reference to six years after commencement a reference to eight years after commencement.

Definitions For 'association', 'commencement', 'company', 'Crown service', 'Crown service under the government of the United Kingdom' 'minor' and 'United Kingdom', see s 50(1) (and see also, as to 'commencement', s 53(2); as to 'date of the application', see s 50(8); as to 'from' or 'to' a date, see s 50(10)(*a*); as to 'full age', see s 50(11)(*a*). Note as to 'relevant service', sub-s (4) above.

[A.1.89]
8 Registration by virtue of marriage
(1) A woman who immediately before commencement was the wife of a citizen of the United Kingdom and Colonies shall be entitled, on an application for her registration as a British citizen made within five years after commencement, to be registered as a British citizen if:

(*a*) immediately before commencement she would (if she had applied for it) have been entitled under section 6(2) of the 1948 Act to be registered as a citizen of the United Kingdom and Colonies by virtue of her marriage to the man who was then her husband; and

(*b*) that man became a British citizen at commencement and did not at any time in the period from commencement to the date of the application under this subsection cease to be such a citizen as a result of a declaration of renunciation; and

(*c*) she remained married to him throughout that period.

(2) On an application for her registration as a British citizen made within five years after commencement, the Secretary of State may, if he thinks fit, cause a woman to be registered as such a citizen if:

(*a*) immediately before commencement she would (if she had applied for it) have been entitled under section 6(2) of the 1948 Act to be registered as a citizen of the United Kingdom and Colonies by virtue of having been married to a man to whom she is no longer married on the date of the application under this subsection; and

(*b*) that man became a British citizen at commencement or would have done so but for his death.

(3) On an application for her registration as a British citizen made within five years after commencement by a woman who at the time of the application is married, the Secretary of State may, if he thinks fit, cause her to be registered as such a citizen if:

(*a*) immediately before commencement she would (if she had applied for it) have been entitled under section 6(2) of the 1948 Act to be registered as a citizen of the United Kingdom and Colonies by virtue of her being or having been married to the man who is her husband on the date of the application under this subsection; and

(*b*) that man either:

(i) became a British citizen at commencement but has ceased to be such a citizen as a result of a declaration of renunciation; or

(ii) would have become a British citizen at commencement but for his having ceased to be a citizen of the United Kingdom and Colonies as a result of a declaration of renunciation.

Definitions For 'commencement', see ss 50(1), 53(2); as to 'date of the application', see s 50(8); as to 'from' or 'to' a date, see s 50(10)(*a*).

[A.1.90]
9 Right to registration by virtue of father's citizenship etc
(1) A person born in a foreign country within five years after commencement shall be entitled, on an application for his registration as a British citizen made within the period of twelve months from the date of the birth, to be registered as such a citizen if:

(*a*) the requirements specified in subsection (2) are fufilled in the case of that person's father; and

(*b*) had that person been born before commencement and become a citizen of the United Kingdom and Colonies by virtue of section 5 of the 1948 Act (citizenship by descent) as a result of the registration of his birth at a United Kingdom consulate under paragraph (*b*) of the proviso to section 5(1) of that Act, he would immediately before commencement have had the right of abode in the United Kingdom by virtue of section 2(1)(*b*) of the Immigration Act 1971 as then in force (connection with United Kingdom through parent or grandparent).

(2) The requirements referred to in subsection (1)(*a*) are that the father of the person to whom the application relates:

(*a*) immediately before commencement or his death (whichever was earlier):

(i) was a citizen of the United Kingdom and Colonies by virtue of section 5 of the 1948 Act (citizenship by descent) or was a person who, under any provision of the British Nationality Acts 1948 to 1965, was deemed for the purposes of the proviso to section 5(1) of the 1948 Act to be a citizen of the United Kingdom and colonies by descent only; and

(ii) was married to that person's mother; and

(iii) was ordinarily resident in a foreign country (no matter which) within the meaning of the 1948 Act; and

(*b*) either:

(i) became a British citizen at commencement and remained such a citizen throughout the period from commencement to the date of the application or, if he died during that period, throughout the period from commencement to his death; or

(ii) would have become a British citizen at commencement but for his death.

Definitions For 'commencement', 'foreign country', 'the United Kingdom' and 'United Kingdom consulate', see s 50(1) (and see also, as to 'commencement', s 53(2); as to 'date of the application' see s 50(8); as to 'father' and 'mother', see s 50(9) (but see s 47); as to 'from' or 'to' a date, see s 50(10)(*a*).

[A.1.91]
10 Registration following renunciation of citizenship of UK and Colonies
(1)   Subject to subsection (3), a person shall be entitled, on an application for his registration as a British citizen, to be registered as such a citizen if immediately before commencement he would (had he applied for it) have been entitled under section 1(1) of the British Nationality Act 1964 (resumption of citizenship) to be registered as a citizen of the United Kingdom and Colonies by virtue of having an appropriate qualifying connection with the United Kingdom or, if a woman, by virtue of having been married before commencement to a person who has, or would if living have, such a connection.

(2)   On an application for his registration as a British citizen made by a person of full capacity who had before commencement ceased to be a citizen of the United Kingdom and Colonies as a result of a declaration of renunciation, the Secretary of State may, if he thinks fit, cause that person to be registered as a British citizen if that person:
(*a*) has an appropriate qualifying connection with the United Kingdom; or
(*b*) if a woman, has been married to a person who has, or would if living have, such a connection.

(3)   A person shall not be entitled to registration under subsection (1) on more than one occasion.
(4)   For the purposes of this section a person shall be taken to have an appropriate qualifying connection with the United Kingdom if he, his father or his father's father:

(*a*) was born in the United Kingdom; or
(*b*) is or was a person naturalised in the United Kingdom; or
(*c*) was registered as a citizen of the United Kingdom and Colonies in the United Kingdom or in a country which at the time was mentioned in section 1(3) of the 1948 Act.

Definitions   For 'commencement' and 'United Kingdom', see s 50(1) (and see also, as to 'commencement', s 53(2); as to 'father', see s 50(9) (but see s 47); as to 'full capacity', see s 50(11)(*a*); as to 'person naturalised in the United Kingdom', see s 50(6)(*a*). Note as to 'appropriate qualifying connection with the United Kingdom, sub-s(4) above.

Acquisition at commencement

[A.1.92]
11 Citizens of UK and Colonies who are to become British citizens at commencement
(1)   Subject to subsection (2), a person who immediately before commencement:

(*a*) was a citizen of the United Kingdom and Colonies; and
(*b*) had the right of abode in the United Kingdom under the Immigration Act 1971 as then in force,

shall at commencement become a British citizen.

(2) A person who was registered as a citizen of the United Kingdom and Colonies under section 1 of the British Nationality (No 2) Act 1964 (stateless persons) on the ground mentioned in subsection (1)(*a*) of that section (namely that his mother was a citizen of the United Kingdom and Colonies at the time when he was born) shall not become a British citizen under subsection (1) unless:

(*a*) his mother becomes a British citizen under subsection (1) or would have done so but for her death; or

(*b*) immediately before commencement he had the right of abode in the United Kingdom by virtue of section 2(1)(*c*) of the Immigration Act 1971 as then in force (settlement in United Kingdom, combined with five or more years' ordinary residence there as a citizen of the United Kingdom and Colonies).

(3) A person who:

(*a*) immediately before commencement was a citizen of the United Kingdom and Colonies by virtue of having been registered under subsection (6) of section 12 of the 1948 Act (British subjects before commencement of 1948 Act becoming citizens of United Kingdom and Colonies) under arrangements made by virtue of subsection (7) of that section (registration in independent Commonwealth country by United Kingdom High Commissioner); and

(*b*) was so registered on an application under the said subsection (6) based on the applicant's descent in the male line from a person ('the relevant person') possessing one of the qualifications specified in subsection (1)(*a*) and (*b*) of that section (birth or naturalisation in the United Kingdom and Colonies),

shall at commencement become a British citizen if the relevant person was born or naturalised in the United Kingdom.

Definitions For 'commencement' and 'United Kingdom', see s 50(1) (and see also, as to 'commencement', s 53(2); as to 'mother', see s 50(9); as to 'naturalised in the United Kingdom', see s 50(6)(*a*).

Renunciation and resumption

[A.1.93]
12 Renunciation

(1) If any British citizen of full age and capacity makes in the prescribed manner a declaration of renunciation of British citizenship, then, subject to subsections (3) and (4), the Secretary of State shall cause the declaration to be registered.

(2) On the registration of a declaration made in pursuance of this section the person who made it shall cease to be a British citizen.

(3) A declaration made by a person in pursuance of this section shall not be registered unless the Secretary of State is satisfied that the person who made it will after the registration have or acquire some citizenship or nationality other than British citizenship; and if that person does not have any such citizenship

or nationality on the date of registration and does not acquire some such citizenship or nationality within six months from that date, he shall be, and be deemed to have remained, a British citizen notwithstanding the registration.

(4) The Secretary of State may withhold registration of any declaration made in pursuance of this section if it is made during any war in which Her Majesty may be engaged in right of Her Majesty's government in the United Kingdom.

(5) For the purposes of this section any person who has been married shall be deemed to be of full age.

Definitions As to 'from' a date, see s 50(10)(*a*); as to 'full age' and 'full capacity', see s 50(11)(*a*) (and note also as to 'full-age', sub-s (5) above).

[A.1.94]
13 Resumption
(1) Subject to subsection (2), a person who has ceased to be a British citizen as a result of a declaration of renunciation shall be entitled, on an application for his registration as a British citizen, to be registered as such a citizen if:

(*a*) he is of full capacity; and

(*b*) his renunciation of British citizenship was necessary to enable him to retain or acquire some other citizenship or nationality.

(2) A person shall not be entitled to registration under subsection (1) on more than one occasion.

(3) If a person of full capacity who has ceased to be a British citizen as a result of a declaration of renunciation (for whatever reason made) makes an application for his registration as such a citizen, the Secretary of State may, if he thinks fit, cause him to be registered as such a citizen.

Supplementary

[A.1.95]
14 Meaning of British citizen 'by descent'
(1) For the purposes of this Act a British citizen is a British citizen 'by descent' if and only if:

(*a*) he is a person born outside the United Kingdom after commencement who is a British citizen by virtue of section (2)(1)(*a*) only or by virtue of registration under section 3(2) or 9; or

(*b*) subject to subsection (2), he is a person born outside the United Kingdom before commencement who became a British citizen at commencement and immediately before commencement:
  (i) was a citizen of the United Kingdom and Colonies by virtue of section 5 of the 1948 Act (citizenship by descent); or
  (ii) was a person who, under any provision of the British Nationality Acts 1948 to 1965, was deemed for the purposes of the proviso to section 5(1) of the 1948 Act to be a citizen of the United Kingdom and Colonies by descent only, or would have been so deemed if male; or
  (iii) had the right of abode in the United Kingdom by virtue only of paragraph (*b*) of subsection (1) of section 2 of the Immigration Act 1971 as then in force (connection with United Kingdom through parent or

grandparent), or by virtue only of that paragraph and paragraph (*c*) of that subsection (settlement in United Kingdom with five years' ordinary residence there), or by virtue only of being or having been the wife of a person who immediately before commencement had that right by virtue only of the said paragraph (*b*) or the said paragraphs (*b*) and (*c*); or

(iv) being a woman, was a citizen of the United Kingdom and Colonies as a result of her registration as such a citizen under section 6(2) of the 1948 Act by virtue of having been married to a man who at commencement became a British citizen by descent or would have done so but for having died or ceased to be a citizen of the United Kingdom and Colonies as a result of a declaration of renunciation; or

(*c*) he is a British citizen by virtue of registration under section 3(1) and either:

(i) his father or mother was a British citizen at the time of the birth; or

(ii) his father or mother was a citizen of the United Kingdom and Colonies at that time and became a British citizen at commencement, or would have done so but for his or her death; or

(*d*) he is a British citizen by virtue of registration under section 5; or

(*e*) subject to subsection (2), being a woman born outside the United Kingdom before commencement, she is a British as a result of her registration as such a citizen under section 8 by virtue of being or having been married to a man who at commencement became a British citizen by descent or would have done so but for his having died or ceased to be a citizen of the United Kingdom and Colonies as a result of a declaration of renunciation; or

(*f*) he is a British citizen by virtue of registration under section 10 who, having before commencement ceased to be a citizen of the United Kingdom and Colonies as a result of a declaration of renunciation, would, if he had not so ceased, have at commencement become a British citizen by descent by virtue of paragraph (*b*); or

(*g*) he is a British citizen by virtue of registration under section 13 who, immediately before he ceased to be a British citizen as a result of a declaration of renunciation, was such a citizen by descent; or

(*h*) he is a person born in a dependent territory after commencement who is a British citizen by virtue of paragraph 2 of Schedule 2.

(2)   A person born outside the United Kingdom before commencement is not a British citizen 'by descent' by virtue of subsection (1)(*b*) or (*e*) if his father was at the time of his birth serving outside the United Kingdom:

(*a*) in service of a description mentioned in subsection (3), his recruitment for the service in question having taken place in the United Kingdom; or

(*b*) in service under a Community institution, his recruitment for that service having taken place in a country which at the time of the recruitment was a member of the Communities.

(3)   The description of service referred to in subsection (2) are:

(*a*) Crown service under the government of the United Kingdom; and

(*b*) service of any description at any time designated under section 2(3).

Definitions   For 'commencement', 'Crown service', 'Crown service under the government of the United Kingdom', 'dependent territory' and 'the United Kingdom', see s 50(1) (and see also, as to 'commencement' s 53(2)); as to 'father' and 'mother', see s 50(9) (but see s 47).

PART II

BRITISH DEPENDENT TERRITORIES CITIZENSHIP

Acquisition after commencement

[A.1.96]
15 Acquisition by birth or adoption
(1)   A person born in a dependent territory after commencement shall be a British Dependent Territories citizen if at the time of the birth his father or mother is:

(*a*) a British Dependent Territories citizen; or
(*b*) settled in a dependent territory.

(2)   A new-born infant who, after commencement, is found abandoned in a dependent territory shall, unless the contrary is shown, be deemed for the purposes of subsection (1):

(*a*) to have been born in that territory after commencement; and
(*b*) to have been born to a parent who at the time of the birth was a British Dependent Territories citizen or settled in a dependent territory.

(3)   A person born in a dependent territory after commencement who is not a British Dependent Territories citizen by virtue of subsection (1) or (2) shall be entitled to be registered as such a citizen if, while he is a minor:

(*a*) his father or mother becomes such a citizen or becomes settled in a dependent territory; and
(*b*) an application is made for his registration as such a citizen.

(4)   A person born in a dependent territory after commencement who is not a British Dependent Territories citizen by virtue of subsection (1) or (2) shall be entitled, on an application for registration as a British Dependent Territories citizen made at any time after he has attained the age of ten years, to be registered as such a citizen if, as regards each of the first ten years of that person's life, the number of days on which he was absent from that territory in that year does not exceed 90.
(5)   Where after commencement an order authorising the adoption of a minor who is not a British Dependent Territories citizen is made by a court in any dependent territory, he shall be a British Dependent Territories citizen as from the date on which the order is made if the adopter or, in the case of a joint adoption, one of the adopters, is a British Dependent Territories citizen on that date.
(6)   Where an order in consequence of which any person became a British Dependent Territories citizen by virtue of subsection (5) ceases to have effect, whether on annulment or otherwise, the cesser shall not affect the status of that person as such a citizen.
(7)   If in the special circumstances of any particular case the Secretary of State thinks fit, he may for the purposes of subsection (4) treat the person to

whom the application relates as fulfilling the requirements specified in that subsection although, as regards any one or more of the first ten years of that person's life, the number of days on which he was absent from the dependent territory there mentioned in that year or each of the years in question exceeds 90.

Definitions For 'commencement', 'dependent territory' and 'minor', see s 50(1) (and see also, as to 'commencement', s 53(2); as to 'father', 'mother' and 'parent', see s 50(9) (but see s 47); as to 'settled', see s 1(8) and s 50.

[A.1.97]
16 Acquisition by descent
(1) A person born outside the dependent territories after commencement shall be a British Dependent Territories citizen if at the time of the birth his father or mother:

(*a*) is such a citizen otherwise than by descent; or

(*b*) is such a citizen and is serving outside the dependent territories in service to which this paragraph applies, his or her recruitment for that service having taken place in a dependent territory.

(2) Paragraph (*b*) of subsection (1) applies to:

(*a*) Crown service under the government of a dependent territory; and

(*b*) service of any description for the time being designated under subsection (3).

(3) For the purposes of this section the Secretary of State may by order made by statutory instrument designate any description of service which he considers to be closely associated with the activities outside the dependent territories of the government of any dependent territory.

(4) Any order made under subsection (3) shall be subject to annulment in pursuant of a resolution of either House of Parliament.

Definitions For 'British Dependent Territories citizen by descent', see s 25; for 'commencement', 'Crown service' and 'dependent territory', see s 50(1) (and see also, as to 'commencement', s 53(2)); as to 'father' and 'mother', see s 50(9) (but see s 47).

[A.1.98]
17 Acquisition by registration: minors
(1) If while a person is a minor an application is made for his registration as a British Dependent Territories citizen the Secretary of State may, if he thinks fit, cause him to be registered as such a citizen.

(2) A person born outside the dependent territories shall be entitled, on an application for his registration as a British Dependent Territories citizen made within the period of twelve months from the date of the birth, to be registered as such a citizen if the requirements specified in subsection (3) or, in the case of a person born stateless, the requirements specified in paragraphs (a) and (b) of that subsection, are fulfilled in the case of either that person's father or mother ('the parent in question').

(3)   The requirements referred to in subsection (2) are:

(*a*) that the parent in question was a British Dependent Territories citizen by descent at the time of the birth; and

(*b*) that the father or mother of the parent in question:

  (i)   was a British Dependent Territories citizen otherwise than by descent at the time of birth of the parent in question; or

  (ii) became a British Dependent Territories citizen otherwise than by descent at commencement, or would have become such a citizen otherwise than by descent at commencement but for his or her death; and

(*c*) that, as regards some period of three years ending with a date not later than the date of the birth:

  (i)   the parent in question was in a dependent territory at the beginning of that period; and

  (ii) the number of days on which the parent in question was absent from that territory in that period does not exceed 270.

(4)   If in the special circumstances of any particular case the Secretary of State thinks fit, he may treat subsection (2) as if the reference to twelve months were a reference to six years.

(5)   A person born outside the dependent territories shall be entitled, on an application for his registration as a British Dependent Territories citizen made while he is a minor, to be registered as such a citizen if the following requirements are satisfied, namely:

(*a*) that at the time of that person's birth his father or mother was a British Dependent Territories citizen by descent; and

(*b*) subject to subsection (6), that that person and his father and mother were in one and the same dependent territory (no matter which) at the beginning of the period of three years ending with the date of the application and that,in the case of each of them, the number of days on which the person in question was absent from the last mentioned territory in that period does not exceed 270; and

(*c*) subject to subsection (6), that the consent of his father and mother to the registration has been signified in the prescribed manner.

(6)   In the case of an application under subsection (5) for the registration of a person as a British Dependent Territories citizen:

(*a*) if his father or mother died, or their marriage was terminated, on or before the date of the application, or his father and mother were legally separated on that date, the references to his father and mother in paragraph (*b*) of that subsection shall be read either as references to his father or as references to his mother;

(*b*) if his father or mother died on or before that date, the reference to his father and mother in paragraph (*c*) of that subsection shall be read as a reference to either of them; and

(*c*) if he was born illegitimate, all those reference shall be read as references to his mother.

Definition   For 'British Dependent Territories citizen by descent', see s 25; for 'commencement', 'dependent territory', 'minor' and 'prescribed', see s 50(1) (and see also, as to 'commencement', s 53(2); as to 'date of the application', see s 50(8); as to 'father', 'mother' and 'parent', see s 50(9) (but see s 47); as 'from' a date, see s 50(10)(*a*). Note as to the 'parent in question', sub-s (2) above.

[A.1.99]
18 Acquisition by naturalisation
(1)   If, on an application for naturalisation as a British Dependent Territories citizens made by a person of full age and capacity, the Secretary of State is satisfied that the applicant fulfils the requirements of Schedule 1 for naturalisation as such a citizen under this subsection, he may, if he thinks fit, grant to him a certificate of naturalisation as such a citizen.

(2)   If, on an application for naturalisation as a British Dependent Territories citizen made by a person of full age and capacity who on the date of the application is married to such a citizen, the Secretary of State is satisfied that the applicant fulfils the requirements of Schedule 1 for naturalisation as such a citizen under this subsection, he may, if he thinks fit, grant to him a certificate of naturalisation as such a citizen.

(3)   Every application under this section shall specify the dependent territory which is to be treated as the relevant territory for the purposes of that application; and, in relation to any such application, references in Schedule 1 to the relevant territory shall be construed accordingly.

Definitions   As to 'date of the application', see s 50(8); for 'dependent territory', see s 50(1); as to 'full age' and 'full capacity', see s 50(11)(*a*).

Acquisition after commencement: special cases

[A.1.100]
19 Right to registration by virtue of residence in dependent territory
(1)   A person shall be entitled, on an application for his registration as a British Dependent Territories citizen made within five years after commencement, to be registered as such a citizen if, had paragraphs 2 to 5 of Schedule 1 to the Immigration Act 1971 remained in force, he would (had he applied for it) have been, on the date of the application under this subsection, entitled under the said paragraph 2 to be registered in a dependent territory as a citizen of the United Kingdom and Colonies.
(2)   In the case of any person who is a minor at commencement, the reference to five years after commencement in subsection (1) shall be treated as a reference to five years from the date on which he attains full age.
(3)   If in the special circumstances of any particular case the Secretary of State thinks fit, he may treat subsection (1) as if:
(*a*)   the reference to five years after commencement were a reference to eight years after commencement; or
(*b*)   where subsection (2) applies, as if the reference to five years from the date on which the person to whom the application relates attains full age were a reference to eight years from that date.

Definitions For 'commencement', 'dependent territory' and 'minor' see s 50(1) (and see also, as to 'commencement', s 53(2); as to 'date of the application', see s 50(8); as to 'from' a date, see s 50(10)(*a*); as to 'full age', see s 50(11)(*a*).

[A.1.101]
20 Registration by virtue of marriage

(1)   A woman who immediately before commencement was the wife of a citizen of the United Kingdom and Colonies shall be entitled, on an applications for her registration as a British Dependent Territories citizen made within five years after commencement, to be registered as a British Dependent Territories citizen if:

(*a*) immediately before commencement she would (if she had applied for it) have been entitled under section 6(2) of the 1948 Act to be registered as a citizen of the United Kingdom and Colonies by virtue of her marriage to the man who was then her husband; and

(*b*) that man became a British Dependent Territories citizen at commencement and did not at any time in the period from commencement to the date of the application under this subsection cease to be such a citizen as a result of a declaration of renunciation; and

(*c*) she remained married to him throughout that period.

(2)   On such an application for her registration as a British Dependent Territories citizen made within five years after commencement the Secretary of State may, if he thinks fit, cause a woman to be registered as such a citizen if:

(*a*) immediately before commencement she would (if she had applied for it) have been entitled under section 6(2) of the 1948 Act to be registered as a citizen of the United Kingdom and Colonies by virtue of having been married to a man to whom she is no longer married on the date of the application under this subsection; and

(*b*) that man became a British Dependent Territories citizen at commencement or would have done so but for his death.

(3)   On an application for her registration as a British Dependent Territories citizen made within five years of commencement by a woman who at the time of the application is married, the Secretary of State, shall if he thinks fit, cause her to be registered as such a citizen if:

(*a*) immediately before commencement she would (if she had applied for it) have been entitled under section 6(2) of the 1948 Act to be registered as a citizen of the United Kingdom and Colonies by virtue of her being or having been married to the man who is her husband on the date of the application under this subsection; and

(*b*) that man either:
   (i) became a British Dependent Territories citizen at commencement but has ceased to be such a citizen as a result of a declaration of renunciation; or
   (ii) would have become a British Dependent Territories citizen at commencement but for his having ceased to be a citizen of the United Kingdom and Colonies as a result of a declaration of renunciation.

Definitions   For 'commencement', see ss 50(1) and 53(2); as to 'date of the application', see s 50(8); as to 'from' or 'to' a date, see s 50(10)(*a*).

[A.1.102]
21 Right to registration by virtue of father's citizenship etc
A person born in a foreign country within five years after commencement shall
be entitled, on an application for his registration as a British Dependent
Territories citizen made within the period of twelve months from the date of
the birth, to be registered as such a citizen if:

(*a*) the requirements referred to in subsection (1)(*a*) of section 9 are fulfilled
in the case of that person's father, subsection (2)(*b*) of that section being
for the purposes of this paragraph read as if any reference to becoming or
remaining a British citizen were a reference to becoming or, as the case
may be, remaining a British Dependent Territories citizen; and

(*b*) had that person been born before commencement and become a citizen of
the United Kingdom and Colonies as mentioned in subsection (1)(*b*) of
that section, he would at commencement have become a British
Dependent Territories citizen by virtue of section 23(1)(*b*).

Definitions   For 'commencement' and 'foreign country', see s 50(1) (and see also, as
to 'commencement', s 53(2); as to 'father', see s 50(9) (but see s 47); as to 'from' a
date, see s 50(10)(*a*).

[A.1.103]
22 Right to registration replacing right to resume citizenship of UK and colonies
(1)   Subject to subsection (3), a person shall be entitled, on an application for
his registration as a British Dependent Territories citizen, to be registered as such
a citizen if immediately before commencement he would (had he applied for it)
have been entitled under section 1(1) of the British Nationality Act 1964
(resumption of citizenship) to be registered as a citizen of the United Kingdom
and Colonies by virtue of having an appropriate qualifying connection with a
dependent territory or, if a woman, by virtue of having been married before commencement to a person who has, or would if living have, such a connection.

(2)   On an application for his registration as a British Dependent Territories
citizen made by a person of full capacity who had before commencement
ceased to be a citizen of the United Kingdom and Colonies as a result of a declaration of renunciation, the Secretary of State may, if he thinks fit, cause that
person to be registered as a British Dependent Territories citizen if that person:

(*a*) has an appropriate qualifying connection with a dependent territory; or
(*b*) if a woman, has been married to a person who has, or would if living have,
such a connection.

(3)   A person shall not be entitled to registration under subsection (1) on more
than one occasion.

(4)   For the purposes of this section a person shall be taken to have an appropriate qualifying connection with a dependent territory if he, his father or his
father's father:

(*a*) was born in that territory; or

(*b*) is or was a person naturalised in that territory; or

(*c*) was registered as a citizen of the United Kingdom and Colonies in that territory; or

(*d*) became a British subject by reason of the annexation of any territory included in that territory.

Definitions For 'commencement' and 'dependent territory', see s 50(1) (and see also as to 'commencement', s 53(2); as to 'father' see s 50(9) (but see s 47); as to 'full capacity', see s 50(11)(*a*); as to 'naturalised in a dependent territory', see s 50(6)(*b*). Note as to 'appropriate qualifying connection with a dependent territory', sub-s (4) above.

Acquisition at commencement

[A.1.104]
23 Citizens of UK and Colonies who are to become British Dependent Territories citizens at commencement

(1)   A person shall at commencement become a British Dependent Territories citizen if:

(*a*) immediately before commencement he was a citizen of the United Kingdom and Colonies who had that citizenship by his birth, naturalisation or registration in a dependent territory; or

(*b*) he was immediately before commencement a citizen of the United Kingdom and Colonies, and was born to a parent:
   (i)   who at the time of the birth ('the material time') was a citizen of the United Kingdom and Colonies; and
   (ii) who either had that citizenship at the material time by his birth; naturalisation or registration in a dependent territory or was himself born to a parent who at the time of that birth so had that citizenship; or

(*c*) being a woman, she was immediately before commencement a citizen of the United Kingdom and Colonies and either was then, or had at any time been, the wife of a man who under paragraph (*a*) or (*b*) becomes a British Dependent Territories citizen at commencement or would have done so but for his death.

(2)   A person shall at commencement become a British Dependent Territories citizen if:

(*a*) immediately before commencement he was a citizen of the United Kingdom and Colonies by virtue of registration under section 7 of the 1948 Act (minor children) or section 1 of the British Nationality (No 2) Act 1964 (stateless persons); and

(*b*) he was so registered otherwise than in a dependent territory; and

(*c*) his father or mother (in the case of a person registered under the said section 7) or his mother (in the case of a person registered under the said section 1):
   (i)   was a citizen of the United Kingdom and Colonies at the time of the

registration or would have been such a citizen at that time but for his or
her death; and

(ii) becomes a British Dependent Territories citizen at commencement or
would have done so but for his or her death.

(3)   A person who:

(*a*) immediately before commencement was a citizen of the United Kingdom
and Colonies by virtue of having been registered under subsection (6) of
section 12 of the 1948 Act (British subjects before commencement of 1948
Act becoming citizens of United Kingdom and Colonies) otherwise than
in a dependent territory; and

(*b*) was so registered on an application under that subsection based on the
applicant's descent in the male line from a person ('the relevant person')
possessing one of the qualifications specified in subsection (1) of that section (birth or naturalisation in the United Kingdom and Colonies, or acquisition of the status of British subject by reason of annexation of territory),

shall at commencement become a British Dependent Territories citizen if the
relevant person:

(i)   was born or naturalised in a dependent territory; or

(ii) became a British subject by reason of the annexation of any territory
included in a dependent territory.

(4)   A person who:

(*a*) immediately before commencement was a citizen of the United Kingdom
and Colonies by virtue of registration under section 1 of the British
Nationality Act 1964 (resumption of citizenship); and

(*b*) was so registered otherwise than in a dependent territory; and

(*c*) was so registered by virtue of having an appropriate qualifying connection
with a dependent territory or, if a woman, by virtue of having been married to a person who at the time of the registration had or would, if then
living, have had such a connection.

shall at commencement become a British Dependent Territories citizen.

(5)   For the purposes of subsection (4) a person shall be taken to have an
appropriate qualifying connection with a dependent territory if he, his father or
his father's father:

(*a*) was born in a dependent territory; or

(*b*) is or was a person naturalised in a dependent territory; or

(*c*) was registered as a citizen of the United Kingdom and Colonies in a
dependent territory; or

(*d*) became a British subject by reason of the annexation of any territory
included in a dependent territory.

(6)   For the purposes of subsection (1)(*b*) references to citizenship of the
United Kingdom and Colonies shall, in relation to a time before the year 1949,
be construed as references to British nationality.

Definitions   For 'commencement' and 'dependent territory', see s 50(1) (and see also,
as to 'commencement', s 53(2); as to 'father', 'mother' and 'parent', see s 50(9) (but
see s 47); as to 'naturalised in a dependent territory', see s 50(6)(*b*). Note as to 'the
material time', sub-s (1)(*b*)(i) above; as to 'the relevant person', sub-s (3)(*b*) above; and

as to 'appropriate qualifying connection with a dependent territory', sub-s (5) above.

Renunciation and resumption

[A.1.105]
24 Renunciation and resumption
The provisions of sections 12 and 13 shall apply in relation to British Dependent Territories citizens and British Dependent Territories citizenship as they apply in relation to British citizens and British citizenship.

Supplementary

[A.1.106]
25 Meaning of British Dependent Territories citizen 'by descent'
(1)   For the purposes of this Act a British Dependent Territories citizen is such a citizen 'by descent' of and only if:

(*a*) he is a person born outside the dependent territories after commencement who is a British Dependent Territories citizen by virtue by section 16(1)(*a*) only or by virtue of registration under section 17(2) or 21; or
(*b*) subject to subsection (2), he is a person born outside the dependent territories before commencement who became a British Dependent Territories citizen at commencement and immediately before commencement:
   (i) was a citizen of the United Kingdom and Colonies by virtue of section 5 of the 1948 Act (citizenship by descent); or
   (ii) was a person who, under any provision of the British Nationality Acts 1948 to 1965, was deemed for the purposes of the proviso to section 5(1) of the 1948 Act to be a citizen of the United Kingdom and Colonies by descent only, or would have been so deemed if male; or
(*c*) he is a British Dependent Territories citizen by virtue of registration under section 17(1) and either:
   (i) his father or mother was a British Dependent Territories citizen at the time of the birth; or
   (ii) his father or mother was a citizen of the United Kingdom and Colonies at that time and become a British Dependent Territories citizen at commencement, or would have done so but for his or her death; or
(*d*) subject to subsection (2), he is a person born outside the dependent territories before commencement who became a British Dependent Territories citizen at commencement under section 23(1)(*b*) only; or
(*e*) subject to subsection (2), being a woman, she became a British Dependent Territories citizen at commencement under section 23(1)(*c*) only, and did so only by virtue of having been, immediately after commencement or earlier, the wife of a man who immediately before commencement or earlier, the wife of a man who immediately after commencement was, or would but for his death have been, a British Dependent Territories citizen by descent by virtue of paragraph (*b*) or (*d*) of this subsection; or
(*f*) subject to subsection (2), being a woman born outside the dependent territories before commencement, she is a British Dependent Territories citizen as a result of her registration as such a citizen under section 20 by

virtue of being or having been married to a man who at commencement became such a citizen by descent or would have done so but for his having died or ceased to be a citizen of the United Kingdom and Colonies as a result of a declaration of renunciation; or

(*g*) he is a British Dependent Territories citizen by virtue of registration under section 22 who, having before commencement ceased to be a citizen of the United Kingdom and Colonies as a result of a declaration of renunciation, would, if he had so ceased, have at commencement become a British Dependent Territories citizen by descent by virtue of paragraph (*b*), (*d*) or (*e*);

(*h*) he is a British Dependent Territories citizen by virtue of registration under section 13 (as applied by section 24) who, immediately before he ceased to be a British Dependent Territories citizen as a result of a declaration of renunciation, was such a citizen by descent; or

(*i*) he is a person born in the United Kingdom after commencement who is a British Dependent Territories citizen by virtue of paragraph 1 of Schedule 2.

(2) A person born outside the dependent territories before commencement is not a British Dependent Territories citizen 'by descent' by virtue of subsection (1)(*b*), (*d*), (*e*) or (*f*) if his father was at the time of his birth serving outside the dependent territories in service of a description mentioned in subsection (3), his recruitment for the service in question having taken place in a dependent territory.

(3) The descriptions of service referred to in subsection (2) are:

(*a*) Crown service under the government of a dependent territory; and

(*b*) service of any description at any time designated under section 16(3).

Definitions For 'commencement', 'Crown service' and 'dependent territory', see s 50(1) (and see also, as to 'commencement', s 53(2); as to 'father' and 'mother', see s 50(9) (but see s 47).

PART III
BRITISH OVERSEAS CITIZENSHIP

[A.1.107]
26 Citizens of UK and Colonies who are to become British Overseas citizens at commencement
Any person who was a citizen of the United Kingdom and Colonies immediately before commencement and who does not at commencement become either a British citizen or a British Dependent Territories citizen shall at commencement become a British Overseas citizen.

[A.1.108]
27 Registration of minors
(1) If while a person is a minor an application is made for his registration as a British Overseas citizen, the Secretary of State may, if he thinks fit, cause him to be registered as such a citizen.

(2) A person born in a foreign country within five years after commencement

shall be entitled, on an application for his registration as a British Overseas citizen made within the period of twelve months from the date of the birth, to be registered as such a citizen if:

(*a*) the requirements referred to in subsection (1)(*a*) of section 9 are fulfilled in the case of that person's father, subsection (2)(*b*) of that section being for the purposes of this paragraph read as if:
  (i) any reference to becoming a British citizen were a reference to becoming a citizen of any of the following descriptions, namely a British citizen, a British Dependent Territories citizen and a British Overseas citizen; and
  (ii) the reference to remaining a British citizen throughout any period were a reference to being throughout that period a citizen of at least one of those descriptions (though not necessarily the same one) throughout that period; and

(*b*) had that person been born before commencement and become a citizen of the United Kingdom and Colonies as mentioned in subsection (1)(*b*) of that section, he would at commencement have become a British Overseas citizen by virtue of section 26.

Definitions For 'commencement', 'foreign country' and 'minor', see s 50(1) (and see also, as to 'commencement', s 53(2)); as to 'father', see s 50(9) (but see s 47); as to 'from' a date, see s 50(10)(*a*).

[A.1.109]
28 Registration by virtue of marriage
(1) A woman who immediately before commencement was the wife of a citizen of the United Kingdom and Colonies shall be entitled, on an application for her registration as a British Overseas citizen made within five years after commencement, to be registered as a British Overseas citizen if:

(*a*) immediately before commencement she would (if she had applied for it) have been entitled under section 6(2) of the 1948 Act to be registered as a citizen of the United Kingdom and Colonies by virtue of her marriage to the man who was then her husband; and

(*b*) that man became a British Overseas citizen at commencement and did not at any time in the period from commencement to the date of application under this subsection cease to be such a citizen as a result of a declaration of renunciation; and

(*c*) she remained married to him throughout that period.

(2) On an application for her registration as a British Overseas citizen made within five years after commencement, the Secretary of State may, if he thinks fit, cause a woman to be registered as such a citizen if:

(*a*) immediately before commencement she would (if she had applied for it) have been entitled under section 6(2) of the 1948 Act to be registered as a citizen of the United Kingdom and Colonies by virtue of having been married to a man to whom she is no longer married on the date of the application under this subsection; and

(*b*) that may became a British Overseas citizen at commencement or would have done so but for his death.

(3) On an application for her registration as a British Overseas citizen made within five years after commencement by a woman who at the time of the application is married, the Secretary of State may, if he thinks fit, cause her to be registered as such a citizen if:

(*a*) immediately before commencement she would (if she had applied for it) have been entitled under section 6(2) of the 1948 Act to be registered as a citizen of the United Kingdom and Colonies by virtue or her being or having been married to the man who is her husband on the date of the application under this subsection; and

(*b*) that man either:
  (i) became a British Overseas citizen at commencement but has ceased to be such a citizen as a result of a declaration of renunciation; or
  (ii) would have become a British Overseas citizen at commencement but for his having ceased to be a citizen of the United Kingdom and Colonies as a result of a declaration of renunciation.

Definitions For 'commencement', see ss 50(1) and 53(2); as to 'date of the application', see s 50(8); as to 'from' or 'to' a date, see s 50(10)(*a*)

[A.1.110]
29 Renunciation
The provisions of section 12 shall apply in relation to British Overseas citizens and British Overseas citizenship as they apply in relation to British citizens and British citizenship.

PART IV
BRITISH SUBJECTS

[A.1.111]
30 Continuance as British subjects of existing British subjects of certain descriptions
A person who immediately before commencement was:

(*a*) a British subject without citizenship by virtue of section 13 to 16 of the 1948 Act; or

(*b*) a British subject by virtue of section 1 of the British Nationality Act 1965 (registration of alien women who have been married to British subjects of certain descriptions),

shall as from commencement be a British subject by virtue of this section.

[A.1.112]
31 Continuance as British subjects of certain former citizens of Eire
(1) A person is within this subsection if immediately before 1st January 1949 he was both a citizen of Eire and a British subject.
(2) A person within subsection (1) who immediately before commencement was a British subject by virtue of section 2 of the 1948 Act (continuance of certain citizens of Eire as British subjects) shall as from commencement be a

British subject by virtue of this subsection.

(3)   If at any time after commencement a citizen of the Republic of Ireland who is within subsection (1) but is not a British subject by virtue of subsection (2) gives notice in writing to the Secretary of State claiming to remain a British subject on either or both of the following grounds, namely:

(*a*) that he is or has been in Crown Service under the government of the United Kingdom; and

(*b*) that he has associations by way of descent, resident or otherwise with the United Kingdom or with any dependent territory,

he shall as from that time be a British subject by virtue of this subsection.

(4)   A person who is a British subject by virtue of subsection (2) or (3) shall be deemed to have remained a British subject from 1st January 1949 to the time when (whether already a British subject by virtue of the said section 2 or not) he became a British subject by virtue of that subsection.

Definitions   For 'commencement', 'Crown service', 'Crown service under the government of the United Kingdom', 'dependent territory' and 'the United Kingdom', see s 50(1) (and see also, as to 'commencement', s 53(2)).

[A.1.113]
32 Registration of minors
If while a person is a minor an application is made for his registration as a British subject, the Secretary of State may, if he thinks fit, cause him to be registered as a British subject.

[A.1.114]
33 Registration of certain alien women entitled to registration as British subjects immediately before commencement
A woman who immediately before commencement was the wife of a British subject shall be entitled, on an application for her registration as a British subject made within five years after commencement, to be registered as a British subject if:

(*a*) immediately before commencement she would (if she had applied for it) have been entitled under section 1 of the British Nationality Act 1965 to be registered as a British subject by virtue of her marriage to the man who was then her husband; and

(*b*) on the date of the application under this section that man is a British subject; and

(*c*) she remained married to him throughout the period from commencement to that date.

Definitions   For 'commencement', see ss 50(1) and 53(2); as to 'date of the application', see 50(8); as to 'from' or 'to' a date, see 50(10)(*a*).

[A.1.115]
34 Renunciation
The provisions of section 12 shall apply in relation to British subjects and the status of a British subject as they apply in relation to British citizens and British citizenship.

[A.1.116]
35 Circumstances in which British subjects are to lose that status
A person who under this Act is a British subject otherwise than by virtue of section 31 shall cease to be such a subject if, in whatever circumstances and whether under this Act or otherwise, he acquires any other citizenship or nationality whatever.

PART V

MISCELLANEOUS AND SUPPLEMENTARY

[A.1.117]
36 Provisions for reducing statelessness
The provisions of Schedule 2 shall have effect for the purpose of reducing statelessness.

[A.1.118]
37 Commonwealth citizenship
(1)   Every person who:

(*a*) under [the British Nationality Acts 1981 and 1983] is a British citizen, a British Dependent Territories citizen, [a British National (Overseas),] a British Overseas citizen or a British subject; or

(*b*) under any enactment for the time being in force in any country mentioned in Schedule 3 is a citizen of that country.

shall have the status of a Commonwealth citizen.

(2)   Her Majesty may by Order in Council amend Schedule 3 by the alteration of any entry, the removal of any entry, or the insertion of any additional entry.

(3)   Any Order in Council made under this section shall be subject to annulment in pursuance of a resolution of either House of Parliament.

(4)   After commencement no person shall have the status of a Commonwealth citizen or the status of a British subject otherwise than under this Act.

Notes   Words in first square brackets in sub-s (1) substituted by the British Nationality (Falkland Islands) Act 1983, s 4(3); words in second square brackets inserted by the Hong Kong (British Nationality) Order 1986, SI 1986/948, as from 1 July 1987.
Definitions   For 'British National (Overseas)', and 'British Overseas citizen', see s 50(1).

[A.1.119]
38 British protected persons
(1)   Her Majesty may by Order in Council made in relation to any territory which was at any time before commencement:

(*a*) a protectorate or protected state for the purposes of the 1948 Act; or
(*b*) a United Kingdom trust territory within the meaning of that Act,

declare to be British protected persons for the purposes of this Act any class of person who are connected with that territory and are not citizens of any country mentioned in Schedule 3 which consists of or includes that territory.
(2)   Any Order in Council made under this section shall be subject to annulment in pursuance of a resolution of either House of Parliament.

[A.1.120]
39 Amendment of Immigration Act 1971
(1)–(5)   . . .
(6)   Schedule 4 (which contains further amendments of the Immigration Act 1971) shall have effect.
(7)   . . .
(8)   A certificate of patriality issued under the Immigration Act 1971 and in force immediately before commencement shall have effect after commencement as if it were a certificate of entitlement issued under that Act [as in force after commencement], unless at commencement the holder ceases to have right of abode in the United Kingdom.

Notes   Sub-ss (1), (2), (4) amend the Immigration Act 1971, ss 2, 8.
   Sub-ss (3), (5) repealed, and words in square brackets in sub-s (8) substituted, by the Immigration Act 1988, s 3(3).
   Sub-s (7) amended the Mental Health Act 1959, s 90 (consolidated in the MentaL Health Act 1983, s 86), and amend, the Mental Health (Scotland) Act 1960, s 82.

[A.1.121]
40 Deprivation of citizenship
(1)   Subject to the provisions of this section, the Secretary of State may by order deprive any British citizen to whom this subsection applies of his British citizenship if the Secretary of State is satisfied that the registration or certificate of naturalisation by virtue of which he is such a citizen was obtained by means of fraud, false representation or the concealment of any material fact.
(2)   Subsection (1) applies to any British citizen who:

(*a*) became a British citizen after commencement by virtue of:
    (i) his registration as a British citizen under any provision of [the British Nationality Acts 1981 and 1983]; or
    (ii) a certificate of naturalisation granted to him under section 6; or
(*b*) being immediately before commencement a citizen of the United Kingdom and Colonies by virtue of registration as such a citizen under any provision of the British Nationality Acts 1948 to 1964, became at commencement a British citizen; or
(*c*) at any time before commencement became a British subject (within the meaning of that expression at that time), or a citizen of Eire or of the

Republic of Ireland, by virtue of a certificate of naturalisation granted to him or in which his name was included.

(3)   Subject to the provisions of this section, the Secretary of State may by order deprive any British citizen to whom this subsection applies of his British citizenship if the Secretary of State is satisfied that that citizen:

(*a*) has shown himself by act or speech to be disloyal or disaffected towards Her Majesty; or

(*b*) has, during any way in which Her Majesty was engaged, unlawfully traded or communicated with an enemy or been engaged in or associated with any business that was to his knowledge carried on in such a manner as to assist an enemy in that war; or

(*c*) has, within the period of five years from the relevant date, been sentenced in any country to imprisonment for a term of not less than twelve months.

(4)   Subsection (3) applies to any British citizen who falls within paragraph (*a*) or (*c*) of subsection (2); and in subsection (3) 'the relevant date', in relation to a British citizen to whom subsection (3) applies, means the date of the registration by virtue of which he is such a citizen or, as the case may be, the date of the grant of the certificate of naturalisation by virtue of which he is such a citizen.

(5)   The Secretary of State:

(*a*) shall not deprive a person of British citizenship under this section unless he is satisfied that it is not conducive to the public good that that person should continue to be a British citizen; and

(*b*) shall not deprive a person of British citizenship under subsection (3) on the ground mentioned in paragraph (*c*) of that subsection if it appears to him that that person would thereupon become stateless.

(6)   Before making an order under this section the Secretary of State shall give the person against whom the order is proposed to be made notice in writing informing him of the ground or grounds on which it is proposed to be made and of his right to an inquiry under this section.

(7)   If the person against whom the order is proposed to be made applies in the prescribed manner for an inquiry, the Secretary of State shall, and in any other case the Secretary of State may, refer the case to a committee of inquiry consisting of a chairman, being a person possessing judicial experience, appointed by the Secretary of State and of such other members appointed by the Secretary of State as he thinks proper.

(8)   The Secretary of State may make rules for the practice and procedure to be followed in connection with references under subsection (7) to a committee of inquiry; and such rules may, in particular, provide for conferring on any such committee any powers, rights or privileges of any court, and for enabling any powers so conferred to be exercised by one or more members of the committee.

(9)   The power of the Secretary of State to make rules under subsection (8) shall be exercisable by statutory instrument subject to annulment in pursuance of a resolution of either House of Parliament.

(10)   The preceding provisions of this section shall apply in relation to British Dependent Territories citizens and British Dependent Territories citizenship as they apply in relation to British citizens and British citizenship, but as if in subsection (2)(*a*)(ii) the reference to section 6 were a reference to section 18.

Notes Words in square brackets in sub-s (2) substituted by the British Nationality (Falkland Islands) Act 1983, s 4(3).

Definitions For 'commencement' and 'prescribed', see s 50(1) (and see also, as to 'commencement', s 53(2)); as to 'from' a date, see s 50(10)(*a*). Note as to 'the relevant date', sub-s(4) above.

[A.1.122]
41 Regulations and Orders in Council

(1)   The Secretary of State may by regulations make provision generally for carrying into effect the purposes of this Act, and in particular provision:

(*a*) for prescribing anything which under this Act is to be prescribed;

(*b*) for prescribing he manner in which, and the persons to and by whom, applications for registration or naturalisation under any provision of this Act may or must be made;

(*c*) for the registration of anything required or authorised by or under this Act to be registered;/

(*d*) for the administration and taking of oaths of allegiance under this Act, as to the time within which oaths of allegiance must be taken, and for the registration of oaths of allegiance;

(*e*) for the giving of any notice required or authorised to be given to any person under this Act;

(*f*) for the cancellation of the registration of, and the cancellation and amendment of certificates of naturalisation relating to, persons deprived of citizenship [or of the status of a British National (Overseas)] under this Act, and for requiring such certificates to be delivered up for those purposes;

(*g*) for the births and deaths of persons of any class or description born or dying in a country mentioned in Schedule 3 to be registered there by the High Commissioner for Her Majesty's government in the United Kingdom or by members of his official staff;

(*h*) for the births and deaths of persons of any class or description born or dying in a foreign country to be registered there by consular officers or other officers in the service of Her Majesty's government in the United Kingdom;

(*i*) for enabling the births and deaths of British citizens, British Dependent Territories citizens, [British Nationals (Overseas)] British Overseas citizens, British subjects and British protected persons born or dying in any country in which Her Majesty's government in the United Kingdom has for the time being no diplomatic or consular representatives to be registered:

(i)   by persons serving in the diplomatic, consular or other foreign service of any country which, by arrangement with Her Majesty's government in the United Kingdom, has undertaken to represent that government's interest in that country, or

(ii) by a person authorised in that behalf by the Secretary of State.(2) The Secretary of State may with the consent of the Treasury by regulations make provision for the imposition, recovery and application of fees in connection with any of the following matters, namely:

(*a*) any application made to the Secretary of State under this Act [other than

an application for the purpose of acquiring the status of a British National (Overseas)];
(*b*) the effecting in the United Kingdom of any registration authorised by or under this Act [other than registration as a British National (Overseas)];
(*c*) the making in the United Kingdom of any declaration, the grant there of any certificate, or the taking there of any oath or allegiance authorised to be made, granted or taken by or under this Act;
(*d*) the supplying in the United Kingdom of a certified or other copy of any notice, certificate, order, declaration or entry given, granted or made under or by virtue of this Act or any of the former nationality Acts;
(*e*) the carrying out of searches in or of any registers or other records, being registers or records held in the United Kingdom by or on behalf of the Secretary of State, which are or may be relevant for the purpose of determining the status of any person under this Act or any of the former nationality Acts;
(*f*) the supplying by or on behalf of the Secretary of State of an opinion in writing concerning the status of any person under this Act or any of the former nationality Acts, or a certified or other copy of such an opinion.

(3)   Regulations under subsection (1) or (2) may make different provision for different circumstances; and:

(*a*) regulations under subsection (1) may provide for the extension of any time-limit for the taking of oaths of allegiance; and
(*b*) regulations under subsection (2) may provide for any fees imposed by the regulations to be payable at such times as may be prescribed.

(4)   Her Majesty may by Order in Council provide for any Act or Northern Ireland legislation to which this subsection applies to apply, with such adaptations and modifications as appear to Her necessary, to births and deaths registered:

(*a*) in accordance with regulations made in pursuance of subsection (1)(*g*) to (*i*) of this section or subsection (1)(*f*) and (*g*) of section 29 of the 1948 Act; or
(*b*) at a consulate of Her Majesty in accordance with regulations made under the British Nationality and Status of Aliens Act 1914 to 1943 or in accordance with instructions of the Secretary of State; or
(*c*) by a High Commissioner of Her Majesty's government in the United Kingdom or members of his official staff in accordance with instructions of the Secretary of State;

and an Order in Council under this subsection may exclude, in relation to births and deaths so registered, any of the provisions of section 45.
(5)   Subsection (4) applies to:

(*a*) the Births and Deaths Registration Act 1953, the Registration Service Act 1953 and the Registration of Births, Deaths and Marriages (Scotland) Act 1965; and
(*b*) so much of any Northern Ireland legislation for the time being in force (whether passed or made before or after commencement) as relates to the registration of births and deaths.

(6)   The power to make regulations under subsection (1) or (2) shall be exercisable by statutory instrument.

(7)   Any regulations or Order in Council made under this section shall be subject to annulment in pursuance of a resolution of either House of Parliament.

Notes   Words in square brackets in sub-ss (1)(*f*), (*i*), (2)(*a*), (*b*) inserted by the Hong Kong (British Nationality) Order 1986, SI 1986/948, art 4(*b*)–(*d*).

For fees imposed under sub-s (2) see British Nationality (Fees) (Amendment) Order 1997, SI 1997/1328 amending SI 1996/444.

Definitions   For 'British National (Overseas)', 'British Overseas citizen', 'British protected person', 'commencement', 'foreign country', 'the former nationality Acts', 'High Commissioner', 'status of a British National (Overseas)' and 'the United Kingdom', see s 50(1) (and see also, as to 'commencement', s 53(2)).

[A.1.123]
42 Registration and naturalisation: general provisions
(1)   Subject to subsection (2):

(*a*) a person shall not be registered under any provision of this Act as a citizen of any description or as a British subject; and

(*b*) a certificate of naturalisation shall not be granted to a person under any provision of this Act,

unless:

(i)   any fee payable by virtue of this Act in connection with the registration or, as the case may be, the grant of the certificate has been paid; and

(ii) the person concerned has within the prescribed time taken an oath of allegiance in the form indicated in Schedule 5.

(2)   So much of subsection (1) as required the taking of an oath of allegiance shall not apply to a person who:

(*a*) is not of full age; or

(*b*) is already a British citizen, a British Dependent Territories citizen, [a British National (Overseas),] a British Overseas citizen, a British subject, or a citizen of any country of which Her Majesty is Queen.

(3)   Any provision of this Act which provides for a person to be entitled to registration as a citizen of any description or as a British subject shall have effect subject to the preceding provisions of this section.

(4)   A person registered under any provision of this Act as a British citizen, or as a British Dependent Territories citizen [, or as a British National (Overseas),] or as a British Overseas citizen, or as a British subject, shall be a citizen of that description or, as the case may be, [a British National (Overseas) or] a British subject as from the date on which he is so registered.

(5)   A person to whom a certificate of naturalisation as a British citizen or as a British Dependent Territories citizen is granted under any provision of this Act shall be a citizen of that description as from the date on which the certificate is granted.

[(6)   A person who applies for registration or naturalisation as a British Dependent Territories citizen under any provision of this Act by virtue (wholly or partly) of his having a connection with Hong Kong, may not be naturalised or registered, as the case may be, unless he makes his application on or before 31st March 1996.

Notes   Words in square brackets in sub-ss (2)(*b*), (4) inserted by the Hong Kong (British Nationality) Order 1986, SI 1986/948, as from 1 July 1987.

Sub-s (6) added by the Hong Kong (British Nationality) (Amendment) Order 1993, SI 1993/1795, art 3.

Definition   For 'British National (Overseas)' and 'British Overseas citizen', see s 50(1).

[A.1.124]
43 Exercise of functions of Secretary of State by Governors and others
(1)   Subject to subsection (3), the Secretary of State may, in the case of any of his functions under this Act with respect to any of the matters mentioned in subsection (2), make arrangements for that function to be exercised:

(*a*)   in any of the Islands, by the Lieutenant-Governor in cases concerning British citizens or British citizenship;

(*b*)   in any dependent territory which is for the time being a colony, by the Governor in cases concerning British Dependent Territories citizens or British Dependent Territories citizenship [and in cases concerning British Nationals (Overseas) or the status of a British National (Overseas)].

(2)   The said matters are:

(*a*)   registration and naturalisation; and

(*b*)   renunciation, resumption and deprivation of British citizenship or British Dependent Territories citizenship;

[(*c*)   renunciation and deprivation of the status of a British National (Overseas)].

(3)   Nothing in this section applies in the case of any power to make regulations or rules conferred on the Secretary of State by this Act.
(4)   Arrangements under subsection (1) may provide for any such function as is there mentioned to be exercisable only with the approval of the Secretary of State.

Notes   Words in square brackets in sub-s (1)(*b*), and sub-s (2)(*c*), added by the Hong Kong (British Nationality) Order 1986, SI 1986/948, as from 1 July 1987.

Definitions   For 'British National (Overseas)', 'British Overseas citizen', 'dependent territory', 'Governor' and 'the Islands', see s 50(1).

[A.1.125]
44 Decisions involving exercise of discretion
(1)   Any discretion vested by or under this Act in the Secretary of State, a Governor or a Lieutenant-Governor shall be exercised without regard to the race, colour or religion of any person who may be affected by its exercise.
(2)   The Secretary of State, a Governor or a Lieutenant-Governor, as the case

may be, shall not be required to assign any reason for the grant or refusal of any application under this Act the decision on which is at his discretion; and the decision of the Secretary of State or a Governor or Lieutenant-Governor on any such application shall not be subject to appeal to, or review in, any court.

(3) Nothing in this section affects the jurisdiction of any court to entertain proceedings of any description concerning the rights of any person under any provision of this Act.

[A.1.126]
45 Evidence
(1) Every document purporting to be a notice, certificate, order or declaration, or an entry in a register, or a subscription of an oath of allegiance, given, granted or made under this Act or any of the former nationality Acts shall be received in evidence and shall, unless the contrary is provided, be deemed to have been given, granted or made by or on behalf of the person by whom or on whose behalf it purports to have been given, granted or made.

(2) Prima facie evidence of any such document may be given by the production of a document purporting to be certified as a true copy of it by such person and in such manner as may be prescribed.

(3) Any entry in a register made under this Act or any of the former nationality Acts shall be received as evidence (and in Scotland as sufficient evidence) of the matters stated in the entry.

(4) A certificate given by or on behalf of the Secretary of State that a person was at any time in Crown service under the government of the United Kingdom or that a person's recruitment for such service took place in the United Kingdom shall, for the purposes of this Act, be conclusive evidence of that fact.

Definitions For 'Crown service', 'Crown service under the government of the United Kingdom', 'the former nationality Acts', 'prescribed' and 'the United Kingdom', see s 50(1).

[A.1.127]
46 Offences and proceedings
(1) Any person who for the purpose of procuring anything to be done or not to be done under this Act:

(*a*) makes any statement which he knows to be false in a material particular; or

(*b*) recklessly makes any statement which is false in a material particular,

shall be liable on summary conviction in the United Kingdom to imprisonment for a term not exceeding three months or to a fine [not exceeding level 5 on the standard scale], or both.

(2) Any person who without reasonable excuse fails to comply with any requirement imposed on him by regulations made under this Act with respect to the delivering up of certificates of naturalisation shall be liable on summary conviction in the United Kingdom to a fine [not exceeding level 4 on the standard scale].

(3) In the case of an offence under subsection (1):

(*a*) any information relating to the offence may in England and Wales be tried by a magistrates' court if it is laid within six months after the commission of the offence, or if it is laid within three years after the commission of the offence and not more than two months after the date certified by a chief officer of police to be the date on which evidence sufficient to justify proceedings came to the notice of an officer of his police force; and

(*b*) summary proceedings for the offence may in Scotland be commenced within six months after the commission of the offence, or within three years after the commission of the offence and not more than two months after the date on which evidence sufficient in the opinion of the Lord Advocate to justify proceedings came to his knowledge; and

(*c*) a complaint charging the commission of the offence may in Northern Ireland be heard and determined by a magistrates' court if it is made within six months after the commission of the offence, or if it is made within three years after the commission of the offence and not more than two months after the date certified by an officer of police not below the rank of assistant chief constable to be the date on which evidence sufficient to justify the proceedings came to the notice of the police in Northern Ireland.

(4) For the purposes of subsection (3)(*b*) proceedings shall be deemed to be commenced on the date on which a warrant to apprehend or to cite the accused is granted, if such warrant is executed without undue delay; and a certificate of the Lord Advocate as to the date on which such evidence as is mentioned in subsection 3(*b*) came to his knowledge shall be conclusive evidence.

(5) For the purposes of the trial of a person for an offence under sub-section (1) or (2), the offence shall be deemed to have been committed either at the place at which it actually was committed or at any place at which he may be.

(6) In their application to the Bailiwick of Jersey subsections (1) and (2) shall have effect with the omission of the words 'on summary conviction'.

Notes Words in square brackets in sub-ss (1), (2) substituted by virtue of the Criminal Justice Act 1982, s 46.

[A.1.128]
47 Legitimated children
(1) A person born out of wedlock and legitimated by the subsequent marriage of his parents shall, as from the date of the marriage, be treated for the purposes of this Act as if he had been born legitimate.

(2) A person shall be deemed for the purposes of this section to have been legitimated by the subsequent marriage of his parents if by the law of the place in which his father was domiciled at the time of the marriage the marriage operated immediately or subsequently to legitimate him, and not otherwise.

[A.1.129]
48 Posthumous children
Any reference in this Act to the status or description of the father or mother of a person at the time of that person's birth shall, in relation to a person born after the death of his father or mother, be construed as a reference to the sta-

tus or description of the parent in question at the time of that parent's death; and where that death occurred before, and the birth occurs after, commencement, the status or description which would have been applicable to the father or mother had he or she died after commencement shall be deemed to be the status or description applicable to him or her at the time of his or her death.

[A.1.130]
49 *(Repealed by s 52(8), Sch 9 post, as from 1 January 1983.)*

[A.1.131]
50 Interpretation
(1)   In this Act, unless the context otherwise requires:

'the 1948 Act' means the British Nationality Act 1948;
'alien' means a person who is neither a Commonwealth citizen nor a British protected person nor a citizen of the Republic of Ireland;
'association' means an unincorporated body of persons;
['British National (Overseas)' means a person who is a British National (Overseas) under the Hong Kong (British Nationality) Order 1986, and 'status of a British National (Overseas)' shall be construed accordingly;
'British Overseas citizen' includes a person who is a British Overseas citizen under the Hong Kong (British Nationality) Order 1986;]
'British protected person' means a person who is a member of any class of person declared to be British protected persons by an Order in Council for the time being in force under section 38 or is a British protected person by virtue of the Soloman Islands Act 1978;
'commencement', without more, means the commencement of this Act;
'Commonwealth citizen' means a person who has the status of a Commonwealth citizen under this Act;
'company' means a body corporate;
'Crown service' means the service of the Crown, whether within Her Majesty's dominions or elsewhere;
'Crown service under the government of the United Kingdom' means Crown service under Her Majesty's government in the United Kingdom or under Her Majesty's government in Northern Ireland [or under the Scottish Administration];
'dependent territory' means a territory mentioned in Schedule 6;
'enactment' includings an enactment comprised in Northern Ireland legislation;
'foreign country' means a country other than the United Kingdom, a dependent territory, a country mentioned in Schedule 3 and the Republic of Ireland;
'the former nationality Acts' means:

(a) the British Nationality Acts 1948 to 1965;
(b) the British Nationality and Status of Aliens Acts 1914 to 1943; and
(c) any Act repealed by the said Acts of 1914 to 1943 or by the Naturalisation Act 1870;

'Governor', in relation to a dependent territory, includes the officer for the time being administering the government of that territory;
'High Commissioner' includes an acting High Commissioner;

'immigration laws':

(*a*) in relation to the United Kingdom, means the Immigration Act 1971 and any law for purposes similar to that Act which is for the time being or has at any time been in force in any part of the United Kingdom;

(*b*) in relation to a dependent territory, means any law for purposes similar to the Immigration Act 1971 which is for the time being or has at any time been in force in that territory;

'the Islands' means the Channel Islands and the Isle of Man;
'minor' means a person who has not attained the age of eighteen years;
'prescribed' means prescribed by regulations made under section 41;
'settled' shall be construed in accordance with subsections (2) to (4);
'ship' includes a hovercraft;
'statutory provision' means any enactment or any provision contained in:

(*a*) subordinate legislation (as defined in section 21(1) of the Interpretation Act 1978); or

(*b*) any instrument of a legislative character made under any Northern Ireland legislation;

'the United Kingdom' means Great Britain, Northern Ireland and the Islands, taken together;
'United Kingdom consulate' means the office of a consular officer of Her Majesty's government in the United Kingdom where a register of births is kept or, where there is no such office, such office as may be prescribed.

(2) Subject to subsection (3), references in this Act to a person being settled in the United Kingdom or in a dependent territory are references to his being ordinarily resident in the United Kingdom or, as the case may be, in that territory without being subject under the immigration laws to any restriction on the period for which he may remain.

(3) Subject to subsection (4), a person is not to be regarded for the purposes of this Act:

(*a*) as having been settled in the United Kingdom at any time when he was entitled to an exemption under section 8(3) or (4)(*b*) or (*c*) of the Immigration Act 1971 or, unless the order under section 8(2) of that Act conferring the exemption in question provides otherwise, to an exemption under the said section 8(2), or to any corresponding exemption under the former immigration laws; or

(*b*) as having been settled in a dependent territory at any time when he was under the immigration laws entitled to any exemption corresponding to any such exemption as is mentioned in paragraph (*a*) (that paragraph being for the purposes of this paragraph read as if the words from 'unless' to 'otherwise' were omitted).

(4) A person to whom a child is born in the United Kingdom after commencement is to be regarded for the purposes of section 1(1) as being settled in the United Kingdom at the time of the birth if:

(*a*) he would fall to be so regarded but for being at that time entitled to an exemption under section 8(3) of the Immigration Act 1971; and

(*b*) immediately before he became entitled to that exemption he was settled in the United Kingdom; and (*c*) he was ordinarily resident in the United Kingdom from the time when he became entitled to that exemption to the time of the birth;

but this subsection shall not apply if at the time of the birth the child's father or mother is a person on whom any immunity from jurisdiction is conferred by or under the Diplomatic Privileges Act 1964.

(5) It is hereby declared that a person is not to be treated for the purpose of any provision of this Act as ordinarily resident in the United Kingdom or in a dependent territory at a time when he is in the United Kingdom or, as the case may be, in that territory in breach of the immigration laws.

(6) For the purposes of this Act:

(*a*) a person shall be taken to have been naturalised in the United Kingdom if but only if, he is:

(i) a person to whom a certificate of naturalisation was granted under any of the former nationality Acts by the Secretary of State or, in any of the Islands, by the Lieutenant-Governor; or

(ii) a person who by virtue of section 27(2) of the British Nationality and Status of Aliens Act 1914 was deemed to be a person to whom a certificate of naturalisation was granted, if the certificate of naturalisation in which his name was included was granted by the Secretary of State; or

(iii) a person who by virtue of section 10(5) of the Naturalisation Act 1870 was deemed to be a naturalised British subject by reason of his residence with his father or mother;

(*b*) a person shall be taken to have been naturalised in a dependent territory if, but only if, he is:

(i) a person to whom a certificate of naturalisation was granted under any of the former nationality Acts by the Governor of that territory or by a person for the time being specified in a direction given in relation to that territory under paragraph 4 of Schedule 3 to the West Indies Act 1967 or for the time being holding an office so specified; or

(i) a person who by virtue of the said section 27(2) was deemed to be a person to whom a certificate of naturalisation was granted, if the certificate of naturalisation in which his name was included was granted by the Governor of that territory; or

(iii) a person who by the law in force in that territory enjoyed the privileges of naturalisation within that territory only;

and references in this Act to naturalisation in the United Kingdom or in a dependent territory shall be construed accordingly.

(7) For the purposes of this Act a person born outside the United Kingdom aboard a ship or aircraft:

(*a*) shall be deemed to have been born in the United Kingdom if:

(i) at the time of the birth his father or mother was a British citizen; or

(ii) he would, but for this subsection, have been born stateless.

and (in either case) at the time of the birth the ship or aircraft was registered in the United Kingdom or was an unregistered ship or aircraft of the government of the United Kingdom; but

(*b*) subject to paragraph (*a*), is to be regarded as born outside the United Kingdom, whoever was the owner of the ship or aircraft at the time, and irrespective of whether or where it was then registered.

The preceding provisions of this subsection shall apply in relation to each dependent territory with the substitution for the references to the United Kingdom and to a British citizen of references to that territory and to a British Dependent Territories citizen respectively.

(8) For the purposes of this Act an application under any provision thereof shall be taken to have been made at the time of its receipt by a person authorised to receive it on behalf of the person to whom it is made; and references in this Act to the date of such an application are references to the date of its receipt by a person so authorised.

(9) For the purposes of this Act:

(*a*) the relationship of mother and child shall be taken to exist between a woman and any child (legitimate or illegitimate) born to her; but

(*b*) subject to section 47, the relationship of father and child shall be taken to exist only between a man and any legitimate child born to him;

and the expressions 'mother', 'father', 'parent', 'child' and 'descended' shall be construed accordingly.

(10) For the purposes of this Act:

(*a*) a period 'from' or 'to' a specified date includes that date; and

(*b*) any reference to a day on which a person was absent from the United Kingdom or from a dependent territory or from the dependent territories is a reference to a day for the whole of which he was so absent.

(11) For the purposes of this Act:

(*a*) a person is of full age if he has attained the age of eighteen years, and of full capacity if he is not of unsound mind; and

(*b*) a person attains any particular age at the beginning of the relevant anniversary of the date of his birth.

(12) References in this Act to any country mentioned in Schedule 3 include references to the dependencies of that country.

(13) Her Majesty may by Order in Council subject to annulment in pursuance of a resolution of either House of Parliament amend Schedule 6 in any of the following circumstances, namely:

(*a*) where the name of any territory mentioned in it is altered; or

(*b*) where any territory mentioned in it is divided into two or more territories.

Notes Definitions 'British National (Overseas)' and 'British Overseas citizen' in sub-s (1) inserted by the Hong Kong (British Nationality) Order 1986, SI 1986/948, as from 1 July 1987.

Words in square brackets in definition 'Crown service under the government of the United Kingdom' in sub-s (1) inserted by SI 1999/1042, art 3, Sch 1, para 10.

[A.1.132]
51 Meaning of certain expressions relating to nationality in other Acts and instruments
(1) Without prejudice to subsection (3)(*c*), in any enactment or instrument whatever passed or made before commencement 'British subject' and 'Commonwealth citizen' have the same meaning, that is:

(*a*) in relation to any time before commencement:

     (i) a person who under the 1948 Act was at that time a citizen of the United Kingdom and Colonies or who, under any enactment then in force in a country mentioned in section 1(3) of that Act as then in force, was at that time a citizen of that country; and

    (ii) any other person who had at that time the status of a British subject under that Act or any other enactment then in force;

(*b*) in relation to any time after commencement, a person who has the status of a Commonwealth citizen under this Act.

(2)   In any enactment or instrument whatever passed or made after commencement:

'British subject' means a person who has the status of a British subject under this Act;

'Commonwealth citizen' means a person who has the status of a Commonwealth citizen under this Act.

(3)   In any enactment or instrument whatever passed or made before commencement:

(*a*) 'citizen of the United Kingdom and Colonies':

     (i) in relation to any time before commencement, means a person who under the 1948 Act was at that time a citizen of the United Kingdom and Colonies;

    (ii) in relation to any time after commencement, means a person who under [the British Nationality Acts 1981 and 1983] is a British citizen, a British Dependent Territories citizen or a British Overseas citizen [or who under the Hong Kong (British Nationality) Order 1986 is a British National (Overseas)];

(*b*) any reference to ceasing to be a citizen of the United Kingdom and Colonies shall, in relation to any time after commencement, be construed as a reference to becoming a person who is neither a British citizen nor a British Dependent Territories citizen [nor a British National (Overseas)] nor a British Overseas citizen;

(*c*) any reference to a person who is a British subject (or a British subject without citizenship) by virtue of section 2, 13 or 16 of the 1948 Act or by virtue of, or of section 1 of, the British Nationality Act 1965 shall, in relation to any time after commencement, be construed as a reference to a person who under this Act is a British subject.

(4)   In any statutory provision, whether passed or made before or after commencement, and in any other instrument whatever made after com-mencement 'alien', in relation to any time after commencement, means a person who is neither a Commonwealth citizen nor a British protected person nor a citizen of the Republic of Ireland.

(5)   The preceding provisions of this section:

(*a*) shall not apply in cases where the context otherwise requires; and

(*b*) shall not apply to this Act or to any instrument made under this Act.

Notes Words in first square brackets in sub-s (3)(*a*)(ii) substituted by the British Nationality (Falkland Islands) Act 1983, s 4(3)

    Words in second square brackets in sub-s (3)(*a*)(ii), and those in square brackets in sub-s (3)(*b*), inserted by the Hong Kong (British Nationality) Order 1986, SI 1986/948, as from 1 July 1987.

Definitions For 'British National (Overseas)', and 'British Overseas citizen', British protected person', 'commencement', 'enactment' and 'statutory provison', see s 50(1) and see also, as to 'commencement', s 53(2).

[A.1.133]
52 Consequential amendments, transitional provisions, repeals and savings

(1)   In any enactment or instrument whatever passed or made before commencement, for any reference to section 1(3) of the 1948 Act (list of countries whose citizens are Commonwealth citizens under that Act) there shall be substituted a reference to Schedule 3 to this Act, unless the context makes that substitution inappropriate.

(2)   Subject to subsection (3), Her Majesty may by Order in Council make such consequential modifications of:

(*a*) any enactment of the Parliament of the United Kingdom passed before commencement;

(*b*) any provision contained in any Northern Ireland legislation passed or made before commencement; or

(*c*) any instrument made before commencement under any such enactment or provision,

as appear to Her necessary or expedient for preserving after commencement the substantive effect of that enactment, provision or instrument.

(3)   Subsection (2) shall not apply in relation to:

(*a*) the Immigration Act 1971; or

(*b*) any provision of this Act not contained in Schedule 7.

(4)   Any Order in Council made under subsection (2) shall be subject to annulment in pursuance of a resolution of either House of Parliament.

(5)   Any provision made by Order in Council under subsection (2) after commencement may be made with retrospective effect as from commencement or any later date.

(6)   The enactments specified in Schedule 7 shall have effect subject to the amendments there specified, being amendments consequential on the provisions of this Act.

(7)   This Act shall have effect subject to the transitional provisions contained in Schedule 8.

(8)   The enactments mentioned in Schedule 9 are hereby repealed to the extent specified in the third column of that Schedule.

(9)   Without prejudice to section 51, nothing in this Act affects the operation, in relation to any time before commencement, of any statutory provision passed or made before commencement.

(10)   Nothing in this Act shall be taken as prejudicing the operation of sections 16 and 17 of the Interpretation Act 1978 (which relate to the effect of repeals).

(11)   In this section 'modifications' includes additions, omissions and alterations.

Definitions   For 'commencement', 'enactment' and 'statutory provision', see s 50(1) (and see also, as to 'commencement', s 53(2)). Note as to 'modifications', sub-s (11) above.

[A.1.134]
53 Citation, commencement and extent
(1)   This Act may be cited as the British Nationality Act 1981.
(2)   This Act, except the provisions mentioned in subsection (3), shall lcome into force on such day as the Secretary of State may by order made by statutory instrument appoint; and references to the commencement of this Act shall be construed as references to the beginning of that day.
(3)   Section 49 and this section shall come into force on the passing of this Act.
(4)   This Act extends to Northern Ireland.
(5)   The provisions of this Act, except those mentioned in subsection (7), extend to the Islands and all dependent territories; and section 36 of the Immigration Act 1971 (power to extend provisions of that Act to Islands) shall apply to the said excepted provisions as if they were provisions of that Act.
(6)   . . .
(7)   The provisions referred to in subsections (5) . . . are:

(*a*) section 39 and Schedule 4;
(*b*) section 52(7) and Schedule 8 so far as they relate to the Immigration Act 1971; and
(*c*) section 52(8) and Schedule 9 so far as they relate to provisions of the Immigration Act 1971 other than Schedule 1.

Notes   Sub-s (6): repealed by the Statute Law (Repeals) Act 1995.
Sub-s (7): words omitted repealed by the Statute Law (Repeals) Act 1995.

Definitions   For 'dependent territory' and 'the Islands', see s 50(1).

Schedules

SCHEDULE 1   REQUIREMENTS FOR NATURALISATION
(SECTIONS 6, 18)

[A.1.135]

Naturalisation as a British citizen under section 6(1)

1—(1)   Subject to paragraph 2, the requirements for naturalisation as a British citizen under section 6(1) are, in the case of any person who applies for it:

(*a*) the requirements specified in sub-paragraph (2) of this paragraph, or the alternative requirement specified in sub-paragraph (3) of this paragraph; and

(b) that he is of good character; and

(c) that he has a sufficient knowledge of the English, Welsh or Scottish Gaelic language; and

(d) that either:

    (i) his intentions are such that, in the event of a certificate of naturalisation as a British citizen being granted to him, his home or (if he has more than one) his principal home will be in the United Kingdom; or

    (ii) he intends, in the event of such a certificate being granted to him, to enter into, or continue in, Crown service under the government of the United Kingdom, or service under an international organisation of which the United Kingdom or Her Majesty's government therein is a member, or service in the employment of a company or association established in the United Kingdom.

(2)   The requirements referred to in sub-paragraph (1)(a) of this paragraph are:

(a) that the applicant was in the United Kingdom at the beginning of the period of five years ending with the date of the application, and that the number of days on which he was absent from the United Kingdom in that period does not exceed 450; and

(b) that the number of days on which he was absent from the United Kingdom in the period of twelve months so ending does not exceed 90; and

(c) that he was not at any time in the period of twelve months so ending subject under the immigration laws to any restriction on the period for which he might remain in the United Kingdom; and

(d) that he was not at any time in the period of five years so ending in the United Kingdom in breach of the immigration laws.

(3)   The alternative requirement referred to in sub-paragraph (1)(a) of this paragraph is that on the date of the application he is serving outside the United Kingdom in Crown service under the government of the United Kingdom.

2   If in the special circumstances of any particular case the Secretary of State thinks fit, he may for the purposes of paragraph 1 do all or any of the following things, namely:

(a) treat the applicant as fulfilling the requirement specified in paragraph 1(2)(a) or paragraph 1(2)(b), or both, although the number of days on which he was absent from the United Kingdom in the period there mentioned exceeds the number there mentioned;

(b) treat the applicant as having been in the United Kingdom for the whole or any part of any period during which he would otherwise fall to be treated under paragraph 9(1) as having been absent;

(c) disregard any such restriction as is mentioned in paragraph 1(2)(c), not being a restriction to which the applicant was subject on the date of the application;

(d) treat the applicant as fulfilling the requirement specified in paragraph 1(2)(d) although he was in the United Kingdom in breach of the immigration laws in the period there mentioned;

(e) waive the need to fulfil the requirement specified in paragraph 1(1)(c) if he considers that because of the applicant's age or physical or mental condition it would be unreasonable to expect him to fulfil it.

Naturalisation as a British citizen under section 6(2)

3 Subject to paragraph 4, the requirements for naturalisation as a British citizen under section 6(2) are, in the case of any person who applies for it:

(*a*) that he was in the United Kingdom at the beginning of the period of three years ending with the date of the application, and that the number of days on which he was absent from the United Kingdom in that period does not exceed 270; and

(*b*) that the number of days on which he was absent from the United Kingdom in the period of twelve months so ending does not exceed 90; and

(*c*) that on the date of the application he was not subject under the immigration laws to any restriction on the period for which he might remain in the United Kingdom; and

(*d*) that he was not at any time in the period of three years ending with the date of the application in the United Kingdom in breach of the immigration laws; and

(*e*) the requirement specified in paragraph 1(1)(*b*).

4 Paragraph 2 shall apply in relation to paragraph 3 with the following modifications namely:

(*a*) the reference to the purposes of paragraph 1 shall be read as a reference to the purposes of paragraph 3;

(*b*) the references to paragraphs 1(2)(*a*), 1(2)(*b*) and 1(2)(*d*) shall be read as references to paragraphs 3(*a*), 3(*b*) and 3(*d*) respectively;

(*c*) paragraph 2(*c*) and (*e*) shall be omitted; and

(*d*) after paragraph (*e*) there shall be added:

'(*f*) waive the need to fulfil all or any of the requirements specified in paragraph 3(*a*) and (*b*) if on the date of the application the person to whom the applicant is married is serving in service to which section 2(1)(*b*) applies, that person's recruitment for that service having taken place in the United Kingdom'.

Naturalisation as a British Dependent Territories citizen under section 18(1)

5—(1) Subject to paragraph 6, the requirements for naturalisation as a British Dependent Territories citizen under section 18(1) are, in the case of any person who applies for it:

(*a*) the requirements specified in sub-paragraph (2) of this paragraph, or the alternative specified in sub-paragraph (3) of this paragraph; and

(*b*) that he is of good character; and

(*c*) that he has a sufficient knowledge of the English language or any other language recognised for official purposes in the relevant territory; and

(*d*) that either:

(i) his intentions are such that, in the event of a certificate of naturalisation as a British Dependent Territories citizen being granted to him, his home or (if he has more than one) his principal home will be in the relevant territory; or

(ii) he intends, in the event of such a certificate being granted to him, to enter into, or continue in, Crown service under the government of that territory, or service under an international organisation of which that territory

or the government of that territory is a member, or service in the employment of a company or association established in that territory.

(2)   The requirements referred to in sub-paragraph (1)(*a*) of this paragraph
are:

(*a*) that he was in the relevant territory at the beginning of the period of five
years ending with the date of the application, and that the number of days
on which he was absent from that territory in that period does not exceed
450; and

(*b*) that the number of days on which he was absent from the territory in the
period of twelve months so ending does not exceed 90; and

(*c*) that he was not at any time in the period of twelve months so ending subject under the immigration laws to any restriction on the period for which
he might remain in that territory; and

(*d*) that he was not at any time in the period of five years so ending in the territory in breach of the immigration laws.

(3)   The alternative requirement referred to in sub-paragraph (1)(*a*) of this
paragraph is that on the date of the application he is serving outside the relevant territory in Crown service under the government of that territory.

6   If in the special circumstances of any particular case the Secretary of State
thinks fit, he may for the purposes of paragraph 5 do all or any of the following things, namely:

(*a*) treat the applicant as fulfilling the requirement specified in paragraph
5(2)(*a*) or paragraph 5(2)(*b*), or both, although the number of days on
which he was absent from the relevant territory in the period there mentioned exceeds the number there mentioned;

(*b*) treat the applicant as having been in the relevant territory for the whole or
any part of any period during which he would otherwise fall to be treated
under paragraph 9(2) as having been absent;

(*c*) disregard any such restriction as is mentioned in paragraph 5(2)(*c*), not
being a restriction to which the applicant was subject on the date of the
application;

(*d*) treat the applicant as fulfilling the requirement specified in paragraph
5(2)(*d*) although he was in the relevant territory in breach of the immigration laws in the period there mentioned;

(*e*) waive the need to fulfil the requirement specified in paragraph 5(1)(*c*) if
he considers that because of the applicant's age or physical or mental condition it would be unreasonable to expect him to fulfil it.

Naturalisation as a British Dependent Territories citizen under section 18(2)

7   Subject to paragraph 8 the requirements for naturalisation as a British
Dependent Territories citizen under section 18(2) are, in the case of any person who applies for it:

(*a*) that he was in the relevant territory at the beginning of the period of three
years ending with the date of the application, and that the number of days
on which he was absent from that territory in that period does not exceed
270; and

(*b*) that the number of days on which he was absent from that territory in the period of twelve months so ending does not exceed 90; and

(*c*) that on the date of the application he was not subject under the immigration laws to any restriction on the period for which he might remain in that territory; and

(*d*) that he was not at any time in the period of thee years ending with the date of the application in that territory in breach of the immigration laws; and

(*e*) the requirement specified in paragraph 5(1)(*b*).

8 Paragraph 6 shall apply in relation to paragraph 7 with the following modifications, namely:

(*a*) the reference to the purposes of paragraph 5 shall be read as a reference to the purposes of paragraph 7;

(*b*) the references to paragraphs 5(2)(*a*), 5(2)(*b*) and 5(2)(*d*) shall be read as references to paragraph 7(*a*), 7(*b*) and 7(*d*) respectively;

(*c*) paragraph 6(*c*) and (*e*) shall be omitted; and

(*d*) after paragraph (*e*) there shall be added:

'(*f*) waive the need to fulfil all or any of the requirements specified in paragraph 7(*a*) and (*b*) if on the date of the application the person to whom the applicant is married is serving in service to which section 16(1)(*b*) applies, that person's recruitment for that service having taken place in a dependent territory'.

Periods to be treated as periods of absence from UK or a dependent territory

9—(1) For the purposes of this Schedule a person shall (subject to paragraph 2(*b*)) be treated as having been absent from the United Kingdom during any of the following periods, that is to say:

(*a*) any period when he was in the United Kingdom and either was entitled to an exemption under section 8(3) or (4) of the Immigration Act 1971 (exemptions for diplomatic agents etc and members of the forces) or was a member of the family and formed part of the household of a person so entitled;

(*b*) any period when he was detained:

(i) in any place of detention in the United Kingdom in pursuance of a sentence passed on him by a court in the United Kingdom or elsewhere for any offence;

(ii) in any hospital in the United Kingdom under a hospital order made under [Part III of the Mental Health Act 1983] or section 175 or 376 of the Criminal Procedure (Scotland) Act 1975 or Part III of the Mental Health [(Northern Ireland) Order 1986], being an order made in connection with his conviction of an offence; or

(iii) under any power of detention conferred by the immigration laws of the United Kingdom;

(*c*) any period when, being liable to be detained as mentioned in paragraph (*b*)(i) or (ii) of this sub-paragraph, he was unlawfully at large or absent without leave and for that reason liable to be arrested or taken into custody;

(*d*) any period when, his actual detention under any such power as is mentioned in paragraph (*b*)(iii) of this sub-paragraph being required or specifically authorised, he was unlawfully at large and for that reason liable to be arrested.

(2) For the purposes of this Schedule a person shall (subject to paragraph 6(*b*)) be treated as having been absent from any particular dependent territory during any of the following periods, that is to say:

(*a*) any period when he was in that territory and either was entitled to an exemption under the immigration laws of that territory corresponding to any such exemption as is mentioned in sub-paragraph (1)(*a*) or was a member of the family and formed part of the household of a person so entitled;

(*b*) any period when he was detained:

(i) in any place of detention in the relevant territory in pursuance of a sentence passed on him by a court in that territory or elsewhere for any offence;

(ii) in any hospital in that territory under a direction (however described) made under any law for purposes similar to [Part III of the Mental Health Act 1983] which was for the time being in force in that territory, being a direction made in connection with his conviction of an offence and corresponding to a hospital order under that Part; or

(iii) under any power of detention conferred by the immigration laws of that territory;

(*c*) any period when, being liable to be detained as mentioned in paragraph (*b*)(i) or (ii) of this sub-paragraph, he was unlawfully at large or absent without leave and for that reason liable to be arrested or taken into custody;

(*d*) any period when, his actual detention under any such power as is mentioned in paragraph (*b*)(iii) of this sub-paragraph being required or specifically authorised, he was unlawfully at large and for that reason liable to be arrested.

Interpretation

10 In this Schedule 'the relevant territory' has the meaning given by section 18(3).

Notes Words in first square brackets in para 9(1)(*b*) and words in square brackets in para 9(2)(*b*) substituted by the Mental Health Act 1983, s 148, Sch 4, para 60; words in second square brackets in para 9(1)(*b*) substituted by the Mental Health (Northern Ireland Consequential Amendments) Order 1986, SI 1986/596.

Definitions For 'the relevant territory', see s 18(3); for 'association', 'company', 'Crown service under the government of the United Kingdom', 'dependent territory', 'immigration laws' and 'the United Kingdom', see s 50(1); as to 'date of the application', see s 50(8).

SCHEDULE 2   PROVISIONS FOR REDUCING STATELESSNESS
(SECTION 36)

[A.1.136]

Persons born in the United Kingdom after commencement

1 — (1)   Where a person born in the United Kingdom after commencement would, but for this paragraph, be born stateless, then, subject to sub-paragraph (3):

(*a*) if at the time of the birth his father or mother is a citizen or subject of a description mentioned in sub-paragraph (2), he shall be a citizen or subject of that description; and accordingly

(*b*) if he is born legitimate and at the time of the birth each of his parents is a citizen or subject of a different description so mentioned, he shall be a citizen or subject of the same description so mentioned as each of them is respectively at that time.

(2)   The descriptions referred to in sub-paragraph (1) are a British Dependent Territories citizen, a British Overseas citizen and a British subject under this Act.

(3)   A person shall not be a British subject by virtue of this paragraph if by virtue of it he is a citizen of a description mentioned in sub-paragraph (2).

Persons born in a dependent territory after commencement

2—(1)   Where a person born in a dependent territory after commencement would, but for this paragraph, be born stateless, the, subject to sub-paragraph (3):

(*a*) if at the time of the birth his father or mother is a citizen or subject of a description mentioned in sub-paragraph (2), he shall be a citizen or subject of that description; and accordingly

(*b*) if he is born legitimate and at the time of the birth each of his parents is a citizen or subject of a different description so mentioned, he shall be a citizen or subject of the same description so mentioned as each of them is respectively at that time.

(2)   The description referred to in sub-paragraph (1) are a British citizen, a British overseas citizen and a British subject under this Act.

(3)   A person shall not be a British subject by virtue of this paragraph if by virtue of it he is a citizen of a description mentioned in sub-paragraph (2).

Persons born in the United Kingdom or a dependent territory after commencement

3—(1)   A person born in the United Kingdom or a dependent territory after commencement shall be entitled, on an application for his registration under this paragraph, to be so registered if the following requirements are satisfied in his case, namely:

(*a*) that he is and always has been stateless; and

(*b*) that on the date of the application he had attained the age of ten but was under the age of twenty-two; and

(*c*) that he was in the United Kingdom or a dependent territory (no matter which) at the beginning of the period of five years ending with that date and that (subject to paragraph 6) the number of days on which he was absent from both the United Kingdom and the dependent territories in that period does not exceed 450.

(2)   A person entitled to registration under this paragraph:

(*a*) shall be registered under it as a British citizen if, in the period of five years mentioned in sub-paragraph (1), the number of days wholly or partly spent by him in the United Kingdom exceeds the number of days wholly or partly spent by him in the dependent territories;

(*b*) in any other case, shall be registered under it as a British Dependent Territories citizen.

Persons born outside the United Kingdom and the dependent territories after commencement

4—(1)   A person born outside the United Kingdom and the dependent territories after commencement, shall be entitled, on an application for his registration under this paragraph, to be so registered if the following requirements are satisfied, namely:

(*a*) that that person is and always has been stateless; and

(*b*) that at the time of that person's birth his father or mother was a citizen or subject of a description mentioned in sub-paragraph (4); and

(*c*) that that person was in the United Kingdom or a dependent territory (no matter which) at the beginning of the period of three years ending with the date of the application and that (subject to paragraph 6) the number of days on which he was absent from both the United Kingdom and the dependent territories in that period does not exceed 270.

(2)   A person entitled to registration under this paragraph:

(*a*) shall be registered under it as a citizen or subject of a description available to him in accordance with sub-paragraph (3); and

(*b*) if more than one description is so available to him, shall be registered under this paragraph as a citizen of whichever one or more of the descriptions available to him is or are stated in the application under this paragraph to be wanted.

(3)   For the purposes of this paragraph the descriptions of citizen or subject available to a person entitled to registration under this paragraph are:

(*a*) in the case of a person whose father or mother was at the time of that person's birth a citizen of a description mentioned in sub-paragraph (4), any description of citizen so mentioned which applied to his father or mother at that time;

(*b*) in any other case, a British subject under this Act.

(4)   The descriptions referred to in sub-paragraphs (1) to (3) are a British citizen, a British Dependent Territories citizen, a British Overseas citizen and a British subject under this Act.

Persons born stateless before commencement

5—(1) A person born before commencement shall be entitled, on an application for his registration under this paragraph, to be so registered if the circumstances are such that, if:

(*a*) this Act had not been passed, and the enactments repealed or amended by this Act had continued in force accordingly; and

(*b*) an application for the registration of that person under section 1 of the British Nationality (No 2) Act 1964 (stateless persons) as a citizen of the United Kingdom and Colonies had been made on the date of the application under this paragraph,

that person would have been entitled under that section to be registered as such a citizen.

(2) A person entitled to registration under this paragraph shall be registered under it as such a citizen as he would have become at commencement if, immediately before commencement, he had been registered as a citizen of the United Kingdom and Colonies under section 1 of the British Nationality (No 2) Act 1964 on whichever of the grounds mentioned in subsection (1)(*a*) to (*c*) of that section he would have been entitled to be so registered on in the circumstances described in sub-paragraph (1)(*a*) and (*b*) of this paragraph.

Supplementary

6 If in the special circumstances of any particular case the Secretary of State thinks fit, he may for the purposes of paragraph 3 or 4 treat the person who is the subject of the application as fulfilling the requirement specified in sub-paragraph (1)(*c*) of that paragraph although the number of days on which he was absent from both the United Kingdom and the dependent territories in the period there mentioned exceeds the number there mentioned.

Definitions For 'commencement', 'dependent territory', and 'the United Kingdom', see s 50(1) (and see also as to 'commencement', s 53(2); as to 'date of the application', see s 50(8); as to 'father' and 'mother', see s 50(9) (but see s 47).

SCHEDULE 3 COUNTRIES WHOSE CITIZENS ARE COMMONWEALTH CITIZENS (SECTION 37)

[A.1.137]

Antigua and Barbuda	[Mozambique]
Australia	[Namibia]
The Bahamas	Nauru
Bangladesh	New Zealand
Barbados	Nigeria
Belize	[Pakistan]
Botswana	Papua New Guinea
[Brunei]	[Saint Christopher and Nevis]

[Cameroon]
Canada
Republic of Cyprus
Dominica
Fiji
The Gambia
Ghana
Grenada
Guyana
India
Jamaica
Kenya
Kiribati
Lesotho
Malawi
Malaysia
[Maldives]
Malta
Mauritius

Saint Lucia
Saint Vincent and the Grenadines
Seychelles
Sierra Leone
Singapore
Solomon Islands
[South Africa]
Sri Lanka
Swaziland
Tanzania
Tonga
Trinidad and Tobago
Tuvalu
Uganda
Vanuatu
Western Samoa
Zambia
Zimbabwe

Notes   Word 'Brunei' inserted by the British Nationality (Brunei) Order 1983, SI 1983/1699; word 'Maldives' inserted by the Brunei and Maldives Act 1985, s 1, Schedule, para 8; word 'Pakistan' inserted by the British Nationality (Pakistan) Order 1989, SI 1989/1331; words 'Saint Christopher and Nevis' inserted by the Saint Christopher and Nevis Modification of Enactments Order 1983, SI 1983/882. Word 'Namibia' inserted by the British Nationality (Namibia) Order 1990, SI 1990/1502; entry 'South Africa' inserted by SI 1994/1634. Words 'Cameroon' and 'Mozambique' inserted by the British Nationality (Cameroon and Mozambique) Order 1998, SI 1998/3161.

(Sch 4 amends the Immigration Act 1971, ss 3–6, 8, 9, 13, 14, 22, 24–26, 29, 33, Schs 2, 4.)

SCHEDULE 5   FORM OF OATH OF ALLEGIANCE (SECTION 42(1))

[A.1.138]
The form of the oath of allegiance is as shown below, with the insertion after the words 'on becoming', of whichever of the following expressions is appropriate, namely —

'a British citizen'
'a British Dependent Territories citizen'
'a British Overseas citizen'
'a British subject'.

Oath of allegiance

I, A.B., swear by Almighty God that, on becoming .... I will be faithful and bear true allegiance to Her Majesty Queen Elizabeth the Second Her Heirs and Successors according to law.

SCHEDULE 6   BRITISH DEPENDENT TERRITORIES (SECTION 50(1))

[A.1.139]
Anguilla
Bermuda
British Antarctic Territory
British Indian Ocean Territory
Cayman Islands
Falkland Islands and Dependencies
Gibraltar

. . . . .

Montserrat
Pitcairn, Henderson, Ducie and Oeno Islands

. . . . .

St Helena and Dependencies
The Sovereign Base Areas of Akrotiri and Dhekelia (that is to say the areas
    mentioned in section 2(1) of the Cyprus Act 1960)
Turks and Caicos Islands
Virgin Islands

Notes   Words omitted repealed by the Hong Kong (British Nationality) Order 1986, SI
1986/948, as from 1 July 1987, and by the Saint Christopher and Nevis Modification of
Enactments Order 1983, SI 1983/882.

---

*(Sch 7 makes minor and consequential amendments to provisions outside the
scope of this work.)*

SCHEDULE 8   TRANSITIONAL PROVISIONS (SECTION 52(7))

[A.1.140]

*Applications for naturalisation or registration pending at commence-
ment*

1—(1)   This paragraph applies to any application:

(*a*) for registration under any provision of the British Nationality Acts 1948 to
    1965 as a citizen of the United Kingdom and Colonies or as a British sub-
    ject; or

(*b*) for a certificate of naturalisation under section 10 of the 1948 Act,

which is received before commencement by a person authorised to receive it
on behalf of the person to whom it is made but which at commencement has
not been determined.

(2)   In relation to any application to which this paragraph applies:

(*a*) the British Nationality Acts 1948 to 1965 and all regulations and arrangements in force under them immediately before commencement shall (so far as applicable) continue to apply; and

(*b*) this Act shall not apply;

but on the granting of such an application and the taking under those Acts of such other steps as are necessary for the person in question to become:

(i) a citizen of the United Kingdom and Colonies by virtue of any provision of those Acts; or

(ii) a British subject by virtue of registration under any provision of those Acts;

that person, instead of becoming a citizen or subject of that description, shall become under this Act such a citizen or subject as he would have become at commencement if, immediately before commencement, he had been such a citizen or subject as is mentioned in paragraph (i) or (ii), as the case may be.

(3)   Sub-paragraph (2) shall have effect as if the references in it to the British Nationality Acts 1948 to 1965 did, and as if the reference in paragraph (*b*) of it to this Act did not, include section 49 of this Act.

2   Where a person who had been registered or to whom a certificate of naturalisation has been granted before the passing of this Act has at commencement not yet taken the oath of allegiance, paragraph 1(2) shall apply as if the application on which he was registered or the certificate was granted were an application to which paragraph 1 applies.

Registration at UK consulate, after commencement, of certain births occurring in foreign countries less than a year before commencement

3—(1)   This paragraph applies to a person born less than a year before commencement if:

(*a*) the birth occurred in a place in a foreign country (within the meaning of the 1948 Act); and

(*b*) at the time of the birth his father was a citizen of the United Kingdom and Colonies by descent only; and

(*c*) the birth was not registered at a United Kingdom consulate before commencement.

(2)   If the birth of a person to whom this paragraph applies is registered at a United Kingdom consulate within one year of its occurrence, he shall be deemed for the purposes of this Act to have been, immediately before commencement, a citizen of the United Kingdom and Colonies by virtue of section 5 of the 1948 Act (citizenship by descent).

(3)   References in this paragraph to the 1948 Act are references to that Act as in force at the time of the birth in question.

Declarations by certain persons who by virtue of an Order in Council under section 4 of the Cyprus Act 1966 have ceased to be citizens of the United Kingdom and Colonies

4—(1)   Where:

(*a*) a person has before commencement duly made a declaration under section 4(2) of the Cyprus Act 1960 of his intention to resume citizenship of the United Kingdom and Colonies; but

(*b*) at commencement the declaration has not been registered,

the Secretary of State shall cause the declaration to be registered.

(2)   If:

(*a*) a person who in consequence of anything done before he attained the age of sixteen years ceased by virtue of an Order in Council under section 4 of the Cyprus Act 1960 to be a citizen of the United Kingdom and Colonies makes, in such a manner as the Secretary of State may direct, a declaration of his intention to accept the citizenship available to him under this paragraph; and

(*b*) the declaration is made by him after commencement and within one year after his attaining the age of twenty-one years,

the Secretary of State shall cause the declaration to be registered.

(3)   On the registration under sub-paragraph (1) or (2) of any such declaration as is there mentioned the person who made it shall become under this Act such a citizen as he would have become at commencement if,immediately before commencement, he had been a citizen of the United Kingdom and Colonies by virtue of section 4(2) of the Cyprus Act 1960.

Applications for certificates of patriality pending at commencement

5   Any application for a certificate of patriality under the Immigration Act 1971 duly made but not determined before commencement shall be treated as if it were an application for a certificate of entitlement under that Act as amended by this Act.

Appeals under Part II of Immigration Act 1971

6   Where a person who has been refused a certificate of patriality under the Immigration Act 1971 before commencement has immediately before commencement a right of appeal under Part II (appeals of that Act against the refusal, the provisions of that Part shall have effect in relation to the refusal as if he had applied for, and been refused, a certificate of entitlement under that Act as amended by this Act.

7   Any appeal under Part II of the Immigration Act 1971 against a refusal of a certificate of patriality under that Act which is pending immediately before commencement shall be treated as if it were an appeal against a refusal of a certificate of entitlement under that Act as amended by this Act.

8   In relation to appeals against any decision taken or other thing done under the Immigration Act 1971 before commencement, other than a refusal of a certificate of partiality under that Act, the provisions of that Act shall continue to apply as in force immediately before commencement, and not as amended by this Act.

Modification   Sch 8 modified in relation to the Isle of Man by SI 1991/2630, see E[561]ff.

Definitions   For 'commencement' and 'United Kingdom consulate', see s 50(1) (and see also, as to 'commencement', s 53(2)); as to 'father', see s 50(9) (but see s 47).

SCHEDULE 9   REPEALS (SECTION 52(8))

[A.1.141]

Chapter	Short Title	Extent of Repeal
11 & 12 Geo 6 c 3	Burmah Independence Act 1947	Section 2. Schedule 1.
11 & 12 Geo 6 c 56	British Nationality Act 1948	The whole Act except— (a) section 3; (b) section 32(3); (c) section 33(1) from the beginning to the words 'Isle of Man'; and (d) section 34(1).
12, 13 & 14 Geo 6 c 41	Ireland Act 1949	Section 5.
14 Geo 6 c 5	Newfoundland (Consequential Provisions Act 1950	The whole Act.
15 & 16 Geo 6 & 1 Eliz 2	Visiting Forces Act 1952	Section 15(3)(c) and (d).
5 & 6 Eliz 2 c 6	Ghana Independence Act 1957	Section 2.
5 & 6 Eliz 2 c 60	Federation of Malaya Independence Act 1957	In Schedule 1, paragraph 1.
6 & 7 Eliz 2 c 10	British Nationality Act 1958	The whole Act.
7 & 8 Eliz 2 c 5	Adoption Act 1958	Section 19. In section 60(2), the words 'section nineteen, and'.
8 & 9 Eliz 2 c 52	Cyprus Act 1960	Section 4(2) to (4) and (7), In the Schedule, paragraph 1.
8 & 9 Eliz 2 c 55	Nigeria Independence Act 1960	Section 2.
9 & 10 Eliz 2 c 16	Sierra Leone Independence Act 1961	Section 2.
10 Eliz 2 c 1	Tanganyika Independence Act 1961	Section 2.

10 & 11 Eliz 2 c 8	Civil Aviation (Eurocontrol) Act 1961	Section 9(2).
10 & 11 Eliz 2 c 21	Commonwealth Immigrants Act 1962	Section 12(2) and (4).
10 & 11 Eliz 2 c 23	South Africa Act 1962	Section 1(2). Schedule 1.
10 & 11 Eliz 2 c 40	Jamaica Independence Act 1962	Section 2.
10 & 11 Eliz 2 c 54	Trinidad and Tobago Independence Act 1962	Section 2.
10 & 11 Eliz 2 c 57	Uganda Independence Act 1962	Section 2.
1963 c 35	Malaysia Act 1963	Section 2. Schedule 1.
1963 c 54	Kenya Independence Act 1963	Sections 2 and 3.
1963 c 55	Zanzibar Act 1963	Section 2. Schedule 2.
1964 c 5	International Headquarters and Defence Organisations Act 1964	Section 2(1)(c). In section 2(1)(d), the reference to paragraph (c).
1964 c 22	British Nationality Act 1964	The whole Act.
1964 c 46	Malawi Independence Act 1964	Sections 2 and 3.
1964 c 54	British Nationality (No 2) Act 1964	The whole Act.
1964 c 57	Adoption Act 1964	Section 1(3). In section 4(4), the words from 'except' to '1958'.
1964 c 65	Zambia Independence Act 1964	Sections 3 and 4.
1964 c 81	Diplomatic Privileges Act 1964	Section 5(2).
1964 c 86	Malta Independence Act 1964	Sections 2 and 3.
1964 c 93	Gambia Independence Act 1964	Sections 2 and 3.
1965 c 34	British Nationality Act 1965	The whole Act.
1966 c 14	Guyana Independence Act 1966	Sections 2 and 3.
1966 c 23	Botswana Independence Act 1966	Sections 3 and 4.
1966 c 24	Lesotho Independence Act 1966	Sections 3 and 4.
1966 c 29	Singapore Act 1966	In the Schedule, paragraph 1.
1966 c 37	Barbados Independece Act 1966	Sections 2 and 3.

1967 c 4	West Indies Act 1967	Section 12.
		In Schedule 3,
		  paragraphs 1 to 3, 5
		  and 7 and, in
		  paragraph 4(1), the
		  words from '(subject'
		  to 'Schedule)'.

1967 c 71	Aden, Perim and Kuria Muria Islands Act 1967	Section 2. Schedule.
1968 c 8	Mauritius Independence Act 1968	Sections 2 and 3.
1968 c 18	Consular Relations Act 1968	Section 7.

1968 c 53	Adoption Act 1968	Section 9(5).
		In section 14(3), the
		  words 'except sections
		  9(5) and this section'.

1968 c 56	Swaziland Independence Act 1968	Sections 3 and 4.
1968 c 59	Hovercraft Act 1968	In the Schedule, paragraph 1(*d*).
1969 c 29	Tanzania Act 1969	Section 1. Section 7(1)(*a*) and (2).

1969 c 46	Family Law Reform Act
	  1969
		Section 28(4)(*a*).
		In Schedule 1, the entry
		  relating to the British
		  Nationality Act 1948.

1970 c 22	Tonga Act 1970	Section 2.
1970 c 50	Fiji Independence Act 1970	Sections 2 and 3.

1971 c 62	Tribunals and Inquiries
	  Act 1971
		In section 14(3), the
		  words from 'affect' to
		  '1948 or'.

1971 c 77	Immigration Act 1971	In section 9(5), the
		  words from 'other' to
		  'section 2'.
		Section 30(1).
		In section 31(*a*), the
		  words from
		  '(including' to 'Act)'.
		Schedule 1 (including
		  Appendices A to C).

1972 c 55	Sri Lanka Republic Act 1972	Section 1(3) and (5).

1973 c 27	Bahamas Independence
	  Act 1973
		Section 2(1), (2) and
		  (6).

1973 c 48	Pakistan Act 1973	Section 1. Schedules 1 and 2.
1973 c 49	Bangladesh Act 1973	Section 2.
1975 c 31	Malta Republic Act 1975	Section 1(3)

1975 c 72	Children Act 1975	In section 109(2)(*b*), the
		  words 'and 63' and
		  'and'.
		Section 109(2)(*c*).

		In Schedule 3, paragraph 63.
1976 c 19	Seychelles Act 1976	Sections 3 and 4. Section 5(3).
1976 c 36	Adoption Act 1976	Section 40. In section 47(2), the words 'Without prejudice to section 40'. In section 74(4), the words from 'except' to '1968'.
1976 c 54	Trinidad and Tobago Republic Act 1976	Section 1(3).
1978 c 15	Solomon Islands Act 1978	Section 2(1). Sectino 4(5). Section 5(1) and (3).
1978 c 20	Tuvalu Act 1978	Sections 2, 3 and 5(2).
1978 c 23	Judicature (Northern Ireland) Act 1978	Section 22(2)(*a*).
1978 c 28	Adoption (Scotland) Act 1978	Section 40. In section 41(2), the words 'Without prejudice to section 40'.
1978 c 30	Interpretation Act 1978	In section 24(4), the words 'British subject and Commonwealth citizen'. In Schedule 1, the entry defining 'British subject' and 'Commonwealth citizen'. In Schedule 2, in paragraph 6, the words 'British subject and Commonwealth citizen.'
1979 c 27	Kiribati Act 1979	Section 3(3). Sections 4 and 5. Section 7(2).
1979 c 60	Zimbabwe Act 1979	Section 2. In section 5(2)— (*a*) paragraph (*a*); and (*b*) in paragraph (*b*), the words '1 or'. Schedule 1.
1980 c 2	Papua New Guinea, Western Samoa and Nauru (Miscellaneous Provisions) Act 1980	In section 1, subsection (1) and, in subsection (3), the reference to section 3(2). Section 2. Section 3(2).

1980 c 16	New Hebrides Act 1980	Section 1. In section 4(2), the reference to section 1(2).
1981 c 52	Belize Act 1981	Section 4(1).
1981 c 61	British Nationality Act 1981	Section 49.

IMMIGRATION ACT 1988
(1988 c 14)

Arrangement of sections

References in bold are to paragraph numbers

An Act to make further provision for the regulation of immigration into the United Kingdom; and for connected purposes   [10 May 1988]

Isle of Man   Ss 2, 7(2), (3), 8, 9, 11 and 12 of the Act and s 7(1) when brought into force are modified in relation to the Isle of Man by SI 1991/2630.

[A.1.142]
1 Termination of saving in respect of Commonwealth citizens settled before 1973
Section 1(5) of the Immigration Act 1971 (in this Act referred to as 'the principal Act') is hereby repealed.

Commencement   1 August 1988 (except in relation to a wife or child of a Commonwealth citizen settled in the United Kingdom on 1 January 1973 if the application of the wife or child for an entry clearance to come to the United Kingdom for settlement was made before 1 August 1988).

[A.1.143]
2 Restriction on exercise of right of abode in cases of polygamy
(1)   This section applies to any woman who:

(*a*) has the right of abode in the United Kingdom under section 2(1)(*b*) of the principal Act as, or has having been, the wife of a man ('the husband'):
  (i) to whom she is or was polygamously married; and
  (ii) who is or was such a citizen of the United Kingdom and Colonies, Commonwealth citizen or British subject as is mentioned in section 2(2)(*a*) or (*b*) of that Act as in force immediately before the commencement of the British Nationality Act 1981; and
(*b*) has not before the coming into force of this section and since her marriage to the husband been in the United Kingdom.

(2) A woman to whom this section applies shall not be entitled to enter the United Kingdom in the exercise of the right of abode mentioned in subsection (1)(*a*) above or to be granted a certificate of entitlement in respect of that right if there is another woman living (whether or not one to whom this section applies) who is the wife or widow of the husband and who:

(*a*) is, or at any time since her marriage to the husband has been, in the United Kingdom; or
(*b*) has been granted a certificate of entitlement in respect of the right of abode mentioned in subsection (1)(*a*) above or an entry clearance to enter the United Kingdom as the wife of the husband.

(3) So long as a woman is precluded by subsection (2) above from entering the United Kingdom in the exercise of her right of abode or being granted a certificate of entitlement in respect of that right the principal Act shall apply to her as it applies to a person not having a right of abode.
(4) Subsection (2) above shall not preclude a woman from re-entering the United Kingdom if since her marriage to the husband she has at any time previously been in the United Kingdom and there was at that time no such other woman living as is mentioned in that subsection.
(5) Where a woman claims that this section does not apply to her because she had been in the United Kingdom before the coming into force of this section and since her marriage to the husband it shall be for her to prove that fact.
(6) For the purposes of this section a marriage may be polygamous although at its inception neither party has any spouse additional to the other.
(7) For the purposes of subsections (1)(*b*), (2)(*a*), (4) and (5) above there shall be disregarded presence in the United Kingdom as a visitor or an illegal entrant and presence in circumstances in which a person is deemed by section 11(1) of the principal Act not to have entered the United Kingdom.
(8) In subsection (2)(*b*) above the reference to a certificate of entitlement includes a reference to a certificate treated as such a certificate by virtue of section 39(8) of the British Nationality Act 1981.
(9) No application by a woman for a certificate of entitlement in respect of such a right of abode as is mentioned in subsection (1)(*a*) above or for an entry clearance shall be granted if another application for such a certificate or clearance is pending and that application is made by a woman as the wife or widow of the same husband.
(10) For the purposes of subsection (9) above an application shall be regarded as pending so long as it and any appeal proceedings relating to it have not been finally determined.

Commencement   1 August 1988 (except in relation to a woman who has made an application for a certificate of entitlement in respect of the right of abode mentioned in sub-s (1)(*a*)).

Definitions   For 'certificate of entitlement' and 'entry clearance', see, by virtue of s 12(2), the Immigration Act 1971, s 33(1).

[A.1.144]
3 *(Amends the Immigration Act 1971, ss 2(2), (8), 3(9), (9A), 13(3); the British Nationality Act 1981, s 39.)*

[A.1.145]
4 *(Amends the Immigration Act 1971, s 8.)*

[A.1.146]
5 Restricted right of appeal against deportation in cases of breach of limited leave

. . .

Notes   Repealed by the Immigration and Asylum Act 1999, s 169(1), (3), Sch 14, paras 83, 84, Sch 16.

[A.1.147]
6 *(Amends the Immigration Act 1971, s 24.)*

[A.1.148]
7 Persons exercising Community rights and nationals of member States
(1)   A person shall not under the principal Act require leave to enter or remain in the United Kingdom in any case in which he is entitled to do so by virtue of an enforceable Community right or of any provision made under section 2(2) of the European Communities Act 1972.
(2)   The Secretary of State may by order made by statutory instrument give leave to enter the United Kingdom for a limited period to any class of persons who are nationals of member States but who are not entitled to enter the United Kingdom as mentioned in subsection (1) above; and any such order may give leave subject to such conditions as may be imposed by the order.
(3)   References in the principal Act to limited leave shall include references to leave given by an order under subsection (2) above and a person having leave by virtue of such an order shall be treated as having been given that leave by a notice given to him by an immigration officer within the period specified in paragraph 6(1) of Schedule 2 to that Act.

Commencement   Sub-s (1): Came into force on 20 July 1994 — SI 1994/1923, c 35, as did the Immigration (European Economic Area) Order, SI 1994/1895, made under the European Communities Act 1972, s 2(2); see **[B.1.2]**; sub-ss (2), (3): 10 July 1988.

[A.1.149]
8 Examination of passengers prior to arrival

. . .

***

Notes   Repealed by the Immigration and Asylum Act 1999, s 169(1), (3), Sch 14, paras 83, 85, Sch 16.

***

[A.1.150]
9 Charges

. . .

***

Note   Repealed by the Immigration and Asylum Act 1999, s 169(1), (3), Sch 14, paras 83, 86, Sch 16.

***

[A.1.151]
10 Miscellaneous minor amendments
The principal Act shall have effect with the amendments specified in the Schedule to this Act.

***

Commencement   10 July 1988.

***

[A.1.152]
11 Expenses and receipts
(1) There shall be paid out of money provided by Parliament any expenses incurred by the Secretary of State in consequence of this Act.
(2) Any sums received by the Secretary of State by virtue of this Act shall be paid into the Consolidated Fund.

***

Commencement   10 July 1988.

***

[A.1.153]
12 Short title, interpretation, commencement and extent
(1)   This Act may be cited as the Immigration Act 1988.
(2)   In this Act 'the principal Act' means the Immigration Act 1971 and any expression which is also used in that Act has the same meaning as in that Act.
(3)   Except as provided in subsection (4) below this Act shall come into force at the end of the period of two months beginning with the day on which it is passed.
(4)   Sections 1, 2, 3, 4, 5 and 7(1) and paragraph 1 of the Schedule shall come into force on such day as may be appointed by the Secretary of State by an

order made by statutory instrument; and such an order may appoint different days for different provisions and contain such transitional provisions and savings as the Secretary of State thinks necessary or expedient in connection with any provision brought into force.

(5)   This Act extends to Northern Ireland and section 36 of the principal Act (power to extend any of its provisions to the Channel Islands or the Isle of Man) shall apply also to the provisions of this Act.

[A.1.154]
Schedule (section 10)   (*Amends the Immigration Act 1971.*)

ASYLUM AND IMMIGRATION APPEALS ACT 1993
(1993 c 23)

Arrangement of sections

References in bold are to paragraph numbers

INTRODUCTORY

An Act to make provision about persons who claim asylum in the United Kingdom and their dependants; to amend the law with respect to certain rights of appeal under the Immigration Act 1971; and to extend the provisions of the Immigration (Carriers' Liability) Act 1987 to transit passengers. [1st July 1993]

INTRODUCTORY

[A.1.155]
1 Interpretation
In this Act :
    'the 1971 Act' means the Immigration Act 1971;
    'claim for asylum' means a claim made by a person (whether before or after the coming into force of this section) that it would be contrary to the United Kingdom's obligations under the Convention for him to be removed from, or required to leave, the United Kingdom; and
    'the Convention' means the Convention relating to the Status of Refugees done at Geneva on 28th July 1951 and the Protocol to that Convention.

Notes   *UK's obligations*: See art 33(1) of the Convention. See also the Convention Determining the State Responsible for Examining Applications for Asylum Lodged in One of the Member States of the European Communities signed in Dublin on 15 June 1990 ('the 1990 Dublin Convention' [**B.3.97**]), arts 4–8 in particular.

Commencement   In so far as it relates to ss 4–11, 26 July 1993 (SI 1993/1655); otherwise, 1 July 1993.

[A.1.156]
2 Primacy of Convention
Nothing in the immigration rules (within the meaning of the 1971 Act) shall lay down any practice which would be contrary to the Convention.

Notes   The immigration rules are rules of practice made pursuant to s 3(2) of the 1971 Act. At present they are contained in the Statement of Changes in Immigration Rules (HC 251) laid before Parliament on 23 March 1990, as amended. Section 2 of this Act has the effect, so far as immigration law is concerned, of incorporating the Convention and Protocol into UK domestic law.

Commencement   1 July 1993.

TREATMENT OF PERSONS WHO CLAIM ASYLUM

[A.1.157]
3 Fingerprinting
(1)   Where a person ('the claimant') has made a claim for asylum, an immigration officer, constable, prison officer or officer of the Secretary of State authorised for the purposes of this section, may :

(*a*) take such steps as may be reasonably necessary for taking the claimant's fingerprints; or
(*b*) by notice in writing require the claimant to attend at a place specified in the notice in order that such steps may be taken.
(2)   The powers conferred by subsection (1) above may be exercised not only in relation to the claimant but also in relation to any dependant of his; but in

the exercise of the power conferred by paragraph (*a*) of that subsection, fingerprints shall not be taken from a person under the age of sixteen ('the child') except in the presence of a person of full age who is:

(*a*) the child's parent or guardian; or

(*b*) a person who for the time being takes responsibility for the child and is not an immigration officer, constable, prison officer or officer of the Secretary of State.

(3) Where the claimant's claim for asylum has been finally determined or abandoned:

(*a*) the powers conferred by subsection (1) above shall not be exercisable in relation to him or any dependant of his; and

(*b*) any requirement imposed on him or any dependant of his by a notice under subsection (1)(*b*) above shall no longer have effect.

(4) A notice given to any person under paragraph (*b*) of subsection (1) above:

(*a*) shall give him a period of at least seven days within which he is to attend as mentioned in that paragraph; and

(*b*) may require him so to attend at a specified time of day or between specified times of day.

(5) Any immigration officer or constable may arrest without warrant a person who has failed to comply with a requirement imposed on him by a notice under subsection (1)(*b*) above (unless the requirement no longer has effect) and, where a person is arrested under this subsection,:

(*a*) he may be removed to a place where his fingerprints may conveniently be taken, and

(*b*) (whether or not he is so removed) there may be taken such steps as may be reasonably necessary for taking his fingerprints,

before he is released.

(6) Fingerprints of a person which are taken by virtue of this section must be destroyed not later than the earlier of:

(*a*) the end of the period of one month beginning with any day on which he is given indefinite leave under the 1971 Act to enter or remain in the United Kingdom; and

(*b*) the end of the period of ten years beginning with the day on which the fingerprints are taken.

(7) Where fingerprints taken by virtue of this section are destroyed:

(*a*) any copies of the fingerprints shall also be destroyed; and

(*b*) if there are any computer data relating to the fingerprints, the Secretary of State shall, as soon as it is practicable to do so, make it impossible for access to be gained to the data.

(8) If:

(*a*) subsection (7)(*b*) above falls to be complied with, and

(*b*) the person to whose fingerprints the data relate asks for a certificate that it has been complied with,

such a certificate shall be issued to him by the Secretary of State not later than the end of the period of three months beginning with the day on which he asks for it.

(9) In this section:

(a) 'immigration officer' means an immigration officer appointed for the purposes of the 1971 Act; and

(b) 'dependant', in relation to the claimant, means a person:
  (i) who is his spouse or a child of his under the age of eighteen; and
  (ii) who has neither a right of abode in the United Kingdom nor indefinite leave under the 1971 Act to enter or remain in the United Kingdom.

(10)   Nothing in this section shall be taken to limit the power conferred by paragraph 18(2) of Schedule 2 to the 1971 Act.

Notes   For a comparison of fingerprinting in criminal cases, see PACE 1984, ss 27, 61 and 64   and D3 (identification by fingerprints) of the Code of Practice, *Archbold* (1993), p 1/1627. Subsection (10) above seems to suggest that the power to fingerprint already exists under Sch 2, para 18(2) to the 1971 Act.   See now *Ex p Irawo-Osan* [1992] Imm AR 337 which establishes that Sch 2, para 18(2) authorises the taking of fingerprints but note the limits of the power referred to in the commentary. It is submitted that para 18(2) was not thought wide enough to enable fingerprints to be taken for the purpose of defeating possible personation by asylum–seekers in social security claims.   Note also that, although sub-s (5)(b) above clearly authorises the use of force to obtain fingerprints, in practice under the rules what is going to happen is that adverse inferences will be drawn if a person fails to attend to be fingerprinted: see para 180F of HC 251 as inserted by HC 725 of 5 July 1993.

Commencement   1 July 1993.

[A.1.158]
4   Housing of asylum-seekers and their dependants
. . .

Notes   Repealed, in relation to England and Wales, by the Housing Act 1996, s 227, Sch 19, Part VIII.
  Repealed, in relation to Scotland and Northern Ireland, by the Immigration and Asylum Act 1999, ss 120(6), 121(3), 169(1), (3), Sch 14, paras 99, 101, Sch 16.

[A.1.159]
5   Housing: interpretative provisions
. . .

Notes   Repealed, in relation to England and Wales, by the Housing Act 1996, s 227, Sch 19, Part VIII.
  Repealed, in relation to Scotland and Northern Ireland, by the Immigration and Asylum Act 1999, ss 120(6), 121(3), 169(1), (3), Sch 14, paras 99, 101, Sch 16.

[A.1.160]
. . .

Note   Repealed by the Immigration and Asylum Act 1999, Sch 14, paras 99, 102.

[A.1.161]
7 Curtailment of leave to enter or remain

. . .

Notes Repealed by the Immigration and Asylum Act 1999, Sch 14, paras 99, 102. In force 2 Ocotber 2000; for transitional provisions see SI 2000/2444, art 3, Sch 2, para 3.

RIGHTS OF APPEAL

[A.1.162]
8 Appeals to special adjudicator

. . .

Notes Repealed by the Immigration and Asylum Act 1999, s 169(1), (3), Sch 14, paras 99, 104, Sch 16. In force 2 October 2000 (except in relation to events which took place before that date): see SI 2000/2444, art 2, Sch; for transitional provisions see art 3, Sch 2, para 3 thereof.

[A.1.163]
9 Appeals from Immigration Appeal Tribunal

. . .

Notes Repealed by the Immigration and Asylum Act 1999, s 169(1), (3), Sch 14, paras 99, 104, Sch 16. In force 2 October 2000 (except in relation to events which took place before that date): see SI 2000/2444, art 2, Sch 1; for transitional provisions see art 3, Sch 2, para 3 thereof.

[A.1.164]
[9A Bail pending appeal from Immigration Appeal Tribunal]
[(1) Where a person ('an appellant'):

[(*a*) has an appeal under Part IV of the Immigration and Asylum Act 1999 which is pending by reason of an appeal;]
(*b*) is for the time being detained under Part I of Schedule 2 to that Act (general provisions as to control on entry etc),

he may be released on bail in accordance with this section.
(2)   An immigration officer not below the rank of chief immigration officer, a police officer not below the rank of inspector or an adjudicator may release an appellant on his entering into a recognizance or, in Scotland, bail bond conditioned for his appearance before the appropriate appeal court at a time and place named in the recognizance or bail bond.
(3)   The Immigration Appeal Tribunal may release an appellant on his entering into a recognizance or, in Scotland, bail bond conditioned for his appearance before the appropriate appeal court at a time and place named in the recognizance or bail bond; and where:

(*a*) the appeal, or the application for leave to appeal, under section 9 above is by the Secretary of State; or (*b*) the appellant has been granted leave to appeal under that section, and has duly given notice of appeal,

the Tribunal shall, if the appellant so requests, exercise its powers under this subsection.

(4) Sub-paragraphs (5) and (6) of paragraph 29 (grant of bail pending appeal) of Schedule 2 to the 1971 Act shall apply for the purposes of this section as they apply for the purposes of that paragraph.

(5) Paragraphs 30 to 33 of that Schedule shall apply as if:

(*a*) any reference to paragraph 29 included a reference to this section;

(*b*) the reference in paragraph 30(2) to paragraph 29(3) or (4) included a reference to subsection (3) above; and

(*c*) any reference in paragraphs 31 to 33 to the Immigration Appeal Tribunal included a reference to the appropriate appeal court.

(6) In this section 'the appropriate appeal court' has the same meaning as in [paragraph 23 of Schedule 4 of the Immigration and Asylum Act 1999].

Notes Section 9A inserted by the Asylum and Immigration Act 1996, Sch 3, para 3.

Sub-s (1), para (a) and words in square brackets in sub-s (6) substituted by the Immigration and Asylum Act 1999, s 169(1). In force 2 October 2000 (except in relation to events which took place before that date): see SI 2000/2444, art 2, Sch 1; for transitional provisions see art 3, Sch 12, para 3 therefore.

Commencement 1 September 1996 (SI 1996/2053).

[A.1.165]
10 Visitors, short-term and prospective students and their dependants
. . .

Notes Repealed by the Immigration and Asylum Act 1999, s 169(1), (3), Sch 14, paras 99, 104, Sch 16. In force 2 October 2000 (except in relation to events which took place before that date): see SI 2000/2444, art 3, Sch 2, para 3 for transitional provisions.

[A.1.166]
11 Refusals which are mandatory under immigration rules
. . .

Notes Repealed by the Immigration and Asylum Act 1999, s 169(1), (3), Sch 14, paras 99, 104, Sch 16. In force 2 October 2000 (except in relation to events which took place before that date): see SI 2000/2444, art 3, Sch 2, para 3 for transitional provisions.

VISAS FOR TRANSIT PASSENGERS

[A.1.167]
12 Carrier's liability for transit passengers
. . .

Notes   Repealed by the Immigration and Asylum Act 1999, s 169(1), (3), Sch 14, paras 99, 107, Sch 16. In force 2 October 2000: see SI 2000/2444, art 3, Sch 2, para 3 for transitional provisions.

SUPPLEMENTARY

[A.1.168]
13   Financial provision
(1)   There shall be paid out of money provided by Parliament:

(*a*)   any expenditure incurred by the Secretary of State under this Act; and

(*b*)   any increase attributable to this Act in the sums payable out of such money under any other enactment.

(2)   Any sums received by the Secretary of State by virtue of this Act shall be paid into the Consolidated Fund.

Commencement   1 July 1993.

[A.1.169]
14   Commencement
(1)   Sections 4 to 11 above (and section 1 above so far as it relates to those sections) shall not come into force until such day as the Secretary of State may by order appoint, and different days may be appointed for different provisions or for different purposes.

(2)   An order under subsection (1) above:

(*a*)   shall be made by statutory instrument; and

(*b*)   may contain such transitional and supplemental provisions as the Secretary of State thinks necessary or expedient.

(3)   Without prejudice to the generality of subsections (1) and (2) above, with respect to any provision of section 4 above an order under subsection (1) above may appoint different days in relation to different descriptions of asylum-seekers and dependants of asylum-seekers; and any such descriptions may be framed by reference to nationality, citizenship, origin or other connection with any particular country or territory, but not by reference to race, colour or religion.

[A.1.170]
15   Extent
(1)   Her Majesty may by Order in Council direct that any of the provisions of this Act shall extend, with such modifications as appear to Her Majesty to be appropriate, to any of the Channel Islands or the Isle of Man.

(2)   This Act extends to Northern Ireland.

Commencement   1 July 1993.

Order made   SI 1997/275 amending SI 1991/2630.

[A.1.171]
16 Short title
This Act may be cited as the Asylum and Immigration Appeals Act 1993.

Commencement 1 July 1993.

Schedules

SCHEDULE 1   HOUSING OF ASYLUM-SEEKERS AND THEIR DEPENDANTS: SUPPLEMENTARY   (SECTION 4(5))

[A.1.172]

. . .

Notes Repealed, in relation to England and Wales, by the Housing Act 1996, s 227, Sch 19, Part VIII.

Repealed, in relation to Scotland and Northern Ireland, by the Immigration and Asylum Act 1999, ss 120(6), 121(3), 161(1), (3), Sch 14, paras 99, 101, Sch 16.

SCHEDULE 2   APPEALS TO SPECIAL ADJUDICATOR: SUPPLEMENTARY   (SECTION 8(6))

[A.1.173]

. . .

Notes Repealed by the Immigration and Asylum Act 1999, s 169(1), (3), Sch 14, paras 99, 104, Sch 16. In force 2 October 2000 (except in relation to events which took place before that date): see SI 2000/2444, art 2, Sch 1; for transitional provisions see art 3, Sch 2, para 3.

ASYLUM AND IMMIGRATION ACT 1996

Arrangement of sections

ASYLUM CLAIMS

An Act to amend and supplement the Immigration Act 1971 and the Asylum and Immigration Appeals Act 1993; to make further provision with respect to persons subject to immigration control and the employment of such persons; and for connected purposes. [24th July 1996]

BE IT ENACTED by the Queen's most Excellent Majesty, by and with the advice and consent of the Lords Spiritual and Temporal, and Commons, in this present Parliament assembled, and by the authority of the same, as follows—

ASYLUM CLAIMS

[A.1.174]
1   Extension of Special Appeals Procedures

. . .

Note   Repealed by the Immigration and Asylum Act 1999, s 169(3), Sch 16.

[A.1.175]
2   Removal etc of asylum claimants to safe third countries

. . .

Note   Repealed by the Immigration and Asylum Act 1999, s 169(3), Sch 16. In force 2 October 2000 (except in relation to events which took place before that date): see SI 2000/2444, art 2, Sch 1; for transitional provisions see art 3, Sch 2, para 4 thereof.

[A.1.176]
3   Appeals against certificates under section 2

. . .

Note   Repealed by the Immigration and Asylum Act 1999, s 169(3), Sch 16. In force 2 October 2000 (except in relation to events which took place before that date): see SI 2000/2444, art 2, Sch 1; for transitional provisions see art 3, Sch 2, para 4 thereof.

IMMIGRATION OFFENCES

[A.1.177]
4   Obtaining leave by deception

. . .

Note   Repealed by the Immigration and Asylum Act 1999, s 169(3), Sch 16.

[A.1.178]
5   Assisting asylum claimants, and persons seeking to obtain leave by deception

. . .

Note   Amends the Immigration Act 1971, s 25.

Commencement   1 October 1996 (Asylum and Immigration Act 1996 (Commencement No 1) Order 1996 (1996/2053)).

[A.1.179]
6   Increased penalties

. . .

Note   Amends the Immigration Act 1971, ss 24, 26 and 27.

Commencement   1 October 1996 (Asylum and Immigration Act 1996 (Commencement No 1) Order 1996 (1996/2053)).

[A.1.180]
7   Power of arrest and search warrants

. . .

Note   Repealed by the Immigration and Asylum Act 1999, s 169(1), (3), Sch 14, paras 108, 109, Sch 16.

PERSONS SUBJECT TO IMMIGRATION CONTROL
[A.1.181]
8   Restrictions on employment
(1) Subject to subsection (2) below, if any person ('the employer') employs a person subject to immigration control ('the employee') who has attained the age of 16, the employer shall be guilty of an offence if:

(*a*) the employee has not been granted leave to enter or remain in the United Kingdom; or
(*b*) the employee's leave is not valid and subsisting, or is subject to a condition precluding him from taking up the employment,
and (in either case) the employee does not satisfy such conditions as may be specified in an order made by the Secretary of State.

(2) Subject to subsection (3) below, in proceedings under this section, it shall be a defence to prove that:

(*a*) before the employment began, there was produced to the employer a document which appeared to him to relate to the employee and to be of a description specified in an order made by the Secretary of State; and
(*b*) either the document was retained by the employer, or a copy or other record of it was made by the employer in a manner specified in the order in relation to documents of that description.

(3) The defence afforded by subsection (2) above shall not be available in any case where the employer knew that his employment of the employee would constitute an offence under this section.
(4) A person guilty of an offence under this section shall be liable on summary conviction to a fine not exceeding level 5 on the standard scale.
(5) Where an offence under this section committed by a body corporate is

proved to have been committed with the consent or connivance of, or to be attributable to any neglect on the part of:

(*a*) any director, manager, secretary or other similar officer of the body corporate; or

(*b*) any person who was purporting to act in any such capacity, he as well as the body corporate shall be guilty of the offence and shall be liable to be proceeded against and punished accordingly.

(6) Where the affairs of a body corporate are managed by its members, subsection (5) above shall apply in relation to the acts and defaults of a member in connection with his functions of management as if he were a director of the body corporate.

(7) An order under this section shall be made by statutory instrument which shall be subject to annulment in pursuance of a resolution of either House of Parliament.

(8) In this section:

'contract of employment' means a contract of service or apprenticeship, whether express or implied, and (if it is express) whether it is oral or in writing;

'employ' means employ under a contract of employment and 'employment' shall be construed accordingly.

Commencement   The order made under this section came into force on 27 January 1997: Immigration (Restriction on Employment) Order 1996, SI 1996/3225.

General   Employers will be liable to prosecution if they employ persons not granted leave to enter or remain in the UK who are not entitled to work. It will apply only to those employees who start work after the coming into force of the section. This new offence was the subject of bitter criticism. The *Times*, the TUC, the Institute of Directors, the Association of British Chambers of Commerce, the Federation of Small Businesses, the Institute of Management and the Institute of Personnel and Development stated that:

> As well as placing an unjustifiable burden on employers, the proposal threatens to damage race relations. There would be every incentive not to hire black staff or people with foreign sounding names; and to concentrate checks on ethnic minority employees.

(Reference in *Hansard* HL, vol 571, col 1854).

An order has now been made specifying the conditions to be met by employees and the documents to establish a defence: SI 1996/3225. The conditions specified are that the employee's claim for asylum or appeal under Part II of the Immigration Act 1971 is pending and that he is permitted to work. The list of documents includes documents issued by a previous employer, the Benefits Agency or other agency indicating the National Insurance Number of the person named; a passport describing the holder as a British citizen or having the right of abode; a certificate of registration or naturalisation; a UK birth certificate; a passport or identity document issued by a party to the European Economic Area Agreement describing the holder as a national; a passport to show the holder is exempt from immigration control or has indefinite leave or an endorsement showing the person has leave to remain not subject to an employment prohibition; or a letter from IND indicating that the person is permitted to work.

[A.1.182]

[8A   Code of practice]

[(1) The Secretary of State must issue a code of practice as to the measures which an employer is to be expected to take, or not to take, with a view to securing that, while avoiding the commission of an offence under section 8, he also avoids unlawful discrimination.

(2) 'Unlawful discrimination' means—

(*a*) discrimination in contravention of section 4(1) of the Race Relations Act 1976 ('the 1976 Act'); or

(*b*) in relation to Northern Ireland, discrimination in contravention of Article 6(1) of the Race Relations (Northern Ireland) Order 1997 ('the 1997 Order').

(3) Before issuing the code, the Secretary of State must—

(*a*) prepare and publish a draft of the proposed code; and

(*b*) consider any representations about it which are made to him.

(4) In preparing the draft, the Secretary of State must consult—

(*a*) the Commission for Racial Equality;

(*b*) the Equality Commission for Northern Ireland; and

(*c*) such organisations and bodies (including organisations or associations of organisations representative of employers or of workers) as he considers appropriate.

(5) If the Secretary of State decides to proceed with the code, he must lay a draft of the code before both Houses of Parliament.

(6) The draft code may contain modifications to the original proposals made in the light of representations to the Secretary of State.

(7) After laying the draft code before Parliament, the Secretary of State may bring the code into operation by an order made by statutory instrument.

(8) An order under subsection (7)—

(*a*) shall be subject to annulment in pursuance of a resolution of either House of Parliament;

(*b*) may contain such transitional provisions or savings as appear to the Secretary of State to be necessary or expedient in connection with the code.

(9) A failure on the part of any person to observe a provision of the code does not of itself make him liable to any proceedings.

(10) But the code is admissible in evidence—

(*a*) in proceedings under the 1976 Act before an employment tribunal;

(*b*) in proceedings under the 1997 Order before an industrial tribunal.

(11) If any provision of the code appears to the tribunal to be relevant to any question arising in such proceedings, that provision is to be taken into account in determining the question.

(12) The Secretary of State may from time to time revise the whole or any part of the code and issue the code as revised.

(13) The provisions of this section also apply (with appropriate modifications) to any revision, or proposed revision, of the code.]

Note Inserted by the Immigration and Asylum Act 1999, s 22.

Commencement 19 February 2001 (for certain purposes: see SI 2001/239, art 2, Sch); for other purposes see the Immigration and Asylum Act 1999, s 170(4).

[A.1.183]
9   Entitlement to housing accommodation and assistance

. . .

Note   Repealed by the Immigration and Asylum Act 1999, s 169(1), (3), Sch 14, paras 108, 110, Sch 16.

[A.1.184]
10   Entitlement to child benefit

. . .

Note   Repealed by the Immigration and Asylum Act 1999, s 169(1), (3), Sch 14, paras 108, 111, Sch 16.

[A.1.185]
11   Saving for social security regulations

. . .

Note   Repealed by the Immigration and Asylum Act 1999, s 169(1), (3), Sch 14, paras 108, 112, Sch 16.

MISCELLANEOUS AND SUPPLEMENTAL

[A.1.186]
12   Other amendments and repeals
(1) Schedule 2 to this Act (which contains amendments of the 1971 Act and a related amendment of the Immigration Act 1988) shall have effect.
(2) Schedule 3 to this Act (which contains amendments of the 1993 Act) shall have effect.
(3) The enactments specified in Schedule 4 to this Act are hereby repealed to the extent specified in the third column of that Schedule.

[A.1.187]
13   Short title, interpretation, commencement and extent
(1) This Act may be cited as the Asylum and Immigration Act 1996.
(2) In this Act:
'the 1971 Act' means the Immigration Act 1971;
'the 1993 Act' means the Asylum and Immigration Appeals Act 1993;
'person subject to immigration control' means a person who under the 1971
    Act requires leave to enter or remain in the United Kingdom (whether or not
    such leave has been given).
(3) This Act, except section 11 and Schedule 1, shall come into force on such day as the Secretary of State may by order made by statutory instrument appoint, and different days may be appointed for different purposes.
(4) An order under subsection (3) above may make such transitional and supplemental provision as the Secretary of State thinks necessary or expedient.
(5) Her Majesty may by Order in Council direct that any of the provisions of this Act shall extend, with such modifications as appear to Her Majesty to be appropriate, to any of the Channel Islands or the Isle of Man.

(6) This Act extends to Northern Ireland.

Schedules

[A.1.188]
SCHEDULE 1 MODIFICATIONS OF SOCIAL SECURITY
REGULATIONS (SECTION 11 (4))

. . .

Note Repealed by the Immigration and Asylum Act 1999, s 169(1), (3), Sch 14, paras 108, 113.

[A.1.189]
SCHEDULE 2 AMENDMENTS OF THE 1971 ACT AND THE
IMMIGRATION ACT 1988 (SECTION12(1))

. . .

Notes This Schedule amends the Immigration Act 1988, s 5(1), the Immigrations Act 1971, ss 3(1), (5), 5(4), 14, 33(1), (4), Sch 2, paras 4, 9, 17, 19–22, Sch 3, para 2, and adds Sch 2, para 34.

Repealed in part by the Immigration and Asylum Act 1999, s 169(1), (3), Sch 14, paras 108, 114, Sch 16.

[A.1.190]
SCHEDULE 3 AMENDMENTS OF THE 1993 ACT (SECTION 12(2))

. . .

Notes This Schedule amends the Asylum and Immigration Appeals Act 1993, ss 7, 8, Sch 1, para 6, Sch 2, para 4(2) and adds s 94.

Paras 1, 2, 5, repealed by the Immigration and Asylum Act 1999, s 169(1), (3), Sch 14, paras 99, 115, Sch 16.

SCHEDULE 4   REPEALS (SECTION 12(3))

[A.1.191]

. . .

Note Amends the Asylum and Immigration Appeals Act 1993 and the Immigration Act 1971.

Commencement Repeals relating to Asylum and Immigration Appeals Act 1993 on 1 September 1996; repeals relating to Immigration Act 1971 on 1 October 1996 (Asylum and Immigration Act 1996 (Commencement No 1) Order 1996 (1996/2053)).

SPECIAL IMMIGRATION APPEALS COMMISSION ACT 1997
(1997 c 68)

Arrangement of sections

[A.1.192]
An Act to establish the Special Immigration Appeals Commission; to make provision with respect to its jurisdiction; and for connected purposes.
[17th December 1997]

[A.1.193]
1 Establishment of the Commission
(1)   There shall be a commission, known as the Special Immigration Appeals Commission, for the purpose of exercising the jurisdiction conferred by this Act.
(2)   Schedule 1 to this Act shall have effect in relation to the Commission.

Notes   This section establishes the body known as the Special Immigration Appeals Commission. The character of such body is spelt out by Schedule 1. Members of the Commission are appointed by the Lord Chancellor – with one member appointed as Chairman by the Lord Chancellor (Sch 1, para 1 refers). At third reading on 26 November 1997 the Government Minister Mike O'Brien MP informed the House that the Lord Chancellor had decided to appoint Mr Justice Potts as chairman of the Commission when it is established (*Hansard* HC Vol 301, col 1033). The Commission will be 'duly constituted' if it consists of three members of whom at least one holds or has held high judicial office (*vis* a High Court judge – Potts J) and at least one 'is or has been' chief adjudicator or a legally qualified member of the Immigration Appeals Tribunal (Sch 1, para 5 refers). The Act is silent as to the qualifications of the third member. During second reading Mr O'Brien stated (*Hansard* HC Vol 299, col 1055) 'it is intended that the person will have some experience of national security matters and will be familiar with the evidence that is likely to be presented to the commission' an observation justified by reference to the fact that 'the Lord Chancellor takes the view that those arrangements will best represent a proper balance of knowledge and experience for the commission' (*ibid*). At third reading Mr O'Brien elaborated further: 'the third member will be someone who has experience of dealing with security matters, not necessarily someone who is a member of the Security Service'.

In *Shafiq ur Rehman* (Special Immigration Appeals Commission, 7 September 1999) the Commission noted '. . . we are reassured by the nature and constitution of the panel presently constituting the Commission. We have as a member a person with long experience and expertise in the evaluation of intelligence material of a kind not normally produced in a court of law or administrative tribunal.'

[A.1.194]
2 Jurisdiction: appeals

[(1)   A person may appeal to the Special Immigration Appeals Commission against a decision which he would be entitled to appeal against under any provision (other than section 59(2)) of Part IV of the Immigration and Asylum Act 1999 ('the 1999 Act') or the Immigration (European Economic Area) Order 1994 ('the 1994 Order') but for a public interest provision.

(1A)   'Public interest provision' means any of:

(*a*) sections 60(9), 62(4), 64(1) or (2) or 70(1) to (6) of the 1999 Act; or

(*b*) paragraphs (b), (c) or (d) of Article 20(2) of the 1994 Order.]

(2)   A person may appeal to the Special Immigration Appeals Commission against the refusal of an entry clearance if he would be entitled to appeal against the refusal under [section 59(2) of the 1999 Act but for section 60(9) of that Act] (exclusion conducive to public good), and:

(*a*) he seeks to rely on an enforceable Community right or any provision made under section 2(2) of the European Communities Act 1972, or

(*b*) he seeks to enter the United Kingdom under immigration rules making provision about entry:

  (i) to exercise rights of access to a child resident there,

  (ii) as the spouse or fiance of a person present and settled there, or

  (iii) as the parent, grandparent or other dependent relative of a person present and settled there.

(3)   Schedule 2 to this Act (which makes supplementary provision relating to appeals under this section) shall have effect.

(4)   In this section, 'immigration rules' has the same meaning as in the Immigration Act 1971.

Notes   Sub-s (1) substituted by sub-ss (1), (1A), by the Immigration and Asylum Act 1999, s 169(1), Sch 14, paras 118, 119.

    Sub-s (2), words in italics substituted by the Immigration and Asylum Act 1999, s 169(1), Sch 14, paras 118, 120.

Section 2 identifies the categories of cases in which a person may appeal to the Special Immigration Appeals Commission. The categories are largely reflective of the provisions of the 1971 Act where persons are not entitled to appeal, in broad terms, on the grounds that the decision is based on conducive to public good grounds in national security and/or political cases (Immigration Act 1971, ss 13(5), 14(3), 15(3) refer). Subsection (1)(*a*) to (*c*) refers. The provision of the right of appeal to the Special Immigration Appeals Commission in the various categories of case otherwise excluded by the Article 20 of the Immigration (European Economic Area) Order 1994 (SI 1994/1895) (subsection (1)(*d*) to (*f*) refers) was prompted by the decision of European Court of Justice in *ex p Shingara and Radiom* [1997] All ER (EC) 577 which makes clear that there must be an effective merits review, including proportionality, to satisfy the requirements of Community law. And subsection (1)(*g*) covers asylum cases where persons are otherwise prevented from appealing under section 8 of the 1993 Act by virtue of paragraph 6 of Schedule 2 to that Act (the 'national security' exception).

Despite the breadth of these provisions there are certain *lacunae*.There is no appeal where there has been a refusal to revoke a deportation order (s 15(4) *ibid*), nor in a refusal of entry clearance case (s 13(5) *ibid*) unless the person seeks to rely on an enforceable Community right or seeks entry in circumstances relating to the exercise of article 8 ECHR rights (1997 Act, s 2(2) refers). Such *lacunae* were sought to be justified by Lord Williams (*Hansard* HL Vol 581, col 481) on the basis that the Government 'wish to ensure that there is a proper review in those cases where detention is an issue (which) for the most part . . . means that a right of appeal is required in those cases where there is an in-country right of appeal which is precluded only by the existing provisions restricting right of appeal in national security cases'. The *general* absence of appeal rights in entry clearance cases is thereby sought to be justified on the basis that 'there is no question of detention or an Article 3 risk'.

The Article 8 limb of section 2 (subs (2)(*b*)(i) to (iii) refers) was a Government amendment introduced at report stage in the House of Lords. Lord Williams (*ibid* at cols 481–2) stated as follows:

> Article 8 allows that national security considerations can justify interference with this right, but there is nevertheless a need to provide for an effective review of any decision to ensure that any interference is in accordance with the law and is necessary.
>
> For the ECHR rights arising from Article 8 considerations to be properly dealt with, the national security case underlying the refusal of entry clearance would need to be examined. If we do not provide a right of appeal to the new commission there would be a strong likelihood, following incorporation of the convention at least, that a court of judicial review would insist on seeing the national security details . . . We believe . . . That it would be preferable for any consideration of the national security case to be dealt with by a commission which has been set up especially to deal with any such issue.

Such reasoning would apply *mutatis mutandis* in a 'family' revocation case and there would seem little justification for such omission. Indeed, if such a person is not entitled to appeal against a refusal to revoke a deportation order s/he will in practice not be in a position to apply for an entry clearance, let alone rely on the section 2(2) right of appeal.

Subsection (3) gives effect to Schedule 2 which contains various supplementary provisions applying Immigration Act 1971 'caveats' and 'stays' to section 2 appeals (suspension of variation of limited leave and not being required to leave pending appeal; deportation order not to be made while appeal pending; stay or removal directions pending appeal and bail; construction of references to pending appeal *etc*).

Particular mention should be made of paragraph 5 of Schedule 2. This provides that asylum appeals before the Special Immigration Appeals Commission (ie where a person would be entitled to appeal under the Asylum and Immigration Appeals Act 1993, section 8 but for the 'national security' element – subsection (1)(*g*) of section 2 of the Act refers) 'shall in the same proceedings' deal with any other Immigration Act 1971 or Immigration (European Economic Area) Order 1994 appeal. One obvious *disadvantage* of such 'mixed' appeal will be that in respect of any other such appeal right there would be no further right of appeal to the Immigration Appeal Tribunal. At report stage an amendment moved by Baroness Anelay had sought to prevent the commission considering such 'mixed' appeals by requiring the appeal (if allowed) to be remitted to an adjudicator or special adjudicator as appropriate 'to determine the remaining issues'. Such approach might have had much to commend it – although in the view of Lord Morris and others this would have resulted in 'fractured jurisdiction' which was said not to be 'an efficient use of resources or an efficient way of coming to these difficult decisions' (*Hansard* HL vol 581 cols 483–489). Such amendment was ultimately withdrawn. Given the loss of appeal rights to the Tribunal identified and the limited numbers of cases anticipated such argument based on 'resources' hardly bears close scrutiny.

[A.1.195]
[2A   Jurisdiction: [racial discrimination and] human rights]
[(1)   A person who alleges that an authority has, in taking an appealable decision, [racially discriminated against him or] acted in breach of his human rights may appeal to the Commission against that decision.

(2)   For the purposes of this section [—

(*a*) an authority racially discriminates against a person if he acts, or fails to act, in relation to that other person in a way which is unlawful by virtue of Section 19B of the Race Relations Act 1976; and

(*b*) an authority acts in breach of a person's human rights if he acts, or fails to act, in relation to that other person in a way which is made unlawful by section 6(1) of the Human Rights Act 1998.

(3)   Subsections (4) and (5) apply if, in any appellate proceedings being heard by the Commission, a question arises as to whether an authority has, in taking a decision which is the subject of the proceedings, [racially discriminated against the appellant or] acted in breach of the appellant's human rights.

(4)   The Commission has jurisdiction to consider the question.

(5)   If the Commission decides that the authority concerned [—

(*a*) racially discriminated against the appellant; or

(*b*) acted in breach of the appellant's human rights, the appeal may be allowed on [the ground in question].

(6)   'Authority' means:

(*a*) the Secretary of State;

(*b*) an immigration officer;

(*c*) a person responsible for the grant or refusal of entry clearance.

(7)   'Appealable decision' means a decision against which a person would be entitled to appeal under Part IV of the 1999 Act or the 1994 Order but for a public interest provision.

(8)   'The 1999 Act', 'the 1994 Order' and 'public interest provision' have the same meaning as in section 2.

(9)   A reference in this Act to an appeal under this section includes a reference to an appeal under regulation 29(1) of the Immigration (European Economic Area) Regulations 2000, on the ground mentioned in paragraph (2) of that regulation, which lies to the Commission as a result of regulation 31 of those Regulations.]

Note   Inserted by the Immigration and Asylum Act 1999, s 169(1), Sch 14, paras 118, 121. Other words in square brackets inserted by the Race Relations (Amendment) Act 2000, s 9(1), Sch 2, for commencement see s 10(2) of that Act.

Sections (7)–(9) substituted by the Immigration (European Economic Area) Regulations 2000 (SI 2000/2326).

[A.1.196]
3 Jurisdiction: bail
(1)   In the case of a person to whom subsection (2) below applies, the provisions of Schedule 2 to the Immigration Act 1971 specified in Schedule 3 to this Act shall have effect with the modifications set out there.

(2)   This subsection applies to a person who is detained under the Immigration Act 1971 if:

(*a*)   the Secretary of State certifies that his detention is necessary in the interests of national security,

(*b*)   he is detained following a decision to refuse him leave to enter the United Kingdom on the ground that his exclusion is in the interests of national security, or

(*c*)   he is detained following a decision to make a deportation order against him on the ground that his deportation is in the interests of national security.

Notes   Section 3 provides a bail jurisdiction in respect of the persons detained in any of the three situations described in subsection (2). The jurisdiction is spelt out in Schedule 2 to the 1971 Act – with Schedule 3 to the Special Immigration Appeals Commission Act 1997 making the necessary modifications to the Immigration Act 1971 in this respect.

[A.1.197]
4 Determination of appeals
(1)   The Special Immigration Appeals Commission on an appeal to it under this Act:

(*a*)   shall allow the appeal if it considers:
   (i)   that the decision or action against which the appeal is brought was not in accordance with the law or with any immigration rules applicable to the case, or
   (ii)   where the decision or action involved the exercise of a discretion by the Secretary of State or an officer, that the discretion should have been exercised differently, and

(*b*)   in any other case, shall dismiss the appeal.

[(1A)   If a certificate under section 70(4)(b) of the Immigration and Asylum Act 1999 has been issued, the Commission on an appeal to it under this Act may, instead of determining the appeal, quash the certificate and remit the appeal to an adjudicator.]

(2)   Where an appeal is allowed, the Commission shall give such directions for giving effect to the determination as it thinks requisite, and may also make recommendations with respect to any other action which it considers should be

taken in the case under the Immigration Act 1971; and it shall be the duty of the Secretary of State and of any officer to whom directions are given under this subsection to comply with them.

(3) In this section, 'immigration rules' has the same meaning as in the Immigration Act 1971.

Notes Sub-s (1A) inserted by the Immigration and Asylum Act 1999, s 169(1), Sch 14, paras 118, 122.

The crucial provision is reflective of the jurisdiction of the immigration appellate authorities under the Immigration Act 1971, section 19(1). The bill as originally drafted entirely omitted *any* provision dealing with determination of appeals by the commission, albeit that Lord Williams was unequivocal at second reading that 'the intention of the Government is that the commission should have the same jurisdiction as the existing appeal bodies, which means a full appeal on the merits' (*Hansard* HL vol 580 col 752). The 'not in accordance with the law' jurisdiction is wide and covers principles of administrative law (see *DS Abdi v Secretary of State for the Home Department* [1996] Imm AR 148), although not at present ECHR. The section was introduced by the Government at committee stage in the Lords (*Hansard* HL Vol 580 col 1431) with Lord Williams accepting the suggestion made during second reading that 'it was not clear on the face of the Bill whether or not the commission would be in a position to make decisions which would be binding has plainly been achieved. Where an appeal is allowed the commission 'shall give directions for giving effect to the determination as it thinks requisite' with which the Secretary of State is obliged to comply (*cf* section 19(3) of the 1971 Act).

At the same time Lord Williams also stated expressly that 'those who believe that their rights under Article 3 have been or would be violated will be able to rely on Article 3 in domestic proceedings once incorporation has been achieved'.

[A.1.198]
5 Procedure in relation to jurisdiction under sections 2 and 3

(1) The Lord Chancellor may make rules:

(*a*) for regulating the exercise of the rights of appeal conferred by section 2 [or 2A] above,

(*b*) for prescribing the practice and procedure to be followed on or in connection with appeals under [section 2 or 2A above], including the mode and burden of proof and admissibility of evidence on such appeals, and

(*c*) for other matters preliminary or incidental to or arising out of such appeals, including proof of the decisions of the Special Immigration Appeals Commission.

(2) Rules under this section shall provide that an appellant has the right to be legally represented in any proceedings before the Commission on an appeal under section 2 [or 2A] above, subject to any power conferred on the Commission by such rules.

(3) Rules under this section may, in particular:

(*a*) make provision enabling proceedings before the Commission to take place without the appellant being given full particulars of the reasons for the decision which is the subject of the appeal,

(*b*) make provision enabling the Commission to hold proceedings in the absence of any person, including the appellant and any legal representative appointed by him,

(*c*) make provision about the functions in proceedings before the Commission of persons appointed under section 6 below, and

(*d*) make provision enabling the Commission to give the appellant a summary of any evidence taken in his absence.

(4) Rules under this section may also include provision:

(*a*) enabling any functions of the Commission which relate to matters preliminary or incidental to an appeal, or which are conferred by Part II of Schedule 2 to the Immigration Act 1971, to be performed by a single member of the Commission, or

(*b*) conferring on the Commission such ancillary powers as the Lord Chancellor thinks necessary for the purposes of the exercise of its functions.

(5) The power to make rules under this section shall include power to make rules with respect to applications to the Commission under paragraphs 22 to 24 of Schedule 2 to the Immigration Act 1971 and matters arising out of such applications.

(6) In making rules under this section, the Lord Chancellor shall have regard, in particular, to:

(*a*) the need to secure that decisions which are the subject of appeals are properly reviewed, and

(*b*) the need to secure that information is not disclosed contrary to the public interest.

(7) . . .

(8) The power to make rules under this section shall be exercisable by statutory instrument.

(9) No rules shall be made under this section unless a draft of them has been laid before and approved by resolution of each House of Parliament.

Commencement Brought into force on 11 June 1998 by SI 1998/1336.

Notes Words in square brackets inserted by the Race Relations (Amendment) Act 2000, s 9(1), Sch 2 (for commencement see s 10(2) of that Act).

Sub-s (7) repealed by the Regulation of Investigatory Powers Act 2000, s 82(2), Sch 5.

This section which empowers the Lord Chancellor to make rules for appeals under the 1997 Act reflects the starting point for the procedures of the commission. The right to legal representation guaranteed by subsection (2) taken together with the binding nature of the commission's decisions (section 4(2) refers) begins to meet the concerns of the European Court of Human Rights in Chahal. However, such rules may also enable proceedings to take place without full particulars being given to the appellant (subsection 3(a)), enable proceedings to be held in the absence of any person including the appellant's legal representative (subsection (3)(b)) and enable the commission 'to give the appellant a summary of any evidence taken in his absence' (subsection (3)(d)). In making rules the Lord Chancellor is obliged to have regard to 'the need to secure that decisions which are the subject of appeals are properly reviewed' and 'the need to secure that information is not disclosed contrary to the public interest'. Some may feel that these powers tilt the 'balance' against the appellant – although such concerns may be said to be met by the use of the security vetted 'special advocate' – who despite the power in subsection (3)(b) to exclude 'any person' was expressly stated by Lord Williams to be someone who would probably need to be present throughout (see commentary on section 6 below).

See Special Immigration Appeal Commission (Procedure) Rules 1998 (SI 1998/1881) which came into force on 31 July 1998 (see **[A.3.1]**).

[A.1.199]
6 Appointment of person to represent the appellant's interests
(1)   The relevant law officer may appoint a person to represent the interests of an appellant in any proceedings before the Special Immigration Appeals Commission from which the appellant and any legal representative of his are excluded.
(2)   For the purposes of subsection (1) above, the relevant law officer is:

(*a*) in relation to proceedings before the Commission in England and Wales, the Attorney General,
(*b*) in relation to proceedings before the Commission in Scotland, the Lord Advocate, and
(*c*) in relation to proceedings before the Commission in Northern Ireland, the Attorney General for Northern Ireland.

(3)   A person appointed under subsection (1) above:

(*a*) if appointed for the purposes of proceedings in England and Wales, shall have a general qualification for the purposes of section 71 of the Courts and Legal Services Act 1990,
(*b*) if appointed for the purposes of proceedings in Scotland, shall be:
  (i) an advocate, or
  (ii) a solicitor who has by virtue of section 25A of the Solicitors (Scotland) Act 1980 rights of audience in the Court of Session and the High Court of Justiciary, and
(*c*) if appointed for the purposes of proceedings in Northern Ireland, shall be a member of the Bar of Northern Ireland.

(4)   A person appointed under subsection (1) above shall not be responsible to the person whose interests he is appointed to represent.

Notes   The provision for the appointment of a 'special advocate' was moved as a Government amendment at committee stage in the Lords by Lord Williams – although the intention to amend the Bill was mentioned at second reading on 5 June 1997. Lord Williams then described such person as 'security vetted counsel to the commission who will be able to act as though for the appellant' albeit that they would not disclose material to the appellant (Hansard HL Vol 580 at cols 755–6). More detail was provided in committee. Lord Williams explained that 'the role of the special advocate should be to represent the interests of the appellant in those parts of the proceedings from which he and his legal representative are excluded. That will probably mean that he or she will need to be present throughout the whole proceedings. . . . (I)t would be the same sort of vetted person as one who prosecutes for the Treasury in important, delicate, sensitive national security matters' (*Hansard* HL vol 580 col 1437).
    Mr O'Brien on second reading in the House of Commons described the relationship of the special advocate and appellant as 'like a person who is appointed by a court to represent a minor – a child – or someone with a psychiatric or mental problem. That person does not take instructions from the client and he is not obliged to do what the client says. A special advocate is not obliged to disclose information that he may become privy to. He does not have the lawyer-client relationship that one commonly expects, so the special advocate will not take any instructions from the appellant' (*Hansard* HC vol 299 cols 1071–1071). Such 'special advocate' system operates in Canada (see *Chahal* judgment at paragraph 144) and as Mr O'Brien states was a relationship 'commended' by the European Court.

[A.1.200]
7 Appeals from the Commission
(1)   Where the Special Immigration Appeals Commission has made a final determination of an appeal, any party to the appeal may bring a further appeal to the appropriate appeal court on any question of law material to that determination.
(2)   An appeal under this section may be brought only with the leave of the Commission or, if such leave is refused, with the leave of the appropriate appeal court.
(3)   In this section 'the appropriate appeal court' means:

(*a*)   in relation to a determination made by the Commission in England and Wales, the Court of Appeal,
(*b*)   in relation to a determination made by the Commission in Scotland, the Court of Session, and
(*c*)   in relation to a determination made by the Commission in Northern Ireland, the Court of Appeal in Northern Ireland.

(4)   . . .

Notes   Sub-s (4) repealed by the Immigration and Asylum Act 1999, s 169(1), (3), Sch 14, paras 118, 123, Sch 16.
    The provision of a right of appeal to the Court of Appeal on a question of law was introduced at committee stage in the commons – although Mr O'Brien gave notice of such intention during second reading in the commons (Standing Committee D, Tuesday 11 November 1997 col 11). This provision reflects that in the Asylum and Immigration Appeals Act 1993, section 9. Subsection (4) is a consequential amendment of section 33(4) of the Immigration Act 1971 defining when an appeal is 'pending'.

[A.1.201]
[7A   Pending appeals]
[(1)   For the purposes of this Act, an appeal to the Commission is to be treated as pending during the period beginning when notice of appeal is given and ending when the appeal is finally determined, withdrawn or abandoned.
(2)   An appeal is not to be treated as finally determined while a further appeal may be brought.
(3)   If a further appeal is brought, the original appeal is not to be treated as finally determined until the further appeal is determined, withdrawn or abandoned.
(4)   A pending appeal to the Commission is to be treated as abandoned if the appellant leaves the United Kingdom.
(5)   A pending appeal to the Commission is to be treated as abandoned if the appellant is granted leave to enter or remain in the United Kingdom.
(6)   But subsection (5) does not apply to an appeal brought under section 2(1) as a result of section 70(4) of the Immigration and Asylum Act 1999.
(7)   A pending appeal brought under section 2(1) as a result of section 62(3) of that Act is to be treated as abandoned if a deportation order is made against the appellant.]

Note   Inserted by the Immigration and Asylum Act 1999, s 169(1), Sch 14, paras 118, 124.

[A.1.202]
8 Procedure on applications to the Commission for leave to appeal
(1)   The Lord Chancellor may make rules regulating, and prescribing the procedure to be followed on, applications to the Special Immigration Appeals Commission for leave to appeal under section 7 above.
(2)   Rules under this section may include provision enabling an application for leave to appeal to be heard by a single member of the Commission.
(3)   The power to make rules under this section shall be exercisable by statutory instrument.
(4)   No rules shall be made under this section unless a draft of them has been laid before and approved by resolution of each House of Parliament.

Commencement   Brought into force on 11 June 1998 by SI 1998/1336.

Notes   This section enables the Lord Chancellor to make rules regulating the procedure to be followed on applications for leave to appeal under section 7 above. Again, such rules must be 'approved by resolution of each House of Parliament' (subsection (4)).

[A.1.203]
9 Short title, commencement and extent
(1)   This Act may be cited as the Special Immigration Appeals Commission Act 1997.
(2)   This Act, except for this section, shall come into force on such day as the Secretary of State may by order made by statutory instrument appoint; and different days may be so appointed for different purposes.
(3)   Her Majesty may by Order in Council direct that any of the provisions of this Act shall extend, with such modifications as appear to Her Majesty to be appropriate, to any of the Channel Islands or the Isle of Man.
(4)   This Act extends to Northern Ireland.

Notes   SI 1998/1336 brought sections 5 and 8 into force on 11 June 1998. All other provisions of the Act were brought into force on 3 August 1998 by SI 1998/1892.

Schedules

SCHEDULE 1   THE COMMISSION (Section 1)

[A.1.204]

Members

1—(1)   The Special Immigration Appeals Commission shall consist of such number of members appointed by the Lord Chancellor as he may determine.
(2)   A member of the Commission shall hold and vacate office in accordance with the terms of his appointment and shall, on ceasing to hold office, be eligible for re-appointment.
(3)   A member of the Commission may resign his office at any time by notice in writing to the Lord Chancellor.

Chairman

2 The Lord Chancellor shall appoint one of the members of the Commission to be its chairman.

Payments to members

3—(1) The Lord Chancellor may pay to the members of the Commission such remuneration and allowances as he may determine.
(2) The Lord Chancellor may, if he thinks fit in the case of any member of the Commission pay such pension, allowance or gratuity to or in respect of the member, of such sums towards the provision of such pension, allowance or gratuity, as he may determine.
(3) If a person ceases to be a member of the Commission and it appears to the Lord Chancellor that there are special circumstances which make it right that the person should receive compensation, he may pay to that person a sum of such amount as he may determine.

Proceedings

4 The Commission shall sit at such times and in such places as the Lord Chancellor may direct and may sit in two or more divisions.
5 The Commission shall be deemed to be duly constituted if it consists of three members of whom:

(*a*) at least one holds or has held high judicial office (within the meaning of the Appellate Jurisdiction Act 1876), and
(*b*) at least one is or has been:
    (i) appointed as chief adjudicator under [section 57(2) of the Immigration and Asylum Act 1999], or
    (ii) a member of the Immigration Appeal Tribunal qualified as mentioned in [paragraph 1(3) of Schedule 2 to that Act].

6 The chairman or, in his absence, such other member of the Commission as he may nominate, shall preside at sittings of the Commission and report its decisions.

Staff

7 The Lord Chancellor may appoint such officers and servants for the Commission as he thinks fit.

Expenses

8 The Lord Chancellor shall defray the remuneration of persons appointed under paragraph 7 above and such expenses of the Commission as he thinks fit.

Notes See section 1 above.
Paragraph 5 amended by Immigration and Asylum Act 1999, Sch 14, para 125.

SCHEDULE 2   APPEALS: SUPPLEMENTARY (Section 2)

[A.1.205]

[Stay on directions for removal

1   If a person in the United Kingdom appeals under section 2(1) above on being refused leave to enter, any directions previously given by virtue of the refusal for his removal from the United Kingdom cease to have effect, except in so far as they have already been carried out, and no directions may be so given so long as the appeal is pending.

2   If a person in the United Kingdom appeals under section 2(1) above against any directions given under Part I of Schedule 2 or Schedule 3 to the 1971 Act for his removal from the United Kingdom, those directions except in so far as they have already been carried out, have no effect while the appeal is pending.

3   But the provisions of Part I of Schedule 2 or, as the case may be, Schedule 3 to the 1971 Act with respect to detention and persons liable to detention apply to a person appealing under section 2(1) above as if there were in force directions for his removal from the United Kingdom, except that he may not be detained on board a ship or aircraft so as to compel him to leave the United Kingdom while the appeal is pending.

3A   In calculating the period of two months limited by paragraph 8(2) of Schedule 2 to the 1971 Act for the giving of directions under that paragraph for the removal of a person from the United Kingdom and for the giving of a notice of intention to give such directions, any period during which there is pending an appeal by him under section 2(1) above is to be disregarded.

3B   If directions are given under Part I of Schedule 2 or Schedule 3 to the 1971 Act for anyone's removal from the United Kingdom, and directions are also so given for the removal with him of persons belonging to his family, then if any of them appeals under section 2(1) above, the appeal has the same effect under paragraphs 1 to 3A in relation to the directions given in respect of each of the others as it has in relation to the directions given in respect of the appellant.

Suspension of variation of limited leave

3C   A variation is not to take effect while an appeal is pending under section 2(1) above against the variation.

Continuation of leave

3D—(1)   While an appeal under section 2(1) above is pending, the leave to which the appeal relates, and any conditions subject to which it was granted continue to have effect.

(2) A person may not make an application for a variation of his leave to enter or remain while that leave is treated as continuing to have effect as a result of sub-paragraph (1).

(3) For the purposes of section 2(1), in calculating whether, as a result of a decision, a person may be required to leave the United Kingdom within twenty-eight days, a continuation of leave under this paragraph is to be disregarded.

Deportation orders

3E A deportation order is not to be made against a person under section 5 of the 1971 Act while an appeal duly brought under section 2(1) above against the decision to make it is pending.

3F In calculating the period of eight weeks set by section 5(3) of the 1971 Act for making a deportation order against a person as belonging to the family of another person, there is to be disregarded any period during which an appeal under section 2(1) above against the decision to make the order is pending.

Appeals under section 2A

3G—(1) A person is not to be required to leave, or be removed from, the United Kingdom if an appeal under section 2A is pending against the decision on which that requirement or removal would otherwise be based.

(2) That does not prevent:

(*a*) directions for his removal being given during that period;

(*b*) a deportation order being made against him during that period.

(3) But no such direction or order is to have effect during that period.]

Construction of references to pending appeal

4 For the purposes of [this Schedule], an appeal under section 2 [or 2A] above shall be treated as pending during the period beginning when notice of appeal is duly given and ending when the appeal is finally determined or withdrawn; and an appeal shall not be treated as finally determined so long as a further appeal can be brought by virtue of section 7 above, not, if such an appeal is duly brought, until it is determined or withdrawn.

Appeals involving asylum

5 . . .

[*Notice of appealable decisions and statement of appeal rights etc*

6 Paragraph 1 of Schedule 4 to the Immigration and Asylum Act 1999 has effect as if section 2 [and 2A] of this Act were contained in Part IV of that Act.

Financial support for organisations helping persons with rights of appeal

7 Section 81 of the Immigration and Asylum Act 1999 shall have effect as if section 2 [and 2A] above were contained in Part IV of that Act.]

Notes Paras 1–3: substituted, by subsequent paras 1–3, 3A–3G, by the Immigration and Asylum Act 1999, s 169(1), Sch 14, paras 118, 126.

Para 4: words 'the Immigration Act 1971 as applied by paragraphs 1 to 3 above' in italics repealed and subsequent words in square brackets substituted by the Immigration and Asylum Act 1999, s 169(1), Sch 14, paras 118, 127.

Para 5: repealed by the Immigration and Asylum Act 1999, s 169(1), (3), Sch 14, paras 118, 128, Sch 16.

Paras 6, 7: substituted by the Immigration and Asylum Act 1999, s 169(1), Sch 14, paras 118, 129.

See section 2 above.]

Words relating to section 2A in paras 4, 6 and 7 inserted by the Race Relations (Amendment) Act 2000, s 9(1), Sch 2.

SCHEDULE 3   BAIL: MODIFICATIONS OF SCHEDULE 2 TO THE IMMIGRA-TION ACT 1971 (Section 3)

[A.1.206]
1—(1) Paragraph 22 shall be amended as follows.
(2) In sub-paragraph (1A), for the words from the beginning to 'adjudicator' there shall be substituted 'The Special Immigration Appeals Commission'.
(3) In sub-paragraph (2):

(*a*) for the words 'immigration officer or adjudicator' there shall be substituted 'Special Immigration Appeals Commission'.
(*b*) for the words 'officer or adjudicator' there shall be substituted 'Commission'.

(4) In sub-paragraph (3):

(*a*) for 'an immigration officer or adjudicator' there shall be substituted 'the Special Immigration Appeals Commission', and
(*b*) for the words 'officer or adjudicator', in both places, there shall be substituted 'Commission'.

2—(1) Paragraph 23 shall be amended as follows.
(2) In sub-paragraph (1):

(*a*) for 'an adjudicator' there shall be substituted 'the Special Immigration Appeals Commission', and
(*b*) for 'the adjudicator', in each place, there shall be substituted 'the Commission',

(3) In sub-paragraph (2):

(*a*) for 'an adjudicator' there shall be substituted 'the Special Immigration

Appeals Commission', and

(*b*) for 'the adjudicator' there shall be substituted 'the Commission'.

3—(1)   Paragraph 24 shall be amended as follows.

(2)   For sub-paragraph (2), there shall be substituted:

'(2) A person arrested under this paragraph shall be brought before the Special Immigration Appeals Commission within twenty-four hours.

(3)   In sub-paragraph (3), for the words from the beginning to 'above' there shall be substituted 'Where a person is brought before the Special Immigration Appeals Commission by virtue of sub-paragraph (2) above, the Commission—'.

4—(1)   Paragraph 29 shall be amended as follows.

(2)   For sub-paragraphs (2) to (4) there shall be substituted:

'(2) The Special Immigration Appeals Commission may release an appellant on his entering into a recognizance or, in Scotland, bail bond conditioned for his appearance before the Commission at a time and place named in the recognizance or bail bond.'

(3)   For sub-paragraph (6) there shall be substituted:

'(6) In any case in which the Special Immigration Appeals Commission has power to release an appellant on bail, the Commission may, instead of taking the bail, fix the amount and conditions of the bail (including the amount in which any sureties are to be bound) with a view to its being taken subsequently by any such person as may be specified by the Commission; and on the recognizance or bail bond being so taken the appellant shall be released'.

5   Paragraph 30(2) shall be omitted.

6—(1)   Paragraph 31 shall be amended as follows.

(2)   In sub-paragraph (1):

(*a*) for 'an adjudicator or the Tribunal' there shall be substituted 'the Special Immigration Appeals Commissions',

(*b*) for 'the adjudicator or the Tribunal, as the case may be,' there shall be substituted 'the Commission', and

(*c*) for 'the adjudicator or Tribunal', in both places, there shall be substituted 'the Commission'.

(3)   In sub-paragraph (3):

(*a*) for 'an adjudicator or the Tribunal' there shall be substituted 'the Special Immigration Appeals Commission', and

(*b*) for 'the adjudicator or Tribunal' there shall be substituted 'it'.

7   Paragraph 32 shall be amended as follows:

(*a*) for 'an adjudicator or the Tribunal' there shall be substituted 'the Special Immigration Appeals Commission', and

(*b*) for 'the adjudicator or Tribunal' there shall be substituted 'the Commission', and

(*c*) for 'the adjudicator or the Tribunal' there shall be substituted 'the Commission'.

8—(1)   Paragraph 33 shall be amended as follows.

(2)   For sub-paragraph (2), there shall be substituted:

'(2) A person arrested under this paragraph shall be brought before the Special Immigration Appeals Commission within twenty-four hours.'

(3)   In sub-paragraph (3), for the words from the beginning to 'above' there shall be substituted 'Where a person is brought before the Special Immigration Appeals Commission by virtue of sub-paragraph (2) above, the Commission—'.

Notes   See section 3 above.

HUMAN RIGHTS ACT 1998
(1998 c 42)

Arrangement of sections

INTRODUCTION

[A.1.207]
1   The Convention Rights
(1)   In this Act 'the Convention rights' means the rights and fundamental freedoms set out in—

(a)   Articles 2 to 12 and 14 of the Convention,
(b)   Articles 1 to 3 of the First Protocol, and
(c)   Articles 1 and 2 of the Sixth Protocol,

as read with Articles 16 to 18 of the Convention.
(2)   Those Articles are to have effect for the purposes of this Act subject to any designated derogation or reservation (as to which see sections 14 and 15).
(3)   The Articles are set out in Schedule 1.
(4)   The Secretary of State may by order make such amendments to this Act as he considers appropriate to reflect the effect, in relation to the United Kingdom, of a protocol.
(5)   In subsection (4) 'protocol' means a protocol to the Convention—

(a)   which the United Kingdom has ratified; or
(b)   which the United Kingdom has signed with a view to ratification.

(6)   No amendment may be made by an order under subsection (4) so as to come into force before the protocol concerned is in force in relation to the United Kingdom.

Commencement   2 October 2000: see SI 2000/1851, art 2.

[A.1.208]
2   Interpretation of Convention rights
(1)   A court or tribunal determining a question which has arisen in connection with a Convention right must take into account any—

(a)   judgment, decision, declaration or advisory opinion of the European Court of Human Rights,
(b)   opinion of the Commission given in a report adopted under Article 31 of the Convention,
(c)   decision of the Commission in connection with Article 26 or 27(2) of the Convention, or
(d)   decision of the Committee of Ministers taken under Article 46 of the Convention,

whenever made or given, so far as, in the opinion of the court or tribunal, it is relevant to the proceedings in which that question has arisen.
(2)   Evidence of any judgment, decision, declaration or opinion of which account may have to be taken under this section is to be given in proceedings before any court or tribunal in such manner as may be provided by rules.
(3)   In this section 'rules' means rules of court or, in the case of proceedings before a tribunal, rules made for the purposes of this section—

(a)   by the Lord Chancellor or the Secretary of State, in relation to any proceedings outside Scotland;

(b) by the Secretary of State, in relation to proceedings in Scotland; or
(c) by a Northern Ireland department, in relation to proceedings before a tribunal in Northern Ireland—
  (i) which deals with transferred matters; and
  (ii) for which no rules made under paragraph (a) are in force.

Commencement 2 October 2000: see SI 2000/1851, art 2.

LEGISLATION

[A.1.209]
3 Interpretation of legislation
(1) So far as it is possible to do so, primary legislation and subordinate legislation must be read and given effect in a way which is compatible with the Convention rights.
(2) This section—

(a) applies to primary legislation and subordinate legislation whenever enacted;
(b) does not affect the validity, continuing operation or enforcement of any incompatible primary legislation; and
(c) does not affect the validity, continuing operation or enforcement of any incompatible subordinate legislation if (disregarding any possibility of revocation) primary legislation prevents removal of the incompatibility.

Commencement 2 October 2000: see SI 2000/1851, art 2.

[A.1.210]
4 Declaration of incompatibility
(1) Subsection (2) applies in any proceedings in which a court determines whether a provision of primary legislation is compatible with a Convention right.
(2) If the court is satisfied that the provision is incompatible with a Convention right, it may make a declaration of that incompatibility.
(3) Subsection (4) applies in any proceedings in which a court determines whether a provision of subordinate legislation, made in the exercise of a power conferred by primary legislation, is compatible with a Convention right.
(4) If the court is satisfied—

(a) that the provision is incompatible with a Convention right, and
(b) that (disregarding any possibility of revocation) the primary legislation concerned prevents removal of the incompatibility,

it may make a declaration of that incompatibility.
(5) In this section 'court' means—

(a) the House of Lords;
(b) the Judicial Committee of the Privy Council;
(c) the Courts-Martial Appeal Court;

(d) in Scotland, the High Court of Justiciary sitting otherwise than as a trial court or the Court of Session;
(e) in England and Wales or Northern Ireland, the High Court or the Court of Appeal.

(6)   A declaration under this section ('a declaration of incompatibility')—

(a) does not affect the validity, continuing operation or enforcement of the provision in respect of which it is given; and
(b) is not binding on the parties to the proceedings in which it is made.

Commencement   2 October 2000: see SI 2000/1851, art 2.

[A.1.211]
5   Right of Crown to intervene
(1)   Where a court is considering whether to make a declaration of incompatibility, the Crown is entitled to notice in accordance with rules of court.
(2)   In any case to which subsection (1) applies—

(a) a Minister of the Crown (or a person nominated by him),
(b) a member of the Scottish Executive,
(c) a Northern Ireland Minister,
(d) a Northern Ireland department,

is entitled, on giving notice in accordance with rules of court, to be joined as a party to the proceedings.
(3)   Notice under subsection (2) may be given at any time during the proceedings.
(4)   A person who has been made a party to criminal proceedings (other than in Scotland) as the result of a notice under subsection (2) may, with leave, appeal to the House of Lords against any declaration of incompatibility made in the proceedings.
(5)   In subsection (4)—

'criminal proceedings' includes all proceedings before the Courts-Martial Appeal Court; and
'leave' means leave granted by the court making the declaration of incompatibility or by the House of Lords.

Commencement   2 October 2000: see SI 2000/1851, art 2.

Transfer of Functions   The function under sub-s (2) shall be exercisable by the National Assembly for Wales concurrently with any Minister of the Crown by whom it is exercisable, in so far as it relates to any proceedings in which a court is considering whether to make a declaration of incompatibility within the meaning of s 4 of this Act, in respect of subordinate legislation made by the National Assembly, and subordinate legislation made, in relation to Wales, by a Minister of the Crown in the exercise of a function which is exercisable by the National Assembly: see the National Assembly for Wales (Transfer of Functions) (No 2) Order 2000, SI 2000/1830, art 2.

PUBLIC AUTHORITIES

[A.1.212]
6   Acts of public authorities
(1)   It is unlawful for a public authority to act in a way which is incompatible with a Convention right.
(2)   Subsection (1) does not apply to an act if—

(a) as the result of one or more provisions of primary legislation, the authority could not have acted differently; or
(b) in the case of one or more provisions of, or made under, primary legislation which cannot be read or given effect in a way which is compatible with the Convention rights, the authority was acting so as to give effect to or enforce those provisions.

(3)   In this section 'public authority' includes—

(a) a court or tribunal, and
(b) any person certain of whose functions are functions of a public nature,

but does not include either House of Parliament or a person exercising functions in connection with proceedings in Parliament.
(4)   In subsection (3) 'Parliament' does not include the House of Lords in its judicial capacity.
(5)   In relation to a particular act, a person is not a public authority by virtue only of subsection (3)(b) if the nature of the act is private.
(6)   'An act' includes a failure to act but does not include a failure to—

(a) introduce in, or lay before, Parliament a proposal for legislation; or
(b) make any primary legislation or remedial order.

Commencement   2 October 2000: see SI 2000/1851, art 2.

[A.1.213]
7   Proceedings
(1)   A person who claims that a public authority has acted (or proposes to act) in a way which is made unlawful by section 6(1) may—

(a) bring proceedings against the authority under this Act in the appropriate court or tribunal, or
(b) rely on the Convention right or rights concerned in any legal proceedings,

but only if he is (or would be) a victim of the unlawful act.
(2)   In subsection (1)(a) 'appropriate court or tribunal' means such court or tribunal as may be determined in accordance with rules; and proceedings against an authority include a counterclaim or similar proceeding.
(3)   If the proceedings are brought on an application for judicial review, the applicant is to be taken to have a sufficient interest in relation to the unlawful act only if he is, or would be, a victim of that act.
(4)   If the proceedings are made by way of a petition for judicial review in Scotland, the applicant shall be taken to have title and interest to sue in relation to the unlawful act only if he is, or would be, a victim of that act.
(5)   Proceedings under subsection (1)(a) must be brought before the end of—

(a) the period of one year beginning with the date on which the act complained of took place; or

(b) such longer period as the court or tribunal considers equitable having regard to all the circumstances,

but that is subject to any rule imposing a stricter time limit in relation to the procedure in question.

(6)   In subsection (1)(b) 'legal proceedings' includes—

(a) proceedings brought by or at the instigation of a public authority; and

(b) an appeal against the decision of a court or tribunal.

(7)   For the purposes of this section, a person is a victim of an unlawful act only if he would be a victim for the purposes of Article 34 of the Convention if proceedings were brought in the European Court of Human Rights in respect of that act.

(8)   Nothing in this Act creates a criminal offence.

(9)   In this section 'rules' means—

(a) in relation to proceedings before a court or tribunal outside Scotland, rules made by the Lord Chancellor or the Secretary of State for the purposes of this section or rules of court,

(b) in relation to proceedings before a court or tribunal in Scotland, rules made by the Secretary of State for those purposes,

(c) in relation to proceedings before a tribunal in Northern Ireland—
   (i)   which deals with transferred matters; and
   (ii) for which no rules made under paragraph (a) are in force,

rules made by a Northern Ireland department for those purposes,and includes provision made by order under section 1 of the Courts and Legal Services Act 1990.

(10)   In making rules, regard must be had to section 9.

(11)   The Minister who has power to make rules in relation to a particular tribunal may, to the extent he considers it necessary to ensure that the tribunal can provide an appropriate remedy in relation to an act (or proposed act) of a public authority which is (or would be) unlawful as a result of section 6(1), by order add to—

(a) the relief or remedies which the tribunal may grant; or

(b) the grounds on which it may grant any of them.

(12)   An order made under subsection (11) may contain such incidental, supplemental, consequential or transitional provision as the Minister making it considers appropriate.

(13)   'The Minister' includes the Northern Ireland department concerned.

Commencement   2 October 2000: see SI 2000/1851, art 2.

[A.1.214]
8   Judicial remedies
(1)   In relation to any act (or proposed act) of a public authority which the court finds is (or would be) unlawful, it may grant such relief or remedy, or make such order, within its powers as it considers just and appropriate.

(2)   But damages may be awarded only by a court which has power to award damages, or to order the payment of compensation, in civil proceedings.

(3)   No award of damages is to be made unless, taking account of all the circumstances of the case, including—

(a) any other relief or remedy granted, or order made, in relation to the act in question (by that or any other court), and

(b) the consequences of any decision (of that or any other court) in respect of that act,

the court is satisfied that the award is necessary to afford just satisfaction to the person in whose favour it is made.

(4)   In determining—

(a) whether to award damages, or

(b) the amount of an award,

the court must take into account the principles applied by the European Court of Human Rights in relation to the award of compensation under Article 41 of the Convention.

(5)   A public authority against which damages are awarded is to be treated—

(a) in Scotland, for the purposes of section 3 of the Law Reform (Miscellaneous Provisions) (Scotland) Act 1940 as if the award were made in an action of damages in which the authority has been found liable in respect of loss or damage to the person to whom the award is made;

(b) for the purposes of the Civil Liability (Contribution) Act 1978 as liable in respect of damage suffered by the person to whom the award is made.

(6)   In this section—

'court' includes a tribunal;
'damages' means damages for an unlawful act of a public authority; and
'unlawful' means unlawful under section 6(1).

Commencement   2 October 2000: see SI 2000/1851, art 2.

[A.1.215]
9   Judicial acts
(1)   Proceedings under section 7(1)(a) in respect of a judicial act may be brought only—

(a) by exercising a right of appeal;

(b) on an application (in Scotland a petition) for judicial review; or

(c) in such other forum as may be prescribed by rules.

(2)   That does not affect any rule of law which prevents a court from being the subject of judicial review.

(3)   In proceedings under this Act in respect of a judicial act done in good faith, damages may not be awarded otherwise than to compensate a person to the extent required by Article 5(5) of the Convention.

(4)   An award of damages permitted by subsection (3) is to be made against the Crown; but no award may be made unless the appropriate person, if not a party to the proceedings, is joined.

(5)   In this section—

'appropriate person' means the Minister responsible for the court concerned, or a person or government department nominated by him;

'court' includes a tribunal;

'judge' includes a member of a tribunal, a justice of the peace and a clerk or other officer entitled to exercise the jurisdiction of a court;

'judicial act' means a judicial act of a court and includes an act done on the instructions, or on behalf, of a judge; and

'rules' has the same meaning as in section 7(9).

Commencement   2 October 2000: see SI 2000/1851, art 2.

Remedial action

[A.1.216]
10   Power to take remedial action
(1)   This section applies if—

(a)   a provision of legislation has been declared under section 4 to be incompatible with a Convention right and, if an appeal lies—
  (i)   all persons who may appeal have stated in writing that they do not intend to do so;
  (ii)   the time for bringing an appeal has expired and no appeal has been brought within that time; or
  (iii)   an appeal brought within that time has been determined or abandoned; or
(b)   it appears to a Minister of the Crown or Her Majesty in Council that, having regard to a finding of the European Court of Human Rights made after the coming into force of this section in proceedings against the United Kingdom, a provision of legislation is incompatible with an obligation of the United Kingdom arising from the Convention.

(2)   If a Minister of the Crown considers that there are compelling reasons for proceeding under this section, he may by order make such amendments to the legislation as he considers necessary to remove the incompatibility.

(3)   If, in the case of subordinate legislation, a Minister of the Crown considers—

(a)   that it is necessary to amend the primary legislation under which the subordinate legislation in question was made, in order to enable the incompatibility to be removed, and
(b)   that there are compelling reasons for proceeding under this section,
he may by order make such amendments to the primary legislation as he considers necessary.

(4)   This section also applies where the provision in question is in subordinate legislation and has been quashed, or declared invalid, by reason of incompatibility with a Convention right and the Minister proposes to proceed under paragraph 2(b) of Schedule 2.

(5)   If the legislation is an Order in Council, the power conferred by subsection (2) or (3) is exercisable by Her Majesty in Council.

(6)   In this section 'legislation' does not include a Measure of the Church Assembly or of the General Synod of the Church of England.

(7)   Schedule 2 makes further provision about remedial orders.

Commencement   2 October 2000: see SI 2000/1851, art 2.

Other rights and proceedings

[A.1.217]
11   Safeguard for existing human rights
A person's reliance on a Convention right does not restrict—

(a)   any other right or freedom conferred on him by or under any law having effect in any part of the United Kingdom; or
(b)   his right to make any claim or bring any proceedings which he could make or bring apart from sections 7 to 9.

Commencement   2 October 2000: see SI 2000/1851, art 2.

[A.1.218]
12   Freedom of expression
(1)   This section applies if a court is considering whether to grant any relief which, if granted, might affect the exercise of the Convention right to freedom of expression.
(2)   If the person against whom the application for relief is made ('the respondent') is neither present nor represented, no such relief is to be granted unless the court is satisfied—

(a)   that the applicant has taken all practicable steps to notify the respondent; or
(b)   that there are compelling reasons why the respondent should not be notified.

(3)   No such relief is to be granted so as to restrain publication before trial unless the court is satisfied that the applicant is likely to establish that publication should not be allowed.
(4)   The court must have particular regard to the importance of the Convention right to freedom of expression and, where the proceedings relate to material which the respondent claims, or which appears to the court, to be journalistic, literary or artistic material (or to conduct connected with such material), to—

(a)   the extent to which—
     (i)   the material has, or is about to, become available to the public; or
     (ii)   it is, or would be, in the public interest for the material to be published;
(b)   any relevant privacy code.

(5)   In this section—
'court' includes a tribunal; and
'relief' includes any remedy or order (other than in criminal proceedings).

Commencement   2 October 2000: see SI 2000/1851, art 2.

[A.1.219]
13 Freedom of thought, conscience and religion
(1) If a court's determination of any question arising under this Act might affect the exercise by a religious organisation (itself or its members collectively) of the Convention right to freedom of thought, conscience and religion, it must have particular regard to the importance of that right.
(2) In this section 'court' includes a tribunal.

Commencement   2 October 2000: see SI 2000/1851, art 2.

Derogations and reservations

[A.1.220]
14 Derogations
(1) In this Act 'designated derogation' means—

(a) the United Kingdom's derogation from Article 5(3) of the Convention; and
(b) any derogation by the United Kingdom from an Article of the Convention, or of any protocol to the Convention, which is designated for the purposes of this Act in an order made by the Secretary of State.

(2) The derogation referred to in subsection (1)(a) is set out in Part I of Schedule 3.
(3) If a designated derogation is amended or replaced it ceases to be a designated derogation.
(4) But subsection (3) does not prevent the Secretary of State from exercising his power under subsection (1)(b) to make a fresh designation order in respect of the Article concerned.
(5) The Secretary of State must by order make such amendments to Schedule 3 as he considers appropriate to reflect—

(a) any designation order; or
(b) the effect of subsection (3).

(6) A designation order may be made in anticipation of the making by the United Kingdom of a proposed derogation.

Commencement   2 October 2000: see SI 2000/1851, art 2.

[A.1.221]
15 Reservations
(1) In this Act 'designated reservation' means—

(a) the United Kingdom's reservation to Article 2 of the First Protocol to the Convention; and
(b) any other reservation by the United Kingdom to an Article of the Convention, or of any protocol to the Convention, which is designated for the purposes of this Act in an order made by the Secretary of State.

(2) The text of the reservation referred to in subsection (1)(a) is set out in Part II of Schedule 3.

(3)　If a designated reservation is withdrawn wholly or in part it ceases to be a designated reservation.

(4)　But subsection (3) does not prevent the Secretary of State from exercising his power under subsection (1)(b) to make a fresh designation order in respect of the Article concerned.

(5)　The Secretary of State must by order make such amendments to this Act as he considers appropriate to reflect—

(a)　any designation order; or

(b)　the effect of subsection (3).

Commencement　2 October 2000: see SI 2000/1851, art 2.

[A.1.222]
16　Period for which designated derogations have effect

(1)　If it has not already been withdrawn by the United Kingdom, a designated derogation ceases to have effect for the purposes of this Act—

(a)　in the case of the derogation referred to in section 14(1)(a), at the end of the period of five years beginning with the date on which section 1(2) came into force;

(b)　in the case of any other derogation, at the end of the period of five years beginning with the date on which the order designating it was made.

(2)　At any time before the period—

(a)　fixed by subsection (1)(a) or (b), or

(b)　extended by an order under this subsection,

comes to an end, the Secretary of State may by order extend it by a further period of five years.

(3)　An order under section 14(1)(b) ceases to have effect at the end of the period for consideration, unless a resolution has been passed by each House approving the order.

(4)　Subsection (3) does not affect—

(a)　anything done in reliance on the order; or

(b)　the power to make a fresh order under section 14(1)(b).

(5)　In subsection (3) 'period for consideration' means the period of forty days beginning with the day on which the order was made.

(6)　In calculating the period for consideration, no account is to be taken of any time during which—

(a)　Parliament is dissolved or prorogued; or

(b)　both Houses are adjourned for more than four days.

(7)　If a designated derogation is withdrawn by the United Kingdom, the Secretary of State must by order make such amendments to this Act as he considers are required to reflect that withdrawal.

Commencement　2 October 2000: see SI 2000/1851, art 2.

[A.1.223]
17 Periodic review of designated reservations
(1) The appropriate Minister must review the designated reservation referred to in section 15(1)(a)—

(a) before the end of the period of five years beginning with the date on which section 1(2) came into force; and
(b) if that designation is still in force, before the end of the period of five years beginning with the date on which the last report relating to it was laid under subsection (3).

(2) The appropriate Minister must review each of the other designated reservations (if any)—

(a) before the end of the period of five years beginning with the date on which the order designating the reservation first came into force; and
(b) if the designation is still in force, before the end of the period of five years beginning with the date on which the last report relating to it was laid under subsection (3).

(3) The Minister conducting a review under this section must prepare a report on the result of the review and lay a copy of it before each House of Parliament.

Commencement   2 October 2000: see SI 2000/1851, art 2.

Judges of the European Court of Human Rights

[A.1.224]
18 Appointment to European Court of Human Rights
(1) In this section 'judicial office' means the office of—

(a) Lord Justice of Appeal, Justice of the High Court or Circuit judge, in England and Wales;
(b) judge of the Court of Session or sheriff, in Scotland;
(c) Lord Justice of Appeal, judge of the High Court or county court judge, in Northern Ireland.

(2) The holder of a judicial office may become a judge of the European Court of Human Rights ('the Court') without being required to relinquish his office.
(3) But he is not required to perform the duties of his judicial office while he is a judge of the Court.
(4) In respect of any period during which he is a judge of the Court—

(a) a Lord Justice of Appeal or Justice of the High Court is not to count as a judge of the relevant court for the purposes of section 2(1) or 4(1) of the Supreme Court Act 1981 (maximum number of judges) nor as a judge of the Supreme Court for the purposes of section 12(1) to (6) of that Act (salaries etc);
(b) a judge of the Court of Session is not to count as a judge of that court for the purposes of section 1(1) of the Court of Session Act 1988 (maximum number of judges) or of section 9(1)(c) of the Administration of Justice Act 1973 ('the 1973 Act') (salaries etc);

(c) a Lord Justice of Appeal or judge of the High Court in Northern Ireland is not to count as a judge of the relevant court for the purposes of section 2(1) or 3(1) of the Judicature (Northern Ireland) Act 1978 (maximum number of judges) nor as a judge of the Supreme Court of Northern Ireland for the purposes of section 9(1)(d) of the 1973 Act (salaries etc);

(d) a Circuit judge is not to count as such for the purposes of section 18 of the Courts Act 1971 (salaries etc);

(e) a sheriff is not to count as such for the purposes of section 14 of the Sheriff Courts (Scotland) Act 1907 (salaries etc);

(f) a county court judge of Northern Ireland is not to count as such for the purposes of section 106 of the County Courts Act (Northern Ireland) 1959 (salaries etc).

(5) If a sheriff principal is appointed a judge of the Court, section 11(1) of the Sheriff Courts (Scotland) Act 1971 (temporary appointment of sheriff principal) applies, while he holds that appointment, as if his office is vacant.

(6) Schedule 4 makes provision about judicial pensions in relation to the holder of a judicial office who serves as a judge of the Court.

(7) The Lord Chancellor or the Secretary of State may by order make such transitional provision (including, in particular, provision for a temporary increase in the maximum number of judges) as he considers appropriate in relation to any holder of a judicial office who has completed his service as a judge of the Court.

Commencement 9 November 1998: see s 22(2).

Parliamentary procedure

[A.1.225]
19 Statements of compatibility
(1) A Minister of the Crown in charge of a Bill in either House of Parliament must, before Second Reading of the Bill—

(a) make a statement to the effect that in his view the provisions of the Bill are compatible with the Convention rights ('a statement of compatibility'); or

(b) make a statement to the effect that although he is unable to make a statement of compatibility the government nevertheless wishes the House to proceed with the Bill.

(2) The statement must be in writing and be published in such manner as the Minister making it considers appropriate.

Commencement 24 November 1998: see SI 1998/2882, art 2.

Supplemental

[A.1.226]
20 Orders etc under this Act
(1) Any power of a Minister of the Crown to make an order under this Act is exercisable by statutory instrument.

(2)   The power of the Lord Chancellor or the Secretary of State to make rules (other than rules of court) under section 2(3) or 7(9) is exercisable by statutory instrument.

(3)   Any statutory instrument made under section 14, 15 or 16(7) must be laid before Parliament.

(4)   No order may be made by the Lord Chancellor or the Secretary of State under section 1(4), 7(11) or 16(2) unless a draft of the order has been laid before, and approved by, each House of Parliament.

(5)   Any statutory instrument made under section 18(7) or Schedule 4, or to which subsection (2) applies, shall be subject to annulment in pursuance of a resolution of either House of Parliament.

(6)   The power of a Northern Ireland department to make—

(a) rules under section 2(3)(c) or 7(9)(c), or
(b) an order under section 7(11),

is exercisable by statutory rule for the purposes of the Statutory Rules (Northern Ireland) Order 1979.

(7)   Any rules made under section 2(3)(c) or 7(9)(c) shall be subject to negative resolution; and section 41(6) of the Interpretation Act (Northern Ireland) 1954 (meaning of 'subject to negative resolution') shall apply as if the power to make the rules were conferred by an Act of the Northern Ireland Assembly.

(8)   No order may be made by a Northern Ireland department under section 7(11) unless a draft of the order has been laid before, and approved by, the Northern Ireland Assembly.

Commencement   9 November 1998: see s 22(2).

[A.1.227]
21   Interpretation, etc
(1)   In this Act—

'amend' includes repeal and apply (with or without modifications);

'the appropriate Minister' means the Minister of the Crown having charge of the appropriate authorised government department (within the meaning of the Crown Proceedings Act 1947);

'the Commission' means the European Commission of Human Rights;

'the Convention' means the Convention for the Protection of Human Rights and Fundamental Freedoms, agreed by the Council of Europe at Rome on 4th November 1950 as it has effect for the time being in relation to the United Kingdom;

'declaration of incompatibility' means a declaration under section 4;

'Minister of the Crown' has the same meaning as in the Ministers of the Crown Act 1975;

'Northern Ireland Minister' includes the First Minister and the deputy First Minister in Northern Ireland;

'primary legislation' means any—

(a) public general Act;
(b) local and personal Act;
(c) private Act;
(d) Measure of the Church Assembly;
(e) Measure of the General Synod of the Church of England;

(f) Order in Council—
    (i) made in exercise of Her Majesty's Royal Prerogative;
    (ii) made under section 38(1)(a) of the Northern Ireland Constitution Act 1973 or the corresponding provision of the Northern Ireland Act 1998; or
    (iii) amending an Act of a kind mentioned in paragraph (a), (b) or (c);

and includes an order or other instrument made under primary legislation (otherwise than by the National Assembly for Wales, a member of the Scottish Executive, a Northern Ireland Minister or a Northern Ireland department) to the extent to which it operates to bring one or more provisions of that legislation into force or amends any primary legislation;

'the First Protocol' means the protocol to the Convention agreed at Paris on 20th March 1952;

'the Sixth Protocol' means the protocol to the Convention agreed at Strasbourg on 28th April 1983;

'the Eleventh Protocol' means the protocol to the Convention (restructuring the control machinery established by the Convention) agreed at Strasbourg on 11th May 1994;

'remedial order' means an order under section 10;

'subordinate legislation' means any—

(a) Order in Council other than one—
    (i) made in exercise of Her Majesty's Royal Prerogative;
    (ii) made under section 38(1)(a) of the Northern Ireland Constitution Act 1973 or the corresponding provision of the Northern Ireland Act 1998; or
    (iii) amending an Act of a kind mentioned in the definition of primary legislation;
(b) Act of the Scottish Parliament;
(c) Act of the Parliament of Northern Ireland;
(d) Measure of the Assembly established under section 1 of the Northern Ireland Assembly Act 1973;
(e) Act of the Northern Ireland Assembly;
(f) order, rules, regulations, scheme, warrant, byelaw or other instrument made under primary legislation (except to the extent to which it operates to bring one or more provisions of that legislation into force or amends any primary legislation);
(g) order, rules, regulations, scheme, warrant, byelaw or other instrument made under legislation mentioned in paragraph (b), (c), (d) or (e) or made under an Order in Council applying only to Northern Ireland;
(h) order, rules, regulations, scheme, warrant, byelaw or other instrument made by a member of the Scottish Executive, a Northern Ireland Minister or a Northern Ireland department in exercise of prerogative or other executive functions of Her Majesty which are exercisable by such a person on behalf of Her Majesty;

'transferred matters' has the same meaning as in the Northern Ireland Act 1998; and

'tribunal' means any tribunal in which legal proceedings may be brought.

(2) The references in paragraphs (b) and (c) of section 2(1) to Articles are to Articles of the Convention as they had effect immediately before the coming into force of the Eleventh Protocol.

(3)   The reference in paragraph (d) of section 2(1) to Article 46 includes a reference to Articles 32 and 54 of the Convention as they had effect immediately before the coming into force of the Eleventh Protocol.

(4)   The references in section 2(1) to a report or decision of the Commission or a decision of the Committee of Ministers include references to a report or decision made as provided by paragraphs 3, 4 and 6 of Article 5 of the Eleventh Protocol (transitional provisions).

(5)   Any liability under the Army Act 1955, the Air Force Act 1955 or the Naval Discipline Act 1957 to suffer death for an offence is replaced by a liability to imprisonment for life or any less punishment authorised by those Acts; and those Acts shall accordingly have effect with the necessary modifications.

Commencement   Sub-ss (1)–(4): 2 October 2000: see SI 2000/1851, art 2.

Sub-s (5): 9 November 1998: see s 22(2).

[A.1.228]
22   Short title, commencement, application and extent
(1)   This Act may be cited as the Human Rights Act 1998.
(2)   Sections 18, 20 and 21(5) and this section come into force on the passing of this Act.
(3)   The other provisions of this Act come into force on such day as the Secretary of State may by order appoint; and different days may be appointed for different purposes.
(4)   Paragraph (b) of subsection (1) of section 7 applies to proceedings brought by or at the instigation of a public authority whenever the act in question took place; but otherwise that subsection does not apply to an act taking place before the coming into force of that section.
(5)   This Act binds the Crown.
(6)   This Act extends to Northern Ireland.
(7)   Section 21(5), so far as it relates to any provision contained in the Army Act 1955, the Air Force Act 1955 or the Naval Discipline Act 1957, extends to any place to which that provision extends.

Commencement   9 November 1998: see s 22(2).

Schedules

SCHEDULE 1 THE ARTICLES

[A.1.229]

Section 1(3)

PART I   THE CONVENTION
RIGHTS AND FREEDOMS

Article 2   Right to life
1   Everyone's right to life shall be protected by law. No one shall be deprived of his life intentionally save in the execution of a sentence of a court following his conviction of a crime for which this penalty is provided by law.

2 Deprivation of life shall not be regarded as inflicted in contravention of this Article when it results from the use of force which is no more than absolutely necessary:

(a) in defence of any person from unlawful violence;
(b) in order to effect a lawful arrest or to prevent the escape of a person lawfully detained;
(c) in action lawfully taken for the purpose of quelling a riot or insurrection.

Article 3 Prohibition of torture
No one shall be subjected to torture or to inhuman or degrading treatment or punishment.

Article 4 Prohibition of slavery and forced labour
1 No one shall be held in slavery or servitude.
2 No one shall be required to perform forced or compulsory labour.
3 For the purpose of this Article the term 'forced or compulsory labour' shall not include:

(a) any work required to be done in the ordinary course of detention imposed according to the provisions of Article 5 of this Convention or during conditional release from such detention;
(b) any service of a military character or, in case of conscientious objectors in countries where they are recognised, service exacted instead of compulsory military service;
(c) any service exacted in case of an emergency or calamity threatening the life or well-being of the community;
(d) any work or service which forms part of normal civic obligations.

Article 5 Right to liberty and security
1 Everyone has the right to liberty and security of person. No one shall be deprived of his liberty save in the following cases and in accordance with a procedure prescribed by law:

(a) the lawful detention of a person after conviction by a competent court;
(b) the lawful arrest or detention of a person for non-compliance with the lawful order of a court or in order to secure the fulfilment of any obligation prescribed by law;
(c) the lawful arrest or detention of a person effected for the purpose of bringing him before the competent legal authority on reasonable suspicion of having committed an offence or when it is reasonably considered necessary to prevent his committing an offence or fleeing after having done so;
(d) the detention of a minor by lawful order for the purpose of educational supervision or his lawful detention for the purpose of bringing him before the competent legal authority;
(e) the lawful detention of persons for the prevention of the spreading of infectious diseases, of persons of unsound mind, alcoholics or drug addicts or vagrants;
(f) the lawful arrest or detention of a person to prevent his effecting an unauthorised entry into the country or of a person against whom action is being taken with a view to deportation or extradition.

2   Everyone who is arrested shall be informed promptly, in a language which he understands, of the reasons for his arrest and of any charge against him.

3   Everyone arrested or detained in accordance with the provisions of paragraph 1(c) of this Article shall be brought promptly before a judge or other officer authorised by law to exercise judicial power and shall be entitled to trial within a reasonable time or to release pending trial. Release may be conditioned by guarantees to appear for trial.

4   Everyone who is deprived of his liberty by arrest or detention shall be entitled to take proceedings by which the lawfulness of his detention shall be decided speedily by a court and his release ordered if the detention is not lawful.

5   Everyone who has been the victim of arrest or detention in contravention of the provisions of this Article shall have an enforceable right to compensation.

Article 6   Right to a fair trial

1   In the determination of his civil rights and obligations or of any criminal charge against him, everyone is entitled to a fair and public hearing within a reasonable time by an independent and impartial tribunal established by law. Judgment shall be pronounced publicly but the press and public may be excluded from all or part of the trial in the interest of morals, public order or national security in a democratic society, where the interests of juveniles or the protection of the private life of the parties so require, or to the extent strictly necessary in the opinion of the court in special circumstances where publicity would prejudice the interests of justice.

2   Everyone charged with a criminal offence shall be presumed innocent until proved guilty according to law.

3   Everyone charged with a criminal offence has the following minimum rights:

(a)   to be informed promptly, in a language which he understands and in detail, of the nature and cause of the accusation against him;

(b)   to have adequate time and facilities for the preparation of his defence;

(c)   to defend himself in person or through legal assistance of his own choosing or, if he has not sufficient means to pay for legal assistance, to be given it free when the interests of justice so require;

(d)   to examine or have examined witnesses against him and to obtain the attendance and examination of witnesses on his behalf under the same conditions as witnesses against him;

(e)   to have the free assistance of an interpreter if he cannot understand or speak the language used in court.

Article 7   No punishment without law

1   No one shall be held guilty of any criminal offence on account of any act or omission which did not constitute a criminal offence under national or international law at the time when it was committed. Nor shall a heavier penalty be imposed than the one that was applicable at the time the criminal offence was committed.

2   This Article shall not prejudice the trial and punishment of any person for

any act or omission which, at the time when it was committed, was criminal according to the general principles of law recognised by civilised nations.

Article 8   Right to respect for private and family life
1   Everyone has the right to respect for his private and family life, his home and his correspondence.
2   There shall be no interference by a public authority with the exercise of this right except such as is in accordance with the law and is necessary in a democratic society in the interests of national security, public safety or the economic well-being of the country, for the prevention of disorder or crime, for the protection of health or morals, or for the protection of the rights and freedoms of others.

Article 9   Freedom of thought, conscience and religion
1   Everyone has the right to freedom of thought, conscience and religion; this right includes freedom to change his religion or belief and freedom, either alone or in community with others and in public or private, to manifest his religion or belief, in worship, teaching, practice and observance.
2   Freedom to manifest one's religion or beliefs shall be subject only to such limitations as are prescribed by law and are necessary in a democratic society in the interests of public safety, for the protection of public order, health or morals, or for the protection of the rights and freedoms of others.

Article 10   Freedom of expression
1   Everyone has the right to freedom of expression. This right shall include freedom to hold opinions and to receive and impart information and ideas without interference by public authority and regardless of frontiers. This Article shall not prevent States from requiring the licensing of broadcasting, television or cinema enterprises.
2   The exercise of these freedoms, since it carries with it duties and responsibilities, may be subject to such formalities, conditions, restrictions or penalties as are prescribed by law and are necessary in a democratic society, in the interests of national security, territorial integrity or public safety, for the prevention of disorder or crime, for the protection of health or morals, for the protection of the reputation or rights of others, for preventing the disclosure of information received in confidence, or for maintaining the authority and impartiality of the judiciary.

Article 11   Freedom of assembly and association
1   Everyone has the right to freedom of peaceful assembly and to freedom of association with others, including the right to form and to join trade unions for the protection of his interests.
2   No restrictions shall be placed on the exercise of these rights other than such as are prescribed by law and are necessary in a democratic society in the interests of national security or public safety, for the prevention of disorder or crime, for the protection of health or morals or for the protection of the rights and freedoms of others. This Article shall not prevent the imposition of lawful

restrictions on the exercise of these rights by members of the armed forces, of the police or of the administration of the State.

Article 12   Right to marry

Men and women of marriageable age have the right to marry and to found a family, according to the national laws governing the exercise of this right.

Article 14   Prohibition of discrimination

The enjoyment of the rights and freedoms set forth in this Convention shall be secured without discrimination on any ground such as sex, race, colour, language, religion, political or other opinion, national or social origin, association with a national minority, property, birth or other status.

Article 16   Restrictions on political activity of aliens

Nothing in Articles 10, 11 and 14 shall be regarded as preventing the High Contracting Parties from imposing restrictions on the political activity of aliens.

Article 17   Prohibition of abuse of rights

Nothing in this Convention may be interpreted as implying for any State, group or person any right to engage in any activity or perform any act aimed at the destruction of any of the rights and freedoms set forth herein or at their limitation to a greater extent than is provided for in the Convention.

Article 18   Limitation on use of restrictions on rights

The restrictions permitted under this Convention to the said rights and freedoms shall not be applied for any purpose other than those for which they have been prescribed.

Commencement   2 October 2000: see SI 2000/1851, art 2.

PART II   THE FIRST PROTOCOL

Article 1   Protection of property

Every natural or legal person is entitled to the peaceful enjoyment of his possessions. No one shall be deprived of his possessions except in the public interest and subject to the conditions provided for by law and by the general principles of international law.

The preceding provisions shall not, however, in any way impair the right of a State to enforce such laws as it deems necessary to control the use of property in accordance with the general interest or to secure the payment of taxes or other contributions or penalties.

Article 2   Right to education
No person shall be denied the right to education. In the exercise of any functions which it assumes in relation to education and to teaching, the State shall respect the right of parents to ensure such education and teaching in conformity with their own religious and philosophical convictions.

Article 3   Right to free elections
The High Contracting Parties undertake to hold free elections at reasonable intervals by secret ballot, under conditions which will ensure the free expression of the opinion of the people in the choice of the legislature.

Commencement   2 October 2000: see SI 2000/1851, art 2.

PART III   THE SIXTH PROTOCOL

Article 1   Abolition of the death penalty
The death penalty shall be abolished. No one shall be condemned to such penalty or executed.

Article 2   Death penalty in time of war
A State may make provision in its law for the death penalty in respect of acts committed in time of war or of imminent threat of war; such penalty shall be applied only in the instances laid down in the law and in accordance with its provisions. The State shall communicate to the Secretary General of the Council of Europe the relevant provisions of that law.

Commencement   2 October 2000: see SI 2000/1851, art 2.

SCHEDULE 2   REMEDIAL ORDERS
Section 10

[A.1.230]
Orders
1   (1)   A remedial order may—

(a) contain such incidental, supplemental, consequential or transitional provision as the person making it considers appropriate;
(b) be made so as to have effect from a date earlier than that on which it is made;
(c) make provision for the delegation of specific functions;
(d) make different provision for different cases.

(2)   The power conferred by sub-paragraph (1)(a) includes—

(a) power to amend primary legislation (including primary legislation other than that which contains the incompatible provision); and

(b) power to amend or revoke subordinate legislation (including subordinate legislation other than that which contains the incompatible provision).

(3) A remedial order may be made so as to have the same extent as the legislation which it affects.

(4) No person is to be guilty of an offence solely as a result of the retrospective effect of a remedial order.

Procedure

2   No remedial order may be made unless—

(a) a draft of the order has been approved by a resolution of each House of Parliament made after the end of the period of 60 days beginning with the day on which the draft was laid; or

(b) it is declared in the order that it appears to the person making it that, because of the urgency of the matter, it is necessary to make the order without a draft being so approved.

Orders laid in draft

3   (1)   No draft may be laid under paragraph 2(a) unless—

(a) the person proposing to make the order has laid before Parliament a document which contains a draft of the proposed order and the required information; and

(b) the period of 60 days, beginning with the day on which the document required by this sub-paragraph was laid, has ended.

(2)   If representations have been made during that period, the draft laid under paragraph 2(a) must be accompanied by a statement containing—

(a) a summary of the representations; and

(b) if, as a result of the representations, the proposed order has been changed, details of the changes.

Urgent cases

4   (1)   If a remedial order ('the original order') is made without being approved in draft, the person making it must lay it before Parliament, accompanied by the required information, after it is made.

(2)   If representations have been made during the period of 60 days beginning with the day on which the original order was made, the person making it must (after the end of that period) lay before Parliament a statement containing—

(a) a summary of the representations; and

(b) if, as a result of the representations, he considers it appropriate to make changes to the original order, details of the changes.

(3)   If sub-paragraph (2)(b) applies, the person making the statement must—

(a) make a further remedial order replacing the original order; and

(b) lay the replacement order before Parliament.

(4)   If, at the end of the period of 120 days beginning with the day on which the original order was made, a resolution has not been passed by each House approving the original or replacement order, the order ceases to have effect

(but without that affecting anything previously done under either order or the power to make a fresh remedial order).

Definitions

5   In this Schedule—

'representations' means representations about a remedial order (or proposed remedial order) made to the person making (or proposing to make) it and includes any relevant Parliamentary report or resolution; and

'required information' means—

(a) an explanation of the incompatibility which the order (or proposed order) seeks to remove, including particulars of the relevant declaration, finding or order; and

(b) a statement of the reasons for proceeding under section 10 and for making an order in those terms.

Calculating periods

6   In calculating any period for the purposes of this Schedule, no account is to be taken of any time during which—

(a) Parliament is dissolved or prorogued; or

(b) both Houses are adjourned for more than four days.

Commencement   2 October 2000: see SI 2000/1851, art 2.

SCHEDULE 3   DEROGATION AND RESERVATION
Sections 14 and 15

PART I   DEROGATION

[A.1.231]
The 1988 notification
The United Kingdom Permanent Representative to the Council of Europe presents his compliments to the Secretary General of the Council, and has the honour to convey the following information in order to ensure compliance with the obligations of Her Majesty's Government in the United Kingdom under Article 15(3) of the Convention for the Protection of Human Rights and Fundamental Freedoms signed at Rome on 4 November 1950.

There have been in the United Kingdom in recent years campaigns of organised terrorism connected with the affairs of Northern Ireland which have manifested themselves in activities which have included repeated murder, attempted murder, maiming, intimidation and violent civil disturbance and in bombing and fire raising which have resulted in death, injury and widespread destruction of property. As a result, a public emergency within the meaning of Article 15(1) of the Convention exists in the United Kingdom.

The Government found it necessary in 1974 to introduce and since then, in cases concerning persons reasonably suspected of involvement in terrorism connected with the affairs of Northern Ireland, or of certain offences under the legislation, who have been detained for 48 hours, to exercise powers enabling further detention without charge, for periods of up to five days, on the authority of the Secretary of State. These powers are at present to be found in Section 12 of the Prevention of Terrorism (Temporary Provisions) Act 1984, Article 9 of the Prevention of Terrorism (Supplemental Temporary Provisions) Order 1984 and Article 10 of the Prevention of Terrorism (Supplemental Temporary Provisions) (Northern Ireland) Order 1984.

Section 12 of the Prevention of Terrorism (Temporary Provisions) Act 1984 provides for a person whom a constable has arrested on reasonable grounds of suspecting him to be guilty of an offence under Section 1, 9 or 10 of the Act, or to be or to have been involved in terrorism connected with the affairs of Northern Ireland, to be detained in right of the arrest for up to 48 hours and thereafter, where the Secretary of State extends the detention period, for up to a further five days. Section 12 substantially re-enacted Section 12 of the Prevention of Terrorism (Temporary Provisions) Act 1976 which, in turn, substantially re-enacted Section 7 of the Prevention of Terrorism (Temporary Provisions) Act 1974.

Article 10 of the Prevention of Terrorism (Supplemental Temporary Provisions) (Northern Ireland) Order 1984 (SI 1984/417) and Article 9 of the Prevention of Terrorism (Supplemental Temporary Provisions) Order 1984 (SI 1984/418) were both made under Sections 13 and 14 of and Schedule 3 to the 1984 Act and substantially re-enacted powers of detention in Orders made under the 1974 and 1976 Acts. A person who is being examined under Article 4 of either Order on his arrival in, or on seeking to leave, Northern Ireland or Great Britain for the purpose of determining whether he is or has been involved in terrorism connected with the affairs of Northern Ireland, or whether there are grounds for suspecting that he has committed an offence under Section 9 of the 1984 Act, may be detained under Article 9 or 10, as appropriate, pending the conclusion of his examination. The period of this examination may exceed 12 hours if an examining officer has reasonable grounds for suspecting him to be or to have been involved in acts of terrorism connected with the affairs of Northern Ireland.

Where such a person is detained under the said Article 9 or 10 he may be detained for up to 48 hours on the authority of an examining officer and thereafter, where the Secretary of State extends the detention period, for up to a further five days.

In its judgment of 29 November 1988 in the Case of Brogan and Others, the European Court of Human Rights held that there had been a violation of Article 5(3) in respect of each of the applicants, all of whom had been detained under Section 12 of the 1984 Act. The Court held that even the shortest of the four periods of detention concerned, namely four days and six hours, fell outside the constraints as to time permitted by the first part of Article 5(3). In addition, the Court held that there had been a violation of Article 5(5) in the case of each applicant.

Following this judgment, the Secretary of State for the Home Department informed Parliament on 6 December 1988 that, against the background of the terrorist campaign, and the over-riding need to bring terrorists to justice, the Government did not believe that the maximum period of detention should be reduced. He informed Parliament that the Government were examining the matter with a view to responding to the judgment. On 22 December 1988, the Secretary of State further informed Parliament that it remained the Government's wish, if it could be achieved, to find a judicial process under which extended detention might be reviewed and where appropriate authorised by a judge or other judicial officer. But a further period of reflection and consultation was necessary before the Government could bring forward a firm and final view.

Since the judgment of 29 November 1988 as well as previously, the Government have found it necessary to continue to exercise, in relation to terrorism connected with the affairs of Northern Ireland, the powers described above enabling further detention without charge for periods of up to 5 days, on the authority of the Secretary of State, to the extent strictly required by the exigencies of the situation to enable necessary enquiries and investigations properly to be completed in order to decide whether criminal proceedings should be instituted. To the extent that the exercise of these powers may be inconsistent with the obligations imposed by the Convention the Government has availed itself of the right of derogation conferred by Article 15(1) of the Convention and will continue to do so until further notice.

Dated 23 December 1988.

The 1989 notification
The United Kingdom Permanent Representative to the Council of Europe presents his compliments to the Secretary General of the Council, and has the honour to convey the following information.

In his communication to the Secretary General of 23 December 1988, reference was made to the introduction and exercise of certain powers under section 12 of the Prevention of Terrorism (Temporary Provisions) Act 1984, Article 9 of the Prevention of Terrorism (Supplemental Temporary Provisions) Order 1984 and Article 10 of the Prevention of Terrorism (Supplemental Temporary Provisions) (Northern Ireland) Order 1984.

These provisions have been replaced by section 14 of and paragraph 6 of Schedule 5 to the Prevention of Terrorism (Temporary Provisions) Act 1989, which make comparable provision. They came into force on 22 March 1989. A copy of these provisions is enclosed.

The United Kingdom Permanent Representative avails himself of this opportunity to renew to the Secretary General the assurance of his highest consideration.

23 March 1989.

Commencement 2 October 2000: see SI 2000/1851, art 2.

PART II RESERVATION

[A.1.232]
At the time of signing the present (First) Protocol, I declare that, in view of certain provisions of the Education Acts in the United Kingdom, the principle affirmed in the second sentence of Article 2 is accepted by the United Kingdom only so far as it is compatible with the provision of efficient instruction and training, and the avoidance of unreasonable public expenditure.

Dated 20 March 1952. Made by the United Kingdom Permanent Representative to the Council of Europe.

Commencement 2 October 2000: see SI 2000/1851, art 2.

SCHEDULE 4   JUDICIAL PENSIONS

Section 18(6)

[A.1.233]
Duty to make orders about pensions
1   (1)   The appropriate Minister must by order make provision with respect to pensions payable to or in respect of any holder of a judicial office who serves as an ECHR judge.
(2)   A pensions order must include such provision as the Minister making it considers is necessary to secure that—

(a) an ECHR judge who was, immediately before his appointment as an ECHR judge, a member of a judicial pension scheme is entitled to remain as a member of that scheme;
(b) the terms on which he remains a member of the scheme are those which would have been applicable had he not been appointed as an ECHR judge; and
(c) entitlement to benefits payable in accordance with the scheme continues to be determined as if, while serving as an ECHR judge, his salary was that which would (but for section 18(4)) have been payable to him in respect of his continuing service as the holder of his judicial office.

Contributions
2   A pensions order may, in particular, make provision—

(a) for any contributions which are payable by a person who remains a member of a scheme as a result of the order, and which would otherwise be payable by deduction from his salary, to be made otherwise than by deduction from his salary as an ECHR judge; and
(b) for such contributions to be collected in such manner as may be determined by the administrators of the scheme.

Amendments of other enactments
3   A pensions order may amend any provision of, or made under, a pensions Act in such manner and to such extent as the Minister making the order considers necessary or expedient to ensure the proper administration of any scheme to which it relates.

Definitions
4   In this Schedule—

'appropriate Minister' means—

(a) in relation to any judicial office whose jurisdiction is exercisable exclusively in relation to Scotland, the Secretary of State; and
(b) otherwise, the Lord Chancellor;

'ECHR judge' means the holder of a judicial office who is serving as a judge of the Court;

'judicial pension scheme' means a scheme established by and in accordance
   with a pensions Act;
'pensions Act' means—

(a) the County Courts Act (Northern Ireland) 1959;
(b) the Sheriffs' Pensions (Scotland) Act 1961;
(c) the Judicial Pensions Act 1981; or
(d) the Judicial Pensions and Retirement Act 1993; and

'pensions order' means an order made under paragraph 1.

Commencement   9 November 1998: see s 22(2).

IMMIGRATION AND ASYLUM ACT 1999
(1999 c 33)

Arrangement of Sections

Procedure
51   Procedure   **[A.1.284]**
52   Use of live television links at bail in hearings   **[A.1.285]**

Bail hearings under other enactments
53   Applications for bail in immigration cases   **[A.1.286]**
54   Extension of right to apply for bail hearings   **[A.1.287]**

Grants
55   Grants to voluntary organisations   **[A.1.288]**

PART IV
APPEALS

The appellate authorities
56   The Immigration Appeal Tribunal   **[A.1.289]**
57   Adjudicators   **[A.1.290]**

Appeals
58   General   **[A.1.291]**

Leave to enter
59   Leave to enter the United Kingdom   **[A.1.292]**
60   Limitations on rights of appeal under section 59   **[A.1.293]**

Variation of limited leave to enter or remain
61   Variation of limited leave to enter or remain   **[A.1.294]**
62   Limitations of rights of appeal under section 61   **[A.1.295]**

Deportation
63   Deportation orders   **[A.1.296]**
64   Limitations on rights or appeal under section 63   **[A.1.297]**

Human rights
65   Acts made unlawful by section 6(1) of the Human Rights Act 1998 **[A.1.298]**

Directions for removal
66   Validity of directions for removal   **[A.1.299]**

Objection to destination
67   Removal on objection to destination   **[A.1.300]**
68   Limitations on rights of appeal under section 67   **[A.1.301]**

Asylum
69   Claims for Asylum   **[A.1.302]**
70   Limitations on rights of appeal under section 69   **[A.1.303]**

Removal to safe countries
71   Removal of asylum claimants to safe third countries   **[A.1.304]**

Miscellaneous
72   Miscellaneous limitations on rights of appeal   **[A.1.305]**

PART VII
POWER TO ARREST, SEARCH AND FINGERPRINT

PART I
IMMIGRATION: GENERAL

Leave to enter, or remain in, the United Kingdom

[A.1.234]
1 *(Amends the Immigration Act 1971, s 3.)*

[A.1.235]
2 *(Amends the Immigration Act 1971, s 3.)*

[A.1.236]
3 *(Amends the Immigration Act 1971, s 3.)*

[A.1.237]
4 Accommodation for those temporarily admitted or released from detention
The Secretary of State may provide, or arrange for the provision of, facilities for the accommodation of persons—

(a) temporarily admitted to the United Kingdom under paragraph 21 of Schedule 2 to the 1971 Act;
(b) released from detention under that paragraph; or
(c) released on bail from detention under any provision of the Immigration Acts.

Commencement   On Royal Assent (section 170(3)).

Note   Debates on this section during the passage of the Act bear witness to considerable confusion, with the result that there was little clarification as to how the powers under this section might be used in practice. The section, introduced at Report stage in the House of Lords on 18 October 1999 (*Hansard* HL Report vol 605, no 136, cols 752 to 724), was first debated fully on Third Reading there on 2 November 1999 (*Hansard* HL Report vol 606, no 147, cols 724 to 743). Much of that debate proceeded on the basis that the section was designed to be used to hold new arrivals who had applied for asylum in a centre in Oakington in Cambridge until Ministers clarified that Oakington would be a detention centre under the powers now set out in Part VIII of this Act (Lord Williams of Mostyn, vol 606, no 47, col 733). Section 4 was debated with the powers now contained in the amendments to paragraph 21 of Schedule 2 to the 1971 Immigration Act made under paragraph 62 of Schedule 14 of this Act, for which see the note on that section. These powers could be used independently of the powers under Section 4. However, the new paragraph 21(2B)(b) would allow the Secretary of State to make regulations requiring a person to reside in section

4 accommodation and 'prohibiting him from being absent from that accommodation except in accordance with the restrictions imposed on him' (new paragraph 21(2B)(b)). The House of Lords Select Committee on Delegated Powers and Deregulation in their 27th Report of 27 October characterised this as 'amounting to a power to impose house arrest'. Lord Falconer's comment that 'People will be free to come and go, subject to any conditions imposed' (vol 605, no 136, col 753) did not illuminate how it was envisaged that section 4 accommodation will operate in practice.

It is not just merely the practical operation of the powers that is in question. The legal rights and obligations of the parties, and their relationship to rights and obligations under immigration detention and under the Human Rights Act 1998, is also unclear. Of particular relevance is the case of *Guzzardi v Italy* [1980] 3 EHRR 333 (European Court of Human Rights) where an individual confined to a small island and limited as to the number and types of his social contacts was found to have been deprived of his liberty.

[A.1.238]

5 Charges

(1)   The Secretary of State may, with the approval of the Treasury, make regulations prescribing fees to be paid in connection with applications for—

(a) leave to remain in the United Kingdom;

(b) the variation of leave to enter, or remain in, the United Kingdom;

(c) an indefinite leave stamp to be fixed on the applicant's passport (or travel document) as the result of the renewal or replacement of his previous passport (or travel document).

(2)   If a fee prescribed in connection with an application of a particular kind is payable, no such application is to be entertained by the Secretary of State unless the fee has been paid in accordance with the regulations.

(3)   But—

(a) a fee prescribed in connection with such an application is not payable if the basis on which the application is made is that the applicant is—

(i)   a person making a claim for asylum which claim either has not been determined or has been granted; or

(ii)   a dependant of such a person; and

(b) the regulations may provide for no fee to be payable in prescribed circumstances.

(4)   If no fee is payable in respect of some part of the application, the Secretary of State must entertain that part of the application.

(5)   'Indefinite leave stamp' means a stamp which indicates that the applicant has been granted indefinite leave to enter, or remain in, the United Kingdom.

(6)   'Claim for asylum' has the meaning given in subsection (1) of section 94; and subsection (3) of that section applies for the purposes of this section as it applies for the purposes of Part VI.

(7)   'Dependant' has such meaning as may be prescribed.

Exemption from immigration control

[A.1.239]
6 *(Amends the Immigration Act 1971, s 8(3A).)*

[A.1.240]
7 *(Amends the Immigration Act 1971, s 8.)*

[A.1.241]
8 *(Amends the Immigration Act 1971, s 8).*

Removal from the United Kingdom

[A.1.242]
9 Treatment of certain overstayers
(1)   During the regularisation period overstayers may apply, in the prescribed manner, for leave to remain in the United Kingdom.
(2)   The regularisation period begins on the day prescribed for the purposes of this subsection and is not to be less than three months.
(3)   The regularisation period ends—

(a) on the day prescribed for the purposes of this subsection; or
(b) if later, on the day before that on which section 65 comes into force.

(4)   Section 10 and paragraph 12 of Schedule 15 come into force on the day after that on which the regularisation period ends.
(5)   The Secretary of State must publicise the effect of this section in the way appearing to him to be best calculated to bring it to the attention of those affected.
(6) 'Overstayer' means a person who, having only limited leave to enter or remain in the United Kingdom, remains beyond the time limited by the leave.

Commencement   On Royal Assent (section 170(3)).

Note   See Immigration (Regularisation Period for Overstayers) Regulations 2000 (SI 2000/265), made 7 February 2000 and commenced 8 February 2000. The Regulations set how an application is to be made and include, in Regulation 4(h), a non-exhaustive list of factors to be taken into account in deciding whether to grant the person leave to remain.

Section 10 of this Act makes overstayers subject to administrative removal rather than deportation. This will have the effect of removing their rights of appeal against the decision, save where this appeal is on asylum or Human Rights Act grounds. Section 9 deals with those who will lose existing rights of appeal that have accrued before section 10 comes into effect. These people can apply for leave to remain in the UK during the regularisation period, which commences 1 February 2000 and ends on 2 October 2000 (SI 2000/2444).

Existing rights of appeal are preserved. Thus a full right of appeal against deportation will only exist for those who last entered the UK less than 7 years before the decision to deport (see the Immigration Act 1988, section 5(2), but see also the Asylum and Immigration Appeals Act 1993 and the Immigration (Restricted Right of Appeal Against Deportation) (Exemption) Order 1993, SI 1993/1656)). In other cases there will be a restricted right of appeal against deportation only.

Section 65 provides for a new right of appeal on the grounds that removal would breach the appellant's human rights, and overstayers who do not apply during the regulation period would have a right of appeal under this section. See Immigration (European Economic Area) Regulations 2000 (SI 2000/2326), as amended by SI 2001/865, regulation 36(3)(a) for transitional provisions in relation to those with a right of appeal under SI 2000/2326, as amended.

See also SI 2000/2444, Schedule 2, paragraph 2 .

9(1) The effect of the wording of this section is that the application must be made during the regularisation period – an application made earlier does not bring the applicant within the terms of section 9. Such an applicant is thus at risk of losing appeal rights if the application is not decided before appeal rights are lost.

[A.1.243]
10 Removal of certain persons unlawfully in the United Kingdom
(1) A person who is not a British citizen may be removed from the United Kingdom, in accordance with directions given by an immigration officer, if—

(a) having only a limited leave to enter or remain, he does not observe a condition attached to the leave or remains beyond the time limited by the leave;
(b) he has obtained leave to remain by deception; or
(c) directions ('the first directions') have been given for the removal, under this section, of a person ('the other person') to whose family he belongs.

(2) Directions may not be given under subsection (1)(a) if the person concerned has made an application for leave to remain in accordance with regulations made under section 9.
(3) Directions may not be given under subsection (1)(c) unless the Secretary of State has given the person concerned written notice, not more than eight weeks after the other person left the United Kingdom in accordance with the first directions, that he intends to remove the person concerned from the United Kingdom.
(4) If such a notice is sent by the Secretary of State by first class post, addressed to the person concerned's last known address, it is to be taken to have been received by that person on the second day after the day on which it was posted.
(5) Directions for the removal of a person under subsection (1)(c) cease to have effect if he ceases to belong to the family of the other person.
(6) Directions under this section—

(a) may be given only to persons falling within a prescribed class;
(b) may impose any requirements of a prescribed kind.

(7) In relation to any such directions, paragraphs 10, 11, 16 to 18, 21 and 22 to 24 of Schedule 2 to the 1971 Act (administrative provisions as to control of entry), apply as they apply in relation to directions given under paragraph 8 of that Schedule.
(8) Directions for the removal of a person given under this section invalidate any leave to enter or remain in the United Kingdom given to him before the directions are given or while they are in force.

(9) The costs of complying with a direction given under this section (so far as reasonably incurred) must be met by the Secretary of State.

Commencement   *Subsection 10(6)* 22 May 2000 (SI 2000/1282) otherwise 2 October 2000 (section 9(4) and SI 2000/2444).

Note   See the Immigration (Regularisation Period for Overstayers) Regulations 2000 (SI 2000/265) and the note to section 9 above.

See SI 2000/2444, the 6th Commencement Order, which provides that section 10 does not apply where the Secretary of State has served notice of intention to deport before 2 October 2000, or where the person has applied for leave to remain in accordance with the Immigration (Regularisation Period for Overstayers) Regulations 2000. In such circumstances the deportation will be governed by Sections 5 and 15 of the Immigration Act 1971 and Section 5 of the Immigration Act 1988. See paragraphs 1, 11 and 12 of Schedule 2 to this Act. The Order also makes a consequential amendment to section 46(3)(a) of the Criminal Justice Act 1991 reflecting the change in the position of those persons who were previously liable to deportation under section 3(5) of the Immigration Act 1971 and are now liable to removal under this Section.

See also Immigration (Removal Directions) Regulations 2000 (SI 2000/2243) made 16 August 2000, laid before parliament 24 August 2000 and into force 2 October 2000.

See Immigration (European Economic Area) Regulations 2000 (SI 2000/2326), as amended by SI 2001/865, regulation 26, for the application of this section to those whom it has been decided to remove from the UK in accordance with regulation 23 of SI 2000/2326, as amended.

10(6)(a) See regulation 3 of SI 2000/2243 which prescribes the owners and agents of ships, and the captains of ships about to leave the UK; the owners and agents of aircraft, and the captains of aircraft about to leave the UK; and persons operating an international service (as defined in section 13(6) of the Channel Tunnel Act 1987).

10(6)(b) See regulation 4 of SI 2000/2243 which prescribe the requirements that may be imposed by directions in respect of a person who may be removed from the UK in accordance with section 10(1) (see regulation 4(4)). The requirements prescribed apply only if the directions specify that the person is being removed to a country or territory of which s/he is a national or a citizen or to which there is 'reason to believe' (regulation 4(2)(ii)) that s/he will be admitted. In all cases there is a requirement to remove the person in accordance with arrangements made by an immigration officer (regulation 4(d)). Where the directions are given to owners or agents of ships or aircraft the requirement is to make arrangements for the removal of the person in a ship or aircraft 'specified or indicated' (regulation 4) in the directions. Where the directions are given to a captain of a ship or aircraft about to leave the UK the requirements are to remove the person from the UK in that ship or aircraft. Directions can require a person operating an international service (see note to 10(6)(a) above) to make arrangements for the removal of the person through the tunnel system, but only where the person arrived in the UK through the tunnel system (regulations 4(1)(b) and 4(3)). The Explanatory Note to SI 2000/2243 (Immigration (Removal Directions) Regulations 2000) states that the regulations mirror paragraph 1(1) of Schedule 3 to the Immigration Act 1971.

[A.1.244]
11 Removal of asylum claimants under standing arrangements with member States

(1)   In determining whether a person in relation to whom a certificate has been issued under subsection (2) may be removed from the United Kingdom, a member State is to be regarded as—

(a) a place where a person's life and liberty is not threatened by reason of his race, religion, nationality, membership of a particular social group, or political opinion; and

(b) a place from which a person will not be sent to another country otherwise than in accordance with the Refugee Convention.

(2) Nothing in section 15 prevents a person who has made a claim for asylum ('the claimant') from being removed from the United Kingdom to a member State if—

(a) the Secretary of State has certified that—
   (i) the member State has accepted that, under standing arrangements, it is the responsible State in relation to the claimant's claim for asylum; and
   (ii) in his opinion, the claimant is not a national or citizen of the member State to which he is to be sent;

(b) the certificate has not been set aside on an appeal under section 65.

(3) Unless a certificate has been issued under section 72(2)(a) in relation to a person, he is not to be removed from the United Kingdom—

(a) if he has an appeal under section 65 against the decision to remove him in accordance with this section pending; or
(b) before the time for giving notice of such an appeal has expired.

(4) 'Standing arrangements' means arrangements in force as between member States for determining which state is responsible for considering applications for asylum.

Commencement 2 October 2000 (SI 2444/2000).

[A.1.245]
12 Removal of asylum claimants in other circumstances

(1) Subsection (2) applies if the Secretary of State intends to remove a person who has made a claim for asylum ('the claimant') from the United Kingdom to—

(a) a member State, or a territory which forms part of a member State, otherwise than under standing arrangements; or
(b) a country other than a member State which is designated by order made by the Secretary of State for the purposes of this section.

(2) Nothing in section 15 prevents the claimant's removal if—

(a) the Secretary of State has certified that, in his opinion, the conditions set out in subsection (7) are fulfilled;
(b) the certificate has not been set aside on an appeal under section 65.

(3) Unless a certificate has been issued under section 72(2)(a) in relation to a person, he is not to be removed from the United Kingdom—

(a) if he has an appeal under section 65 against the decision to remove him in accordance with subsection (2) pending; or
(b) before the time for giving notice of such an appeal has expired.

(4) Subsection (5) applies if the Secretary of State intends to remove a person who has made a claim for asylum ('the claimant') from the United Kingdom to a country which is not—

(a) a member State; or

(b) a country designated under subsection (1)(b).

(5)   Nothing in section 15 prevents the claimant's removal if—

(a) the Secretary of State has certified that, in his opinion, the conditions set out in subsection (7) are fulfilled;

(b) the certificate has not been set aside on an appeal under section 65 or 71; and

(c) the time for giving notice of such an appeal has expired and no such appeal is pending.

(6)   For the purposes of subsection (5)(c), an appeal under section 65 is not to be regarded as pending if the Secretary of State has issued a certificate under section 72(2)(a) in relation to the allegation on which it is founded.

(7)   The conditions are that—

(a) he is not a national or citizen of the country to which he is to be sent;

(b) his life and liberty would not be threatened there by reason of his race, religion, nationality, membership of a particular social group, or political opinion; and

(c) the government of that country would not send him to another country otherwise than in accordance with the Refugee Convention.

(8)   'Standing arrangements' has the same meaning as in section 11.

Commencement   Subsection 12(1) 22 May 2000 for the purposes of enabling subordinate legislation to be made under it (SI 2000/1282). Section 12 in full 2 October 2000 (SI 2444/2000).

Note   See The Asylum (Designated Safe Third Countries) Order 2000 (SI 2000/2245) made 16 August 2000, laid before parliament 24 August 2000 and coming into force 2 October 2000. The countries designated in the Order for the purposes of section 12(1)(b) are Canada, Norway, Switzerland and the United States of America. The order replaces the Asylum (Designated Countries of Destination and Designated Safe Third Countries) Order 1996 (SI 1996/2671).

See section 72(2) which limits in country rights of appeal under Section 71 where an asylum claimant has been removed (or is to be removed) to one of these countries or to a Member State of the European Union. The asylum claimant facing such a removal continues to enjoy the 'human rights' appeal rights set out in section 65, save, as set out in section 12(3) and 12(6) and (7), in those cases where the Secretary of State has certified the claim as 'manifestly unfounded' under 72(2)(a). While the aim of sections 11 and 12 is to limit the number of judicial reviews of decisions to remove an asylum claimant to a Member State or designated safe third country, the decision to issue a section 72(2)(a) certificate still remains susceptible to a challenge by judicial review. The limitations on rights of appeal imposed by section 72(2) do not apply to removals to the countries defined in section 11(4).

[A.1.246]
13   Proof of identity of persons to be removed or deported

(1)   This section applies if a person—

(a) is to be removed from the United Kingdom to a country of which he is a national or citizen; but

(b) does not have a valid passport or other document establishing his identity and nationality or citizenship and permitting him to travel.

(2)   If the country to which the person is to be removed indicates that he will not be admitted to it unless identification data relating to him are provided by the Secretary of State, he may provide them with such data.

(3)   In providing identification data, the Secretary of State must not disclose whether the person concerned has made a claim for asylum.

(4)   For the purposes of paragraph 4(1) of Schedule 4 to the Data Protection Act 1998, the provision under this section of identification data is a transfer of personal data which is necessary for reasons of substantial public interest.

(5)   'Identification data' means—

(a)   fingerprints taken under section 141; or
(b)   data collected in accordance with regulations made under section 144.

(6)   'Removed' means removed as a result of directions given under section 10 or under Schedule 2 or 3 to the 1971 Act.

Commencement   11 December 2000 (SI 2000/3099).

Note   See ss 141 and 144 of this Act, and the notes thereto.

[A.1.247]
14 Escorts for persons removed from the United Kingdom under directions

(1)   Directions for, or requiring arrangements to be made for, the removal of a person from the United Kingdom may include or be amended to include provision for the person who is to be removed to be accompanied by an escort consisting of one or more persons specified in the directions.

(2)   The Secretary of State may by regulations make further provision supplementing subsection (1).

(3)   The regulations may, in particular, include provision—

(a)   requiring the person to whom the directions are given to provide for the return of the escort to the United Kingdom;
(b)   requiring him to bear such costs in connection with the escort (including, in particular, remuneration) as may be prescribed;
(c)   as to the cases in which the Secretary of State is to bear those costs;
(d)   prescribing the kinds of expenditure which are to count in calculating the costs incurred in connection with escorts.

Commencement   1 March 2000 (SI 2000/168).

[A.1.248]
15 Protection of claimants from removal or deportation

(1)   During the period beginning when a person makes a claim for asylum and ending when the Secretary of State gives him notice of the decision on the claim, he may not be removed from, or required to leave, the United Kingdom.

(2)   Subsection (1) does not prevent—

(a)   directions for his removal being given during that period;
(b)   a deportation order being made against him during that period.

(3)   But no such direction or order is to have effect during that period.

(4)   This section is to be treated as having come into force on 26 July 1993.

Commencement On Royal Assent (section 170(3)).

Note Given limited retrospective effect by subsection (4). This section replaces section 6 of the Asylum and Immigration Appeals Act 1993. That section had given rise to litigation as to whether the Secretary of State had power to serve decisions on asylum applications and removal directions or a deportation order simultaneously, as occurred when service was effected by post. The dispute was decided in the Secretary of State's favour subsequent to the passage of this Act by the judgment of *Vladic v Secretary of State for the Home Department* [1998] AR 542, CA, but against him in *Sanusii* [1999] INLR 198, CA.

This was the mischief that this section was stated to address. However, the terms of the section are much broader and it is perhaps inappropriately named. It would allow removal directions to be given or a deportation order made prior to a decision being made on the asylum application. Ministers have stated that it will not be used in this manner. Lord Williams of Mostyn, on 18 October concluding the debate at Report stage in House of Lords, where the section was first introduced, stated 'The directions will not be served until there is a decision on the claim' (*Hansard* HL Report, vol 605, no 136, col 785). He reaffirmed this at Third Reading on 2 November 1999 when it was put to him again, and stated 'where someone has applied for asylum a deportation order will not be signed, let alone served, unless and until we have concluded that he is not a refugee . . . what we want is a sensible opportunity to provide both documents in one envelope' (vol 606, no 147, cols 766 to 767). It remain unclear why, given these assurances, the government rejected amendments that would have provided for the simultaneous service of the decision and the removal directions but precluded the service of the removal directions or decision to deport prior to the service of the decision on the asylum application (vol 605, no 136, cols 778 to 788).

15(4) gives the section retrospective effect to the date when the disputed section 6 of the 1993 Act first came into force. This covers cases where the refusal of asylum and the removal directions or deportation order were served simultaneously but in the light of Ministerial undertakings it must be doubtful whether this section would serve to regularise a situation where the removal directions or deportation order had been served prior to the refusal of the asylum claim.

See paragraph 102 of Schedule 14 for consequential amendments.

Provision of financial security

[A.1.249]
16   Security on grant of entry clearance
(1)   In such circumstances as may be specified, the Secretary of State may require security to be given, with respect to a person applying for entry clearance, before clearance is given.
(2)   In such circumstances as may be specified—

(a) the Secretary of State may accept security with respect to a person who is applying for entry clearance but for whom security is not required; and
(b) in determining whether to give clearance, account may be taken of any security so provided.

(3)   'Security' means—

(a) the deposit of a sum of money by the applicant, his agent or any other person, or

(b) the provision by the applicant, his agent or any other person of a financial guarantee of a specified kind,

with a view to securing that the applicant will, if given leave to enter the United Kingdom for a limited period, leave the United Kingdom at the end of that period.

(4)   Immigration rules must make provision as to the circumstances in which a security provided under this section—

(a) is to be repaid, released or otherwise cancelled; or
(b) is to be forfeited or otherwise realised by the Secretary of State.

(5)   No security provided under this section may be forfeited or otherwise realised unless the person providing it has been given an opportunity, in accordance with immigration rules, to make representations to the Secretary of State.

(6)   Immigration rules may, in particular—

(a) fix the maximum amount that may be required, or accepted, by way of security provided under this section;
(b) specify the form and manner in which such a security is to be given or may be accepted;
(c) make provision, where such a security has been forfeited or otherwise realised, for the person providing it to be reimbursed in such circumstances as may be specified;
(d) make different provision for different cases or descriptions of case.

(7)   'Specified' means specified by immigration rules.

(8)   Any security forfeited or otherwise realised by the Secretary of State under this section must be paid into the Consolidated Fund.

[A.1.250]
17   Provision of further security on extension of leave
(1)   This section applies if security has been provided under section 16(1) or (2) with respect to a person who, having entered the United Kingdom (with leave to do so), applies—

(a) to extend his leave to enter the United Kingdom; or
(b) for leave to remain in the United Kingdom for a limited period.

(2)   The Secretary of State may refuse the application if security of such kind as the Secretary of State considers appropriate is not provided, or continued, with respect to the applicant.

(3)   Immigration rules must make provision as to the circumstances in which a security provided under this section—

(a) is to be repaid, released or otherwise cancelled; or
(b) is to be forfeited or otherwise realised by the Secretary of State.

(4)   No security provided under this section may be forfeited or otherwise realised unless the person providing it has been given an opportunity, in accordance with immigration rules, to make representations to the Secretary of State.

(5)   Subsection (7) of section 16 applies in relation to this section as it applies in relation to that section.

(6)   Any security forfeited or otherwise realised by the Secretary of State under this section must be paid into the Consolidated Fund.

Information

[A.1.251]
18 *(Amends the Immigration Act 1971, Sch 2, para 27.)*

[A.1.252]
19 *(Amends the Immigration Act 1971, Sch 2, para 27.)*

[A.1.253]
20 Supply of information to Secretary of State
(1)   This section applies to information held by—

(a) a chief officer of police;
(b) the Director General of the National Criminal Intelligence Service;
(c) the Director General of the National Crime Squad;
(d) the Commissioners of Customs and Excise, or a person providing services to them in connection with the provision of those services;
(e) a person with whom the Secretary of State has made a contract or other arrangements under section 95 or 98 or a sub-contractor of such a person; or
(f) any specified person, for purposes specified in relation to that person.

(2)   The information may be supplied to the Secretary of State for use for immigration purposes.
(3)   'Immigration purposes' means any of the following—

(a) the administration of immigration control under the Immigration Acts;
(b) the prevention, detection, investigation or prosecution of criminal offences under those Acts;
(c) the imposition of penalties or charges under Part II;
(d) the provision of support for asylum-seekers and their dependants under Part VI;
(e) such other purposes as may be specified.

(4)   'Chief officer of police' means—

(a) the chief officer of police for a police area in England and Wales;
(b) the chief constable of a police force maintained under the Police (Scotland) Act 1967;
(c) the Chief Constable of the Royal Ulster Constabulary.

(5)   'Specified' means specified in an order made by the Secretary of State.
(6) This section does not limit the circumstances in which information may be supplied apart from this section.

Commencement   1 January 2000 (SI 1999/3190).

Note   *20(1)* No extra persons have yet been specified under subsection (f). Subsection (e) allows information to be provided by those with whom the Secretary of State has contracted, and their sub-contractors, under the support provisions of Part VI. Section 95(1) states that the Secretary of State 'may provide, or arrange for the provision of support' for asylum seekers and/or their dependants but makes no express provision as to the contracts into which he may enter. Nor does it set out the persons with whom he may contract.

Similarly with section 98, which is concerned with temporary or emergency support until a person's eligibility for support under section 95 has been determined. Given that section 20(2) states that information 'may' be provided, and imposes no duty, it would not appear to override any express or implied terms in these contracts as to provision of information to the Secretary of State.

20(3) No extra purposes have yet been specified under subsection (e). The scope of the provisions in force is unclear, particularly with respect to the persons specified in subsection 1(e).

[A.1.254]
21 Supply of information by Secretary of State

(1)   This section applies to information held by the Secretary of State in connection with the exercise of functions under any of the Immigration Acts.

(2)   The information may be supplied to—

(a) a chief officer of police, for use for police purposes;
(b) the Director General of the National Criminal Intelligence Service, for use for NCIS purposes;
(c) the Director General of the National Crime Squad, for use for NCS purposes;
(d) the Commissioners of Customs and Excise, or a person providing services to them, for use for customs purposes; or
(e) any specified person, for use for purposes specified in relation to that person.

(3)   'Police purposes' means any of the following—

(a) the prevention, detection, investigation or prosecution of criminal offences;
(b) safeguarding national security;
(c) such other purposes as may be specified.

(4)   'NCIS purposes' means any of the functions of the National Criminal Intelligence Service mentioned in section 2 of the Police Act 1997.

(5)   'NCS purposes' means any of the functions of the National Crime Squad mentioned in section 48 of that Act.

(6)   'Customs purposes' means any of the Commissioners' functions in relation to—

(a) the prevention, detection, investigation or prosecution of criminal offences;
(b) the prevention, detection or investigation of conduct in respect of which penalties which are not criminal penalties are provided for by or under any enactment;
(c) the assessment or determination of penalties which are not criminal penalties;
(d) checking the accuracy of information relating to, or provided for purposes connected with, any matter under the care and management of the Commissioners or any assigned matter (as defined by section 1(1) of the Customs and Excise Management Act 1979);
(e) amending or supplementing any such information (where appropriate);
(f) legal or other proceedings relating to anything mentioned in paragraphs (a) to (e);
(g) safeguarding national security; and
(h) such other purposes as may be specified.

(7) 'Chief officer of police' and 'specified' have the same meaning as in section 20.

(8) This section does not limit the circumstances in which information may be supplied apart from this section.

Commencement 1 January 2000 (SI 1999/3190).

Note See notes on section 20, which deals with provision of information to the Secretary of State. This section deals with supply of information by him. Providers of support under Part VI have not been expressly mentioned in this section and no persons or purposes other than those set out on the face of the Act have yet been specified.

Employment: code of practice

[A.1.255]
22 *(Amends the Immigration and Asylum Act 1996, s 8.)*

Monitoring entry clearance

[A.1.256]
23 Monitoring refusals of entry clearance

(1) The Secretary of State must appoint a person to monitor, in such a manner as the Secretary of State may determine, refusals of entry clearance in cases where there is, as a result of section 60(5), no right of appeal.

(2) But the Secretary of State may not appoint a member of his staff.

(3) The monitor must make an annual report on the discharge of his functions to the Secretary of State.

(4) The Secretary of State must lay a copy of any report made to him under subsection (3) before each House of Parliament.

(5) The Secretary of State may pay to the monitor such fees and allowances as he may determine.

Commencement 2 October 2000 (SI 2000/2444).

Reporting suspicious marriages

[A.1.257]
24 Duty to report suspicious marriages
(1) Subsection (3) applies if—

(a) a superintendent registrar to whom a notice of marriage has been given under section 27 of the Marriage Act 1949,

(b) any other person who, under section 28(2) of that Act, has attested a declaration accompanying such a notice,

(c) a district registrar to whom a marriage notice or an approved certificate has been submitted under section 3 of the Marriage (Scotland) Act 1977, or

(d) a registrar or deputy registrar to whom notice has been given under section 13 of the Marriages (Ireland) Act 1844 or section 4 of the Marriage Law (Ireland) Amendment Act 1863,

has reasonable grounds for suspecting that the marriage will be a sham marriage.

(2)   Subsection (3) also applies if—

(a) a marriage is solemnized in the presence of a registrar of marriages or, in relation to Scotland, an authorised registrar (within the meaning of the Act of 1977); and

(b) before, during or immediately after solemnization of the marriage, the registrar has reasonable grounds for suspecting that the marriage will be, or is, a sham marriage.

(3)   The person concerned must report his suspicion to the Secretary of State without delay and in such form and manner as may be prescribed by regulations.

(4)   The regulations are to be made—

(a) in relation to England and Wales, by the Registrar General for England and Wales with the approval of the Chancellor of the Exchequer;

(b) in relation to Scotland, by the Secretary of State after consulting the Registrar General of Births, Deaths and Marriages for Scotland;

(c) in relation to Northern Ireland, by the Secretary of State after consulting the Registrar General in Northern Ireland.

(5)   'Sham marriage' means a marriage (whether or not void)—

(a) entered into between a person ('A') who is neither a British citizen nor a national of an EEA State other than the United Kingdom and another person (whether or not such a citizen or such a national); and

(b) entered into by A for the purpose of avoiding the effect of one or more provisions of United Kingdom immigration law or the immigration rules.

Commencement   1 January 2001 (SI 2000/2698).

Note   See also Part IX of this Act and the notes thereto. As explained therein, the transitional provisions of The Immigration and Asylum Act 1999 (Commencement No 8 and Transitional Provisions) Order 2000 (SI 2000/3099) mean that this section applies only to marriages of which notice had been entered into the marriage notice book before 1 January 2001. To marriages entered into the book before that date, the provisions of the Marriage Act 1949 continue to apply.

Immigration control: facilities and charges

[A.1.258]
25   Provision of facilities for immigration control at ports
(1)   The person responsible for the management of a control port ('the manager') must provide the Secretary of State free of charge with such facilities at the port as the Secretary of State may direct as being reasonably necessary for, or in connection with, the operation of immigration control there.

(2)   Before giving such a direction, the Secretary of State must consult such persons likely to be affected by it as he considers appropriate.

(3)   If the Secretary of State gives such a direction, he must send a copy of it to the person appearing to him to be the manager.

(4)   If the manager persistently fails to comply with the direction (or part of it), the Secretary of State may—

(a)   in the case of a control port which is not a port of entry, revoke any approval in relation to the port given under paragraph 26(1) of Schedule 2 to the 1971 Act;

(b)   in the case of a control port which is a port of entry, by order revoke its designation as a port of entry.

(5)   A direction under this section is enforceable, on the application of the Secretary of State—

(a)   by injunction granted by a county court; or

(b)   in Scotland, by an order under section 45 of the Court of Session Act 1988.

(6)   'Control port' means a port in which a control area is designated under paragraph 26(3) of Schedule 2 to the 1971 Act.

(7)   'Facilities' means accommodation, facilities, equipment and services of a class or description specified in an order made by the Secretary of State.

[A1.259]
26   Charges: immigration control

(1)   The Secretary of State may, at the request of any person and in consideration of such charges as he may determine, make arrangements—

(a)   for the provision at any control port of immigration officers or facilities in addition to those (if any) needed to provide a basic service at the port;

(b)   for the provision of immigration officers or facilities for dealing with passengers of a particular description or in particular circumstances.

(2)   'Control port' has the same meaning as in section 25.

(3)   'Facilities' includes equipment.

(4)   'Basic service' has such meaning as may be prescribed.

Charges: travel documents

[A.1.260]
27   Charges: travel documents

(1)   The Secretary of State may, with the approval of the Treasury, make regulations prescribing fees to be paid in connection with applications to him for travel documents.

(2)   If a fee is prescribed in connection with an application of a particular kind, no such application is to be entertained by the Secretary of State unless the fee has been paid in accordance with the regulations.

(3)   In respect of any period before the coming into force of this section, the Secretary of State is to be deemed always to have had power to impose charges in connection with—

(a) applications to him for travel documents; or

(b) the issue by him of travel documents.

(4) 'Travel document' does not include a passport.

Commencement On Royal Assent (section 170(3)).

Note *27(2)* The use of the word 'always' in sub-section (2) gives the section unusually broad retrospective effect.

The Secretary of State has always charged fees for travel documents, but as the Explanatory Notes delicately put it 'there has not previously been an express power to do so which covered the full range of travel documents'. This lacuna had led to the setting up of a refund scheme for a limited period in 1999 and the history of the matter is set out in Hansard for 18 October 1999, the Report stage debate in the House of Lords where this section was introduced (HL report, vol 605, no 136, cols 839 to 841).

This section should be read with section 166, which allows for the imposition of different fees in different cases.

Offences

[A1.261]
28 *(Amends the Immigration Act 1971, s 24.)*

[A1.262]
29 *(Amends the Immigration Act 1971, s 25.)*

[A.1.263]
30 *(Amends the Immigration Act 1971, s 26.)*

[A.1.264]
31 Defences based on Article 31(1) of the Refugee Convention
(1) It is a defence for a refugee charged with an offence to which this section applies to show that, having come to the United Kingdom directly from a country where his life or freedom was threatened (within the meaning of the Refugee Convention), he—

(a) presented himself to the authorities in the United Kingdom without delay;

(b) showed good cause for his illegal entry or presence; and

(c) made a claim for asylum as soon as was reasonably practicable after his arrival in the United Kingdom.

(2) If, in coming from the country where his life or freedom was threatened, the refugee stopped in another country outside the United Kingdom, subsection (1) applies only if he shows that he could not reasonably have expected to be given protection under the Refugee Convention in that other country.

(3) In England and Wales and Northern Ireland the offences to which this section applies are any offence, and any attempt to commit an offence, under—

(a) Part I of the Forgery and Counterfeiting Act 1981 (forgery and connected offences);

(b) section 24A of the 1971 Act (deception); or

(c) section 26(1)(d) of the 1971 Act (falsification of documents).

(4)   In Scotland, the offences to which this section applies are those—

(a) of fraud,

(b) of uttering a forged document,

(c) under section 24A of the 1971 Act (deception), or

(d) under section 26(1)(d) of the 1971 Act (falsification of documents),

and any attempt to commit any of those offences.

(5)   A refugee who has made a claim for asylum is not entitled to the defence provided by subsection (1) in relation to any offence committed by him after making that claim.

(6)   'Refugee' has the same meaning as it has for the purposes of the Refugee Convention.

(7)   If the Secretary of State has refused to grant a claim for asylum made by a person who claims that he has a defence under subsection (1), that person is to be taken not to be a refugee unless he shows that he is.

(8)   A person who—

(a) was convicted in England and Wales or Northern Ireland of an offence to which this section applies before the commencement of this section, but

(b) at no time during the proceedings for that offence argued that he had a defence based on Article 31(1),

may apply to the Criminal Cases Review Commission with a view to his case being referred to the Court of Appeal by the Commission on the ground that he would have had a defence under this section had it been in force at the material time.

(9)   A person who—

(a) was convicted in Scotland of an offence to which this section applies before the commencement of this section, but

(b) at no time during the proceedings for that offence argued that he had a defence based on Article 31(1),

may apply to the Scottish Criminal Cases Review Commission with a view to his case being referred to the High Court of Justiciary by the Commission on the ground that he would have had a defence under this section had it been in force at the material time.

(10)   The Secretary of State may by order amend—

(a) subsection (3), or

(b) subsection (4),

by adding offences to those for the time being listed there.

(11) Before making an order under subsection (10)(b), the Secretary of State must consult the Scottish Ministers.

Commencement   On Royal Assent (section 170(3)).

Note   During the passage of the Act, judgment was given in *Adimi, Sorani and Kaizu* [1999] TLR 596, High Court which examined the United Kingdom's obligations under Article 31(1) of the United Nations Convention on the Status of Refugees. Article 31(1) states:

'The Contracting States shall not impose penalties, on account of their illegal entry or presence, on refugees who, coming directly from a territory where their life or freedom was threatened in the sense of Article 1, enter or are present in their territory without authorisation, provided they present themselves without delay to the authorities and show good cause for their illegal entry or presence.'

The court in *Adimi* held that the United Kingdom, in prosecuting 'presumptive refugees' travelling on false documents for offences of deception, was in breach of its obligations under this Article. The court left open to the government the means by which it would bring its practice into line with its international obligations. Ministers state that their approach is twofold. First, they have issued guidance to the Crown Prosecution Service as to when charges should be brought in the first place. Lord Williams of Mostyn stated on 18 October 1999 during the Report stage debate in the House of Lords that 'The bulk of prospective prosecutions will be dealt with by the administrative guidance. However, there will be cases where administrative arrangements are not perfect . . . It is important, as it seems to us, to have the defence available' (Hansard HL report vol 605, no 606, col 855) and further 'If inappropriate prosecutions get through the sieve, the defence exists' (col 857). This section provides for that defence. The *Adimi* case has led to successful applications for compensation for those imprisoned in violation of the UK's obligations under Article 31. *The Guardian* newspaper of 14 March 2001 carried details of one such case, including an interview with the applicants' representative, Fiona Lindsley of Birnberg Pierce solicitors. In that case a married couple were prosecuted in 1998 for travelling on false documents. They were advised to plead guilty by a duty solicitor on the basis that they had no defence to the charge. They were convicted, and each spent six months in prison, he in Wormwood Scrubs, she in Holloway. They were subsequently recognised as refugees. Ms Lindsley indicates in the article that she drew on official reports detailing conditions in Wormwood Scrubs in making the applications for compensation. The couple were awarded £40,000 each. The payments were made from the Home Office *ex gratia* compensation scheme, the fund used for miscarriages of justice cases.

31(1) and 31(6) provide that the defence is only available to a refugee. The section does not prescribe the procedure to be followed where a prosecution is brought against an asylum seeker whose application for refugee status has yet to be determined.

31(1) subsections (a) to (c) limit those who can invoke the defence by reference to the timing and circumstances of the claim for asylum. Subsections (1)(a) and 1(b) reflect the wording of Article 31. The High Court in *Adimi* considered the interpretation of the phrases 'without delay' and 'good cause' in Article 31. They rejected the argument that 'without delay' necessarily meant as soon as the asylum seeker arrived at passport control but left open the precise scope of the phrase. They stated that the need to show 'good cause' 'will be satisfied by a genuine refugee showing that he was reasonably travelling on false papers'. Article 31 contains no equivalent to subsection 31(1)(c) but the scope of the meaning of 'without delay' as addressed by the High Court in *Adimi* is relevant to this sub-section also.

31(2) and 31(7) A procedural problem could also arise in respect of this subsection. There is a risk that the question of whether the asylum seeker could have been expected to be given protection in the third country will arise both in the criminal proceedings and before those dealing with the application for asylum, whether in the context of deciding whether the person can be removed to a third country or in determining the asylum claim. Sub-section (7) appears expressly to envisage such a conflict, without making clear how it is to be resolved. The Explanatory Notes state 'where the Secretary of State has refused to grant a claim for asylum that person is taken not to be a refugee unless he can show that he is, eg by means of other legal proceedings, including an appeal to the Immigration Appellate Authority'.

Article 31 uses the phrase 'coming directly' from a country where the refugee's life or freedom was threatened. The court in *Adimi* examined the meaning of this phrase and concluded that 'any merely short-term stopover en route to such intended sanctuary cannot forfeit the protection of the Article . . . the main touchstones by which exclusion from protection should be judged are the length of stay in the intermediate country, the reasons for delaying there (even a substantive delay in an unsafe third country would be reasonable were the time spent trying to acquire the means of travelling on) and whether or not the refugee sought or found there protection de jure or de facto from the persecution they were fleeing'. Subsection (2) does not use the phrase 'coming directly' but employs a novel term of phrase 'stopped in'. The interpretation of this phrase raises important questions, particularly in the light of Lord Williams' statement at Third Reading on 2 November 1999 that the government had employed a narrower definition than the court in *Adimi* (*Hansard* HL Report, vol 606, no 147, col 784).

Is the defence to be denied a person who has not been returned to a third country, and whose asylum application the UK has agreed to consider substantively, for example in accordance with the provisions of The Dublin Convention, the convention determining the state responsible for examining applications for asylum lodged in one of the member states of the EU? If so in what circumstances? The interaction of this provision with the UK's approach to persons who remained airside in the third country is also in doubt. In the debates on the Bill which became the 1996 Asylum and Immigration Act, the then Minister stated '*where we are satisfied that an applicant had remained airside during any transit period in a third country, we would not normally seek removal to that country*' (House of Commons, *Hansard* 23 January 1996, Report of Standing Committee D, col 260). This statement reflects the contents of the *Airside Transits* Circular to Immigration Staff of 13 01 94.

See *R v Crown Prosecution Service on application by (1) MS. 2(SG), (3) RSD & (4) MH* (CO/1754/00, CO/1755/00, CO/1756/00, CO/1922/00). These were applications for judicial review of the decision of the Crown Prosecution to prosecute the applicants. The applicants had been charged with using false travel documents. They were asylum seekers. The Immigration Service and the Crown Prosecution Service contended that the applicants could not avail themselves of defences based on Article 31(1). The applicants sought judicial review of the decision on the grounds that the prosecutions were unlawful and in breach of Article 31 and/or the Draft Memorandum of Good Practice in respect of such cases. Subsequent to the applications for judicial review, the CPS agreed to review the decisions to prosecute and decided to discontinue all the prosecutions. The judicial review proceedings were thus settled with a consent order.

31(5) appears to distinguish between the person who presents a false document, is found out and then makes an application for asylum and a person who claims asylum on arrival but then denies to the Immigration Officer that the document s/he is carrying is false, in favour of the former.

31(7) and (8) The provision has retrospective effect. These subsections provide the mechanism by which those previously convicted may seek to have their cases re-examined.

PART II
CARRIERS' LIABILITY

Clandestine entrants

[A.1.265]
32 Penalty for carrying clandestine entrants
(1)   A person is a clandestine entrant if—

(a) he arrives in the United Kingdom concealed in a vehicle, ship or aircraft,
(b) he passes, or attempts to pass, through immigration control concealed in a vehicle, or
(c) he arrives in the United Kingdom on a ship or aircraft, having embarked—
  (i)   concealed in a vehicle; and
  (ii) at a time when the ship or aircraft was outside the United Kingdom,

and claims, or indicates that he intends to seek, asylum in the United Kingdom or evades, or attempts to evade, immigration control.
(2)   The person (or persons) responsible for a clandestine entrant is (or are together) liable to—

(a) a penalty of the prescribed amount in respect of the clandestine entrant; and
(b) an additional penalty of that amount in respect of each person who was concealed with the clandestine entrant in the same transporter.

(3)   A penalty imposed under this section must be paid to the Secretary of State before the end of the prescribed period.
(4)   Payment of the full amount of a penalty by one or more of the persons responsible for the clandestine entrant discharges the liability of each of the persons responsible for that entrant.
(5)   In the case of a clandestine entrant to whom subsection (1)(a) applies, each of the following is a responsible person—

(a) if the transporter is a ship or aircraft, the owner or captain;
(b) if it is a vehicle (but not a detached trailer), the owner, hirer or driver of the vehicle;
(c) if it is a detached trailer, the owner, hirer or operator of the trailer.

(6)   In the case of a clandestine entrant to whom subsection (1)(b) or (c) applies, each of the following is a responsible person—

(a) if the transporter is a detached trailer, the owner, hirer or operator of the trailer;
(b) if it is not, the owner, hirer or driver of the vehicle.

(7)   Subject to any defence provided by section 34, it is immaterial whether a responsible person knew or suspected—

(a) that the clandestine entrant was concealed in the transporter; or
(b) that there were one or more other persons concealed with the clandestine entrant in the same transporter.

(8)   Subsection (9) applies if a transporter ('the carried transporter') is itself being carried in or on another transporter.
(9)   If a person is concealed in the carried transporter, the question whether

any other person is concealed with that person in the same transporter is to be determined by reference to the carried transporter and not by reference to the transporter in or on which it is carried.

(10) 'Immigration control' means United Kingdom immigration control and includes any United Kingdom immigration control operated in a prescribed control zone outside the United Kingdom.

Commencement Subsections 2(a), (3) and (10) 6 December 1999 (SI 1999/3190) for the purposes of enabling subordinate legislation to be made under them. 3 April 2000 for the purposes of clandestine entrants within the meaning of section 32(1) other than those who (a) within the meaning of Part II of the Act arrive in the United Kingdom concealed otherwise than in a vehicle, and (b) are clandestine entrants by virtue of section 32(1)(a) of this Act (SI 2000/464).

18 September 2000 (SI 2000/2444) in so far as not already in force for the purposes of section 39 (Rail freight) and any regulations made under it.

Note The Carriers' Liability (Clandestine Entrants and the Sale of Transporters) Regulations 2001 (SI 2001/685) were modified before coming into force by the Carriers' Liability (Clandestine Entrants and the Sale of Transporters) (Amendment) Regulations (SI 2001/311) which came into force 1 March 2001. All the amendments were consequential upon the extension of the regulations to cover rail freight, as described in the following paragraph. The Regulations, as modified, came into force 3 April 2001. See also the Carriers' Liability (Clandestine Entrants) (Code of Practice) Order 2001 (2001/684), into force 3 April 2001 and the note to section 33 below.

See also the Carriers' Liability (Clandestine Entrants) (Application to Rail Freight) Regulations 2001 (SI 2001/280), regulation 3. The regulations apply only to those who arrive in the UK concealed in a rail freight wagon and who claim, or indicate that they intend to seek asylum in the UK or evade, or attempt to evade, immigration control. In other words, in applying carriers' liability in respect of rail freight, the regulations track section 32(1)(a), but contain no equivalent of 32(1)(b) or 32(1)(c). Where rail freight is concerned, the carrier is not liable for the person concealed at an earlier stage of the journey, but who is not concealed at the time of arrival in the UK and who makes no attempt to evade immigration control. Regulation 4 applies sections 32(2)-(5), (7) and (10), with modifications, to rail freight.

32(2) 'liable to a penalty'. See *R v Secretary of State for the Home Department ex p Balbo B & C Auto Transporti Internazionali* (2001) Times, 22 March, QBD, reasons for refusal on a preliminary issue, given 22 March 2001, in which this phrase was construed. The case decided that the owner of a vehicle in which clandestine entrants were found had an alternative remedy to judicial review of the Secretary of State's decision to issue a notice of liability. The remedy available to an owner contending that s/he has a defence under this Section is to defend proceedings brought by the Secretary of State after the time prescribed for payment of the penalty had expired. The owners served a notice of objection to the Secretary of State's penalty notice served on them under section 35(7), but the Secretary of State maintained that the penalty was payable. The penalty notice gave a deadline for payment, and made no mention of the penalty being recoverable by the Secretary of State through the courts. The owners therefore believed that their only recourse was judicial review. Lord Justice Brooke, giving the reasons of the court, disagreed. Were the owners' reading correct, then this would make the Secretary of State the sole arbiter of whether the owner had a viable defence. This could not have been parliament's intention: it would be a clear breach of Article 6(1) ECHR, because it would make the Secretary of State judge in his own cause. The owners should instead wait until the Secretary of State sued for payment, and plead section 34 in their defence in those proceedings. The court paid special attention to the words 'liable to a penalty'. The issue in the proceedings would be whether the owners were indeed 'liable to a penalty' or whether they had a defence under section 34. If they were not liable to penalty, that would be the end of the section 35 procedure. Leave to sell the vehicle under section 37, if sought, would only be given if it were proven that the owner of the vehicle was 'liable to a penalty': ie that s/he did not have a section 34 defence.

The amount prescribed is £2000 (SI 2000/685, reg 3).

32(3) The period prescribed is 60 days from the date on which the responsibility person, or the first responsible person served, where there is more than one, was served with the penalty notice. No account is taken of any period during which the Secretary of State is in receipt of a notice of objection but has not notified his determination under section 35(8) to the person who objects (SI 2000/685, regulation 4).

32(7) See SI 2000/684 and the note to section 33 below.

32(10) The control zone at Coquelles in France has been prescribed as a control zone for the purposes of this section (see SI 2000/685, regulation 5(1)).

[A.1.266]
33 Code of practice
(1)   The Secretary of State must issue a code of practice to be followed by any person operating a system for preventing the carriage of clandestine entrants.

(2)   Before issuing the code, the Secretary of State must—

(a) consult such persons as he considers appropriate; and

(b) lay a draft before both Houses of Parliament.

(3)   The requirement of subsection (2)(a) may be satisfied by consultation before the passing of this Act.
(4)   After laying the draft code before Parliament, the Secretary of State may bring the code into operation by an order.
(5)   The Secretary of State may from time to time revise the whole or any part of the code and issue the code as revised.
(6)   Subsections (2) and (4) also apply to any revision, or proposed revision, of the code.

Commencement   6 December 1999 (SI 1999/3190).

Note   The Immigration and Asylum Act 1999: Civil Penalty: Code of Practice for Vehicles was laid before parliament in draft on 3 March 2000 and brought into operation on 3 April 2000, by SI 2000/685, as amended by SI 2001/311. See SI 2001/280, regs 4 and 5, applying this section, with modifications, to rail freight. See the Carriers' Liability (Clandestine Entrants) (Code of Practice for Rail Freight) Order 2001 (SI 2001/312), into force 1 March 2001. The Civil Penalty: Code of Practice for Rail Freight Wagons was laid in draft before both Houses of Parliament on 6 February 2001 and came into operation on 1 March 2001, by operation of SI 2001/301.

Copies of the Codes of Practice for both road vehicles and rail freight may be found on the Home Office website.

[A.1.267]
34 Defences to claim that penalty is due under section 32
(1)   This section applies if it is alleged that a person ('the carrier') is liable to a penalty under section 32.

(2)   It is a defence for the carrier to show that he, or an employee of his who was directly responsible for allowing the clandestine entrant to be concealed, was acting under duress.

(3)   It is also a defence for the carrier to show that—

(a) he did not know, and had no reasonable grounds for suspecting, that a clandestine entrant was, or might be, concealed in the transporter;
(b) an effective system for preventing the carriage of clandestine entrants was in operation in relation to the transporter; and
(c) that on the occasion in question the person or persons responsible for operating that system did so properly.

(4)   In determining, for the purposes of this section, whether a particular system is effective, regard is to be had to the code of practice issued by the Secretary of State under section 33.

(5)   If there are two or more persons responsible for a clandestine entrant, the fact that one or more of them has a defence under subsection (3) does not affect the liability of the others.

(6)   But if a person responsible for a clandestine entrant has a defence under subsection (2), the liability of any other person responsible for that entrant is discharged.

Commencement   3 April 2000 for the purposes of clandestine entrants, within the meaning of section 32(1) other than those who (a) within the meaning of Part II of the Act arrive in the United Kingdom concealed otherwise than in a vehicle and (b) are clandestine entrants by virtue of section 32(1)(a) of this Act (SI 2000/464).

18 September 2000 (SI 2000/2444) in so far as not already in force for the purposes of section 39 (Rail freight) and any regulations made under it.

Note   *34(4)* See The Carriers' Liability (Clandestine Entrants) (Code of Practice) Order 2000 (SI 2000/684), into force 3 April 2000, and note to section 33 above. See SI 2001/280, regs 4 and 6, applying this section, with modifications, to rail freight.

[A.1.268]
35 Procedure
(1)   If the Secretary of State decides that a person ('P') is liable to one or more penalties under section 32, he must notify P of his decision.

(2)   A notice under subsection (1) (a 'penalty notice') must—

(a) state the Secretary of State's reasons for deciding that P is liable to the penalty (or penalties);
(b) state the amount of the penalty (or penalties) to which P is liable;
(c) specify the date before which, and the manner in which, the penalty (or penalties) must be paid; and
(d) include an explanation of the steps—
    (i)   that P must take if he objects to the penalty;
    (ii) that the Secretary of State may take under this Part to recover any unpaid penalty.

(3)   Subsection (4) applies if more than one person is responsible for a clandestine entrant.

(4)   If a penalty notice is served on one of the responsible persons, the Secretary of State is to be taken to have served the required penalty notice on each of them.

(5)   The Secretary of State must nevertheless take reasonable steps, while the penalty remains unpaid, to secure that the penalty notice is actually served on each of those responsible persons.

(6)   If a person on whom a penalty notice is served, or who is treated as having had a penalty notice served on him, alleges that he is not liable for one or more, or all, of the penalties specified in the penalty notice, he may give written notice of his allegation to the Secretary of State.

(7)   Notice under subsection (6) ('a notice of objection') must—

(a)   give reasons for the allegation; and
(b)   be given before the end of such period as may be prescribed.

(8)   If a notice of objection is given before the end of the prescribed period, the Secretary of State must consider it and determine whether or not any penalty to which it relates is payable.

(9)   The Secretary of State may by regulations provide, in relation to detached trailers, for a penalty notice which is served in such manner as may be prescribed to have effect as a penalty notice properly served on the responsible person or persons concerned under this section.

(10)   Any sum payable to the Secretary of State as a penalty under section 32 may be recovered by the Secretary of State as a debt due to him.

Commencement   Subsections *35(7)* to *(9)* 6 December 1999 (SI 1999/3190) for the purposes of enabling subordinate legislation to be made under them. 3 April 2000 for the purposes of clandestine entrants, within the meaning of section 32(1) other than those who (a) within the meaning of Part II of the Act arrive in the United Kingdom concealed otherwise than in a vehicle and (b) are clandestine entrants by virtue of section 32(1)(a) of this Act (SI 2000/464).

18 September 2000 (SI 2000/2444) in so far as not already in force for the purposes of section 39 (Rail freight) and any regulations made under it.

Note   See SI 2000/685. In relation to a detached trailer, a penalty notice is properly served by being fixed to a conspicuous part of the trailer (SI 2000/685, regulation 7), as amended by SI 2001/311.

See SI 2001/280, regs 4 and 7, applying sub-ss (1), (2), (6)–(8) and (10), with modifications, to rail freight.

35(7) and 35(8) The period prescribed is 30 days from the date on which the responsible person, or the first responsible person served, where there is more than one, was served with the penalty notice.

See *R v Secretary of State for the Home Department ex p Balbo B & C Auto Transporti Internazionali* (2001) Times, 22 March, QBD, discussed in the note s 32(2) above.

[A.1.269]
36 Power to detain vehicles etc in connection with penalties under section 32
(1)   If a penalty notice has been given under section 35, a senior officer may detain any relevant—

(a)   vehicle,
(b)   small ship, or
(c)   small aircraft,

until all penalties to which the notice relates, and any expenses reasonably incurred by the Secretary of State in connection with the detention, have been paid.

(2)   That power—

(a) may be exercised only if, in the opinion of the senior officer concerned, there is a significant risk that the penalty (or one or more of the penalties) will not be paid before the end of the prescribed period if the transporter is not detained; and

(b) may not be exercised if alternative security which the Secretary of State considers is satisfactory, has been given.

(3)   If a transporter is detained under this section, the owner, consignor or any other person who has an interest in any freight or other thing carried in or on the transporter may remove it, or arrange for it to be removed, at such time and in such way as is reasonable.

(4)   The detention of a transporter under this section is lawful even though it is subsequently established that the penalty notice on which the detention was based was ill-founded in respect of all or any of the penalties to which it related.

(5) But subsection (4) does not apply if the Secretary of State was acting unreasonably in issuing the penalty notice.

Commencement   Subsection *36(2)(a)* 6 December 1999 (SI 1999/3190) for the purposes of enabling subordinate legislation to be made under it. 3 April 2000 for the purposes of clandestine entrants, within the meaning of section 32(1) other than those who (a) within the meaning of Part II of the Act arrive in the United Kingdom concealed otherwise than in a vehicle and (b) are clandestine entrants by virtue of section 32(1)(a) of this Act (SI 2000/464).

18 September 2000 (SI 2000/2444) in so far as not already in force for the purposes of section 39 (Rail freight) and any regulations made under it.

Note   *36(2)* The period prescribed is 60 days (SI 2000/685, regulation 4). See note to section 32(2).

See SI 2001/280, regs 4 and 8, applying this section, with modifications, to rail freight.

[A.1.270]
37 Effect of detention
(1)   This section applies if a transporter is detained under section 36.
(2)   The person to whom the penalty notice was addressed, or the owner or any other person claiming an interest in the transporter, may apply to the court for the transporter to be released.
(3)   The court may release the transporter if it considers that—

(a) satisfactory security has been tendered in place of the transporter for the payment of the penalty alleged to be due and connected expenses;
(b) there is no significant risk that the penalty (or one or more of the penalties) and any connected expenses will not be paid; or
(c) there is a significant doubt as to whether the penalty is payable and the applicant has a compelling need to have the transporter released.

(4)   If the court has not ordered the release of the transporter, the Secretary of State may sell it if the penalty in question and connected expenses are not paid

before the end of the period of 84 days beginning with the date on which the detention began.

(5) 'Connected expenses' means expenses reasonably incurred by the Secretary of State in connection with the detention.

(6) Schedule 1 applies to the sale of transporters under this section.

Commencement Subsection 37(6) 6 December 1999 (SI 1999/3190) insofar as it relates to those paragraphs to Schedule 1 commenced by SI 1999/3190. 3 April 2000 for the purposes of clandestine entrants, within the meaning of section 32(1) other than those who (a) within the meaning of Part II of the Act arrive in the United Kingdom concealed otherwise than in a vehicle and (b) are clandestine entrants by virtue of section 32(1)(a) of this Act (SI 2000/464).

18 September 2000 (SI 2000/2444) in so far as not already in force for the purposes of section 39 (Rail freight) and any regulations made under it.

Note See SI 2000/685, as amended by SI 2001/311. Regulation 10 of SI 2000/685 deals with the application of the proceeds of any sale under this section.

See SI 2001/280, reg 4, applying this section to rail freight.

See *R v Secretary of State for the Home Department ex p Balbo B & C Auto Transporti Internazionali* (2001) Times, 22 March, QBD, discussed in the note to s 32(2) above.

[A.1.271]
38 *(Amends the Immigration Act 1971, s 25.)*

[A.1.272]
39 Rail freight

(1) The Secretary of State may make regulations applying (with or without modification) any provision of this Part for the purpose of enabling penalties to be imposed in respect of a person ('a clandestine entrant') who—

(a) arrives in the United Kingdom concealed in a rail freight wagon; and
(b) claims, or indicates that he intends to seek, asylum in the United Kingdom or evades, or attempts to evade, immigration control.

(2) The regulations may, in particular, make provision—

(a) enabling additional penalties to be imposed in respect of persons concealed with the clandestine entrant;
(b) as to which person is (or which persons are together) liable to penalties in respect of the clandestine entrant;
(c) for conferring on a senior officer a power to detain any relevant rail freight wagon in prescribed circumstances;
(d) for conferring on the Secretary of State a power to sell in prescribed circumstances a rail freight wagon which has been detained.

(3) Before making any regulations under this section, the Secretary of State must consult, in the way he considers appropriate, persons appearing to him to be likely to be affected by the imposition of penalties under the regulations.

Commencement 6 December 1999 (SI 1999/3190).

Note *39(1)* The Carriers' Liability (Clandestine Entrants) (application to Rail Freight) Regulations 2001 (SI 2001/280) made 5 February 2001, laid before parliament 6

February 2001, into force 1 March 2001 subject to the provisions of reg 1(2). Regulation 1(2) provides for some provisions of the regulations to come into force on an earlier date, 7 February 2001. The regulations apply certain provisions of Part II, with modifications, for the purposes of enabling penalties to be imposed in respect of 'clandestine entrants' arriving in the UK concealed in a rail freight wagon. See the note to section 32 for a note on who is a clandestine entrant for the purposes of the Regulations. 'Rail freight wagon' is defined in reg 2 for the purposes of this Part (see section 43 and the note thereto) and the regulations. In summary: sections 32, 35 and 43 are applied in part and modified, sections 33, 34 and 36 are applied as modified, section 37 is applied. Regulation 5 is a transitional provision which states that no penalty shall be imposed pursuant to the regulations in respect of a train which made its last scheduled stop, before arriving in the UK, prior to 1 March 2001. The Home Office has prepared a regulatory impact assessment in respect of the regulations and details of how to obtain it are contained in the Explanatory Note to the Regulations.

39(3) See SI 2001/280. These regulations simply state 'Whereas the Secretary of State, in satisfaction of the requirements of section 39(3) of the Immigration and Asylum Act 1999, has consulted, in the way he considers appropriate, persons appearing to him to be likely to be affected by the imposition of penalties under regulations made under section 39(1)...'. No further details are given.

Passengers without proper documents

[A.1.273]
40 Charges in respect of passengers without proper documents
(1) This section applies if a person requiring leave to enter the United Kingdom arrives in the United Kingdom by ship, aircraft, road passenger vehicle or train and, on being required to do so by an immigration officer, fails to produce—

(a) a valid passport with photograph or some other document satisfactorily establishing his identity and nationality or citizenship; and
(b) if he requires a visa, a valid visa of the required kind.

(2) The Secretary of State may charge the owner of the ship, aircraft or vehicle or the train operator, in respect of that person, the sum of £2,000 or such other sum as may be prescribed.
(3) The charge is payable to the Secretary of State on demand.
(4) No charge is payable in respect of any person who is shown by the owner or train operator to have produced the required document or documents to him or his representative when embarking—

(a) on the ship or aircraft for the voyage or flight to the United Kingdom; or
(b) on the vehicle or train for the journey to the United Kingdom.

(5) No charge is payable by a train operator, or by the owner of a road passenger vehicle, in respect of a person ('A'), if he shows that—

(a) neither he nor his representative was permitted, under the law applicable to the place where A embarked on the journey to the United Kingdom, to require A to produce to him when embarking the required document or documents;
(b) he had in place satisfactory arrangements (including, where appropriate, arrangements with other persons) designed to ensure that he did not carry

passengers who did not, or might not, have documents of the required kind;

(c) all such steps as were practicable were taken in accordance with the arrangements to establish whether A had the required document or documents; and

(d) all such steps as were practicable were taken in accordance with the arrangements to prevent A's arrival in the United Kingdom where—

    (i) A refused to produce the required document or documents to a person acting in accordance with the arrangements; or

    (ii) for other reasons it appeared to that person that A did not, or might not, have the required document or documents.

(6) For the purposes of subsections (4) and (5), a document—

(a) is to be regarded as being what it purports to be unless its falsity is reasonably apparent; and

(b) is to be regarded as relating to the person producing it unless it is reasonably apparent that it relates to another person.

(7) Subsection (8) applies if—

(a) a person arrives in the United Kingdom in circumstances in which the Secretary of State is entitled to impose on the owner of a road passenger vehicle a charge under this section in respect of that person; and

(b) the vehicle arrived in the United Kingdom in a ship or aircraft.

(8) The Secretary of State may impose a charge in respect of the arrival of the vehicle, or a charge in respect of the arrival of the ship or aircraft, but not in respect of both.

(9) The Secretary of State may by order provide that this section is not to apply in relation to passengers arriving in the United Kingdom on a train who embarked on the journey to the United Kingdom—

(a) in a country specified in the order; or

(b) at places so specified within a country so specified.

(10) The Secretary of State may make an order under subsection (9) only if he is satisfied that there is in force between the United Kingdom and the country concerned an agreement providing for the operation of United Kingdom immigration control in that country or for the checking of passports and visas there.

(11) 'Road passenger vehicle' means a vehicle—

(a) which is adapted to carry more than eight passengers and is being used for carrying passengers for hire or reward; or

(b) which is not so adapted but is being used for carrying passengers for hire or reward at separate fares in the course of a business of carrying passengers.

(12) For the purposes of this section a person requires a visa if—

(a) under the immigration rules he requires a visa for entry into the United Kingdom; or

(b) as a result of section 41 he requires a visa for passing through the United Kingdom.

(13) 'Representative', in relation to a person, means an employee or agent of his.

Commencement *40(9)* and *40(10)* 6 December 1999 (SI 1999/3190).

Note No orders have yet been made under this section.

40(1)(b) See The Immigration (European Economic Area) Regulations 2000 (SI 2000/2326), as amended by SI 2001/285, regulation 7 which provides that 'a valid visa of the required kind' includes a family or resident document required for admission as a visa national under regulation 12 of those regulations. See notes to section 80.

[A.1.274]
41 Visas for transit passengers
(1) The Secretary of State may by order require transit passengers to hold a transit visa.
(2) 'Transit passengers' means persons of any description specified in the order who on arrival in the United Kingdom pass through to another country without entering the United Kingdom; and 'transit visa' means a visa for that purpose.
(3) The order—

(a) may specify a description of persons by reference to nationality, citizenship, origin or other connection with any particular country but not by reference to race, colour or religion;
(b) may not provide for the requirement imposed by the order to apply to any person who under the 1971 Act has the right of abode in the United Kingdom;
(c) may provide for any category of persons of a description specified in the order to be exempt from the requirement imposed by the order;
(d) may make provision about the method of application for visas required by the order.

Passengers without proper documents

[A.1.275]
42 Power to detain vehicles etc in connection with charges under section 40
(1) A senior officer may, pending payment of any charge imposed under section 40, detain—

(a) the transporter in which the person in respect of whom the charge was imposed was carried; or
(b) any other transporter used (on any route) in the course of providing a service of carriage of passengers by sea, air or land by the person on whom the charge was imposed.

(2) If a transporter is detained under subsection (1) it may continue to be detained pending payment of any connected expenses.
(3) The court may release the transporter if it considers that—

(a) satisfactory security has been tendered in place of the transporter for the payment of the charge alleged to be due and connected expenses;
(b) there is no significant risk that the charge and any connected expenses will not be paid; or

(c) there is a significant doubt as to whether the charge is payable and the applicant has a compelling need to have the transporter released.

(4)   If the court has not ordered the release of the transporter, the Secretary of State may sell it if the charge in question and connected expenses are not paid before the end of the period of 84 days beginning with the date on which the detention began.

(5)   The detention of a transporter under this section is lawful even though it is subsequently established that the imposition of the charge on which the detention was based was ill-founded.

(6)   But subsection (5) does not apply if the Secretary of State was acting unreasonably in imposing the charge.

(7)   'Connected expenses' means expenses reasonably incurred by the Secretary of State in connection with the detention.

(8)   Schedule 1 applies to the sale of transporters under this section.

Commencement   42(8) 6 December 1999 (SI 1999/3190) insofar as it relates to those paragraphs of Schedule 1 commenced by that instrument.

Note   See SI 2000/465, as amended by SI 2001/311.

Regulation 10 of SI 2000/465 deals with the application of any proceeds of sale under this section.

Interpretation

[A.1.276]
43 Interpretation of Part II
In this Part—

'aircraft' includes hovercraft;
'captain' means the master of a ship or commander of an aircraft;
'concealed' includes being concealed in any freight, stores or other thing carried in or on the vehicle, ship or aircraft concerned;
'court' means—

(a) in England and Wales, the county court or the High Court;
(b) in Scotland, the sheriff or the Court of Session;
(c) in Northern Ireland, the county court or the High Court;

'detached trailer' means a trailer, semi-trailer, caravan or any other thing which is designed or adapted for towing by a vehicle but which has been detached for transport—

(a) in or on the vehicle concerned; or
(b) in the ship or aircraft concerned (whether separately or in or on a vehicle);

'equipment', in relation to an aircraft, includes—

(a) any certificate of registration, maintenance or airworthiness of the aircraft;
(b) any log book relating to the use of the aircraft; and
(c) any similar document;

'hirer', in relation to a vehicle, means any person who has hired the vehicle from another person;
'operating weight', in relation to an aircraft, means the maximum total weight

of the aircraft and its contents at which the aircraft may take off anywhere in the world, in the most favourable circumstances, in accordance with the certificate of airworthiness in force in respect of the aircraft;

'owner' includes—

(a) in relation to a ship or aircraft, the agent or operator of the ship or aircraft; and

(b) in relation to a road passenger vehicle, the operator of the vehicle; and

in relation to a transporter which is the subject of a hire-purchase agreement, includes the person in possession of it under that agreement;

'penalty notice' has the meaning given in section 35(2);

'rail freight wagon' has such meaning as may be prescribed;

'senior officer' means an immigration officer not below the rank of chief immigration officer;

'ship' includes every description of vessel used in navigation;

'small aircraft' means an aircraft which has an operating weight of less than 5,700 kilogrammes;

'small ship' means a ship which has a gross tonnage of less than 500 tonnes;

'train' means a train which—

(a) is engaged on an international service as defined by section 13(6) of the Channel Tunnel Act 1987; but

(b) is not a shuttle train as defined by section 1(9) of that Act;

'train operator', in relation to a person arriving in the United Kingdom on a train, means the operator of trains who embarked that person on that train for the journey to the United Kingdom;

'transporter' means a vehicle, ship or aircraft together with—

(a) its equipment; and

(b) any stores for use in connection with its operation;

'vehicle' includes a trailer, semi-trailer, caravan or other thing which is designed or adapted to be towed by another vehicle.

Commencement 6 December 1999 (SI 1999/3190).

Note 'rail freight wagon' is defined in reg 2 of the Carriers' Liability (Clandestine Entrants) (Application to Rail Freight) Regulations 2001 (SI 2001/280) to mean 'any rolling stock, other than a locomotive, which forms part of a train.' The definitions of 'rolling stock' and 'locomotive' for these purposes are stated in reg 1(3) to be those given in section 83 of the Railways Act 1993. Regulation 1(3) also defines train to mean any train other than a train engaged on a service for the carriage of passengers or a train which is a shuttle train as defined by section 1(9) of the Channel Tunnel Act 1987. Regulation 4 applies the definitions of 'concealed' 'court' 'penalty notice' 'senior officer', with modifications, to rail freight, along with the definition of 'train', modified as detailed above.

PART III

BAIL

Note See SI 2000/2333 the Immigration and Asylum (Appeals) Procedure Rules 2000 **[A.3.29]** for new provisions as to elective bail hearings before adjudicators.

See also the Bail: Guidance Notes for Adjudicators from the Chief Adjudicator issued in September 2000. These deal *inter alia* with the implications of the European Convention on Human Rights for bail hearings. Current notices and forms for bail hearings are appended to them.

Routine bail hearings

[A.1.277]
44   Bail hearings for detained persons
(1)   This section applies if a person is detained under any provision of the 1971 Act.
(2)   The Secretary of State must arrange a reference to the court for it to determine whether the detained person should be released on bail.
(3)   The duty under this section to arrange a reference does not apply if the detained person—

(a) is also detained otherwise than under a provision of the 1971 Act;
(b) is liable (under section 3(6) of that Act) to deportation as a result of the recommendation of a court; or
(c) has given to the Secretary of State, and has not withdrawn, written notice that he does not wish his case to be referred to a court under this section.

(4)   The Secretary of State must secure that a first reference to the court is made—

(a) in the case of a reference to the Commission, in accordance with rules; and
(b) in any other case, no later than the eighth day following that on which the detained person was detained.

(5)   If the detained person remains in detention, the Secretary of State must secure that a second reference to the court is made—

(a) in the case of a reference to the Commission, in accordance with rules; and
(b) in any other case, no later than the thirty-sixth day following that on which the detained person was detained.

(6)   A reference under subsection (5) may not be heard by the court before the thirty-third day following that on which the detained person was detained.
(7)   The court hearing a case referred to it under this section must proceed as if the detained person had made an application to it for bail.
(8)   The court must determine the matter—

(a) in the case of a reference to the Commission, in accordance with rules; and
(b) in any other case—
    (i)   on a first reference, before the tenth day following that on which the person concerned was detained; and
    (ii) on a second reference, before the thirty-eighth day following that on which he was detained.

(9)   Subsection (8) does not apply if the detained person has been released or has given notice under subsection (3)(c).
(10)   If it appears to the Secretary of State that there has been a failure to comply with subsection (4) or (5), he must refer the matter to the court, and the court must deal with the reference, as soon as is reasonably practicable.

(11)   If it appears to the Secretary of State that there has been a failure to comply with subsection (8), he must notify the court concerned, and the court must deal with the matter, as soon as is reasonably practicable.

(12)   In this Part 'court' means—

(a) if the detained person has brought an appeal under the Immigration Acts, the court or other appellate authority dealing with his appeal;
(b) in the case of a detained person to whom section 3(2) of the Special Immigration Appeals Commission Act 1997 applies (jurisdiction in relation to bail for persons detained on grounds of national security), the Commission; and
(c) in any other case, such magistrates' court as the Secretary of State considers appropriate or, in Scotland, an adjudicator.

(13)   Rules made by the Lord Chancellor under section 5 of the Special Immigration Appeals Commission Act 1997 may include provision made for the purposes of this section; and in subsections (4), (5) and (8) 'rules' means rules made by virtue of this subsection.

(14)   The Secretary of State may by regulations make provision modifying the application of this section in relation to cases where the proceedings on a reference under this section are adjourned to enable medical or other reports to be obtained or for any other reason.

(15)   The regulations may, in particular, provide for the requirement for there to be a second reference not to apply in prescribed circumstances.

(16)   This section does not affect any other provision under which the detained person may apply for, or be released on, bail.

[A.1.278]
45   Location of bail hearings
(1)   The Secretary of State may, in relation to a particular case or class of case, direct that the hearing of a reference under section 44 is to be at a specified place.

(2)   The places that may be specified include, in particular—

(a) any place at which a court sits;
(b) any place at which appeals under this Act are heard;
(c) detention centres;
(d) prisons; or
(e) any particular premises or rooms within a place of a kind mentioned in paragraphs (a) to (d).

(3)   A direction under subsection (1) has effect notwithstanding any other direction which may be given as to the place in which the court is to sit.

(4)   A direction under subsection (1) requires the approval of the Lord Chancellor.

(5)   'Specified' means specified in the direction.

[A.1.279]
46   General right to be released on bail

(1)   On a reference under section 44, the court must release the detained person on bail unless—

(a) subsection (2), (3) or (4) applies; or

(b) the court has imposed a requirement under section 47(1) which has not been complied with.

(2) The detained person need not be granted bail if the court is satisfied that there are substantial grounds for believing that if released on bail he would—

(a) fail to comply with one or more of the conditions of bail or of any recognizance or bail bond;
(b) commit an offence while on bail which is punishable with imprisonment;
(c) be likely to cause danger to public health; or
(d) alone or with others, be a serious threat to the maintenance of public order.

(3) The detained person need not be granted bail if the court is satisfied that—

(a) he is or has been knowingly involved with others in a concerted attempt by all or some of them to enter the United Kingdom in breach of immigration law;
(b) he is suffering from mental disorder and his continued detention is necessary in his own interests or for the protection of any other person;
(c) he is under the age of 18 and, while arrangements ought to be made for his care in the event of his release from detention, no satisfactory arrangements have been made;
(d) he is required to submit to an examination by an immigration officer under paragraph 2 or 2A of Schedule 2 to the 1971 Act and there is no relevant decision which the officer is in a position to take; or
(e) directions for his removal from the United Kingdom are in force.

(4) The detained person need not be granted bail if the court is satisfied that he is a person to whom section 3(2) of the Special Immigration Appeals Commission Act 1997 (national security cases) applies.

(5) For the purposes of this section, the question whether an offence is one which is punishable with imprisonment is to be determined without regard to any enactment prohibiting or restricting the imprisonment of young offenders or first offenders.

(6) 'Immigration law' means any provision of the Immigration Acts or any similar provision in force in any part of the British Islands.

(7) Each of the following is a relevant decision—

(a) a decision as to whether, and if so how, to exercise the powers conferred by paragraph 21 of Schedule 2 to the 1971 Act;
(b) a decision as to whether to grant the person concerned leave to enter, or remain in, the United Kingdom;
(c) a decision as to whether to cancel his leave to enter the United Kingdom under paragraph 2A(8) of that Schedule.

(8) The Secretary of State may by order amend subsection (2) or (3) by adding to or restricting the circumstances in which the subsection applies.

(9) If bail is granted under this section, the appropriate court may, on an application by or on behalf of the person released, vary any condition on which it was granted.

(10) If bail is granted under this section, the appropriate court may, on an application by or on behalf of the Secretary of State, vary any condition on which it was granted or impose conditions on it.

(11) 'Appropriate court' means—

(a) if the person released has brought an appeal under the Immigration Acts, the court or other appellate body dealing with his appeal;

(b) in any other case, the court which released the person concerned on bail.

[A.1.280]
47 Powers exercisable on granting bail
(1)   Before releasing a person on bail under section 46, the court may require—

(a) a recognizance or, in Scotland, a bail bond to be entered into; or

(b) security to be given by the person bailed or on his behalf.

(2)   The court may impose a requirement under subsection (1) only if it considers that its imposition is necessary to secure compliance with any condition to which bail granted under section 46 will be subject as a result of subsection (3), (4) or (5).
(3)   Bail granted under section 46 by the Commission is subject to a condition requiring the person bailed to appear before it at a specified time and place.
(4)   Bail granted under section 46 by a court or other appellate authority (other than the Commission) dealing with an appeal by the person bailed is subject to a condition requiring him—

(a) to appear before the court or authority at a time and place specified by it; and

(b) if the appeal is dismissed, withdrawn or abandoned, to appear before an immigration officer at such time and place as may be notified to him in writing by an immigration officer.

(5)   In any other case, bail granted under section 46 is subject to a condition requiring the person bailed to appear before an immigration officer—

(a) at a time and place specified by the court; or

(b) at such other time and place as may be notified to him in writing by an immigration officer.

(6)   Bail granted under section 46 may be subject to such other conditions as appear to the court to be likely to result in the appearance of the person bailed at the required time and place.
(7)   A recognizance taken under this section may be with or without sureties, as the court may determine.
(8)   Subsections (9) and (10) apply if, on a reference under section 44, the court has power to release the detained person on bail but is not required to do so by section 46.
(9)   The court may, instead of releasing him—

(a) fix the amount of any recognizance, bail bond or security to be taken on his release on bail (including the amount in which any sureties are to be bound); and

(b) settle the terms of any conditions to be imposed on his release on bail.

(10)   The person concerned must be released on bail on the recognizance or bond being taken, or the security being given.
(11)   A person released on bail under section 46 is to be subject to such restrictions (if any) as to his employment or occupation while he is in the United Kingdom as may from time to time be notified to him in writing by an immigration officer.

(12)   Any restriction imposed on a person under subsection (11) has effect for the purposes of this Part as a condition of his bail.

[A.1.281]
48   Forfeiture

(1)   If it appears to a court that a mandatory bail condition has been broken, it may—

(a) by order declare the recognizance to be forfeited; and
(b) order any person bound by the recognizance (whether as principal or surety) to pay the sum in which he is bound or such part of that sum, if any, as the court thinks fit.

(2)   'Mandatory bail condition' means a condition—

(a) to which bail granted under section 46 is subject as a result of section 47(3), (4) or (5); and
(b) in relation to which the court has taken a recognizance under section 47.

(3)   If the court which makes an order under subsection (1) is not a magistrates' court, it must—

(a) specify a magistrates' court which is, for the purposes of collection, enforcement and remission of the sum forfeited, to be treated as the court which ordered the forfeiture; and
(b) as soon as practicable give particulars of the recognizance to—
   (i)   in England and Wales, the justices' chief executive appointed by the magistrates' court committee whose area includes the petty sessions area, or
   (ii) in Northern Ireland, the clerk of petty sessions for the petty sessions district,
   for which the specified court acts.

(4)   Any sum collected as a result of subsection (3)(a) must be paid to the Lord Chancellor.
(5)   The Lord Chancellor may, with the approval of the Treasury, make regulations as to the times at which and the manner in which accounts for, and payments of, sums collected as a result of subsection (3)(a) must be made and for the keeping and auditing of accounts in relation to such sums.
(6)   If a person fails to comply with any of the conditions of a bail bond taken by a court under section 47, the court may declare the bail to be forfeited.
(7)   Any bail forfeited by a court under subsection (6)—

(a) must be transmitted to the sheriff court having jurisdiction in the area where the proceedings took place; and
(b) is to be treated as having been forfeited by that court.

[A.1.282]
49   Forfeiture of securities
(1)   If a court is satisfied that a person ('A') by whom, or on whose behalf, security has been given under section 47 has broken a mandatory bail condition, it may order the security to be forfeited unless it appears that A had reasonable cause for breaking the condition.

(2)   The order may provide for the forfeiture to extend to a specified amount which is less than the value of the security.

(3)   An order under subsection (1) takes effect, unless previously revoked, at the end of the period of 21 days beginning with the day on which it is made.

(4)   Any sum forfeited as a result of this section must be paid to the Lord Chancellor.

(5)   Subsection (6) applies if a court which has made an order under subsection (1) is satisfied, on an application made by or on behalf of the person who gave the security, that A did after all have reasonable cause for breaking the condition.

(6)   The court may by order—

(a) remit the forfeiture; or
(b) provide for it to extend to a specified amount which is less than the value of the security.

(7)   An application under subsection (5)—

(a) may be made before or after the order for forfeiture has taken effect; but
(b) may not be entertained unless the court is satisfied that the Secretary of State was given reasonable notice of the applicant's intention to make the application.

(8)   The Lord Chancellor may, with the approval of the Treasury, make regulations as to the times at which and the manner in which accounts for, and payments of, sums forfeited as a result of this section must be made and for keeping and auditing of accounts in relation to such sums.

(9)   'Mandatory bail condition' means a condition—

(a) to which bail granted under section 46 is subject as a result of section 47(3), (4) or (5); and
(b) in relation to which a person has given security under section 47.

[A.1.283]
50   Power of arrest

(1)   An immigration officer or constable who has reasonable grounds for believing that a person released on a reference under section 44 has broken or is likely to break any condition on which he was bailed, may arrest him without a warrant.

(2)   Subsection (3) applies if a person other than the person bailed ('a third party')—

(a) has agreed to act as a surety in relation to a recognizance entered into under section 47; or
(b) has given security on behalf of the person bailed under that section.

(3)   If an immigration officer or constable is notified in writing by a third party—

(a) of his belief that a person released on a reference under section 44 is likely to break the condition that he must appear at the time and place required; and
(b) of the third party's wish, for that reason, to be relieved of his obligations as a surety or to have the security given returned to him,

the officer or constable may arrest the person released without a warrant.

(4)   Subsection (5) applies if—

(a) a justice of the peace is, by written information on oath, satisfied that there are reasonable grounds for suspecting that a person liable to be arrested under this section is to be found on any premises;
(b) in Scotland, the sheriff or a justice of the peace is by evidence on oath so satisfied; or
(c) in Northern Ireland, a justice of the peace is by written complaint on oath so satisfied.

(5)   The justice of the peace or the sheriff may grant a warrant authorising any immigration officer or constable to enter, if need be by reasonable force, the premises named in the warrant for the purpose of searching for and arresting the person concerned.

(6)   A person arrested under this section must, if required by a condition on which he was released to appear before an immigration officer within 24 hours after his arrest, be brought before an immigration officer within that period.

(7)   A person arrested under this section must, if he was released under section 46 by the Commission, be brought before it within twenty-four hours after his arrest.

(8)   Subsection (9) applies if a person has been arrested under this section and—

(a) neither subsection (6) nor subsection (7) applies to him; or
(b) he has been brought before an immigration officer under subsection (6) but has not been released.

(9)   The arrested person must be brought before—

(a) a justice of the peace acting for the petty sessions area in which he was arrested;
(b) in Scotland, an adjudicator or, if that is not practicable within 24 hours after his arrest, the sheriff; or
(c) in Northern Ireland, a magistrates' court acting for the county court division in which he was arrested.

(10)   If subsection (9) applies, the arrested person must be brought before the person or court concerned—

(a) as soon as is practicable after his arrest; and
(b) if subsection (9)(a) or (c) applies, in any event within 24 hours after his arrest.

(11)   Subsections (12) and (13) apply in relation to an arrested person dealt with under subsection (7) or (9).

(12)   The court or person dealing with the matter may, if of the opinion that the arrested person has broken or is likely to break any condition on which he was released—

(a) give a direction that the arrested person be detained under the authority of the person by whom he was arrested;
(b) release him on his original bail; or
(c) release him on a new recognizance (with or without sureties) or on new bail.

(13)   If not of that opinion, that court or person must release the arrested person on his original bail.

(14)   In reckoning any period of 24 hours for the purposes of this section, no account is to be taken of Christmas Day, Good Friday or any Sunday.

Procedure

[A.1.284]
51   Procedure
(1)   Any rules made in connection with bail hearings resulting from any provision of, or made under, this Part must include provision requiring the Secretary of State to notify—

(a)   the detained person who is the subject of the hearing of a reference under section 44, and
(b)   if the Secretary of State is aware that that person will be represented at the hearing (whether or not by an authorised advocate), the person who will be representing him at the hearing,

of the date, place and time of the hearing as soon as is reasonably practicable after the Secretary of State is given that information by the magistrates' court.
(2)   If a person has been refused bail—

(a)   on a reference under section 44, or
(b)   on an application under the 1971 Act, the Asylum and Immigration Appeals Act 1993 or the Special Immigration Appeals Commission Act 1997,

he may, on the first subsequent such reference or application, advance any argument as to fact or law.
(3)   But on any subsequent such reference or application the court need not hear any argument as to fact or law that that court has heard previously.
(4)   A magistrates' court dealing with a reference under section 44 must sit in open court unless—

(a)   the detained person has made a claim for asylum and the court considers that there are compelling reasons why it should sit in private; or
(b)   the court considers that the interests of the administration of justice require it to sit in private.

(5)   Any proceedings before a magistrates' court or the sheriff under this Part may be conducted—

(a)   on behalf of the Secretary of State, by a person authorised by him, or
(b)   on behalf of the detained person, by a person nominated by him,

even though that person is not an authorised advocate.
(6)   'Authorised advocate'—

(a)   in relation to England and Wales, has the meaning given by section 119 of the Courts and Legal Services Act 1990;
(b)   in relation to Scotland, means an advocate or solicitor;
(c)   in relation to Northern Ireland, means a barrister or solicitor.

(7)   'Rules' means rules made by the Lord Chancellor under section 144 of the Magistrates' Courts Act 1980 or under any corresponding provision having effect in Northern Ireland.

[A.1.285]
52 Use of live television links at bail hearings
(1) On a reference under section 44, the court may, after hearing representations from the parties, direct that the detained person is to be treated as being present in the court if he is able (whether by means of a live television link or otherwise) to see and hear the court and to be seen and heard by it.
(2) If the detained person wishes to make representations under subsection (1) he must do so by using the facilities that will be used if the court decides to give the proposed direction.
(3) If, after hearing representations from the parties, the court decides not to give a direction, it must give its reasons for refusing.
(4) The court may not give a direction unless—

(a) it has been notified by the Secretary of State that facilities are available in the relevant institution which will enable the detained person to see and hear the court and to be seen and heard by it; and
(b) the notice has not been withdrawn.

(5) 'Relevant institution' means the institution in which the detained person will be detained at the time of the bail hearing.

Bail hearings under other enactments

[A.1.286]
53 Applications for bail in immigration cases
(1) The Secretary of State may by regulations make new provision in relation to applications for bail by persons detained under the 1971 Act.
(2) The regulations may confer a right to be released on bail in prescribed circumstances.
(3) The regulations may, in particular, make provision—

(a) creating or transferring jurisdiction to hear an application for bail by a person detained under the 1971 Act;
(b) as to the places in which such an application may be held;
(c) as to the procedure to be followed on, or in connection with, such an application;
(d) as to circumstances in which, and conditions (including financial conditions) on which, an applicant may be released on bail;
(e) amending or repealing any enactment so far as it relates to such an application.

(4) The regulations must include provision for securing that an application for bail made by a person who has brought an appeal under any provision of this Act or the Special Immigration Appeals Commission Act 1997 is heard by the appellate authority hearing that appeal.
(5) When exercising his power under subsection (1), the Secretary of State must have regard to the desirability, in relation to applications for bail by persons detained under the 1971 Act, of making provision similar to that which is made by this Part in relation to references to the court under section 44.
(6) Regulations under this section require the approval of the Lord Chancellor.
(7) In so far as regulations under this section relate to the sheriff or the Court

of Session, the Lord Chancellor must obtain the consent of the Scottish Ministers before giving his approval.

[A.1.287]
54 *(Amends the Immigration Act 1971, Sch 3, para 2.)*

Grants

[A.1.288]
55   Grants to voluntary organisations
(1)   The Secretary of State may, with the approval of the Treasury, make grants to any voluntary organisation which provides advice or assistance for detained persons in connection with proceedings under this Part.
(2)   Grants may be made on such terms, and subject to such conditions, as the Secretary of State may determine.

PART IV
APPEALS

Note   In the Second Reading debate in the House of Commons on the Immigration and Asylum Bill, now this Act, the Home Secretary described the intention behind Part IV of the Act thus:

'The existing structure of successive rights of appeal will therefore be replaced by a one-stop comprehensive appeal that will cover all the appealable aspects of a case at one go. When an application is refused, the applicant will be invited to set out all the grounds on which he wishes to remain in the United Kingdom, including asylum, the European Convention on Human Rights or compassionate grounds.

The subsequent appeal will then consider all the factors in the case on which an appeal may be brought. Unless a ground for staying in the United Kingdom has been set out at this stage, it cannot form the basis of any appeal by the applicant unless he had reasonable excuse for not mentioning it when invited to do so, or in asylum and ECHR cases, provided the claim is not being made to frustrate removal' Hansard HC Report 22 February 1999, Cols 40-41.

It proved to be a matter of some complexity to give effect to this clearly stated aim, and the provisions of Part IV of the Bill were the subject of numerous government amendments right up to the last stages of its passage through parliament. A complex edifice has resulted, the provisions of which are to be found not only in Part IV, but in Part I (sections 3, 9-12 and 15) and in Schedules 2,3,4 14 and 15, supplemented by the transitional provisions and statutory instruments detailed below. It remains to be seen how far these will in practice deliver the 'one-stop comprehensive appeal' aspired to.

Transitional Provisions relating to Part IV

See Immigration and Asylum Act 1999 (Commencement No 5 and Transitional Provisions) Order 2000 (SI 2000/1985), section 3, and the Immigration and Asylum Act 1999 (Commencement No 6, Transitional and Consequential Provisions) Order 2000 (SI 2000/2444). The transitional provisions under Commencement Order No 5 preserve appeal rights under Part II of the 1971 Immigration Act, section 8 of, and Schedule 2 to, the Asylum and Immigration Act 1993 and section 3 of the Asylum and Immigration Act 1996 for the decisions taken prior to the commencement of Part IV, but provide that new procedural regulations and rules, as detailed in SI 2000/1985 are (see the Explanatory Note to SI 2000/1985 'in the interests of simplicity') to apply to all appeals, whether brought under Part IV or under the earlier legislation by virtue of these transitional provisions.

The 'interests of simplicity' were found to require something more than Commencement Order No 6. Its transitional provisions as they relate to appeals under section 14 of the 1971 Act and section 8 of the 1993 Act had themselves to be amended for the purposes of sections 61 and 69(2) of this Act by further transitional provisions. These are set out in article 5 of the Immigration and Asylum Act (Commencement and Transitional Provisions) Order No 8 2000 (SI 2000/3099). Commencement Order No 8, and in particular the Explanatory Note to article 5, threw the interests of simplicity to the winds in the interests of protecting the 'one-stop' appeal.

The provisions of Commencement Order No 6 created problems where a person has applied to vary his/her leave both on asylum and on other grounds, and was refused before 2 October 2000 on one element of the application and the other ground after that date. Without the transitional provisions of Commencement Order No 8, the second refusal would not have attracted a right of appeal, because it would not have had the effect of requiring the person to leave within 28 days. Why not? Because the person would already be protected from removal by the outstanding right of appeal against the pre-2 October 2000 refusal.

Commencement Order No 6 brings Part IV, save for section 79, fully into force on 2 October 2000. It makes complex transitional provisions, among which the most controversial is to be found in paragraph 7 of Schedule 1: 'Section 65 (human rights appeals) is not to have effect where the decision under the Immigration Acts was taken before 2 October 2000'. Generally, SI 2000/2444 sets out to make provision for the appeal rights in this Part not to apply (see SI 2000/2444, article 3(1)(a)) to 'events' (as defined in article 4(2) of SI 2000/2444) before 2 October 2000, with the relevant provisions in the Immigration Act 1971, the Asylum and Immigration Appeals Act 1993 and the Asylum and Immigration Act 1996 to continue to apply to decisions taken before that date. At the same time, the provisions of Part IV relating to procedure are to apply to all appeal rights, whichever is the governing Act. The definition of an 'event' in article 4(2) is curious as a cumulative list including the (a) service of a notice, (b) the making or taking or a decision, (c) the giving of directions and (d) the issuing of a certificate. The word 'and' appears between each of these parts of 4(1), suggesting that, for example, where no certificate is issued, there is no event. Similarly, this suggests that if any of (a) to (d) took place after the 2nd of October, there is no pre-2nd October event, and therefore the new appeals provisions must apply. However, this sits oddly with the transitional provisions set out in Schedule 2 of the Order.

The transitional provisions were considered in the 'starred' Immigration Appeals Tribunal judgment in *Pardeepan v Secretary of State for the Home Department* (HX/73829/97, 00/TH/2514), heard 5 October 2000. The question before the IAT was whether the terms of the transitional provisions in Commencement Order No 6 meant that it could not hear human rights issues. The IAT held that the effect of the Commencement Order was to preclude it from considering human rights issues in appeals brought before 2 October 2000. It rejected the argument that it had power to disregard the terms of a statutory instrument, even where these appeared to be in conflict with the Human Rights Act 1998, considering that the Commencement Order was not manifestly ultra vires, that the vires of the Order should be a matter for the High Court, and not for the IAT, and that it would proceed on the basis that the order was intra vires. The appellant sought to rely on section 7(1) of the Human Rights Act 1998, arguing that under that section, it is unlawful for a public authority to act in a way which is incompatible with a right under the European Convention on Human Rights and that the IAT therefore had an independent jurisdiction to consider the matter under the Human Rights Act 1998. The Tribunal rejected this argument, stating that:

'If we were persuaded that the result of our decision not to consider human rights would mean that the Secretary of State was enabled to remove without the human rights question being considered then, as it seems to us, we would be permitting the Secretary of State to act in a way which was unlawful under section 6(1) [of the Human Rights Act 1998] and that would at least arguably mean that we ourselves were acting in breach of Section 6(1) . . .'

The IAT did not consider that the Secretary of State could remove without consideration of the human rights issues because of assurances they were given by the Secretary of State, which they described thus:

'we are assured by Mr Thompson, on behalf of the Secretary of State, that those whose appeals are refused . . . will be given the opportunity to raise, if they think fit, human rights objections to removal, should the Secretary of State decide to remove them. We are equally assured that the Secretary of State will not seek to argue that they do not have a right of appeal under section 65 in respect of such a subsequent decision to remove.'

These assurances are extremely problematic, given the terms of the Immigration and Asylum Appeals (Notices) Regulations 2000 (SI 2000/2246), which, as discussed in the note to section 65 below, ensure that people need not be told that they can appeal on human rights grounds unless and until they allege a breach of their human rights. This issued was pursued in the House of Lords by the Lord Lester of Herne Hill, See *Hansard* HL Official Report written answers cols *12* and *14* (23 October 2000). In the exchange, at WA14:

'Lord Lester of Herne Hill asked Her Majesty's Government:

Why the United Kingdom Immigration Service is continuing to send to the representatives of asylum seekers standard notifications of removal indicating that the individual concerned has "exhausted all rights of appeal" without making it clear that there is an opportunity to ask the Secretary of State to reconsider on human rights grounds. [HL4183]

Lord Bassam of Brighton:

The form in question is a locally produced form, the wording of which has now been amended. However the right of appeal only arises where an allegation is made to the effect that a decision breaches a person's human rights and is made unlawful by Section 6(1) of the Human Rights Act 1998.'

Thus it is clear that while the Secretary of State will not tell an asylum that s/he has no further rights of appeal, neither will the Secretary of State inform the asylum seeker of his/her rights under the Human Rights Act 1998 and under section 65 of this Act.

The matter was considered by the Court of Appeal in *Amjad Mahood* (8 December 2000, CO/2000/0385), an immigration, not an asylum, case, which involved consideration of Article 8 EHCR, the right to family life. The parties accepted that since the decision to remove the applicant, taken before 2 October 2000, would not be implemented until after that date, then the Court of Appeal could review the legality of the decision under the Human Rights Act 1998. The judges did not agree. Laws LH held that the task of the court in this case was to review the administrative decision already made and not 'the legality of the decision-maker's carrying the decision into effect at some future date'. The Master of the Rolls did not dissent from this view, although on the facts of the case he considered that the court should review the legality of the decision under the Human Rights Act 1998 because the Secretary of State, in his decision, had stated that he had had regard to Article 8.

The effect of these judgments on the 'one-stop' appeals procedure should be noted. In cases where the decision was taken before 2 October 2000 the appellant who is aware of his/her rights and who alleges that his/her human rights are violated by a decision to remove, will have not one appeal, but two. The caveat 'who is aware of his/her rights' is however, a significant one as was made clear in the Lord Bassam's written answer to the Lord Lester of Hill set out in Hansard HL Official Report written answers cols *153* to *154* (20 March 2001):

'Asylum Seekers: Appeal Conditions

Lord Lester of Herne Hill asked Her Majesty's Government:

Whether they will ensure that asylum seekers who inform the Immigration Service of their intention to appeal against removal from the United Kingdom on human rights grounds under Section 65 of the Immigration Appeal Act 1999 are permitted to remain in the United Kingdom pending the determination of their appeal.

Lord Bassam of Brighton:

There is a right of appeal under Section 65 of the Immigration and Asylum Act 1999 against a decision relating to entitlement to leave to enter or remain in the United Kingdom, which is exercisable if that decision was taken on or after 2 October 2000, when that section came into force. The right of appeal is normally suspensive. That is to say, anyone who has made an appeal cannot be removed while the appeal is pending. However, the right of appeal is not triggered until an allegation is made that the decision breaches the person's human rights. Once the appeal right has been triggered, there is a 10 working day period for lodging the appeal and the person will not be removed during that period unless he or she agrees to depart voluntarily. A statement indicating a possible intention to make an allegation or to appeal at some point in the future is not sufficient to trigger an appeal and therefore does not prevent removal. People appealing against immigration decisions made before 2 October 2000 cannot benefit from Section 65 of the Immigration and Asylum Act 1999, which is not retrospective. We have given assurances that such people, if they have human rights concerns, may make a separate human rights claim and will have an opportunity to appeal. We wish to make it clear that we will not provide an opportunity for an appeal on human rights grounds where the human rights issue has been fully considered at an earlier appeal or by the courts or where the human rights claim is based solely on facts which the adjudicator at an earlier appeal or the Immigration Appeal Tribunal or higher court has not accepted. We expect claims by those who wish to benefit from an independent review of their case from a human rights perspective to give some clear indication of how their human rights arguments could result in a different decision. Alternatively, they may of course present a claim based on relevant evidence or circumstances which have arisen since the earlier appeal was dismissed.'

SI 2000/2333 The Immigration and Asylum (Appeals) Procedure Rules 2000 makes transitional provision for the application of the procedure rules in rule 4. See also the notes to Sections 3 and 10 of Part I of this Act.

Statutory Instruments relating to Part IV

Apart from the transitional provisions noted above, the key instruments are:

Immigration and Asylum Appeals (One Stop Procedure) Regulations 2000 (SI 2000/2244), as amended by the Immigration and Asylum Appeals (One Stop Procedure) (Amendment) Regulations 2001 (SI 2001/867), see **[A.3.80]**;

Immigration and Asylum Appeals (Notices) Regulations 2000 (SI 2000/2246), as amended by the Immigration and Asylum Appeals (Notices) (Amendment) Regulations 2001 (SI 2001/868), see [A.3.89];

Immigration (European Economic Area) Regulations 2000 (SI 2000/2326), as amended by the Immigration (European Economic Area) (Amendment) Regulations 2001 (SI 2001/865), see [A.4.58];

Immigration and Asylum Appeals (Procedure) Rules 2000 (SI 2000/2333) see [A.3.29].

Regard should also be had to:

- the *Practice Direction* issued on 11 September 2000 by the Chief Adjudicator and coming into effect on 2 October 2000. This deals with the allocation of appeals to either the 'first hearing track' or the 'fast track'.
- Immigration Appellate Authority's *Asylum Gender Guidelines* published in November 2000.

Note that for the purposes of these regulations, a representative is defined as a person not prohibited from acting as such by section 84 of this Act (see SI 2000/2246, regulation 2.

The appellate authorities

[A.1.289]
56 The Immigration Appeal Tribunal
(1)   There is to continue to be an Immigration Appeal Tribunal.
(2)   Schedule 2 makes further provision about the Tribunal.

Commencement   14 February 2000 (SI 2000/168).

[A.1.290]
57 Adjudicators
(1)   There are to be such number of adjudicators for the purposes of this Act as the Lord Chancellor may determine.
(2)   The Lord Chancellor must appoint one of the adjudicators as Chief Adjudicator.
(3) Schedule 3 makes further provision about the adjudicators.

Commencement   14 February 2000 (SI 2000/168).

Appeals

[A.1.291]
58 General
(1)   The right of appeal given by a particular provision of this Part is to be read with any other provision of this Part which restricts or otherwise affects that right.
(2)   Part I of Schedule 4 makes provision with respect to the procedure applicable in relation to appeals under this Part.

(3)   Part II of Schedule 4 makes provision as to the effect of appeals.

(4)   Part III of Schedule 4 makes provision—

(a) with respect to the determination of appeals under this Part; and

(b) for further appeals.

(5)   For the purposes of the Immigration Acts, an appeal under this Part is to be treated as pending during the period beginning when notice of appeal is given and ending when the appeal is finally determined, withdrawn or abandoned.

(6)   An appeal is not to be treated as finally determined while a further appeal may be brought.

(7)   If such a further appeal is brought, the original appeal is not to be treated as finally determined until the further appeal is determined, withdrawn or abandoned.

(8)   A pending appeal under this Part is to be treated as abandoned if the appellant leaves the United Kingdom.

(9)   A pending appeal under any provision of this Part other than section 69(3) is to be treated as abandoned if the appellant is granted leave to enter or remain in the United Kingdom.

(10)   A pending appeal under section 61 is to be treated as abandoned if a deportation order is made against the appellant.

Commencement   *58(2)* 14 February 2000 (SI 2000/168) for the purposes of Part I of Schedule 4. as commenced by SI 2000/168, viz paragraphs 3 to 5 of that Part of the Schedule, and 22 May 2000 (SI 2000/1282) for the purposes of the provisions of paragraph 1 of Schedule 4, which is commenced by SI 2000/1282. Commenced in full 2 October 2000 (SI 2000/2444).

Note   For transitional provisions applying 58(5) to (10) to appeals under sections 13 to 17 of the Immigration Act 1971, section 8 of the Asylum and Immigration Appeals Act 1993 and section 3(1) and (2) of the Asylum and Immigration Act 1976 see SI 2000/2444, articles 3(1)(b) and 4(1)(c)(i) and paragraph 1(3) of Schedule 2.

58(2) See SI 2000/2333 The Immigration and Asylum (Procedure) Rules 2000. One set of procedure rules now cover both immigration and asylum appeals.

58(8) This insertion of this sub-section settled the question of whether a departure from the UK always resulted in the abandonment of a pending appeal, which had remained a live issue under the wording of s 33(4) of the Immigration Act 1971 as amended by paragraph 4(2) of Schedule 2 to the Asylum and Immigration Act 1996. In the event, the decision of the Court of Appeal in Dupouac (IATRF/1999/0151/C, 22 January 2000) favoured an interpretation of section 33(4) that accords with the wording of this, now unambiguous, sub-section.

58(9) Subsection 69(3) allows a person granted limited leave to enter or remain to appeal on asylum grounds, that is to say, to seek to 'upgrade' the limited leave to full refugee status. Prior to the coming into force of this Act, the situation of a pending appeal where an appellant was granted limited leave to remain had been problematic. These problems were considered by the Court of Appeal in *Massaquoi v Secretary of State for the Home Department* (C/2000/0622, 20 December 2000).

Leave to enter

[A.1.292]
59 Leave to enter the United Kingdom

(1)   A person who is refused leave to enter the United Kingdom under any provision of the 1971 Act may appeal to an adjudicator against—

(a) the decision that he requires leave; or
(b) the refusal.

(2)   A person who, on an application duly made, is refused a certificate of entitlement or an entry clearance may appeal to an adjudicator against the refusal.

(3)   Subsection (4) applies if a person appeals under this section on being refused leave to enter the United Kingdom and—

(a) before he appeals, directions have been given for his removal from the United Kingdom; or
(b) before or after he appeals, the Secretary of State or an immigration officer serves on him notice that any directions which may be given for his removal as a result of the refusal will be for his removal to a country or one of several countries specified in the notice.

(4)   The appellant may—

(a) object to the country to which he would be removed in accordance with the directions, or
(b) object to the country specified in the notice (or to one or more of those specified),

and claim that he ought to be removed (if at all) to a different country specified by him.

Commencement   2 October 2000 (SI 2000/2444).

Note For transitional provisions see SI 2000/2444, articles 3(1) and 4(1) and Schedule 2, paragraph 1(4), which provides that this section is not to have effect where the decision to refuse leave to enter, or to refuse a certificate of entitlement or entry clearance, was made before 2 October 2000.

See notes to section 60 below and SI 2000/2333, Rule 894) of SI 2000/2333 specifies that when an appeal is made under this section in relation to a family visitor appeal, the appellant shall specify in, or attach to, the notice of appeal all matters s/he wishes to be considered for the purposes of the appeal.

59(1) Reflecting sub-sections 13(1), (2) of the Immigration Act 1971.

59(2) 'Certificate of entitlement' and 'entry clearance' are defined in section 167(2) to have the same meaning as under section 33(1) of the Immigration Act 1971.

59(3)(b) 'country' is defined in section 167(1).

59(4) Reflecting section 17(2) of the Immigration Act 1971. See notes to sections 67 and 68 below.

[A.1.293]
60 Limitations on rights of appeal under section 59

(1)   Section 59 does not entitle a person to appeal, on the ground that he has

a right of abode in the United Kingdom, against a decision that he requires leave to enter the United Kingdom if he does not hold—

(a) a United Kingdom passport describing him as a British citizen or as a citizen of the United Kingdom and Colonies having the right of abode in the United Kingdom; or
(b) a certificate of entitlement.

(2)   Section 59 does not entitle a person to appeal, on the ground that he does not require leave to enter the United Kingdom, against a decision that he does require such leave if he is required by immigration rules or an order under section 8(2) of the 1971 Act to hold a specified document but does not do so.

(3)   Section 59 does not entitle a person to appeal against a refusal of leave to enter while he is in the United Kingdom unless, at the time of the refusal, he held a current entry clearance or was a person named in a current work permit.

(4)   Subsection (5) applies to a person who seeks to enter the United Kingdom—

(a) as a visitor;
(b) in order to follow a course of study of not more than six months' duration for which he has been accepted;
(c) with the intention of studying but without having been accepted for any course of study; or
(d) as a dependant of a person within paragraph (a), (b) or (c).

(5)   That person—

(a) is not entitled to appeal under section 59 against a refusal of an entry clearance unless he is a family visitor; and
(b) is not entitled to appeal against a refusal of leave to enter if he does not hold a current entry clearance at the time of the refusal.

(6)   The Secretary of State may by regulations make provision—

(a) requiring a family visitor appealing under section 59 to pay such fee as may be fixed by the regulations;
(b) for such an appeal not to be entertained unless the required fee has been paid by the appellant;
(c) for the repayment of any such fee if the appeal is successful.

(7)   Section 59 does not entitle a person to appeal against a refusal of leave to enter, or against a refusal of an entry clearance, if the refusal is on the ground that he or any person whose dependant he is—

(a) does not hold a relevant document required by the immigration rules;
(b) does not satisfy a requirement of the immigration rules as to age or nationality or citizenship; or
(c) seeks entry for a period exceeding that permitted by the immigration rules.

(8)   The following are relevant documents—
(a) entry clearances;
(b) passports or other identity documents; and
(c) work permits.

(9)   Section 59 does not entitle a person to appeal against a refusal of leave to enter, or against a refusal of an entry clearance, if—

(a) the Secretary of State certifies that directions have been given by the Secretary of State (and not by a person acting under his authority) for the appellant not to be given entry to the United Kingdom on the ground that his exclusion is conducive to the public good; or

(b) the leave to enter, or entry clearance, was refused in compliance with any such directions.

(10) 'Family visitor' has such meaning as may be prescribed.

Commencement   Subsections 60(6) and (10) 22 May 2000 (SI 2000/1282). In full 2 October 2000 (SI 2000/2444).

Note   Reflecting section 13 of the Immigration Act 1971. See the note to section 59 above on definitions. See SI 2000/2333 the Immigration and Asylum (Appeals) Procedure Rules.

60(1) Reflecting Immigration Act 1971, section 13(3).

60(2) This restriction on the right of appeal has no parallel in the Immigration Act 1971. See the Immigration (Exemption from Control) Order 1972 (SI 1972/1613).

See also the Immigration (European Economic Area) Regulations 2000 (SI 2000/2326), as amended by the Immigration (European Economic Area) (Amendment) Regulations 2001 (SI 2001/865), and the note to section 80 for the position of those relying on European Community law rights.

60(3) Reflecting section 13(3) of the Immigration Act 1971.

60(4) Reflecting section 13(3A) of the Immigration Act 1971, save that as set out in 60(5)(a) rights of appeal have been restored to 'family visitors' (see subsection 10).

60(5)(a) Section 10 of the Asylum and Immigration Act 1993 abolished rights of appeal in family visitor cases. This section restores them.

60(6) See the Immigration Appeals (Family Visitor) (No 2) Regulations 2000 SI 2000/2446, in force 2 October 2000 and replacing and revoking the Immigration Appeals (Family Visitor) Regulations 2000 (SI 2000/2302). These define a 'family visitor' (see note to 60(10) below) and prescribe fees for those wishing to exercise their right of appeal as a family visitor. Following widespread protest, the level of fees was reduced by the Immigration Appeals (Family Visitor) (Amendment) Regulations 2001 (SI 20001/52), in force 12 January 2001. Under SI 2000/152 the fees are set at £125 for an oral hearing (the figure was previously £500) and £50 in all other cases (the figure was previously £150). The fee must be repaid if the appeal succeeds (SI 2000/2446, regulation 3(3)).

60(7) Reflecting section 13(3B) of the Immigration Act 1971.

60(8) Reflecting section 13 (3C) of the Immigration Act 1971.

60(9) Reflecting section 13(5) of the Immigration Act 1971. For appeals to the Special Immigration Appeals Commission see Regulation 32(4)(a) of the Immigration (European Economic Area) Regulations 2000 (SI 2000/2326), as amended by SI 2001/865 and the notes to the (now repealed) paragraph 119 of Schedule 14 of this Act.

60(10) See SI 2000/2446 (see note to 60(6) above). Regulation 2(2) of that instrument defines a family visitor as a person visiting his/her spouse, father, mother, child, grandparent, grandchild, brother, sister, uncle, aunt, nephew, niece or first cousin (regulation 2(2)(a)); a person visiting the father, mother, brother or sister of his/her spouse (regulation 2(2)(b)); a person visiting the following step- relations - father, mother, son, daughter, brother or sister (regulation 2(2)(c)); or a person visiting a person with whom s/he has lived as a member of an unmarried couple for at least two of the three years prior to the date of making the application for entry clearance (regulation 2(2)(d)).

Variation of limited leave to enter or remain

[A.1.294]
61 Variation of limited leave to enter or remain
A person may appeal against a decision to vary, or to refuse to vary, any limited leave to enter or remain in the United Kingdom which he has if, as a result of that decision, he may be required to leave the United Kingdom within 28 days of being notified of the decision.

Commencement   2 October 2000 (SI 2000/2444).

Note   For transitional provisions see SI 2000/2444, 3(1) and 4(1) and Schedule 2, paragraph 1(5) which provides that this section is not to have effect where the decision to vary, or to refuse to vary, the limited leave to enter or remain was made before 2 October 2000. See the Note at the beginning of Part IV on Transitional Provisions relating to Part IV for the amendments to the transitional provisions of SI 2000/2444, Commencement Order No 6, effected by the further transitional provisions of SI 2000/3099, Commencement Order No 8, for the purposes of this section.

Modelled on section 14 of the Immigration Act 1971, but with some important changes, notably in the insertion of the 28 days requirement and the lack of any appeal against the conditions to which leave is subject. This is intentional, as set out in paragraph 198 of the Explanatory Notes to this Act; it is based on 'the principle that a right of appeal should exist only for the most adverse immigration decisions and that there should be no right of appeal unless a decision requires the person's departure from the United Kingdom'. This paragraph of course expresses two principles, not one. Section 14(2) of the 1971 Act is not replicated. This section does not replicate the requirement of section 14(1) of the 1971 Act that a person have limited leave at the time of appealing. The provisions in respect of VOLO have in any event been tidied up, with the Immigration (Variation of Leave) Order 1976 (SI 1976/1572) being replaced by section 3 of this Act, and the Immigration (Variation of Leave) Amendment Order 2000 (SI 2000/2445).

See also Schedule 4, paragraph 17(1) and the note thereto.

[A.1.295]
62 Limitations on rights of appeal under section 61
(1)   Section 61 does not entitle a person or a person whose dependant he is to appeal against a refusal to vary leave if the refusal is on the ground that—

(a) a relevant document which is required by the immigration rules has not been issued;
(b) the person does not satisfy a requirement of the immigration rules as to age or nationality or citizenship;
(c) the variation would result in the duration of a person's leave exceeding that permitted by the immigration rules; or
(d) any fee required by or under any enactment has not been paid.

(2)   The following are relevant documents—

(a) entry clearances;
(b) passports or other identity documents; and
(c) work permits or equivalent documents issued after entry.

(3)   Section 61 does not entitle a person to appeal against a refusal to vary leave if either of the following conditions is satisfied.

(4)   The conditions are—

(a) that the Secretary of State has certified that the appellant's departure from the United Kingdom would be conducive to the public good as being in the interests of national security, the relations between the United Kingdom and any other country or for other reasons of a political nature; or
(b) that the decision questioned by the appeal was taken on that ground by the Secretary of State (and not by a person acting under his authority).

(5)   A person is not entitled to appeal under section 61 against—

(a) a variation made by statutory instrument; or
(b) a refusal of the Secretary of State to make a statutory instrument.

Commencement   2 October 2000 (SI 2000/2444).

Note
62(3) See the Immigration (European Economic Area) Regulations 2000 (SI 2000/2326), as amended by SI 2001/865, Regulation 36(4) for transitional provisions in respect of those with a right of appeal under SI 2000/2326.

Deportation

[A.1.296]
63 Deportation orders
(1)   A person may appeal to an adjudicator against—

(a) a decision of the Secretary of State to make a deportation order against him under section 5(1) of the 1971 Act as a result of his liability to deportation under section 3(5) of that Act; or
(b) a refusal by the Secretary of State to revoke a deportation order made against him.

(2)   A deportation order is not to be made against a person under section 5(1) of the 1971 Act while an appeal may be brought against the decision to make it.
(3)   Subsection (4) applies if—

(a) a person appeals under this section; and
(b) before or after he appeals, the Secretary of State serves on him notice that any directions which may be given for his removal as a result of the deportation order will be for his removal to a country or one of several countries specified in the notice.

(4)   The appellant may object to the country specified in the notice (or to one or more of those specified), and claim that he ought to be removed (if at all) to a different country specified by him.

Commencement   2 October 2000 (SI 2000/2444).

Note   For transitional provisions see SI 2000/2444, 3(1) and 4(1) and Schedule 2, paragraph 1(6), which provides that this section is not to have effect where the decision to make a deportation order, or the decision to refuse to revoke a deportation order, was made before 2 October 2000.

63(1)(a) See Schedule 14 paragraph 44(2) for amendments to section 3(5) of the Immigration Act 1971, limiting the circumstances in which there will be rights of appeal against deportation and reflecting the changes to the deportation regime effected by section 10 of this Act.

The wording of this sub-section reflects that of the original version of the Immigration and Asylum Bill (Bill 42). It was subsequently amended by the government in the Special Standing Committee to encompass section 3(6) of the Immigration Act 1971 (*Hansard* Offical Report of the Special Standing Committee Immigration and Asylum Bill 15th Sitting 27 April 1999 Cols 1135–1138). This would have given a person who had been recommended for deportation by a court and in respect of whom a deportation order had been made a new right of appeal against that decision to the IAA. However, in the House of Lords the government re-amended the Act to restore the Bill 42 version (*Hansard* HL Report Vol 604 Col 794). The legislative history is set out by the Lord Avebury, who sought a further amendment to reverse the re-amendment (see Hansard HL Report Vol 65 No 136 Cols 918 to 921 and Vol 65 No 147 cols 794 to 799). The government declined to change the Bill again, prompting the Lord Avebury's exasperated response to the Lord Williams of Mostyn: 'My lords, the Minister said he could see no reason for including this amendment in the Bill. Why then did the government see fit to include the provision in the first instance? I often think governments include provisions in Bills for which there is no good reason, but this is the first time I have heard a plain admission from a Minister on the floor of the House that they have actually done so' (Vol 65 No 147, Col 798).

63(2) Reflecting, when read with paragraph 18 of Schedule 4 to this Act, section 15(2) of the Immigration Act 1971.

63(4) See notes to sections 59 and 67.

[A.1.297]
64 Limitations on rights of appeal under section 63

(1)   Section 63 does not entitle a person to appeal against a decision to make a deportation order against him if the ground of the decision was that his deportation is conducive to the public good as being in the interests of national security or of the relations between the United Kingdom and any other country or for other reasons of a political nature.

(2)   Section 63 does not entitle a person to appeal against a refusal to revoke a deportation order, if—

(a) the Secretary of State has certified that the appellant's exclusion from the United Kingdom would be conducive to the public good; or

(b) revocation was refused on that ground by the Secretary of State (and not by a person acting under his authority).

(3)   Section 63 does not entitle a person to appeal against a refusal to revoke a deportation order while he is in the United Kingdom, whether because he has not complied with the requirement to leave or because he has contravened the prohibition on entering.

(4)   Subsection (5) applies to—

(a) an appeal against a decision to make a deportation order against a person as belonging to the family of another person; or

(b) an appeal against a refusal to revoke a deportation order so made.

(5)   The appellant is not to be allowed, for the purpose of showing that he does not or did not belong to another person's family, to dispute any statement

made with a view to obtaining leave for the appellant to enter or remain in the United Kingdom (including any statement made to obtain an entry clearance).

(6)   But subsection (5) does not apply if the appellant shows—

(a) that the statement was not so made by him or by any person acting with his authority; and

(b) that, when he took the benefit of the leave, he did not know any such statement had been made to obtain it or, if he did know, he was under the age of eighteen.

Commencement   2 October 2000 (SI 2000/2444).

Note   *64(1)* See Immigration (European Economic Area) Regulations 2000 (SI 2000/2326), as amended by SI 2001/865, regulation 36(4) for transitional provisions in respect of those with a right of appeal under SI 2000/2326 and the note to the (now repealed) paragraph 119 of Schedule 14 to this Act.

64(3) Reflecting the Immigration and Asylum Act 1971 section 15(5).

64(4)–(6) Reflecting section 15(6) of the Immigration Act 1971.

Human rights

[A.1.298]
65 [Racial discrimination and breach of human rights]
(1)   A person who alleges that an authority has, in taking any decision under the Immigration Acts relating to that person's entitlement to enter or remain in the United Kingdom, [racially discriminated against him or] acted in breach of his human rights may appeal to an adjudicator against that decision unless he has grounds for bringing an appeal against the decision under the Special Immigration Appeals Commission Act 1997.

(2)   For the purposes of this Part [:

(a) an authority racially discriminates against a person if he acts, or fails to act, in relation to that other person in a way which is unlawful by virtue of section 19B of the Race Relations Act 1976; and

(b)] acts in breach of a persons human rights if he acts, or fails to act, in relation to that other person in a way which is made unlawful by section 6(1) of the Human Rights Act 1998.

(3)   Subsections (4) and (5) apply if, in proceedings before an adjudicator or the Immigration Appeal Tribunal on an appeal, a question arises as to whether an authority has, in taking any decision under the Immigration Acts relating to the appellant's entitlement to enter or remain in the United Kingdom, [racially discriminated against the appelant or] acted in breach of the appellant's human rights.

(4)   The adjudicator, or the Tribunal, has jurisdiction to consider the question.

(5)   If the adjudicator, or the Tribunal, decides that the authority concerned acted in breach of the appellant's human rights, the appeal may be allowed on [the ground in question].

(6)   No appeal may be brought under this section by any person in respect of a decision if—

(a) that decision is already the subject of an appeal brought by him under the Special Immigration Appeals Commission Act 1997; and

(b) the appeal under that Act has not been determined.

(7) 'Authority' means—

(a) the Secretary of State;

(b) an immigration officer;

(c) a person responsible for the grant or refusal of entry clearance.

Commencement   2 October 2000 (SI 2000/2444). The section was subsequently amended, as detailed in the notes to *65(1)* and *65(2)* and set out in full in paragraphs 32 to 34 of Schedule 2 to the Race Relations (Amendment) Act 2001. The amendments came into force on 2 April 2001 (Race Relations (Amendment) Act 2000 section 10(2) and The Race Relations (Amendment) Act 2000 (Commencement) Order 2001 (SI 2001/566)).

Note   See the introductory note to this section in respect of the impact of the transitional provisions of SI 2000/2444, and in particular paragraph 1(7) of Schedule 2 on this section. See also SI 2000/2444, 3(1) and 4(1).

This section provides new rights of appeal in respect of breaches of the appellant's human rights and, subsequent to the amendment of the section by the Race Relations (Amendment) Act 2000, on the grounds of racial discrimination. Words in square brackets inserted by the Race Relations (Amendment) Act 2000 (for commencement see s 10(2) of that Act). The coming into force of that Act led to amendments to the regulations made under this part. The Immigration and Asylum Appeals (One Stop Procedure) (Amendment) Regulations 2001 (SI 2001/868) amends SI 2000/2444, primarily, although not solely, to take account of the Race Relations (Amendment) Act. The Immigration and Asylum Appeals (Notices) (Amendment) Regulations 2001 (SI 2001/868) amends SI 2000/2246, again primarily, but not solely, to take account of the Race Relations (Amendment) Act.

It is often forgotten (although not by the editor of the BILS March 1999 Special Bulletin on the Human Rights Act – see note 15 at page 29 of the Special Bulletin) that this is essentially a section about jurisdiction. Section 7 of the Human Rights Act 1998 gives a 'victim' (see section 7(1)) the right to bring proceedings against a public authority which 'has acted (or proposes to act) in a way which is made unlawful by section 6(1)'. Section 65 does not create the right of a person in the circumstances set out in 65(1) to bring proceedings, it simply designates the forum in which such proceedings should be brought and the procedures to be followed. This is important, because it means that any restrictions placed upon the exercise of section 65 appeal rights, for example under paragraph (7) of Schedule 2 of SI 2000/2444, as described above, are restrictions on the right to appeal to the adjudicator under these procedures. In such cases the would-be appellant may retain rights to bring proceedings in the courts. The same is true in respect of the Race Relations (Amendment) Act 2000. Section 65 of this Act is about jurisdiction to hear claims of race discrimination; it does not create the right to bring proceedings but simply designates forum and procedures.

See SI 2000/2246, as amended by SI 2001/868. Under regulation 4(1) of SI 2000/2246, as amended, written notice must be given to a person of any decision or action taken in respect of that person which is appealable. However, regulation 4(4), as amended, provides that no such notice is required 'by reason only of the fact that the decision could be appealed under' this section or under the corresponding provision of the Special Immigration Appeals Commission Act 1997(section 2A) 'if the person in question were to make an allegation that an authority had acted in breach of his human rights or racially discriminated against him in taking it; but such notice must be given upon such allegation being made'. In other words, people need not be told that they can appeal under section 65 unless and until they make an allegation that the decision breaches their human rights. Contrast the statement of the Home Secretary on Second Reading of the Immigration and Asylum Bill in the House of Commons 'when an application is refused, the applicant will be invited to set out all the grounds on which he wishes to remain in the United Kingdom, including asylum, the European Convention on Human Rights, or compassionate grounds' Hansard HC Report 22 February 1999, Col 40. The regulation seems to rely on 'allegation' being a term of art, distinct from 'claim'. Yet neither word is defined in the primary legislation, where the word 'alleges' in used in section 65(1), 'allegation' in 72(2)(a), and 'claim' in 73(2), 74(7) and 75(1) and 76(3). It is difficult to see a distinction between, for example, the use of 'alleges' in 65(1) and 'making a claim' in 73(2). Neither word is defined for the purposes of Part IV, SI 2000/2246, as amended, or SI 2000/2333. SI 2000/2244, as amended, is of little assistance in this regard; it defines 'claim' but only for the purposes of those regulations and only to mean a claim to which section 75 applies (regulation 2(1)). SI 2000/2244, as amended, does not define 'allegation'. The situation is further complicated by the use of a third phrase 'a question arises' in 65(3) and the jurisdiction and powers accorded to the adjudicator or Tribunal, when a question arises as to whether an authority has acted in breach of the appellant's human rights arises, by subsections 65(4) and 65(5).

See the Note on Transitional Provisions Relating to Part IV at the beginning of this Part for details of the assurances given by the Secretary of State in the *Pardeepan* case and subsequent written exchanges in the House of Lords as to how those assurances will work in practice and the effect of the notice regulations on the appellant's ability to exercise his/her rights under section 65.

Since this section came into force, the European Court of Human Rights has given judgement in the case of *Maaouia v France* (00/39652, 15 October 2000) in which it held that Article 6(1) of the European Convention on Human Rights did not apply to procedures for the expulsion of aliens, in that they were not proceedings that concerned the determination of a 'civil right or obligation' or of a criminal charge. The judgement in *Maaouia* is in line with previous decisions of the European Commission on Human Rights. The scope of the *Maaouia* judgment remains to be tested. However, regard should be had to the 'starred' decision of the Immigration Appeals Tribunal in *MNM* (OO/TH/02423, 1 November 2000), in which the *Maaouia* judgment was considered. The IAT followed *Maaouia* in holding that Article 6(1) did not apply but observed that this would make 'little if any difference' because in considering the fairness of the proceedings they would 'apply the same tests as would be applicable if Article 6(1) applied'.

This section, and section 69, are the only ones under which an adjudicator is prohibited by Rule 11(3) of SI 2000/2333 from giving leave to vary the grounds of appeal without needing to be satisfied that it is just to do so because of special circumstances.

65(1) 'alleges' see note above. The words 'racially discriminates against him or' were inserted into this Act by section 6(3) of the Race Relations (Amendment) Act 2000. Section 6 also amends section 57 of the Race Relations Act 1976 to ensure that appeals on the ground of racial discrimination are heard as part of the 'one-stop- appeal and not in other fora. Once again, section 65 is revealed as a section about jurisdiction. Note that section 6 also makes provision for claims of race discrimination to be heard by the Special Immigration Appeals Commission under the 1997 Act.

65(2) Subsection (a) was added by section 6(4) of the Race Relations (Amendment) Act 2000. Note that the Immigration Appellate Authority is not empowered to award damages, but where an appeal on the ground of racial discrimination is won before the IAA, it will be possible to bring proceedings in the county or sheriff's court to claim damages.

It is important to note the limitations on the rights of appeal against racial discrimination. The Race Relations (Amendment) Act 2000, which inserted these rights of appeal into section 65, makes special provision for 'immigration and nationality functions' as defined by new section 19D it inserts into the Race Relations Act 1976. Section 1 of the 2000 Act inserts a new section 19B into the 1976 Act, making it unlawful for a public authority in carrying out its functions to do any act which constitutes discrimination. However, 19D(1) provides that 'Section 19B does not make it unlawful for a relevant person to discriminate against another person on grounds of nationality or ethnic or national origins in carrying out immigration and nationality functions.' This provision was extremely controversial during the passage of the 2000 Act. It was argued that to discriminate is to go beyond treating people differently, to treating them differently without an objective justification and that there was therefore no need to exempt immigration and nationality functions. Indeed it was argued that to do so was to make express provision for those exercising immigration and nationality functions to treat people differently without objective justification. In recognition of this controversy, Section 19E provides for the Secretary of State to appoint a person to monitor the operation of this exception.

Directions for removal

[A.1.299]
66 Validity of directions for removal
(1)   This section applies if directions are given for a person's removal from the United Kingdom—

(a) on the ground that he is an illegal entrant;
(b) under section 10; or
(c) under the special powers conferred by Schedule 2 to the 1971 Act in relation to members of the crew of a ship or aircraft or persons coming to the United Kingdom to join a ship or aircraft as a member of the crew.

(2)   That person may appeal to an adjudicator against the directions on the ground that on the facts of his case there was in law no power to give them on the ground on which they were given.
(3)   This section does not entitle a person to appeal while he is in the United Kingdom unless he is appealing under section 65 or 69(5).
(4)   If a person appeals under this section against directions given by virtue of a deportation order, he may not dispute the original validity of that order.

Commencement   2 October 2000 (SI 2000/2444).

Note   For transitional provisions see SI 2000/2444, 3(1) and 4(1) and Schedule 2, paragraph 1(8) which provides that this section is not to have effect where removal directions were given before 2 October 2000.

Objection to destination

[A.1.300]
67 Removal on objection to destination
(1)   This section applies if directions are given under the 1971 Act for a person's removal from the United Kingdom—

(a) on his being refused leave to enter,
(b) on a deportation order being made against him, or

(c) on his having entered the United Kingdom in breach of a deportation order.

(2) That person may appeal to an adjudicator against the directions on the ground that he ought to be removed (if at all) to a different country specified by him.

Commencement   2 October 2000 (SI 2000/2444).

Note   For transitional provisions see SI 2000/2444, 3(1) and 4(1) and Schedule 2, paragraph 1(9), which provides that this section is not to have effect where removal directions were given before 2 October 2000.

See The Immigration (European Economic Area) Regulations 2000 (SI 2000/2326), as amended by SI 2001/865, regulation 25 for the application of this section to persons in the UK but refused admission in accordance with those regulations.

See sections 59, 63 and 68. Section 59 provides for the appellant to object to destination in the course of appeal against refusal of leave to enter. This section provides for a free-standing appeal against the destination to which the person is to be removed, like the appeal right in section 17(1) of the Immigration Act 1971. Thus far it is an exception to the 'one-stop' principle (see introductory note to this Part). However, the circumstances in which this appeal right is available are tightly circumscribed by section 68. Only those who meet the 68(1)(b) and 68(2) criteria will have a free-standing right of appeal against destination and without administrative error, it is difficult to see how there could be any such persons.

67(2) Seer v Immigration Appeal Tribunal ex p Murunganadarajah & Sureshkumar [1986] Imm AR 382, CA. The appeal right does not mean that there will be a review of the decision to remove.

[A.1.301]
68 Limitations on rights of appeal under section 67
(1)   Section 67 does not entitle a person to appeal against directions given on his being refused leave to enter the United Kingdom unless—

(a) he is also appealing under section 59(1) against the decision that he requires leave to enter; or
(b) he was refused leave at a time when he held a current entry clearance or was a person named in a current work permit.

(2)   If a person is entitled to object to a country on an appeal under section 59 or 63 and—

(a) he does not object to it on that appeal, or
(b) his objection to it on that appeal is not sustained,

section 67 does not entitle him to appeal against any directions subsequently given as a result of the refusal or order in question, if their effect will be his removal to that country.

(3)   A person who claims that he ought to be removed to a country other than one he has objected to on an appeal under section 59, 63 or 67 must produce evidence, if he is not a national or citizen of that other country, that that country will admit him.

Commencement   2 October 2000 (SI 2000/2444).

Note For transitional provisions see SI 2000/2444, 3(1) and 4(1).

See the note to section 67 above. See The Immigration (European Economic Area) Regulations 2000 (SI 2000/2326, as amended by 2001/865), regulation 25 and the note to section 67 above.

68(2) See SI 2000/2444, Schedule 2, paragraph 1(10) which makes transitional provision applying the reference to an appeal herein to appeals under section 17(2) and (3) of the Immigration Act 1971.

68(3) This requirement to produce evidence that the country will admit the applicant gives statutory effect to the decision in *Mounciffe v Secretary of State for the Home Department* [1996] Imm AR 265, CA, and paragraph 385 of HC 395.

Asylum

[A.1.302]
69 Claims for asylum
(1)   A person who is refused leave to enter the United Kingdom under the 1971 Act may appeal against the refusal to an adjudicator on the ground that his removal in consequence of the refusal would be contrary to the Convention.
(2)   If, as a result of a decision to vary, or to refuse to vary, a person's limited leave to enter or remain in the United Kingdom, he may be required to leave the United Kingdom within 28 days of being notified of the decision, he may appeal against the decision to an adjudicator on the ground that such a requirement would be contrary to the Convention.
(3)   A person who—

(a)   has been refused leave to enter or remain in the United Kingdom on the basis of a claim for asylum made by him, but
(b)   has been granted (whether before or after the decision to refuse leave) limited leave to enter or remain,

may, if that limited leave will not expire within 28 days of his being notified of the decision, appeal to an adjudicator against the refusal on the ground that requiring him to leave the United Kingdom after the time limited by that leave would be contrary to the Convention.

(4)   If the Secretary of State—

(a)   has decided to make a deportation order against a person under section 5(1) of the 1971 Act, or
(b)   has refused to revoke such an order,

that person may appeal to an adjudicator against the decision or refusal on the ground that his removal in pursuance of the order would be contrary to the Convention.
(5)   If directions are given as mentioned in section 66(1) for the removal of a person from the United Kingdom, he may appeal to an adjudicator on the ground that his removal in pursuance of the directions would be contrary to the Convention.
(6)   'Contrary to the Convention' means contrary to the United Kingdom's obligations under the Refugee Convention.

Commencement   2 October 2000 (SI 2000/2444).

Note   For transitional provisions see SI 2000/2444, 3(1) and 4(1), as amended by the further transitional provisions of SI 2000/3099. See SI 2000/2333 Rule 4(6) for transitional provision applying references to this section in Rule 11(3) to appeals under section 8 of the Asylum and Immigration (Appeals) Act 1993. This section, and section 65, are the only ones under which an adjudicator is prohibited by Rule 11(3) of SI 2000/2333 from giving leave to vary the grounds of appeal without needing to be satisfied that it is just to do so because of special circumstances.See the note on 'Transitional Provisions relating to Part IV' at the beginning of this Part.

69(1) See SI 2000/2444, Schedule 2, paragraph 1(11)(a), which provides that 69(1) is not to have effect where the decision to refuse to leave to enter or remain was made before 2 October 2000.

69(2) See Schedule 4, paragraph 17(1). See SI 2000/2444, paragraph Schedule 2, paragraph 1(11)(b), which provides that 69(2) is not to have effect where the decision to vary or to refuse to vary leave was made before 2 October 2000. As set out in the second paragraph of the note on 'Transitional Provisions relating to Part IV' at the beginning of this Part, SI 2000/2444 had further to be amended by SI 2000/3099 in order to make this sub-section work as intended.

69(3) See SI 2000/2444, paragraph Schedule 2, paragraph 1(11)(c), which provides that 69(3) is not to have effect where the decision to refuse leave was made before 2 October 2000.

69(4) See SI 2000/2444, paragraph Schedule 2, paragraph 1(11)(d), which provides that 69(4) is not to have effect where the decision to make, or to refuse to revoke, a deportation order was made before 2 October 2000.

69(5) See SI 2000/2444, paragraph Schedule 2, paragraph 1(11)(e), which provides that 69(5) is not to have effect where the removal directions were given before 2 October 2000.

[A.1.303]
70 Limitations on rights of appeal under section 69
(1)   Section 69(1) does not entitle a person to appeal against a refusal of leave to enter if—

(a) the Secretary of State certifies that directions have been given by the Secretary of State (and not by a person acting under his authority) for the appellant not to be given entry to the United Kingdom on the ground that his exclusion is in the interests of national security; or
(b) the leave to enter was refused in compliance with any such directions.

(2)   Section 69(2) does not entitle a person to appeal against—

(a) a variation of his leave which reduces its duration, or
(b) a refusal to enlarge or remove the limit on its duration,

if either of the following conditions is satisfied.
(3)   The conditions are—

(a) that the Secretary of State has certified that the appellant's departure from the United Kingdom would be in the interests of national security; or
(b) that the decision questioned by the appeal was taken on that ground by the Secretary of State (and not by a person acting under his authority).

(4)   Section 69(3) does not entitle a person to appeal against a refusal mentioned in paragraph (a) of that subsection if—

(a) the reason for the refusal was that he was a person to whom the Refugee Convention did not apply by reason of Article 1(F) of that Convention; and

(b) the Secretary of State has certified that the disclosure of material on which the refusal was based is not in the interests of national security.

(5)   Section 69(4)(a) does not entitle a person to appeal against a decision to make a deportation order against him if the ground of the decision was that his deportation is in the interests of national security.

(6)   Section 69(4)(b) does not entitle a person to appeal against a refusal to revoke a deportation order, if—

(a) the Secretary of State has certified that the appellant's exclusion from the United Kingdom would be in the interests of national security; or

(b) if revocation was refused on that ground by the Secretary of State (and not by a person acting under his authority).

(7)   A person may not bring an appeal on any of the grounds mentioned in subsections (1) to (5) of section 69—

(a) if, before the time of the refusal, variation, decision or directions (as the case may be) he has not made a claim for asylum;

(b) otherwise than under that section.

(8)   A person may not appeal under section 69(4)(b) if he has had the right to appeal under section 69(4)(a) (whether or not he has exercised it).

Commencement   2 October 2000 (SI 2000/2444).

Note   *74(4)* See SI 2000/2333, rule 8(7) which provides that where a notice has been served on an appellant under this section, the appellant shall attach to the notice of appeal a statement form, on which additional grounds s/he has or may have for wishing to enter or remain in the UK may be stated, whether or not that form has been completed.

70(8) See SI 2000/2444, Schedule 2, paragraph 1(12) extending the reference to a right to appeal to appeals under section 8(3)(a) of the Asylum and Immigration Appeals Act 1993.

Removal to safe countries

[A.1.304]
71 Removal of asylum claimants to safe third countries
(1)   This section applies if a certificate has been issued under section 11 or 12.
(2)   The person in respect of whom the certificate was issued may appeal against it to an adjudicator on the ground that any of the conditions applicable to that certificate was not satisfied when it was issued, or has since ceased to be satisfied.

Commencement   2 October 2000 (SI 2000/2444).

Note   See SI 2000/2244 as amended and the notes to ss 74 and 75 below.

Miscellaneous

[A.1.305]
72 Miscellaneous limitations on rights of appeal
(1)   Unless a certificate issued under section 11 or 12 has been set aside on an appeal under section 65 or 71 or otherwise ceases to have effect, the person in respect of whom the certificate was issued is not entitled to appeal under this Act as respects any matter arising before his removal from the United Kingdom.
(2)   A person who has been, or is to be, sent to a member State or to a country designated under section 12(1)(b) is not, while he is in the United Kingdom, entitled to appeal—

(a)   under section 65 if the Secretary of State certifies that his allegation that a person acted in breach of his human rights [or racially discriminated against him] is manifestly unfounded; or
(b)   under section 71.

(3)   No appeal under this Part may be made in relation to a decision made on an application if—

(a)   the application was required to be made in a prescribed form but was not made in that form; or
(b)   the applicant was required to take prescribed steps in relation to the application, or to take such steps at a prescribed time or within a prescribed period, but failed to do so.

Commencement   Subsection 72(3) 22 May 2000 (SI 2000/1282 (C 38)) for the purposes of enabling subordinate legislation to be made under it. The section was subsequently amended, as detailed in the note to *72(2)*.   The amendment took effect on 2 April 2001 (Race Relations (Amendment) Act 2000, section 10(2) and the Race Relations (Amendment) Act 2000 (Commencement) Order 2001 (SI 2001/566)).

Note   *72(2)* See section 12 of this Act and note thereto, and Asylum (Designated Safe Third Countries) Order 2000 (SI 2000/2245). See also SI 2000/2333, Rule 9 which provides that where an appellant is treated as appealing on additional grounds by virtue of this section, the appellant must serve on the person and at the address specified in the supplementary grounds of refusal any variation of his/her grounds of appeal not later than 5 days after receiving the supplementary grounds of refusal.

Words in square brackets in subsection (2)(a) inserted by the Race Relations (Amendment) Act 2000, Sch 2, para 36.

[A.1.306]
73 Limitation on further appeals
(1)   This section applies where a person ('the appellant') has appealed under the Special Immigration Appeals Commission Act 1997 or this Act and that appeal ('the original appeal') has been finally determined.

(2)   If the appellant serves a notice of appeal making a claim that [in taking a decision, a decision-maker racially discriminated against the appellant or that] a decision of a decision-maker was in breach of the appellant's human rights, the Secretary of State may certify that in his opinion—

(a) the appellant's claim—
   (i) could reasonably have been included in a statement required from him under section 74 but was not so included, or
   (ii) could reasonably have been made in the original appeal but was not so made;
(b) one purpose of such a claim would be to delay the removal from the United Kingdom of the appellant or of any member of his family; and
(c) the appellant had no other legitimate purpose for making the claim.

(3) On the issuing of a certificate by the Secretary of State under subsection (2), the appeal, so far as relating to that claim, is to be treated as finally determined.

(4) Subsection (5) applies if a notice under section 74 was served on the appellant before the determination of his original appeal and the appellant has served a further notice of appeal.

(5) The Secretary of State may certify that grounds contained in the notice of appeal were considered in the original appeal.

(6) On the issuing of a certificate by the Secretary of State under subsection (5), the appeal, so far as relating to those grounds, is to be treated as finally determined.

(7) Subsection (8) applies if, on the application of the appellant, an immigration officer or the Secretary of State makes a decision in relation to the appellant.

(8) The immigration officer or, as the case may be, the Secretary of State may certify that in his opinion—

(a) one purpose of making the application was to delay the removal from the United Kingdom of the appellant or any member of his family; and
(b) the appellant had no other legitimate purpose for making the application.

(9) No appeal may be brought under the Special Immigration Appeals Commission Act 1997 or this Act against a decision on an application in respect of which a certificate has been issued under subsection (8).

(10) Nothing in section 58(6) affects the operation of subsections (3) and (6).

Commencement 2 October 2000 (SI 2444/2000). The section was subsequently amended, as detailed in the note to *73(2)*. The section as amended came into force on 2 April 2001 (Race Relations (Amendment) Act 2000, section 10(2) and the Race Relations (Amendment) Act 2000 (Commencement) Order 2001 (SI 2001/566)).

Note See regulation 5(3) of Immigration and Asylum Appeals (One-Stop Procedure) Regulations 2000, SI 2000/2244, as amended by SI 2001/867, making this section applicable, with the modifications set out in those regulations, to appeals pursuant to service of notices under section 75. New forms of the notice, set out in the Schedules to SI 2001/867 make express reference to certification under this section. See note to section 75.

Words in square brackets in subsection (2) inserted by the Race Relations (Amendment) Act 2000, Sch 2, para 36.

73(2) 'claim' see note to section 65 above.

'One-stop' procedure

[A.1.307]
74 Duty to disclose the grounds for appeal etc
(1) This section applies if—

(a) the decision on an application for leave to enter or remain in the United Kingdom is that the application be refused; and
(b) the applicant, while he is in the United Kingdom, is entitled to appeal against the refusal under the Special Immigration Appeals Commission Act 1997 or this Act.

(2) This section also applies if—

(a) as a result of a decision to vary, or to refuse to vary, any limited leave to enter or remain in the United Kingdom which a person has, he may be required to leave the United Kingdom within 28 days of being notified of the decision; and
(b) that person is entitled to appeal against the decision under the Special Immigration Appeals Commission Act 1997 or this Act.

(3) This section also applies if—

(a) the Secretary of State has decided to make a deportation order against a person under section 5(1) of the 1971 Act as a result of his liability to deportation under section 3(5) of that Act; and
(b) that person, while he is in the United Kingdom, is entitled to appeal against that decision under the Special Immigration Appeals Commission Act 1997 or this Act.

(4) The decision-maker must serve on the applicant and on any relevant member of his family a notice requiring the recipient of the notice to state any additional grounds which he has or may have for wishing to enter or remain in the United Kingdom.
(5) 'Decision-maker' means the Secretary of State or (as the case may be) an immigration officer.

(6) The statement must be—

(a) in writing; and
(b) served on the Secretary of State before the end of such period as may be prescribed.

(7) A statement required under this section must—

(a) if the person making it wishes to claim asylum, include a claim for asylum;
[(aa) if he claims that he was racially discriminated against, include notice of that claim;] and
(b) if he claims that an act breached his human rights, include notice of that claim.

(8) Regulations may prescribe the persons who, in relation to an applicant, are relevant members of his family.
(9) Regulations may prescribe the procedure to be followed in connection with notices given and statements made in accordance with this section and, in

particular, may prescribe the form in which such notices and statements are to be given or made.

Commencement   22 May 2000 (SI 2000/1282) for the purposes of enabling subordinate legislation to be made under it . In full 2 October 2000 (SI 2000/2444). The section was subsequently amended, as detailed in the note to *74(7)*. The section as amended came into force on 2 April 2001 (Race Relations (Amendment) Act 2000, section 10(2) and the Race Relations (Amendment) Act 2000 (Commencement) Order 2001 (SI 2001/566)).

Note   See Immigration and Asylum Appeals (One-Stop Procedure) Regulations 2000 (SI 2000/2244), as amended by SI 2001/867, and the note to section 75 of this Act. See also the Immigration and Asylum Appeals (Notices) Regulations 2000 (2000/2246, as amended by SI 2001/868) made under section 166(3) of, and paragraph 1 of Schedule 4 to, this Act.

74(4) The form of the notice is set out in Part I of the Schedule to SI 2001/867, replacing the form of notice previously set out in Part I of the Schedule to SI 2000/2244.

74(6)(b) Regulation 4(3) of SI 2000/2244, as amended, prescribes the periods. 4(3)(a) prescribes a period of 10 days where the person is entitled to appeal under this Act. Regulation 4(3)(b) prescribes a period of 5 days where the person is entitled to appeal under the Special Immigration Appeals Act 1997. Regulation 4 sets out how these periods are to be calculated.

74(7) 'claim' see note to section 65 above. Words in square brackets (subsection (7)(aa)) inserted by the Race Relations (Amendment) Act 2000, Sch 2, para 37.

74(8) The definition of a relevant member of the applicant's family for the purposes of this section is set out in SI 2000/2244, as amended, regulation 6. A 'relevant member' is a person who is not themselves an applicant for the purposes of 74(4) but is the subject of a decision mentioned in 74(1)(a), 74(2)(a) or 74(3)(a) and 'appears to the decision maker to be' (regulation 6(b)) the applicant's spouse; a child of the applicant or of the applicant's spouse; a person who has been living with the applicant as a member of an unmarried couple for at least two of the three years before the day on which the decision was made; a person who is dependent on the applicant or a person on whom the applicant is dependant.

[A.1.308]
75 Duty to disclose grounds for entering etc the United Kingdom
(1)   This section applies if a person who—

(a) is an illegal entrant,
(b) is liable to be removed under section 10, or
(c) has arrived in the United Kingdom without—
    (i)   leave to enter;
    (ii) an entry clearance; or
    (iii) a current work permit in which he is named,

makes a claim for asylum or a claim that it would be contrary to the United Kingdom's obligations under the Human Rights Convention for him to be removed from, or required to leave, the United Kingdom.
(2)   The person responsible for the determination of the claim must serve on the claimant and on any relevant member of his family a notice requiring the recipient of the notice to state any additional grounds which he has or may have for wishing to enter or remain in the United Kingdom.
(3)   The statement must be—

(a) in writing; and

(b) served on the person who is responsible for the determination of the claim before the end of such period as may be prescribed.

(4) Regulations may prescribe the procedure to be followed in connection with notices given and statements made in accordance with this section and, in particular, may prescribe the form in which such notices and statements are to be given or made.

(5) Regulations may prescribe the persons who, in relation to a claimant, are relevant members of his family.

(6) Regulations may provide that, if a claim is determined against the claimant, prescribed provisions of section 73, 76, or 77 are to apply to an appeal against that determination by a person on whom a notice has been served under subsection (2), with such modifications (if any) as may be prescribed.

Commencement   22 May 2000 (SI 2000/1282 (C 38)) for the purposes of enabling subordinate legislation to be made under it. In full 2 October 2000 (SI 2000/2444).

Note   See SI 2000/2244, as amended by SI 2001/867, and the note to section 74 above. The Explanatory Note to SI 2000/2244 states:

'These regulations set out the procedure for the serving of notices and statements. Apart from the fact that the form of the notice (which is shown in the Schedule to the Regulations) differs according to whether it is a section 74 or a section 75 notice, and in some cases the time limit for serving the statement differs, the Regulations make no distinction between section 74 and section 75 of the Act.'

SI 2001/867 provides for new notices to replace those appended as Schedules to SI 2000/2244.   These new notices reflect amendments made to this Act by the Race Relations (Amendment) Act 2000.   They also insert a new paragraph dealing with the issue of certificates under section 73 above.   The notices in the Schedules to SI 2000/2244 made no reference to such certificates.   The notices in the Schedules to 2001/867 state 'if you have already appealed under the Immigration and Asylum Act 1999 against an earlier decision we may issue a certificate under section 73 of the Act which cuts off or limits your appeal against this new decision.   This is likely to happen if your grounds for appeal were dealt with at the earlier appeal or could have been mentioned then'.

Regulation 5 of SI 2000/2244 sets out the application of section 73 to appeals pursuant to notices given under section 75. Sections 73, 76 and 77 are made applicable to claims that are not determined within the period of 10 days prescribed by regulation 4(4) – see note to 75(3)(b).

75(1) 'claim' see note to section 65 above.

75(3)(b) Regulation 4(4) of SI 2000/1282 prescribes a period of 10 days. Regulation 4 sets out how that period is to be calculated.

75(4) The form of the notice is set out in Part II of the Schedule to SI 2001/867, replacing the form of notice set out in Part II of the Schedule to SI 2000/2244.

75(5) Regulation 7 of SI 2000/2244, as amended, defines a relevant member of a claimant's family for the purposes of this section as a person who is not a claimant for the purposes of section 75(2) but has made an application for leave to enter or remain in the UK and 'appears to the decision-taker to be' (regulation 7(b)) the claimant's spouse; a child of the claimant or spouse, a person who has been living with the claimant as a member of an unmarried couple for at least two of the three years before the day on which the claim was made; a person who is dependent on the claimant or a person on whom the claimant is dependent.

[A.1.309]
76 Result of failure to comply with section 74
(1)   In this section—

(a) 'the applicant' means the person on whom a notice has been served under section 74(4);
(b) 'notice' means a notice served under that section; and
(c) 'statement' means the statement which the notice requires the applicant to make to the Secretary of State.

(2)   If the applicant's statement does not mention a particular ground—

(a) on which he wishes to enter or remain in the United Kingdom, and
(b) of which he is aware at the material time,

he may not rely on that ground in any appeal under the Special Immigration Appeals Commission Act 1997 or this Part.

(3)   Subsection (2) does not apply if—

(a) the ground is a claim for asylum or a claim that an act [racially discriminated against the applicant or breached his] human rights; or
(b) the Secretary of State considers that the applicant had a reasonable excuse for the omission.

(4)   Subsection (5) applies if the applicant's statement does not include a claim for asylum.
(5)   If the applicant claims asylum after the end of the period prescribed under section 74(6)(b), no appeal may be made under section 69 if the Secretary of State has certified that in his opinion—

(a) one purpose of making the claim for asylum was to delay the removal from the United Kingdom of the applicant or of any member of his family; and
(b) the applicant had no other legitimate purpose for making the application.

(6)   'Member of the family' has such meaning as may be prescribed.

Commencement   Sub-section 76(6) 22 May 2000 (SI 2000/1282). In full 2 October 2000 (SI 2000/2444). The section was subsequently amended, as detailed in the note to 76(3).   The section as amended came into force on 2 April 2001 (Race Relations (Amendment) Act 2000, section 10(2) and the Race Relations (Amendment) Act 2000 (Commencement) Order 2001 (SI 2001/566)).

Note   See SI 2000/2244, as amended by SI 2001/865 and the notes to sections 74 and 75 above. Regulation 5(6) of SI 2000/2244 makes provision for section 73 to apply to appeals pursuant to service of notices under section 75.

76(3) 'claim' see note to section 65 above. Words in square brackets inserted by the Race Relations (Amendment) Act 2000, Sch 2, para 38, replacing the words 'breached the applicant's'.

76(6) 'member of the family' for the purposes of this section is defined in Regulation 8 of SI 2000/2244, as amended, as a person on whom the applicant is dependent or the applicant's spouse; the child of the applicant or the spouse; a person who has been living with the applicant as a member of an unmarried couple for at least two of the three years before the day on which the applicant claimed asylum, or a person who is dependent on the applicant.

[A.1.310]
77 'One-stop' appeals
(1)   This section applies in relation to—

(a) an appeal brought on any of the grounds mentioned in section 69;
(b) any other appeal against a decision—
> (i) to refuse an application for leave to enter or remain in the United Kingdom;
> (ii) to vary, or to refuse to vary, any limited leave to enter or remain in the United Kingdom, which has the result mentioned in section 74(2)(a); or
> (iii) to make a deportation order against a person under section 5(1) of the 1971 Act as a result of his liability to deportation under section 3(5) of that Act.

(2)   Subject to section 72(2), the appellant is to be treated as also appealing on any additional grounds—

(a) which he may have for appealing against the refusal, variation, decision or directions in question under any other provision of this Act; and
(b) which he is not prevented (by any provision of section 76) from relying on.

(3)   In considering—

(a) any ground mentioned in section 69, or
(b) any question relating to the appellant's rights under Article 3 of the Human Rights Convention,

the appellate authority may take into account any evidence which it considers to be relevant to the appeal (including evidence about matters arising after the date on which the decision appealed against was taken).

(4)   In considering any other ground, the appellate authority may take into account only evidence—

(a) which was available to the Secretary of State at the time when the decision appealed against was taken; or
(b) which relates to relevant facts as at that date.

(5)   'Additional grounds', in relation to an appeal, means any grounds specified in a statement made to the Secretary of State under section 74(4) other than those on which the appeal has been brought.
(6)   'Appellate authority' means an adjudicator, the Tribunal or the Special Immigration Appeals Commission.

Commencement   2 October 2000 (SI 2000/2444).

Note   See SI 2000/2244 and the note to sections 74 and 75 above. Regulation 5(6) of SI 2000/2244 sets out the application of this section, with the modifications set out in that regulation to appeals pursuant to service of notices under section 75.

77(3) This provision of the statute reflects the decision in *Sandralingham & Ravichandran v Secretary of State for the Home Department* [1996] Imm AR 97.

77(4) This provision reflects the decision in *R v Immigration Appeals Tribunal ex p Kotecha* [1983] All ER 289.

[A.1.311]
78 Transfer of appellate proceedings

(1)   Subsection (3) applies if—

(a) a person who has brought an appeal under this Part has been notified of the Secretary of State's decision to make a deportation order against him; and

(b) as a result of section 64(1), he is not entitled to appeal against that decision under section 63.

(2)   Subsection (3) also applies if—

(a) a person who has brought an appeal under this Part has been notified of the Secretary of State's decision to refuse to revoke a deportation order made against him; and

(b) as a result of section 64(2), he is not entitled to appeal against that refusal under section 63.

(3)   If he appeals against that decision under section 2(1) or 2A of the Special Immigration Appeals Commission Act 1997, any appeal under this Part is transferred to, and must be heard by, the Commission.

(4)   Subsection (5) applies if a person, in a statement required by a notice under section 74 or 75, states an additional ground which relates to a matter which may be the subject of an appeal under section 2(1) or 2A of the Special Immigration Appeals Commission Act 1997.

(5)   The appeal under this Part is transferred to, and must be heard by, the Commission.

Commencement   2 October 2000 (SI 2000/2444).

Appeals without merit

[A.1.312]
79 Penalty on continuing an appeal without merit

(1)   If, at any time before it determines an appeal, the Immigration Appeal Tribunal considers that the appeal has no merit it may notify the appellant of its opinion.

(2)   A notice under subsection (1) must—

(a) include an explanation of the Tribunal's powers under this section; and
(b) be made in such form as may be required by rules made under paragraph 3 of Schedule 4.

(3)   Subsection (1) does not apply if leave for appeal to the Tribunal was required.

(4)   Subsection (5) applies if an appeal which has been continued by the appellant after he has been given a notice under subsection (1) is dismissed.

(5)   The Tribunal may impose on the appellant, or on his representative, a penalty of the specified amount.

(6)   'Specified' means specified by an order made by the Lord Chancellor.

(7)   The Lord Chancellor may by order make such provision as he considers appropriate as to—

(a) the enforcement in England and Wales and Northern Ireland, and

(b) the payment and application,

of penalties imposed under this section.

(8) Such an order may, in particular, make provision similar to that made by sections 129 and 130 of the County Courts Act 1984.

(9) An order imposing a penalty under subsection (5) may be enforced in Scotland as if it were an extract registered decree arbitral bearing a warrant for execution issued by the sheriff court of any sheriffdom in Scotland.

EEA nationals

[A.1.313]
80 EEA nationals
(1) The Secretary of State may by regulations make provision for appeals against any immigration decision in relation to—

(a) an EEA national;
(b) a member of the family of an EEA national;
(c) a member of the family of a United Kingdom national who is neither such a national nor an EEA national.

(2) 'Immigration decision' means a decision concerning a person's removal from the United Kingdom or his entitlement—

(a) to be admitted to the United Kingdom;
(b) to reside, or to continue to reside, in the United Kingdom; or
(c) to be issued with, or not to have withdrawn, a residence permit.

(3) The regulations may also make provision for appeals against any decision concerning the matters mentioned in subsection (1) taken in relation to a citizen of any other State on whom any such entitlement has been conferred by an agreement to which the United Kingdom is a party or by which it is bound.

(4) An appeal under the regulations lies to an adjudicator or, in such circumstances as may be prescribed, to the Commission.

(5) The regulations may provide for appeals from the adjudicator or the Commission.

(6) The regulations may prescribe cases, or classes of case, in which a person is not entitled to appeal while he is in the United Kingdom.

(7) The regulations may make provision under which an appellant may be required to state, in such manner as may be prescribed, any grounds he has or may have for wishing to be admitted to, or to remain in, the United Kingdom additional to those on which he is appealing and for the consequences of such a requirement.

(8) The regulations may—

(a) amend sections 2 and 2A of the Special Immigration Appeals Commission Act 1997 (appellate jurisdiction of the Commission);
(b) amend or revoke the Immigration (European Economic Area) Order 1994.

(9) Part IV has effect subject to any regulations made under this section.

(10) 'EEA national' means a person who is, or claims to be, a national of an EEA State (other than the United Kingdom).

(11) 'United Kingdom national' means a person who falls to be treated as a national of the United Kingdom for the purposes of the Community Treaties.

(12)   If a person claims to be an EEA national, he may not appeal under the regulations unless he produces—

(a) a valid national identity card, or
(b) a valid passport,

issued by an EEA State other than the United Kingdom.

(13)   For the purposes of subsection (12), a document—

(a) is to be regarded as being what it purports to be unless its falsity is reasonably apparent; and
(b) is to be regarded as relating to the person producing it unless it is reasonably apparent that it relates to another person.

(14)   The regulations may—

(a) prescribe the persons who, for the purposes of this section, are the members of a person's family; and
(b) make provision as to the manner in which membership of a person's family is to be established.

(15)   'Residence permit' means any permit or other document issued by the Secretary of State as proof of the holder's right of residence in the United Kingdom.

Commencement   22 May 2000 (SI 2000/1282).

Note   See Immigration (European Economic Area) Regulations 2000 (SI 2000/2326) made under this section and under section 2(2) of the European Communities Act 1972, in force 2 October 2000. Like so many of the regulations made under this Part, these have been amended, see the Immigration (European Economic Area) (Amendment) Regulations 2001 (SI 2001/285), in force 2 April 2001. The Regulations revoke, re-enact and amend the provisions of the Immigration (European Economic Area) Order 1994 (SI 1994/1895, as amended by SI 1997/2981). They implement the following European Community Council directives: 64/221/EEC, 68/360/EEC. 72/194/EEC, 73/148/EEC, 75/34/EEC. 75/35/EEC, 90/364/EEC, 90/365/EEC and 93/96/EEC. The rights they give should be read and considered with the directly applicable rights set out in Commission Regulation 1251/70/EEC.

The major change from SI 1994/1895 is that the Regulations create new free-standing rights of appeal, as set out in Part VII of the regulations. These rights extend to nationals of Iceland, Liechtenstein and Norway, States part to the Eureopan Economic Area Agreement. Where a decision on removal or admission, or the issue, renewal or revocation of residence permits or other documents is taken under these regulations or under Commission Regulation 1251/70/EEC, there is provision for a right of appeal (Regulation 29 as amended). Under Regulation 35 these provisions are only to have effect in relation to decisions taken on or after 2 October 2000. Transitional provision is made. See regulation 30 for those appeals against decisions concerning admission that can only be made from outside the UK.

The other main changes are:

For the purposes of the Immigration Act 1971 and the British Nationality Act 1981, people with rights to remain in the UK under Commission Regulation 1251/70 and directive 75/34/EC, and EEA nationals and family members granted permission to remain under UK immigration law, are to be regarded as being in the UK without being subject to any restriction on the period for which they may remain (Regulation 8).

A new power to treat extended family members as set out in Regulation 10 as 'family members' for the purposes of the rights given by the regulations (see Regulation 10), subject to the amendments effected by regulation 5 of SI 2001/285 as set out below.

The extension of community rights to family members of a UK national in order to give effect to the judgment of the ECJ in *R v Immigration Appeal Tribunal and Surinder Singh, ex p Secretary of State for the Home Department* [1992] ECR I-4265.

Powers for an immigration officer to revoke an EEA family permit on the grounds of public policy, public security or public health, and where the family member who is not an EEA national arrives in the UK at a time when s/he is not the family member of a qualified person (Regulation 22).

The provisions for the grant of an EEA family permit, previously found in the Immigration Rules, now appear in Regulation 13. The regulations cover procedural and transitional matters.

SI 2000/2326 came into force on 2 October 2000. SI 2001/285, amending it to correct errors and make changes, came into force on 2 April 2001. It was considered necessary to amend reg 4 to make clear that references to the activity of a self-employed person were references to such activity in the UK. Regulation 10(4) of SI 2000/2326 was amended by reg 5 of SI 2001/285 to limit the potential beneficiaries of that regulation to relatives of the relevant EEA national or his/her spouse, in accordance with Article 10(2) of Council Regulation (EEC) 1612/68 and Article 1(2) of Council Directive 73/148/EEC. Other amendments effected by 20001/285 are to take account of the coming into force of the Race Relations (Amendment) Act 2001. They make provision for EEA nationals appealing under this section to appeal under section 65 of this Part on the grounds of racial discrimination. They also make provision for the certification of such appeals as manifestly unfounded, by the insertion of a new paragraph 9A into Schedule 4 of this Act.

See also Immigration and Asylum Appeals (Notices) Regulations (SI 2000/2246), as amended by SI 2001/2246, regulation 2, defining an appeal for the purposes of Part IV of this Act to encompass an appeal under SI 2000/2326, as amended, and SI 2000/2333 Immigration and Asylum Appeals (Procedure) Rules 2000. Rule 12(1)(ii) provides for an allegation that an appellant is not entitled to appeal by virtue of this section to be dealt with as a preliminary issue on appeal.

Grants

[A.1.314]
81 Grants to voluntary organisations
(1)   The Secretary of State may, with the approval of the Treasury, make grants to any voluntary organisation which provides advice or assistance for, or other services for the welfare of, persons who have rights of appeal under this Act.

(2)   Grants may be made on such terms, and subject to such conditions, as the Secretary of State may determine.

Commencement   2 October 2000 (SI 2000/2444).

Note   SI 2000/2333, Rule 4(b) provides that a person appointed by voluntary organisation in receipt of a grant under this section can represent an appellant before the Immigration Appellate Authority prior to the coming into force of section 84.

PART V
IMMIGRATION ADVISERS AND IMMIGRATION SERVICE PROVIDERS

Note on Part V   John Scampion has been appointed as the Immigration Services Commissioner, with Linda Allan as his Deputy. In October 2000, the Office of the

Immigration Services Commissioner issued four documents, following a period of consultation. The first three, the *Code of Standards, The Commissioner's Rules*, and the
Complaints Scheme are all envisaged in this Act. The fourth, *Guidance to Advisors:
Competencies*, has, as the Commissioner explains in his introduction, been produced 'to
assist advisers in their approaches to the Commissioner for registration or exemption'. The
Commissioner goes on to note that the guidance will be subject to review and amendment
in 2001 and notes 'Advisers should understand that such a review and resulting amend-
ments may result in a stricter regime.' All these documents are available on the
Commissioner's website www.oisc.org.uk. See also The Immigration Services Tribunal
Rules 2000 (SI 2000/2739), and the Immigration Services Commissioner (Registration
Fee) Order 2000 (SI 2000/2735). The fee payable for registration by a sole immigration
adviser has been set at £1,800 (SI 2000/2735, article 3). Fees for groups of more than one
adviser, as defined in article 2 of the order, are on a sliding scale from £2,675 to £6,000,
as set out in the Schedule to SI 2000/2735. Those providing immigration advice or immigration services as employees or under the supervision of the adviser, count towards the
calculation of the fee, as set out in article 2 of the order. Qualified persons within the meaning of sections 84(2)(c)-(f) and persons to whom section 84(4) applies, are not advisors
within the meaning of article 2.

Interpretation

[A.1.315]
82 Interpretation of Part V
(1)   In this Part—

'claim for asylum' means a claim that it would be contrary to the United
    Kingdom's obligations under—

(a) the Refugee Convention, or
(b) Article 3 of the Human Rights Convention,

for the claimant to be removed from, or required to leave, the United Kingdom;

'the Commissioner' means the Immigration Services Commissioner;
'the complaints scheme' means the scheme established under paragraph 5(1)
    of Schedule 5;
'designated judge' has the same meaning as in section 119(1) of the Courts and
    Legal Services Act 1990;
'designated professional body' has the meaning given by section 86;
'immigration advice' means advice which—

(a) relates to a particular individual;
(b) is given in connection with one or more relevant matters;
(c) is given by a person who knows that he is giving it in relation to a par-
    ticular individual and in connection with one or more relevant matters;
    and
(d) is not given in connection with representing an individual before a court in
    criminal proceedings or matters ancillary to criminal proceedings;

'immigration services' means the making of representations on behalf of a par-
    ticular individual—

(a) in civil proceedings before a court, tribunal or adjudicator in the United
    Kingdom, or

    (b) in correspondence with a Minister of the Crown or government department,

in connection with one or more relevant matters;

'Minister of the Crown' has the same meaning as in the Ministers of the Crown
    Act 1975;
'qualified person' means a person who is qualified for the purposes of section 84;
'registered person' means a person who is registered with the Commissioner
    under section 85;
'relevant matters' means any of the following—

    (a) a claim for asylum;
    (b) an application for, or for the variation of, entry clearance or leave to
        enter or remain in the United Kingdom;
    (c) unlawful entry into the United Kingdom;
    (d) nationality and citizenship under the law of the United Kingdom;
    (e) citizenship of the European Union;
    (f) admission to Member States under Community law;
    (g) residence in a Member State in accordance with rights conferred by or
        under Community law;
    (h) removal or deportation from the United Kingdom;
    (i) an application for bail under the Immigration Acts or under the Special
        Immigration Appeals Commission Act 1997;
    (j) an appeal against, or an application for judicial review in relation to,
        any decision taken in connection with a matter referred to in paragraphs
        (a) to (i); and

'the Tribunal' means the Immigration Services Tribunal.

(2) In this Part, references to the provision of immigration advice or immigration services are to the provision of such advice or services by a person—

(a) in the United Kingdom (regardless of whether the persons to whom they
    are provided are in the United Kingdom or elsewhere); and
(b) in the course of a business carried on (whether or not for profit) by him or
    by another person.

Commencement   22 May 2000 (SI 2000/1282).

The Immigration Services Commissioner

[A.1.316]
83 The Commissioner
(1) There is to be an Immigration Services Commissioner (referred to in this
Part as 'the Commissioner').
(2) The Commissioner is to be appointed by the Secretary of State after consulting the Lord Chancellor and the Scottish Ministers.
(3) It is to be the general duty of the Commissioner to promote good practice
by those who provide immigration advice or immigration services.
(4) In addition to any other functions conferred on him by this Part, the
Commissioner is to have the regulatory functions set out in Part I of Schedule
5.
(5) The Commissioner must exercise his functions so as to secure, so far as

is reasonably practicable, that those who provide immigration advice or immigration services—

(a) are fit and competent to do so;

(b) act in the best interests of their clients;

(c) do not knowingly mislead any court, tribunal or adjudicator in the United Kingdom;

(d) do not seek to abuse any procedure operating in the United Kingdom in connection with immigration or asylum (including any appellate or other judicial procedure);

(e) do not advise any person to do something which would amount to such an abuse.

(6) The Commissioner—

(a) must arrange for the publication, in such form and manner and to such extent as he considers appropriate, of information about his functions and about matters falling within the scope of his functions; and

(b) may give advice about his functions and about such matters.

(7) Part II of Schedule 5 makes further provision with respect to the Commissioner.

Commencement Subsections 83(4) and (5) commenced 22 May 2000 (SI 2000/1282 (C 38)) for the purposes of the provisions of Schedule 5 commenced by SI 2000/1282, viz paragraphs 1(1),(2) and (4), 2 (1)-(4) and (6)-(8), 3(1)-(3), (5)-(7), 4, 5(1) to (3), 6(1) and 11 to 25, and in full 30 October 2000 (SI 2000/1985).

The general prohibition

[A.1.317]
84 Provision of immigration services
(1) No person may provide immigration advice or immigration services unless he is a qualified person.
(2) A person is a qualified person if—

(a) he is registered with the Commissioner or is employed by, or works under the supervision of, such a person;

(b) he is a member or employee of a body which is a registered person, or works under the supervision of such a member or employee;

(c) he is authorised by a designated professional body to practise as a member of the profession whose members are regulated by that body, or works under the supervision of such a person;

(d) he is registered with, or authorised by, a person in another EEA State responsible for regulating the provision in that EEA State of advice or services corresponding to immigration advice or immigration services or would be required to be so registered or authorised were he not exempt from such a requirement;

(e) he is authorised by a body regulating the legal profession, or any branch of it, in another EEA State to practise as a member of that profession or branch; or

(f) he is employed by a person who falls within paragraph (d) or (e) or works under the supervision of such a person or of an employee of such a person.

(3)   If a registered person's registration has limited effect (by virtue of paragraph 2(2) of Schedule 6), neither paragraph (a) nor (b) of subsection (2) authorises the provision of advice or services falling outside the scope of that registration.

(4)   Subsection (1) does not apply to a person who—

(a) is certified by the Commissioner as exempt ('an exempt person');
(b) is employed by an exempt person;
(c) works under the supervision of an exempt person or an employee of an exempt person; or
(d) who falls within a category of person specified in an order made by the Secretary of State for the purposes of this subsection.

(5)   A certificate under subsection (4)(a) may relate only to a specified description of immigration advice or immigration services.

(6)   Subsection (1) does not apply to a person—

(a) holding an office under the Crown, when acting in that capacity;
(b) employed by, or for the purposes of, a government department, when acting in that capacity;
(c) acting under the control of a government department; or
(d) otherwise exercising functions on behalf of the Crown.

(7)   An exemption given under subsection (4) may be withdrawn by the Commissioner.

Commencement   84(2)(a) and (b), 4(a) and (d), (5) and (7) 30 October 2000 (SI 2000/1985).

Note   For transitional provisions relating to representation before the Immigration Appellate Authority prior to the coming into force of this section, see SI 2000/2333 rules 4(1)) and 35(1)(a).

[A.1.318]
85 Registration exemption by the Commissioner
(1)   The Commissioner must prepare and maintain a register for and the purposes of section 84(2)(a) and (b).
(2)   The Commissioner must keep a record of the persons to whom he has issued a certificate of exemption under section 84(4)(a).
(3)   Schedule 6 makes further provision with respect to registration.

Commencement   Section 85(3) 1 August 2000 (SI 2000/1985) for the purposes of the provisions of Schedule 6 commenced on 1 August 2000 by SI 2000/1985, viz paragraph 5(1) (which is commenced on that date for the purposes of enabling subordinate legislation to be made under it).

Section 85 in full 30 October 2000 (SI 2000/1985).

Note   See Schedule 6 and the Immigration Services (Commissioner (Registration Fee) Order 2000 (SI 2000/2735), in force 30 October 2000.

[A.1.319]
86 Designated professional bodies
(1)   'Designated professional body' means—

(a) The Law Society;
(b) The Law Society of Scotland;
(c) The Law Society of Northern Ireland;
(d) The Institute of Legal Executives;
(e) The General Council of the Bar;
(f) The Faculty of Advocates; or
(g) The General Council of the Bar of Northern Ireland.

(2) If the Secretary of State considers that a designated professional body has consistently failed to provide effective regulation of its members in their provision of immigration advice or immigration services, he may by order amend subsection (1) to remove the name of that body.

(3) If a designated professional body asks the Secretary of State to amend subsection (1) so as to remove its name, the Secretary of State may by order do so.

(4) If the Secretary of State is proposing to act under subsection (2) he must, before doing so—

(a) consult the Commissioner;
(b) consult the Legal Services Ombudsman, if the proposed order would affect a designated professional body in England and Wales;
(c) consult the Scottish Legal Services Ombudsman, if the proposed order would affect a designated professional body in Scotland;
(d) consult the lay observers appointed under Article 42 of the Solicitors (Northern Ireland) Order 1976, if the proposed order would affect a designated professional body in Northern Ireland;
(e) notify the body concerned of his proposal and give it a reasonable period within which to make representations; and
(f) consider any representations so made.

(5) An order under subsection (2) requires the approval of—

(a) the Lord Chancellor, if it affects a designated professional body in England and Wales or Northern Ireland;
(b) the Scottish Ministers, if it affects a designated professional body in Scotland.

(6) Before deciding whether or not to give his approval under subsection (5)(a), the Lord Chancellor must consult—

(a) the designated judges, if the order affects a designated professional body in England and Wales;
(b) the Lord Chief Justice of Northern Ireland, if it affects a designated professional body in Northern Ireland.

(7) Before deciding whether or not to give their approval under subsection (5)(b), the Scottish Ministers must consult the Lord President of the Court of Session.

(8) If the Secretary of State considers that a body which—

(a) is concerned (whether wholly or in part) with regulating the legal profession, or a branch of it, in an EEA State,
(b) is not a designated professional body, and
(c) is capable of providing effective regulation of its members in their provision of immigration advice or immigration services,

ought to be designated, he may by order amend subsection (1) to include the name of that body.

(9)   The Commissioner must—

(a) keep under review the list of designated professional bodies set out in sub-section (1); and

(b) report to the Secretary of State if he considers that a designated professional body is failing to provide effective regulation of its members in their provision of immigration advice or immigration services.

(10)   For the purpose of meeting the costs incurred by the Commissioner in discharging his functions under this Part, each designated professional body must pay to the Commissioner, in each year and on such date as may be specified, such fee as may be specified.

(11)   Any unpaid fee for which a designated professional body is liable under subsection (10) may be recovered from that body as a debt due to the Commissioner.

(12)   'Specified' means specified by an order made by the Secretary of State.

Commencement   86(1) to (9) 22 May 2000 (SI (2000/1282). 86(10) to (12), 30 October 2000 (SI 2000/1985) for the purposes of making subordinate legislation under them.

The Immigration Services Tribunal

[A.1.320]
87 The Tribunal
(1)   There is to be a tribunal known as the Immigration Services Tribunal (referred to in this Part as 'the Tribunal').

(2)   Any person aggrieved by a relevant decision of the Commissioner may appeal to the Tribunal against the decision.

(3)   'Relevant decision' means a decision—

(a) to refuse an application for registration made under paragraph 1 of Schedule 6;

(b) to withdraw an exemption given under section 84(4)(a);

(c) under paragraph 2(2) of that Schedule to register with limited effect;

(d) to refuse an application for continued registration made under paragraph 3 of that Schedule;

(e) to vary a registration on an application under paragraph 3 of that Schedule; or

(f) which is recorded under paragraph 9(1)(a) of Schedule 5.

(4)   The Tribunal is also to have the function of hearing disciplinary charges laid by the Commissioner under paragraph 9(1)(e) of Schedule 5.

(5)   Schedule 7 makes further provision with respect to the Tribunal and its constitution and functions.

Commencement   30 October 2000 (SI 2000/1985).

Note   See Schedule 7 and the notes thereto, and the Immigration Service Tribunal Rules 2000 (SI 2000/2739).

[A.1.321]
88 Appeal upheld by the Tribunal

(1)   This section applies if the Tribunal allows an appeal under section 87.
(2)   If the Tribunal considers it appropriate, it may direct the Commissioner—

(a) to register the applicant or to continue the applicant's registration;
(b) to make or vary the applicant's registration so as to have limited effect in any of the ways mentioned in paragraph 2(2) of Schedule 6;
(c) to restore an exemption granted under section 84(4)(a); or
(d) to quash a decision recorded under paragraph 9(1)(a) of Schedule 5 and the record of that decision.

Commencement   30 October 2000 (SI 2000/1985).

[A.1.322]
89 Disciplinary charge upheld by the Tribunal
(1)   This section applies if the Tribunal upholds a disciplinary charge laid by the Commissioner under paragraph 9(1)(e) of Schedule 5 against a person ('the person charged').
(2)   Subsection (3) applies if the person charged is—

(a) a registered person;
(b) a person employed by, or working under the supervision of, a registered person;
(c) a member or employee of a body which is a registered person; or
(d) a person working under the supervision of such a member or employee.

(3)   The Tribunal may—

(a) direct the Commissioner to record the charge and the Tribunal's decision on it for consideration when the registered person next applies for continued registration; or
(b) direct the registered person to apply to the Commissioner for continued registration without delay.

(4)   If the person charged is certified by the Commissioner as exempt under section 84(4)(a), the Tribunal may direct the Commissioner to consider whether to withdraw his exemption.
(5)   If the person charged is found to have charged unreasonable fees for immigration advice or immigration services, the Tribunal may direct him to repay to the clients concerned such portion of those fees as it may determine.
(6)   The Tribunal may direct the person charged to pay a penalty to the Commissioner of such sum as it considers appropriate.
(7)   A direction given by the Tribunal under subsection (5) (or under subsection (6)) may be enforced by the clients concerned (or by the Commissioner)—

(a) as if it were an order of a county court; or
(b) in Scotland, as if it were an extract registered decree arbitral bearing a warrant for execution issued by the sheriff court of any sheriffdom in Scotland.

(8)   The Tribunal may direct that the person charged or any person employed by him or working under his supervision is to be—

(a) subject to such restrictions on the provision of immigration advice or immigration services as the Tribunal considers appropriate;
(b) suspended from providing immigration advice or immigration services for such period as the Tribunal may determine; or
(c) prohibited from providing immigration advice or immigration services indefinitely.

(9)   The Commissioner must keep a record of the persons against whom there is in force a direction given by the Tribunal under subsection (8).

Commencement   30 October 2000 (SI 2000/1985).

[A.1.323]
90 Orders by disciplinary bodies
(1)   A disciplinary body may make an order directing that a person subject to its jurisdiction is to be—

(a) subject to such restrictions on the provision of immigration advice or immigration services as the body considers appropriate;
(b) suspended from providing immigration advice or immigration services for such period as the body may determine; or
(c) prohibited from providing immigration advice or immigration services indefinitely.

(2)   'Disciplinary body' means any body—

(a) appearing to the Secretary of State to be established for the purpose of hearing disciplinary charges against members of a designated professional body; and
(b) specified in an order made by the Secretary of State.

(3)   The Secretary of State must consult the designated professional body concerned before making an order under subsection (2)(b).
(4)   For the purposes of this section, a person is subject to the jurisdiction of a disciplinary body if he is an authorised person or works under the supervision of an authorised person.
(5)   'Authorised person' means a person who is authorised by the designated professional body concerned to practise as a member of the profession whose members are regulated by that body.

Commencement   1 August 2000 (SI 2000/1985) for the purposes of enabling subordinate legislation to be made under it.

Enforcement

[A.1.324]
91   Offences
(1)   A person who provides immigration advice or immigration services in contravention of section 84 or of a restraining order is guilty of an offence and liable—

(a) on summary conviction, to imprisonment for a term not exceeding six months or to a fine not exceeding the statutory maximum, or to both; or

(b) on conviction on indictment, to imprisonment for a term not exceeding two years or to a fine, or to both.

(2)   'Restraining order' means—

(a) a direction given by the Tribunal under section 89(8) or paragraph 9(3) of Schedule 5; or

(b) an order made by a disciplinary body under section 90(1).

(3)   If an offence under this section committed by a body corporate is proved—

(a) to have been committed with the consent or connivance of an officer, or
(b) to be attributable to neglect on his part,

the officer as well as the body corporate is guilty of the offence and liable to be proceeded against and punished accordingly.

(4)   'Officer', in relation to a body corporate, means a director, manager, secretary or other similar officer of the body, or a person purporting to act in such a capacity.

(5)   If the affairs of a body corporate are managed by its members, subsection (3) applies in relation to the acts and defaults of a member in connection with his functions of management as if he were a director of the body corporate.

(6)   If an offence under this section committed by a partnership in Scotland is proved—

(a) to have been committed with the consent or connivance of a partner, or
(b) to be attributable to neglect on his part,

the partner as well as the partnership is guilty of the offence and liable to be proceeded against and punished accordingly.

(7)   'Partner' includes a person purporting to act as a partner.

[A.1.325]
92   Enforcement
(1)   If it appears to the Commissioner that a person—

(a) is providing immigration advice or immigration services in contravention of section 84 or of a restraining order, and
(b) is likely to continue to do so unless restrained,

the Commissioner may apply to a county court for an injunction, or to the sheriff for an interdict, restraining him from doing so.

(2)   If the court is satisfied that the application is well-founded, it may grant the injunction or interdict in the terms applied for or in more limited terms.

(3)   'Restraining order' has the meaning given by section 91.

Miscellaneous

[A.1.326]
93 Information
(1)   No enactment or rule of law prohibiting or restricting the disclosure of information prevents a person from—

(a) giving the Commissioner information which is necessary for the discharge of his functions; or

(b) giving the Tribunal information which is necessary for the discharge of its functions.

(2)   No relevant person may at any time disclose information which—

(a) has been obtained by, or given to, the Commissioner under or for purposes of this Act,

(b) relates to an identified or identifiable individual or business, and

(c) is not at that time, and has not previously been, available to the public from other sources,

unless the disclosure is made with lawful authority.

(3)   For the purposes of subsection (2), a disclosure is made with lawful authority only if, and to the extent that—

(a) it is made with the consent of the individual or of the person for the time being carrying on the business;

(b) it is made for the purposes of, and is necessary for, the discharge of any of the Commissioner's functions under this Act or any Community obligation of the Commissioner;

(c) it is made for the purposes of any civil or criminal proceedings arising under or by virtue of this Part, or otherwise; or

(d) having regard to the rights and freedoms or legitimate interests of any person, the disclosure is necessary in the public interest.

(4)   A person who knowingly or recklessly discloses information in contravention of subsection (2) is guilty of an offence and liable—

(a) on summary conviction, to a fine not exceeding the statutory maximum; or

(b) on conviction on indictment, to a fine.

(5)   'Relevant person' means a person who is or has been—

(a) the Commissioner;

(b) a member of the Commissioner's staff; or

(c) an agent of the Commissioner.

Commencement   22 May 2000 (SI 2000/1282).

PART VI
SUPPORT FOR ASYLUM-SEEKERS

For General Note see A.5 Support for Asylum Seekers, paragraph **[A.5.1]**.

Interpretation

[A.1.327]
94 Interpretation of Part VI
(1)   In this Part—
'adjudicator' has the meaning given in section 102(2);
'asylum-seeker' means a person who is not under 18 and has made a claim for
    asylum which has been recorded by the Secretary of State but which has
    not been determined;
'claim for asylum' means a claim that it would be contrary to the United
Kingdom's obligations under the Refugee Convention, or under Article 3 of
the Human Rights Convention, for the claimant to be removed from, or
required to leave, the United Kingdom;
'the Department' means the Department of Health and Social Services for
    Northern Ireland;
'dependant', in relation to an asylum-seeker or a supported person, means a
    person in the United Kingdom who—

(a) is his spouse;
(b) is a child of his, or of his spouse, who is under 18 and dependent on him;
     or
(c) falls within such additional category, if any, as may be prescribed;

'the Executive' means the Northern Ireland Housing Executive;
'housing accommodation' includes flats, lodging houses and hostels;
'local authority' means—

(a) in England and Wales, a county council, a county borough council, a dis-
     trict council, a London borough council, the Common Council of the City
     of London or the Council of the Isles of Scilly;
(b) in Scotland, a council constituted under section 2 of the Local Government
     etc (Scotland) Act 1994;

'supported person' means—

(a) an asylum-seeker, or
(b) a dependant of an asylum-seeker,
     who has applied for support and for whom support is provided under sec-
     tion 95.

(2)   References in this Part to support provided under section 95 include references to support which is provided under arrangements made by the
Secretary of State under that section.

(3) For the purposes of this Part, a claim for asylum is determined at the end of such period beginning—

(a) on the day on which the Secretary of State notifies the claimant of his decision on the claim, or

(b) if the claimant has appealed against the Secretary of State's decision, on the day on which the appeal is disposed of,

as may be prescribed.

(4) An appeal is disposed of when it is no longer pending for the purposes of the Immigration Acts or the Special Immigration Appeals Commission Act 1997.

(5) If an asylum-seeker's household includes a child who is under 18 and a dependant of his, he is to be treated (for the purposes of this Part) as continuing to be an asylum-seeker while—

(a) the child is under 18; and

(b) he and the child remain in the United Kingdom.

(6) Subsection (5) does not apply if, on or after the determination of his claim for asylum, the asylum-seeker is granted leave to enter or remain in the United Kingdom (whether or not as a result of that claim).

(7) For the purposes of this Part, the Secretary of State may inquire into, and decide, the age of any person.

(8) A notice under subsection (3) must be given in writing.

(9) If such a notice is sent by the Secretary of State by first class post, addressed—

(a) to the asylum-seeker's representative, or

(b) to the asylum-seeker's last known address,

  it is to be taken to have been received by the asylum-seeker on the second day after the day on which it was posted.

Commencement On Royal Assent (section 170(3)).

Note This complex interpretation section serves to define eligibility for support under Part VI of the Act and in so doing contains much of the architecture of the new support scheme. It must be contextualised by a brief consideration of the operation of Part VI as a whole.

  The 'Exclusions' provisions of Part VI, sections 115 to 123, set out the extent of the exclusion of 'persons under immigration control' as defined in section 115(9) from a large number of benefits or other forms of social assistance.

  For some, although not all, of those so excluded, alternative provision is made. There are two forms of alternative provision, the 'interim provisions' and the Part VI scheme which will eventually replace it entirely. The only people for whom provision is made under either scheme are those who have made a claim for asylum and their dependants. Neither scheme extends to all such people.

  Section 94 sets out eligibility for this alternative provision. The issue is one of eligibility, not entitlement, for under section 95(1) the Secretary of State has a power, not a duty, to support asylum seekers.

  However, a duty can be imposed by means of regulations. The Asylum Support (Interim Provisions) Regulations 1999 (SI 1999/3056) impose duties upon local authorities to support certain asylum seekers and their dependants, as set out in the notes to Schedule 9 and the Asylum Support Regulations 2000 (SI 2000/704) and the Immigration (Eligibility for Assistance) (Scotland and Northern Ireland) Regulations 2000 (SI 2000/705) impose duties upon the Secretary of State in this regard, as set out in the notes to Schedule 8.

Section 94 alone does not provide an exhaustive definition of eligibility. Under section 95(1), for example, support may only be provided to an asylum seeker who appears to the Secretary of State to be 'destitute' as defined in and under section 95.

The 'interim provisions' governed by Schedule 9 of this Act, took effect on 6 December 1999 (SI 1999/3056). Within this statutory framework, the scheme operates on the basis of voluntary agreements between local authorities. While the interim provisions are in force they operate as transitional provisions. Those who applied for asylum at port before 3 April 2000 retain their entitlement to specified benefits until the first negative decision or until the main scheme is brought into force for everyone (SI 2000/636 regulation 12(4)). SI 2000/636 contains other transitional and saving provisions affecting limited classes of asylum-seekers, most with very long-outstanding claims. See for example regulations 12(11) and 12(7)(b)).

The main Part VI scheme was to have come into force in April 2000. However, implementation on 3 April 2000 was partial. The scheme was implemented on 3 April 2000 only for those claiming asylum on arrival in England and Wales on or after that date, including those detained in the detention centre at Oakington, and for all those claiming asylum (at whatever time relative to arrival) in Scotland and Northern Ireland on or after 3 April 2000. Over the period 24 July 2000 to 25 September 2000 the main Part VI scheme was extended. For the timetable of the extensions, many of which were determined by geographical area, see Home Office Press Release 191/2000 of 11 July 2000. Post September 25, all new in-country asylum claimants and all those who lose their entitlement to benefits following a negative decision on their asylum claim fall under the main scheme. It is important to note that the relevant date for determining whether an asylum seeker is entitled to benefits, to support under the main scheme, or to support under the interim scheme is the date of the claim for asylum and not of the claim for support. Perhaps the greatest confusion has been caused in situations where family members have joined an asylum-seeker already present and supported, either by benefits, under the interim scheme or by NASS. NASS *Policy Bulletin 11: Mixed Households Version 1* issued as part of the NASS Casework instructions on 30/07/00 clarifies the position. It makes clear that the question of whether or not the family members claim asylum in their own right is irrelevant to the question of who is responsible for supporting them, as is the date of their arrival. In broad terms, where the asylum-seeker first present in the UK is in receipt of benefits, the family should look to an increase in benefits (urgent cases payments) to cover the family members. Where the asylum seeker first present in the UK is supported under the interim scheme, the family should look to the local authority concerned to support the family members under the interim scheme. Where the asylum seeker first present in the UK is supported by NASS, the family should look to NASS under the main scheme. The main scheme will run concurrently with the interim scheme but must finally replace it by 1 April 2002 when the interim scheme comes to an end (SI 1999/3056, regulation 5). See the Directions made by the Minister of State, Barbara Roche, for the extension of the NASS scheme, Direction 1 of 13 March 2000, Direction 2 of 10 April 2000, Direction 2A of 10 April 2000 and Direction 3 of 11 July 2000. Thanks to Simon Cox, Barrister, for uncovering this, and much other information which has informed these notes, on the operation of the Part VI scheme.

Ministers have given undertakings relating the introduction of the main scheme to the average time taken to process asylum applications. The Home Secretary stated on 16 June 1999:

'The undertaking I am giving is that there will be an average target of two months in which to process a claim... It will be in nobody's interest... to press the start button and then to discover that applications are routinely taking not two months, but four. ...for that reason, I also give the subsidiary but very important undertaking that if we cannot achieve those targets for families with children, and if I am not satisfied that they can be achieved, we will not introduce those applications into the new support arrangements in April 2000. The existing arrangements will continue until we are so satisfied.' (Hansard HC Report vol 333 no104, col 475).

The interim scheme is closely modelled on the main scheme but differs from it in retaining a number of the arrangements in force prior to 6 December 1999, albeit on a different statutory basis, see the notes on Schedule 9.

The definitions in section 94 apply equally to the interim and main schemes, save insofar as the regulation-making powers under the section are used differently in respect of each scheme.

The definitions in section 94 at times appears subject to an infinite regress. In summary:

• The scheme does not cover unaccompanied minors seeking asylum.
• It is intended that asylum-seeking families with dependant children under 18 be eligible for support until they are granted leave to enter or remain, or until removal. Other asylum-seekers are to be given a notice of termination of support at the end of a fixed period commencing:
— when the Secretary of State notifies them of his decision on their claim for asylum, as defined in this section, or
— when the time limit for appealing against the most recent negative decision on any appeal ends,
— or when they withdraw or abandon their appeal,
— or when their appeal is finally determined in that there is no further appeal open to them.

Thus unsuccessful applicants without dependants under 18 are not necessarily eligible for support until removal or grant of status. Nor will an application for judicial review of a decision in respect of their claim for asylum entitle them to support. During the debates in parliament on these provisions, Ministers stated that a grant would be provided to voluntary organisations (see section 111) to provide for 'hard cases' among those losing all eligibility to support. Debate centred upon those who could not be removed, particularly where this was through no fault of their own, and those pursuing applications for judicial review (see *Hansard* HL Report, vol 605, no 138, cols 1130 to 1137). For example, on 20 October 1999, Lord Falconer of Thoroton (of those who could not be removed) 'Where there are genuine problems, the voluntary sector would be able to deploy a hard cases grant to assist such people. The support arrangements that we propose in this part are eminently fair and reasonable for anyone with a genuine claim for asylum.' (vol 605, no 138, col 1136). Lord Falconer went on to state of those granted leave to move for judicial review 'we believe that those cases can be dealt with by the substantial sums that will be given to the voluntary sector to help with hard cases' (col 1137).

The hard cases fund has not been made the responsibility of any voluntary organisation, but instead is held within NASS. A letter from the Director of NASS, dated 27 March 2000 states that:

'"Hard cases" support will mean basic full board accommodation outside of London. The ex- asylum seeker will have no access to other vouchers or cash. The ex-asylum seeker must also subject themselves to regular monthly reviews in which they will be expected to demonstrate the steps they have taken to enable themselves to leave the country. If there is not sufficient evidence that this has happened then hard cases support will be terminated. Nor will an application for judicial review of a decision in respect of their claim for asylum entitle them to support.'

The letter goes on to set out the criteria of eligibility for support from the fund. This states that support from the fund will not normally be made available unless the circumstances of the case are exceptional and there is some physical/health impediment to immediate travel.

94(1) 'adjudicator' Section 102 makes provision for new Asylum Support Adjudicators to hear appeals against refusal of support. See the note on that section.

'asylum seeker' This definition encompasses both the commencement and the termination of entitlement to support. The former is self contained within this section, the latter requires reference to the other subsections in this section which define when a

claim is determined. Unaccompanied children seeking asylum are not part of the scheme and thus retain eligibility for support from local authorities under the Children Act 1989, the Children Act (Scotland) 1995 or the Children (Northern Ireland) Order 1995. See note on 94(7) in relation to disputes as to age.

The definition of an asylum seeker is not limited to those who have claimed that they should be recognised as refugees under Article 1 of the 'Refugee Convention' (as defined in section 167).

'recorded' This has given rise to difficulties under the interim provisions where an application for asylum has been made, but no acknowledgement of receipt has been received from the Home Office. The question of whether a local authority can refuse assistance in these circumstances was raised but not decided in *R v London Borough of Camden, ex p Diirshe* CO/5069/99 heard 25 February 2000. The case also raised but did not decide the question of whether the local authority must make its own enquiries of the Home Office in these circumstances.

Similar issues arise where an unsuccessful applicant makes a fresh 'claim for asylum' during the period in which the Secretary of State is deciding whether or not to treat it as a fresh application.

When the 'claim to asylum' is a claim that return would breach Article 3, how is an Article 3 claim recorded? Under subsections (3) and 4(4) of Section 65 of this Act, an adjudicator or the Immigration Appeal Tribunal will have jurisdiction to consider a Human Rights Act claims arising. This reflects section 2 of the Human Rights Act 1998 which also uses the word 'arising'. If the facts give rise to a question of a breach of human rights, the adjudicator, court or tribunal is seized of the matter. By analogy the Secretary of State would appear to be seized of an Article 3 application when the facts raise the issue of torture, inhuman or degrading treatment if the person is returned or removed.

'determined' see subsections (3) and (4) of this section. Note that the determination of the claim only triggers loss of eligibility to support. This actually takes place at the end of the period prescribed under 94(3).

94(5) operates by modifying the definition of an asylum seeker. In the case of unsuccessful applicants with minor dependants, it is the age of the child which determines whether they are still asylum-seekers and is nothing to do with the decision on the claim for asylum or any subsequent appeals.

'claim for asylum' With reference to the Refugee Convention, a 'claim for asylum' extends beyond a claim under Article 1 of the Convention to any claim that it would be contrary to the UK's obligations under the Convention to remove the person from the UK, or to require them to leave.

The definition of a claim for asylum extends to a claim that to remove the person from the UK, or to require them to leave, would be in breach of the Article 3 of the 'Human Rights Convention' (as defined in section 167). This is narrower than the new appeal right in section 65, which includes all provisions of the Human Rights Convention incorporated by the Human Rights Act 1998. Thus a person appealing against removal on the grounds that it would breach Human Rights Convention rights other than rights under Article 3 would not have a claim for asylum or be eligible for support under the Part VI schemes. Article 3 states 'No one shall be subject to torture, inhuman or degrading treatment or punishment'. The classic example of a claim that removal would breach this article is a claim that the person would face torture in the place to which it is proposed to remove him/her, see *Chahal v United Kingdom* (1996) 23 EHRR 413. A claim that s/he would face inhuman or degrading treatment or punishment would also breach Article 3, see *Ireland v United Kingdom* (1978) 2 EHRR 25. The threat of torture, inhuman or degrading treatment can be a threat once returned, or attendant upon the circumstances of removal, or a combination of the two, see *East African Asians v United Kingdom* (1973) 3 EHRR 76 and *Giama v Belgium* 23 YB 428 (1980).

'dependant' Additional categories of dependant are prescribed for the purposes of the interim provisions in regulation 2(1) of SI 1995/3056. See notes to Schedule 9, paragraph 1 and for the purposes of the main scheme by regulation 2(4) of SI 2000/704 as

glossed by regulation 2(1) and 2(7) and 2(8) of those regulations, see notes to Schedule 8. The two definitions are not identical; for example SI 2000/704 specifically excludes same sex partners from the definition of an unmarried couple but SI 1999/3056 does not. Under section 95(1), the primary claimant for support can be the asylum seeker or a dependant. The dependency relationship is the relationship to the primary claimant for support. See also note on 94(7) below.

'*supported person*' Under section 95(1) support can be provided to asylum seekers and/or to their dependants. The Explanatory Notes state that this 'reflects the ability of the Secretary of State to provide support for an asylum seeker's dependants even though he may not be supporting the principal asylum seeker, for example because he is detained'. This appears to envisage that where the household of an asylum seeker are all together, the asylum seeker will be the primary claimant for support. However, there is nothing in the Act that demands this.

In contrast to the definition of an asylum-seeker, there is no reference to an age limit in this section. There appears to be no legal barrier to the minor dependant of the asylum seeker being the primary claimant for support.

'support provided under Part VI' includes support provided under the interim scheme under 95(13)

94(3) 'such period' See notes on the meaning of 'determined' in the definition of a claim for asylum. See SI 2000/704, regulation 2(2) which prescribes a period of 14 days.

'*notifies*' The end of eligibility for support depends not upon the decision on the claim but on notification of that decision. In respect of a claim of a breach of Article 3, see the notes on the definition of a 'claim for asylum' above. Where the applicant claims that s/he should be recognised as a refugee, but the facts give rise to a claim under Article 3 also, then eligibility for support appears to cease only when the Secretary of State notifies the applicant of the decision on both claims. Those who do not appeal a negative decision lose their eligibility for support regardless of whether or not they are removed, subject to the provisions of subsection (5) below.

No provision equivalent to that for appeals imported into this section by subsection (4) exists to cover the situation where the applicant withdraws or abandons his/her claim for asylum prior to a decision by the Secretary of State. Notification of a decision on the claim by the Secretary of State is needed to terminate eligibility for support in these circumstances.

'*has appealed*' It is unclear how the provision will be interpreted in cases where an applicant fails to make an appeal in time but later seeks to appeal out of time. The wording of this subsection, read with section 58(5), appears to indicate that where such an appeal is made, eligibility for support revives.

'*disposed of*' see notes to subsection (4) below.

'*as may be prescribed*' for the purposes of the interim provisions, the period is 14 days (SI 1999/3056, regulation 6).

These provisions apply equally to those whose applications are unsuccessful and to those who are recognised as refugees or given exceptional leave to remain. Those who succeed in their applications cease to be eligible for support under the scheme regardless of whether or not they have been able to access alternative means of support during the 14 day period.

Where there is no appeal in the case, because the Secretary of State recognises the person as a refugee or grants exceptional leave to remain, or because the person does not appeal the Secretary of State's decision, the key date is the date on which the Secretary of State's decision is notified to the applicant. In the case of a person who is recognised as a refugee or given exceptional leave to remain, it would thus appear that they cease to be eligible for support under the scheme regardless of whether or not they have been able to access alternative means of support during the 14 day period. Those who succeed on appeal are arguably at the greatest risk of such a hiatus because there may be a time lag between final determination of the appeal and the receipt of the papers from the Secretary of State confirming their new status which are often demanded before alternative support is provided.

94(4) 'pending under the Immigration Acts' 'Immigration Acts' are defined in section 167. The Special Immigration Appeals Act 1997 and section 58(5)-(10) and paragraph 23 of Schedule 4, Part III (appeals to the Court of Appeal and the Court of Sessions) of this Act define the circumstances in which an appeal is pending for the purposes of this part. The appeal is no longer pending when it is finally determined, withdrawn or abandoned (section 58(5) and see paragraph 23 of Schedule 4 Part III).

While subsection (10) of section 58 reflects the provision in section 14(5) of the 1971 Act on treating an appeal as abandoned, subsections (8) and (9) make new provision for when an appeal is to be so treated.

Until the period for lodging a further appeal ends, the appeal is not finally determined (section 58(6)). See the decision of the Social Security Commissioner in CIS/3418/1998. This case considered the date on which an appeal against a pre-5 February 1996 refusal of asylum is determined for the purposes of the Income Support (General) Regulations 1987 (SI 1987/1967), Regulation 70(3A)(b)(2). The Commissioner held that on the facts of that case, and for the purposes of that regulation, the appeal was determined on the date of the first decision made on the appeal, in this case the first instance appeal to the special adjudicator, and that further appeal to the Immigration Appeal Tribunal was excluded.

Under these provisions, eligibility for support does not continue while the applicant seeks judicial review of a refusal of leave to appeal to the Immigration Appeal Tribunal. Where judicial review proceedings are successful (or conceded) however, the appeal is once again pending and eligibility for support revives. If the judicial review proceedings can be completed within the 94(3) notice period, the applicant who succeeds in the judicial review will not experience any break in eligibility for support. If the judicial review proceedings take any longer, then without successful applications for interlocutory relief, the applicant will lose support while they are still ongoing.

94(5) This subsection establishes that families with dependent children under 18 who are not granted leave to enter or remain (see 94(6)) will remain eligible for support until removal. The effect of subsection (a) is that when the child turns 18, or when the youngest child does so if there is more than one child in the family, the family only continue to receive support if the asylum seeker remains eligible for support under the other provisions governing eligibility, as set out below. There is no provision comparable to the provision made in 94(3) for a notice period in these circumstances.

See *R v London Borough of Waltham Forest ex p Tietie* CO/2083/00. A decision was said to have made on the applicant's claim, but nothing had been received from the Home Office. Waltham Forest withdrew support because the applicant could not provide documentation to prove that she was still an asylum seeker. A letter from her representatives was not accepted. The applicant relied on 94(5). She further asserted that the local authority ha a duty to make enquiries of the Home Office to determine her status and further that they retained obligations toward her under the Children Act (see section 122). Permission to move for judicial review and interim relief were granted.

94(6) See note on subsection 94(3). Where an asylum-seeker with dependant children is granted leave to enter or remain, the provisions of section 122(5) would allow assistance to be provided to them in these circumstances by a local authority under the 'child welfare provisions' as defined in section 122(7).

94(7) This allows the Secretary of State to decide questions of age dispute, but the Act is silent on how those whose age is disputed are to be supported until a decision is made.

In the case of unaccompanied disputed minors seeking asylum, then because of the definition of an 'asylum-seeker' if they are not over 18 in fact then they are not eligible for support as asylum seekers. The Children Acts define a child as 'a person under the age of 18' and are silent on the question of disputed age. Section 20(5) of the Children Act 1989 and the equivalent provisions of the Children (Scotland) Act 1999 and the Children (Northern Ireland) Order 1995 allow support to be provided for those under 21 and may thus be relevant where it is not disputed that the person is over 21.

Similar problems arise where the age dispute is in respect of a dependant of a supported person because of the effect of the existence of such dependants upon eligibility under subsection (5) above. The age of a child is also relevant to the definition of dependency, see section on *'dependant'* in this note.

Provision of support

[A.1.328]
95 Persons for whom support may be provided
(1)   The Secretary of State may provide, or arrange for the provision of, support for—

(a) asylum-seekers, or
(b) dependants of asylum-seekers,

who appear to the Secretary of State to be destitute or to be likely to become destitute within such period as may be prescribed.

(2)   In prescribed circumstances, a person who would otherwise fall within subsection (1) is excluded.
(3)   For the purposes of this section, a person is destitute if—

(a) he does not have adequate accommodation or any means of obtaining it (whether or not his other essential living needs are met); or
(b) he has adequate accommodation or the means of obtaining it, but cannot meet his other essential living needs.

(4)   If a person has dependants, subsection (3) is to be read as if the references to him were references to him and his dependants taken together.
(5)   In determining, for the purposes of this section, whether a person's accommodation is adequate, the Secretary of State—

(a) must have regard to such matters as may be prescribed for the purposes of this paragraph; but
(b) may not have regard to such matters as may be prescribed for the purposes of this paragraph or to any of the matters mentioned in subsection (6).

(6)   Those matters are—

(a) the fact that the person concerned has no enforceable right to occupy the accommodation;
(b) the fact that he shares the accommodation, or any part of the accommodation, with one or more other persons;
(c) the fact that the accommodation is temporary;
(d) the location of the accommodation.

(7)   In determining, for the purposes of this section, whether a person's other essential living needs are met, the Secretary of State—

(a) must have regard to such matters as may be prescribed for the purposes of this paragraph; but
(b) may not have regard to such matters as may be prescribed for the purposes of this paragraph.

(8)   The Secretary of State may by regulations provide that items or expenses of such a description as may be prescribed are, or are not, to be treated as being an essential living need of a person for the purposes of this Part.

(9)   Support may be provided subject to conditions.

(10)   The conditions must be set out in writing.

(11)   A copy of the conditions must be given to the supported person.

(12)   Schedule 8 gives the Secretary of State power to make regulations supplementing this section.

(13)   Schedule 9 makes temporary provision for support in the period before the coming into force of this section.

Commencement   Subsections *(3) to (8)* 6 December 1999 (SI 1999/3190) for the purposes of sections 116 and 117(1) and (2), the amendments to other legislation effected by those sections, and paragraph 3 of Schedule 9 to the Act.

Subsection (12) 1 January 2000 (SI 1999/3190).

Subsection (13) on Royal Assent (section 170 (3)).

All remaining subsections 1 January 2000 (SI 1999/3190) for the purposes of making subordinate legislation under this subsection (8). In full 3 April 2000 (SI 2000/464).

Note   Section 95 introduces the interim support scheme by means of 95(13) and sets up the main support scheme, as described in the note to section 94 above. The provisions of sub-paragraphs (3) to (8) which provide a test of 'destitution' as a further criterion for eligibility to support apply to the interim provisions.

See the Asylum Support Regulations 2000, SI 200/704, into force 3 April 2000. See also The Immigration (Eligibility for Assistance) (Scotland and Northern Ireland) Regulations 2000, (SI 2000/705) into force 3 April 2000. The Asylum Support (Interim Provisions) Regulations 1999, SI 1999/3056 have been made under Schedule 9. See notes on that Schedule for the extent to which these provisions reflect the provisions of section 95.

95(1) See SI 2000/705, regulations 5 and 7. In applying section 95(1) the Secretary of State must take the applicant and all those who are dependants, or whom the applicant puts forward as dependants together. Destitution is assessed in respect of the asylum seeker and any dependants. Regulation 7(a) prescribes a period of 14 days in the case of a person applying for support. Regulation 7(b) prescribes a period of 56 days where the person is a person already in receipt of support. These periods are essentially academic, the key issue is the amount of income, assets or support a person has. For example, a person deemed not to be eligible for support because s/he would not become destitute within 14 days, who was then robbed or otherwise lost this income, support or assets, would become eligible for support provided s/he did not fall foul of the test of intentionally making oneself destitute contained in regulation 20(2) of SI 2000/705.

In deciding whether a person is destitute the Secretary of State must ignore any support provided under section 95 or section 98, see SI 2000/705, regulation 6(3). The Secretary of State must take into account income, assets and support set out in regulation 6(4) of SI 2000/705 – see notes to Schedule 8. The assets in question are cash, savings, land, investments, cars and other vehicles, and goods held for the purposes of a trade or business. Other assets must be ignored.

95(2) See SI 2000/705, regulation 4. Under regulation 4(4) and 4(5) a person is excluded from support if s/he is eligible for support under the interim scheme (see notes to Schedule 8). The regulations governing the interim scheme (SI 1999/3046) were not amended when SI 2000/705 was promulgated. A person is excluded from support if s/he is entitled to the benefits set out in regulation 6 of SI 2000/705. A person who has not made a claim for asylum is excluded from support by regulation 4(4)(c) of SI 2000/705.

95(3)–(8) provide a framework for the definition of destitution which functions to determine eligibility for support, with powers to amplify the definition in regulations. See SI 2000/704 and notes to Schedule 8 below. For interim scheme, see SI 1999/3056 and notes to Schedule 9 below.

'adequate accommodation or any means of obtaining it' See *Westminster City Council v NASS* [2001] EWHC ADMIN 138, CO/4738/2000, QBD, judgment of 27 February 2001 and the note to section 116 below. Leave has been granted to appeal to

the Court of Appeal. The Hon Mr Justice Stanley Burton, giving judgment for NASS stated

'I am therefore driven to the conclusion that accommodation to which an asylum-seeker is entitled from a local authority under section 21 [of the National Assistance Act 1948] is a "means" of obtaining accommodation for the purposes of section 95 (3).'

95(3) 'essential living needs' Regulation 9 of SI 2000/704 makes further provision with respect to essential living needs. See note to 95(8) below. In SI 1999/3056, governing the interim period, essential living needs are not defined.

'adequate' See regulation 8 of SI 2000/704 and notes to Schedule 8. Regulation 8(2) provides that the matters set out therein are prescribed only where the Secretary of State is determining an application for accommodation under the scheme. They are not prescribed for cases where the person applies for support for essential living needs only. The application form for support and notes form a schedule to Regulation SI 2000/704 and give further details relevant to whether accommodation is adequate. Asylum Support Adjudicators have considered the question of when accomodation is adequate. See in particular the decision No 00/09/0063, which is discussed in the notes to paragraph 8 of Schedule 8 to this Act.

Addressing the use of the word 'adequate' in this provision in contrast to the use of the word 'suitable' in the Housing Act 1996 the Minister stated 'The distinction between 'adequate' and 'suitable' is that the test is different but not lower . . . The term 'suitable' is used for someone seeking permanent accommodation under the homelessness legislation, and 'adequate' level of accommodation will be available to someone seeking temporary accommodation while his case is being considered' (*Hansard* HC Report Immigration and Asylum Bill Special Standing Committee Nineteenth Sitting, Tuesday, 4 May 1999, col 1292).

95(5)(a) See SI 2000/704, regulation 8. Whether it would be reasonable for the person to continue to occupy the accommodation. Regulation 8(4) provides that the Secretary of State may have regard to the general circumstances in relation to housing in the district where the accommodation is, in deciding whether it would be reasonable for the person to continue to occupy the accommodation. Whether the accommodation is affordable. Regulation 8(5) provides that in assessing this the Secretary of State must have regard to the persons income or assets, other than support under section 98, the costs in respect of the accommodation and the person's other reasonable living expenses. Whether the accommodation is provided under section 98 or otherwise on an emergency basis only while the claim for asylum is being decided. Whether the person can secure entry to the accommodation. Whether the accommodation is a moveable structure and whether there is any place where the person is entitled to place it and reside in it. Whether the accommodation is available for occupation by the person together with any dependants. Whether it is 'probable' that continued occupation of the property will lead to domestic violence against the person. Regulation 6(a) defines domestic violence as 'violence from a person who is or has been a close family member, or threats of violence from such a person which are likely to be carried out'. A further gloss as to the meaning of 'adequate' is provided by the notes to the application form for support which form a schedule to SI 2000/704. These refer to overcrowding in relation to other property in the area. They also refer to violence wider than domestic violence, viz racial harassment or attacks, physical violence, sexual abuse or harassment and harassment because of religion. The coming to an end of a licence is also mentioned.

95(6) See note to 95(5)(a) above.

95(6)(b) 'shared' The Minister stated 'The fact that sharing cannot be taken into account does not mean that overcrowding cannot' ((*Hansard* HC Report Immigration and Asylum Bill Special Standing Committee, Nineteenth Sitting, Tuesday, 4 May 1999, col 1299). Overcrowding can mean that the accommodation is not 'adequate' for the purposes of 95(3). The other provisions in 95(6) occasioned similar debate. Thus for example, while the temporary nature of accommodation would not in and of itself make the accommodation inadequate (95(6)(c), the need to quit it within a very short time could do so. By analogy, while location by itself would not make accommodation inadequate, difficulties attendant on location have the potential to do so. The location of accommodation was a recurring theme in the debates and the assurances repeatedly given as to the services that would be made available to supported persons dispersed throughout the country under the Part VI scheme are relevant to consideration of whether the location of their existing accommodation makes it 'adequate' under the provisions of this section. (see for example Lord Williams of Mostyn on 20 October 1999 (*Hansard* HL Report, vol 605, no 138, cols 1163 and 1164).

95(7)(b) See SI 2000/705, regulation 9(2). The Secretary of State may not have regard to the asylum seeker's personal preference as to clothing.

95(8) Regulation 9(4) sets out matters expressly excluded from the definition of essential living needs. These are the cost of faxes; computers and the cost of computer facilities; the cost of photocopying; travel expenses save for the initial journey to the location at which support is to be provided; toys and other recreational items and entertainment expenses. See also notes to Schedule 8.

95(9) See SI 2000/705, regulations 16(4) and 19. Prompt payment of any contributions required under regulation 16 may be made a condition of support. Regulation 19 sets out what is to happen where conditions are breached.

95(12) See SI 2000/704 and notes to Schedule 8.

95(13) See SI 1999/3056 and notes to Schedule 9.

See Council Tax (Liability for Owners) (Amendment) (England) Regulations (SI 2000/537); Council Tax (Liability of Owners) (Amendment) (Scotland) Regulations 2000 (SI 2000/715, (S1)) and Council Tax (Liability for Owners) (Wales) Regulations 2000 (SI 2000/1024 (W60)), all in force from 3 April 2000. These provide that council tax liability for any accommodation provided under section 95 will fall on the owner of the accommodation as opposed to the asylum seeker living there. Under the provisions of section 115 and regulations made under that section, asylum seekers will not be eligible for council tax benefit. Note that the regulations deal only with accommodation provided by the Secretary of State. The general rules covering liability for Council Tax are thus applicable to those who accommodate asylum seekers receiving support but not accommodation from the Secretary of State. In these cases also, the asylum seeker him/herself is not eligible for Council Tax Benefit.

See also The Income-related benefits and Job-seekers' Allowance (Amendment) Regulations 2000 (SI 2000/979) which amend the definition of "person from abroad" for the purposes of *inter alia* the Council Tax Benefit (General) Regulations 1992 (SI 19992/1814). See also the note to see 115(9).

[A.1.329]

96 Ways in which support may be provided

(1) Support may be provided under section 95—

(a) by providing accommodation appearing to the Secretary of State to be adequate for the needs of the supported person and his dependants (if any);

(b) by providing what appear to the Secretary of State to be essential living needs of the supported person and his dependants (if any);

(c) to enable the supported person (if he is the asylum-seeker) to meet what appear to the Secretary of State to be expenses (other than legal expenses or other expenses of a prescribed description) incurred in connection with his claim for asylum;

(d) to enable the asylum-seeker and his dependants to attend bail proceedings in connection with his detention under any provision of the Immigration Acts; or

(e) to enable the asylum-seeker and his dependants to attend bail proceedings in connection with the detention of a dependant of his under any such provision.

(2)   If the Secretary of State considers that the circumstances of a particular case are exceptional, he may provide support under section 95 in such other ways as he considers necessary to enable the supported person and his dependants (if any) to be supported.

(3)   Unless the circumstances of a particular case are exceptional, support provided by the Secretary of State under subsection (1)(a) or (b) or (2) must not be wholly or mainly by way of payments made (by whatever means) to the supported person or to his dependants (if any).

(4)   But the Secretary of State may by order provide for subsection (3) not to apply—

(a)   in all cases, for such period as may be specified;
(b)   in such circumstances as may be specified;
(c)   in relation to specified categories of person; or
(d)   in relation to persons whose accommodation is in a specified locality.

(5)   The Secretary of State may by order repeal subsection (3).

(6)   'Specified' means specified in an order made under subsection (4).

Commencement   3 April 2000 (SI 2000/464).

Note   *96(1)(b)* Note that under the main support scheme, support for essential living needs may be provided to a person who has their own accommodation. Under the interim scheme, single people who have their own accommodation cannot receive any support for essential living needs, see SI 1999/3056, regulation 5.

96(1)(c)-(e) and 96(2) and (3) These subsections are not amplified in SI 2000/705.

96(4)–(6) No orders have been made under these sub-sections.

[A.1.330]
97 Supplemental
(1)   When exercising his power under section 95 to provide accommodation, the Secretary of State must have regard to—

(a)   the fact that the accommodation is to be temporary pending determination of the asylum-seeker's claim;
(b)   the desirability, in general, of providing accommodation in areas in which there is a ready supply of accommodation; and
(c)   such other matters (if any) as may be prescribed.

(2)   But he may not have regard to—

(a)   any preference that the supported person or his dependants (if any) may have as to the locality in which the accommodation is to be provided; or
(b)   such other matters (if any) as may be prescribed.

(3)   The Secretary of State may by order repeal all or any of the following—

(a)   subsection (1)(a);
(b)   subsection (1)(b);
(c)   subsection (2)(a).

(4)   When exercising his power under section 95 to provide essential living needs, the Secretary of State—

(a) must have regard to such matters as may be prescribed for the purposes of this paragraph; but

(b) may not have regard to such other matters as may be prescribed for the purposes of this paragraph.

(5)   In addition, when exercising his power under section 95 to provide essential living needs, the Secretary of State may limit the overall amount of the expenditure which he incurs in connection with a particular supported person—

(a) to such portion of the income support applicable amount provided under section 124 of the Social Security Contributions and Benefits Act 1992, or

(b) to such portion of any components of that amount,

as he considers appropriate having regard to the temporary nature of the support that he is providing.

(6)   For the purposes of subsection (5), any support of a kind falling within section 96(1)(c) is to be treated as if it were the provision of essential living needs.

(7)   In determining how to provide, or arrange for the provision of, support under section 95, the Secretary of State may disregard any preference which the supported person or his dependants (if any) may have as to the way in which the support is to be given.

Commencement   1 January 2000 (SI 1999/3190) for the purposes of enabling subordinate legislation to be made under it. 3 April 2000 (SI 2000/464) in full.

Note   See The Asylum Support Regulations 2000, SI 2000/704 into force 3 April 2000 and the Immigration (Eligibility for Assistance) (Scotland and Northern Ireland) Regulations 2000, (SI 2000/705) into force 3 April 2000.
  See the notes to Schedule 9 for the extent to which the provisions of Asylum Support (Interim Provisions) Regulations, SI 1999/3056 reflect the provisions of section 97.
  See notes to Schedule 8.
  97(1)(c) No matters have been prescribed.
  97(2)(b) See SI 2000/704, regulation 13(2). Regulation 13(2)(a) provides that the asylum seekers' personal preference as to the nature of the accommodation to be provided shall not be taken into account; regulation 13(2)(b) provides that his/her personal preference as to the nature and standard of fixtures and fittings shall not be taken into account. However, regulation 13(2) does provide that the person's individual circumstances as they relate to his/her accommodation needs can be taken into account.
  97(3) No orders have been made under this section.
  97(4) See SI 2000/704.
  97(5) See SI 2000/704. The limitations have been made not by reference to the income support applicable amount, but in a free-standing table set out in regulation 10 of that instrument, as amended by The Asylum Support (Amendment) Regulations 2000 (SI 2000/3053) in respect of persons under 16. The figures in the table have been amended in one respect. The Asylum Support (Amendment) Regulations 2000 (SI 2000/3053) increase the sum to be paid for support for essential living needs for a person under 16, from the £26.60 to £30.95.

[A.1.331]
98 Temporary support
(1)   The Secretary of State may provide, or arrange for the provision of, support for—

(a) asylum-seekers, or

(b) dependants of asylum-seekers,

who it appears to the Secretary of State may be destitute.

(2)   Support may be provided under this section only until the Secretary of State is able to determine whether support may be provided under section 95.

(3)   Subsections (2) to (11) of section 95 apply for the purposes of this section as they apply for the purposes of that section.

Commencement   Section 98(3) 1 March 2000 for the purposes of enabling supporting legislation to be made under section 95 of the Act as applied by section 98(3) and 3 April 2000 in full (SI 2000/464).

Note   NASS has contracted with a number of voluntary organisations, the main ones being the Refuge Council, the Refuge Arrivals Project, Migrant Helpline and Refugee Action, to provide this 'temporary' or 'emergency' support. However, these cases do not extend to cover persons previously in receipt of social security benefits who make an application to NASS when these benefits are terminated because a negative decision is made on their applications. There has been confusion as to whether the Secretary of State is using the powers under this section so that emergency accommodation can be provided by NASS itself pending its decision on the application for support. Following, inter alia the application for judicial review in the case of *Paulo* (CO/4769/00), NASS has issued a Policy Bulletin, No 53 *Temporary Support for the Disbenefited*, clarifying the issue. NASS is grant funding local authorities to provide section 98 support to asylum seekers who have been refused asylum on or after September 25 2000 if their household contains dependant minor children. NASS itself will provide section 98 support to those without dependant children 'within a reasonable time period, if requested, provided that an application form is completed in full and submitted to NASS' (letter of Richard Honeyman of NASS 22 January 2001 submitted in the case of *Paulo*. Thanks to Stefan Vnuk of Lloyd and Associates for this information). In contrast to the letter submitted in *Paulo*, Policy Bulletin No 53 demands that the application form has *been* submitted, before NASS will provide this support.

98(3) See notes to 95(2) to (11) above. 98(3) introduces an element of circularity. 95(2) to (11) set out a test of destitution. Section 98 applies while NASS are ascertaining whether or not the person is destitute in accordance with these tests, as it reflected in the words 'may be destitute' in 95(1). Yet 98(3) imports those very same tests of destitution into the criteria of eligibility of section 98 support. See SI 2000/705, *inter alia*, regulation 8, excluding from temporary support those eligible for local authority support or for benefits, or who have not made a claim for asylum.

Support and assistance by local authorities etc

[A.1.332]
99 Provision of support by local authorities
(1)   A local authority may provide support for asylum-seekers and their dependants (if any) in accordance with arrangements made by the Secretary of State under section 95.

(2)   Such support may be provided by the local authority—

(a) in one or more of the ways mentioned in section 96(1) and (2);
(b) whether the arrangements in question are made with the authority or with another person.

(3)   The Executive may provide support by way of accommodation for asy-

lum-seekers and their dependants (if any) in accordance with arrangements made by the Secretary of State under section 95, whether the arrangements in question are made with the Executive or with another person.

(4) A local authority may incur reasonable expenditure in connection with the preparation of proposals for entering into arrangements under section 95.

(5) The powers conferred on a local authority by this section include power to—

(a) provide services outside their area;
(b) provide services jointly with one or more bodies who are not local authorities;
(c) form a company for the purpose of providing services;
(d) tender for contracts (whether alone or with any other person).

Commencement Sub-sections (4) and (5) commenced on Royal Assent (section 170(3)). In full 3 April 2000 (SI 2000/464).

Note *'arrangements under section 95'* includes arrangements for the interim scheme under Schedule 9, introduced by section 95(13).

99(5)(a) This provision facilities the operation of consortia, see 95(b).

99(5)(b) Under both the main support scheme and the interim provisions it is intended that local authorities, or groups of local authorities form "consortia" in their area with other interested parties, for example voluntary organisations, registered social landlords, housing associations in order to bid for contracts to provide support and to manage the dispersal of asylum seekers to different parts of the country. The powers to do so are provided by this section.

99(5)(d) This provision allows local authorities to tender for contracts from the National Asylum Support Service to provide support to asylum seekers under the main support scheme.

[A.1.333]
100 Local authority and other assistance for Secretary of State

(1) This section applies if the Secretary of State asks—

(a) a local authority;
(b) a registered social landlord,
(c) a registered housing association in Scotland or Northern Ireland, or
(d) the Executive,

to assist him to exercise his power under section 95 to provide accommodation.

(2) The person to whom the request is made must co-operate in giving the Secretary of State such assistance in the exercise of that power as is reasonable in the circumstances.

(3) Subsection (2) does not require a registered social landlord to act beyond its powers.

(4) A local authority must supply to the Secretary of State such information about their housing accommodation (whether or not occupied) as he may from time to time request.

(5) The information must be provided in such form and manner as the Secretary of State may direct.

(6) 'Registered social landlord' has the same meaning as in Part I of the Housing Act 1996.

(7) 'Registered housing association' has the same meaning—

(a) in relation to Scotland, as in the Housing Associations Act 1985; and
(b) in relation to Northern Ireland, as in Part II of the Housing (Northern Ireland) Order 1992.

Commencement 3 April 2000 (SI 2000/464).

[A.1.334]
101 Reception zones
(1) The Secretary of State may by order designate as reception zones—

(a) areas in England and Wales consisting of the areas of one or more local authorities;
(b) areas in Scotland consisting of the areas of one or more local authorities;
(c) Northern Ireland.

(2) Subsection (3) applies if the Secretary of State considers that—

(a) a local authority whose area is within a reception zone has suitable housing accommodation within that zone; or
(b) the Executive has suitable housing accommodation.

(3) The Secretary of State may direct the local authority or the Executive to make available such of the accommodation as may be specified in the direction for a period so specified—

(a) to him for the purpose of providing support under section 95; or
(b) to a person with whom the Secretary of State has made arrangements under section 95.

(4) A period specified in a direction under subsection (3)—

(a) begins on a date so specified; and
(b) must not exceed five years.

(5) A direction under subsection (3) is enforceable, on an application made on behalf of the Secretary of State, by injunction or in Scotland an order under section 45(b) of the Court of Session Act 1988.

(6) The Secretary of State's power to give a direction under subsection (3) in respect of a particular reception zone must be exercised by reference to criteria specified for the purposes of this subsection in the order designating that zone.

(7) The Secretary of State may not give a direction under subsection (3) in respect of a local authority in Scotland unless the Scottish Ministers have confirmed to him that the criteria specified in the designation order concerned are in their opinion met in relation to that authority.

(8) Housing accommodation is suitable for the purposes of subsection (2) if it—

(a) is unoccupied;
(b) would be likely to remain unoccupied for the foreseeable future if not made available; and

(c) is appropriate for the accommodation of persons supported under this Part or capable of being made so with minor work.

(9) If housing accommodation for which a direction under this section is, for the time being, in force—

(a) is not appropriate for the accommodation of persons supported under this Part, but
(b) is capable of being made so with minor work,

the direction may require the body to whom it is given to secure that that work is done without delay.

(10) The Secretary of State must make regulations with respect to the general management of any housing accommodation for which a direction under subsection (3) is, for the time being, in force.

(11) Regulations under subsection (10) must include provision—

(a) as to the method to be used in determining the amount of rent or other charges to be payable in relation to the accommodation;
(b) as to the times at which payments of rent or other charges are to be made;
(c) as to the responsibility for maintenance of, and repairs to, the accommodation;
(d) enabling the accommodation to be inspected, in such circumstances as may be prescribed, by the body to which the direction was given;
(e) with respect to the condition in which the accommodation is to be returned when the direction ceases to have effect.

(12) Regulations under subsection (10) may, in particular, include provision—

(a) for the cost, or part of the cost, of minor work required by a direction under this section to be met by the Secretary of State in prescribed circumstances;
(b) as to the maximum amount of expenditure which a body may be required to incur as a result of a direction under this section.

(13) The Secretary of State must by regulations make provision ('the dispute resolution procedure') for resolving disputes arising in connection with the operation of any regulations made under subsection (10).

(14) Regulations under subsection (13) must include provision—

(a) requiring a dispute to be resolved in accordance with the dispute resolution procedure;
(b) requiring the parties to a dispute to comply with obligations imposed on them by the procedure; and
(c) for the decision of the person resolving a dispute in accordance with the procedure to be final and binding on the parties.

(15) Before—

(a) designating a reception zone in Great Britain,
(b) determining the criteria to be included in the order designating the zone, or
(c) making regulations under subsection (13),

the Secretary of State must consult such local authorities, local authority associations and other persons as he thinks appropriate.

(16)   Before—

(a) designating Northern Ireland as a reception zone, or
(b) determining the criteria to be included in the order designating Northern Ireland, the Secretary of State must consult the Executive and such other persons as he thinks appropriate.

(17)   Before making regulations under subsection (10) which extend only to Northern Ireland, the Secretary of State must consult the Executive and such other persons as he thinks appropriate.

(18)   Before making any other regulations under subsection (10), the Secretary of State must consult—

(a) such local authorities, local authority associations and other persons as he thinks appropriate; and
(b) if the regulations extend to Northern Ireland, the Executive.

Commencement   3 April 2000 (SI 2000/464).

Appeals

[A.1.335]
102 Asylum Support Adjudicators
(1)   There are to be adjudicators to hear appeals under this Part.
(2)   A person appointed as an adjudicator under this Part is to be known as an Asylum Support Adjudicator (but is referred to in this Part as 'an adjudicator').
(3)   Schedule 10 makes further provision with respect to adjudicators.

Commencement   3 April 2000 (SI 2000/464).

Note   See Schedule 10 and Asylum Support (Appeals) Procedure Rules 2000, SI 2000/541 made 2 March 2000, laid before Parliament 10 March 2000, into force 3 April 2000.

[A.1.336]
103 Appeals
(1)   If, on an application for support under section 95, the Secretary of State decides that the applicant does not qualify for support under that section, the applicant may appeal to an adjudicator.
(2)   If the Secretary of State decides to stop providing support for a person under section 95 before that support would otherwise have come to an end, that person may appeal to an adjudicator.
(3)   On an appeal under this section, the adjudicator may—

(a) require the Secretary of State to reconsider the matter;
(b) substitute his decision for the decision appealed against; or
(c) dismiss the appeal.

(4)   The adjudicator must give his reasons in writing.
(5)   The decision of the adjudicator is final.

(6)   If an appeal is dismissed, no further application by the appellant for support under section 95 is to be entertained unless the Secretary of State is satisfied that there has been a material change in the circumstances.

(7)   The Secretary of State may by regulations provide for decisions as to where support provided under section 95 is to be provided to be appealable to an adjudicator under this Part.

(8)   Regulations under subsection (7) may provide for any provision of this section to have effect, in relation to an appeal brought by virtue of the regulations, subject to such modifications as may be prescribed.

(9)   The Secretary of State may pay any reasonable travelling expenses incurred by an appellant in connection with attendance at any place for the purposes of an appeal under this section.

Commencement   3 April 2000 (SI 2000/464).

Note   See Schedule 10 and SI 2000/541.

103(4) The written reasons of Asylum Support Adjudicators are entitled 'Reasons Statement'. The statements are made in accordance with rule 13 of SI 2000/541. Reasons statements are, at the time of writing, fairly detailed documents, covering the relevant issues of fact and law.

103(7) No regulations have been made under this section. The jurisdiction of Asylum Support Adjudicators is limited to refusals of support – refusal of any support, or refusal to give either the accommodation or essential living needs element of the support package. Judicial review continues to be the mechanism by which the location, nature or level of support provided is to be challenged.

[A.1.337]
104 Secretary of State's rules
(1)   The Secretary of State may make rules regulating—

(a) the bringing of appeals under this Part; and
(b) the practice and procedure of the adjudicators.

(2)   The rules may, in particular, make provision—

(a) for the period within which an appeal must be brought;
(b) as to the burden of proof on an appeal;
(c) as to the giving and admissibility of evidence;
(d) for summoning witnesses;
(e) for an appeal to be heard in the absence of the appellant;
(f) for determining an appeal without a hearing;
(g) requiring reports of decisions of adjudicators to be published;
(h) conferring such ancillary powers on adjudicators as the Secretary of State considers necessary for the proper discharge of their functions.

(3)   In making the rules, the Secretary of State must have regard to the desirability of securing, so far as is reasonably practicable, that appeals are brought and disposed of with the minimum of delay.

Commencement   1 January 2000 (SI 1999/3190).

Note   See Asylum Support (Appeals) Procedure Rules 2000, SI 2000/541 into force 3 April 2000. Asylum Support Adjudicators have jurisdiction only to hear appeals against refusal of support by the Secretary of State; judicial review continues to be the means by which refusals of support by local authorities under the interim scheme are to be challenged. Decisions of Asylum Support Adjudicators themselves are subject to challenge by means of judicial review.

104(2)(a) See SI 2000/541, regulation 3(3). The notice of appeal must be received by the adjudicator not later than 2 days after the day on which the decision letter was received. Regulation 3(4) makes provision for this time limit to be extended where the applicant or any representative was prevented from complying due to circumstances beyond his/her control.

104(2)(b) SI 2000/541 makes no provision as to the burden of proof.

104(2)(c) See SI 2000/541, regulations 8 and 10.

104(2)(d) See SI 2000/541, regulation 10.

104(2)(e) and (f) See SI 2000/541, regulations 5 and 9. Where the appellant requests an oral hearing, such a hearing must be given, unless the appellant and/or his/her representative, if any, have been duly notified of the hearing and fail to attend. The adjudicator has power to hold an oral hearing even where the appellant does not request one, if the adjudicator considers that this is necessary for the just disposal of the appeal.

104(2)(h) See SI 2000/541.

Offences

[A.1.338]
105 False representations
(1) A person is guilty of an offence if, with a view to obtaining support for himself or any other person under any provision made by or under this Part, he—

(a) makes a statement or representation which he knows is false in a material particular;

(b) produces or gives to a person exercising functions under this Part, or knowingly causes or allows to be produced or given to such a person, any document or information which he knows is false in a material particular;

(c) fails, without reasonable excuse, to notify a change of circumstances when required to do so in accordance with any provision made by or under this Part; or

(d) without reasonable excuse, knowingly causes another person to fail to notify a change of circumstances which that other person was required to notify in accordance with any provision made by or under this Part.

(2) A person guilty of an offence under this section is liable on summary conviction to imprisonment for a term not exceeding three months or to a fine not exceeding level 5 on the standard scale, or to both.

Commencement Royal Assent (section 170(3)).

Note The provision is modelled on section 112 of the Social Security Administration Act 1992.

See SI 2000/704, regulation 3. Under the main scheme applications for support must be made on the form which appears as a schedule to these regulations, or any replacement form issued by the Secretary of State. Regulation 3 provides that the form must be completed 'in full and in English'. Under the interim provisions it is left to the local authority to determine the manner in which such applications are dealt with. The scope of what is a 'material particular' is broad. The Asylum Support (Interim Provisions) Regulations (SI 1999/3056) are, inevitably concerned in a large part to identify what is material to a decision to provide support. However, the procedure used by a particular local authority for collecting information about applicants is likely to determine whether the asylum-seeker 'knows' the information to be false in a 'material particular'.

[A.1.339]
106 Dishonest representations
(1)   A person is guilty of an offence if, with a view to obtaining any benefit or other payment or advantage under this Part for himself or any other person, he dishonestly—

(a) makes a statement or representation which is false in a material particular;
(b) produces or gives to a person exercising functions under this Part, or causes or allows to be produced or given to such a person, any document or information which is false in a material particular;
(c) fails to notify a change of circumstances when required to do so in accordance with any provision made by or under this Part; or
(d) causes another person to fail to notify a change of circumstances which that other person was required to notify in accordance with any provision made by or under this Part.

(2)   A person guilty of an offence under this section is liable—

(a) on summary conviction, to imprisonment for a term not exceeding six months or to a fine not exceeding the statutory maximum, or to both; or
(b) on conviction on indictment, to imprisonment for a term not exceeding seven years or to a fine, or to both.

(3)   In the application of this section to Scotland, in subsection (1) for 'dishonestly' substitute 'knowingly'.

Commencement   On Royal Assent (170(3)).

Note   The provision is modelled on the Social Security Administration Act 1992. The Explanatory Notes state 'This section is directed at cases of serious and calculated fraud, such as where a person makes a plan to extract as much from the Home Office as possible by deception'.

[A.1.340]
107 Delay or obstruction
(1)   A person is guilty of an offence if, without reasonable excuse, he—

(a) intentionally delays or obstructs a person exercising functions conferred by or under this Part; or
(b) refuses or neglects to answer a question, give any information or produce a document when required to do so in accordance with any provision made by or under this Part.

(2)   A person guilty of an offence under subsection (1) is liable on summary conviction to a fine not exceeding level 3 on the standard scale.

Commencement   On Royal Assent (section 170(3)).

Note   The provision is modelled section 111 of the Social Security Administration Act 1992.

[A.1.341]
108 Failure of sponsor to maintain
(1) A person is guilty of an offence if, during any period in respect of which he has given a written undertaking in pursuance of the immigration rules to be responsible for the maintenance and accommodation of another person—

(a) he persistently refuses or neglects, without reasonable excuse, to maintain that person in accordance with the undertaking; and
(b) in consequence of his refusal or neglect, support under any provision made by or under this Part is provided for or in respect of that person.

(2) A person guilty of an offence under this section is liable on summary conviction to imprisonment for a term not exceeding 3 months or to a fine not exceeding level 4 on the standard scale, or to both.
(3) For the purposes of this section, a person is not to be taken to have refused or neglected to maintain another person by reason only of anything done or omitted in furtherance of a trade dispute.

Commencement On Royal Assent (section 170(3)).

Note *108(2)(b)* envisages the situation where a sponsored immigrant receives support under Part VI – which could only be where s/he claimed asylum and was found to be destitute within the meaning of section 95. It thus provides an interesting commentary on paragraph 2 of Schedule 8, which provides in 2(1)(b) that 'The regulations may provide…for the Secretary of State to take into account…support which is…or might reasonably be expected to be available' to a person applying for support. This section clearly envisages circumstances in which a sponsorship agreement would not be treated as providing support which might reasonably be expected to be available to the sponsored person. The Minister stated in the Special Standing Committee that 'it is not our intention to catch people who might become ill, or be unable to support the person for a genuine reason.' (*Hansard* HC Report, Immigration and Asylum Bill Special Standing Committee Twenty-first Sitting, Tuesday, 11 May 1999, col 1422). The matter was put beyond doubt when the government accepted Lord Brightman's amendment to add the words 'without reasonable excuse' at Report Stage in the House of Lords on 2 November 1999, Lord Williams having rejected all the arguments he was proffered to present against the amendment as 'not marvellously convincing to me' (HL Report, vol 606, no 147, cols 839 to 842). The words added do not appear in section 105 of the Social Security Administration Act on which the provision is modelled.

[A.1.342]
109 Supplemental
(1) If an offence under section 105, 106, 107 or 108 committed by a body corporate is proved—

(a) to have been committed with the consent or connivance of an officer, or
(b) to be attributable to neglect on his part,

the officer as well as the body corporate is guilty of the offence and liable to be proceeded against and punished accordingly.
(2) 'Officer', in relation to a body corporate, means a director, manager, secretary or other similar officer of the body, or a person purporting to act in such a capacity.
(3) If the affairs of a body corporate are managed by its members, subsection (1) applies in relation to the acts and defaults of a member in connection with his functions of management as if he were a director of the body corporate.

(4)   If an offence under section 105, 106, 107 or 108 committed by a partnership in Scotland is proved—

(a) to have been committed with the consent or connivance of a partner, or
(b) to be attributable to neglect on his part,

the partner as well as the partnership is guilty of the offence and liable to be proceeded against and punished accordingly.
(5)   'Partner' includes a person purporting to act as a partner.

Commencement   On Royal Assent (section 170(3)).

Expenditure

[A.1.343]
110 Payments to local authorities
(1)   The Secretary of State may from time to time pay to any local authority or Northern Ireland authority such sums as he considers appropriate in respect of expenditure incurred, or to be incurred, by the authority in connection with—

(a) persons who are, or have been, asylum-seekers; and
(b) their dependants.

(2)   The Secretary of State may from time to time pay to any—

(a) local authority,
(b) local authority association, or
(c) Northern Ireland authority,

such sums as he considers appropriate in respect of services provided by the authority or association in connection with the discharge of functions under this Part.
(3)   The Secretary of State may make payments to any local authority towards the discharge of any liability of supported persons or their dependants in respect of council tax payable to that authority.
(4)   The Secretary of State must pay to a body to which a direction under section 101(3) is given such sums as he considers represent the reasonable costs to that body of complying with the direction.
(5)   The Secretary of State must pay to a directed body sums determined to be payable in relation to accommodation made available by that body under section 101(3)(a).
(6)   The Secretary of State may pay to a directed body sums determined to be payable in relation to accommodation made available by that body under section 101(3)(b).
(7)   In subsections (5) and (6)—
'determined' means determined in accordance with regulations made by virtue
       of subsection (11)(a) of section 101, and
'directed body' means a body to which a direction under subsection (3) of sec-
       tion 101 is given.

(8)   Payments under subsection (1), (2) or (3) may be made on such terms, and subject to such conditions, as the Secretary of State may determine.

(9)   'Northern Ireland authority' means—

(a) the Executive; or

(b) a Health and Social Services Board established under Article 16 of the Health and Personal Social Services (Northern Ireland) Order 1972.

Commencement   Subsections (1) and (2), and subsection (8) insofar as it relates to those subsections commenced on Royal Assent (section 170(3)).
Subsection 9 commenced 6 December 1999 (SI 1999/3190).
In full 3 April 2000 (SI 2000/464).

[A.1.344]
111 Grants to voluntary organisations
(1)   The Secretary of State may make grants of such amounts as he thinks appropriate to voluntary organisations in connection with—

(a) the provision by them of support (of whatever nature) to persons who are, or have been, asylum-seekers and to their dependants; and

(b) connected matters.

(2)   Grants may be made on such terms, and subject to such conditions, as the Secretary of State may determine.

Commencement   On Royal Assent (section 170(3)).

Note   See note on section 94 above on the 'hard cases fund'.

[A.1.345]
112 Recovery of expenditure on support: misrepresentations etc
(1)   This section applies if, on an application made by the Secretary of State, the court determines that—

(a) a person ('A') has misrepresented or failed to disclose a material fact (whether fraudulently or otherwise); and

(b) as a consequence of the misrepresentation or failure, support has been provided under section 95 or 98 (whether or not to A).

(2)   If the support was provided by the Secretary of State, the court may order A to pay to the Secretary of State an amount representing the monetary value of the support which would not have been provided but for A's misrepresentation or failure.

(3)   If the support was provided by another person ('B') in accordance with arrangements made with the Secretary of State under section 95 or 98, the court may order A to pay to the Secretary of State an amount representing the payment to B which would not have been made but for A's misrepresentation or failure.

(4)   'Court' means a county court or, in Scotland, the sheriff.

Commencement   3 April 2000 (SI 2000/464).

[A.1.346]
113 Recovery of expenditure on support from sponsor
(1)   This section applies if—

(a) a person ('the sponsor') has given a written undertaking in pursuance of the immigration rules to be responsible for the maintenance and accommodation of another person; and
(b) during any period in relation to which the undertaking applies, support under section 95 is provided to or in respect of that other person.

(2)   The Secretary of State may make a complaint against the sponsor to a magistrates' court for an order under this section.

(3)   The Court—

(a) must have regard to all the circumstances (and in particular to the sponsor's income); and
(b) may order him to pay to the Secretary of State such sum (weekly or otherwise) as it considers appropriate.

(4)   But such a sum is not to include any amount attributable otherwise than to support provided under section 95.
(5)   In determining—

(a) whether to order any payments to be made in respect of support provided under section 95 for any period before the complaint was made, or
(b) the amount of any such payments,

the court must disregard any amount by which the sponsor's current income exceeds his income during that period.
(6)   An order under this section is enforceable as a magistrates' court maintenance order within the meaning of section 150(1) of the Magistrates' Courts Act 1980.
(7)   In the application of this section to Scotland—

(a) omit subsection (6);
(b) for references to a complaint substitute references to an application; and
(c) for references to a magistrates' court substitute references to the sheriff.

(8)   In the application of this section to Northern Ireland, for references to a magistrates' court substitute references to a court of summary jurisdiction and for subsection (6) substitute—

'(6) An order under this section is an order to which Article 98(11) of the Magistrates' Courts (Northern Ireland) Order 1981 applies.'

Commencement   3 April 2000 (SI 2000/464).

[A.1.347]
114 Overpayments
(1)   Subsection (2) applies if, as a result of an error on the part of the Secretary of State, support has been provided to a person under section 95 or 98.
(2)   The Secretary of State may recover from a person who is, or has been, a supported person an amount representing the monetary value of support provided to him as a result of the error.

(3) An amount recoverable under subsection (2) may be recovered as if it were a debt due to the Secretary of State.

(4) The Secretary of State may by regulations make provision for other methods of recovery, including deductions from support provided under section 95.

Commencement 1 January 1999 (SI 1999/3190).

Note Modelled on provisions for recovery of overpayment under social security legislation. Section 95 governs support for eligible asylum seekers found to be destitute. Section 98 deals with temporary support to be provided for the period during which eligibility is being determined. The Explanatory Notes to the Act state that this section 'extends to recovery by the Secretary of State of the monetary value of support given by a contractor on the Secretary of State's behalf'. See SI 2000/704, regulation 18.

Exclusions

[A.1.348]
115 Exclusion from benefits
(1) No person is entitled to income-based jobseeker's allowance under the Jobseekers Act 1995 or to—

(a) attendance allowance,
(b) severe disablement allowance,
(c) invalid care allowance,
(d) disability living allowance,
(e) income support,
(f) working families' tax credit,
(g) disabled person's tax credit,
(h) a social fund payment,
(i) child benefit,
(j) housing benefit, or
(k) council tax benefit,

under the Social Security Contributions and Benefits Act 1992 while he is a person to whom this section applies.

(2) No person in Northern Ireland is entitled to—

(a) income-based jobseeker's allowance under the Jobseekers (Northern Ireland) Order 1995, or
(b) any of the benefits mentioned in paragraphs (a) to (j) of subsection (1),
under the Social Security Contributions and Benefits (Northern Ireland) Act 1992 while he is a person to whom this section applies.

(3) This section applies to a person subject to immigration control unless he falls within such category or description, or satisfies such conditions, as may be prescribed.

(4) Regulations under subsection (3) may provide for a person to be treated for prescribed purposes only as not being a person to whom this section applies.

(5) In relation to the benefits mentioned in subsection (1)(f) or (g), 'prescribed' means prescribed by regulations made by the Treasury.

(6) In relation to the matters mentioned in subsection (2) (except so far as it

relates to the benefits mentioned in subsection (1)(f) or (g)), 'prescribed' means prescribed by regulations made by the Department.

(7) Section 175(3) to (5) of the Social Security Contributions and Benefits Act 1992 (supplemental powers in relation to regulations) applies to regulations made by the Secretary of State or the Treasury under subsection (3) as it applies to regulations made under that Act.

(8) Sections 133(2), 171(2) and 172(4) of the Social Security Contributions and Benefits (Northern Ireland) Act 1992 apply to regulations made by the Department under subsection (3) as they apply to regulations made by the Department under that Act.

(9) 'A person subject to immigration control' means a person who is not a national of an EEA State and who—

(a) requires leave to enter or remain in the United Kingdom but does not have it;
(b) has leave to enter or remain in the United Kingdom which is subject to a condition that he does not have recourse to public funds;
(c) has leave to enter or remain in the United Kingdom given as a result of a maintenance undertaking; or
(d) has leave to enter or remain in the United Kingdom only as a result of paragraph 17 of Schedule 4.

(10) 'Maintenance undertaking', in relation to any person, means a written undertaking given by another person in pursuance of the immigration rules to be responsible for that person's maintenance and accommodation.

Commencement   1 January 1999 (SI 1999/3190) for the purposes of allowing subordinate legislation to be made under it. Commenced in full 3 April 2000 See also paragraphs 5 to 10 of Schedule 15.

Note   This section is the first in the 'Exclusions' section of Part VI. With the provisions in sections 116 to 123 it removes or in other circumstances limits the entitlement to state support of 'persons under immigration control' as defined in section 115(9). These sections operate independently of the schemes for support under Part VI and logically precede them. First entitlement to State support is removed or limited under the 'Exclusions' section, then alternative schemes are set up to support some although not all of those so excluded as described in the General Note on Support and the notes to section 94.

The effect of SI 2000/636, SI 2000/704, SI 2000/705 and SI 1999/3056 is that certain limited categories of asylum seeker retain their entitlement to benefits for the time being. For example, asylum-seekers who were entitled to benefit before coming into force of the interim provisions on 6 December 1999 retain that entitlement, including an entitlement to apply for other benefits, until the first negative decision after that date, and asylum-seekers who claimed asylum on arrival before 3 April 2000 are entitled to make applications for benefits. The key date is the date of the asylum claim, not the date of the applicant for benefits itself.

As described in the General Note on Support, a broad range of statutory instruments have been promulgated, not under this Act but under the relevant governing legislation, to effect the exclusion of persons under immigration control from a wide range of benefits and other social assistance. Key instruments are SI 2000/636 and SI 2000/705, but as indicated in the General Note on Support, a much broader range of statutory instruments impact upon the entitlements of asylum seekers.

115(9) This is a key provision. It provides a free-standing definition of persons under immigration control for the purposes of Part VI. It is narrower than definitions used for other purposes; a number of persons requiring (whether or not benefiting from) leave to enter or remain in the UK are not persons under immigration control for the purposes of this section. However, it is much broader than the persons for whom alternative support schemes are set up under part VI (ie asylum seekers and their dependants) and excludes categories of other immigrants who would previously have been able to access benefits.

EEA nationals are never persons under immigration control. Nor are recognised refugees or persons with ELR, who escape the definition because no restriction on access to public funds is made a provision of their leave.

See also the Income-related Benefits and Job-seeker's Allowance (Amendment) Regulations 2000 (SI 2000/979). These amend the definition of 'person from abroad' as it is used in the Income Support (General) Regulations 1987 (SI 1987/1967), the Jobseeker's Allowance Regulations 1996 (SI 19996/207), the Housing Benefit (General) Regulations 1987 (SI 1987/1971) and the Council Tax Benefit (General) Regulations 1992 (SI 1992/1814) to exclude persons who are excluded from being treated as not habitually resident in the UK to cover persons who have been deported, expelled or otherwise removed by compulsion of law from another country to the United Kingdom.

[A.1.349]
116 Amendment of section 21 of the National Assistance Act 1948

In section 21 of the National Assistance Act 1948 (duty of local authorities to provide accommodation), after subsection (1), insert—

(1A)   A person to whom section 115 of the Immigration and Asylum Act 1999 (exclusion from benefits) applies may not be provided with residential accommodation under subsection (1)(a) if his need for care and attention has arisen solely—

(a)   because he is destitute; or

(b)   because of the physical effects, or anticipated physical effects, of his being destitute.

(1B)   Subsections (3) and (5) to (8) of section 95 of the Immigration and Asylum Act 1999, and paragraph 2 of Schedule 8 to that Act, apply for the purposes of subsection (1A) as they apply for the purposes of that section, but for the references in subsections (5) and (7) of that section and in that paragraph to the Secretary of State substitute references to a local authority.

Commencement   6 December 1999 (SI 1999/3190).

Note   On 6 December 1999, entitlement to support under section 21 of the National Assistance Act 1948 ceased for those falling within the scope of the exclusion in this section. However, by Regulation 11 of Asylum Support (Interim Provisions) Regulations 1999, SI 1999/3056, asylum seekers and their dependants who had been receiving support under section 21 of that Act on that date were deemed to have been accepted for support under the interim scheme by the local authority in question. There are no powers parallel to the support schemes for asylum seekers that would allow alternative provision to be made for other persons under immigration control as defined in section 115(9) who have lost their National Assistance Act support.

Before focusing on alternative entitlements for people affected by this section, it is important to note that the exclusion is not absolute. It applies only to those need arises 'solely' for the reasons set out in the new subsections 1(A)(b) and (a) of section 21 of the National Assistance Act – destitution and the physical or anticipated physical effects of destitution. Thus, for example, where one reason for the need is the mental or anticipated mental effects of destitution, the exclusion does not apply.

See *Westminster City Council v NASS* [2001] EWHC ADMIN 138, CO/4738/2000, QBD, judgment of 27 February 2001. Leave has been granted to appeal to the Court of Appeal. The Hon Mr Justice Stanley Burton gave judgment for NASS, agreeing with their contention that the entire responsibility for meeting all the needs of a person who needs did not arise solely from destitution or the physical effects of destitution, fell to the local authority, in this case Westminster City Council. A person with needs arising other than from destitution or the physical effects of destitution was a person with the 'means of obtaining' accommodation (from the local authority, under section 21 of the NAA 1948) for the purposes of section 95(3) and was therefore excluded from NASS support. The applicant for support, A, was an Iraqi Kurdish asylum-seeker suffering from spinal myeloma. Confined to a wheelchair and she required 'in addition to her essential living needs, accommodation which is wheelchair accessible, with enough space for her, her daughter, and her family carers, and within reach of the hospital treating her'. It was accepted that her needs did not arise solely from destitution or its physical effects.

Readers will feel some sympathy for the judge, who commented 'I have to say... that one would expect the legislation I have to consider to have been sufficiently clearly drafted to make the answer to the question before me obvious'. This the legislation did not do, and the judgment goes on to construe section 95 of this Act and this section in reaching the conclusion that the applicant was entitled to support under the NAA 1948. It appears to have been accepted by the parties to the case that whichever of them was responsible for supporting A was also responsible for supporting her minor daughter, although this is not expressly considered in the judgment.

The effect of this section on those who are not eligible for support from NASS because they are not asylum seekers within the meaning of s 94 has also been considered. See *R v Wandsworth Borough Council ex p O and R v Leicester City Council ex p Bhikha* (2000) Times, 18 July, (CA) (C/1999/0747, C/1999/7342, C/1999/7696). The Secretary of State for the Home Department intervened in these cases, at the request of the Court of Appeal which addressed the question of the construction of s 116. The Court of Appeal took note of the 'harsh new regime' (Lord Justice Simon Brown) under s 115. O is a Nigerian overstayer suffering severe depression with psychotic features and physical illness. She was awaiting a decision on an application for ELR on health grounds and was therefore without support. Mr Bhikha, suffering from cancer, was refused ELR on health grounds and had a restricted appeal under section 15(1)(a) of the Immigration Act 1971, as restricted by s 5 of the Immigration Act 1988. Thus he too was without support. The judges preferred the appellant's construction of the new section 21(2A) as inserted by this section, viz that 'if an applicant's need for care and attention is to any material extent made more acute by some circumstance other than mere lack of accommodation and funds, then, despite being subject to immigration control, he qualifies for assistance. Other relevant circumstances include, of course, age, illness and disability. If for example, an immigrant, as well as being destitute, is old, ill or disabled, he is likely to become yet more vulnerable and less well able to survive than if he were merely destitute'. Lord Justice Simon Brown observed 'if there are to be immigrant beggars on our streets, then let them at least not be ill, old or disabled'. The court also rejected a suggestion that illegality should bar a claim for support. Lord Justice Simon Brown declared 'a local authority has no business with the applicant's immigration status save only for the purpose of learning why the care and attention is not otherwise available to them'. He observed that 'it should be for the Home Office to decide (and decide speedily) any claim for ELR and to ensure that those unlawfully here are promptly removed, rather than for local authorities to, so to speak, starve immigrants out of the country by withholding last resort support from those who today will by definition be not merely destitute but for other reasons too in need of urgent care and assistance'. Destitution is defined in the new subsection (1B) by reference to section 95, with the interesting effect that any attempt to narrow the range of asylum seekers entitled to support under Part VI schemes, resulting in a corresponding broad ening of the range of those persons under immigration control, including but not limited to asylum seekers, who will not be excluded by this section.

See notes to paragraphs 5 to 10 of Schedule 15.

See SI 2000/704, regulation 23(1)(a) which imports the definition of 'destitute' in those regulations into the new section 21(1A) of the National Assistance Act inserted by this section.

[A.1.350]

117 (*Amends the Health Services and Public Health Act 1963, s 45.*)

[A.1.351]

118 Housing authority accommodation

(1)   Each housing authority must secure that, so far as practicable, a tenancy of, or licence to occupy, housing accommodation provided under the accommodation provisions is not granted to a person subject to immigration control unless—

(a) he is of a class specified in an order made by the Secretary of State; or
(b) the tenancy of, or licence to occupy, such accommodation is granted in accordance with arrangements made under section 95.

(2)   'Housing authority' means—

(a) in relation to England and Wales, a local housing authority within the meaning of the Housing Act 1985;
(b) in relation to Scotland, a local authority within the meaning of the Housing (Scotland) Act 1987; and
(c) in relation to Northern Ireland, the Executive.

(3)   'Accommodation provisions' means—

(a) in relation to England and Wales, Part II of the Housing Act 1985;
(b) in relation to Scotland, Part I of the Housing (Scotland) Act 1987;
(c) in relation to Northern Ireland, Part II of the Housing (Northern Ireland) Order 1981.

(4)   'Licence to occupy', in relation to Scotland, means a permission or right to occupy.

(5)   'Tenancy', in relation to England and Wales, has the same meaning as in the Housing Act 1985.

(6)   'Person subject to immigration control' means a person who under the 1971 Act requires leave to enter or remain in the United Kingdom (whether or not such leave has been given).

(7)   This section does not apply in relation to any allocation of housing to which Part VI of the Housing Act 1996 (allocation of housing accommodation) applies.

Commencencement   1 January 1999 (SI 1999/3190) for the purposes of allowing subordinate legislation to be made under it. Commenced in full 1 March 2000 (SI 2000/464).

Note   This section and secondary legislation, have the effect of replacing section 9(1) of the Asylum and Immigration Act 1996. Paragraphs 73, 81 and 88 of Schedule 14 have the effect of removing asylum seekers supported under Part VI, under both the main and the interim scheme, from the security of tenure provisions in housing legislation. These have paved the way for the Housing Accommodation (Persons subject to Immigration Control) (Amendment) Order (SI 1999/3057) made under section 9 of the Asylum and Immigration Act 1996 and commencing 6 December 1999. This instrument amends the Housing Accommodation and Homelessness (Persons Subject to Immigration Control) Order 1996 to insert persons to whom a local authority is required to provide accomodation in accordance with The Asylum Support (Interim Provisions) Regulations 1999 (SI 1999/3126) into article 3 of that order. The effect is that of removing restrictions on the granting of tenancies of local authority housing to asylum seekers.

See also the Homelessness (Asylum Seekers) (Interim Period) Order 1999 (SI 1999/3126), which came into force 6 December 1999. It was made under s 166(3) and paragraph 13 of this Act which modifies Part VIII of the Housing Act 1996 for the period that the interim scheme for support for asylum seekers is in force. See the (Social Security) (Immigration and Asylum) Consequential Amendments Regulations 2000, (SI 2000/636), and the Council Tax (Liability of Owners) (Scotland) Regulations 2000.

See also The Allocation of Housing (England) Regulations 2000 (SI 2000/702) made in the exercise of powers under the Housing Act 1996. The regulations replace the Allocation of Housing Regulations 1996 insofar as they extend to England and make provision for cases where the allocation of housing accommodation by local housing authorities are not subject to Part VI of the Housing Act 1996. The main change is that from now on only those persons under immigration who are nationals of states who have ratified the European Convention on Social and Medical Assistance, or the European Social Charter, will be eligible for housing assistance by virtue of that ratification. Previously nationals of states who had signed the Convention or Charter were eligible, regardless of whether their states had ratified these instruments.

See also Persons Subject to Immigration Control (Housing Authority Accommodation and Homelessness) Order 2000 (SI 2000/706). The order revokes all extant orders made under section 9 of the Asylum and Immigration Act 1996. The order amends the classes of person who may be granted housing authority accommodation in England, Scotland and Northern Ireland. See the Persons Subject to Immigration Control (Housing Authority Accommodation) (Wales) Order 2000 (SI 2000/1036 (W 67)). This order provides for the class of persons specified in relation to England by SI 2000/706 to be specified in relation to Wales also.

[A.1.352]
119 Homelessness: Scotland and Northern Ireland
(1)   A person subject to immigration control—

(a) is not eligible for accommodation or assistance under the homelessness provisions, and
(b) is to be disregarded in determining for the purposes of those provisions, whether another person—
   (i)   is homeless or is threatened with homelessness, or
   (ii)   has a priority need for accommodation,

unless he is of a class specified in an order made by the Secretary of State.
(2)   An order under subsection (1) may not be made so as to include in a specified class any person to whom section 115 applies.
(3)   'The homelessness provisions' means—

(a) in relation to Scotland, Part II of the Housing (Scotland) Act 1987; and

(b) in relation to Northern Ireland, Part II of the Housing (Northern Ireland) Order 1988.

(4)   'Person subject to immigration control' has the same meaning as in section 118.

Commencement   1 January 1999 (SI 1999/3190) for the purposes of allowing subordinate legislation to be made under it. Commenced in full 1 March 2000 (SI 2000/464).

Note   This section has the effect of replacing section 9(2) of the Asylum and Immigration Act 1996. See the Immigration (Eligibility for Assistance) (Scotland and Northern Ireland) Regulations 2000, SI 2000/705.

During the passage of the Act there was much debate as to the effect of the provisions of Part VI in Scotland. Ministers took the view that because immigration is a reserved matter, matters dealing with the support of persons under immigration control were within the competence of the Westminster parliament. The opposing view was that the legislation being amended by Part VI, and in particular the Exclusions section, related to devolved matters and that some of the amendments fell out with the reserved category of immigration. The issues have yet to be tested.

See SI 2000/706 and the notes under section 118 above. SI 2000/706, in addition to amending the classes of person who may be granted housing authority accommodation in Scotland and Northern Ireland, amends the classes of person who are eligible for homelessness assistance in Scotland and Northern Ireland. The provisions with relation to the two regions are not identical.

[A.1.353]
120 *(Amends the Social Work (Scotland) Act 1968, ss 12, 13A, 13B; the Mental Health (Scotland) Act 1984, ss 7 and 8 and the Asylum and Immigration Appeals Act 1993, ss 4 and 5 and Sch 1.)*

[A.1.354]
121 *(Amends the Health and Personal Services (Northern Ireland) Order 1972, arts 7, 15 and the Asylum and Immigration Appeals Act 1993, ss 4 and 5 and Sch 1.)*

[A.1.355]
122 Support for children
(1)   In this section 'eligible person' means a person who appears to the Secretary of State to be a person for whom support may be provided under section 95.
(2)   Subsections (3) and (4) apply if an application for support under section 95 has been made by an eligible person whose household includes a dependant under the age of 18 ('the child').
(3)   If it appears to the Secretary of State that adequate accommodation is not being provided for the child, he must exercise his powers under section 95 by offering, and if his offer is accepted by providing or arranging for the provision of, adequate accommodation for the child as part of the eligible person's household.
(4)   If it appears to the Secretary of State that essential living needs of the child are not being met, he must exercise his powers under section 95 by offer-

ing, and if his offer is accepted by providing or arranging for the provision of, essential living needs for the child as part of the eligible person's household.

(5)   No local authority may provide assistance under any of the child welfare provisions in respect of a dependant under the age of 18, or any member of his family, at any time when—

(a) the Secretary of State is complying with this section in relation to him; or
(b) there are reasonable grounds for believing that—
    (i) the person concerned is a person for whom support may be provided under section 95; and
    (ii) the Secretary of State would be required to comply with this section if that person had made an application under section 95.

(6)   'Assistance' means the provision of accommodation or of any essential living needs.
(7)   'The child welfare provisions' means—

(a) section 17 of the Children Act 1989 (local authority support for children and their families);
(b) section 22 of the Children (Scotland) Act 1995 (equivalent provision for Scotland); and
(c) Article 18 of the Children (Northern Ireland) Order 1995 (equivalent provision for Northern Ireland).

(8)   Subsection (9) applies if accommodation provided in the discharge of the duty imposed by subsection (3) has been withdrawn.
(9)   Only the relevant authority may provide assistance under any of the child welfare provisions in respect of the child concerned.
(10) 'Relevant authority' means—

(a) in relation to Northern Ireland, the authority within whose area the withdrawn accommodation was provided;
(b) in any other case, the local authority within whose area the withdrawn accommodation was provided.

(11) In such circumstances as may be prescribed, subsection (5) does not apply.

Commencement   1 March 2000 for the purposes of enabling subordinate legislation to be made under it. In full 3 April 2000 (SI 2000/464).

Note   Under regulation 11 of Asylum Support (Interim Provisions) Regulations 1999, SI 1999/3056 asylum seekers and/or their dependants receiving assistance from a local authority under the section 17 of the Children Act 1989 immediately before 6 December 1999 were deemed to have been accepted by the local authority providing assistance for support under the interim scheme from that date. Thus accommodation and essential living needs would be provided under the interim scheme from 6 December. Regulation 12 provides that a person entitled to support under these regulations is not entitled to assistance under section 17 of the Children Act 1989. Assistance under section 17 of the Children Act 1989 is defined in regulation 2(5) as being a reference to the provision of accommodation or any essential living needs. The exclusion only affects section 17 support. Unaccompanied asylum-seeking children continue to be eligible for support under section 20 of the Children Act 1989. Upon turning 18 and leaving care such children are eligible for support under section 24 of the Children Act 1989 and the provisions of this section do not affect that entitlement. Because, unlike the other provisions of the 'Exclusions' section, this provision affects only those for whom support may be provided under section 95, it does not affect families who are persons under immigration control as defined in section 115(9), but are not seeking asylum. Such families, for example in circumstances where a sponsorship arrangement breaks down, continue to be eligible for support under the child welfare provisions as defined.

See *R v London Borough of Bromley ex p Badzo* CO/2571/2000, 21 July 2000. The applicants had been granted leave to enter to care for their grandchildren, who had ELR. The grandparents had no funds and were staying with relatives, a total of 5 adults and five children in a two bed-roomed flat. Bromley provided cash payments under section 17 of the Children Act 1989 but refused to reaccommodate. The grandparents applied for permission for judicial review arguing that the refusal to accommodate was unlawful because of over-crowding and the importance of keeping the family together. This was granted, and an interim ex parte injunction made requiring Bromley to accommodate the children and grandparents together within 10 days. On the 10th day the grandparents and their grandchildren were accommodated by Bromley in a three bedroom house.

See notes to Schedules 8 and 9. See the Asylum Support Regulations 2000, SI 2000/74 and SI 2000/705.

[A.1.356]
123 Back-dating of benefits where person recorded as refugee
(1)   This section applies if—

(a) a person is recorded by the Secretary of State as a refugee within the meaning of the Refugee Convention; and
(b) before the refugee was so recorded, he or his dependant was a person to whom section 115 applied.

(2)   Regulations may provide that a person mentioned in subsection (1)(b) may, within a prescribed period, claim the whole, or any prescribed proportion, of any benefit to which he would have been entitled had the refugee been so recorded when he made his claim for asylum.

(3)   Subsections (5) and (6) apply if the refugee has resided in the areas of two or more local authorities and he or his dependant makes a claim under the regulations in relation to housing benefit.

(4)   Subsections (5) and (6) also apply if the refugee has resided in the areas of two or more local authorities in Great Britain and he or his dependant makes a claim under the regulations in relation to council tax benefit.

(5)   The claim must be investigated and determined, and any benefit awarded must be paid or allowed, by such one of those authorities as may be prescribed by the regulations ('the prescribed authority').

(6)   The regulations may make provision requiring a local authority who are not the prescribed authority to supply that authority with such information as they may reasonably require in connection with the exercise of their functions under the regulations.

(7)   The regulations may make provision in relation to a person who has received support under this Part or who is a dependant of such a person—

(a) for the determination, or for criteria for the calculation, of the value of that support; and
(b) for the sum which he would be entitled to claim under the regulations to be reduced by the whole, or any prescribed proportion, of that valuation.

(8)   The reductions permitted by subsection (7) must not exceed the amount of the valuation.

(9)   'Regulations' means—

(a)   in relation to jobseeker's allowance under the Jobseekers Act 1995, regulations made by the Secretary of State under that Act or the Social Security Administration Act 1992;
(b)   in relation to jobseeker's allowance under the Jobseekers (Northern Ireland) Order 1995, regulations made by the Department under that Order or the Social Security Administration (Northern Ireland) Act 1992;
(c)   in relation to a benefit under the Social Security Contributions and Benefits Act 1992, regulations made by the Secretary of State under that Act or the Social Security Administration Act 1992;
(d)   in relation to a benefit under the Social Security Contributions and Benefits (Northern Ireland) Act 1992, regulations made by the Department under that Act or the Social Security Administration (Northern Ireland) Act 1992.

Commencement   1 January 1999 (SI 1999/3190) for the purposes of allowing subordinate legislation to be made under it. In full 3 April 2000 (SI 2000/464).

Note   See SI 2000/636, regulatiom 3(5) inserting a new subsection 21 ZB into the Income Support (General) Regulations 1987 (SI 1987/1967).

Miscellaneous

[A.1.357]
124 Secretary of State to be corporation sole for purposes Part VI
(1)   For the purpose of exercising his functions under this Part, the Secretary of State is a corporation sole.
(2)   Any instrument in connection with the acquisition, management or of disposal of property, real or personal, heritable or moveable, by the Secretary of State under this Part may be executed on his behalf by a person authorised by him for that purpose.
(3)   Any instrument purporting to have been so executed on behalf of the Secretary of State is to be treated, until the contrary is proved, to have been so executed on his behalf.

Note   Commenced on Royal Assent under section 170(3)2.

[A.1.358]
125 Entry of premises
(1)   This section applies in relation to premises in which accommodation has been provided under section 95 or 98 for a supported person.
(2)   If, on an application made by a person authorised in writing by the Secretary of State, a justice of the peace is satisfied that there is reason to believe that—

(a)   the supported person or any dependants of his for whom the accommodation is provided is not resident in it,
(b)   the accommodation is being used for any purpose other than the accommodation of the asylum-seeker or any dependant of his, or
(c)   any person other than the supported person and his dependants (if any) is residing in the accommodation,

he may grant a warrant to enter the premises to the person making the application.

(3)   A warrant granted under subsection (2) may be executed—

(a) at any reasonable time;
(b) using reasonable force.

(4)   In the application of subsection (2) to Scotland, read the reference to a justice of the peace as a reference to the sheriff or a justice of the peace.

Commencement   3 April 2000 (SI 2000/464).

[A.1.359]
126   Information from property owners
(1)   The power conferred by this section is to be exercised with a view to obtaining information about premises in which accommodation is or has been provided for supported persons.

(2)   The Secretary of State may require any person appearing to him—

(a) to have any interest in, or
(b) to be involved in any way in the management or control of,

such premises, or any building which includes such premises, to provide him with such information with respect to the premises and the persons occupying them as he may specify.

(3)   A person who is required to provide information under this section must do so in accordance with such requirements as may be prescribed.

(4)   Information provided to the Secretary of State under this section may be used by him only in the exercise of his functions under this Part.

Commencement   3 April 2000 (SI 2000/464).

[A.1.360]
127   Requirement to supply information about redirection of post
(1)   The Secretary of State may require any person conveying postal packets to supply redirection information to the Secretary of State—

(a) for use in the prevention, detection, investigation or prosecution of criminal offences under this Part;
(b) for use in checking the accuracy of information relating to support provided under this Part; or
(c) for any other purpose relating to the provision of support to asylum-seekers.

(2)   The information must be supplied in such manner and form, and in accordance with such requirements, as may be prescribed.
(3)   The Secretary of State must make payments of such amount as he considers reasonable in respect of the supply of information under this section.
(4)   'Postal packet' has the same meaning as in the Post Office Act 1953.

(5) 'Redirection information' means information relating to arrangements made with any person conveying postal packets for the delivery of postal packets to addresses other than those indicated by senders on the packets.

Commencement   3 April 2000 (SI 2000/464).

PART VII
POWER TO ARREST, SEARCH AND FINGERPRINT

Power to arrest

[A.1.361]
128 *(Amends the Immigration Act 1971, s 28.)*

Power to search and arrest

[A.1.362]
129 *(Amends the Immigration Act 1971, s 28.)*

[A.1.363]
130 *(Amends the Immigration Act 1971, s 28.)*

Power to enter and search premises

[A.1.364]
131 *(Amends the Immigration Act 1971, s 28.)*

[A.1.365]
132 *(Amends the Immigration Act 1971, s 28 and Sch 2, para 25.)*

[A.1.366]
133 *(Amends the Immigration Act 1971, s 28.)*

Power to search persons

[A.1.367]
134 *(Amends the Immigration Act 1971, s 28 and Sch 2, para 25.)*

[A.1.368]
135 *(Amends the Immigration Act 1971, s 28 and Sch 2, para 25).*

Seized material: access and copying

[A.1.369]
136 *(Amends the Immigration Act 1971, s 28 and Sch 2, para 25.)*

Search warrants

[A.1.370]
137 *(Amends the Immigration Act 1971, s 28.)*

[A.1.371]
138 *(Amends the Immigration Act 1971, s 28.)*

[A.1.372]
139 *(Amends the Immigration Act 1971, s 28.)*

Detention

[A.1.373]
140 *(Amends the Immigration Act 1971, Sch 2, paras 16 and 17.)*

Fingerprinting

[A.1.374]
141   Fingerprinting
(1)   Fingerprints may be taken by an authorised person from a person to whom this section applies.
(2)   Fingerprints may be taken under this section only during the relevant period.
(3)   Fingerprints may not be taken under this section from a person under the age of sixteen ('the child') except in the presence of a person of full age who is—

(a) the child's parent or guardian; or
(b) a person who for the time being takes responsibility for the child.

(4)   The person mentioned in subsection (3)(b) may not be—

(a) an officer of the Secretary of State who is not an authorised person;
(b) an authorised person.

(5)   'Authorised person' means—

(a) a constable;
(b) an immigration officer;
(c) a prison officer;
(d) an officer of the Secretary of State authorised for the purpose; or
(e) a person who is employed by a contractor in connection with the discharge of the contractor's duties under a detention centre contract.

(6) In subsection (5)(e) 'contractor' and 'detention centre contract' have the same meaning as in Part VIII.

(7) This section applies to—

(a) any person ('A') who, on being required to do so by an immigration officer on his arrival in the United Kingdom, fails to produce a valid passport with photograph or some other document satisfactorily establishing his identity and nationality or citizenship;

(b) any person ('B') who has been refused leave to enter the United Kingdom but has been temporarily admitted under paragraph 21 of Schedule 2 to the 1971 Act if an immigration officer reasonably suspects that B might break any condition imposed on him relating to residence or as to reporting to the police or an immigration officer;

(c) any person ('C') in respect of whom—

   (i) an immigration officer has given directions under paragraph 9(1) of Schedule 2 to the 1971 Act or under section 10;

   (ii) the Secretary of State has given directions under paragraph 10(1) of Schedule 2 to the 1971 Act (but only in a case where it appears to the Secretary of State that the person is a person in respect of whom directions under paragraph 9 of that Schedule might be given); or

   (iii) the Secretary of State has given directions under paragraph 1(1) of Schedule 3 to that Act;

(d) any person ('D') who has been arrested under paragraph 17 of Schedule 2 to the 1971 Act;

(e) any person ('E') who has made a claim for asylum;

(f) any person ('F') who is a dependant of any of those persons.

(8) 'The relevant period' begins—

(a) for A, on his failure to produce the passport or other document;

(b) for B, on the decision to admit him temporarily;

(c) for C, on the direction being given;

(d) for D, on his arrest;

(e) for E, on the making of his claim for asylum; and

(f) for F, at the same time as for the person whose dependant he is.

(9) 'The relevant period' ends on the earliest of the following—

(a) the grant of leave to enter or remain in the United Kingdom;

(b) for A, B, C or D, his removal or deportation from the United Kingdom;

(c) for C, if a deportation order has been made against him, its revocation or otherwise ceasing to have effect;

(d) for D, his release if he is no longer liable to be detained under paragraph 16 of Schedule 2 to the 1971 Act;

(e) for E, the final determination or abandonment of his claim for asylum; and

(f) for F, at the same time as for the person whose dependant he is.

(10) No fingerprints may be taken from A if the immigration officer considers that A has a reasonable excuse for the failure concerned.

(11) No fingerprints may be taken from B unless the decision to take them has been confirmed by a chief immigration officer.

(12) An authorised person may not take fingerprints from a person under the age of sixteen unless his decision to take them has been confirmed—

(a) if he is a constable, by a person designated for the purpose by the chief constable of his police force;
(b) if he is a person mentioned in subsection (5)(b) or (e), by a chief immigration officer;
(c) if he is a prison officer, by a person designated for the purpose by the governor of the prison;
(d) if he is an officer of the Secretary of State, by a person designated for the purpose by the Secretary of State.

(13)   Neither subsection (3) nor subsection (12) prevents an authorised person from taking fingerprints if he reasonably believes that the person from whom they are to be taken is aged sixteen or over.
(14)   For the purposes of subsection (7)(f), a person is a dependant of another person if—

(a) he is that person's spouse or child under the age of eighteen; and
(b) he does not have a right of abode in the United Kingdom or indefinite leave to enter or remain in the United Kingdom.

(15)   'Claim for asylum' has the same meaning as in Part VI.

Commencement In force 11 December 2000 (SI 2000/3099).

Note Powers to take fingerprints were previously set out in paragraph 18(2) of Schedule 2 to the Immigration Act 1971, paragraph 2(4) of Schedule 3 to that Act and section 3 of the Asylum and Immigration Appeals Act 1993. This section consolidates and extends those powers, primarily where immigrants other than asylum-seekers are concerned. The persons listed in 141(5)(a)-(d) have enjoyed, by virtue of this section, wider powers both to take and to retain fingerprints, while one new category of persons is authorised to take fingerprints: those employed pursuant to a detention centre contract (see 141(5)(e)).

In the debates on the clause that became this section, Mike O'Brien, Under-Secretary of State for the Home Department, stated 'We intend to introduce safeguards to the system and we will publish the instructions to be issued to immigration staff before the provisions come into force' . . . (*Hansard*, HC Report, Immigration and Asylum Bill Special Standing Committee 13 May 1999 col 1521). It is unclear whether he is referring to the system of fingerprinting as a whole, or to the powers to fingerprint children.

See The Immigration (PACE Codes of Practice No 2 and Amendment) Direction 2000, into operation 20 November 2000. This reflects the categories set out in section 141, but also includes reference to the powers in paragraphs 16 to 18 of Schedule 2 to the Immigration Act 1971.

141(5)(a) 'Any detention centre staff who carry out this duties will need to be specifically trained to do so' (Mike O'Brien, *Hansard*, as above, col 1527).

141(7)(a) 'In the case of inadequately documented arrivals, instructions to those authorised to take fingerprints will make clear that they should only be taken when there is no reasonable excuse for failing to produce adequate documentation' (Mike O'Brien, *Hansard*, as above, col 1520).

141(12) '. . . I should stress that we have no intention of routinely fingerprinting children. We intend to fingerprint children under the age of 16 only when there are doubts as to their identity.' (Mike O'Brien, *Hansard*, as above, col 1521). The question of disputes as to age was raised, and Mr O'Brien stated 'The usual intention is to err on the side on caution, particularly when there is power to require the person to come back in seven days.' (col 1528). This would suggest that the safeguards of 141(12) should be applied to those whose age is in dispute at the time when the fingerprints are taken.

141(15) See Section 94(1). A claim for asylum is defined therein to mean both a claim under the Refugee Convention and a claim that removal would be in breach of the UK's obligations under Article 3 ECHR.

[A.1.375]
142   Attendance for fingerprinting
(1)   The Secretary of State may, by notice in writing, require a person to whom section 141 applies to attend at a specified place for fingerprinting.
(2)   The notice—

(a)   must give the person concerned a period of at least seven days within which to attend, beginning not earlier than seven days after the date of the notice; and
(b)   may require him to attend at a specified time of day or during specified hours.

(3)   A constable or immigration officer may arrest without warrant a person who has failed to comply with a requirement imposed on him under this section (unless the requirement has ceased to have effect).
(4)   Before a person arrested under subsection (3) is released—

(a)   he may be removed to a place where his fingerprints may conveniently be taken; and
(b)   his fingerprints may be taken (whether or not he is so removed).

(5)   A requirement imposed under subsection (1) ceases to have effect at the end of the relevant period (as defined by section 141).

Commencement   11 December 2000 (SI 2000/3099).

[A.1.376]
143   Destruction of fingerprints
(1)   If they have not already been destroyed, fingerprints must be destroyed before the end of the specified period beginning with the day on which they were taken.
(2)   If a person from whom fingerprints were taken proves that he is—

(a)   a British citizen, or
(b)   a Commonwealth citizen who has a right of abode in the United Kingdom as a result of section 2(1)(b) of the 1971 Act,

the fingerprints must be destroyed as soon as reasonably practicable.

(3)   If a person from whom fingerprints were taken—

(a)   in the case of E, is given indefinite leave to enter or remain in the United Kingdom, or
(b)   in any other case, is given leave to enter or remain in the United Kingdom,

the fingerprints must be destroyed as soon as reasonably practicable.
(4)   Fingerprints taken from B must be destroyed as soon as reasonably practicable after his removal from the United Kingdom.
(5)   But subsection (4) does not apply if it appears to the Secretary of State

that B has failed to comply with a restriction imposed on him under paragraph 21(2) of Schedule 2 to the 1971 Act.

(6)   Fingerprints taken from C must, if the directions cease to have effect, be destroyed as soon as reasonably practicable.

(7)   If a deportation order made against C is revoked, any fingerprints taken from him must be destroyed as soon as reasonably practicable.

(8)   If D ceases to be liable to be detained under paragraph 16 of Schedule 2 to the 1971 Act, fingerprints taken from him must be destroyed as soon as reasonably practicable.

(9)   Fingerprints taken from F must be destroyed when fingerprints taken from the person whose dependant he is have to be destroyed.

(10)   The obligation to destroy fingerprints under this section applies also to copies of fingerprints.

(11)   The Secretary of State must take all reasonably practicable steps to secure—

(a)   that data which are held in electronic form and which relate to fingerprints which have to be destroyed as a result of this section are destroyed or erased; or

(b)   that access to such data is blocked.

(12)   The person to whom the data relate is entitled, on request, to a certificate issued by the Secretary of State to the effect that he has taken the steps required by subsection (11).

(13)   A certificate under subsection (12) must be issued within three months of the date of the request for it.

(14)   'Fingerprints' means fingerprints taken under section 141 and references to B, C, D, E and F are to the persons so described in that section.

(15)   'Specified period' means—

(a)   such period as the Secretary of State may specify by order;

(b)   if no period is so specified, ten years.

Commencement   In force 11 December 2000 (SI 2000/3099).

Note   See the Immigration (PACE Codes of Practice No 2 and Amendment) Direction 2000, into operation 20 November 2000, which modifies Annex E of Code D of PACE as applied to immigration with respect to the destruction of fingerprints.

143(15)(a) No maximum period for the retention of fingerprints is specified on the face of the Act. The Secretary of State is free to make an order under this subsection specifying a period longer than the 10 years set out in 143(15)(b). However, such orders will be subject to the affirmative resolution procedure in parliament, see section 166(3)(g).

[A.1.377]

144   Other methods of collecting data about physical characteristics

The Secretary of State may make regulations containing provisions equivalent to sections 141, 142 and 143 in relation to such other methods of collecting data about external physical characteristics as may be prescribed.

Commencement   In force 11 December 2000 (SI 2000/3099).

Note   Any order made under this section is subject to the affirmative resolution procedure in parliament, see 160(4)(d). Methods envisaged in the debates in parliament included systems based upon the recognition of the iris of the eye and palm prints (*Hansard* HC Report SSC 13 May 1999 col 1523).

Codes of practice

[A.1.378]
145 Codes of practice
(1)   An immigration officer exercising any specified power to—

(a) arrest, question, search or take fingerprints from a person,
(b) enter and search premises, or
(c) seize property found on persons or premises,

must have regard to such provisions of a code as may be specified.
(2)   Subsection (1) also applies to an authorised person exercising the power to take fingerprints conferred by section 141.
(3)   Any specified provision of a code may have effect for the purposes of this section subject to such modifications as may be specified.
(4)   'Specified' means specified in a direction given by the Secretary of State.
(5)   'Authorised person' has the same meaning as in section 141.
(6)   'Code' means—

(a) in relation to England and Wales, any code of practice for the time being in force under the Police and Criminal Evidence Act 1984;
(b) in relation to Northern Ireland, any code of practice for the time being in force under the Police and Criminal Evidence (Northern Ireland) Order 1989.

(7)   This section does not apply to any person exercising powers in Scotland.

Commencement   On Royal Assent (section 170(3)).

Note   See the Immigration (PACE Codes of Practice) Direction 2000 and the Immigration (PACE Codes of Practice No 2 and Amendment) Direction (made 19 November 2000, into operation 20 November 2000). These are discussed further in the notes to section 148.

The second Direction modifies the provisions 3.1, 3.2 and 3.4 of the PACE Code D, and the equivalent provisions for Northern Ireland, as they are applied to immigration matters. This second Direction is concerned with matters relating to fingerprinting, see the notes to sections 141 and 143 above. It also amendments the provisions of Schedule 2 to The Immigration (PACE Codes of Practice) Direction 2000, inserting reference to an immigration officer in the modifications to Annexe E of PACE Code D effected by that schedule.

Use of force

[A.1.379]
146 Use of force
(1) An immigration officer exercising any power conferred on him by the
1971 Act or this Act may, if necessary, use reasonable force.
(2) Any person exercising a power conferred by section 141 or 142 or regulations under section 144 may, if necessary, use reasonable force.

Commencement Subsection (1) on Royal Assent (section 170(3)).

Note The breadth of this provision was debated at length during the passage of Act,
where attempts were made to limit it so that immigration officers could only use reasonable force in respect of the powers given to them under Part VII. The amendment
was rejected, Ministers stating that in respect of some duties the use of force would
never be reasonable in any event, and thus the provision extends to the exercise of any
powers under any of the Immigration Acts.
  'Immigration Acts' is defined in section 167.
  As set out in the notes to section 128, it is intended that the use of Part VII powers
be piloted in the first instance. There is thus at the very least an expectation that immigration officers outside the pilot will not be using force under the powers given in this
section from 14 February 2000.

PART VIII
DETENTION CENTRES AND DETAINED PERSONS

[A.1.380]
147 Interpretation of Part VIII
In this Part—

'certificate of authorisation' means a certificate issued by the Secretary of
    State under section 154;
'certified prisoner custody officer' means a prisoner custody officer certified
    under section 89 of the Criminal Justice Act 1991, or section 114 of the
    Criminal Justice and Public Order Act 1994, to perform custodial duties;
'contract monitor' means a person appointed by the Secretary of State under
    section 149(4);
'contracted out detention centre' means a detention centre in relation to which
    a detention centre contract is in force;
'contractor', in relation to a detention centre which is being run in accordance
    with a detention centre contract, means the person who has contracted to
    run it;
'custodial functions' means custodial functions at a detention centre;
'detained persons' means persons detained or required to be detained under the
    1971 Act;
'detainee custody officer' means a person in respect of whom a certificate of
    authorisation is in force;
'detention centre' means a place which is used solely for the detention of

detained persons but which is not a short-term holding facility, a prison or part of a prison;

'detention centre contract' means a contract entered into by the Secretary of State under section 149;

'detention centre rules' means rules made by the Secretary of State under section 153;

'directly managed detention centre' means a detention centre which is not a contracted out detention centre;

'escort arrangements' means arrangements made by the Secretary of State under section 156;

'escort functions' means functions under escort arrangements;

'escort monitor' means a person appointed under paragraph 1 of Schedule 13;

'prisoner custody officer'—

(a) in relation to England and Wales, has the same meaning as in the Criminal Justice Act 1991;

(b) in relation to Scotland, has the meaning given in section 114(1) of the Criminal Justice and Public Order Act 1994;

(c) in relation to Northern Ireland, has the meaning given in section 122(1) of that Act of 1994;

'short-term holding facility' means a place used solely for the detention of detained persons for a period of not more than seven days or for such other period as may be prescribed.

Commencement   1 August 2000 (SI 2000/1985).

Detention centres

[A.1.381]
148 Management of detention centres
(1)   A manager must be appointed for every detention centre.
(2)   In the case of a contracted out detention centre, the person appointed as manager must be a detainee custody officer whose appointment is approved by the Secretary of State.
(3)   The manager of a detention centre is to have such functions as are conferred on him by detention centre rules.
(4)   The manager of a contracted out detention centre may not—

(a) enquire into a disciplinary charge laid against a detained person;
(b) conduct the hearing of such a charge; or
(c) make, remit or mitigate an award in respect of such a charge.

(5)   The manager of a contracted out detention centre may not, except in cases of urgency, order—

(a) the removal of a detained person from association with other detained persons;
(b) the temporary confinement of a detained person in special accommodation; or
(c) the application to a detained person of any other special control or restraint (other than handcuffs).

Commencement   Sub-section 148(3) 1 August 2000 (SI 2000/1985) for the purpose of enabling subordinate legislation to be made under it; in full, 2 April 2001 (SI 2001/239).

Note   See the Detention Centre Rules 2001 (SI 2001/238).

[A.1.382]
149 Contracting out of certain detention centres
(1)   The Secretary of State may enter into a contract with another person for the provision or running (or the provision and running) by him, or (if the contract so provides) for the running by sub-contractors of his, of any detention centre or part of a detention centre.
(2)   While a detention centre contract for the running of a detention centre or part of a detention centre is in force—

(a) the detention centre or part is to be run subject to and in accordance with the provisions of or made under this Part; and
(b) in the case of a part, that part and the remaining part are to be treated for the purposes of those provisions as if they were separate detention centres.

(3)   If the Secretary of State grants a lease or tenancy of land for the purposes of a detention centre contract, none of the following enactments applies to the lease or tenancy—

(a) Part II of the Landlord and Tenant Act 1954 (security of tenure);
(b) section 146 of the Law of Property Act 1925 (restrictions on and relief against forfeiture);
(c) section 19(1), (2) and (3) of the Landlord and Tenant Act 1927 and the Landlord and Tenant Act 1988 (covenants not to assign etc);
(d) the Agricultural Holdings Act 1986;
(e) sections 4 to 7 of the Law Reform (Miscellaneous Provisions) (Scotland) Act 1985 (irritancy clauses);
(f) the Agricultural Holdings (Scotland) Act 1991;
(g) section 14 of the Conveyancing Act 1881;
(h) the Conveyancing and Law of Property Act 1892;
(i) the Business Tenancies (Northern Ireland) Order 1996.

(4)   The Secretary of State must appoint a contract monitor for every contracted out detention centre.
(5)   A person may be appointed as the contract monitor for more than one detention centre.
(6)   The contract monitor is to have—

(a) such functions as may be conferred on him by detention centre rules;
(b) the status of a Crown servant.

(7)   The contract monitor must—

(a) keep under review, and report to the Secretary of State on, the running of a detention centre for which he is appointed; and
(b) investigate, and report to the Secretary of State on, any allegations made against any person performing custodial functions at that centre.

(8)   The contractor, and any sub-contractor of his, must do all that he reason-

ably can (whether by giving directions to the officers of the detention centre or otherwise) to facilitate the exercise by the contract monitor of his functions.

(9)   'Lease or tenancy' includes an underlease, sublease or sub-tenancy.

(10)   In relation to a detention centre contract entered into by the Secretary of State before the commencement of this section, this section is to be treated as having been in force at that time.

Commencement   Subsections 149(1), (3), 6(a) and 9, 1 August 2000; in full, 2 April 2001 (SI 2001/239).

Note   See the Detention Centre Rules 2001 (SI 2001/238). The section does not replace any existing statutory provisions, raising the interesting question why this statutory power was felt to be necessary and of the powers under which privately run detention centres operated prior to commencement of this section.

[A.1.383]
150   Contracted out functions at directly managed detention centres

(1)   The Secretary of State may enter into a contract with another person—

(a)   for functions at, or connected with, a directly managed detention centre to be performed by detainee custody officers provided by that person; or

(b)   for such functions to be performed by certified prisoner custody officers who are provided by that person.

(2)   For the purposes of this section 'detention centre' includes a short-term holding facility.

Commencement   2 April 2001 (SI 2001/239).

[A.1.384]
151   Intervention by Secretary of State

(1)   The Secretary of State may exercise the powers conferred by this section if it appears to him that—

(a)   the manager of a contracted out detention centre has lost, or is likely to lose, effective control of the centre or of any part of it; or

(b)   it is necessary to do so in the interests of preserving the safety of any person, or of preventing serious damage to any property.

(2)   The Secretary of State may appoint a person (to be known as the Controller) to act as manager of the detention centre for the period—

(a)   beginning with the time specified in the appointment; and

(b)   ending with the time specified in the notice of termination under subsection (5).

(3)   During that period—

(a)   all the functions which would otherwise be exercisable by the manager or the contract monitor are to be exercisable by the Controller;

(b)   the contractor and any sub-contractor of his must do all that he reasonably can to facilitate the exercise by the Controller of his functions; and

(c) the staff of the detention centre must comply with any directions given by the Controller in the exercise of his functions.

(4)   The Controller is to have the status of a Crown servant.

(5)   If the Secretary of State is satisfied that a Controller is no longer needed for a particular detention centre, he must (by giving notice to the Controller) terminate his appointment at a time specified in the notice.

(6)   As soon as practicable after making an appointment under this section, the Secretary of State must give notice of the appointment to those entitled to notice.

(7)   As soon as practicable after terminating an appointment under this section, the Secretary of State must give a copy of the notice of termination to those entitled to notice.

(8)   Those entitled to notice are the contractor, the manager, the contract monitor and the Controller.

Commencement   2 April 2001 (SI 2001/239).

[A.1.385]

152 Visiting Committees and inspections

(1)   The Secretary of State must appoint a committee (to be known as the Visiting Committee) for each detention centre.

(2)   The functions of the Visiting Committee for a detention centre are to be such as may be prescribed by the detention centre rules.

(3)   Those rules must include provision—

(a) as to the making of visits to the centre by members of the Visiting Committee;

(b) for the hearing of complaints made by persons detained in the centre;

(c) requiring the making of reports by the Visiting Committee to the Secretary of State.

(4)   Every member of the Visiting Committee for a detention centre may at any time enter the centre and have free access to every part of it and to every person detained there.

(5)   In section 5A of the Prison Act 1952 (which deals with the appointment and functions of Her Majesty's Chief Inspector of Prisons), after subsection (5), insert—

'(5A)   Subsections (2) to (5) apply to detention centres (as defined by section 147 of the Immigration and Asylum Act 1999 and including any in Scotland) and persons detained in such detention centres as they apply to prisons and prisoners.'

Commencement   Subsections 152(2) and (3) 1 August 2000 for the purposes of enabling subordinate legislation to be made under them; in full, 2 April 2001 (SI 2001/239.

Note   See the Detention Centre Rules 2001 (SI 2001/238).

[A.1.386]
153 Detention centre rules
(1)   The Secretary of State must make rules for the regulation and management of detention centres.
(2)   Detention centre rules may, among other things, make provision with respect to the safety, care, activities, discipline and control of detained persons.

Commencement   1 August 2000 for the purposes of enabling subordinate legislation to be made under it; in full, 2 April 2001 (SI 2001/239).

Note   See the Detention Centre Rules 2001 (SI 2001/238) made 29 January 2001, laid before Parliament 6 February 2001, into force 2 April 2001. The Rules will be amplified by more detailed 'Operating Standards' which are in development. See *Hansard* HL Report 27 March 2001 Cols 240 to 257 where the Lord Avebury's prayer for the annulment of the rules, and hence the Rules themselves, were debated in some detail.

Custody and movement of detained persons

[A.1.387]
154 Detainee custody officers
(1)   On an application made to him under this section, the Secretary of State may certify that the applicant—

(a) is authorised to perform escort functions; or
(b) is authorised to perform both escort functions and custodial functions.

(2)   The Secretary of State may not issue a certificate of authorisation unless he is satisfied that the applicant—

(a) is a fit and proper person to perform the functions to be authorised; and
(b) has received training to such standard as the Secretary of State considers appropriate for the performance of those functions.

(3)   A certificate of authorisation continues in force until such date, or the occurrence of such event, as may be specified in the certificate but may be suspended or revoked under paragraph 7 of Schedule 11.
(4)   A certificate which authorises the performance of both escort functions and custodial functions may specify one date or event for one of those functions and a different date or event for the other.
(5)   If the Secretary of State considers that it is necessary for the functions of detainee custody officers to be conferred on prison officers or prisoner custody officers, he may make arrangements for that purpose.
(6)   A prison officer acting under arrangements made under subsection (5) has all the powers, authority, protection and priveleges of a constable.
(7)   Schedule 11 makes further provision about detainee custody officers.

Commencement   Section 154(7) 3 April 2000 for the purposes of paragraphs 1 and 7(1) of Schedule 11 (SI 2000/464), and 1 August 2000 (SI 2000/1985) for the purposes of the provisions of Schedule 11 commenced by SI 2000/1985, viz paragraphs 2(1)(a) and 7(2), (3) for the purposes of enabling subordinate legislation to be made under them. Subsections (1)–(6), and for remaining purposes, subs (7), 2 April 2001 (SI 2001/239).

Note   See notes to Sch 11 and the Immigration (Suspension of Detainee Custody Order Certificate) Regulations 2001 (SI 2001/241).

[A.1.388]
155 Custodial functions and discipline etc at detention centres
(1)   Custodial functions may be discharged at a detention centre only by—

(a) a detainee custody officer authorised, in accordance with section 154(1), to perform such functions; or
(b) a prison officer, or a certified prisoner custody officer, exercising functions in relation to the detention centre—
  (i)   in accordance with arrangements made under section 154(5); or
  (ii) as a result of a contract entered into under section 150(1)(b).

(2)   Schedule 12 makes provision with respect to discipline and other matters at detention centres and short-term holding facilities.

Commencement   Subsection 155(2) 1 August 2000 (SI 2000/1985) for the purposes of the provisions of Schedule 12 commenced by SI 2000/1985, viz paragraphs 1, 2 and 3(7) for the purposes of enabling subordinate legislation to be made under them. Subsection (1), and for remaining purposes, subs (2), 2 April 2001 (SI 2001/239).

[A.1.389]
156 Arrangements for the provision of escorts and custody
(1)   The Secretary of State may make arrangements for—

(a) the delivery of detained persons to premises in which they may lawfully be detained;
(b) the delivery of persons from any such premises for the purposes of their removal from the United Kingdom in accordance with directions given under the 1971 Act or this Act;
(c) the custody of detained persons who are temporarily outside such premises;
(d) the custody of detained persons held on the premises of any court.

(2)   Escort arrangements may provide for functions under the arrangements to be performed, in such cases as may be determined by or under the arrangements, by detainee custody officers.
(3)   'Court' includes—

(a) adjudicators;
(b) the Immigration Appeal Tribunal;
(c) the Commission.

(4)   Escort arrangements may include entering into contracts with other persons for the provision by them of—

(a) detainee custody officers; or
(b) prisoner custody officers who are certified under section 89 of the Criminal Justice Act 1991, or section 114 or 122 of the Criminal Justice and Public Order Act 1994, to perform escort functions.

(5)   Schedule 13 makes further provision about escort arrangements.

(6)   A person responsible for performing a function of a kind mentioned in subsection (1), in accordance with a transfer direction, complies with the direction if he does all that he reasonably can to secure that the function is performed by a person acting in accordance with escort arrangements.

(7)   'Transfer direction' means a transfer direction given under—

(a)   section 48 of the Mental Health Act 1983 or section 71 of the Mental Health (Scotland) Act 1984 (removal to hospital of, among others, persons detained under the 1971 Act); or

(b)   in Northern Ireland, article 54 of the Mental Health (Northern Ireland) Order 1986 (provision corresponding to section 48 of the 1983 Act).

Commencement   Subsection (5), 1 August 2000 (SI 2000/1985) for the purposes of the provisions of Schedule 13 commenced by SI 2000/1985, viz paragraphs 2(1)(a) and 2(4) for the purposes of enabling subordinate legislation to be made under them. Subsections (1)–(4), (6)–(7), and for remaining purposes, 2 April 2001 (SI 2001/239).

[A.1.390]
157 Short-term holding facilities
(1)   The Secretary of State may by regulations extend any provision made by or under this Part in relation to detention centres (other than one mentioned in subsection (2)) to short-term holding facilities.

(2)   Subsection (1) does not apply to section 150.

(3)   The Secretary of State may make rules for the regulation and management of short-term holding facilities.

Commencement   1 August 2000 for the purposes of enabling subordinate legislation to be made under it. 2 April 2001 (SI 2001/239) for remaining purposes.

[A.1.391]
158   Wrongful disclosure of information
(1)   A person who is or has been employed (whether as a detainee custody officer, prisoner custody officer or otherwise)—

(a)   in accordance with escort arrangements,
(b)   at a contracted out detention centre, or
(c)   to perform contracted out functions at a directly managed detention centre,

is guilty of an offence if he discloses, otherwise than in the course of his duty or as authorised by the Secretary of State, any information which he acquired in the course of his employment and which relates to a particular detained person.

(2)   A person guilty of such an offence is liable—

(a)   on conviction on indictment, to imprisonment for a term not exceeding two years or to a fine or to both;
(b)   on summary conviction, to imprisonment for a term not exceeding

six months or to a fine not exceeding the statutory maximum or to both.

(3) 'Contracted out functions' means functions which, as the result of a contract entered into under section 150, fall to be performed by detainee custody officers or certified prisoner custody officers.

Commencement   2 April 2001 (SI 2001/239).

[A.1.392]
159 Power of constable to act outside his jurisdiction
(1)   For the purpose of taking a person to or from a detention centre under the order of any authority competent to give the order, a constable may act outside the area of his jurisdiction.
(2)   When acting under this section, the constable concerned retains all the powers, authority, protection and privileges of his office.

Commencement   2 April 2001 (SI 2001/239).

PART IX
REGISTRAR'S CERTIFICATES: PROCEDURE

Note   For transitional provisions relating to this part, see the Immigration and Asylum Act 1999 (Commencement No 8 and Transitional Provisions) Order 2000 (SI 2000/3099). By the unwieldy method of amending Commencement Order No 7 (SI 2000/2698), Commencement Order No 8 ensured that the provisions of sections 24 and 160 to 163 of this Act apply only to marriages of which notice had been entered into the marriage notice book before 1 January 2001. To marriages entered into the book before that date, the provisions of the Marriage Act 1949 continue to apply.

[A.1.393]
160   *(Amends the Marriage Act 1949, ss 26–27. 31–32.)*

[A.1.394]
161   *(Amends the Marriage Act 1949, ss 26–27 and the Marriage Law (Ireland) Amendment Act 1863, s 2.)*

[A.1.395]
162   *(Amends the Marriage Act 1949, s 28 and the Marriage Law (Ireland) Amendment Act 1863, s 3.)*

[A.1.396]
163   *(Amends the Marriage Act 1949, s 31 and the Marriages (Ireland) Act 1844, s 16.)*

PART X
MISCELLANEOUS AND SUPPLEMENTAL

[A.1.397]
164 *(Amends the Prosecution of Offences Act 1985, s 3.)*

[A.1.398]
165 *(Amends the Immigration Act 1971, s 31.)*

[A.1.399]
166 Regulations and orders
(1)   Any power to make rules, regulations or orders conferred by this Act is exercisable by statutory instrument.
(2)   But subsection (1) does not apply in relation to rules made under paragraph 1 of Schedule 5 or immigration rules.
(3)   Any statutory instrument made as a result of subsection (1) may—

(a) contain such incidental, supplemental, consequential and transitional provision as the person making it considers appropriate;
(b) make different provision for different cases or descriptions of case; and
(c) make different provision for different areas.

(4)   No order is to be made under—

(a) section 20,
(b) section 21,
(c) section 31(10),
(d) section 86(2),
(e) section 96(5),
(f) section 97(3),
(g) section 143(15), or
(h) paragraph 4 of Schedule 5,

unless a draft of the order has been laid before Parliament and approved by a resolution of each House.

(5)   No regulations are to be made under—

(a) section 9,
(b) section 46(8),
(c) section 53, or
(d) section 144,

unless a draft of the regulations has been laid before Parliament and approved by a resolution of each House.
(6)   Any statutory instrument made under this Act, apart from one made—

(a) under any of the provisions mentioned in subsection (4) or (5), or
(b) under section 24(3) or 170(4) or (7),

shall be subject to annulment by a resolution of either House of Parliament.

Commencement   On Royal Assent (section 170(3))

Note   *166(4)* affirmative resolution procedure in parliament
   166(5) affirmative resolution procedure in parliament.
   166(6) negative resolution procedure in parliament

166(6) No parliamentary approval is required. Regulations under section 24(3) will prescribe the form and manner in which registrars shall report their suspicions as to sham marriages to the Secretary of State. Section 170(4) deals with the making of commencement orders. Those orders so far made are set out in the notes to Section 170. Section 170(7) allows for the extension of the provisions of the Act, with modifications, to the Channel Islands and the Isle of Man.

[A.1.400]
167 Interpretation
(1)   In this Act—

'the 1971 Act' means the Immigration Act 1971;
'adjudicator' (except in Part VI) means an adjudicator appointed under section 57;
'Chief Adjudicator' means the person appointed as Chief Adjudicator under section 57(2);
'claim for asylum' (except in Parts V and VI and section 141) means a claim that it would be contrary to the United Kingdom's obligations under the Refugee Convention for the claimant to be removed from, or required to leave, the United Kingdom;
'the Commission' means the Special Immigration Appeals Commission;
'country' includes any territory;
'EEA State' means a State which is a Contracting Party to the Agreement on the European Economic Area signed at Oporto on 2nd May 1992 as it has effect for the time being;
'the Human Rights Convention' means the Convention for the Protection of Human Rights and Fundamental Freedoms, agreed by the Council of Europe at Rome on 4th November 1950 as it has effect for the time being in relation to the United Kingdom;
'the Immigration Acts' means—

(a) the 1971 Act;
(b) the Immigration Act 1988;
(c) the Asylum and Immigration Appeals Act 1993;
(d) the Asylum and Immigration Act 1996; and
(e) this Act;

'prescribed' means prescribed by regulations made by the Secretary of State;
'the Refugee Convention' means the Convention relating to the Status of Refugees done at Geneva on 28 July 1951 and the Protocol to the Convention;
'voluntary organisations' means bodies (other than public or local authorities) whose activities are not carried on for profit.

(2)   The following expressions have the same meaning as in the 1971 Act—

'certificate of entitlement';
'entry clearance';
'illegal entrant';
'immigration officer';
'immigration rules';

'port';
'United Kingdom passport';
'work permit'.

Commencement   On Royal Assent (section 170(3)).

[A.1.401]
168 Expenditure and receipts
(1)   There is to be paid out of money provided by Parliament—

(a)   any expenditure incurred by the Secretary of State or the Lord Chancellor in consequence of this Act; and

(b)   any increase attributable to this Act in the sums so payable by virtue of any other Act.

(2)   Sums received by the Secretary of State under section 5, 32, 40, 112 or 113 or by the Lord Chancellor under section 48(4) or 49(4) must be paid into the Consolidated Fund.

Commencement   On Royal Assent (170(3)).

[A.1.402]
169 Minor and consequential amendments, transitional provisions and repeals
(1)   Schedule 14 makes minor and consequential amendments.
(2)   Schedule 15 contains transitional provisions and savings.
(3)   The enactments set out in Schedule 16 are repealed.

Commencement   Subsections (1) and (2) insofar as they relate to the paragraphs of Schedule 14 and 15 commenced on Royal Assent by section 170(3) and by SI 1999/3190, 6 December 1999 (SI 1999/3190). The rest of the section insofar as it relates to the provisions of schedules 14 to 16, 14 February 2000 (SI 2000/168). Subsections (1) and (3) insofar as they relate to those provisions of Schedules 14 and 16 commenced by SI 2000/464 on 1 March 2000 and in full on 3 April 2000 (SI 2000/464).

Subsection 169(1) 1 August 2000 (SI 2000/1985) for the purposes of the provisions of Schedule 14 commenced by SI 2000/1985, viz paragraph 118 to the extent that it refers to paragraph 129, Section 169 commenced 2 October 2000 (SI 2000/2444) for the purposes of the provisions of Schedules 14 to 16 commenced by SI 2000/2444.

Subsections 169(1) and 169(3) 11 December 2000 for the purposes of the provisions of Schedules 14 and 16 commenced by SI 2000/3099 and 1 January 2001 for the purposes of the provisions of Schedules 15 and 16 commenced by SI 2000/2698.

Note   Schedule 14 deals with Consequential amendments and Schedule 15 with Transitional Provisions and Savings. Schedule 16 deals with repeals.

[A.1.403]
170 Short title, commencement and extent
(1)   This Act may be cited as the Immigration and Asylum Act 1999.

(2)   Subsections (1) and (2) of section 115 come into force on the day on which the first regulations made under Schedule 8 come into force.

(3)   The following provisions come into force on the passing of this Act—

(a) section 4;
(b) section 9;
(c) section 15;
(d) section 27;
(e) section 31;
(f) section 94;
(g) section 95(13);
(h) section 99(4) and (5);
(i) sections 105 to 109;
(j) section 110(1), (2) and (8) (so far as relating to subsections (1) and (2));
(k) section 111;
(l) section 124;
(m) section 140;
(n) section 145;
(o) section 146(1);
(p) sections 166 to 168;
(q) this section;
(r) Schedule 9;
(s) paragraphs 62(2), 73, 78, 79, 81, 82, 87, 88 and 102 of Schedule 14;
(t) paragraphs 2 and 13 of Schedule 15.

(4)   The other provisions of this Act, except section 10 and paragraph 12 of Schedule 15 (which come into force in accordance with section 9), come into force on such day as the Secretary of State may by order appoint.

(5)   Different days may be appointed for different purposes.

(6)   This Act extends to Northern Ireland.

(7)   Her Majesty may by Order in Council direct that any of the provisions of this Act are to extend, with such modifications (if any) as appear to Her Majesty to be appropriate, to any of the Channel Islands or the Isle of Man.

Commencement   On Royal Assent (170(3)).

Note   Nine subsequent commencement orders have been made: Immigration and Asylum Act (Commencement No 1) Order 1999 (SI 1999/3190), Immigration and Asylum Act 1999 (Commencement No 2 and Transitional Provisions) Order 1999 (SI 1999/3190), Immigration and Asylum Act 1999 (Commencement No 3) Order 2000 (SI 2000/464), Immigration and Asylum Act 1999 (Commencement No 4) Order 2000 (SI 2000/1282), Immigration and Asylum Act 1999 (Commencement No 5 and Transitional Provisions) Order 2000 (SI 2000/1985), Immigration and Asylum Act 1999 (Commencement No 6, Transitional and Consequential Provisions) Order 2000 (SI 2000/2444), Immigration and Asylum Act (Commencement No 7) Order 2000 (SI 2000/2698), Immigration and Asylum Act (Commencement No 8 and Transitional Provisions) Order 2000 (SI 2000/3099) and Immigration and Asylum Act 1999 (Commencement No 9) Order 2001 (SI 2001/239).

SCHEDULE 1
SALE OF TRANSPORTERS

Sections 37(6) and 42(8)

[A.1.404]

Leave of court required

1
(1) The sale of a transporter requires the leave of the court.
(2) The court is not to give its leave except on proof—

(a) that the penalty or charge is or was due;
(b) that the person liable to pay it or any connected expenses has failed to do so; and
(c) that the transporter which the Secretary of State seeks leave to sell is liable to sale.

Commencement 3 April 2000 for the purposes of section 37 of this Act (SI 2000/464).

Notice of proposed sale

2 Before applying for leave to sell a transporter, the Secretary of State must take such steps as may be prescribed—

(a) for bringing the proposed sale to the notice of persons whose interests may be affected by a decision of the court to grant leave; and
(b) for affording to any such person an opportunity of becoming a party to the proceedings if the Secretary of State applies for leave.

Commencement 6 December 1999 (SI 1999/3190).

Note See The Carrier's Liability (Clandestine Entrants and Sale of Transporters) Regulations 2000 (SI 2000/685), as amended by the Carrier's Liability (Clandestine Entrants and Sale of Transporters) (Amendment) Regulations 2001 (SI 2001/311). See regulations 8 and 9.

Duty to obtain best price

3 If leave for sale is given, the Secretary of State must secure that the transporter is sold for the best price that can reasonably be obtained.

Commencement 3 April 2000 (SI 2000/464).

Effect of failure to comply with paragraph 2 or 3

4 Failure to comply with any requirement of paragraph 2 or 3 in respect of any sale—

(a) is actionable against the Secretary of State at the suit of any person suffering loss in consequence of the sale; but
(b) after the sale has taken place, does not affect its validity.

Commencement 3 April 2000 (SI 2000/464).

Application of proceeds of sale

5—(1) Any proceeds of sale arising from a sale under section 37 or 42 must be applied—

(a) in making prescribed payments; and
(b) in accordance with such provision as to priority of payments as may be prescribed.
(2) The regulations may, in particular, provide for proceeds of sale to be applied in payment—

(a) of customs or excise duty,
(b) of value added tax,
(c) of expenses incurred by the Secretary of State,
(d) of any penalty or charge which the court has found to be due,
(e) in the case of the sale of an aircraft, of charges due as a result of regulations made under section 73 of the Civil Aviation Act 1982,
(f) of any surplus to or among the person or persons whose interests in the transporter have been divested as a result of the sale,

but not necessarily in that order of priority.

Commencement 6 December 1999 (SI 1999/3190).

Note See Carrier's Liability (Clandestine Entrants and Sale of Transporters) Regulation 2000, SI 2000/685, as amended by the Carrier's Liability (Cleandestine Entrants and Sale of Transporters) (Amendment) Regulations 2001 (SI 2001/311).

See paragraph 12. The proceeds of sale shall be applied first in payment of expenses reasonably incurred by the Secretary of State in connection with the detention and sale, including expenses in connection with the application to court, then to the payment of penalties, then in the payment of any duty, then, where the transporter is an aircraft, in payment of any charge due by virtue of regulations under section 73 of the Civil Aviation Act 1982. Any surplus is then to be paid to those whose interests in the transporter have, to the knowledge of the Secretary of State, been divested by reason of the sale.

SCHEDULE 2
THE IMMIGRATION APPEAL TRIBUNAL

Section 56(2)

[A.1.405]

Commencement   14 February 2000 (SI 2000/168).

Members

1—(1)   The members of the Tribunal are to be appointed by the Lord Chancellor.
(2)   The Lord Chancellor may appoint such number of legally qualified members and of other members as he considers appropriate.
(3)   A person is legally qualified if—

(a) he has a 7 year general qualification, within the meaning of section 71 of the Courts and Legal Services Act 1990;
(b) he is an advocate or solicitor in Scotland of at least 7 years' standing;
(c) he is a member of the Bar of Northern Ireland or solicitor of the Supreme Court of Northern Ireland of at least 7 years' standing; or
(d) he has such legal and other experience as appears to the Lord Chancellor to make him suited for appointment as a legally qualified member.

President and Deputy President

2—(1)   The Lord Chancellor must appoint one legally qualified member to be President of the Tribunal and another such member to be Deputy President.
(2)   The Deputy President is to have such functions in relation to the Tribunal as the President may assign to him.
(3)   If the President is temporarily absent or otherwise unable to act, the Deputy President may act on his behalf.

Term of office

3—(1)   Each member of the Tribunal—

(a) is to hold and vacate his office in accordance with the terms of his appointment;
(b) is, on ceasing to hold office, eligible for re-appointment;
(c) may resign his office at any time by giving written notice to the Lord Chancellor;
(d) must vacate his office on the day on which he reaches the age of 70.

(2)   But sub-paragraph (1)(d) is subject to subsections (4) to (6) of section 26

375

of the Judicial Pensions and Retirement Act 1993 (power to authorise continuance in office up to the age of 75).

Remuneration

4   The Lord Chancellor must pay to the members such remuneration and allowances as he may determine.

Compensation

5   If a person ceases to be a member and it appears to the Lord Chancellor that there are special circumstances which make it right that he should receive compensation, the Lord Chancellor may pay him a sum of such amount as the Lord Chancellor may determine.

Proceedings

6—(1)   For the purpose of hearing and determining appeals under this Act or any matter preliminary or incidental to such an appeal, the Tribunal must sit at such times and in such place or places as the Lord Chancellor may direct.
(2)   The Tribunal may sit in two or more divisions.
(3)   The jurisdiction of the Tribunal may be exercised by such number of members as the President may direct.
(4)   A direction under sub-paragraph (3) may—

(a)   be given in relation to a specified case or category of case;
(b)   provide for the jurisdiction to be exercised by a single member;
(c)   require the member exercising the jurisdiction, or a specified number of the members exercising the jurisdiction, to be legally qualified;
(d)   be varied at any time by a further direction given by the President.

(5)   'Specified' means specified in the direction.

Staff

7—(1)   The Lord Chancellor may appoint such staff for the Tribunal as he may determine.
(2)   The remuneration of the Tribunal's staff is to be defrayed by the Lord Chancellor.
(3)   Such expenses of the Tribunal as the Lord Chancellor may determine are to be defrayed by the Lord Chancellor.

SCHEDULE 3
ADJUDICATORS

Section 57(3)

[A.1.406]

Commencement   14 February 2000 (SI 2000/168).

Deputy Chief Adjudicator and Regional Adjudicators

1—(1)   The Lord Chancellor may appoint one of the adjudicators as Deputy
Chief Adjudicator.
(2)   The Lord Chancellor may appoint as Regional Adjudicators such number
of the adjudicators as he may determine.
(3)   A person appointed under sub-paragraph (1) or (2) is to have such functions as the Chief Adjudicator may assign to him.
(4)   If the Chief Adjudicator is temporarily absent or otherwise unable to act,
the Deputy Chief Adjudicator may act on his behalf.

Qualification for appointment

2   A person is qualified for appointment as an adjudicator only if—

(a)   he has a 7 year general qualification, within the meaning of section 71 of
the Courts and Legal Services Act 1990;
(b)   he is an advocate or solicitor in Scotland of at least 7 years' standing;
(c)   he is a member of the Bar of Northern Ireland or solicitor of the Supreme
Court of Northern Ireland of at least 7 years' standing; or
(d)   he has such legal and other experience as appears to the Lord Chancellor
to make him suited for appointment as an adjudicator.

Term of office

3—(1)   Each adjudicator—

(a)   is to hold and vacate his office in accordance with the terms of his appointment;
(b)   is, on ceasing to hold office, eligible for re-appointment;
(c)   may resign his office at any time by giving written notice to the Lord
Chancellor;
(d)   must vacate his office on the day on which he reaches the age of 70.

(2)   But sub-paragraph (1)(d) is subject to subsections (4) to (6) of section 26
of the Judicial Pensions and Retirement Act 1993 (power to authorise continuance in office up to the age of 75).

Note *6(2)(a)* See SI 2000/2333 Immigration and Asylum Appeals (Procedure) Rules, rule 2 which provides that the reference to Chief Adjudicator in the Rules includes an adjudicator nominated by the Chief Adjudicator under this section.

Remuneration

4 The Lord Chancellor must pay to the adjudicators such remuneration and allowances as he may determine.

Compensation

5 If a person ceases to be an adjudicator and it appears to the Lord Chancellor that there are special circumstances which make it right that he should receive compensation, the Lord Chancellor may pay him a sum of such amount as the Lord Chancellor may determine.

Proceedings

6—(1) The adjudicators must sit at such times and at such places as the Lord Chancellor may direct.

(2) The Chief Adjudicator—

(a) must allocate duties among the adjudicators; and

(b) is to have such other functions as may be conferred on him by the Lord Chancellor.

(3) The Chief Adjudicator may direct that, in a specified case or category of case, an appeal to an adjudicator is to be heard by such number of adjudicators as may be specified.

(4) 'Specified' means specified in the direction.

Staff

7—(1) The Lord Chancellor may appoint such staff for the adjudicators as he may determine.

(2) The remuneration of the adjudicators' staff is to be defrayed by the Lord Chancellor.

(3) Such expenses of the adjudicators as the Lord Chancellor may determine are to be defrayed by the Lord Chancellor.

SCHEDULE 4
APPEALS

Section 58(2) to (4)

Note   SI 2000/2444 makes transitional provisions with regard to this Schedule. See also SI 2000/3099. See the general note to Part IV of this Act.

Note that nothing in the new procedures allows the 'section 21 reference' of the Immigration Act 1971 whereby under section 21 of that Act cases could be referred back to the IAT after all other appeal rights had been exhausted, in the circumstances set out in that section. However, references made prior to 2 October 2000 are protected by the transitional provision set out in paragraph 2(9) of Schedule 2 to SI 2000/2444.

For the application of the provisions of this schedule to those appealing under section 80 of this Act, see that section, the notes thereto and the Immigration (European Economic Area) Regulations 2000 (SI 2000/2326), as amended by the Immigration (European Economic Area) (Amendment) Regulations 2001 (SI 2001/285), in particular Regulation 29(4) and Schedule 2 thereto.

See also SI 2000/2244 Immigration and Asylum Appeals (One Stop Procedure) Regulations 2000, as amended by the Immigration and Asylum Appeals (One Stop Procedure) (Amendment) Regulations 2001 (SI 2001/867), SI 2000/2246 Immigration and Asylum Appeals (Notices) Regulations 2000, as amended by the Immigration and Asylum Appeals (Notices) (Amendment) Regulations 2001 (SI 2001/868), and SI 2000/2333 Immigration and Asylum Appeals (Procedure) Rules 2000 and see the note at the beginning of Part IV of this Act.

[A.1.407]

PART I
PROCEDURE

Notice of appealable matters

1—(1) The Secretary of State may by regulations provide—

(a) for written notice to be given to a person of any such decision or action taken in respect of him as is appealable under Part IV (whether or not in his particular case he is entitled to appeal) or would be so appealable but for the ground on which it was taken;

(b) for any such notice to include a statement of the reasons for the decision or action and, where the action is the giving of directions for the removal of the person from the United Kingdom, of the country to which he is to be removed;

(c) for any such notice to be accompanied by a statement containing particulars of the rights of appeal available under Part IV and of the procedure by which those rights may be exercised;

(d) for the form of any such notice or statement and the way in which a notice is to be, or may be, given.

(2) For the purpose of any proceedings under Part IV, a statement included in a notice in accordance with the regulations is conclusive as to the person by whom and the ground on which any decision or action was taken.

Commencement   22 May 2000 (SI 2000/1282).

Note   See SI 2000/2244, as amended by SI 2001/867, and SI 2000/2246, as amended by SI 2001/868, and the note at the beginning of Part IV herein.

For EEA appeals, see introductory note to this section and SI 2000/2326, Schedule 2, paragraph 2, as amended by reg 6(3) of SI 2001/865.

Service of notices

2   If a notice given under regulations made under paragraph 1 is sent by first class post, addressed to the person to whom the notice is required to be given, it is to be taken to have been received by that person on the second day after the day on which it was posted unless the contrary is proved.

Commencement   2 October 2000 (SI 2000/2444).

Note   See SI 2000/2246, regulation 6, for notices deemed to comply with those regulations.

See also SI 2001/868, reg 8, which provides that where a notice is sent outside the UK, it is deemed to have been received on the twenty-eighth day after the day on which it is posted. Unlike service under paragraph 2, the deeming provisions of reg 8 are not stated to be rebuttable.

For EEA appeals, see introductory note to this section and SI 2000/2326 Schedule 2, paragraph 2, as amended by reg 6(3) of SI 2001/285.

Lord Chancellor's rules of procedure

3   The Lord Chancellor may make rules—

(a) for regulating the exercise of the rights of appeal conferred by Part IV;
(b) for prescribing the practice and procedure to be followed on or in connection with appeals under Part IV, including the mode and burden of proof and admissibility of evidence on such an appeal; and
(c) for other matters preliminary or incidental or arising out of such appeals, including proof of the decisions of the adjudicator or the Immigration Appeal Tribunal.

Commencement   14 February 2000 (SI 2000/168).

Note   See the Immigration and Asylum Appeals (Procedure) Rules (SI 2000/2333). One set of procedure rules now cover both immigration and asylum appeals. The notices and forms to be used appear as schedules to the rules. Under Rule 30(2) 'The overriding objective shall be to secure the just, timely and effective disposal of appeals and, in order to further that objective, the appellate authority may give directions which control the conduct of any appeal'. All the powers and in particular discretionary powers given to the Tribunal under SI 2000/2333 should be read in the light of this 'overriding' objective. However, the limits of this principle must be noted. See for example the case of *Maimuna* (01/TH/0121) 14 February 2001, IAT. This case concerned rules 46 and 48, which deal with deemed service of the notice of hearing. Notification of the date for the full hearing of the case before the adjudicator was sent by recorded delivery. The appellant was not served with the notice and the appellant's representatives said that they had not received the notice. However, when the case came before the IAT the representatives had not produced evidence of this. They asked for an adjournment in order to obtain such evidence. The IAT held that in the absence of proof to the contrary rule 48(2) meant that the representatives were deemed to have received notice of the hearing. The IAT further held that rule 46(2) meant that the appellant was deemed to have notice of the hearing by the service of notice on the representatives. It was argued that because there was no fault on the part of the appellant herself, to deny an adjournment for the representatives to seek to obtain evidence that they had not received the notice of hearing would prevent the just disposal of the appeal. The IAT rejected this argument, stating that 'the just disposal of the appeal includes also the requirement that the rules which govern the conduct of those appeals should be met'. In the *Maimuna* case the applicant would have the possibility of making a Human Rights Act claim before any removal to Somalia, thus there was no danger of returning her to face persecution even if the adjournment was refused. In those circumstances, the IAT held, to refuse the adjournment did not prevent the just disposal of the appeal. It should be noted that in determination, the notion of the 'just disposal of appeal' appears to have been conflated with the notion of the just disposal of the *case*. Note that under Rule 30(3) directions under Rule 30 may be given orally or in writing. Rule 30 deals with directions and includes powers to limit the documents to be produced and the length of oral submissions (30(4)(e)). However, directions may not be given to an unrepresented appellant unless the appellate authority is satisfied that the unrepresented appellant is able to comply with those directions (30(6)). Rule 34 makes provision for bail and applies during the period while Part III is not yet in force.

For EEA appeals, see introductory note to this section and SI 2000/2326 Schedule 2, paragraph 2, as amended by reg 6(3) of SI 2001/285.

See SI 2000/2333 Rule 6 for time limits. 6(1) provides that 10 days shall be given for an appeal from within the UK. In earlier drafts of the rules, a period of five days was set, but this was changed following consultation. When the appeal is made from outside the UK, the appellant has 28 days to appeal, running from the date when the decision was received, if the appellant was in the UK at that time (6(2)(a)) and from the date when the decision was received if the appellant was outside the UK at that time (6(2)(b)). Under 7(1) late appeals can be treated as in time if the person to whom the notice of appeal is given is satisfied that because of 'special' circumstances, it is just for the appeal to be treated in that way. Earlier drafts of the Rules referred to 'exceptional' circumstances; the requirement in the Rules as enacted is less stringent. A restricted power for the adjudicator to extend time was added following consultation. Rule 8 provides for the method of giving notice of appeal, rule 10 for the despatch of documents to the adjudicator and rule 11 for variation of the notice of appeal. Preliminary issues are dealt with by rule 12. Rule 13 deals with notification of hearings. Rule 15 provides for written notice of the adjudicator's determination to be sent to every party and to the appellant's representative (if any).

3(b) SI 2000/2333 Rule 39 makes provision for the burden of proof. Rules 22 and 37 make provision as to evidence and rule 36 makes provision for the summoning of witnesses. See *Kesse v SSHD* (C/2000/2955), CA, 7 February 2001. This case determined that under rule 27(1) of the Immigration Procedure Rules 1984 the IAT has power to summon witnesses of its own motion if the evidence of the witness relates to a matter in issue at the appeal, but that it should consider carefully before exercising this power against the wishes of the parties. The case may be of persuasive authority in the interpretation of the Immigration and Asylum (Appeals) Procedure Rules 2000. Under Rule 19(11), when considering an application for leave to appeal, the Tribunal is not required to consider evidence that was not submitted to the adjudicator unless satisfied that there were good reasons why it was not submitted to an adjudicator. Evidence may be given by electronic means (14(2) and 24(2)). The actual use of electronic methods and whether the consent of the parties will be required for this is likely to be the subject of a future practice direction. On a full hearing before the Tribunal, the Tribunal can consider evidence that was not before the adjudicator, whether on the application of a party or of its own motion (Rule 22(2)). It is necessary to give written notice that such evidence is to be adduced, see Rule 22(5).

4—(1)   The rules may include provision—

(a) enabling appeals to be determined without a hearing;

(b) enabling an adjudicator or the Tribunal to allow or dismiss an appeal without considering its merits—

    (i)   if there has been a failure by one of the parties to comply with a provision of the rules or with a direction given under the rules; or

    (ii) if one of the parties has failed to attend at a hearing;

(c) enabling or requiring an adjudicator or the Tribunal to treat an appeal as abandoned in specified circumstances;

(d) enabling the Tribunal, on an appeal from an adjudicator, to remit the appeal to an adjudicator for determination by him in accordance with any directions of the Tribunal, or for further evidence to be obtained with a view to determination by the Tribunal;

(e) as to the circumstances in which—

    (i)   a decision of an adjudicator may be set aside by an adjudicator; or

    (ii) a decision of the Tribunal may be set aside by the Tribunal;

(f) conferring on adjudicators or the Tribunal such ancillary powers as the Lord Chancellor thinks necessary for the purposes of the exercise of their functions;

(g) as to the procedure to be followed on applications to the Tribunal for leave to appeal under paragraph 23.

(2)   The rules must provide that any appellant is to have the right to be legally represented at any hearing of his appeal.

(3)   Nothing in this paragraph affects the scope of the power conferred by paragraph 3.

(4)   In this Schedule 'rules' means rules under this paragraph.

Commencement   14 February 2000 (SI 2000/168).

Note   For transitional provisions applying this paragraph to appeals under sections 13 to 17 of the Immigration Act 1971, section 8 of the Asylum and Immigration Appeals Act 1993 and section 3(1) and (2) of the Asylum and Immigration Act 1976 see SI 2000/2444, articles 3(1)(b) and 4(1)(c)(i).

See the Immigration and Asylum Appeals (Procedure) Rules (SI 2000/2333). For EEA appeals, see introductory note to this section and SI 2000/2326 Schedule 2, paragraph 2, as amended by reg 6(3) of SI 2001/285.

4(1)(a) See SI 2000/2333, rules 43 and 44 for the circumstances in which an appeal may be determined without a hearing. In no other circumstances can this be done. However, under rule 18(4), applications for leave to appeal are to be determined without a hearing. Rule 14(1) provides for hearings to be conducted or given or representations made by video link or other electronic means.

4(1)(b) See rule 33(2). These include a power under 33(2)(a) to allow the appeal without considering its merits in a case of a failure by the respondent. Rule 44 makes further provision for the summary determination of an appeal.

4(1)(c) Powers to treat appeals as abandoned are set out in rule 32. Failure to comply with a direction, a provision of the rules or to appear at a hearing of which the party had notice, the lack of a satisfactory explanation for such failure and the appellate authority's being satisfied in all the circumstances that the party is not pursuing the appeal, are all required before the appeal is to be treated as abandoned.

4(1)(e) Note that rule 16 of SI 2000/2333 also provides for the circumstances in which the Chief Adjudicator can review a determination of an adjudicator and either confirm it, or set it aside and direct a re-hearing of the appeal. These rights exist only in respect of determinations to which there is not right of appeal to the Tribunal. Rule 19 provides for circumstances in which the Tribunal can review its decision to refuse leave to appeal , if the appellant alleges that this was as a result of a procedural or administrative error. In these circumstances, the Tribunal can either reaffirm the refusal of leave, or set it aside and re-consider the decision.

4(1) (f) Rules on adjournments appear in rule 31(1).

4(2) See rule 35 on representation.

Practice directions

5—(1)   The President of the Tribunal may give directions as to the practice and procedure to be followed by the Tribunal in relation to appeals and applications to it.
(2)   The Chief Adjudicator may give directions as to the practice and procedure to be followed by adjudicators in relation to appeals and applications to them.

Commencement   14 February 2000 (SI 2000/168).

Hearings in private

6—(1)   Sub-paragraph (2) applies if, on an appeal under Part IV, it is alleged—

(a)   that a passport or other travel document, certificate of entitlement, entry clearance or work permit (or any part of it or entry in it) on which a party relies is a forgery, and
(b)   that the disclosure to that party of any matters relating to the method of detection would be contrary to the public interest.

(2)   The adjudicator or Tribunal must arrange—

(a)   for the proceedings to take place in the absence of that party and his representatives while the allegation mentioned in sub-paragraph (1)(b) is inquired into by the adjudicator or Tribunal; and
(b)   if it appears to the adjudicator or Tribunal that the allegation is made out, for such further period as appears necessary in order to ensure that those matters can be presented to the adjudicator or Tribunal without any disclosure being directly or indirectly made contrary to the public interest.

Commencement   2 October 2000 (SI 2000/2444).

Note   For transitional provisions applying this paragraph to appeals under sections 13 to 17 of the Immigration Act 1971, section 8 of the Asylum and Immigration Appeals Act 1993 and section 3(1) and (2) of the Asylum and Immigration Act 1976 see SI 2000/2444, articles 3(1)(b) and 4(1)(c)(i) and Schedule 2, paragraph 1(13)(a).

For EEA appeals, see introductory note to this section and SI 2000/2326 Schedule 2, paragraph 2, as amended by reg 6(3) of SI 2001/285. Note that Rule 40 of SI 2000/2333 makes further provision for the exclusion of the public, moving beyond this paragraph to provide for the exclusion of the public where this is necessary in the interests of morals, public order, national security, the interests of minors or the protection of the private life of the parties or in special circumstances where publicity would prejudice the interests of justice. This is the only explicit mention of minors in the rules. This rule did not appear in earlier drafts but was added following consultation with interested parties including UNHCR, the IAA and appellants' representatives. Provisions as to hearings in the absence of a party are contained in Rule 40, provisions for determination without a hearing in Rule 43. Note in particular that where the fee has not been paid for a family visit appeal at the time of appealing, the appeal is to be determined without a hearing (Rule 43(2)).

Leave to appeal

7 If, under the rules, leave to appeal to the Tribunal is required in cases in which an adjudicator dismisses an appeal under section 59, the authority having power to grant leave must grant it—

(a) if the appeal was against a decision that the appellant required leave to enter the United Kingdom and the authority is satisfied that at the time of the decision he held a certificate of entitlement; and

(b) if the appeal was against a refusal of leave to enter and the authority is satisfied that—

   (i) at the time of the refusal the appellant held an entry clearance; and

   (ii) the dismissal of the appeal was not required by paragraph 24.

Commencement   2 October 2000 (SI 2000/2444).

Note   For transitional provisions applying this paragraph to appeals under sections 13 to 17 of the Immigration Act 1971, section 8 of the Asylum and Immigration Appeals Act 1993 and section 3(1) and (2) of the Asylum and Immigration Act 1976 see SI 2000/2444, articles 3(1)(b) and 4(1)(c)(i) and Schedule 2, paragraph 1(13)(b) and 1(14).

For EEA appeals, see introductory note to this section and SI 2000/2326 Schedule 2, paragraph 2, as amended by reg 6(3) of SI 2001/285.

Under SI 2000/2333 leave is indeed required for an appeal where an adjudicator dismisses an appeal under section 59. See Rule 18(1).

Offences

8   A person who is required under or in accordance with the rules to attend and give evidence or produce documents before an adjudicator or the Tribunal, and fails without reasonable excuse to comply with the requirement is guilty of an offence and liable on summary conviction to a fine not exceeding level three on the standard scale.

Commencement   2 October 2000 (SI 2000/2444).

Note   For transitional provisions applying this paragraph to appeals under sections 13 to 17 of the Immigration Act 1971, section 8 of the Asylum and Immigration Appeals Act 1993 and section 3(1) and (2) of the Asylum and Immigration Act 1976 see SI 2000/2444, articles 3(1)(b) and 4(1)(c)(i) and Schedule 2, paragraph 1(13).

For EEA appeals, see introductory note to this section and SI 2000/2326 Schedule 2, paragraph 2, as amended by reg 6(3) of SI 2001/285.

Convention cases

9—(1)   This paragraph applies to an appeal under Part IV of this Act by a person who claims that it would be contrary to the Convention for him to be removed from, or to be required to leave, the United Kingdom, if the Secretary of State has certified that, in his opinion, that claim is one to which—

(a)   sub-paragraph (3), (4), (5) or (6) applies; and
(b)   sub-paragraph (7) does not apply.

(2)   If, on an appeal to which this paragraph applies, the adjudicator agrees [with the opinion expressed in the Secretary of State's certificate, paragraph 22 does not confer on the appellant any right to appeal to the Immigration Appeal Tribunal.

(3)   This sub-paragraph applies to a claim if, on his arrival in the United Kingdom, the appellant was required by an immigration officer to produce a valid passport and—

(a)   he failed to do so, without giving a reasonable explanation for his failure; or
(b)   he produced an invalid passport and failed to inform the officer that it was not valid.

(4)   This sub-paragraph applies to a claim under the Refugee Convention if—

(a)   it does not show a fear of persecution by reason of the appellant's race, religion, nationality, membership of a particular social group, or political opinion; or
(b)   it shows a fear of such persecution, but the fear is manifestly unfounded or the circumstances which gave rise to the fear no longer subsist.

(5)   This sub-paragraph applies to a claim under the Human Rights Convention if—

(a)   it does not disclose a right under the Convention; or
(b)   it does disclose a right under the Convention, but the claim is manifestly unfounded.

(6)   This sub-paragraph applies to a claim if—

(a)   it is made at any time after the appellant—
    (i)   has been refused leave to enter the United Kingdom under the 1971 Act;
    (ii)   has been recommended for deportation by a court empowered by that Act to do so;
    (iii)   has been notified of the Secretary of State's decision to make a deportation order against him under section 5(1) of the 1971 Act as a result of his liability to deportation; or
    (iv)   has been notified of his liability to removal under paragraph 9 of Schedule 2 to that Act;
(b)   it is manifestly fraudulent, or any of the evidence adduced in its support is manifestly false; or
(c)   it is frivolous or vexatious.

(7)   This sub-paragraph applies to a claim if the evidence adduced in its sup-

port establishes a reasonable likelihood that the appellant has been tortured in the country to which he is to be sent.

(8) 'Contrary to the Convention' means contrary to the United Kingdom's obligations under the Refugee Convention or the Human Rights Convention.

Commencement 2 October 2000 (SI 2000/2444). The paragraph was subsequently amended, as detailed in the note to *9(2)*. The paragraph as amended came into force on 2 April 2001 (Race Relations (Amendment) Act 2000, section 10(2) and the Race Relations (Amendment) Act 2000 (Commencement) Order 2001 (SI 2001/566)).

Note For transitional provisions applying this paragraph to appeals under sections 13 to 17 of the Immigration Act 1971, section 8 of the Asylum and Immigration Appeals Act 1993 and section 3(1) and (2) of the Asylum and Immigration Act 1976 see SI 2000/2444, articles 3(1)(b) and 4(1)(c)(i).

For EEA appeals, see introductory note to this section and SI 2000/2326 Schedule 2, paragraph 2, as amended by reg 6(3) of SI 2001/285.

9(2) The words 'with the opinion expressed in the Secretary of State's certificate' were inserted by the Race Relations (Amendment) Act 2000, Schedule 2, paragraph 39, replacing the previous wording 'that the claim is one to which this paragraph applies'.

[Racial discrimination

9A (1) This paragraph applies to an appeal under Part IV of this Act by a person who claims that he has been racially discriminated against, if the Secretary of State has certified that, in his opinion, the claim is manifestly unfounded.

(2) If, on an appeal to which this paragraph applies, the adjudicator agrees with the opinion expressed in the Secretary of State's certificate, paragraph 22 does not confer on the appellant any right to appeal to the Immigration Appeal Tribunal.]

Commencement 2 April 2001 (Race Relations (Amendment) Act 2000 (Commencement) Order 2001 (SI 2001/566)).

Notes This paragraph was inserted into the Act by the Race Relations (Amendment) Act 2001, Schedule 2, paragraph 40. The effect is that when a person brings an appeal on race discrimination grounds, the Secretary of State may certify that the appeal is manifestly unfounded. If the Adjudicator agrees with the certificate, the person is prevented from appealing against the adjudicator's decision to the IAT. The only recourse is then by way of a judicial review of the decision to agree with the certificate. See SI 2001/285, amending SI 2001/2326 which applies the certification procedure to appeals on the grounds of racial discrimination brought by those appealing against EEA decisions.

PART II
EFFECT OF APPEALS

Stay on directions for removal

10 If a person in the United Kingdom appeals under section 59 or 69(1) on being refused leave to enter, any directions previously given by virtue of the refusal for his removal from the United Kingdom cease to have effect, except in so far as they have already been carried out, and no directions may be so given while the appeal is pending.

11 If a person in the United Kingdom appeals under section 66, 67 or 69(5) against any directions given under—

(a) section 10,

(b) Part I of Schedule 2 to the 1971 Act, or

(c) Schedule 3 to that Act,

for his removal from the United Kingdom, those directions except in so far as they have already been carried out, are to have no effect while the appeal is pending.

12 But the provisions of Part I of Schedule 2 or, as the case may be, Schedule 3 to the 1971 Act with respect to detention and persons liable to detention apply to a person appealing under section 59, 66, 67 or 69(1) or (5), as if there were in force directions for his removal from the United Kingdom, except that he may not be detained on board a ship or aircraft so as to compel him to leave the United Kingdom while the appeal is pending.

13 In calculating the period of two months limited by paragraph 8(2) of Schedule 2 to the 1971 Act for—

(a) the giving of directions under that paragraph for the removal of a person from the United Kingdom, and

(b) the giving of a notice of intention to give such directions,

any period during which there is pending an appeal by him under section 59, 67 or 69(1) of this Act is to be disregarded.

14 For the purposes of paragraphs 10 to 12 (but not for purposes of paragraph 13), except in so far as those paragraphs apply to appeals under section 69, where an appeal to an adjudicator is dismissed, an appeal is not to be regarded as pending unless immediately after the dismissal—

(a) the appellant gives notice of appeal against the determination of the adjudicator; or

(b) in a case in which leave to appeal against that determination is required and the adjudicator has power to grant leave, the appellant applies for and obtains the leave of the adjudicator.

15 If directions are given under Part I of Schedule 2 or Schedule 3 to the 1971 Act for a person's removal from the United Kingdom, and directions are also so given for the removal with him of persons belonging to his family, then if any of them appeals under section 59, 63, 66, 67 or 69(1) or (5), the appeal is to have the same effect under paragraphs 10 to 14 in relation to the directions given in respect of each of the others as it has in relation to the directions given in respect of the appellant.

Suspension of variation of limited leave

16 A variation is not to take effect while an appeal against the variation is pending under section 61 or 69(2).

Commencement Paragraphs 10–16 2 October 2000 (SI 2000/2444).

Continuation of leave

17—(1) While an appeal under section 61 or 69(2) is pending, the leave to which the appeal relates and any conditions subject to which it was granted continue to have effect.

(2)   A person may not make an application for a variation of his leave to enter or remain while that leave is treated as continuing to have effect as a result of sub-paragraph (1).

(3)   For the purposes of section 61 or 69(2), in calculating whether, as a result of a decision, a person may be required to leave the United Kingdom within 28 days, a continuation of leave under this paragraph is to be disregarded.

Commencement   2 October 2000 (SI 2000/2444).

Note   Because the same leave and the same conditions continue while an appeal is pending, a person who breaches the conditions of his/her leave during this period will be liable to removal under section 10. See notes to that section.

Deportation orders

18   A deportation order is not to be made against a person under section 5 of the 1971 Act while an appeal duly brought under section 63(1)(a) or 69(4)(a) against the decision to make it is pending.

19   In calculating the period of 8 weeks set by section 5(3) of the 1971 Act for making a deportation order against a person as belonging to the family of another person, there is to be disregarded any period during which an appeal under section 63(1)(a) or 69(4)(a) against the decision to make the order is pending.

Appeals under section 65

20—(1)   A person is not to be required to leave, or be removed from, the United Kingdom if an appeal under section 65 is pending against the decision on which that requirement or removal would otherwise be based.

(2)   That does not prevent—

(a) directions for his removal being given during that period;
(b) a deportation order being made against him during that period.

(3)   But no such direction or order is to have effect during that period.

Commencement   Paragraphs 18–20, 2 October 2000 (SI 2000/2444).

PART III
DETERMINATION OF APPEALS

Determination of appeals

21—(1)   On an appeal to him under Part IV, an adjudicator must allow the appeal if he considers—

(a) that the decision or action against which the appeal is brought was not in accordance with the law or with any immigration rules applicable to the case, or

(b) if the decision or action involved the exercise of a discretion by the Secretary of State or an officer, that the discretion should have been exercised differently,

but otherwise must dismiss the appeal.

(2)   Sub-paragraph (1) is subject to paragraph 24 and to any restriction on the grounds of appeal.

(3)   For the purposes of sub-paragraph (1), the adjudicator may review any determination of a question of fact on which the decision or action was based.

(4)   For the purposes of sub-paragraph (1)(b), no decision or action which is in accordance with the immigration rules is to be treated as having involved the exercise of a discretion by the Secretary of State by reason only of the fact that he has been requested by or on behalf of the appellant to depart, or to authorise an officer to depart, from the rules and has refused to do so.

(5)   If an appeal is allowed, the adjudicator—

(a) must give such directions for giving effect to the determination as he thinks are required; and

(b) may also make recommendations with respect to any other action which he considers should be taken in the case under any of the Immigration Acts.

(6)   The duty to comply with directions given under this paragraph is subject to paragraph 22.

Commencement   2 October 2000 (SI 2000/2444).

Note   For transitional provisions applying this paragraph to appeals under sections 13 to 17 of the Immigration Act 1971, section 8 of the Asylum and Immigration Appeals Act 1993 and section 3(1) and (2) of the Asylum and Immigration Act 1976 see SI 2000/2444, as amended by SI 2001/867, articles 3(1)(b) and 4(1)(c)(I) and Schedule 2 thereto, paragraphs 1(13)(d) and 1(15).

For EEA appeals, see introductory note to this section and SI 2000/2326, as amended by SI 2001/868, Schedule 2, paragraph 2.

Appeals to Immigration Appeal Tribunal

22—(1)   Subject to any requirement of rules made under paragraph 3 as to leave to appeal, any party to an appeal, other than an appeal under section 71, to an adjudicator may, if dissatisfied with his determination, appeal to the Immigration Appeal Tribunal.

(2)   The Tribunal may affirm the determination or make any other determination which the adjudicator could have made.

(3)   Sub-paragraphs (4) to (6) apply if directions have been given by an adjudicator under paragraph 21.

(4)   The directions need not be complied with—

(a) so long as an appeal can be brought against his determination; and

(b) if such an appeal is duly brought, so long as the appeal is pending.

(5) If the Tribunal affirm the adjudicator's determination allowing the appeal, they may alter or add to his directions and recommendations under paragraph 21 or replace them with their own directions and recommendations.

(6) The provisions of paragraph 21 are to apply accordingly.

(7) If an appeal is dismissed by an adjudicator but allowed by the Tribunal, paragraph 21 applies with the substitution of references to the Tribunal for references to the adjudicator.

Commencement   2 October 2000 (SI 2000/2444).

Note   For transitional provisions applying this paragraph to appeals under sections 13 to 17 of the Immigration Act 1971, section 8 of the Asylum and Immigration Appeals Act 1993 and section 3(1) and (2) of the Asylum and Immigration Act 1976 see SI 2000/2444, articles 3(1)(b) and 4(1)(c)(i) and Schedule 2, paragraph 1(13)(e), 1(16) and 1(17). Paragraph 1(17) provides that where an appeal has been determined before 2 October 2000 on the grounds that it has been abandoned, it is to continue to be treated as determined for the purposes of this paragraph.

See SI 2000/2333 Immigration and Asylum Appeals (Procedure) Rules 2000, Part III on appeals to the Tribunal. The time limit for appealing is 10 days (rule 18(2)), or 28 days if the appeal is made from outside the United Kingdom. The Tribunal has power to extend these time limits 'where it is satisfied because of special circumstances, it is just for the time limit to be extended' (rule 18(2)). The Tribunal is given powers under rule 19 to review its decision to refuse to grant leave at the behest of an appellant, where the appellant contends that the decision to refuse leave was due to an administrative or procedural error by the Tribunal. An appellant has 10 days to make such an application.

For EEA appeals, see introductory note to this section and SI 2000/2326, as amended by SI 2001/865, Schedule 2, paragraph 2.

22(1) Leave is required to appeal to the tribunal (SI 2000/2333, rule 18(1)). Rule 18 sets out the procedure for applying for leave. The form is prescribed. Leave to appeal is only to be granted where the Tribunal is satisfied that the appeal would have a real prospect of success or there is some other compelling reason why the appeal should be heard (rule 18(7)).

Appeals from Immigration Appeal Tribunal

23—(1)   If the Immigration Appeal Tribunal has made a final determination of an appeal brought under Part IV, any party to the appeal may bring a further appeal to the appropriate appeal court on a question of law material to that determination.

(2)   An appeal under this section may be brought only with the leave of the Immigration Appeal Tribunal or, if such leave is refused, of the appropriate appeal court.

(3)   'Appropriate appeal court' means—

(a) if the appeal is from the determination of an adjudicator made in Scotland, the Court of Session; and

(b) in any other case, the Court of Appeal.

Commencement   2 October 2000 (SI 2000/2444).

Note   For transitional provisions applying this paragraph to appeals under sections 13 to 17 of the Immigration Act 1971, section 8 of the Asylum and Immigration Appeals Act 1993 and section 3(1) and (2) of the Asylum and Immigration Act 1976 see SI 2000/2444, articles 3(1)(b) and 4(1)(c)(i) and Schedule 2, paragraph 1(13)(f), and 1(17). Paragraph 1(17) provides that where an appeal has been determined before 2 October 2000 on the grounds that it has been abandoned, it is to continue to be treated as determined for the purposes of this paragraph.

See SI 2000/2333 Part IV for provisions as to appeals from the Tribunal.

For EEA appeals, see introductory note to this section and SI 2000/2326, as amended by SI 2001/867, Schedule 2, paragraph 2.

23(2) A time of limit of 10 days is imposed for making an application to the Tribunal for leave to appeal (See 27(1)). The prescribed form for appealing appears as a schedule to SI 2000/2333. Such applications are to be decided by a legally qualified member without a hearing. Under 27(5) a Tribunal intending to grant leave to appeal may instead, having given every party an opportunity to make representations, set aside the determination appealed against and direct that the appeal to the Tribunal be reheard.

Appeals which must be dismissed

24—(1)   An appeal against a refusal of leave to enter the United Kingdom must be dismissed by the adjudicator if he is satisfied that the appellant was at the time of the refusal an illegal entrant.

(2)   An appeal against a refusal of an entry clearance must be dismissed by the adjudicator if he is satisfied that a deportation order was at the time of the refusal in force in respect of the appellant.

(3)   An appeal under section 66 against directions given as mentioned in subsection (1)(c) of that section must be dismissed by the adjudicator, even though the ground of appeal is made out, if he is satisfied that there was power to give the same directions on the ground that the appellant was an illegal entrant.

Commencement   2 October 2000 (SI 2000/2444).

Note   For transitional provisions applying this paragraph to appeals under sections 13 to 17 of the Immigration Act 1971, section 8 of the Asylum and Immigration Appeals Act 1993 and section 3(1) and (2) of the Asylum and Immigration Act 1976 see SI 2000/2444, articles 3(1)(b) and 4(1)(c)(i) and Schedule 2, paragraphs 1(13)(g) and 1(18).

24(2) For EEA appeals, see introductory note to this section and SI 2000/2326, as amended by SI 2001/867, Schedule 2, paragraph 2.

SCHEDULE 5
THE IMMIGRATION SERVICES COMMISSIONER

Section 83

[A.1.408]

Note   See the introductory note to Part V of this Act for details of the Commissioner's scheme.

PART I
REGULATORY FUNCTIONS

Commencement This Part of Schedule 5 commenced in full 30 October 2000 (SI 2000/1985). Notes to individual paragraphs indicate where they commenced earlier.

The Commissioner's rules

1—(1) The Commissioner may make rules regulating any aspect of the professional practice, conduct or discipline of—

(a) registered persons, and
(b) those employed by, or working under the supervision of, registered persons,

in connection with the provision of immigration advice or immigration services.

(2) Before making or altering any rules, the Commissioner must consult such persons appearing to him to represent the views of persons engaged in the provision of immigration advice or immigration services as he considers appropriate.

(3) In determining whether a registered person is competent or otherwise fit to provide immigration advice or immigration services, the Commissioner may take into account any breach of the rules by—

(a) that person; and
(b) any person employed by, or working under the supervision of, that person.

(4) The rules may, among other things, make provision requiring the keeping of accounts or the obtaining of indemnity insurance.

Commencement Sub-paragraphs (1) (2) and (4), 22 May 2000 (SI 2000/1282). Commenced in full 30 October 2000 (SI 2000/1985).

Note *The Commissioner's Rules* were published in October 2000. See introductory note to Part V of this Act.

2—(1) The Commissioner's rules must be made or altered by an instrument in writing.

(2) Such an instrument must specify that it is made under this Schedule.

(3) Immediately after such an instrument is made, it must be printed and made available to the public.

(4) The Commissioner may charge a reasonable fee for providing a person with a copy of the instrument.

(5) A person is not to be taken to have contravened a rule made by the Commissioner if he shows that at the time of the alleged contravention the instrument containing the rule had not been made available in accordance with this paragraph.

(6) The production of a printed copy of an instrument purporting to be made by the Commissioner on which is endorsed a certificate signed by an officer of the Commissioner authorised by him for that purpose and stating—

(a) that the instrument was made by the Commissioner,
(b) that the copy is a true copy of the instrument, and
(c) that on a specified date the instrument was made available to the public in accordance with this paragraph,

is evidence (or in Scotland sufficient evidence) of the facts stated in the certificate.

(7) A certificate purporting to be signed as mentioned in sub-paragraph (6) is to be treated as having been properly signed unless the contrary is shown.

(8) A person who wishes in any legal proceedings to rely on an instrument containing the Commissioner's rules may require him to endorse a copy of the instrument with a certificate of the kind mentioned in sub-paragraph (6).

Commencement Sub-paragraphs (1) to (4) and (6) to (8), 22 May 2000 (SI 2000/1282). Commenced in full 30 October 2000 (SI 2000/1985).

Code of Standards

3—(1) The Commissioner must prepare and issue a code setting standards of conduct which those to whom the code applies are expected to meet.

(2) The code is to be known as the Code of Standards but is referred to in this Schedule as 'the Code'.

(3) The Code is to apply to any person providing immigration advice or immigration services other than—

(a) a person who is authorised by a designated professional body to practise as a member of the profession whose members are regulated by that body;
(b) a person who works under the supervision of such a person; or
(c) a person mentioned in section 84(6).

(4) It is the duty of any person to whom the Code applies to comply with its provisions in providing immigration advice or immigration services.

(5) If the Commissioner alters the Code, he must re-issue it.

(6) Before issuing the Code or altering it, the Commissioner must consult—

(a) each of the designated professional bodies;
(b) the designated judges;
(c) the Lord President of the Court of Session;
(d) the Lord Chief Justice of Northern Ireland; and
(e) such other persons appearing to him to represent the views of persons engaged in the provision of immigration advice or immigration services as he considers appropriate.

(7) The Commissioner must publish the Code in such form and manner as the Secretary of State may direct.

Commencement Sub-paragraphs (1) to (3) and (5) to (7), 22 May 2000 (SI 2000/1282). Commenced in full 30 October 2000 (SI 2000/1985).

Note The *Code of Standards* was published in October 2000. See introductory note to Part V of this Act.

Extension of scope of the Code

4—(1)   The Secretary of State may by order provide for the provisions of the Code, or such provisions of the Code as may be specified by the order, to apply to—

(a) persons authorised by any designated professional body to practise as a member of the profession whose members are regulated by that body; and
(b) persons working under the supervision of such persons.

(2)   If the Secretary of State is proposing to act under sub-paragraph (1) he must, before doing so, consult—

(a) the Commissioner;
(b) the Legal Services Ombudsman, if the proposed order would affect a designated professional body in England and Wales;
(c) the Scottish Legal Services Ombudsman, if the proposed order would affect a designated professional body in Scotland;
(d) the lay observers appointed under Article 42 of the Solicitors (Northern Ireland) Order 1976, if the proposed order would affect a designated professional body in Northern Ireland.

(3)   An order under sub-paragraph (1) requires the approval of—

(a) the Lord Chancellor, if it affects a designated professional body in England and Wales or Northern Ireland;
(b) the Scottish Ministers, if it affects a designated professional body in Scotland.

(4)   Before deciding whether or not to give his approval under sub-paragraph (3)(a), the Lord Chancellor must consult—

(a) the designated judges, if the order affects a designated professional body in England and Wales;
(b) the Lord Chief Justice of Northern Ireland, if it affects a designated professional body in Northern Ireland.

(5)   Before deciding whether or not to give their approval under sub-paragraph (3)(b), the Scottish Ministers must consult the Lord President of the Court of Session.

Commencement   22 May 2000 (SI 2000/1282). Commenced in full 30 October 2000 (SI 2000/1985).

Investigation of complaints

5—(1)   The Commissioner must establish a scheme ('the complaints scheme') for the investigation by him of relevant complaints made to him in accordance with the provisions of the scheme.

(2)   Before establishing the scheme or altering it, the Commissioner must consult—

(a) each of the designated professional bodies; and
(b) such other persons appearing to him to represent the views of persons

engaged in the provision of immigration advice or immigration services as he considers appropriate.

(3)   A complaint is a relevant complaint if it relates to—

(a) the competence or fitness of a person to provide immigration advice or Immigration services,
(b) the competence or fitness of a person employed by, or working under the supervision of, a person providing immigration advice or immigration services,
(c) an alleged breach of the Code,
(d) an alleged breach of one or more of the Commissioner's rules by a person to whom they apply, or
(e) an alleged breach, by a person who falls within paragraph (c), (d), (e) or (f) of section 84(2), of one or more of the rules of the relevant regulatory body,

but not if it relates to a person who is excluded from the application of sub-section (1) of section 84 by subsection (6) of that section.

(4)   The Commissioner may, on his own initiative, investigate any matter which he would have power to investigate on a complaint made under the com-plaints scheme.

(5) In investigating any such matter on his own initiative, the Commissioner must proceed as if his investigation were being conducted in response to a complaint made under the scheme.

Commencement   Sub-paragraphs (1) to (3), 22 May 2000 (SI 2000/1282). Commenced in full 30 October 2000 (SI 2000/1985).

Note   The *Complaint's Scheme* was made in October 2000. See introductory note to Part V of this Act.

6—(1)   The complaints scheme must provide for a person who is the subject of an investigation under the scheme to be given a reasonable opportunity to make representations to the Commissioner.

(2)   Any person who is the subject of an investigation under the scheme must—

(a) take such steps as are reasonably required to assist the Commissioner in his investigation; and
(b) comply with any reasonable requirement imposed on him by the Commissioner.

(3)   If a person fails to comply with sub-paragraph (2)(a) or with a require-ment imposed under sub-paragraph (2)(b) the Commissioner may—

(a) in the case of a registered person, cancel his registration;
(b) in the case of a person certified by the Commissioner as exempt under sec-tion 84(4)(a), withdraw his exemption; or
(c) in the case of a person falling within paragraph (c), (d), (e) or (f) of sec-tion 84(2), refer the matter to the relevant regulatory body.

Power to enter premises

7—(1)   This paragraph applies if—

(a) the Commissioner is investigating a complaint under the complaints scheme;

(b) the complaint falls within paragraph 5(3)(a), (b) or (d); and

(c) there are reasonable grounds for believing that particular premises are being used in connection with the provision of immigration advice or immigration services by a registered person.

(2) The Commissioner, or a member of his staff authorised in writing by him, may enter the premises at reasonable hours.

(3) Sub-paragraph (2) does not apply to premises to the extent to which they constitute a private residence.

(4) A person exercising the power given by sub-paragraph (2) ('the investigating officer') may—

(a) take with him such equipment as appears to him to be necessary;

(b) require any person on the premises—

    (i) to produce any document which he considers relates to any matter relevant to the investigation; and

    (ii) if the document is produced, to provide an explanation of it;

(c) require any person to state, to the best of his knowledge and belief, where any such document is to be found;

(d) take copies of, or extracts from, any document which is produced;

(e) require any information which is held in a computer and is accessible from the premises and which the investigating officer considers relates to any matter relevant to the investigation, to be produced in a form—

    (i) in which it can be taken away; and

    (ii) in which it is visible and legible.

(5) Instead of exercising the power under sub-paragraph (2), the Commissioner may require such person as he may determine ('his agent') to make a report on the provision of immigration advice or immigration services from the premises.

(6) If the Commissioner so determines, his agent may exercise the power conferred by sub-paragraph (2) as if he were a member of the Commissioner's staff appropriately authorised.

(7) If a registered person fails without reasonable excuse to allow access under sub-paragraph (2) or (6) to any premises under his occupation or control, the Commissioner may cancel his registration.

(8) The Commissioner may also cancel the registration of a registered person who—

(a) without reasonable excuse fails to comply with a requirement imposed on him under sub-paragraph (4);

(b) intentionally delays or obstructs any person exercising functions under this paragraph; or

(c) fails to take reasonable steps to prevent an employee of his from obstructing any person exercising such functions.

Determination of complaints

8—(1) On determining a complaint under the complaints scheme, the Commissioner must give his decision in a written statement.

(2)   The statement must include the Commissioner's reasons for his decision.

(3)   A copy of the statement must be given by the Commissioner to—

(a) the person who made the complaint; and
(b) the person who is the subject of the complaint.

9—(1) On determining a complaint under the complaints scheme, the Commissioner may—

(a) if the person to whom the complaint relates is a registered person or a person employed by, or working under the supervision of, a registered person, record the complaint and the decision on it for consideration when that registered person next applies for his registration to be continued;
(b) if the person to whom the complaint relates is a registered person or a person employed by, or working under the supervision of, a registered person and the Commissioner considers the matter sufficiently serious to require immediate action, require that registered person to apply for continued registration without delay;
(c) if the person to whom the complaint relates falls within paragraph (c), (d), (e) or (f) of section 84(2), refer the complaint and his decision on it to the relevant regulatory body;
(d) if the person to whom the complaint relates is certified by the Commissioner as exempt under section 84(4)(a) or is employed by, or working under the supervision of, such a person, consider whether to withdraw that person's exemption;
(e) lay before the Tribunal a disciplinary charge against a relevant person.

(2)   Sub-paragraph (3) applies if—

(a) the Tribunal is considering a disciplinary charge against a relevant person; and
(b) the Commissioner asks it to exercise its powers under that sub-paragraph.

(3)   The Tribunal may give directions (which are to have effect while it is dealing with the charge)—

(a) imposing such restrictions in connection with the provision—
     (i)   by the relevant person, or
     (ii) by any person employed by him or working under his supervision,
     of immigration advice or immigration services as the directions may specify; or
(b) prohibiting him, or any person employed by him or working under his supervision, from providing immigration advice or immigration services.

(4)   'Relevant person' means a person providing immigration advice or immigration services who is—

(a) a registered person;
(b) a person employed by, or working under the supervision of, a registered person;
(c) a member or employee of a body which is a registered person;
(d) a person working under the supervision of a member or employee of such a body;
(e) a person certified by the Commissioner as exempt under section 84(4)(a);
(f) a person to whom section 84(4)(d) applies; or

(g) a person employed by, or working under the supervision of, a person to whom paragraph (e) or (f) applies.

Note See the Immigration Services Tribunal Rules 2000 (SI 2000/2739).

Complaints referred to designated professional bodies

10—(1) This paragraph applies if the Commissioner refers a complaint to a designated professional body under paragraph 9(1)(c).

(2) The Commissioner may give directions setting a timetable to be followed by the designated professional body—

(a) in considering the complaint; and
(b) if appropriate, in taking disciplinary proceedings in connection with the complaint.

(3) In making his annual report to the Secretary of State under paragraph 21, the Commissioner must take into account any failure of a designated professional body to comply (whether wholly or in part) with directions given to it under this paragraph.

(4) Sub-paragraph (5) applies if the Commissioner or the Secretary of State considers that a designated professional body has persistently failed to comply with directions given to it under this paragraph.

(5) The Commissioner must take the failure into account in determining whether to make a report under section 86(9)(b) and the Secretary of State must take it into account in determining whether to make an order under section 86(2).

PART II
COMMISSIONER'S STATUS, REMUNERATION AND STAFF ETC

Commencement This Part of Schedule 5 commenced 22 May 2000 (SI 2000/1282) (c 38).

Status

11—(1) The Commissioner is to be a corporation sole.

(2) The Commissioner and the members of the Commissioner's staff are not to be regarded as the servants or agents of the Crown or as having any status, privilege or immunity of the Crown.

Period of office

12—(1) The Commissioner—

(a) is to hold office for a term of five years; but
(b) may resign at any time by notice in writing given to the Secretary of State.

(2) The Secretary of State may dismiss the Commissioner—

(a) on the ground of incapacity or misconduct; or
(b) if he is satisfied—
  (i) that he has been convicted of a criminal offence; or
  (ii) that a bankruptcy order has been made against him, or his estate has been sequestrated, or he has made a composition or arrangement with, or granted a trust deed for, his creditors.

(3) The Commissioner is eligible for re-appointment when his term of office ends.

Terms and conditions of appointment

13 Subject to the provisions of this Schedule, the Commissioner is to hold office on such terms and conditions as the Secretary of State may determine.

Remuneration, expenses and pensions

14—(1) There is to be paid to the Commissioner such remuneration and expenses as the Secretary of State may determine.
(2) The Secretary of State may pay, or provide for the payment of, such pensions, allowances or gratuities to or in respect of the Commissioner as he may determine.

Compensation

15 If a person ceases to be the Commissioner, otherwise than when his term of office ends, and it appears to the Secretary of State that there are special circumstances which make it right for him to receive compensation, the Secretary of State may make a payment to him of such amount as the Secretary of State may determine.

Deputy Commissioner

16—(1) The Secretary of State must appoint a person to act as Deputy Commissioner.
(2) During any vacancy in the office of Commissioner, or at any time when he is unable to discharge his functions, the Deputy Commissioner may act in his place.
(3) Paragraphs 11(2) and 12 to 15 apply to the Deputy Commissioner as they apply to the Commissioner.

Staff

17—(1) Subject to obtaining the approval of the Secretary of State as to numbers and terms and conditions of service, the Commissioner may appoint such staff as he considers appropriate.
(2) Subject to obtaining the approval of the Secretary of State, the Commissioner may pay, or provide for the payment of, such pensions, allowances or gratuities (including by way of compensation for loss of office or employment) to or in respect of his staff as he considers appropriate.
(3) Any functions of the Commissioner may, to the extent authorised by him, be performed by the Deputy Commissioner or any of his staff.

(4) The Employers' Liability (Compulsory Insurance) Act 1969 is not to require insurance to be effected by the Commissioner.

Expenditure

18 The Secretary of State may pay to the Commissioner—

(a) any expenses incurred or to be incurred by the Commissioner in respect of his staff; and
(b) with the approval of the Treasury, such other sums for enabling the Commissioner to perform his functions as the Secretary of State thinks fit.

Receipts

19—(1) Subject to any general or specific directions given to him by the Secretary of State, sums received by the Commissioner in the exercise of his functions must be paid to the Secretary of State.
(2) Sums received by the Secretary of State under this paragraph must be paid into the Consolidated Fund.
(3) The approval of the Treasury is required for any direction given under this paragraph.

Accounts and records

20—(1) The Commissioner must—

(a) keep proper accounts and proper records in relation to his accounts;
(b) prepare a statement of accounts for each financial year; and
(c) send copies of the statement to the Secretary of State and to the Comptroller and Auditor General on or before the specified date.

(2) The statement of accounts must be in such form as the Secretary of State may, with the approval of the Treasury, direct.
(3) The Comptroller and Auditor General must—

(a) examine, certify and report on each statement received by him under this paragraph; and
(b) lay copies of each statement and of his report before each House of Parliament.

(4) 'Financial year' means the period of 12 months beginning with 1st April.
(5) 'Specified date' means—

(a) 31st August next following the end of the year to which the statement relates; or
(b) such earlier date after the end of that year as the Treasury may direct.

Annual report

21—(1) The Commissioner must, as soon as is practicable after the end of each financial year, report to the Secretary of State on the performance of his functions in that year.
(2) The report must, in particular, set out the Commissioner's opinion as to the extent to which each designated professional body has provided effective

regulation of its members in their provision of immigration advice or immigration services.

(3) The Secretary of State must lay a copy of the report before each House of Parliament.

(5) 'Financial year' has the same meaning as in paragraph 20.

Proof of instruments

22 A document purporting to be an instrument issued by the Commissioner and to be signed by or on behalf of the Commissioner is to be received in evidence and treated as such an instrument unless the contrary is shown.

Disqualification for House of Commons

23 In Part III of Schedule 1 to the House of Commons Disqualification Act 1975 (offices disqualifying for membership), insert at the appropriate place—

'The Immigration Services Commissioner
The Deputy Immigration Services Commissioner'.

Disqualification for Northern Ireland Assembly

24 In Part III of Schedule 1 to the Northern Ireland Assembly Disqualification Act 1975 (offices disqualifying for membership), insert at the appropriate place—

'The Immigration Services Commissioner
The Deputy Immigration Services Commissioner'.

The Parliamentary Commissioner Act 1967 (c 13)

25 In Schedule 2 of the Parliamentary Commissioner Act 1967 (departments and authorities subject to investigation) insert, at the appropriate place, 'The Immigration Services Commissioner'.

SCHEDULE 6
REGISTRATION

[A.1.409]

Commencement   Schedule 6 in full 30 August 2000 (SI 2000/1985). Notes to individual paragraphs indicate where they commenced earlier.

Note   See the introductory note to Part V of this Act.

Section 85(3)

Applications for registration

1—(1)   An application for registration under section 84(2)(a) or (b) must—

(a) be made to the Commissioner in such form and manner, and
(b) be accompanied by such information and supporting evidence,

as the Commissioner may from time to time determine.

(2)   When considering an application for registration, the Commissioner may

require the applicant to provide him with such further information or supporting evidence as the Commissioner may reasonably require.

Registration

2—(1)   If the Commissioner considers that an applicant for registration is competent and otherwise fit to provide immigration advice and immigration services, he must register the applicant.

(2)   Registration may be made so as to have effect—

(a) only in relation to a specified field of advice or services;

(b) only in relation to the provision of advice or services to a specified category of person;

(c) only in relation to the provision of advice or services to a member of a specified category of person; or

(d) only in specified circumstances.

Review of qualifications

3   (1)   At such intervals as the Commissioner may determine, each registered person must submit an application for his registration to be continued.

(2)   Different intervals may be fixed by the Commissioner in relation to different registered persons or descriptions of registered person.

(3)   An application for continued registration must—

(a) be made to the Commissioner in such form and manner, and

(b) be accompanied by such information and supporting evidence,

as the Commissioner may from time to time determine.

(4)   When considering an application for continued registration, the Commissioner may require the applicant to provide him with such further information or supporting evidence as the Commissioner may reasonably require.

(5)   If the Commissioner considers that an applicant for continued registration is no longer competent or is otherwise unfit to provide immigration advice or immigration services, he must cancel the applicant's registration.

(6)   Otherwise, the Commissioner must continue the applicant's registration but may, in doing so, vary the registration—

(a) so as to make it have limited effect in any of the ways mentioned in paragraph 2(2); or

(b) so as to make it have full effect.

(7)   If a registered person fails, without reasonable excuse—

(a) to make an application for continued registration as required by sub-paragraph (1) or by a direction given by the Tribunal under section 89(3)(b), or

(b) to provide further information or evidence under sub-paragraph (4),

the Commissioner may cancel the person's registration as from such date as he may determine.

Disqualification of certain persons

4   A person convicted of an offence under section 25 or 26(1)(d) or (g) of the 1971 Act is disqualified for registration under paragraph 2 or for continued registration under paragraph 3.

Fees

5—(1)   The Secretary of State may by order specify fees for the registration or continued registration of persons on the register.

(2) No application under paragraph 1 or 3 is to be entertained by the Commissioner unless it is accompanied by the specified fee.

Commencement   5(1) 1 August 2000 for the purposes of enabling subordinate legislation to be made under it (SI 2000/1985). Paragraph 5 commenced in full 30 October 2000 (SI 2000/1985).

Note   See the Immigration Services Commissioner (Registration Fee) Order 2000 (SI 2000/2735). The fee payable for registration by a sole immigration adviser has been set at £1,800 (SI 2000/2735, article 3). Fees for groups of more than one adviser are on a sliding scale from £2,675 to £6,000, as set out in the Schedule to SI 2000/2735.

Open registers

6   (1)   The register must be made available for inspection by members of the public in a legible form at reasonable hours.

(2)   A copy of the register or of any entry in the register must be provided—

(a)   on payment of a reasonable fee;
(b)   in written or electronic form; and
(c)   in a legible form.

(3)   Sub-paragraphs (1) and (2) also apply to—

(a)   the record kept by the Commissioner of the persons to whom he has issued a certificate of exemption under section 84(4)(a); and
(b)   the record kept by the Commissioner of the persons against whom there is in force a direction given by the Tribunal under section 89(8).

SCHEDULE 7
THE IMMIGRATION SERVICES TRIBUNAL

[A.1.410]

Commencement   Schedule 7 in full 30 August 2000 (SI 2000/1985). Notes to individual paragraphs indicate where they commenced earlier.

Note   See the introductory note to Part V of this Act. See the Immigration Services Tribunal Rules 2000 (SI 2000/2729), which came into force 30 October 2000.

Section 87(5)

Members

1—(1)   The Tribunal is to consist of such number of members as the Lord Chancellor may determine.

(2)   The members are to be appointed by the Lord Chancellor.

(3)   A person may be appointed as a member only if—

(a)   he is legally qualified; or

(b)   he appears to the Lord Chancellor to have had substantial experience in immigration services or in the law and procedure relating to immigration.

The President

2   The Tribunal is to have a President appointed by the Lord Chancellor from among those of its members who are legally qualified.

Terms and conditions of appointment

3—(1)   Each member is to hold and vacate office in accordance with the terms of his appointment.

(2)   A member is eligible for re-appointment when his term of office ends.

(3)   A member may resign at any time by notice in writing given to the Lord Chancellor.

(4)   The Lord Chancellor may dismiss a member on the ground of incapacity or misconduct.

Remuneration and expenses

4   The Lord Chancellor may pay to any member such remuneration and expenses as he may determine.

Proceedings

5   The Tribunal is to sit at such times and in such places as the Lord Chancellor may direct.

6—(1)   The Commissioner is entitled to be represented before the Tribunal, in relation to the hearing of appeals or disciplinary charges, by such persons as he may authorise.

(2)   The Commissioner may authorise a person to represent him before the Tribunal in relation to—

(a)   specified proceedings; or

(b)   all or specified categories of proceedings.

(3)   'Specified' means specified by the Commissioner.

Rules of procedure

7—(1)   The Lord Chancellor may make rules as to the procedure and practice to be followed in relation to the exercise of the Tribunal's functions.

(2)   Before making or altering any such rules, the Lord Chancellor must consult the Scottish Ministers.

(3)   Subject to the provisions of this Schedule and the rules, the Tribunal may determine its own procedure.

(4)   The rules must make provision for any person appealing to the Tribunal or otherwise subject to its jurisdiction to be entitled to be legally represented.

(5)   The rules may, in particular, make provision—

(a) as to the mode and burden of proof and the giving and admissibility of evidence;

(b) for proceedings before the Tribunal to be capable of being determined in the absence of any party to the proceedings if that party has failed, without reasonable excuse, to appear before the Tribunal or has failed to comply with any reasonable directions given by the Tribunal as to the conduct of the proceedings;

(c) with respect to other matters preliminary or incidental to, or arising out of, any matter with respect to which the Tribunal is or may be exercising functions;

(d) as to the period within which an appeal against a decision of the Commissioner can be brought;

(e) authorising such functions of the Tribunal as may be specified in the rules to be exercised by a single member.

Commencement   1 August 2000 (SI 2000/1985).

Note   See the Immigration Services Tribunal Rules 2000 (SI 2000/2729).

7(4) See Rule 21.

7(5)(a) See Rule 22. The standard of proof is the balance of probabilities, save where it is alleged that a person has been guilty of criminal or fraudulent conduct, when the standard is that of beyond reasonable doubt.

7(5)(b) See Rules 19 and 20. There will normally be an oral hearing.

7(5)(d) See Rule 8. 28 days from notification of the decision are given for appealing.

7(5)(e) See Rule 3. At the hearing of an appeal or charge, the Tribunal shall consist of a legally qualified member and two other members. The legally qualified member sitting alone has power to give permission for out of time appeals, to make cancel or vary directions under paragraph 8 of this Schedule, to make directions under paragraph 9(3) of this Schedule, to make procedural directions or to deal with consent orders. See also Rule 3(4).

Suspending the effect of a relevant decision

8—(1)   A relevant decision of the Commissioner is not to have effect while the period within which an appeal may be brought against the decision is running.

(2)   If the appellant applies to the Tribunal under this paragraph, the Tribunal may direct that while the appeal is being dealt with—

(a) no effect is to be given to the decision appealed against; or

(b) only such limited effect is to be given to it as may be specified in the direction.

(3)   Rules under paragraph 7 must include provision requiring the Tribunal to consider applications by the Commissioner for the cancellation or variation of directions given under this paragraph.

Commencement   Sub-paragraph 8(3) 1 August 2000 (SI 2000/1985). Paragraph 8 in full 30 October 2000 (SI 2000/1985).

Note   *8(3)* See SI 2000/2739, Rule 11.

Staff

9—(1)   The Lord Chancellor may appoint such staff for the Tribunal as he considers appropriate.

(2)   The Lord Chancellor may pay, or provide for the payment of, such pensions, allowances or gratuities (including by way of compensation for loss of office or employment) to or in respect of the Tribunal's staff as he considers appropriate.

Expenditure

10   The Lord Chancellor may pay such other expenses of the Tribunal as he considers appropriate.

Meaning of 'legally qualified'

11   A person is legally qualified for the purposes of this Schedule if—

(a)   he has a 7 year general qualification, within the meaning of section 71 of the Courts and Legal Services Act 1990;
(b)   he is an advocate or solicitor in Scotland of at least 7 years' standing; or
(c)   he is a member of the Bar of Northern Ireland or solicitor of the Supreme Court of Northern Ireland of at least 7 years' standing.

Disqualification for House of Commons

12   In Part I of Schedule 1 to the House of Commons Disqualification Act 1975 (offices disqualifying for membership), insert at the appropriate place—

'Member of the Immigration Services Tribunal'.

Disqualification for Northern Ireland Assembly

13   In Part I of Schedule 1 to the Northern Ireland Assembly Disqualification Act 1975 (offices disqualifying for membership), insert at the appropriate place—

'Member of the Immigration Services Tribunal'.

SCHEDULE 8
PROVISION OF SUPPORT: REGULATIONS

Section 95(12)

[A.1.411]

Commencement   1 January 2000 (SI 1999/3190).

Note   The Asylum Support Regulations 2000 (SI 2000/704) have been made under this Schedule. The application form for support and the notes thereto form a schedule to the regulations. The regulations were made on 6 March 2000, laid before parliament on 11 March 2000 and came into force on 3 April 2000. The regulations were subject to the negative resolution procedure, whereby they come into force unless challenged. It is a mark of the controversy surrounding the regulations that, unusually for legislation subject to negative procedures, they were the made the subject of a challenge, brought by the Lord Dholakia, the Liberal Democrat peer. They were the subject of a full debate in the House of Lords, see *Hansard*, HL Report Vol 612, No 80, 20 April 2000, cols 893 to 920. All references in the notes to this schedule are to this instrument as amended by the Asylum Support (Amendment) Regulations 2000 (see note to paragraph 3(a) below), unless otherwise stated. The notes should be read with the notes to sections 94, 95 and 96.

General regulation-making power

1 The Secretary of State may by regulations make such further provision with respect to the powers conferred on him by section 95 as he considers appropriate.

Determining whether a person is destitute

2—(1) The regulations may provide, in connection with determining whether a person is destitute, for the Secretary of State to take into account, except in such circumstances (if any) as may be prescribed—

(a) income which the person concerned, or any dependant of his, has or might reasonably be expected to have, and

(b) support which is, or assets of a prescribed kind which are, or might reasonably be expected to be, available to him or to any dependant of his,

otherwise than by way of support provided under section 95.

(2) The regulations may provide that in such circumstances (if any) as may be prescribed, a person is not to be treated as destitute for the purposes of section 95.

Note   See regulations 5 to 9.

2(1) See regulation 6.

2(1)(a) See regulation 6(4)(a). The incomes of the person applying for support and dependants are to be taken into account. There remains considerable confusion as to the meaning of 'might reasonably be expected to have'. For example, in respect of a person entitled to work, would this mean that the Secretary of State could consider his/her earning power? How would the likelihood of obtaining employment, and the remuneration the person could then be expected to receive, be calculated?

2(1)(b) See regulation 6(4)(b). The same confusion as to the meaning of 'might reasonably be expected' arises under this section also. Debate around these provisions has focused on the extent to which donations from charities and individuals can be taken into account. The problem was summarised in the debates on the Act by Conservative peer, the Lord Cope of Berkeley:

'I can think of no other instance where, if a charity gives money to a deserving person, that person then has their social security or other benefit taken away from them. But that is contemplated here.' (See *Hansard* HL Report 20 October 1999, col 1196)

The matter was further discussed in the debate on the regulations in the House of Lords. See *Hansard* HL Report Vol 612 No 80 cols 895-898 and 906 to 907, 920. Ministerial responses have failed to provide clarification. The Lord Bach, speaking for the government suggested that gifts in kind would not be taken into account, but that gifts in cash would (col 920). However, subsequent Ministerial statements in letters and speeches have suggested that this is not the government's final word on the issue. The Minister of State, Ms Roche, speaking at the Catholic Refugee Forum on 11 May 2000, envisaged certain gifts in cash not being taken into account. The Lord Bach indicated that he would provide further written clarification (col 920). This has not yet appeared.

The prescribed assets are cash, savings, investments, land, cars or other vehicles and goods held for the purposes of a trade or business, see regulation 6(4). Regulation 6(5) provides that other assets must be ignored. The Secretary of State must also ignore any support given under section 95 or 98 of the Act (see regulation 6(3)).

2(2) The regulations do not provide for circumstances in which a person who would otherwise be treated as destitute is not to be so treated. However, they do make provision as the circumstances to be taken into account when assessing destitution. Regulation 4 deals with those excluded from support for the purposes of section 95(2). These include persons to whom interim support or benefits 'apply', as defined in regulation 4(5) and 4(6) and those who have not made an asylum claim. Regulation 8 sets out the test by which the adequacy of existing accommodation is to be judged for the purposes of section 95(5)(a). Regulation 9 sets out matters to be treated as essential living needs when deciding whether or not a person is to be treated as destitute. Regulation 9(4) expressly excludes from the definition of essential living needs the cost of faxes, of computers and computer facilities, the cost of photocopying, travel expenses other than the expense of the initial journey to the location at which support is to be provided, toys and other recreational items and entertainment expenses. A person who cannot meet these expenses is nonetheless not to be considered destitute. Thus the Secretary of State, the Rt Hon Jack Straw MP in a letter of 13 April 2000 to the Director of the Medical Foundation for the Care of Victims of Torture, stating that the purpose of regulation 9(4)(e), excluding toys from essential living needs 'is to ensure that families are not regarded as destitute simply because they cannot afford toys for their children.'

Prescribed levels of support

3   The regulations may make provision—

(a) as to the circumstances in which the Secretary of State may, as a general rule, be expected to provide support in accordance with prescribed levels or of a prescribed kind;
(b) as to the circumstances in which the Secretary of State may, as a general rule, be expected to provide support otherwise than in accordance with the prescribed levels.

Note   See regulations 5 to 14. The dependants of the person claiming support for the purposes of the regulations are set out in regulation 2(4). These are:

2(4)(a) the spouse;

2(4)(b) dependent children under 18 of the person claiming support or the spouse;

2(4)(c) children under 18 who are a member of the his/her or his/her spouse's close family. There is no requirement of dependency in this provision;

2(4)(d) children under 18 who have been living as part of his/her household for at least six of 12 months before the date of the application for support or since birth if this is shorter;

2(4)(e) persons over 18 in need of care and attention from the him/her or a member of his/her household by reason of a disability who have been living with him/her for at least six of the 12 months before the date of the application;

2(4)(f) unmarried partners who have been living with him/her for at least 2 of the 3 years preceding the date of the claim for support. The interpretation section of the regulations defines unmarried partners to demand that they are a man and a woman, thus excluding same-sex partners. SI 1999/3046, governing the interim arrangements, imposes no such express limitation, see notes to Schedule 9;

2(4)(g) persons living as part of his/her household and receiving assistance from a local authority under section 17 of the Children Act 1989 immediately before the beginning of the interim period (6 December 1999);

2(4)(h) persons living as part of his/her household and receiving assistance from a local authority under section 22 of the Children (Scotland) Act 1995 or Article 18 of the Children (Northern Ireland) Order 1995 immediately before the beginning of the interim period;

2(4) a dependant on the asylum application.

In *R v London Borough of Camden ex p Diirshe* CO/5069/99, an application for judicial review brought under the interim scheme of SI 1999/3046 held that there was no requirement for the dependant biological children of an asylum seeker to show a financial dependency.

3(a) See regulation 10(2). Levels of support to be provided 'As a general rule' are prescribed therein. These are, per week: for a qualifying couple £57.37; for a lone parent over 18 £36.54, for a single person aged 25 or over £36.54; for a single person aged 18 to 24 £28.95 and for a child aged 16-17 £31.75. The Asylum Support (Amendment) Regulations 2000 (SI 2000/3053), into force 4 December 2000, increased the sum in respect of a child under 16 from £26.60 to £30.95. The increase reflects that effected by the Social Security Amendment (Personal Allowances for Children) Regulations 2000. The terms 'qualifying couple' 'lone parent' and 'single person' are defined in regulation 10(4). Of these sums a maximum of £10 per person, £20 per qualifying couple, may 'as a general rule' be paid in vouchers redeemable for cash (regulation 10(6). The remaining sum to be paid to the asylum seeker must be reduced where the asylum seeker receives support in kind as part of full-board accommodation. The regulations do not set out how the value of such support in kind is to be calculated.

3(b) See regulation 11. This makes provision 'as a general rule' for a one-off payment of £50 worth of vouchers redeemable for cash for each six months for those who have been in the support system under section 95 for 6 months or more. Such payments are only made if the supported person applies for them (regulation 11(5)). Regulation 11(6) provides that any period of delay incurred by a person responsible without reasonable excuse for delay in the determination of his/her claim may be added to the six month period before a payment is made. No other provision is made for circumstances in which support will be provided other than in accordance with the prescribed levels, although the use of the phrase 'as a general rule' in the regulations as in this schedule, means that the regulations provide no bar to the making of such payments. It remains to be seen whether applicants with special needs, for example arising from a disability, would receive support for essential living needs at higher rate than those set out in regulation 10, or whether support would be provided to them under the separate powers contained in section 96(2) to provide support where the circumstances of a particular case are exceptional. In this regard, see the notes to Sections 95 and 116 discussing the case of *Westminster City Council v NASS*.

See also NASS Policy Bulletin 37 'Maternity Payments'. NASS has made provision for a discretionary one-off payment of £300, in vouchers with an expiry date of approximately four weeks from the date of issue, to asylum-seekers who have a baby while on NASS support. There are a number of eligibility criteria. In particular, an application must be received between one month before the birth of the child and two weeks after. There is also provision for the payment to be made when the baby was born outside the United Kingdom and is less than 3 months old when the family qualify for NASS support.

Provision of items and services

4 The regulations may make provision for prescribed items or services to be provided or made available to persons receiving support under section 95 for such purposes and in such circumstances as may be prescribed.

Note See regulation 14. The services for which regulation 14(2) makes provision are education, including English language classes and sport or other developmental activities. However, regard should be had to 14(1) which states 'The services mentioned in paragraph 2 may be provided or made available by way of asylum support to persons who are otherwise receiving such support, but may be so provided only for the purpose of maintaining good order amongst such persons.' At the time of writing no court has been called upon to undertake the curious task of deciding whether an English language class or free access to swimming pool has been provided only for the maintenance of good order or for some other illegal purpose.

Support and assets to be taken into account

5 The regulations may make provision requiring the Secretary of State, except in such circumstances (if any) as may be prescribed, to take into account, when deciding the level or kind of support to be provided—

(a) income which the person concerned, or any dependant of his, has or might reasonably be expected to have, and

(b) support which is, or assets of a prescribed kind which are, or might reasonably be expected to be, available to him or to any dependant of his,

otherwise than by way of support provided under section 95.

Note This paragraph mirrors paragraph 2 and the same issues and difficulties arise and await further clarification. Whereas paragraph 2 dealt with the issue of entitlement to support, and thus with the income or assets which the asylum seeker had before becoming supported, this paragraph deals with level of support and thus what an asylum seeker whom the Secretary of State has agreed to support can receive by way of such support. Regulation 12 addresses these matters. The list of assets to be taken into account is as for paragraph 2, regulation 12(3)(c) importing a reference to regulation 6(5).

Valuation of assets

6 The regulations may make provision as to the valuation of assets.

Note The regulations do not make any provision for the valuation of assets. However the notes to the application form appended as a schedule to the regulations allot the task of valuing assets to the asylum seeker. In this regard, attention should be drawn to sections 105 and 106 of this Act, which deal with the making of false or dishonest representations. These sections do not appear to catch the asylum seeker who unwittingly makes an inaccurate estimation of the value of an asset, due to the requirement in section 105 that the person knows the statement to be false, and in 106 the requirement of dishonesty, as elements of the offence. There may nonetheless be circumstances in which an asylum seeker declines to seek to value an asset because s/he does not feel capable of doing so, and the regulations do not make provision for how this situation is to be dealt with.

Breach of conditions

7 The regulations may make provision for the Secretary of State to take into account, when deciding—

(a) whether to provide, or to continue to provide, support under section 95, or

(b) the level or kind of support to be provided,

the extent to which any condition on which support is being, or has previously been, provided has been complied with.

Note See regulation 9. Little more appears in the regulations than is already set out in paragraph 7 – there are no details as to how a breach of conditions might be taken into account.

Suspension or discontinuation of support

8—(1) The regulations may make provision for the suspension or discontinuance of support under section 95 in prescribed circumstances (including circumstances in which the Secretary of State would otherwise be under a duty to provide support).

(2) The circumstances which may be prescribed include the cessation of residence—

(a) in accommodation provided under section 95; or

(b) at an address notified to the Secretary of State in accordance with the regulations.

Note See regulation 20. This regulation provides that support may be discontinued, for one or more of those supported, if the Secretary of State has reasonable grounds to suspect that the person has failed without reasonable excuse to comply with the conditions of support or reasonable grounds to suspect that the person has intentionally made him/herself and/or any dependants destitute. The meaning of making oneself intentionally destitute is prescribed in regulation 20(2). Support may also be suspended or discontinued if any supported person ceases to reside at the authorised address for more than 7 consecutive days and nights, and for a total of more than 15 days and nights in any six month period, without the permission of the Secretary of State. The reference to 'days and nights' is unusual. It appears to suggest that an asylum seeker can sleep away from home without falling foul of these conditions, providing s/he returns to the accommodation during the day.

The question of what constitutes a reasonable excuse has arisen in appeals to Asylum Support Adjudicators in cases where the appellant left the accommodation because of racial harassment. In appeal no 000/07/0024 (26 July 2000) the appellant left his NASS accommodation in Gateshead following racial attacks in respect of which the police had been called. The appellant detailed persistent racial harassment and racial attacks during his three month stay in Gateshead, including attacks on the shared accommodation in which he was living in which windows were broken and the building stoned. He had been robbed and racially insulted in the context of this. On the facts of the case the Adjudicator found that the appellant had given notice of his departure and in the circumstances of the cases had provided a reasonable explanation for not returning. NASS were directed to continue to support the appellant and to allocate him accommodation in a place other than Gateshead. See also appeals nos 00/07/0031, 00/08/0036 and 00/09/0044. In general, Adjudicators have treated racial harassment as a 'reasonable excuse' where there has been inadequate NASS investigation or response, where the harassment has been sustained or of particular severity, but not in other cases.

In 00/01/0106 the appellants were found to have had a 'reasonable excuse' for leaving their accommodation because that accommodation was not 'adequate' (see section 95(3)). The regime in the accommodation was found to constitute inhuman and degrading treatment, in breach of Article 3 ECHR, for a man with a suspected heart condition.

Adjudicators have dealt with cases in which appellants have failed to travel to NASS accommodation, or failed to comply with the conditions on which support is provided. They have required that sufficient warning of failure to comply be communicated to the appellant. See for example case no 00/10/0087 where the appellant had not understood the letter from NASS. The adjudicator found that the appellant had not failed to comply with the conditions. In 00/06/0020 the appellant had not been warned of the consequences of sending money back to the home country (Iran). No finding of intentional destitution was made in that case.

Notice to quit

9—(1)   The regulations may provide that if—

(a) as a result of support provided under section 95, a person has a tenancy or a licence to occupy accommodation,

(b) one or more of the conditions mentioned in sub-paragraph (2) are satisfied, and

(c) he is given such notice to quit as may be prescribed by the regulations,

his tenancy or licence is to be treated as ending with the period specified in that notice, regardless of when it could otherwise be brought to an end.

(2)   The conditions are that—

(a) the support provided under section 95 is suspended or discontinued as a result of any provision of a kind mentioned in paragraph 8;

(b) the relevant claim for asylum has been determined;

(c) the supported person has ceased to be destitute;

(d) he is to be moved to other accommodation.

Note   See regulation 22. Regulation 22(3) provides that a notice to quit must be in writing. In cases where the reason to quit is that support is being discontinued or suspended in accordance with regulation 20 (see notes to paragraph 8 above), or that the asylum claim has finally been determined, or that the person is to be moved to other accommodation, at least 7 days notice must be given. Where the notice to quit is given because the Secretary of State has notified his decision on the claim to asylum the notice period is at least 7 days. If the period beginning with the date of service of the notice to quit and ending with the date of determination of the claim to asylum (see section 94(3) is longer, this is the relevant period. Under regulation 20(4)(c) a notice to quit is only a notice in accordance with paragraph 20 if the circumstances of the case are such that the 7 day notice period is justified.

Contributions to support

10   The regulations may make provision requiring a supported person to make payments to the Secretary of State, in prescribed circumstances, by way of contributions to the cost of the provision of that support.

Note   See regulation 16. This gives the Secretary of State power to set the support for a person at a level which does not reflect the person's income, support or assets, and then require from that person payments by way of contributions toward the cost of provision of support. Under regulation 16(4) prompt payment of contributions may be made a condition of support. This regulation gives scope for a measure of flexibility where, for example, the asylum seeker is able to obtain a small income, perhaps for a temporary period, which would not be sufficient to support him/her. The regulations make no provision as to the amount of contribution that might be demanded in such circumstances, nor as to how the cost of provision of support is to be calculated.

Recovery of sums by Secretary of State

11—(1)   The regulations may provide for the recovery by the Secretary of State of sums representing the whole or part of the monetary value of support provided to a person under section 95 where it appears to the Secretary of State—

(a) that that person had, at the time when he applied for support, assets of any kind in the United Kingdom or elsewhere which were not capable of being realised; but

(b) that those assets have subsequently become, and remain, capable of being realised.

(2)   An amount recoverable under regulations made by virtue of sub-paragraph (1) may be recovered—

(a) as if it were a debt due to the Secretary of State; or

(b) by such other method of recovery, including by deduction from support provided under section 95 as may be prescribed.

Note   See regulation 17. The regulation applies 'where it appears to the Secretary of State at any time' that when a person applied for support s/he had assets anywhere which were not capable of being realised and that they have subsequently become, and remain, capable of being realised. Then the Secretary of State has a discretion to recover sums from the person. The maximum sum may be recovered is the value of the assets, or the value of all asylum support provided, whichever is the lesser. The Secretary of State has a discretion as to whether recover this maximum sum. The sum may be recovered as a debt (see sub-paragraph 2(a) of this paragraph) or by deduction from asylum support. Regulation 18 also makes provision for the recovery of overpayments; see section 114(3).

Procedure

12   The regulations may make provision with respect to procedural requirements including, in particular, provision as to—

(a) the procedure to be followed in making an application for support;

(b) the information which must be provided by the applicant;

(c) the circumstances in which an application may not be entertained;

(d) the making of further enquiries by the Secretary of State;

(e) the circumstances in which, and person by whom, a change of circumstances of a prescribed description must be notified to the Secretary of State.

Note   Regulation 3 makes provision with regard to the making of an application for support. Regulation 15 makes provision with regard to a supported person's notifying the Secretary of State of a change of circumstances. Under regulation 3 the procedure is set out in detail. There is no prescribed form for notification of a change of circumstances. There is no requirement that the change be notified in writing. The only requirement is that notification be made 'without delay'. Nonetheless, regulation 15 places considerable demands upon supported persons. The list of circumstances to be notified is long. It is unclear what would constitute notification 'without delay' in the circumstance envisaged by regulation 16(2)(j), that the asylum seeker becomes pregnant. And supported persons without dependants are sure to find themselves defeated by regulation 16(2)(r), which requires them to notify the Secretary of State, 'without delay' if they die.

The Schedule to the regulations serves to deal with other procedural matters in some detail.

12(a) See regulation 3. This prescribes that support must be made on the prescribed form, which must be completed 'in full and in English' (Regulation 3(3)). The form currently in use, and the notes to it, appear as a schedule to the regulations. Regulation 3(4) provides that there is no requirement to complete the form where a supported person is seeking to add a dependant to those supported. In such circumstances, regulation 15 applies.

12(b) This is set out in the form and notes thereto appended as a schedule to the regulations. These present a considerable challenge to an asylum seeker seeking to complete the form 'in full and in English'.

12(c) Paragraph 3(4) provides that the application may not be entertained by the Secretary of State unless it is made in accordance with regulation 3(3).

12(d) Regulation 3(5) simply provides that the Secretary of State may make further enquiries 'about any matter connected with the application.'

SCHEDULE 9
ASYLUM SUPPORT: INTERIM PROVISIONS

Section 95(13)

Commencement   On Royal Assent (section 170(3)).

Note   Regulations have been made under paragraph 1(1) and all references in the notes on this schedule are to those regulations: Asylum Support (Interim Provisions) Regulations 1999 (SI 1999/3056).

[A.1.412]

1—(1)   The Secretary of State may by regulations make provision requiring prescribed local authorities or local authorities falling within a prescribed description of authority to provide support, during the interim period, to eligible persons.

(2)   'Eligible persons' means—

(a) asylum-seekers, or

(b) their dependants,

who appear to be destitute or to be likely to become destitute within such period as may be prescribed.

(3)   For the purposes of sub-paragraph (1), in Northern Ireland, a Health and Social Services Board established under Article 16 of the Health and Personal Social Services (Northern Ireland) Order 1972 is to be treated as a local authority.

Note   1(1) See regulation 2. The regulations apply to local authorities in England and Wales. Scotland and Northern Ireland have not been brought into the interim scheme. Under regulation 3, local authorities are placed under a duty to provide support to eligible persons.

1(2) Regulation 2 repeats the definition and prescribes a period of 14 days. Under regulation 3(2) it is for the local authority concerned, as defined in regulation 3(3) to determine whether a person is an eligible person. Regulation 4 applies to support to be provided before a decision has been made on eligibility and regulation 4(2) provides that 'Temporary support is to be provided to a person claiming support' by a local authority during the period preceding determination of eligibility.

In *R v London Borough of Lambeth ex p Amanuel Tekeste* Co/77/00, 11 January 2000 an Eritrean national who had exhausted all asylum appeals but had then made an application for ELR on the grounds that return would breach article 3 ECHR was refused support on the ground that the Immigration Service had said there was no outstanding asylum claim. The applicant argued *inter alia* that Lambeth should have accommodated him under regulation 4 pending the result of those enquires. Interim relief was granted on an ex p hearing. Subsequently the Immigration Service were added as a proposed respondent. The applicant was given ELR and the case did not go further.

Regulation 2(1) defines dependants to be people in the following relationships to the asylum claimant or dependant claiming of an asylum seeker claiming support:

2(1)(c) children under 18 who are a member of the his/her or his/her spouse's close family;

2(1)(d) children under 18 who have been living as part of his/her household for at least six of 12 months before the date of the application for support 2(1)(d)(i)), or since birth ((2)(1)(d)(ii))if this is shorter;

2(1)(e) persons over 18 in need of care and attention from the him/her or a member of his/her household by reason of a disability who have been living with him/her for at least six of the 12 months before the date of the application;

2(1)(f) unmarried partners who have been living with him/her for at least 2 of the 3 years preceding the date of the claim for support. The wording of the regulation would appear to be broad enough to cover same-sex partners although this is not expressly stated;

2(1)(g) persons living as part of his/her household and receiving assistance from a local authority under section 17 of the Children Act 1989 immediately before the beginning of the interim period;

2(1)(h) dependants on the application for asylum or the asylum seeker in respect of whom the person claiming support is a dependant;

Regulations 2(1)(a) and 2(1)(b) repeat for the purposes of the interim period the definitions (a) and (b) respectively of dependant in section 94 of the Act. In *R v London Borough of Camden ex p Diirshe* CO/5069/99 it was held that the minor children of a supported person do not have to show a financial dependency.

Diirshe also raises the question of whether the children of the asylum seeker can rely on regulations 2(1)(c) and (d), which do not include a test of dependency.

1(3) The regulations do not extend to Northern Ireland.

2—(1) The regulations must provide for the question whether a person is an eligible person to be determined by the local authority concerned.

(2) The regulations may make provision for support to be provided, before the determination of that question, to a person making a claim for support under the regulations by the Secretary of State or such local authority as may be prescribed.

(3) 'The local authority concerned' has such meaning as may be prescribed.

Note 2(1) See regulation 3 which repeats this provision. Regulation 3(3) identifies the local authority concerned as the local authority to whom an application for support is made, or to whom it is transferred under regulation 9.

2(2) Regulation 4 makes such provision. Local authorities are obliged to provide such support. The local authority which must provide such support is the local authority to whom the claim is made unless the claim is transferred under regulation

2(3) Regulation 1 prescribes that local authority means:

(a) in England a country council, metropolitan district council, district council, the common council of the City of London or the Council of the Isles of Scilly;

(b) in Wales, a county council or a country borough council.

The effect of the definition is to that the interim scheme does not extend to Scotland or to Northern Ireland.

---

3 Subsections (3) to (8) of section 95 apply for the purposes of the regulations as they apply for the purposes of that section, but for the references in subsections (5) and (7) to the Secretary of State substitute references to the ocal authority concerned.

Note   This paragraph has the effect of applying the test of destitution set out in section 95 (see notes on that section) to the interim scheme.

---

4   The regulations may prescribe circumstances in which support for an eligible person—

(a) must be provided;
(b) must or may be refused; or
(c) must or may be suspended or discontinued.

Note   *4(a)* Regulation 3 provides that the local authority must provide to support to eligible persons for which see the note on paragraph 1(2) above.

   4(b) Regulation 7 sets out the circumstances in which support must be refused. No provisions have been made as to circumstances in which support may be refused. Support must be refused if the person:

— 7(1)(a) the person has made him/herself intentionally destitute, defined in regulation 7(2) to be where the person appears to be, or likely within 14 days to become destitute as a result of a deliberate act or omission done by him or by a dependant without reasonable excuse.
— 7(1)(b) has made a claim for support to another local authority save where the two authorities have agreed to a transfer (see regulation 9).
— 7(1)(c) has made a claim for support to another local authority under section 21 of the National Assistance Act 1948 or under section 17 of the Children Act 1989 in the past 12 months. Note that regulation 11 provided for the transfer of existing National Assistance Act and Children Act cases to the interim scheme on 6 December 1999. Thus where support was given under these acts the cases fall to be treated in the same way as cases under regulation 7(1)(b). Where such applications were refused, the effect of this regulation appears to be that the person must return to the local authority who refused the National Assistance Act or Children Act support, if s/he now wishes to make an application under the interim scheme. No guidance is given as to what should be done with anyone who, in the past 12 months, made unsuccessful applications to more than one local authority.
— 7(1)(d) is entitled to benefits. The entitlements in question are set out in 7(1)(d). This is provision at first sight appears otiose, given that those in receipt of benefits would not satisfy the destitution test in any event. However, it has the function of ensuring that those entitled to benefits cannot instead opt for support under the scheme.

4(c) Regulation 8 sets out the circumstances in which support must be suspended or discontinued. Regulation 8(1) provides that support must be discontinued as soon as the local authority becomes aware of any circumstance which would have led to the application being refused under 7(1)(a). There is no provision for notice to be given in these circumstances.

Regulation 8(2) provides that support may be suspended or discontinued:

— 8(2)(a) where the person assisted, or any dependant fails without reasonable excuse to comply with a condition on which support is provided. See note on paragraph 6 below.

— 8(2)(b) where the assisted person or any dependant of his leaves the accommodation provided 'as part of such support' for more than seven consecutive days without reasonable excuse. Note that under regulation 5(1), a person without dependant children under 18 can only receive support under the scheme in the form of accommodation and essential living needs. In the cases of such people, their accommodation will thus always have been provided 'as part of such support'. However, where the supported person has dependants under 18, regulation 5(2) provides that the family can receive support in the form of either accommodation only, or support for essential living needs, or a package with both. Thus regulation 8(2)(b) does not appear to cover the situation where a family supplying its own accommodation leaves that accommodation, even though it is receiving support for essential living needs at that address. Contrast in this regard the Asylum Support Regulations 2000, SI 2000/704, regulation 22(3)(b).

---

5 The regulations may provide that support—

(a) is to be provided in prescribed ways;
(b) is not to be provided in prescribed ways.

Note Regulation 5 provides that those without dependent children can be provided with a package including accommodation appearing to the local authority to be adequate for the assisted person and any dependants (regulation 5(1)(a)) and what appear to the local authority to be the essential living needs (regulation 5(1)(b)). A maximum of £10 per week can be given in cash (regulation 5(5)). For those with dependent children under 18, the situation is different. They can be provided with support for essential living needs and/or accommodation (regulation 5(2) and there is no limit on how much of the support can be provided in cash (regulation 5(5)(a)). The local authority is not obliged to provide cash to any supported person. There is a further provision in section 5(5)(b) that where the circumstances of the particular case are exceptional, the £10 limit on cash support can be exceeded. Under regulation 5(3)(b) the local authority is obliged to ensure that an asylum seeker can meet the reasonable expenses of travelling to interviews 'requested by the Secretary of State' 'in connection with the claim for asylum'. This is broad enough to cover Home Office interviews and interviews at ports and is not limited to substantive asylum interviews or otherwise. Regulation 5(3)(b) makes the same provision in respect of travel to 'a hearing of his appeal'. The use of the indefinite article appears to make this provision sufficiently broad to cover interlocutory hearings. There is no provision to pay dependants to travel to interviews or hearings, nor to enable the asylum seeker to attend these other than for his/her own case, for example as a witness. Nor is any reference made to payment of travel to attend bail hearings, either by asylum seekers or their dependants (contrast the powers under section 96(1)(d)).

There is no definition of 'essential living needs' in the regulations and it remains to be seen whether or not it will be accepted that the need to travel to a bail hearing, or to travel to see a legal representative, is an 'essential living need' of an asylum seeker. The Consultation Document on main regulations under Part VI of the Immigration and Asylum Act 1999 (National Asylum Support Service, November 1999) dealt with them expressly (favouring payment of travel to bail hearings, but not payment of travel to legal representatives). However, the Asylum Support Regulations 2000 (SI 2000/704) make provision only for the initial journey to a dispersal location (regulation 9 of SI 2000/704) and regulation 9(4)(d) of SI 2000/705 expressly excludes other travel expenses from the definition of essential living needs for the purposes of those regulations. Finally regulation 5(4) provides for support to be provided 'in such other ways as are necessary' where 'the circumstances of a particular case are exceptional'. This is in addition to the power to give more than £10 per week in cash under regulation 5(5)(b).

---

6 The regulations may include provision—

(a) as to the level of support that is to be provided;
(b) for support to be provided subject to conditions;
(c) requiring any such conditions to be set out in writing;

requiring a copy of any such conditions to be given to such person as may be prescribed.

Note *6 (a)* No regulations have been made as to the level of support.

6(b) to (d) See regulation 5 which reflects these provisions. Under regulation 5(6) the local authority is not obliged to place conditions on the support it provides. If it chooses to do so then the conditions must be set out in writing (5(7)) and a copy given to the supported person (5(8)).

A number of cases have been commenced where local authorities have cut the level of support, or paid less than the prescribed NASS levels under SI 2000/704. Most have been resolved before reaching court. In *R v London Borough of Camden ex p Kwiek* 12 April 2000, Camden had cut support of £85 per week plus rent to £64 per week plus rent (thus removing the payment in respect of the mother) and then to nothing for an asylum seeker and her children on the basis of suspicions that the applicant was sub-letting and because of equipment found on the property. A mandatory injunction forced Camden to restore the payments of £64 per week. Although on the facts of the case the judge refused leave on the basis that Camden was entitled to reduce support because of evidence of other income, during the leave hearing payment was restored to £85 per week plus rent.

---

7 The regulations may make provision that, in providing support, a local authority—

(a) are to have regard to such matters as may be prescribed;
(b) are not to have regard to such matters as may be prescribed.

Note *7(a)* Regulation 6(1) provides that the local authority must have regard to:
  — 6(1)(a) income,
  — (6(1)(b) support or assets
which the assisted person or dependants have or might reasonably be expected to have. The question of income which a person has, and in particular that which s/he might reasonably be expected to have, was the subject of much debate during the passage of the Act. Particular concern was expressed that support might be reduced on the basis that voluntary organisations, for example faith groups, had provided clothing, food or other goods, and there was felt to be a lack of clarity as to what might constitute a 'reasonable expectation' that they would provide such goods. Ministers stated that they would not seek to force voluntary organisations to provide such support, by denying support under the scheme on the expectation that voluntary organisations could provide. However, the concern of voluntary organisations was somewhat different. They feared that they would not be free to top up what they perceived to be an inadequate level of support, because statutory support would be reduced to take account of this (see *Hansard*, HC Report, Special Standing Committee on the Immigration and Asylum Bill, Twentieth Sitting, Tuesday, 11 May 1999, cols 1378 to 1387 and HL Report, vol 605, no 138, cols 1165 to 1177 and 1193 to 1200). See the notes to Schedule 8, paragraph 2(1)(b).

There was also much debate on the question of assets (see for example, Hansard, HC Report, Special Standing Committee on the Immigration and Asylum Bill, Twentieth Sitting, Tuesday, 11 May 1999, cols 1382 to 1390) much of it concerned with whether people would denied support if they possessed personal jewellery of any value, and thus forced to sell it or remain destitute. Under SI 2000/705, governing the main support scheme, personal jewellry is valued but is not taken into consideration until sold. See the notes to the application form which appear as a schedule to SI 2000/705. See now SI 2000/464.

— 6(1)(c) provides that the local authority must take into account the welfare of the assisted person and any dependant

— 6(1)(d) provides that it must taken into account the cost of providing support.

The welfare of the supported person is potentially a term with very broad scope. See *R v Waltham Forest ex p Haile* CO/4756. Permission to apply for judicial review was granted and the Secretary of State joined to the proceedings. The local authority subsequently conceded that it was not lawful for it to disperse without its considering the welfare of the asylum seeker and dependants, and the how the dispersal would impact upon these, and the case went no further.

7(b) Regulation 6(2) provides that the local authority must not have regard to the assisted person or his dependants' preferences as to the location or nature of the accommodation or as to the nature or standard of fixtures and fittings in that accommodation. During the passage of the Act, Ministers were at pains to state during the debates on a similar provision, now 97(2)(a) that a prohibition on taking into account preferences was not a prohibition on taking into account circumstances (see for example, Hansard, HC Report, Special Standing Committee on the Immigration and Asylum Bill, Nineteenth Sitting, Tuesday 24 May 1999, cols 1346 to 1349). A 'preference' for a certain town because one's cousin lived there could not be taken into account, but the fact that one's cousin lived there could be taken into account as a 'circumstance'.

8   The regulations may include provision—

(a) prescribing particular areas, or descriptions of area, (which may include a locality within their own area) in which a local authority may not place asylum-seekers while providing support for them;

(b) prescribing circumstances in which a particular area, or description of area, (which may include a locality within their own area) is to be one in which a local authority may not place asylum-seekers while providing support for them;

(c) as to the circumstances (if any) in which any such provision is not to apply.

Note   No regulations have been made reflecting this paragraph. However, a letter of 19 November 1999 from the Director of the National Asylum Support Service to all Chief Executives of Local Authorities in England and Wales enclosed as an annexe a draft of regulations that could be made to reflect paragraphs 8 and 9 of this Schedule.

The letter states that it is at the request of the Local Government Association that these regulations have not been made, but that if the voluntary arrangements between local authorities on which the interim scheme is based do not have the desired effect (of dispersal) 'Ministers will not hesitate to bring into force new regulations that rely on those powers, possibly at short notice'.

9—(1)   The regulations may make provision for the referral by one local authority to another of a claim for support made under the regulations if the local authority to whom the claim is made consider that it is not manifestly unfounded but—

(a) they are providing support for a number of asylum-seekers equal to, or greater than, the maximum number of asylum-seekers applicable to them; or

(b) they are providing support for a number of eligible persons equal to, or greater than, the maximum number of eligible persons applicable to them.

(2) For the purposes of any provision made as a result of sub-paragraph (1), the regulations may make provision for the determination by the Secretary of State of—

(a) the applicable maximum number of asylum-seekers;
(b) the applicable maximum number of eligible persons.

(3) The regulations may make provision for any such determination to be made—

(a) for local authorities generally;
(b) for prescribed descriptions of local authority; or
(c) for particular local authorities.

(4) The regulations may provide that a referral may not be made—

(a) to a prescribed local authority;
(b) to local authorities of a prescribed description; or
(c) in prescribed circumstances.

(5) The regulations may make provision for the payment by a local authority of any reasonable travel or subsistence expenses incurred as a result of a referral made by them.

(6) The regulations may make provision for the transfer of a claim for support, or responsibility for providing support, under the regulations from one local authority to another on such terms as may be agreed between them.

(7) In exercising any power under the regulations to refer or transfer, a local authority must have regard to such guidance as may be issued by the Secretary of State with respect to the exercise of the power.

Note The only regulation that has been made reflecting this paragraph is regulation 9 which provides that a local authority may transfer a claim for support, or responsibility for providing support to another local authority on such terms as may be agreed between them. The consent of both local authorities is required. The interim scheme for support thus operates on the basis of voluntary arrangements made between local authorities. See the note on paragraph 8 above.

See *R v London Borough Newham ex p Ally* CO/220/2000 21 January 2000. Newham proposed to move an asylum seeker whom they were accommodating in Great Yarmouth without consulting the asylum seeker. A telephone injunction was granted prohibiting this (Jackson J). Newham subsequently consulted and the application was withdrawn. Newham was not ordered to pay the applicants costs.

In *R v City of Westminster ex p Guimares* 17 April 2000 Westminster evicted two boys aged 19 and 21 on the grounds of fighting with other applicants and having visitors without permission. Westminster subsequently agreed to reconsider the allegations and to accommodate the two boys in the interim, but proposed to house them in Liverpool. Westminster asserted that no accommodation was available in London. The applicants, who did not claim to have special needs, argued that the decision that there was no accommodation for them in London was perverse. They obtained an ex p interim injunction obliging Westminster to accommodate in London, which they did. The *inter partes* hearing never took place because the boys were granted Exceptional Leave to Remain in the meantime.

See *R v Hammersmith & Fulham Borough Council ex p Isik* (CO/00/1945, CA3813/00, CA, 15 August 2000 (permission), 19 September 2000 3813/00). In this case the Court of Appeal granted permission to apply for judicial review, the High Court having refused it. Permission was accompanied by an order that Hammersmith and Fulham support the family in London the interim. The family had lived in London for nearly a year and a half when Hammersmith and Fulham sought to disperse them to Hull. The children were settled in school and the family benefited from non-pecuniary support in London. There was evidence before the Court of Appeal from the school to suggest that the children were traumatised. Following the permission hearing Hammersmith and Fulham agreed to continue to accommodate the family in London. At the full hearing, the Court of Appeal determined that the point was now academic and held that they had no power to award pecuniary damages in the context of the judicial review.

10—(1)   The regulations may make provision for the referral of claims for support made to the Secretary of State to prescribed local authorities or local authorities of a prescribed description.

(2)   The regulations may make provision for the payment by the Secretary of State of any reasonable travel or subsistence expenses incurred as a result of a referral made by him as a result of provision made by virtue of sub-paragraph (1).

11   The regulations may make provision requiring prescribed local authorities or other prescribed bodies to give reasonable assistance to local authorities providing support under the regulations.

Note   Regulation 11 provides that reasonable assistance must be provided on request by district councils for an area where part of the area covered by the district council falls within the areas of the local authority providing support and by registered social landlords (see Part I of the Housing Act 1996) within the area of that local authority.

12   The regulations may make provision for the procedure for making and determining claims for support.

13   The regulations may make provision for an asylum-seeker or a dependant of an asylum-seeker who has received, or is receiving, any prescribed description of support from a local authority to be taken to have been accepted for support under the regulations by a prescribed local authority.

Note   Regulation 11 provides that those who were being supported by the local authority under section 21 of the National Assistance Act 1948 or section 17 of the Children Act 1989 immediately before the beginning of the interim period are to be taken to have been accepted for support by the local authority who was supporting them under these Acts. The extent to which the transitional provision in regulation 11 protects those to whom it applies from having their support terminated in accordance with the provisions of the interim scheme has been considered by the Social Security Commissioners in a number of decisions. See CIS/115/99, CIS/3955/97 and CIS/4609/97. All these cases were considered by the Commissioner in CIS/6258/99. Leave to appeal to the Court of Appeal from that decision was granted.

14   A person entitled to support under the regulations is not entitled to any prescribed description of support, except to such extent (if any) as may be prescribed.

Note   This extremely obscure provision appears to be otiose. Note however regulation 12 which provides that a person entitled to support under the regulations is not entitled to assistance under section 17 of the Children Act 1989. Under regulation 2(4) the reference to assistance under section 17 of the Children Act is to be read for the purposes of the regulations as a reference to 'the provision of accommodation or essential living needs'. The intention behind regulation 12 would appear to be that a family cannot elect for support under section 17 as an alternative to making an application for support under Part VI. Ministers gave assurances during the passage of the Act that where needs that would otherwise fall to be met under section 17 were not being provided for under the support schemes, they would be provided under section 17 (see eg *Hansard* HC Report vol 605, no 138, col 982).

15   'The interim period' means the period—

(a) beginning on such day as may be prescribed for the purposes of this paragraph; and
(b) ending on such day as may be so prescribed.

Note   'The interim period began on 6 December 1999 and ends on 1 April 2002, see regulation 2(5). This would allow the support under the interim scheme and support under the main scheme to overlap for a period of approximately two years, as described in the note on section 94. See also the note to paragraph 14 of Schedule 9 to this Act.

SCHEDULE 10
ASYLUM SUPPORT ADJUDICATORS

[A.1.413]

Commencement   Schedule 10 commenced in full 3 April 2000 (SI 2000/464).

Note   See the Asylum Support Appeals (Procedure) Rules 2000, SI 2000/541) made under section 104 of this Act and the notes to section 104.

Section 102(3)

Adjudicators

1—(1)   The Secretary of State must—

(a) appoint such number of adjudicators as he considers necessary;
(b) appoint one of the adjudicators to be the Chief Asylum Support Adjudicator; and
(c) appoint one of the adjudicators to be the Deputy Chief Asylum Support Adjudicator ('the Deputy').

(2)   The adjudicators are to exercise their functions under the direction of the Chief Asylum Support Adjudicator.
(3)   The Chief Asylum Support Adjudicator is to have such other functions as the Secretary of State may from time to time direct.

(4)   During any vacancy in the office of Chief Asylum Support Adjudicator, or at any time when he is unable to discharge his functions, the Deputy may act in his place.

Note   *1(b)* Mrs Seba Haroon Storey has been appointed as the Chief Asylum Support Adjudicator.

Terms and conditions of appointment

2—(1)   Each adjudicator is to hold and vacate office in accordance with the terms of his appointment.
(2)   An adjudicator is eligible for re-appointment when his term of office ends.
(3)   An adjudicator may resign at any time by notice in writing given to the Secretary of State.

Remuneration, expenses and pensions

3—(1)   The Secretary of State may pay to any adjudicator such remuneration and expenses as he may determine.
(2)   The Secretary of State may pay, or provide for the payment of, such pensions, allowances or gratuities to or in respect of any adjudicator as he may determine.

Compensation

4   If a person ceases to be an adjudicator, otherwise than when his term of office ends, and it appears to the Secretary of State that there are special circumstances which make it right for him to receive compensation, the Secretary of State may make a payment to him of such amount as the Secretary of State may determine.

Staff

5—(1)   The Secretary of State may appoint such staff for the adjudicators as he considers appropriate.
(2)   The Secretary of State may pay, or provide for the payment of, such pensions, allowances or gratuities (including by way of compensation for loss of office or employment) to or in respect of the adjudicators' staff as he considers appropriate.

Expenditure

6   The Secretary of State may pay such other expenses of the adjudicators as he considers appropriate.

Proceedings

7   For the purpose of discharging their functions, adjudicators are to sit at such times and in such places as the Secretary of State may direct.

Commencement   Paragraphs 1–7, 3 April 2000 (SI 2000/464).

SCHEDULE 11
DETAINEE CUSTODY OFFICERS

Section 154(7)

[A.1.414]

Obtaining certificates of authorisation by false pretences

1   A person who, for the purpose of obtaining a certificate of authorisation for himself or for any other person—

(a) makes a statement which he knows to be false in a material particular, or
(b) recklessly makes a statement which is false in a material particular,

is guilty of an offence and liable on summary conviction to a fine not exceeding level 4 on the standard scale.

Commencement   3 April 2000 (SI 2000/464).

Powers and duties of detainee custody officers

2—(1)   A detainee custody officer exercising custodial functions has power—

(a) to search (in accordance with rules made by the Secretary of State) any detained person in relation to whom the officer is exercising custodial functions; and
(b) to search any other person who is in, or is seeking to enter, any place where any such detained person is or is to be held, and any article in the possession of such a person.

(2)   The power conferred by sub-paragraph (1)(b) does not authorise requiring a person to remove any of his clothing other than an outer coat, jacket or glove.
(3)   As respects a detained person in relation to whom he is exercising custodial functions, it is the duty of a detainee custody officer—

(a) to prevent that person's escape from lawful custody;
(b) to prevent, or detect and report on, the commission or attempted commission by him of other unlawful acts;
(c) to ensure good order and discipline on his part; and
(d) to attend to his wellbeing.

(4)   The powers conferred by sub-paragraph (1), and the powers arising by virtue of sub-paragraph (3), include power to use reasonable force where necessary.

***

Commencement   Sub-paragraph 2(1)(a) 1 August 2000 for the purposes of enabling subordinate legislation to be made under it; in full 2 April 2001 (SI 2001/239).

Note   See the Detention Centre Rules 2001 (SI 2001/238), Part IV.

***

Short-term holding facilities

3—(1)   A detainee custody officer may perform functions of a custodial nature at a short-term holding facility (whether or not he is authorised to perform custodial functions at a detention centre).

(2)   When doing so, he is to have the same powers and duties in relation to the facility and persons detained there as he would have if the facility were a detention centre.

***

Commencement   2 April 2001 (SI 2001/239).

***

Assaulting a detainee custody officer

4   A person who assaults a detainee custody officer who is—

(a) acting in accordance with escort arrangements,
(b) performing custodial functions, or
(c) performing functions of a custodial nature at a short-term holding facility,

is guilty of an offence and liable on summary conviction to a fine not exceeding level 5 on the standard scale or to imprisonment for a term not exceeding six months or to both.

***

Commencement   2 April 2001 (SI 2001/239).

***

Obstructing detainee custody officers

5   A person who resists or wilfully obstructs a detainee custody officer who is—

(a) acting in accordance with escort arrangements,
(b) performing custodial functions, or
(c) performing functions of a custodial nature at a short-term holding facility,

is guilty of an offence and liable on summary conviction to a fine not exceeding level 3 on the standard scale

***

Commencement   2 April 2001 (SI 2001/239).

***

Uniforms and badges

6   For the purposes of paragraphs 4 and 5, a detainee custody officer is not to
be regarded as acting in accordance with escort arrangements at any time when
he is not readily identifiable as such an officer (whether by means of a uniform
or badge which he is wearing or otherwise).

Commencement   2 April 2001 (SI 2001/239).

Suspension and revocation of certificates of authorisation

7—(1)   If it appears to the Secretary of State that a detainee custody officer
is not a fit and proper person to perform escort functions or custodial functions, he may revoke that officer's certificate so far as it authorises the performance of those functions.
(2)   If it appears to the escort monitor that a detainee custody officer is not a
fit and proper person to perform escort functions, he may—

(a)   refer the matter to the Secretary of State; or
(b)   in such circumstances as may be prescribed, suspend the officer's certificate pending a decision by the Secretary of State as to whether to revoke
it.

(3)   If it appears to the contract monitor for the detention centre concerned
that a detainee custody officer is not a fit and proper person to perform custodial functions, he may—

(a)   refer the matter to the Secretary of State; or
(b)   in such circumstances as may be prescribed, suspend the officer's certificate pending a decision by the Secretary of State as to whether to revoke
it.

Commencement   Sub-paragraph 7(1), 3 April 2000 (SI 2000/464). Sub-paragraphs
7(2) and (3) 1 August 2000 for the purposes of enabling subordinate legislation to be
made under them. In full 2 April 2001 (SI 2001/239).

Note   See the Immigration (Suspension of Detainee Custody Officer) Regulations
2001 (SI 2001/241), made 28 January 2001, laid before parliament 6 February 2001.

7(2)(b) For the prescribed circumstances, see SI 2001/241, regulation 3. The circumstances are that an allegation has been made a detainee custody officer acting in pursuance of escort arrangements or performing functions at a contracted-out detention
centre, or that the officer has been charged with a criminal offence, or that disciplinary
action is being taken against the officer by his/her employer, or that it appears to the
escort monitor that the officer is, by reason by physical or mental illness, or for any
other reason, incapable of satisfactorily carrying out his duties. For the details of escort
monitors see sections 147 and 156 of this Act.

7(3)(b) The prescribed circumstances are as for 7(2)(b), save that the reference in regulation 3 for the purposes of this sub-paragraph is to the contract monitor, and not the
escort monitor. For details of contract monitors see sections 147 and 149 of this Act.

SCHEDULE 12
DISCIPLINE ETC AT DETENTION CENTRES

[A.1.415]

Section 155(2)

Measuring and photographing detained persons

1—(1)   Detention centre rules may (among other things) provide for detained persons to be measured and photographed.
(2)   The rules may, in particular, prescribe—

(a) the time or times at which detained persons are to be measured and photographed;
(b) the manner and dress in which they are to be measured and photographed; and
(d) the numbers of copies of measurements or photographs that are to be made and the persons to whom they are to be sent.

Commencement   1 August 2000 (SI 2000/1985) for the purposes of allowing subordinate legislation to be made under it; in full 2 April 2001 (SI 2001/239).

Testing for drugs or alcohol

2—(1)   If an authorisation is in force, a detainee custody officer may, at the centre to which the authorisation applies and in accordance with detention centre rules, require a detained person who is confined in the centre to provide a sample for the purpose of ascertaining—

(a) whether he has a drug in his body; or
(b) whether he has alcohol in his body.

(2)   The sample required may be one or more of the following—

(a) a sample of urine;
(b) a sample of breath;
(c) a sample of a specified description.

(3)   Sub-paragraph (2)(c)—

(a) applies only if the authorisation so provides; and
(b) does not authorise the taking of an intimate sample.

(4)   'Authorisation' means an authorisation given by the Secretary of State for the purposes of this paragraph in respect of a particular detention centre.
(5)   'Drug' means a drug which is a controlled drug for the purposes of the Misuse of Drugs Act 1971.
(6)   'Specified' means specified in the authorisation.
(7)   'Intimate sample'—

(a) in relation to England and Wales, has the same meaning as in Part V of the Police and Criminal Evidence Act 1984;
(b) in relation to Scotland, means—
   (i) a sample of blood, semen or any other tissue fluid, urine or pubic hair;
   (ii) a dental impression;
   (iii) a swab taken from a person's body orifice other than the mouth; and
(c) in relation to Northern Ireland, has the same meaning as in Part VI of the Police and Criminal Evidence (Northern Ireland) Order 1989.

Commencement 1 August 2000 (SI 2000/1985) for the purposes of allowing subordinate legislation to be made under it; in full 2 April 2001 (SI 2001/239).

Medical examinations

3—(1) This paragraph applies if—

(a) an authorisation is in force for a detention centre; and
(b) there are reasonable grounds for believing that a person detained in the centre is suffering from a disease which is specified in an order in force under sub-paragraph (7).

(2) A detainee custody officer may require the detained person to submit to a medical examination at the centre.
(3) The medical examination must be conducted in accordance with detention centre rules.
(4) A detained person who fails, without reasonable excuse, to submit to a medical examination required under this paragraph is guilty of an offence.
(5) A person guilty of an offence under sub-paragraph (4) is liable on summary conviction to imprisonment for a term not exceeding six months or to a fine not exceeding level 5 on the standard scale.
(6) 'Authorisation' means an authorisation given by the manager of the detention centre for the purpose of this paragraph.
(7) The Secretary of State may by order specify any disease which he considers might, if a person detained in a detention centre were to suffer from it, endanger the health of others there.

Commencement Sub-paragraph (7), 1 August 2000 (SI 2000/1985) for the purposes of allowing subordinate legislation to be made under it. Sub paragraphs (1)–(6), 2 April 2001 (SI 2001/239.)

Note See the Detention Centre (Specified Diseases) Order 2001 (SI 2001/240) made 28 January 2001, laid before parliament 6 February 2001, into force 2 April 2001.

3(7) The Schedule to SI 2001/240 specifies some 33 diseases, ranging from yellow fever, plague and cholera through measles and mumps to food poisoning and relapsing fever.

Assisting detained persons to escape

4—(1) A person who aids any detained person in escaping or attempting to escape from a detention centre or short-term holding facility is guilty of an offence.

(2)   A person who, with intent to facilitate the escape of any detained person from a detention centre or short-term holding facility—

(a) conveys any thing into the centre or facility or to a detained person,
(b) sends any thing (by post or otherwise) into the centre or facility or to a person detained there,
(c) places any thing anywhere outside the centre or facility with a view to its coming into the possession of a person detained there,

is guilty of an offence.

(3)   A person guilty of an offence under this section is liable—

(a) on summary conviction, to imprisonment for a term not exceeding six months or to a fine not exceeding the statutory maximum or to both; or
(b) on conviction on indictment, to imprisonment for a term not exceeding two years or to a fine or to both.

Commencement   2 April 2001 (SI 2001/239).

Alcohol

5—(1)   A person who, contrary to detention centre rules, brings or attempts to bring any alcohol into a detention centre, or to a detained person, is guilty of an offence.

(2)   A person who places alcohol anywhere outside a detention centre, intending that it should come into the possession of a detained person there, is guilty of an offence.

(3)   A detainee custody officer or any other person on the staff of a detention centre who, contrary to detention centre rules, allows alcohol to be sold or used in the centre is guilty of an offence.

(4)   A person guilty of an offence under this paragraph is liable on summary conviction to imprisonment for a term not exceeding six months or to a fine not exceeding level 3 on the standard scale or to both.

(5)   'Alcohol' means any spirituous or fermented liquor.

Commencement   2 April 2001 (SI 2001/239).

Introduction of other articles

6—(1)   A person who—

(a) conveys or attempts to convey any thing into or out of a detention centre or to a detained person, contrary to detention centre rules, and
(b) is not as a result guilty of an offence under paragraph 4 or 5,

is guilty of an offence under this paragraph.

(2)   A person who—

(a) places any thing anywhere outside a detention centre, intending it to come into the possession of a detained person, and
(b) is not as a result guilty of an offence under paragraph 4 or 5,

is guilty of an offence under this paragraph.

(3)   A person guilty of an offence under this paragraph is liable on summary conviction to a fine not exceeding level 3 on the standard scale.

Commencement   2 April 2001 (SI 2001/239).

Notice of penalties

7—(1)   In the case of a contracted out detention centre, the contractor must cause a notice setting out the penalty to which a person committing an offence under paragraph 4, 5 or 6 is liable to be fixed outside the centre in a conspicuous place.

(2)   In the case of any other detention centre, the Secretary of State must cause such a notice to be fixed outside the centre in a conspicuous place.

Commencement   2 April 2001 (SI 2001/239)

8—(1)   In the case of a contracted out short-term holding facility, the contractor must cause a notice setting out the penalty to which a person committing an offence under paragraph 4 is liable to be fixed outside the facility in a conspicuous place.

(2)   In the case of any other short-term holding facility, the Secretary of State must cause such a notice to be fixed outside the facility in a conspicuous place.

Commencement   2 April 2001 (SI 2001/239).

SCHEDULE 13
ESCORT ARRANGEMENTS

[A.1.416]

Section 156(5)

Monitoring of escort arrangements

1—(1)   Escort arrangements must include provision for the appointment of a Crown servant as escort monitor.

(2)   The escort monitor must—

(a) keep the escort arrangements under review and report on them to the Secretary of State as required in accordance with the arrangements;

(b) from time to time inspect the conditions in which detained persons are transported or held in accordance with the escort arrangements;

(c) make recommendations to the Secretary of State, with a view to improving those conditions, whenever he considers it appropriate to do so;

(d) investigate, and report to the Secretary of State on, any allegation made against a detainee custody officer or prisoner custody officer in respect of any act done, or failure to act, when carrying out functions under the arrangements;

(3)   Paragraph (d) of sub-paragraph (2) does not apply in relation to—

(a) detainee custody officers employed as part of the Secretary of State's staff; or

(b) an act or omission of a prisoner custody officer so far as it falls to be investigated by a prisoner escort monitor under section 81 of the Criminal Justice Act 1991 or under section 103 or 119 of the Criminal Justice and Public Order Act 1994.

Commencement   2 April 2001 (SI 2001/239).

Powers and duties of detainee custody officers

2—(1)   A detainee custody officer acting in accordance with escort arrangements has power—

(a) to search (in accordance with rules made by the Secretary of State) any detained person for whose delivery or custody the officer is responsible in accordance with the arrangements; and

(b) to search any other person who is in, or is seeking to enter, any place where any such detained person is or is to be held, and any article in the possession of such a person.

(2)   The power conferred by sub-paragraph (1)(b) does not authorise requiring a person to remove any of his clothing other than an outer coat, jacket or glove.

(3)   As respects a detained person for whose delivery or custody he is responsible in accordance with escort arrangements, it is the duty of a detainee custody officer—

(a) to prevent that person's escape from lawful custody;

(b) to prevent, or detect and report on, the commission or attempted commission by him of other unlawful acts;

(c) to ensure good order and discipline on his part; and

(d) to attend to his wellbeing.

(4)   The Secretary of State may make rules with respect to the performance by detainee custody officers of their duty under sub-paragraph (3)(d).

(5)   The powers conferred by sub-paragraph (1), and the powers arising by virtue of sub-paragraph (3), include power to use reasonable force where necessary.

Commencement   Subparagraphs 2(1)(a) and 2(4), 1 August 2000 for the purposes of enabling subordinate legislation to be made under them. For remaining purposes 2 April 2001 (SI 2001/239).

Breaches of discipline

3—(1)   Sub-paragraph (2) applies if a detained person for whose delivery or custody a person ('A') has been responsible in accordance with escort arrangements is delivered to a detention centre.

(2)   The detained person is to be treated, for the purposes of such detention

centre rules as relate to disciplinary offences, as if he had been in the custody of the director of the detention centre at all times while A was so responsible.
(3)   Sub-paragraph (4) applies if a detained person for whose delivery or custody a person ('B') has been responsible in accordance with escort arrangements is delivered to a prison.
(4)   The detained person is to be treated, for the purposes of such prison rules as relate to disciplinary offences, as if he had been in the custody of the governor or controller of the prison at all times while B was so responsible.
(5)   'Director' means—

(a) in the case of a contracted out detention centre, the person appointed by the Secretary of State in relation to the centre under section 149 or such other person as the Secretary of State may appoint for the purposes of this paragraph;
(b) in the case of any other detention centre, the manager of the detention centre.

(6)   This paragraph does not authorise the punishment of a detained person under detention centre rules or prison rules in respect of any act or omission of his for which he has already been punished by a court.
(7)   'Prison rules' means—

(a) rules made under section 47 of the Prison Act 1952;
(b) rules made under section 19 of the Prisons (Scotland) Act 1989;
(c) rules made under section 13 of the Prison Act (Northern Ireland) 1953.

Commencement   2 April 2001 (SI 2001/239).

SCHEDULE 14
CONSEQUENTIAL AMENDMENTS

Section 169(1)

[A.1.417]

Note   See SI 2000/1985 Immigration and Asylum Act 1999 (Consequential and Transitional Provisions) Order 2000 and SI 2000/2444 Immigration and Asylum Act 1999 (Commencement No 6, Transitional and Consequential Provisions) Order 2000, for important transitional provisions, in particular relating to the 1971 Immigration Act, the Asylum and Immigration Appeals Act 1993, and the Asylum and Immigration Act 1996. See also SI 2000/2333 Immigration and Asylum Appeals (Procedure) Rules, Rule 4 for transitional provisions with regard to the procedure rules applicable to appeals.

See also SI 2000/3099 The Immigration and Asylum Act 1999 (Commencement No 8 and Transitional Provisions) Order 2000 inserting a transitional provision into Commencement Order No 7 (SI 2000/2698) for marriages where notice had been entered in the marriage notice book before 1 January 2001. Commencement Order No 8 also makes further transitional provisions relating to appeals, for which see the notes at the beginning of Part IV.

(Makes consequential amendments to The Marriages (Ireland) Act 1844, The Marriage Law (Ireland) Amendment Act 1863, The Marriage Act 1949, The Prison Act 1952, The Firearms Act 1968, The Family Law Reform Act 1969,

The Marriage (Registrar General's Licence) Act 1970, The Immigration Act 1971, The House of Commons Disqualification Act 1975, The Northern Ireland Assembly Disqualification Act 1975, The Protection from Eviction Act 1977, The Education (Scotland) Act 1980, The Firearms (Northern Ireland) Order 1981 (SI 1981/ISS (NI 2)), The Magistrates' Courts (Northern Ireland) Order 1981 (SI 1981/1675 (NI 26)), The Marriage Act 1983, The Housing (Northern Ireland) Order 1983 (SI 1983/1118 (NI 15). The Rent (Scotland) Act 1984, The Police and Criminal Evidence Act 1984, The Housing Act 1985, The Housing (Scotland) Act 1987, The Immigration Act 1988, The Prevention of Terrorism (Temporary Provisions) Act 1989, The Police and Criminal Evidence (Northern Ireland) Order 1989 (SI 1989/1341 (NI 12)), The Courts and Legal Services Act 1990, The Social Security Contributions and Benefits Act 1992, The Social Security Contributions and Benefits (Northern Ireland) Act 1992, The Tribunals and Inquiries Act 1992, The Judicial Pensions and Retirement Act 1993, The Asylum and Immigration Appeals Act 1993, The Asylum and Immigration Act 1996, The Housing Act 1996, The Education Act 1996, The Special Immigration Appeals Commission Act 1997.)

SCHEDULE 15
TRANSITIONAL PROVISIONS AND SAVINGS

Section 169(2)

[A.1.418]

Note   See SI 2000/1985 The Immigration and Asylum Act 1999 (Consequential and Transitional Provisions) Order 2000 and SI 2000/2444 The Immigration and Asylum Act 1999 (Commencement No 6, Transitional and Consequential Provisions) Order 2000, for important transitional provisions, in particular relating to the 1971 Immigration Act, the Asylum and Immigration Appeals Act 1993, and the Asylum and Immigration Act 1996. See also SI 2000/2333 The Immigration and Asylum Appeals (Procedure) Rules, Rule 4 for transitional provisions with regard to the procedure rules applicable to appeals.

See also the Immigration and Asylum Act (Commencement No 2 and Transitional Provisions) Order1999 (SI 1999/3190).

See also Immigration and Asylum Act 1999 (Commencement No 8 and Transitional Provisions) Order 2000 (SI 2000/3099) inserting a transitional provision into Commencement Order No 7 (SI 2000/2698) for marriages where notice had been entered in the marriage notice book before 1 January 2001. Commencement Order No 8 also made further transitional provisions relating to appeals, for which see the notes at the beginning of Part IV above.

Leave to enter or remain

1—(1)   An order made under section 3A of the 1971 Act may make provision with respect to leave given before the commencement of section 1.
(2)   An order made under section 3B of the 1971 Act may make provision with respect to leave given before the commencement of section 2.

Commencement   14 February 2000 (SI 2000/168).

Section 2 of the Asylum and Immigration Act 1996

2—(1) This paragraph applies in relation to any time before the commencement of the repeal by this Act of section 2 of the Asylum and Immigration Act 1996.
(2) That section has effect, and is to be deemed always to have had effect, as if the reference to section 6 of the Asylum and Immigration Appeals Act 1993 were a reference to section 15, and any certificate issued under that section is to be read accordingly.

Commencement On Royal Assent (section 170(3)).

Adjudicators and the Tribunal

3—(1) Each existing member of the Tribunal is to continue as a member of the Tribunal as if he had been duly appointed by the Lord Chancellor under Schedule 2.
(2) Each existing adjudicator is to continue as an adjudicator as if he had been duly appointed by the Lord Chancellor under Schedule 3.
(3) The terms and conditions for a person to whom sub-paragraph (1) or (2) applies remain those on which he held office immediately before the appropriate date.
(4) The provisions of Schedule 7 to the Judicial Pensions and Retirement Act 1993 (transitional provisions for retirement dates), so far as applicable in relation to an existing member or adjudicator immediately before the appropriate date, continue to have effect.
(5) The repeal by this Act of Schedule 5 to the 1971 Act (provisions with respect to adjudicators and the Tribunal) does not affect any entitlement which an existing member or adjudicator had immediately before the appropriate date as a result of a determination made under paragraph 3(1)(b) or 9(1)(b) of that Schedule.
(6) 'The appropriate date' means—

(a) in relation to existing members of the Tribunal, the date on which section 56 comes into force; and
(b) in relation to existing adjudicators, the date on which section 57 comes into force.

(7) 'Existing member' means a person who is a member of the Tribunal immediately before the appropriate date.
(8) 'Existing adjudicator' means a person who is an adjudicator immediately before the appropriate date.

Commencement 14 February 2000 (SI 2000/168).

References to justices' chief executive

4 At any time before the coming into force of section 90 of the Access to Justice Act 1999—

(a) the reference in section 48(3)(b) to the justices' chief executive appointed by the magistrates' court committee whose area includes the petty sessions area for which the specified court acts is to be read as a reference to the clerk of that court; and

(b) the reference in section 28K(9)(a) and (10) of the 1971 Act (inserted by section 138) to the justices' chief executive appointed by the magistrates' court committee whose area includes the petty sessions area for which the justice acts is to be read as a reference to the clerk to the justices for the petty sessions area for which the justice acts.

Commencement   Paragraph 4(b) 14 February 2000 (SI 2000/168).

Duties under National Assistance Act 1948

5   Section 116 has effect, in relation to any time before section 115 is brought into force, as if section 115 came into force on the passing of this Act.

Commencement   6 December 1999 (SI 1999/3190).

Duties under Health Services and Public Health Act 1968

6   Section 117(1) has effect, in relation to any time before section 115 is brought into force, as if section 115 came into force on the passing of this Act.

Commencement   6 December 1999 (SI 1999/3190).

Duties under Social Work (Scotland) Act 1968

7   Subsections (1) to (3) of section 120 have effect, in relation to any time before section 115 is brought into force, as if section 115 came into force on the passing of this Act.

Duties under Health and Personal Social Services (Northern Ireland) Order 1972

8   Subsections (1) and (2) of section 121 have effect, in relation to any time before section 115 is brought into force, as if section 115 came into force on the passing of this Act.

Duties under National Health Service Act 1977

9   Section 117(2) has effect, in relation to any time before section 115 is brought into force, as if section 115 came into force on the passing of this Act.

Commencement   6 December 1999 (SI 1999/3190).

Duties under Mental Health (Scotland) Act 1984

10 Subsections (4) and (5) of section 120 have effect, in relation to any time before section 115 is brought into force, as if section 115 came into force on the passing of this Act.

Appeals relating to deportation orders

11 Section 15 of the 1971 Act, section 5 of the Immigration Act 1988 and the Immigration (Restricted Right of Appeal against Deportation) (Exemption) Order 1993 are to continue to have effect in relation to any person on whom the Secretary of State has, before the commencement of the repeal of those sections, served a notice of his decision to make a deportation order.

Commencement   2 October 2000 (SI 2000/2444).

Appeals relating to deportation orders

12—(1)   Sub-paragraph (2) applies if, on the coming into force of section 10, sections 15 of the 1971 Act and 5 of the Immigration Act 1988 have been repealed by this Act.
(2)   Those sections are to continue to have effect in relation to any person—

(a) who applied during the regularisation period fixed by section 9, in accordance with the regulations made under that section, for leave to remain in the United Kingdom, and
(b) on whom the Secretary of State has since served a notice of his decision to make a deportation order.

Commencement   On Royal Assent (section 170(3)) in accordance with section 9. See also SI 2000/2444.

Note   See notes to sections 9 and 10 of this Act. See also The Immigration and Asylum Appeals (Notices) Regulations 2000 (SI 2000/2246), as amended by SI 2001/868, regulation 3 for transitional provision.

Assistance under Part VII of the Housing Act 1996

13—(1)   The Secretary of State may by order provide for any provision of Part VII of the Housing Act 1996 (homelessness) to have effect in relation to section 185(2) persons, during the interim period, with such modifications as may be specified in the order.
(2)   An order under this paragraph may, in particular, include provision—

(a) for the referral of section 185(2) persons by one local housing authority to another by agreement between the authorities;
(b) as to the suitability of accommodation for such persons;
(c) as to out-of-area placements of such persons.

(3)   'Interim period' means the period beginning with the passing of this Act and ending on the coming into force of the repeal of section 186 of the Act of

1996 (asylum-seekers and their dependants) by this Act (as to which see section 117(5)).

(4) 'Local housing authority' has the same meaning as in the Act of 1996.

(5) 'Section 185(2) person' means a person who—

(a) is eligible for housing assistance under Part VII of the Act of 1996 as a result of regulations made under section 185(2) of that Act; and

(b) is not made ineligible by section 186 (or any other provision) of that Act.

(6) The fact that an order may be made under this paragraph only in respect of the interim period does not prevent it from containing provisions of a kind authorised under section 166(3)(a) which are to have continuing effect after the end of that period.

Commencement On Royal Assent (section 170(3))

Note See the Homelessness (Asylum Seekers) (Interim Period) (England) Order 1999 (SI 1999/3126). All references in this note are to this order.

4(2) Article 3(b) adds new subsections 4A and 4B to section 198 of the Housing Act 1996, specifying additional circumstances in which the conditions for referral may be satisfied. These circumstances are that there is a voluntary agreement between the two local housing authorities party to the transfer, confirmed in writing by the receiving authority, and that there is no risk of domestic violence in the area of the receiving authority (new sub-section 4A). Domestic violence is specified, no reference is made to risk of any other type of violence. The new sub-section 4B provides that the authorities need have no regard to the preference of the applicant or 'any person who might reasonably be expected to reside with him' as to the location of accommodation provided, nor to any 'local connection' of the applicant or any such person.

(3) 'Interim Period' See note to paragraph 15 of Schedule 9 to this Act.

Provision of support

14—(1) The Secretary of State may, by directions given to a local authority to whom Schedule 9 applies, require the authority to treat the interim period fixed for the purposes of that Schedule as coming to an end—

(a) for specified purposes,

(b) in relation to a specified area or locality, or

(c) in relation to persons of a specified description,

on such earlier day as may be specified.

(2) The Secretary of State may, by directions given to an authority to whom an amended provision applies, provide for specified descriptions of person to be treated—

(a) for specified purposes, or

(b) in relation to a specified area or locality,

as being persons to whom section 115 applies during such period as may be specified.

(3) Directions given under this paragraph may—

(a) make such consequential, supplemental or transitional provision as the Secretary of State considers appropriate; and

(b) make different provision for different cases or descriptions of case.

(4) 'Specified' means specified in the directions.

(5) 'Amended provision' means any provision amended by—

(a) section 116;

(b) section 117(1) or (2);

(c) section 120; or

(d) section 121.

Commencement   14 February 2000 (SI 2000/168).

Note   See note to paragraph 15 of Schedule 9 to this Act on the end of the interim period, for which see the note to section 94. This paragraph makes clear that the date provided for under that paragraph is a 'long-stop' date.

SCHEDULE 16
REPEALS

[A.1.419]

Section 169(3)

Chapter	Short title	Extent of repeal
1949 c 76	The Marriage Act 1949	In section 3(1), 'whether by licence or without licence,'.
		Section 26(2).
		In section 27, in subsection (1) 'without licence', subsection (2), in subsection (3)(a) 'in the case of a marriage intended to be solemnized without licence,' and subsection (3)(b).
		In section 27B, in subsections (4) and (6) 'or licence', and in subsection (5) 'or certificate and licence,'.
		In section 28(1), 'or licence'.
		In section 29, every 'or licence'.
		In section 31, in subsection (1) 'without licence', and in subsection (4) 'without licence'.
		Section 32.
		In section 35, in subsection (1) ', or if the marriage is to be by licence, a certificate and a licence,' in subsections (2) and (4) 'or, if the marriage is to be by licence, a certificate and a licence,' and in subsections (2A) and (2B) 'or, if the marriage is to be by licence, a certificate and licence,'
		Section 36.
		In section 37(1), 'without licence'.
		In section 38(1), 'without licence'.
		In section 39(1), 'without licence'.
		Section 40(2).
		Section 49(c).
		In section 50, in subsection (1) 'the certificate or, if notice of marriage has been given to more than one superintendent registrar', and subsection (2).
		In section 51(1), from first 'the sum' to 'case,'.
		In section 75(3), in paragraph (b) 'or licence'.
		In Schedule 4, in Part III, 'The proviso to subsection (2) of section twenty-six'.
1969 c 46	The Family Law Reform Act 1969	In section 2(3), 'or licence' in both cases

Chapter	Short title	Extent of repeal
1970 c 34	The Marriage (Registrar General's Licence) Act 1970	In section 5, 'or licence'
		Section 13(b).
1971 c 77	The Immigration Act 1971	In section 10(1), from 'and any such Order' to the end.
		Part II.
		In section 24, subsections (1)(aa) and (2).
		Section 25(3).
		In Schedule 2, in paragraph 21(4)(a) 'under paragraph 2 above', in paragraph 26(1) 'and have not been given leave' and paragraph 28.
		In Schedule 3, in paragraph3, 'in paragraph 28(2), (3) and (6) and'.
		Schedule 5.
1975 c 24	The House of Commons Disqualification Act 1975	In Schedule 1, in Part III, 'Adjudicator appointed for the purposes of the Immi gration Act 1971'.
1975 c 25	The Northern Ireland Assembly Disqualification Act 1975	In Schedule 1, in Part III, 'Adjudicator appointed for the purposes of the Immi-gration Act 1971'.
1987 c 24	The Immigration (Carriers' Liability) Act 1987	The whole Act.
1988 c 14	The Immigration Act 1988	Section 5.
		Section 8.
		Section 9.
1990 c 41	The Courts and Legal Services Act 1990	In Schedule 10, paragraph 34.
		In Schedule 11, in the entry relating to the Immigration Appeal Tribunal, 'appointed under Schedule 5 to the Immigration Act 1971'.
1992 c 4	The Social Security and Benefits Act Contributions 1992	Section 146A.
1992 c 7	The Social Security Contributions and Benefits (Northern Ireland) Act 1992	Section 142A.

Chapter	Short title	Extent of repeal
1993 c 8	The Judicial Pensions and Retirement Act 1993	In Schedule 6, paragraphs 37 and 38.
1993 c 23	The Asylum and Immigration Appeals Act 1993	Section 3.
		Section 4.
		Section 5.
		Section 6.
		Section 7.
		Section 8.
		Section 9.
		Section 10.
		Section 11.
		Section 12.
		Schedule 1.
		Schedule 2.
1996 c 49	The Asylum and Immigration Act 1996	Section 1.
		Section 2.
		Section 3.
		Section 4.
		Section 7.
		Section 9.
		Section 10.
		Section 11.
		In Schedule 2, paragraphs 1(2) and (3), 3 and 4(2).
		In Schedule 3, paragraphs 1, 2 and 5.
1996 c 52	The Housing Act 1996	In section 183(2), in the definition 'eligible for assistance', 'or section 186 (asylum seekers and their dependants)'.
		Section 186.
		In Schedule 16, paragraph 3.
1997 c 68	The Special Immigration Appeals Commission Act 1997	Section 7(4).
		In Schedule 2, paragraph 5.

Notes

1949 c 76	Commencement (Date of Repeal) 1 January 2000 (SI 2000/2698).
1969 c 46	Commencement (Date of Repeal) 1 January 2000 (SI 2000/2698).
1970 c 34	Commencement (Date of Repeal) 1 January 2000 (SI 2000/2698).
1971 c 77	Commencement (Date of repeal) Part II insofar as it repeals section 12 of the 1971 Act, sections 24 and 25, Schedule 2 (insofar as it repeals words in paragraphs 21 and 26 of that Schedule), Schedule 5

	14 February 2000 (SI 2000/168). All remaining entries relating to Part II and Schedules 2 and 2, save for section 22 insofar as that section has effect for the purposes of paragraph 25 of Schedule 2 to the Immigration Act 1971, 2 October 2000 (SI 2000/2444).
1975 c 24	Commencement (Date of Repeal) All repeals 14 February 2000 (SI 2000/168).
1975 c 25	Commencement (Date of Repeal) All repeals 14 February 2000 (SI 2000/168).
1988 c 14	Commencement (Date of Repeal) Section 5 2 October 2000 (SI 2000/2444)
1990 c 41	Commencement (Date of Repeal) All repeals 14 February 2000 (SI 2000/168).
1992 c 4	Commencement (Date of Repeal) 3 April 2000 (SI 2000/464).
1992 c 7	Commencement (Date of Repeal) 3 April 2000 (SI 2000/464).
1993 c 8	Commencement (Date of Repeal) Section 7 14 February 2000 (SI 2000/168); sections 4 and 5 and Sch 1, 3 April 2000 (SI 2000/464). Sections 7,8,9,10 and 11a and Schedule 2, 2 October 2000 (SI 2000/2444). Section 3, 11 December 2000 (SI 2000/3099).
1996 c 49	Commencement (Date of Repeal) Section 9, 1 March 2000 (SI 2000/464). Sections 1,2, 3 and schedules 2 and 3, 2 October 2000 (SI 2000/2444).
1996 c 52	Commencement (Date of Repeal) Paragraph 3 of Schedule 16, 1 March 2000 (SI 2000/464).
1997 c 68	Commencement (Date of Repeal) Section 7(4) and Schedule 2, paragraph 5, 2 October 2000 (SI 2000/2444).

The other provisions set out in this Schedule have yet to be repealed.

A2   Immigration Rules

STATEMENT OF CHANGES IN IMMIGRATION RULES (HC 395)

Date   Laid before Parliament 23 May 1994.

Authority   Immigration Act 1971, s 3(2).

Note   This incorporates amending Statements laid before, or presented to, Parliament on 20 September 1994 (Cmnd 2663), 26 October 1995 (HC 797), 4 January 1996 (Cmnd 3073), 7 March 1996 (HC 274), 2 April 1996 (HC 329), 30 August 1996 (Cmnd 3365), 31 October 1996 (HC 31), 27 February 1997 (HC 338), 29 May 1997 (Cmnd 3669), 5 June 1997 (HC 26), 30 July 1997 (HC 161), 11 May 1998 (Cmnd 3953), October 1998 (Cmnd 4065), 18 November 1999 (HC 22), 28 July 2000 (HC 704) and 2 October 2000 (Cmnd 4851).

Contents

References in bold are to paragraph numbers

Part 1:   General provisions regarding leave to enter or remain in the United Kingdom

INTRODUCTION

[A.2.1]
1   The Home Secretary has made changes in the Rules laid down by him as to the practice to be followed in the administration of the Immigration Acts for regulating entry into and the stay of persons in the United Kingdom and contained in the statement laid before Parliament on 23 March 1990 (HC 251) (as amended). This statement contains the Rules as changed and replaces the provisions of HC 251 (as amended).

2   Immigration Officers, Entry Clearance Officers and all staff of the Home Office Immigration and Nationality [Directorate] will carry out their duties without regard to the race, colour or religion of persons seeking to enter or remain in the United Kingdom [and in compliance with the provisions of the Human Rights Acts 1998].

3   In these Rules words importing the masculine gender include the feminine unless the contrary intention appears.

Note   Words in square brackets inserted by CM 4851.

[A.2.2]
Implementation and transitional provisions
4   These Rules come into effect on 1 October 1994 and will apply to all decisions taken on or after that date save that any application made before 1 October 1994 for entry clearance, leave to enter or remain or variation of leave to enter or remain [, other than an application for leave by a person seeking asylum,] shall be decided under the provisions of HC 251, as amended, as if these Rules had not been made.

[A.2.3]
Application
[5   Save where expressly indicated, these Rules do not apply to those persons who are entitled to enter or remain in the United Kingdom by virtue of the provisions of the Immigration (European Economic Area) Regulations 2000 or Commission Regulation 1251/70. But any person who is not entitled to rely on the provisions of those Regulations is covered by these Rules.]

Note   Substituted by CM 4851.

[A.2.4]
Interpretation
6   In these Rules the following interpretations apply:
'the Immigration Acts' mean the Immigration Act 1971 and the Immigration Act 1988.
'the 1993 Act' is the Asylum and Immigration Appeals Act 1993.
['the 1996 Act' is the Asylum and Immigration Act 1996.]
['the 2000 EEA Regulations' are the Immigration (European Area) Regulations 2000.]

'United Kingdom passport' bears the meaning it has in the Immigration Act 1971.

'Immigration Officer' includes a Customs Officer acting as an Immigration Officer.

['public funds' means:

    (*a*) housing under Part II or III of the Housing Act 1985, Part I or II of the Housing (Scotland) Act 1987, Part II of the Housing (Northern Ireland) Order 1988;

    (*b*) attendance allowance, severe disablement allowance, invalid care allowance and disability living allowance under Part III, income support, family credit, council tax benefit, disability working allowance and housing benefit under Part VII and child benefit under Part IX of the Social Security Contribution and Benefits Act 1992;

    (*c*) attendance allowance, severe disablement allowance, invalid care allowance and disability living allowance under Part III, income support, family credit, disability working allowance, housing benefit under Part VII and child benefit under Part IX of the Social Security Contributions and Benefits (Northern Ireland) Act 1992; and

    (*d*) income-based jobseeker's allowance under the Jobseekers Act 1995.]

['Department of Employment' means the Department for Education and Employment and includes, where appropriate, the equivalent Government Department for Northern Ireland;]

'settled in the United Kingdom' means that the person concerned:

    (*a*) is free from any restriction on the period for which he may remain save that a person entitled to an exemption under Section 8 of the Immigration Act 1971 (otherwise than as a member of the home forces) is not to be regarded as settled in the United Kingdom except in so far as Section 8(5A) so provides; and

    (*b*) is either:

        (i) ordinarily resident in the United Kingdom without having entered or remained in breach of the immigration laws; or

        (ii) despite having entered or remained in breach of the immigration laws, has subsequently entered lawfully or has been granted leave to remain and is ordinarily resident.

'a parent' includes:

    (*a*) the stepfather of a child whose father is dead;

    (*b*) the stepmother of a child whose mother is dead;

    (*c*) the father as well as the mother of an illegitimate child where he is proved to be the father;

    (*d*) an adoptive parent but only where a child was adopted in accordance with a decision taken by the competent administrative authority or court in a country whose adoption orders are recognised by the United Kingdom (except where an application for leave to enter or remain is made under paragraphs 310–316);

    (*e*) in the case of a child born in the United Kingdom who is not a British citizen, a person to whom there has been a genuine transfer of parental responsibility on the ground of the original parent(s)' inability to care for the child.

'visa nationals' are the persons specified in the [Appendix 1] to these Rules who need a visa for the United Kingdom.

'employment', unless the contrary intention appears, includes paid and unpaid employment, self-employment and engaging in business or any professional activity.

[. . .]

['the Human Rights Convention' means the Convention for the Protection of Human Rights and Fundamental Freedoms, agreed by the Council of Europe at Rome on 4th November 1950 as it has effect for the time being in relation to the United Kingdom.]

Note Frequent amendments to this paragraph makes it important to note the following. Before 4 April 1996 the definition covered: housing under the Housing Act 1985; income support family credit, council tax benefit and housing benefit. After 3 April 1996, HC 329 added: attendance allowance, severe disablement allowance, invalid care allowance, disability living allowance, disability working allowance. The position (as at March 1997) is that since 30 October 1996 HC 31 has added child benefit. It also replaces income support with income-based jobseeker's allowance (JSA). This definition does not include contributions-based JSA. The definition of 'visa national' was amended with effect from 11 May 1998 (Cmnd 3953). On each occasion the definitions have included the equivalent provisions under legislation for Scotland and Northern Ireland.

Words in square brackets beginning 'the 2000 EEA Regulations' substituted by CM 4851.

Definitions of 'EEA national' and 'family member' following the definition of 'employment' omitted by CM 4851.

Words in square brackets beginning 'the Human Rights Convention' inserted by CM 4851.

[6A   For the purpose of these Rules, a person is not to be regarded as having (or potentially having) recourse to public funds merely because he is (or will be) reliant in whole or in part on public funds provided to his sponsor, unless, as a result of his presence in the United Kingdom, the sponsor is (or would be) entitled to increased or additional public funds).]

Note Inserted by CM 4851.

Part 1:   General provisions regarding leave to enter or remain in the United Kingdom

[A.2.5]
Leave to enter the United Kingdom

[7   A person who is neither a British citizen nor a Commonwealth citizen with the right of abode nor a person who is entitled to enter or remain in the United Kingdom by virtue of the provisions of the Immigration (European Economic Area) Regulations 2000 or Commission Regulation 1251/70 requires leave to enter the United Kingdom.]

Note Substituted by CM 4851.

[8   Under Sections 3 and 4 of the Immigration Act 1971 an Immigration Officer when admitting to the United Kingdom a person subject to control under that Act may give leave to enter for a limited period and, if he does, may impose all or any of the following conditions:

  (i) a condition restricting employment or occupation in the United Kingdom;
  (ii) a condition requiring the person to maintain and accommodate himself, and any dependants of his, without recourse to public funds; and

(iii) a condition requiring the person to register with the police.

He may also require him to report to the appropriate Medical Officer of Environmental Health. Under Section 24 of the 1971 Act it is an offence knowingly to remain beyond the time limit or to fail to comply with such a condition or requirement.]

[9   The time limit and any conditions attached will normally be made known to the person concerned:

(i) by written notice given to him or endorsed by the immigration officer in his passport or travel document; or

(ii) in any other manner permitted by the Immigration (Leave to Enter and Remain) Order 2000.]

Note   Paragraph 9 substituted by HC 704.

[A.2.6]
[Exercise of the power to refuse leave to enter the United Kingdom or to cancel leave to enter or remain which is in force]
10   The power to refuse leave to enter the United Kingdom [or to cancel leave to enter or remain which is already in force] is not to be exercised by an Immigration Officer acting on his own. The authority of a Chief Immigration Officer or of an Immigration Inspector must always be obtained.

[A.2.7]
[Suspension of leave to enter or remain in the United Kingdom
10A   Where a person has arrived in the United Kingdom with leave to enter or remain which is in force but which was given to him before his arrival he may be examined by an Immigration Officer under paragraph 2A of Schedule 2 to the Immigration Act 1971. An Immigration Officer examining a person under paragraph 2A may suspend that person's leave to enter or remain in the United Kingdom until the examination is completed.

[A.2.8]
Cancellation of leave to enter or remain in the United Kingdom
10B   Where a person arrived in the United Kingdom with leave to enter or remain in the United Kingdom which is already in force, an Immigration Officer may cancel that leave.]

Note   Sub-heading of paragraph 10 substituted, words in square brackets in para 10 inserted and paragraphs 10A and B inserted by HC 704.

[A.2.9]
Requirement for persons arriving in the United Kingdom or seeking entry through the Channel Tunnel to produce evidence of identity and nationality
11   A person must, on arrival in the United Kingdom or when seeking entry through the Channel Tunnel, produce on request by the Immigration Officer:

(i) a valid national passport or other document satisfactorily establishing his identity and nationality; and

(ii) such information as may be required to establish whether he requires leave to enter the United Kingdom and, if so, whether and on what terms leave to enter should be given.

Note   This para reproduces the powers of Immigration Officers contained in the Immigration Act 1971, Sch 2, para 4.

[A.2.10]
Requirement for a person not requiring leave to enter the United Kingdom to prove that he has the right of abode
12   A person claiming to be a British citizen must prove that he has the right of abode in the United Kingdom by producing either:

(i) a United Kingdom passport describing him as a British citizen or as a citizen of the United Kingdom and Colonies having the right of abode in the United Kingdom; or

(ii) a certificate of entitlement duly issued by or on behalf of the Govern-ment of the United Kingdom certifying that he has the right of abode.

Note   This para reproduces the requirements of the Immigration Act 1971, s 3(9) as substituted by the British Nationality Act 1981 and the Immigration Act 1988.

---

13   A person claiming to be a Commonwealth citizen with the right of abode in the United Kingdom must prove that he has the right of abode by producing a certificate of entitlement duly issued to him by or on behalf of the Government of the United Kingdom certifying that he has the right of abode.

14   A Commonwealth citizen who has been given limited leave to enter the United Kingdom may later claim to have the right of abode. The time limit on his stay may be removed if he is able to establish a claim to the right of abode, for example by showing that:

(i) immediately before the commencement of the British Nationality Act 1981 he was a Commonwealth citizen born to or legally adopted by a parent who at the time of his birth had citizenship of the United Kingdom and Colonies by his birth in the United Kingdom or any of the Islands; and

(ii) he has not ceased to be a Commonwealth citizen in the meanwhile.

[A.2.11]
Common Travel Area
15   The United Kingdom, the Channel Islands, the Isle of Man and the Republic of Ireland collectively form a common travel area. A person who has been examined for the purpose of immigration control at the point at which he entered the area does not normally require leave to enter any other part of it. However certain persons subject to the Immigration (Control of Entry through the Republic of Ireland) Order 1972 (as amended) who enter the United Kingdom through the Republic of Ireland do require leave to enter. This includes:

   (i)   those who merely passed through the Republic of Ireland;

  (ii)   persons requiring visas;

 (iii)   persons who entered the Republic of Ireland unlawfully;

 (iv)   persons who are subject to directions given by the Secretary of State for their exclusion from the United Kingdom on the ground that their exclusion is conducive to the public good;

  (v)   persons who entered the Republic from the United Kingdom and Islands after entering there unlawfully or overstaying their leave.

[A.2.12]
Admission of certain British passport holders

16   A person in any of the following categories may be admitted freely to the United Kingdom on production of a United Kingdom passport issued in the United Kingdom and Islands or the Republic of Ireland prior to 1 January 1973, unless his passport has been endorsed to show that he was subject to immigration control:

   (i)   a British Dependent Territories citizen;

  (ii)   a British National (Overseas);

 (iii)   a British Overseas citizen;

 (iv)   a British protected person;

  (v)   a British subject by virtue of Section 30(*a*) of the British Nationality Act 1981, (who, immediately before the commencement of the 1981 Act, would have been a British subject not possessing citizenship of the United Kingdom and Colonies or the citizenship of any other Commonwealth country or territory).

17   British Overseas citizens who hold United Kingdom passports wherever issued and who satisfy the Immigration Officer that they have, since 1 March 1968, been given indefinite leave to enter or remain in the United Kingdom may be given indefinite leave to enter.

[A.2.13]
[Persons outside the United Kingdom

17A   Where a person is outside the United Kingdom but wishes to travel to the United Kingdom an Immigration Officer may give or refuse him leave to enter. An Immigration Officer may exercise these powers whether or not he is, himself, in the United Kingdom. However, an Immigration Officer is not obliged to consider an application for leave to enter from a person outside the United Kingdom.

17B   Where a person, having left the common travel area, has leave to enter the United Kingdom which remains in force under article 13 of the Immigration (Leave to Enter and Remain) Order 2000, an Immigration Officer may cancel that leave. An Immigration Officer may exercise these powers whether or not he is, himself, in the United Kingdom. If a person outside the United Kingdom has leave to remain in the United Kingdom which is in force in this way, the Secretary of State may cancel that leave.]

Note   Paragraphs 17A and B inserted by HC 704.

[A.2.14]
Returning residents

18   A person seeking leave to enter the United Kingdom as a returning resident may be admitted for settlement provided the Immigration Officer is satisfied that the person concerned:

  (i)   had indefinite leave to enter or to remain in the United Kingdom when he last left; and
 (ii)   has not been away from the United Kingdom for more than 2 years; and
(iii)   did not receive assistance from public funds towards the cost of leaving the United Kingdom; and
 (iv)   now seeks admission for the purpose of settlement.

19   A person who does not benefit from the preceding paragraph by reason only of having been away from the United Kingdom too long may nevertheless be admitted as a returning resident if, for example, he has lived here for most of his life.

[19A   Where a person who has infinite leave to enter or remain in the United Kingdom accompanies, on a tour of duty abroad, a spouse who is a member of HM Forces serving overseas, or a permanent member of HM Diplomatic Service or a comparable UK-based staff member of the British Council, sub-paragraphs (ii) and (iii) of paragraph 18 shall not apply.]

Note   Paragraph 19A inserted by CM 4851.

20   The leave of a person whose stay in the United Kingdom is subject to a time limit lapses on his going to a country or territory outside the common travel area [if the leave was given for a period of six months or less or conferred by a visit visa. In other cases, leave lapses on the holder remaining outside the United Kingdom for a continuous period of more than two years]. [A person whose leave has lapsed and] who returns after a temporary absence abroad within the period of this earlier leave has no claim to admission as a returning resident. His application to re-enter the United Kingdom should be considered in the light of all the relevant circumstances. The same time limit and any conditions attached will normally be reimposed if he meets the requirements of these Rules, unless he is seeking admission in a different capacity from the one in which he was last given leave to enter or remain.

Note   Words in first set of square brackets in paragraph 20 inserted and those in second set of square brackets substituted by HC 704.

[A.2.15]
[Non-lapsing leave

20A   Leave to enter or remain in the United Kingdom will usually lapse on the holder going to a country or territory outside the common travel area. However, under article 13 of the Immigration (Leave to Enter and Remain) Order 2000 such leave will not lapse where it was given for a period exceeding six months or where it was conferred by means of an entry clearance (other than a visit visa).]

Note   Inserted by HC 704.

[A.2.16]
Holders of restricted travel documents and passports
21　The leave to enter or remain in the United Kingdom of the holder of a passport or travel document whose permission to enter another country has to be exercised before a given date may be restricted so as to terminate at least 2 months before that date.

22　If his passport or travel document is endorsed with a restriction on the period for which he may remain outside his country of normal residence, his leave to enter or remain in the United Kingdom may be limited so as not to extend beyond the period of authorised absence.

23　The holder of a travel document issued by the Home Office should not be given leave to enter or remain for a period extending beyond the validity of that document. This paragraph and paragraphs 21–22 do not apply to a person who is eligible for admission for settlement or to a spouse who is eligible for admission under paragraph 282 or to a person who qualifies for the removal of the time limit on his stay.

[A.2.17]
Entry clearance
24　A visa national and any other person who is seeking entry for a purpose for which prior entry clearance is required under these Rules must produce to the Immigration Officer a valid passport or other identity document endorsed with a United Kingdom entry clearance issued to him for the purpose for which he seeks entry. Such a person will be refused leave to enter if he has no such current entry clearance. Any other person who wishes to ascertain in advance whether he is eligible for admission to the United Kingdom may apply for the issue of an entry clearance.

25　Entry clearance takes the form of a visa (for visa nationals) or an entry certificate (for non-visa nationals). These documents are to be taken as evidence of the holder's eligibility for entry into the United Kingdom, and accordingly accepted as 'entry clearances' within the meaning of the Immigration Act 1971.

[25A　An entry clearance which satisfies the requirements set out in article 3 of the Immigration (Leave to Enter and Remain) Order 2000 will have effect as leave to enter the United Kingdom. The requirements are that the entry clearance must specify the purpose for which the holder wants to enter the United Kingdom and should be endorsed with the conditions to which it is subject or with a statement that it has effect as indefinite leave to enter the United Kingdom. The holder of such an entry clearance will not require leave to enter on arrival in the United Kingdom and, for the purposes of the Rules, will be treated as a person who has arrived in the United Kingdom with leave to enter the United Kingdom which is in force but which was given to him before his arrival.]

Note　Inserted by HC 704.

26　An application for entry clearance will be considered in accordance with the provisions in these Rules governing the grant or refusal of leave to enter. Where appropriate, the term 'Entry Clearance Officer' should be substituted for 'Immigration Officer'.

27   An application of entry clearance is to be decided in the light of the circumstances existing at the time of the decision, except that an applicant will not be refused an entry clearance where entry is sought in one of the categories contained in paragraphs 296–316 solely on account of his attaining the age of 18 years between receipt of his application and the date of the decision on it.

28   An applicant for an entry clearance must be outside the United Kingdom and Islands at the time of the application. An applicant for an entry clearance who is seeking entry as a visitor must apply to a post designated by the Secretary of State to accept applications for entry clearance for that purpose and from that category of applicant. Any other application must be made to the post in the country or territory where the applicant is living which has been designated by the Secretary of State to accept applications for entry clearance for that purpose and from that category of applicant. Where there is no such post the applicant must apply to the appropriate designated post outside the country or territory where he is living.

29   For the purposes of paragraph 28 'post' means a British Diplomatic Mission, British Consular post or the office of any person outside the United Kingdom and Islands who has been authorised by the Secretary of State to accept applications for entry clearance. A list of designated posts is published by the Foreign and Commonwealth Office.

30   An application for an entry clearance is not made until any fee required to be paid under the Consular Fees Act 1980 (including any Regulations or Orders made under that Act) has been paid.

[30A   An entry clearance may be revoked if the Entry Clearance Officer is satisfied that:

(i)   whether or not to the holder's knowledge, false representations were employed or material facts were not disclosed, either in writing or orally, for the purpose of obtaining the entry clearance; or

(ii)   a change in circumstances since the entry clearance was issued has removed the basis of the holder's claim to be admitted to the United Kingdom, except where the change of circumstances amounts solely to his exceeding the age for entry in one of the categories contained in paragraphs 296–316 of these Rules since the issue of the entry clearance; or

(iii)   the holder's exclusion from the United Kingdom would be conducive to the public good.]

[30B   An entry clearance shall cease to have effect where the entry clearance has effect as leave to enter and an Immigration Officer cancels that leave in accordance with paragraph 2A(8) of Schedule 2 to the Immigration Act 1971.

30C   An Immigration Officer may cancel an entry clearance which is capable of having effect as leave to enter if the holder arrives in the United Kingdom before the day on which the entry clearance becomes effective of if the holder seeks to enter the United Kingdom for a purpose other than the purpose specified in the entry clearance.]

Note   Paragraph 30A inserted by HC 31 and paragraphs 30B and 30C inserted by HC 704.

[A.2.18]
Variation of leave to enter or remain in the United Kingdom
31   Under Section 3(3) of the 1971 Act a limited leave to enter or remain in the United Kingdom may be varied by extending or restricting its duration, by adding, varying or revoking conditions or by removing the time limit (whereupon any condition attached to the leave ceases to apply). When leave to enter or remain is varied an entry is to be made in the applicant's passport or travel document (and his registration certificate where appropriate) or the decision may be made known in writing or some other appropriate way.

[31A   Where a person has arrived in the United Kingdom with leave to enter or remain in the United Kingdom which is in force but was given to him before his arrival, he may apply, on arrival at a port of entry in the United Kingdom, for variation of that leave. An Immigration Officer acting on behalf of the Secretary of State may vary the leave at the port of entry but is not obliged to consider an application for variation made at the port of entry. If an Immigration Officer acting on behalf of the Secretary of State has declined to consider an application for variation of leave at a port of entry but the leave has not been cancelled under paragraph 2A(8) of Schedule 2 to the Immigration Act 1971, the person seeking variation should apply to the Home Office under paragraph 32.]

Note   Paragraph 31A inserted by HC 704.

32   After admission to the United Kingdom any application for an extension of the time limit on or variation of conditions attached to a person's stay in the United Kingdom must be made to the Home Office before the applicant's current leave to enter or remain expires.

[With the exception of applications made under [paragraph 31A (applications at the port of entry),] paragraph 33 (work permits), [33A (applications made outside the United Kingdom),] paragraphs 255 to 257 (EEA nationals) and Part 11 (asylum), all applications for variation of leave to enter or remain must be made using the form prescribed for the purpose by the Secretary of State, which must be completed in the manner required by the form and be accompanied by the documents and photographs specified in the form. An application for such a variation made in any other way is not valid.]

33   Where the application is in respect of employment for which a work permit or a permit for training or work experience is required or is in respect of the spouse or child or a person who is making such an application, the application should be made direct to the Department of Employment Overseas Labour Service.

[33A   Where a person, having left the common travel area, has leave to enter or remain in the United Kingdom which remains in force under article 13 of the Immigration (Leave to Enter and Remain) Order 2000, his leave may be varied (including any conditions to which it is subject) in such form and manner as permitted for the giving of leave to enter. However, the Secretary of State is not obliged to consider an application for variation of leave to enter or remain from a person outside the United Kingdom.]

Note Words in first set of square brackets in para 32 added by HC 329, para 2 with effect from 3 June 1996. The forms, which had been withdrawn for amendment as a result of judicial review (7 June 1996) were reintroduced after having been revised, on 25 November 1996. Words in square brackets within first set in para 32, and the whole of para 33A, inserted by HC 704.

[A.2.19]
Withdrawn applications for variation of leave to enter or remain in the United Kingdom
34 Where a person whose application for variation of leave to enter or remain is being considered requests the return of his passport for the purpose of travel outside the common travel area, the application for variation of leave shall, provided it has not already been determined, be treated as withdrawn as soon as the passport is returned in response to that request [. . .]

Note Words deleted by CM 4851.

[A.2.20]
Undertakings
35 A sponsor of a person seeking leave to enter or variation of leave to enter or remain in the United Kingdom may be asked to give an undertaking in writing to be responsible for that person's maintenance and accommodation for the period of any leave granted, including any further variation. Under the Social Security Administration Act 1992 and the Social Security Administration (Northern Ireland) Act 1992, the Department of Social Security or, as the case may be, the Department of Health and Social Services in Northern Ireland may seek to recover from the person giving such an undertaking any income support paid to meet the needs of the person in respect of whom the undertaking has been given.

[Under the Immigration and Asylum Act 1999 the Home Office may seek to recover from the person giving such an undertaking amounts attributable to any support provided under section 95 of the Immigration and Asylum Act 1999 (support for asylum seekers) to, or in respect of, the person in respect of whom the undertaking has been given. Failure by the sponsor to maintain that person on accordance with the undertaking, may also be an offence under section 105 of the Social Security Administration Act 1992 and/or under section 108 of the Immigration and Asylum Act 1999 if, as a consequence asylum support and/or income support is provided to or in respect of, that person.]

Note Words in square brackets inserted by CM 4851.

[A.2.21]
Medical
36 A person who intends to remain in the United Kingdom for more than 6 months should normally be referred to the Medical Inspector for examination. If he produces a medical certificate he should be advised to hand it to the Medical Inspector. Any person seeking entry who mentions health or medical treatment as a reason for his visit, or who appears not to be in good mental or physical health, should also be referred to the Medical Inspector; and the

Immigration Officer has discretion, which should be exercised sparingly, to refer for examination in any other case.

37 Where the Medical Inspector advises that a person seeking entry is suffering from a specified disease or condition which may interfere with his ability to support himself or his dependants, the Immigration Officer should take account of this, in conjunction with other factors, in deciding whether to admit that person. The Immigration Officer should also take account of the Medical Inspector's assessment of the likely course of treatment in deciding whether a person seeking entry for private medical treatment has sufficient means at his disposal.

38 A returning resident should not be refused leave to enter [or have existing leave to enter or remain cancelled] on medical grounds. But where a person would be refused leave to enter [or have existing leave to enter or remain cancelled] on medical grounds if he were not a returning resident, or in any case where it is decided on compassionate grounds not to exercise the power to refuse leave to enter [or to cancel existing leave to enter or remain], or in any other case where the Medical Inspector so recommends, the Immigration Officer should give the person concerned a notice requiring him to report to the Medical Officer of Environmental Health designated by the Medical Inspector with a view to further examination and any necessary treatment.

39 The Entry Clearance Officer has the same discretion as an Immigration Officer to refer applicants for entry clearance for medical examination and the same principles will apply to the decision whether or not to issue an entry clearance.

Note Paras 7–39 replace HC 251, paras 6–21 and 58–60.

Words in square brackets in paragraph 38 inserted by HC 704.

[A.2.22]
[Students
39A An application for a variation of leave to enter or remain made by a student who is sponsored by a government or international sponsorship agency may be refused if the sponsor has not given written consent to the proposed variation.]

Part 2: Persons seeking to enter or remain in the United Kingdom for visits

VISITORS

[A.2.23]
Requirements for leave to enter as a visitor
40 For the purpose of paragraphs 41–46 a visitor includes a person living and working outside the United Kingdom who comes to the United Kingdom to

transact business (such as attending meetings and briefings, fact finding, negotiating or making contracts with United Kingdom businesses to buy or sell goods or services). A visitor seeking leave to enter or remain for private medical treatment must meet the requirements of paragraphs 51 or 54.

41   The requirements to be met by a person seeking leave to enter the United Kingdom as a visitor are that he:

  (i) is genuinely seeking entry as a visitor for a limited period as stated by him, not exceeding 6 months; and
 (ii) intends to leave the United Kingdom at the end of the period of the visit as stated by him; and
(iii) does not intend to take employment in the United Kingdom; and
 (iv) does not intend to produce goods or provide services within the United Kingdom, including the selling of goods or services direct to members of the public; and
  (v) does not intend to study at a maintained school; and
 (vi) will maintain and accommodate himself and any dependants adequately out of resources available to him without recourse to public funds or taking employment; or will, with any dependants, be maintained and accommodated adequately by relatives or friends; and
(vii) can meet the cost of the return or onward journey.

[A.2.24]
Leave to enter as a visitor
42   A person seeking leave to enter the United Kingdom as a visitor may be admitted for a period not exceeding 6 months, subject to a condition prohibiting employment, provided the Immigration Officer is satisfied that each or the requirements of paragraph 41 is met.

[A.2.25]
Refusal of leave to enter as a visitor
43 Leave to enter as a visitor is to be refused if the Immigration Officer is not satisfied that each of the requirements of paragraph 41 is met.

[A.2.26]
Requirements for an extension of stay as a visitor
44   Six months is the maximum permitted leave which may be granted to a visitor. The requirements for an extension of stay as a visitor are that the applicant:

  (i) meets the requirements of paragraph 41(ii)–(vii); and
 (ii) has not already spent, or would not as a result of an extension of stay spend, more than 6 months in total in the United Kingdom as a visitor.

Any period spent as a seasonal agricultural worker is to be counted as a period spent as a visitor.

[A.2.27]
Extension of stay as a visitor
45   An extension of stay as a visitor may be granted, subject to a condition prohibiting employment, provided the Secretary of State is satisfied that each of the requirements of paragraph 44 is met.

[A.2.28]
Refusal of extension of stay as a visitor
46   An extension of stay as a visitor is to be refused if the Secretary of State is not satisfied that each of the requirements of paragraph 44 is met.

Note   Paras 40–46 replace HC 251, paras 22, 24, 104 and 105.

It is important to remember that apart from in family visitor cases there is no right of appeal against refusal of an entry clearance as a visitor, or refusal of leave to enter as a visitor unless he holds a current entry clearance as a visitor at the time of his refusal. See Immigration and Asylum Act 1999 s 60(4) and (5).

VISITORS IN TRANSIT

[A.2.29]
Requirements for admission as a visitor in transit to another country
47   The requirements to be met by a person (not being a member of the crew of a ship, aircraft, hovercraft, hydrofoil or train) seeking leave to enter the United Kingdom as visitor in transit to another country are that he:

  (i) is in transit to a country outside the common travel area; and
 (ii) has both the means and the intention of proceeding at once to another country; and
(iii) is assured of entry there; and
 (iv) intends and is able to leave the United Kingdom within 48 hours.

[A.2.30]
Leave to enter as a visitor in transit
48   A person seeking leave to enter the United Kingdom as a visitor in transit may be admitted for a period not exceeding 48 hours with a prohibition on employment provided the Immigration Officer is satisfied that each of the requirements of paragraph 47 is met.

[A.2.31]
Refusal of leave to enter as a visitor in transit
49   Leave to enter as a visitor in transit is to be refused if the Immigration Officer is not satisfied that each of the requirements of paragraph 47 is met.

[A.2.32]
Extension of stay as a visitor in transit
50   The maximum permitted leave which may be granted to a visitor in transit is 48 hours. An application for an extension of stay beyond 48 hours from a person admitted in this category is to be refused.

Note   See HC 251, paras 25 and 105.

These paras introduce a separate category for visitors admitted in transit for up to 48 hours.

VISITORS SEEKING TO ENTER OR REMAIN FOR PRIVATE MEDICAL TREATMENT

[A.2.33]
Requirements for leave to enter as a visitor for private medical treatment
51   The requirements to be met by a person seeking leave to enter the United Kingdom as a visitor for private medical treatment are that he:

  (i) meets the requirements set out in paragraph 41(iii)–(vii) for entry as a visitor; and
 (ii) in the case of a person suffering from a communicable disease, has satisfied the Medical Inspector that there is no danger to public health; and
(iii) can show, if required to do so, that any proposed course of treatment is of finite duration; and
 (iv) intends to leave the United Kingdom at the end of his treatment; and
  (v) can produce satisfactory evidence, if required to do so, of:
         (*a*) the medical condition requiring consultation or treatment; and
         (*b*) satisfactory arrangements for the necessary consultation or treatment at his own expense; and
         (*c*) the estimated costs of such consultation or treatment; and
         (*d*) the likely duration of his visit; and
         (*e*) sufficient funds available to him in the United Kingdom to meet the estimated costs of his undertaking to do so.

[A.2.34]
Leave to enter as a visitor for private medical treatment
52   A person seeking leave to enter the United Kingdom as a visitor for private medical treatment may be admitted for a period not exceeding 6 months, subject to a condition prohibiting employment, provided the Immigration Officer is satisfied that each of the requirements of paragraph 51 is met.

[A.2.35]
Refusal of leave to enter as a visitor for private medical treatment
53   Leave to enter as a visitor for private medical treatment is to be refused if the Immigration Officer is not satisfied that each of the requirements of paragraph 51 is met.

[A.2.36]
Requirements for an extension of stay as a visitor for private medical treatment
54   The requirements for an extension of stay as a visitor to undergo or continue private medical treatment are that the applicant:

  (i) meets the requirements set out in paragraph 41(ii)–(vii) and paragraph 51(ii)–(v); and
 [(ii) has produced evidence from a registered medical practitioner who holds an NHS consultant post or who appears in the Specialist Register of the General Medical Council of satisfactory arrangements for private medical consultation or treatment and its likely duration; and, where treatment has already begun, evidence as to its progress; and]

(iii) can show that he has met, out of the resources available to him, any costs and expenses incurred in relation to his treatment in the United Kingdom; and

(iv) has sufficient funds available to him in the United Kingdom to meet the likely costs of his treatment and intends to meet those costs.

Note   Para 54(ii) substituted by CM 4851.

[A.2.37]
Extension of stay as a visitor for private medical treatment

55   An extension of stay to undergo or continue private medical treatment may be granted, with a prohibition on employment, provided the Secretary of State is satisfied that each of the requirements of paragraph 54 is met.

[A.2.38]
Refusal of extension of stay as a visitor for private medical treatment

56   An extension of stay as a visitor to undergo or continue private medical treatment is to be refused if the Secretary of State is not satisfied that each of the requirements of paragraph 54 is met.

[PARENT OF A CHILD AT SCHOOL

[A.2.39]
Requirements for leave to enter or remain as the parent of a child at school

56A   The requirements to be met by a person seeking leave to enter or remain in the United Kingdom as the parent of a child at school are that:

(i)   the parent meets the requirements set out in paragraph 41 (ii)-(iv); and

(ii) the child is attending an independent fee paying day school and meets the requirements set out in paragraph 57 (i)-(vi); and

(iii) the child is under 12 years of age; and

(iv) the parent can provide satisfactory evidence of adequate and reliable funds for maintaining a second home in the United Kingdom; and

(v)   the parent is not seeking to make the United Kingdom his main home.

[A.2.40]
Leave to enter or remain as the parent of a child at school

56B   A person seeking leave to enter or remain in the United Kingdom as the parent of a child at school may be admitted or allowed to remain for a period not exceeding 12 months, subject to a condition prohibiting employment, providing the Immigration Officer or, in the case of an application for limited leave to remain, the Secretary of State is satisfied that each of the requirements of paragraph 56A is met.

[A.2.41]
Refusal of leave to enter or remain as the parent of a child at school
56C   Leave to enter or remain in the United Kingdom as the parent of a child at school is to be refused if the Immigration Office or, in the case of an application for limited leave to remain, the Secretary of State, is not satisfied that each of the requirements of paragraph 56A is met.]

Notes   Paras 51–56 replace HC 251, paras 23 and 106.

Words in square brackets inserted by CM 4851.

It is necessary for the applicant to show, if required to do so, that any proposed course of treatment is for a finite period.

Part 3:   Persons seeking to enter or remain in the United Kingdom for studies

STUDENTS

[A.2.42]
Requirements for leave to enter as a student
57   The requirements to be met by a person seeking leave to enter the United Kingdom as a student are that he:

  (i) has been accepted for a course of study at:
    (*a*) a publicly funded institution of further or higher education; or
    (*b*) a *bona fide* private education institution which maintains satisfactory records of enrolment and attendance; or
    (*c*) an independent fee paying school outside the maintained sector; and
  (ii) is able and intends to follow either:
    (*a*) a recognised full-time degree course at a publicly funded institution of further or higher education; or
    (*b*) a weekday full-time course involving attendance at a single institution for a minimum of 15 hours organised daytime study per week of a single subject or directly related subjects; or
    (*c*) a full-time course of study at an independent fee paying school; and
  (iii) if under the age of 16 years is enrolled at an independent fee paying school on a full-time course of studies which meets the requirements of the Education Act 1944; and
  (iv) intends to leave the United Kingdom at the end of his studies; and
  (v) does not intend to engage in business or to take employment, except part-time or vacation work undertaken with the consent of the Secretary of State for Employment; and
  (vi) is able to meet the costs of his course and accommodation and the maintenance of himself and any dependants without taking employment or engaging in business or having recourse to public funds.

Note   Paras 57–62 replace HC 251, paras 26, 27 and 108–112.

Each of the requirements of para 57(i) to (vi) must be met. Thus the view taken by the

House of Lords in *Alexander v Immigration Appeal Tribunal* [1982] 2 All ER 766 that if the Immigration Officer was satisfied of an applicant's genuine and realistic intention to study, there was a discretion to admit that applicant even though he could not satisfy an immigration officer of an intention to leave the country at the end of his studies is no longer good law.

It is important to notice that the applicant under para 57 must be able to show that he or she 'is able and intends' to follow the particular course of study.

[A.2.43]
Leave to enter as a student
58   A person seeking leave to enter the United Kingdom as a student may be admitted for an appropriate period depending on the length of his course of study and his means, and with a condition restricting his freedom to take employment, provided the Immigration Officer is satisfied that each of the requirements of paragraph 57 is met.

[A.2.44]
Refusal of leave to enter as a student
59   Leave to enter as a student is to be refused if the Immigration Officer is not satisfied that each of the requirements of paragraph 57 is met.

[A.2.45]
Requirements for an extension of stay as student
60   The requirements for an extension of stay as a student are that the applicant:
- (i) was admitted to the United Kingdom with a valid student entry clearance if he is a person specified in [Appendix 1] to these Rules; and
- (ii) meets the requirements for admission as a student set out in paragraph 57(i)–(vi); and
- (iii) has produced evidence of his enrolment on a course which meets the requirements of paragraph 57; and
- (iv) can produce satisfactory evidence of regular attendance during any course which he has already begun; or any other course for which he has been enrolled in the past; and
- (v) can show evidence of satisfactory progress in his course of study including the taking and passing of any relevant examinations; and
- (vi) would not, as a result of an extension of stay, spend more than 4 years on short courses (ie courses of less than 2 years duration, or longer courses broken off before completion); and
- (vii) has not come to the end of a period of government or international scholarship agency sponsorship, or has the written consent of his [official] sponsor for a further period of study in the United Kingdom and satisfactory evidence that sufficient sponsorship funding is available.

Note   All parts of para 60 must be satisfied in order to obtain an extension of stay. Attendance and progress must be satisfactory. To that extent *Remi Adekola Durojaiye v Secretary of State for the Home Department* [1991] Imm AR 307 remains good law.
Paragraph 60(i) shall not apply to any application for an extension of stay for the purpose of studying made by a national of Bahrain, the Dominican Republic, Fiji, Guyana, Kuwait, the Maldives, Mauritius, Niger, Papua New Guinea, Peru, Qatar, Surinam,

United Arab Emirates or Zambia where current leave to enter or remain was granted before 4 April 1996.

Paragraph 60(i) of HC 395 of 1994 shall not apply to any application for an extension of stay for the purpose of studying made by a national of Colombia whose current leave to enter or remain was granted before 29 May 1997, a national of Ecuador whose current leave to enter or remain was granted before 1 August 1997 or a national of the Slovak Republic whose current leave to enter or remain was granted before 8 October 1998 or a national of the Republic of Croatia whose current leave to enter or remain was granted before 19 November 1999.

Paragraph 60(i) amended with effect from 11 May 1998 (Cmnd 3953)

Words in square brackets in paragraph 60(vii) substituted by CM 4851.

[A.2.46]
Extension of stay as a student
61   An extension of stay as a student may be granted, subject to a restriction on his freedom to take employment, provided the Secretary of State is satisfied that the applicant meets each of the requirements of paragraph 60.

[A.2.47]
Refusal of extension of stay as a student
62   an extension of stay as a student is to be refused if the Secretary of State is not satisfied that each of the requirements of paragraph 60 is met.

STUDENT NURSES

[A.2.48]
Definition of student nurse
63   For the purposes of these Rules the term student nurse means a person accepted for training as a student nurse or midwife leading to a registered nursing qualification; or an overseas nurse or midwife who has been accepted on an adaptation course leading to registration as a nurse with the United Kingdom Central Council for Nursing, Midwifery and Health Visiting.

[A.2.49]
Requirements for leave to enter as a student nurse
64   The requirements to be met by a person seeking leave to enter the United Kingdom as a student nurse are that the person:
  (i) comes within the definition set out in paragraph 63 above; and
  (ii) has been accepted for a course of study in a recognised nursing educational establishment offering nursing training which meets the requirements of the United Kingdom Central Council for Nursing, Midwifery and Health Visiting; and
  (iii) did not obtain acceptance by misrepresentation; and
  (iv) is able and intends to follow the course; and
  (v) does not intend to engage in business or take employment except in connection with the training course; and
  (vi) intends to leave the United Kingdom at the end of the course; and
  (vii) has sufficient funds available for accommodation and maintenance for himself and any dependants without engaging in business or taking employment (except in connection with the training course) or having recourse to public funds. The possession of a Department of Health bursary may be taken into account in assessing whether the student meets the maintenance requirement.

[A.2.50]
Leave to enter the United Kingdom as a student nurse
65 A person seeking leave to enter the United Kingdom as a student nurse may be admitted for the duration of the training course, with a restriction on his freedom to take employment, provided the Immigration Officer is satisfied that each of the requirements of paragraph 64 is met.

[A.2.51]
Refusal of leave to enter as a student nurse
66 Leave to enter as a student nurse is to be refused if the Immigration Officer is not satisfied that each of the requirements of paragraph 64 is met.

[A.2.52]
Requirements for an extension of stay as a student nurse
67 The requirements for an extension of stay as a student nurse are that the applicant:

(i) was admitted to the United Kingdom with a valid student entry clearance if he is a person specified in [Appendix 1] to these Rules; and

(ii) meets the requirements set out in paragraphs 64(i)–(vii); and

(iii) has produced evidence of enrolment at a recognised nursing educational establishment; and

(iv) can provide satisfactory evidence of regular attendance during any course which he has already begun; or any other course for which he has been enrolled in the past; and

(v) would not, as a result of an extension of stay, spend more than 4 years in obtaining the relevant qualification; and

(vi) has not come to the end of a period of government or international scholarship agency sponsorship, or has the written consent of his [official] sponsor for a further period of study in the United Kingdom and evidence that sufficient sponsorship funding is available.

Note Paragraph 67(i) amended with effect from 11 May 1998 (Cmnd 3953). Paragraph 67(i) of HC 395 shall not apply to any application for an extension of stay for the purpose of studying made by a national of the Slovak Republic whose current leave to enter and remain was granted before 8 October 1998 or by a national of the Republic of Croatia whose current leave to enter or remain was granted before 19 November 1999.

Words in square brackets in para 67(vi) substituted by CM 4851.

[A.2.53]
Extension of stay as a student nurse
68 An extension of stay as a student nurse may be granted, subject to a restriction on his freedom to take employment, provided the Secretary of State is satisfied that the applicant meets each of the requirements of paragraph 67.

[A.2.54]
Refusal of extension of stay as student nurse
69 An extension of stay as a student nurse is to be refused if the Secretary of State is not satisfied that each of the requirements of paragraph 67 is met.

[A.2.55]
Requirements for leave to enter to re-sit an examination
69A The requirements to be met by a person seeking leave to enter the United Kingdom in order to re-sit an examination are that the applicant:

(i) (*a*) meets the requirements for admission as a student set out in paragraph 57 (i)-(vi); or

(*b*) met the requirements for admission as a student set out in paragraph 57 (i)-(iii) in the previous academic year and continues to meet the requirements of paragraph 57 (iv)-(vi); and

(ii) has produced written confirmation from the education institution or independent fee paying school which he attends or attended in the previous academic year that he is required to re-sit an examination; and

(iii) can provide satisfactory evidence of regular attendance during any course which he has already begun; or any other course for which he has been enrolled in the past; and

(iv) has not come to the end of a period of government or international scholarship agency sponsorship, or has the written consent of his official sponsor for a further period of study in the United Kingdom and satisfactory evidence that sufficient sponsorship funding is available; and

(v) has not previously been granted leave to re-sit the examination.

[A.2.56]
Leave to enter to re-sit an examination
69B A person seeking leave to enter the United Kingdom in order to re-sit an examination may be admitted for a period sufficient to enable him to re-sit the examination at the first available opportunity with a condition restricting his freedom to take employment, provided the Immigration Officer is satisfied that each of the requirements of paragraph 69A is met.

[A.2.57]
Refusal of leave to enter to re-sit an examination
69C Leave to enter to re-sit an examination is to be refused if the Immigration Officer is not satisfied that each of the requirements of paragraph 69A is met.

[A.2.58]
Requirements for an extension of stay to re-sit an examination
69D The requirements for an extension of stay to re-sit an examination are that the applicant:

(i) was admitted to the United Kingdom with a valid student entry clearance if he was then a visa national; and

(ii) meets the requirements set out in paragraph 69A (i)-(v).

[A.2.59]
Extension of stay to re-sit an examination
69E An extension of stay to re-sit an examination may be granted for a period sufficient to enable the applicant to re-sit the examination at the first available opportunity, subject to a restriction on his freedom to take employment, provided the Secretary of State is satisfied that the applicant meets each of the requirements of paragraph 69D.

[A.2.60]
Refusal of extension of stay to re-sit an examination
69F   An extension of stay to re-sit an examination is to be refused if the Secretary of State is not satisfied that each of the requirements of paragraph 69D is met.

WRITING UP A THESIS

[A.2.61]
Requirements for leave to enter to write up a thesis
69G   The requirements to be met by a person seeking leave to enter the United Kingdom in order to write up a thesis are that the applicant:

   (i) (a meets the requirements for admission as a student set out in paragraph 57 (i)-(vi); or
      (b) met the requirements for admission as a student set out in paragraph 57 (i)-(iii) in the previous academic year and continues to meet the requirements of paragraph 57 (iv)-(vi); and
  (ii) can provide satisfactory evidence that he is a postgraduate student enrolled at an education institution as either a full time, part time or writing up student; and
 (iii) can demonstrate that his application is supported by the education institution; and
 (iv) has not come to the end of a period of government or international scholarship agency sponsorship, or has the written consent of his official sponsor for a further period of study in the United Kingdom and satisfactory evidence that sufficient sponsorship funding is available; and
  (v) has not previously been granted 12 months leave to write up the same thesis.

[A.2.62]
Leave to enter to write up a thesis
69H   A person seeking leave to enter the United Kingdom in order to write up a thesis may be admitted for 12 months with a condition restricting his freedom to take employment, provided the Immigration Officer is satisfied that each of the requirements of paragraph 69G is met.

[A.2.63]
Refusal of leave to enter to write up a thesis
69I   Leave to enter to write up a thesis is to be refused if the Immigration Officer is not satisfied that each of the requirements of paragraph 69G is met.

[A.2.64]
Requirements for an extension of stay to write up a thesis
69J   The requirements for an extension of stay to write up a thesis are that the applicant:

   (i) was admitted to the United Kingdom with a valid student entry clearance if he was then a visa national; and
  (ii) meets the requirements set out in paragraph 69G (i)-(v).

[A.2.65]
Extension of stay to write up a thesis
69K   An extension of stay to write up a thesis may be granted for 12 months subject to a restriction on his freedom to take employment, provided the Secretary of State is satisfied that the applicant meets each of the requirements of paragraph 69J.

[A.2.66]
Refusal of extension of stay to write up a thesis
69L   An extension of stay to write up a thesis is to be refused if the Secretary of State is not satisfied that each of the requirements of paragraph 69J is met.]

Note   *[Paras 63–69 replace HC 251, para 29.]*

Paragraphs 69A to 69L inserted by CM 4851.

POSTGRADUATE DOCTORS AND DENTISTS

[A.2.67]
Requirements for leave to enter as a postgraduate doctor or dentist
[70   The requirements for leave to enter the United Kingdom for the purpose of training as a postgraduate doctor or dentist are that the applicant:

- (i) (*a*) is a graduate from a medical school, who is eligible for provisional or limited registration with the General Medical Council, and who
  - (1) intends to undertake Pre-Registration House Officer employment for up to 12 months, and
  - (2) has not spent more than 12 months in aggregate in Pre-Registration House Officer employment; or
  - (*b*) is a doctor or dentist eligible for full or limited registration with the General Medical Council or the General Dental Council, who intends to undertake post-graduate training in a hospital or the Community Health Services or both;
- (ii) intends to leave the United Kingdom on completion of his training period; and
- (iii) is able to maintain and accommodate himself and any dependants without recourse to public funds.]

Note   Substituted by HC 338, r 1 with effect from 1 April 1997.

[A.2.68]
[Leave to enter as a postgraduate doctor or dentist
71   A person seeking leave to enter the United Kingdom to undertake:

- (*a*) Pre-Registration House Officer employment may be admitted for a period not exceeding 12 months; and
- (*b*) postgraduate training as a doctor or dentist in a hospital or the Community Health services, or both, may be admitted for a period not exceeding three years,

if the Immigration Officer is satisfied that each of the requirements of paragraph 70 is met.]

Note   Substituted by HC 338, r 1 with effect from 1 April 1997.

[A.2.69]
Refusal of leave to enter as a postgraduate doctor or dentist
72   Leave to enter as a postgraduate doctor or dentist is to be refused if the Immigration Officer is not satisfied that each of the requirements of paragraph 70 is met.

[A.2.70]
Requirements for extension of stay as a postgraduate doctor or dentist
[73   The requirements for an extension of stay as a postgraduate doctor or dentist are that the applicant:

  (i) (*a*) is a graduate from a medical school who is eligible for provisional or limited registration with the General Medical Council, and who
    (1) intends to undertake Pre-Registration House Officer employment for up to 12 months, and
    (2) would not, as a result of an extension of stay, spend more than 12 months in aggregate in Pre-Registration House Officer employment; or
  (*b*) is a doctor or dentist, who can provide evidence of limited or full registration with the General Medical Council or registration with the General Dental Council and who—
    (1) intends to undertake or continue postgraduate training in a hospital or the Community Health Services or both, and
    (2) can show evidence of satisfactory progress in his postgraduate training including the passing of any relevant examinations.
  (ii) intends to leave the United Kingdom on completion of his training period; and
  (iii) is able to maintain and accommodate himself and any dependants without recourse to public funds.]

Note   Substituted by HC 338, r 1 with effect from 1 April 1997.

[A.2.71]
Extension of stay as a postgraduate doctor or dentist
[74   An extension of stay may be granted—

(*a*) as a Pre-Registration House Officer for a period not exceeding 12 months, and
(*b*) as a doctor or dentist undertaking postgraduate training in a hospital or the Community Health Service or both for a period not exceeding three years,
if the Secretary of State is satisfied that—
 (i) each of the requirements of paragraph 73 is met, and
 (ii) no more than four years in aggregate will be spent in Senior House Officer (basic specialist training) or equivalent posts.]

Note   Substituted by HC 338, r 1 with effect from 1 April 1997.

[A.2.72]
Refusal of extension of stay as a postgraduate doctor or dentist
75   An extension of stay as a postgraduate doctor or dentist is to be refused if the Secretary of State is not satisfied that each of the requirements of paragraph 73 is met.

[A.2.73]
Requirements for leave to enter or remain as the spouse of a student [or prospective student]
76 The requirements to be met by a person seeking leave to enter or remain in the United Kingdom as the spouse of a student are that:

  (i) the applicant is married to a person admitted to or allowed to remain in the United Kingdom under paragraphs 57–75 [or 82–87]; and
  (ii) each of the parties intends to live with the other as his or her spouse during the applicant's stay and the marriage is subsisting; and
  (iii) there will be adequate accommodation for the parties and any dependants without recourse to public funds; and
  (iv) the parties will be able to maintain themselves and any dependants adequately without recourse to public funds; and
  (v) the applicant does not intend to take employment except as permitted under paragraph 77 below; and
  (vi) the applicant intends to leave the United Kingdom at the end of any period of leave granted to him.

[A.2.74]
Leave to enter or remain as the spouse of a student [or prospective student]
77 A person seeking leave to enter or remain in the United Kingdom as the spouse of a student may be admitted or allowed to remain for a period not in excess of that granted to the student provided the Immigration Officer or, in the case of an application for limited leave to remain, the Secretary of State, is satisfied that each of the requirements of paragraph 76 is met. [Employment may be permitted] where the period of leave being granted is [, or was,] 12 months or more.

Note Words in square brackets substituted and inserted by CM 4851.

[A.2.75]
Refusal of leave to enter or remain as the spouse of a student [or prospective student]
78 Leave to enter or remain as the spouse of a student is to be refused if the Immigration Officer or, in the case of an application for limited leave to remain, the Secretary of State is not satisfied that each of the requirements of paragraph 76 is met.

[A.2.76]
Requirements for leave to enter or remain as the child of a student [or prospective student]
79 The requirements to be met by a person seeking leave to enter or remain in the United Kingdom as the child of a student are that he:

  (i) is the child of a parent admitted to or allowed to remain in the United Kingdom as a student under the paragraphs 57–75 [or 82–87]; and
  (ii) is under the age of 18 or has current leave to enter or remain in this capacity; and

(iii) is unmarried, has not formed an independent family unit and is not leading an independent life; and

(iv) can, and will, be maintained and accommodated adequately without
recourse to public funds; and

(v) will not stay in the United Kingdom beyond any period of leave granted
to his parent.

[A.2.77]
Leave to enter or remain as the child of a student [or prospective student]

[80   A person seeking leave to enter or remain in the United Kingdom as the
child of a student may be admitted or allowed to remain for a period not in
excess of that granted to the student provided the Immigration Officer or, in
the case of an application for limited leave to remain, the Secretary of State is
satisfied that each of the requirements of paragraph 79 is met. Employment
may be permitted where the period of leave being granted is, or was, 12
months or more.]

Note   Substituted by CM 4851.

[A.2.78]
**Refusal of leave to enter or remain as the child of a student [or prospec-
tive student]**

81   Leave to enter or remain in the United Kingdom as the child of a student
is to be refused if the Immigration Officer or, in the case of an application for
limited leave to remain, the Secretary of State, is not satisfied that each of the
requirements of paragraph 79 is met.

Note   Paras 76–81 replace HC 251, paras 31 and 116.
The husband of a female student is able to qualify as a dependant spouse in the same
way as a wife of a male student. Spouses and children are prohibited from taking
employment unless the leave to enter or remain is for 12 months or more.

PROSPECTIVE STUDENTS

[A.2.79]
Requirements for leave to enter as a prospective student

82   The requirements to be met by a person seeking leave to enter the United
Kingdom as a prospective student are that he:

(i) can demonstrate a genuine and realistic intention of undertaking, within
6 months of his date of entry, a course of study which would meet the
requirements for an extension of stay as a student set out in paragraphs
60 or 67; and

(ii) intends to leave the United Kingdom on completion of his studies or on the
expiry of his leave to enter if he is not able to meet the requirements for an
extension of stay as a student set out in paragraphs 60 or 67; and

(iii) is able without working or recourse to public funds to meet the costs of
his intended course and accommodation and the maintenance of himself
and any dependants while making arrangements to study and during the
course of his studies.

[A.2.80]
Leave to enter as a prospective student
83   A person seeking leave to enter the United Kingdom as a prospective student may be admitted for a period not exceeding 6 months with a condition prohibiting employment, provided the Immigration Officer is satisfied that each of the requirements of paragraph 82 is met.

[A.2.81]
Refusal of leave to enter as a prospective student
84   Leave to enter as a prospective student is to be refused if the Immigration Officer is not satisfied that each of the requirements of paragraph 82 is met.

[A.2.82]
Requirements for extension of stay as a prospective student
85   Six months is the maximum permitted leave which may be granted to a prospective student. The requirements for an extension of stay as a prospective student are that the applicant:

  (i) was admitted to the United Kingdom with a valid prospective student entry clearance if he is a person specified in [Appendix 1] to these Rules; and
 (ii) meets the requirements of paragraph 82; and
(iii) would not, as a result of an extension of stay, spend more than 6 months in the United Kingdom.

Note   Paragraph 85(i) amended with effect from 11 May 1998 (Cmnd 3953).
Paragraph 85(i) of HC 395 of 1994 shall not apply to any application for an extension of stay for the purpose of studying made by a national of the Slovak Republic whose current leave to enter and remain was granted before 8 October 1998 or by a national of the Republic of Croatia whose current leave to enter and remain was granted before 19 November 1999.

[A.2.83]
Extension of stay as a prospective student
86   An extension of stay as a prospective student may be granted, with a prohibition on employment, provided the Secretary of State is satisfied that each of the requirements of paragraph 85 is met.

[A.2.84]
Refusal of extension of stay as a prospective student
87   An extension of stay as a prospective student is to be refused if the Secretary of State is not satisfied that each of the requirements of paragraph 85 is met.

Note   Paras 82–87 replace HC 251, paras 28 and 109.

It is important to note that the applicant must demonstrate a genuine and realistic intention to undertake the course of study within six months and that he can accommodate and maintain himself and his dependents while making the arrangements.

[STUDENTS' UNIONS SABBATICAL OFFICERS

[A.2.85]
Requirements for leave to enter as a sabbatical officer
87A   The requirements to be met by a person seeking leave to enter the United Kingdom as a sabbatical officer are that the person:

   (i) has been elected to a full-time salaried post as a sabbatical officer at an educational establishment at which he is registered as a student;

  (ii) meets the requirements set out in paragraph 57 (i)-(ii) or met the requirements set out in paragraph 57 (i)-(ii) in the academic year prior to the one in which he took up or intends to take up sabbatical office; and

 (iii) does not intend to engage in business or take employment except in connection with his sabbatical post; and

 (iv) is able to maintain and accommodate himself and any dependants adequately without recourse to public funds; and

  (v) at the end of the sabbatical post he intends to:

      (*a*) complete a course of study which he has already begun; or

      (*b*) take up a further course of study which has been deferred to enable the applicant to take up the sabbatical post; or

      (*c*) leave the United Kingdom; and

 (vi) has not come to the end of a period of government or international scholarship agency sponsorship, or has the written consent of his official sponsor to take up a sabbatical post in the United Kingdom; and

(vii) has not already completed 2 years as a sabbatical officer.

[A.2.86]

Leave to enter the United Kingdom as a sabbatical officer

87B   A person seeking leave to enter the United Kingdom as a sabbatical officer may be admitted for a period not exceeding 12 months on conditions specifying his employment provided the Immigration Officer is satisfied that each of the requirements of paragraph 87A is met.

[A.2.87]

Refusal of leave to enter the United Kingdom as a sabbatical officer

87C   Leave to enter as a sabbatical officer is to be refused if the Immigration Officer is not satisfied that each of the requirements of paragraph 87A is met.

[A.2.88]

Requirements for an extension of stay as a sabbatical officer

87D   The requirements for an extension of stay as a sabbatical officer are that the applicant:

   (i) was admitted to the United Kingdom with a valid student entry clearance if he was then a visa national; and

  (ii) meets the requirements set out in paragraph 87A (i)-(vi); and

 (iii) would not, as a result of an extension of stay, remain in the United Kingdom as a sabbatical officer to a date beyond 2 years from the date on which he was first given leave to enter the United Kingdom in this capacity.

[A.2.89]

Extension of stay as a sabbatical officer

87E   An extension of stay as a sabbatical officer may be granted for a period not exceeding 12 months on conditions specifying his employment provided the Secretary of State is satisfied that the applicant meets each of the requirements of paragraph 87D.

[A.2.90]
Refusal of extension of stay as a sabbatical officer
87F   An extension of stay as a sabbatical officer is to be refused if the Secretary of State is not satisfied that each of the requirements of paragraph 87D is met.]

Note   Paragraphs 87A–87F inserted by CM 4851.

Part 4:   Persons seeking to enter or remain in the United Kingdom in an 'au pair' placement, as a working holidaymaker, or for training or work experience

'AU PAIR' PLACEMENTS

[A.2.91]
Definition of an 'au pair' placement
88   For the purposes of these Rules an 'au pair' placement is an arrangement whereby a young person:
(*a*) comes to the United Kingdom for the purpose of learning the English language; and
(*b*) lives for a time as a member of an English speaking family with appropriate opportunities for study; and
(*c*) helps in the home for a maximum of 5 hours per day in return for a reasonable allowance and with two free days per week.

[A.2.92]
Requirements for leave to enter as an 'au pair'
89   The requirements to be met by a person seeking leave to enter the United Kingdom as an 'au pair' are that he:

(i)   is seeking entry for the purpose of taking up an arranged placement which can be shown to fall within the definition set out in paragraph 88; and
(ii) is aged between 17–27 inclusive or was so aged when first given leave to enter in this capacity; and
(iii) is unmarried; and
(iv) is without dependants; and
(v)   is a national of one of the following countries: Andorra, Bosnia-Herzegovina, Croatia, Cyprus, Czech Republic, [The Faroes], Greenland, Hungary, . . . Macedonia, Malta, Monaco, San Marino, Slovak Republic, Slovenia, Switzerland, or Turkey; and
(vi) does not intend to stay in the United Kingdom for more than 2 years as an 'au pair'; and
(vii) intends to leave the United Kingdom on completion of his stay as an 'au pair'; and
(viii) if he has previously spent time in the United Kingdom as an 'au pair', is not seeking leave to enter to a date beyond 2 years from the date on which he was first given leave to enter the United Kingdom in this capacity.
[; and
(ix) is able to maintain and accommodate himself without recourse to public funds.]

474

[A.2.93]
Leave to enter as an 'au pair'
90 A person seeking leave to enter the United Kingdom as an 'au pair' may be admitted for a period not exceeding 2 years with a prohibition on employment except as an 'au pair', provided the Immigration Officer is satisfied that each of the requirements of paragraph 89 is met. (A non-visa national who wishes to ascertain in advance whether a proposed 'au pair' placement is likely to meet the requirements of paragraph 89 is advised to obtain entry clearance before travelling to the United Kingdom).

[A.2.94]
Refusal of leave to enter as an 'au pair'
91 An application for leave to enter as an 'au pair' is to be refused if the Immigration Officer is not satisfied that each of the requirements of paragraph 89 is met.

[A.2.95]
Requirements for an extension of stay as an 'au pair'
92 The requirements for an extension of stay as an 'au pair' are that the applicant:

(i) was given leave to enter the United Kingdom as an 'au pair' under paragraph 90; and
(ii) is undertaking an arranged 'au pair' placement which can be shown to fall within the definition set out in paragraph 88; and
(iii) meets the requirements of paragraph [89(ii)–(ix)]; and
(iv) would not, as a result of an extension to stay, remain in the United Kingdom as an 'au pair' to a date beyond 2 years from the date on which he was first given leave to enter the United Kingdom in this capacity.

[A.2.96]
Extension of stay as an 'au pair'
93 An extension of stay as an 'au pair' may be granted with a prohibition on employment except as an 'au pair', provided the Secretary of State is satisfied that each of the requirements of paragraph 92 is met.

[A.2.97]
Refusal of extension of stay as an 'au pair'
94 An extension of stay as an 'au pair' is to be refused if the Secretary of State is not satisfied that each of the requirements of paragraph 92 is met.

Note Paras 88–94 replace HC 251, paras 33 and 121 as amended by HC 725.

There is now a detailed definition of an 'au pair' placement. See para 88 above. The new rules no longer discriminate against men. Whether families will continue to prefer woman 'au pairs' remains to be seen. Also note the change from 'au pair' to '"au pair" placement'.

EEA countries have been deleted from the list of countries participating in the 'au pair' scheme because nationals of states which are parties to the EEA Agreement, which came into force on 1 January 1994, do not require leave to enter or remain in the United Kingdom.

See now Immigration (European Economic Area) Regulations 2000 (SI 2000/2326).

WORKING HOLIDAYMAKERS

[A.2.98]
Requirements for leave to enter as a working holidaymaker
95   The requirements to be met by a person seeking leave to enter the United Kingdom as a working holidaymaker are that he:

(i) is a Commonwealth citizen; and

(ii) is aged 17–27 inclusive or was so aged when first given leave to enter in this capacity; and

(iii) is unmarried or is married to a person who meets the requirements of this paragraph and the parties to the marriage intend to take a working holiday together; and

(iv) has the means to pay for his return or onward journey; and

(v) is able and intends to maintain and accommodate himself without recourse to public funds; and

(vi) is intending to take employment incidental to a holiday but not to engage in business, provide services as a professional sportsman or entertainer or pursue a career in the United Kingdom; and

(vii) does not have dependent children any of whom are 5 years of age or over or who will reach 5 years of age before the applicant completes his working holiday; or commitments which would require him to earn a regular income; and

(viii) intends to leave the United Kingdom at the end of his working holiday; and

(ix) if he has previously spent time in the United Kingdom as a working holidaymaker, is not seeking leave to enter to a date beyond 2 years from the date he was first given leave to enter in this capacity; and

(x) holds a valid United Kingdom entry clearance for entry in this capacity.

[A.2.99]
Leave to enter as a working holidaymaker
96   A person seeking leave to enter the United Kingdom as a working holidaymaker may be admitted for a period not exceeding 2 years with a condition restricting his freedom to take employment, provided he is able to produce to the Immigration Officer, on arrival, a valid United Kingdom entry clearance for entry in this capacity.

[A.2.100]
Refusal of leave to enter as a working holidaymaker
97   Leave to enter as a working holidaymaker is to be refused if a valid United Kingdom entry clearance for entry in this capacity is not produced to the Immigration Officer on arrival.

[A.2.101]
Requirements for an extension of stay as a working holidaymaker
98   The requirements for an extension of stay as a working holidaymaker are that the applicant:

(i) entered the United Kingdom with a valid United Kingdom entry clearance as a working holidaymaker; and

(ii) meets the requirements of paragraph 95(i)–(viii); and

(iii) would not, as a result of an extension of stay, remain in the United Kingdom as a working holidaymaker to a date beyond 2 years from the date on which he was first given leave to enter the United Kingdom in this capacity.

[A.2.102]
Extension of stay as a working holidaymaker
99 An extension of stay as a working holidaymaker may be granted with a condition restricting his freedom to take employment, provided the Secretary of State is satisfied that the applicant meets each of the requirements of paragraph 98.

[A.2.103]
Refusal of extension of stay as a working holidaymaker
100 An extension of stay as a working holidaymaker is to be refused if the Secretary of State is not satisfied that each of the requirements of paragraph 98 is met.

CHILDREN OF WORKING HOLIDAYMAKERS

[A.2.104]
Requirements for leave to enter or remain as the child of a working holidaymaker
101 The requirements to be met by a person seeking leave to enter or remain in the United Kingdom as the child of a working holidaymaker are that:

(i) he is the child of a parent admitted to or allowed to remain in the United Kingdom as a working holidaymaker; and

(ii) he is under the age of 5 and will leave the United Kingdom before reaching that age; and

(iii) he can and will be maintained and accommodated adequately without recourse to public funds or without his parent(s) engaging in business or taking employment except as provided by paragraph 95 above; and

(iv) both parents are being or have been admitted to or allowed to remain in the United Kingdom save where:

(*a*) the parent he is accompanying or joining is his sole surviving parent; or

(*b*) the parent he is accompanying or joining has had the sole responsibility for his upbringing; or

(*c*) there are serious and compelling family or other considerations which make exclusion from the United Kingdom undesirable and suitable arrangements have been made for his care; and

(v) if seeking leave to enter, he holds a valid United Kingdom entry clearance for entry in this capacity or, if seeking leave to remain, was admitted with a valid United Kingdom entry clearance for entry in this capacity.

[A.2.105]
Leave to enter or remain as the child of a working holidaymaker
102   A person seeking leave to enter or remain in the United Kingdom as the child of a working holidaymaker may be admitted or allowed to remain for the same period of leave as that granted to the working holidaymaker provided that, in relation to an application for leave to enter, a valid United Kingdom entry clearance for entry in this capacity is produced to the Immigration Officer on arrival or, in the case of an application for leave to remain, he was admitted with a valid United Kingdom entry clearance for entry in this capacity and is able to satisfy the Secretary of State that each of the requirements of paragraph 101(i)–(iv) is met.

[A.2.106]
Refusal of leave to enter or remain as the child of a working holiday-maker
103   Leave to enter or remain in the United Kingdom as the child of a working holidaymaker is to be refused if, in relation to an application for leave to enter, a valid United Kingdom entry clearance for entry in this capacity is not produced to the Immigration Officer on arrival or, in the case of an application for leave to remain, the applicant was not admitted with a valid United Kingdom entry clearance for entry in this capacity or is unable to satisfy the Secretary of State that each of the requirements of paragraph 101(i)–(iv) is met.

Note   Paras 95–103 replace HC 251, paras 37 and 107.

Entry clearance is now mandatory and there is no 'switching' to working holidaymaker status in-country. The maximum period of 2 years during which a working holidaymaker can stay will no longer be aggregated. Working holidaymakers must intend to take employment incidental to a holiday and the employment available to them has been severely restricted (see para 95(vi)). In addition there are now restrictions on spouses and children of working holidaymakers see para 95(iii) and 101–103.

SEASONAL WORKERS AT AGRICULTURAL CAMPS

[A.2.107]
Requirements for leave to enter as a seasonal worker at an agricultural camp
104   The requirements to be met by a person seeking leave to enter the United Kingdom as a seasonal worker at an agricultural camp are that he:

  (i) is a student in full-time education aged between 18–25 years inclusive, except if returning for another season at the specific invitation of a farmer; and
 (ii) holds a valid Home Office work card issued by the operator of a scheme approved by the Secretary of State; and
(iii) intends to leave the United Kingdom at the end of his period of leave as a seasonal worker; and
(iv) does not intend to take employment except in the terms of this paragraph.
     [; and
 (v) is able to maintain and accommodate himself and any dependants without recourse to public funds.]

[A.2.108]
Leave to enter as a seasonal worker at an agricultural camp
[105   A person seeking leave to enter the United Kingdom as a seasonal worker at an agricultural camp may be admitted with a condition restricting his freedom to take employment, until 30 November of the year in question, if the Immigration Officer is satisfied that each of the requirements of paragraph 104 is met.]

Note   Substituted by HC 338, r 2 with effect from 1 April 1997.

[A.2.109]
Refusal of leave to enter as a seasonal worker at an agricultural camp
106   Leave to enter the United Kingdom as a seasonal worker at an agricultural camp is to be refused if the Immigration Officer is not satisfied that each of the requirements of paragraph 104 is met.

[A.2.110]
Requirements for extension of stay as a seasonal worker at an agricultural camp
107   The requirements for an extension of stay as a seasonal worker at an agricultural camp are that the applicant:

 (i) entered the United Kingdom as a seasonal worker with a valid Home Office work card under paragraph 105; and
 (ii) meets the requirements of paragraph [104(iii)–(v)]; and
 (iii) can show that there is further farm work available under the approved scheme; and
 (iv) would not, as a result of an extension of stay, remain in the United Kingdom as a seasonal worker for longer than 6 months in aggregate or beyond 30 November of the year in question, whichever is the shorter period.

[A.2.111]
Extension of stay as a seasonal worker at an agricultural camp
108   An extension of stay as a seasonal worker may be granted with a condition restricting his freedom to take employment for a further period not exceeding 3 months or until 30 November of the year in question, whichever is the shorter period, provided the Secretary of State is satisfied that the applicant meets each of the requirements of paragraph 107.

[A.2.112]
Refusal of extension of stay as a seasonal worker in an agricultural camp
109   An extension of stay as a seasonal worker at an agricultural camp is to be refused if the Secretary of State is not satisfied that each of the requirements of paragraph 107 is met.

Note   Paras 104–109 replace HC 251, paras 40(f) and 123.

The Rules now formalise the arrangements for seasonal agricultural workers and clarify the requirements to be met. Seasonal workers can no longer bring dependants to the United Kingdom.

TEACHERS AND LANGUAGE ASSISTANTS COMING TO THE UNITED KINGDOM UNDER
APPROVED EXCHANGE SCHEMES

[A.2.113]
Requirements for leave to enter as a teacher or language assistant under an approved exchange scheme

110   The requirements to be met by a person seeking leave to enter the United Kingdom as a teacher or language assistant on an approved exchange scheme are that he:

(i) is coming to an educational establishment in the United Kingdom under an exchange scheme approved by the Education Departments or administered by the Central Bureau for Educational Visits and Exchanges or the League for the Exchange of Commonwealth Teachers; and

(ii) intends to leave the United Kingdom at the end of his exchange period; and

(iii) does not intend to take employment except in the terms of this paragraph; and

(iv) is able to maintain and accommodate himself and any dependants without recourse to public funds; and

(v) holds a valid United Kingdom entry clearance for entry in this capacity.

[A.2.114]
Leave to enter as a teacher or language assistant under an exchange scheme

111   A person seeking leave to enter the United Kingdom as a teacher or language assistant under an approved exchange scheme may be given leave to enter for a period not exceeding 12 months provided he is able to produce to the Immigration Officer, on arrival, a valid United Kingdom entry clearance for entry in this capacity.

[A.2.115]
Refusal of leave to enter as a teacher or language assistant under an approved exchange scheme

112   Leave to enter the United Kingdom as a teacher or language assistant under an approved exchange scheme is to be refused if a valid United Kingdom entry clearance for entry in this capacity is not produced to the Immigration Officer on arrival.

[A.2.116]
Requirements for extension of stay as a teacher or language assistant under an approved exchange scheme

113   The requirements for an extension of stay as a teacher or language assistant under an approved exchange scheme are that the applicant:

(i) entered the United Kingdom with a valid United Kingdom entry clearance as a teacher or language assistant; and

(ii) is still engaged in the employment for which his entry clearance was granted; and

(iii) is still required for the employment in question, as certified by the employer; and

(iv) meets the requirements of paragraph 110(ii)–(iv); and

(v) would not, as a result of an extension of stay, remain in the United Kingdom as an exchange teacher or language assistant for more than 2 years from the date on which he was first given leave to enter the United Kingdom in this capacity.

[A.2.117]
Extension of stay as a teacher or language assistant under an approved exchange scheme
114   An extension of stay as a teacher or language assistant under an approved exchange scheme may be granted for a further period not exceeding 12 months provided the Secretary of State is satisfied that each of the requirements of paragraph 113 is met.

[A.2.118]
Refusal of extension of stay as a teacher or language assistant under an approved exchange scheme
115   An extension of stay as a teacher or language assistant under an approved exchange scheme is to be refused if the Secretary of State is not satisfied that each of the requirements of paragraph 113 is met.

Note   Paras 110–115 replace HC 251, para 40(c) and 123.

The Rules now introduce a mandatory entry clearance requirement and detailed provision for dependants are found in paras 122–127.

DEPARTMENT OF EMPLOYMENT APPROVED TRAINING OR WORK EXPERIENCE

[A.2.119]
Requirements for leave to enter for Department of Employment approved training or work experience
116   The requirements to be met by a person seeking leave to enter the United Kingdom for Department of Employment approved training or work experience are that he:

(i) holds a valid work permit from the Department of Employment issued under the Training and Work Experience Scheme; and

(ii) is not of an age which puts him outside the limits for employment; and

(iii) is capable of undertaking the training or work experience as specified in his work permit; and

(iv) intends to leave the United Kingdom on the completion of his training or work experience; and

(v) does not intend to take employment except as specified in his work permit; and

(vi) is able to maintain and accommodate himself and any dependants adequately without recourse to public funds.

[A.2.120]
Leave to enter for Department of Employment approved training or work experience
117   A person seeking leave to enter the United Kingdom for approved training may be admitted to the United Kingdom for a period not exceeding 3 years and a person seeking entry for approved work experience may be admitted for a period not exceeding 12 months, provided the Immigration Officer is satisfied that each of the requirements of paragraph 116 is met. Leave to enter is to be subject to a condition permitting the person to take or change employment only with the permission of the Department of Employment.

[A.2.121]
Refusal of leave to enter for Department of Employment approved training or work experience
118   Leave to enter the United Kingdom for Department of Employment approved training or work experience is to be refused if the Immigration Officer is not satisfied that each of the requirements of paragraph 116 is met.

[A.2.122]
Requirements for extension of stay for Department of Employment approved training or work experience
119   The requirements for an extension of stay for Department of Employment approved training or work experience are that the applicant:

(i) entered the United Kingdom with a valid work permit under paragraph 117 or was admitted or allowed to remain in the United Kingdom as a student; and

(ii) has written approval from the Department of Employment for an extension of stay in this category; and

(iii) meets the requirements of paragraph 116(ii)–(vi); and

(iv) would not as a result of an extension of stay spend more than 2 years in the United Kingdom for Department of Employment approved work experience.

[A.2.123]
Extension of stay for Department of Employment approved training or work experience
120   An extension of stay for approved training may be granted for a further period not exceeding 3 years; and an extension of stay for approved work experience may be granted for a further period not exceeding 12 months provided the Secretary of State is satisfied that each of the requirements of paragraph 119 is met. An extension of stay is to be subject to a condition permitting the applicant to take or change employment only with the permission of the Department of Employment.

[A.2.124]
Refusal of extension of stay for Department of Employment approved training or work experience
121 An extension of stay for Department of Employment approved training or work experience is to be refused if the Secretary of State is not satisfied that each of the requirements of paragraph 119 is met.

Note Paras 116–121 replace HC 251, paras 34, 35 and 117–120.

Visitors can no longer 'switch' to the Training and Work Permit Scheme although students may continue to do so.

SPOUSES OF PERSONS WITH LIMITED LEAVE TO ENTER OR REMAIN UNDER
PARAGRAPHS 110–121

[A.2.125]
Requirements for leave to enter or remain as the spouse of a person with limited leave to enter or remain in the United Kingdom under paragraphs 110–121
122 The requirements to be met by a person seeking leave to enter or remain in the United Kingdom as the spouse of a person with limited leave to enter or remain in the United Kingdom under paragraphs 110–121 are that:

   (i) the applicant is married to a person with limited leave to enter or remain in the United Kingdom under paragraphs 110–121; and
  (ii) each or the parties intends to live with the other as his or her spouse during the applicant's stay and the marriage is subsisting; and
 (iii) there will be adequate accommodation for the parties and any dependants without recourse to public funds in accommodation which they own or occupy exclusively; and
  (iv) the parties will be able to maintain themselves and any dependants adequately without recourse to public funds; and
   (v) the applicant does not intend to stay in the United Kingdom beyond any period of leave granted to his spouse; and
  (vi) if seeking leave to enter, the applicant holds a valid United Kingdom entry clearance for entry in this capacity or, if seeking leave to remain, was admitted with a valid United Kingdom entry clearance for entry in this capacity.

[A.2.126]
Leave to enter or remain as the spouse of a person with limited leave to enter or remain in the United Kingdom under paragraphs 110–121
123 A person seeking leave to enter or remain in the United Kingdom as the spouse of a person with limited leave to enter or remain in the United Kingdom under paragraphs 110–121 may be given leave to enter or remain in the United Kingdom for a period of leave not in excess of that granted to the person with limited leave to enter or remain under paragraphs 110–121 provided that, in relation to an application for leave to enter, he is able, on arrival, to produce to the Immigration Officer a valid United Kingdom entry clearance for entry in this capacity or, in the case of an application for limited leave to remain, was admitted with a valid United Kingdom entry clearance for entry in this capacity and is able to satisfy the Secretary of State that each of the requirements of paragraph 122(i)–(v) is met.

[A.2.127]
Refusal of leave to enter or remain as the spouse of a person with limited leave to enter or remain in the United Kingdom under paragraphs 110–121

124   Leave to enter or remain in the United Kingdom as the spouse of a person with limited leave to enter or remain in the United Kingdom under paragraphs 110–121 is to be refused if, in relation to an application for leave to enter, a valid United Kingdom entry clearance for entry in this capacity is not produced the the Immigration Officer on arrival or, in the case of an application for limited leave to remain, if the applicant was not admitted with a valid United Kingdom entry clearance for entry in this capacity or is unable to satisfy the Secretary of State that each of the requirements of paragraph 122(i)–(v) is met.

CHILDREN OF PERSONS ADMITTED OR ALLOWED TO REMAIN UNDER PARAGRAPHS 110–121

[A.2.128]
Requirements for leave to enter or remain as the child of a person with limited leave to enter or remain in the United Kingdom under paragraphs 110–121

125   The requirements to be met by a person seeking leave to enter or remain in the United Kingdom as the child of a person with limited leave to enter or remain in the United Kingdom under paragraphs 110–121 are that:

   (i) he is the child of a parent who has limited leave to enter or remain in the United Kingdom under paragraphs 110–121; and
   (ii) he is under the age of 18 or has current leave to enter or remain in this capacity; and
   (iii) he is unmarried, has not formed an independent family unit and is not leading an independent life; and
   (iv) he can, and will, be maintained and accommodated adequately without recourse to public funds in accommodation which his parent(s) own or occupy exclusively; and
   (v) he will not stay in the United Kingdom beyond any period of leave granted to his parent(s); and
   (vi) both parents are being or have been admitted to or allowed to remain in the United Kingdom save where:
      (*a*) the parent he is accompanying or joining is his sole surviving parent; or
      (*b*) the parent he is accompanying or joining has had sole responsibility for his upbringing; or
      (*c*) there are serious and compelling family or other considerations which make exclusion from the United Kingdom undesirable and suitable arrangements have been made for his care; and
   (vii) if seeking leave to enter, he holds a valid United Kingdom entry clearance for entry in this capacity of, if seeking leave to remain, was admitted with a valid United Kingdom entry clearance for entry in this capacity.

[A.2.129]
Leave to enter or remain as the child of a person with limited leave to enter or remain in the United Kingdom under paragraphs 110–121
126   A person seeking leave to enter or remain in the United Kingdom as the child of a person with limited leave to enter or remain in the United Kingdom under paragraphs 110–121 may be given leave to enter or remain in the United Kingdom for a period of leave not in excess of that granted to the person with limited leave to enter or remain under paragraphs 110–121 provided that, in relation to an application for leave to enter, he is able, on arrival, to produce to the Immigration Officer a valid United Kingdom entry clearance for entry in this capacity or, in the case of an application for limited leave to remain, he was admitted with a valid United Kingdom entry clearance for entry in this capacity and is able to satisfy the Secretary of State that each of the requirements of paragraph 125(i)–(vi) is met.

[A.2.130]
Refusal of leave to enter or remain as the child of a person with limited leave to enter or remain in the United Kingdom under paragraphs 110–121
127   Leave to enter or remain in the United Kingdom as the child of a person with limited leave to enter or remain in the United Kingdom under paragraphs 110–121 is to be refused if, in relation to an application for leave to enter, a valid United Kingdom entry clearance for entry in this capacity is not produced to the Immigration Officer on arrival or, in the case of an application for limited leave to remain, if the applicant was not admitted with a valid United Kingdom entry clearance for entry in this capacity or is unable to satisfy the Secretary of State that each of the requirements of paragraph 125(i)–(vi) is met.

Part 5:   Persons seeking to enter or remain in the United Kingdom for employment

WORK PERMIT EMPLOYMENT

[A.2.131]
Requirements for leave to enter the United Kingdom for work permit employment
128   The requirements to be met by a person coming to the United Kingdom to seek or take employment (unless he is otherwise eligible for admission for employment under these Rules or is eligible for admission as a seaman under contract to join a ship due to leave British waters) are that he:

  (i)   holds a valid Department of Employment work permit; and
 (ii)   is not of an age which puts him outside the limits for employment; and
(iii)   is capable of undertaking the employment specified in the work permit; and
 (iv)   does not intend to take employment except as specified in his work permit; and
  (v)   is able to maintain and accommodate himself and any dependants adequately without recourse to public funds; and

(vi) in the case of a person in possession of a work permit which is valid for a period of 12 months or less, intends to leave the United Kingdom at the end of his approved employment.

[A.2.132]
Leave to enter for work permit employment
129   A person seeking leave to enter the United Kingdom for the purpose of work permit employment may be admitted for a period not exceeding 4 years (normally as specified in his work permit), subject to a condition restricting him to employment approved by the Department of Employment, provided the Immigration Officer is satisfied that each of the requirements of paragraph 128 is met.

[A.2.133]
Refusal of leave to enter for employment
130   Leave to enter for the purpose of employment is to be refused if the Immigration Officer is not satisfied that each of the requirements of paragraph 128 is met (unless he is otherwise eligible for admission for employment under these Rules or is eligible for admission as a seaman under contract to join a ship due to leave British waters).

[A.2.134]
Requirements for an extension of stay for work permit employment
131   The requirements for an extension of stay to seek or take employment (unless the applicant is otherwise eligible for an extension of stay for employment under these Rules) are that the applicant:

(i) entered the United Kingdom with a valid work permit under paragraph 129; and
(ii) has written approval from the Department of Employment for the continuation of his employment; and
(iii) meets the requirements of paragraph 128(ii)–(v).

[A.2.135]
Extension of stay for work permit employment
132   An extension of stay for work permit employment may be granted for a period not exceeding the period of approved employment recommended by the Department of Employment provided the Secretary of State is satisfied that each of the requirements of paragraph 131 is met. An extension of stay is to be subject to a condition restricting the applicant to employment approved by the Department of Employment.

[A.2.136]
Refusal of extension of stay for employment
133   An extension of stay for employment is to be refused if the Secretary of State is not satisfied that each of the requirements of paragraph 131 is met (unless the applicant is otherwise eligible for an extension of stay for employment under these Rules).

[A.2.137]
Indefinite leave to remain for a work permit holder
134   Indefinite leave to remain may be granted, on application, to a person admitted as a work permit holder provided:

   (i) he has spent a continuous period of 4 years in the United Kingdom in this capacity; and
   (ii) he has met the requirements of paragraph 131 throughout the 4 year period; and
   (iii) he is still required for the employment in question, as certified by his employer.

[A.2.138]
Refusal of indefinite leave to remain for a work permit holder
135   Indefinite leave to remain in the United Kingdom for a work permit holder is to be refused if the Secretary of State is not satisfied that each of the requirements of paragraph 134 is met.

Note   Paras 128–135 replace HC 251, paras 34, 35, 122 and 139(a).

The rules have an additional requirement that a holder of a short-term work permit (valid for 12 months or less) must not intend to stay beyond the validity of his permit. However, an extension of stay is possible if the Department of Employment gives written approval. The Rules also take away the discretion of an immigration officer to admit, in certain circumstances, a work permit holder who is holding an expired permit.

REPRESENTATIVES OF OVERSEAS NEWSPAPERS, NEWS AGENCIES AND BROADCASTING ORGANISATIONS

[A.2.139]
Requirements for leave to enter as a representative of an overseas newspaper, news agency or broadcasting organisation
136   The requirements to be met by a person seeking leave to enter the United Kingdom as a representative of an overseas newspaper, news agency or broadcasting organisation are that he:

   (i) has been engaged by that organisation outside the United Kingdom and is being posted to the United Kingdom on a long-term assignment as a representative; and
   (ii) intends to work full-time as a representative of that overseas newspaper, news agency or broadcasting organisation; and
   (iii) does not intend to take employment except within the terms of this paragraph; and
   (iv) can maintain and accommodate himself and any dependants adequately without recourse to public funds; and
   (v) holds a valid United Kingdom entry clearance for entry in this capacity.

[A.2.140]
Leave to enter as a representative of an overseas newspaper, news agency or broadcasting organisation

137   A person seeking leave to enter the United Kingdom as a representative of an overseas newspaper, news agency or broadcasting organisation may be admitted for a period not exceeding 12 months provided he is able to produce to the Immigration Officer, on arrival, a valid United Kingdom entry clearance for entry in this capacity.

[A.2.141]
Refusal of leave to enter as a representative of an overseas newspaper, news agency or broadcasting organisation

138   Leave to enter as a representative of an overseas newspaper, news agency or broadcasting organisation is to be refused if a valid United Kingdom entry clearance for entry in this capacity is not produced to the Immigration Officer on arrival.

[A.2.142]
Requirements for an extension of stay as a representative of an overseas newspaper, news agency or broadcasting organisation

139   The requirements for an extension of stay as a representative of an overseas newspaper, news agency or broadcasting organisation are that the applicant:

  (i) entered the United Kingdom with a valid United Kingdom entry clearance as a representative of an overseas newspaper, news agency or broadcasting organisation; and
 (ii) is still engaged in the employment for which his entry clearance was granted; and
(iii) is still required for the employment in question, as certified by his employer; and
 (iv) meets the requirements of paragraph 136(ii)–(iv).

[A.2.143]
Extension of stay as a representative of an overseas newspaper, news agency or broadcasting organisation

140   An extension of stay as a representative of an overseas newspaper, news agency or broadcasting organisation may be granted for a period not exceeding 3 years provided the Secretary of State is satisfied that each of the requirements of paragraph 139 is met.

[A.2.144]
Refusal of extension of stay as a representative of an overseas newspaper, news agency or broadcasting organisation

141   An extension of stay as a representative of an overseas newspaper, news agency or broadcasting organisation is to be refused if the Secretary of State is not satisfied that each of the requirements of paragaph 139 is met.

[A.2.145]
Indefinite leave to remain for a representative of an overseas newspaper, news agency or broadcasting organisation
142   Indefinite leave to remain may be granted, on application, to a representative of an overseas newspaper, news agency or broadcasting organisation provided:

(i) he has spent a continuous period of 4 years in the United Kingdom in this capacity; and

(ii) he has met the requirements of paragraph 139 throughout the 4 year period; and

(iii) he is still required for the employment in question, as certified by his employer.

[A.2.146]
Refusal of indefinite leave to remain for a representative of an overseas newspaper, news agency or broadcasting organisation
143   Indefinite leave to remain in the United Kingdom for a representative of an overseas newspaper, news agency or broadcasting organisation is to be refused if the Secretary of State is not satisfied that each of the requirements of paragraph 142 is met.

REPRESENTATIVES OF OVERSEAS FIRMS WHICH HAVE NO BRANCH, SUBSIDIARY OR OTHER
REPRESENTATIVE IN THE UNITED KINGDOM (SOLE REPRESENTATIVES)

[A.2.147]
Requirements for leave to enter as a sole representative
144   The requirements to be met by a person seeking leave to enter the United Kingdom as a sole representative are that he:

(i) has been recruited and taken on as an employee outside the United Kingdom as a representative of a firm which has its headquarters and principal place of business outside the United Kingdom and which has no branch, subsidiary or other representative in the United Kingdom; and

(ii) seeks entry to the United Kingdom as a senior employee with full authority to take operational decisions on behalf of the overseas firm for the purpose of representing it in the United Kingdom by establishing and operating a registered branch or wholly owned subsidiary of that overseas firm; and

(iii) intends to be employed full time as a representative of that overseas firm; and

(iv) is not a majority shareholder in that overseas firm; and

(v) does not intend to take employment except within the terms of this paragraph; and

(vi) can maintain and accommodate himself and any dependants adequately without recourse to public funds; and

(vii) holds a valid United Kingdom entry clearance for entry in this capacity.

[A.2.148]
Leave to enter as a sole representative
145   A person seeking leave to enter the United Kingdom as a sole representative may be admitted for a period not exceeding 12 months provided he is able to produce to the Immigration Officer, on arrival, a valid United Kingdom entry clearance for entry in this capacity.

[A.2.149]
Refusal of leave to enter as a sole representative
146   Leave to enter as a sole representative is to be refused if a valid United Kingdom entry clearance for entry in this capacity is not produced to the Immigration Officer on arrival.

[A.2.150]
Requirements for an extension of stay as a sole representative
147   The requirements for an extension of stay as a sole representative are that the applicant:

(i) entered the United Kingdom with a valid United Kingdom entry clearance as a sole representative of an overseas firm; and

(ii) can show that the overseas firm still has its headquarters and principal place of business outside the United Kingdom; and

(iii) is employed full-time as a representative of that overseas firm and has established and is in charge of its registered branch or wholly-owned subsidiary; and

(iv) is still required for the employment in question, as certified by his employer; and

(v) meets the requirements of paragraph 144(iii)–(vi).

[A.2.151]
Extension of stay as a sole representative
148   An extension of stay not exceeding 3 years as a sole representative may be granted provided the Secretary of State is satisfied that each of the requirements of paragraph 147 is met.

[A.2.152]
Refusal of extension of stay as a sole representative
149   An extension of stay as a sole representative is to be refused if the Secretary of State is not satisfied that each of the requirements of paragraph 147 is met.

[A.2.153]
Indefinite leave to remain for a sole representative
150   Indefinite leave to remain may be granted, on application, to a sole representative provided:

(i) he has spent a continuous period of 4 years in the United Kingdom in this capacity; and

(ii) he has met the requirements of paragraph 147 throughout the 4 year period; and

(iii) he is still required for the employment in question, as certified by his employer.

[A.2.154]
Refusal of indefinite leave to remain for a sole representative
151   Indefinite leave to remain in the United Kingdom for a sole representative is to be refused if the Secretary of State is not satisfied that each of the requirements of paragraph 150 is met.

Note   Paras 144–151 replace HC 251, paras 39, 124 and 139(b).

The current rules provide a detailed definition of sole representatives and the criteria under which they may be permitted to operate. Majority shareholders can no longer become sole representatives and the overseas firm must establish a registered branch or a wholly-owned subsidiary in the United Kingdom. *Lokko v Secretary of State for the Home Department* ([1990] Imm AR 111) and the cases mentioned in that decision are therefore only relevant to cases to be decided under the old rules, HC 251, paras 39 and 124 and to the extent that current rules incorporate anything decided in them.

PRIVATE SERVANTS IN DIPLOMATIC HOUSEHOLDS

[A.2.155]
Requirements for leave to enter as a private servant in a diplomatic household
152   The requirements to be met by a person seeking leave to enter the United Kingdom as a private servant in a diplomatic household are that he:

  (i) is aged 18 or over; and
 (ii) is employed as a private servant in the household of a member of staff of a diplomatic or consular mission who enjoys diplomatic privileges and immunity within the meaning of the Vienna Convention on Diplomatic and Consular Relations or a member of the family forming part of the household of such a person; and
(iii) intends to work full-time as a private servant within the terms of this paragraph; and
(iv) does not intend to take employment except within the terms of this paragraph; and
 (v) can maintain and accommodate himself and any dependants adequately without recourse to public funds; and
(vi) holds a valid United Kingdom entry clearance for entry in this capacity.

[A.2.156]
Leave to enter as a private servant in a diplomatic household
153   A person seeking leave to enter the United Kingdom as a private servant in a diplomatic household may be given leave to enter for a period not exceeding 12 months provided he is able to produce to the Immigration Officer, on arrival, a valid United Kingdom entry clearance for entry in this capacity.

[A.2.157]
Refusal of leave to enter as a private servant in a diplomatic household
154   Leave to enter as a private servant in a diplomatic household is to be refused if a valid United Kingdom entry clearance for entry in this capacity is not produced to the Immigration Officer on arrival.

[A.2.158]
Requirements for an extension of stay as a private servant in a diplomatic household
155   The requirements for an extension of stay as a private servant in a diplomatic household are that the applicant:

  (i) entered the United Kingdom with a valid United Kingdom entry clearance as a private servant in a diplomatic household; and
 (ii) is still engaged in the employment for which his entry clearance was granted; and
(iii) is still required for the employment in question, as certified by the employer; and
(iv) meets the requirements of paragraph 152(iii)–(v).

[A.2.159]
Extension of stay as a private servant in a diplomatic household
156   An extension of stay as a private servant in a diplomatic household may be granted for a period not exceeding 12 months provided the Secretary of State is satisfied that each of the requirements of paragraph 155 is met.

[A.2.160]
Refusal of extension of stay as a private servant in a diplomatic household
157   An extension of stay as a private servant in a diplomatic household is to be refused if the Secretary of State is not satisfied that each of the requirements of paragraph 155 is met.

[A.2.161]
Indefinite leave to remain for a servant in a diplomatic household
158   Indefinite leave to remain may be granted, on application, to a private servant in a diplomatic household provided:

  (i) he has spent a continuous period of 4 years in the United Kingdom in this capacity; and
 (ii) he has met the requirements of paragraph 155 throughout the 4 year period; and
(iii) he is still required for the employment in question, as certified by his employer.

[A.2.162]
Refusal of indefinite leave to remain for a servant in a diplomatic household
159   Indefinite leave to remain in the United Kingdom for a private servant in a diplomatic household is to be refused if the Secretary of State is not satisfied that each of the requirements of paragraph 158 is met.

Note   Paras 152–159 replace HC 251, paras 40(a) and 123.
The age has been raised from 16 to 18 and now private servants can qualify for settlement.

[A.2.163]
Requirements for leave to enter as an overseas government employee
160 For the purposes of these Rules an overseas government employee means a person coming for employment by an overseas government or employed by the United Nations Organisation or other international organisation of which the United Kingdom is a member.

161 The requirements to be met by a person seeking leave to enter the United Kingdom as an overseas government employee are that he:

(i) is able to produce either a valid United Kingdom entry clearance for entry in this capacity or satisfactory documentary evidence of his status as an overseas government employee; and

(ii) intends to work full time for the government or organisation concerned; and

(iii) does not intend to take employment except within the terms of this paragraph; and

(iv) can maintain and accommodate himself and any dependants adequately without recourse to public funds.

[A.2.164]
Leave to enter as an overseas government employee
162 A person seeking leave to enter the United Kingdom as an overseas government employee may be given leave to enter for a period not exceeding 12 months, provided he is able, on arrival, to produce to the Immigration Officer a valid United Kingdom entry clearance for entry in this capacity or satisfy the Immigration Officer that each of the requirements of paragraph 161 is met.

[A.2.165]
Refusal of leave to enter as an overseas government employee
163 Leave to enter as an overseas government employee is to be refused if a valid United Kingdom entry clearance for entry in this capacity is not produced to the Immigration Officer on arrival or if the Immigration Officer is not satisfied that each of the requirements of paragraph 161 is met.

[A.2.166]
Requirements for an extension of stay as an overseas government employee
164 The requirements to be met by a person seeking an extension of stay as an overseas government employee are that the applicant:

(i) was given leave to enter the United Kingdom under paragraph 162 as an overseas government employee; and

(ii) is still engaged in the employment in question; and

(iii) is still required for the employment is question, as certified by the employer; and

(iv) meets the requirements of paragraph 161(ii)–(iv).

[A.2.167]
Extension of stay as an overseas government employee
165   An extension of stay as an overseas government employee may be grant-ed for a period not exceeding 3 years provided the Secretary of State is satis-fied that each of the requirements of paragraph 164 is met.

[A.2.168]
Refusal of extension of stay as an overseas government employee
166   An extension of stay as an overseas government employee is to be refused if the Secretary of State is not satisfied that each of the requirements of paragraph 164 is met.

[A.2.169]
Indefinite leave to remain for an overseas government employee
167   Indefinite leave to remain may be granted, on application, to an overseas government employee provided:

(i)   he has spent a continuous period of 4 years in the United Kingdom in this capacity; and
(ii) he has met the requirements of paragraph 164 throughout the 4 year peri-od; and
(iii) he is still required for the employment in question, as certified by his employer.

[A.2.170]
Refusal of indefinite leave to remain for an overseas government employee
168   Indefinite leave to remain in the United Kingdom for an overseas gov-ernment employee is to be refused if the Secretary of State is not satisfied that each of the requirements of paragraph 167 is met.

Note   Paras 160–168 replace HC 251, paras 40(b), 123 and 139(b).

The new Rules provide a more detailed definition of the requirements to be met for this category.

MINISTERS OF RELIGION, MISSIONARIES AND MEMBERS OF RELIGIOUS ORDERS

[A.2.171]
169   For the purposes of these Rules:

(i)   a minister of religion means a religious functionary whose main regular duties comprise the leading of a congregation in performing the rites and rituals of the faith and in preaching the essentials of the creed;
(ii) a missionary means a person who is directly engaged in spreading a reli-gious doctrine and whose work is not in essence administrative or cleri-cal;
(iii) a member of a religious order means a person who is coming to live in a community run by that order.

[A.2.172]
Requirements for leave to enter as a minister or religion, missionary or member of a religious order
170   The requirements to be met by a person seeking leave to enter the United Kingdom as a minister of religion, missionary or member of a religious order are that he:

   (i) (*a*) if seeking leave to enter as a minister of religion has either been work-ing for at least one year as a minister of religion or, where ordination is prescribed by a religious faith as the sole means of entering the min-istry, has been ordained as a minister of religion following at least one year's full-time or two years' part-time training for the ministry; or
   (*b*) if seeking leave to enter as a missionary has been trained as a mis-sionary or has worked as a missionary and is being sent to the United Kingdom by an overseas organisation; or
   (*c*) if seeking leave to enter as a member of a religious order is coming to live in a community maintained by the religious order of which he is a member and, if intending to teach, does not intend to do so save at an establishment maintained by his order; and
   (ii) intends to work full-time as a minister of religion, missionary or for the religious order of which he is a member; and
   (iii) does not intend to take employment except within the terms of this para-graph; and
   (iv) can maintain and accommodate himself and any dependants adequately without recourse to public funds; and
   (v) holds a valid United Kingdom entry clearance for entry in this capacity.

[A.2.173]
Leave to enter as a minister or religion, missionary or member of a religious order
171   A person seeking leave to enter the United Kingdom as a minister of religion, missionary or member of a religious order may be admitted for a peri-od not exceeding 12 months provided he is able to produce to the Immigration Officer, on arrival, a valid United Kingdom entry clearance for entry in this capacity.

[A.2.174]
Refusal of leave to enter as a minister of religion, missionary or member of a religious order
172   Leave to enter as a minister of religion, missionary or member of a reli-gious order is to be refused if a valid United Kingdom entry clearance for entry in this capacity is not produced to the Immigration Officer on arrival.

[A.2.175]
Requirements for an extension to stay as a minister of religion, missionary or member of a religious order
173   The requirements for an extension of stay as a minister of religion, mis-sionary or member of a religious order are that the applicant:

   (i) entered the United Kingdom with a valid United Kingdom entry clearance as a minister of religion, missionary or member of a religious order; and

   (ii) is still engaged in the employment for which his entry clearance was granted; and

   (iii) is still required for the employment in question as certified by the leadership of his congregation, his employer or the head of his religious order; and

   (iv) meets the requirements of paragraph 170(ii)–(iv).

[A.2.176]
Extension of stay as a minister of religion, missionary or member of a religious order

174   An extension of stay as a minister of religion, missionary or member of a religious order may be granted for a period not exceeding 3 years provided the Secretary of State is satisfied that each of the requirements of paragraph 173 is met.

[A.2.177]
Refusal of extension of stay as a minister of religion, missionary or member of a religious order

175   An extension of stay as a minister of religion, missionary or member of a religious order is to be refused if the Secretary of State is not satisfied that each of the requirements of paragraph 173 is met.

[A.2.178]
Indefinite leave to remain for a minister of religion, missionary or member of a religious order

176   Indefinite leave to remain may be granted, on application, to a person admitted as a minister of religion, missionary or member of a religious order provided:

   (i) he has spent a continuous period of 4 years in the United Kingdom in this capacity; and

   (ii) he has met the requirements of paragraph 173 throughout the 4 year period; and

   (iii) he is still required for the employment in question as certified by the leadership of his congregation, his employer or the head of the religious order to which he belongs.

[A.2.179]
Refusal of indefinite leave to remain for a minister of religion, missionary or member of a religious order

177   Indefinite leave to remain in the United Kingdom for a minister of religion, missionary or member of a religious order is to be refused if the Secretary of State is not satisfied that each of the requirements of paragraph 176 is met.

Note   Paras 169–177 replace HC 251, paras 38(a), 123 and 139(b).

There is now a definition of minister of religion, missionary and member of a religious order. An ordained minister is now expected to have followed a period of one year full-time study or two years part-time study before ordination.

AIRPORT-BASED OPERATIONAL GROUND STAFF OF OVERSEAS-OWNED AIRLINES

[A.2.180]
Requirements for leave to enter the United Kingdom as a member of the operational ground staff of an overseas-owned airline

178　The requirements to be met by a person seeking leave to enter the United Kingdom as a member of the operational ground staff of an overseas-owned airline are that he:

  (i) has been transferred to the United Kingdom by an overseas-owned airline operating services to and from the United Kingdom to take up duty at an international airport as station manager, security manager or technical manager; and

  (ii) intends to work full-time for the airline concerned; and

  (iii) does not intend to take employment except within the terms of this paragraph; and

  (iv) can maintain and accommodate himself and any dependants without recourse to public funds; and

  (v) holds a valid United Kingdom entry clearance for entry in this capacity.

[A.2.181]
Leave to enter as a member of the operational ground staff of an overseas-owned airline

179　A person seeking leave to enter the United Kingdom as a member of the operational staff of an overseas-owned airline may be given leave to enter for a period not exceeding 12 months, provided he is able to produce to the Immigration Officer, on arrival, a valid United Kingdom entry clearance for entry in this capacity.

[A.2.182]
Refusal of leave to enter as a member of the operational ground staff of an overseas-owned airline

180　Leave to enter as a member of the operational ground staff of an overseas-owned airline is to be refused if a valid United Kingdom entry clearance for entry in this capacity is not produced to the Immigration Officer on arrival.

[A.2.183]
Requirements for an extension of stay as a member of the operational ground staff of an overseas-owned airline

181　The requirements to be met by a person seeking an extension of stay as a member of the operational ground staff of an overseas-owned airline are that the applicant:

  (i) entered the United Kingdom with a valid United Kingdom entry clearance as a member of the operational ground staff of an overseas-owned airline; and

  (ii) is still engaged in the employment for which entry was granted; and

  (iii) is still required for the employment in question, as certified by the employer; and

  (iv) meets the requirements of paragraph 178(ii)–(iv).

[A.2.184]
Extension of stay as a member of the operational ground staff of an overseas-owned airline
182   An extension of stay as a member of the operational ground staff of an overseas-owned airline may be granted for a period not exceeding 3 years, provided the Secretary of State is satisfied that each of the requirements of paragraph 181 is met.

[A.2.185]
Refusal of extension of stay as a member of the operational ground staff of an overseas-owned airline
183   An extension of stay as a member of the operational staff of an overseas-owned airline is to be refused if the Secretary of State is not satisfied that each of the requirements of paragraph 181 is met.

[A.2.186]
Indefinite leave to remain for a member of the operational ground staff of an overseas-owned airline
184   Indefinite leave to remain may be granted, on application, to a member of the operational ground staff of an overseas-owned airline provided:

   (i) he has spent a continuous period of 4 years in the United Kingdom in this capacity; and
   (ii) he has met the requirements of paragraph 181 throughout the 4 year period; and
   (iii) he is still required for the employment in question, as certified by the employer.

[A.2.187]
Refusal of indefinite leave to remain for a member of the operational ground staff of an overseas-owned airline
185   Indefinite leave to remain in the United Kingdom for a member of the operational ground staff of an overseas-owned airline is to be refused if the Secretary of State is not satisfied that each of the requirements of paragraph 184 is met.

Note   Paras 178–185 replace HC 251, paras 40(e), 123 and 139(b).
The new Rules clarify the requirements to be met and limit the posts to certain managerial grades.

PERSONS WITH UNITED KINGDOM ANCESTRY

[A.2.188]
Requirements for leave to enter on the grounds of United Kingdom ancestry
186   The requirements to be met by a person seeking leave to enter the United Kingdom on the grounds of his United Kingdom ancestry are that he:

   (i) is a Commonwealth citizen; and

   (ii)   is aged 17 or over; and

  (iii)   is able to provide proof that one of his grandparents was born in the United Kingdom and Islands; and

  (iv)   is able to work and intends to take or seek employment in the United Kingdom; and

   (v)   will be able to maintain and accommodate himself and any dependants adequately without recourse to public funds; and

  (vi)   holds a valid United Kingdom entry clearance for entry in this capacity.

[A.2.189]
Leave to enter the United Kingdom on the grounds of United Kingdom ancestry
187   A person seeking leave to enter the United Kingdom on the grounds of his United Kingdom ancestry may be given leave to enter for a period not exceeding 4 years provided he is able to produce to the Immigration Officer, on arrival, a valid United Kingdom entry clearance for entry in this capacity.

[A.2.190]
Refusal of leave to enter on the grounds of United Kingdom ancestry
188   Leave to enter the United Kingdom on the grounds of United Kingdom ancestry is to be refused if a valid United Kingdom entry clearance for entry in this capacity is not produced to the Immigration Officer on arrival.

[A.2.191]
Requirements for an extension of stay on the grounds of United Kingdom ancestry
189   The requirements to be met by a person seeking an extension of stay on the grounds of United Kingdom ancestry are that he is able to meet each of the requirements of paragraph 186(i)–(v).

[A.2.192]
Extension of stay on the grounds of United Kingdom ancestry
190   An extension of stay on the grounds of United Kingdom ancestry may be granted for a period not exceeding 4 years provided the Secretary of State is satisfied that each of the requirements of paragraph 186(i)–(v) is met.

[A.2.193]
Refusal of extension of stay on the grounds of United Kingdom ancestry
191   An extension of stay on the grounds of United Kingdom ancestry is to be refused if the Secretary of State is not satisfied that each of the requirements of paragraph 186(i)–(v) is met.

[A.2.194]
Indefinite leave to remain on the grounds of United Kingdom ancestry
192   Indefinite leave to remain may be granted, on application, to a Commonwealth citizen with a United Kingdom born grandparent provided:

(i) he meets the requirements of paragraph 186(i)–(v); and

(ii) he has spent a continuous period of 4 years in the United Kingdom in this capacity.

[A.2.195]
Refusal of indefinite leave to remain on the grounds of United Kingdom ancestry

193 Indefinite leave to remain in the United Kingdom on the grounds of a United Kingdom born grandparent is to be refused if the Secretary of State is not satisfied that each of the requirements of paragraph 192 is met.

Note Paras 186–193 replace HC 251, paras 36 and 139(g).

The new rules specify that an applicant must be at least 17 and is 'able to work' and intends to take or seek employment in the United Kingdom. Applicants are likely to be asked to provide their current curriculum vitae to ascertain their ability to work and to ensure they will be able to maintain and accommodate themselves without recourse to public funds. It is still possible to switch in-country to this category (see para 189).

SPOUSES OF PERSONS WITH LIMITED LEAVE TO ENTER OR REMAIN UNDER PARAGRAPHS 128–193

[A.2.196]
Requirements for leave to enter or remain as the spouse of a person with limited leave to enter or remain in the United Kingdom under paragraphs 128–193

194 The requirements to be met by a person seeking leave to enter or remain in the United Kingdom as the spouse of a person with limited leave to enter or remain in the United Kingdom under paragraphs 128–193 are that:

(i) the applicant is married to a person with limited leave to enter or remain in the United Kingdom under paragraphs 128–193; and

(ii) each of the parties intends to live with the other as his or her spouse during the applicant's stay and the marriage is subsisting; and

(iii) there will be adequate accommodation for the parties and any dependants without recourse to public funds in accommodation which they own or occupy exclusively; and

(iv) the parties will be able to maintain themselves and any dependants adequately without recourse to public funds; and

(v) the applicant does not intend to stay in the United Kingdom beyond any period of leave granted to his spouse; and

(vi) if seeking leave to enter, the applicant holds a valid United Kingdom entry clearance for entry in this capacity or, if seeking leave to remain, was admitted with a valid United Kingdom entry clearance for entry in this capacity.

[A.2.197]
Leave to enter or remain as the spouse of a person with limited leave to enter or remain in the United Kingdom under paragraphs 128–193

195 A person seeking leave to enter or remain in the United Kingdom as the spouse of a person with limited leave to enter or remain in the United Kingdom

under paragraphs 128–193 may be given leave to enter or remain in the United Kingdom for a period of leave not in excess of that granted to the person with limited leave to enter or remain under paragraphs 128–193 provided that, in relation to an application for leave to enter, he is able, on arrival, to produce to the Immigration Officer a valid United Kingdom entry clearance for entry in this capacity or, in the case of an application for limited leave to remain, he was admitted with a valid United Kingdom entry clearance for entry in this capacity and is able to satisfy the Secretary of State that each of the requirements of paragraph 194(i)–(v) is met. An application for indefinite leave to remain in this category may be granted provided the applicant was admitted with a valid United Kingdom entry clearance for entry in this capacity and is able to satisfy the Secretary of State that each of the requirements of paragraph 194(i)–(v) is met and provided indefinite leave to remain is, at the same time, being granted to the person with limited leave to enter or remain under paragraphs 128–193.

[A.2.198]
Refusal of leave to enter or remain as the spouse of a person with limited leave to enter or remain in the United Kingdom under paragraphs 128–193
196   Leave to enter or remain in the United Kingdom as the spouse of a person with limited leave to enter or remain in the United Kingdom under paragraphs 128–193 is to be refused if, in relation to an application for leave to enter, a valid United Kingdom entry clearance for entry in this capacity is not produced to the Immigration Officer on arrival or, in the case of an application for limited leave to remain, if the applicant was not admitted with a valid United Kingdom entry clearance for entry in this capacity or is unable to satisfy the Secretary of State that each of the requirements of paragraph 194(i)–(v) is met. An application for indefinite leave to remain in this category is to be refused if the applicant was not admitted with a valid United Kingdom entry clearance for entry in this capacity or is unable to satisfy the Secretary of State that each of the requirements of paragraph 194(i)–(v) is met or if indefinite leave to remain is not, at the same time, being granted to the person with limited leave to enter or remain under paragraphs 128–193.

CHILDREN OF PERSONS WITH LIMITED LEAVE TO ENTER OR REMAIN IN THE UNITED KINGDOM UNDER PARAGRAPHS 128–193

[A.2.199]
Requirements for leave to enter or remain as the child of a person with limited leave to enter or remain in the United Kingdom under paragraphs 128–193
197   The requirements to be met by a person seeking leave to enter or remain in the United Kingdom as a child of a person with limited leave to enter or remain in the United Kingdom under paragraphs 128–193 are that:

(i) he is the child of a parent with limited leave to enter or remain in the United Kingdom under paragraphs 128–193; and

(ii) he is under the age of 18 or has current leave to enter or remain in this capacity; and

(iii) he is unmarried, has not formed an independent family unit and is not leading an independent life; and

(iv) he can and will be maintained and accommodated adequately without recourse to public funds in accommodation which his parent(s) own or occupy exclusively; and

(v) he will not stay in the United Kingdom beyond any period of leave granted to his parent(s); and

(vi) both parents are being or have been admitted to or allowed to remain in the United Kingdom save where:

    (*a*) the parent he is accompanying or joining is his sole surviving parent; or

    (*b*) the parent he is accompanying or joining has had sole responsibility for his upbringing; or

    (*c*) there are serious and compelling family or other considerations which make exclusion from the United Kingdom undesirable and suitable arrangements have been made for his care; and

(vii) if seeking leave to enter, he holds a valid United Kingdom entry clearance for entry in this capacity or, if seeking leave to remain, was admitted with a valid United Kingdom entry clearance for entry in this capacity.

[A.2.200]
Leave to enter or remain as the child of a person with limited leave to enter or remain in the United Kingdom under paragraphs 128–193

198 A person seeking leave to enter or remain in the United Kingdom as the child of a person with limited leave to enter or remain in the United Kingdom under paragraphs 128–193 may be given leave to enter or remain in the United Kingdom for a period of leave not in excess of that granted to the person with limited leave to enter or remain under paragraphs 128–193 provided that, in relation to an application for leave to enter, he is able to produce to the Immigration Officer, on arrival, a valid United Kingdom entry clearance for entry in this capacity or, in the case of an application for limited leave to remain, he was admitted with a valid United Kingdom entry clearance for entry in this capacity and is able to satisfy the Secretary of State that each of the requirements of paragraph 197(i)–(vi) is met. An application for indefinite leave to remain in this category may be granted provided the applicant was admitted with a valid United Kingdom entry clearance for entry in this capacity and is able to satisfy the Secretary of State that each of the requirements of paragraph 197(i)–(vi) is met and provided indefinite leave to remain is, at the same time, being granted to the person with limited leave to enter or remain under paragraphs 128–193.

[A.2.201]
Refusal of leave to enter or remain as the child of a person with limited leave to enter or remain in the United Kingdom under paragraphs 128–193

199 Leave to enter or remain in the United Kingdom as the child of a person with limited leave to enter or remain in the United Kingdom under paragraphs 128–193 is to be refused if, in relation to an application for leave to enter, a valid United Kingdom entry clearance for entry in this capacity is not produced to the Immigration Officer on arrival or, in the case of an application for

limited leave to remain, if the applicant was not admitted with a valid United Kingdom entry clearance for entry in this capacity or is unable to satisfy the Secretary of State that each of the requirements of paragraph 197(i)–(vi) is met. An application for indefinite leave to remain in this category is to be refused if the applicant was not admitted with a valid United Kingdom entry clearance for entry in this capacity or is unable to satisfy the Secretary of State that each of the requirements of paragraph 197(i)–(vi) is met or if indefinite leave to remain is not, at the same time, being granted to the person with limited leave to enter or remain under paragraphs 128–193.

Part 6: Persons seeking to enter or remain in the United Kingdom as a businessman, self-employed person, investor, writer, composer or artist

PERSONS INTENDING TO ESTABLISH THEMSELVES IN BUSINESS

[A.2.202]
Requirements for leave to enter the United Kingdom as a person intending to establish himself in business
200   For the purpose of paragraphs 201–210 a business means an enterprise as:

– a sole trader; or
– a partnership; or
– a company registered in the United Kingdom.

201   The requirements to be met by a person seeking leave to enter the United Kingdom to establish himself in business are:

(i) that he satisfies the requirements of either paragraph 202 or paragraph 203; and
(ii) that he has not less than £200,000 of his own money under his control and disposable in the United Kingdom which is held in his own name and not by a trust or other investment vehicle and which he will be investing in the business in the United Kingdom; and
(iii) that until his business provides him with an income he will have sufficient additional funds to maintain and accommodate himself and any dependants without recourse to employment (other than his work for the business) or to public funds; and
(iv) that he will be actively involved full-time in trading or providing services on his own account or in partnership, or in the promotion and management of the company as a director; and
(v) that his level of financial investment will be proportional to his interest in the business; and
(vi) that he will have either a controlling or equal interest in the business and that any partnership or directorship does not amount to disguised employment; and
(vii) that he will be able to bear his share of liabilities; and
(viii) that there is a genuine need for his investment and services in the United Kingdom; and
(ix) that his share of the profits of the business will be sufficient to maintain and accommodate himself and any dependants without recourse to employment (other than his work for the business) or to public funds; and

(x) that he does not intend to supplement his business activities by taking or seeking employment in the United Kingdom other than his work for the business; and

(xi) that he holds a valid United Kingdom entry clearance for entry in this capacity.

202   Where a person intends to take over or join as a partner or director an existing business in the United Kingdom he will need, in addition to meeting the requirements at paragraph 201, to produce:

(i) a written statement of the terms on which he is to take over or join the business; and

(ii) audited accounts for the business for previous years; and

(iii) evidence that his services and investment will result in a net increase in the employment provided by the business to persons settled here to the extent of creating at least 2 new full-time jobs.

203   Where a person intends to establish a new business in the United Kingdom he will need, in addition to meeting the requirements at paragraph 201 above, to produce evidence:

(i) that he will be bringing into the country sufficient funds of his own to establish a business; and

(ii) that the business will create full-time paid employment for at least 2 persons already settled in the United Kingdom.

[A.2.203]
Leave to enter the United Kingdom as a person seeking to establish himself in business
204   A person seeking leave to enter the United Kingdom to establish himself in business may be admitted for a period not exceeding 12 months with a condition restricting his freedom to take employment provided he is able to produce to the Immigration Officer, on arrival, a valid United Kingdom entry clearance for entry in this capacity.

[A.2.204]
Refusal of leave to enter the United Kingdom as a person seeking to establish himself in business
205   Leave to enter the United Kingdom as a person seeking to establish himself in business is to be refused if a valid United Kingdom entry clearance for entry in this capacity is not produced to the Immigration Officer on arrival.

[A.2.205]
Requirements for an extension of stay in order to remain in business
206   The requirements for an extension to stay in order to remain in business in the United Kingdom are that the applicant can show:

(i) that he entered the United Kingdom with a valid United Kingdom entry clearance as a businessman; and

(ii) audited accounts which show the precise financial position of the business and which confirm that he has invested not less than £200,000 of his own money directly into the business in the United Kingdom; and

  (iii) that he is actively involved on a full-time basis in trading or providing services on his own account or in partnership or in the promotion and management of the company as a director; and

  (iv) that his level of financial investment is proportional to his interest in the business; and

  (v) that he has either a controlling or equal interest in the business and that any partnership or directorship does not amount to disguised employment; and

  (vi) that he is able to bear his share of any liability the business may incur; and

  (vii) that there is a genuine need for his investment and services in the United Kingdom; and

(viii) (*a*) that where he has established a new business, new full-time paid employment has been created in the business for at least 2 persons settled in the United Kingdom; or

     (*b*) that where he has taken over or joined an existing business, his services and investment have resulted in a net increase in the employment provided by the business to persons settled here to the extent of creating at least 2 new full-time jobs; and

  (ix) that his share of the profits of the business is sufficient to maintain and accommodate him and any dependants without recourse to employment (other than his work for the business) or to public funds; and

  (x) that he does not and will not have to supplement his business activities by taking or seeking employment in the United Kingdom other than his work for the business.

[A.2.206]
Extension of stay in order to remain in business
207   An extension of stay in order to remain in business with a condition restricting his freedom to take employment may be granted for a period not exceeding 3 years provided the Secretary of State is satisfied that each of the requirements of paragraph 206 is met.

[A.2.207]
Refusal of extension of stay in order to remain in business
208   An extension of stay in order to remain in business is to be refused if the Secretary of State is not satisfied that each of the requirements of paragraph 206 is met.

[A.2.208]
Indefinite leave to remain for a person established in business
209   Indefinite leave to remain may be granted, on application, to a person established in business provided he:

  (i) has spent a continuous period of 4 years in the United Kingdom in this capacity and is still engaged in the business in question; and

  (ii) has met the requirements of paragraph 206 throughout the 4 year period; and

  (iii) submits audited accounts for the first 3 years of trading and management accounts for the 4th year.

[A.2.209]
Refusal of indefinite leave to remain for a person established in business
210   Indefinite leave to remain in the United Kingdom for a person established in business is to be refused if the Secretary of State is not satisfied that each of the requirements of paragraph 209 is met.

PERSONS INTENDING TO ESTABLISH THEMSELVES IN BUSINESS UNDER PROVISIONS OF
EC ASSOCIATION AGREEMENTS

[A.2.210]
Requirements for leave to enter the United Kingdom as a person intending to establish himself in business under the provisions of an EC Association Agreement
211   For the purpose of paragraphs 212–223 a business means an enterprise as:

– a sole trader; or
– a partnership; or
– a company registered in the United Kingdom.

212   The requirements to be met by a person seeking leave to enter the United Kingdom to establish himself in business are that:

(i) he satisfies the requirements of either paragraph 213 or paragraph 214; and
(ii) the money he is putting into the business is under his control and sufficient to establish himself in business in the United Kingdom; and
(iii) until his business provides him with an income he will have sufficient additional funds to maintain and accommodate himself and any dependants without recourse to employment (other than his work for the business) or to public funds; and
(iv) his share of the profits of the business will be sufficient to maintain and accommodate himself and any dependants without recourse to employment (other than his work for the business) or to public funds; and
(v) he does not intend to supplement his business activities by taking or seeking employment in the United Kingdom other than his work for the business; and
(vi) he holds a valid United Kingdom entry clearance for entry in this capacity.

213   Where a person intends to establish himself in a company in the United Kingdom which he effectively controls he will need, in addition to meeting the requirements at paragraph 212, to show:

[(i) that he is a national of Bulgaria, the Czech Republic, Estonia, Hungary, Latvia, Poland, Romania, Slovakia or Slovenia; and]
(ii) that he will have a controlling interest in the company; and
(iii) that he will be actively involved in the promotion and management of the company; and
(iv) that the company will be registered in the United Kingdom and be trading or providing services in the United Kingdom; and
(v) that the company will be the owner of the assets of the business; and
(vi) where he is taking over an existing company, a written statement of the

terms on which he is to take over the business and audited accounts for the business for previous years.

Note   Paragraph 213(i) substituted by CM 4851.

---

214   Where a person intends to establish himself in self-employment or in partnership in the United Kingdom he will need, in addition to meeting the requirements at 212 above, to show:

[(i) that he is a national of Bulgaria, the Czech Republic, Estonia, Hungary, Latvia, Lithuania, Poland, Romania or Slovakia; and]
(ii) that he will be actively involved in trading or providing services on his own account or in partnership in the United Kingdom; and
(iii) that he, or he together with his partners, will be the owner of the assets of the business; and
(iv) in the case of a partnership, that his part in the business will not amount to disguised employment; and
(v) where he is taking over or joining an existing business a written statement of the terms on which he is to take over or join the business and audited accounts for the business for previous years.

Note   Paragraph 214(i) substituted by CM 4851.

[A.2.211]
Leave to enter the United Kingdom as a person seeking to establish himself in business under the provisions of an EC Association Agreement
215   A person seeking leave to enter the United Kingdom to establish himself in business may be admitted for a period not exceeding 12 months with a condition restricting his freedom to take employment provided he is able to produce to the Immigration Officer, on arrival, a valid United Kingdom entry clearance for entry in this capacity.

[A.2.212]
Refusal of leave to enter the United Kingdom as a person seeking to establish himself in business under the provisions of an EC Association Agreement
216   Leave to enter the United Kingdom as a person seeking to establish himself in business is to be refused if a valid United Kingdom entry clearance for entry in this capacity is not produced to the Immigration Officer on arrival.

[A.2.213]
Requirements for an extension of stay in order to remain in business under the provisions of an EC Association Agreement
217   The requirements for an extension of stay in order to remain in business in the United Kingdom are that the applicant can show that:

(i) he has established himself in business in the United Kingdom; and
(ii) his share of the profits of the business is sufficient to maintain and accommodate himself and any dependants without recourse to employment (other than his work for the business) or to public funds; and

(iii) he does not and will not supplement his business activities by taking or seeking employment in the United Kingdom other than his work for the business; and

(iv) in addition he satisfies the requirements of either paragraph 218 or paragraph 219.

218   Where a person has established himself in a company in the United Kingdom which he effectively controls he will need, in addition to meeting the requirements at paragraph 217 above, to show:

[(i) that he is a national of Bulgaria, the Czech Republic, Estonia, Hungary, Latvia, Lithuania, Poland, Romania, Slovakia or Slovenia; and]

(ii) that he is actively involved in the promotion and management of the company; and

(iii) that he has a controlling interest in the company; and

(iv) that the company is registered in the United Kingdom and trading or providing services in the United Kingdom; and

(v) that the company is the owner of the assets of the business; and

(vi) the current financial position in the form of audited accounts for the company.

Note   Paragraph 218(i) substituted by CM 4851.

219   Where a person has established himself as a sole trader or in partnership in the United Kingdom he will need, in addition to meeting the requirements at 217 above, to show:

[(i) that he is a national of Bulgaria, the Czech Republic, Estonia, Hungary, Latvia, Lithuania, Poland, Romania or Slovakia; and]

(ii) that he is actively involved in trading or providing services on his own account or in partnership in the United Kingdom; and

(iii) that he, or he together with his partners, is the owner of the assets of the business; and

(iv) in the case of a partnership, that his part in the business does not amount to disguised employment; and

(v) the current financial position in the form of audited accounts for the business.

Note   Paragraph 219(i) substituted by CM 4851.

[A.2.214]
Extension of stay in order to remain in business under the provisions of an EC Association Agreement
220   An extension of stay in order to remain in business with a condition restricting his freedom to take employment may be granted for a period not exceeding 3 years provided the Secretary of State is satisfied that each of the requirements of paragraphs 217 and 218 or 219 is met.

[A.2.215]
Refusal of extension of stay in order to remain in business under the provisions of an EC Association Agreement
221   An extension of stay in order to remain in business is to be refused if the Secretary of State is not satisfied that each of the requirements of paragraphs 217 and 218 or 219 is met.

[A.2.216]
Indefinite leave to remain for a person established in business under the provisions of an EC Association Agreement
222   Indefinite leave to remain may be granted, on application, to a person established in business provided he:

(i) has spent a continuous period of 4 years in the United Kingdom in this capacity and is still so engaged; and
(ii) has met the requirements of paragraphs 217 and 218 or 219 throughout the 4 years; and
(iii) submits audited accounts for the first 3 years of trading and management accounts for the 4th year.

[A.2.217]
Refusal of indefinite leave to remain for a person established in business under the provisions of an EC Association Agreement
223   Indefinite leave to remain in the United Kingdom for a person established in business is to be refused if the Secretary of State is not satisfied that each of the requirements of paragraph 222 is met.

Note   Paras 200–223 replace HC 251, paras 41–43 and 125–127.

INVESTORS

[A.2.218]
Requirements for leave to enter the United Kingdom as an investor
224   The requirements to be met by a person seeking leave to enter the United Kingdom as an investor are that he:

(i) has money of his own under his control and disposable in the United Kingdom amounting to no less than £1 million; and
(ii) intends to invest not less than £750,000 of his capital in the United Kingdom by way of United Kingdom Government bonds, share capital or loan capital in active and trading United Kingdom registered companies (other than those principally engaged in property investment and excluding investment by the applicant by way of deposits with a bank, building society or other enterprise whose normal course of business includes the acceptance of deposits); and
(iii) intends to make the United Kingdom his main home; and
(iv) is able to maintain and accommodate himself and any dependants without taking employment (other than self-employment or business) or recourse to public funds; and
(v) holds a valid United Kingdom entry clearance for entry in this capacity.

[A.2.219]
Leave to enter as an investor
225   A person seeking leave to enter the United Kingdom as an investor may be admitted for a period not exceeding 12 months with a restriction on his right to take employment, provided he is able to produce to the Immigration Officer, on arrival, a valid United Kingdom entry clearance for entry in this capacity.

[A.2.220]
Refusal of leave to enter as an investor
226   Leave to enter as an investor is to be refused if a valid United Kingdom entry clearance for entry in this capacity is not produced to the Immigration Officer on arrival.

[A.2.221]
Requirements for an extension of stay as an investor
227   The requirements for an extension of stay as an investor are that the applicant:

(i)   entered the United Kingdom with a valid United Kingdom entry clearance as an investor; and

(ii) has no less than £1 million of his own money under his control in the United Kingdom; and

(iii) has invested not less than £750,000 of his capital in the United Kingdom on the terms set out in paragraph 224(ii) above and intends to maintain that investment on the terms set out in paragraph 224(ii); and

(iv) has made the United Kingdom his main home; and

(v)   is able to maintain and accommodate himself and any dependants without taking employment (other than his self-employment or business) or recourse to public funds.

[A.2.222]
Extension of stay as an investor
228   An extension of stay as an investor, with a restriction on the taking of employment, may be granted for a maximum period of 3 years, provided the Secretary of State is satisfied that each of the requirements of paragraph 227 is met.

[A.2.223]
Refusal of extension of stay as an investor
229   An extension of stay as an investor is to be refused if the Secretary of State is not satisfied that each of the requirements of paragraph 227 is met.

[A.2.224]
Indefinite leave to remain for an investor
230   Indefinite leave to remain may be granted, on application, to a person admitted as an investor provided he:

(i) has spent a continuous period of 4 years in the United Kingdom in this capacity; and

(ii) has met the requirements of paragraph 227 throughout the 4 year period including the requirement as to the investment of £750,000 and continues to do so.

[A.2.225]
Refusal of indefinite leave to remain for an investor
231 Indefinite leave to remain in the United Kingdom for an investor is to be refused if the Secretary of State is not satisfied that each of the requirements of paragraph 230 is met.

Note This is a new category (paras 224–231). Formerly (under HC 251) persons with £500,000 or more could qualify for leave to enter as persons of independent means under the 'general interests' provisions, however, from 1 October 1994, that category has been restricted to retired persons aged 60 or over with a close connection to the United Kingdom (see HC 395 paras 263–376). There is no age restriction on the new investor category and, unlike the old independent means, investors are permitted to engage in business. The investment, however, must be substantial and the applicant can only invest in certain specified investments. The applicant must also intend to make his 'main home' in the United Kingdom.

WRITERS, COMPOSERS AND ARTISTS

[A.2.226]
Requirements for leave to enter the United Kingdom as a writer,
composer or artist
232 The requirements to be met by a person seeking leave to enter the United Kingdom as a writer, composer or artist are that he:

(i) has established himself outside the United Kingdom as a writer, composer or artist primarily engaged in producing original work which has been published (other than exclusively in newspapers or magazines), performed or exhibited for its literary, musical or artistic merit; and

(ii) does not intend to work except as related to his self-employment as a writer, composer or artist; and

(iii) has for the preceding year been able to maintain and accommodate himself and any dependants from his own resources without working except as a writer, composer or artist; and

(iv) will be able to maintain and accommodate himself and any dependants from his own resources without working except as a writer, composer or artist and without recourse to public funds; and

(v) holds a valid United Kingdom entry clearance for entry in this capacity.

[A.2.227]
Leave to enter as a writer, composer or artist
233 A person seeking leave to enter the United Kingdom as a writer, composer or artist may be admitted for a period not exceeding 12 months, subject

to a condition restricting his freedom to take employment, provided he is able to produce to the Immigration Officer, on arrival, a valid United Kingdom entry clearance for entry in this capacity.

[A.2.228]
Refusal of leave to enter as a writer, composer or artist
234 Leave to enter as a writer, composer or artist is to be refused if a valid United Kingdom entry clearance for entry in this capacity is not produced to the Immigration Officer on arrival.

[A.2.229]
Requirements for an extension of stay as a writer, composer or artist
235 The requirements for an extension of stay as a writer, composer or artist are that the applicant:

(i) entered the United Kingdom with a valid United Kingdom entry clearance as a writer, composer or artist; and
(ii) meets the requirements of paragraph 232(ii)–(iv).

[A.2.230]
Extension of stay as a writer, composer or artist
236 An extension of stay as writer, composer or artist may be granted for a period not exceeding 3 years with a restriction on his freedom to take employment, provided the Secretary of State is satisfied that each of the requirements of paragraph 235 is met.

[A.2.231]
Refusal of extension of stay as a writer, composer or artist
237 An extension of stay as a writer, composer or artist is to be refused if the Secretary of State is not satisfied that each of the requirements of paragraph 235 is met.

[A.2.232]
Indefinite leave to remain for a writer, composer or artist
238 Indefinite leave to remain may be granted, on application, to a person admitted as a writer, composer or artist provided he:

(i) has spent a continuous period of 4 years in the United Kingdom in this capacity; and
(ii) has met the requirements of paragraph 235 throughout the 4 year period.

[A.2.233]
Refusal of indefinite leave to remain for a writer, composer or artist
239 Indefinite leave to remain for a writer, composer or artist is to be refused

if the Secretary of State is not satisfied that each of the requirements of paragraph 238 is met.

Note   Paras 232–239 replace HC 251, paras 45, 128 and 139(e).

Composers have been included along with writers and artists; and there are more detailed rules including a requirement that a person seeking leave to enter or remain as either a composer, writer or artist must have first established himself in his particular field abroad.

SPOUSES OF PERSONS WITH LIMITED LEAVE TO ENTER OR REMAIN UNDER PARAGRAPHS 200–239

[A.2.234]
Requirements for leave to enter or remain as the spouse of a person with limited leave to enter or remain under paragraphs 200–239
240   The requirements to be met by a person seeking leave to enter or remain in the United Kingdom as the spouse of a person with limited leave to enter or remain in the United Kingdom under paragraphs 200–239 are that:

 (i) the applicant is married to a person with limited leave to enter or remain in the United Kingdom under paragraphs 200–239; and
 (ii) each of the parties intends to live with the other as his or her spouse during the applicant's stay and the marriage is subsisting; and
 (iii) there will be adequate accommodation for the parties and any dependants without recourse to public funds in accommodation which they own or occupy exclusively; and
 (iv) the parties will be able to maintain themselves and any dependants adequately without recourse to public funds; and
 (v) the applicant does not intend to stay in the United Kingdom beyond any period of leave granted to his spouse; and
 (vi) if seeking leave to enter, the applicant holds a valid United Kingdom entry clearance for entry in this capacity or, if seeking leave to remain, was admitted with a valid United Kingdom entry clearance for entry in this capacity.

[A.2.235]
Leave to enter or remain as the spouse of a person with limited leave to enter or remain in the United Kingdom under paragraphs 200–239
241   A person seeking leave to enter or remain in the United Kingdom as the spouse of a person with limited leave to enter or remain in the United Kingdom under paragraphs 200–239 may be given leave to enter or remain in the United Kingdom for a period of leave not in excess of that granted to the person with limited leave to enter or remain under paragraphs 200–239 provided that, in relation to an application for leave to enter, he is able, on arrival, to produce to the Immigration Officer a valid United Kingdom entry clearance for entry in this capacity or, in the case of an application for limited leave to remain, he was admitted with a valid United Kingdom entry clearance for entry in this

capacity and is able the satisfy the Secretary of State that each of the requirements of paragraph 240(i)–(v) is met. An application for indefinite leave to remain in this category may be granted provided the applicant was admitted with a valid United Kingdom entry clearance for entry in this capacity and is able to satisfy the Secretary of State that each of the requirements of paragraph 240(i)–(v) is met and provided indefinite leave to remain is, at the same time, being granted to the person with limited leave to remain under paragraphs 200–239.

[A.2.236]
Refusal of leave to enter or remain as the spouse of a person with limited leave to enter or remain in the United Kingdom under paragraphs 200–239

242   Leave to enter or remain in the United Kingdom as the spouse of a person with limited leave to enter or remain in the United Kingdom under paragraphs 200–239 is to be refused if, in relation to an application for leave to enter, a valid United Kingdom entry clearance for entry in this capacity is not produced to the Immigration Officer on arrival or, in the case of an application for limited leave to remain, if the applicant was not admitted with a valid United Kingdom entry clearance for entry in this capacity or is unable to satisfy the Secretary of State that each of the requirements of paragraph 240(i)–(v) is met. An application for indefinite leave to remain in this category is to be refused if the applicant was not admitted with a valid United Kingdom entry clearance for entry in this capacity or is unable to satisfy the Secretary of State that each of the requirements of paragraph 240(i)–(v) is met or if indefinite leave to remain is not, at the same time, being granted to the person with limited leave to remain under paragraphs 200–239.

CHILDREN OF PERSONS WITH LIMITED LEAVE TO ENTER OR REMAIN UNDER
PARAGRAPHS 200–239

[A.2.237]
Requirements for leave to enter or remain as the child of a person with limited leave to enter or remain in the United Kingdom under paragraphs 200–239

243   The requirements to be met by a person seeking leave to enter or remain in the United Kingdom as a child of a person with limited leave to enter or remain in the United Kingdom under paragraphs 200–239 are that:

  (i) he is the child of a parent who has leave to enter or remain in the United Kingdom under paragraphs 200–239; and
 (ii) he is under the age of 18 or has current leave to enter or remain in this capacity; and
(iii) he is unmarried, has not formed an independent family unit and is not leading an independent life; and
 (iv) he can and will be maintained and accommodated adequately without recourse to public funds in accommodation which his parent(s) own or occupy exclusively; and

   (v) he will not stay in the United Kingdom beyond any period of leave granted to his parent(s); and

  (vi) both parents are being or have been admitted to or allowed to remain in the United Kingdom save where:

        (*a*) the parent he is accompanying or joining is his sole surviving parent; or

        (*b*) the parent he is accompanying or joining has had sole responsibility for his upbringing; or

        (*c*) there are serious and compelling family or other considerations which make exclusion from the United Kingdom undesirable and suitable arrangements have been made for his care; and

  (vii) if seeking leave to enter, he holds a valid United Kingdom entry clearance for entry in this capacity or, if seeking leave to remain, was admitted with a valid United Kingdom entry clearance for entry in this capacity.

[A.2.238]

Leave to enter or remain as the child of a person with limited leave to enter or remain in the United Kingdom under paragraphs 200–239

244   A person seeking leave to enter or remain in the United Kingdom as the child of a person with limited leave to enter or remain in the United Kingdom under paragraphs 200–239 may be admitted to or allowed to remain in the United Kingdom for the same period of leave as that granted to the person given limited leave to enter or remain under paragraphs 200–239 provided that, in relation to an application for leave to enter, he is able to produce to the Immigration Officer, on arrival, a valid United Kingdom entry clearance for entry in this capacity or, in the case of an application for limited leave to remain, he was admitted with a valid United Kingdom entry clearance for entry in this capacity and is able the satisfy the Secretary of State that each of the requirements of paragraph 243(i)–(vi) is met. An application for indefinite leave to remain in this category may be granted provided the applicant was admitted with a valid United Kingdom entry clearance for entry in this capacity and is able to satisfy the Secretary of State that each of the requirements of paragraph 243(i)–(vi) is met and provided indefinite leave to remain is, at the same time, being granted to the person with limited leave to remain under paragraphs 200–239.

[A.2.239]

Refusal of leave to enter or remain as the child of a person with limited leave to enter or remain in the United Kingdom under paragraphs 200–239

245   Leave to enter or remain in the United Kingdom as the child of a person with limited leave to enter or remain in the United Kingdom under paragraphs 200–239 is to be refused if, in relation to an application for leave to enter, a valid United Kingdom entry clearance for entry in this capacity is not produced to the Immigration Officer on arrival or, in the case of an application for limited leave to remain, if the applicant was not admitted with a valid United Kingdom entry clearance for entry in this capacity or is unable to satisfy the Secretary of State that each of the requirements of paragraph 243(i)–(vi) is met. An application for indefinite leave to remain in this capacity is to be refused if the applicant was not admitted with a valid United Kingdom entry clearance for

entry in this capacity or is unable to satisfy the Secretary of State that each of the requirements of paragraph 243(i)–(vi) is met or if indefinite leave to remain is not, at the same time, being granted to the person with limited leave to remain under paragraphs 200–239.

Part 7: Other categories

PERSONS EXERCISING RIGHTS OF ACCESS TO A CHILD RESIDENT IN THE UNITED KINGDOM

[A.2.240]
[Requirements for leave to enter the United Kingdom as a person exercising rights of access to a child resident in the United Kingdom
246   The requirements to be met by a person seeking leave to enter the United Kingdom to exercise access rights to a child resident in the United Kingdom are that:

  (i)   the applicant is the parent of a child who is resident in the United Kingdom; and
  (ii)   the parent or carer with whom the child permanently resides is resident in the United Kingdom; and
  (iii)   the applicant produces evidence that he has access rights to the child in the form of:
          (*a*) a Residence Order or a Contact Order granted by a Court in the United Kingdom; or
          (*b*) a certificate issued by a district judge confirming the applicant's intention to maintain contact with the child; and
  (iv)   the applicant intends to continue to take an active role in the child's upbringing; and
  (v)   the child is under the age of 18; and
  (vi)   there will be adequate accommodation for the applicant and any dependants without recourse to public funds in accommodation which the applicant owns or occupies exclusively; and
  (vii)   the applicant will be able to maintain himself and any dependants adequately without recourse to public funds; and
  (viii) the applicant holds a valid United Kingdom entry clearance for entry in this capacity.

[A.2.241]
Leave to enter the United Kingdom as a person exercising rights of access to a child resident in the United Kingdom
247   Leave to enter as a person exercising access rights to a child resident in the United Kingdom may be granted for 12 months in the first instance, provided that a valid United Kingdom entry clearance for entry in this capacity is produced to the Immigration Officer on arrival.

[A.2.242]
Refusal of leave to enter the United Kingdom as a person exercising rights of access to a child resident in the United Kingdom
248   Leave to enter as a person exercising rights of access to a child resident in the United Kingdom is to be refused if a valid United Kingdom entry clearance for entry in this capacity is not produced to the Immigration Officer on arrival.]

[A.2.243]
[Requirements for leave to remain in the United Kingdom as a person exercising rights of access to a child resident in the United Kingdom
248A   The requirements to be met by a person seeking leave to remain in the United Kingdom to exercise access rights to a child resident in the United Kingdom are that:

(i)   the applicant is the parent of a child who is resident in the United Kingdom; and

(ii)   the parent or carer with whom the child permanently resides is resident in the United Kingdom; and

(iii)   the applicant produces evidence that he has access rights to the child in the form of:

(*a*) a Residence Order or a Contact Order granted by a Court in the United Kingdom; or

(*b*) a certificate issued by a district judge confirming the applicant's intention to maintain contact with the child; or

(*c*) a statement from the child's other parent (or, if contact is supervised, from the supervisor) that the applicant is maintaining contact with the child; and

(iv)   the applicant takes and intends to continue to take an active role in the child's upbringing; and

(v)   the child visits or stays with the applicant on a frequent and regular basis and the applicant intends this to continue; and

(vi)   the child is under the age of 18; and

(vii)   the applicant has limited leave to remain in the United Kingdom as the spouse or unmarried partner of a person present and settled in the United Kingdom who is the other parent of the child; and

(viii) the applicant has not remained in breach of the immigration laws; and

(ix)   there will be adequate accommodation for the applicant and any dependants without recourse to public funds in accommodation which the applicant owns or occupies exclusively; and

(x)   the applicant will be able to maintain himself and any dependants adequately without recourse to public funds.

[A.2.244]
Leave to remain in the United Kingdom as a person exercising rights of access to a child resident in the United Kingdom
248B   Leave to remain as a person exercising access rights to a child resident in the United Kingdom may be granted for 12 months in the first instance, provided the Secretary of State is satisfied that each of the requirements of paragraph 248A is met.

[A.2.245]
Refusal of leave to remain in the United Kingdom as a person exercising rights of access to a child resident in the United Kingdom
248C   Leave to remain as a person exercising rights of access to a child resident in the United Kingdom is to be refused if the Secretary of State is not satisfied that each of the requirements of paragraph 248A is met.

[A.2.246]
Indefinite leave to remain in the United Kingdom as a person exercising rights of access to a child resident in the United Kingdom
248D The requirements for indefinite leave to remain in the United Kingdom as a person exercising rights of access to a child resident in the United Kingdom are that:

(i) the applicant was admitted to the United Kingdom or granted leave to remain in the United Kingdom for a period of 12 months as a person exercising rights of access to a child and has completed a period of 12 months as a person exercising rights of access to a child; and

(ii) the applicant takes and intends to continue to take an active role in the child's upbringing; and

(iii) the child visits or stays with the applicant on a frequent and regular basis and the applicant intends this to continue; and

(iv) there will be adequate accommodation for the applicant and any dependants without recourse to public funds in accommodation which the applicant owns or occupies exclusively; and

(v) the applicant will be able to maintain himself and any dependants adequately without recourse to public funds; and

(vi) the child is under 18 years of age.

[A.2.247]
Indefinite leave to remain as a person exercising rights of access to a child resident in the United Kingdom
248E Indefinite leave to remain as a person exercising rights of access to a child may be granted provided the Secretary of State is satisfied that each of the requirements of paragraph 248D is met.

[A.2.248]
Refusal of indefinite leave to remain in the United Kingdom as a person exercising rights of access to a child resident in the United Kingdom
248F Indefinite leave to remain as a person exercising rights of access to a child is to be refused if the Secretary of State is not satisfied that each of the requirements of paragraph 248D is met.]

Note Paragraphs 246–248 substituted by CM 4851.

Paragraphs 248A–248F inserted by CM 4851.

These rules are not only going to be helpful to persons exercising rights of access to their children, but also to the United Kingdom government in the event of a human rights challenge by a parent excluded from the UK, see s 65 Immigration and Asylum Act 1999. Such a parent will, arguably, no longer be able to claim a violation of his or the child's right to family life contrary to the European Convention on Human Rights, art 8: see *Berrehab v The Netherlands* (1988) 11 EHRR 322.

It is to be noted that the rules only cover orders for contact made by UK courts presumably on the footing that it will normally be in those kinds of cases that the need for access to a child will arise in the UK.

HOLDERS OF SPECIAL VOUCHERS

[A.2.249]
Requirements for indefinite leave to enter as the holder of a special voucher
249   The requirements for indefinite leave to enter as the holder of a special voucher are that the person concerned:

(i) is a British Overseas citizen; and

(ii) is in possession of a special voucher issued to him by a British Government representative overseas or a valid United Kingdom entry clearance for settlement in the United Kingdom in this capacity.

[A.2.250]
Indefinite leave to enter as the holder of a special voucher
250   A British Overseas citizen may be granted indefinite leave to enter the United Kingdom provided he is able to produce to the Immigration Officer, on arrival, either a special voucher issued to him by a British Government representative or a valid United Kingdom entry clearance for settlement in this capacity.

[A.2.251]
Refusal of indefinite leave to enter as the holder of a special voucher
251   Indefinite leave to enter as the holder of a special voucher is to be refused if neither a special voucher issued by a British Government representative nor a valid United Kingdom entry clearance for settlement in this capacity is produced to the Immigration Officer on arrival.

[A.2.252]
Requirements for indefinite leave to enter as the spouse or child of a special voucher holder
252   The requirements for indefinite leave to enter the United Kingdom as the spouse or child of a special voucher holder are that the person concerned:

(i) is in possession of a valid United Kingdom entry clearance for settlement in the United Kingdom in this capacity; and

(ii) can and will be maintained and accommodated adequately by the special voucher holder without recourse to public funds.

[A.2.253]
Indefinite leave to enter as the spouse or child of a special voucher holder
253   Indefinite leave to enter as the spouse or child of a special voucher holder may be granted provided a valid United Kingdom entry clearance for settlement is produced to the Immigration Officer on arrival.

[A.2.254]
Refusal of indefinite leave to enter as the spouse or child of a special voucher holder
254   Indefinite leave to enter as the spouse or child of a special voucher holder is to be refused if a valid United Kingdom entry clearance for settlement is

not produced to the Immigration Officer on arrival.

Note   Paras 249–254 replace HC 251, paras 49 and 52.

No substantive change has taken place as a result of what, in effect, is a consolidation of the requirements of the previous rules. Moreover, under HC 395, para 250, the entitlement to indefinite leave to enter is made express.

EEA NATIONALS AND THEIR FAMILIES

[A.2.255]
Settlement
[255   Any person (other than a student) who under, either the Immigration (European Economic Area) Order 1994, or the 2000 EEA Regulations has been issued with a residence permit or residence document valid for 5 years, and who has remained in the United Kingdom in accordance with the provisions of that Order or those Regulations (as the case may be) for 4 years and continues to do so may, on application, have his residence permit or residence document (as the case may be) endorsed to show permission to remain in the United Kingdom indefinitely.]

Note   Substituted by CM 4851.

256   [. . .].

Note   Paragraph 256 deleted by CM 4851.

257   In addition, the following persons will be permitted to remain in the United Kingdom indefinitely [in accordance with Commission Regulation 1251/70]:

  (i) an EEA national who has been continuously resident in the United Kingdom for at least 3 years, has been in employment in the United Kingdom or any other Member State of the EEA for the preceding 12 months, and has reached the age of entitlement to a state retirement pension;

  (ii) an EEA national who has ceased to be employed owing to a permanent incapacity for work arising out of an accident at work or an occupational disease entitling him to a state disability pension;

  (iii) an EEA national who has been continuously resident in the United Kingdom for at least 2 years, and who has ceased to be employed owing to a permanent incapacity for work;

  (iv) a member of the family of an EEA national [. . .] to whom (i), (ii) or (iii) above applies;

(v) a member of the family of an EEA national [. . .] who dies during his working life after having resided continuously in the United Kingdom for at least 2 years, or whose death results from an accident at work or an occupational disease.

[For the purposes of this paragraph:

'EEA national' means a national of a State other than the United Kingdom which is a Contracting Party to the European Economic Area Agreement, but for the purposes of (iv) and (v) includes a national of the United Kingdom where the conditions set out in regulation 11 of the 2000 EEA Regulations are satisfied.

A 'member of the family' is a family member as defined in regulation 6 of the 2000 EEA Regulations, or a person whom it has been decided to treat as a family member in accordance with the principles set out in regulation 10 of those Regulations.]

Notes   Words deleted and words in square brackets inserted by CM 4851.

258–261 [. . .].

Note   Paragraphs 258–281deleted by CM 4851.

[A.2.256]
Registration with the police for family members of EEA nationals
262   [*Deleted with effect from 11 May 1998 by Cmnd 3953.*]

RETIRED PERSONS OF INDEPENDENT MEANS

[A.2.257]
Requirements for leave to enter the United Kingdom as a retired person of independent means
263   The requirements to be met by a person seeking leave to enter the United Kingdom as a retired person of independent means are that he:
  (i) is at least 60 years old; and
 (ii) has under his control and disposable in the United Kingdom an income of his own of not less than £25,000 per annum; and
(iii) is able and willing to maintain and accommodate himself and any dependants indefinitely in the United Kingdom from his own resources with no assistance from any other person and without taking employment or having recourse to public funds; and
 (iv) can demonstrate a close connection with the United Kingdom; and
  (v) intends to make the United Kingdom his main home; and
 (vi) holds a valid United Kingdom entry clearance for entry in this capacity.

[A.2.258]
Leave to enter as a retired person of independent means
264   A person seeking leave to enter the United Kingdom as a retired person of independent means may be admitted subject to a condition prohibiting employment for a period not exceeding 4 years, provided he is able to produce to the Immigration Officer, on arrival, a valid United Kingdom entry clearance for entry in this capacity.

[A.2.259]
Refusal of leave to enter as a retired person of independent means
265   Leave to enter as a retired person of independent means is to be refused if a valid United Kingdom entry clearance for entry in this capacity is not produced to the Immigration Officer on arrival.

[A.2.260]
Requirements for an extension of stay as a retired person of independent means
266   The requirements for an extension of stay as a retired person of independent means are that the applicant:

(i) entered the United Kingdom with a valid United Kingdom entry clearance as a retired person of independent means; and
(ii) meets the requirements of paragraph 263(ii)–(iv); and
(iii) has made the United Kingdom his main home.

[A.2.261]
Extension of stay as a retired person of independent means
267   An extension of stay as a retired person of independent means, with a prohibition on the taking of employment, may be granted so as to bring the person's stay in this category up to a maximum of 4 years in aggregate, provided the Secretary of State is satisfied that each of the requirements of paragraph 266 is met.

[A.2.262]
Refusal of extension of stay as a retired person of independent means
268   An extension of stay as a retired person of independent means is to be refused if the Secretary of State is not satisfied that each of the requirements of paragraph 266 is met.

[A.2.263]
Indefinite leave to remain for a retired person of independent means
269   Indefinite leave to remain may be granted, on application, to a person admitted as a retired person of independent means provided he:

(i) has spent a continuous period of 4 years in the United Kingdom in this capacity; and
(ii) has met the requirements of paragraph 266 throughout the 4 year period and continues to do so.

[A.2.264]
Refusal of indefinite leave to remain for a retired person of independent means
270   Indefinite leave to remain in the United Kingdom for a retired person of independent means is to be refused if the Secretary of State is not satisfied that each of the requirements of paragraph 26[9] is met.

SPOUSES OF PERSONS WITH LIMITED LEAVE TO ENTER OR REMAIN IN THE UNITED KINGDOM
AS RETIRED PERSONS OF INDEPENDENT MEANS

[A.2.265]
Requirements for leave to enter or remain as the spouse of a person with limited leave to enter or remain in the United Kingdom as a retired person of independent means
271   The requirements to be met by a person seeking leave to enter or remain in the United Kingdom as the spouse of a person with limited leave to enter or remain in the United Kingdom as a retired person of independent means are that:
  (i) the applicant is married to a person with limited leave to enter or remain in the United Kingdom as a retired person of independent means; and
 (ii) each of the parties intends to live with the other as his or her spouse during the applicant's stay and the marriage is subsisting; and
(iii) there will be adequate accommodation for the parties and any dependants without recourse to public funds in accommodation which they own or occupy exclusively; and
 (iv) the parties will be able to maintain themselves and any dependants adequately without recourse to public funds; and
  (v) the applicant does not intend to stay in the United Kingdom beyond any period of leave granted to his spouse; and
 (vi) if seeking leave to enter, the applicant holds a valid United Kingdom entry clearance for entry in this capacity or, if seeking leave to remain, was admitted with a valid United Kingdom entry clearance for entry in this capacity.

[A.2.266]
Leave to enter or remain as the spouse of a person with limited leave to enter or remain in the United Kingdom as a retired person of independent means
272   A person seeking leave to enter or remain in the United Kingdom as the spouse of a person with limited leave to enter or remain in the United Kingdom as a retired person of independent means may be given leave to enter or remain in the United Kingdom for a period not in excess of that granted to the person given limited leave to enter or remain as a retired person of independent means provided that, in relation to an application for leave to enter, he is able to produce to the Immigration Officer, on arrival, a valid United Kingdom entry clearance for entry in this capacity, or, in the case of an application for limited leave to remain, he was admitted with a valid United Kingdom entry clearance for entry in this capacity and is able to satisfy the Secretary of State that each of the requirements of paragraph 271(i)–(v) is met. An application for indefinite leave to remain in this category may be granted provided the appli-

cant was admitted with a valid United Kingdom entry clearance for entry in this capacity and is able to satisfy the Secretary of State that each of the requirements of paragraph 271(i)–(v) is met and provided indefinite leave to remain is, at the same time, being granted to the person with limited leave to enter or remain as a retired person of independent means. Leave to enter or remain is to be subject to a condition prohibiting employment except in relation to the grant of indefinite leave to remain.

[A.2.267]

Refusal of leave to enter or remain as the spouse of a person with limited leave to enter or remain in the United Kingdom as a retired person of independent means

273   Leave to enter or remain in the United Kingdom as the spouse of a person with limited leave to enter or remain in the United Kingdom as a retired person of independent means is to be refused if, in relation to an application for leave to enter, a valid United Kingdom entry clearance for entry in this capacity is not produced to the Immigration Officer on arrival or, in the case of an application for limited leave to remain, if the applicant was not admitted with a valid United Kingdom entry clearance for entry in this capacity or is unable to satisfy the Secretary of State that each of the requirements of paragraph 271(i)–(v) is met. An application for indefinite leave to remain in this category is to be refused if the applicant was not admitted with a valid United Kingdom entry clearance for entry in this capacity or is unable to satisfy the Secretary of State that each of the requirements of paragraph 271(i)–(v) is met or if indefinite leave to remain is not, at the same time, being granted to the person with limited leave to enter or remain as a retired person of independent means.

CHILDREN OF PERSONS WITH LIMITED LEAVE TO ENTER OR REMAIN IN THE UNITED KINGDOM AS RETIRED PERSONS OF INDEPENDENT MEANS

[A.2.268]

Requirements for leave to enter or remain as the child of a person with limited leave to enter or remain in the United Kingdom as a retired person of independent means

274   The requirements to be met by a person seeking leave to enter or remain in the United Kingdom as the child of a person with limited leave to enter or remain in the United Kingdom as a retired person of independent means are that:

(i) he is the child of a parent who has been admitted to or allowed to remain in the United Kingdom as a retired person of independent means; and

(ii) he is under the age of 18 or has current leave to enter or remain in this capacity; and

(iii) he is unmarried, has not formed an independent family unit and is not leading an independent life; and

(iv) he can, and will, be maintained and accommodated adequately without recourse to public funds in accommodation which his parent(s) own or occupy exclusively; and

(v) he will not stay in the United Kingdom beyond any period of leave granted to his parent(s); and

(vi) both parents are being or have been admitted to or allowed to remain in the United Kingdom save where:

(*a*) the parent he is accompanying or joining is his sole surviving parent; or

(*b*) the parent he is accompanying or joining has had sole responsibility for his upbringing; or

(*c*) there are serious and compelling family or other considerations which make exclusion from the United Kingdom undesirable and suitable arrangements have been made for his care; and

(vii) if seeking leave to enter, he holds a valid United Kingdom entry clearance for entry in this capacity or, if seeking leave to remain, was admitted with a valid United Kingdom entry clearance for entry in this capacity.

[A.2.269]
Leave to enter or remain as the child of a person with limited leave to enter or remain in the United Kingdom as a retired person of independent means

275   A person seeking leave to enter or remain in the United Kingdom as the child of a person with limited leave to enter or remain in the United Kingdom as a retired person of independent means may be given leave to enter or remain in the United Kingdom for a period of leave not in excess of that granted to the person with limited leave to enter or remain as a retired person of independent means provided that, in relation to an application for leave to enter, he is able to produce to the Immigration Officer, on arrival, a valid United Kingdom entry clearance for entry in this capacity or, in the case of an application for limited leave to remain, he was admitted with a valid United Kingdom entry clearance for entry in this capacity and is able to satisfy the Secretary of State that each of the requirements of paragraph 274(i)–(vi) is met. An application for indefinite leave to remain in this category may be granted provided the applicant was admitted to the United Kingdom with a valid United Kingdom entry clearance for entry in this capacity and is able to satisfy the Secretary of State that each of the requirements of paragraph 274(i)–(vi) is met and provided indefinite leave to remain is, at the same time, being granted to the person with limited leave to enter or remain as a retired person of independent means. Leave to enter or remain is to be subject to a condition prohibiting employment except in relation to the grant of indefinite leave to remain.

[A.2.270]
Refusal of leave to enter or remain as the child of a person with limited leave to enter or remain in the United Kingdom as a retired person of independent means

276   Leave to enter or remain in the United Kingdom as the child of a person with limited leave to enter or remain in the United Kingdom as a retired person of independent means is to be refused if, in relation to an application for leave to enter, a valid United Kingdom entry clearance for entry in this capacity is not produced to the Immigration Officer on arrival, or in the case of an application for limited leave to remain, if the applicant was not admitted with a valid United Kingdom entry clearance for entry in this capacity or is unable to satisfy the Secretary of State that each of the requirements of paragraph 274(i)–(vi) is met. An application for indefinite leave to remain in this category is to be refused if the applicant was not admitted with a valid United Kingdom entry clearance for entry in this capacity or is unable to satisfy the

Secretary of State that each of the requirements of paragraph 274(i)–(vi) is met or if indefinite leave to remain is not, at the same time, being granted to the person with limited leave to enter or remain as a retired person of independent means.

Note   Paras 263–276 replace HC 251, paras 44, 129 and 139(f).

The former category of person of independent means is now restricted to *retired* persons aged 60 years or over who have a 'close connection' with the UK. There is now no provision for applicants without a 'close connection' whose presence in the UK would be in the 'general interest' of the UK. In addition, applicants must have under their control and disposable in the UK an *income* of not less than £25,000. This is a substantial increase in the old financial requirement of £200,000 capital or £20,000 income. In order to demonstrate an income of £25,000 at current interest rates the applicant's capital would have to be at least double the former capital requirement. Applicants must also intend to make the UK their 'main home'.

Part 8: Family members

SPOUSES

[A.2.271]
277   Nothing in these Rules shall be construed as permitting a person to be granted entry clearance, leave to enter, leave to remain or variation of leave as a spouse of another if either party to the marriage will be aged under 16 on the date of arrival in the United Kingdom or (as the case may be) on the date on which the leave to remain or variation of leave would be granted.

[278   Nothing in these Rules shall be construed as allowing a person to be granted entry

clearance, leave to enter, leave to remain or variation of leave as the spouse of a man or woman (the sponsor) if:

  (i) his or her marriage to the sponsor is polygamous; and
 (ii) there is another person living who is the husband or wife of the sponsor and who:
    (*a*) is, or at any time since his or her marriage to the sponsor has been, in the United Kingdom; or
    (*b*) has been granted a certificate of entitlement in respect of the right of abode mentioned in Section 2(1)(a) of the Immigration Act 1988 or an entry clearance to enter the United Kingdom as the husband or wife of the sponsor.

For the purpose of this paragraph a marriage may be polygamous although at its inception neither party had any other spouse.]

Note   Paragraph 278 substituted by CM 4851.

[279   Paragraph 278 does not apply to any person who seeks entry clearance, leave to enter, leave to remain or variation of leave where:

(i) he or she has been in the United Kingdom before 1 August 1988 having been admitted for the purpose of settlement as the husband or wife of the sponsor; or

(ii) he or she has, since their marriage to the sponsor, been in the United Kingdom at any time when there was no such other spouse living as is mentioned in paragraph 278 (ii).

But where a person claims that paragraph 278 does not apply to them because they have been in the United Kingdom in circumstances which cause them to fall within sub-paragraphs (i) or (ii) of that paragraph, it shall be for them to prove that fact.]

Note   Paragraph 279 substituted by CM 4851.

[280   For the purposes of paragraphs 278 and 279 the presence of any wife or husband in the United Kingdom in any of the following circumstances shall be disregarded:

(i)   as a visitor; or

(ii) an illegal entrant; or

(iii) in circumstances whereby a person is deemed by Section 11(1) of the Immigration Act 1971 not to have entered the United Kingdom.]

Note   Paragraph 280 substituted by CM 4851.

SPOUSES OF PERSONS PRESENT AND SETTLED IN THE UNITED KINGDOM OR BEING ADMITTED ON THE SAME OCCASION FOR SETTLEMENT

[A.2.272]
Requirements for leave to enter the United Kingdom with a view to settlement as the spouse of a person present and settled in the United Kingdom or being admitted on the same occasion for settlement
[281   The requirements to be met by a person seeking leave to enter the United Kingdom with a view to settlement as the spouse of a person present and settled in the United Kingdom or who is on the same occasion being admitted for settlement are that:

(i)   the applicant is married to a person present and settled in the United Kingdom or who is on the same occasion being admitted for settlement; and

(ii) the parties to the marriage have met; and

(iii) each of the parties intends to live permanently with the other as his or her spouse and the marriage is subsisting; and

(iv) there will be adequate accommodation for the parties and any dependants without recourse to public funds in accommodation which they own or occupy exclusively; and

(v)   the parties will be able to maintain themselves and any dependants adequately without recourse to public funds; and

(vi) the applicant holds a valid United Kingdom entry clearance for entry in this capacity.

[For the purposes of this paragraph and paragraphs 282-289 a member of HM Forces serving overseas, or a permanent member of HM Diplomatic Service or a comparable UK-based staff member of the British Council on a tour of duty abroad, is to be regarded as present and settled in the United Kingdom.]

Note   As with all references in the rules to 'public funds' it will be essential to note here the dates of changes in the definition as contained in para 6: see note at para **[A.2.4]**.
 Substituted by HC 26, para 1 with effect from 5 June 1997.
 Words in second set of square brackets substituted by CM 4851.

[A.2.273]
Leave to enter as the spouse of a person present and settled in the
United Kingdom or being admitted for settlement on the same occasion
282   A person seeking leave to enter the United Kingdom as the spouse of a person present and settled in the United Kingdom or who is on the same occasion being admitted for settlement may be admitted for an initial period not exceeding 12 months provided a valid United Kingdom entry clearance for entry in this capacity is produced to the Immigration Officer on arrival.

[A.2.274]
Refusal of leave to enter as the spouse of a person present and settled in
the United Kingdom or being admitted on the same occasion for
settlement
283   Leave to enter the United Kingdom as the spouse of a person present and settled in the United Kingdom or who is on the same occasion being admitted for settlement is to be refused if a valid United Kingdom entry clearance for entry in this capacity is not produced to the Immigration Officer on arrival.

[A.2.275]
Requirements for an extension of stay as the spouse of a person present
and settled in the United Kingdom
[284   The requirements for an extension of stay as the spouse of a person present and settled in the United Kingdom are that:

  (i) the applicant has limited leave to remain in the United Kingdom; and
  (ii) is married to a person present and settled in the United Kingdom; and
  (iii) the parties to the marriage have met; and
  (iv) the applicant has not remained in breach of the immigration laws; and
  (v) the marriage has not taken place after a decision has been made to deport the applicant or he has been recommended for deportation or been given notice under Section 6(2) of the Immigration Act 1971; and
  (vi) each of the parties intends to live permanently with the other as his or her spouse and the marriage is subsisting; and
  (vii) there will be adequate accommodation for the parties and any dependants without recourse to public funds in accommodation which they own or occupy exclusively; and
  (viii) the parties will be able to maintain themselves and any dependants adequately without recourse to public funds.]

Note   Substituted by HC 26, para 2 with effect from 5 June 1997.

[A.2.276]
Extension of stay as the spouse of a person present and settled in the United Kingdom
285   An extension of stay as the spouse of a person present and settled in the United Kingdom may be granted for a period of 12 months in the first instance, provided the Secretary of State is satisfied that each of the requirements of paragraph 284 is met.

[A.2.277]
Refusal of extension of stay as the spouse of a person present and settled in the United Kingdom
286   An extension of stay as the spouse of a person present and settled in the United Kingdom is to be refused if the Secretary of State is not satisfied that each of the requirements of paragraph 284 is met.

[A.2.278]
Requirements for indefinite leave to remain for the spouse of a person present and settled in the United Kingdom
[287(*a*) The requirements for indefinite leave to remain for the spouse of a person present and settled in the United Kingdom are that:

(i)   the applicant was admitted to the United Kingdom or given an extension of stay for a period of 12 months and has completed a period of 12 months as the spouse of a person present and settled in the United Kingdom; and

(ii)   the applicant is still the spouse of the person he or she was admitted or granted an extension of stay to join and the marriage is subsisting; and

(iii)   each of the parties intends to live permanently with the other as his or her spouse; and

(iv)   there will be adequate accommodation for the parties and any dependants without recourse to public funds in accommodation which they own or occupy exclusively; and

(v)   the parties will be able to maintain themselves and any dependants adequately without recourse to public funds.

(*b*)   The requirements for indefinite leave to remain for the bereaved spouse of a person who was present and settled in the United Kingdom are that:

(i)   the applicant was admitted to the United Kingdom or given an extension of stay for a period of 12 months as the spouse of a person present and settled in the United Kingdom; and

(ii)   the person whom the applicant was admitted or granted an extension of stay to join died during that 12 month period; and

(iii)   the applicant was still the spouse of the person he or she was admitted or granted an extension of stay to join at the time of the death; and

(iv)   each of the parties intended to live permanently with the other as his or her spouse and the marriage was subsisting at the time of the death.]

Note   Paragraph 287 substituted by CM 4851.

[A.2.279]
Indefinite leave to remain for the spouse of a person present and settled in the United Kingdom
288   Indefinite leave to remain for the spouse of a person present and settled in the United Kingdom may be granted provided the Secretary of State is satisfied that each of the requirements of paragraph 287 is met.

[A.2.280]
Refusal of indefinite leave to remain for the spouse of a person present and settled in the United Kingdom
289   Indefinite leave to remain for the spouse of a person present and settled in the United Kingdom is to be refused if the Secretary of State is not satisfied that each of the requirements of paragraph 287 is met.

FIANCE(E)S

[A.2.281]
Requirements for leave to enter the United Kingdom as a fiance(e) (ie with a view to marriage and permanent settlement in the United Kingdom)
[290   The requirements to be met by a person seeking leave to enter the United Kingdom as a fiance(e) are that:

   (i) the applicant is seeking leave to enter the United Kingdom for marriage to a person present and settled in the United Kingdom or who is on the same occasion being admitted for settlement; and
   (ii) the parties to the proposed marriage have met; and
   (iii) each of the parties intends to live permanently with the other as his or her spouse after the marriage; and
   (iv) adequate maintenance and accommodation without recourse to public funds will be available for the applicant until the date of the marriage; and
   (v) there will, after the marriage, be adequate accommodation for the parties and any dependants without recourse to public funds in accommodation which they own or occupy exclusively; and
   (vi) the parties will be able after the marriage to maintain themselves and any dependants adequately without recourse to public funds; and
   (vii) the applicant holds a valid United Kingdom entry clearance for entry in this capacity.]

Note   Substituted by HC 26, para 3 with effect from 5 June 1997.

[A.2.282]
Leave to enter as a fiance(e)
291   A person seeking leave to enter the United Kingdom as a fiance(e) may be admitted, with a prohibition on employment, for a period not exceeding 6 months to enable the marriage to take place provided a valid United Kingdom entry clearance for entry in this capacity is produced to the Immigration Officer on arrival.

[A.2.283]
Refusal of leave to enter as a fiance(e)
292   Leave to enter the United Kingdom as a fiance(e) is to be refused if a valid United Kingdom entry clearance for entry in this capacity is not produced to the Immigration Officer on arrival.

[A.2.284]
Requirements for an extension of stay as a fiance(e)
293   The requirements for an extension of stay as a fiance(e) are that:

(i) the applicant was admitted to the United Kingdom with a valid United Kingdom entry clearance as a fiance(e); and

(ii) good cause is shown why the marriage did not take place within the initial period of leave granted under paragraph 291; and

(iii) there is satisfactory evidence that the marriage will take place at an early date; and

(iv) the requirements of paragraph 290(ii)–(vi) are met.]

Note   Sub-para (iv) substituted by HC 26, para 4 with effect from 5 June 1997.

[A.2.285]
Extension of stay as a fiance(e)
294   An extension of stay as a fiance(e) may be granted for an appropriate period with a prohibition on employment to enable the marriage to take place provided the Secretary of State is satisfied that each of the requirements of paragraph 293 is met.

[A.2.286]
Refusal of extension of stay as a fiance(e)
295   An extension of stay is to be refused if the Secretary of State is not satisfied that each of the requirements of paragraph 293 is met.

Note   Paras 290–295 replace HC 251, paras 2–4, 50–51, 131–132, 47 and 130.

[LEAVE TO ENTER AS THE UNMARRIED PARTNER OF A PERSON PRESENT AND SETTLED IN THE UNITED KINGDOM OR BEING ADMITTED ON THE SAME OCCASION FOR SETTLEMENT

[A.2.287]
Requirements for leave to enter the United Kingdom with a view to settlement as the unmarried partner of a person present and settled in the United Kingdom or being admitted on the same occasion for settlement
295A   The requirements to be met by a person seeking leave to enter the United Kingdom with a view to settlement as the unmarried partner of a person present and settled in the United Kingdom or being admitted on the same occasion for settlement, are that:

(i) the applicant is the unmarried partner of a person present and settled in the United Kingdom or who is on the same occasion being admitted for settlement; and

(ii) any previous marriage (or similar relationship) by either partner has permanently broken down; and

(iii) the parties are legally unable to marry under United Kingdom law (other than by reason of consanguineous relationships or age); and

(iv) the parties have been living together in a relationship akin to marriage which has subsisted for two years or more; and

(v) there will be adequate accommodation for the parties and any dependants without recourse to public funds in accommodation which they own or occupy exclusively; and

(vi) the parties will be able to maintain themselves and any dependants adequately without recourse to public funds; and

(vii) the parties intend to live together permanently; and

(viii) the applicant holds a valid United Kingdom entry clearance for entry in this capacity.

[A.2.288]
Leave to enter the United Kingdom with a view to settlement as the unmarried partner of a person present and settled in the United Kingdom or being admitted on the same occasion for settlement

295B   Leave to enter the United Kingdom with a view to settlement as the unmarried partner of a person present and settled in the United Kingdom or being admitted on the same occasion for settlement, may be granted for an initial period not exceeding 2 years provided that a valid United Kingdom entry clearance for entry in this capacity is produced to the Immigration Officer on arrival.

[A.2.289]
Refusal of leave to enter the United Kingdom with a view to settlement as the unmarried partner of a person present and settled in the United Kingdom or being admitted on the same occasion for settlement

295C Leave to enter the United Kingdom with a view to settlement as the unmarried partner of a person present and settled in the United Kingdom or being admitted on the same occasion for settlement, is to be refused if a valid United Kingdom entry clearance for entry in this capacity is not produced to the Immigration Officer on arrival.

LEAVE TO REMAIN AS THE UNMARRIED PARTNER OF A PERSON PRESENT AND SETTLED IN THE UNITED KINGDOM

[A.2.290]
Requirements for leave to remain as the unmarried partner of a person present and settled in the United Kingdom

295D   The requirements to be met by a person seeking leave to remain as the unmarried partner of a person present and settled in the United Kingdom are that:

(i) the applicant has limited leave to remain in the United Kingdom; and

(ii) any previous marriage (or similar relationship) by either partner has permanently broken down; and

(iii) the applicant is the unmarried partner of a person who is present and settled in the United Kingdom; and

(iv) the applicant has not remained in breach of the immigration laws; and

(v) the parties are legally unable to marry under United Kingdom law (other than by reason of consanguineous relationships or age); and

(vi) the parties have been living together in a relationship akin to marriage which has subsisted for two years or more; and

(vii) the parties' relationship pre-dates any decision to deport the applicant, recommend him for deportation, give him notice under Section 6(2) of the Immigration Act 1971, or give directions for his removal under section 10 of the Immigration and Asylum Act 1999; and

(viii) there will be adequate accommodation for the parties and any dependants without recourse to public funds in accommodation which they
own or occupy exclusively; and -
(ix) the parties will be able to maintain themselves and any dependants adequately without recourse to public funds; and
(x) the parties intend to live together permanently.

[A.2.291]
**Leave to remain as the unmarried partner of a person present and settled
in the United Kingdom**
295E   Leave to remain as the unmarried partner of a person present and settled in the United Kingdom may be granted for a period of 2 years in the first
instance provided that the Secretary of State is satisfied that each of the
requirements of paragraph 295D are met.

[A.2.292]
**Refusal of leave to remain as the unmarried partner of a person present
and settled in the United Kingdom**
295F   Leave to remain as the unmarried partner of a person present and settled in the United Kingdom is to be refused if the Secretary of State is not satisfied that each of the requirements of paragraph 295D is met.

INDEFINITE LEAVE TO REMAIN AS THE UNMARRIED PARTNER OF A PERSON PRESENT AND
SETTLED IN THE UNITED KINGDOM

[A.2.293]
**Requirements for indefinite leave to remain as the unmarried partner of
a person present and settled in the United Kingdom**
295G   The requirements to be met by a person seeking indefinite leave to
remain as the unmarried partner of a person present and settled in the United
Kingdom are that:

(i)   the applicant was admitted to the United Kingdom or given an extension
of stay for a period of 2 years and has completed a period of 2 years as
the unmarried partner of a person present and settled here; and
(ii)   the applicant is still the unmarried partner of the person he was admitted
or granted an extension of stay to join and the relationship is still subsisting; and
(iii)   each of the parties intends to live permanently with the other as his partner; and
(iv)   there will be adequate accommodation for the parties and any dependants without recourse to public funds in accommodation which they
own or occupy exclusively; and
(v)   the parties will be able to maintain themselves and any dependants adequately without recourse to public funds.

[A.2.294]
**Indefinite leave to remain as the unmarried partner of a person present
and settled in the United Kingdom**
295H   Indefinite leave to remain as the unmarried partner of a person present
and settled in the United Kingdom may be granted provided that the Secretary
of State is satisfied that each of the requirements of paragraph 295G is met.

[A.2.295]
Refusal of indefinite leave to remain as the unmarried partner of a person present and settled in the United Kingdom
295I   Indefinite leave to remain as the unmarried partner of a person present and settled in the United Kingdom is to be refused if the Secretary of State is not satisfied that each of the requirements of paragraph 295G is met.

LEAVE TO ENTER OR REMAIN AS THE UNMARRIED PARTNER OF A PERSON WITH LIMITED
LEAVE TO ENTER OR REMAIN IN THE UNITED KINGDOM UNDER PARAGRAPHS 128-193; 200-239;
OR 263-270

[A.2.296]
Requirements for leave to enter or remain as the unmarried partner of a person with limited leave to enter or remain in the United Kingdom under paragraphs 128-193; 200-239; or 263-270
295J   The requirements to be met by a person seeking leave to enter or remain as the unmarried partner of a person with limited leave to enter or remain in the United Kingdom under paragraphs 128-193; 200-239; or 263-270; are that:

  (i) the applicant is the unmarried partner of a person who has limited leave to enter or remain in the United Kingdom under paragraphs 128-193; 200-239; or 263-270; and
 (ii) any previous marriage (or similar relationship) by either partner has permanently broken down; and
(iii) the parties are legally unable to marry under United Kingdom law (other than by reason of consanguineous relationship or age); and
 (iv) the parties have been living together in a relationship akin to marriage which has subsisted for 2 years or more; and
  (v) each of the parties intends to live with the other as his partner during the applicant's stay; and
 (vi) there will be adequate accommodation for the parties and any dependants without recourse to public funds in accommodation which they own or occupy exclusively; and
(vii) the parties will be able to maintain themselves and any dependants adequately without recourse to public funds; and
(viii) the applicant does not intend to stay in the United Kingdom beyond any period of leave granted to his partner; and
 (ix) if seeking leave to enter, the applicant holds a valid United Kingdom entry clearance for entry in this capacity or, if seeking leave to remain, was admitted with a valid United Kingdom entry clearance for entry in this capacity.

[A.2.297]
Leave to enter or remain as the unmarried partner of a person with limited leave to enter or remain in the United Kingdom under paragraphs 128-193; 200-239; or 263-270
295K   Leave to enter as the unmarried partner of a person with limited leave to enter or remain in the United Kingdom under paragraphs 128-193; 200-239; or 263-270; may be granted provided that a valid United Kingdom entry clearance for entry in this capacity is produced to the Immigration Officer on arrival. Leave to remain as the unmarried partner of a person with limited leave to enter or remain in the United Kingdom under paragraphs 128-193; 200-239; or 263-270; may be granted provided that the Secretary of State is satisfied that each of the requirements of paragraph 295J is met.

[A.2.298]
Refusal of leave to enter or remain as the unmarried partner of a person with limited leave to enter or remain in the United Kingdom under paragraphs 128-193; 200-239; or 263-270
295L   Leave to enter as the unmarried partner of a person with limited leave to enter or remain in the United Kingdom under paragraphs 128-193; 200-239; or 263-270; is to be refused if a valid United Kingdom entry clearance for entry in this capacity is not produced to the Immigration Officer on arrival. Leave to remain as the unmarried partner of a person with limited leave to enter or remain in the United Kingdom under paragraphs 128-193; 200-239; or 263-270; is to be refused if the Secretary of State is not satisfied that each of the requirements of paragraph 295J is met.

INDEFINITE LEAVE TO REMAIN FOR THE BEREAVED UNMARRIED PARTNER OF A PERSON PRESENT AND SETTLED IN THE UNITED KINGDOM

[A.2.299]
Requirements for indefinite leave to remain for the bereaved unmarried partner of a person present and settled in the United Kingdom
295M   The requirements to be met by a person seeking indefinite leave to remain as the bereaved unmarried partner of a person present and settled in the United Kingdom, are that:

  (i)   the applicant was admitted to the United Kingdom or given an extension of stay for a period of 2 years as the unmarried partner of a person present and settled in the United Kingdom; and
 (ii)   the person whom the applicant was admitted or granted an extension of stay to join died during that 2 year period; and
(iii)   the applicant was still the unmarried partner of the person he was admitted or granted extension of stay to join at the time of the death; and
 (iv)   each of the parties intended to live permanently with the other as his partner and the relationship was subsisting at the time of the death.

[A.2.300]
Indefinite leave to remain for the bereaved unmarried partner of a person present and settled in the United Kingdom
295N   Indefinite leave to remain for the bereaved unmarried partner of a person present and settled in the United Kingdom, may be granted provided that the Secretary of State is satisfied that each of the requirements of paragraph 295M is met.

[A.2.301]
Refusal of indefinite leave to remain for the bereaved unmarried partner of a person present and settled in the United Kingdom
295O   Indefinite leave to remain for the bereaved unmarried partner of a person present and settled in the United Kingdom, is to be refused if the Secretary of State is not satisfied that each of the requirements of paragraph 295M is met.]

Note   Paragraphs 295A–295O inserted by CM 4851.

CHILDREN

[A.2.302]
[296   Nothing in these Rules shall be construed as permitting a child to be granted entry clearance, leave to enter or remain, or variation of leave where his mother is party to a polygamous marriage and any application by that parent for admission or leave to remain for settlement or with a view to settlement would be refused pursuant to paragraphs 278 or 278A].

Note   Paragraphs 296 substituted by CM 4851.

Leave to enter or remain in the United Kingdom as the child of a parent, parents or a relative present and settled or being admitted for settlement in the United Kingdom

[A.2.303]
Requirements for indefinite leave to enter the United Kingdom as the child of a parent, parents or a relative present and settled or being admitted for settlement in the United Kingdom
297   The requirements to be met by a person seeking indefinite leave to enter the United Kingdom as the child of a parent, parents or a relative present and settled or being admitted for settlement in the United Kingdom are that he:
  (i)   is seeking leave to enter to accompany or join a parent, parents or a relative in one of the following circumstances:
    (*a*)   both parents are present and settled in the United Kingdom; or
    (*b*)   both parents are being admitted on the same occasion for settlement; or
    (*c*)   one parent is present and settled in the United Kingdom and the other is being admitted on the same occasion for settlement; or
    (*d*)   one parent is present and settled in the United Kingdom or being admitted on the same occasion for settlement and the other parent is dead; or
    (*e*)   one parent is present and settled in the United Kingdom or being admitted on the same occasion for settlement and has had sole responsibility for the child's upbringing; or
    (*f*)   one parent or a relative is present and settled in the United Kingdom or being admitted on the same occasion for settlement and there are serious and compelling family or other considerations which make exclusion of the child undesirable and suitable arrangements have been made for the child's care; and
  (ii)   is under the age of 18; and
  (iii)   is not leading an independent life, is unmarried, and has not formed an independent family unit; and
  [(iv)   can, and will, be accommodated adequately by the parent, parents or relative the child is seeking to join without recourse to public funds in accommodation which the parent, parents or relative the child is seeking to join, own or occupy exclusively; and
  (v)   can, and will, be maintained adequately by the parent, parents or relative the child is seeking to join, without recourse to public funds; and
  (vi)   holds a valid United Kingdom entry clearance for entry in this capacity.]

Note   Paragraph 297 (iv)-(v) substituted and paragraph 297 (vi) inserted by CM 4851.

[A.2.304]
Requirements for indefinite leave to remain in the United Kingdom as the child of a parent, parents or a relative present and settled or being admitted for settlement in the United Kingdom
298   The requirements to be met by a person seeking indefinite leave to remain in the United Kingdom as the child of a parent, parents or a relative present and settled in the United Kingdom are that he:

(i)   is seeking to remain with a parent, parents or a relative in one of the following circumstances:
   (*a*)   both parents are present and settled in the United Kingdom; or
   (*b*)   one parent is present and settled in the United Kingdom and the other parent is dead; or
   (*c*)   one parent is present and settled in the United Kingdom and has had sole responsibility for the child's upbringing; or
   (*d*)   one parent or a relative is present and settled in the United Kingdom and there are serious and compelling family or other considerations which make exclusion of the child undesirable and suitable arrangements have been made for the child's care; and

(ii)   has limited leave to enter or remain in the United Kingdom, and
   (*a*)   is under the age of 18; or
   (*b*)   was given leave to enter or remain with a view to settlement under paragraph 302; and

(iii)   is not leading an independent life, is unmarried, and has not formed an independent family unit; and

[(iv)   can, and will, be accommodated adequately by the parent, parents or relative the child was admitted to join, without recourse to public funds in accommodation which the parent, parents or relative the child was admitted to join, own or occupy exclusively; and

(v)   can, and will, be maintained adequately by the parent, parents or relative the child was admitted to join, without recourse to public funds.]

Note   Paragraph 298 (iv) substituted and paragraph 298 (v) inserted by CM 4851.

[A.2.305]
Indefinite leave to enter or remain in the United Kingdom as the child of a parent, parents or a relative present and settled or being admitted for settlement in the United Kingdom
299   Indefinite leave to enter the United Kingdom as the child of a parent, parents or a relative present and settled or being admitted for settlement in the United Kingdom may be granted provided a valid United Kingdom entry clearance for entry in this capacity is produced to the Immigration Officer on arrival. Indefinite leave to remain in the United Kingdom as the child of a parent, parents or a relative present and settled in the United Kingdom may be granted provided the Secretary of State is satisfied that each of the requirements of paragraph 298 is met.

[A.2.306]
Refusal of indefinite leave to enter or remain in the United Kingdom as the child of a parent, parents or a relative present and settled or being admitted for settlement in the United Kingdom
300   Indefinite leave to enter the United Kingdom as the child of a parent, parents or a relative present and settled or being admitted for settlement in the

United Kingdom is to be refused if a valid United Kingdom entry clearance for entry in this capacity is not produced to the Immigration Officer on arrival. Indefinite leave to remain in the United Kingdom as the child of a parent, parents or a relative present and settled in the United Kingdom is to be refused if the Secretary of State is not satisfied that each of the requirements of paragraph 298 is met.

[A.2.307]

Requirements for limited leave to enter or remain in the United Kingdom with a view to settlement as the child of a parent or parents given limited leave to enter or remain in the United Kingdom with a view to settlement

301   The requirements to be met by a person seeking limited leave to enter or remain in the United Kingdom with a view to settlement as the child of a parent or parents given limited leave to enter or remain in the United Kingdom with a view to settlement are that he:

(i)   is seeking leave to enter to accompany or join or remain with a parent or parents in one of the following circumstances:

    (*a*)   one parent is present and settled in the United Kingdom or being admitted on the same occasion for settlement and the other parent is being or has been given limited leave to enter or remain in the United Kingdom with a view to settlement; or

    (*b*)   one parent is being or has been given limited leave to enter or remain in the United Kingdom with a view to settlement and has had sole responsibility for the child's upbringing; or

    (*c*)   one parent is being or has been given limited leave to enter or remain in the United Kingdom with a view to settlement and there are serious and compelling family or other considerations which make exclusion of the child undesirable and suitable arrangements have been made for the child's care; and

(ii)   is under the age of 18; and

(iii)   is not leading an independent life, is unmarried, and has not formed an independent family unit; and

[(iv)   can, and will, be accommodated adequately without recourse to public funds, in accommodation which the parent or parents own or occupy exclusively; and

(iva)   can, and will, be maintained adequately by the parent or parents without recourse to public funds; and]

(v)   (where an application is made for limited leave to remain with a view to settlement) has limited leave to enter or remain in the United Kingdom; and

(vi)   if seeking leave to enter, holds a valid United Kingdom entry clearance for entry in this capacity or, if seeking leave to remain, was admitted with a valid United Kingdom entry clearance for entry in this capacity.

Note   Paragraph 301(iv) substituted and paragraph 301(iva) inserted by CM 4851.

[A.2.308]
Limited leave to enter or remain in the United Kingdom with a view to settlement as the child of a parent or parents given limited leave to enter or remain in the United Kingdom with a view to settlement
302   A person seeking limited leave to enter the United Kingdom with a view to settlement as the child of a parent or parents given limited leave to enter or remain in the United Kingdom with a view to settlement may be admitted for a period not exceeding 12 months provided he is able, on arrival, to produce to the Immigration Officer a valid United Kingdom entry clearance for entry in this capacity. A person seeking limited leave to remain in the United Kingdom with a view to settlement as the child of a parent or parents given limited leave to enter or remain in the United Kingdom with a view to settlement may be given limited leave to remain for a period not exceeding 12 months provided the Secretary of State is satisfied that each of the requirements of paragraph 301(i)–(v) is met.

[A.2.309]
Refusal of limited leave to enter or remain in the United Kingdom with a view to settlement as the child of a parent or parents given limited leave to enter or remain in the United Kingdom with a view to settlement
303   Limited leave to enter the United Kingdom with a view to settlement as the child of a parent or parents given limited leave to enter or remain in the United Kingdom with a view to settlement is to be refused if a valid United Kingdom entry clearance for entry in this capacity is not produced to the Immigration Officer on arrival. Limited leave to remain in the United Kingdom with a view to settlement as the child of a parent or parents given limited leave to enter or remain in the United Kingdom with a view to settlement is to be refused if the Secretary of State is not satisfied that each of the requirements of paragraph 301(i)–(v) is met.

[LEAVE TO ENTER AND EXTENSION OF STAY IN THE UNITED KINGDOM AS THE CHILD OF A PARENT WHO IS BEING, OR HAS BEEN ADMITTED TO THE UNITED KINGDOM AS A FIANCÉ(E)]

[A.2.310]
Requirements for limited leave to enter the United Kingdom as the child of a fiancé(e)
303A   The requirements to be met by a person seeking limited leave to enter the United Kingdom as the child of a fiancé(e), are that:

  (i)   he is seeking to accompany or join a parent who is, on the same occasion that the child seeks admission, being admitted as a fiancé(e), or who has been admitted as a fiancé(e); and
 (ii)   he is under the age of 18; and
(iii)   he is not leading an independent life, is unmarried, and has not formed an independent family unit; and
 (iv)   he can, and will, be maintained and accommodated adequately without recourse to public funds with the parent admitted or being admitted as a fiancé(e); and

(v) there are serious and compelling family or other considerations which make the child's exclusion undesirable, that suitable arrangements have been made for his care in the United Kingdom, and there is no other person outside the United Kingdom who could reasonably be expected to care for him; and

(vi) he holds a valid United Kingdom entry clearance for entry in this capacity.

[A.2.311]
Limited leave to enter the United Kingdom as the child of a parent who is being, or has been admitted to the United Kingdom as a fiancé(e)

303B   A person seeking limited leave to enter the United Kingdom as the child of a fiancé(e), may be granted limited leave to enter the United Kingdom for a period not in excess of that granted to the fiancé(e), provided that a valid United Kingdom entry clearance for entry in this capacity is produced to the Immigration Officer on arrival. Where the period of limited leave granted to a fiancé(e) will expire in more than 6 months, a person seeking limited leave to enter as the child of the fiancé(e) should be granted leave for a period not exceeding six months.

[A.2.312]
Refusal of limited leave to enter the United Kingdom as the child of a parent who is being, or has been admitted to the United Kingdom as a fiancé(e)

303C   Limited leave to enter the United Kingdom as the child of a fiancé(e), is to be refused if a valid United Kingdom entry clearance for entry in this capacity is not produced to the Immigration Officer on arrival.

[A.2.313]
Requirements for an extension of stay in the United Kingdom as the child of a fiancé(e)

303D   The requirements to be met by a person seeking an extension of stay in the United Kingdom as the child of a fiancé(e) are that:

(i) the applicant was admitted with a valid United Kingdom entry clearance as the child of a fiancé(e); and

(ii) the applicant is the child of a parent who has been granted limited leave to enter, or an extension of stay, as a fiancé(e); and

(iii) the requirements of paragraph 303A (ii)-(v) are met.

[A.2.314]
Extension of stay in the United Kingdom as the child of a fiancé(e)

303E   An extension of stay as the child of a fiancé(e) may be granted provided that the Secretary of State is satisfied that each of the requirements of paragraph 303D is met.

[A.2.315]
Refusal of an extension of stay in the United Kingdom as the child of a fiancé(e)
303F An extension of stay as the child of a fiancé(e) is to be refused if the Secretary of State is not satisfied that each of the requirements of paragraph 303D is met.]

Note Paragraphs 303A-303F inserted by CM 4851.

Children born in the United Kingdom who are not British citizens

[A.2.316]
304 This paragraph and paragraphs 305–309 apply only to unmarried dependent children under 18 years of age who were born in the United Kingdom on or after 1 January 1983 (when the British Nationality Act 1981 came into force) but who, because neither of their parents was a British citizen or settled in the United Kingdom at the time of their birth, are not British citizens and are therefore subject to immigration control. Such a child requires leave to enter where admission to the United Kingdom is sought, and leave to remain where permission is sought for the child to be allowed to stay in the United Kingdom. If he qualifies for entry clearance, leave to enter or leave to remain under any other part of these Rules, a child who was born in the United Kingdom but is not a British citizen may be granted entry clearance, leave to enter or leave to remain in accordance with the provisions of that other part.

[A.2.317]
Requirements for leave to enter or remain in the United Kingdom as the child of a parent or parents given leave to enter or remain in the United Kingdom
305 The requirements to be met by a child born in the United Kingdom who is not a British citizen who seeks leave to enter or remain in the United Kingdom as the child of a parent or parents given leave to enter or remain in the United Kingdom are that he:

    (i) (*a*) is accompanying or seeking to join or remain with a parent or parents who have, or are given, leave to enter or remain in the United Kingdom; or

        (*b*) is accompanying or seeking to join or remain with a parent or parents one of whom is a British citizen or has the right of abode in the United Kingdom; or

        (*c*) is a child in respect of whom the parental rights and duties are vested solely in a local authority; and

    (ii) is under the age of 18; and

    (iii) was born in the United Kingdom; and

    (iv) is not leading an independent life, is unmarried, and has not formed an independent family unit; and

    (v) (where an application is made for leave to enter) has not been away from the United Kingdom for more than 2 years.

[A.2.318]
Leave to enter or remain in the United Kingdom
306   A child born in the United Kingdom who is not a British citizen and who requires leave to enter or remain in the circumstances set out in paragraph 304 may be given leave to enter for the same period as his parent or parents where paragraph 305(i)(*a*) applies, provided the Immigration Officer is satisfied that each of the requirements of paragraph 305(ii)–(v) is met. Where leave to remain in sought, the child may be granted leave to remain for the same period as his parent or parents where paragraph 305(i)(*a*) applies, provided the Secretary of State is satisfied that each of the requirements of paragraph 305(ii)–(iv) is met. Where the parent or parents have or are given periods of leave of different duration, the child may be given leave to whichever period is longer except that if the parents are living apart the child should be given leave for the same period as the parent who has day to day responsibility for him.

307   If a child does not qualify for leave to enter or remain because neither of his parents has a current leave (and neither of them is a British citizen or has the right of abode), he will normally be refused leave to enter or remain, even if each of the requirements of paragraph 305(ii)–(v) has been satisfied. However, he may be granted leave to enter or remain for a period not exceeding 3 months if both of his parents are in the United Kingdom and it appears unlikely that they will be removed in the immediate future, and there is no other person outside the United Kingdom who could reasonably be expected to care for him.

308   A child born in the United Kingdom who is not a British citizen and who requires leave to enter or remain in the United Kingdom in the circumstances set out in paragraph 304 may be given indefinite leave to enter where paragraph 305(i)(*b*) or (i)(*c*) applies provided the Immigration Officer is satisfied that each of the requirements of paragraph 305(ii)–(v) is met. Where an application is for leave to remain, such a child may be granted indefinite leave to remain where paragraph 305(i)(*b*) or (i)(*c*) applies, provided the Secretary of State is satisfied that each of the requirements of paragraph 305(ii)–(iv) is met.

[A.2.319]
Refusal of leave to enter or remain in the United Kingdom
309   Leave to enter the United Kingdom where the circumstances set out in paragraph 304 apply is to be refused if the Immigration Officer is not satisfied that each of the requirements of paragraph 305 is met. Leave to remain for such a child is to be refused if the Secretary of State is not satisfied that each of the requirements of paragraph 305(i)–(iv) is met.

Adopted children

[A.2.320]
Requirements for indefinite leave to enter the United Kingdom as the adopted child of a parent or parents present and settled or being admitted for settlement in the United Kingdom
310   The requirements to be met in the case of a child seeking indefinite leave to enter the United Kingdom as the adopted child of a parent or parents present and settled or being admitted for settlement in the United Kingdom are that he:

  (i) is seeking leave to enter to accompany or join an adoptive parent or parents in one of the following circumstances:

    (*a*) both parents are present and settled in the United Kingdom; or

    (*b*) both parents are being admitted on the same occasion for settlement; or

    (*c*) one parent is present and settled in the United Kingdom and the other is being admitted on the same occasion for settlement; or

    (*d*) one parent is present and settled in the United Kingdom or being admitted on the same occasion for settlement and the other parent is dead; or

    (*e*) one parent is present and settled in the United Kingdom or being admitted on the same occasion for settlement and has had sole responsibility for the child's upbringing; or

    (*f*) one parent is present and settled in the United Kingdom or being admitted on the same occasion for settlement and there are serious and compelling family or other considerations which make exclusion of the child undesirable and suitable arrangements have been made for the child's care; and

  (ii) is under the age of 18; and

  (iii) is not leading an independent life, is unmarried, and has not formed an independent family unit; and

  [(iv) can, and will, be accommodated adequately without recourse to public funds in accommodation which the adoptive parent or parents own or occupy exclusively; and

  (v) can, and will, be maintained adequately by the adoptive parent or parents without recourse to public funds; and]

  (vi) was adopted in accordance with a decision taken by the competent administrative authority or court in his country of origin or the country in which he is resident; and

  (vii) was adopted at a time when:

    (*a*) both adoptive parents were resident together abroad; or

    (*b*) either or both adoptive parents were settled in the United Kingdom; and

  (viii) has the same rights and obligations as any other child of the marriage; and

  (ix) was adopted due to the inability of the original parent(s) or current carer(s) to care for him and there has been a genuine transfer of parental responsibility to the adoptive parents; and

  (x) has lost or broken his ties with his family of origin; and

  (xi) was adopted, but the adoption is not one of convenience arranged to facilitate his admission to or remaining in the United Kingdom; and

  (xii) holds a valid United Kingdom entry clearance for entry in this capacity.

Note Paragraph 310(iv) substituted, paragraph 310(v) inserted and subsequent paragraphs renumbered by CM 4851.

[A.2.321]

Requirements for indefinite leave to remain in the United Kingdom as the adopted child of a parent or parents present and settled in the United Kingdom

311   The requirements to be met in the case of a child seeking indefinite leave to remain in the United Kingdom as the adopted child of a parent or parents

present and settled in the United Kingdom are that he:

(i) is seeking to remain with an adoptive parent or parents in one of the following circumstances:

  (*a*) both parents are present and settled in the United Kingdom; or

  (*b*) one parent is present and settled in the United Kingdom and the other parent is dead; or

  (*c*) one parent is present and settled in the United Kingdom and has had sole responsibility for the child's upbringing; or

  (*d*) one parent is present and settled in the United Kingdom and there are serious and compelling family or other considerations which make exclusion of the child undesirable and suitable arrangements have been made for the child's care; and

(ii) has limited leave to enter or remain in the United Kingdom, and

  (*a*) is under the age of 18; or

  (*b*) was given leave to enter or remain with a view to settlement under paragraph 315 [or paragraph 316B]; and

(iii) is not leading an independent life, is unmarried, and has not formed an independent family unit; and

[(iv) can, and will, be accommodated adequately without recourse to public funds in accommodation which the adoptive parent or parents own or occupy exclusively; and

(v) can, and will, be maintained adequately by the adoptive parent or parents without recourse to public funds; and]

(vi) was adopted in accordance with a decision taken by the competent administrative authority or court in his country of origin or the country in which he is resident; and

(vii) was adopted at a time when:

  (*a*) both adoptive parents were resident together abroad; or

  (*b*) either or both adoptive parents were settled in the United Kingdom; and

(viii) has the same rights and obligations as any other child of the marriage; and

(ix) was adopted due to the inability of the original parent(s) or current carer(s) to care for him and there has been a genuine transfer of parental responsibility to the adoptive parents; and

(x) has lost or broken his ties with his family of origin; and

(ix) was adopted, but the adoption is not one of convenience arranged to facilitate his admission to or remaining in the United Kingdom.

Note Words in square brackets in paragraph 311(ii)(b) and paragraph 311(v) inserted, paragraph 311(iv) substituted and subsequent paragraphs renumbered by CM 4851.

[A.2.322]
Indefinite leave to enter or remain in the United Kingdom as the adopted child of a parent or parents present and settled or being admitted for settlement in the United Kingdom
312   Indefinite leave to enter the United Kingdom as the adopted child of a parent or parents present and settled or being admitted for settlement in the United Kingdom may be granted provided a valid United Kingdom entry clearance for entry in this capacity is produced to the Immigration Officer on arrival. Indefinite leave to remain in the United Kingdom as the adopted child

of a parent or parents present and settled in the United Kingdom may be granted provided the Secretary of State is satisfied that each of the requirements of paragraph 311 is met.

[A.2.323]
Refusal of indefinite leave to enter or remain in the United Kingdom as the adopted child of a parent or parents present and settled or being admitted for settlement in the United Kingdom
313   Indefinite leave to enter the United Kingdom as the adopted child of a parent or parents present and settled or being admitted for settlement in the United Kingdom is to be refused if a valid United Kingdom entry clearance for entry in this capacity is not produced to the Immigration Officer on arrival. Indefinite leave to remain in the United Kingdom as the adopted child of a parent or parents present and settled in the United Kingdom is to be refused if the Secretary of State is not satisfied that each of the requirements of paragraph 311 is met.

[A.2.324]
Requirements for limited leave to enter or remain in the United Kingdom with a view to settlement as the adopted child of a parent or parents given limited leave to enter or remain in the United Kingdom with a view to settlement
314   The requirements to be met in the case of a child seeking limited leave to enter or remain in the United Kingdom with a view to settlement as the adopted child of a parent or parents given limited leave to enter or remain in the United Kingdom with a view to settlement are that he:

   (i) is seeking leave to enter to accompany or join or remain with a parent or parents in one of the following circumstances:
      (*a*) one parent is present and settled in the United Kingdom or being admitted on the same occasion for settlement and the other parent is being or has been given limited leave to enter or remain in the United Kingdom with a view to settlement; or
      (*b*) one parent is being or has been given limited leave to enter or remain in the United Kingdom with a view to settlement and has had sole responsibility for the child's upbringing; or
      (*c*) one parent is being or has been given limited leave to enter or remain in the United Kingdom with a view to settlement and there are serious and compelling family or other considerations which make exclusion of the child undesirable and suitable arrangements have been made for the child's care; and
   (ii) is under the age of 18; and
   (iii) is not leading an independent life, is unmarried, and has not formed an independent family unit; and
   [(iv) can, and will, be accommodated adequately without recourse to public funds in accommodation which the adoptive parent or parents own or occupy exclusively; and
   (iva) can, and will, be maintained adequately by the adoptive parent or parents without recourse to public funds; and]
   (v) was adopted in accordance with a decision taken by the competent administrative authority or court in his country of origin or the country in which he is resident; and

   (vi) was adopted at a time when:
      (*a*) both adoptive parents were resident together abroad; or
      (*b*) either or both adoptive parents were settled in the United Kingdom; and
  (vii) has the same rights and obligations as any other child of the marriage; and
 (viii) was adopted due to the inability of the original parent(s) or current carer(s) to care for him and there has been a genuine transfer of parental responsibility to the adoptive parents; and
   (ix) has lost or broken his ties with his family of origin; and
    (x) was adopted, but the adoption is not one of convenience arranged to facilitate his admission to the United Kingdom; and
   (xi) (where an application is made for limited leave to remain with a view to settlement) has limited leave to enter or remain in the United Kingdom; and
  (xii) if seeking leave to enter, holds a valid United Kingdom entry clearance for entry in this capacity.

Note   Paragraph 314(iv) substituted and paragraph 314(iva) inserted by CM 4851.

[A.2.325]
Limited leave to enter or remain in the United Kingdom with a view to settlement as the adopted child of a parent or parents given limited leave to enter or remain in the United Kingdom with a view to settlement
315   A person seeking limited leave to enter the United Kingdom with a view to settlement as the adopted child of a parent or parents given limited leave to enter or remain in the United Kingdom with a view to settlement may be admitted for a period not exceeding 12 months provided he is able, on arrival, to produce to the Immigration Officer a valid United Kingdom entry clearance for entry in this capacity. A person seeking limited leave to remain in the United Kingdom with a view to settlement as the adopted child of a parent or parents given limited leave to enter or remain in the United Kingdom with a view to settlement may be granted limited leave for a period not exceeding 12 months provided the Secretary of State is satisfied that each of the requirements of paragraph 314(i)–(xi) is met.

[A.2.326]
Refusal of limited leave to enter or remain in the United Kingdom with a view to settlement as the adopted child of a parent or parents given limited leave to enter or remain in the United Kingdom with a view to settlement
316   Limited leave to enter the United Kingdom with a view to settlement as the adopted child of a parent or parents given limited leave to enter or remain in the United Kingdom with a view to settlement is to be refused if a valid United Kingdom entry clearance for entry in this capacity is not produced to the Immigration Officer on arrival. Limited leave to remain in the United Kingdom with a view to settlement as the adopted child of a parent or parents given limited leave to enter or remain in the United Kingdom with a view to settlement is to be refused if the Secretary of State is not satisfied that each of the requirements of paragraph 314(i)–(xi) is met.

Note   Paras 310–316 replace HC 251, paras 53–55, 133–137 and 139.

The concession in HC 251, para 55 relating to fully dependent daughters over 18 and under 21 has been removed.

Paras 310–316 have been introduced to take account of European harmonisation in this area. Article 2 of The Resolution on the Harmonisation of National Policies on Family Reunification agreed by EC Ministers (Copenhagen, 1993) states that Member States will normally grant admission to 'children adopted by both the resident and his or her spouse while they were resident together in a third country . . . and where the adopted children have the same rights and obligations as the other children and there has been a definitive break with the family of origin.' The adoption must have taken place in accordance 'with a decision taken by the competent administrative authority or court in his country of origin or country in which he is resident.' – paras 310(v), 311(v), and 314(v).

Defacto adoption arrangements (see *Ex p Tohur Ali* [1988] Imm AR 237) no longer can be considered under these provisions although it is still possible for the admission of such a child to be permitted under para 297(*f*) if the sponsor is a relative 'and there are serious and compelling family or other considerations which make exclusion of the child undesirable and suitable arrangements have been made for the child's care.'

[A.2.327]
[Requirements for limited leave to enter the United Kingdom with a view to settlement as a child for adoption
316A   The requirements to be satisfied in the case of a child seeking limited leave to enter the United Kingdom for the purpose of being adopted in the United Kingdom are that he:

(i)   is seeking limited leave to enter to accompany or join a person or persons who wish to adopt him in the United Kingdom (the 'prospective parent(s)'), in one of the following circumstances:
  (*a*)   both prospective parents are present and settled in the United Kingdom; or
  (*b*)   both prospective parents are being admitted for settlement on the same occasion that the child is seeking admission; or
  (*c*)   one prospective parent is present and settled in the United Kingdom and the other is being admitted for settlement on the same occasion that the child is seeking admission; or
  (*d*)   one prospective parent is present and settled in the United Kingdom and the other is being given limited leave to enter or remain in the United Kingdom with a view to settlement on the same occasion that the child is seeking admission, or has previously been given such leave; or
  (*e*)   one prospective parent is being admitted for settlement on the same occasion that the other is being granted limited leave to enter with a view to settlement, which is also on the same occasion that the child is seeking admission; or
  (*f*)   one prospective parent is present and settled in the United Kingdom or is being admitted for settlement on the same occasion that the child is seeking admission, and has had sole responsibility for the child's upbringing; or

    (*g*) one prospective parent is present and settled in the United Kingdom or is being admitted for settlement on the same occasion that the child is seeking admission, and there are serious and compelling family or other considerations which would make the child's exclusion undesirable, and suitable arrangements have been made for the child's care; and

(ii) is under the age of 18; and

(iii) is not leading an independent life, is unmarried, and has not formed an independent family unit; and

(iv) can, and will, be maintained and accommodated adequately without recourse to public funds in accommodation which the prospective parent or parents own or occupy exclusively; and

(v) will have the same rights and obligations as any other child of the marriage; and

(vi) is being adopted due to the inability of the original parent(s) or current carer(s) (or those looking after him immediately prior to him being physically transferred to his prospective parent or parents) to care for him, and there has been a genuine transfer of parental responsibility to the prospective parent or parents; and

(vii) has lost or broken or intends to lose or break his ties with his family of origin; and

(viii) will be adopted in the United Kingdom by his prospective parent or parents, but the proposed adoption is not one of convenience arranged to facilitate his admission to the United Kingdom.

[A.2.328]
Limited leave to enter the United Kingdom with a view to settlement as a child for adoption

316B   A person seeking limited leave to enter the United Kingdom with a view to settlement as a child for adoption may be admitted for a period not exceeding 12 months provided he is able, on arrival, to produce to the Immigration Officer a valid United Kingdom entry clearance for entry in this capacity.

[A.2.329]
Refusal of limited leave to enter the United Kingdom with a view to settlement as a child for adoption

316C   Limited leave to enter the United Kingdom with a view to settlement as a child for adoption is to be refused if a valid United Kingdom entry clearance for entry in this capacity is not produced to the Immigration Officer on arrival.]

Note   Paragraphs 316A–316C inserted by CM 4851.

PARENTS, GRANDPARENTS AND OTHER DEPENDENT RELATIVES OF PERSONS PRESENT AND SETTLED IN THE UNITED KINGDOM

[A.2.330]
Requirements for indefinite leave to enter or remain in the United Kingdom as the parent, grandparent or other dependent relative of a person present and settled in the United Kingdom

317   The requirements to be met by a person seeking indefinite leave to enter or remain in the United Kingdom as the parent, grandparent or other depend-

ent relative of a person present and settled in the United Kingdom are that the person:

(i) is related to a person present and settled in the United Kingdom in one of the following ways:

    (*a*) mother or grandmother who is a widow aged 65 years or over; or

    (*b*) father or grandfather who is a widower aged 65 years or over; or

    (*c*) parent or grandparents travelling together of whom at least one is aged 65 or over; or

    (*d*) a parent or grandparent aged 65 or over who has remarried but cannot look to the spouse or children of the second marriage for financial support; and where the person settled in the United Kingdom is able and willing to maintain the parent or grandparent and any spouse or child of the second marriage who would be admissible as a dependent; or

    (*e*) a parent or grandparent under the age of 65 if living alone outside the United Kingdom in the most exceptional compassionate circumstances and mainly dependent financially on relatives settled in the United Kingdom; or

    (*f*) the son, daughter, sister, brother, uncle or aunt over the age of 18 if living alone outside the United Kingdom in the most exceptional compassionate circumstances and mainly dependent financially on relatives settled in the United Kingdom; and

(ii) is joining or accompanying a person who is present and settled in the United Kingdom or who is on the same occasion being admitted for settlement; and

(iii) is financially wholly or mainly dependent on the relative present and settled in the United Kingdom; and

[(iv) can, and will, be accommodated adequately, together with any dependants, without recourse to public funds, in accommodation which the sponsor owns or occupies exclusively; and

(iva) can, and will, be maintained adequately, together with any dependants, without recourse to public funds; and]

(v) has no other close relatives in his own country to whom he could turn for financial support; and

(vi) if seeking leave to enter, holds a valid United Kingdom entry clearance for entry in this capacity.

Note Paragraph 317(iv) substituted and paragraph 317(iva) inserted by CM 4851.

[A.2.331]

Indefinite leave to enter or remain as the parent, grandparent or other dependent relative of a person present and settled in the United Kingdom

318   Indefinite leave to enter the United Kingdom as the parent, grandparent or other dependent relative of a person present and settled in the United Kingdom may be granted provided a valid United Kingdom entry clearance for entry in this capacity is produced to the Immigration Officer on arrival. Indefinite leave to remain in the United Kingdom as the parent, grandparent or other dependent relative of a person present and settled in the United Kingdom may be granted provided the Secretary of State is satisfied that each of the requirements of paragraph 317(i)–(v) is met.

[A.2.332]
Refusal of indefinite leave to enter or remain in the United Kingdom as the parent, grandparent or other dependent relative of a person present and settled in the United Kingdom
319   Indefinite leave to enter the United Kingdom as the parent, grandparent or other dependent relative of a person settled in the United Kingdom is to be refused if a valid United Kingdom entry clearance for entry in this capacity is not produced to the Immigration Officer on arrival. Indefinite leave to remain in the United Kingdom as the parent, grandparent or other dependent relative of a person present and settled in the United Kingdom is to be refused if the Secretary of State is not satisfied that each of the requirements of paragraph 317(i)–(v) is met.

Note   Paras 317–319 replace HC 251, paras 56–57 and 139.

The only change of policy is that the admission of widowed parents and grandparents is now limited to those of 65 years of age, unless he or she, although under 65, is 'living alone outside the UK in the most exceptional compassionate circumstances and mainly dependent financially on relatives settled in the UK.' Other relatives who can qualify for admission under this paragraph, if they are living alone in the most exceptional compassionate circumstances and mainly dependent financially on relatives in the UK, are sons, daughters, sisters, brothers, uncles and aunts.

Part 9:   General grounds for the refusal of entry clearance, leave to enter or variation of leave to enter or remain in the United Kingdom

REFUSAL OF ENTRY CLEARANCE OR LEAVE TO ENTER THE UNITED KINGDOM

[A.2.333]
320   In addition to the grounds for refusal of entry clearance or leave to enter set out in Parts 2–8 of these Rules, and subject to paragraph 321 below, the following grounds for the refusal of entry clearance or leave to enter apply:

[A.2.334]
Grounds on which entry clearance or leave to enter the United Kingdom is to be refused
(1)   the fact that entry is being sought for a purpose not covered by these Rules;
(2)   the fact that the person seeking entry to the United Kingdom is currently the subject of a deportation order;
(3)   failure by the person seeking entry to the United Kingdom to produce to the Immigration Officer a valid national passport or other document satisfactorily establishing his identity and nationality;
(4)   failure to satisfy the Immigration Officer, in the case of a person arriving in the United Kingdom or seeking entry through the Channel Tunnel with the intention of entering any other part of the common travel area, that he is acceptable to the immigration authorities there;
(5)   failure, in the case of a visa national, to produce to the Immigration Officer a passport or other identity document endorsed with a valid and current United Kingdom entry clearance issued for the purpose for which entry is sought;

(6)   where the Secretary of State has personally directed that the exclusion of a person from the United Kingdom is conducive to the public good;

(7)   save in relation to a person settled in the United Kingdom or where the Immigration Officer is satisfied that there are strong compassionate reasons justifying admission, confirmation from the Medical Inspector that, for medical reasons, it is undesirable to admit a person seeking leave to enter the United Kingdom.

[A.2.335]
Grounds on which entry clearance or leave to enter the United Kingdom should normally be refused

(8)   failure by a person arriving in the United Kingdom to furnish the Immigration Officer with such information as may be required for the purpose of deciding whether he requires leave to enter and, if so, whether and on what terms leave should be given;

[(8A) where the person seeking leave is outside the United Kingdom, failure by him to supply any information, documents, copy documents or medical report requested by an Immigration Officer;]

(9)   failure by a person seeking leave to enter as a returning resident to satisfy the Immigration Officer that he meets the requirements of paragraph 18 of these Rules [or that he seeks leave to enter for the same purpose as that for which his earlier leave was granted];

(10)   production by the person seeking leave to enter the United Kingdom of a national passport or travel document issued by a territorial entity or authority which is not recognised by Her Majesty's Government as a state or is not dealt with as a government by them, or which does not accept valid United Kingdom passports for the purpose of its own immigration control; or a passport or travel document which does not comply with international passport practice;

(11)   failure to observe the time limit or conditions attached to any grant of leave to enter or remain in the United Kingdom;

(12)   the obtaining of a previous leave to enter or remain by deception;

(13)   failure, except by a person eligible for admission to the United Kingdom for settlement or a spouse eligible for admission under paragraph 282, to satisfy the Immigration Officer that he will be admitted to another country after a stay in the United Kingdom;

(14)   refusal by a sponsor of a person seeking leave to enter the United Kingdom to give, if requested to do so, an undertaking in writing to be responsible for that person's maintenance and accommodation for the period of any leave granted;

(15)   whether or not to the holder's knowledge, the making of false representations or the failure to disclose any material fact for the purpose of obtaining a work permit;

(16)   failure, in the case of a child under the age of 18 years seeking leave to enter the United Kingdom otherwise than in conjunction with an application made by his parent(s) or legal guardian, to provide the Immigration Officer, if required to do so, with written consent to the application from his parent(s) or legal guardian; save that the requirement as to written consent does not apply in the case of a child seeking admission to the United Kingdom as an asylum seeker;

(17) save in relation to a person settled in the United Kingdom, refusal to undergo a medical examination when required to do so by the Immigration Officer;
(18) save where the Immigration Officer is satisfied that admission would be justified for strong compassionate reasons, conviction in any country including the United Kingdom of an offence which, if committed in the United Kingdom, is punishable with imprisonment for a term of 12 months or any greater punishment or, if committed outside the United Kingdom, would be so punishable if the conduct constituting the offence had occurred in the United Kingdom;
(19) where from information available to the Immigration Officer, it seems right to refuse leave to enter on the ground that exclusion from the United Kingdom is conducive to the public good; if, for example, in the light of the character, conduct or associations of the person seeking leave to enter it is undesirable to give him leave to enter.

Note Para 320, sub-paras (10) and (16) are new although discretionary refusal of cases covered by these sub-paras would be possible under HC 251, albeit on different grounds. Sub-para (10) is designed to cater for the creation of the number of new States following the break up of the Soviet Union and former Yugoslavia. The UK formally recognises States but not, since 1980, governments. Where there is an issue of recognition, it is proved by a certificate from the Foreign and Commonwealth Office. As to whether a government is dealt with as a government by HM Government, it will be for the courts to decide the meaning of this expression. For example, will immigration officers accept the government of the 'Turkish Republic of Northern Cyprus' as one with which HM Government has dealt with as a government even though the UK does not recognise the 'TRNC'.
Sub-paragraph 8A inserted by HC 704.

[A.2.336]
Refusal of leave to enter in relation to a person in possession of an entry clearance
321 A person seeking leave to enter the United Kingdom who holds an entry clearance which was duly issued to him and is still current may be refused leave to enter only where the Immigration Officer is satisfied that:

(i) whether or not to the holder's knowledge, false representations were employed or material facts were not disclosed, either in writing or orally, for the purpose of obtaining the entry clearance; or
(ii) a change of circumstances since it was issued has removed the basis of the holder's claim to admission, except where the change of circumstances amounts solely to the person becoming over age for entry in one of the categories contained in paragraphs 296–316 of these Rules since the issue of the entry clearance; or
(iii) refusal is justified on grounds of restricted returnability; on medical grounds; on grounds of criminal record; because the person seeking leave to enter is the subject of a deportation order or because exclusion would be conducive to the public good.

Note Para 321 replaces HC 251, para 17, which did not come under the sub-heading General in Pt IX of HC 251.

[A.2.337]
[Grounds on which leave to enter or remain which is in force is to be cancelled at port or while the holder is outside the United Kingdom
321A   The following grounds for the cancellation of a person's leave to enter or remain which is in force on his arrival in, or whilst he is outside, the United Kingdom apply:

(1)   there has been such a change in the circumstances of that person's case, since the leave was given, that it should be cancelled; or
(2)   the leave was obtained as a result of false information given by that person or by that person's failure to disclose material facts; or
(3)   save in relation to a person settled in the United Kingdom or where the Immigration Officer or the Secretary of State is satisfied that there are strong compassionate reasons justifying admission, where it is apparent that, for medical reasons, it is undesirable to admit that person to the United Kingdom; or
(4)   where the Secretary of State has personally directed that the exclusion of that person from the United Kingdom is conducive to the public good; or
(5)   where from information available to the Immigration officer or the Secretary of State, it seems right to cancel leave on the ground that exclusion from the United Kingdom is conducive to public good; if, for example, in the light of the character, conduct or associations of that person it is undesirable for him to have leave to enter the United Kingdom; or
(6)   where that person is outside the United Kingdom, failure by that person to supply any information, documents, copy documents or medical report requested by an Immigration Officer or the Secretary of State.]

Note   Para 321A inserted by HC 704.

REFUSAL OF VARIATION OF LEAVE TO ENTER OR REMAIN OR CURTAILMENT OF LEAVE

[A.2.338]
322   In addition to the grounds for refusal of extension of stay set out in Parts 2–8 of these Rules, the following provisions apply in relation to the refusal of an application for variation of leave to enter or remain or, where appropriate, the curtailment of leave:

[A.2.339]
Grounds on which an application to vary leave to enter or remain in the United Kingdom is to be refused
(1)   the fact that variation of leave to enter or remain is being sought for a purpose not covered by these Rules.

[A.2.340]
Grounds on which an application to vary leave to enter or remain in the United Kingdom should normally be refused
(2)   the making of false representations or the failure to disclose any material fact for the purpose of obtaining leave to enter or a previous variation of leave;

(3) failure to comply with any conditions attached to the grant of leave to enter or remain;

(4) failure by the person concerned to maintain or accommodate himself and any dependants without recourse to public funds;

(5) the undesirability of permitting the person concerned to remain in the United Kingdom in the light of his character, conduct or associations or the fact that he represents a threat to national security;

(6) refusal by a sponsor of the person concerned to give, if requested to do so, an undertaking in writing to be responsible for his maintenance and accommodation in the United Kingdom or failure to honour such an undertaking once given;

(7) failure by the person concerned to honour any declaration or undertaking given orally or in writing as to the intended duration and/or purpose of his stay;

(8) failure, except by a person who qualifies for settlement in the United Kingdom or by the spouse of a person settled in the United Kingdom, to satisfy the Secretary of State that he will be returnable to another country if allowed to remain in the United Kingdom for a further period;

(9) failure by an applicant to produce within a reasonable time documents or other evidence required by the Secretary of State to establish his claim to remain under these Rules;

(10) failure, without providing a reasonable explanation, to comply with a request made on behalf of the Secretary of State to attend for interview;

(11) failure, in the case of a child under the age of 18 years seeking a variation of his leave to enter or remain in the United Kingdom otherwise than in conjunction with an application by his parent(s) or legal guardian, to provide the Secretary of State, if required to do so, with written consent to the application from his parent(s) or legal guardian; save that the requirement as to written consent does not apply in the case of a child who has been admitted to the United Kingdom as an asylum seeker.

Note Sub-para (1) is new. It does not directly affect the power of the Secretary of State to grant permission to remain outside the rules although it will no longer be possible to argue that the Secretary of State failed to consider a case outside the immigration rules.

Sub-paras (10) and (11) are also new.

[A.2.341]
Grounds on which leave to enter or remain may be curtailed
[323 A person's leave to enter or remain may be curtailed:

(i) on any of the grounds set out in paragraph 322 (2)–(5) above; or

(ii) if he ceases to meet the requirements of the Rules under which his leave to enter or remain was granted; or

(iii) if he is the dependant, or is seeking leave to remain as the dependant, of an asylum applicant whose claim has been refused and whose leave has been curtailed under section 7 of the 1993 Act, and he does not qualify for leave to remain in his own right.]

[A.2.342]
Crew members
324   A person who has been given leave to enter to join a ship, aircraft, hovercraft, hydrofoil or international train service as a member of its crew, or a crew member who has been given leave to enter for hospital treatment, repatriation or transfer to another ship, aircraft, hovercraft, hydrofoil or international train service in the United Kingdom, is to be refused leave to remain unless an extension of stay is necessary to fulfil the purpose for which he was given leave to enter or unless he meets the requirements for an extension of stay as a spouse in paragraph 284.

Note   Paras 320–324 replace HC 251, paras 78–86, 99–102.

Part 10:   Registration with the police

[A.2.343]
[324A   For the purposes of paragraphs 325 and 326, a 'relevant foreign national' is a person aged 16 years or over who is:

  (i) a national or citizen of a country or territory listed in Appendix 2 to these Rules;
 (ii) a stateless person; or
(iii) a person holding a non-national travel document.

325   (1) A condition requiring registration with the police should normally be imposed on any relevant foreign national who is given limited leave to enter the United Kingdom:

  (i) for employment for longer than 6 months unless he has been admitted for permit free employment as:
      (*a*) a seasonal worker at an agricultural camp;
      (*b*) a private servant in a diplomatic household; or
      (*c*) a minister of religion, missionary or member of a religious order; or
 (ii) for longer than 6 months under the following categories of these Rules:
      (*a*) students;
      (*b*) 'au pair';
      (*c*) businessmen and self-employed persons;
      (*d*) investors or persons of independent means;
      (*e*) creative artists; or
(iii) as the spouse or child of a person required to register with the police.

  (2)   Such a condition should also be imposed on any foreign national aged 16 years or over who is given limited leave to enter the United Kingdom where, exceptionally, the Immigration Officer considers it necessary to ensure that he complies with the terms of the leave.

326   A condition requiring registration with the police should also normally be imposed when a relevant foreign national on whom a registration requirement was not imposed on arrival is granted an extension of stay which has the effect of allowing him to remain in the United Kingdom for longer than 6

months, reckoned from the date of his arrival, save where the extension of stay
was granted:

   (i) as a private servant in a diplomatic household;
   (ii) as a minister of religion, missionary or member of a religious order;
   (iii) on the basis of marriage to a person settled in the United Kingdom; or
   (iv) following the grant of asylum.]

Note Paras 325–326 replace HC 251, paras 76–77, 142–143; substituted with effect
from 11 May 1998 by Cmnd 3953.

There are no substantive changes.

Part 11:   Asylum

[A.2.344]
Definition of asylum applicant
327   Under these Rules an asylum applicant is a person who claims that it
would be contrary to the United Kingdom's obligations under the United
Nations Convention and Protocol relating to the Status of Refugees for him to
be removed from or required to leave the United Kingdom. All such cases are
referred to in these Rules as asylum applications.

Note Para 327 reproduces the definition of asylum claimant contained in AIAA
1993, s 1.

[A.2.345]
Applications for asylum
328   All asylum applications will be determined by the Secretary of State in
accordance with the United Kingdom's obligations under the United Nations
Convention and Protocol relating to the Status of Refugees. Every asylum
application made by a person at a port or airport in the United Kingdom will
be referred by the Immigration Officer for determination by the Secretary of
State in accordance with these Rules.

Note Para 328 reflects the AIAA 1993, s 6.

[329   Until an asylum application has been determined by the Secretary of
State or the Secretary of State has issued a certificate under section 2(1)(a) of
the 1996 Act, no action will be taken to require the departure of the asylum
applicant or his dependants from the United Kingdom.]

330   If the Secretary of State decides to grant asylum and the person has not
yet been given leave to enter, the Immigration Officer will grant limited leave
to enter.

331 [If a person seeking leave to enter is refused asylum, the Immigration Officer will consider whether or not he is in a position to decide to give or refuse leave to enter without interviewing the person further. If the Immigration Officer decides that a further interview is not required he may serve the notice giving or refusing leave to enter by post. If the Immigration Officer decides that a further interview is required, he will then resume his examination to determine whether or not to grant the person] leave to enter without interviewing the person further. If the Immigration Officer decides that a further interview is not required he may serve the notice giving or refusing leave to enter by post. If the Immigration Officer decides that a further interview is required, he will then resume his examination to determine whether or not to grant the person leave to enter under any other provision of these Rules. If the person fails at any time to comply with a requirement to report to an Immigration Officer for examination, the Immigration Officer may direct that the person's examination shall be treated as concluded at that time. The Immigration Officer will then consider any outstanding applications for entry on the basis of any evidence before him.

Note Paragraph 331 substituted by CM 3365. Words in square brackets in para 331 substituted by HC 704.

332 If a person who has been refused leave to enter applies for asylum and that application is refused, leave to enter will again be refused unless the applicant qualifies for admission under any other provision of these Rules.

[333 A person who is refused leave to enter following the refusal of an asylum application will be provided with a notice informing him of the decision and of the reasons for refusal. The notice of refusal will also explain any rights of appeal available to the applicant and will inform him of the means by which he may exercise those rights. Subject to paragraph 356(ii) below, the applicant will not be removed from the United Kingdom so long as any appeal which he may bring or pursue in the United Kingdom is pending.]

[A.2.346]
Grant of asylum
334 An asylum applicant will be granted asylum in the United Kingdom if the Secretary of State is satisfied that:

(i) he is in the United Kingdom or has arrived at a port of entry in the United Kingdom; and

(ii) he is a refugee, as defined by the Convention and Protocol; and

(iii) refusing his application would result in his being required to go (whether immediately or after the time limited by an existing leave to enter or remain) in breach of the Convention and Protocol, to a country in which his life or freedom would be threatened on account of his race, religion, nationality, political opinion or membership of a particular social group.

335 If the Secretary of State decides to grant asylum to a person who has been given leave to enter (whether or not the leave has expired) or to a person who has entered without leave, the Secretary of State will vary the existing leave or grant limited leave to remain.

Note Paras 334 and 335: The right to asylum provided for by these paragraphs is new. It is not an obligation arising out of the Convention and Protocol.

[A.2.347]
Refusal of asylum
336 An application which does not meet the criteria set out in paragraph 334 will be refused.

337 . . .

338 When a person in the United Kingdom is notified that asylum has been refused he may, if he is liable to removal as an illegal entrant or to deportation, at the same time be notified of removal directions, served with a notice of intention to make a deportation order, or served with a deportation order, as appropriate.

[339 When a person's leave is curtailed under Section 7(1) or 7(1A) of the Asylum and Immigration Appeals Act 1993, he may at the same time be served with a notice of the Secretary of State's intention to make a deportation order against him. Full account will be taken of all relevant circumstances known to the Secretary of State, including those listed in paragraph 364.]

[A.2.348]
Consideration of cases
[340 A failure, without reasonable explanation, to make a prompt and full disclosure of material facts, either orally or in writing, or otherwise to assist the Secretary of State in establishing the facts of the case may lead to refusal of an asylum application. This includes failure to comply with a notice issued by the Secretary of State or an Immigration Officer requiring the applicant to report to a designated place to be fingerprinted, or failure to complete an asylum questionnaire, or failure to comply with a request to attend an interview concerning the application, or failure to comply with a requirement to report to an Immigration Officer for examination.]

Note Para 340: The adverse inference that may be drawn from a failure to report for fingerprinting suggests that asylum seekers will not be forced to provide fingerprints under the AIAA 1993, s 3(5)(*b*).

[341 In determining an asylum application the Secretary of State will have regard to matters which may damage an asylum applicant's credibility. Among such matters are:

  (i) that the applicant has failed without reasonable explanation to apply forthwith upon arrival in the United Kingdom, unless the application is founded on events which have taken place since his arrival in the United Kingdom;
  (ii) that the application is made after the applicant has been refused leave to enter under the 1971 Act, or has been recommended for deportation by a court empowered by the 1971 Act to do so, or has been notified of the

Secretary of State's decision to make a deportation order against him or
has been notified of his liability for removal;
(iii) that the application has adduced manifestly false evidence in support of
his application, or has otherwise made false representations, either orally or in writing;
(iv) that on his arrival in the United Kingdom the applicant was required to
produce a passport in accordance with paragraph 11(i) and either:
   (*a*)   failed to do so without providing a reasonable explanation; or
   (*b*)   produced a passport which was not in fact valid, and failed to
          inform the immigration officer of that fact;
 (v) that the applicant has otherwise, without reasonable explanation,
destroyed, damaged or disposed of any passport, other document, or ticket relevant to his claim;

(vi) that the applicant has undertaken any activities in the United Kingdom
before or after lodging his application which are inconsistent with his
previous beliefs and behaviour and calculated to create or substantially
enhance his claim to refugee status;

(vii) that the applicant has lodged concurrent applications for asylum in the
United Kingdom or in another country.

If the Secretary of State concludes for these or any other reasons that an asylum applicant's account is not credible, the application will be refused.]

Note   Para 341: It is significant that the matters referred to in para 341(i)–(v) above
come under the heading 'Consideration of cases'. This means that they should not constitute reasons for holding that a claim is without foundation within the IAA 1999, Sch,
para 9.

---

342   The actions of anyone acting as an agent of the asylum applicant may also
be taken into account in regard to the matters set out in paragraphs 340 and 341.

343   If there is a part of the country from which the applicant claims to be a
refugee in which he would not have a well-founded fear of persecution, and to
which it would be reasonable to expect him to go, the application may be
refused.

Note   Para 343: This para reflects the previous position in UK law. For further background see article by H H Storey '*The Internal Flight Alternative (IFA) Test: a Re-
examination*' in Immigration and Nationality Law and Practice, vol 11 No 2, 1997. See
now *R v SSHD, ex p Robinson* [1998] QB 929, [1999] INLR 182 and *Karanakaran v
SSHD* [2000] INLR 122. The test is whether it would be 'unduly harsh' to expect the
claimant to relocate.

---

344   Cases will normally be considered on an individual basis but if an applicant is part of a group whose claims are clearly not related to the criteria for
refugee status in the Convention and Protocol he may be refused without
examination of his individual claim. However, the Secretary of State will have
regard to any evidence produced by an individual to show that his claim should
be distinguished from those of the rest of the group.

Note Para 344: It seems that a person refused under this category will not be caught by the IAA 1999, Sch, para 9 either: see the notes to para 341 above.

[A.2.349]
Third country cases
[345 (1) In a case where the Secretary of State is satisfied that the conditions set out in section 2(2) of the 1996 Act are fulfilled, he will normally refuse the asylum application and issue a certificate under section 2(1) of the 1996 Act without substantive consideration of the applicant's claim to refugee status. The conditions are:

  (i) that the applicant is not a national or citizen of the country or territory to which he is to be sent;
 (ii) that the applicant's life and liberty would not be threatened in that country by reason of his race, religion, nationality, membership of a particular social group, or political opinion; and
(iii) that the government of that country or territory would not send him to another country or territory otherwise than in accordance with the Convention.

(2) The Secretary of State shall not remove an asylum applicant without substantive consideration of his claim unless:

  (i) the asylum applicant has not arrived in the United Kingdom directly from the country in which he claims to fear persecution and has had an opportunity at the border or within the third country or territory to make contact with the authorities of that third country or territory in order to seek their protection; or
 (ii) there is other clear evidence of his admissibility to a third country or territory.

Provided that he is satisfied that a case meets these criteria, the Secretary of State is under no obligation to consult the authorities of the third country or territory before the removal of an asylum applicant to that country or territory.]

Note The regime is now that contained in sections 11 and 12 of the Immigration and Asylum Act 1999. The 1996 provisions here referred to have been repealed: Schedule 16, 1999 Act refers. The necessary consequential changes in the immigration rules have not yet all been made.

[A.2.350]
Previously rejected applications
[346 Where an asylum applicant has previously been refused asylum during his stay in the United Kingdom, the Secretary of State will determine whether any further representations should be treated as a fresh application for asylum. The Secretary of State will treat representations as a fresh application for asylum if the claim advanced in the representations is sufficiently different from the earlier claim that there is a realistic prospect that the conditions set out in paragraph 334 will be satisfied. In considering whether to treat the representations as a fresh claim, the Secretary of State will disregard any material which:

  (i) is not significant; or

(ii)   is not credible; or
(iii)   was available to the applicant at the time when the previous application was refused or when any appeal was determined.]

347   . . .

[A.2.351]
Rights of appeal
[348   Special provisions governing appeals in asylum cases are set out in the Asylum and Immigration Appeals Act 1993, the Asylum and Immigration Act 1996 and the Asylum Appeals (Procedure) Rules 1996. Where asylum is refused, the applicant will be provided with a notice informing him of the decision and of the reasons for refusal. At the same time that asylum is refused, the applicant may be notified of removal directions, or served with a notice of the Secretary of State's intention to deport him, as appropriate. The notice of refusal of asylum will also explain any rights of appeal available to the applicant and will inform him of the means by which he may exercise those rights.]

Note   For the references to the regime contained in the 1993 and 1996 Acts and the 1993 Procedure Rules, see now Part IV and Schedule IV of the 1999 Act and the Immigration and Asylum (Procedure) Rules 2000. See also note to rule 342 above.

[A.2.352]
Dependants
[349   A husband or wife or minor children accompanying a principal applicant may be included in an application for asylum. If the principal applicant is granted asylum any such dependants will be granted leave to enter or remain for the same duration. The case of any dependant who claims asylum in his own right and who would otherwise be refused leave to enter or remain will be considered individually in accordance with paragraph 334 above. If the dependant has a claim in his own right, it should be made at the earliest opportunity. Any failure to do so will be taken into account and may damage credibility if no reasonable explanation for it is given. Where the principal applicant is refused asylum and the dependant has previously been refused asylum in his own right, the dependant may be removed forthwith, notwithstanding any outstanding right of appeal that may be available to the principal applicant. At the same time that asylum is refused the applicant may be notified of removal directions or served with a notice of the Secretary of State's intention to deport him, as appropriate. The notice of refusal of asylum will also explain any rights of appeal available to the applicant and will inform him of the means by which he may exercise those rights.]
   [In this paragraph and paragraphs 350–352, a child means a person who is under 18 years of age or who, in the absence of documentary evidence, appears to be under that age.]

[A.2.353]
Unaccompanied children
350   Unaccompanied children may also apply for asylum and, in view of their potential vulnerability, particular priority and care is to be given to the handling of their cases.

351   A person of any age may qualify for refugee status under the Convention and the criteria in paragraph 334 apply to all cases. However, account should be taken of the applicant's maturity and in assessing the claim of a child more weight should be given to objective indications of risk than to the child's state of mind and understanding of his situation. An asylum application made on behalf of a child should not be refused solely because the child is too young to understand his situation or to have formed a well-founded fear of persecution. Close attention should be given to the welfare of the child at all times.

352   A child will not be interviewed about the substance of his claim to refugee status if it is possible to obtain by written enquiries or from other sources sufficient information properly to determine the claim. When an interview is necessary it should be conducted in the presence of a parent, guardian, representative or another adult who for the time being takes responsibility for the child and is not an Immigration Officer, an officer of the Secretary of State or a police officer. The interviewer should have particular regard to the possibility that a child will feel inhibited or alarmed. The child should be allowed to express himself in his own way and at his own speed. If he appears tired or distressed, the interview should be stopped.

Note   Paras 327–352 replace HC 725, para 180.

Paras 350–352: These have seemingly been included in the rules as a result of amendment 1 concerning young unaccompanied asylum seekers proposed by the House of Lords but which was rejected by the House of Commons for, it was said, lack of funds. The spirit of these paragraphs suggests that the fast track appeals procedures referred to above will not be used in such cases.

[352A   The requirements to be met by a person seeking leave to enter or remain in the United Kingdom as the spouse of a refugee are that:

(i)   the applicant is married to a person granted asylum in the United Kingdom; and
(ii)   the marriage did not take place after the person granted asylum had left the country of his former habitual residence in order to seek asylum; and
(iii) the applicant would not be excluded from protection by virtue of article 1F of the United Nations Convention and Protocol relating to the Status of Refugees if he were to seek asylum in his own right; and
(iv)   if seeking leave to enter, the applicant holds a valid United Kingdom entry clearance for entry in this capacity.

352B   Limited leave to enter the United Kingdom as the spouse of a refugee may be granted provided a valid United Kingdom entry clearance for entry in this capacity is produced to the Immigration Officer on arrival. Limited leave to remain in the United Kingdom as the spouse of a refugee may be granted provided the Secretary of State is satisfied that each of the requirements paragraph 352A (i)-(iii) are met.

352C   Limited leave to enter the United Kingdom as the spouse of a refugee is to be refused if a valid United Kingdom entry clearance for entry in this capacity is not produced to the Immigration Officer on arrival. Limited leave to remain as the spouse of a refugee is to be refused if the Secretary of State is not satisfied that each of the requirements of paragraph 352A (i)-(iii) are met.

352D   The requirements to be met by a person seeking leave to enter or remain in the United Kingdom as the child of a refugee are that the applicant:

(i)   is the child of a parent who has been granted asylum in the United Kingdom; and

(ii)   is under the age of 18; and

(iii)   is not leading an independent life, is unmarried, and has not formed an independent family unit; and

(iv)   was part of the family unit of the person granted asylum at the time that the person granted asylum left the country of his habitual residence in order to seek asylum; and

(v)   would not be excluded from protection by virtue of article 1F of the United Nations Convention and Protocol relating to the Status of Refugees if he were to seek asylum in his own right; and

(vi)   if seeking leave to enter, holds a valid United Kingdom entry clearance for entry in this capacity.

352E   Limited leave to enter the United Kingdom as the child of a refugee may be granted provided a valid United Kingdom entry clearance for entry in this capacity is produced to the Immigration Officer on arrival. Limited leave to remain in the United Kingdom as a child of a refugee may be granted provided the Secretary of State is satisfied that each of the requirements of paragraph 352D (i)-(v) are met.

352F   Limited leave to enter the United Kingdom as the child of a refugee is to be refused if a valid United Kingdom entry clearance for entry in this capacity is not produced to the Immigration Officer on arrival. Limited leave to remain as the child of a refugee is to be refused if the Secretary of State is not satisfied that each of the requirements of paragraph 352D (i)-(v) are met.

Note   Paragraphs 352A-352F inserted by Cm 4851.

Part 12:   Rights of appeal

[A.2.354]
353–361   [. . .]

Note   Paragraphs 353 to 361 deleted by CM 4851.

Part 13: Deportation [and Administrative Removal under Section 10 of the 1999 Act]

[A.2.355]
A deportation order

362 A deportation order requires the subject to leave the United Kingdom and authorises his detention until he is removed. It also prohibits him from re-entering the country for as long as it is in force and invalidates any leave to enter or remain in the United Kingdom given him before the order was made or while it is in force.

[363 The circumstances in which a person is liable to deportation include:

(i) where the Secretary of State deems the person's deportation to be conducive the public good;

(ii) where the person is the spouse or child under 18 of a person ordered to be deported; and

(iii) where a court recommends deportation in the case of a person over the age of 17 who has been convicted of an offence punishable with imprisonment.]

[363A Prior to 2 October 2000, a person would have been liable to deportation in certain circumstances in which he is now liable to administrative removal. These circumstances are listed in paragraph 394B below. However, such a person remains liable to deportation, rather than administrative removal where:

(i) a decision to make a deportation order against him was taken before 2 October 2000; or

(ii) the person has made a valid application under the Immigration (Regularisation Period for Overstayers) Regulations 2000.]

364 [Subject to paragraph 380] in considering whether deportation is the right course on the merits, the public interest will be balanced against any compassionate circumstances of the case. While each case will be considered in the light of the particular circumstances, the aim is an exercise of the power of deportation which is consistent and fair as between one person and another, although one case will rarely be identical with another in all material respects.

[In the cases detailed in paragraph 363A,] deportation will normally be the proper course where a person has failed to comply with or has contravened a condition or has remained without authority. Before a decision to deport is reached the Secretary of State will take into account all relevant factors known to him including:

(i) age;

(ii) length of residence in the United Kingdom;

(iii) strength of connections with the United Kingdom;

(iv) personal history, including character, conduct and employment record;

(v) domestic circumstances;

(vi) previous criminal record and the nature of any offence of which the person has been convicted;

(vii) compassionate circumstances;

(viii) any representations received on the person's behalf.

Notes Words in square brackets in the title to Part 13 inserted by CM 4851.

Paragraph 363 substituted and paragraph 363A and words in square brackets in paragraph 364 inserted by CM 4851.

[A.2.356]
Deportation of family members
[365 Section 5 of the Immigration Act 1971 gives the Secretary of State power in certain circumstances to make a deportation order against the spouse or child of a person against whom a deportation order has been made. The Secretary of State will not normally decide to deport the spouse of a deportee where:

  (i) he has qualified for settlement in his own right; or
 (ii) he has been living apart from the deportee.]

[366 The Secretary of State will not normally decide to deport the child of a deportee where:

  (i) he and his mother or father are living apart from the deportee; or
 (ii) he has left home and established himself on an independent basis; or
(iii) he married before deportation came into prospect.]

[367 In considering whether to require a spouse or child to leave with the deportee, the Secretary of State will take account of the factors listed in paragraph 364 as well as the following:

  (i) the ability of the spouse to maintain herself and any children in the United Kingdom, or to be maintained by relatives or friends without charge to public funds, not merely for a short period but for the foreseeable future; and
 (ii) in the case of a child of school age, the effect of removal on his education; and
(iii) the practicability of any plans for a child's care and maintenance in this country if one or both of his parents were deported; and
(iv) any representations made by or on behalf of the spouse or child.]

368 Where the Secretary of State decides that it would be appropriate to deport a member of a family as such, the decision, and the right of appeal, will be notified and it will at the same time be explained that it is open to the member of the family to leave the country voluntarily if he does not wish to appeal or if he appeals and his appeal is dismissed.

[A.2.357]
369–374 [. . .].

Note Paragraph 369 to 374 deleted by CM 4851.

[A.2.358]
Hearing of appeals
376 . . .

377 [. . .]

[378   A deportation order may not be made while it is still open to the person to appeal against the Secretary of State's decision, or while an appeal is pending. There is no appeal within the immigration appeal system against the making of a deportation order on the recommendation of a court; but there is a right of appeal to a higher court against the recommendation itself. A deportation order may not be made while it is still open to the person to appeal against the relevant conviction, sentence or recommendation, or while such an appeal is pending.]

Note   Paragraph 377 deleted and paragraph 378 substituted by CM 4851.

[A.2.359]
Persons who have claimed asylum
379–379A   [. . .]:

Note   Paragraphs 379 and 379A deleted by CM 4851.

380   A deportation order will not be made against any person if his removal in pursuance of the order would be contrary to the United Kingdom's obligations under the Convention and Protocol relating to the Status of Refugees [or the Human Rights Convention].

Note   Words in square brackets inserted by CM 4851.

[A.2.360]
Procedure
381   When a decision to make a deportation order has been taken (otherwise than on the recommendation of a court) a notice will be given to the person concerned informing him of the decision and of his right of appeal [. . .].

382   [Following the issue of such a notice the Secretary of State may authorise detention or make an order restricting a person as to residence, employment or occupation and requiring him to report to the police, pending the making of a deportation order.]

383   [. . .].

384   If a notice of appeal is given within the period allowed, a summary of the facts of the case on the basis of which the decision was taken will be sent to the [appropriate] appellate authorities, who will notify the appellant of the arrangements for the appeal to be heard.

Notes   Words in paragraph 381 deleted, paragraph 382 substituted, paragraph 383 deleted and words in square brackets in paragraph 384 inserted by CM 4851.

[A.2.361]
Arrangements for removal
385   A person against whom a deportation order has been made will normally be removed from the United Kingdom. The power is to be exercised so as to secure the person's return to the country of which he is a national, or which

has most recently provided him with a travel document, unless he can show that another country will receive him. In considering any departure from the normal arrangements, regard will be had to the public interest generally, and to any additional expense that may fall on public funds.

386   The person will not be removed as the subject of a deportation order while an appeal may be brought against the removal directions or such an appeal is pending.

[A.2.362]
Supervised departure
387   [. . .].

Note   Paragraph 387 deleted by CM 4851.

[A.2.363]
Returned deportees
388   Where a person returns to this country when a deportation order is in force against him, he may be deported under the original order. The Secretary of State will consider every such case in the light of all the relevant circumstances before deciding whether to enforce the order.

[A.2.364]
Returned family members
389   Persons deported in the circumstances set out in paragraph 365–368 above (deportation of family members) may be able to seek re-admission to the United Kingdom under the Immigration Rules where:

(i) a child reaches 18 (when he ceases to be subject to the deportation order); or

(ii) in the case of a wife, the marriage comes to an end.

[A.2.365]
Revocation of deportation order
390   An application for revocation of a deportation order will be considered in the light of all the circumstances including the following:

(i) the grounds on which the order was made;

(ii) any representations made in support of revocation;

(iii) the interests of the community, including the maintenance of an effective immigration control;

(iv) the interests of the applicant, including any compassionate circumstances.

391   In the case of an applicant with a serious criminal record continued exclusion for a long term of years will normally be the proper course. In other cases revocation of the order will not normally be authorised unless the situation has been materially altered, either by a change of circumstances since the order was made, or by fresh information coming to light which was not before the court which made the recommendation or the appellate authorities or the Secretary of State. The passage of time since the person was deported may also

in itself amount to such a change of circumstances as to warrant revocation of the order. However, save in the most exceptional circumstances, the Secretary of State will not revoke the order unless the person has been absent from the United Kingdom for a period of at least 3 years since it was made.

392   Revocation of a deportation order does not entitle the person concerned to re-enter the United Kingdom; it renders him eligible to apply for admission under the Immigration Rules. Application for revocation of the order may be made to the Entry Clearance Officer or direct to the Home Office.

[A.2.366]
Rights of appeal in relation to a decision not to revoke a deportation order
393–394   [. . .].

395   [There may be a right of appeal against refusal to revoke a deportation order.] Where an appeal does lie the right of appeal will be notified at the same time as the decision to refuse to revoke the order.

[A.2.367]
[Administrative Removal
395A   A person is now liable to administrative removal in certain circumstances in which he would, prior to 2 October 2000, have been liable to deportation.

395B   These circumstances are set out in section 10 of the 1999 Act. They are:
  (i) failure to comply with a condition attached to his leave to enter or remain, or remaining beyond the time limited by the leave;
  (ii) where the person has obtained leave to remain by deception; and
  (iii) where the person is the spouse or child under 18 of someone in respect of whom directions for removal have been given under section 10.

395C   Before directions for removal under section 10 are given, regard will be had to any compassionate circumstances of the case, taking into account all the relevant factors known to the Secretary of State, as listed in paragraph 364. In the case of family members, the factors listed in paragraphs 365—368 will also be taken into account.

395D   No one shall be removed under section 10 if his removal' would be contrary to the United Kingdom's obligations under the Convention and Protocol relating to the Status of Refugees or under the Human Rights Convention.

[A.2.368]
Procedure
395E   When directions for a person's removal under section 10 have been given, a notice will be given to the person concerned informing him of the decision.

395F   Following the issue of such a notice an Immigration Officer may authorise detention or make an order restricting a person as to residence, employment or occupation and requiring him to report to the police, pending the removal.]

Note Paras 362–395 replace HC 251, paras 155–180. Paragraphs 393 and 394 deleted, words in square brackets in paragraph 395 inserted and paragraphs 395A to 395F inserted by CM 4851.

[Appendix 1]
[A.2.369]
[Visa requirements for the United Kingdom
1   Subject to paragraph 2 below the following persons need a visa for the United Kingdom:

(*a*) Nationals or citizens of the following countries or territorial entities:

Afghanistan	Fiji	Peru
Albania	Gabon	Philippines
Algeria	Georgia	Qatar
Angola	Ghana	Romania
Armenia	Guinea	Russia
Azerbaijan	Guinea-Bissau	Rwanda
Bahrain	Guyana	Sao Tome e Principe
Bangladesh	Haiti	Saudi Arabia
Belarus	India	Senegal
Benin	Indonesia	Sierra Leone
Bhutan	Iran	[Slovak Republic]
Bosnia-Herzegovina	Iraq	Somalia
Bulgaria	Ivory Coast	Sri Lanka
Burkina Faso	Jordan	Sudan
Burma	Kazakhstan	Surinam
Burundi	Kenya	Syria
Cambodia	Kirgizstan	Taiwan
Cameroon	Korea (North)	Tajikistan
Cape Verde	Laos	Tanzania
Central African	Lebanon	Thailand
Republic	Liberia	Togo
Chad	Libya	Tunisia
China	Macedonia	Turkey
[Colombia]	Madagascar	Turkmenistan
Comoros	Maldives	Uganda
Congo	Mali	Ukraine
[Republic of Croatia]	Mauritania	United Arab Emirates
Cuba	Moldova	Uzbekistan
[Democratic Republic of	Mongolia	Vietnam
the Congo (Zaire)]	Morocco	Yemen
Djibouti	Mozambique	The territories
Dominican Republic	Nepal	formerly comprising
Ecuador	Niger	the Socialist Federal
Egypt	Nigeria	Republic of Yugo-
Equatorial Guinea	Oman	slavia excluding
Eritrea	Pakistan	Croatia and Slovenia
Ethiopia	Papua New Guinea	

(*b*) Persons who hold passports or travel documents issued by the former Soviet Union or by the former Socialist Federal Republic of Yugoslavia.

(*c*) Stateless persons.

(*d*) Persons who hold non-national documents.

2   The following persons do not need a visa for the United Kingdom:

(*a*) those who qualify for admission to the United Kingdom as returning residents in accordance with paragraph 18;

[(*b*) those who seek leave to enter the United Kingdom within the period of their earlier leave and for the same purpose as that for which leave was granted, unless it:

(i) was for a period of six months or less; or

(ii) was extended by statutory instrument;]

(*c*) those holding refugee travel documents issued under the 1951 Convention relating to the Status of Refugees by countries which are signatories of the Council of Europe Agreement of 1959 on the Abolition of Visas for Refugees if coming on visits of 3 months or less.]

Note   Appendix amended by Statement of Changes in Immigration Rules with effect from 4 April 1996. Renamed Appendix 1 with effect from 11 May 1998 (Cmnd 3953). Republic of Croatia added by HC 22.

Readers are warned that in relation to this Appendix in particular amendments are made periodically and often without prior warning.

[Appendix 2   (Paragraph 324A)
[A.2.370]
Countries or territories whose nationals or citizens are relevant foreign nationals for the purposes of Part 10 of these rules (registration with the police)

Afghanistan	Iran	Qatar
Algeria	Iraq	Russia
Argentina	Israel	Saudi Arabia
Armenia	Jordan	Sudan
Azerbaijan	Kazakhstan	Syria
Bahrain	Kirgizstan	Tajikistan
Belarus	Kuwait	Tunisia
Bolivia	Lebanon	Turkey
Bhutan	Libya	Turkmenistan
Brazil	Moldova	United Arab Emirates
China	Morocco	Ukraine
Colombia	North Korea	Uzbekistan
Cuba	Oman	Yemen]
Egypt	Palestine	
Georgia	Peru	

Note   Appendix 2 added with effect from 11 May 1998 by Cmnd 3953.

A3 Procedure Rules

SPECIAL IMMIGRATION APPEALS COMMISSION (PROCEDURE) RULES 1998
SI 1998/1881

Date   30 July 1998
Coming into force   31 July 1998

Arrangement of Rules

PART I
GENERAL PROVISIONS

Note These Rules came into force on 31 July 1998.

[A.3.1]
Citation and commencement
1 These Rules may be cited as the Special Immigration Appeals Commission (Procedure) Rules 1998 and shall come into force on the day after the day on which they are made.

Note The Special Immigration Appeals Commission (Procedure) Rules 1998 came into force on 31 July 1998.

[A.3.2]
Interpretation
2 In these Rules—
'the 1971 Act' means the Immigration Act 1971;
'the 1997 Act' means the Special Immigration Appeals Commission Act 1997;
['the 1999 Act' means the Immigration and Asylum Act 1999;]
'the chairman' means the chairman of the Commission;
'the Commission' means the Special Immigration Appeals Commission; and
'the special advocate' means a person appointed under section 6(1) of the 1997
    Act to represent the interests of the appellant.

Notes For the Immigration Act 1971 see **[A1.1]** et seq For the Special Immigration Appeals Commission Act 1997 see **[A.1.192]** et seq. The Chairman of the Commission is Mr Justice Potts. Words in square brackets inserted by SI 2000/1849.

[A.3.3]
General duty of Commission
3—(1) When exercising its functions, the Commission shall secure that information is not disclosed contrary to the interests of national security, the international relations of the United Kingdom, the detection and prevention of crime, or in any other circumstances where disclosure is likely to harm a public interest.

(2) Where the Rules require information not to be disclosed contrary to the public interest, the requirement shall be construed in accordance with paragraph (1).

(3) Subject to paragraphs (1) and (2), the Commission must satisfy itself that the material available to it enables it properly to review decisions.

[A.3.4]
Delegated powers
4—(1) The powers of the Commission under the following provisions may be exercised by the chairman or by any other member of the Commission who falls within paragraph 5(*a*) or (*b*) of Schedule 1 to the 1997 Act:

(*a*) rule 12(1) and (3) (amendment and supplementary grounds);
(*b*) rule 13 (directions);
(*c*) rule 25 (application for leave to appeal);
(*d*) rules 26 and 27 (bail proceedings).

(2) Instead of exercising a power under paragraph (1), the chairman or member may remit the matter to be dealt with by the Commission.

(3) Where the chairman or member exercises any power of the Commission, references to the Commission in the Rules shall as appropriate include references to him.

Note The delegated powers of the Commission may not be exercised by the third member of the Commission. The third member is expected to have experience of dealing with security matters.

[A.3.5]
Notices etc
5—(1) Any document required or authorised to be given or sent to—

(*a*) the Commission, shall be directed to the Secretary to the Commission;
(*b*) the Secretary of State, shall be directed to [an address or fax number specified by him].

(2) The appellant must inform the Commission if an address given under rule 9(3) changes.

Note Words in square brackets substituted by SI 2000/1849.

PART II
APPEALS

[A.3.6]
[Application of Part II]
[**6** —(1) Subject to paragraph (2), this Part applies to appeals brought under section 2 of the 1997 Act and to appeals transferred to the Commission under subsection (3) or (5) of section 78 of the 1999 Act where an appeal has been or may be made under section 2(1) of the 1997 Act.

(2)   The provisions of this Part shall not—

(*a*) prejudice steps already taken in respect of an appeal transferred under either of those subsections, or
(*b*) require any step to be taken under these Rules which is equivalent to a step which has already been taken in respect of such an appeal.]

Note Substituted by SI 2000/1849.

[A.3.7]
The special advocate
7—(1) On receiving [. . .] the notice of appeal, the Secretary of State shall inform the relevant law officer of the proceedings before the Commission,

with a view to the law officer, if he thinks fit to do so, appointing a special advocate to represent the interests of the appellant in the proceedings.

(2) Paragraph (1) applies unless—

(*a*) the Secretary of State does not intend to oppose the appeal, or
(*b*) he does not intend to object to the disclosure of material to the appellant.

(3) If at any stage in proceedings before the Commission, paragraph (2)(*b*) ceases to apply, the Secretary of State shall immediately notify the relevant law officer as in paragraph (1).

(4) The function of the special advocate is to represent the interests of the appellant by—

(*a*) making submissions to the Commission in any proceedings from which the appellant and his representative are excluded;
(*b*) cross-examining witnesses at any such proceedings; and
(*c*) making written submissions to the Commission.

(5) Except in accordance with paragraphs (6) to (9), the special advocate may not communicate directly with the appellant or his representative on any matter connected with proceedings before the Commission.

(6) The special advocate may communicate with the appellant and his representative at any time before the Secretary of State makes material available to him under rule 10(3).

(7) At any time after the Secretary of State has made material available under rule 10(3), the special advocate may seek directions from the Commission authorising him to seek information in connection with the proceedings from the appellant or his representative.

(8) The Commission shall notify the Secretary of State of a request for directions under paragraph (7) and the Secretary of States must, within a period specified by the Commission, give the Commission notice of any objection which he has to the request for information being made or to the form in which it is proposed to be made.

(9) Where the Secretary of State makes an objection under paragraph (8), rule 11 shall apply as appropriate.

Notes Section 6 of the 1997 Act enables the relevant law officer to appoint the special advocate to represent the appellant's interests: see **[A.1.192]** et seq. The special advocate's ability to communicate with the appellant is restricted by r 7(5). Words omitted from para (1) by SI 2000/1849.

[A.3.8]
[Time limit for appealing
[8—(1) The appellant shall give notice of an appeal no later than—

(a) 5 days after receiving the notice of the decision being appealed against, where the appellant appeals in the United Kingdom; or
(b) 28 days after receiving the notice of the decision being appealed against, where the appellant appeals from outside the United Kingdom.

(2) The period specified in paragraph (1) shall begin from the end of the day

on which the notice of the decision being appealed against was received.

(3) Where the period specified under paragraph (1) expires on an excluded day, the notice of appeal shall be taken to have been served as required if served on the next day that is not an excluded day.

(4) Where the period specified under paragraph (1)(a) includes an excluded day, that day shall be discounted.

(5) The notice of appeal shall be taken to have been served as required on the day on which it is received at the address or fax number specified in the notice of the decision against which the appeal is made.

(6) 'Excluded day' means a Saturday, a Sunday, a bank holiday, Christmas Day, 27th to 31st December or Good Friday.

(7) 'Bank holiday' means a day that is specified in, or appointed under, the Banking and Financial Dealings Act 1971.]

Note   Substituted by SI 2000/1849, r 7.

[A.3.9]
[Notice of appeal]
[**9**—(1) An appeal to the Commission shall be made by sending to the Secretary of State a notice of appeal by hand, by fax or by post to the address or fax number specified in the document which informed him of the decision against which he is appealing.

(2) The notice of appeal shall set out the grounds for the appeal.

(3) The notice of appeal shall state the name and address of the appellant and the name and address of any representative of the appellant.

(4) The appellant or his representative shall sign the notice of appeal.

(5) The appellant shall attach to the notice of appeal—

(*a*) a copy of the document which informed him of the decision against which he is appealing; and

(*b*) where a notice has been served on the appellant under section 74(4) of the 1999 Act, a statement form, on which additional grounds which he has or may have for wishing to enter or remain in the United Kingdom may be stated, whether or not that form has been completed.

(6)   As soon as practicable after he receives a notice of appeal in a case where no such grounds have been stated, the Secretary of State shall send that notice, together with any documents attached to it under paragraph (5), to the Commission.]

Note   Substituted by SI 2000/1849, r 8.

[A.3.10]
[Additional grounds for appealing]
[**9A**—(1) Where the appellant is treated as appealing on additional grounds by virtue of section 77(2) of the 1999 Act, he shall serve any variation of his grounds of appeal on the Secretary of State no later than 5 days after he

received the supplementary grounds of refusal.

(2) As soon as practicable after this period, the Secretary of State shall send to the Commission—

(a) the notice of appeal, together with any documents attached to it under rule 9(5),
(b) any supplementary grounds for refusal, and
(c) any variation of the grounds of appeal.

(3) For the purpose of calculating the period specified in paragraph (1), paragraphs (2) to (7) of rule 8 shall apply as if the variation of grounds of appeal were a notice of appeal and the supplementary grounds of refusal were the notice of the decision against which the appeal is made.

(4) In this rule, 'supplementary grounds of refusal' means the reasons given by the Secretary of State for maintaining the decision being appealed against after consideration by him of the additional grounds.]

Note Inserted by SI 2000/1849.

[A.3.11]
Secretary of State's reply
10—(1) If the Secretary of State intends to oppose the appeal, he must [. . .],—

(*a*) provide the Commission with a summary of the facts relating to decision being appealed and the reasons for the decision;
(*b*) inform the Commission of the grounds on which he opposes the appeal; and
(*c*) provide the Commission with a statement of the evidence which he relies upon in support of those grounds.

(2) Where the Secretary of State objects to material referred to in paragraph (1) being disclosed to the appellant or his representative, he must also—

(*a*) state the reasons for his objection; and
(*b*) if and to the extent it is possible to do so without disclosing information contrary to the public interest, provide a statement of that material in a form which can be shown to the appellant.

(3) Where he makes an objection under paragraph (2), the Secretary of State must make available to the special advocate, as soon as it is practicable to do so, the material which he has provided to the Commission under paragraphs (1) and (2).

Note Words omitted from para (1) by SI 2000/1849.

[A.3.12]
Consideration of Secretary of State's objection
11—(1) Proceedings under this rule shall take place in the absence of the appellant and his representative.

(2) The Commission shall decide whether to uphold the Secretary of State's objection.

(3) Before doing so, it must invite the special advocate to make written representations.

(4) After considering representations made under paragraph (3), the Commission may—

(*a*) invite the special advocate to make oral representations; or
(*b*) uphold the Secretary of State's objection without requiring further representations from the special advocate.

(5) Where the Commission is minded to overrule the Secretary of State's objection, or to require him to provide material in a different form from that in which he has provided it under rule 10(2)(*b*), the Commission must invite the Secretary of State and the special advocate to make oral representations.

(6) Where—

(*a*) the Commission overrules the Secretary of State's objection or requires him to provide material in a different form from that which he has provided under rule 10(2)(*b*), and
(*b*) the Secretary of State wishes to continue to oppose the appeal,

he shall not be required to disclose any material which was the subject of his unsuccessful objection if he chooses not to rely upon it in opposing the appeal.

[A.3.13]
Amendment and supplementary grounds
12 [(1) Subject to paragraph (1A), the appellant may amend his notice of appeal or deliver supplementary grounds of appeal.

(1A) Where the Secretary of State has provided material under rule 10, the appellant shall obtain the leave of the Commission before amending his notice of appeal or delivering supplementary grounds of appeal under paragraph (1).

(2) The appellant shall send any proposed amended notice of appeal or supplementary grounds of appeal to the Secretary of State who shall, as soon as practicable, send a copy to the Commission.]

(3) With the leave of the Commission, the Secretary of State may amend or supplement the material which he has provided under rule 10.

(4) Where the Secretary of State provides further objections under paragraph 3, the Commission shall consider them in accordance with rule 11.

Note Paragraphs (1)–(2) substituted by SI 2000/1849.

[A.3.14]
Directions
13—(1) Subject to any decision which it makes under rule 11 and to the need to secure that information is not disclosed contrary to the public interest, the Commission may give directions for the conduct of proceedings.

(2) Directions may—

(*a*) provide for a particular matter to be dealt with as a preliminary issue and for a pre-hearing review to be held;

(*b*) limit the length of oral submissions and the time allowed for the examination and cross-examination of witnesses;

(*c*) require any party to the appeal to give to the Commission—

    (i) statements of facts and statements of the evidence which will be called at any hearing, including such statements provided in a modified or edited form;

    (ii) a skeleton argument which summarises the submissions which will be made and cites all the authorities which will be relied upon, identifying any particular passages to be relied upon;

    (iii) an estimate of the time which will be needed for any hearing;

    (iv) a list of the witnesses who will be called to give evidence;

    (v) a chronology of events;

    (vi) a statement of any interpretation requirements,

and to serve any such material on the other parties to the appeal.

[(3) The Commission may—

(*a*) subject to any specific provisions of the Rules, specify time limits for steps to be taken in the proceedings; and

(*b*) extend any time limit.]

(4) The power to give directions may be exercised in the absence of the parties.

Note   Paragraph (3) substituted by SI 2000/1849.

[A.3.15]
Failure to comply with directions
14—(1) Where a party fails to comply with a direction, the Commission may send him a notice which states—

(*a*) the respect in which he has failed to comply with the relevant direction;

(*b*) the time limit for complying with the direction; and

(*c*) that the Commission may proceed to determine the appeal on the material available to it if the party fails to comply with the relevant direction within the time specified.

(2) Where the party in default fails to comply with the notice under paragraph (1), the Commission may proceed in accordance with paragraph (1)(*c*).

[A.3.16]
Applications by Secretary of State
15—(1) This rule applies to the notification to the appellant by the Commission of—

(*a*) any order or direction made or given in the absence of the Secretary of State,

(*b*) any summary prepared under rule 22, and

(*c*) its determination under rule 23.

(2) Before the Commission notifies the appellant as mentioned in paragraph (1), it must first notify the Secretary of State.

(3) If the Secretary of State considers that compliance by him with an order or direction or notification to the appellant of any matter under paragraph (1)

would cause information to be disclosed contrary to the public interest, he may apply to the Commission to reconsider the order or direction or to review the proposed summary or determination.

(4) At the same time as he makes his application, or as soon as practicable afterwards, the Secretary of State must send a copy of it to the special advocate.

(5) An application by the Secretary of State must be made within 14 days of receipt of notification under paragraph (2), and the Commission shall notify the appellant as mentioned in paragraph (1) before the time for applying has expired.

(6) Rule 11 shall apply as appropriate to the Commission's consideration of the Secretary of State's application.

[A.3.17]
Notification of hearing
16 The Secretary to the Commission must send notice of the date, time and place fixed for any hearing to the special advocate and every party entitled to attend that hearing.

[A.3.18]
Parties
17—(1) The parties to an appeal shall be the appellant and the Secretary of State.

(2) If the United Kingdom Representative of the United Nations High Commissioner for Refugees (the 'United Kingdom Representative') gives written notice that he wishes to be treated as a party to the appeal, he shall be so treated from the date of the notice.

(3) Any restriction imposed by or under these Rules in relation to the appellant as to the disclosure of material, attendance at hearings, notification of directions or decisions and communications with the special advocate, applies to the United Kingdom Representative.

[A.3.19]
Representation of parties
18—(1) The appellant may act in person or be represented or appear by—

(*a*) a person having a qualification referred to in section 6(3) of the 1997 Act,
(*b*) a person appointed by any voluntary organisation for the time being in receipt of a grant under section 23 of the 1971 Act, or
(*c*) with the leave of the Commission, any other person.

(2) The Secretary of State and the United Kingdom Representative may be represented by any person appointed by them respectively for that purpose.

[A.3.20]
Proceedings in private
19—(1) Where the Commission considers it necessary for the appellant and his representative to be excluded from the proceedings or any part of them in order to secure that information is not disclosed contrary to the public interest, it must—

(*a*) direct accordingly, and
(*b*) hear the proceedings, or that part of it from which the appellant and his representative are excluded, in private.

(2) The Commission may hear the proceedings or part of them in private for any other good reason.

[A.3.21]
Evidence
20—(1) In any proceedings on an appeal, the evidence of witnesses may be given either—

(*a*) orally, before the Commission, or
(*b*) in writing, in which case it shall be given in such a manner and at such time as the Commission has directed.

(2) The Commission may also receive evidence in documentary or any other form.

(3) The Commission may receive evidence that would not be admissible in a court of law.

(4) No person shall be compelled to give evidence or produce a document which he could not be compelled to give or produce on the trial of an action in the part of the United Kingdom in which the proceedings before the Commission are taking place.

(5) Every party shall be entitled to adduce evidence and to cross-examine witnesses during any part of the hearing of the appeal from which he and his representative are not excluded.

(6) The Commission may require a witness to give evidence on oath.

[A.3.22]
Summoning of witnesses
21—(1) Subject to rules 3 and 20(4) and paragraph (2) of this rule, the Commission may require any person in the United Kingdom to attend as a witness at any proceedings before the Commission and to answer any questions or produce any documents in his custody or under his control which relate to any matter in question in the appeal.

(2) No person shall be required to travel more than 16 kilometres from his place of residence unless the necessary expenses of his attendance are paid or tendered to him.

(3) Where a party requests the attendance of a witness, that party must pay or tender those expenses.

[A.3.23]
Notification to appellant before determination
22—(1) Where the appellant or his representative have been excluded from the hearing of the appeal or any part of it, the Commission must, before it [determines the appeal], give the appellant a summary of the submissions and evidence received in his absence if and to the extent it is possible to do so without disclosing information contrary to the public interest.

(2) Where the Commission provides such a summary, it shall afford the special advocate and the parties an opportunity to make representations and adduce evidence or further evidence to the Commission in respect of the material contained in it.

Note Words in square brackets substituted by SI 2000/1849.

[A.3.24]
Promulgation of determination
23—(1) The Commission must record its determination and, if and to the extent it is possible to do so without disclosing information contrary to the public interest, the reasons for it.

(2) The Commission shall publish its determination and send written notice of it to the special advocate and the parties.

PART III
LEAVE TO APPEAL FROM COMMISSION

[A.3.25]
Application of Part III
24 This Part applies to applications for leave to appeal, on a question of law, to the Court of Appeal, the Court of Session or the Court of Appeal in Northern Ireland, as the case may be, from a final determination of an appeal by the Commission.

[A.3.26]
Application for leave to appeal
25—(1) An application to the Commission for leave to appeal shall be made not later than 10 days after the party seeking to appeal has received written notice of the determination.

(2) The Commission may decide an application for leave without a hearing unless it considers there are special circumstances which make a hearing necessary or desirable.

PART IV
BAIL APPLICATIONS

[A.3.27]
Application for bail: procedure
26—(1) Subject to the provisions of this rule and rule 27, these Rules apply to—

(*a*) applications for bail by a person who brings an appeal under section 2 of the 1997 Act, and
(*b*) applications to the Commission under paragraphs 22 to 24 of Schedule 2 to the 1971 Act,

with appropriate modifications.

(2) References in the Rules to the appellant shall be read, in relation to bail applications, as if they were references to the applicant.

[(3) Rules 8, 9 and 9A shall not apply to bail applications.]

(4) . . .

(5) An application to the Commission to be released on bail must be made in writing and shall contain the following particulars—

(*a*) the full name of the applicant;
(*b*) the address of the place where, and the reason why, the applicant is detained at the time when the application is made;
(*c*) the date of any notice of appeal which has been given;
(*d*) the address where the applicant would reside if his application for bail were to be granted;
(*e*) the amount of the recognizance in which he would agree to be bound;
(*f*) the full names, addresses and occupations of two persons who might act as sureties for the applicant if his application for bail were to be granted, and the amounts of the recognizances in which those persons might agree to be bound; and
(*g*) the grounds on which the application is made and, where a previous application has been refused, particulars of any change in circumstances which has occurred since that refusal.

(6) In its application to Scotland, this rule shall have effect as if, for paragraph (5)(*e*) and (*f*), there were substituted—

'(*e*) the amount, if any, to be deposited if bail is granted;
(*f*) the full names, addresses and occupations of such persons if any, who offer to act as cautioners if the applicant's application for bail were to be granted;'.

(7) A bail application shall be signed by the applicant or by a person duly authorised by him for that purpose or, in the case of an applicant who is a minor or who is for any reason incapable of acting, by any person acting on his behalf.

(8) The application must be delivered, or sent by post, to the Commission.

Note Paragraph (3) substituted for paras (3) and (4) by SI 2000/1849.

[A.3.28]
Release on bail
27—(1) Where the Commission directs the release of an applicant on bail and the taking of the recognizance is postponed under paragraph 22(3) or 29(6) of Schedule 2 to the 1971 Act, it shall certify in writing that the applicant has been granted bail and shall include in the certificate—

(*a*) particulars of the conditions to be endorsed on the recognizance with a view to the recognizance being taken subsequently;
(*b*) the amounts in which the applicant and any sureties are to be bound; and
(*c*) the date of issue of the certificate.

(2) The person having custody of an applicant shall release him—

(*a*) on receipt of a certificate signed by the Commission stating that the recognizances of any sureties required have been taken or on being otherwise satisfied that all such recognizances have been taken, and
(*b*) on being satisfied that the applicant has entered into his recognizance.

(3) In its application to Scotland, this rule shall have effect as if for paragraph (2), there were substituted—

'(2) The person having custody of an appellant shall release him—

(*a*) on receipt of a certified copy of the decision to grant bail, and
(*b*) on being satisfied that the amount, if any, to be deposited has been so deposited.'.

IMMIGRATION AND ASYLUM APPEALS (PROCEDURE) RULES 2000
SI 2000/2333

Made   21 August 2000
Laid before Parliament   1 September 2000
Coming into force   2 October 2000

Arrangement of Rules

PART I
INTRODUCTION

[A.3.29]
1   Citation, commencement and revocation
(1)   These Rules may be cited as the Immigration and Asylum Appeals (Procedure) Rules 2000 and shall come into force on 2nd October 2000.

(2)   Subject to rule 4, the following Rules:

(a)   the Immigration Appeals (Procedure) Rules 1984;
(b)   the Immigration Appeals (Procedure) (Amendment) Rules 1991;
(c)   the Immigration Appeals (Procedure) (Amendment) Rules 1993; and
(d)   the Asylum Appeals (Procedure) Rules 1996;

shall be revoked.

[A.3.30]
2   Interpretation
(1)   In these Rules:

'the 1971 Act' means the Immigration Act 1971;

'the 1993 Act' means the Asylum and Immigration Appeals Act 1993;

'the 1996 Act' means the Asylum and Immigration Act 1996;

'the 1999 Act' means the Immigration and Asylum Act 1999;

'appellate authority' means the adjudicator or the Tribunal, as the case may be;

'appeal' means, subject to rule 4, any appeal under Part IV of the 1999 Act;

'appellant' has the meaning given in Parts II and III of these Rules and includes an applicant for bail;

'appropriate prescribed form' means the appropriate form in the Schedule to these Rules and those forms, or similar forms, may be used with any variations that the circumstances may require;

'authorised advocate':

(a)   in relation to England and Wales, has the meaning given in section 119(1) of the Courts and Legal Services Act 1990;
(b)   in relation to Scotland, means a solicitor or advocate; and
(c)   in relation to Northern Ireland, means a solicitor or barrister;

'Chief Adjudicator' includes an adjudicator nominated by the Chief Adjudicator under paragraph 6(2)(a) of Schedule 3 to the 1999 Act;

'determination' means the decision of the appellate authority to allow or dismiss an appeal and the reasons for that decision;

'entry clearance officer' means a person having authority to grant an entry clearance on behalf of the Government of the United Kingdom;

'family visitor appeal' means an appeal made under section 59 by a person who is a family visitor as defined by regulations made under section 60;

'member' means a member of the Tribunal;

'officer' means an immigration officer or an entry clearance officer;

'party' has the meaning given in rule 29;

'President' means the President of the Tribunal;

'previous appeals provisions' means Part II of the 1971 Act, section 8 of the 1993 Act or section 3 of the 1996 Act;

'supplementary grounds of refusal' means the reasons given for maintaining the decision being appealed against after consideration of the additional grounds required under section 74(4); and

'Tribunal' means the Immigration Appeal Tribunal.

(2)   In these Rules, a section referred to by number alone is a reference to a section of the 1999 Act.

[A.3.31]
3   Application of Rules
Subject to rule 4, these Rules shall apply to:

(a)   appeals to an adjudicator;
(b)   applications to the Tribunal for leave to appeal to the Tribunal and appeals to the Tribunal;
(c)   applications for bail; and
(d)   applications to the Tribunal for leave to appeal to the Court of Appeal or in Scotland, to the Court of Session.

[A.3.32]
4   Transitional provisions
(1)   Subject to paragraphs (3) to (9), these Rules shall apply, with appropriate modifications, to any appeal made under the previous appeals provisions pending on 2nd October 2000 or made on or after that date.

(2)   Anything done or any direction given under the Immigration Appeals (Procedure) Rules 1984 ('the 1984 Rules') or the Asylum Appeals (Procedure) Rules 1996 ('the 1996 Rules') in relation to an appeal made under the previous appeals provisions pending on 2nd October 2000 or made on or after that date, shall be treated as if done or given under these Rules.

(3)   Where an appeal is made under Part II of the 1971 Act, the time limits for giving notice of appeal shall be those in rule 4 of the 1984 Rules and the reference to rule 6 in paragraphs (1)(b), (5) and (6) of rule 12 of these Rules shall be read as a reference to rule 4 of the 1984 Rules.

(4)   Where an appeal is made under section 8 of the 1993 Act or section 3 of the 1996 Act, the time limits for giving notice of appeal shall be those in rule 5 of the 1996 Rules and the reference to rule 6 in paragraphs (1)(b), (5) and (6) of rule 12 of these Rules shall be read as a reference to rule 5 of the 1996 Rules.

(5)   Where an appeal made under Part II of the 1971 Act has been determined by an adjudicator before 2nd October 2000, the time limits for making an application to the Tribunal for leave to appeal shall be those in paragraphs (2) to (4) of rule 15 of the 1984 Rules.

(6)   Where an appeal is made under section 8 of the 1993 Act, the reference in rule 11(3) of these Rules to section 69 of the 1999 Act shall be read as a reference to section 8 of the 1993 Act.

(7)   Where an appeal is made under the previous appeals provisions, the reference in rule 12(1)(a)(i) of these Rules to a provision of the 1999 Act shall be read as a reference to a provision of the 1971 Act, the 1993 Act or the 1996 Act specified by the respondent.

(8)   Where an appeal is made to the Tribunal at first instance under section 15(7) of the 1971 Act as provided by rule 3 of the 1984 Rules, Part II of these Rules shall apply as if the appeal had been made to an adjudicator at first instance.

(9)   Rule 41 of the 1984 Rules shall continue to apply to a reference made by the Secretary of State under section 21 of the 1971 Act.

(10)   In rule 35(1)(a) of these Rules, before the coming into force of section 84, a person appealing against an immigration decision may be represented by:

(a) a solicitor, barrister, advocate or a person who is a Fellow of the Institute of Legal Executives;
(b) a person appointed by a voluntary organisation in receipt of a grant under section 23 of the 1971 Act or section 81 of the 1999 Act; or
(c) with the leave of the appellate authority, any other person.

PART II
APPEALS TO ADJUDICATORS

[A.3.33]
5   Application of Part II
(1)   This Part applies to appeals to an adjudicator.

(2)   In this Part, 'appellant' means a person appealing against an immigration decision.

[A.3.34]
6   Time limit for giving notice of appeal
(1)   Where an appellant makes an appeal within the United Kingdom, notice of appeal shall be given not later than 10 days after the notice of the decision was received.

(2)   Where the appellant makes an appeal outside the United Kingdom, notice of appeal shall be given:

(a)   in a case where the appellant is in the United Kingdom when the decision is made, not later than 28 days after his departure from the United Kingdom; or

(b)   in a case where the appellant is not in the United Kingdom when the decision is made, not later than 28 days after the notice of the decision was received.

(3)   In this rule, 'decision' means the decision against which the appellant is appealing.

[A.3.35]
7   Late notice of appeal
(1)   Where any notice of appeal is not given within the appropriate time limit, it shall nevertheless be treated for all purposes as having been given within that time limit if the person to whom it was given is satisfied that, because of special circumstances, it is just for the notice to be treated in that way.

(2)   An adjudicator shall not extend the time limit for giving notice of appeal unless he is satisfied that because of special circumstances, it is just for the notice to be treated in that way.

[A.3.36]
8   Method of giving notice of appeal
(1)   Subject to paragraph (2), an appeal to an adjudicator shall be made by sending to the person, and at the address, specified in the notice of the decision which is the subject of the appeal, a notice of appeal in the appropriate prescribed form.

(2)   In any case where an appellant is in custody, service under paragraph (1) may be upon the person having custody of him.

(3)   The notice of appeal shall set out the grounds for the appeal.

(4)   Where the appeal is made under section 59, in relation to a family visitor appeal, the appellant shall specify in, or attach to, the notice of appeal all matters he wishes to be considered for the purposes of the appeal.

(5)   The notice of appeal shall state the name and address of the appellant and the name and address of his representative (if he has one).

(6)   The appellant or his representative (if he has one) shall sign the notice of appeal.

(7)   The appellant shall attach to the notice of appeal:

(a) a copy of any document which informed him of the decision against which he is appealing and any reasons for that decision; and
(b) where a notice has been served on the appellant under section 74(4), a statement form, on which additional grounds which he has or may have for wishing to enter or remain in the United Kingdom may be stated, whether or not that form has been completed.

[A.3.37]
9   Additional grounds for appealing
Where the appellant is treated as appealing on additional grounds by virtue of section 77(2), he shall serve on the person, and at the address, specified in the supplementary grounds of refusal, any variation of his grounds of appeal not later than 5 days after he received the supplementary grounds of refusal.

[A.3.38]
10   Despatch of documents to adjudicator
(1)   Whether or not the notice of appeal was given within the time limit specified, the respondent shall send to an adjudicator, the appellant and the appellant's representative:

(a) the notice of appeal, together with any documents attached to it under rule 8;
(b) any supplementary grounds of refusal;
(c) any variation of the grounds of appeal;
(d) any notes of an asylum interview; and
(e) any other document (except statutory or public materials) referred to in the decision which is the subject of appeal.

(2)   In this rule, 'statutory or public materials' means an enactment or a provision made under an enactment, a convention or other provisions of a similar nature or other documents which are published or publicly available.

[A.3.39]
11   Variation of notice of appeal
(1)   This rule applies where the documents have been sent to the adjudicator in accordance with rule 10.

(2)   The grounds of the appeal may be varied by the appellant with the leave of the adjudicator.

(3)   Except in the case of an appeal under section 65 or 69, the adjudicator shall not give leave to vary the grounds of appeal unless he is satisfied that because of special circumstances, it is just to allow the variation.

[A.3.40]
12 Preliminary issues
(1)   When the respondent alleges that:

(a) the appellant is not entitled to appeal:

  (i)   by virtue of a provision of the 1999 Act specified by the respondent;
  (ii) by virtue of a provision of Regulations made under section 2(2) of the European Communities Act 1972 and section 80 of the 1999 Act specified by the respondent;
  (iii) by reason that a passport or other travel document, certificate of entitlement, entry clearance or work permit on which the appellant relies is a forgery or was issued to, and relates to, another person; or
  (iv) by reason that notice of appeal has not been signed by the appellant or by his representative (if he has one) or, in the case of an appellant who is a minor or who is for any reason incapable of acting, by any person acting on his behalf; or

(b) the notice of appeal was not given within the period specified by rule 6; the respondent shall send to the adjudicator with the documents required under rule 8, and to the appellant and his representative (if he has one), a written statement setting out the allegation, the reasons for it and any relevant facts relating to it.

(2)   The appellant may send a written statement in reply to the respondent's statement given in accordance with paragraph (1) to the adjudicator and the respondent.

(3)   Where a written statement has been given in accordance with paragraph (1), the adjudicator may, and at the request of the respondent shall, determine the validity of the allegation as a preliminary issue.

(4)   At a hearing before the adjudicator in accordance with paragraph (3):

(a) the respondent shall be given an opportunity to explain the allegation contained in his statement and any matters relating to it; and
(b) the appellant shall be given an opportunity to respond to the matters raised under sub-paragraph (a).

(5)   Where the adjudicator determines as a preliminary issue that the notice of appeal was not given within the period specified by rule 6, then, except where a deportation order is in force in respect of the appellant, the adjudicator may allow the appeal to proceed if he is satisfied that by reason of special circumstances, it is just to do so.

(6)   Where the adjudicator allows the appeal to proceed in accordance with paragraph (5), the notice of appeal shall be treated for all purposes as if it had been given in accordance with rule 6.

[A.3.41]
13 Notification of hearing
Notice of the date, time and place fixed for the hearing and any directions given under rule 30 shall be served on the appellant or his representative (if he has one) and any other party.

[A.3.42]
14   Determining an appeal
(1)   Except where rule 43 or 44 applies, a hearing shall be conducted to determine the appeal.

(2)   A hearing may be conducted or evidence given or representations made
by video link or by other electronic means.

[A.3.43]
15   Giving of determination
Written notice of the adjudicator's determination shall be sent to every party
and the appellant's representative (if he has one).

[A.3.44]
16   Adjudicator's review of determination
(1)   Where a party receives written notice of a determination to which there
is no right of appeal to the Tribunal, he may apply to the Chief Adjudicator to
review that determination on the ground that it was wrongly made as a result
of an administrative or procedural error by the adjudicator.

(2)   An application under paragraph (1) shall:

(a) be made not later than 10 days after written notice of the determination
     was received by the party;
(b) be in writing;
(c) identify all matters relied on; and
(d) be accompanied by copies of all relevant documents.

(3)   In addition to his power to review a determination on an application
made under paragraph (1), the Chief Adjudicator may, of his own motion, if
satisfied that the interests of justice so require, not later than 10 days after
written notice of the determination has been sent to the parties, review that
determination on the ground that it was wrongly made as a result of an administrative or procedural error by the adjudicator.

(4)   Where the Chief Adjudicator reviews the determination, he may:

(a) confirm it; or
(b) set it aside and direct a re-hearing of the appeal.

(5)   Where the Chief Adjudicator confirms the determination, written notice
shall be sent to the parties.

(6)   Where the Chief Adjudicator sets aside the determination, written notice
shall be sent to the parties, together with the date, time and place, and any
directions, for the re-hearing of the appeal.

(7)   Any notice given under paragraphs (5) and (6) shall contain, in summary form, the reasons for the decision.

PART III
APPEALS TO TRIBUNAL FROM ADJUDICATOR

[A.3.45]
17   Application of Part III
(1)   This Part applies to:

(a) applications to the Tribunal for leave to appeal to the Tribunal; and

(b) appeals to the Tribunal from the determination of an adjudicator.

(2)   In this Part, 'appellant' means a party appealing against an adjudicator's determination and includes an applicant for leave to appeal under rule 18 and an applicant for a review under rule 19.

[A.3.46]
18   Leave to appeal
(1)   An appeal from the determination of an adjudicator may be made only with the leave of the Tribunal.

(2)   An application for leave to appeal shall be made not later than 10 days, or in the case of an application made from outside the United Kingdom, 28 days, after the appellant has received written notice of the determination against which he wishes to appeal.

(3)   A time limit set out in paragraph (2) may be extended by the Tribunal where it is satisfied that because of special circumstances, it is just for the time limit to be extended.

(4)   An application for leave to appeal shall be made by serving upon the Tribunal the appropriate prescribed form, which shall:

(a) be signed by the appellant or his representative (if he has one);

(b) be accompanied by the adjudicator's determination;

(c) identify the alleged errors of fact or law in the adjudicator's determination which would have made a material difference to the outcome, together with all the grounds relied on for the appeal; and

(d) state whether a hearing of the appeal is desired.

(5)   When an application for leave to appeal has been made, the Tribunal shall notify the other parties.

(6)   The Tribunal shall not be required to consider any grounds other than those included in that application.

(7)   Leave to appeal shall be granted only where:

(a) the Tribunal is satisfied that the appeal would have a real prospect of success; or

(b) there is some other compelling reason why the appeal should be heard.

(8)   An application for leave to appeal shall be decided by a legally qualified member without a hearing.

(9)   When an application for leave to appeal has been decided, written notice of the Tribunal's decision on the application shall be sent to the parties and, if granted, the grounds upon which the appellant may appeal.

(10)   Where the application for leave to appeal is refused, the notice referred to in paragraph (9) shall include, in summary form, the reasons for the refusal.

(11)   Subject to section 77, where evidence which was not submitted to the adjudicator is relied upon in an application for leave to appeal, the Tribunal shall not be required to consider that evidence in deciding whether to grant leave to appeal, unless it is satisfied that there were good reasons why it was not submitted to the adjudicator.

[A.3.47]
19 Tribunal's review of decision to refuse leave to appeal
(1)   Where the Tribunal has refused an application for leave to appeal, the appellant may apply to the Tribunal to review its decision on the ground that it was wrongly made as a result of an administrative or procedural error by the Tribunal.

(2)   An application under paragraph (1) shall:

(a) be made not later than 10 days after written notice of the decision refusing leave to appeal was received by the appellant;
(b) be in writing;
(c) identify all matters relied on; and
(d) be accompanied by copies of all relevant documents.

(3)   In addition to its power to review a decision on an application made under paragraph (1), the Tribunal may, of its own motion, if satisfied that the interests of justice so require, not later than 10 days after sending to the appellant the notice of its decision, review its decision on the ground that it was wrongly made as a result of an administrative or procedural error by the Tribunal.

(4)   A review under this rule shall be conducted by a legally qualified member without a hearing.

(5)   Where the Tribunal reviews the decision, it may:

(a) confirm it; or
(b) set it aside and re-consider the decision.

(6)   Written notice of the Tribunal's decision shall be sent to the parties and shall contain, in summary form, the reasons for the decision.

[A.3.48]
20 Notice of appeal
(1)   Where an application for leave to appeal is granted, it shall be deemed to be the notice of appeal.

(2)   Where leave to appeal is granted, written notice of the date, time and place fixed for any hearing shall be sent to:

(a) every party; and
(b) every party's representative, except where the representative is acting for the Secretary of State, an officer or the United Kingdom Representative of the United Nations High Commissioner for Refugees.

[A.3.49]
21 Variation of notice of appeal
The grounds of appeal may be varied by the appellant with the leave of the Tribunal.

[A.3.50]
22 Evidence
(1)   The Tribunal may consider as evidence any note or record made by the adjudicator of any proceedings before him in connection with the appeal.

(2)   Subject to paragraph (3), the Tribunal may, of its own motion or on the application of any party, consider evidence further to that which was submitted to the adjudicator.

(3)   The Tribunal shall not consider any evidence which is not served in accordance with time limits set out in these Rules or directions given under rule 30, unless the Tribunal is satisfied that there are good reasons to do so.

(4)   Subject to rule 38, the Tribunal shall not in its determination rely on any evidence which was not disclosed to all the parties.

(5)   Where any party wishes to adduce further evidence before the Tribunal in accordance with paragraph (2), he shall give written notice to that effect to the Tribunal indicating the nature of the evidence.

(6)   The notice referred to in paragraph (5) shall be given as soon as practicable after the parties have been notified that leave to appeal has been granted.

(7)   Where the Tribunal decides to admit any evidence under this rule, it may direct that it be given, either:

(a)   orally, in which case the Tribunal may take the evidence itself or remit the appeal to the same or another adjudicator for the taking of that evidence; or

(b)   in writing, in which case it shall be given in any manner and at any time that the Tribunal may direct.

[A.3.51]
23   Appeals remitted by Tribunal to adjudicator
Unless it considers:

(a)   that it is necessary in the interests of justice, and
(b)   that it would save time and avoid expense

to remit the case to the same or another adjudicator for determination by him in accordance with any directions given to him by the Tribunal, the Tribunal shall determine the appeal itself.

[A.3.52]
24   Determining an appeal
(1)   Except where rule 43 or 44 applies, a hearing shall be conducted to determine an appeal.

(2)   A hearing may be conducted or evidence given or representations made by video link or by other electronic means.

[A.3.53]
25   Giving of determination
(1)   Written notice of the Tribunal's determination shall be sent to:

(a)   every party; and
(b)   every party's representative, except where the representative is acting for the Secretary of State, an officer or the United Kingdom Representative of the United Nations High Commissioner for Refugees.

(2)   Where an appeal is determined by a panel of more than one member, the determination may be given by a legally qualified member of that panel or, if the panel contains no legally qualified member, by such member as the President may direct.

PART IV
APPEALS FROM TRIBUNAL

[A.3.54]
26   Application of Part IV
This Part applies to applications to the Tribunal for leave to appeal, on a question of law, to the Court of Appeal or, in Scotland, to the Court of Session, from a final determination of an appeal by the Tribunal.

[A.3.55]
27   Leave to appeal
(1)   An application to the Tribunal for leave to appeal shall be made not later than 10 days after the party seeking to appeal has received written notice of the determination.

(2)   An application for leave to appeal shall be made by serving upon the Tribunal and any other party a notice of application for leave to appeal on the appropriate prescribed form and shall include the grounds of appeal.

(3)   The appropriate prescribed form shall be signed by the party seeking leave to appeal or his representative (if he has one).

(4)   An application for leave to appeal shall be decided by a legally qualified member without a hearing.

(5)   Where the Tribunal intends to grant leave to appeal, it may, having given every party an opportunity to make representations, instead, set aside the determination appealed against and direct that the appeal to the Tribunal be reheard.

(6)   Written notice of the Tribunal's decision shall be sent to the parties.

(7)   Any notice given under paragraph (6) shall contain, in summary form, the reasons for the decision.

PART V
GENERAL PROVISIONS

[A.3.56]
28   Application of Part V
This Part applies to:

(a) proceedings to which Part II applies (appeals to adjudicator);
(b) proceedings to which Part III applies (appeals to the Tribunal from adjudicator);

(c) proceedings to which Part IV applies (applications to the Tribunal for leave to appeal from the Tribunal); and

(d) applications for bail.

[A.3.57]
29   Parties
(1)   Subject to paragraph (2), the parties to the appeal shall be the appellant and the respondent.

(2)   Where, in the case of a claim for asylum, the United Kingdom Representative of the United Nations High Commissioner for Refugees gives written notice to the appellate authority at any time during the course of an appeal that he wishes to be treated as a party, he shall be so treated from the date of the notice.

[A.3.58]
30   Conduct of appeals
(1)   The appellate authority may, subject to the provisions of these Rules, regulate the procedure to be followed in relation to the conduct of any appeal.

(2)   The overriding objective shall be to secure the just, timely and effective disposal of appeals and, in order to further that objective, the appellate authority may give directions which control the conduct of any appeal.

(3)   The appellate authority may give directions under this rule orally or in writing and notice of any written directions given shall be served on the appellant or his representative (if he has one) and any other party.

(4)   Directions given under this rule may, in particular:

(a) relate to any matter concerning the preparation for a hearing and may specify the length of time allowed for anything to be done;

(b) specify the place at which the appeal shall be heard;

(c) provide for:

(i)   a particular matter to be dealt with as a preliminary issue;

(ii)   a pre-hearing review to be held;

(iii) the furnishing of any particulars which appear to be requisite for the determination of the appeal;

(iv) whether there should be a hearing of the appeal;

(v)   the witnesses, if any, to be heard;

(vi) the manner in which any evidence may be given; and

(vii) in the case of the Tribunal, times to be prescribed within which leave must be sought to submit any evidence or call any witnesses;

(d) require any party to file:

(i)   statements of the evidence which will be called at the hearing specifying in what respect the services of an interpreter will be required;

(ii)   a paginated and indexed bundle of all the documents which will be relied on at the hearing;

(iii) a skeleton argument which summarises succinctly the submissions which will be made at the hearing and cites all the authorities which will be relied on, identifying any particular passages to be relied on;

   (iv) an estimate of the time which will be needed for the hearing of the appeal;

   (v) a list of the witnesses whom any party wishes to call to give evidence; and

   (vi) a chronology of events;

(e) limit:

   (i) the number or length of documents produced by, for example, requiring a party to specify to another party the passage or part of any document on which he will rely, especially if the document has to be translated into English for the hearing;

   (ii) the length of oral submissions;

   (iii) the time allowed for the examination and cross examination of witnesses by, for example, allowing a witness statement to stand as evidence in chief; and

   (iv) the issues which will be addressed at the hearing;

(f) facilitate the holding of combined hearings under rule 42.

(5) A party shall provide to every other party a copy of any document which he is directed to file under paragraph (4).

(6) In an appeal in which a party is unrepresented, the appellate authority may not give directions under this rule where it is necessary for the party to comply, unless it is satisfied that he is able to comply with those directions.

[A.3.59]
31   Adjournment of hearings
(1) Where an adjournment of the appeal is requested, the appellate authority shall not adjourn the hearing unless it is satisfied that refusing the adjournment would prevent the just disposal of the appeal.

(2) Where a party applies for an adjournment of a hearing, he shall, where practicable, notify all other parties of the application and:

(a) show good reason why an adjournment is necessary;
(b) establish any fact or matter relied on in support of the application; and
(c) offer a new date for the hearing.

(3) Where a hearing is adjourned, the appellate authority shall give any further directions which it considers to be necessary for the future conduct of the appeal.

(4) Written notice of the date, time and place of the adjourned hearing shall be sent to:

(a) every party; and
(b) every party's representative, except where the representative is acting for the Secretary of State, an officer or the United Kingdom Representative of the United Nations High Commissioner for Refugees.

[A.3.60]
32   Abandoned appeals
(1) Where a party has, without a satisfactory explanation, failed:

(a) to comply with a direction given under these Rules;

(b) to comply with a provision of these Rules; or

(c) to appear at a hearing of which he had notice in accordance with these Rules;

and the appellate authority is satisfied in all the circumstances, including the extent of the failure and any reasons for it, that the party is not pursuing his appeal, the appellate authority may treat the appeal as abandoned.

(2)   Where the appellate authority treats an appeal as abandoned, it shall send a notice to the parties which shall:

(a) inform the parties that the appeal is being treated as abandoned; and

(b) include the reasons.

[A.3.61]
33   Failure to comply with these Rules
(1)   Where a party has failed:

(a) to comply with a direction given under these Rules; or

(b) to comply with a provision of these Rules;

and the appellate authority is satisfied in all the circumstances, including the extent of the failure and any reasons for it, that it is necessary to have regard to the overriding objective in rule 30(2), the appellate authority may dispose of the appeal in accordance with paragraph (2).

(2)   The appellate authority may:

(a) in the case of a failure by the appellant, dismiss the appeal or, in the case of a failure by the respondent, allow the appeal, without considering its merits;

(b) determine the appeal without a hearing in accordance with rule 43; or

(c) in the case of a failure by a party to send any document, evidence or statement of any witness, prohibit that party from relying on that document, evidence or statement at the hearing.

[A.3.62]
34   Bail
(1)   An application to be released on bail may be made orally or in writing to an immigration officer, a police officer or the appellate authority.

(2)   In an application for bail, an applicant may be represented by any person listed in rule 35(1)(a).

(3)   A written application made in accordance with paragraph (1) shall contain the following particulars:

(a) the full name of the applicant and his date of birth;

(b) the address of the place where the applicant is detained at the time when the application is made;

(c) whether an appeal is pending at the time when the application is made;

(d) the address where the applicant would reside if his application for bail were to be granted;

(e) the amount of the recognizance in which he would agree to be bound;

(f) the full names, addresses and occupations of two persons who might act as sureties for the applicant if his application for bail were to be granted, and the amounts of the recognizance in which those persons might agree to be bound; and

(g) the grounds on which the application is made and, where a previous application has been refused, full particulars of any change in circumstances which has occurred since the refusal.

(4)   A written application made in accordance with paragraph (1) shall be signed by the applicant or by a person authorised by him to act or, in the case of an applicant who is a minor or who is for any reason incapable of acting, by a person acting on his behalf.

(5)   The recognizance of an applicant and that of a surety shall be on the appropriate prescribed forms.

(6)   Where the appellate authority directs the release of an applicant on bail and the taking of the recognizance is postponed, it shall certify in writing that bail has been granted in respect of the applicant, and shall include in the certificate particulars of the conditions to be endorsed on the recognizance with a view to the recognizance being taken subsequently, the amounts in which the applicant and any sureties are to be bound and the date of issue of the certificate.

(7)   The person having custody of an applicant shall:

(a) on receipt of a certificate signed by or on behalf of the appellate authority stating that the recognizances of any sureties required have been taken, or on being otherwise satisfied that all such recognizances have been taken; and

(b) on being satisfied that the applicant has entered into his recognizance;

release the applicant.

(8)   Where the appellate authority directs the release of an applicant on bail and does not require the taking of a recognizance from the applicant or a surety, the person having custody of the applicant shall release him.

(9)   Paragraphs (5) and (6) shall not apply to Scotland, and in its application to Scotland, this rule shall have effect as if:

(a) for paragraph (3)(e) and (f), there were substituted:

'(e) the amount, if any, to be deposited if bail is granted;
(f) the full names, addresses and occupations of such persons, if any, who offer to act as cautioners if the application for bail were to be granted;'; and

(b) for paragraph (7), there were substituted:

'(7)   The person having custody of an applicant shall, on receipt of a certified copy of the decision to grant bail and on being satisfied that the amount, if any, to be deposited has been deposited, release the applicant.'.

[A.3.63]
35   Representation
(1)   In any proceedings in an appeal, a party may act in person or be represented:

(a) in the case of a person appealing against an immigration decision, by any person not prohibited by section 84;

(b) in the case of the Secretary of State or any officer, by an authorised advocate or any officer of the Secretary of State; and

(c) in the case of the United Kingdom Representative of the United Nations High Commissioner for Refugees in an asylum appeal, by a person appointed by him.

(2) A person representing a party may do anything relating to the proceedings that the person whom he represents is by these Rules required or authorised to do.

(3) Each party shall have a duty to maintain contact with his representative (if he has one) until the appeal is finally determined and notify the representative of any change of address.

(4) Where a representative referred to in paragraph (1)(a) ('the first representative') ceases to act, he and the party he was representing, shall forthwith notify the appellate authority and any other party of that fact and of the name and address of any new representative (if known).

(5) Until the appellate authority is notified that the first representative has ceased to act by either the first representative or the party he was representing, any document served on the first representative shall be deemed to be properly served on the party he was representing.

(6) Where a representative begins acting for a party to which these Rules apply, he shall forthwith notify the appellate authority of that fact.

[A.3.64]
36   Summoning of witnesses
(1) Subject to paragraph (2), the appellate authority may, for the purposes of any appeal, by summons on the appropriate prescribed form, require any person in the United Kingdom to attend as a witness at a hearing of the appeal at the time and place specified in the form and, subject to the provisions of rule 37(2), at the hearing to answer any questions or produce any documents in his custody or under his control which relate to any matter in question in the appeal.

(2) A person shall not be required, in obedience to a summons referred to in paragraph (1), to travel unless the necessary expenses of his attendance are paid or tendered to him, and when the summons is issued at the request of a party, those expenses are paid or tendered by that party.

[A.3.65]
37   Mode of giving evidence
(1) The appellate authority may receive oral, documentary or other evidence of any fact which appears to that authority to be relevant to the appeal, even though that evidence would be inadmissible in a court of law.

(2) In any proceedings before the appellate authority, a person shall not be compelled to give any evidence or produce any document which he could not be compelled to give or produce on the trial of an action in that part of the United Kingdom in which the proceedings are conducted.

(3) The appellate authority may require any witness to give evidence on oath

or affirmation or without either, and for that purpose, in a case where an oath or affirmation is required, an oath or affirmation in due form may be administered.

[A.3.66]
38 Inspection of documentary evidence
Subject to paragraph 6 of Schedule 4 to the 1999 Act, when the appellate authority takes into consideration documentary evidence, every party shall be given an opportunity of inspecting that evidence and taking copies if copies have not been provided pursuant to rule 30.

[A.3.67]
39 Burden of proof
(1)   If in any proceedings before the appellate authority a party asserts that a decision or action taken against him under any statutory provision ought not to have been taken on the grounds that he is not a person to whom the provision applies, it shall lie on him to prove that he is not such a person.

(2)   If in any proceedings before the appellate authority a party asserts any fact of a kind that, if the assertion were made to the Secretary of State or any officer for the purposes of any statutory provisions or any immigration rules, it would by virtue of those provisions or rules be for him to satisfy the Secretary of State or officer of the truth thereof, it shall lie on that party to prove that the assertion is true.

(3)   In this rule, 'immigration rules' means the rules referred to in section 3(2) of the 1971 Act and a reference to 'statutory provisions' includes a reference to any provision made under an enactment.

[A.3.68]
40 Exclusion of public
(1)   Subject to the provisions of this rule, any hearing by the appellate authority shall take place in public.

(2)   Where the appellate authority is considering an allegation referred to in paragraph 6(1) of Schedule 4 to the 1999 Act in accordance with paragraph 6(2) of that Schedule, all members of the public shall be excluded from that hearing.

(3)   Subject to paragraph (4), the appellate authority may exclude any member of the public or members of the public generally from any hearing or from any part of a hearing where:

(a) in the opinion of that authority, it is necessary in the interests of morals, public order or national security;
(b) in the opinion of that authority, the interests of minors or the protection of the private life of the parties so require; or
(c) in special circumstances publicity would prejudice the interests of justice, but only to the extent strictly necessary in the opinion of that authority.

(4)   Nothing in this rule shall prevent a member of the Council on Tribunals or of its Scottish Committee from attending a hearing in that capacity.

[A.3.69]
41   Hearing of appeal in absence of a party
(1)   The appellate authority may, where in the circumstances of the case it appears just so to do, hear an appeal in the absence of a party if satisfied that:

(a)   he is not in the United Kingdom;
(b)   he is suffering from a communicable disease or from a mental disorder;
(c)   by reason of illness or accident he cannot attend the hearing;
(d)   it is impracticable to give him notice of the hearing and that no person is authorised to represent him at the hearing; or
(e)   he has notified the appellate authority that he does not wish to attend the hearing.

(2)   Without prejudice to paragraph (1) but subject to paragraph (3), the appellate authority may proceed with the hearing of an appeal in the absence of a party if satisfied that, in the case of that party, notice of the date, time and place of the hearing, or of the adjourned hearing, has been given in accordance with these Rules.

(3)   Where the absent party has not furnished the appellate authority with a satisfactory explanation of his absence, it shall proceed with the hearing in pursuance of paragraph (2).

(4)   Where in pursuance of this rule the appellate authority hears an appeal or proceeds with a hearing in the absence of a party, it shall determine the appeal on the evidence which has been received.

(5)   Any reference to a party in paragraphs (2) to (4) includes a reference to his representative.

[A.3.70]
42   Combined hearings
Where in the case of two or more appeals it appears to the appellate authority that:

(a)   some common question of law or fact arises in both or all of them;
(b)   they relate to decisions or action taken in respect of persons who are members of the same family; or
(c)   for some other reason it is desirable to proceed with the appeals under this rule,

the appellate authority may, after giving all the parties an opportunity of being heard, decide that the appeals should be heard together.

[A.3.71]
43   Determination without hearing
(1)   An appeal may be determined without a hearing under this rule if:

(a)   the appellate authority has decided, after giving every other party an opportunity of replying to any representations submitted in writing by or on behalf of the appellant, to allow the appeal;
(b)   the appellate authority is satisfied that the appellant, except where the appellant is the Secretary of State or an officer, is outside the United

Kingdom or that it is impracticable to give him notice of a hearing and, in either case, that no person is authorised to represent him at a hearing;
(c) a preliminary issue has arisen under rule 12 and, the appellant having been given an opportunity to submit a written statement rebutting the respondent's allegation:

   (i)   the appellant has not submitted such a statement, or
   (ii) the appellate authority is of the opinion that matters put forward by the appellant in such a statement do not warrant a hearing;

(d) the appellate authority is satisfied, having given every party an opportunity to make representations and having regard to:

   (i)   the material before it; and
   (ii) the nature of the issues raised;

   that the appeal could be so disposed of justly;
(e) no party has requested a hearing; or
(f) the appellate authority is proceeding in accordance with rule 33(2)(b).

(2)   Where, in a family visitor appeal, the appellant has not paid the fee for a hearing at the time he made the appeal, the appellate authority shall determine the appeal without a hearing.

(3)   The appellate authority shall send written notice of the determination to:

(a) every party; and
(b) every party's representative, except where the representative is acting for the Secretary of State, an officer or the United Kingdom Representative of the United Nations High Commissioner for Refugees.

[A.3.72]
44   Summary determination of appeals
(1)   Subject to paragraph (2), where it appears to the appellate authority that the issues raised in an appeal have been determined:

(a) in the case of an appeal before an adjudicator, by the same or another adjudicator or by the Tribunal, or
(b) in the case of an appeal before the Tribunal, by the Tribunal,

in previous proceedings to which the appellant, or a family member, was a party, on the basis of facts which did not materially differ from those to which the appeal relates, the appellate authority may determine the appeal summarily without a hearing.

(2)   Before the appellate authority determines an appeal summarily in accordance with paragraph (1), it shall give the parties an opportunity of making representations to the effect that the appeal ought not to be determined in that way.

(3)   Where an appeal is determined summarily in accordance with paragraph (1), the appellate authority shall send to the parties written notice of that fact, and that notice shall:

(a) contain a statement of the issues raised in the appeal; and
(b) specify the previous proceedings in which those issues were determined.

(4)   In this rule, 'family member' means a person on whom a notice was served under section 74(4) at the same time in relation to the previous proceedings referred to in paragraph (1) that such a notice was served on the appellant.

[A.3.73]
45   Transfer of proceedings
(1)   Where any proceedings before an adjudicator have not been disposed of by him and the Chief Adjudicator, or any person for the time being carrying out the functions of the Chief Adjudicator, is of the opinion that:

(a)   it is not practicable without undue delay for the proceedings to be completed by that adjudicator, or
(b)   for some other good reason the proceedings cannot be completed justly by that adjudicator,

he shall make arrangements for the appeal to be heard by another adjudicator.

(2)   Where any proceedings are transferred to another adjudicator in accordance with paragraph (1):

(a)   any notice or other document which is sent or given to or by the adjudicator from whom the proceedings were transferred shall be deemed to have been sent or given to or by the adjudicator to whom the appeal is transferred; and
(b)   any adjudicator to whom an appeal is transferred shall have power to deal with it as if it had been commenced before him.

(3)   The powers of the Chief Adjudicator under this rule shall, with the appropriate modifications, also apply to the President in relation to proceedings before the Tribunal.

(4)   Where the Secretary of State notifies the Chief Adjudicator or the President, as the case may be, that section 78 applies, the Chief Adjudicator or the President shall transfer the proceedings to the Special Immigration Appeals Commission and shall notify the parties and their representatives (if any) of the transfer.

[A.3.74]
46   Notices etc
(1)   Any notice or other document required or authorised by these Rules to be sent or given to any person or authority may be delivered or sent by post to an address, or sent by fax to a fax number, specified by the person or authority to whom the notice or document is directed.

(2)   If any notice or other document is sent or given to a person appearing to the authority or person sending it to represent that party, it shall be deemed to have been sent or given to that party.

[A.3.75]
47   Notification of address
(1)   A party shall inform the appellate authority of the address at which doc-

uments may be served on him ('his address for service') and of any changes to that address.

(2)   Until a party gives notice to the appellate authority that his address for service has changed, any document served on him at the most recent address he has given to the appellate authority shall be deemed to have been properly served on him.

(3)   A person representing a party shall inform the appellate authority of his address for service and of any changes to that address.

(4)   Until a person representing a party gives notice to the appellate authority that his address for service has changed, any document served on him at the most recent address he has given to the appellate authority shall be deemed to have been properly served on him.

[A.3.76]
48   Calculation of time
(1)   This rule applies to any notice or other document sent, served or given under these Rules.

(2)   Subject to paragraphs (3) and (4), any notice or other document that is sent shall, unless the contrary is proved, be deemed to have been received:

(a) where the notice or other document is sent by post to a place within the United Kingdom, on the second day after it was sent;
(b) where the notice or other document is sent by post to a place outside the United Kingdom, on the twenty-eighth day after it was sent; and
(c) in any other case, on the day on which the notice or other document was sent.

(3)   Where a notice or other document is sent by post to the appellate authority, it shall be deemed to have been received on the day on which it was received by that authority.

(4)   Where a notice of appeal is sent by post or by fax to the address or fax number specified in the notice of decision, it shall be deemed to have been given on the day on which it was received at that address or fax number.

(5)   A notice or other document is received by the appellate authority when it is received by any person employed as a clerk to that authority.

(6)   Where an act is to be done not later than a specified period after any event, the period shall be calculated from the end of the day on which the event occurred.

(7)   Where the time provided by these Rules by which any act must be completed ends on a Saturday, a Sunday, a bank holiday, Christmas Day, 27th to 31st December or Good Friday, the act shall be completed in time if completed on the next day which is not excluded under this paragraph.

(8)   Where, apart from this paragraph, the period in question, being a period of 10 days or less, would include a Saturday, a Sunday, a bank holiday, Christmas Day, 27th to 31st December or Good Friday, that day shall be excluded.

(9)   In this rule, 'bank holiday' means a day that is specified in, or appointed under, the Banking and Financial Dealings Act 1971 as a bank holiday.

[A.3.77]
49 Irregularities
(1) Any irregularity resulting from failure to comply with these Rules before the appellate authority has reached a decision shall not by itself render the proceedings void.

(2) Where the appellate authority considers that any person may have been prejudiced by that irregularity, it shall take any steps that it considers necessary to cure it, whether by the amendment of any document, the giving of any notice or otherwise.

[A.3.78]
50 Correction of accidental errors
(1) Clerical mistakes in any determination or notice of determination, or errors arising therein from any accidental slip or omission, may at any time be corrected and any correction made to, or to a record of, a determination shall be deemed to be part of that determination or record and written notice of it shall be given as soon as practicable to every party.

(2) The Tribunal may, after consulting the adjudicator concerned, correct errors in a determination given by an adjudicator and any correction made to, or to a record of, a determination shall be deemed to be part of that determination or record and written notice of it shall be given as soon as practicable to every party and to the adjudicator.

[A.3.79]

SCHEDULE

The Immigration and Asylum Act 1999 Notice of appeal (United Kingdom) Form 1

Decision-Maker's Reference Number

1   Appeal Notice

   a Your surname/family name

   b Your other names

   c Your address (where you can be contacted)

   d Telephone number (where you can be contacted during the day)

   e Your date of birth

   f Your nationality or citizenship

   g Have you ever made any other appeal about either asylum or immigration?   ☐ **No**   ☐ **Yes (please tick a box)**

   h If you have said **YES**; when did you appeal?

   i the case number: if you know it

   j what did you appeal about?

The Immigration and Asylum Act 1999 Notice of appeal (United Kingdom) Form 1

2   Help with your appeal

   a Do you have a
      representative to help
      you?

☐ **No**   ☐ **Yes (please tick a box)**

   b If you have said **YES**,
      please give:

      ◆ the person's name

      ◆ address

      ◆ reference

      ◆ telephone number

      ◆ fax number

SPECIMEN

You must let us know if:

     a you change your address
     b you change your representative

     To do this, please use the last page of this form

The Immigration and Asylum Act 1999 Notice of appeal (United Kingdom) Form 1

For help with this part of the form please refer to your Guidance Notes

3 The grounds on which you are appealing to an adjudicator

  a Please explain why you are appealing and why you think the decision was wrong.

  b You need to tell us all of the grounds for your appeal. If you do not do this <u>now,</u> then you may not be allowed to mention any further grounds at a later time.

    [Note: you may use additional sheets of paper if you need to]

The Immigration and Asylum Act 1999 Notice of appeal (United Kingdom) Form 1

4   Declaration

YOU OR YOUR REPRESENTATIVE (IF YOU HAVE ONE) <u>MUST</u> SIGN BELOW

> "I, the appellant, declare that the information I have given is true and complete to the best of my knowledge and belief."

Signed (appellant)

Print name in **BLOCK LETTERS**

Dated

> "I, the representative, declare that the contents of the notice have been explained to, and agreed by, the appellant."

Signed (representative)

Print name in **BLOCK LETTERS**

Dated

5   The documents you are sending with this form

Please list **every** document you are sending with this form

The Immigration and Asylum Act 1999 Notice of appeal (United Kingdom) Form 1

6 At the hearing of your appeal by an adjudicator

a Do you want to attend the hearing ?

☐ No ☐ Yes (please tick a box)

b If <u>you are not</u> attending the hearing, will your representative be attending?

☐ No ☐ Yes

c If you attend the hearing, will you need an interpreter?

☐ No ☐ Yes

d If you do need an interpreter, which language will you need?

(i) Language

(ii) Dialect (if any)

e Do you use a wheelchair, or have a hearing difficulty, or have any other disability that you would like us to make arrangements for at the hearing?

☐ No ☐ Yes

f If you have said **YES**, please explain the nature of your disability and how we can help you.

WHAT TO DO NEXT:
Please keep a copy of this form for your own use and send or deliver the original to:

611

The Immigration and Asylum Act 1999 Notice of appeal (United Kingdom) Form 1

ONLY COMPLETE THIS PART OF THE FORM IF YOU CHANGE YOUR ADDRESS OR CHANGE YOUR REPRESENTATIVE

7   About you

   a   Your surname/family name

   b   Your other names

   c   Your case number

8   Change of address

   a   Your <u>new</u> address (where you are living now)

   b   Telephone number

9   Change of representative

   If you have changed your representative, or your representative has changed address, please tell us:

   a   the new representative's name (if any)

   b   address (or new address)

   c   reference

   d   telephone number

   e   fax number

WHAT TO DO NEXT: WHEN YOU HAVE FILLED IN THIS PART OF THE FORM, PLEASE SEND OR DELIVER IT TO THE IMMIGRATION APPELLATE AUTHORITY AND THE HOME OFFICE.

The Immigration and Asylum Act 1999	Application to the Immigration Appeal Tribunal for leave to appeal (United Kingdom) Form 1A (Tribunal)

Your surname/family name	
Your case reference number	

1.   Your grounds for asking for leave to appeal to the Immigration Appeal Tribunal

Do you want to appeal against an
adjudicator's determination?   ☐ **No**   ☐ **Yes (please tick a box)**

If you have ticked **Yes** please provide below full details of the grounds on which you believe
that the adjudicator's determination was wrong.
or
Do you want to appeal against a
determination of the Tribunal?   ☐ **No**   ☐ **Yes**

If you have ticked **Yes**, please identify the error of law that you believe has been made.

> "I believe that the adjudicator's/Tribunal's* determination was wrong because . . .
>
>
>
>
>
>
>
>
>
> **Please delete as appropriate*   **Note**: *You may use additional sheets of paper if you need to.*

2.   Appeals to the Tribunal

If your application for leave to appeal against the adjudicator's determination is granted, do you
wish to attend any hearing of your appeal?

                         ☐ **No**   ☐ **Yes**

3.   Declaration

YOU OR YOUR REPRESENTATIVE (IF YOU HAVE ONE) <u>MUST</u> SIGN BELOW

> "I declare that the information I have given is true and complete to the best of my knowledge
> and belief."

Signed (appellant/representative)	
Print name in **BLOCK LETTERS**	
Dated	

> **WHAT TO DO NEXT:** YOU MUST RETURN THIS FORM AND A COPY OF THE
> DETERMINATION YOU ARE APPEALING AGAINST. PLEASE REFER TO YOUR
> GUIDANCE NOTES WHICH TELL YOU HOW TO DO THIS.

The Immigration and Asylum Act 1999   **Notice of appeal (Overseas)**   **Form 2**

Decision-Maker's Reference Number

1 Appeal Notice

a Your surname/family
name →

b Your other names

c Your address (where you
can be contacted)

d Your date of birth

e Your nationality or
citizenship

f Have you ever made any
other appeal about either
asylum or immigration?   ☐ **No**   ☐ **Yes (please tick a box)**

g If you have said **YES**:
when did you appeal?

h the case number: if you
know it

i what did you appeal
about?

The Immigration and Asylum Act 1999   **Notice of appeal (Overseas)**   **Form 2**

2   Help with your appeal

  a   Do you have a representative to help you?

    ☐ **No**   ☐ **Yes (please tick a box)**

  b   If you have said **YES**, please give:

  ◆   the person's name

  ◆   address

  ◆   company name

  ◆   reference

  ◆   telephone number

  ◆   fax number

  c   Is there anyone else who will be acting for you in the United Kingdom?

    ☐ **No**   ☐ **Yes**

  d   If you have said **YES**, please give:

  ◆   the person's family name

  ◆   the person's other names

  ◆   their relationship with you

  ◆   their United Kingdom address (where they can be contacted)

You must let us know if:

    a   you change you address
    b   you change your representative

To do this, please use the last page of this form

The Immigration and Asylum Act 1999   **Notice of appeal (Overseas)**   **Form 2**

FOR HELP WITH THIS PART OF THE FORM PLEASE REFER TO YOUR GUIDANCE NOTES

3   The grounds on which you are appealing to an adjudicator

a   Please explain why you are appealing and why you think the decision was wrong.

b   You need to tell us all of the grounds for your appeal. If you do not do this <u>now</u>, then you may not be allowed to mention any further grounds at a later time.

[Note: you may use additional sheets of paper if you need to]

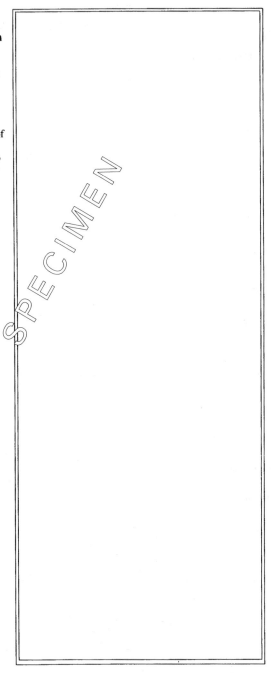

The Immigration and Asylum Act 1999   **Notice of appeal (Overseas)**   **Form 2**

4   Declaration

YOU <u>OR</u> YOUR REPRESENTATIVE (IF YOU HAVE ONE) <u>MUST</u> SIGN BELOW

"I, the appellant, declare that the information I have given is true and complete to the best of my knowledge and belief."

Signed (appellant)

Print name in **BLOCK LETTERS**

Dated

"I, the representative, declare that the contents of the notice have been explained to, and agreed by, the appellant."

Signed (representative)

Print name in **BLOCK LETTERS**

Dated

5   The documents you are sending with this form

Please list **every** document you are sending with this form

617

The Immigration and Asylum Act 1999   **Notice of appeal (Overseas)**   **Form 2**

ONLY COMPLETE THIS PART OF THE FORM IF YOU CHANGE YOUR ADDRESS OR CHANGE YOUR REPRESENTATIVE

6 About you

    a Your surname/family name

    b Your other names

    c Your case number

7 Change of address

    a Your <u>new</u> address (where you are living now)

    b Telephone number (where you can be contacted)

8 Change of representative

If you have changed your representative, or your representative has changed address, please tell us:

    a the new representative's name (if any)

    b address (or new address)

    c reference

    d telephone number

    e fax number

WHAT TO DO NEXT: WHEN YOU HAVE FILLED IN THIS PART OF THE FORM, PLEASE SEND OR DELIVER IT TO THE ENTRY CLEARANCE OFFICER.

The Immigration and Asylum Act 1999   **Application to the Immigration Appeal Tribunal for leave to appeal (Overseas)**   **Form 2A (Tribunal)**

Your surname/family name	
Your case reference number	

1. Your grounds for asking for leave to appeal to the Immigration Appeal Tribunal

Do you want to appeal against an adjudicator's determination?   **No** [ ]   **Yes (please tick a box)**

If you have ticked **Yes**, please provide below, full details of the grounds on which you believe that the adjudicator's determination was wrong.

or

Do you want to appeal against a determination of the Tribunal? [ ] **No** [ ] **Yes**

If you have ticked **Yes**, please identify the error of law that you believe has been made.

"I believe that the adjudicator's/Tribunal's* determination was wrong because . . .

*Please delete as appropriate   *Note: You may use additional sheets of paper if you need to.*

2. Appeals to the Tribunal

If your application for leave to appeal against the adjudicator's determination is granted, do you wish for the person named in Form 2 Part 2d to attend any hearing of your appeal?

No [ ] **Yes** [ ]

3. Declaration

YOU OR YOUR REPRESENTATIVE (IF YOU HAVE ONE) MUST SIGN BELOW

"I declare that the information I have given is true and complete to the best of my knowledge and belief."

Signed (appellant/representative)	
Print name in **BLOCK LETTERS**	
Dated	

WHAT TO DO NEXT: YOU MUST RETURN THIS FORM AND A COPY OF THE DETERMINATION YOU ARE APPEALING AGAINST. PLEASE REFER TO YOUR GUIDANCE NOTES WHICH TELL YOU HOW TO DO THIS.

The Immigration and Asylum Act 1999   Notice of appeal (Family Visitor)   Form 3

1   Appeal Notice

    a Your family name

    b Your other names

    c Your address (where you can be contacted)

    d Your date of birth

    e Your nationality or citizenship

2   Help with your Family Visitor Appeal

    a Who will be acting for you in the United Kingdom? Please give details of:

	Your representative (if any)	The family member you are visiting
◆ the person's family name		
◆ the person's other names		
◆ company name (representative only)		
◆ the person's address in the United Kingdom		
◆ postcode		
◆ telephone number		
◆ fax number		

    b If you are paying for a hearing of your appeal, do you want your family member (named above) to attend the hearing?

                Yes   No (please tick a box)

    c If an interpreter is needed, what language (and dialect, if any) is required?

The Immigration and Asylum Act 1999   Notice of appeal (Family Visitor)   Form 3

**FOR HELP WITH THIS PART OF THE FORM PLEASE REFER TO YOUR
GUIDANCE NOTES**

3   The grounds on which you are appealing to an adjudicator

Please explain, in English, why you are appealing and why you think the decision was wrong.
You must tell us all of the grounds on which you are appealing. If you do not do this now, then you
may not be allowed to mention any further grounds at a later time.

[Note: *you may use additional sheets of paper if you need to.]*

The Immigration and Asylum Act 1999   Notice of appeal (Family Visitor)   Form 3

4   How your appeal is dealt with

Please choose one of these two options:

a   your appeal will be decided only on the basis of the information you have provided in this
        form (and any other information you may have attached)

OR   (please tick a box)

b   your appeal will be decided at a hearing

Make sure that you pay the right fee. Once you have paid for one of these options you cannot later
change to another option.

5   The documents you are sending with this form

Please list **every** document you
are sending with this form

Make sure you provide an English
translation of any documents not
originally written in English

6   What to do next

Please send or deliver this form, together with the appropriate fee and any supporting documents
you wish to submit, to the Entry Clearance Officer at:

This form and any documents attached to it, will be sent to an adjudicator in the United Kingdom
for consideration of your appeal. You will be informed of the adjudicator's determination.

The Immigration and Asylum Act 1999   Notice of appeal (Family Visitor)   Form 3

7   Declaration (You <u>must</u> sign below)

> "I declare that the information I have given is true and complete to the best of my knowledge and belief."

Signed

Name in **BLOCK LETTERS**

Dated

TO BE COMPLETED BY ENTRY CLEARANCE MANAGER

Reference Number

Type of appeal   **Paper**   **Hearing**

Date appeal received

Fee paid (amount)

Declaration by Entry Clearance Manager:

> "I have considered the grounds of appeal set out in **Part 3** of this form and the attached supporting documentation, and uphold the decision to refuse the applicant entry as a visitor."

Signed

Name in **BLOCK LETTERS**

Date

The Immigration and Asylum Act 1999   **Application to the Immigration Appeal Tribunal for leave to appeal (Family Visitor)**   **Form 3A (Tribunal)**

Your surname/family name	
Your case reference number	

1.   Your grounds for asking for leave to appeal to the Immigration Appeal Tribunal

Please explain why you believe the adjudicator's determination was wrong.

"I believe that the adjudicator's determination was wrong because . . .

Note: You may use additional sheets of paper if you need to.

2.   If your appeal to the adjudicator was decided at a hearing, do you also want your appeal to the Tribunal to be decided at a hearing?

☐ No   ☐ Yes (please tick a box)

3.   Declaration

YOU <u>MUST</u> SIGN BELOW

"I declare that the information I have given is true and complete to the best of my knowledge and belief."

Your signature	
Print name in **BLOCK LETTERS**	
Dated	

WHAT TO DO NEXT: YOU MUST RETURN THIS FORM, AND A COPY OF THE ADJUDICATOR'S DETERMINATION TO THE IMMIGRATION APPEAL TRIBUNAL

The Immigration and Asylum Act 1999   **Recognizance of applicant**   **Form 4**

1   About you

a   Your surname/family
    name

→

b   Your other names

c   Your address (where you
    can be contacted)

2   Your undertaking

I promise to pay the sum of

if I do not comply with the following conditions.   £

3   The condition[s] [is] [are] that

I, the applicant, appear before
the Authorities at

or, at any other place and time that may be ordered

on (which date?),

at (please state am or pm),

I, the applicant, reside at
(your address)

I, the applicant, will report to the
police station at:

◆   every

◆   between the hours of   and

◆   beginning on

Signed   Date

For official use

The applicant was detained because

Taken before me on   at   . Signed

The Immigration and Asylum Act 1999 Recognizance of applicant's surety Form 5

1 About the applicant

 a The applicant's name →

 b The applicant's address
  (where he/she can be
  contacted)

2 About you (the surety)

 a Your full name
  BLOCK LETTERS

 b Your address

3 About your undertaking

When you sign the undertaking below you agree to pay a sum of money if the applicant does not comply with the conditions which follow. If that happens, but you think you should not have to pay, you will be allowed to tell the Immigration Appellate Authorities why not. The Immigration Appellate Authorities may then order you to pay the whole sum, part of the sum, or excuse you from paying any money.

Undertaking

I promise to pay the sum of
if the applicant does not comply with the following con   £

4 The condition[s] [is] [are] that

the applicant appear before the
Authorities at

 Or, at any other place and time that may be ordered

on (which date?),

at (please state am or pm),

the applicant reside at
(your address)

 Or, at any other address that may be approved

the applicant will report to the
police station at

 ◆   every

 ◆   between the hours of   and

 ◆   beginning on

 Signed   Date

For official use

The applicant was detained because

Taken before me on   at   Signed

The Immigration and Asylum Act 1999   **Witness Summons**   **Form 6**

1   Immigration Appellate Authorities

Appeal Number

to   →

of

2   Witness Summons

You are summoned to be a witness at the appeal of

   a   You must attend

      on

      at (time)

      at (where)

   b   You must bring to the appeal the documents

3   Warning

If you do not attend the hearing according to this summons, you may have to pay a fine.

4   Notice

This summons does not oblige you to show a document to anyone without the permission of the Immigration Appellate Authorities.

5   About the appeal   of

   a   The appellant has appealed against the [decision] [action] [determination]   that

   b   I am satisfied that your evidence is necessary

Signed   **Date**

   [President]   **[Chairman of Tribunal]**   **[Adjudicator]**

IMMIGRATION AND ASYLUM APPEALS (ONE-STOP PROCEDURE) REGULATIONS 2000
SI 2000/2244

Made   16 August 2000
Laid before Parliament   24 August 2000
Coming into force   2 October 2000

Arrangement of Regulations

1 Citation and commencement   **[A.3.80]**
2 Interpretation   **[A.3.81]**
3 The notice   **[A.3.82]**
4 The statement   **[A.3.83]**
5 Application of sections 73, 76 and 77 to section 75 notices   **[A.3.84]**
6 Relevant member of the applicant's family: section 74   **[A.3.85]**
7 Relevant member of the claimant's family: section 75   **[A.3.86]**
8 Member of the family: section 76   **[A.3.87]**

Schedule   **[A.3.88]**

[A.3.80]
1   Citation and commencement
These Regulations may be cited as the Immigration and Asylum Appeals (One-Stop Procedure) Regulations 2000 and shall come into force on 2nd October 2000.

[A.3.81]
2   Interpretation
(1)   In these Regulations—

'the Act' means the Immigration and Asylum Act 1999;
'the 1997 Act' means the Special Immigration Appeals Commission Act 1997;
'claim' means a claim to which section 75 applies;
'decision-taker' means the Secretary of State or an immigration officer, as the case may be;
'notice' means a section 74 or section 75 notice, as the case may be;
'representative' means a person who appears to the decision-taker—

(a) to be the representative of a requisite person; and
(b) not to be prohibited from acting as a representative by section 84 of the Act;

'requisite person' means the person on whom the notice is required to be served;
'section 74 notice' means a notice which is required to be served under section 74(4);
'section 75 notice' means a notice which is required to be served under section 75(2);
'statement' means the statement specifying additional grounds which the requisite person has or may have for wishing to enter or remain in the United Kingdom; and

'statement form' means the form shown in Part III of the Schedule to these Regulations.

(2)   Where reference is made in these Regulations to a form shown in the Schedule to these Regulations, that form, or a form to like effect, may be used with such variations as the circumstances may require.

(3)   In these Regulations, a section referred to by number alone is a reference to a section of the Act.

One-stop procedure

[A.3.82]
3   The notice
(1)   A section 74 notice is to be in the form shown in Part I of the Schedule to these Regulations.

(2)   A section 75 notice is to be in the form shown in Part II of the Schedule to these Regulations.

(3)   The notice is to—

(a)   provide a postal address to which the statement may be returned by post;
(b)   provide an address to which the statement may be returned by hand;
(c)   provide a fax number which may be used to return the statement by fax; and
(d)   be accompanied by a copy of the statement form.

(4)   The notice may be served—

(a)   by hand;
(b)   by fax; or
(c)   by sending it by postal service in which delivery or receipt is recorded to—

(i)   the last known or usual place of abode of the requisite person or his representative; or
(ii)   an address provided by him or his representative for correspondence.

(5)   The notice may be served on the requisite person by serving it on his representative.

(6)   If the notice is served by post, addressed to the requisite person, it is to be taken to have been received by the requisite person on the second day after the day on which it was posted, unless the contrary is proved.

[A.3.83]
4   The statement
(1)   The statement is to be made by completing in full, and in English, a statement form.

(2)   The statement form must be signed by the requisite person or his representative.

(3)   For the purposes of section 74(6)(b) (the period before the end of which a statement must be served in response to a section 74 notice)—

(a) the period of ten days is prescribed, where the applicant is entitled to appeal under the Act;

(b) the period of five days is prescribed, where the applicant is entitled to appeal under the 1997 Act.

(4) For the purposes of section 75(3)(b) (the period before the end of which the statement must be served in response to a section 75 notice), the period of ten days is prescribed.

(5) For the purposes of paragraphs (3) and (4)—

(a) the prescribed period is to be calculated from the expiry of the day on which the notice was received by the requisite person or his representative; and

(b) where the prescribed period—

(i) expires on an excluded day, the statement is to be taken to have been served as required if served on the next day that is not an excluded day;

(ii) includes an excluded day, that day is to be discounted.

(6) The statement may be served—

(a) by hand;

(b) by post; or

(c) by fax;

using the address or fax number specified in the notice.

(7) The statement is to be taken to have been served as required on the day on which it is received at the address or fax number specified in the notice.

(8) Unless paragraph (9) applies, where the requisite person is in custody, the statement may also be served by giving it to the person who has custody of the requisite person.

(9) This paragraph applies where a section 74 notice has been served and the requisite person is entitled to appeal under the 1997 Act.

(10) 'Bank holiday' means a day that is specified in, or appointed under, the Banking and Financial Dealings Act 1971.

(11) 'Excluded day' means a Saturday, a Sunday, a bank holiday, Christmas Day, 27th to 31st December or Good Friday.

Applications of sections 73, 76 and 77 to section 75 notices

[A.3.84]
5   Application of sections 73, 76 and 77 to section 75 notices
(1) Subject to paragraph (2), this regulation applies if a claim is determined against a person on whom a section 75 notice has been served and that person appeals against the determination.

(2) With the exception of the modification to section 77(5), this regulation does not apply if the claim is determined before the expiry of the period prescribed in regulation 4(4).

(3) Section 73 applies to the appeal subject to the following modification.

(4) In subsections (2)(a)(i) and (4) of section 73, the references to 'section 74' are to be read as references to 'section 75'.

(5) Section 76 applies to the appeal subject to the following modifications—

(a) in subsection (1)—

(i) the reference to 'section 74(4)' is to be read as a reference to 'section 75(2)'; and
(ii) the reference to 'the Secretary of State' is to be read as a reference to 'the person who is responsible for the determination of the claim';

(b) in subsection (5)—

(i) the reference to 'section 74(6)(b)' is to be read as a reference to 'section 75(3)(b)'; and
(ii) the reference to 'the Secretary of State' is to be read as a reference to 'the Secretary of State or an immigration officer'.

(6)   Section 77 applies to the appeal subject to the following modifications—

(a) in subsection (2)(b), the reference to 'any provision of section 76' is to be read as a reference to 'any provision of section 76 as applied and modified by regulations made under section 75(6)};
(b) in subsection (5)—

(i) the reference to 'the Secretary of State' is to be read as a reference to 'the person who is responsible for the determination of the claim'; and
(ii) the reference to 'section 74(4)' is to be read as a reference to 'section 75(2)'.

Family member definitions

[A.3.85]
6   Relevant member of the applicant's family: section 74
For the purposes of section 74(8), a relevant member of an applicant's family is a person—

(a) who is the subject of a decision mentioned in subsection (1)(a), (2)(a) or 3(a) of section 74, but is not himself an applicant for the purposes of section 74(4); and
(b) who appears to the decision-taker to be—

(i) his spouse;
(ii) a child of his or of his spouse;
(iii) a person who has been living with him as a member of an unmarried couple for at least two of the three years before the day on which the decision was made;
(iv) a person who is dependent on him; or
(v) a person on whom he is dependent.

[A.3.86]
7   Relevant member of the claimant's family: section 75
For the purposes of section 75(5), a relevant member of a claimant's family is a person—

(a) who has made an application for leave to enter or remain in the United Kingdom, but is not himself a claimant for the purposes of section 75(2); and
(b) who appears to the decision-taker to be—

(i)   his spouse;
(ii) a child of his or of his spouse;
(iii) a person who has been living with him as a member of an unmarried cou-
      ple for at least two of the three years before the day on which the claim
      was made;
(iv) a person who is dependent on him; or
(v)   a person on whom he is dependent.

[A.3.87]
8   Member of the family: section 76
(1)   For the purposes of section 76(6), 'member of the family' means—

(a)   a person on whom the applicant is dependent; or
(b)   a person who, in relation to the applicant—

(i)   is his spouse;
(ii) is a child of his or of his spouse;
(iii) has been living with him as a member of an unmarried couple for at least
      two of the three years before the day on which the applicant claimed asy-
      lum; or
(iv) is dependent on him.

SCHEDULE

[A.3.88]

PART I

REGULATION 2(2)

ONE-STOP NOTICE

Section 74, Immigration and Asylum Act 1999

To:
   You have been given a **notice of decision**; you have, or a member of your
family has, a right to appeal that decision to an adjudicator. Under section 74
of the Immigration and Asylum Act 1999 I must also give you this one-stop
notice. It requires you to state any **additional grounds** which you have or may
have for wishing to enter or remain in the United Kingdom.

   <u>If you have not yet taken advice on your position, I strongly advise you
to do so now.</u>

**The STATEMENT OF ADDITIONAL GROUNDS should be completed
and returned to arrive within 10 working days of receipt by you or your
representative**

Additional grounds

The **notice of decision** takes into account the reasons you gave for wishing to enter or remain in the United Kingdom. *You are now required to state any reasons you think you have or may have for staying in the United Kingdom which you have not previously disclosed: these will be your 'additional grounds'.* The decision will be reviewed in the light of what you say. It is in your own interest to now disclose all your grounds for staying in the United Kingdom. But you should not make false claims: do not, for example, apply for asylum unless you have genuine reasons for believing that you qualify in the terms of the 1951 Convention.

Section 74(7) of the Immigration and Asylum Act 1999 says that, if you wish to claim asylum, you must do so in your statement. And if you wish to claim that in taking the decision, the decision maker breached your human rights or racially discriminated against you, you must give notice of your claim in your statement.

Your statement

You must use the form STATEMENT OF ADDITIONAL GROUNDS which accompanies this notice.

The form must be:

—completed in English

—completed in full

—signed by yourself or your representative if you have one

— returned as instructed below so as to arrive within 10 working days of when you or your representative received it. Saturdays, Sundays and bank and public holidays are not included when counting the 10 days.

Consequences of failure to disclose additional grounds

The purpose of this procedure is to make sure that there is no unnecessary delay in dealing with your case. Where you have a right of appeal already, it is important that the adjudicator should be able to deal with all the aspects of your case which he is entitled to consider on one single occasion. If you believe you qualify to stay in the United Kingdom, then it is clearly of benefit to you to have a final and comprehensive decision as quickly as possible.

If you raise additional grounds after the period allowed to return the statement, you may lose the chance to have any decision on them reviewed by an independent adjudicator. It may be concluded that they were put forward late to delay your removal from the United Kingdom or the removal of a member of your family. Even if you still have an opportunity to appeal, the appeal may be limited and the fact that you had not disclosed your grounds when required to do so would not be in your favour.

There are safeguards for exceptional circumstances: for example if you only became aware of a reason for staying in the United Kingdom after you returned the statement or if you can give a reasonable excuse for not mentioning additional grounds when asked to do so.

If you have already appealed under the Immigration and Asylum Act 1999 against an earlier decision, we may issue a certificate under section 73 of the Act which cuts off or limits your appeal against this new decision. This is likely to happen if your grounds for appeal were dealt with at the earlier appeal or could have been mentioned then.

The consequences of raising additional grounds late may be serious: you should always disclose your reasons for wishing to stay here and any change of circumstances without delay.

Your right to appeal the decision

*If you have been given this form because you are a member of the family of someone who has a right of appeal, but you do not yourself have a right of appeal, this paragraph does not apply to you. The **notice of decision** tells you if you can appeal the decision. If you do have a right of appeal, a **notice of appeal** form will be attached to the **statement of additional** grounds.*

— If you do not agree with the reason given for my decision in the **notice of decision**, then you should explain why in your **notice of appeal**. What you say there is your '**grounds of appeal**'. The statement of additional grounds is for matters different from those which have already been considered.

— If you make a valid **appeal** and submit **additional grounds**, arguments provided in support of those grounds will be considered. If the decision is maintained in the light of those arguments you will be told why. If the **additional grounds** could have formed part of your appeal if you had disclosed them earlier then the grounds will be included in the material which the adjudicator can consider and you can add to your **grounds of appeal** in the light of our reasons for maintaining the decision before your papers are sent to the adjudicator. If the **additional grounds** could not have formed part of your appeal if you had disclosed them earlier then the adjudicator cannot consider those grounds and you will not be able to add to your **grounds of appeal**. Remember that if you have already appealed under the Immigration and Asylum Act 1999, we may issue a certificate under section 73 of the Act which cuts off or limits your right of appeal. Please do not separate the **statement of additional grounds** form and the **notice of appeal** form. There is also a copy of the **notice of decision** attached to the appeal form: this is for the use of the adjudicator if you appeal, and appeal procedures require you to return it with the appeal form. If you make a photocopy of these papers, or send them by fax, please ensure that all the pages are kept together and in the correct order.

—You may, if you wish, put forward additional grounds without making an appeal. Likewise you should not put forward additional grounds with your appeal if you genuinely have none to suggest. But in either case, please return both forms together. If you submit neither an appeal nor additional grounds then you should comply with any instructions to leave the United Kingdom which you have been given.

Service of statement of additional grounds

The statement may be returned by post to the following address:

[to be inserted by signatory]

The statement may be returned by hand to the following address:

[to be inserted by signatory]

The statement may be sent by fax to the following fax number:

[to be inserted by signatory]

If you are **detained** the statement may be served by giving it to the person who has custody of you.

Please remember:

— keep any evidence of posting or receipt which you are given

— use a reliable postal service which offers speedy delivery if you can

— if you have been given a **notice of appeal** make sure it is attached to your **statement of additional grounds**

— keep this notice with your copy of the notice of refusal

Family applications

If you have received this notice in a package of notices and forms relating to yourself and other members of your family, please return all the statement and appeals forms together if possible. An envelope was enclosed with the package.

[Signature]

[Immigration Officer/On behalf of the Secretary of State]

[Date]

If you have not seen, or need a further copy of the guidance on how to obtain help ('Getting advice on Immigration Matters') your nearest Citizen's Advice Bureau can assist. The leaflet is also available at the Immigration and Nationality Directorate's website: http://www.homeoffice.gov.uk/ind/hpg.htm

PART II

REGULATION 2(3)

ONE-STOP NOTICE

Section 75, Immigration and Asylum Act 1999

To:

You have made a claim for asylum, or a claim that it would be in breach of your human rights for you to be removed from, or required to leave, the United Kingdom.

You are also one of the following:

— an illegal entrant, **or**

— a person who is liable to be removed as an overstayer under section 10 of the Immigration and Asylum Act 1999, **or**

— a person who has arrived in the United Kingdom without leave to enter, an entry clearance, or a current work permit in which you are named.

Alternatively you have applied for leave to enter or remain in the United Kingdom as the spouse or dependent of such a person, or because such a person is dependent on you.

Under section 75 of the Immigration and Asylum Act 1999 I must give you this **one-stop notice**. It requires you to state any **additional grounds** which you have or may have for wishing to enter or remain in the United Kingdom.

If you have not yet taken advice on your position, I strongly advise you to do so now.

The STATEMENT OF ADDITIONAL GROUNDS should be completed and returned to arrive within 10 working days of receipt by you or your representative.

Additional grounds

You are now required to state any reasons you think you have or may have for staying in the United Kingdom which you have not previously disclosed when making your application: these will be your "additional grounds". They will be considered together with the application which you have already made.

If you are claiming asylum personally you should now put forward any human rights arguments you may have. If you have made a claim based on your own human rights, you should now put forward any reasons you have for thinking that you qualify for asylum. If your overall claim is refused, you will have the opportunity to appeal that decision to an adjudicator. Your appeal would address both issues at once. You should also mention any other reasons you have for wishing to stay here, but you may not be entitled to raise them at an appeal.

If you are not the person who has made an asylum or human rights claim, but are the spouse or dependant of such a person or they are dependent on you, and their application is refused, your application will also be refused. If you have any reason to think that you have grounds to make an asylum or human rights claim in your own individual right, you should give them now. If your claim is refused you will have the chance to appeal to an independent adjudicator. You should also mention any other reasons you have for wishing to stay here, but you may not be entitled to raise them at an appeal.

If you have already appealed under the Immigration and Asylum Act 1999 against an earlier decision, we may issue a certificate under section 73 of the Act which cuts off or limits any appeal against a decision on the claim you are now making. This is likely to happen if we think that you made the claim in order to delay your removal from the United Kingdom.

Your statement

You must use the form **STATEMENT OF ADDITIONAL GROUNDS** which accompanies this notice.

The form must be:

— completed in English

— completed in full

— signed by yourself or your representative if you have one

— returned as instructed below so as to arrive within 10 working days of when you or your representative received it. Saturdays, Sundays, bank and public holidays are not included when counting the 10 days.

Consequence of failure to disclose additional grounds

The purpose of this procedure is to make sure that there is no unnecessary delay in dealing with your case. Where you have a right of appeal, it is important that the adjudicator should be able to deal with all the aspects of your case which he is entitled to consider on one single occasion. If you believe you qualify to stay in the United Kingdom, then it is clearly of benefit to you to have a final and comprehensive decision as quickly as possible.

If you raise additional grounds after the period allowed, you may lose the chance to have any decision on them reviewed by an independent adjudicator. It may be concluded that they were put forward late to delay your removal from the United Kingdom or the removal of a member of your family. Even if you still have an opportunity to appeal, the appeal may be limited and the fact that you had not disclosed your grounds when required to do so would not be in your favour.

There are safeguards for exceptional circumstances: for example if you only became aware of a reason for staying in the United Kingdom after you return the statement or you can give a reasonable excuse for not mentioning additional grounds when asked to do so.

The consequences of raising additional grounds late may be serious: you should always disclose your reasons for wishing to stay here and any change of circumstances without delay.

Service of statement of additional grounds

The statement may be returned by post to the following address:

[to be inserted by signatory]

The statement may be returned by hand to the following address:

[to be inserted by signatory]

The statement may be sent by fax to the following fax number:

[to be inserted by signatory]

If you are detained the statement may be served by giving it to the person who has custody of you.

Please remember:

—keep any evidence of posting or receipt which you are given

—use a reliable postal service which offers speedy delivery if you can

—keep this notice

Family applications

If you have received this notice in a package of notices and forms relating to yourself and other members of your family, please return all the statements together if possible. An envelope was enclosed with the package.

[Signature]

Immigration Officer/On behalf of the Secretary of State]

[Date]

If you have not seen, or need a further copy of the guidance on how to obtain help ("Getting advice on Immigration Matters") your nearest Citizen's Advice Bureau can assist. The leaflet is also available at the Immigration and Nationality Directorate's website: http//www.homeoffice.gov.uk/ind/hpg.htm.

PART III

REGULATION 2(1)

STATEMENT OF ADDITIONAL GROUNDS
Section 74 of 75, Immigration and Asylum Act 1999

You should fully complete this form in English and return it as explained in the **ONE-STOP NOTICE**.

[If the following details have already been printed on the form for you, please amend them if they are wrong]

Your reference number:

(as given in the **notice of decision**)

Your family name:

Your other names:

Your date of birth:

Your nationality:

— Please state clearly any reasons which you have or may have for wishing to enter or remain in the United Kingdom and which you have not previously disclosed.
— Continue on the reverse of this page or a separate sheet of paper if necessary.
— Attach any documentary evidence you have which supports your grounds. If you need more time to obtain evidence, please say what it is, and how long it is likely to take.

You or your representative if you have one must now make a declaration. If you are not capable of making the declaration, for example if you are too young, someone may make it on your behalf, using the box marked 'APPLICANT'.

APPLICANT

I declare that the information I have given is **true** and **complete** to the best of my knowledge and belief.

Signature: Date:

If signed on behalf of the applicant please give your full name, relationship to the applicant and address if it is different.

Applicant's address for correspondence if this has changed:
REPRESENTATIVE

I declare that the information I have given is true and complete to the best of my knowledge and belief; and that the contents of this statement have been explained to and agreed by the applicant.

Signature: Date:

Organisation:

Please give your full name, address and telephone number if you have not previously notified us that you are acting in this case:

Note   Schedule, Parts I and II substituted by SI 2001/867, in force 2 April 2001.

IMMIGRATION AND ASYLUM APPEALS (NOTICES) REGULATIONS 2000
SI 2000/2246

Made   16 August 2000
Laid before Parliament   24 August 2000
Coming into force   2 October 2000

[A.3.89]
1   Citation and commencement
(1)   These Regulations may be cited as the Immigration and Asylum Appeals (Notices) Regulations 2000 and shall come into force on 2nd October 2000.
(2)   The Immigration Appeals (Notices) Regulations 1984 are hereby revoked.

[A.3.90]
2   Interpretation
In these Regulations—

'the 1971 Act' means the Immigration Act 1971;
'the 1997 Act' means the Special Immigration Appeals Commission Act 1997;
'the 1999 Act' means the Immigration and Asylum Act 1999;
'appeal' means an appeal under—

(a)   Part IV of the 1999 Act (including any regulations made under section 80 of the 1999 Act, whether or not such regulations are also made under section 2(2) of the European Communities Act 1972);
(b)   the 1997 Act;

and 'appealable' is to be construed accordingly, unless the context otherwise requires;
'decision-maker' means—

(a)   the Secretary of State;
(b)   an immigration officer;
(c)   an entry clearance officer;
'entry clearance officer' means a person responsible for the grant or refusal of entry clearance;
'representative' means a person who appears to the decision-maker—

(a)   to be the representative of a requisite person; and
(b)   not to be prohibited from acting as a representative by section 84 of the 1999 Act;
'requisite person' has the meaning given to it by regulation 4(1).

[A.3.91]
3   Transitional provision
These Regulations apply to a decision to make a deportation order which, by virtue of paragraph 12 of Schedule 15 to the 1999 Act,—

(a) is appealable under section 15 of the 1971 Act (appeals in respect of deportation orders);

(b) would be appealable under section 15 of the 1971 Act, but for section 15(3) (deportation conducive to public good), and is appealable under section 2(1)(c) of the 1997 Act (appeal to Special Immigration Appeals Commission against a decision to make a deportation order).

[A.3.92]
4   Notice of appealable decisions and actions
(1)   Subject to the provisions of this regulation and to regulation 6, the decision-maker must give written notice to a person (the 'requisite person') of any decision or action taken in respect of him which is appealable.
(2)   If the notice is given to the representative of the requisite person, it is to be taken to have been given to the requisite person.
(3)   Where the notice is given as required by paragraph (1) of a decision to refuse leave to a person to enter the United Kingdom, it is not necessary in addition for notice to be given of the decision that he requires leave unless he claims or has claimed that leave is not required.
(4)   No notice of decision is required to be given under paragraph (1) by reason only of the fact that the decision could be appealed under section 65 of the 1999 Act or section 2A of the 1997 Act if the person in question were to make an allegation that an authority had acted in breach of his human rights [or racially discriminated against him] in taking it; but such notice must be given upon such allegation being made.
(5)   In paragraph (4), 'authority' has the meaning given to it by section 65(7) of the 1999 Act.

Note   Words in square brackets inserted by SI 2001/868, in force 2 April 2001.

[A.3.93]
5   Contents of notice
(1)   A notice given under regulation 4 is to—

(a) include a statement of the reasons for the decision or action to which it relates; and

(b) if it relates to the giving of directions for the removal of the person from the United Kingdom, include a statement of the country to which he is to be removed.

(2)   The notice is also to include, or to be accompanied by, a statement informing the requisite person of—

(a) his right of appeal and the statutory provision on which his right of appeal is based;

(b) the manner in which the appeal is to be brought;

(c) a postal address to which a notice of appeal may be returned by post;

(d) an address to which a notice of appeal may be returned by hand;

(e) a fax number which may be used to return a notice of appeal by fax;

(f) the time within which an appeal is to be brought; and

(g) the facilities available for advice and assistance in connection with the appeal.

641

[A.3.94]
6   Certain notices under the 1971 Act deemed to comply with Regulations
(1)   This regulation applies where the power to—

(a) refuse leave to enter; or
(b) vary leave to enter or remain in the United Kingdom;

is exercised by notice in writing under section 4 of, or paragraph 6(2) of Schedule 2 to, the 1971 Act (notice of decisions as to leave to enter or remain).
(2)   If—

(a) the statements required by regulation 5 are included in or accompany that notice; and
(b) the notice is given in accordance with the provisions of regulation 7;

the notice is to be taken to have been given under regulation 4(1) for the purposes of these Regulations, and for the purposes of paragraph 2 of Schedule 4 to the 1999 Act.

[A.3.95]
7   Service of notice
A notice required to be given by regulation 4 may be—

(a) given by hand;
(b) sent by fax;
(c) sent by postal service in which delivery or receipt is recorded to—

   (i) the last known or usual place of abode of the requisite person or his representative; or
   (ii) an address provided by him or his representative for correspondence.

[A.3.96]
[8
Where a notice required to be given by regulation 4 is sent by postal service under regulation 7(c) to a place outside the United Kingdom, it shall, unless the contrary is proved, be deemed to have been received on the twenty-eighth day after the day on which it was posted.]

Note   Regulation 8 inserted by SI 2001/868, in force 2 April 2001.

A4   Statutory Instruments

IMMIGRATION (CONTROL OF ENTRY THROUGH REPUBLIC OF IRELAND) ORDER 1972
SI 1972/1610

Date   23 October 1972
Authority   Immigration Act 1971, s 9(2), (6)
Commencement   1 January 1973 (art 1)

[A.4.1]
1   This Order may be cited as the Immigration (Control of Entry through Republic of Ireland) Order 1972 and shall come into operation on 1 January 1973.

[A.4.2]
2   (1) In this Order:

'the Act' means the Immigration Act 1971; and
'visa national' means a person who, in accordance with the immigration rules, is required on entry into the United Kingdom to produce a passport or other document of identity endorsed with a United Kingdom visa and includes a stateless person.

(2) In this Order any reference to an Article shall be construed as a reference to an Article of this Order and any reference in an Article to a paragraph as a reference to a paragraph of that Article.

(3) The Interpretation Act 1889 shall apply to the interpretation of this Order as it applies to the interpretation of an Act of Parliament.

[A.4.3]
3   (1) This Article applies to:

(*a*) any person (other than a citizen of the Republic of Ireland) who arrives in the United Kingdom on an aircraft which began its flight in that Republic if he entered that Republic in the course of a journey to the United Kingdom which began outside the common travel area and was not given leave to land in that Republic in accordance with the law in force there;
(*b*) any person (other than a person to whom sub-paragraph (*a*) of this paragraph applies) who arrives in the United Kingdom on a local journey from the Republic of Ireland if he satisfies any of the following conditions, that is to say:

    (i) he is a visa national who has no valid visa for his entry into the United Kingdom,

    (ii) he entered that Republic unlawfully from a place outside the common travel area,

    (iii) he entered that Republic from a place in the United Kingdom and Islands after entering there unlawfully, [or, if he had a limited leave to enter or remain there, after the expiry of the leave, provided that in either case] he has not subsequently been given leave to enter or remain in the United Kingdom or any of the Islands, or

    (iv) he is a person in respect of whom directions have been given by the Secretary of State for him not to be given entry to the United Kingdom on the ground that his exclusion is conducive to the public good.

(2) In relation only to persons to whom this Article applies, the Republic of Ireland shall be excluded from section 1(3) of the Act (provisions relating to persons travelling on local journeys in the common travel area).

Notes   Words in square brackets in para 1(1)(*b*)(iii) substituted by SI 1979/730.

[A.4.4]

4   (1) Subject to paragraph (2), this Article applies to [any person who does not have the right of abode in the United Kingdom under section 2 of the Act] and is not a citizen of the Republic of Ireland and who enters the United Kingdom on a local journey from the Republic of Ireland after having entered that Republic:

(*a*) on coming from a place outside the common travel area; or

(*b*) after leaving the United Kingdom whilst having a limited leave to enter or remain there which has since expired.

(2) This Article shall not apply to any person [who arrives in the United Kingdom with leave to enter or remain in the United Kingdom which is in force but which was given to him before his arrival or] who requires leave to enter the United Kingdom by virtue of Article 3 or section 9(4) of the Act.

(3) A person to whom this Article applies by virtue only of paragraph (1)(*a*) shall, unless he is a visa national who has a visa containing the words 'short visit', be subject to the restriction and to the condition set out in paragraph (4).

(4) The restriction and the condition referred to in paragraph (3) are—

(*a*) the period for which he may remain in the United Kingdom shall not be more than three months from the date on which he entered the United Kingdom; and

[(*b*) unless he is a national of a state which is a member of the European Economic Community, he shall not engage in any occupation for reward; and

(*c*) unless he is a national of a state which is a member of the European

Economic Community other than . . . [,Portugal or Spain] he shall not engaged in any employment.]

(5) In relation to a person who is a visa national and has a visa containing the words 'short visit' the restriction and the conditions set out in paragraph (6) shall have effect instead of the provisions contained in paragraph (4).

(6) The restriction and the conditions referred to in paragraph (5) are:

(*a*) the period for which he may remain in the United Kingdom shall not be more than one month from the date on which he entered the United Kingdom;

(*b*) he shall not engage in any occupation for reward or any employment; and

(*c*) he shall, unless he is under the age of 16 years, be required to register with the police.

(7) The preceding provisions of this Article shall have effect in relation to a person to whom this Article applies by virtue of sub-paragraph (*b*) of paragraph (1) (whether or not he is also a person to whom this Article applies by virtue of sub-paragraph (*a*) thereof) as they have effect in relation to a person to whom this Article applies by virtue only of the said sub-paragraph (*a*), but as if for the references in paragraphs (4) and (6) to three months and one month respectively there were substituted a reference to seven days.

Notes Words in square brackets in para (1) substituted by SI 1982/1028.
Words in square brackets in para (2) inserted by SI 2000/1776, art 2.
Para (4)(*b*), (*c*) substituted for the original para 4(*b*) by SI 1980/1859, and the words 'Portugal or Spain' in square brackets in para (4)(*c*) inserted by SI 1985/1854. Words omitted from para (4)(*c*) revoked by SI 1987/2092.

IMMIGRATION (EXEMPTION FROM CONTROL) ORDER 1972
SI 1972/1613

Date   24 October 1972
Authority Immigration Act 1971, s 8(2)
Commencement   1 January 1973 (art 1)

[A.4.5]
1   This Order may be cited as the Immigration (Exemption from Control) Order 1972 and shall come into operation on 1 January 1973.

[A.4.6]
2   (1) In this Order—

'the Act' means the Immigration Act 1971; and
'consular employee' and 'consular officer' have the meanings respectively assigned to them by Article 1 of the Vienna Convention on Consular Relations as set out in Schedule 1 to the Consular Relations Act 1968.

(2) In this Order any reference to an Article or to the Schedule shall be construed as a reference to an Article of this Order or, as the case may be, to the Schedule thereto and any reference in an Article to a paragraph as a reference to a paragraph of that Article.

(3) In this Order any reference to an enactment is a reference to it as amended, and includes a reference to it as applied, by or under any other enactment and any reference to an instrument made under or by virtue of any enactment is a reference to any such instrument for the time being in force.

(4) The Interpretation Act 1889 shall apply to the interpretation of this Order as it applies to the interpretation of an Act of Parliament.

[A.4.7]
3   (1) The following persons shall be exempt from any provision of the Act relating to those who are not [British citizens], that is to say—

(a) any consular officer in the service of any of the states specified in the Schedule (being states with which consular conventions have been concluded by Her Majesty);
(b) any consular employee in such service as is mentioned in subparagraph (a) of this paragraph; and
(c) any member of the family of a person exempted under sub-paragraph (a) or (b) of this paragraph forming part of his household.

(2) In paragraph (1) and to Article 4 any reference to a consular employee shall be construed as a reference to such an employee who is in full-time serv-

ice of the state concerned and is not engaged in the United Kingdom in any private occupation for gain.

Notes   Words in square brackets in para (1) substituted by SI 1982/1649.

[A.4.8]
4   The following persons shall be exempt from any provision of the Act relating to those who are not [British citizens] except any provision relating to deportation that is to say—

(*a*) unless the Secretary of State otherwise directs, any member of the government of a country or territory outside the United Kingdom and Islands who is visiting the United Kingdom on the business of that government;

(*b*) any person entitled to immunity from legal process with respect to acts performed by him in his official capacity under any Order in Council made under section 3(1) of the Bretton Woods Agreement Act 1945 (which empowers Her Majesty by Order in Council to make provision relating to the immunities and privileges of the governors, executive directors, alternates, officers and employees of the International Monetary Fund and the International Bank for Reconstruction and Development);

(*c*) any person entitled to immunity from legal process with respect to acts performed by him in his official capacity under any Order in Council made under section 3(1) of the International Finance Corporation Act 1955 (which empowers Her Majesty by Order in Council to make provision relating to the immunities and privileges of the governors, directors, alternates, officers and employees of the International Finance Corporation);

(*d*) any person entitled to immunity from legal process with respect to acts performed by him in his official capacity under any Order in Council made under section 3(1) of the International Development Association Act 1960 (which empowers Her Majesty by Order in Council to make provision relating to the immunities and privileges of the governors, directors, alternates, officers and employees of the International Development Association);

(*e*) any person (not being a person to whom section 8(3) of the Act applies) who is the representative or a member of the official staff of the representative of the government of a country to which section 1 of the Diplomatic Immunities (Conferences with Commonwealth Countries and Republic of Ireland) Act 1961 applies (which provides for representatives of certain Commonwealth countries and their staff attending conferences in the United Kingdom to be entitled to diplomatic immunity) so long as he is included in a list compiled and published in accordance with that section;

(*f*) any person on whom any immunity from jurisdiction is conferred by any Order in Council made under section 12(1) of the Consular Relations Act 1968 (which empowers Her Majesty by Order in Council to confer on certain persons connected with the service of the government of Commonwealth countries or the Republic of Ireland all or any of the immunities and privileges which are conferred by or may be conferred under that Act on persons connected with consular posts);

(*g*) any person (not being a person to whom section 8(3) of the Act applies) on whom any immunity from suit and legal process is conferred by any Order in Council made under section 1(2), 5(1) or 6(2) of the International Organisations Act 1968 (which empowers Her Majesty by Order in Council to confer certain immunities and privileges on persons connected with certain international organisations and international tribunals and on representatives of foreign countries and their staffs attending certain conferences in the United Kingdom) except any such person as is mentioned in section 5(2)(*c*) to (*e*) of the said Act of 1968 [or by any Order in Council continuing to have effect by virtue of section 12(5) of the said Act of 1968];

(*h*) any consular officer (not being an honorary consular officer) in the service of a state other than such a state as is mentioned in the Schedule;

(*i*) any consular employee in such service as is mentioned in paragraph (*h*);

[(*j*) any officer or servant of the Commonwealth Secretariat falling within paragraph 6 of the Schedule to the Commonwealth Secretariat Act 1966 (which confers certain immunities on those members of the staff of the Secretariat who are not entitled to full diplomatic immunity);]

[(*k*) any person on whom any immunity from suit and legal process is conferred by the European Communities (Immunities and Privileges of the North Atlantic Salmon Conservation Organisation) Order 1985 (which confers certain immunities and privileges on the representatives and officers of the North Atlantic Salmon Conservation Organisation);]

[(*l*) any member of the Hong Kong Economic and Trade Office as defined by paragraph 8 of the Schedule to the Hong Kong Economic and Trade Office Act 1996,

(*m*) (i) Any member or servant of the Independent International Commission on Decommissioning ("the Commission") established under an Agreement between the Government of the United Kingdom of Great Britain and Northern Ireland and the Government of the Republic of Ireland concluded on 26th August 1997,

(ii) in sub paragraph (i) above, "servant" includes any agent of or person carrying out work for or giving advice to the Commission,

(*n*) any member of the family of a person exempted under any of the preceding paragraphs forming part of his household.]

Notes Words 'British citizen' in square brackets substituted by SI 1982/1649.
Words in square brackets at the end of para (*g*) were added, and para (*j*) substituted by SI 1977/693. SI 1977/693 also added para (*k*), which was later substituted, and para (*l*) added, by SI 1985/1809.
Para (*l*) substituted and (*m*) added by SI 1997/1402.
Para (*m*) substituted and (*n*) added by SI 1997/2207.

[A.4.9]

5 (1) Subject to the provisions of this Article the following persons who are not [British citizens] shall, on arrival in the United Kingdom, be exempt from the provisions of section 3(1)(*a*) of the Act (which requires persons who are not [British citizens] to obtain leave to enter the United Kingdom), that is to say—

(*a*) any citizen of the United Kingdom and Colonies who holds a passport issued to him in the United Kingdom and Islands and expressed to be a British Visitor's Passport;

(*b*) any Commonwealth citizen who is included in a passport issued in the United Kingdom by the Government of the United Kingdom or in one of the Islands by the Lieutenant-Governor thereof which is expressed to be a Collective Passport;

(c) any Commonwealth citizen or citizen of the Republic of Ireland returning to the United Kingdom from an excursion to France or Belgium [or the Netherlands] who holds a valid document of identity issued in accordance with arrangements approved by the United Kingdom Government and in a form authorised by the Secretary of State and enabling him to travel on such an excursion without a passport;

(d) any Commonwealth citizen who holds a British seaman's card or any citizen of the Republic of Ireland if (in either case) he was engaged as a member of the crew of a ship in a place within the common travel area and, on arrival in the United Kingdom, is or is to be, discharged from his engagement;

(e) any person who, having left the United Kingdom after having been given a limited leave to enter, returns to the United Kingdom within the period for which he had leave as a member of the crew of an aircraft under an engagement requiring him to leave on that or another aircraft as a member of its crew within a period exceeding seven days.

(2) Paragraph (1) shall not apply so as to confer any exemption on any person against whom there is a deportation order in force or who has previously entered the United Kingdom unlawfully and has not subsequently been given leave to enter or remain in the United Kingdom and subparagraphs (*d*) and (*e*) of that paragraph shall not apply to a person who is required by an immigration officer to submit to examination in accordance with Schedule 2 to the Act.

(3) In this Article any reference to a Commonwealth citizen shall be construed as including a reference to a British protected person and in paragraph (1)(*d*) 'British seaman's card' means a valid card issued under any regulations in force under section 70 of the Merchant Shipping Act 1970 or any card having effect by virtue of the said regulations as a card so issued and 'holder of a British seaman's card' has the same meaning as in the said regulations.

Notes Words 'British citizens' in square brackets substituted by SI 1982/1649. Words in square brackets in para 1(*c*) added by SI 1975/617.

[A.4.10]

[6 (1) For the purposes of section 1(1) of the British Nationality Act 1981 (which relates to acquisition of British citizenship by birth in the United Kingdom), a person to whom a child is born in the United Kingdom on or after 1 January 1983 is to be regarded (notwithstanding the preceding provisions of this Order) as settled in the United Kingdom at the time of birth if—

(*a*) he would fall to be so regarded but for his being at that time entitled to an exemption by virtue of this Order; and

(*b*) immediately before he became entitled to that exemption he was settled in the United Kingdom; and

(*c*) he was ordinarily resident in the United Kingdom from the time when he became entitled to that exemption to the time of birth,

but this Article shall not apply if at the time of the birth the child's father or mother is a person on whom any immunity from jurisdiction is conferred by or under the Diplomatic Privileges Act 1964.

(2)   Expressions used in this Article shall be construed in accordance with section 50 of the British Nationality Act 1981.]

Notes   Article 6 inserted by SI 1982/1649.

SCHEDULE
STATES WITH WHICH CONSULAR CONVENTIONS HAVE BEEN
CONCLUDED BY HER MAJESTY

[A.4.11]

Austria
Belgium
Bulgaria
[Czechoslovakia]
Denmark
France
[German Democratic Republic]
Greece
Federal Republic of Germany
Hungary
Italy

Japan
Mexico
[Mongolia]
Norway
Poland
Romania
Sweden
Spain
Union of Soviet Socialist Republics
United States of America
Yugoslavia

Notes   The references to Czechoslovakia, the German Democratic Republic and Mongolia added by SI 1977/693.

IMMIGRATION (REGISTRATION WITH POLICE) REGULATIONS 1972
SI 1972/1758

Date   14 November 1972
Authority   Immigration Act 1971, s 4(3)
Commencement   1 January 1973 (reg 1)

[A.4.12]
1   Citation and commencement
These Regulations may be cited as the Immigration (Registration with Police) Regulations 1972 and shall come into operation on 1 January 1973.

[A.4.13]
2   Interpretation and transitional provisions
(1) In these Regulations, except where the context otherwise requires, the following expressions have the meanings hereby respectively assigned to them, that is to say –

'the Act' means the Immigration Act 1971;
'alien' has the same meaning as in the [British Nationality Act 1981];
'certificate of registration' means a certificate issued in pursuance of Regulation 10(1) to the alien concerned;
'local register' means a register kept in pursuance of Regulation 4;
'nationality' includes the status of a stateless alien;
'registration officer' and 'appropriate registration officer' have the meanings assigned thereto by Regulation 4;
'a residence' means a person's private dwelling-house or other premises in which he is ordinarily resident but does not include any premises in which he is not ordinarily resident.

(2) In these Regulations any reference to a Regulation is a reference to a Regulation contained therein and any reference in a Regulation to a paragraph is a reference to a paragraph of that Regulation.

(3) Where an alien has failed to comply with any requirement made by a provision of these Regulations within a period specified in that provision he shall, without prejudice to any liability in respect of that failure under section 26(1)(*f*) of the Act, continue to be subject to that requirement notwithstanding the expiry of that period.

(4) The Interpretation Act 1889 shall apply to the interpretation of these Regulations as it applies to the Interpretation of an Act of Parliament.

(5) Anything done, or having effect as if done, under or for the purposes of, any provision of the Aliens Order 1953, as amended, corresponding to a provision of these Regulations shall have effect as if done under, or for the purposes of, that corresponding provision and, in particular–

(*a*) any register kept under the Article 13 of the said Order shall be treated as part of the local register kept under Regulation 4(2);

(*b*) particulars furnished under Article 14(2) of the said Order shall be treated as furnished under Regulation 5; and

(*c*) a certificate of registration supplied in pursuance of Article 13(3)(*b*) of the said Order shall be treated as a certificate of registration issued in pursuance of Regulation 10(1).

Notes Words in square brackets in para (1) substituted by SI 1982/1024.

[A.4.14]
3 Application of Regulations
These Regulations shall apply in the case of an alien who has a limited leave to enter or remain in the United Kingdom which is for the time being subject to a condition requiring him to register with the police and in the case of an alien who, by virtue of section 34 of the Act or paragraph 1 of Schedule 4 thereto, is treated as having such a limited leave.

[A.4.15]
4 Registration officers etc
(1) For the purposes of these Regulations the chief officer of police for each police area shall be the registration officer for that area, and the police area shall be the registration area; and any reference to the appropriate registration officer is a reference–

(*a*) in the case of an alien who has a residence in the United Kingdom to the registration officer for the area in which that residence is situated;
(*b*) in any other case, to the registration officer for the area in which, for the time being, he happens to be.

(2) Every registration officer shall keep for his registration district a local register of aliens containing the particulars specified in the Schedule hereto:

Provided that if a registration officer is not satisfied as to the nationality of an alien he may describe that alien in the local register as being of uncertain nationality or may describe him as having such nationality as appears to that officer to be the probable nationality of the alien.

(3) Anything required or authorised by these Regulations to be done by or to a registration officer may be done by or to any constable or other person who is authorised by that officer to act for the purposes of these Regulations.

[A.4.16]
5 Duty to register etc
(1) Within 7 days of these Regulations becoming applicable to him, an alien shall, subject to Regulation 6, attend at the office of the appropriate registration officer and furnish to that officer such information, documents and other particulars (including a recent photograph) relating to him as are required by

that officer for the purposes of the local register kept by him or the issue of a certificate of registration to the alien.

(2) Without prejudice to the generality of paragraph (1) an alien attending as aforesaid shall either–

(*a*) produce to the appropriate registration officer a passport furnished with a photograph of himself or some other document satisfactorily establishing his identity and nationality; or

(*b*) give to that officer a satisfactory explanation of the circumstances which prevent him from producing such a passport or document.

[A.4.17]
6 Exemption from registration in certain cases
(1) An alien shall not be required to attend and furnish particulars under Regulation 5 if–

(*a*) immediately before these Regulations becoming applicable to him, he was ordinarily resident in the United Kingdom; and

(*b*) he had previously, during that period of ordinary residence, attended and furnished particulars under Regulation 5.

(2) Without prejudice to paragraph (1) or the provisions of Regulation 2(5), an alien shall not be required to attend and furnish particulars under Regulation 5 if–

(*a*) on the coming into operation of these Regulations they become applicable to him;

(*b*) immediately before their coming into operation he was resident in the United Kingdom; and

(*c*) he had previously, during that period of residence, attended and furnished particulars under Article 14(2) of the Aliens Order 1953, as amended.

[A.4.18]
7 Duty to notify changes of residence or address etc
(1) Every alien to whom these Regulations apply who has furnished particulars under Regulation 5 shall be under a duty to notify any changes therein in accordance with this Regulation.

(2) Such an alien who for the time being has a residence in the United Kingdom shall, if he adopts a new residence within the United Kingdom, report his arrival at his new residence to the appropriate registration officer before the expiration of the period of 7 days beginning with the day of his arrival.

(3) Such an alien who for the time being has a residence in the United Kingdom, if he is absent from his residence for a continuous period exceeding 2 months (without adopting a new residence):

(*a*) shall forthwith notify the appropriate registration officer of his address for the time being (whether within or outside the United Kingdom);

(*b*) subject to paragraph (5), shall notify the appropriate registration officer of any subsequent change of address within the United Kingdom before the expiration of 8 days beginning with the day of his arrival at the new address; and

(*c*) shall, on returning to his residence, notify the appropriate registration officer of his return (whether or not he has throughout the period of absence remained in the United Kingdom).

(4) Subject to paragraphs (5) and (6), such an alien who for the time being has not a residence in the United Kingdom shall, if he moves from one address to another (in the same or a different registration district), notify the appropriate registration officer of his arrival thereat before the expiration of 8 days beginning with the day of his arrival.

(5) Such an alien need not, under paragraph (3)(*b*) or (4), notify the appropriate registration officer of his address unless he remains or intends to remain at that address for a longer period than 7 days beginning with the day of his arrival thereat.

(6) If such an alien who for the time being has not a residence in the United Kingdom supplies to a registration officer the name and address of a referee, being a person resident within the United Kingdom who is willing to act, and in the opinion of that officer is a suitable person to act, as a referee under this paragraph, the officer shall include the referee's name and address among the entries relating to the alien in the local register kept by him; and in such case, the following provisions shall apply in substitution for those of paragraph (4), that is to say—

(*a*) the alien shall keep the referee informed as to his address from time to time and shall notify the registration officer of any change in the referee's address; and

(*b*) the referee shall, if so required by the registration officer, furnish to that officer any information in his possession as to the alien which is required by that officer for the purposes of his duties under these Regulations.

[A.4.19]
8   Duty to notify other changes in particulars etc
Every alien to whom these Regulations apply who has furnished particulars under Regulation 5:

(*a*) shall notify the appropriate registration officer of any change in his case in the particulars specified as items 1, 3, 5, 6, 7 and 14 in the Schedule hereto, before the expiration of 8 days beginning with that on which the change, or the event occasioning this change, occurs; and

(*b*) if so required by the appropriate registration officer, shall furnish to that officer by such date as he may specify such information, documents and other particulars (including, where so required, a recent photograph) relating to him which are required by that officer for the purposes of his duties under these Regulations.

[A.4.20]
9 Provisions supplemental to Regulations 5, 7 and 8
(1) An alien required under Regulation 5(1) or 8(*b*) to furnish a photograph of himself shall furnish 2 copies of the same photograph; and, if he fails to furnish such copies, the registration officer may cause him to be photographed.

(2) An alien required under Regulation 7 or 8(*a*) to notify the appropriate registration officer of any change in his residence or address or of any change in his case in the particulars mentioned in Rule 8(*a*) shall either attend for the purpose at the office of the registration officer or send written notice of the change to that officer by post so, however, that where written notice is given the alien shall also send to the registration officer his certificate of registration.

(3) An alien required under Regulation 8(*b*) to furnish information, documents or other particulars to the appropriate registration officer (whether or not in connection with a change of which written notice has been given in pursuance of paragraph (2)) shall attend for the purposes at the office of the registration officer if that officer so requires.

[A.4.21]
[**10** (1) Every registration officer shall issue certificates of registration to aliens of whom particulars are entered in the local register kept by him.

(2) A certificate of registration shall be independent of, and shall not be included in, any other document.

(3) An alien to whom a certificate of registration is issued shall pay to the registration officer concerned a fee of [£34] except where the requirement to register is a condition of leave granted to an alien after an absence from the United Kingdom of a period of less than one year immediately following an earlier period of leave which was subject to the same condition.]

Notes Reg 10 substituted by SI 1990/400 (superseding previous amendments made by SI 1975/999, SI 1976/2018, SI 1978/24, SI 1979/196, SI 1980/451, SI 1981/534, SI 1982/502, SI 1983/442).
   Reg 10(3): Figures in square brackets substituted by SI 1995/2928, reg 2.

[A.4.22]
11 Production of registration certificates
(1) On the making of any alteration or addition to the local register, the registration officer may require the alien concerned to produce his certificate of registration in order that any necessary amendment may be made thereto.

(2) Any immigration officer or constable may –

(*a*) require an alien to whom these Regulations apply, forthwith, to either produce a certificate of registration or to give to the officer or constable a satisfactory reason for his failure to produce it;

(*b*) where the alien fails to produce a certificate of registration in pursuance of such a requirement (whether or not he gives a satisfactory reason for his failure), require him, within the following 48 hours, to produce a certificate of registration at a police station specified by the officer or constable,

so, however, that a requirement under sub-paragraph (*b*) to produce a certificate of registration at a police station shall have effect in substitution for the requirement under sub-paragraph (*a*) so as to cause that previous requirement to cease to have effect.

SCHEDULE
PARTICULARS TO BE ENTERED IN LOCAL REGISTER

[A.4.23]
1. Name in full.
2. Sex.
3. Matrimonial status (married or single).
4. (*a*) Date of birth.
   (*b*) Country of birth.
5. (*a*) Present nationality.
   (*b*) How and when acquired.
   (*c*) Previous nationality (if any).
6. Particulars of passport or other document establishing nationality.
7. Business, profession or occupation.
8. Residence in the United Kingdom (or address if no residence).
9. Name and address of referee (if any) supplied under Regulation 7(*b*).
10. Last residence outside the United Kingdom.
11. (*a*) Date of arrival in the United Kingdom.
    (*b*) Place of arrival in the United Kingdom.
    (*c*) Mode of arrival in the United Kingdom.
12. Duration of limited leave and conditions attached thereto.
13. Restrictions or conditions, if any, applicable by virtue of section 9(2) of the Act.
14. (*a*) If employed in the United Kingdom –
        (i) name and address of employer;
        (ii) address at which employed, if different.
    (*b*) If engaged in business or profession in the United Kingdom –
        (i) name under which business or profession is carried on;
        (ii) address at which business or profession is carried on.
15. Signature (or fingerprints if unable to write in the characters of the English language).
16. Photograph.

IMMIGRATION (VARIATION OF LEAVE) ORDER 1976
SI 1976/1572

Date 22 September 1976
Authority Immigration Act 1971, s 4(1)
Commencement 27 September 1976 (art 1)

[A.4.24]
1 Citation and Operation
This Order may be cited as the Immigration (Variation of Leave) Order 1976 and shall come into operation on 27 September 1976.

[A.4.25]
2 Interpretation
The Interpretation Act 1889 shall apply to the interpretation of this Order as it applies to the interpretation of an Act of Parliament.

[A.4.26]
3 Variation of limited leave to enter or remain in the United Kingdom
(1) Where a person has leave to enter or remain in the United Kingdom for a limited period and applies to the Secretary of State before the expiry of that period for such limited leave to be varied, then, except in a case falling within paragraph (2) below, the duration of his leave shall, by virtue of this Order, be extended until the expiration of the twenty-eighth day after [either the date of the decision on the application or, if the application is withdrawn, the date of the withdrawal of the application.]

(2) Paragraph (1) above shall not apply –

(*a*) in a case in which the date of the decision is earlier than 28 days before the expiration of the period of limited leave;
(*b*) in a case in which the period of limited leave had expired before the coming into operation of this Order;
(*c*) in a case in which the application is made at a time when, by virtue of the previous operation of this Order, an extension of the applicant's period of leave is taking effect [and he has no other concurrent period for leave];
[(*d*) in a case in which the duration of a person's limited leave to enter or remain has been curtailed by the Secretary of State under section 7(1) of the Asylum and Immigration Appeals Act 1993];
[(*e*) in a case in which the date of the decision is 2nd October 2000 or later].

(3) For the purposes of this Article the date of the decision shall have the same meaning as in Rule 4 (11) of the Immigration Appeals (Procedure) Rules 1972, that is to say, shall –

(*a*) where notice of the decision is sent by post, be deemed to be the day on which such notice is sent;

(*b*) in any other case, be deemed to be the day on which notice of the decision is served.

Notes   Words in square brackets in para (1) substituted, and words at end of para (2)(*c*) added, by SI 1989/1005.

Para 2(*d*) added by SI 1993/1657 with effect from 26 July 1993.

Para 2(*e*) inserted by SI 2000/2445, art 2(*a*).

[A.4.27]

[4 Where –

(*a*) the duration of a person's limited leave to enter or remain in the UK has been extended by the operation of article 3(1); and
(*b*) the duration of that leave has been curtailed by the Secretary of State under section 7(1) of the Asylum and Immigration Appeals Act 1993,

the extension shall not have effect beyond the date to which the leave is curtailed.]

Note   Article 4 added by SI 1993/1657 with effect from 26 July 1993.

IMMIGRATION (PORTS OF ENTRY) ORDER 1987
SI 1987/177

Date   10 February 1987
Authority   Immigration Act 1971, s 33(3)
Commencement   1 March 1987 (art 1(1))

[A.4.28]
1 (1) This Order may be cited as the Immigration (Ports of Entry) Order 1987 and shall come into force on 1 March 1987.

(2) The Immigration (Ports of Entry) Order 1972, the Immigration (Ports of Entry) (Amendment) Order 1975 and the Immigration (Ports of Entry) (Amendment) Order 1979 are hereby revoked.

[A.4.29]
2 The ports specified in the Schedule to this Order shall be ports of entry for the purposes of the Immigration Act 1971.

SCHEDULE
PORTS OF ENTRY

[A.4.30]
Seaports and Hoverports

Dover	Plymouth
Felixstowe	Portsmouth
Folkestone	Ramsgate
Harwich	Sheerness
Hull	Southampton
London	Tyne
Newhaven	

Airports

Aberdeen	Leeds/Bradford
Belfast	Liverpool
Birmingham	Luton
Bournemouth (Hurn)	Manchester
Bristol	Newcastle
Cardiff (Wales)	Norwich
East Midlands	Prestwick
Edinburgh	Southampton
Gatwick-London	Southend
Glasgow	Stansted-London
Heathrow-London	Tees-side

IMMIGRATION (TRANSIT VISA) ORDER 1993
SI 1993/1678

Made   2 July 1993
Authority   Immigration (Carriers' Liability) Act 1987, s 1A(1) and (2)
Coming into force   22 July 1993
Note   As amended by SIs 1996/2065, 1998/55, 1998/1014, 1998/2483.

[A.4.31]
1   This Order may be cited as the Immigration (Transit Visa) Order 1993 and shall come into force on 22nd July 1993.

[A.4.32]
[In this Order, 'EEA State' means a country which is a Contracting Party to the Agreement on the European Economic Area signed at Oporto on 2nd May 1992 as adjusted by the Protocol signed at Brussels on 17th March 1993.]

Note   Inserted by SI 2000/1381, art 2(1).

[A.4.33]
2   A national or citizen of one or more of the countries or territories specified in the Schedule to this Order [,or a person holding a travel document issued by the purported 'Turkish Republic of Northern Cyprus' [or the former Socialist Federal Republic of Yugoslavia,]] who on arrival in the United Kingdom passes through to another country or territory without entering the United Kingdom shall hold a visa for that purpose (a transit visa) unless he:

(*a*) has the right of abode in the United Kingdom under the Immigration Act 1971; or
(*b*) is also a national of [an EEA State].

Notes   Words ', or a person holding a travel document issued by the purported "Turkish Republic of Northern Cyprus",' in square brackets inserted by SI 1998/55, art 2.
Words 'or the former Socialist Federal Republic of Yugoslavia,' in square brackets inserted by SI 1998/1014, art 3.
In para (b) words 'an EEA State' in square brackets substituted by SI 2000/1381, art 2(2).

[A.4.34]
3   An application for a transit visa shall be made to any British High Commission, Embassy or Consulate which accepts such applications.

[SCHEDULE   COUNTRIES OR TERRITORIES WHOSE NATIONALS OR CITIZENS NEED A VISA FOR PASSING THROUGH THE UNITED KINGDOM] (art 3)

[A.4.35]

[Afghanistan
Colombia
Democratic Republic of Congo
Ecuador
Eritrea
Ethiopia
Federal Republic of Yugoslavia
Ghana
Iran
Iraq

Libya
Nigeria
People's Republic of China
Republic of Croatia
Slovak Republic
Somalia
Sri Lanka
Turkey
Uganda]

Note   Schedule substituted by SI 2000/1381, art 3, Schedule

IMMIGRATION (PASSENGER INFORMATION) ORDER 2000
SI 2000/912

Made 29 March 2000
Laid before Parliament 6 April 2000
Coming into force 28 April 2000

[A.4.36]
1 This Order may be cited as the Immigration (Passenger Information) Order 2000 and shall come into force on 28th April 2000.

[A.4.37]
2 (1) Subject to paragraph (2), the information listed in the Schedule to this Order is specified for the purposes of paragraph 27B(9) of Schedule 2 to the Immigration Act 1971 (definition of 'passenger information').
(2) The information listed in Part II of the Schedule to this Order is so specified only to the extent that it is known to the carrier.

SCHEDULE
PASSENGER INFORMATION

[A.4.38]

ARTICLE 2

PART I
INFORMATION RELATING TO A PASSENGER AS GIVEN ON OR SHOWN BY THE PASSENGER'S PASSPORT OR OTHER TRAVEL DOCUMENT

Full name.

Gender.

Date of birth.

Nationality.

The type of travel document held by the passenger and its number.
If the passenger has a United Kingdom visa or other form of United Kingdom entry clearance, its expiry date.

PART II
OTHER INFORMATION RELATING TO A PASSENGER

Name as it appears on the passenger's reservation.

Ticket number.

Date and place of issue of the ticket.

If not the carrier, the identity of the person who made the passenger's reservation on behalf of the carrier.

Method of payment for the ticket.

Travel itinerary.

Names of all other passengers appearing on the passenger's reservation.

If the passenger is travelling with a car or other vehicle, the vehicle registration number and, if the vehicle has a trailer, the trailer registration number (if different to the vehicle registration number).

IMMIGRATION (LEAVE TO ENTER AND REMAIN) ORDER 2000
SI 2000/1161

Made   19 April 2000
Coming into force   Articles 1 to 12, 14 and 15(1) in accordance with article 1(2). Articles 13 and 15(2) 30 July 2000

PART I
GENERAL

[A.4.39]
Citation, commencement and interpretation
1 (1)   This Order may be cited as the Immigration (Leave to Enter and Remain) Order 2000.
(2)   Articles 1 to 12, 14 and 15(1) of this Order shall come into force on 28th April 2000 or, if later, on the day after the day on which it is made and articles 13 and 15(2) shall come into force on 30th July 2000.
(3)   In this Order—

'the Act' means the Immigration Act 1971;
'control port' means a port in which a control area is designated under paragraph 26(3) of Schedule 2 to the Act;
'the Immigration Acts' means:

(a) the Act;
(b) the Immigration Act 1988;
(c) the Asylum and Immigration Appeals Act 1993;
(d) the Asylum and Immigration Act 1996; and
(e) the Immigration and Asylum Act 1999;

'responsible third party' means a person appearing to an immigration officer to be:

(*a*) in charge of a group of people arriving in the United Kingdom together or intending to arrive in the United Kingdom together;
(*b*) a tour operator;
(*c*) the owner or agent of a ship, aircraft, train, hydrofoil or hovercraft;
(*d*) the person responsible for the management of a control port or his agent; or
(*e*) an official at a British Diplomatic Mission or at a British Consular Post or at the office of any person outside the United Kingdom and Islands who has been authorised by the Secretary of State to accept applications for entry clearance;

'tour operator' means a person who, otherwise than occasionally, organises and provides holidays to the public or a section of it; and
'visit visa' means an entry clearance granted for the purpose of entry to the United Kingdom as a visitor under the immigration rules.

PART II
ENTRY CLEARANCE AS LEAVE TO ENTER

[A.4.40]
Entry clearance as Leave to Enter
2 Subject to article 6(3), an entry clearance which complies with the requirements of article 3 shall have effect as leave to enter the United Kingdom to the extent specified in article 4, but subject to the conditions referred to in article 5.

[A.4.41]
Requirements
3 (1) An entry clearance shall not have effect as leave to enter unless it complies with the requirements of this article.
(2) The entry clearance must specify the purpose for which the holder wishes to enter the United Kingdom.
(3) The entry clearance must be endorsed with:

(*a*) the conditions to which it is subject; or
(*b*) a statement that it is to have effect as indefinite leave to enter the United Kingdom.

[A.4.42]
Extent to which Entry Clearance is to be Leave to Enter
4 (1) A visit visa, during its period of validity, shall have effect as leave to enter the United Kingdom on an unlimited number of occasions, in accordance with paragraph (2).
(2) On each occasion the holder arrives in the United Kingdom, he shall be treated for the purposes of the Immigration Acts as having been granted, before arrival, leave to enter the United Kingdom for a limited period beginning on the date of arrival, being:

(*a*) six months if six months or more remain of the visa's period of validity; or
(*b*) the visa's remaining period of validity, if less than six months.

(3) In the case of any other form of entry clearance, it shall have effect as leave to enter the United Kingdom on one occasion during its period of validity; and, on arrival in the United Kingdom, the holder shall be treated for the purposes of the Immigration Acts as having been granted, before arrival, leave to enter the United Kingdom:

(*a*) in the case of an entry clearance which is endorsed with a statement that it is to have effect as indefinite leave to enter the United Kingdom, for an indefinite period; or
(*b*) in the case of an entry clearance which is endorsed with conditions, for a limited period, being the period beginning on the date on which the holder arrives in the United Kingdom and ending on the date of expiry of the entry clearance.

(4) In this article 'period of validity' means the period beginning on the day

on which the entry clearance becomes effective and ending on the day on which it expires.

[A.4.43]
Conditions
5   An entry clearance shall have effect as leave to enter subject to any conditions, being conditions of a kind that may be imposed on leave to enter given under section 3 of the Act, to which the entry clearance is subject and which are endorsed on it.

[A.4.44]
Incidental, supplementary and consequential provisions
6   (1)   Where an immigration officer exercises his power to cancel leave to enter under paragraph 2A(8) of Schedule 2 to the Act or article 13(7) below in respect of an entry clearance which has effect as leave to enter, the entry clearance shall cease to have effect.
(2)   If the holder of an entry clearance—

(*a*)   arrives in the United Kingdom before the day on which it becomes effective; or

(*b*)   seeks to enter the United Kingdom for a purpose other than the purpose specified in the entry clearance,

an immigration officer may cancel the entry clearance.
(3)   If the holder of an entry clearance which does not, at the time, have effect as leave to enter the United Kingdom seeks leave to enter the United Kingdom at any time before his departure for, or in the course of his journey to, the United Kingdom and is refused leave to enter under article 7, the entry clearance shall not have effect as leave to enter.

PART III
FORM AND MANNER OF GIVING AND REFUSING LEAVE TO ENTER

[A.4.45]
Grant and refusal of leave to enter before arrival in the United Kingdom
7   (1)   An immigration officer, whether or not in the United Kingdom, may give or refuse a person leave to enter the United Kingdom at any time before his departure for, or in the course of his journey to, the United Kingdom.
(2)   In order to determine whether or not to give leave to enter under this article (and, if so, for what period and subject to what conditions), an immigration officer may seek such information, and the production of such documents or copy documents, as an immigration officer would be entitled to obtain in an examination under paragraph 2 or 2A of Schedule 2 to the Act.
(3)   An immigration officer may also require the person seeking leave to supply an up to date medical report.
(4)   Failure by a person seeking leave to supply any information, documents, copy documents or medical report requested by an immigration officer under this article shall be a ground, in itself, for refusal of leave.

[A.4.46]
Grant or refusal of leave otherwise than by notice in writing
8   (1)   A notice giving or refusing leave to enter may, instead of being given in writing as required by section 4(1) of the Act, be given as follows.
(2)   The notice may be given by facsimile or electronic mail.
(3)   In the case of a notice giving or refusing leave to enter the United Kingdom as a visitor, it may be given orally, including by means of a telecommunications system.
(4)   In paragraph (3), 'leave to enter the United Kingdom as a visitor' means leave to enter as a visitor under the immigration rules for a period not exceeding six months, subject to conditions prohibiting employment and recourse to public funds (within the meaning of the immigration rules).

[A.4.47]
Grant or refusal of leave by notice to a responsible third party
9   (1)   Leave to enter may be given or refused to a person by means of a notice given (in such form and manner as permitted by the Act or this Order for a notice giving or refusing leave to enter) to a responsible third party acting on his behalf.
(2)   A notice under paragraph (1) may refer to a person to whom leave is being granted or refused either by name or by reference to a description or category of persons which includes him.

[A.4.48]
Notice of refusal of leave
10   (1)   Where a notice refusing leave to enter to a person is given under article 8(3) or 9, an immigration officer shall as soon as practicable give to him a notice in writing stating that he has been refused leave to enter the United Kingdom and stating the reasons for the refusal.
(2)   Where an immigration officer serves a notice under the Immigration (Appeals) Notices Regulations 1984 or under regulations made under paragraph 1 of Schedule 4 to the Immigration and Asylum Act 1999 in respect of the refusal, he shall not be required to serve a notice under paragraph (1).
(3)   Any notice required by paragraph (1) to be given to any person may be delivered, or sent by post to—

(*a*)   that person's last known or usual place of abode; or
(*b*)   any address provided by him for receipt of the notice.

[A.4.49]
Burden of proof
11   Where any question arises under the Immigration Acts as to whether a person has leave to enter the United Kingdom and he alleges that he has such leave by virtue of a notice given under article 8(3) or 9, the onus shall lie upon him to show the manner and date of his entry into the United Kingdom.

[A.4.50]
12   (1)   This article applies where—

(*a*) an immigration officer has commenced examination of a person ('the applicant') under paragraph 2(1)(c) of Schedule 2 to the Act (examination to determine whether or not leave to enter should be given);

(*b*) that examination has been adjourned, or the applicant has been required (under paragraph 2(3) of Schedule 2 to the Act) to submit to a further examination, whilst further inquiries are made (including, where the applicant has made an asylum claim, as to the Secretary of State's decision on that claim); and

(*c*) upon the completion of those inquiries, an immigration officer considers he is in a position to decide whether or not to give or refuse leave to enter without interviewing the applicant further.

(2)   Where this article applies, any notice giving or refusing leave to enter which is on any date thereafter sent by post to the applicant (or is communicated to him in such form or manner as is permitted by this Order) shall be regarded, for the purposes of the Act, as having been given within the period of 24 hours specified in paragraph 6(1) of Schedule 2 to the Act (period within which notice giving or refusing leave to enter must be given after completion of examination).

PART IV
LEAVE WHICH DOES NOT LAPSE ON TRAVEL OUTSIDE COMMON TRAVEL AREA

[A.4.51]
13
(1)   In this article 'leave' means—

(*a*) leave to enter the United Kingdom (including leave to enter conferred by means of an entry clearance under article 2); and

(*b*) leave to remain in the United Kingdom.

(2)   Subject to paragraph (3), where a person has leave which is in force and which was:

(*a*) conferred by means of an entry clearance (other than a visit visa) under article 2; or

(*b*) given by an immigration officer or the Secretary of State for a period exceeding six months,

such leave shall not lapse on his going to a country or territory outside the common travel area.
(3)   Paragraph (2) shall not apply:

(*a*) where a limited leave has been varied by the Secretary of State; and
(*b*) following the variation the period of leave remaining is six months or less.

(4)   Leave which does not lapse under paragraph (2) shall remain in force either indefinitely (if it is unlimited) or until the date on which it would otherwise have expired (if limited), but—

(*a*) where the holder has stayed outside the United Kingdom for a continuous period of more than two years, the leave (where the leave is unlimited) or any leave then remaining (where the leave is limited) shall thereupon lapse; and

(*b*) any conditions to which the leave is subject shall be suspended for such time as the holder is outside the United Kingdom.

(5)   For the purposes of paragraphs 2 and 2A of Schedule 2 to the Act (examination by immigration officers, and medical examination), leave to remain which remains in force under this article shall be treated, upon the holder's arrival in the United Kingdom, as leave to enter which has been granted to the holder before his arrival.

(6)   Without prejudice to the provisions of section 4(1) of the Act, where the holder of leave which remains in force under this article is outside the United Kingdom, the Secretary of State may vary that leave (including any conditions to which it is subject) in such form and manner as permitted by the Act or this Order for the giving of leave to enter.

(7)   Where a person is outside the United Kingdom and has leave which is in force by virtue of this article, that leave may be cancelled:

(*a*) in the case of leave to enter, by an immigration officer; or

(*b*) in the case of leave to remain, by the Secretary of State.

(8)   In order to determine whether or not to vary (and, if so, in what manner) or cancel leave which remains in force under this article and which is held by a person who is outside the United Kingdom, an immigration officer or, as the case may be, the Secretary of State may seek such information, and the production of such documents or copy documents, as an immigration officer would be entitled to obtain in an examination under paragraph 2 or 2A of Schedule 2 to the Act and may also require the holder of the leave to supply an up to date medical report.

(9)   Failure to supply any information, documents, copy documents or medical report requested by an immigration officer or, as the case may be, the Secretary of State under this article shall be a ground, in itself, for cancellation of leave.

(10)   Section 3(4) of the Act (lapsing of leave upon travelling outside the common travel area) shall have effect subject to this article.

PART V
CONSEQUENTIAL AND TRANSITIONAL PROVISIONS

[A.4.52]
14   Section 9(2) of the Act (further provisions as to common travel area: conditions applicable to certain arrivals on a local journey) shall have effect as if, after the words 'British Citizens', there were inserted 'and do not hold leave to enter or remain granted to them before their arrival'.

[A.4.53]
15   (1)   Article 12 shall apply where an applicant's examination has begun before the date that article comes into force, as well as where it begins on or after that date.

(2) Article 13 shall apply with respect to leave to enter or remain in the United Kingdom which is in force on the date that article comes into force, as well as to such leave given after that date.

IMMIGRATION (REMOVAL DIRECTIONS) REGULATIONS 2000
SI 2000/2243

Made   16 August 2000
Laid before Parliament   24 August 2000
Coming into force   2 October 2000

[A.4.54]
1   Citation and commencement
These Regulations may be cited as the Immigration (Removal Directions) Regulations 2000 and shall come into force on 2nd October 2000.

[A.4.55]
2   Interpretation
(1)   In these Regulations—

'the Act' means the Immigration and Asylum Act 1999;
'aircraft' includes hovercraft;
'captain' means master (of a ship) or commander (of an aircraft);
'international service' has the meaning given by section 13(6) of the Channel Tunnel Act 1987;
'ship' includes every description of vessel used in navigation; and
'the tunnel system' has the meaning given by section 1(7) of the Channel Tunnel Act 1987.

(2)   In these Regulations, a reference to a section number is a reference to a section of the Act.

[A.4.56]
3   Persons to whom directions may be given
For the purposes of section 10(6)(a) (classes of person to whom directions may be given), the following classes of person are prescribed—

(a) owners of ships;
(b) owners of aircraft;
(c) agents of ships;
(d) agents of aircraft;
(e) captains of ships about to leave the United Kingdom;
(f) captains of aircraft about to leave the United Kingdom; and
(g) persons operating an international service.

[A.4.57]
4   Requirements that may be imposed by directions
(1)   For the purposes of section 10(6)(b) (requirements that may be imposed by directions), the following kinds of requirements are prescribed—

(a) in the case where directions are given to a captain of a ship or aircraft about to leave the United Kingdom, a requirement to remove the relevant person from the United Kingdom in that ship or aircraft;

(b)   in the case where directions are given to a person operating an international service, a requirement to make arrangements for the removal of the relevant person through the tunnel system;

(c)   in the case where directions are given to any other person who falls within a class prescribed in regulation 3, a requirement to make arrangements for the removal of the relevant person in a ship or aircraft specified or indicated in the directions; and

(d)   in all cases, a requirement to remove the relevant person in accordance with arrangements to be made by an immigration officer.

(2)   Paragraph (1) only applies if the directions specify that the relevant person is to be removed to a country or territory being—

(i)   a country of which he is a national or citizen; or

(ii)   a country or territory to which there is reason to believe that he will be admitted.

(3)   Paragraph (1)(b) only applies if the relevant person arrived in the United Kingdom through the tunnel system.

(4)   'Relevant person' means a person who may be removed from the United Kingdom in accordance with section 10(1).

IMMIGRATION (EUROPEAN ECONOMIC AREA) REGULATIONS 2000
SI 2000/2326

Made   30 August 2000
Laid before Parliament   1 September 2000
Coming into force   2 October 2000

PART I
INTERPRETATION ETC

[A.4.58]
1   Citation, commencement and revocation
(1)   These Regulations may be cited as the Immigration (European Economic Area) Regulations 2000 and shall come into force on 2nd October 2000.

(2)   Subject to paragraph (3), the Immigration (European Economic Area) Order 1994 is hereby revoked.

(3)   Article 19 of the Order continues to have effect until the commencement of the repeal by the 1999 Act of the Immigration (Carriers' Liability) Act 1987.

Interpretation of Regulations

[A.4.59]
2   General
(1)   In these Regulations:

'the 1971 Act' means the Immigration Act 1971;

'the 1999 Act' means the Immigration and Asylum Act 1999;

'decision-maker' means the Secretary of State, an immigration officer or an entry clearance officer (as the case may be);

'EEA family permit' means a document issued to a person, in accordance with regulation 10 or 13, in connection with his admission to the United Kingdom;

'EEA national' means a national of an EEA State;

'EEA State' means a State, other than the United Kingdom, which is a Contracting Party to the Agreement on the European Economic Area signed at Oporto on 2nd May 1992 as adjusted by the Protocol signed at Brussels on 17th March 1993;

'economic activity' means activity as a worker or self-employed person, or as a provider or recipient of services;

'entry clearance officer' means a person responsible for the grant or refusal of entry clearances;

'military service' means service in the armed forces of an EEA State;

'Regulation 1251/70' means Commission Regulation (EEC) No 1251/70 on the right of workers to remain in the territory of a Member State after having been employed in that State;

'residence document' means a document issued to a person who is not an EEA national, in accordance with regulation 10 or 15, as proof of the holder's right of residence in the United Kingdom;

'residence permit' means a permit issued to an EEA national, in accordance with regulation 10 or 15, as proof of the holder's right of residence in the United Kingdom;

'spouse' does not include a party to a marriage of convenience;

'United Kingdom national' means a person who falls to be treated as a national of the United Kingdom for the purposes of the Community Treaties;

'visa national' means a person who requires a visa for the United Kingdom because he is a national or citizen of one of the countries or territorial entities for the time being specified in the immigration rules.

(2)   In these Regulations unless the context otherwise requires a reference to a regulation is a reference to a regulation of these Regulations; and within a regulation a reference to a paragraph is to a paragraph of that regulation.

[A.4.60]
3   'Worker', 'self-employed person', 'provider' and 'recipient' of services, 'self-sufficient person', 'retired person' and 'student'
(1)   In these Regulations:

(a) 'worker' means a worker within the meaning of Article 39 of the EC Treaty;
(b) 'self-employed person' means a person who establishes himself in order to pursue activity as a self-employed person in accordance with Article 43 of the EC Treaty, or who seeks to do so;
(c) 'provider of services' means a person who provides, or seeks to provide, services within the meaning of Article 50 of the EC Treaty;
(d) 'recipient of services' means a person who receives, or seeks to receive, services within the meaning of Article 50 of the EC Treaty;
(e) 'self-sufficient person' means a person who:

    (i)   has sufficient resources to avoid his becoming a burden on the social assistance system of the United Kingdom; and
    (ii) is covered by sickness insurance in respect of all risks in the United Kingdom;

(f) 'retired person' means a person who:

    (i)   has pursued an activity as an employed or self-employed person;
    (ii) is in receipt of:

        (aa) an invalidity or early retirement pension;
        (bb) old age benefits;

(cc) survivor's benefits; or

(dd) a pension in respect of an industrial accident or disease;

sufficient to avoid his becoming a burden on the social security system of the United Kingdom; and

(iii) is covered by sickness insurance in respect of all risks in the United Kingdom;

(g) 'student' means a person who:

(i) is enrolled at a recognised educational establishment in the United Kingdom for the principal purpose of following a vocational training course;

(ii) assures the Secretary of State by means of a declaration, or by such alternative means as he may choose that are at least equivalent, that he has sufficient resources to avoid him becoming a burden on the social assistance system of the United Kingdom; and

(iii) is covered by sickness insurance in respect of all risks in the United Kingdom.

(2)   For the purposes of paragraph (1)(e) and (f), resources or income are to be regarded as sufficient if they exceed the level in respect of which the recipient would qualify for social assistance.

[A.4.61]
4 'Self-employed person who has ceased activity'
(1)   In these Regulations, 'self-employed person who has ceased activity' means:

(a) a person who:

(i) on the day on which he terminates his activity as a self-employed person has reached the age at which he is entitled to a state pension;

(ii) has pursued such activity in the United Kingdom for at least the twelve months prior to its termination; and

(iii) has resided continuously in the United Kingdom for more than three years;

(b) a person who:

(i) has resided continuously in the United Kingdom for more than two years; and

(ii) has terminated his activity [there] as a self-employed person as a result of a permanent incapacity to work;

(c) a person who:

(i) has resided and pursued activity as a self-employed person in the United Kingdom;

(ii) has terminated that activity as a result of a permanent incapacity to work; and

(iii) such incapacity is the result of an accident at work or an occupational illness which entitles him to a pension payable in whole or in part by the state;

(d) a person who:

    (i) has been continuously resident and continuously active as a self-employed person in the United Kingdom for three years; and

    (ii) is active as a self-employed person in the territory of an EEA State but resides in the United Kingdom and returns to his residence at least once a week.

(2) But, if the person is the spouse of a United Kingdom national:

(a) the conditions as to length of residence and activity in paragraph (1)(a) do not apply; and

(b) the condition as to length of residence in paragraph (1)(b) does not apply.

(3) For the purposes of [paragraph (1)(a), (b) and (c)] periods of activity completed in an EEA State by a person to whom paragraph (1)(d)(ii) applies are to be considered as having been completed in the United Kingdom.

(4) For the purposes of paragraph (1):

(a) periods of absence from the United Kingdom which do not exceed three months in any year or periods of absence from the United Kingdom on military service are not to be taken into account; and

(b) periods of inactivity caused by circumstances outside the control of the self-employed person and periods of inactivity caused by illness or accident are to be treated as periods of activity as a self-employed person.

Note Words in square brackets in para (1)(b)(ii) inserted and those in para (3) substituted by SI 2001/865 in force 2 April 2001.

[A.4.62]
5 'Qualified person'
(1) In these Regulations, 'qualified person' means a person who is an EEA national and in the United Kingdom as:

(a) a worker;
(b) a self-employed person;
(c) a provider of services;
(d) a recipient of services;
(e) a self-sufficient person;
(f) a retired person;
(g) a student; or
(h) a self-employed person who has ceased activity;

or who is a person to whom paragraph (4) applies.

(2) A worker does not cease to be a qualified person solely because:

(a) he is temporarily incapable of work as a result of illness or accident; or

(b) he is involuntarily unemployed, if that fact is duly recorded by the relevant employment office.

(3) A self-employed person does not cease to be a qualified person solely because he is temporarily incapable of work as a result of illness or accident.

(4)   This paragraph applies to:

(a)   the family member of a qualified person referred to in paragraph (1)(h), if:

    (i)   the qualified person has died; and

    (ii)   the family member was residing with him in the United Kingdom immediately before his death;

(b)   the family member of a qualified person referred to in paragraph 1(b) where:

    (i)   the qualified person has died;

    (ii)   the family member resided with him immediately before his death; and

    (iii)   either:

        (aa)   the qualified person had resided continuously in the United Kingdom for at least the two years immediately before his death; or

        (bb)   the death was the result of an accident at work or an occupational disease; or

        (cc)   his surviving spouse is a United Kingdom national.

(5)   For the purposes of paragraph (4)(b), periods of absence from the United Kingdom which do not exceed three months in any year or periods of absence from the United Kingdom on military service are not to be taken into account.

[A.4.63]
6   'Family member'
(1)   In these Regulations, paragraphs (2) to (4) apply in order to determine the persons who are family members of another person.

(2)   If the other person is a student, the persons are:

(a)   his spouse; and

(b)   his dependent children.

(3)   [. . .]

(4)   In any other case, the persons are:

(a)   his spouse;

(b)   descendants of his or of his spouse who are under 21 or are their dependants;

(c)   dependent relatives in his ascending line or that of his spouse.

Note   Paragraph (3) omitted by SI 2001/865 in force 2 April 2001.

Interpretation of other legislation

[A.4.64]
7 Carriers' liability
For the purposes of satisfying a requirement to produce a visa under section 40(1)(b) of the 1999 Act (charges to carriers in respect of passengers without proper documents), a 'valid visa of the required kind' includes a family permit or residence document required for admission as a visa national under regulation 12.

[A.4.65]
8 Persons not subject to restriction on the period for which they may remain
(1) For the purposes of the 1971 Act and the British Nationality Act 1981, the following are to be regarded as persons who are in the United Kingdom without being subject under the immigration laws to any restriction on the period for which they may remain:

(a) a self-employed person who has ceased activity;
(b) the family member of such a person who was residing with that person in the United Kingdom immediately before that person ceased his activity in the United Kingdom;
(c) a family member to whom regulation 5(4) applies;
(d) a person who has rights under Regulation 1251/70;
(e) a person who has been granted permission to remain in the United Kingdom indefinitely.

(2) However, a qualified person or family member who is not mentioned in paragraph (1) is not, by virtue of his status as a qualified person or the family member of a qualified person, to be so regarded for those purposes.

PART II
SCOPE OF REGULATIONS

[A.4.66]
9 General
Subject to regulations 10 and 11 (and to regulations 24(1), 25(1), 26(1) and 28) these Regulations apply solely to EEA nationals and their family members.

[A.4.67]
10 Dependants and members of the household of EEA nationals
(1) If a person satisfies any of the conditions in paragraph (4), and if in all the circumstances it appears to the decision-maker appropriate to do so, the decision-maker may issue to that person an EEA family permit, a residence permit or a residence document (as the case may be).

(2) Where a permit or document has been issued under paragraph (1), these

Regulations apply to the holder of the permit or document as if he were the family member of an EEA national and the permit or document had been issued to him under regulation 13 or 15.

(3)   Without prejudice to regulation 22, a decision-maker may revoke (or refuse to renew) a permit or document issued under paragraph (1) if he decides that the holder no longer satisfies any of the conditions in paragraph (4).

(4)   The conditions are that the person [is a relative of an EEA national or his spouse and]:

(a)   is dependent on the EEA national or his spouse;
(b)   is living as part of the EEA national's household outside the United Kingdom; or
(c)   was living as part of the EEA national's household before the EEA national came to the United Kingdom.

(5)   However, for those purposes 'EEA national' does not include:

(a)   an EEA national who is in the United Kingdom as a self-sufficient person, a retired person or a student;
(b)   an EEA national who, when he is in the United Kingdom, will be a person referred to in sub-paragraph (a).

Note   Words in square brackets in para(4) inserted by SI 2001/865 in force 2 April 2001.

[A.4.68]
11   Family members of United Kingdom nationals
(1)   If the conditions in paragraph (2) are satisfied, these Regulations apply to a person who is the family member of a United Kingdom national returning to the United Kingdom as if that person were the family member of an EEA national.

(2)   The conditions are that:

(a)   after leaving the United Kingdom, the United Kingdom national resided in an EEA State and:

(i)   was employed there (other than on a transient or casual basis); or
(ii)   established himself there as a self-employed person;

(b)   the United Kingdom national did not leave the United Kingdom in order to enable his family member to acquire rights under these Regulations and thereby to evade the application of United Kingdom immigration law;
(c)   on his return to the United Kingdom, the United Kingdom national would, if he were an EEA national, be a qualified person; and
(d)   if the family member of the United Kingdom national is his spouse, the marriage took place, and the parties lived together in an EEA State, before the United Kingdom national returned to the United Kingdom.

PART III
EEA RIGHTS

[A.4.69]
12   Right of admission to the United Kingdom
(1)   Subject to regulation 21(1), an EEA national must be admitted to the United Kingdom if he produces, on arrival, a valid national identity card or passport issued by an EEA State.

(2)   Subject to regulation 21(1) and (2), a family member of an EEA national who is not himself an EEA national must be admitted to the United Kingdom if he produces, on arrival:

(a)   a valid national identity card issued by an EEA State, or a valid passport; and
(b)   either:

    (i)   where the family member is a visa national or a person who seeks to be admitted to instal himself with a qualified person, a valid EEA family permit or residence document; or
    (ii)   in all other cases (but only where required by an immigration officer) a document proving that he is a family member of a qualified person.

[A.4.70]
13   Issue of EEA family permit
(1)   An entry clearance officer must issue an EEA family permit, free of charge, to a person who applies for one if he is a family member of:

(a)   a qualified person; or
(b)   a person who is not a qualified person, where that person:

    (i)   will be travelling to the United Kingdom with the person who has made the application within a year of the date of the application; and
    (ii)   will be a qualified person on arrival in the United Kingdom.

(2)   But paragraph (1) does not apply if:

(a)   the applicant; or
(b)   the person whose family member he is

fails to be excluded from the United Kingdom on grounds of public policy, public security or public health.

[A.4.71]
14   Right of residence
(1)   A qualified person is entitled to reside in the United Kingdom, without the requirement for leave to remain under the 1971 Act, for as long as he remains a qualified person.

(2)   A family member of a qualified person is entitled to reside in the United Kingdom, without the requirement for such leave, for as long as he remains the family member of a qualified person.

(3)   A qualified person and the family member of such a person may reside and pursue economic activity in the United Kingdom notwithstanding that his application for a residence permit or residence document (as the case may be) has not been determined by the Secretary of State.

(4)   However, this regulation is subject to regulation 21(3)(b).

PART IV
RESIDENCE PERMITS AND DOCUMENTS

[A.4.72]
15   Issue of residence permits and residence documents
(1)   Subject to regulations 16 and 22(1), the Secretary of State must issue a residence permit to a qualified person on application and production of:

(a) a valid identity card or passport issued by an EEA State; and
(b) the proof that he is a qualified person.

(2)   Subject to regulation 22(1), the Secretary of State must issue a residence permit to a family member of a qualified person (or, where the family member is not an EEA national, a residence document) on application and production of:

(a) a valid identity card issued by an EEA State or a valid passport;
(b) in the case of a family member who required an EEA family permit for admission to the United Kingdom, such a permit; and
(c) in the case of a person not falling within sub-paragraph (b), proof that he is a family member of a qualified person.

(3)   In the case of a worker, confirmation of the worker's engagement from his employer or a certificate of employment is sufficient proof for the purposes of paragraph (1)(b).

[A.4.73]
16   Where no requirement to issue residence permit
(1)   The Secretary of State is not required to grant a residence permit to:

(a) a worker whose employment in the United Kingdom is limited to three months and who holds a document from his employer certifying that his employment is so limited;
(b) a worker who is employed in the United Kingdom but who resides in the territory of an EEA State and who returns to his residence at least once a week;
(c) a seasonal worker whose contract of employment has been approved by the Department for Education and Employment; or
(d) a provider or recipient of services if the services are to be provided for no more than three months.

(2)   The requirement in paragraph (1)(a) to hold a document does not apply to workers coming within the provisions of Council Directive 64/224/EEC of

25 February 1964 concerning the attainment of freedom of establishment and freedom to provide services in respect of activities of intermediaries in commerce, industry and small craft industries.

[A.4.74]
17 Form of residence permit and residence document
(1)   The residence permit issued to a worker or a worker's family member who is an EEA national must be in the following form:

'Residence Permit for a National of an EEA State

This permit is issued pursuant to Regulation (EEC) No 1612/68 of the Council of the European Communities of 15 October 1968 and to the measures taken in implementation of the Council Directive of 15 October 1968.

In accordance with the provisions of the above-mentioned Regulation, the holder of this permit has the right to take up and pursue an activity as an employed person in the territory of the United Kingdom under the same conditions as United Kingdom national workers.'.

(2)   A residence document issued to a family member who is not an EEA national may take the form of a stamp in that person's passport.

[A.4.75]
18 Duration of residence permit
(1)   Subject to the following paragraphs and to regulations 20 and 22(2), a residence permit must be valid for at least five years from the date of issue.

(2)   In the case of a worker who is to be employed in the United Kingdom for less than twelve but more than three months, the validity of the residence permit may be limited to the duration of the employment.

(3)   In the case of a seasonal worker who is to be employed for more than three months, the validity of the residence permit may be limited to the duration of the employment if the duration is indicated in the document confirming the worker's engagement or in a certificate of employment.

(4)   In the case of a provider or recipient of services, the validity of the residence permit may be limited to the period during which the services are to be provided.

(5)   In the case of a student, the residence permit is to be valid for a period which does not exceed the duration of the course of study; but where the course lasts for more than one year the validity of the residence permit may be limited to one year.

(6)   In the case of a retired person or a self-sufficient person, the Secretary of State may, if he deems it necessary, require the revalidation of the residence permit at the end of the first two years of residence.

(7)   The validity of a residence permit is not to be affected by absence from

the United Kingdom for periods of no more than six consecutive months or absence from the United Kingdom on military service.

[A.4.76]
19   Renewal of residence permit
(1)   Subject to paragraphs (2) and (3) and to regulations 20 and 22(2), a residence permit must be renewed on application.

(2)   On the occasion of the first renewal of a worker's residence permit the validity may be limited to one year if the worker has been involuntarily unemployed in the United Kingdom for more than one year.

(3)   In the case of a student whose first residence permit is limited to one year by virtue of regulation 18(5), renewal may be for periods limited to one year.

[A.4.77]
20   Duration and renewal of residence permit or residence document granted to a family member
The family member of an EEA national is entitled to a residence permit or residence document of the same duration as the residence permit granted to the qualified person of whose family he is a member; and the family member's residence permit or residence document is subject to the same terms as to renewal.

PART V
WITHDRAWAL OF EEA RIGHTS

[A.4.78]
21   Exclusion and removal from the United Kingdom
(1)   A person is not entitled to be admitted to the United Kingdom by virtue of regulation 12 if his exclusion is justified on grounds of public policy, public security or public health.

(2)   A person is not entitled to be admitted to the United Kingdom by virtue of regulation 12(2) if, at the time of his arrival, he is not the family member of a qualified person.

(3)   A person may be removed from the United Kingdom:

(a)   if he is not, or has ceased to be:

(i)   a qualified person; or
(ii)   the family member of a qualified person;

(b)   if he is a qualified person or the family member of such a person, but the Secretary of State has decided that his removal is justified on the grounds of public policy, public security or public health.

[A.4.79]
22   Refusal to issue or renew residence permit or residence document, and revocation of residence permit, residence document or EEA family permit
(1)   The Secretary of State may refuse to issue a residence permit or residence document (as the case may be) if the refusal is justified on grounds of public policy, public security or public health.

(2)   The Secretary of State may revoke, or refuse to renew, a residence permit or residence document if:

(a)   the revocation or refusal is justified on grounds of public policy, public security or public health; or
(b)   the person to whom the residence permit or residence document was issued:

    (i)   is not, or has ceased to be, a qualified person;
    (ii)   is not, or has ceased to be, the family member of a qualified person.

(3)   An immigration officer may, at the time of the arrival in the United Kingdom of a person who is not an EEA national, revoke that person's residence document if he is not at that time the family member of a qualified person.

(4)   An immigration officer may, at the time of a person's arrival in the United Kingdom, revoke that person's EEA family permit if:

(a)   the revocation is justified on grounds of public policy, public security or public health; or
(b)   the person is not at that time the family member of a qualified person.

[A.4.80]
23   Public policy, public security and public health
Decisions taken on grounds of public policy, public security or public health ('the relevant grounds') must be taken in accordance with the following principles:

(a)   the relevant grounds must not be invoked to secure economic ends;
(b)   a decision taken on one or more of the relevant grounds must be based exclusively on the personal conduct of the individual in respect of whom the decision is taken;
(c)   a person's previous criminal convictions do not, in themselves, justify a decision on grounds of public policy or public security;
(d)   a decision to refuse admission to the United Kingdom, or to refuse to grant the first residence permit or residence document, to a person on the grounds that he has a disease or disability may be justified only if the disease or disability is of a type specified in Schedule 1 to these Regulations;
(e)   a disease or disability contracted after a person has been granted a first residence permit or first residence document does not justify a decision to refuse to renew the permit or document or a decision to remove him;
(f)   a person is to be informed of the grounds of public policy, public security or public health upon which the decision taken in his case is based unless it would be contrary to the interests of national security to do so.

PART VI
APPLICATION OF THE 1971 ACT AND THE 1999 ACT

[A.4.81]
24 Persons claiming right of admission
(1)   This regulation applies to a person who claims a right of admission to the United Kingdom under regulation 12 as:

(a) the family member of an EEA national, where he is not himself an EEA national; or
(b) an EEA national, where there is reason to believe that he may fall to be excluded from the United Kingdom on grounds of public policy, public security or public health.

(2)   A person to whom this regulation applies is to be treated as if he were a person seeking leave to enter the United Kingdom under the 1971 Act and paragraphs 2 to 4, 7, 16 to 18 and 21 to 24 of Schedule 2 to the 1971 Act (administrative provisions as to control on entry etc) apply accordingly, except that:

(a) the reference in paragraph 2(1) to the purpose for which the immigration officer may examine any persons who have arrived in the United Kingdom is to be read as a reference to the purpose of determining whether he is a person who is to be granted admission under these Regulations; and
(b) the references in paragraph 4(2A) and in paragraph 7 to a person who is, or may be, given leave to enter are to be read as references to a person who is, or may be, granted admission under these Regulations.

(3)   For so long as a person to whom this regulation applies is detained, or temporarily admitted or released while liable to detention, under the powers conferred by Schedule 2 to the 1971 Act, he is deemed not to have been admitted to the United Kingdom.

[A.4.82]
25 Persons refused admission
(1)   This regulation applies to a person who is in the United Kingdom and has been refused admission to the United Kingdom:

(a) because he does not meet the requirements of regulation 12 (including where he does not meet those requirements because his residence document or EEA family permit has been revoked by an immigration officer in accordance with regulation 22); or
(b) in accordance with regulation 21(1) or (2).

(2)   A person to whom this regulation applies is to be treated as if he were a person refused leave to enter under the 1971 Act, and the provisions set out in paragraph (3) apply accordingly.

(3)   Those provisions are:

(a) paragraphs 8, 10, 11, 16 to 18 and 21 to 24 of Schedule 2 to the 1971 Act;
(b) paragraph 19 of Schedule 2 to the 1971 Act, except that the reference in

that paragraph to a certificate of entitlement, entry clearance or work permit is to be read as a reference to an EEA family permit or residence document; and

(c) sections 67 and 68 of the 1999 Act (appeal concerning objection to removal destination), except that the reference in section 68(1)(b) to a person who held a current entry clearance or was a person named in a current work permit is to be read as a reference to a person who held an EEA family permit or residence document.

[A.4.83]
26   Persons subject to removal
(1)   This regulation applies to a person whom it has been decided to remove from the United Kingdom in accordance with regulation 21(3).

(2)   Where the decision is under sub-paragraph (a) of regulation 21(3), the person is to be treated as if he were a person to whom section 10(1)(a) of the 1999 Act applied, and section 10 of that Act (removal of certain persons unlawfully in the United Kingdom) is to apply accordingly.

(3)   Where the decision is under sub-paragraph (b) of regulation 21(3), the person is to be treated as if he were a person to whom section 3(5)(a) of the 1971 Act (liability to deportation) applied, and section 5 of that Act (procedure for deportation) and Schedule 3 to that Act (supplementary provisions as to deportation) are to apply accordingly.

PART VII
APPEALS

[A.4.84]
27   Interpretation of Part VII
(1)   In this Part:

'the 1997 Act' means the Special Immigration Appeals Commission Act 1997;

'adjudicator' and 'Commission' have the same meaning as in the 1999 Act;

'Refugee Convention' has the same meaning as in the 1999 Act.

(2)   In this Part, 'EEA decision' means a decision under these Regulations, or under Regulation 1251/70, which concerns a person's:

(a) removal from the United Kingdom;
(b) entitlement to be admitted to the United Kingdom; or
(c) entitlement to be issued with or to have renewed, or not to have revoked, a residence permit or residence document.

(3)   For the purposes of this Part [—

(a) a decision-maker racially discriminates against a person if he acts, or fails to act, in relation to that other person in a way which is unlawful by virtue of section 19B of the Race Relations Act 1976; and (b)] a decision-maker acts in breach of a person's human rights if he acts, or fails to act, in relation to that other person in a way which is made unlawful by section 6(1) of the Human Rights Act 1998.

Note   Words in square brackets in para (3) inserted by SI 2001/865 in force 2 April 2001.

[A.4.85]
28   Scope of Part VII
This Part applies to persons who have, or who claim to have, rights under these Regulations or under Regulation 1251/70.

[A.4.86]
29   Appeal rights
(1)   Subject to section 80(12) of the 1999 Act (requirement to produce a valid national identity card or passport), and to regulation 33, a person may appeal under these Regulations against an EEA decision.

(2)   Such an appeal may in particular be made on the ground that, in taking the decision, the decision-maker acted in breach of that person's human rights [or racially discriminated against that person].

(3)   Except where an appeal lies to the Commission as a result of regulation 31, an appeal under these Regulations lies to an adjudicator.

(4)   Schedule 4 to the 1999 Act (appeals), to the extent (and with the modifications) set out in Schedule 2 to these Regulations, has effect in relation to appeals to the adjudicator under these Regulations.

Note   Words in square brackets in para (2) inserted by SI 2001/865 in force 2 April 2001.

[A.4.87]
30   Out-of-country appeals
(1)   Regulation 29 does not entitle a person to appeal while he is in the United Kingdom against an EEA decision:

(a)   to refuse to admit him to the United Kingdom;
(b)   to refuse to revoke a deportation order made against him;
(c)   to refuse to issue him with an EEA family permit.

(2)   Paragraph (1) also applies to a decision to remove someone from the United Kingdom which is consequent upon a refusal to admit him.

(3)   But paragraphs (1)(a) and (2) do not apply:

(a)   where the right of appeal is to the Commission;
(b)   where a ground of the appeal is that, in taking the decision, the decision-maker acted in breach of the appellant's human rights; or

(c) where the person held an EEA family permit, or a residence permit or residence document, on his arrival in the United Kingdom.

[A.4.88]
31 Appeals to the Commission
(1) An appeal in respect of an EEA decision mentioned in regulation 27(2)(a) lies to the Commission where paragraph (2) applies.

(2) This paragraph applies if the ground of the decision to remove the person concerned was that his removal is conducive to the public good as being in the interests of national security or of the relations between the United Kingdom and any other country or for other reasons of a political nature.

(3) An appeal in respect of an EEA decision mentioned in regulation 27(2)(b) lies to the Commission where paragraph (4) applies.

(4) This paragraph applies if:

(a) the Secretary of State certifies that directions have been given by the Secretary of State (and not by a person acting under his authority) for the person concerned not to be admitted to the United Kingdom on the ground that his exclusion is conducive to the public good; or
(b) admission was refused in compliance with any such directions.

(5) An appeal in respect of an EEA decision mentioned in regulation 27(2)(c) lies to the Commission where paragraph (6) applies.

(6) This paragraph applies where the decision was taken in connection with an EEA decision mentioned in regulation 27(2)(a) or (b) in respect of which an appeal lies to the Commission in accordance with this regulation.

[A.4.89]
32 *(Amends the Special Immigration Appeals Commission Act 1997, ss 2 and 2A and the Immigration and Asylum Act 1999, Sch 14.)*

[A.4.90]
33 Proof of family membership
Where for the purposes of an appeal under these Regulations a person claims to be the family member of another person, he must produce:

(a) an EEA family permit; or
(b) other proof that he is related as claimed to that other person.

[A.4.91]
34 Effects of appeals to the adjudicator
(1) If a person in the United Kingdom appeals under regulation 29 against an EEA decision to refuse to admit him to the United Kingdom, any directions previously given by virtue of the refusal for his removal from the United

Kingdom cease to have effect, except in so far as they have already been carried out, and no directions may be so given while the appeal is pending.

(2)　If a person appeals under regulation 29 against an EEA decision to remove him from the United Kingdom, any directions given under section 10 of the 1999 Act or Schedule 3 of the 1971 Act for his removal from the United kingdom are to have no effect, except in so far as they have already been carried out, while the appeal is pending.

(3)　But the provisions of Part I of Schedule 2, or as the case may be, Schedule 3 to the 1971 Act with respect to detention and persons liable to detention apply to a person appealing under regulation 29 against a refusal to admit him or a decision to remove him as if there were in force directions for his removal from the United Kingdom, except that he may not be detained on board a ship or aircraft so as to compel him to leave the United Kingdom while the appeal is pending.

(4)　In calculating the period of two months limited by paragraph 8(2) of Schedule 2 to the 1971 Act for:

(a)　the giving of directions under that paragraph for the removal of a person from the United Kingdom, and

(b)　the giving of a notice of intention to give such directions,

any period during which there is pending an appeal by him under regulation 29 is to be disregarded.

(5)　If a person appeals under regulation 29 against an EEA decision to remove him from the United Kingdom, a deportation order is not to be made against him under section 5 of the 1971 Act while the appeal is pending.

(6)　Paragraph 29 of Schedule 2 to the 1971 Act (grant of bail pending appeal) applies to a person who has an appeal pending under regulation 29 as it applies to a person who has an appeal pending under section 59, 65, 66, 67, 69(1) or (5) or 71 of the 1999 Act.

(7)　For the purposes of this regulation, and subject to paragraphs (8) and (9), an appeal is to be treated as pending during the period beginning when notice of appeal is given and ending when the appeal is finally determined, withdrawn or abandoned.

(8)　An appeal is not to be treated as finally determined while a further appeal may be brought; and, if such a further appeal is brought, the original appeal is not to be treated as finally determined until the further appeal is determined, withdrawn or abandoned.

(9)　A pending appeal is not to be treated as abandoned solely because the appellant leaves the United Kingdom.

(10)　This regulation does not apply to an appeal which lies to the Commission as a result of regulation 31.

[A.4.92]
35   Transitional provisions (EEA decisions)
(1)   Regulation 29 does not have effect in relation to an EEA decision made before 2nd October 2000.

(2)   Notwithstanding the revocation of the Immigration (European Economic Area) Order 1994 by regulation 1(2):

(a)   articles 15(1) and 20(2)(b) of the Order continue to have effect where the decision to exclude a person from the United Kingdom was made before 2nd October 2000;
(b)   articles 15(2) and 20(2)(d) continue to have effect where the decision to remove a person from the United Kingdom was made before 2nd October 2000;
(c)   articles 18 and 20(2)(c) continue to have effect where the decision to refuse or withdraw a residence permit or residence document was made before 2nd October 2000.

[A.4.93]
36   Transitional provisions (the 1997 Act)
(1)   Regulation 32 does not have effect in relation to any decision made before 2nd October 2000.

(2)   In relation to such decisions, section 2(1) of the 1997 Act continues to have effect without the amendments made by regulation 32.

(3)   Section 2(1)(c) of the 1997 Act (appeals against a decision to make a deportation order) continues to have effect without the amendments made by regulation 32 in relation to any person:

(a)   who applied during the regularisation period fixed by section 9 of the 1999 Act, in accordance with the Immigration (Regularisation Period for Overstayers) Regulations 2000, for leave to remain in the United Kingdom; and
(b)   on whom the Secretary of State has since served a notice of his decision to make a deportation order.

(4)   In the case of an appeal in respect of which section 2(1)(b) of the 1997 Act (appeals against variation of limited leave or refusal to vary it) continues to have effect in accordance with paragraph (2), section 7A(7) of the 1997 Act (pending appeals) applies as if the reference to section 62(3) of the 1999 Act were a reference to section 14(3) of the 1971 Act.

(5)   In the case of an appeal in respect of which section 2(1) of the 1997 Act continues to have effect in accordance with paragraph (2) or (3), Schedule 2 of the 1997 Act (supplementary provisions as to appeals) has effect without the amendments made by the 1999 Act.

SCHEDULE 1
SPECIFIED DISEASES AND DISABILITIES

Regulation 23(d)

[A.4.94]
1 The following diseases may justify a decision taken on grounds of public health:

(a) diseases subject to quarantine listed in International Health Regulation No 2 of the World Health Organisation of 25th May 1951;
(b) tuberculosis of the respiratory system in an active state or showing a tendency to develop;
(c) syphilis;
(d) other infectious diseases or contagious parasitic diseases, if they are the subject of provisions for the protection of public health in the United Kingdom.

2 The following diseases or disabilities may justify a decision taken on grounds of public policy or public security:

(a) drug addiction;
(b) profound mental disturbance; manifest conditions of psychotic disturbance with agitation, delirium, hallucinations or confusion.

SCHEDULE 2
APPEALS TO THE ADJUDICATOR

Regulation 29(4)

[A.4.95]
1 In this Schedule, unless the context otherwise requires, a reference to a paragraph is a reference to a paragraph of Schedule 4 to the 1999 Act.

2 Subject to paragraph 3 of this Schedule:

[paragraphs 1 to 9A];

paragraphs 21 to 23; and

paragraph 24(2)

have effect in relation to appeals to the adjudicator under these Regulations.

3 (1) *(Amends the Immigration and Asylum Act 1999.)*

(2) *(Amends the Immigration and Asylum Act 1999.)*

(3) Paragraph 9 has effect only to the etent that it relates to a claim under the Human Rights Convention.

(4) *(Amends the Immigration and Asylum Act 1999.)*

Note Words in square brackets in para (2) inserted by SI 2001/865, in force 2 April 2001.

IMMIGRATION APPEALS (FAMILY VISITOR) (NO 2) REGULATIONS 2000
SI 2000/2446

Made   11 September 2000
Laid before Parliament   13 September 2000
Coming into force   2 October 2000

[A.4.96]
1   Citation, commencement and revocation
(1)   These Regulations may be cited as the Immigration Appeals (Family Visitor) (No 2) Regulations 2000 and shall come into force on 2nd October 2000.

(2)   The Immigration Appeals (Family Visitor) Regulations 2000 are hereby revoked.

[A.4.97]
2   Interpretation
(1)   In these Regulations:

'the Act' means the Immigration and Asylum Act 1999;

'entry clearance officer' means a person responsible for the grant or refusal of entry clearance;

'fee' means the fee required to be paid in accordance with regulation 3(1);

'first cousin' means, in relation to a person, the son or daughter of his uncle or aunt;

'repayment' means any repayment required to be made in accordance with regulation 3(3).

(2)   For the purposes of section 60(10) of the Act, a 'family visitor' is a person who applies for entry clearance to enter the United Kingdom as a visitor, in order to visit:

(a)   his spouse, father, mother, son, daughter, grandfather, grandmother, grandson, granddaughter, brother, sister, uncle, aunt, nephew, niece or first cousin;
(b)   the father, mother, brother or sister of his spouse;
(c)   the spouse of his son or daughter;
(d)   his stepfather, stepmother, stepson, stepdaughter, stepbrother or stepsister; or
(e)   a person with whom he lived as a member of an unmarried couple for at least two of the three years before the day on which his application for entry clearance was made.

[A.4.98]
3   Fees
(1)   A family visitor who appeals under section 59 of the Act ('the appellant') must pay to an entry clearance officer at the place where his application for entry clearance was made:

(a)   [£125], if he elects a hearing;
(b)   [£50], in all other cases.

(2)   The appeal is not to be entertained unless the fee has been paid by the appellant.

(3)   If the appeal is successful, the fee is to be repaid to the appellant by an entry clearance officer.

Note   Sums in square brackets substituted by SI 2001/52, in force 12 January 2001.

[A.4.99]
4   Method of payment
(1)   The fee is to be paid, and the repayment made, in currency circulating at the place of payment.

(2)   The rate of exchange to be used for calculating the equivalent of the fee or repayment in foreign currency is to be based on the rate of exchange which is generally prevailing on the date, and at the place, of payment of the fee.

IMMIGRATION (DESIGNATION OF TRAVEL BANS) ORDER 2000
SI 2000/2724

Made 3 October 2000
Laid before Parliament 9 October 2000
Coming into force 10 October 2000

[A.4.100]
1 This Order may be cited as the Immigration (Designation of Travel Bans) Order 2000 and shall come into force on 10th October 2000.

[A.4.101]
2 The instruments listed in the Schedule to this Order are designated for the purposes of section 8B(4) and (5) of the Immigration Act 1971.

[A.4.102]
3 Section 8B(1), (2) and (3) of the Immigration Act 1971 shall not apply in any case where:

(a) failure to apply these provisions would not be contrary to the United Kingdom's obligations under any of the instruments designated by article 2 of this Order,

(b) to apply these provisions would be contrary to the United Kingdom's obligations under the Convention for the Protection of Human Rights and Fundamental Freedoms, agreed by the Council of Europe at Rome on 4th November 1950, or

(c) to apply these provisions would be contrary to the United Kingdom's obligations under the Convention relating to the Status of Refugees done at Geneva on 28th July 1951 and the Protocol to that Convention.

SCHEDULE
DESIGNATED INSTRUMENTS

[A.4.103]

Article 2

[PART 1
RESOLUTIONS OF THE SECURITY COUNCIL OF THE UNITED NATIONS

Resolution 1127 (1997) of 28th August 1997 (Angola)

Resolution 1171 (1998) of 5th June 1998 (Sierra Leone)]

Note Substituted by SI 2000/3338, in force 21 December 2000.

[PART 2
INSTRUMENTS MADE BY THE COUNCIL OF THE EUROPEAN UNION

Common Position 97/759/CFSP of 30th October 1997 (Angola)

Common Position 96/635/CFSP of 28th October 1996 (Burma)

Common Position 2000/346/CFSP of 26th April 2000 (Burma)

Common Position 98/240/CFSP of 19th March 1998 (Federal Republic of Yugoslavia)

Common Position 98/725/CFSP of 14th December 1998 (Federal Republic of Yugoslavia)

Common Position 99/318/CFSP of 10th May 1999 (Federal Republic of Yugoslavia)

Common Position 2000/56/CFSP of 24th January 2000 (Federal Republic of Yugoslavia)

Common Position 2000/696/CFSP of 10th November 2000 (Federal Republic of Yugoslavia)

Common Position 98/409/CFSP of 29th June 1998 (Sierra Leone)]

Note Substituted by SI 2000/3338, in force 21 December 2000.

IMMIGRATION SERVICES COMMISSIONER (REGISTRATION FEE) ORDER 2000
SI 2000/2735

Made   5 October 2000
Laid before Parliament   9 October 2000
Coming into force   30 October 2000

[A.4.104]
Citation and commencement
1   This Order may be cited as the Immigration Services Commissioner (Registration Fee) Order 2000 and shall come into force on 30th October 2000.

[A.4.105]
Interpretation
2   In this Order:

'the Act' means the Immigration and Asylum Act 1999;

'registration' means registration or (as the case may be) continued registration, under section 84(2)(a) or (b) of the Act;

'relevant advisers' means, in respect of:

(a)   an individual, that individual together with:

(i)   the number of employees of that individual who provide immigration advice or immigration services, excluding such employees who are qualified persons under sections 84(2)(c) to (f) of the Act, or who are persons to whom section 84(4) of the Act applies; and

(ii)   the number of persons who provide immigration advice or immigration services who work under the supervision of that individual and his employees, excluding such persons who are qualified persons under sections 84(2)(c) to (f) of the Act, or who are persons to whom section 84(4) of the Act applies;

(b)   a body corporate or unincorporate:

(i)   the number of members and employees of that body who provide immigration advice or immigration services, excluding such members and employees who are qualified persons under sections 84(2)(c) to (f) of the Act, or who are persons to whom section 84(4) of the Act applies; and

(ii)   the number of persons who provide immigration advice or immigration services who work under the supervision of such members and employees, excluding such persons who are qualified persons under sections 84(2)(c) to (f) of the Act, or who are persons to whom section 84(4) of the Act applies;

'sole immigration adviser' means an individual who does not employ any other person to provide immigration advice or immigration services and who does not have any person who works under his supervision or the supervision of any of his employees who provides immigration advice or immigration services.

[A.4.106]
Fee for registration
3 The fee payable by a sole immigration adviser for registration shall be £1,800.

[A.4.107]
4 The fee payable by any other person for registration shall be determined by the number of relevant advisers in respect of that person at the date of his application for registration, and shall be the sum specified for such number of relevant advisers in the Schedule to this Order.

SCHEDULE

Article 4

[A.4.108]

Number of relevant advisers	*Fee payable for registration*
1	£1,800
2 to 4	£2,675
5 to 9	£3,475
10 to 19	£4,275
20 or over	£6,000

IMMIGRATION SERVICES TRIBUNAL RULES 2000
SI 2000/2739

Made 4 October 2000
Laid before Parliament 9 October 2000
Coming into force 30 October 2000

[A.4.109]
1   Citation and commencement
These Rules may be cited as the Immigration Services Tribunal Rules 2000 and shall come into force on 30th October 2000.

[A.4.110]
2   Interpretation
In these Rules:

'appeal' means an appeal under section 87(2) against a decision of the Commissioner, and 'appellant' shall be construed accordingly;

'charge' means a disciplinary charge laid by the Commissioner under paragraph 9(1)(e) of Schedule 5 and 'person charged' shall be construed accordingly;

'procedural direction' means a direction relating to any of the following matters:

(a)   the suspension of the effect of the decision appealed against pending determination of the appeal (rule 10);

(b)   the cancellation or variation of a direction suspending the effect of a decision (rule 11);

(c)   restrictions on or prohibition of the provision of immigration advice or immigration services pending determination of a charge (rule 15);

(d)   the consolidation of the proceedings with any other proceedings before the Tribunal, whether involving the same or different parties (rule 16(2)(a));

(e)   the hearing of any two or more sets of proceedings together (rule 16(2)(b));

(f)   the extension of the time limited by these Rules for any step in the proceedings (rule 16(2)(c));

(g)   what witnesses are to be heard at the full hearing of an appeal or charge (rule 17);

(h)   the provision of information, or disclosure of documents, by any party to the proceedings to any other party or to the Tribunal (rule 18);

(i)   the date for the full hearing of an appeal or charge (rule 19);

(j)   who may represent any party to an appeal or charge (rule 21(d));

(k)   the setting aside of a decision made in the absence of a party and the re-listing of the proceedings for hearing (rule 25);

(l)   any other arrangement which, in the opinion of the Tribunal, may facilitate the determination of the appeal or charge (rule 16(2)(d));

a section or Schedule cited by number alone means the section or Schedule so numbered in the Immigration and Asylum Act 1999;

all words and expressions defined in section 82 shall have the same meaning in these Rules.

[A.4.111]
3   Composition of the Tribunal
(1)   At the hearing of an appeal or charge, the Tribunal shall consist of a legally qualified member and two other members.

(2)   The Tribunal shall consist of a legally qualified member alone when considering or deciding, at a hearing or otherwise, whether:

(a)   to give a person permission to appeal out of time;
(b)   to make, cancel or vary a direction under paragraph 8 of Schedule 7 (suspending the effect of a relevant decision);
(c)   to make a direction under paragraph 9(3) of Schedule 5 (restricting or prohibiting the provision of immigration advice or immigration services while the Tribunal deals with a charge);
(d)   to make any other procedural direction; or
(e)   to give effect to a draft order settling proceedings by consent.

(3)   At a preliminary hearing, the Tribunal shall consist of a legally qualified member sitting alone if the hearing relates solely to procedural directions, and of a legally qualified member and two other members otherwise.

(4)   Subject to the preceding paragraphs of this rule and to rule 4, every function of the Tribunal may be exercised by such member of the Tribunal or of its staff as the President shall direct, either generally or in relation to a specified case or description of cases.

[A.4.112]
4   The Register
(1)   There shall be a Register of proceedings pending or concluded before the Tribunal.

(2)   That Register shall record:

(a)   every appeal commenced and every charge laid before the Tribunal, together with the number allotted to it;
(b)   a brief statement of the way in which each appeal or charge was determined.

(3)   That Register shall be open to inspection by the public during normal office hours.

[A.4.113]
5   Notice of appeal
(1)   An appeal shall be commenced by sending to the Tribunal written notice

of appeal, together with a copy of the decision against which the appeal is brought.

(2)   Every notice of appeal shall be signed and dated, and contain the following information:

(a)   the name and address of the appellant;
(b)   the name and address of any person representing the appellant;
(c)   the nature and date of the decision against which the appeal is brought;
(d)   the grounds of the appeal; and
(e)   where the appeal is out of time, the reason for the delay.

[A.4.114]
6   Acknowledgment of appeal
As soon as practicable after receiving the notice of appeal, the Tribunal shall:

(a)   allot a number to the appeal and enter it in the Register mentioned in rule 4; and
(b)   send an acknowledgment to the appellant and a copy of the notice of appeal to the Commissioner.

[A.4.115]
7   Reply to notice of appeal
(1)   Within the period specified in paragraph (2) below, the Commissioner may send to the appellant and the Tribunal a notice in reply, containing the Commissioner's reasons for opposing the appeal.

(2)   The notice in reply may be sent at any time within 28 days from:

(a)   where the appeal is out of time, the Tribunal's decision to permit the appellant to appeal out of time;
(b)   otherwise, the sending to the Commissioner of the copy of the notice of appeal.

[A.4.116]
8   Time for appealing
The period within which an appeal against any relevant decision of the Commissioner as defined in section 87(3) can be brought is 28 days after the decision is notified to the person aggrieved; and where the decision is notified in writing, the decision shall be deemed to be notified as soon as written notice of it is sent.

[A.4.117]
9   Permission to appeal out of time
(1)   A person aggrieved by a decision of the Commissioner may appeal against it after the expiry of the period limited by rule 8 with the permission of the Tribunal.

(2)   An application for permission under this rule shall be made in the notice

of appeal, and this notice shall be acknowledged, and a copy sent to the Commissioner, in accordance with rule 6; but no further steps in the appeal shall be taken until the application for permission has been granted.

(3)   The Commissioner may, within 14 days after the sending to him of a copy of a notice of appeal containing an application for permission under paragraph (2) above, send the Tribunal a written statement consenting or objecting to the grant of permission; and whether or not he sends such a statement the Tribunal shall decide on the application as soon as practicable after the expiry of those 14 days.

(4)   Where the Tribunal gives permission to appeal out of time, it may concurrently make an interim direction suspending the effect of the decision appealed against.

(5)   The Tribunal may decide on an application under this rule either:

(a)   without a hearing, by consideration of the written application for permission, together with the notice from the Commissioner under paragraph (3) if any, or
(b)   at a hearing at which the applicant and the Commissioner are given the opportunity to be heard.

[A.4.118]
10   Applications for suspension of effect of decision
(1)   An application for a direction under paragraph 8 of Schedule 7 (suspending the effect of a relevant decision) shall be made by sending to the Tribunal written notice of the application; and this written notice may:

(a)   be combined with the written notice of appeal against the decision to which the direction sought relates, or
(b)   be sent after the notice of appeal and refer to that notice

and in either case shall state the grounds of the application.

(2)   As soon as practicable after receiving a notice of application under paragraph (1), the Tribunal shall send an acknowledgement to the applicant and a copy of the notice of application to the Commissioner.

(3)   Before deciding any application under this rule, the Tribunal may if it sees fit invite representations in writing from the Commissioner or hold a hearing.

(4)   Where a direction is made other than at a hearing at which both parties were present or represented, the Tribunal shall as soon as practicable notify both parties in writing of the terms of the direction.

[A.4.119]
11   Cancellation or variation of direction for suspension
(1)   An application by the Commissioner for the cancellation or variation of a direction given under paragraph 8(2) of Schedule 7 shall be made by send-

ing to the Tribunal written notice of the application, which shall state the grounds of the application.

(2) As soon as practicable after receiving a notice of application under paragraph (1), the Tribunal shall send an acknowledgement to the Commissioner and a copy of the notice of application to the appellant.

(3) Before deciding any application under this rule, the Tribunal shall either invite representations in writing from the appellant or hold a hearing at which both parties may be heard.

(4) Where a decision on an application under this rule is made other than at a hearing at which both parties were present or represented, the Tribunal shall as soon as practicable notify both parties in writing of the decision.

[A.4.120]
12 Notice of charge
(1) A charge shall be laid by sending a written notice of charge to the Tribunal.

(2) Every notice of charge shall contain the following information:

(a) the name and address for service of the person charged;
(b) the nature of the complaint giving rise to the charge;
(c) the directions under section 89 which, in the Commissioner's opinion, the Tribunal ought to make in relation to the person charged

and shall be accompanied by a copy of the written statement of the Commissioner's decision on the complaint given under paragraph 8 of Schedule 5.

[A.4.121]
13 Acknowledgement of notice of charge

As soon as practicable after receiving the notice of charge, the Tribunal shall:

(a) allot a number to the charge and enter it in the Register mentioned in rule 4; and
(b) send an acknowledgment to the Commissioner and a copy of the notice to the person charged.

[A.4.122]
14 Reply to notice of charge
Within 28 days after the sending to him of his copy of the notice of charge, the person charged may send to the Tribunal and the Commissioner a notice in reply, containing his answer to the complaint giving rise to the charge and any representations about the directions sought by the Commissioner.

[A.4.123]
15   Interim directions restricting or prohibiting provision of immigration advice or immigration services
(1)   The Commissioner may apply for a direction under paragraph 9(3) of Schedule 5 (restricting or prohibiting the provision of immigration advice or immigration services while the Tribunal deals with a charge) by sending to the Tribunal written notice of the application; and this written notice may:

(a) be combined with the written notice of charge to which the direction sought relates, or
(b) be sent after the notice of charge and refer to that notice

and in either case shall state the grounds of the application.

(2)   As soon as practicable after receiving a notice of application under paragraph (1), the Tribunal shall send an acknowledgement to the Commissioner and a copy of the notice of application to the person charged.

(3)   Before deciding any application under this rule, the Tribunal shall either invite representations in writing from the person charged or hold a hearing at which all parties may be heard.

[A.4.124]
16   Procedural directions in general
(1)   Any procedural direction provided for by these Rules may be made by the Tribunal either of its own motion or on the application of either party to the proceedings.

(2)   In addition to every other power to make directions conferred by these Rules, the Tribunal may at any time make directions providing for:

(a) the consolidation of the proceedings with any other proceedings before the Tribunal, whether involving the same or different parties;
(b) two or more sets of proceedings to be heard together;
(c) the extension of the time limited by these Rules for any step in the proceedings; or
(d) any other arrangement which, in the opinion of the Tribunal, may facilitate the determination of the appeal or charge.

(3)   Before making any procedural directions, the Tribunal may invite representations in writing or hold a hearing.

[A.4.125]
17   Witnesses
(1)   Within 42 days after the Tribunal has sent an acknowledgement under rule 6(b) or 13(b), each party shall notify the Tribunal in writing of the names of all witnesses whom he proposes to call in the proceedings.

(2)   The Tribunal may invite any person to appear as a witness at the hearing of an appeal or charge.

(3)   At or before the time when it makes arrangements for the hearing, the Tribunal shall notify all parties to the proceedings of the names of all witnesses who are due to appear at the hearing.

[A.4.126]
18   Documents
(1)   Within 42 days after the Tribunal has sent an acknowledgement under rule 6(b) or 13(b), each party shall:

(a)   send to the Tribunal copies of all documents on which he proposes to rely in the proceedings; and
(b)   send to the Tribunal a list of all other documents in his possession or control which may be relevant to issues in the proceedings, stating which he is willing to produce and which he objects to producing, with the ground of any objection.

(2)   The Tribunal, upon receiving the information and documents referred to in paragraph (1) above from any party to the proceedings, shall send copies to all other parties.

(3)   The Tribunal may at any time direct a party to the proceedings to disclose a specified document or documents of a specified description to the other party or parties and to the Tribunal.

(4)   At or before the time when he makes arrangements for the hearing, the Tribunal shall send to each party to the proceedings copies of such of the following documents as are not already in that party's possession:

(a)   all documents furnished to the Tribunal by any party in response to procedural directions;
(b)   in the case of an appeal, the decision appealed against;
(c)   in the case of a charge, the Commissioner's statement of his decision on the complaint underlying the charge; and
(d)   any other documents in the Tribunal's possession which it considers relevant.

[A.4.127]
19   Arrangements for the hearing
(1)   The Tribunal shall make arrangements for the hearing of an appeal or charge as soon as it is satisfied that:

(a)   all outstanding procedural directions have been complied with and there is sufficient information to allow a fair determination of the issues; or
(b)   a party has failed to comply with any reasonable directions as to the conduct of the proceedings and it is expedient for the proceedings to be determined.

(2)   In selecting a date for the hearing, the Tribunal shall consult each party to the proceedings, except that if the circumstance set out in paragraph (1)(b) obtains, the hearing may be arranged so as to take place in the absence of the party in default.

(3)   The President may direct that there shall be one or more preliminary hearings, either on a question of law or for any other purpose.

[A.4.128]
20   The hearing
(1)   Every hearing of an appeal or charge shall be open to the public unless the Tribunal directs otherwise.

(2)   A hearing may be held in the absence of a party either:

(a) in the circumstance set out in rule 19(1)(b), or
(b) if the party has been notified of the date of the hearing but has failed, with-out reasonable excuse, to appear before the Tribunal.

(3)   At any time in the course of the hearing the Tribunal may make proce-dural directions, including a direction that the hearing be adjourned.

(4)   At the conclusion of a hearing, the members of the Tribunal shall retire to consider their determination.

(5)   Any member or representative of the Council on Tribunals shall be allowed to be present at the hearing, including any part of the hearing from which the public is excluded.

(6)   If the members considering an appeal or charge disagree, they shall decide by a majority.

[A.4.129]
21   Representation
At the hearing of an appeal or charge, the appellant or person charged may appear in person or be represented by:

(a) a person with a general qualification within the meaning of section 71 of the Courts and Legal Services Act 1990;
(b) an advocate or solicitor in Scotland;
(c) a member of the Bar of Northern Ireland or solicitor of the Supreme Court of Northern Ireland; or
(d) with the permission of the Tribunal, any other person.

[A.4.130]
22   Evidence
(1)   Oral evidence may be given either on oath or affirmation or unsworn, as the Tribunal may decide.

(2)   Subject to paragraph (3) below, the appellant in appeal proceedings, and the Commissioner in charge proceedings, shall have the burden of proving the facts on which he relies; and in either case proof shall be on a balance of prob-abilities and the strict rules of evidence shall not apply.

(3)   The burden of proving that any person has been guilty of criminal or

fraudulent conduct shall be on the party so alleging, and proof shall be beyond reasonable doubt; but the fact that a person has been convicted of an offence shall be sufficient evidence that he committed it.

[A.4.131]
23   Withdrawal of proceedings
(1)   An appellant may withdraw his appeal, or the Commissioner may withdraw a charge, by sending written notice to that effect to the Tribunal at any time between the sending of the notice of appeal or charge and the date of the main hearing.

(2)   The Tribunal shall send a copy of a notice under paragraph (1) to every other party to the proceedings.

(3)   The parties to any proceedings may at any time apply to settle them by sending an agreed draft order to the Tribunal.

(4)   On receiving an agreed draft order, the Tribunal shall either:

(a)   make an order in the terms of that draft, or
(b)   state its reasons for not making an order in those terms;

and the Tribunal shall send the order, or as the case may be a letter recording its reasons for not making an order, to the parties.

[A.4.132]
24   Determination of the appeal or charge
(1)   The Tribunal may either announce its decision on any appeal or charge at the conclusion of the main hearing or reserve its decision.

(2)   In either case, as soon as possible after the decision the Tribunal shall draw up a formal order, stating:

(a)   whether the appeal or charge is upheld or dismissed; and
(b)   any direction made by the Tribunal under section 88 or 89.

(3)   The order shall be sent to all parties to the proceedings and shall be accompanied by a statement of the reasons for the Tribunal's decision, and both the order and the statement of reasons shall be signed by the member presiding at the hearing (or if he is unavailable, by another member who was present at the hearing).

[A.4.133]
25   Reopening of determination made in absence of party
(1)   Where a decision is made following a hearing in the absence of one of the parties, that party may apply to the Tribunal to set aside its decision and re-list the proceedings for hearing.

(2)   An application under paragraph (1) above shall not be granted unless the applicant satisfies the Tribunal that he had a reasonable excuse for failing to comply with the direction, or to attend the hearing, as the case may be.

[A.4.134]
26 Irregularities

(1)   Any irregularity resulting from failure to comply with any provision of these Rules before the Tribunal has reached its decision shall not of itself render the proceedings void.

(2)   In any such case the Tribunal shall, if it considers that any person may have been prejudiced, take such steps as it thinks fit to cure the irregularity before reaching its decision.

(3)   Clerical mistakes in any document recording a decision of the Tribunal, or errors arising in such a document from an accidental slip or omission, may be corrected by a legally qualified member.

[A.4.135]
27 Notices etc

(1)   Any notice or other document required or authorised by these Rules to be sent or given to any person or authority may be delivered or sent by post to an address, or sent by fax to a fax number, specified by the person or authority to whom the notice or document is directed.

(2)   If any notice or other document is sent or given to a person appearing to the authority or person sending it to represent that party, it shall be deemed to have been sent or given to that party.

[A.4.136]
28 Time

Where the time limited by these Rules for doing any thing expires on a Saturday, Sunday, Christmas day, Good Friday or bank holiday, the time limit shall be deemed to have been complied with if that thing is done on the next succeeding working day.

IMMIGRATION AND ASYLUM ACT 1999 (COMMENCE-MENT NO 6, TRANSITIONAL AND CONSEQUENTIAL PROVISIONS) ORDER 2000
SI 2000/2444

Made 11 September 2000

[A.4.137]

1 Citation and interpretation

(1) This Order may be cited as the Immigration and Asylum Act 1999 (Commencement No 6, Transitional and Consequential Provisions) Order 2000.

(2) In this Order:

'the 1971 Act' means the Immigration Act 1971;

'the 1993 Act' means the Asylum and Immigration Appeals Act 1993;

'the 1996 Act' means the Asylum and Immigration Act 1996;

'the 1997 Act' means the Special Immigration Appeals Commission Act 1997;

'the 1999 Act' means the Immigration and Asylum Act 1999.

[A.4.138]
2 Commencement
The provisions of the 1999 Act specified in column 1 of Schedule 1 to this Order shall come into force on the date specified in column 2 of that Schedule, subject to the transitional provisions contained in this Order, but where a particular purpose is specified in relation to any such provision in column 3 of that Schedule, the provision concerned shall come into force on that date only for that purpose.

[A.4.139]
3 Transitional provisions
(1) Subject to Schedule 2:

(a) the new appeals provisions are not to have effect in relation to events which took place before 2nd October 2000 and, notwithstanding their repeal by the provisions of the 1999 Act commenced by this Order, the old appeals provisions are to continue to have effect in relation to such events;
(b) the new procedural provisions are to apply to appeals under the old appeals provisions as well as the new appeals provisions; and
(c) references in the new procedural provisions to the new appeal rights (however expressed) are to be construed as including a reference to the equivalent provision of the old appeal rights.

(2)   Schedule 2, which makes further transitional provision in respect of the 1999 Act, has effect.

[A.4.140]
4   Definitions for transitional provisions
(1)   In article 3:

(a) 'the new appeals provisions' means sections 59, 61, 63, 65, 66, 67 and 69 of the 1999 Act; together with any provision (including subordinate legislation) of:

    (i)   the 1999 Act; and
    (ii) the 1971 and 1993 Acts (as amended by the 1999 Act);

which refers to those provisions;
(b) 'the old appeals provisions' means:

    (i)   sections 13 (but not subsections (3AA) and (3AB)), 14, 15, 16, 17 of the 1971 Act;
    (ii) subsections (1) to (4) of section 8 of the 1993 Act; and
    (iii) subsections (1) and (2) of section 3 of the 1996 Act;

together with:

    (iv) any subordinate legislation which applies to those provisions; and
    (v) any provision of the old Immigration Acts (including subordinate legislation) which refers to those provisions;

(c) 'the new procedural provisions' means:

    (i)   subsections (5) to (10) of section 58 of the 1999 Act; and
    (ii) paragraphs 6 to 8 and 21 to 24 of Schedule 4 to the 1999 Act.

(2)   For the purposes of article 3, an event takes place when:

(a) a notice is served;
(b) a decision is made or taken;
(c) directions are given; and
(d) a certificate is issued.

(3)   For the purposes of article 3 and Schedule 2:

(a) a notice is served;
(b) a decision is made or taken;
(c) directions are given; and
(d) a certificate is issued;

on the day on which it is or they are sent to the person concerned, if sent by post or by fax, or delivered to that person, if delivered by hand.

(4)   In this article:

(a) 'the old Immigration Acts' means the 1971 Act, the 1993 Act and the 1996 Act, all without the amendments made by the 1999 Act;
(b) 'the person concerned' means the person who is the subject of the notice,

decision, directions or certificate or the person who appears to be his representative; and

(c) a reference to the issue of a certificate is a reference to the issue of a certificate in relation to the removal of asylum claimants to safe third countries.

[A.4.141]
5   Consequential provision
The reference in section 46(3)(a) of the Criminal Justice Act 1991 to a person who is liable to deportation under section 3(5) of the 1971 Act is to be read, from 2nd October 2000, as including a reference to a person who may be removed from the United Kingdom in accordance with section 10 of the 1999 Act.

SCHEDULES 1 AND (2)

[A.4.142]
(*Omitted for the purposes of this work.*)

IMMIGRATION AND ASYLUM ACT 1999 (COMMENCEMENT NO 8 AND TRANSITIONAL PROVISIONS) ORDER 2000
SI 2000/3099

Made 19 November 2000

[A.4.143]
Citation and interpretation
1 This Order may be cited as the Immigration and Asylum Act 1999 (Commencement No 8 and Transitional Provisions) Order 2000.
2 In this Order 'the 1999 Act' means the Immigration and Asylum Act 1999.

[A.4.144]
Commencement
3 The provisions of the 1999 Act specified in column 1 of the Schedule to this Order shall come into force on 11th December 2000, but where a particular purpose is specified in relation to any such provision in column 2 of that Schedule, the provision shall come into force on that date only for that purpose.

[A.4.145]
Amendment
4 (*Amends the Asylum and Immigration Act 1999.*)

5 With effect from 27th November 2000, the limitations on the taking effect of a variation and on a requirement to leave the United Kingdom contained in section 14(1) of the Immigration Act 1971 and in paragraph 7 of Schedule 2 to the Asylum and Immigration Appeals Act 1993 (as continued in force by paragraphs 2(5) and 3(4) of Schedule 2 to the Immigration and Asylum Act 1999 (Commencement No 6 and Consequential Provisions) Order 2000) are to be disregarded in calculating, for the purposes of section 61 or 69(2) of the 1999 Act, whether, as a result of a decision, a person may be required to leave the United Kingdom within 28 days.

SCHEDULE
Article 2

[A.4.146]

Column 1	Column 2
Section 13 (Proof of identity of persons to be removed or deported).	
Sections 141 to 144 (Fingerprinting, Attendance for fingerprinting, Destruction of fingerprints and other methods of collecting data about physical characteristics).	
Section 169(1) and (3).	So far as relating to the provisions of Schedules 14 and 16 commenced by this Order.
In Schedule 14, paragraph 61.	
In Schedule 16 (Repeals), the entry relating to section 3 of the Asylum and Immigration Appeals Act 1993.	

IMMIGRATION (REGULARISATION PERIOD FOR OVERSTAYERS) REGULATIONS 2000
SI 2000/265

Date   7 February 2000
Coming into force   8 February 2000

[A.4.147]
1 Citation, commencement and interpretation
(1)   These Regulations may be cited as the Immigration (Regularisation Period for Overstayers) Regulations 2000 and shall come into force on the day after the day on which they are made.
(2)   In these Regulations 'the Act' means the Immigration and Asylum Act 1999.

[A.4.148]
2 Manner of application
(1)   An application under section 9(1) of the Act shall be made in the following manner.
(2)   The application shall be made in writing, setting out the information required by paragraph (4), and attaching the material required by paragraph (5).
(3)   The application shall either:

(*a*)   be sent by post to the following address:

> Regularisation Scheme for Overstayers
> Initial Consideration Unit
> Immigration and Nationality Directorate
> Block C
> Whitgift Centre
> Croydon
> CR9 1AT; or

(*b*)   be delivered by hand to the Home Office at:

> The Public Caller Unit
> Immigration and Nationality Directorate
> Block C
> Whitgift Centre
> Wellesley Road
> Croydon.

(4)   The information referred to in paragraph (2) is:

(*a*)   the applicant's full name, date of birth and nationality;
(*b*)   the applicant's home address or, if none, an address where he may be contacted;
(*c*)   the name and address of any representative who is acting on behalf of the applicant;

(*d*) the date of each occasion on which leave to enter or remain has been granted to the applicant since his first arrival in the United Kingdom, if known;

(*e*) in relation to each date specified in accordance with sub-paragraph (d), the period for which leave was granted, if known;

(*f*) the applicant's Home Office reference, if known;

(*g*) the fact that the application is made under section 9 of the Act; and

(*h*) all the circumstances which the applicant wishes the Secretary of State to take into account when considering his application, including:

  (i)   his length of residence in the United Kingdom;

  (ii)   the strength of his connections with the United Kingdom;

  (iii) his personal history, including character, conduct and employment record;

  (iv) his domestic circumstances; and

  (v)   any compassionate circumstances.

(5)   The material referred to in paragraph (2) is:

(*a*) the applicant's current passport, if he has one and it is available to him;

(*b*) any other passports (whether expired or not) which have been used by the applicant and which are available to him; and

(*c*) any document or copy document which the applicant considers is evidence supporting his application.

[A.4.149]
3 Prescribed days
(1)   The day prescribed for the purposes of section 9(2) of the Act (the start of the regularisation period) is the day on which these Regulations come into force or, if later, 1st February 2000.

(2)   The day prescribed for the purposes of section 9(3) of the Act (the end of the regularisation period in certain circumstances) is 1st October 2000.

[A.4.150]
4 Delivery of applications
(1)   Paragraph (2) applies to an application sent by recorded delivery, addressed to the address set out in regulation 2(3)(a).

(2)   Such an application shall be taken to have been delivered for the purposes of these Regulations and section 9 of the Act on the second day after the day on which it was posted, if not received earlier.

A5   Support for Asylum Seekers

SUPPORT FOR ASYLUM-SEEKERS

[A.5.1]

General Note: *Part VI of the Immigration and Asylum Act 1999 and secondary legislation*

As explained in the note to section 94 of the Immigration and Asylum Act 1999 (see A.1 Statutes, paragraph **A.1.327**), Part VI operates by excluding persons under immigration control from large number of benefits or other forms of social assistance and then goes on to make alternative provision for some, although not all, of those so excluded. The process of exclusion is one of enormous legislative complexity, requiring regulations to be made under a whole range of social welfare legislation. It is difficult for a practitioner to track these developments, which are ongoing, and therefore the main statutory instruments of relevance are listed below. The list is not exhaustive. Several instruments have been omitted. One example of an omission, Statutory Rule 2000 No 91. The Social Fund Winter Fuel Payment Regulations (Northern Ireland) 2000, provides a glimpse of the range of issues being addressed. Practitioners should check for recent regulations pertaining to the social welfare legislation on which they seek to rely to satisfy themselves that it has not been changed subsequent to the coming into force of Part VI.

Main statutory instruments of relevance to working of Part VI

1999/3056	Asylum Support (Interim Provisions) Regulations 1999
1999/3126	Homelessness (Asylum Seekers) (Interim Period) (England) Order 1999
2000/537	Council Tax (Liability of Owners) (Amendment) (England) Regulations 2000
2000/541	Asylum Support (Appeals) (Procedure) Rules 2000
2000/621	National Health Service (Travelling Expenses and Remission of Charges) Amendment Regulations 2000
2000/636	Social Security (Immigration and Asylum) Consequential Amendments Regulations 2000
2000/701	Homelessness (England) Regulations 2000
2000/702	Allocation of Housing (England) Regulations 2000
2000/704	Asylum Support Regulations 2000
2000/705	Immigration (Eligibility for Assistance) (Scotland and Northern Ireland) Regulations 2000
2000/706	Persons subject to immigration control (Housing Authority Accommodation and Homelessness) Order 2000
2000/715	Council Tax (Liability of Owners) (Amendment) (Scotland) Regulations 2000
2000/1024	Council Tax (Liability for Owners) (Amendment) (Wales) Regulations 2000
2000/979	Income Related Benefits and Jobseekers Allowance (Amendment) Regulations 2000
2000/1036 (W67)	Persons Subject to Immigration Control (Housing Authority Accommodation) (Wales) Order 2000 (made 30 March 2000, came into force 1 April 2000)
2000/1079 (W72)	The Homelessness (Wales) Regulations 2000 (made 20 March 2000, came into force 1 April 2000)

2000/1080   Allocation of Housing (Wales) Regulations 2000
(W78)
2000/3053   Asylum Support (Amendment) Regulations 2000

Also: Statutory Rule 2000 No 71 The Social Security (Immigration and Asylum) Consequential Amendments Regulations (Northern Ireland) 2000;
Statutory Rule 2000 No 102 Travelling Expenses and Remission of Charges (Amendment) Regulations (Northern Ireland) 2000.

The texts of the majority of these Statutory Instruments can be found in *Butterworths Immigration Law Service*.

ASYLUM SUPPORT APPEALS (PROCEDURE) RULES 2000
SI 2000/541

Made   2 March 2000
Coming into force   3 April 2000

General

[A.5.2]
1   Title and commencement
These Rules may be cited as the Asylum Support Appeals (Procedure) Rules 2000 and shall come into force on 3rd April 2000.

[A.5.3]
2 Interpretation
(1)   In these Rules—

'the Act' means the Immigration and Asylum Act 1999;

'adjudication' means a decision of an adjudicator made in accordance with section 103(3) of the Act;

'appeal bundle' means a bundle prepared by the Secretary of State containing copies of the following documents:

(a)   the form on which the appellant made a claim for support under section 95 of the Act, if the appeal is made under section 103(1) of the Act;
(b)   any supporting documentation attached to that form;
(c)   the decision letter; and
(d)   other material relied on by the Secretary of State in reaching his decision;

'appellant' means a person who appeals under section 103 of the Act against a decision of the Secretary of State;

'bank holiday' means a day that is specified in, or appointed under, the Banking and Financial Dealings Act 1971;

'consideration day' has the meaning given to it by rule 4(4);

'decision letter' means a letter from the Secretary of State giving notice of a decision that gives rise to a right to appeal under section 103;

'excluded day' means a Saturday, a Sunday, a bank holiday, Christmas Day or Good Friday;

'member of the adjudicators' staff' means a person appointed by the Secretary of State under paragraph 5(1) of Schedule 10 to the Act;

'notice of appeal' has the meaning given to it by rule 3(1); and

'party' includes the appellant and the Secretary of State.

(2)   Any reference in these Rules:

(*a*)   to an adjudicator, in relation to the sending, giving or receiving of notices or other documents, whether by an adjudicator or a party to the appeal, includes a reference to a member of the adjudicators' staff;

(*b*) to an adjudicator, in relation to the receiving of a notice of appeal by him, includes a reference to the offices occupied by the adjudicators;

(*c*) to the appellant, in relation to the sending or giving of notices or other documents by the adjudicator or the Secretary of State, is also a reference to his representative, if he has one; and

(*d*) to a representative is to be construed in accordance with rule 15.

(3) For the purposes of these Rules, an appeal is determined when an adjudicator gives his adjudication.

Procedure before determination of appeal

[A.5.4]
3 Notice of appeal
(1) A person who wishes to appeal under section 103 of the Act must give notice to an adjudicator by completing in full, and in English, the form for the time being issued by the Secretary of State for the purpose ('notice of appeal'); and any form so issued is to be in the form shown in the Schedule to these Rules or a form to like effect.
(2) The notice of appeal must be signed by the appellant or his representative.
(3) Subject to paragraph (4), the notice of appeal must be received by the adjudicator not later than 2 days after the day on which the appellant received the decision letter.
(4) The adjudicator may extend the time limit for receiving the notice of appeal (either before or after its expiry) if:

(*a*) he considers that it is in the interests of justice to do so; and
(*b*) he is satisfied that:
    (i)   the appellant; or
    (ii) his representative (if he has one);

was prevented from complying with the time limit by circumstances beyond his control.

[A.5.5]
4 Procedure after receiving notice of appeal
(1) On the day that the adjudicator receives notice of appeal or, if not reasonably practicable, as soon as possible on the following day, he must send a copy of the notice of appeal, and any supporting documents, to the Secretary of State by fax.
(2) On the day after the day on which the adjudicator receives notice of appeal, the Secretary of State must send the appeal bundle to the adjudicator by fax or by hand and to the appellant by first class post or by fax.
(3) On consideration day, the adjudicator must:

(*a*) decide in accordance with rule 5 whether there should be an oral hearing;
(*b*) set the date for determining the appeal in accordance with rule 6;
(*c*) if there is to be an oral hearing, give notice to the Secretary of State and the appellant, in accordance with rule 7, of the date on which it is to be held.

(4) 'Consideration day' means the day after the day on which the Secretary of State sends the appeal bundle to the adjudicator in accordance with paragraph (2).

[A.5.6]

5   Whether there should be an oral hearing

(1)   The adjudicator must decide to hold an oral hearing:

(*a*) where the appellant has requested an oral hearing in his notice of appeal; or

(*b*) if the adjudicator considers that it is necessary for the appeal to be disposed of justly.

(2)   In all other cases, the appeal may be determined without an oral hearing.

[A.5.7]

6   Date for determination of appeal

(1)   If there is to be an oral hearing, the hearing must be held and the appeal determined 4 days after consideration day.

(2)   In all other cases, the appeal must be determined on consideration day, or as soon as possible thereafter, but in any event not later than 4 days after consideration day.

[A.5.8]

7   Notification of date of oral hearing

If there is to be an oral hearing, the adjudicator must send a notice to the appellant and to the Secretary of State informing them of the date, time and place of the hearing.

[A.5.9]

8   Further evidence provided before the determination of the appeal

(1)   Where the appellant sends to the adjudicator evidence to which this paragraph applies, the appellant must at the same time send a copy of such evidence to the Secretary of State.

(2)   Paragraph (1) applies to evidence which is sent after the appellant has sent notice of appeal to the adjudicator but before the appeal has been determined.

(3)   Where the Secretary of State sends to the adjudicator evidence to which this paragraph applies, the Secretary of State must at the same time send a copy of such evidence to the appellant.

(4)   Paragraph (3) applies to evidence which is sent after the Secretary of State has sent the appeal bundle to the adjudicator but before the appeal has been determined.

Determination of appeal

[A.5.10]
9   Hearing of appeal in absence of either party
(1)   If an appellant has indicated in his notice of appeal that he does not want
to attend, or be represented at, an oral hearing, the hearing may proceed in his
absence.
(2)   Where:

(*a*)   an appellant has indicated in his notice of appeal that he wants to attend,
      or be represented at, an oral hearing;
(*b*)   he has been notified of the date, time and place of the hearing in accor-
      dance with rule 7; and
(*c*)   neither he nor his representative (if he has one) attends the hearing;

the hearing may proceed in his absence.
(3)   Where neither the Secretary of State nor his representative (if he has one)
attends the hearing, it may proceed in his absence.

[A.5.11]
10   Evidence
(1)   Paragraph (2) applies to all appeals.
(2)   The adjudicator may take into account any matters which he considers to
be relevant to the appeal (including matters arising after the date on which the
decision appealed against was taken).
(3)   Paragraphs (4) to (6) apply to oral hearings only.
(4)   No person may be compelled to give any evidence or produce any document which he could not be compelled to give or produce on the trial of an
action.
(5)   The adjudicator may require any witness to give evidence on oath or
affirmation, and for that purpose an oath or affirmation in due form may be
administered.
(6)   When the adjudicator takes into consideration documentary evidence at an
oral hearing, a party present at the hearing is to be given an opportunity of
inspecting and considering that evidence and taking copies if copies have not
been provided previously to that party in accordance with these Rules.

[A.5.12]
11   Record of proceedings
A record of the proceedings at an oral hearing before the adjudicator is to be
made.

[A.5.13]
12   Exclusion of public
(1)   Subject to the provisions of this rule, oral hearings are to take place in
public.
(2)   Subject to the provisions of paragraph (3), the adjudicator may exclude a
member of the public or members of the public generally from a hearing or

from part of a hearing if, and to the extent that, he considers it necessary to do so in the public interest.

(3) But nothing in this rule is to prevent a member of the Council on Tribunals, a member of the Scottish Committee of that Council, the Chief Asylum Support Adjudicator or the Deputy Chief Asylum Support Adjudicator, in their capacity as such, from attending an oral hearing.

[A.5.14]
13 Adjudication
(1) Where an oral hearing is held:

(*a*) the adjudicator must inform all persons present of his adjudication at the conclusion of the hearing;

(*b*) if neither the appellant nor his representative (if he has one) is present at the conclusion of the hearing, the adjudicator must send notice of his adjudication on the same day to the appellant;

(*c*) if the Secretary of State is not present at the conclusion of the hearing, the adjudicator must send notice of his adjudication on the same day to the Secretary of State; and

(*d*) not later than 2 days after the day on which the appeal is determined, the adjudicator must send a reasons statement to the appellant and the Secretary of State.

(2) Where there is no oral hearing, the adjudicator must on the day that the appeal is determined:

(*a*) send notice of his adjudication to the appellant and the Secretary of State; and

(*b*) send a reasons statement to them.

(3) An adjudication takes effect from the day on which it is made.
(4) A 'reasons statement' is a written statement giving reasons for the adjudication.

Miscellaneous

[A.5.15]
14 Directions
The adjudicator may give directions on any matter arising in connection with an appeal if he considers it necessary or desirable to do so in the interests of justice.

[A.5.16]
15 Representation
A party to the appeal may be represented by any other person.

[A.5.17]
16 Withdrawal of decision
(1) Where the Secretary of State withdraws the decision which is appealed against, he must give notice to the adjudicator and the appellant forthwith.

(2)   Where the appellant withdraws his appeal, he must give notice to the adjudicator and the Secretary of State forthwith.

(3)   Where paragraph (1) or (2) applies, the appeal is to be treated for all purposes as at an end.

[A.5.18]
17   Notices
In the absence of express provision, any notice or other document required or authorised by these Rules to be sent or given by any party may be sent by first class post, by fax or by hand.

[A.5.19]
18   Time
(1)   Subject to paragraph (2), for the purposes of these Rules, a notice or other document is to be taken to have been received on the day on which it was in fact received.

(2)   Where a notice or other document is sent by first class post by the Secretary of State or by the adjudicator, it is to be taken to have been received 2 days after the day on which it was sent, unless the contrary is proven.

(3)   Where reference is made in these Rules to a specified number of days after an event, the number of days is to be calculated from the expiry of the day on which the event occurred.

(4)   Where these Rules provide that an act is to be done or to be taken to have been done:

(*a*)   not later than a specified number of days after an event; or

(*b*)   a specified number of days after an event;

and that number of days:

(*c*)   expires on an excluded day, the act is to be taken to have been done as required if done on the next working day;

(*d*)   includes an excluded day, that day is to be discounted.

(5)   Where these Rules provide that an act is to be done or to be taken to have been done on a certain day and that day is an excluded day, the act is to be taken to have been done as required if done on the next working day.

[A.5.20]
19   Irregularities
(1)   Any irregularity resulting from failure to comply with these Rules before the adjudicator has determined the appeal is not by itself to render the proceedings void.

(2)   But the adjudicator must, if he considers that either party may have been prejudiced, take such steps as he thinks fit to remove or reduce the prejudice.

[A.5.21]
SCHEDULE
NOTICE OF APPEAL

Rule 3(1)

Asylum Support Adjudicators
Notice of Appeal

Section one

Give your personal details

Full Name: ....

Date of Birth: .... Nationality ....

Your NASS reference number:...

Section two

Give an address in the United Kingdom

where we can contact you: ....

....

....

....

Give a daytime fax or telephone number in the UK

where we can contact you (if you have one):...

Section three

Give the date of the decision letter against which

you are appealing:..

Section four

Do you want an oral hearing of your appeal?	Yes/No
Do you want to attend any oral hearing of your appeal?	Yes/No
If you want to attend the hearing, will you need an interpreter?	Yes/No
If so, in what language?	....
Are you to be represented in this appeal?	Yes/No
If so you must give full details of your representative: name and address, and telephone and fax numbers if available, together with any reference number the representative has given your case	....
Will your representative attend any oral hearing of your appeal?	Yes/No

Section five

What are the grounds of your appeal?

What matters in the decision letter do you dispute?

Signed: ....Date: ....

[Appellant/Representative]

If you have further information which you would like the Adjudicator to take into account when making a decision about your appeal, you should send copies of any documents with this form.

Return this form to:

Asylum Support Adjudicator
Christopher Wren House
113 High Street
Croydon CR0 1GQ

ASYLUM SUPPORT REGULATIONS 2000
SI 2000/704

Made   6 March 2000
Coming into force   3 April 2000

General

[A.5.22]
1   Citation and commencement
These Regulations may be cited as the Asylum Support Regulations 2000 and shall come into force on 3rd April 2000.

[A.5.23]

2   Interpretation
(1)   In these Regulations—

'the Act' means the Immigration and Asylum Act 1999;
'asylum support' means support provided under section 95 of the Act;
'dependant' has the meaning given by paragraphs (4) and (5);
'the interim Regulations' means the Asylum Support (Interim Provisions) Regulations 1999;
'married couple' means a man and woman who are married to each other and are members of the same household; and
'unmarried couple' means a man and woman who, though not married to each other, are living together as if married.

(2)   The period of 14 days is prescribed for the purposes of section 94(3) of the Act (day on which a claim for asylum is determined).
(3)   Paragraph (2) does not apply in relation to a case to which the interim Regulations apply (for which case, provision corresponding to paragraph (2) is made by regulation 2(6) of those Regulations).
(4)   In these Regulations 'dependant', in relation to an asylum-seeker, a supported person or an applicant for asylum support, means, subject to paragraph (5), a person in the United Kingdom ('the relevant person') who—

(*a*)   is his spouse;
(*b*)   is a child of his or of his spouse, is dependant on him and is, or was at the relevant time, under 18;
(*c*)   is a member of his or his spouse's close family and is, or was at the relevant time, under 18;
(*d*)   had been living as part of his household—
   (i)   for at least six of the twelve months before the relevant time, or
   (ii)   since birth,
   and is, or was at the relevant time, under 18;

(*e*) is in need of care and attention from him or a member of his household by reason of a disability and would fall within sub-paragraph (c) or (d) but for the fact that he is not, and was not at the relevant time, under 18;

(*f*) had been living with him as a member of an unmarried couple for at least two of the three years before the relevant time;

(*g*) is living as part of his household and was, immediately before 6th December 1999 (the date when the interim Regulations came into force), receiving assistance from a local authority under section 17 of the Children Act 1989;

(*h*) is living as part of his household and was, immediately before the coming into force of these Regulations, receiving assistance from a local authority under—

(i)   section 22 of the Children (Scotland) Act 1995; or

(ii) Article 18 of the Children (Northern Ireland) Order 1995; or

(*i*) has made a claim for leave to enter or remain in the United Kingdom, or for variation of any such leave, which is being considered on the basis that he is dependant on the asylum-seeker;

and in relation to a supported person, or an applicant for asylum support, who is himself a dependant of an asylum-seeker, also includes the asylum-seeker if in the United Kingdom.

(5)   Where a supported person or applicant for asylum support is himself a dependant of an asylum-seeker, a person who would otherwise be a dependant of the supported person, or of the applicant, for the purposes of these Regulations is not such a dependant unless he is also a dependant of the asylum-seeker or is the asylum-seeker.

(6)   In paragraph (4), 'the relevant time', in relation to the relevant person, means—

(*a*) the time when an application for asylum support for him was made in accordance with regulation 3(3); or

(*b*) if he has joined a person who is already a supported person in the United Kingdom and sub-paragraph (a) does not apply, the time when he joined that person in the United Kingdom.

(7)   Where a person, by falling within a particular category in relation to an asylum-seeker or supported person, is by virtue of this regulation a dependant of the asylum-seeker or supported person for the purposes of these Regulations, that category is also a prescribed category for the purposes of paragraph (c) of the definition of 'dependant' in section 94(1) of the Act and, accordingly, the person is a dependant of the asylum-seeker or supported person for the purposes of Part VI of the Act.

(8)   Paragraph (7) does not apply to a person who is already a dependant of the asylum-seeker or supported person for the purposes of Part VI of the Act because he falls within either of the categories mentioned in paragraphs (a) and (b) of the definition of 'dependant' in section 94(1) of the Act.

(9)   Paragraph (7) does not apply for the purposes of any reference to a 'dependant' in Schedule 9 to the Act.

Initial application for support

[A.5.24]
3   Initial application for support: individual and group applications
(1)   Either of the following—

(*a*) an asylum-seeker, or
(*b*) a dependant of an asylum-seeker,

may apply to the Secretary of State for asylum support.
(2)   An application under this regulation may be—

(*a*) for asylum support for the applicant alone; or
(*b*) for asylum support for the applicant and one or more dependants of his.

(3)   The application must be made by completing in full and in English the form for the time being issued by the Secretary of State for the purpose; and any form so issued shall be the form shown in the Schedule to these Regulations or a form to the like effect.
(4)   The application may not be entertained by the Secretary of State unless it is made in accordance with paragraph (3).
(5)   The Secretary of State may make further enquiries of the applicant about any matter connected with the application.
(6)   Paragraphs (3) and (4) do not apply where a person is already a supported person and asylum support is sought for a dependant of his for whom such support is not already provided (for which case, provision is made by regulation 15).

[A.5.25]
4   Persons excluded from support
(1)   The following circumstances are prescribed for the purposes of subsection (2) of section 95 of the Act as circumstances where a person who would otherwise fall within subsection (1) of that section is excluded from that subsection (and, accordingly, may not be provided with asylum support).
(2)   A person is so excluded if he is applying for asylum support for himself alone and he falls within paragraph (4) by virtue of any sub-paragraph of that paragraph.
(3)   A person is so excluded if—

(*a*) he is applying for asylum support for himself and other persons, or he is included in an application for asylum support made by a person other than himself;
(*b*) he falls within paragraph (4) (by virtue of any sub-paragraph of that paragraph); and
(*c*) each of the other persons to whom the application relates also falls within paragraph (4) (by virtue of any sub-paragraph of that paragraph).

(4)   A person falls within this paragraph if at the time when the application is determined—

(*a*) he is a person to whom interim support applies; or
(*b*) he is a person to whom social security benefits apply; or
(*c*) he has not made a claim for leave to enter or remain in the United

Kingdom, or for variation of any such leave, which is being considered on the basis that he is an asylum-seeker or dependent on an asylum-seeker.

(5)   For the purposes of paragraph (4), interim support applies to a person if—

(*a*) at the time when the application is determined, he is a person to whom, under the interim Regulations, support under regulation 3 of those Regulations must be provided by a local authority;

(*b*) sub-paragraph (*a*) does not apply, but would do so if the person had been determined by the local authority concerned to be an eligible person; or

(*c*) sub-paragraph (*a*) does not apply, but would do so but for the fact that the person's support under those Regulations was (otherwise than by virtue of regulation 7(1)(*d*) of those Regulations) refused under regulation 7, or suspended or discontinued under regulation 8, of those Regulations;

and in this paragraph 'local authority', 'local authority concerned' and 'eligible person' have the same meanings as in the interim Regulations.

(6)   For the purposes of paragraph (4), a person is a person to whom social security benefits apply if he is—

(*a*) a person who by virtue of regulation 2 of the Social Security (Immigration and Asylum) Consequential Amendments Regulations 2000 is not excluded by section 115(1) of the Act from entitlement to—
  (i)   income-based jobseeker's allowance under the Jobseekers Act 1995; or
  (ii) income support, housing benefit or council tax benefit under the Social Security Contributions and Benefits Act 1992;

(*b*) a person who, by virtue of regulation 2 of the Social Security (Immigration and Asylum) Consequential Amendments Regulations (Northern Ireland) 2000 is not excluded by section 115(2) of the Act from entitlement to—
  (i)   income-based jobseeker's allowance under the Jobseekers (Northern Ireland) Order 1995; or
  (ii) income support or housing benefit under the Social Security Contributions and Benefits (Northern Ireland) Act 1992;

(7)   A person is not to be regarded as falling within paragraph (2) or (3) if, when asylum support is sought for him, he is a dependant of a person who is already a supported person.

(8)   The circumstances prescribed by paragraphs (2) and (3) are also prescribed for the purposes of section 95(2), as applied by section 98(3), of the Act as circumstances where a person who would otherwise fall within subsection (1) of section 98 is excluded from that subsection (and, accordingly, may not be provided with temporary support under section 98).

(9)   For the purposes of paragraph (8), paragraphs (2) and (3) shall apply as if any reference to an application for asylum support were a reference to an application for support under section 98 of the Act.

Determining whether persons are destitute

[A.5.26]
5 Determination where application relates to more than one person, etc
(1) Subject to paragraph (2), where an application in accordance with regulation 3(3) is for asylum support for the applicant and one or more dependants of his, in applying section 95(1) of the Act the Secretary of State must decide whether the applicant and all those dependants, taken together, are destitute or likely to become destitute within the period prescribed by regulation 7.
(2) Where a person is a supported person, and the question falls to be determined whether asylum support should in future be provided for him and one or more other persons who are his dependants and are—

(*a*) persons for whom asylum support is also being provided when that question falls to be determined; or
(*b*) persons for whom the Secretary of State is then considering whether asylum support should be provided,

in applying section 95(1) of the Act the Secretary of State must decide whether the supported person and all those dependants, taken together, are destitute or likely to become destitute within the period prescribed by regulation 7.

[A.5.27]
6 Income and assets to be taken into account
(1) This regulation applies where it falls to the Secretary of State to determine for the purposes of section 95(1) of the Act whether—

(*a*) a person applying for asylum support, or such an applicant and any dependants of his, or
(*b*) a supported person, or such a person and any dependants of his,

is or are destitute or likely to become so within the period prescribed by regulation 7.
(2) In this regulation 'the principal' means the applicant for asylum support (where paragraph (1)(*a*) applies) or the supported person (where paragraph (1)(b) applies).
(3) The Secretary of State must ignore—

(*a*) any asylum support, and
(*b*) any support under section 98 of the Act,

which the principal or any dependant of his is provided with or, where the question is whether destitution is likely within a particular period, might be provided with in that period.
(4) But he must take into account—

(*a*) any other income which the principal, or any dependant of his, has or might reasonably be expected to have in that period;
(*b*) any other support which is available to the principal or any dependant of his, or might reasonably be expected to be so available in that period; and
(*c*) any assets mentioned in paragraph (5) (whether held in the United Kingdom or elsewhere) which are available to the principal or any depen-

dant of his otherwise than by way of asylum support or support under section 98, or might reasonably be expected to be so available in that period.

(5)   Those assets are—

(*a*) cash;
(*b*) savings;
(*c*) investments;
(*d*) land;
(*e*) cars or other vehicles; and
(*f*) goods held for the purpose of a trade or other business.

(6)   The Secretary of State must ignore any assets not mentioned in paragraph (5).

[A.5.28]
7   Period within which applicant must be likely to become destitute
The period prescribed for the purposes of section 95(1) of the Act is—

(*a*) where the question whether a person or persons is or are destitute or likely to become so falls to be determined in relation to an application for asylum support and sub-paragraph (b) does not apply, 14 days beginning with the day on which that question falls to be determined;
(*b*) where that question falls to be determined in relation to a supported person, or in relation to persons including a supported person, 56 days beginning with the day on which that question falls to be determined.

[A.5.29]
8   Adequacy of existing accommodation
(1)   Subject to paragraph (2), the matters mentioned in paragraph (3) are prescribed for the purposes of subsection (5)(*a*) of section 95 of the Act as matters to which the Secretary of State must have regard in determining for the purposes of that section whether the accommodation of—

(*a*) a person applying for asylum support, or
(*b*) a supported person for whom accommodation is not for the time being provided by way of asylum support,

is adequate.
(2)   The matters mentioned in paragraph (3)(*a*) and (*d*) to (*g*) are not so prescribed for the purposes of a case where the person indicates to the Secretary of State that he wishes to remain in the accommodation.
(3)   The matters referred to in paragraph (1) are—

(*a*) whether it would be reasonable for the person to continue to occupy the accommodation;
(*b*) whether the accommodation is affordable for him;
(*c*) whether the accommodation is provided under section 98 of the Act, or otherwise on an emergency basis, only while the claim for asylum support is being determined;
(*d*) whether the person can secure entry to the accommodation;
(*e*) where the accommodation consists of a moveable structure, vehicle or

vessel designed or adapted for human habitation, whether there is a place where the person is entitled or permitted both to place it and reside in it;

(*f*) whether the accommodation is available for occupation by the person's dependants together with him;

(*g*) whether it is probable that the person's continued occupation of the accommodation will lead to domestic violence against him or any of his dependants.

(4) In determining whether it would be reasonable for a person to continue to occupy accommodation, regard may be had to the general circumstances prevailing in relation to housing in the district of the local housing authority where the accommodation is.

(5) In determining whether a person's accommodation is affordable for him, the Secretary of State must have regard to:

(*a*) any income, or any assets mentioned in regulation 6(5) (whether held in the United Kingdom or elsewhere), which is or are available to him or any dependant of his otherwise than by way of asylum support or support under section 98 of the Act, or might reasonably be expected to be so available;

(*b*) the costs in respect of the accommodation; and

(*c*) the person's other reasonable living expenses.

(6) In this regulation:

(*a*) 'domestic violence' means violence from a person who is or has been a close family member, or threats of violence from such a person which are likely to be carried out; and

(*b*) 'district of the local housing authority' has the meaning given by section 217(3) of the Housing Act 1996.

(7) The reference in paragraph (1) to subsection (5)(a) of section 95 of the Act does not include a reference to that provision as applied by section 98(3) of the Act.

[A.5.30]
9   Essential living needs
(1) The matter mentioned in paragraph (2) is prescribed for the purposes of subsection (7)(*b*) of section 95 of the Act as a matter to which the Secretary of State may not have regard in determining for the purposes of that section whether a person's essential living needs (other than accommodation) are met.
(2) That matter is his personal preference as to clothing (but this shall not be taken to prevent the Secretary of State from taking into account his individual circumstances as regards clothing).
(3) None of the items and expenses mentioned in paragraph (4) is to be treated as being an essential living need of a person for the purposes of Part VI of the Act.
(4) Those items and expenses are:

(*a*) the cost of faxes;
(*b*) computers and the cost of computer facilities;
(*c*) the cost of photocopying;
(*d*) travel expenses, except the expense mentioned in paragraph (5);
(*e*) toys and other recreational items;

(*f*) entertainment expenses.

(5) The expense excepted from paragraph (4)(*d*) is the expense of an initial journey from a place in the United Kingdom to accommodation provided by way of asylum support or (where accommodation is not so provided) to an address in the United Kingdom which has been notified to the Secretary of State as the address where the person intends to live.

(6) Paragraph (3) shall not be taken to affect the question whether any item or expense not mentioned in paragraph (4) or (5) is, or is not, an essential living need.

(7) The reference in paragraph (1) to subsection (7)(*b*) of section 95 of the Act includes a reference to that provision as applied by section 98(3) of the Act and, accordingly, the reference in paragraph (1) to 'that section' includes a reference to section 98.

Provision of support

[A.5.31]
10 Kind and levels of support for essential living needs
(1) This regulation applies where the Secretary of State has decided that asylum support should be provided in respect of the essential living needs of a person.

(2) As a general rule, asylum support in respect of the essential living needs of that person may be expected to be provided weekly in the form of vouchers redeemable for goods, services and cash whose total redemption value, for any week, equals the amount shown in the second column of the following Table opposite the entry in the first column which for the time being describes that person.

TABLE

Qualifying couple	£57.37
Lone parent aged 18 or over	£36.54
Single person aged 25 or over	£36.54
Single person aged at least 18 but under 25	£28.95
Person aged at least 16 but under 18 (except a member of a qualifying couple)	£31.75
Person aged under 16	£30.95

(3) In paragraph (1) and the provisions of paragraph (2) preceding the Table, 'person' includes 'couple'.
(4) In this regulation:

(*a*) 'qualifying couple' means a married or unmarried couple at least one of whom is aged 18 or over and neither of whom is aged under 16;
(*b*) 'lone parent' means a parent who is not a member of a married or unmarried couple;
(*c*) 'single person' means a person who is not a parent or a member of a qualifying couple; and
(*d*) 'parent' means a parent of a relevant child, that is to say a child who is aged under 18 and for whom asylum support is provided.
(5) Where the Secretary of State has decided that accommodation should be

provided for a person (or couple) by way of asylum support, and the accommodation is provided in a form which also meets other essential living needs (such as bed and breakfast, or half or full board), the amounts shown in the Table in paragraph (2) shall be treated as reduced accordingly.

(6)   The redemption value of the vouchers redeemable for cash which the Secretary of State may be expected to include in the asylum support provided for any week in accordance with paragraph (2) may, as a general rule, be expected not to exceed £10 per person (or, as the case may be, £20 per qualifying couple).

Note   Sum in square brackets in para (2) substituted by SI 2000/3053.

[A.5.32]
11   Additional single payments in respect of essential living needs
(1)   At the end of each qualifying period, the Secretary of State may as a general rule be expected to provide, or arrange for the provision of, additional support for an eligible person (in respect of his essential living needs) in the form of a single issue of vouchers redeemable for cash whose total redemption value equals £50.

(2)   In paragraph (1) 'eligible person' means a person for whom asylum support has been provided for the whole of the qualifying period.

(3)   Each of the following is a qualifying period:

(*a*)   the period of six months beginning with the day on which asylum support was first provided for the person; and

(*b*)   each period of six months beginning with a re-start day.

(4)   Each of the following is a re-start day:

(*a*)   the day after the day on which the period mentioned in paragraph (3)(a) ends; and

(*b*)   the day after the day on which a period mentioned in paragraph (3)(b) ends.

(5)   Paragraph (1) applies only if an application for the additional support is made to the Secretary of State by or on behalf of the eligible person.

(6)   Where a person is, in the opinion of the Secretary of State, responsible without reasonable excuse for a delay in the determination of his claim for asylum, the Secretary of State may treat any qualifying period as extended by the period of delay.

[A.5.33]
12   Income and assets to be taken into account in providing support
(1)   This regulation applies where it falls to the Secretary of State to decide the level or kind of asylum support to be provided for:

(*a*)   a person applying for asylum support, or such an applicant and any dependants of his; or

(*b*)   a supported person, or such a person and any dependants of his.

(2)   In this regulation 'the principal' means the applicant for asylum support

(where paragraph (1)(*a*) applies) or the supported person (where paragraph (1)(*b*) applies).

(3)   The Secretary of State must take into account:

(*a*) any income which the principal or any dependant of his has or might reasonably be expected to have,

(*b*) support which is or might reasonably be expected to be available to the principal or any dependant of his, and

(*c*) any assets mentioned in regulation 6(5) (whether held in the United Kingdom or elsewhere) which are or might reasonably be expected to be available to the principal or any dependant of his,

otherwise than by way of asylum support.

[A.5.34]
13   Accommodation
(1)   The matters mentioned in paragraph (2) are prescribed for the purposes of subsection (2)(*b*) of section 97 of the Act as matters to which regard may not be had when exercising the power under section 95 of the Act to provide accommodation for a person.
(2)   Those matters are:

(*a*) his personal preference as to the nature of the accommodation to be provided; and

(*b*) his personal preference as to the nature and standard of fixtures and fittings;

but this shall not be taken to prevent the person's individual circumstances, as they relate to his accommodation needs, being taken into account.

[A.5.35]
14   Services
(1)   The services mentioned in paragraph (2) may be provided or made available by way of asylum support to persons who are otherwise receiving such support, but may be so provided only for the purpose of maintaining good order among such persons.
(2)   Those services are:

(*a*) education, including English language lessons,

(*b*) sporting or other developmental activities.

Change of circumstances

[A.5.36]
15   Change of circumstances
(1)   If a relevant change of circumstances occurs, the supported person concerned or a dependant of his must, without delay, notify the Secretary of State of that change of circumstances.

(2) A relevant change of circumstances occurs where a supported person or a dependant of his—

(*a*) is joined in the United Kingdom by a dependant or, as the case may be, another dependant, of the supported person;
(*b*) receives or gains access to any money, or other asset mentioned in regulation 6(5), that has not previously been declared to the Secretary of State;
(*c*) becomes employed;
(*d*) becomes unemployed;
(*e*) changes his name;
(*f*) gets married;
(*g*) starts living with a person as if married to that person;
(*h*) gets divorced;
(*i*) separates from a spouse, or from a person with whom he has been living as if married to that person;
(*j*) becomes pregnant;
(*k*) has a child;
(*l*) leaves school;
(*m*) starts to share his accommodation with another person;
(*n*) moves to a different address, or otherwise leaves his accommodation;
(*o*) goes into hospital;
(*p*) goes to prison or is otherwise held in custody;
(*q*) leaves the United Kingdom; or
(*r*) dies.

(3) If, on being notified of a change of circumstances, the Secretary of State considers that the change may be one—

(*a*) as a result of which asylum support should be provided for a person for whom it was not provided before, or
(*b*) as a result of which asylum support should no longer be provided for a person, or
(*c*) which may otherwise affect the asylum support which should be provided for a person,
he may make further enquiries of the supported person or dependant who gave the notification.

(4) The Secretary of State may, in particular, require that person to provide him with such information as he considers necessary to determine whether, and if so, what, asylum support should be provided for any person.

Contributions

[A.5.37]
16 Contributions
(1) This regulation applies where, in deciding the level of asylum support to be provided for a person who is or will be a supported person, the Secretary of State is required to take into account income, support or assets as mentioned in regulation 12(3).
(2) The Secretary of State may—

(*a*) set the asylum support for that person at a level which does not reflect the income, support or assets; and

(*b*) require from that person payments by way of contributions towards the cost of the provision for him of asylum support.

(3) A supported person must make to the Secretary of State such payments by way of contributions as the Secretary of State may require under paragraph (2).

(4) Prompt payment of such contributions may be made a condition (under section 95(9) of the Act) subject to which asylum support for that person is provided.

Recovery of sums by Secretary of State

[A.5.38]
17 Recovery where assets become realisable
(1) This regulation applies where it appears to the Secretary of State at any time (the relevant time)—

(*a*) that a supported person had, at the time when he applied for asylum support, assets of any kind in the United Kingdom or elsewhere which were not capable of being realised; but

(*b*) that those assets have subsequently become, and remain, capable of being realised.

(2) The Secretary of State may recover from that person a sum not exceeding the recoverable sum.

(3) Subject to paragraph (5), the recoverable sum is a sum equal to whichever is the less of—

(*a*) the monetary value of all the asylum support provided to the person up to the relevant time; and

(*b*) the monetary value of the assets concerned.

(4) As well as being recoverable as mentioned in paragraph 11(2)(*a*) of Schedule 8 to the Act, an amount recoverable under this regulation may be recovered by deduction from asylum support.

(5) The recoverable sum shall be treated as reduced by any amount which the Secretary of State has by virtue of this regulation already recovered from the person concerned (whether by deduction or otherwise) with regard to the assets concerned.

[A.5.39]
18 Overpayments: method of recovery
As well as being recoverable as mentioned in subsection (3) of section 114 of the Act, an amount recoverable under subsection (2) of that section may be recovered by deduction from asylum support.

Breach of conditions and suspension and discontinuation of support

[A.5.40]
19   Breach of conditions: decision whether to provide support
(1)   When deciding—

(*a*) whether to provide, or to continue to provide, asylum support for any person or persons, or
(*b*) the level or kind of support to be provided for any person or persons,

the Secretary of State may take into account the extent to which any relevant condition has been complied with.
(2)   A relevant condition is a condition subject to which asylum support for that person or any of those persons is being, or has previously been, provided.

[A.5.41]
20   Suspension or discontinuation of support
(1)   Asylum support for a supported person and his dependants (if any), or for one or more dependants of a supported person, may be suspended or discontinued if—

(*a*) the Secretary of State has reasonable grounds to suspect that the supported person or any dependant of his has failed without reasonable excuse to comply with any condition subject to which the asylum support is provided;
(*b*) the Secretary of State has reasonable grounds to suspect that the supported person or any dependant of his has committed an offence under Part VI of the Act;
(*c*) the Secretary of State has reasonable grounds to suspect that the supported person has intentionally made himself and his dependants (if any) destitute;
(*d*) the supported person or any dependant of his for whom asylum support is being provided ceases to reside at the authorised address; or
(*e*) the supported person or any dependant of his for whom asylum support is being provided is absent from the authorised address—
   (i)   for more than seven consecutive days and nights, or
   (ii) for a total of more than 14 days and nights in any six month period,

without the permission of the Secretary of State.
(2)   For the purposes of this regulation, a person has intentionally made himself destitute if he appears to be, or to be likely to become within the period prescribed by regulation 7, destitute as a result of an act or omission deliberately done or made by him or any dependant of his without reasonable excuse while in the United Kingdom.
(3)   For the purposes of this regulation, the authorised address is—

(*a*) the accommodation provided for the supported person and his dependants (if any) by way of asylum support; or
(*b*) if no accommodation is so provided, the address notified by the supported person to the Secretary of State in his application for asylum support or, where a change of his address has been notified to the Secretary of State under regulation 15, the address for the time being so notified.

[A.5.42]
21 Effect of previous suspension or discontinuation
(1)   Where—

(*a*) an application for asylum support is made,
(*b*) the applicant or any other person to whom the application relates has previously had his asylum support suspended or discontinued under regulation 20, and
(*c*) there has been no material change of circumstances since the suspension or discontinuation,

the application need not be entertained unless the Secretary of State considers that there are exceptional circumstances which justify its being entertained.
(2)   A material change of circumstances is one which, if the applicant were a supported person, would have to be notified to the Secretary of State under regulation 15.
(3)   This regulation is without prejudice to the power of the Secretary of State to refuse the application even if he has entertained it.

Notice to quit

[A.5.43]
22 Notice to quit
(1)   If—

(*a*) as a result of asylum support, a person has a tenancy or licence to occupy accommodation,
(*b*) one or more of the conditions mentioned in paragraph (2) is satisfied, and
(*c*) he is given notice to quit in accordance with paragraph (3) or (4),

his tenancy or licence is to be treated as ending with the period specified in that notice, regardless of when it could otherwise be brought to an end.
(2)   The conditions are that—

(*a*) the asylum support is suspended or discontinued as a result of any provision of regulation 20;
(*b*) the relevant claim for asylum has been determined;
(*c*) the supported person has ceased to be destitute; or
(*d*) he is to be moved to other accommodation.

(3)   A notice to quit is in accordance with this paragraph if it is in writing and:

(*a*) in a case where sub-paragraph (*a*), (*c*) or (*d*) of paragraph (2) applies, specifies as the notice period a period of not less than seven days; or
(*b*) in a case where the Secretary of State has notified his decision on the relevant claim for asylum to the claimant, specifies as the notice period a period at least as long as whichever is the greater of:
  (i)   seven days; or
  (ii) the period beginning with the date of service of the notice to quit and ending with the date of determination of the relevant claim for asylum (found in accordance with section 94(3) of the Act).

(4)   A notice to quit is in accordance with this paragraph if:

(*a*) it is in writing;

(*b*) it specifies as the notice period a period of less than seven days; and

(*c*) the circumstances of the case are such that that notice period is justified.

Meaning of 'destitute' for certain other purposes

[A.5.44]
23   Meaning of 'destitute' for certain other purposes
(1)   In this regulation 'the relevant enactments' means:

(*a*) section 21(1A) of the National Assistance Act 1948;

(*b*) section 45(4A) of the Health Services and Public Health Act 1968;

(*c*) paragraph 2(2A) of Schedule 8 to the National Health Service Act 1977;

(*d*) sections 12(2A), 13A(4) and 13B(3) of the Social Work (Scotland) Act 1968;

(*e*) sections 7(3) and 8(4) of the Mental Health (Scotland) Act 1984; and

(*f*) Articles 7(3) and 15(6) of the Health and Personal Social Services (Northern Ireland) Order 1972.

(2)   The following provisions of this regulation apply where it falls to an authority, or the Department, to determine for the purposes of any of the relevant enactments whether a person is destitute.

(3)   Paragraphs (3) to (6) of regulation 6 apply as they apply in the case mentioned in paragraph (1) of that regulation, but as if references to the principal were references to the person whose destitution or otherwise is being determined and references to the Secretary of State were references to the authority or (as the case may be) Department.

(4)   The matters mentioned in paragraph (3) of regulation 8 (read with paragraphs (4) to (6) of that regulation) are prescribed for the purposes of subsection (5)(a) of section 95 of the Act, as applied for the purposes of any of the relevant enactments, as matters to which regard must be had in determining for the purposes of any of the relevant enactments whether a person's accommodation is adequate.

(5)   The matter mentioned in paragraph (2) of regulation 9 is prescribed for the purposes of subsection (7)(b) of section 95 of the Act, as applied for the purposes of any of the relevant enactments, as a matter to which regard may not be had in determining for the purposes of any of the relevant enactments whether a person's essential living needs (other than accommodation) are met.

(6)   Paragraphs (3) to (6) of regulation 9 shall apply as if the reference in paragraph (3) to Part VI of the Act included a reference to the relevant enactments.

(7)   The references in regulations 8(5) and 9(2) to the Secretary of State shall be construed, for the purposes of this regulation, as references to the authority or (as the case may be) Department.

[A.5.45]

SCHEDULE
APPLICATION FORM AND NOTES
National Asylum Support Service

Application form

Please read the guidance notes before you fill in this form.

Please fill in this form in BLOCK CAPITALS using black ink.

Section 1	**About you—please read note 1**
Title	Mr ☐ Mrs ☐ Miss ☐ Ms ☐
	Other ☐ Please give details ....
Surname	
Other names	
Names that you have previously used	
Date of birth	
Nationality	
Are you:	male? ☐ female? ☐
Are you:	married? ☐ divorced? ☐ separated? ☐ widowed? ☐
	single? ☐ other? ☐ Please give details............................
Which language is easiest for you to speak and understand?	
Are you reasonably fluent in English?	yes ☐ no ☐
Would you need an interpreter?	yes ☐ no ☐

Section 3 **About your support application—please read note 3**

What type of support are you applying for? Subsistence only ☐ Accommodation only ☐

Both ☐

Have you applied for support before? Yes ☐ No ☐

Are you currently receiving support from the National Asylum Support Service? Yes ☐ No ☐

If you have answered 'Yes' to either of the questions above, please give the following details.

The date you applied for support ⌊___/___/___⌋

Your previous National Asylum Support Service reference number ⌊__｜__｜__｜__｜__｜__｜__｜__⌋

Section 4 **Your address details—please read note 4**

Please give your address in the United Kingdom

Phone number

How long have you lived at this address?

Section 5a **Other people you have included in your application—please read note 5**

Do you have a husband or wife, partner or dependant children or other relatives, who are in the United Kingdom and who you want to include in this application for support?

Yes ☐ Please fill in section 5b.

No ☐ please go to section 6a.

Section 5b	Details about the other people you have included in this application—please read note 5

Dependant 1

Surname:	Other names:

Date of birth: [/ /]	Are they male? ☐ female? ☐	Nationality

Their relationship to you:

Name and address of school, college or university (if this applies)	Address (if different from the main applicant):

How long have they been at this school?

Dependant 2

Surname:	Other names:

Date of birth: [/ /]	Are they male? ☐ female? ☐	Nationality

Their relationship to you:

Name and address of school, college or university (if this applies)	Address (if different from the main applicant):

How long have they been at this school?

Dependant 3

Surname:	Other names:

Date of birth: [/ /]	Are they male? ☐ female? ☐	Nationality

Their relationship to you:

Name and address of school, college or university (if this applies)	Address (if different from the main applicant):

How long have they been at this school?

Dependant 4

Surname:	Other names:

Date of birth: [/ /]	Are they male? ☐ female? ☐	Nationality

Their relationship to you:

Name and address of school, college or university (if this applies)	Address (if different from the main applicant):

How long have they been at this school?

Please tick here if you have continued on another sheet ☐

Section 6a	About your current accommodation—please read note 6			

Are you currently living in 'emergency accommodation'?   Yes ☐   No ☐

Are you staying with a relative or friend (other than your dependants)?   Yes ☐

No ☐

If you are staying with a relative or friend, do you pay?   Yes ☐ Please give details below.

No ☐

Does not apply ☐

Are you are living in rented accommodation?   Yes ☐ Please give details below.

No ☐

How much rent do you pay?   £   every

Name of landlord

Do you live in any other kind of accommodation

Is there any legal reason why you cannot move from your accommodation?   Yes ☐ Please give details below.

No ☐

Can you afford your accommodation?   Yes ☐

No ☐ Please give details below and go to section 7.

Do you want to stay in your current accommodation   Yes ☐ Please go straight to section 7.

No ☐ Please fill in section 6b.

Please tick here if you have continued on another sheet. ☐

Section 6b   More information about your accommodation—please read note 6

You should only fill in this section if you do not want to stay in your current accommodation.

In this section, we may use your answers to decide whether your current accommodation is not adequate for your own needs, and, if you have any, your dependants' needs.

If you are staying with a friend or relative, have they asked you to leave as soon as possible?	Yes ☐	Please give details below and go to section 7.
	No ☐	

Is there any other reason why you do not think your current accommodation is adequate?	Yes ☐	Please give details below.
	No ☐	Go to section 7a.

SPECIMEN

Section 7a   Friends and relatives—please read note 7

We take into account any support (either accommodation, financial support or other support) that your friends and relatives give you when we decide whether or not you are eligible for support. In this section, you should tell us whether or not any friends or relatives can give you support.

Can any friends or relatives in the UK provide you with adequate accommodation? (Please see note 6b for guidance on accommodation.)	Yes ☐	Please give details in section 7b.
	No ☐	

Can any friends or relatives (whether in the UK or elsewhere) provide you with financial support, or support other than accommodation?	Yes ☐	Please give details in section 7b.
	No ☐	

If you have answered "No" to both questions, you should go straight to section 8.

Section 7b	Support from friends, relatives or other sources	
Name:		
Address:		
Their relationship to you:	Occupation:	
Immigration status (if they live in the UK):		
Details of the support they can give you:		
Name:		
Address:		
Their relationship to you:	Occupation:	
Immigration status (if they live in the UK):		
Details of the support they can give you:		
Name:		
Address:		
Their relationship to you:	Occupation:	
Immigration status (if they live in the UK):		
Details of the support they can give you:		
Name:		
Address:		
Their relationship to you:	Occupation:	
Immigration status (if they live in the UK):		
Details of the support they can give you:		
Please tick here if you have continued on another sheet.	☐	

Section 8   **Cash, savings and assets—please read note 8**

We will take into account your cash, savings and certain possessions (see note 8) when we decide whether or not you are eligible for suppport. You should give details of cash, savings and assets in this section.

| Do you, or any of your dependants, have any cash? | Yes ☐ | Please give details below. |
| | No ☐ | |

| Do you, or any of your dependants, have any savings or investments? | Yes ☐ | Please give details below. |
| | No ☐ | |

| Do you, or any of your dependants, have any property, such as a house or vehicle? | Yes ☐ | Please give details below. |
| | No ☐ | |

| Do you, or any of your dependants, have any valuable jewellery? | Yes ☐ | Please give details below. |
| | No ☐ | |

	Value	Description
Cash		
Savings		
Other		

Please tick here if you have continued on another sheet ☐

Section 9   **Income—please read note 9**

We will take into account your income from employment, or any other source we have not already covered, when we decide whether or not you are eligible for support.
You should give details of any income that you have in this section.

| Are you, or any of your dependants, currently employed? | Yes ☐ | Please give details in the box below. |
| | No ☐ | |

| Do you, or any of your dependants, have any other income? | Yes ☐ | Please give details in the box below. |
| | No ☐ | |

If you have a job, please give your national insurance number.

Please tick here if you have continued on another sheet ☐

Section 10   **State benefits—please read note 10**

Are you, or any of your dependants, currently   Yes ☐   No ☐
receiving any benefits?

If 'Yes', please give the following information.

Type of benefit.   [   ]

Amount of benefit.   [£   ]

How often you receive the benefit.   [   ]

Have you, or any of your dependants,   Yes ☐   No ☐
previously been receiving any benefits?

If 'Yes', please give the following information.

Type of benefit.   [   ]

Amount of benefit.   [£   ]

How often you receive the benefit.   [   ]

When and why did these benefits stop? Please give details below.

[   ]
[SPECIMEN   ]
[   ]

Section 11   **Accommodation**

You should only fill in this section if you have asked us for accommodation.

if appropriate, please tell us your ethnic   [   ]
group.

Please tell us your religion and any specific   [   ]
needs connected to your faith.

Section 11 Continued

Do you, or any of your dependants, suffer from any medical condition that you need treatment, medication or counselling for?

Yes ☐   No ☐

If 'Yes', please provide details below of your condition and any treatment or medication you receive.

Name	Condition	Treatment or medication

Who is providing treatment?

Doctor's name

Surgery or hospital address

The date of your next appointment (if this applies)

Do you, or any of your dependants, have a disability that will affect the type of accommodation you are given?

Yes ☐   No ☐

If 'Yes', please give details about the disability and any requirements you may have with regard to your accommodation.

Do you, or any of your dependants, have any special dietary requirements?

Yes ☐   No ☐

If 'Yes', please give details.

Any other information.

Please tick here if you have continued on another sheet. ☐

Section 12   **Other information—please read note 12**

Please give any other information that you feel we should take into account.

Please list the documents you have sent in to support this application, for example, letters, medical certificates and passport sized photographs.

Please tick here if you have continued on another sheet. ☐

Section 13   Warning and declaration—please read note 13

This is my claim for support under the Immigration and Asylum Act 1999. I also want to claim help with health costs for myself and my family listed in section 5 of this form.

Warning and declaration. You must now read the declaration below and sign it.

I confirm that the information I have given on this form is correct and complete. I understand that if I give false information, you may take action against me and I could be prosecuted. I confirm that I will tell you if my circumstances change or there is new information that is relevant to this application. *I agree that you can pass the information on this form to the Prescription Pricing Authority so they can give me and my family listed in section 5 of this form, help towards health costs.* You can also use this information to check I, and my family listed in section 5 on this form, am entitled to help and to prevent or detect fraud.

Your signature:	
Name (please print):	
Date:	/ /

Can we give your details to the local health authority and, if your dependants are under 16, the local education authority in the area where you will be living?

Yes ☐

No ☐   You should read Note 13 before you tick this box.

Section 14   If someone helped you to fill in the form—please read note 14

Did anyone help you to fill in this form?   Yes ☐   No ☐

If 'Yes', please give the following details.

Name of assistant or representative	
Organisation and address	
Phone number	
Reference number	

Did an interpreter help you fill in this form?   Yes ☐   No ☐

If 'Yes', please give the following details.

Name of interpreter	
Organisation	
Contact number	

If you have filled in this form for the applicant, you should sign the declaration below.

I can confirm that I have included all the necessary information in this application. I have accurately recorded the information that the applicant gave me.

I can also confirm that I have signed the enclosed photograph of the main applicant.

Your signature:	
Name (please print):	
Date:	/ /

ASYLUM SUPPORT (INTERIM PROVISIONS) REGULATIONS 1999
SI 1999/3056

Date 13 November 1999
Coming into force 6 December 1999

[A.5.46]
1 Citation, commencement and extent
(1) These Regulations may be cited as the Asylum Support (Interim Provisions) Regulations 1999 and shall come into force on 6th December 1999.
(2) These Regulations do not extend to Scotland or Northern Ireland.

[A.5.47]
2 Interpretation
(1) In these Regulations—

'assisted person' means an asylum-seeker, or a dependant of an asylum-seeker, who has applied for support and for whom support is provided;
'dependant', in relation to an asylum-seeker, an assisted person or a person claiming support, means a person in the United Kingdom who:

(a) is his spouse;
(b) is a child of his, or of his spouse, who is under 18 and dependent on him;
(c) is under 18 and is a member of his, or his spouse's, close family;
(d) is under 18 and had been living as part of his household:

  (i) for at least six of the 12 months before the day on which his claim for support was made; or
  (ii) since birth;

(e) is in need of care and attention from him or a member of his household by reason of a disability and would fall within sub-paragraph (c) or (d) but for the fact that he is not under 18;
(f) had been living with him as a member of an unmarried couple for at least two of the three years before the day on which his claim for support was made;
(g) is a person living as part of his household who was receiving assistance from a local authority under section 17 of the Children Act 1989 immediately before the beginning of the interim period;
(h) has made a claim for leave to enter or remain in the United Kingdom, or for variation of any such leave, which is being considered on the basis that he is dependent on the asylum-seeker; or
(i) in relation to an assisted person or a person claiming support who is himself a dependant of an asylum-seeker, is the asylum-seeker;

'eligible persons' means asylum-seekers or their dependants who appear to be destitute or to be likely to become destitute within 14 days;
'local authority' means:

(a) in England, a county council, a metropolitan district council, a district council with the functions of a county council, a London borough council, the Common Council of the City of London or the Council of the Isles of Scilly;

(b) in Wales, a county council or a county borough council.

(2) Any reference in these Regulations to support is to support under these Regulations.

(3) Any reference in these Regulations to assistance under section 21 of the National Assistance Act 1948 is to assistance, the need for which has arisen solely:

(a) because of destitution; or
(b) because of the physical effects, or anticipated physical effects, of destitution.

(4) Any reference in these Regulations to assistance under section 17 of the Children Act 1989 is to the provision of accommodation or of any essential living needs.

(5) The interim period begins on the day on which these Regulations come into force and ends on 1st April 2002.

(6) For the purposes of section 94(3) of the Immigration and Asylum Act 1999 (day on which a claim for asylum is determined), the period of 14 days is prescribed for any case to which these Regulations apply.

[A.5.48]
3 Requirement to provide support
(1) Subject to regulations 7 and 8:

(a) the local authority concerned, or
(b) the local authority to whom responsibility for providing support is transferred under regulation 9,

must provide support during the interim period to eligible persons.

(2) The question whether a person is an eligible person is to be determined by the local authority concerned.

(3) For the purposes of these Regulations, the local authority concerned are the local authority to whom a claim for support is made, except where a claim for support is transferred by a local authority in accordance with regulation 9, in which case the local authority concerned are the local authority to whom the claim is transferred.

[A.5.49]
4 Temporary support
(1) This regulation applies to support to be provided before it has been determined whether a person is an eligible person ('temporary support').

(2) Temporary support is to be provided to a person claiming support:

(a) by the local authority to whom the claim is made until such time (if any) as the claim is transferred under regulation 9;
(b) where the claim is so transferred, by the local authority to whom the claim is transferred.

(3) Temporary support must appear to the local authority by whom it is provided to be adequate for the needs of the person claiming support and his dependants (if any).

[A.5.50]
5   Provision of support
(1)   Subject to paragraph (2), support is to be provided by providing:

(a)   accommodation appearing to the local authority by whom it is provided to be adequate for the needs of the assisted person and his dependants (if any) ('accommodation'); and
(b)   what appear to the local authority by whom it is provided to be essential living needs of the assisted person and his dependants (if any) ('essential living needs').

(2)   Where an assisted person's household includes a child who is under 18 and a dependant of his, support is to be provided:

(a)   in accordance with paragraph (1);
(b)   by providing accommodation; or
(c)   by providing essential living needs.

(3)   Support is to be provided to enable the assisted person (if he is the asylum-seeker) to meet reasonable travel expenses incurred in attending:

(a)   a hearing of an appeal on his claim for asylum; or
(b)   an interview in connection with his claim for asylum which has been requested by the Secretary of State.

(4)   Where the circumstances of a particular case are exceptional, support is to be provided in such other ways as are necessary to enable the assisted person and his dependants (if any) to be supported.
(5)   Support provided by way of payments made (by whatever means) to the assisted person and his dependants (if any) is not to exceed £10 per person in any one week, unless:

(a)   the assisted person's household includes a child who is under 18 and a dependant of his; or
(b)   the circumstances of a particular case are exceptional.

(6)   A local authority may provide support subject to conditions.
(7)   Such conditions are to be set out in writing.
(8)   A copy of the conditions is to be given to the assisted person.

[A.5.51]
6   Matters to which the local authority are to have regard
(1)   In providing support, the local authority are to have regard to:

(a)   income which the assisted person has, or his dependants (if any) have, or might reasonably be expected to have;
(b)   support which is, or assets which are, or might reasonably be expected to be, available to the assisted person, or to his dependants (if any);
(c)   the welfare of the assisted person and his dependants (if any); and
(d)   the cost of providing support.

(2)   In providing accommodation under these Regulations, the local authority are not to have regard to any preference that the assisted person or his dependants (if any) may have as to:

(a)   the locality in which the accommodation is to be provided;

(b) the nature of the accommodation to be provided; or
(c) the nature and standard of fixtures and fittings in that accommodation.

[A.5.52]
7 Refusal of support
(1)   Unless this paragraph does not apply, support must be refused in the following circumstances:

(a) where the person claiming support has intentionally made himself and his dependants (if any) destitute;
(b) where the person claiming support has made a claim for support to another local authority, except where the claim is one to which regulation 9 applies;
(c) where the claim for support is made by a person to a local authority other than one to whom, in the previous 12 months, he has made a claim for assistance under section 21 of the National Assistance Act 1948 or under section 17 of the Children Act 1989;
(d) where the person claiming support—

    (i)   is an asylum-seeker within the meaning of paragraph (3A)(a) or (aa) of regulation 70 of the Income Support (General) Regulations 1987 who has not ceased to be an asylum-seeker by virtue of sub-paragraph (b) of that paragraph;
    (ii)   is a person who became an asylum-seeker under paragraph (3A)(a) of regulation 70 of the Income Support (General) Regulations 1987 and who has not ceased to be an asylum-seeker by virtue of sub-paragraph (b) of that paragraph, as saved by regulation 12(1) of the Social Security (Persons from Abroad) Miscellaneous Amendments Regulations 1996;
    (iii) is not a person from abroad within the meaning of sub-paragraph (a) of regulation 21(3) of the Income Support (General) Regulations 1987 by virtue of the exclusions specified in that sub-paragraph;

(e) where neither the person claiming support nor any of his dependants is an asylum-seeker or has made a claim for leave to enter or remain in the United Kingdom, or for variation of any such leave, which is being considered on the basis that he is dependent on an asylum-seeker.

(2)   For the purposes of paragraph (1)(a), a person has intentionally made himself destitute if he appears to be, or likely within 14 days to become, destitute as a result of an act or omission deliberately done or made by him or any dependant of his without reasonable excuse while in the United Kingdom.
(3)   Paragraph (1) does not apply where the local authority concerned did not know, or could not with reasonable diligence have known, of any circumstance set out in that paragraph.

[A.5.53]
8 Suspension and discontinuation of support
(1)   Support for the assisted person and his dependants (if any) must be discontinued as soon as the local authority by whom it is provided become aware of any circumstance which, if they had known of it when the claim was made, would have led to the claim being refused in accordance with regulation 7(1).

(2)   Support may be suspended or discontinued:

(a) where the assisted person, or any dependant of his, fails without reasonable excuse to comply with any condition subject to which the support is provided;

(b) where the assisted person, or any dependant of his, leaves accommodation provided as part of such support for more than seven consecutive days without reasonable excuse.

[A.5.54]
9 Transfer of a claim for support or responsibility for providing support by a local authority
A local authority may transfer a claim for support made to them, or responsibility for providing support, to another local authority on such terms as may be agreed between the two authorities.

[A.5.55]
10 Assistance to those providing support
Reasonable assistance to a local authority providing support is to be given by:

(a) any district council for an area any part of which lies within the area of the local authority providing support, and

(b) any registered social landlord, within the meaning of Part I of the Housing Act 1996, which manages any house or other property which is in the area of the local authority providing support,

who is requested to provide such assistance by the local authority providing support.

[A.5.56]
11 Transitional provision
Where an asylum-seeker or a dependant of an asylum-seeker is receiving assistance from a local authority under section 21 of the National Assistance Act 1948 or under section 17 of the Children Act 1989 immediately before the beginning of the interim period, he is to be taken to have been accepted for support by the local authority providing such assistance.

[A.5.57]
12 Entitlement to claim support
A person entitled to support under these Regulations is not entitled to assistance under section 17 of the Children Act 1989.

Part B

European Materials

B1 Statutes and Treaties

EUROPEAN COMMUNITIES ACT 1972
(1972 c 68)

An Act to make provision in connection with the enlargement of the European Communities to include the United Kingdom, together with (for certain purposes) the Channel Islands, the Isle of Man and Gibraltar

[17 October 1972]

Note   Only provisions relevant to this work are printed below.

[B.1.1]
1   Short title and interpretation
(1) This Act may be cited as the European Communities Act 1972.
(2) In this Act . . .—

'the Communities' means the European Economic Community, the European Coal and Steel Community and the European Atomic Energy Community;

'the Treaties' or 'the Community Treaties' means, subject to subsection (3) below, the pre-accession treaties, that is to say, those described in Part I to Schedule I of this Act, taken with—

(a) the treaty relating to the accession of the United Kingdom to the European Economic Community and to the European Atomic Energy Community, signed at Brussels on the 22nd January 1972; and

(b) the decision, of the same date, of the Council of the European Communities relating to the accession of the United Kingdom to the European Coal and Steel Community; [and

(c) the treaty relating to the accession of the Hellenic Republic to the European Economic Community and to the European Atomic Energy Community, signed at Athens on 28th May 1979; and

(d) the decision, of 24th May 1979, of the Council relating to the accession of the Hellenic Republic to the European Coal and Steel Community;] [and

(e) the decisions, of 7th May 1985 and of 24th June 1988, of the Council on the Communities' system of own resources; and

(f) the undertaking by the Representatives of the Governments of the member States, as confirmed at their meeting within the Council on 24th June 1988 in Luxembourg, to make payments to finance the Communities' general budget for the financial year 1988; and]

(g) the treaty relating to the accession of the Kingdom of Spain and the

Portuguese Republic to the European Economic Community and to the European Atomic Energy Community, signed at Lisbon and Madrid on 12th June 1985; and

(*h*) the decision of 11th June 1985, of the Council relating to the accession of the Kingdom of Spain and the Portuguese Republic to the European Coal and Steel Community;] [and

(*j*) the following provisions of the Single European Act signed at Luxembourg and The Hague on 17th and 28th February 1986, namely Title II (amendment of the treaties establishing the Communities) and, so far as they relate to any of the Communities or any Community institution, the preamble and Titles I (common provisions) and IV (general and final provisions);]

(k) Titles II, III and IV of the Treaty on European Union signed at Maastricht on 7th February 1992, together with the other provisions of the Treaty so far as they relate to those Titles, and the Protocols adopted at Maastricht on that date and annexed to the Treaty establishing the European Community with the exception of the Protocol on Social Policy on page 117 of Cm 1934] [and

(l) the decision, of 1st February 1993, of the Council amending the Act concerning the election of the representatives of the European Parliament by direct universal suffrage annexed to Council Decision 76/787/ECSC, EEC, Euratom of 20th September 1976] [and

(m)the Agreement on the European Economic Area signed at Oporto on 2nd May 1992 together with the Protocol adjusting that Agreement signed at Brussels on 17th March 1993] [and

(n) the treaty concerning the accession of the Kingdom of Norway, the Republic of Austria, the Republic of Finland and the Kingdom of Sweden to the European Union, signed at Corfu on 24th June 1994;] [and

(o) the following provisions of the Treaty signed at Amsterdam on 2nd October 1997 amending the Treaty on European Union, the Treaties establishing the European Communities and certain related Acts—

(i) Articles 2 to 9,

(ii) Article 12, and

(iii) the other provisions of the Treaty so far as they relate to those Articles, and the Protocols adopted on that occasion other than the Protocol on Article J.7 of the Treaty on European Union]

and any other treaty entered into by any of the Communities, with or without any of the member States, or entered into, as a treaty ancillary to any of the Treaties, by the United Kingdom;

and any expression defined in Schedule 1 to this Act has the meaning there given to it.

(3) If Her Majesty by Order in Council declares that a treaty specified in the Order is to be regarded as one of the Community Treaties as herein defined, the Order shall be conclusive that it is to be so regarded; but a treaty entered into by the United Kingdom after the 22nd January 1972, other than a pre-accession treaty to which the United Kingdom accedes on terms settled on or before that date, shall not be so regarded unless it is so specified, nor be so specified unless a draft of the Order in Council has been approved by resolution of each House of Parliament.

(4) For purposes of subsections (2) and (3) above, 'treaty' includes any international agreement, and any protocol or annex to a treaty or international agreement.

Notes Sub-s (2): words omitted, repealed by the Interpretation Act 1978, s 25(1), Sch 3; paras (*c*), (*d*) added by the European Communities (Greek Accession) Act 1979, s 1; paras (*e*), (*f*) added by the European Communities (Finance) Act 1985, s 1, substituted by the European Communities (Finance) Act 1988, s 1; paras (*g*), (*h*) added by the European Communities (Spanish and Portuguese Accession) Act 1985, s 1, substituted by the European Communities (Finance) Act 1988, s 1; para (*j*) added by the European Communities (Amendment) Act 1986, s 1; para (*k*) added by the European Communities (Amendment) Act 1993, s 1; para (*l*) added by the European Parliamentary Elections Act 1993, s 3(2); para (*m*) added by the European Economic Area Act 1992, s 1; para (*n*) added by the European Union (Accessions) Act 1994, s 1; para (*o*) added by the European Communities (Amendment) Act 1998, s 8.

[B.1.2]
2 General implementation of Treaties
(1) All such rights, powers, liabilities, obligations and restrictions from time to time created or arising by or under the Treaties, and all such remedies and procedures from time to time provided for, by, or under the Treaties, as in accordance with the Treaties are without further enactment to be given legal effect or used in the United Kingdom shall be recognised and available in law, and be enforced, allowed and followed accordingly; and the expression 'enforceable Community right' and similar expressions shall be read as referring to one to which this subsection applies.
(2) Subject to Schedule 2 to this Act, at any time after its passing Her Majesty may by Order in Council, and any designated Minister or department may by regulations, make provision—

(*a*) for the purpose of implementing any Community obligation of the United Kingdom,or enabling any such obligation to be implemented, or of enabling any rights enjoyed or to be enjoyed by the United Kingdom under or by virtue of the Treaties to be exercised; or
(*b*) for the purpose of dealing with matters arising out of or related to any such obligation or rights or the coming into force, or the operation from time to time, of subsection (2) above;

and in the exercise of any statutory power of duty, including any power to give directions or to legislate by means of orders, rules, regulations or other subordinate instrument, the person entrusted with the power or duty may have regard to the objects of the Communities and to any such obligation or rights as aforesaid.

In this subsection 'designated Minister or department' means such Minister of the Crown or government department as may from to time be designated by Order in Council in relation to any matter or for any purpose, but subject to such restrictions or conditions (if any) as may be specified by the Order in Council.
(3) There shall be charged on and issued out of the Consolidated Fund or, if so determined by the Treasury, the National Loans Fund the amounts required to meet any Community obligation to make payments to any of the

Communities or member States, or any Community obligation in respect of contributions to the capital or reserves of the European Investment Bank or in respect of loans to the Bank, or to redeem any notes or obligations issued or created in respect of any such Community obligation; and, except as otherwise provided by or under any enactment,—

(*a*) any other expenses incurred under or by virtue of the Treaties or this Act by any Minister of the Crown or government department may be paid out of moneys provided by Parliament; and

(*b*) any sums received under or by virtue of the Treaties or this Act by any Minister of the Crown or government department, save for such sums as may be required for disbursements permitted by any other enactment, shall be paid into the Consolidated Fund or, if so determined by the Treasury, the National Loans Fund.

(4) The provision that may be made under subsection (2) above includes, subject to Schedule 2 to this Act, any such provision (of any such extent) as might be made by Act of Parliament, and any enactment passed or to be passed, other than one contained in this Part of this Act, shall be construed and have effect subject to the foregoing provisions of this section; but, except as may be provided by any Act passed after this Act, Schedule 2 shall have effect in connection with the powers conferred by this and the following sections of this Act to make Orders in Council and regulations.

(5) . . .; and the references in that subsection to a Minister of the Crown or government department and to a statutory power or duty shall include a Minister or department of the Government of Northern Ireland and a power or duty arising under or by virtue of an Act of the Parliament of Northern Ireland.

(6) A law passed by the legislature of any of the Channel Islands or of the Isle of Man, or a colonial law (within the meaning of the Colonial Laws Validity Act 1986) passed or made for Gibraltar, if expressed to be passed or made in the implementation of the Treaties and of the obligations of the United Kingdom thereunder, shall not be void or inoperative by reason of any inconsistency with or repugnancy to an Act of Parliament, passed or to be passed, that extends to the Island or Gibraltar or any provision having the force and effect of an Act there (but not including this section), nor by reason of its having some operation under the Island or Gibraltar; and any such Act or provision that extends to the Island or Gibraltar shall be construed and have effect subject to the provisions of any such law.

Note   Sub-s (5): words omitted repealed by the Northern Ireland Constitution Act 1973; s 4(1), Sch 6.

[B.1.3]
3   Decisions on, and proof of, Treaties and Community instruments, etc
(1) For the purposes of all legal proceedings any question as to the meaning or effect of any of the Treaties, or as to the validity, meaning or effect of any Community instrument, shall be treated as a question of law (and, if not referred to the European Court, be for determination as such in accordance with the principles laid down by and any relevant [decision of the European Court or any court attached thereto)].

(2) Judicial notice shall be taken of the Treaties, of the Official Journal of the Communities and of any decision of, or expression of opinion by, the

European Court [or any court attached thereto] on any such question as afore-said; and the Official Journal shall be admissible as evidence of any instrument or other act thereby communicated of any of the Communities or of any Community institution.

(3) Evidence of any instrument issued by a Community institution, including any judgment or order of the European Court [or any court attached thereto], or of any document in the custody of a Community institution, or any entry in or extract from such a document, may be given in any legal proceedings by production of a copy certified as a true copy by an official of that institution; and any document purporting to be such a copy shall be received in evidence without proof of the official position or handwriting of the person signing the certificate.

(4) Evidence of any Community instrument may also be given in any legal proceedings—

(*a*) by production of a copy purporting to be printed by the Queen's Printer;

(*b*) where the instrument is in the custody of a government department (including a department of the Government of Northern Ireland), by pro-duction of a copy certified on behalf of the department to be a true copy by an officer of the department generally or specially authorised so to do;

and any document purporting to be such a copy as is mentioned in paragraph (*b*) above of an instrument in the custody of a department shall be received in evidence without proof of the official position or handwriting of the person signing the certificate, or of his authority to do so, or of the document being in the custody of the department.

(5) . . .

Notes Subsections (1)–(3): amended by the European Communities (Amendment) Act 1986, s 2. Sub-s (5): applies to Scotland only.

---

4 General provision for repeal and amendment

(1) The enactments mentioned in Schedule 3 to this Act (being enactments that are superseded or to be superseded by reason of Community obligations and of the provision made by this Act in relation thereto or are not compatible with Community obligations) are hereby repealed, to the extent specified in column 3 of the Schedule, with effect from the entry date or other date men-tioned in the Schedule; and in the enactments mentioned in Schedule 4 to this Act there shall, subject to any transitional provision there included, be made the amendments provided for by that Schedule.

(2) Where in any Part of Schedule 3 to this Act it is provided that repeals made by that Part are to take effect from a date appointed by order, the orders shall be made by statutory instrument, and an order may appoint different dates for the repeal of different provisions to take effect, or for the repeal of the same provision to take effect for different purposes; and an order appointing a date for a repeal to take effect may included transitional and other supplementary provisions arising out of that repeal, including provisions adapting the opera-tion of other enactments included for repeal but not yet repealed by that Schedule, an may amend or revoke any such provisions included in a previous order.

(3) Where any of the following sections of this Act, or any paragraph of Schedule 4 to this Act, affects or is construed as one with an Act or Part of an Act similar in purpose to provisions having effect only in Northern Ireland, then—

(*a*) unless otherwise provided by Act of the Parliament of Northern Ireland, the Governor of Northern Ireland may by Order in Council make provision corresponding to any made by the section or paragraph, and amend or revoke any provision so made; and

(*b*) . . .

(4) Where Schedule 3 or 4 to this Act provides for the repeal or amendment of an enactment that extends or is capable of being extended to any of the Channel Islands or the Isle of Man, the repeal or amendment shall in like manner extend or be capable of being extended thereto.

Date in force   17 October 1972—1 September 1978 (part); to be appointed remainder.

Note   Subsection (3)(*b*) repealed by the Northern Ireland Constitution Act 1973, s 4(1), Sch 6.

CONSOLIDATED VERSION OF THE TREATY ON EUROPEAN UNION

(as amended by the Treaty of Amsterdam) signed in Maastricht on 7 February 1992, OJ C191, 29 June 1992

Note Only provisions relevant to this work are printed below.

(92/C 191/01)

Title I   Common provisions

[B.1.5]
Article 2 *(ex Article B)*
The Union shall set itself the following objectives:

— to promote economic and social progress and a high level of employment and to achieve balanced and sustainable development, in particular through the creation of an area without internal frontiers, through the strengthening of economic and social cohesion and through the establishment of economic and monetary union, ultimately including a single currency in accordance with the provisions of this Treaty;
— to assert its identity on the international scene, in particular through the implementation of a common foreign and security policy including the progressive framing of a common defence policy, which might lead to a common defence, in accordance with the provisions of Article 17;
— to strengthen the protection of the rights and interests of the nationals of its Member States through the introduction of a citizenship of the Union;
— to maintain and develop the Union as an area of freedom, security and justice, in which the free movement of persons is assured in conjunction with appropriate measures with respect to external border controls, asylum, immigration and the prevention and combating of crime;
— to maintain in full the acquis communautaire and build on it with a view to considering to what extent the policies and forms of cooperation introduced by this Treaty may need to be revised with the aim of ensuring the effectiveness of the mechanisms and the institutions of the Community.

The objectives of the Union shall be achieved as provided in this Treaty and in accordance with the conditions and the timetable set out therein while respecting the principle of subsidiarity as defined in Article 5 of the Treaty establishing the European Community.

[B.1.6]
Article 6 *(ex Article F)*
1.   The Union is founded on the principles of liberty, democracy, respect for human rights and fundamental freedoms, and the rule of law, principles which are common to the Member States.

2.   The Union shall respect fundamental rights, as guaranteed by the

765

European Convention for the Protection of Human Rights and Fundamental Freedoms signed in Rome on 4 November 1950 and as they result from the constitutional traditions common to the Member States, as general principles of Community law.

3.   The Union shall respect the national identities of its Member States.

4.   The Union shall provide itself with the means necessary to attain its objectives and carry through its policies.

Title VI   Provisions on Co-operation in the fields of justice and home affairs

[B.1.7]
Article 29 *(ex Article K1)*
For the purposes of achieving the objectives of the Union, in particular the free movement of persons, and without prejudice to the powers of the European Community, Member States shall regard the following areas as matters of common interest:

— asylum policy;
— rules governing the crossing by persons of the external borders of the Member States and the exercise of controls thereon;
— immigration policy and policy regarding nationals of third countries;

   (a)   conditions of entry and movement by nationals of third countries on the territory of Member States;
   (b)   conditions of residence by nationals of third countries on the territory of Member States, including family reunion and access to employment;
   (c)   combatting unauthorized immigration, residence and work by nationals of third countries on the territory of Member States;

— combating drug addiction in so far as this is not covered by 7 to 9;
— combating fraud on an international scale in so far as this is not covered by 7 to 9;
— judicial cooperation in civil matters;
— judicial cooperation in criminal matters;
— customs cooperation;
— police cooperation for the purposes of preventing and combating terrorism, unlawful drug trafficking and other serious forms of international crime, including if necessary certain aspects of customs cooperation, in connection with the organization of a Union-wide system for exchanging information within a European Police Office (Europol).

CONSOLIDATED VERSION OF THE TREATY ESTABLISHING THE EUROPEAN COMMUNITY

(as amended by the Treaty on European Union and the Treaty of Amsterdam) signed in Rome on 25 March 1957, OJ C340, 10 November 1997

Note   Title as amended by Article G(1) of the Treaty on European Union (hereinafter referred to as 'TEU'). The reader will find in the following pages an amended version of the Treaty establishing the European Economic Community as amended by the Treaty of Amsterdam and the Treaty on European Union. Only provisions relevant to this work are printed below.

PART ONE   PRINCIPLES

[B.1.8]
Article 3 *(ex Article 3)*
1.   For the purposes set out in Article 2, the activities of the Community shall include, as provided in this Treaty and in accordance with the timetable set out therein:

(*a*) the prohibition, as between Member States, of customs duties and quantitative restrictions on the import and export of goods, and of all other measures having equivalent effect;

(*b*) a common commercial policy;

(*c*) an internal market characterised by the abolition, as between Member States, of obstacles to the free movement of goods, persons, services and capital;

(*d*) measures concerning the entry and movement of persons as provided for in Title IV;

(*e*) a common policy in the sphere of agriculture and fisheries;

(*f*) a common policy in the sphere of transport;

(*g*) a system ensuring that competition in the internal market is not distorted;

(*h*) the approximation of the laws of Member States to the extent required for the functioning of the common market;

(*i*) the promotion of coordination between employment policies of the Member States with a view to enhancing their effectiveness by developing a coordinated strategy for employment;

(*j*) a policy in the social sphere comprising a European Social Fund;

(*k*) the strengthening of economic and social cohesion;

(*l*) a policy in the sphere of the environment;

(*m*) the strengthening of the competitiveness of Community industry;

(*n*) the promotion of research and technological development;

(*o*) encouragement for the establishment and development of trans-European networks;

(*p*) a contribution to the attainment of a high level of health protection;

(*q*) a contribution to education and training of quality and to the flowering of the cultures of the Member States;

(*r*) a policy in the sphere of development cooperation;

(*s*) the association of the overseas countries and territories in order to increase trade and promote jointly economic and social development;

(*t*) a contribution to the strengthening of consumer protection;

(*u*) measures in the spheres of energy, civil protection and tourism.

2.   In all the activities referred to in this Article, the Community shall aim to eliminate inequalities, and to promote equality, between men and women.

[B.1.9]

Article 5 *(ex Article 3b)*

The Community shall act within the limits of the powers conferred upon it by this Treaty and of the objectives assigned to it therein.

In areas which do not fall within its exclusive competence, the Community shall take action, in accordance with the principle of subsidiarity, only if and insofar as the objectives of the proposed action cannot be sufficiently achieved by the Member States and can therefore, by reason of the scale or effects of the proposed action, be better achieved by the Community.

Any action by the Community shall not go beyond what is necessary to achieve the objectives of this Treaty.

[B.1.10]

Article 12 *(ex Article 6)*

Within the scope of application of this Treaty, and without prejudice to any special provisions contained therein, any discrimination on grounds of nationality shall be prohibited.

The Council, acting in accordance with the procedure referred to in Article 251, may adopt rules designed to prohibit such discrimination.

[B.1.11]

Article 13 *(ex Article 6a)*

Without prejudice to the other provisions of this Treaty and within the limits of the powers conferred by it upon the Community, the Council, acting unanimously on a proposal from the Commission and after consulting the European Parliament, may take appropriate action to combat discrimination based on sex, racial or ethnic origin, religion or belief, disability, age or sexual orientation.

[B.1.12]

Article 14 *(ex Article 7a)*

1.   The Community shall adopt measures with the aim of progressively establishing the internal market over a period expiring on 31 December 1992, in accordance with the provisions of this Article and of Articles 15, 26, 47(2), 49, 80, 93 and 95 and without prejudice to the other provisions of this Treaty.

2.   The internal market shall comprise an area without internal frontiers in which the free movement of goods, persons, services and capital is ensured in accordance with the provisions of this Treaty.

3. The Council, acting by a qualified majority on a proposal from the Commission, shall determine the guidelines and conditions necessary to ensure balanced progress in all the sectors concerned.

PART TWO   CITIZENSHIP OF THE UNION

[B.1.13]
Article 17 *(ex Article 8)*
1. Citizenship of the Union is hereby established. Every person holding the nationality of a Member State shall be a citizen of the Union. Citizenship of the Union shall complement and not replace national citizenship.

2. Citizens of the Union shall enjoy the rights conferred by this Treaty and shall be subject to the duties imposed thereby.

[B.1.14]
Article 18 *(ex Article 8a)*
1. Every citizen of the Union shall have the right to move and reside freely within the territory of the Member States, subject to the limitations and conditions laid down in this Treaty and by the measures adopted to give it effect.

2. The Council may adopt provisions with a view to facilitating the exercise of the rights referred to in paragraph 1; save as otherwise provided in this Treaty, the Council shall act in accordance with the procedure referred to in Article 251. The Council shall act unanimously throughout this procedure.

Title III   Free movement of persons, services and capital

Chapter 1   Workers

[B.1.15]
Article 39 *(ex Article 48)*
1. Freedom of movement for workers shall be secured within the Community.

2. Such freedom of movement shall entail the abolition of any discrimination based on nationality between workers of the Member States as regards employment, remuneration and other conditions of work and employment.

3. It shall entail the right, subject to limitations justified on grounds of public policy, public security or public health:

(*a*) to accept offers of employment actually made;
(*b*) to move freely within the territory of Member States for this purpose;
(*c*) to stay in a Member State for the purpose of employment in accordance with the provisions governing the employment of nationals of that State laid down by law, regulation or administrative action;
(*d*) to remain in the territory of a Member State after having been employed

769

in that State, subject to conditions which shall be embodied in implementing regulations to be drawn up by the Commission.

4.   The provisions of this Article shall not apply to employment in the public service.

[B.1.16]
Article 40 *(ex Article 49)*

The Council shall, acting in accordance with the procedure referred to in Article 251 and after consulting the Economic and Social Committee, issue directives or make regulations setting out the measures required to bring about freedom of movement for workers, as defined in Article 39, in particular:

(*a*) by ensuring close cooperation between national employment services;

(*b*) by abolishing those administrative procedures and practices and those qualifying periods in respect of eligibility for available employment, whether resulting from national legislation or from agreements previously concluded between Member States, the maintenance of which would form an obstacle to liberalisation of the movement of workers;

(*c*) by abolishing all such qualifying periods and other restrictions provided for either under national legislation or under agreements previously concluded between Member States as imposed on workers of other Member States conditions regarding the free choice of employment other than those imposed on workers of the State concerned;

(*d*) by setting up appropriate machinery to bring offers of employment into touch with applications for employment and to facilitate the achievement of a balance between supply and demand in the employment market in such a way as to avoid serious threats to the standard of living and level of employment in the various regions and industries.

[B.1.17]
Article 41 *(ex Article 50)*

Member States shall, within the framework of a joint programme, encourage the exchange of young workers.

[B.1.18]
Article 42 *(ex Article 51)*

The Council shall, acting in accordance with the procedure referred to in Article 251, adopt such measures in the field of social security as are necessary to provide freedom of movement for workers; to this end, it shall make arrangements to secure for migrant workers and their dependants:

(*a*) aggregation, for the purpose of acquiring and retaining the right to benefit and of calculating the amount of benefit, of all periods taken into account under the laws of the several countries;

(*b*) payment of benefits to persons resident in the territories of Member States.

The Council shall act unanimously throughout the procedure referred to in Article 251.

Chapter 2   Right of establishment

[B.1.19]
Article 43 *(ex Article 52)*
Within the framework of the provisions set out below, restrictions on the freedom of establishment of nationals of a Member State in the territory of another Member State shall be prohibited. Such prohibition shall also apply to restrictions on the setting-up of agencies, branches or subsidiaries by nationals of any Member State established in the territory of any Member State.

Freedom of establishment shall include the right to take up and pursue activities as self-employed persons and to set up and manage undertakings, in particular companies or firms within the meaning of the second paragraph of Article 48, under the conditions laid down for its own nationals by the law of the country where such establishment is effected, subject to the provisions of the Chapter relating to capital.

[B.1.20]
Article 44 *(ex Article 54)*
1.   In order to attain freedom of establishment as regards a particular activity, the Council, acting in accordance with the procedure referred to in Article 251 and after consulting the Economic and Social Committee, shall act by means of directives.

2.   The Council and the Commission shall carry out the duties devolving upon them under the preceding provisions, in particular:

(*a*) by according, as a general rule, priority treatment to activities where freedom of establishment makes a particularly valuable contribution to the development of production and trade;
(*b*) by ensuring close cooperation between the competent authorities in the Member States in order to ascertain the particular situation within the Community of the various activities concerned;
(*c*) by abolishing those administrative procedures and practices, whether resulting from national legislation or from agreements previously concluded between Member States, the maintenance of which would form an obstacle to freedom of establishment;
(*d*) by ensuring that workers of one Member State employed in the territory of another Member State may remain in that territory for the purpose of taking up activities therein as self-employed persons, where they satisfy the conditions which they would be required to satisfy if they were entering that State at the time when they intended to take up such activities;
(*e*) by enabling a national of one Member State to acquire and use land and buildings situated in the territory of another Member State, insofar as this does not conflict with the principles laid down in Article 33(2);
(*f*) by effecting the progressive abolition of restrictions on freedom of establishment in every branch of activity under consideration, both as regards the conditions for setting up agencies, branches or subsidiaries in the territory of a Member State and as regards the subsidiaries in the territory of a Member State and as regards the conditions governing the entry of personnel belonging to the main establishment into managerial or supervisory posts in such agencies, branches or subsidiaries;
(*g*) by coordinating to the necessary extent the safeguards which, for the pro-

tection of the interests of members and other, are required by Member States of companies or firms within the meaning of the second paragraph of Article 48 with a view to making such safeguards equivalent throughout the Community;

(*h*) by satisfying themselves that the conditions of establishment are not distorted by aids granted by Member States.

[B.1.21]
Article 45 *(ex Article 55)*
The provisions of this Chapter shall not apply, so far as any given Member State is concerned, to activities which in that State are connected, even occasionally, with the exercise of official authority.

The Council may, acting by a qualified majority on a proposal from the Commission, rule that the provisions of this Chapter shall not apply to certain activities.

[B.1.22]
Article 46 *(ex Article 56)*
1.   The provisions of this Chapter and measures taken in pursuance thereof shall not prejudice the applicability of provisions laid down by law, regulation or administrative action providing for special treatment for foreign nationals on grounds of public policy, public security or public health.

2.   The Council shall, acting in accordance with the procedure referred to in Article 251, issue directives for the coordination of the abovementioned provisions.

[B.1.23]
Article 47 *(ex Article 57)*
1.   In order to make it easier for persons to take up and pursue activities as self-employed persons, the Council shall, acting in accordance with the procedure referred to in Article 251, issue directives for the mutual recognition of diplomas, certificates and other evidence of formal qualifications.

2.   For the same purpose, the Council shall, acting in accordance with the procedure referred to in Article 251, issue directives for the coordination of the provisions laid down by law, regulation or administrative action in Member States concerning the taking-up and pursuit of activities as self-employed persons. The Council, acting unanimously throughout the procedure referred to in Article 251, shall decide on directives the implementation of which involves in at least one Member State amendment of the existing principles laid down by law governing the professions with respect to training and conditions of access for natural persons. In other cases the Council shall act by qualified majority.

3.   In the case of the medical and allied and pharmaceutical professions, the progressive abolition of restrictions shall be dependent upon coordination of the conditions for their exercise in the various Member States.

[B.1.24]
Article 48 *(ex Article 58)*
Companies or firms formed in accordance with the law of a Member State and having their registered office, central administration or principal place of business within the Community shall, for the purposes of this Chapter, be treated in the same way as natural persons who are nationals of Member States.

'Companies or firms' means companies or firms constituted under civil or commercial law, including cooperative societies, and other legal persons governed by public or private law, save for those which are non-profit-making.

Chapter 3   Services

[B.1.25]
Article 49 *(ex Article 59)*
Within the framework of the provisions set out below, restrictions on freedom to provide services within the Community shall be prohibited in respect of nationals of Member States who are established in a State of the Community other than that of the person for whom the services are intended.

The Council may, acting by a qualified majority on a proposal from the Commission, extend the provisions of the Chapter to nationals of a third country who provide services and who are established within the Community.

[B.1.26]
Article 50 *(ex Article 60)*
Services shall be considered to be 'services' within the meaning of this Treaty where they are normally provided for remuneration, insofar as they are not governed by the provisions relating to freedom of movement for goods, capital and persons.

'Services' shall in particular include:

(*a*) activities of an industrial character;
(*b*) activities of a commercial character;
(*c*) activities of craftsmen;
(*d*) activities of the professions.

Without prejudice to the provisions of the Chapter relating to the right of establishment, the person providing a service may, in order to do so, temporarily pursue his activity in the State where the service is provided, under the same conditions as are imposed by that State on its own nationals.

[B.1.27]
Article 51 *(ex Article 61)*
1.   Freedom to provide services in the field of transport shall be governed by the provisions of the Title relating to transport.

2.   The liberalisation of banking and insurance services connected with movements of capital shall be effected in step with the liberalisation of movement of capital.

[B.1.28]
Article 52 *(ex Article 63)*
1.   In order to achieve the liberalisation of a specific service, the Council shall, on a proposal from the Commission and after consulting the Economic and Social Committee and the European Parliament, issue directives acting by a qualified majority.

2.   As regards the directives referred to in paragraph 1, priority shall as a general rule be given to those services which directly affect production costs or the liberalisation of which helps to promote trade in goods.

[B.1.29]
Article 53 (ex Article 64)
The Member States declare their readiness to undertake the liberalisation of services beyond the extent required by the directives issued pursuant to Article 52(1), if their general economic situation and the situation of the economic sector concerned so permit.

To this end, the Commission shall make recommendations to the Member States concerned.

[B.1.30]
Article 54 *(ex Article 65)*
As long as restrictions on freedom to provide services have not been abolished, each Member State shall apply such restrictions without distinction on grounds of nationality or residence to all persons providing services within the meaning of the first paragraph of Article 49.

[B.1.31]
Article 55 *(ex Article 66)*
The provisions of Articles 45 to 48 shall apply to the matters covered by this Chapter.

Title IV (ex Title IIIa)   Visas, asylum, immigration and other policies related to free movement of persons

[B.1.32]
Article 61 *(ex Article 73i)*
In order to establish progressively an area of freedom, security and justice, the Council shall adopt:

(*a*)   within a period of five years after the entry into force of the Treaty of Amsterdam, measures aimed at ensuring the free movement of persons in accordance with Article 14, in conjunction with directly related flanking measures with respect to external border controls, asylum and immigration, in accordance with the provisions of Article 62(2) and (3) and Article 63(1)(*a*) and (2)(*a*), and measures to prevent and combat crime in accordance with the provisions of Article 31(*e*) of the Treaty on European Union;

(*b*) other measures in the fields of asylum, immigration and safeguarding the rights of nationals of third countries, in accordance with the provisions of Article 63;

(*c*) measures in the field of judicial cooperation in civil matters as provided for in Article 65;

(*d*) appropriate measures to encourage and strengthen administrative cooperation, as provided for in Article 66;

(*e*) measures in the field of police and judicial cooperation in criminal matters aimed at a high level of security by preventing and combating crime within the Union in accordance with the provisions of the Treaty on European Union.

[B.1.33]
Article 62 *(ex Article 73j)*
The Council, acting in accordance with the procedure referred to in Article 67, shall, within a period of five years after the entry into force of the Treaty of Amsterdam, adopt:

(1) measures with a view to ensuring, in compliance with Article 14, the absence of any controls on persons, be they citizens of the Union or nationals of third countries, when crossing internal borders;

(2) measures on the crossing of the external borders of the Member States which shall establish:

   (*a*) standards and procedures to be followed by Member States in carrying out checks on persons at such borders;

   (*b*) rules on visas for intended stays of no more than three months, including:

      (i) the list of third countries whose nationals must be in possession of visas when crossing the external borders and those whose nationals are exempt from that requirement;

      (ii) the procedures and conditions for issuing visas by Member States;

      (iii) a uniform format for visas;

      (iv) rules on a uniform visa;

(3) measures setting out the conditions under which nationals of third countries shall have the freedom to travel within the territory of the Member States during a period of no more than three months.

[B.1.34]
Article 63 *(ex Article 73k)*
The Council, acting in accordance with the procedure referred to in Article 67, shall, within a period of five years after the entry into force of the Treaty of Amsterdam, adopt:

(1) measures on asylum, in accordance with the Geneva Convention of 28 July 1951 and the Protocol of 31 January 1967 relating to the status of refugees and other relevant treaties, within the following areas:

(a)   criteria and mechanisms for determining which Member State is responsible for considering an application for asylum submitted by a national of a third country in one of the Member States,

(b)   minimum standards on the reception of asylum seekers in Member States,

(c)   minimum standards with respect to the qualification of nationals of third countries as refugees,

(d)   minimum standards on procedures in Member States for granting or withdrawing refugee status;

(2) measures on refugees and displaced persons within the following areas:

(a)   minimum standards for giving temporary protection to displaced persons from third countries who cannot return to their country of origin and for persons who otherwise need international protection,

(b)   promoting a balance of effort between Member States in receiving and bearing the consequences of receiving refugees and displaced persons;

(3) measures on immigration policy within the following areas:

(a)   conditions of entry and residence, and standards on procedures for the issue by Member States of long term visas and residence permits, including those for the purpose of family reunion,

(b)   illegal immigration and illegal residence, including repatriation of illegal residents;

(4) measures defining the rights and conditions under which nationals of third countries who are legally resident in a Member State may reside in other Member States.

Measures adopted by the Council pursuant to points 3 and 4 shall not prevent any Member State from maintaining or introducing in the areas concerned national provisions which are compatible with this Treaty and with international agreements.

Measures to be adopted pursuant to points 2(b), 3(a) and 4 shall not be subject to the five year period referred to above.

[B.1.35]
Article 64 *(ex Article 73l)*

1.   This Title shall not affect the exercise of the responsibilities incumbent upon Member States with regard to the maintenance of law and order and the safeguarding of internal security.

2.   In the event of one or more Member States being confronted with an emergency situation characterised by a sudden inflow of nationals of third countries and without prejudice to paragraph 1, the Council may, acting by qualified majority on a proposal from the Commission, adopt provisional measures of a duration not exceeding six months for the benefit of the Member States concerned.

[B.1.36]
Article 65 *(ex Article 73m)*
Measures in the field of judicial cooperation in civil matters having cross-border implications, to be taken in accordance with Article 67 and insofar as necessary for the proper functioning of the internal market, shall include:

(*a*) improving and simplifying:

— the system for cross-border service of judicial and extrajudicial documents;
— cooperation in the taking of evidence;
— the recognition and enforcement of decisions in civil and commercial cases, including decisions in extrajudicial cases;

(*b*) promoting the compatibility of the rules applicable in the Member States concerning the conflict of laws and of jurisdiction;
(*c*) eliminating obstacles to the good functioning of civil proceedings, if necessary by promoting the compatibility of the rules on civil procedure applicable in the Member States.

[B.1.37]
Article 66 *(ex Article 73n)*
The Council, acting in accordance with the procedure referred to in Article 67, shall take measures to ensure cooperation between the relevant departments of the administrations of the Member States in the areas covered by this Title, as well as between those departments and the Commission.

[B.1.38]
Article 67 *(ex Article 73o)*
1. During a transitional period of five years following the entry into force of the Treaty of Amsterdam, the Council shall act unanimously on a proposal from the Commission or on the initiative of a Member State and after consulting the European Parliament.

2. After this period of five years:

— the Council shall act on proposals from the Commission; the Commission shall examine any request made by a Member State that it submit a proposal to the Council;
— the Council, acting unanimously after consulting the European Parliament, shall take a decision with a view to providing for all or parts of the areas covered by this Title to be governed by the procedure referred to in Article 251 and adapting the provisions relating to the powers of the Court of Justice.

3. By derogation from paragraphs 1 and 2, measures referred to in Article 62(2)(*b*) (i) and (iii) shall, from the entry into force of the Treaty of Amsterdam, be adopted by the Council acting by a qualified majority on a proposal from the Commission and after consulting the European Parliament.

4. By derogation from paragraph 2, measures referred to in Article 62(2)(*b*) (ii) and (iv) shall, after a period of five years following the entry into force of

the Treaty of Amsterdam, be adopted by the Council acting in accordance with the procedure referred to in Article 251.

[B.1.39]
Article 68 *(ex Article 73p)*
1.   Article 234 shall apply to this Title under the following circumstances and conditions: where a question on the interpretation of this Title or on the validity or interpretation of acts of the institutions of the Community based on this Title is raised in a case pending before a court or a tribunal of a Member State against whose decisions there is no judicial remedy under national law, that court or tribunal shall, if it considers that a decision on the question is necessary to enable it to give judgment, request the Court of Justice to give a ruling thereon.

2.   In any event, the Court of Justice shall not have jurisdiction to rule on any measure or decision taken pursuant to Article 62(1) relating to the maintenance of law and order and the safeguarding of internal security.

3.   The Council, the Commission or a Member State may request the Court of Justice to give a ruling on a question of interpretation of this Title or of acts of the institutions of the Community based on this Title. The ruling given by the Court of Justice in response to such a request shall not apply to judgments of courts or tribunals of the Member States which have become res judicata.

[B.1.40]
Article 69 *(ex Article 73q)*
The application of this Title shall be subject to the provisions of the Protocol on the position of the United Kingdom and Ireland and to the Protocol on the position of Denmark and without prejudice to the Protocol on the application of certain aspects of Article 14 of the Treaty establishing the European Community to the United Kingdom and to Ireland.

B2   Secondary Legislation

COUNCIL DIRECTIVE (64/221/EEC)

of 25 February 1964 on the co-ordination of special measures concerning the movement and residence of foreign nationals which are justified on grounds of public policy, public security or public health

[B.2.1]

The Council of The European Economic Community,

Having regard to the Treaty establishing the European Economic Community, and in particular Article 56(2) thereof;

Having regard to Council Regulation of 16 August 1961[1] on initial measures to bring about free movement of workers within the Community, and in particular Article 47 thereof;

Having regard to Council Directive of 16 August 1961[2] on administrative procedures and practices governing the entry into and employment and residence in a member state of workers and their families from other member states of the Community;

Having regard to the General Programme[3] for the abolition of restrictions on freedom of establishment and on freedom to provide services, and in particular Title II of each such programme;

Having regard to the Council Directive of 25 February 1964[4] on the abolition of restrictions on movement and residence within the Community for nationals of member states with regard to establishment and the provision of services;

Having regard to the proposal from the Commission;

Having regard to the Opinion of the European Parliament[5];

Having regard to the Opinion of the Economic and Social Committee[6];

Whereas co-ordination of provisions laid down by law, regulation or administrative action which provide for special treatment for foreign nationals on grounds of public policy, public security or public health should in the first place deal with the conditions for entry and residence of nationals of member states moving within the Community either in order to pursue activities as employed or self-employed persons, or as recipients of services;

Whereas such co-ordination presupposes in particular an approximation of the procedures followed in each member state when invoking grounds of public policy, public security or public health in matters connected with the movement or residence of foreign nationals;

Whereas in each member state, nationals of other member states should have adequate legal remedies available to them in respect of the decisions of the administration in such matters;

Whereas it would be of little practical use to compile a list of diseases and disabilities which might endanger public health, public policy or public security and it would be difficult to make such a list exhaustive; whereas it is sufficient to classify such diseases and disabilities in groups;

---

1 OJ No 57, 26.8.1961, p 1073/61.
2 OJ No 80, 13.12.1961, p 1513/61.
3 OJ No 2, 15.1.1962, pp 32/62 and 36/62.
4 OJ No 56, 4.4.1964, p 845/64.
5 OJ No 134,14.12.1967, p2861/62.
6 OJ No 56, 4.4.1964, p 856/64.

Has adopted this Directive:

[B.2.2]
Article 1

1 The provisions of this Directive shall apply to any national of a member state who resides in or travels to another member state of the Community, either in order to pursue an activity as an employed or self-employed person, or as a recipient of services.

2 These provisions shall apply also to the spouse and to members of the family who come within the provisions of the regulations and directives adopted in this field in pursuance of the Treaty.

[B.2.3]
Article 2

1 This Directive relates to all measures concerning entry into their territory, issue or renewal of residence permits, or expulsion from their territory, taken by member states on grounds of public policy, public security or public health.

2 Such grounds shall not be invoked to service economic ends.

[B.2.4]
Article 3

1 Measures taken on grounds of public policy or of public security shall be based exclusively on the personal conduct of the individual concerned.

2 Previous criminal convictions shall not in themselves constitute grounds for the taking of such measures.

3 Expiry of the identity card or passport used by the person concerned to enter the host country and to obtain a residence permit shall not justify expulsion from the territory.

4 The state which issued the identity card or passport shall allow the holder of such document to re-enter its territory without any formality even if the document is no longer valid or the nationality of the holder is in dispute.

[B.2.5]
Article 4
1   The only diseases or disabilities justifying refusal of entry into a territory or refusal to issue a first residence permit shall be those listed in the Annex to this Directive.

2   Diseases or disabilities occurring after a first residence permit has been issued shall not justify refusal to renew the residence permit or expulsion from the territory.

3   Member states shall not introduce new provisions or practices which are more restrictive than those in force at the date of notification of this Directive.

[B.2.6]
Article 5
1   A decision to grant or to refuse a first residence permit shall be taken as soon as possible and in any event not later than six months from the date of application for the permit.
    The person concerned shall be allowed to remain temporarily in the territory pending a decision either to grant or to refuse a residence permit.

2   The host country may, in cases where this is considered essential, request the member state of origin of the applicant, and if need be other member states, to provide information concerning any previous police record. Such enquiries shall not be made as a matter of routine. The member state consulted shall give its reply within two months.

[B.2.7]
Article 6
The person concerned shall be informed of the grounds of public policy, public security, or public health upon which the decision taken in his case is based, unless this is contrary to the interests of the security of the state involved.

[B.2.8]
Article 7
The person concerned shall be officially notified of any decision to refuse the issue or renewal of a residence permit or to expel him from the territory. The period allowed for leaving the territory shall be stated in this notification. Save in cases of urgency, this period shall be not less than fifteen days if the person concerned has not yet been granted a residence permit and not less than one month in all other cases.

[B.2.9]
Article 8
The person concerned shall have the same legal remedies in respect of any decision concerning entry, or refusing the issue or renewal of a residence permit, or ordering expulsion from the territory, as are available to nationals of the state concerned in respect of acts of the administration.

[B.2.10]
Article 9
1   Where there is no right of appeal to a court of law, or where such appeal may be only in respect of the legal validity of the decision, or where the appeal cannot have suspensory effect, a decision refusing renewal of a residence permit or ordering the expulsion of the holder of a residence permit from the territory shall not be taken by the administrative authority, save in cases of urgency, until an opinion has been obtained from a competent authority of the host country before which the person concerned enjoys such rights of defence and of assistance or representation as the domestic law of that country provides for.

This authority shall not be the same as that empowered to take the decision refusing renewal of the residence permit or ordering expulsion.

2   Any decision refusing the issue of a first residence permit or ordering expulsion of the person concerned before the issue of the permit shall, where that person so requests, be referred for consideration to the authority whose prior opinion is required under paragraph 1. The person concerned shall then be entitled to submit his defence in person, except where this would be contrary to the interests of national security.

[B.2.11]
Article 10
1   Member states shall within six months of notification of this Directive put into force the measures necessary to comply with its provisions and shall forthwith inform the Commission thereof.

2   Member states shall ensure that the texts of the main provisions of national law which they adopt in the field governed by this Directive are communicated to the Commission.

[B.2.12]
Article 11
This Directive is addressed to the member states.

Done at Brussels, 25 February 1964.

Annex

[B.2.13]
A   Diseases which might endanger public health:

1   Diseases subject to quarantine listed in International Health Regulation No 2 of the World Health Organisation of 25 May 1951;
2   Tuberculosis of the respiratory system in an active state or showing a tendency to develop;
3   Syphilis;

4   Other infectious diseases or contagious parasitic diseases if they are the subject of provisions for the protection of nationals of the host country.

B   Diseases and disabilities which might threaten public policy or public security:

1   Drug addiction;
2   Profound mental disturbance; manifest conditions of psychotic disturbance with agitation, delirium, hallucinations or confusion.

REGULATION (EEC) 1612/68 OF THE COUNCIL

of 15 October 1968 on freedom of movement for workers within the Community

[B.2.14]

The Council of The European Communities,

Having regard to the Treaty establishing the European Economic Community, and in particular Article 49 thereof;

Having regard to the proposal from the Commission;

Having regard to the Opinion of the European Parliament[1];

Having regard to the Opinion of the Economic and Social Committee[2];

Whereas freedom of movement for workers should be secured within the Community by the end of the transitional period at the latest; whereas the attainment of this objective entails the abolition of any discrimination based on nationality between workers of the member states as regards employment, remuneration and other conditions of work and employment, as well as the right of such workers to move freely within the Community in order to pursue activities as employed persons subject to any limitations justified on grounds of public policy, public security or public health;

Whereas by reason in particular of the early establishment of the customs union and in order to ensure the simultaneous completion of the principal foundations of the Community, provisions should be adopted to enable the objectives laid down in Articles 48 and 49 of the Treaty in the field of freedom of movement to be achieved and to perfect measures adopted successively under Regulation No 15[3] on the first steps for attainment of freedom of movement and under Council Regulation No 38/EEC[4] of 25 March 1964 on freedom of movement for workers within the Community;

Whereas freedom of movement constitutes a fundamental right of workers and their families; whereas mobility of labour within the Community must be one of the means by which the worker is guaranteed the possibility of improving his living and working conditions and promoting his social advancement, while helping to satisfy the requirements of the economies of the member states; whereas the right of all workers in the member states to pursue the activity of their choice within the Community should be affirmed;

Whereas such right must be enjoyed without discrimination by permanent, seasonal and frontier workers and by those who pursue their activities for the purpose of providing services;

Whereas the right of freedom of movement, in order that it may be exercised, by objective standards, in freedom and dignity, requires that equality of treatment shall be ensured in fact and in law in respect of all matters relating to the actual pursuit of activities as employed persons and to eligibility for housing, and also that obstacles to the mobility of workers shall be eliminated, in particular as regards the worker's right to be joined by his family and the conditions for the integration of that family into the host country;

Whereas the principle of non-discrimination between Community workers entails that all nationals of member states have the same priority as regards employment as is enjoyed by national workers;

Whereas it is necessary to strengthen the machinery for vacancy clearance, in particular by developing direct co-operation between the central employment services and also between the regional services, as well as by increasing and co-ordinating the exchange of information in order to ensure in a general way a clearer picture of the labour market; whereas workers wishing to move should also be regularly informed of living and working conditions; whereas, furthermore, measures should be provided for the case where a member state undergoes or foresees disturbances on its labour market which may seriously threaten the standard of living and level of employment in a region or an industry; whereas for this purpose the exchange of information, aimed at discouraging workers from moving to such a region or industry, constitutes the method to be applied in the first place but, where necessary, it should be possible to strengthen the results of such exchange of information by temporarily suspending the abovementioned machinery, any such decision to be taken at Community level;

Whereas close links exist between freedom of movement for workers, employment and vocational training, particularly where the latter aims at putting workers in a position to take up offers of employment from other regions of the Community; whereas such links make it necessary that the problems arising in this connection should no longer be studied in isolation but viewed as inter-dependent, account also being taken of the problems of employment at the regional level; and whereas it is therefore necessary to direct the efforts of member states toward coordinating their employment policies at Community level;

Whereas the Council, by its Decision of 15 October 1968[5] made Article 48 and 49 of the Treaty and also the measures taken in implementation thereof applicable to the French overseas departments;

---

1 OJ No 268, 6.11.1967, p 9.
2 ON No 298, 7.12.1967, p 10.
3 OJ No 57, 26.8.1961, p 1073/61.
4 OJ No 62, 17.4.1964, p 965/64.
5 OJ No 257, 19.10.1968, p 1.

Has adopted this Regulation:

PART I   EMPLOYMENT AND WORKERS' FAMILIES

Title I   Eligibility for employment

[B.2.15]
Article 1
1   Any national of a member state, shall, irrespective of his place of residence, have the right to take up an activity as an employed person, and to pursue such activity, within the territory of another member state in accordance

with the provisions laid down by law, regulation or administrative action governing the employment of nationals of that state.

2   He shall, in particular, have the right to take up available employment in the territory of another member state with the same priority as nationals of that state.

[B.2.16]
Article 2
Any national of a member state and any employer pursuing an activity in the territory of a member state may exchange their applications for and offers of employment, and may conclude and perform contracts of employment in accordance with the provisions in force laid down by law, regulation or administrative action, without any discrimination resulting therefrom.

[B.2.17]
Article 3
1   Under this Regulation, provisions laid down by law, regulation or administrative action or administrative practices of a member state shall not apply:

— where they limit application for and offers of employment, or the right of foreign nationals to take up and pursue employment or subject these to conditions not applicable in respect of their own nationals; or
— where, though applicable irrespective of nationality, their exclusive or principal aim or effect is to keep nationals of other member states away from the employment offered.

This provision shall not apply to conditions relating to linguistic knowledge required by reason of the nature of the post to be filled.

2   There shall be included in particular among the provisions or practices of a member state referred to in the first subparagraph of paragraph 1 those which:

(*a*) prescribe a special recruitment procedure for foreign nationals;
(*b*) limit or restrict the advertising of vacancies in the press or through any other medium or subject it to conditions other than those applicable in respect of employers pursuing their activities in the territory of that member state;
(*c*) subject eligibility for employment to conditions of registration with employment offices or impede recruitment of individual workers, where persons who do not reside in the territory of that state are concerned.

[B.2.18]
Article 4
1   Provisions laid down by law, regulation or administrative action of the member states which restrict by number or percentage the employment of foreign nationals in any undertaking, branch of activity or region, or at a national level, shall not apply to nationals of the other member states.

786

2   When in a member state the granting of any benefit to undertakings is subject to a minimum percentage of national workers being employed, nationals of the other member states shall be counted as national workers, subject to the provisions of the Council Directive of 15 October 1963.[1]

---

1 OJ No 159, 2.11.63, p 2661/63.

[B.2.19]
Article 5
A national of a member state who seeks employment in the territory of another member state shall receive the same assistance there as that afforded by the employment offices in that state to their own nationals seeking employment.

[B.2.20]
Article 6
1   The engagement and recruitment of a national of one member state for a post in another member state shall not depend on medical, vocational or other criteria which are discriminatory on grounds of nationality by comparison with those applied to nationals of the other member state who wish to pursue the same activity.

2   Nevertheless, a national who holds an offer in his name from an employer in a member state other than that of which he is a national may have to undergo a vocational test, if the employer expressly requests this when making his offer of employment.

Title II   Employment and equality of treatment

[B.2.21]
Article 7
1   A worker who is a national of a member state may not, in the territory of another member state, be treated differently from national workers by reason of his nationality in respect of any conditions of employment and work, in particular as regards remuneration, dismissal, and should he become unemployed, reinstatement or re-employment;

2   He shall enjoy the same social and tax advantages as national workers.

3   He shall also, by virtue of the same right and under the same conditions as national workers, have access to training in vocational schools and retraining centres.

4   Any clause of a collective or individual agreement or of any other collective regulation concerning eligibility for employment, employment remuneration and other conditions of work or dismissal shall be null and void in so far as it lays down or authorises discriminatory conditions in respect of workers who are nationals of the other member states.

[B.2.22]
Article 8

1   A worker who is a national of a member state and who is employed in the territory of another member state shall enjoy equality of treatment as regards membership of trade unions and the exercise of rights attaching thereto, including the right to vote [and to be eligible for the administration or management posts of a trade union][1]; he may be excluded from taking part in the management of bodies governed by public law and from holding an office governed by public law. Furthermore, he shall have the right of eligibility for workers' representative bodies in the undertaking. The provisions of this Article shall not affect law or regulations in certain member states which grant more extensive rights to workers coming from the other member states.

---

1   Paragraph deleted by Council Regulation (EEC) 312/76 OJ L39 14.2.76, p 2.

[B.2.23]
Article 9

1   A worker who is a national of a member state and who is employed in the territory of another member state shall enjoy all the rights and benefits accorded to national workers in matters of housing, including ownership of the housing he needs.

2   Such a worker may, with the same right as nationals, put his name down on the housing lists in the region in which he is employed, where such lists exist; he shall enjoy the resultant benefits and priorities.

If his family has remained in the country whence he came, they shall be considered for this purpose as residing in the said region, where national workers benefit from a similar presumption.

Title III   Workers' families

[B.2.24]
Article 10

1   The following shall, irrespective of their nationality, have the right to install themselves with a worker who is a national of one member state and who is employed in the territory of another member state.

(*a*)   his spouse and their descendants who are under the age of 21 years or are dependants;
(*b*)   dependent relatives in the ascending line of the worker and his spouse.

2   Member states shall facilitate the admission of any member of the family not coming within the provisions of paragraph 1 if dependent on the worker referred to above or living under his roof in the country whence he comes.

3   For the purposes of paragraphs 1 and 2, the worker must have available for his family housing considered as normal for national workers in the region

where he is employed; this provision, however must not give rise to discrimination between national workers and workers from the other member states.

[B.2.25]
Article 11
Where a national of a member state is pursuing an activity as an employed or self-employed person in the territory of another member state, his spouse and those of the children who are under the age of 21 years or dependent on him shall have the right to take up any activity as an employed person throughout the territory of that same state, even if they are not nationals of any member state.

[B.2.26]
Article 12
The children of a national of a member state who is or has been employed in the territory of another member state shall be admitted to that state's general educational, apprenticeship and vocational training courses under the same conditions as the nationals of that state, if such children are residing in its territory.

Member states shall encourage all efforts to enable such children to attend these courses under the best possible conditions.

PART II   CLEARANCE OF VACANCIES AND APPLICATIONS FOR
EMPLOYMENT

Title I   Co-operation between the member states and with the Commission

[B.2.27]
Article 13
1   The member states or the Commission shall instigate or together undertake any study of employment or unemployment which they consider necessary for securing freedom of movement for workers within the Community.

The central employment services of the member states shall co-operate closely with each other and with the Commission with a view to acting jointly as regards the clearing of vacancies and applications for employment within the Community and the resultant placing of workers in employment.

2   To this end the member states shall designate specialist services which shall be entrusted with organising work in the fields referred to above and co-operating with each other and with the departments of the Commission.

The member states shall notify the Commission of any change in the designation of such services; the Commission shall publish details thereof for information in the *Official Journal of the European Communities.*

[B.2.28]
Article 14

1   The member states shall send to the Commission information on problems arising in connection with the freedom of movement and employment of workers and particulars of the state and development of employment . . . .[1]

2   [The Commission, taking the utmost account of the opinion of the Technical Committee, shall determine the manner in which the information referred to in paragraph 1 is to be drawn up][2].

3   In accordance with the procedure laid down by the Commission [taking the utmost account of the opinion of the Technical Committee][3], the specialist service of each member state shall send to the specialist services of the other member states and to the European Co-ordination Office such information concerning living and working conditions and the state of the labour market as is likely to be of guidance to workers from the other member states. Such information shall be brought up to date regularly.

The specialist services of the other member states shall ensure that wide publicity is given to such information, in particular by circulating it among the appropriate employment services and by all suitable means of communication for informing the workers concerned.

---

1 Some words deleted in para 1 by Council Regulation (EEC) 2434 OJ L245 26.8.92 p 1.
2 Amended by Council Regulation (EEC) 2434 OJ L245 26.8.92 p 1.
3 Amended by Council Regulation (EEC) 2434 OJ L245 26.8.92 p 1.

Title II   Machinery for vacancy clearance

[B.2.29]
Article 15

1   [The specialist service of each member state shall regularly send to the specialist services of the other member states and to the European Co-ordination Office:

(*a*) details of vacancies which could be filled by nationals of other member states;
(*b*) details of vacancies addressed to non-member states;
(*c*) details of applications for employment by those who have formally expressed a wish to work in another member state;
(*d*) information, by region and by branch of activity, on applicants who have declared themselves actually willing to accept employment in another country.

The specialist service of each member state shall forward this information to the appropriate employment services and agencies as soon as possible.

2   The details of vacancies and applications referred to in paragraph 1 shall be circulated according to a uniform system to be established by the European Coordination Office in collaboration with the Technical Committee.

If necessary, the European Co-ordination Office may adapt this system in collaboration with the Technical Committee][1].

1 Amended by Council Regulation (EEC) 2434 OJ L245 26.8.92 p 1 and p 2.

[B.2.30]
Article 16
1   [Any vacancy within the meaning of Article 15 communicated to the employment services of a member state shall be notified to and processed by the competent employment services of the other member states concerned.

Such services shall forward to the services of the first member state the details of suitable applications.

2   The applications for employment referred to in Article 15(1)(*c*) shall be responded to by the relevant services of the member states within a reasonable period, not exceeding one month.

3   The employment services shall grant workers who are nationals of the member states the same priority as the relevant measures grant to nationals *vis-à-vis* workers from non-member states.]

1 Amended by Council Regulation (EEC) 2434 OJ L245 26.8.92 p 2.

[B.2.31]
Article 17
1   The provisions of Article 16 shall be implemented by the specialist services. However, in so far as they have been authorised by the central services and in so far as the organisation of the employment services of a member state and the placing techniques employed make it possible:

(*a*) the regional employment services of the member states shall:

  (i) on the basis of the [details] referred to in Article 15, on which appropriate action will be taken, directly bring together and clear vacancies and applications for employment;
  (ii) establish direct relations for clearance:

  — of vacancies offered to a named worker;
  — of individual applications for employment sent either to a specific employment service or to an employer pursuing his activity within the area covered by such a service;
  — where the clearing operations concern seasonal workers who must be recruited as quickly as possible;

(*b*) [the services territorially responsible for the border regions of two or more member states shall regularly exchange data relating to vacancies and applications for employment in their area and, acting in accordance with their arrangements with the other employment services of their countries, shall directly bring together and clear vacancies and applications for employment.

If necessary, the services territorially responsible for border regions shall also set up co-operation and service structures to provide:

  — users with as much practical information as possible on the various aspects of mobility; and
  — management and labour, social services (in particular public, private

or those of public interest) and all institutions concerned, with a framework of coordinated measures relating to mobility];[2]

(c) official employment services which specialise in certain occupations or specific categories of persons shall co-operate directly with each other.

2   The member states concerned shall forward to the Commission the list, drawn up by common accord, of services referred to in paragraph 1; the Commission shall publish such list, and any amendment thereto, in the *Official Journal of the European Communities.*

---

1 Amended by Council Regulation (EEC) 2434 OJ L245 26.8.92 p 2.
2 Para 1(*b*) as amended by Council Regulations (EEC) 2434 OJ L245 26.8.92 p 2.

[B.2.32]
Article 18

Adoption of recruiting procedures as applied by the implementing bodies provided for under agreements concluded between two or more member states shall not be obligatory.

Title III   Measures for controlling the balance of the labour market

[B.2.33]
Article 19

[1   On the basis of a report from the Commission drawn up from information supplied by the member states, the latter and the Commission shall at least once a year analyse jointly the results of Community arrangements regarding vacancies and applications.][1]

2   The member states shall examine with the Commission all the possibilities of giving priority to nationals of member states when filing employment vacancies in order to achieve a balance between vacancies and applications for employment within the Community. They shall adopt all measures necessary for this purpose.

[3   Every two years the Commission shall submit a report to the European Parliament, the Council and the Economic and Social Committee on the implementation of Part II of this Regulation, summarising the information required and the data obtained from the studies and research carried out and highlighting any useful points with regard to developments on the Community's labour market.][2]

---

1 Amended by Council Regulation (EEC) 2434 OJ L245 26.8.92 p 2.
2 Added by Council Regulation (EEC) 2434 OJ L245 26.8.92 p 2.

[B.2.34]
Article 20
Article 20 deleted by Council Regulation (EEC) 2434 OJ 245 26.8.92 p 2.

Title IV   European Co-ordination Office

[B.2.35]
Article 21
The European Office for Co-ordinating the Clearance of Vacancies and Applications for Employment, established within the Commission (called in this Regulation the 'European Co-ordination Office', shall have the general task of promoting vacancy clearance at Community level. It shall be responsible in particular for all the technical duties in this field which, under the provisions of this Regulation, are assigned to the Commission, and especially for assisting the national employment services.

It shall summarise the information referred to in Articles 14 and 15 and the data arising out of the studies and research carried out pursuant to Article 13, so as to bring to light any useful facts about foreseeable developments on the Community labour market; such facts shall be communicated to the specialist services of the member states and to the Advisory and Technical Committees.

[B.2.36]
Article 22
1   The European Co-ordination Office shall be responsible, in particular, for:

(*a*) co-ordinating the practical measures necessary for vacancy clearance at Community level and for analysing the resulting movements of workers;
(*b*) contributing to such objectives by implementing, in co-operation with the Technical Committee, joint methods of action at administrative and technical levels;
(*c*) carrying out, where a special need arises, and in agreement with the specialist services, the bringing together of vacancies and applications for employment for clearance by these specialist services.

2   It shall communicate to the specialist services vacancies and applications for employment sent directly to the Commission, and shall be informed of the action taken thereon.

[B.2.37]
Article 23
The Commission may, in agreement with the competent authority of each member state, and in accordance with the conditions and procedures which it shall determine on the basis of the Opinion of the Technical Committee, organise visits and assignments for officials of other member states, and also advanced programmes for specialist personnel.

PART III COMMITTEES FOR ENSURING CLOSE CO-OPERATION BETWEEN THE MEMBER STATES IN MATTERS CONCERNING THE FREE- DOM OF MOVEMENT OF WORKERS AND THEIR EMPLOYMENT

Title I The Advisory Committee

[B.2.38]
Article 24
The Advisory Committee shall be responsible for assisting the Commission in the examination of any questions arising from the application of the Treaty and measures taken in pursuance thereof, in matters concerning the freedom of movement of workers and their employment.

[B.2.39]
Article 25
The Advisory Committee shall be responsible in particular for:

(*a*) examining problems concerning freedom of movement and employment within the framework of national manpower policies, with a view to co-ordinating the employment policies of the member states at Community level, thus contributing to the development of the economies and to an improved balance of the labour market;
(*b*) making a general study of the effects of implementing this Regulation and any supplementary measures;
(*c*) submitting to the Commission any reasoned proposals for revising this Regulation;
(*d*) delivering, either at the request of the Commission or on its own initiative, reasoned opinions on general questions or on questions of principle, in particular on exchange of information concerning developments in the labour market, on the movement of workers between member states, on programmes or measures to develop vocational guidance and vocational training which are likely to increase the possibilities of freedom of movement and employment, and on all forms of assistance to workers and their families, including social assistance and the housing of workers.

[B.2.40]
Article 26
1 The Advisory Committee shall be composed of six members for each member state, two of whom shall represent the government, two the trade unions and two the employers' associations.

2 For each of the categories referred to in paragraph 1, one alternate member shall be appointed by each member state.

3 The term of office of the members and their alternates shall be two years. Their appointments shall be renewable.

On expiry of their term of office, the members and their alternates shall remain in office until replaced or until their appointments are renewed.

[B.2.41]
Article 27
The members of the Advisory Committee and their alternates shall be appointed by the Council which shall endeavour, when selecting representatives of trade unions and employers' associations, to achieve adequate representation on the Committee of the various economic sectors concerned.

The list of members and their alternates shall be published by the Council for information in the *Official Journal of the European Communities*.

[B.2.42]
Article 28
The Advisory Committee shall be chaired by a member of the Commission or his alternate. The Chairman shall not vote. The Committee shall meet at least twice a year. It shall be convened by its Chairman, either on his own initiative, or at the request of at least one third of the members. Secretarial services shall be provided for the Committee by the Commission.

[B.2.43]
Article 29
The chairman may invite individuals or representatives of bodies with wide experience in the field of employment or movement of workers to take part in meetings as observers or as experts. The Chairman may be assisted by expert advisers.

[B.2.44]
Article 30
1   An opinion delivered by the Committee shall not be valid unless two-thirds of the members are present.

2   Opinions shall state the reasons on which they are based; they shall be delivered by an absolute majority of the votes validly cast; they shall be accompanied by a written statement of the views expressed by the minority, when the latter so requests.

[B.2.45]
Article 31
The Advisory Committee shall establish its working methods by rules of procedure which shall enter into force after the Council, having received an opinion from the Commission, has given its approval. The entry into force of any amendment that the Committee decides to make thereto shall be subject to the same procedure.

Title II   The Technical Committee

[B.2.46]
Article 32
The Technical Committee shall be responsible for assisting the Commission to

prepare, promote and follow up all technical work and measures for giving effect to this Regulation and any supplementary measures.

[B.2.47]
Article 33
The Technical Committee shall be responsible in particular for:

(*a*) promoting and advancing co-operation between the public authorities concerned in the member states on all technical questions relating to freedom of movement of workers and their employment;

(*b*) formulating procedures for the organisation of the joint activities of the public authorities concerned;

(*c*) facilitating the gathering of information likely to be of use to the Commission and for the studies and research provided for in this Regulation, and encouraging exchange of information and experience between the administrative bodies concerned;

(*d*) investigating at a technical level the harmonisation of the criteria by which member states assess the state of their labour markets.

[B.2.48]
Article 34
1   The Technical Committee shall be composed of representatives of the Governments of the member states. Each Government shall appoint as member of the Technical Committee one of the members who represent it on the Advisory Committee.

2   Each government shall appoint an alternate from among its other representatives—members or alternates—on the Advisory Committee.

[B.2.49]
Article 35
The Technical Committee shall be chaired by a member of the Commission or his representative. The Chairman shall not vote. The Chairman and the members of the Committee may be assisted by expert advisers.

Secretarial services shall be provided for the Committee by the Commission.

[B.2.50]
Article 36
The proposals and opinions formulated by the Technical Committee shall be submitted to the Commission, and the Advisory Committee shall be informed thereof. Any such proposals and opinions shall be accompanied by a written statement of the views expressed by the various members of the Technical Committee, when the latter so request.

[B.2.51]
Article 37
The Technical Committee shall establish its working methods by rules of pro-

cedure which shall enter into force after the Council, having received an opinion from the Commission, has given its approval. The entry into force of any amendment which the Committee decides to make thereto shall be subject to the same procedure.

PART IV   TRANSITIONAL AND FINAL PROVISIONS

Title I   Transitional provisions

[B.2.52]
Article 38
Until the adoption by the Commission of the uniform system referred to in Article 15(2), the European Co-ordination Office shall propose any measures likely to be of use in drawing up and circulating the returns referred to in Article 15(1).

[B.2.53]
Article 39
The rules of procedure of the Advisory Committee and the Technical Committee in force at the time of entry into force of this Regulation shall continue to apply.

[B.2.54]
Article 40
Until the entry into force of the measures to be taken by member states in pursuance of the Council Directive of 15 October 1968[1] and where, under the measures taken by the member states in pursuance of the Council Directive of 25 March 1964[2] the work permit provided for in Article 22 of Regulation No 38/64/EEC is necessary to determine the period of validity and extension of the residence permit, written confirmation of engagement from the employer or a certificate of employment stating the period of employment may be substituted for such work permit. Any written confirmation by the employer or certificate of employment showing that the worker has been engaged for an indefinite period shall have the same effect as that of a permanent work permit.

1 OJ No 257 19.10.1968, p 13.
2 OJ No 62, 17.4.1964, p 981/64.

[B.2.55]
Article 41
If, by reason of the abolition of the work permit, a member state can no longer compile certain statistics on the employment of foreign nationals such member state may, for statistical purposes, retain the work permit in respect of nationals of the other member states until new statistical methods are introduced, but no later than 31 December 1969. The work permit must be issued

automatically and must be valid until the actual abolition of work permit in such member state.

Title II   Final provisions

[B.2.56]
Article 42
1   This Regulation shall not affect the provisions of the Treaty establishing the European Coal and Steel Community which relate to workers with recognised qualifications in coalmining or steelmaking, nor those of the Treaty establishing the European Atomic Energy Community which deal with eligibility for skilled employment in the field of nuclear energy, nor any measures taken in pursuance of those Treaties.

Nevertheless, this Regulation shall apply to categories of workers referred to in the first subparagraph and to members of their families in so far as their legal position is not governed by the above-mentioned Treaties or measures.

2   This Regulation shall not affect measures taken in accordance with Article 51 of the Treaty.

3   This Regulation shall not affect the obligations of member states arising out of:

— special relations or future agreements with certain non-European countries or territories, based on institutional ties existing at the time of the entry into force of this Regulation; or
— agreements in existence at the time of the entry into force of this Regulation with certain non-European countries or territories, based on institutional ties between them.

Workers from such countries or territories who, in accordance with this provision, are pursuing activities as employed persons in the territory of one of those member states may not invoke the benefit of the provisions of this Regulation in the territory of the other member states.

[B.2.57]
Article 43
Member states shall, for information purposes, communicate to the Commission the texts of agreements, conventions or arrangements concluded between them in the manpower field between the date of their being signed and that of their entry into force.

[B.2.58]
Article 44
The Commission shall adopt measures pursuant to this Regulation for its implementation. To this end it shall act in close co-operation with the central public authorities of the member states.

[B.2.59]
Article 45

The Commission shall submit to the Council proposals aimed at abolishing, in accordance with the conditions of the Treaty, restrictions on eligibility for employment of workers who are nationals of member states, where the absence of mutual recognition of diplomas, certificates or other evidence of formal qualifications may prevent freedom of movement for workers.

[B.2.60]
Article 46

The administrative expenditure of the Committees referred to in Part III shall be included in the budget of the European Communities in the section relating to the Commission.

[B.2.61]
Article 47

This Regulation shall apply to the territories of the member states and to their nationals, without prejudice to Articles 2, 3, 10 and 11.

[B.2.62]
Article 48

Regulation No 38/64/EEC shall cease to have effect when this Regulation enters into force.

This Regulation shall be binding in its entirety and directly applicable in all member states.

Done at Luxembourg, 15 October 1968.

Annex

[B.2.63]
[Annex deleted by Council Regulation (EEC) 2434 OJ L245 36.8.92 p 2.]

COUNCIL DIRECTIVE (68/360/EEC)

on the abolition of restrictions on movement and residence within the Community for workers of member states and their families

[B.2.64]

The Council of The European Communities,

Having regard to the Treaty establishing the European Economic Community, and in particular Article 49 thereof;

Having regard to the proposal from the Commission;

Having regard to the Opinion of the European Parliament;

Having regard to the Opinion of the Economic and Social Committee;

Whereas Council Regulation (EEC) No 1612/68 fixed the provisions governing freedom of movement for workers within the Community; whereas, consequently, measures should be adopted for the abolition of restrictions which still exist concerning movement and residence within the Community, which conform to the rights and privileges accorded by the said Regulation to nationals of any member state who move in order to pursue activities as employed persons and to members of their families;

Whereas the rules applicable to residence should, as far as possible, bring the position of workers from other member states and members of their families into line with that of nationals;

Whereas the co-ordination of special measures relating to the movement and residence of foreign nationals, justified on grounds of public policy, public security or public health, is the subject of the Council Directive of 25 February 1964 adopted in application of Article 56(2) of the Treaty;

Has adopted this Directive:

[B.2.65]
Article 1
Member states shall, acting as provided in this Directive, abolish restrictions on the movement and residence of nationals of the said states and of members of their families to whom Regulation (EEC) No 1612/68 applies.

[B.2.66]
Article 2
1 Member states shall grant the nationals referred to in Article 1 the right to leave their territory in order to take up activities as employed persons and to pursue such activities in the territory of another member state. Such right shall be exercised simply on production of a valid identity card or passport. Members of the family shall enjoy the same right as the national on whom they are dependent.

2 Member states shall, acting in accordance with their laws, issue to such

nationals, or renew, an identity card or passport, which shall state in particular the holder's nationality.

3   The passport must be valid at least for all member states and for countries through which the holder must pass when travelling between member states. Where a passport is the only document on which the holder may lawfully leave the country, its period of validity shall be not less than five years.

4   Member states may not demand from the nationals referred to in Article 1 any exit visa or any equivalent document.

[B.2.67]
Article 3
1   Member states shall allow the persons referred to in Article 1 to enter their territory simply on production of a valid identity card or passport.

2   No entry visa or equivalent document may be demanded save from members of the family who are not nationals of a member state. Member states shall accord to such persons every facility for obtaining any necessary visas.

[B.2.68]
Article 4
1   Member states shall grant the right of residence in their territory to the persons referred to in Article 1 who are able to produce the documents listed in paragraph 3.

2   As proof of the right of residence, a document entitled 'Residence permit for a national of a member state of the EEC' shall be issued. This document must include a statement that it has been issued pursuant to Regulation (EEC) No 1612/68 and to the measures taken by the member states for the implementation of the present Directive. The text of such statement is given in the Annex to this Directive.

3   For the issue of a residence permit for a national of a member state of the EEC, member states may require only the production of the following documents;

— by the worker:

   (*a*)   the document with which he entered their territory;
   (*b*)   a confirmation of engagement from the employer or a certificate of employment;

— by the members of the worker's family:

   (*c*)   the document with which they entered the territory;
   (*d*)   a document issued by the competent authority of the state of origin or the state whence they came, proving their relationship;
   (*e*)   in the cases referred to in Article 10(1) and (2) of Regulation (EEC) No 1612/68, a document issued by the competent authority of the state of origin or the state whence they came, testifying that they are dependent on the worker or that they live under his roof in such country.

4   A member of the family who is not a national of a member state shall be

issued with a residence document which shall have the same validity as that issued to the worker on whom he is dependent.

[B.2.69]
Article 5
Completion of the formalities for obtaining a residence permit shall not hinder the immediate beginning of employment under a contract concluded by the applicants.

[B.2.70]
Article 6
1   The residence permit:

(*a*)   must be valid throughout the territory of the member state which issued it;
(*b*)   must be valid for at least five years from the date of issue and be automatically renewable.

2   Breaks in residence not exceeding six consecutive months and absence on military service shall not affect the validity of a residence permit.

3   Where a worker is employed for a period exceeding three months but not exceeding a year in the service of an employer in the host state or in the employ of a person providing services, the host member state shall issue him a temporary residence permit, the validity of which may be limited to the expected period of the employment.

Subject to the provisions of Article 8(1)(*c*), a temporary residence permit shall be issued also to a seasonal worker employed for a period of more than three months. The period of employment must be shown in the documents referred to in paragraph 4(3)(*b*).

[B.2.71]
Article 7
1   A valid residence permit may not be withdrawn from a worker solely on the grounds that he is no longer in employment, either because he is temporarily incapable of work as a result of illness or accident, or because he is involuntarily unemployed, this being duly confirmed by the competent employment office.

2   When the residence permit is renewed for the first time, the period of residence may be restricted, but not to less than twelve months, where the worker has been involuntarily unemployed in the member state for more than twelve consecutive months.

[B.2.72]
Article 8
1   Member states shall, without issuing a residence permit, recognise the right of residence in their territory of:

(*a*) a worker pursuing an activity as an employed person, where the activity is not expected to last for more than three months. The document with which the person concerned entered the territory and a statement by the employer on the expected duration of the employment shall be sufficient to cover his stay; a statement by the employer shall not, however, be required in the case of workers coming within the provisions of the Council Directive of 25 February 1964 on the attainment of freedom of establishment and freedom to provide services in respect of the activities of intermediaries in commerce, industry and small craft industries.

(*b*) a worker who, while having his residence in the territory of a member state to which he returns as a rule, each day or at least once a week, is employed in the territory of another member state. The competent authority of the state where he is employed may issue such worker with a special permit valid for five years and automatically renewable;

(*c*) a seasonal worker who holds a contract of employment stamped by the competent authority of the member state on whose territory he has come to pursue his activity.

2   In all cases referred to in paragraph 1, the competent authorities of the host member state may require the worker to report his presence in the territory.

[B.2.73]
Article 9
1   The residence documents granted to nationals of a member state of the EEC referred to in this Directive shall be issued and renewed free of charge or on payment of an amount not exceeding the dues and taxes charged for the issue of identity cards to nationals.

2   The visa referred to in Article 3(2) and the stamp referred to in Article 8(1)(*c*) shall be free of charge.

3   Member states shall take the necessary steps to simplify as much as possible the formalities and procedure for obtaining the documents mentioned in paragraph 1.

[B.2.74]
Article 10
Member states shall not derogate from the provisions of this Directive save on grounds of public policy, public security or public health.

[B.2.75]
Article 11
1   This Directive shall not affect the provisions of the Treaty establishing the European Coal and Steel Community which relate to workers with recognised skills in coal mining and steel making, or the provisions of the Treaty establishing the European Atomic Energy Community which deal with the right to take up skilled employment in the field of nuclear energy, or any measures taken in implementation of those Treaties.

2   Nevertheless, this Directive shall apply to the categories of workers referred to in paragraph 1, and to members of their families, in so far as their legal position is not governed by the abovementioned Treaties or measures.

[B.2.76]
Article 12
1   Member states shall, within nine months of notification of this Directive, bring into force the measures necessary to comply with its provisions and shall forthwith inform the Commission thereof.

2   They shall notify the Commission of amendments made to provisions imposed by law, regulation or administrative action for the simplification of the formalities and procedure for issuing such documents as are still necessary for the entry, exit and residence of workers and members of their families.

[B.2.77]
Article 13
1   The Council Directive of 25 March 1964 on the abolition of restrictions on movement and on residence within the Community of workers and their families shall continue to have effect until this Directive is implemented by the member states.

2   Residence permits issued pursuant to the Directive referred to in paragraph 1 shall remain valid until the date on which they next expire.

[B.2.78]
Article 14
This Directive is addressed to the member states

Done at Luxembourg, 15 October 1968.

Annex

[B.2.79]
Text of the statement referred to in Article 4(2):

'This permit is issued pursuant to Regulation (EEC) No 1612/68 of the Council of the European Communities of 15 October 1968 and to the measures taken in implementation of the Council Directive of 15 October 1968.

In accordance with the provisions of the above-mentioned Regulation, the holder of this permit has the right to take up and pursue an activity as an employed person in .... territory under the same conditions as ....* workers.'

* Belgian, Danish, German, Greek, Spanish, French, Irish, Italian, Luxembourg, Dutch, Portuguese, United Kingdom, depending on which country issues the card.

REGULATION (EEC) 1251/70 OF THE COMMISSION

of 29 June 1970 on the right of workers to remain in the territory of a member state after having been employed in that state

[B.2.80]

The Commission of The European Communities,

Having regard to the Treaty establishing the European Economic Community, and in particular Article 48(3)(*d*) thereof, and Article 2 of the Protocol on the Grand Duchy of Luxembourg;

Having regard to the Opinion of the European Parliament[1];

Whereas Council Regulation (EEC) No 1612/68[2] of 15 October 1968 and Council Directive No 68/360/EEC of 15 October 1968[3] enabled freedom of movement for workers to be secured at the end of a series of measures to be achieved progressively; whereas the right of residence acquired by workers in active employment has as a corollary the right, granted by the Treaty to such workers, to remain in the territory of a member state after having been employed in that state; whereas it is important to lay down the conditions for the exercise of such right;

Whereas the said Council Regulation and Council Directive contain the appropriate provisions concerning the right of workers to reside in the territory of a member state for the purposes of employment; whereas the right to remain, referred to in Article 48(3)(*d*) of the Treaty is interpreted therefore as the right of the worker to maintain his residence in the territory of a member state when he ceases to be employed there;

Whereas the mobility of labour in the Community requires that workers may be employed successively in several member states without thereby being placed at a disadvantage;

Whereas it is important, in the first place, to guarantee to the worker residing in the territory of a member state the right to remain in that territory when he ceases to be employed in that state because he has reached retirement age or by reason of permanent incapacity to work; whereas, however, it is equally important to ensure that right for the worker who, after a period of employment and residence in the territory of a member state, works as an employed person in the territory of another member state, while still retaining his residence in the territory of the first state;

Whereas, to determine the conditions under which the right to remain arises, account should be taken of the reasons which have led to the termination of employment in the territory of the member state concerned and, in particular, of the difference between retirement, the normal and foreseeable end of working life, and incapacity to work which leads to a premature and unforeseeable termination of activity; whereas special conditions must be laid down where termination of activity is the result of an accident at work or occupational disease, or where the worker's spouse is or was a national of the member state concerned;

Whereas the worker who has reached the end of his working life should have sufficient time in which to decide where he wishes to establish his final residence;

Whereas the exercise by the worker of the right to remain entails that such right shall be extended to members of his family; whereas in the case of the death of the worker during his working life, maintenance of the right of residence of the members of his family must also be recognised and be the subject of special conditions;

Whereas persons to whom the right to remain applies must enjoy equality of treatment with national workers who have ceased their working lives;

---

1 OJ No C65, 5.6.1970, p 16.
2 OJ No L 257, 19.10.1968, p 2.
3 OJ No L 257, 19.10.1968, p 13.

Has adopted this Regulation:

[B.2.81]
Article 1
The provisions of this Regulation shall apply to nationals of a member state who have worked as employed persons in the territory of another member state and to members of their families, as defined in Article 10 of Council Regulation (EEC) No 1612/68 on freedom of movement for workers within the Community.

[B.2.82]
Article 2
1   The following shall have the right to remain permanently in the territory of a member state:

(*a*) a worker who, at the time of termination of his activity, has reached the age laid down by the law of that member state for entitlement to an old-age pension and who has been employed in that state for at least the last twelve months and has resided there continuously for more than three years;

(*b*) a worker who, having resided continuously in the territory of that state for more than two years, ceases to work there as an employed person as a result of permanent incapacity to work. If such incapacity is the result of an accident at work or an occupational disease entitling him to a pension for which an institution of that state is entirely or partially responsible, no condition shall be imposed as to length of residence;

(*c*) a worker who, after three years' continuous employment and residence in the territory of that state, works as an employed person in the territory of another member state, while retaining his residence in the territory of the first state, to which he returns, as a rule, each day or at least once a week.

Periods of employment completed in this way in the territory of the other member state shall, for the purposes of entitlement to the rights referred to in subparagraphs (*a*) and (*b*), be considered as having been completed in the territory of the state of residence.

2 The conditions as to length of residence and employment laid down in paragraph 1(*a*) and the conditions as to length of residence laid down in paragraph 1(*b*) shall not apply if the worker's spouse is a national of the member state concerned or has lost the nationality of that state by marriage to that worker.

[B.2.83]
Article 3
1 The members of a worker's family referred to in Article 1 of this Regulation who are residing with him in the territory of a member state shall be entitled to remain there permanently if the worker has acquired the right to remain in the territory of that state in accordance with Article 2, and to do so even after his death.

2 If, however, the worker dies during his working life and before having acquired the right to remain in the territory of the state concerned, members of his family shall be entitled to remain there permanently on condition that:

— the worker, on the date of his decease, had resided continuously in the territory of that member state for at least 2 years; or
— his death resulted from an accident at work or an occupational disease; or
— the surviving spouse is a national of the state of residence or lost the nationality of that state by marriage to that worker.

[B.2.84]
Article 4
1 Continuity of residence as provided for in Articles 2(1) and 3(2) may be attested by any means of proof in use in the country of residence. It shall not be affected by temporary absences not exceeding a total of three months per year, nor by longer absences due to compliance with the obligations of military service.

2 Periods of involuntary unemployment, duly recorded by the competent employment office, and absences due to illness or accident shall be considered as periods of employment within the meaning of Article 2(1).

[B.2.85]
Article 5
1 The person entitled to the right to remain shall be allowed to exercise it within two years from the time of becoming entitled to such right pursuant to Article 2(1)(*a*) and (*b*) and Article 3. During such period he may leave the territory of the member state without adversely affecting such right.

2 No formality shall be required on the part of the person concerned in respect of the exercise of the right to remain.

[B.2.86]

Article 6

1 Persons coming under the provisions of this Regulation shall be entitled to a residence permit which:

(a) shall be issued and renewed free of charge or on payment of a sum not exceeding the dues and taxes payable by nationals for the issue or renewal identity documents;

(b) must be valid throughout the territory of the Member State issuing it;

(c) must be valid for at least five years and be renewable automatically.

2 Periods of non-residence not exceeding six consecutive months shall not affect the validity of the residence permit.

[B.2.87]

Article 7

The right to equality of treatment, established by Council Regulation (EEC) No 1612/68, shall apply also to persons coming under the provisions of this Regulation.

[B.2.88]

Article 8

1 This Regulation shall not affect any provisions laid down by law, regulation or administrative action of one Member State which would be more favourable to nationals of other Member States.

2 Member States shall facilitate re-admission to their territories of workers who have left those territories after having resided there permanently for a long period and having been employed there and who wish to return there when they have reached retirement age or are permanently incapacitated for work.

[B.2.89]

Article 9

1 The Commission may, taking account of developments in the demographic situation of the Grand Duchy of Luxembourg, lay down, at the request of that State, different conditions from those provided for in this Regulation, in respect of the exercise of the right to remain in Luxembourg territory.

2 Within two months after the request supplying all appropriate details has been put before it, the Commission shall take a decision, stating the reasons on which it is based.

It shall notify the Grand Duchy of Luxembourg of such decision and inform the other Member States thereof;

This Regulation shall be binding in its entirety and directly applicable in all Member States.

Done at Brussels, 29 June 1970.

COUNCIL DIRECTIVE (72/194/EEC)

of 18 May 1972 extending to workers exercising the right to remain in the territory of a member state after having been employed in that state the scope of the Directive of 25 February 1964 on co-ordination of special measures concerning the movement and residence of foreign nationals which are justified on grounds of public policy, public security or public health

[B.2.90]

The Council of The European Communities,

Having regard to the Treaty establishing the European Economic Community, and in particular Articles 49 and 56(2) thereof;

Having regard to the proposal from the Commission;

Having regard to the Opinion of the European Parliament;

Having regard to the Opinion of the Economic and Social Committee;

Whereas the Council Directive of 25 February 1964[1] co-ordinated special measures concerning the movement and residence of foreign nationals which are justified on grounds of public policy, public security or public health and whereas Commission Regulation (EEC) No 1251/70[2] of 29 June 1970 on the right of workers to remain in the territory of a member state after having been employed in that state laid down conditions for the exercise of such right;

Whereas the Directive of 25 February 1964 should continue to apply to persons to whom that Regulation applies;

---

1 OJ No 56, 4.4.1964, p 850/64.
2 OJ No 142, 30.6.1970, p 24.

Has adopted the following Directive:

[B.2.91]
Article 1
The Council Directive of 25 February 1964 on co-ordination of special measures concerning the movement and residence of foreign nationals which are justified on grounds of public policy, public security or public health shall apply to nationals of member states and members of their families who, pursuant to Regulation (EEC) No 1251/70, exercise the right to remain in the territory of a member state.

[B.2.92]
Article 2
Member states shall put into force the measures needed to comply with this Directive within six months of its notification and shall forthwith inform the Commission thereof.

[B.2.93]
Article 3
This Directive is addressed to the member states.

Done at Brussels, 18 May 1972.

COUNCIL DIRECTIVE (73/148/EEC)

of 21 May 1973 on the abolition of restrictions on movements and residence within the Community for nationals of member states with regard to establishment and the provision of services

[B.2.94]
The Council of The European Economic Community,

Having regard to the Treaty establishing the European Economic Community, and in particular Articles 54(2) and 63(2) thereof;

Having regard to the General Programmes for the abolition of restrictions on freedom of establishment and freedom to provide services[1], and in particular Title II thereof;

Having regard to the proposal from the commission;

Having regard to the Opinion of the European Parliament[2];

Having regard to the Opinion of the Economic and Social Committee[3];

Whereas freedom of movement of persons as provided for in the Treaty and the General Programmes for the abolition of restrictions on freedom of establishment and on freedom to provide services entails the abolition of restrictions on movement and residence within the Community for nationals of member states wishing to establish themselves or to provide services within the territory of another member state;

Whereas freedom of establishment can be fully attained only if a right of permanent residence is granted to the persons who are to enjoy freedom of establishment; whereas freedom to provide services entails that persons providing and receiving services should have the right of residence for the time during which the services are being provided;

Whereas this Directive does not affect measures justified on grounds of public policy, public security or public health; whereas, in pursuance of Article 56(2) of the Treaty, co-ordination of such measures is to be dealt with in a separate Directive;

Whereas Council Directive of 25 February 1964[4] on the abolition of restrictions on movement and residence within the Community for nationals of member states with regard to establishment and the provision of services laid down the rules applicable in this area to activities as self-employed persons;

Whereas Council Directive of 15 October 1968[5] on the abolition of restrictions on movement and residence within the Community for workers of member states and their families, which replaced the Directive of 25 March 1964[6] bearing the same title, has in the meantime amended the rules applicable to employed persons;

Whereas the provisions concerning movement and residence within the Community of self-employed persons and their families should likewise be improved;

Whereas the co-ordination of special measures concerning the movement and residence of foreign nationals, justified on grounds of public policy, public security or public health, is already the subject of the Council Directive of 25 February 1964[7];

---

1 OJ No 2, 15.1.1962, pp 32/62 and 36/62.
2 OJ No 19, 28.2.1972, p 5.
3 OJ No C 67, 24.6.1972, p 7.
4 OJ No 56, 4.4.1964, p 845/64.
5 OJ No L 257, 19.10.1968, p 13.
6 OJ No 62, 17.4.1964, p 981/64.
7 OJ No 56, 4.4.1964, p 850/64.

Has adopted this directive:

[B.2.95]
Article 1
1 Member states shall, acting as provided in this Directive, abolish restrictions on the movement and residence of:

(*a*) nationals of a member state who are established or who wish to establish themselves in another member state in order to pursue activities as self-employed persons, or who wish to provide services in that state;

(*b*) nationals of member states wishing to go to another member state as recipients of services;

(*c*) the spouse and the children under twenty-one years of age of such nationals, irrespective of their nationality;

(*d*) the relatives in the ascending and descending lines of such nationals and of the spouse of such nationals, whose relatives are dependent on them, irrespective of their nationality.

2 Member states shall favour the admission of any other member of the family of a national referred to in paragraph 1(*a*) or (*b*) or of the spouse of that national, which member is dependent on that national or who in the country of origin was living under the same roof.

[B.2.96]
Article 2
1 Member states shall grant the persons referred to in Article 1 the right to leave their territory. Such right shall be exercised simply on production of a valid identity card or passport. Members of the family shall enjoy the same right as the national on whom they are dependent.

2 Member states shall, acting in accordance with their laws, issue to their nationals, or renew, an identity card or passport, which shall state in particular the holder's nationality.

3 The passport must be valid at least for all member states and for countries through which the holder must pass when travelling between member states. Where a passport is the only document on which the holder may lawfully leave the country, its period of validity shall not be less than five years.

4 Member states may not demand from the persons referred to in Article 1 any exit visa or any equivalent requirement.

[B.2.97]
Article 3
1 Member states shall grant to the persons referred to in Article 1 right to enter their territory merely on production of a valid identity card or passport.

2 No entry visa or equivalent requirement may be demanded save in respect of members of the family who do have the nationality of a member state. Member states shall afford to such persons every facility for obtaining any necessary visas.

[B.2.98]
Article 4
1 Each member state shall grant the right of permanent residence to nationals of other member states who establish themselves within its territory in order to pursue activities as self-employed persons, when the restrictions on these activities have been abolished pursuant to the Treaty.

As proof of the right of residence, a document entitled 'Residence Permit for a national of a member state of the European Communities' shall be issued. This document shall be valid for not less than five years from the date of issue and shall be automatically renewable.

Breaks in residence not exceeding six consecutive months and absence on military service shall not affect the validity of a residence permit.

A valid residence permit may not be withdrawn from a national referred to in Article 1(1)(*a*) solely on the grounds that he is no longer in employment because he is temporarily incapable of work as a result of illness or accident.

Any national of a member state who is not specified in the first subparagraph but who is authorised under the laws of another member state to pursue an activity within its territory shall be granted a right of abode for a period not less than that of the authorisation granted for the pursuit of the activity in question.

However, any national referred to in subparagraph 1 and to whom the provisions of the preceding subparagraph apply as a result of a change of employment shall retain his residence permit until the date on which it expires.

2 The right of residence for persons providing and receiving services shall be of equal duration with the period during which the services are provided.

Where such period exceeds three months, the member state in the territory of which the services are performed shall issue a right of abode as proof of the right of residence.

Where the period does not exceed three months, the identity card or passport with which the person concerned entered the territory shall be sufficient to cover his stay. The member state may, however, require the person concerned to report his presence in the territory.

3 A member of the family who is not a national of a member state shall be issued with a residence document which shall have the same validity as that issued to the national on whom he is dependent.

[B.2.99]
Article 5
The right of residence shall be effective throughout the territory of the member state concerned.

[B.2.100]
Article 6
An applicant for a residence permit or right of abode shall not be required by a member state to produce anything other than the following, namely:

(*a*) the identity card or passport with which he or she entered its territory;
(*b*) proof that he or she comes within one of the classes of person referred to in Articles 1 and 4.

[B.2.101]
Article 7
1   The residence documents granted to nationals of a member state shall be issued and renewed free of charge or on payment of an amount not exceeding the dues and taxes charged for the issue of identity cards to nationals. These provisions shall also apply to documents and certificates required for the issue and renewal of such residence documents.

2   The visas referred to in Article 3(2) shall be free of charge.

3   Member states shall take the necessary steps to simplify as much as possible the formalities and the procedure for obtaining the documents mentioned in paragraph 1.

[B.2.102]
Article 8
Member states shall not derogate from the provisions of this Directive save on grounds of public security or public health.

[B.2.103]
Article 9
1   Member states shall within six months of notification of this Directive bring into force the measures necessary to comply with its provisions and shall forthwith inform the Commission thereof.
2   They shall notify the Commission of amendments made to provisions imposed by law, regulation or administrative action for the simplification with regard to establishment and the provision of services of the formalities and procedure for issuing such documents as are still necessary for the movement and residence of persons referred to in Article 1.

[B.2.104]
Article 10
1   The Council Directive of 25 February 1964 on the abolition of restrictions on movement and residence within the Community for nationals of member states with regard to establishment and the provision of services shall remain applicable until this Directive is implemented by the member states.

2   Residence documents issued pursuant to the Directive referred to in paragraph 1 shall remain valid until the date on which they next expire.

[B.2.105]
Article 11
This Directive is addressed to the member states.

Done at Brussels, 21 May 1973.

COUNCIL DIRECTIVE (75/34/EEC)

of 17 December 1974 concerning the right of nationals of a member state to remain in the territory of another member state after having pursued therein an activity in a self-employed capacity

[B.2.106]
The Council of The European Communities,

Having regard to the Treaty establishing the European Economic Community, and in particular Article 235 thereof;

Having regard to the General Programme for the abolition of restrictions on freedom of establishment[1], and in particular Title II thereof;

Having regard to the proposal from the Commission;

Having regard to the Opinion of the European Parliament[2];

Having regard to the Opinion of the Economic and Social Committee[3];

Whereas pursuant to Council Directive No 73/148/EEC[4] of 21 May 1973 on the abolition of restrictions on movement and residence within the Community for nationals of member states with regard to establishment and the provision of services, each member state grants the right of permanent residence to nationals of other member states who establish themselves within its territory in order to pursue activities as self-employed persons, when the restrictions on these activities have been abolished pursuant to the Treaty;

Whereas it is normal for a person to prolong a period of permanent residence in the territory of a member state by remaining there after having pursued an activity there; whereas the absence of a right so to remain in such circumstances is an obstacle to the attainment of freedom of establishment; whereas, as regards employed persons, the conditions under which such a right may be exercised have already been laid down by Regulation (EEC) No 1251/70[5];

Whereas Article 48(3)(*d*) of the Treaty recognises the right of workers to remain in the territory of a member state after having been employed in that state; whereas Article 54(2) does not expressly provide a similar right for self-employed persons; whereas, nevertheless, the nature of establishment, together with attachments formed to the countries in which they have pursued their activities, means that such persons have a definite interest in enjoying the same right to remain as that granted to workers; whereas in justification of this measure reference should be made to the Treaty provision enabling it to be taken;

Whereas freedom of establishment within the Community requires that nationals of member states may pursue self-employed activities in several member states in succession without thereby being placed at a disadvantage;

Whereas a national of a member state residing in the territory of another member state should be guaranteed the right to remain in that territory when he ceases to pursue an activity as a self-employed person in that state because he has reached retirement age or by reason of permanent incapacity to work; whereas such a right should also be guaranteed to the national of a member state who, after a period of activity in a self-employed capacity and residence in the territory of a second member state, while still retaining his residence in the territory of the second state;

Whereas, to determine the conditions under which the right to remain arises, account should be taken of the reasons which have led to the termination of activity in the territory of the member state concerned and, in particular, of the difference between retirement, the normal and foreseeable end of working life, and permanent incapacity to work which leads to a premature and unforeseeable termination of activity; whereas special conditions must be laid down where the spouse is or was a national of the member state concerned, or where termination of activity is the result of an accident at work or occupational illness;

Whereas a national of a member state who has reached the end of his working life, after working in self-employed capacity in the territory of another member state, should have sufficient time in which to decide where he wishes to establish his final residence;

Whereas the exercise of the right to remain by a national of a member state working in a self-employed capacity entails extension of such right to the members of his family; whereas in the case of the death of a national of a member state working in a self-employed capacity during his working life the right of residence of the members of his family must also be recognised and be the subject of special conditions;

Whereas persons to whom the right to remain applies must enjoy equality of treatment with nationals of the state concerned who have reached the end of their working lives;

---

1 OJ No 2, 15.1.1962, p 36/62.
2 OJ No C 14, 27.3.1973, p 20.
3 OJ No C 142, 31.12.1972, p 12.
4 OJ No L 172, 28.6.1973, p 14.
5 OJ No L 142, 30.6.1970, p 24.

Has adopted this Directive:

[B.2.107]
Article 1
Member states shall, under the conditions laid down in this Directive, abolish restrictions on the right to remain in their territory in favour of nationals of another member state who have pursued activities as self-employed persons in their territory, and members of their families, as defined in Article 1 of Directive No 73/148/EEC.

[B.2.108]
Article 2
1 Each member state shall recognise the right to remain permanently in its territory of:

(*a*) any person who, at the time of termination of his activity, has reached the age laid down by the law of that state for entitlement to an old-age pension and who has pursued his activity in that state for at least the previous twelve months and has resided there continuously for more than three years.

   Where the law of that member state does not grant the right to an old-age pension to certain categories of self-employed workers, the age requirement shall be considered as satisfied when the beneficiary reaches 65 years of age;

(*b*) any person who, having resided continuously in the territory of that state for more than two years, ceases to pursue his activity there as a result of permanent incapacity to work.

   If such incapacity is the result of an accident at work or an occupational illness entitling him to a pension which is payable in whole or in part by an institution of that state no condition shall be imposed as to length of residence;

(*c*) any person who, after three years' continuous activity and residence in the territory of that state, pursues his activity in the territory of another member state, while retaining his residence in the territory of the first state, to which he returns, as a rule, each day or at least once a week.

Periods of activity so completed in the territory of the other member state shall, for the purposes of entitlement to the rights referred to in (*a*) and (*b*), be considered as having been completed in the territory of the state of residence.

2   The conditions as to length of residence and activity laid down in paragraph 1(*a*) and the condition as to length of residence laid down in paragraph 1(*b*) shall not apply if the spouse of the self-employed person is a national of the member state concerned or has lost the nationality of that state by marriage to that person.

[B.2.109]
Article 3
1   Each member state shall recognise the right of the members of the self-employed person's family referred to in Article 1 who are residing with him in the territory of that state to remain there permanently, if the person concerned has acquired the right to remain in the territory of that state in accordance with Article 2. This provision shall continue to apply even after the death of the person concerned.

2   If, however, the self-employed person dies during his working life and before having acquired the right to remain in the territory of the state concerned, that state shall recognise the right of the members of his family to remain there permanently on condition that:

— the person concerned, on the date of his decease, had resided continuously in its territory for at least two years; or
— his death resulted from an accident at work or an occupational illness; or
— the surviving spouse is a national of that state or lost such nationality by marriage to the person concerned.

[B.2.110]
Article 4
1   Continuity of residence as provided for in Articles 2(1) and 3(2) may be attested by any means of proof in use in the country of residence. It may not be affected by temporary absences not exceeding a total of three months per year, nor by longer absences due to compliance with the obligations of military service.

2   Periods of inactivity due to circumstances outside the control of the person concerned or of inactivity owing to illness or accident must be considered as periods of activity within the meaning of Article 2(1).

[B.2.111]
Article 5
1   Member states shall allow the person entitled to the right to remain to exercise such right within two years from the time of becoming entitled thereto pursuant to Article 2(1)(*a*) and (*b*) and Article 3. During this period the beneficiary must be able to leave the territory of the member state without adversely affecting such right.

2   Member states shall not require the person concerned to comply with any particular formality in order to exercise the right to remain.

[B.2.112]
Article 6
1   Member states shall recognise the right of persons having the right to remain in their territory to a residence permit, which must:

(*a*) be issued and renewed free of charge or on payment of a sum not exceeding the dues and taxes payable by nationals for the issue or renewal of identity cards;
(*b*) be valid throughout the territory of the member state issuing it;
(*c*) be valid for five years and renewable automatically.

2   Periods of non-residence not exceeding six consecutive months and longer absences due to compliance with the obligations of military service may not affect the validity of a residence permit.

[B.2.113]
Article 7
Member states shall apply to persons having the right to remain in their territory the right of equality of treatment recognised by the Council Directives on the abolition of restrictions on freedom of establishment pursuant to Title III of the General Programme which provides for such abolition.

[B.2.114]
Article 8
1   This Directive shall not affect any provisions laid down by law, regulation or administrative action of any member state which would be more favourable to nationals of other member states.

2   Member states shall facilitate re-admission to their territories of self-employed persons who left those territories after having resided there permanently for a long period while pursuing an activity there and who wish to return when they have reached retirement age as defined in Article 2(1)(*a*) or are permanently incapacitated for work.

[B.2.115]
Article 9
Member states may not derogate from the provisions of this Directive save on grounds of public policy, public security or public health.

[B.2.116]
Article 10
1   Member states shall, within twelve months of notification of this Directive, bring into force the measures necessary to comply with its provisions and shall forthwith inform the Commission thereof.

2   Following notification of this Directive, member states shall further ensure that the Commission is informed, in sufficient time for it to submit its comments, of all proposed laws, regulations or adminsitrative provisions which they intend to adopt in the field covered by this Directive.

[B.2.117]
Article 11
This Directive is addressed to the member states.

Done at Brussels, 17 December 1974.

COUNCIL DIRECTIVE (75/35/EEC)

of 17 December 1974 extending the scope of Directive No 64/221/EEC on the co-ordination of special measures concerning the movement and residence of foreign nationals which are justified on grounds of public policy, public security or public health to include nationals of a member state who exercise the right to remain in the territory of another member state after having pursued therein an activity in a self-employed capacity

[B.2.118]

The Council of The European Communities,

Having regard to the Treaty establishing the European Economic Community, and in particular Article 56(2) and Article 235 thereof;

Having regard to the proposal from the Commission;

Having regard to the Opinion of the European Parliament[1];

Having regard to the Opinion of the Economic and Social Committee[2];

Whereas Directive No 64/221/EEC[3] co-ordinated special measures concerning the movement and residence of foreign nationals which are justified on grounds of public policy, public security or public health and whereas Directive No 75/34/EEC[4] laid down conditions for the exercise of the right of nationals of a member state to remain in the territory of another member state after having pursued therein an activity in a self-employed capacity;

Whereas Directive No 64/221/EEC should therefore apply to persons to whom Directive No 75/34/EEC applies;

---

1 OJ No C 14, 27.3.1973, p 21.
2 OJ No C 142, 31.12.1972, p 10.
3 OJ No 56, 4.4.1964, p 850/64.
4 See p 10 of this Official Journal.

Has adopted this Directive:

[B.2.119]
Article 1
Directive No 64/221/EEC shall apply to nationals of member states and members of their families who have the right to remain in the territory of a member state pursuant to Directive No 75/34/EEC.

[B.2.120]
Article 2
Member states shall, within twelve months of notification of this Directive, bring into force the measures necessary to comply with its provisions and shall forthwith inform the Commission thereof.

[B.2.121]
Article 3
This Directive is addressed to the member states.

Done at Brussels, 17 December 1974.

COUNCIL REGULATION (EEC) 312/76

of 9 February 1976 amending the provisions relating to the trade union rights of workers contained in Regulation (EEC) No 1612/68 on freedom of movement for workers within the Community

[B.2.122]
The Council of The European Communities,

Having regard to the Treaty establishing the European Economic Community, and in particular Article 49 thereof;

Having regard to the proposal from the Commission;

Having regard to the Opinion of the European Parliament[1];

Having regard to the Opinion of the Economic and Social Committee[2];

Whereas it should be specified in Article 8 of Council Regulation (EEC) No 1612/68 of 15 October 1968 on freedom of movement for workers within the Community[3], that workers who are nationals of one member state and who are employed in the territory of another member state shall also enjoy equality of treatment as regards the exercise of trade union rights with respect to eligibility for the administration or management posts of a trade union;

---

1 OJ No C 280, 8.12.1975, p 43.
2 OJ No C 12, 17.1.1976, p 2.
3 OJ No L 257, 19.10.1968, p 2.

Has adopted this Regulation:

[B.2.123]
Article 1
Article 8 of Regulation (EEC) No 1612/68 shall be amended as follows:

1   The following shall be added to the first sentence of paragraph 1 after 'including the right to vote';

'and to be eligible for the administration or management posts of a trade union.'

2   Paragraph 2 is hereby deleted.

[B.2.124]
Article 2
This Regulation shall enter into force on the third day following that of its publication in the *Official Journal of the European Communities.*

This Regulation shall be binding in its entirety and directly applicable in all member states.

Done at Brussels, 9 February 1976.

COUNCIL DIRECTIVE 77/486/EEC

of 25 July 1977 on the education of the children of migrant workers

[B.2.125]

The Council of the European Communities,

Having regard to the Treaty establishing the European Economic Community, and in particular Article 49 thereof,

Having regard to the proposal from the Commission,

Having regard to the opinion of the European Parliament[1],

Having regard to the opinion of the Economic and Social Committee[2],

Whereas in its resolution of 21 January 1974 concerning a social action programme[3], the Council included in its priority actions those designed to improve the conditions of freedom of movement for workers relating in particular to reception and to the education of their children;

Whereas in order to permit the integration of such children into the educational environment and the school system of the host State, they should be able to receive suitable tuition including teaching of the language of the host State;

Whereas host Member States should also take, in conjunction with the Member States of origin, appropriate measures to promote the teaching of the mother tongue and of the culture of the country of origin of the abovementioned children, with a view principally to facilitating their possible reintegration into the Member State of origin,

---

1 OJ No C 280, 8.12.1975, p 48.
2 OJ No C 45, 27.2.1976, p 6.
3 OJ No C 13, 12.2.1974, p 1.

Has adopted this directive:

[B.2.126]
Article 1

This Directive shall apply to children for whom school attendance is compulsory under the laws of the host State, who are dependants of any worker who is a national of another Member State, where such children are resident in the territory of the Member State in which that national carries on or has carried on an activity as an employed person.

[B.2.127]
Article 2

Member States shall, in accordance with their national circumstances and legal systems, take appropriate measures to ensure that free tuition to facilitate initial reception is offered in their territory to the children referred to in Article 1, including, in particular, the teaching – adapted to the specific needs of such children – of the official language or one of the official languages of the host State.

Member States shall take the measures necessary for the training and further training of the teachers who are to provide this tuition.

[B.2.128]
Article 3
Member States shall, in accordance with their national circumstances and legal systems, and in cooperation with States of origin, take appropriate measures to promote, in coordination with normal education, teaching of the mother tongue and culture of the country of origin for the children referred to in Article 1.

[B.2.129]
Article 4
The Member States shall take the necessary measures to comply with this Directive within four years of its notification and shall forthwith inform the Commission thereof.

The Member States shall also inform the Commission of all laws, regulations and administrative or other provisions which they adopt in the field governed by this Directive.

[B.2.130]
Article 5
The Member States shall forward to the Commission within five years of the notification of this Directive, and subsequently at regular intervals at the request of the Commission, all relevant information to enable the Commission to report to the Council on the application of this Directive.

[B.2.131]
Article 6
This Directive is addressed to the Member States.

Done at Brussels, 25 July 1977.

COUNCIL DIRECTIVE (90/364/EEC)

of 28 June 1990 on the right of residence

The Council of The European Communities,

Having regard to the Treaty establishing the European Economic Community, and in particular Article 235 thereof;

Having regard to the proposal from the Commission[1];

Having regard to the Opinion of the European Parliament[2];

Having regard to the Opinion of the Economic and Social Committee[3];

Whereas Article 3(*c*) of the Treaty provides that the activities of the Community shall include, as provided in the Treaty, the abolition, as between member states, of obstacles to freedom of movement for persons;

Whereas Article 8(*a*) of the Treaty provides that the internal market must be established by 31 December 1992; whereas the internal market comprises an area without internal frontiers in which the free movement of goods, persons, services and capital is ensured in accordance with the provisions of the Treaty;

Whereas national provisions on the right of nationals of the member states to reside in a member state other than their own must be harmonised to ensure such freedom of movement;

Whereas beneficiaries of the right of residence must not become an unreasonable burden on the public finances of the host member state;

Whereas this right can only be genuinely exercised if it is also granted to members of the family;

Whereas the beneficiaries of this Directive should be covered by administrative arrangements similar to those laid down in particular in Directive 68/360/EEC[4] and Directive 64/221/EEC[5];

Whereas the Treaty does not provide, for the action concerned, powers other than those of Article 235;

---

1 OJ No C 191, 28.7.1989, p 5; and OJ No C 26, 3.2.1990, p 22.
2 Opinion delivered on 13 June 1990 (not yet published in official Journal).
3 OJ No C 329, 30.12.1989, p 25.
4 OJ No L 257, 19.10.1968, p 13.
5 OJ No 56, 4.4.1964, p 850/40.

Has adopted this Directive:
[B.2.132]
Article 1

1   Member states shall grant the right of residence to nationals of member states who do not enjoy this right under other provisions of Community law and to members of their families as defined in paragraph 2, provided that they themselves and the members of their families are covered by sickness insurance in respect of all risks in the host member state and have sufficient

resources to avoid becoming a burden on the social assistance system of the host member state during their period of residence.

The resources referred to in the first subparagraph shall be deemed sufficient where they are higher than the level of resources below which the host member state may grant social assistance to its nationals, taking into account the personal circumstances of the applicant and, where appropriate, the personal circumstances of persons admitted pursuant to paragraph 2.

Where the second subparagraph cannot be applied in a member state, the resources of the applicant shall be deemed sufficient if they are higher than the level of the minimum social security pension paid by the host member state.

2   The following shall, irrespective of their nationality, have the right to install themselves in another member state with the holder of the right of residence:

(*a*) his or her spouse and their descendants who are dependents;
(*b*) dependent relatives in the ascending line of the holder of the right of residence and his or her spouse.

[B.2.133]
Article 2
1   Exercise of the right of residence shall be evidenced by means of the issue of a document known as a 'Residence permit for a national of a member state of the EEC', the validity of which may be limited to five years on a renewable basis. However, the member states may, when they deem it to be necessary, require revalidation of the permit at the end of the first two years of residence. Where a member of the family does not hold the nationality of a member state, he or she shall be issued with a residence document of the same validity as that issued to the national on whom he or she depends.

For the purpose of issuing the residence permit or document, the member state may require only that the applicant present a valid identity card or passport and provide proof that he or she meets the conditions laid down in Article 1.

2   Articles 2, 3, 6(1)(*a*) and (2) and Article 9 of Directive 68/360/EEC shall apply *mutatis mutandis* to the beneficiaries of this Directive.

The spouse and the dependent children of a national of a member state entitled to the right of residence within the territory of a member state shall be entitled to take up any employed or self-employed activity anywhere within the territory of that member state, even if they are not nationals of a member state.

Member states shall not derogate from the provisions of this Directive save on grounds of public policy, public security or public health. In that event, Directive 64/221/EEC shall apply.

3   This Directive shall not affect existing law on the acquisition of second homes.

[B.2.134]
Article 3
The right of residence shall remain for as long as beneficiaries of that right fulfil the conditions laid down in Article 1.

[B.2.135]
Article 4

The Commission shall, not more than three years after the date of implementation of this Directive, and at three-yearly intervals thereafter, draw up a report on the application of this Directive and submit it to the European Parliament and the Council.

[B.2.136]
Article 5

Member states shall bring into force the laws, regulations and administrative provisions necessary to comply with this Directive not later than 30 June 1992. They shall forthwith inform the Commission thereof.

[B.2.137]
Article 6

This Directive is addressed to the member states.

Done at Luxembourg, 28 June 1990.

COUNCIL DIRECTIVE (90/365/EEC)

of 28 June 1990 on the right of residence for employees and self-employed persons who have ceased their occupational activity

[B.2.138]

The Council of The European Communities,

Having regard to the Treaty establishing the European Economic Community, and in particular Article 235 thereof;

Having regard to the proposal from the Commission[1];

Having regard to the opinion of the European Parliament[2];

Having regard to the opinion of the Economic and Social Committee[3];

Whereas Article 3(*c*) of the Treaty provides that the activities of the Community shall include, as provided in the Treaty, the abolition, as between member states, of obstacles to freedom of movement for persons;

Whereas Article 8(*a*) of the Treaty provides that the internal market must be established by 31 December 1992; whereas the internal market comprises an area without internal frontiers in which the free movement of goods, persons, services and capital is ensured, in accordance with the provisions of the Treaty;

Whereas Articles 48 and 52 of the Treaty provide for freedom of movement for workers and self-employed persons, which entails the right of residence in the member states in which they pursue their occupational activity; whereas it is desirable that this right of residence also be granted to persons who have ceased their occupational activity even if they have not exercised their right to freedom of movement during their working life;

Whereas beneficiaries of the right of residence must not become an unreasonable burden on the public finances of the host member state;

Whereas under Article 10 of Regulation (EEC) No 1408/71[4], as amended by Regulation (EEC) No 1390/81[5], recipients of invalidity or old age cash benefits or pensions for accidents at work or occupational diseases are entitled to continue to receive these benefits and pensions even if they reside in the territory of a member state other than that in which the institution responsible for payment is situated;

Whereas this right can only be genuinely exercised if it is also granted to members of the family;

Whereas the beneficiaries of this Directive should be covered by administrative arrangements similar to those laid down in particular in Directive 68/630/EEC[6] and Directive 64/221/EEC[7];

Whereas the Treaty does not provide, for the action concerned, powers other than those of Article 235;

---

1 OJ No C 191, 28.7.1989, p 3; and OJ No C 26, 3.2.1990, p 19.

2 Opinion delivered on 13 June 1990 (not yet published in Official Journal).
3 OJ No C 329, 30.12.1989, p 25.
4 OJ No L 149, 5.7.1971, p 2.
5 OJ No L 143, 29.5.1981, p 1.
6 OJ No L 257, 19.10.1968, p 13.
7 OJ No 56, 4.4.1964, p 850/64.

Has adopted this Directive:

[B.2.139]
Article 1

1   Member states shall grant the right of residence to nationals of member states who have pursued an activity as an employee or self-employed person and to members of their families as defined in paragraph 2, provided that they are recipients of an invalidity or early retirement pension, or old age benefits, or of a pension in respect of an industrial accident or disease of an amount sufficient to avoid becoming a burden on the social security system of the host member state during their period of residence and provided they are covered by sickness insurance in respect of all risks in the host member state.

The resources of the applicant shall be deemed sufficient where they are higher than the level of resources below which the host member state may grant social assistance to its nationals, taking into account the personal circumstances of persons admitted pursuant to paragraph 2.

Where the second subparagraph cannot be applied in a member state, the resources of the applicant shall be deemed sufficient if they are higher than the level of the minimum social security pension paid by the host member state.

2   The following shall, irrespective of their nationality, have the right to install themselves in another member state with the holder of the right of residence:

(*a*) his or her spouse and their descendants who are dependents;
(*b*) dependent relatives in the ascending line of the holder of the right of residence and his or her spouse.

[B.2.140]
Article 2

1   Exercise of the right of residence shall be evidenced by means of the issue of a document known as a 'Residence permit for a national of a member state of the EEC', whose validity may be limited to five years on a renewable basis. However, the member states may, when they deem it to be necessary, require revalidation of the permit at the end of the first two years of residence. Where a member of the family does not hold the nationality of a member state, he or she shall be issued with a residence document of the same validity as that issued to the national on whom he or she depends.

For the purposes of issuing the residence permit or document, the member state may require only that the applicant present a valid identity card or passport and provide proof that he or she meets the conditions laid down in Article 1.

2   Articles 2, 3, 6(1)(*a*) and (2) and Article 9 of Directive 68/360/EEC shall apply *mutatis mutandis* to the beneficiaries of this Directive.

The spouse and the dependent children of a national of a member state entitled to the right of residence within the territory of a member state shall be entitled to take up any employed or self-employed activity anywhere within the territory of that member state, even if they are not nationals of a member state.

Member states shall not derogate from the provisions of this Directive save on grounds of public policy, public security or public health. In that event, Directive 64/221/EEC shall apply.

3   This Directive shall not affect existing law on the acquisition of second homes.

[B.2.141]
Article 3
The right of residence shall remain for as long as beneficiaries of that right fulfil the conditions laid down in Article 1.

[B.2.142]
Article 4
The Commission shall, not more than three years after the date of implementation of this Directive, and at three-yearly intervals thereafter, draw up a report on the application of this Directive and submit it to the European Parliament and the Council.

[B.2.143]
Article 5
Member states shall bring into force the laws, regulations and administrative provisions necessary to comply with this Directive not later than 30 June 1992. They shall forthwith inform the Commission thereof.

[B.2.144]
Article 6
This Directive is addressed to the member states.

Done at Luxembourg, 28 June 1990.

COUNCIL DIRECTIVE (93/96/EEC)

of 29 October 1993 on the right of residence for students

[B.2.145]

The Council of the European Communities,

Having regard to the Treaty establishing the European Economic Community, and in particular the second paragraph of Article 7 thereof;

Having regard to the proposal from the Commission[1];

In cooperation with the European Parliament[2];

Having regard to the opinion of the Economic and Social Committee[3];

Whereas Article 3(*c*) of the Treaty provides that the activities of the Community shall include, as provided in the Treaty, the abolition, as between member states, of obstacles to freedom of movement for persons;

Whereas Article 8(*a*) of the Treaty provides that the internal market must be established by 31 December 1992; whereas the internal market comprises an area without internal frontiers in which the free movement of goods, persons, services and capital is ensured in accordance with the provisions of the Treaty;

Whereas, as the Court of Justice has held, Articles 128 and 7 of the Treaty prohibit any discrimination between nationals of the member states as regards access to vocational training in the Community; whereas access by a national of one member state to vocational training in another member state implies, for that national, a right of residence in that other member state;

Whereas, accordingly, in order to guarantee access to vocational training, the conditions likely to facilitate the effective exercise of that right of residence should be laid down;

Whereas the right of residence for students forms part of a set of related measures designed to promote vocational training;

Whereas beneficiaries of the right of residence must not become an unreasonable burden on the public finances of the host member state;

Whereas, in the present state of Community law, as established by the case law of the Court of Justice, assistance granted to students, does not fall within the scope of the Treaty within the meaning of Article 7 thereof;

Whereas the right of residence can only be genuinely exercised if it is also granted to the spouse and their dependent children;

Whereas the beneficiaries of this Directive should be covered by administrative arrangements similar to those laid down in particular in Council Directive 68/360/EEC of 15 October 1968 on the abolition of restrictions on movement and residence within the Community for workers of member states and their families[4] and Council Directive 64/221/EEC of 25 February 1964 on the co-ordination of special measures concerning the movement and residence of foreign nationals which are justified on grounds of public policy, public security or public health[5];

Whereas this Directive does not apply to students who enjoy the right of residence by virtue of the fact that they are or have been effectively engaged in economic activities or are members of the family of a migrant worker;

Whereas, by its judgment of 7 July 1992 in Case C–295/90, the Court of Justice annulled Council Directive 90/366/EEC of 28 June 1990 on the right of residence for students 'while maintaining the effects of the annulled Directive until the entry into force of a Directive adopted on the appropriate legal basis';

Whereas the effects of Directive 90/366/EEC should be maintained during the period up to 31 December 1993, the date by which member states are to have adopted the laws, regulations and administrative provisions necessary to comply with this Directive;

---

1 OJ No C166, 17.6.1993, p 16.
2 OJ No C255, 20.9.1993, p 70 and OJ No C315, 22.1.1993.
3 OJ No C304, 10.11.1993, p 1.
4 OJ No L257, 19.10.1968, p 13. Directive as last amended by the Act of Accession of 1985.
5 OJ No 56, 4.4.1964, p 850/64.
6 OJ No L180, 13.7.1990, p 30.

Has adopted this directive:

[B.2.146]
Article 1
In order to lay down conditions to facilitate the exercise of the right of residence and with a view to guaranteeing access to vocational training in a non-discriminatory manner for a national of a member state who has been accepted to attend a vocational training course in another member state, the member states shall recognise the right of residence for any student who is a national of a member state and who does not enjoy that right under other provisions of Community law, and for the student's spouse and their dependent children, where the student assures the relevant national authority, by means of a declaration or by such alternative means as the student may choose that are at least equivalent, that he has sufficient resources to avoid becoming a burden on the social assistance system of the host member state during their period of residence, provided that the student is enrolled in a recognised educational establishment for the principal purpose of following a vocational training course there and that he is covered by sickness insurance in respect of all risks in the host member state.

[B.2.147]
Article 2
1   The right of residence shall be restricted to the duration of the course of studies in question.

The right of residence shall be evidenced by means of the issue of a document known as a 'residence permit for a national of a member state of the

Community', the validity of which may be limited to the duration of the course of studies or to one year where the course lasts longer; in the latter event it shall be renewable annually. Where a member of the family does not hold the nationality of a member state, he or she shall be issued with a residence document of the same validity as that issued to the national on whom he or she depends.

For the purpose of issuing the residence permit or document, the member state may require only that the applicant present a valid identity card or passport and provide proof that he or she meets the conditions laid down in Article 1.

2   Articles 2, 3 and 9 of Directive 68/360/EEC shall apply *mutatis mutandis* to the beneficiaries of this Directive.

The spouse and dependent children of a national of a member state entitled to the right of residence within the territory of a member state shall be entitled to take up any employed or self-employed activity anywhere within the territory of that member state, even if they are not nationals of a member state.

Member states shall not derogate from the provisions of this Directive save on grounds of public policy, public security or public health; in that event, Articles 2 to 9 of Directive 64/221/EEC shall apply.

[B.2.148]
Article 3
This Directive shall not establish any entitlement to the payment of maintenance grants by the host member state on the part of students benefiting from the right of residence.

[B.2.149]
Article 4
The right of residence shall remain for as long as beneficiaries of that right fulfil the conditions laid down in Article 1.

[B.2.150]
Article 5
The Commission shall, not more than three years after the date of implementation of this Directive, and at three-yearly intervals thereafter, draw up a report on the application of this Directive and submit it to the European Parliament and the Council.

The Commission shall pay particular attention to any difficulties which the implementation of Article 1 might give rise in the member states; it shall, if appropriate, submit proposals to the Council with the aim of remedying such difficulties.

[B.2.151]
Article 6
Member states shall bring into force the laws, regulations and administrative provisions necessary to comply with this Directive not later than 31 December 1993. They shall forthwith inform the Commission thereof.

For the period preceding that date, the effects of Directive 90/366/EEC shall be maintained.

When member states adopt those measures, they shall contain a reference to this Directive or shall be accompanied by such a reference on the occasion of their official publication. The methods of making such references shall be laid down by the member states.

[B.2.152]
Article 7
This Directive is addressed to the member states.

Done at Brussels, 29 October 1993.

COUNCIL REGULATION (EC) 574/99

of 12 March 1999 determining the third countries whose nationals must be in possession of visas when crossing the external borders of the Member States

[B.2.153]
The Council of the European Union,

Having regard to the Treaty establishing the European Community, and in particular Article 100c thereof,

Having regard to the proposal from the Commission[1],

Having regard to the opinion of the European Parliament[2],

(1) *Whereas* Article 100c of the Treaty requires the Council to determine the third countries whose nationals must be in possession of a visa when crossing the external borders of the Member States;

(2) *Whereas* the drawing up of the common list annexed to this Regulation represents an important step towards the harmonisation of visa policy; whereas the second subparagraph of Article 7a of the Treaty stipulates in particular that the internal market shall comprise an area without internal frontiers in which the free movement of, inter alia, persons is ensured in accordance with the Treaty; whereas other aspects of the harmonisation of visa policy, including the conditions for the issue of visas, are matters to be determined within the appropriate framework;

(3) *Whereas* risks relating to security and illegal immigration should be given priority consideration when the said common list is drawn up; whereas, in addition, Member States' international relations with third countries also play a role;

(4) *Whereas* the principle that a Member State may not require a visa from a person wishing to cross its external borders if that person holds a visa issued by another Member State which meets the harmonised conditions governing the issue of visas and is valid throughout the Community or if that person holds an appropriate permit issued by a Member State is a matter that should be determined within the appropriate framework;

(5) *Whereas* this Regulation should not prevent a Member State from deciding under what conditions nationals of third countries lawfully resident within its territory may re-enter it after having left the territory of the Member States of the Union during the period of validity of their permits;

(6) *Whereas*, in special cases justifying an exemption where visa requirements would in principle exist, Member States may exempt certain categories of person in keeping with international law or custom;

(7) *Whereas*, since national rules differ on stateless persons, recognised refugees and persons who produce passports or travel documents issued by a territorial entity or authority which is not recognised as a State by all Member

States, Member States may decide on visa requirements for that group of persons, where that territorial entity or authority is not on the said common list;

(8) *Whereas* it is necessary, when new entities are added to the list, to take account of diplomatic implications and guidelines adopted on the matter by the European Union; whereas, at all events, the inclusion of a third country on the common list is entirely without prejudice to its international status;

(9) *Whereas* the determination of third countries whose nationals must be in possession of visas when crossing the external borders of the Member States should be achieved gradually; whereas Member States will constantly endeavour to harmonise their visa policies with regard to third countries not on the common list; whereas the present provisions must not prejudice the achievement of free movement of persons as provided for in Article 7a of the Treaty; whereas the Commission should draw up a progress report on harmonisation in the first half of the year 2001;

(10) *Whereas*, with a view to ensuring that the system is administered openly and that the persons concerned are informed, Member States should communicate to the other Member States and to the Commission the measures which they take pursuant to this Regulation; whereas for the same reasons that information must also be published in the Official Journal of the European Communities,

---

1 OJ C 11, 15. 1. 1994, p. 15.
2 OJ C 128, 9. 5. 1994, p. 350. Opinion of the European Parliament of 10 February 1999.

Has adopted this Regulation:

[B.2.154]
Article 1
1   Nationals of third countries on the common list in the Annex shall be required to be in possession of visas when crossing the external borders of the Member States.

2   Nationals of countries formerly part of countries on the common list shall be subject to the requirements of paragraph 1 unless and until the Council decides otherwise under the procedure laid down in the relevant provision of the Treaty.

[B.2.155]
Article 2
1   Member States shall determine the visa requirements for nationals of third countries not on the common list.

2   Member States shall determine the visa requirements for stateless persons and recognised refugees.

3   Member States shall determine the visa requirements for persons who produce passports or travel documents issued by a territorial entity or authority

which is not recognised as a State by all Member States if that territorial entity or authority is not on the common list.

4   Within 10 working days of the entry into force of this Regulation, Member States shall communicate to the other Member States and the Commission the measures they have taken pursuant to paragraphs 1, 2 and 3.   Any further measures taken pursuant to paragraph 1 shall be similarly communicated within five working days.

The Commission shall publish the measures communicated pursuant to this paragraph and updates thereof in the Official Journal of the European Communities for information.

[B.2.156]
Article 3
During the first half of 2001 the Commission shall draw up a progress report on the harmonisation of Member States' visa policies with regard to third countries not on the common list and, if necessary, submit to the Council proposals for further measures required to achieve the objective of harmonisation laid down in the Treaty.

[B2.157]
Article 4
1   A Member State may exempt nationals of third countries subject to visa requirements under Article 1(1) and (2) from such requirements. This shall apply in particular to civilian air and sea crew, flight crew and attendants on emergency or rescue flights and other helpers in the event of disaster or accident and holders of diplomatic passports, official duty passports and other official passports.
2   Article 2(4) shall apply mutatis mutandis.

[B2.158]
Article 5
For the purposes of this Regulation, 'visa' shall mean an authorisation given or a decision taken by a Member State which is required for entry into its territory with a view to:

— an intended stay in that Member State or in several Member States of no more than three months in all,
— transit through the territory of that Member State or several Member States, except for transit through the international zones of airports and transfers between airports in a Member State.

[B2.159]
Article 6
This Regulation shall be without prejudice to any further harmonisation between individual Member States, going beyond the common list, determining the third countries whose nationals must be in possession of a visa when crossing their external borders.

[B2.160]
Article 7
This Regulation shall enter into force on the day following that of its publication in the Official Journal of the European Communities.

This Regulation shall be binding in its entirety and directly applicable in all Member States.

Done at Brussels, 12 March 1999.

[B.2.161]
Annex

COMMON LIST REFERRED TO IN ARTICLE 1

I. STATES
Afghanistan
Albania
Algeria
Angola
Armenia
Azerbaijan
Bahrain
Bangladesh
Belarus
Benin
Bhutan
Bulgaria
Burkina Faso
Burma/Myanmar
Burundi
Cambodia
Cameroon
Cape Verde
Central African Republic
Chad
China (*)
Comoros
Congo
Côte d'Ivoire
Cuba
Democratic Republic of the Congo
Djibouti
Dominican Republic
Egypt
Equatorial Guinea
Eritrea
Ethiopia
Federal Republic of Yugoslavia (Serbia and Montenegro)
Fiji
Former Yugoslav Republic of Macedonia
Gabon

The Gambia
Georgia
Ghana
Guinea
Guinea-Bissau
Guyana
Haiti
India
Indonesia
Iran
Iraq
Jordan
Kazakhstan
Kyrgyzstan
Kuwait
Laos
Lebanon
Liberia
Libya
Madagascar
Maldives
Mali
Mauritania
Mauritius
Moldavia
Mongolia
Morocco
Mozambique
Nepal
Niger
Nigeria
North Korea
Oman
Pakistan
Papua New Guinea
Peru
Philippines
Qatar
Romania
Russia
Rwanda
Sao Tomé and Principe
Saudi Arabia
Senegal
Sierra Leone
Somalia
Sri Lanka
Sudan
Suriname
Syria
Tajikistan
Tanzania

Thailand
Togo
Tunisia
Turkey
Turkmenistan
Uganda
Ukraine
United Arab Emirates
Uzbekistan
Vietnam
Yemen
Zambia

II. TERRITORIAL ENTITIES AND AUTHORITIES NOT RECOGNISED AS STATES BY ALL THE MEMBER STATES

Taiwan

(*) In respect of China, this does not include holders of the Hong Kong Special Administrative Region passport. Article 2 applies: Member States may decide whether to maintain or review their visa requirements in respect of such persons.

B3   Miscellaneous Agreements and Conventions

THE SCHENGEN AGREEMENT

AGREEMENT BETWEEN THE GOVERNMENTS OF THE STATES OF THE BENELUX ECONOMIC UNION, THE FEDERAL REPUBLIC OF GERMANY AND THE FRENCH REPUBLIC ON THE GRADUAL ABOLITION OF CONTROLS AT THE COMMON FRONTIERS

[B.3.1]
The Governments of the Kingdom of Belgium, the Federal Republic of Germany, the French Republic, the Grand Duchy of Luxembourg and the Kingdom of the Netherlands,
Hereinafter referred to as the parties,

Aware that the increasingly closer union of the peoples of the member states of the European Communities should be manifested through freedom to cross internal frontiers for all nationals of the member states and in the free movement of goods and services,

Anxious to affirm the solidarity between their peoples by removing the obstacles to free movement at the common frontiers between the states of the Benelux Economic Union, the Federal Republic of Germany and the French Republic,

Considering the progress already achieved within the European Communities with a view to ensuring the free movement of persons, goods and services,

Prompted by the will to succeed in abolishing controls at the common frontiers in the movement of nationals of the member states of the European Communities and to facilitate the movement of goods and services,

Considering that application of this Agreement may require legislative measures which will have to be submitted to the national Parliaments in accordance with the constitutions of the signatory states,

Having regard to the Declaration of the Fontainebleau European Council of 25 and 26 June 1984 on the abolition at the internal frontiers of police and customs formalities in the movement of persons and goods,

Having regard to the Agreement concluded at Saarbrücken on 13 July 1984 between the Federal Republic of Germany and the French Republic,

Having regard to the conclusions adopted on 31 May 1984 following the meeting at Neustadt/Aisch of the Ministers of Transport of the Benelux states and the Federal Republic of Germany.

Having regard to the memorandum of the Governments of the Benelux Economic Union of 12 December 1984 forwarded to the Governments of the Federal Republic of Germany and the French Republic,

Have agreed as follows:

Title I   Measures applicable in the short term

[B.3.2]
Article 1
As soon as this Agreement enters into force and until all controls are abolished completely, the formalities at the common frontiers between the States of the Benelux Economic Union, the Federal Republic of Germany and the French Republic shall be completed, for the nationals of the member states of the European Communities, in accordance with the conditions laid down below.

[B.3.3]
Article 2
In regard to the movement of persons, from 15 June 1985 the police and customs authorities shall as a general rule carry out a simple visual check on private vehicles crossing the common frontier at a reduced speed, without requiring such vehicles to stop.

However, they may carry out more thorough controls by means of spot checks. These shall be carried out where possible, in special bays in such a way that the movement of other vehicles crossing the frontier is not hampered.

[B.3.4]
Article 3
To facilitate the visual check, the nationals of the member states of the European Communities presenting themselves at the common frontier in a motor car may affix to the windscreen of the vehicle a green disc measuring at least 8 centimetres in diameter. This disc shall indicate thay they have complied with the rules of the frontier police, are carrying only goods permitted under the duty-free arrangements and have complied with exchange regulations.

[B.3.5]
Article 4
The parties shall endeavour to reduce to a minimum the time spent at common frontiers on account of the checks on the carriage of persons by road for hire or reward.

The parties shall seek solutions enabling them to forego, by 1 January 1986, the systematic control at the common frontiers of the passenger waybill and licences for the carriage of persons by road for hire or reward.

[B.3.6]
Article 5
By 1 January 1986 common control points shall be set up in the adjacent national control offices in so far as that is not already the case and in so far as actual circumstances permit. Consideration shall subsequently be given to the possible introduction of common control points at other frontier posts in the light of local conditions.

[B.3.7]
Article 6
Without prejudice to the application of more favourable arrangements between the parties, the latter shall take the measures required to facilitate the movement of nationals of the member states of the European Communities resident in the municipalities located in the proximity of the common frontiers with a view to allowing them to cross such frontiers outside the approved crossing points and outside the opening times of the control points.

The persons concerned may benefit from these advantages provided that they transport only goods permitted under the duty-free arrangements and comply with exchange regulations.

[B.3.8]
Article 7
The parties shall endeavour to approximate as soon as possible their visa policies in order to avoid any adverse consequences that may result from the easing of controls at the common frontiers in the field of immigration and security. They shall take, if possible by 1 January 1986, the steps necessary with a view, in applying their procedures for the issue of visas and admission to their territory, to taking into account the need to assure the protection of the entire territory of the five states against illegal immigrants and activities which could jeopardize security.

[B.3.9]
Article 8
With a view to easing the controls at the common frontiers and in the light of the significant differences in the laws of the states of the Benelux Economic Union, the Federal Repulic of Germany and the French Republic, the parties shall undertake to combat vigorously on their territories illicit drug trafficking and to coordinate effectively their action in this area.

[B.3.10]
Article 9
The parties shall reinforce the cooperation between their customs and police authorities, notably in fighting crime, particularly illicit traffic in drugs and arms, the unauthorised entry and residence of persons and customs and tax fraud and smuggling. To that end and in accordance wtih their national laws, the parties shall endeavour to improve the exchange of information and reinforce it where information likely to be of interest to the other parties in combating crime is concerned.

The parties shall reinforce in the context of their national laws mutual assistance in respect of irregular capital movements.

[B.3.11]
Article 10
With a view to assuring the cooperation provided for in Articles 6, 7, 8 and 9, meetings between the competent authorities of the parties shall be held at regular intervals.

[B.3.12]
Article 11
In regard to the cross-frontier carriage of goods by road, the parties shall forego, from 1 July 1985, the systematic completion at the common frontiers of the following controls:

— control of driving and rest periods (Council Regulation (EEC) No 543/69 of 25 March 1969 on the harmonisation of certain social legislation relating to road transport and AETR);
— control of the weight and size of commercial vehicles; this provision shall not exclude the introduction of automatic weighing systems with a view to spot checks on weight;
— controls on the technical state of the vehicles.

Measures shall be taken to prevent the duplication of controls within the territories of the parties.

[B.3.13]
Article 12
From 1 July 1985 control of documents giving details of transport operations not carried out under licence or quota pursuant to Community or bilateral rules shall be replaced at the common frontiers by spot checks. The vehicles carrying out the transport under these systems shall be distin-guished when crossing the frontier by means of a visible symbol.

The competent authorities of the Parties shall determine the features of this symbol by common agreement.

[B.3.14]
Article 13
The parties shall endeavour to harmonise by 1 January 1986 the systems for the licensing of commercial road transport in force among them for cross-frontier traffic with the aim of simplifying, easing and possibly replacing licenses for journeys by licenses for a period of time, with a visual check on the crossing of the common frontiers.

The procedures for converting the licenses for journeys into licenses for periods shall be agreed on a bilateral basis, account being taken of the road transport requirements in the different countries concerned.

[B.3.15]
Article 14
The parties shall seek solutions to reduce the waiting times of rail transport at the common frontiers caused by completion of frontier formalities.

[B.3.16]
Article 15
The parties shall recommend to their respective rail transport companies:

— to adapt technical procedures in order to reduce to a minimum the waiting time at the common frontiers;
— to do everything possible to apply to certain types of carriage of goods by rail to be defined by the rail companies, a special routing system such that the common frontiers can be crossed rapidly without any appreciable stops (goods trains with reduced waiting times at frontiers).

[B.3.17]
Article 16
The parties shall harmonise the opening times and dates of customs posts for waterway traffic at the common frontiers.

Title II Measures applicable in the long term

[B.3.18]
Article 17
In regard to the movement of persons, the parties shall endeavour to abolish the controls at the common frontiers and transfer them to their external frontiers. To that end, they shall endeavour to harmonise in advance, where necessary, the laws and administrative provisions concerning the prohibitions and restrictions which form the basis for the controls and to take complementary measures to safeguard security and combat illegal immigration by nationals of states that are not members of the European Communities.

[B.3.19]
Article 18
The parties shall open discussions, notably on the following matters, account being taken of the results of the short-term measures:

(*a*) drawing up arrangements for police cooperation on the prevention of delinquency and on search;
(*b*) examining any difficulties in applying agreements on international judicial assistance and extradition in order to determine the most appropriate solutions for improving cooperation between the parties in those fields;
(*c*) seeking means to permit the joint combating of crime, *inter alia*, by studying possible introduction of a right of pursuit for police officers, taking into account existing means of communication and judicial assistance.

[B.3.20]
Article 19
The parties shall seek to hamonise laws and regulations, in particular on:

— drugs;
— arms and explosives;
— registration of travellers in hotels.

[B.3.21]
Article 20
The parties shall endeavour to harmonise their visa policies and conditions for entry to their territories. In so far as necessary, they shall also prepare for harmonisation of their rules governing certain aspects of the law on aliens in regard to nationals of states that are not members of the European Communities.

[B.3.22]
Article 21
The parties shall undertake common initiatives within the European Communities:

(*a*) to arrive at an increase in the duty-free allowances granted to travellers;
(*b*) to remove in the context of the Community allowances, restrictions which might remain on entry to the member states in respect of goods whose possession is not prohibited for their nationals.

The parties shall take steps within the European Communities to attain harmonised charging in the country of departure of VAT on tourism transport services within the European Communitites.

[B.3.23]
Article 22
The parties shall endeavour both among themselves and within the European Communities:

— to increase the duty-free allowance for fuel to bring it into line with the normal contents of bus and coach tanks (600 litres);
— to harmonise the taxation of diesel fuel and increase the duty-free allowances for the normal contents of lorry tanks.

[B.3.24]
Article 23
The parties shall also endeavour in the area of road transport to reduce, at the adjacent national control offices, waiting times and numbers of stopping points.

[B.3.25]
Article 24
In regard to the movement of goods, the parties shall seek means to transfer to

847

the external frontiers or to within their own territories the controls now carried out at the common frontiers.

To that end, they shall take, where necessary, common steps among themselves and within the European Communities to harmonise the provisions which form the basis for the controls of goods at the common frontiers. They shall ensure that these measures are without prejudice to the necessary protection of the health of persons, animals and plants.

[B.3.26]
Article 25
The parties shall develop their cooperation with a view to facilitating the customs clearance of goods crossing a common frontier, thanks to a systematic, automatic exchange of the necessary data collected by means of the single document.

[B.3.27]
Article 26
The parties shall examine how taxes (VAT and excise duties) can be harmonised in the framework of the European Communities. To that end they shall support the initiatives undertaken by the European Communities.

[B.3.28]
Article 27
The parties shall examine whether, on a reciprocal basis, the limits on the duty-free allowances granted at the common frontiers to frontier-zone residents, as authorised under Community law, can be abolished.

[B.3.29]
Article 28
Any conclusion on a bilateral or multilateral basis of arrangements similar to this Agreement with states that are not parties thereto shall be preceded by consultation between the parties.

[B.3.30]
Article 29
This Agreement shall apply also to the Land of Berlin, unless a declaration to the contrary is made by the Government of the Federal Republic of Germany to the Governments of the states of the Benelux Economic Union and the Government of the French Republic within three months of entry into force of this Agreement.

[B.3.31]
Article 30
The measures provided for in this Agreement which are not applicable as soon as it enters into force shall be applied by 1 January 1986 as regards the meas-

ures provided for in Title I and if possible by 1 January 1990 as regards the measures provided for in Title II, unless other deadlines are fixed in this Agreement.

[B.3.32]
Article 31

This Agreement shall apply subject to the provisions of Articles 5 and 6, and 8 to 16 of the Agreement concluded at Saarbrücken on 13 July 1984 between the Federal Republic of Germany and the French Republic.

[B.3.33]
Article 32

This Agreement shall be signed without being subject to ratification or approval or subject to ratification or approval followed by ratification or approval.

This Agreement shall be applied on a provisional basis from the day following its signature. This Agreement shall enter into force thirty days after deposit of the last instrument of ratification or approval.

[B.3.34]
Article 33

The Government of the Grand Duchy of Luxembourg shall be depository of this Agreement.

In witness whereof, the representatives of the Governments duly empowered to that effect have signed this Agreement.

Done at Schengen, Grand Duchy of Luxembourg, on 14 June 1985, the German, French and Dutch texts of this Agreement being equally authentic.

CONVENTION

Applying the Schengen Agreement of 14 June 1985 between the governments of the states of the Benelux Economic Union, the Federal Republic of Germany and the French Republic, on the gradual abolition of checks at their common borders.

[B.3.35]
The Kingdom of Belgium, the Federal Republic of Germany, the French Republic, the Grand Duchy of Luxembourg and the Kingdom of the Netherlands, herinafter called the Contracting Parties,

Taking as their basis the Schengen Agreement of 14 June 1985 on the gradual abolition of checks at their common borders,

Having decided to implement the intention expressed in that agreement of bringing about the abolition of checks at their common borders on the movement of persons and facilitating the transport and movement of goods,

Whereas the Treaty establishing the European Communities, supplemented by the Single European Act, provides that the internal market shall comprise an area without internal frontiers,

Whereas the aim pursued by the Contracting Parties coincides with that objective, without prejudice to the measures to be taken to implement the provisions of the Treaty,

Whereas the implementation of that intention requires a series of appropriate measures and close co-operation between the Contracting Parties,

Have agreed as follows:

Title I   Definitions

[B.3.36]
Article 1
For the purposes of this Convention:

'Internal borders'   shall mean the common land borders of the Contracting Parties, their airports for internal flights and their sea ports for regular transshipment connections exclusively from or to other ports within the territories of the Contracting Parties not calling at any ports outside those territories.

'External borders'   shall mean the Contracting Parties' land and sea borders and their airports and sea ports, provided they are not internal borders;

'Internal flight'   shall mean any flight exclusively to or from territories of the Contracting Parties not landing within the territory of a Third State;

'Third State'   shall mean any state other than the Contracting Parties;

'Alien'   shall mean any person other than a national of a member state of the European Communities;

'Alien reported as a person not to be permitted entry' shall mean any alien listed reported as a person not to be permitted entry in the Schengen Information System in accordance with Article 96;

'Border crossing point' shall mean any crossing point authorised by the competent authorities for the crossing of external borders;

'Border control' shall mean a check made at a border in response solely to an intention to cross that border regardless of any other consideration.

'Carrier' shall mean any natural or legal person whose occupation it is to provide passenger transport by air, sea or land;

'Residence permit' shall mean an authorisation of any type issued by a Contracting Party giving the right of residence within its territory. This definition shall not inlcude temporary admission to residence within the territory of a Contracting Party for the purpose of the processing of an application for asylum or an application for a residence permit.

'Application for asylum' shall mean any application submitted in writing, orally or otherwise by an alien at an external border or within the territory of a Contracting Party with a view to obtaining recognition as a refugee in accordance with the Geneva Convention of 28 July 1951 relating to the Status of Refugees, as amended by the New York Protocol of 31 January 1967 and as such obtaining the right of residence;

'Applicant for asylum' shall mean any alien who has submitted an application for asylum within the meaning of this Convention, on which no final decision has been taken;

'Processing of an application for asylum' shall mean all the procedures for examining and taking a decision on an application for asylum, including measures taken in implementation of a final decision thereon, with the exception of the determination of the Contracting Party responsible for the processing of an application for asylum under this Convention.

Title II Abolition of checks at internal borders and movement of persons

Chapter 1 Crossing internal frontiers

[B.3.37]
Article 2
1 Internal borders may be crossed at any point without any checks on persons being carried out.

2 Where public policy or national security so require, however, a Contracting Party may, after consulting the other Contracting Parties, decide that for a limited period national border checks appropriate to the situation will be carried out at internal borders. If public policy or national security require immediate action, the Contracting Party concerned shall take the necessary measures and shall inform the other Contracting Parties thereof at the earliest opportunity.

3 The abolition of checks on persons at internal borders shall not affect either Article 22 below or the exercise of police powers by the competent authorities under each Contracting Party's legislation throughout its territory,

or the obligations to hold, carry and produce permits and documents provided for in its legislation.

4   Checks on goods shall be carried out in accordance with the relevant provisions of this Convention.

Chapter 2   *Crossing external borders*

[B.3.38]
Article 3
1   External borders may in principle be crossed only at border crossing points during the fixed opening hours. More detailed provisions, and exceptions and arrangements for minor border traffic, as well as the rules applicable to special categories of maritime traffic such as yachting and coastal fishing, shall be adopted by the Executive Committee.

2   The Contracting Parties undertake to introduce penalties for the unauthorised crossing of external borders at places other than crossing points or at times other than the fixed opening hours.

[B.3.39]
Article 4
1   The Contracting Parties guarantee that as from 1993 passengers on flights from Third States who board internal flights will first be subject, upon arrival, to personal and hand baggage checks in the airport of arrival of their external flight. Passengers on internal flights who board flights bound for Third States will first be subject, on departure, to personal and hand baggage checks in the airport of departure of their external flight.

2   The Contracting Parties shall take the measures required for checks to be carried out in accordance with paragraph 1.

3   Neither paragraph 1 nor paragraph 2 shall affect checks on registered luggage; such checks shall be carried out either in the airport of final destination or in the airport of initial departure.

4   Until the date laid down in paragraph 1, airports shall, by way of derogation from the definition of internal borders, be considered as external borders for internal flights.

[B.3.40]
Article 5
1   For visits not exceeding three months entry into the territories of the Contracting Parties may be granted to an alien who fulfils the following conditions:

(*a*) in possession of a valid document or documents permitting them to cross the border, as determined by the Executive Committee;
(*b*) in possession of a valid visa if required;
(*c*) if applicable, submits documents substantiating the purpose and the conditions of the planned visit and has sufficient means of support, both for the period of the planned visit and to return to their country of origin or to

travel in transit in a Third State, into which their admission is guaranteed, or is in a position to acquire such means legally;

(*d*) has not been reported as a person not to be permitted entry;

(*e*) is not considered to be a threat to public policy, national security or the international relations of any of the Contracting Parties.

2 Entry to the territories of the Contracting Parties must be refused to any alien who does not fulfil all the above conditions unless a Contracting Party considers it necessary to derogate from that principle on humanitarian grounds or in the national interest or because of international obligations. In such cases permission to enter will be restricted to the territory of the Contacting Party concerned, which must inform the other Contracting Parties accordingly.

These rules shall not preclude the application of special provisions concerning the right of asylum or of the provisions of Article 18.

3 An alien who holds a residence permit or a return visa issued by one of the Contracting Parties or, if required, both documents, shall be permitted to enter in transit, unless their name is on the national list of persons reported as not to be refused entry which is held by the Contracting Party at the external borders of which they arrive.

[B.3.41]
Article 6
1 Cross-border movement at external borders shall be subject to checks by the competent authorities. Checks shall be made in accordance with uniform principles, within the scope of national powers and national legislation, account being taken of the interests of all Contracting Parties throughout the Contracting Parties' territories.

2 The uniform principles referred to in paragraph 1 shall be as follows:

(*a*) Checks on persons shall include not only the verification of travel documents and of the other conditions governing entry, residence, work and exit but also checks to detect and prevent threats to the national security and public policy of the Contracting Parties. Such checks shall also cover vehicles and objects in the possession of persons crossing the border. They shall be carried out by each Contracting Party in accordance with its legislation, in particular as regards searches.

(*b*) All persons must be subject to at least one check making it possible to establish their identities on the basis of their presentation of travel documents.

(*c*) On entry aliens must be subject to a thorough check as defined in (*a*).

(*d*) On exit checks shall be carried out as required in the interest of all Contracting Parties under the law on aliens in order to detect and prevent threats to the national security and public policy of the Contracting Parties. Such checks shall be made in all cases in respect of aliens.

(*e*) If such checks cannot be made because of particular circumstances priorities must be established. In this connection, entry checks shall in principle take priority over exit checks.

3 The competent authorities shall use mobile units to exercise surveillance on external borders between crossing points; the same shall apply to border crossing points outside normal hours. This surveillance shall be carried out in

such a way as not to encourage people to circumvent the checks at crossing points. The surveillance procedures shall, where appropriate, be fixed by the Executive Committee.

4   The Contracting Parties undertake to deploy enough appropriate officers to conduct checks and maintain surveillance along external borders.

5   An equivalent level of control shall be exercised at external frontiers.

[B.3.42]
Article 7
The Contracting Parties shall assist each other and shall maintain constant, close co-operation with a view to the effective exercise of checks and surveillance. They shall in particular exchange all relevant, important information, with the exception of data relating to named individuals, unless otherwise provided in this Convention, shall as far as possible harmonise the instructions given to the authorities responsible for checks and shall promote the uniform training and retraining of officers manning checkpoints. Such co-operation may take the form of the exchange of liaison officers.

[B.3.43]
Article 8
The Executive Committee shall take the necessary decisions relating to the practical procedures for implementing border checks and surveillance.

Chapter 3   Visas

SECTION I   VISAS FOR SHORT VISITS

[B.3.44]
Article 9
1   The Contracting Parties undertake to adopt a common policy on the movement of persons and in particular on the arrangements for visas. They shall give each other assistance to that end. The Contracting Parties undertake to pursue by common agreement the harmonisation of their policies on visas.

2   The visa arrangements relating to Third States, the nationals of which are subject to visa arrangements common to all the Contracting Parties at the time when this Convention is signed or later, may be amended only by common agreement of all the Contracting Parties. A Contracting Party may exceptionally derogate from the common visa arrangements with respect to a Third State for over-riding reasons of national policy that require an urgent decision. It must first consult the other Contracting Parties and, in its decision, must take account of their interests and of the consequences of that decision.

[B.3.45]
Article 10
1   A uniform visa valid for the entire territory of the Contracting Parties shall be introduced. This visa, the period of which shall be determined by Article 11, may be issued for visits not exceeding three months.

2   Until this visa is introduced the Contracting Parties shall recognise their respective national visas, insofar as these are issued on the basis of common conditions and criteria determined within the framework of the relevant provisions of this Chapter.

3   By way of derogation from paragraphs 1 and 2 above each Contracting Party shall reserve the right to restrict the territorial validity of the visa in accordance with common arrangements determined in the context of the relevant provisions of this Chapter.

[B.3.46]
Article 11
1   The visa provided for in Article 10 may be:

(*a*) a travel visa valid for one or more entries, provided that neither the length of a continuous visit nor the total length of successive visit may exceed three months in any half year as from the date of first entry;
(*b*) a transit visa allowing its holder to pass through the territories of the Contracting Parties once, twice or exceptionally several times en route to the territory of a Third State, provided that no transit shall last longer than five days.

2   Paragraph 1 shall not preclude a Contracting Party from issuing a new visa, the validity of which is limited to its own territory, within the half year in question if necessary.

[B.3.47]
Article 12
1   The uniform visa provided for in Article 10(1) shall be issued by the diplomatic and consular authorities of the Contracting Parties and, where appropriate, by the authorities of the Contracting Parties designated under Article 17.

2   The Contracting Party competent to issue such a visa shall in principle be that of the principal destination. If this cannot be determined the visa shall in principle be issued by the diplomatic or consular post of the Contracting Party of first entry.

3   The Executive Committee shall specify the implementing arrangements and, in particular, the criteria for determining the principal destination.

[B.3.48]
Article 13
1   No visa shall be apposed on a travel document that has expired.

2   The period of validity of a travel document must be greater than that of the visa, taking account of the period of use of the visa. It must enable an alien to return to his country of origin or to enter a third country.

[B.3.49]
Article 14
1   No visa may be apposed to a travel document if that travel document is

valid for none of the Contracting Parties. If a travel document is valid only for one Contracting Party or for a number of Contracting Parties the visa to be apposed shall be limited to the Contracting Party or Parties in question.

2 If a travel document is not recognised as valid by one or more of the Contracting Parties a visa may be issued in the form of an authorisation in place of a visa.

[B.3.50]
Article 15
In principle the visas referred to in Article 10 may be issued only if an alien fulfils the conditions of entry laid down in Article 5(1)(*a*), (*c*), (*d*) and (*e*).

[B.3.51]
Article 16
If a Contracting Party considers it necessary to derogate, on one of the grounds listed in Article 5(2), from the principle enunciated in Article 15 by issuing a visa to an alien who does not fulfil all of the conditions of entry referred to in Article 5(1), the validity of this visa shall be restricted to the territory of that Contracting Party, which must inform the other Contracting Parties accordingly.

[B.3.52]
Article 17
1 The Executive Committee shall adopt common rules for the examination of applications for a visa, shall ensure their correct implementation and shall adapt them to new situations and circumstances.

2 The Executive Committee shall also specify the cases in which the issue of a visa shall be subject to consultation with the central authority of the Contracting Party to which application is made and, where appropriate, the central authorities of other Contracting Parties.

3 The Executive Committee shall also take the necessary decisions regarding the following points:

(*a*) the travel documents to which a visa may be apposed;
(*b*) the bodies responsible for the issue of visas;
(*c*) the conditions governing the issue of visas at borders;
(*d*) the form, content, and period of validity of visas and the charges to be imposed for their issue;
(*e*) the conditions for the extension and refusal of the visas referred to in (*c*) and (*d*) above, in accordance with the interests of all the Contracting Parties;
(*f*) the procedures for the limitation of the territorial validity of visas;
(*g*) the principles governing the preparation of a common list of aliens reported as not to be permitted entry, without prejudice to Article 96.

SECTION 2   VISAS FOR LONG VISITS

[B.3.53]
Article 18
Visas for visits of more than three months shall be national visas issued by one of the Contracting Parties in accordance with its own legislation. Such a visa shall enable its holder to transit through the territories of the other Contracting Parties in order to proceed to the territory of the Contracting Party which issued the visa, unless he fails to fulfil the conditions of entry referred to in Article 5(1)(*a*), (*d*) and (*e*) or he is on the national reporting list of the Contracting Party through the territory of which he seeks to transit.

Chapter 4   Conditions governing the movement of aliens

[B.3.54]
Article 19
1   Aliens holding a uniform visa who have legally entered the territory of a Contracting Party may move freely within the territories of all the Contracting Parties throughout the period of validity of their visas, provided they fulfil the conditions of entry referred to in Article 5(1)(*a*), (*c*), (*d*) and (*e*).

2   Pending the introduction of a uniform visa, aliens holding a visa issued by one of the Contracting Parties who have legally entered the territory of one Contracting Party may move freely within the territories of all the Contracting Parties during the period of validity of their visa up to a maximum of three months from the date of first entry, provided they fulfil the conditions of entry referred to in Article 5(1)(*a*), (*c*), (*d*), and (*e*).

3   Paragraphs 1 and 2 shall not apply to visas of which the validity is subject to territorial limitation in accordance with Chapter 3 of this Title.

4   This Article shall apply without prejudice to Article 22.

[B.3.55]
Article 20
1   Aliens not subject to a visa requirement may move freely within the territories of the Contracting Parties for a maximum period of three months during the six months following the date of first entry, provided they fulfil the conditions of entry referred to in Article 5(1)(*a*), (*c*), (*d*) and (*e*).

2   Paragraph 1 shall not affect the rights of each Contracting Party to extend beyond three months the visit of an alien within its territory in exceptional circumstances or in implementation of a bilateral agreement concluded before the entry into force of this Convention.

3   This Article shall apply without prejudice to Article 22.

[B.3.56]
Article 21
1   An alien holding a residence permit issued by one of the Contracting Parties may, under cover of that permit and of a travel document, both documents still being valid, move freely for up to three months within the territo-

ries of the other Contracting Parties provided he fulfils the conditions of entry referred to in Article 5(1)(*a*), (*c*) and (*e*) and is not on the national reporting list of the Contracting Party concerned.

2   Paragraph 1 shall also apply to an alien holding a provisional residence permit issued by one of the Contracting Parties and a travel document issued by that Contracting Party.

3   The Contracting Parties shall communicate to the Executive Committee a list of the documents which they issue that are valid as residence permits or provisional residence permits and travel documents within the meaning of this Article.

4   This Article shall apply without prejudice to Article 22.

[B.3.57]
Article 22
1   An alien who has legally entered the territory of one of the Contracting Parties shall be obliged to declare himself, in accordance with the conditions imposed by each Contracting Party, to the competent authorities of the Contracting Party the territory of which he enters. Such declaration may be made, at Contracting Party's choice, either on entry or, within three working days of entry, within the territory of the Contracting Party which he enters.

2   An alien resident within the territory of one of the Contracting Parties who enters the territory of another Contracting Party shall be subject to the obligation to declare himself referred to in paragraph 1.

3   Each Contracting Party shall enact exceptions to paragraphs 1 and 2 and shall communicate them to the Executive Committee.

[B.3.58]
Article 23
1   An alien who does not fulfil or no longer fulfils the short visit conditions applicable within the territory of a Contracting Party must in principle leave the territories of the Contracting Parties without delay.

2   An alien who holds a valid residence permit or temporary residence permit issued by another Contracting Party must enter the territory of that Contracting Party without delay.

3   Where such an alien has not left voluntarily or where it may be assumed that he will not so leave or if his immediate departure is required for reasons of national security or public policy, he must be expelled from the territory of the Contracting Party within which he has been arrested as laid down in the national law of that Contracting Party. If the application of that law does not permit expulsion, the Contracting Party concerned may allow the person concerned to remain within its territory.

4   Expulsion may be effected from the territory of that State to the alien's country of origin or to any other State to which he may be permitted entry, in particular under the relevant provisions of the re-entry agreements concluded by the Contracting Parties.

5   Paragraph 4 shall not preclude the application of national provisions

on the right of asylum, of the Geneva Convention of 28 July 1951 relating to the Status of Refugees as amended by the New York Protocol of 31 January 1967, or of paragraph 2 of this Article or Article 33(1) of this Convention.

[B.3.59]
Article 24
Subject to the Executive Committee's definition of the appropriate practical criteria and arrangements, the Contracting Parties shall compensate each other for any financial imbalances resulting from the compulsory expulsion provided for in Article 23 where such expulsion cannot be effected at the alien's expense.

Chapter 5   Residence permits and reporting as a person not to be permitted entry

[B.3.60]
Article 25
1   Where a Contracting Party considers issuing a residence permit to an alien who has been reported as a person not to be permitted entry it shall first consult the reporting Contracting Party and shall take account of its interests; the residence permit shall be issued only on serious grounds, in particular of a humanitarian nature or pursuant to international obligations.

If a residence permit is issued the reporting Contracting Party shall withdraw the report but may put the alien concerned on its national reporting list of persons not to be permitted entry.

2   Where it emerges that an alien holding a valid residence permit issued by one of the Contracting Parties has been reported as a person not to be permitted entry the reporting Contracting Party shall consult the Party which issued the residence permit in order to determine whether there are sufficient grounds for the withdrawal of the residence permit.

If the residence permit is not withdrawn the reporting Contracting Party shall withdraw the report but may put the alien in question on its national reporting list.

Chapter 6   Measures relating to organised travel

[B.3.61]
Article 26
1   Subject to the obligations arising out or their accession to the Geneva Convention of 28 July 1951 relating to the Status of Refugees, as amended by the New York Protocol of 31 January 1967, the Contracting Parties undertake to incorporate the following rules in their national legislation:

(*a*) If an alien is refused entry into the territory of one of the Contracting Parties the carrier which brought him to the external border by air, sea or land shall be obliged to assume responsibility for him again without delay. At the request of the border surveillance authorities the carrier must return the alien to the Third State from which he was transported, to the Third State which issued the travel document on which he travelled or to any other Third State to which he is guaranteed entry.

(*b*) The carrier shall be obliged to take all necessary measures to ensure that an alien carried by air or sea is in possession of the travel documents required for entry into the territory of the Contracting Parties.

2 The Contracting Parties undertake, subject to the obligations arising out of their accession to the Geneva Convention of 28 July 1951 relating to the Status of Refugees, as amended by the New York Protocol of 31 January 1967, and in accordance with their constitutional law, to impose penalties on carriers who transport aliens who do not possess the necessary travel documents by air or sea from a Third State to their territories.

3 Paragraph 1(*b*) and paragraph 2 shall also apply to carriers of groups by coach over international road links, with the exception of border traffic.

[B.3.62]
Article 27
1 The Contracting Parties undertake to impose appropriate penalties on any person who, for purposes of gain, assists or tries to assist an alien to enter or reside within the territory of one of the Contracting Parties contrary to the laws of that Contracting Party on the entry and residence of aliens.

2 If a Contracting Party is informed of the facts referred to in paragraph 1 which constitute an infringement of the legislation of another Contracting Party, it shall inform the latter accordingly.

3 Any Contracting Party which requests another Contracting Party to prosecute, on the grounds of the infringement of its own legislation, offences such as those referred to in paragraph 1, must specify, by means of an official denunciation or a certificate from the competent authorities, the provisions of law which have been infringed.

Chapter 7 Responsibility for the processing of applications for asylum

[B.3.63]
Article 28
The Contracting Parties hereby reaffirm their obligations under the Geneva Convention of 28 July 1951 relating to the Status of Refugees as amended by the New York Protocol of 31 January 1967, without any geographical restriction on the scope of those instruments, as also their commitment to co-operate with the United Nations High Commissioner for Refugees in the implementation of those instruments.

[B.3.64]
Article 29
1 The Contracting Parties undertake to process any application for asylum lodged by an alien within the territory of any one of them.

2 This obligation shall not bind a Contracting Party to authorise every applicant for asylum to enter or to remain within its territory.

Every Contracting Party shall retain the right to refuse entry or to expel any applicant for asylum to a Third State on the basis of its national provisions and in accordance with its international commitments.

3   Regardless of the Contracting Party to which an alien addresses an application for asylum, only one Contracting Party shall be responsible for processing that application. It shall be determined by the criteria laid down in Article 30.

4   Notwithstanding paragraph 3 every Contracting Party shall retain the right, for special reasons concerning national law in particular, to process an application for asylum even if under this Convention the responsibility for doing so is that of another Contracting Party.

[B.3.65]
Article 30
1   The Contracting Party responsible for the processing of an application for asylum shall be determined as follows:

(*a*) If a Contracting Party has issued to the applicant for asylum a visa of any type, or a residence permit, it shall be responsible for processing the application. If the visa was issued on the authorisation of another Contracting Party, the Contracting Party who gave the authorisation shall be responsible.

(*b*) If two or more Contracting Parties have issued to the applicant for asylum a visa of any type or a residence permit, the Contracting Party responsible shall be the one which issued the visa or the residence permit that will expire last.

(*c*) As long as the applicant for asylum has not left the territory of the Contracting Parties the responsibility defined in accordance with (*a*) and (*b*) shall subsist even if the period of validity of the visa of any type or of the residence permit has expired. If the applicant for asylum has left the territory of the Contracting States after the issue of the visa or the residence permit, these documents shall be the basis for the responsibility as defined in (*a*) and (*b*) unless they have expired in the interval under national provisions.

(*d*) If the Contracting Parties exempt the applicant for asylum from the requirement for a visa, the Contracting Party across the external borders of which the applicant for asylum has entered the territory of the Contracting Parties shall be responsible.

Until the harmonisation of visa policies is completed, and if the applicant for asylum is exempted from the requirement for a visa by certain Contracting Parties only, the Contracting Party across the external border of which the applicant for asylum has entered the territory of the Contracting Parties by means of an exemption from the requirement of a visa shall be responsible, subject to (*a*), (*b*) and (*c*).

If the application for asylum is submitted to a Contracting Party which has issued a transit visa to the applicant – whether the applicant has passed passport checks or not – and if the transit visa was issued after the country of transit had ascertained from the consular or diplomatic authorities of the Contracting Party of destination that the applicant for asylum fulfilled the conditions for entry into the Contracting Party of destination, the Contracting Party of destination shall be responsible for processing the application.

(*e*) If the applicant for asylum has entered the territory of the Contracting Parties without being in possession of one or more documents permitting the crossing of the border, determined by the Executive Committee, the

861

Contracting Party across the external borders of which the applicant for asylum has entered the territory of the Contracting Parties shall be responsible.

(f) If an alien whose application for asylum is already being processed by one of the Contracting Parties submits a new application, the Contracting Party responsible shall be the one that processed the first application.

(g) If an alien on whose previous application for asylum a Contracting Party has already taken a final decision submits a new application, the Contracting Party responsible shall be the one that processed the previous request unless the applicant has left the territory of the Contracting Parties.

2   If a Contracting Party has undertaken the processing of an application for asylum in accordance with Article 29(4) the Contracting Party responsible under paragraph 1 of the present Article shall be relieved of its obligations.

3   If the Contracting Party responsible cannot be determined by means of the criteria laid down in paragraphs 1 and 2 the Contracting Party to which the application for asylum was submitted shall be responsible.

[B.3.66]
Article 31
1   The Contracting Parties shall endeavour to determine as quickly as possible which of them is responsible for the processing of an application for asylum.

2   If an application for asylum is addressed to a Contracting Party which is not responsible under Article 30 by an alien resident within its territory that Contracting Party may request the Contracting Party responsible to take responsibility for the applicant for asylum in order to process his application for asylum.

3   The Contracting Party responsible shall be bound to take responsibility for the applicant for asylum referred to in paragraph 2 if the request is made within six months of the submission of the application for asylum. If the request is not made within that time the Contracting Party to which the application for asylum was submitted shall be responsible for processing the application.

[B.3.67]
Article 32
The Contracting Party responsible for the processing of an application for asylum shall process it in accordance with its national law.

[B.3.68]
Article 33
1   If an applicant for asylum is illegally within the territory of another Contracting Party while the asylum procedure is in progress the Contracting Party responsible shall be bound to take him back.

2   Paragraph 1 shall not apply where the other Contracting Party has issued an applicant for asylum with a residence permit valid for one year or more. In this case responsibility for the processing of the application shall be transferred to the other Contracting Party.

[B.3.69]
Article 34
1   The Contracting Party responsible shall be bound to take back an alien whose application for asylum has been finally rejected and who has entered the territory of another Contracting Party without being authorised to reside there.

2   Paragraph 1 shall not, however, apply where the Contracting Party responsible expelled the alien from the territories of the Contracting Parties.

[B.3.70]
Article 35
1   The Contracting Party which granted an alien the status of refugee and gave him the right of residence shall be bound, provided that those concerned are in agreement, to be responsible for processing any application for asylum made by a member of his family.

2   A family member for the purposes of paragraph 1 shall be the spouse or the unmarried child less than 18 years old of the refugee or, if the refugee is an unmarried child less than 18 years old, his father or mother.

[B.3.71]
Article 36
Any Contracting Party responsible for the processing of an application for asylum may, on humanitarian grounds, based on family or cultural reasons, ask another Contracting Party to assume that responsibility insofar as the person concerned so wishes. The Contracting Party to whom such a request is made shall consider whether it can grant it.

[B.3.72]
Article 37
1   The competent authorities of the Contracting Parties shall at the earliest opportunity send each other details of:
(*a*) any new rules or measures adopted as regards the law of asylum or of the treatment of applicants for asylum no later than their entry into force;
(*b*) statistical data concerning the monthly arrivals for asylum, indicating the principal countries of origin, and decisions on applications for asylum insofar as they are available;
(*c*) the emergence of, or significant increases in, certain groups of applicants for asylum and any information available on this subject;
(*d*) any fundamental decisions as regards the law of asylum.

2   The Contracting Parties shall also guarantee close co-operation in the collection of information on the situation in the countries of origin of applicants for asylum with a view to reaching a common assessment.

3   Any instruction given by a Contracting Party concerning the confidential processing of the information that it communicates must be complied with by the other Contracting Parties.

[B.3.73]
Article 38

1   Every Contracting Party shall send every other Contracting Party that requests it the information it holds on an applicant for asylum that is necessary for purposes of:

— determining the Contracting Party responsible for processing the application for asylum;
— processing the application for asylum;
— implementing the obligations arising under the chapter.

2   Such information may concern only:

(*a*) the identity (name and forename, any previous names, appellations or aliases, date and place of birth, present nationality and any previous nationalities of the applicant for asylum and, where appropriate, the members of his family);

(*b*) the identity and travel documents (references, periods of validity, dates of issue, issuing authorities, place of issue, etc.);

(*c*) any other particulars necessary for establishing the applicant's identity;

(*d*) places of residence and the itineraries of journeys;

(*e*) residence permits of visas issued by a Contracting Party.

(*f*) the place where the application for asylum was submitted;

(*g*) where appropriate, the date of submission of any previous application for asylum, the date of submission of the present application, the point reached in the procedure and the import of the decision taken.

3   In addition, a Contracting Party may ask another Contracting Party to inform it of the grounds invoked by an applicant for asylum in support of his application and, where appropriate, the grounds for the decision taken on it. The Contracting Party requested shall consider whether it can comply with the request made to it. In any case the communication of such information shall be subject to the consent of the applicant for asylum.

4   Exchanges of information shall be effected at the request of a Contrac-ting Party and may be effected only between the authorities the designation of which has been communicated by each Contracting Party to the Executive Committee.

5   The information exchanged may be used only for the purposes set out in paragraph 1. Such information may be communicated only to the authorities and jurisdictions responsible for:

— determining the Contracting Party responsible for the processing of an application for asylum;
— processing an application for asylum;
— implementing obligations arising under this Chapter.

6   A Contracting Party that communicates information shall ensure it is correct and up to date.

If it emerges that this Contracting Party supplied information that was not correct or should not have been communicated the recipient Contracting Parties shall be informed without delay. They shall be bound to correct that information or to delete it.

7   An applicant for asylum shall be entitled to be informed, at his request, of the information exchanged regarding him as long as it is available.

If he ascertains that this information is incorrect or should not have been communicated he shall be entitled to require its correction or deletion. Corrections shall be effected as laid down in paragraph 6.

8   In each Contracting Party concerned the communication and receipt of information exchanged shall be recorded.

9   Information communicated shall be preserved no longer than the time necessary for the purposes for which it was exchanged. The need for its preservation must be assessed in due course by the Contracting Party concerned.

10   Information communicated shall in any case have at least the same protection as that laid down in the law of the recipient Contracting Party for information of a similar nature.

11   If information is not processed automatically but in another manner each Contracting Party must take appropriate measures to ensure that this Article is complied with by means of effective checks. If a Contracting Party has a service of the type referred to in paragraph 12 it may instruct that service to carry out those checks.

12   If one or more Contracting Parties want to computerise the processing of all or part of the information referred to in paragraphs 2 and 3, computerisation shall be authorised only if the Contracting Parties concerned have adopted legislation relating to such processing that implements the principles of the Council of Europe Convention of 28 January 1981 for the Protection of Individuals with regard to Automatic Processing of Personal Data and if they have entrusted an appropriate national body with the independent control of the processing and use of date communicated under this Convention.

Title VIII   Final Provisions

[B.3.74]
Article 134
The provisions of this Convention shall apply only insofar as they are compatible with Community law.

[B.3.75]
Article 135
The provisions of this Convention shall apply subject to the provisions of the Geneva Convention of 28 July 1951 relating to the Status of Refugees, as amended by the New York Protocol of 31 January 1967.

[B.3.76]
Article 136
1   A Contracting Party which envisages conducting negotiations on border checks with a Third State shall inform the other Contracting Parties thereof in good time.

2   No Contracting Party shall conclude with one or more Third States agreements simplifying or abolishing border checks without the prior agreement of the other Contracting Parties, subject to the right of the member states of the European Communities to conclude such agreements jointly.

3   The provisions of paragraph 2 shall not apply to agreements on local border traffic since these agreements comply with the exemptions and arrangements laid down under Article 3(1).

[B.3.77]
Article 137
This Convention shall not be the subject of any reservations, save for those referred to in Article 60.

[B.3.78]
Article 138
As regards the French Republic, the provisions of this Convention shall apply only to the European territory of the French Republic.

As the regards the Kingdom of the Netherlands, the provisions of this Convention shall apply only to the territory of the Kingdom of the Netherlands situated in Europe.

[B.3.79]
Article 139
1   The present Convention shall be subject to ratification, acceptance of approval. The instruments of ratification, acceptance or approval shall be deposited with the Government of the Grand Duchy of Luxembourg, which shall notify all the Contracting Parties thereof.

2   This Convention shall enter into force on the first day of the second month following the deposit of the final instrument of ratification, acceptance or approval. The provisions concerning the setting up, activities and jurisdiction of the Executive Committee shall apply as from the entry into force of this Convention. The other provisions shall apply as from the first day of the third month following the entry into force of this Convention.

3   The Government of the Grand Duchy of Luxembourg shall notify all the Contracting Parties of the date of entry into force.

[B.3.80]
Article 140
1   Any member state of the European Communities may become a Party to this Convention. Such accession shall be the subject of an agreement between that State and the Contracting Parties.

2   Such an agreement shall be subject to ratification, acceptance or approval by the acceeding State and by each of the Contracting Parties. It shall enter into force on the first day of the second month following the deposit of the final instrument of ratification, acceptance or approval.

[B.3.81]
Article 141
1 Any Contracting Party may submit to the depository a proposal to amend this Convention. The depository shall forward that proposal to the other Contracting Parties. At the request of one Contracting Party, the Contracting Parties shall re-examine the provisions of the Convention if, in their opinion, there has been a fundamental change in the conditions obtaining when the Convention entered into force.

2 The Contracting Parties shall adopt amendments to this Convention by mutual consent.

3 Amendments shall enter into force on the first day of the second month following the date of deposit of the final instrument of ratification, acceptance or approval.

[B.3.82]
Article 142
1 When Conventions are concluded between member states of the European Communities with a view to the completion of an area without internal frontiers, the Contracting Parties shall agree on the conditions under which the provisions of the present Convention are to be replaced or amended in the light of the corresponding provisions of such Conventions.

The Contracting Parties shall, to that end, take account of the fact that the provisions of this Convention may provide for more extensive co-operation than that resulting from the provisions of the said Conventions.

Provisions which are in breach of those agreed between the member states of the European Communities shall in any case be adapted in any circumstances.

2 Amendments to this Convention deemed necessary by the Contracting Parties shall be subject to ratification, acceptance or approval. The provision contained in Article 141(3) shall apply, it being understood that the amendments will not enter into force before the said Conventions between the member states of the European Communities comes into force.

[B.3.83]
In witness whereof, the undersigned, duly authorised to that end, have hereunto set their hands.

Done at Schengen, this nineteenth day of June in the year one thousand nine hundred and ninety, in a single original, in the Dutch, French and German languages, all three texts being equally authentic, which shall be deposited in the archives of the Government of the Grand Duchy of Luxembourg, which shall transmit a certified copy to each of the Contracting Parties.

For the Government of the Kingdom of Belgium,

For the Government of the Federal Republic of Germany,

For the Government of the French Republic,

For the Government of the Grand Duchy of Luxembourg.

For the Government of the Kingdom of the Netherlands.

THE DUBLIN CONVENTION

CONVENTION DETERMINING THE STATE RESPONSIBLE FOR EXAMINING APPLICATIONS FOR ASYLUM LODGED IN ONE OF THE MEMBER STATES OF THE EUROPEAN COMMUNITIES

Signed in Dublin on 15 June 1990
Ratified by the United Kingdom and all other member states

[B.3.84]

Having regard to the objective, fixed by the European Council meeting in Strasbourg on 8 and 9 December 1989, of the harmonisation of their asylum policies;

Determined, in keeping with their common humanitarian tradition, to guarantee adequate protection to refugees in accordance with the terms of the Geneva Convention of 28 July 1951, as amended by the New York Protocol of 31 January 1967 relating to the Status of Refugees, hereinafter referred to as the 'Geneva Convention' and the 'New York Protocol' respectively;

Considering the joint objective of an area without internal frontiers in which the free movement of persons shall, in particular, be ensured, in accordance with the provisions of the Treaty establishing the European Economic Community, as amended by the Single European Act;

Aware of the need, in pursuit of this objective, to take measures to avoid any situations arising, with the result that applicants for asylum are left in doubt for too long as regards the likely outcome of their applications and concerned to provide all applicants for asylum with a guarantee that their applications will be examined by one of the member states and to ensure that applicants for asylum are not referred successively from one member state to another without any of these states acknowledging itself to be competent to examine the application for asylum;

Desiring to continue the dialogue with the United Nations High Commissioner for Refugees in order to achieve the above objectives;

Determined to co-operate closely in the application of this Convention through various means, including exchanges of information.

[The representatives of the member states of the EEC]...
Have agreed* as follows:

---

* Denmark has not yet acceded to the Convention.

[B.3.85]
Article 1
1   For the purposes of this Convention:

(*a*) Alien means: any person other than a national of a member state;

(*b*) Application for asylum means: a request whereby an alien seeks from a member state protection under the Geneva Convention by claiming refugee status within the meaning of Article 1 of the Geneva Convention, as amended by the New York Protocol;

(*c*) Applicant for asylum means: an alien who has made an application for asylum in respect of which a final decision has not yet been taken;

(*d*) Examination of an application for asylum means: all the measures for examination, decisions or rulings given by the competent authorities on an application for asylum, except for procedures to determine the state responsible for examining the application for asylum pursuant to this Convention;

(*e*) Residence permit means: any authorization issued by the authorities of a member state authorizing an alien to stay in its territory, with the exception of visas and 'stay permits' issued during examination of an application for a residence permit or for asylum.

(*f*) Entry visa means: authorization or decision by a member state to enable an alien to enter its territory, subject to the other entry conditions being fulfilled;

(*g*) Transit visa means: authorization or decision by a member state to enable an alien to transit through its territory or pass through the transit zone of a port or airport, subject to the other transit conditions being fulfilled.

2   The nature of the visa shall be assessed in the light of the definitions set out in paragraph 1, points (*f*) and (*g*).

[B.3.86]
Article 2
The member states reaffirm their obligations under the Geneva Convention, as amended by the New York Protocol, with no geographic restriction of the scope of these instruments, and their commitment to co-operating with the services of the United Nations High Commissioner for Refugees in applying these instruments.

[B.3.87]
Article 3
1   Member states undertake to examine the application of any alien who applies at the border or in their territory to any one of them for asylum.

2   That application shall be examined by a single member state, which shall be determined in accordance with the criteria defined in this Convention. The criteria set out in Articles 4 to 8 shall apply in the order in which they appear.

3   That application shall be examined by that state in accordance with its national laws and its international obligations.

4   Each member state shall have the right to examine an application for asylum submitted to it by an alien, even if such examination is not its responsibility under the criteria defined in this Convention, provided that the applicant for asylum agrees thereto.

    The member state responsible under the above criteria is then relieved of its obligations, which are transferred to the member state which expressed the wish to examine the application. The latter state shall inform the member state responsible under the said criteria if the application has been referred to it.

5 Any member state shall retain the right, pursuant to its national laws, to send an applicant for asylum to a third state, in compliance with the provisions of the Geneva Convention, as amended by the New York Protocol.

6 The process of determining the member state responsible for examining the application for asylum under this Convention shall start as soon as an application for asylum is first lodged with a member state.

7 An applicant for asylum who is present in another member state and there lodges an application for asylum after withdrawing his or her application during the process of determining the state responsible shall be taken back, under the conditions laid down in Article 13, by the member state with which that application for asylum was lodged, with a view to completing the process of determining the state responsible for examining the application for asylum.

This obligation shall cease to apply if the applicant for asylum has since left the territory of the member states for a period of at least three months or has obtained from a member state a residence permit valid for more than three months.

[B.3.88]
Article 4
Where the applicant for asylum has a member of his family who has been recognized as having refugee status within the meaning of the Geneva Convention, as amended by the New York Protocol, in a member state and is legally resident there, that state shall be responsible for examining the application, provided that the persons concerned so desire.

The family member in question may not be other than the spouse of the applicant for asylum or his or her unmarried child who is a minor of under eighteen years, or his or her father or mother where the applicant for asylum is himself or herself an unmarried child who is a minor of under eighteen years.

[B.3.89]
Article 5
1 Where the applicant for asylum is in possession of a valid residence permit, the member state which issued the permit shall be responsible for examining the application for asylum.

2 Where the applicant for asylum is in possession of a valid visa, the member state which issued the visa shall be responsible for examining the application for asylum, except in the following situations:

(a) if the visa was issued on the written authorization of another member state, that state shall be responsible for examining the application for asylum. Where a member state first consults the central authority of another member state, inter alia for security reasons, the agreement of the latter shall not constitute written authorization within the meaning of this provision.

(b) where the applicant for asylum is in possession of a transit visa and lodges his application in another member state in which he is not subject to a visa requirement, that state shall be responsible for examining the application for asylum.

(c) where the applicant for asylum is in possession of a transit visa and lodges his application in the state which issued him or her with the visa and which has received written confirmation from the diplomatic or consular authorities of the member state of destination that the alien for whom the visa requirement was waived fulfilled the conditions for entry into that state, the latter shall be responsible for examining the application for asylum.

3   Where the applicant for asylum is in possession of more than one valid residence permit or visa issued by different member states, the responsibility for examining the application for asylum shall be assumed by the member states in the following order:

(a) the state which issued the residence permit conferring the right to the longest period of residency or, where the periods of validity of all the permits are identical, the state which issued the residence permit having the latest expiry date;

(b) the state which issued the visa having the latest expiry date where the various visas are of the same type;

(c) where visas are of different kinds, the state which issued the visa having the longest period of validity, or where the periods of validity are identical, the state which issued the visa having the latest expiry date. This provision shall not apply where the applicant is in possession of one or more transit visas, issued on presentation of an entry visa for another member state. In that case, that member state shall be responsible.

4   Where the applicant for asylum is in possession only of one or more residence permits which have expired less than two years previously or one or more visas which have expired less than six months previously and enabled him or her actually to enter the territory of a member state, the provisions of paragraphs 1, 2 and 3 of this Article shall apply for such time as the alien has not left the territory of the member states.

Where the applicant for asylum is in possession of one or more residence permits which have expired more than two years previously or one or more visas which have expired more than six months previously and enabled him or her to enter the territory of a member state and where an alien has not left Community territory, the member state in which the application is lodged shall be responsible.

[B.3.90]
Article 6
When it can be proved that an applicant for asylum has irregularly crossed the border into a member state by land, sea or air, having come from a non-member state of the European Communities, the member state thus entered shall be responsible for examining the application for asylum.

That state shall cease to be responsible, however, if it is proved that the applicant has been living in the member state where the application for asylum was made at least six months before making this application for asylum. In that case it is the latter member state which is responsible for examining the application for asylum.

[B.3.91]
Article 7

1   The responsibility for examining an application for asylum shall be incumbent upon the member state responsible for controlling the entry of the alien into the territory of the member states, except where, after legally entering a member state in which the need for him or her to have a visa is waived, the alien lodges his or her application for asylum in another member state in which the need for him or her to have a visa for entry into the territory is also waived. In this case, the latter state shall be responsible for examining the application for asylum.

2   Pending the entry into force of an agreement between member states on arrangements for crossing external borders, the member state which authorizes transit without a visa through the transit zone of its airports shall not be regarded as responsible for control on entry, in respect of travellers who do not leave the transit zone.

3   Where the application for asylum is made in transit in an airport of a member state, that state shall be responsible for examination.

[B.3.92]
Article 8

Where no member state responsible for examining the application for asylum can be designated on the basis of the other criteria listed in this Convention, the first member state with which the application for asylum is lodged shall be responsible for examining it.

[B.3.93]
Article 9

Any member state, even when it is not responsible under the criteria laid out in this Convention, may, for humanitarian reasons, based in particular on family or cultural grounds, examine an application for asylum at the request of another member state, provided that the applicant so desires.

   If the member state thus approached accedes to the request, responsibility for examining the application shall be transferred to it.

[B.3.94]
Article 10

1   The member state responsible for examining an application for asylum according to the criteria set out in this Convention shall be obliged to:

(a) Take charge under the conditions laid down in Article 11 of an applicant who has lodged an application for asylum in a different member state.
(b) Complete the examination of the application for asylum.
(c) Re-admit or take back under the conditions laid down in Article 13 an applicant whose application is under examination and who is irregularly in another member state.
(d) Take back, under the conditions laid down in Article 13, an applicant who has withdrawn the application under examination and lodged an application in another member state.

872

(*e*) Take back, under the conditions laid down in Article 13, an alien whose application it has rejected and who is illegally in another member state.

2   If a member state issues to the applicant a residence permit valid for more than three months, the obligations specified in paragraph 1, points (*a*) to (*e*) shall be transferred to that member state.

3   The obligations specified in paragraph 1, points (*a*) to (*d*) shall cease to apply if the alien concerned has left the territory of the member states for a period of at least three months.

4   The obligations specified in paragraph 1, points (*d*) and (*e*) shall cease to apply if the state responsible for examining the application for asylum, following the withdrawal or rejection of the application, takes and enforces the necessary measures for the alien to return to his country of origin or to another country which he may lawfully enter.

[B.3.95]
Article 11
1   If a member state with which an application for asylum has been lodged considers that another member state is responsible for examining the application, it may, as quickly as possible and in any case within the six months following the date on which the application was lodged, call upon the other member state to take charge of the applicant.

If the request that charge be taken is not made within the six-month time limit, responsibility for examining the application for asylum shall rest with the state in which the application was lodged.

2   The request that charge be taken shall contain indications enabling the authorities of that other state to ascertain whether it is responsible on the basis of the criteria laid down in this Convention.

3   The state responsible in accordance with those criteria shall be determined on the basis of the situation obtaining when the applicant for asylum first lodged his application with a member state.

4   The member state shall pronounce judgment on the request within three months of receipt of the claim. Failure to act within that period shall be tantamount to accepting the claim.

5   Transfer of the applicant for asylum from the member state where the application was lodged to the member state responsible must take place not later than one month after acceptance of the request to take charge or one month after the conclusion of any proceedings initiated by the alien challenging the transfer decision if the proceedings are suspensory.

6   Measures taken under Article 18 may subsequently determine the details of the process by which applicants shall be taken in charge.

[B.3.96]
Article 12
Where an application for asylum is lodged with the competent authorities of a member state by an applicant who is on the territory of another member state,

the determination of the member state responsible for examining the application for asylum shall be made by the member state on whose territory the applicant is. The latter member state shall be informed without delay by the member state which received the application and shall then, for the purpose of applying this Convention, be regarded as the member state with which the application for asylum was lodged.

[B.3.97]
Article 13
1   An applicant for asylum shall be taken back in the cases provided for in Article 3(7) and in Article 10 as follows:

(*a*) the request for the applicant to be taken back must provide indications enabling the state with which the request is lodged to ascertain that it is responsible in accordance with Article 3(7) and with Article 10;
(*b*) the state called upon to take back the applicant shall give an answer to the request within eight days of the matter being referred to it. Should it acknowledge responsibility, it shall then take back the applicant for asylum as quickly as possible and at the latest one month after it agrees to do so.

2   Measures taken under Article 18 may at a later date set out the details of the procedure for taking the applicant back.

[B.3.98]
Article 14
1   Member states shall conduct mutual exchanges with regard to:

— national legislative or regulatory measures or practices applicable in the field of asylum;
— statistical data on monthly arrivals of applicants for asylum, and their breakdown by nationality. Such information shall be forwarded quarterly through the General Secretariat of the Council of the European Communities, which shall see that it is circulated to the member states and the Commission of the European Communities and to the United Nations High Commissioner for Refugees.

2   The member states may conduct mutual exchanges with regard to:

— general information on new trends in applications for asylum;
— general information on the situation in the countries of origin or of provenance of applicants for asylum.

3   If the member state providing the information referred to in paragraph 2 wants it to be kept confidential, the other member states shall comply with this wish.

[B.3.99]
Article 15
1   Each member state shall communicate to any member state that so requests such information on individual cases as is necessary for:

— determining the member state which is responsible for examining the application for asylum;
— examining the application for asylum;
— implementing any obligation arising under this Convention.

2 This information may only cover:

— personal details of the applicant, and, where appropriate, the members of his family (full name—where appropriate, former name—, nicknames or pseudonyms, nationality—present and former—, date and place of birth);
— identity and travel papers (references, validity, date of issue, issuing authority, place of issue, etc);
— other information necessary for establishing the identity of the applicant;
— places of residence and routes travelled;
— residence permits or visas issued by a member state;
— the place where the application was lodged;
— the date any previous application for asylum was lodged, the date the present application was lodged, the stage reached in the proceedings and the decision taken, if any.

3 Furthermore, one member state may request another member state to let it know on what grounds the applicant for asylum bases his or her application and, where applicable, the grounds for any decisions taken concerning the applicant. It is for the member state from which the information is requested to decide whether or not to impart it. In any event, communication of the information requested shall be subject to the approval of the applicant for asylum.

4 This exchange of information shall be effected at the request of a member state and may only take place between authorities the designation of which by each member state has been communicated to the Committee provided for under Article 18.

5 The information exchanged may only be used for the purposes set out in paragraph 1. In each member state such information may only be communicated to the authorities and courts and tribunals entrusted with:

— determining the member state which is responsible for examining the application for asylum;
— examining the application for asylum;
— implementing any obligation arising under this Convention.

6 The member state that forwards the information shall ensure that it is accurate and up-to-date.
If it appears that this member state has supplied information which is inaccurate or which should not have been forwarded, the recipient member state, shall be immediately informed thereof. They shall be obliged to correct such information or to have it erased.

7 An applicant for asylum shall have the right to receive, on request, the information exchanged concerning him or her, for such time as it remains available.
If he or she establishes that such information is inaccurate or should not have been forwarded, he or she shall have the right to have it corrected or erased. This right shall be exercised in accordance with the conditions laid down in paragraph 6.

8   In each Member State concerned, the forwarding and receipt of exchanged information shall be recorded.

9   Such information shall be kept for a period not exceeding that necessary for the ends for which it was exchanged. The need to keep it shall be examined at the appropriate moment by the Member State concerned.

10   In any event, the information thus communicated shall enjoy at least the same protection as is given to similar information in the Member State which receives it.

11   If data are not processed automatically but are handled in some other form, every Member State shall take the appropriate measures to ensure compliance with this Article by means of effective controls. If a Member State has a monitoring body of the type mentioned in paragraph 12, it may assign the control task to it.

12   If one or more Member States wish to computerise all or part of the information mentioned in paragraphs 2 and 3, such computerisation is only possible if the countries concerned have adopted laws applicable to such processing which implement the principles of the Strasbourg Convention of 28 February 1981 for the Protection of Individuals, with regard to Automatic Processing of Personal Data and if they have entrusted an appropriate national body with the independent monitoring of the processing and use of data forwarded to the Convention.

[B.3.100]
Article 16
1   Any member state may submit to the Committee referred to in Article 18 proposals for revision of this Convention in order to eliminate difficulties in the application thereof.

2   If it proves necessary to revise or amend this Convention pursuant to the achievement of the objectives set out in Article 8a of the Treaty establishing the European Economic Community, such achievement being linked in particular to the establishment of a harmonised asylum and a common visa policy, the member state holding the Presidency of the Council of the European Communities shall organize a meeting of the Committee referred to in Article 18.

3   Any revision of this Convention or amendment hereto shall be adopted by the Committee referred to in Article 18. They shall enter into force in accordance with the provisions of Article 22.

[B.3.101]
Article 17
1   If a member state experiences major difficulties as a result of a substantial change in the circumstances obtaining on conclusion of this Convention, the state in question may bring the matter before the Committee referred to in Article 18 so that the latter may put to the member states measured to deal with the situation or adopt such revisions or amendments to this Convention as appear necessary, which shall enter into force as provided for in Article 16(3).

2   If, after six months, the situation mentioned in paragraph 1 still obtains, the Committee, acting in accordance with Article 18(2), may authorize the member state affected by that change to suspend temporarily the application of the provisions of this Convention, without such suspension being allowed to impede the achievement of the objectives mentioned in Article 8a of the Treaty establishing the European Economic Treaty or contravene other international obligations of the member states.

3   During the period of suspension, the Committee shall continue its discussions with a view to revising the provisions of this Convention, unless it has already reached an agreement.

[B.3.102]
Article 18
1   A Committee shall be set up comprising one representative of the Government of each member state.
   The Committee shall be chaired by the member state holding the Presidency of the Council of the European Communities.
   The Commission of the European Communities may participate in the discussions of the Committee and the working parties referred to in paragraph 4.

2   The Committee shall examine, at the request of one or more member states, any question of a general nature concerning the application or interpretation of this Convention.
   The Committee shall determine the measures referred to in Article 11(6) and Article 13(2) and shall give the authorization referred to in Article 17(2).
   The Committee shall adopt decisions revising or amending the Convention pursuant to Articles 16 and 17.

3   The Committee shall take its decisions unanimously, except where it is acting pursuant to Article 17(2), in which case it shall take its decisions by a majority of two-thirds of the votes of its members.

4   The Committee shall determine its rules of procedure and may set up working parties.
   The Secretariat of the Committee and of the working parties shall be provided by the General Secretariat of the Council of the European Communities.

[B.3.103]
Article 19
As regards the Kingdom of Denmark, the provisions of this Convention shall not apply to the Faroe Islands nor to Greenland unless a declaration to the contrary is made by the Kingdom of Denmark. Such a declaration may be made at any time by a communication to the Government of Ireland which shall inform the Governments of the other member states thereof.
   As regards the French Republic, the provisions of this Convention shall apply only to the European territory of the French Republic.
   As regards the Kingdom of the Netherlands, the provisions of this Convention shall apply only to the territory of the Kingdom of the Netherlands in Europe.
   As regards the United Kingdom the provisions of this Convention sha'
apply only to the United Kingdom of Great Britain and Northern Ireland. T⊦

shall not apply to the European territories for whose external relations the United Kingdom is responsible unless a declaration to the contrary is made by the United Kingdom. Such a declaration may be made at any time by a communication to the Government of Ireland, which shall inform the Governments of the other Member States thereof.

[B.3.104]
Article 20
This Convention shall not be the subject of any reservations.

[B.3.105]
Article 21
1   This Convention shall be open for the accession of any State which becomes a member of the European Convention. The instruments of accession will be deposited with the Government of Ireland.

2   It shall enter into force in respect of any State which accedes thereto on the first day of the third month following the deposit of its instrument of accession.

[B.3.106]
Article 22
1   This Convention shall be subject to ratification, acceptance or approval. The instruments of ratification, acceptance or approval shall be deposited with the Government of Ireland.

2   The Government of Ireland shall notify the Governments of the other member states of the deposit of the instruments of ratification, acceptance or approval.

3   This Convention shall enter into force on the first day of the third month following the deposit of the instrument of ratification, acceptance or approval by the last signatory state to take this step.
   The state with which the instruments of ratification, acceptance or approval are deposited shall notify the member states of the date of entry into force of this Convention.

Part C

Human Rights and International Law

C1 Council of Europe Materials

EUROPEAN CONVENTION FOR THE PROTECTION OF HUMAN RIGHTS AND FUNDAMENTAL FREEDOMS

Signed in Rome on 4 November 1950

Entry into force 3 September 1953, in accordance with Article 66
Text Council of Europe Treaty Series No 5

Note This text is the amended version brought into force by Protocol No 11 as from 1 November 1998.

[C.1.1]
The Governments signatory hereto, being members of the Council of Europe,

Considering the Universal Declaration of Human Rights proclaimed by the General Assembly of the United Nations on 10th December 1948;

Considering that this Declaration aims at securing the universal and effective recognition and observance of the Rights therein declared;

Considering that the aim of the Council of Europe is the achievement of greater unity between its members and that one of the methods by which that aim is to be pursued is the maintenance and further realisation of Human Rights and Fundamental Freedoms;

Reaffirming their profound belief in those Fundamental Freedoms which are the foundation of justice and peace in the world and are best maintained on the one hand by an effective political democracy and on the other by a common understanding and observance of the Human Rights upon which they depend;

Being resolved, as the Governments of European countries which are like-minded and have a common heritage of political traditions, ideals, freedom and the rule of law, to take the first steps for the collective enforcement of certain of the Rights stated in the Universal Declaration;

Have agreed as follows:

[C.1.2]
Article 1 Obligation to respect human rights
The High contracting parties shall secure to everyone within their jurisdiction the rights and freedoms defined in Section I of this Convention.

SECTION I   RIGHTS AND FREEDOMS

[C.1.3]
Article 2   Right to life

1   Everyone's right to life shall be protected by law. No one shall be deprived of his life intentionally save in the execution of a sentence of a court following his conviction of a crime for which this penalty is provided by law.

2   Deprivation of life shall not be regarded as inflicted in contravention of this Article when it results from the use of force which is no more than absolutely necessary:

(*a*) in defence of any person from unlawful violence;
(*b*) in order to effect a lawful arrest or to prevent the escape of a person lawfully detained;
(*c*) in action lawfully taken for the purpose of quelling a riot or insurrection.

[C.1.4]
Article 3   Prohibition of torture

No one shall be subjected to torture or to inhuman or degrading treatment or punishment.

[C.1.5]
Article 4   Prohibition of slavery and forced labour

1   No one shall be held in slavery or servitude.

2   No one shall be required to perform forced or compulsory labour.

3   For the purpose of this Article the term 'forced or compulsory labour' shall not include:

(*a*) any work required to be done in the ordinary course of detention imposed according to the provisions of Article 5 of this Convention or during conditional release from such detention;
(*b*) any service of a military character or, in case of conscientious objectors in countries where they are recognised, service exacted instead of compulsory military service;
(*c*) any service exacted in case of an emergency or calamity threatening the life or well-being of the community;
(*d*) any work or service which forms part of normal civic obligations.

[C.1.6]
Article 5   Right to liberty and security

1   Everyone has the right to liberty and security of person.

No one shall be deprived of his liberty save in the following cases and in accordance with a procedure prescribed by law:

(*a*) the lawful detention of a person after conviction by a competent court;
(*b*) the lawful arrest or detention of a person for non-compliance with the lawful order of a court or in order to secure the fulfilment of any obligation prescribed by law;

(*c*) the lawful arrest or detention of a person effected for the purpose of bringing him before the competent legal authority on reasonable suspicion of having committed an offence or when it is reasonably considered necessary to prevent his committing an offence or fleeing after having done so;

(*d*) the detention of a minor by lawful order for the purpose of educational supervision or his lawful detention for the purpose of bringing him before the competent legal authority;

(*e*) the lawful detention of persons for the prevention of the spreading of infectious diseases, of persons of unsound mind, alcoholics or drug addicts or vagrants;

(*f*) the lawful arrest or detention of a person to prevent his effecting an unauthorised entry into the country or of a person against whom action is being taken with a view to deportation or extradition.

2 Everyone who is arrested shall be informed promptly, in a language which he understands, of the reasons for his arrest and of any charge against him.

3 Everyone arrested or detained in accordance with the provisions of paragraph 1(*c*) of this Article shall be brought promptly before a judge or other officer authorised by law to exercise judicial power and shall be entitled to trial within a reasonable time or to release pending trial. Release may be conditioned by guarantees to appear for trial.

4 Everyone who is deprived of his liberty by arrest or detention shall be entitled to take proceedings by which the lawfulness of his detention shall be decided speedily by a court and his release ordered if the detention is not lawful.

5 Everyone who has been the victim of arrest or detention in contravention of the provisions of this Article shall have an enforceable right to compensation.

[C.1.7]
Article 6   Right to a fair trial
1   In the determination of his civil rights and obligations or of any criminal charge against him, everyone is entitled to a fair and public hearing within a reasonable time by an independent and impartial tribunal established by law. Judgment shall be pronounced publicly but the press and public may be excluded from all or part of the trial in the interests of morals, public order or national security in a democratic society, where the interests of juveniles or the protection of the private life of the parties so require, or to the extent strictly necessary in the opinion of the court in special circumstances where publicity would prejudice the interests of justice.

2   Everyone charged with a criminal offence shall be presumed innocent until proved guilty according to law.

3   Everyone charged with a criminal offence has the following minimum rights:

(*a*) to be informed promptly, in a language which he understands and in detail, of the nature and cause of the accusation against him;

(*b*) to have adequate time and facilities for the preparation of his defence;

(*c*) to defend himself in person or through legal assistance of his own choosing or, if he has not sufficient means to pay for legal assistance, to be given it free when the interests of justice so require;

(*d*) to examine or have examined witnesses against him and to obtain the attendance and examination of witnesses on his behalf under the same conditions as witnesses against him;

(*e*) to have the free assistance of an interpreter if he cannot understand or speak the language used in court.

[C.1.8]
Article 7   No punishment without law

1   No one shall be held guilty of any criminal offence on account of any act or omission which did not constitute a criminal offence under national or international law at the time when it was committed. Nor shall a heavier penalty be imposed than the one that was applicable at the time the criminal offence was committed.

2   This Article shall not prejudice the trial and punishment of any person for any act or omission which, at the time when it was committed, was criminal according to the general principles of law recognized by civilized nations.

[C.1.9]
Article 8   Right to respect for family and private life

1   Everyone has the right to respect for his private and family life, his home and his correspondence.

2   There shall be no interference by a public authority with the exercise of this right except such as is in accordance with the law and is necessary in a democratic society in the interests of national security, public safety or the economic well-being of the country, for the prevention of disorder or crime, for the protection of health or morals, or for the protection of the rights and freedoms of others.

[C.1.10]
Article 9   Freedom of thought, conscience and religion

1   Everyone has the right to freedom of thought, conscience and religion; this right includes freedom to change his relation or belief and freedom, either alone or in community with others and in public or private, to manifest his religion or belief, in worship, teaching, practice and observance.

2   Freedom to manifest one's religion or beliefs shall be subject only to such limitations as are prescribed by law and are necessary in a democratic society in the interests of public safety, for the protection of public order, health or morals, or for the protection of the rights and freedoms of others.

[C.1.11]
Article 10   Freedom of expression

1   Everyone has the right to freedom of expression. This right shall include freedom to hold opinions and to receive and impart information and ideas

without interference by public authority and regardless of frontiers. This Article shall not prevent States from requiring the licensing of broadcasting, television or cinema enterprises.

2   The exercise of these freedoms, since it carries with it duties and responsibilities, may be subject to such formalities, conditions, restrictions or penalties as are prescribed by law and are necessary in a democratic society, in the interests of national security, territorial integrity or public safety, for the prevention of disorder or crime, for the protection of health or morals, for the protection of the reputation or rights of others, for preventing the disclosure of information received in confidence, or for maintaining the authority and impartiality of the judiciary.

[C.1.12]
Article 11   Freedom of assembly and association
1   Everyone has the right to freedom of peaceful assembly and to freedom of association with others, including the right to form and to join trade unions for the protection of his interests.

2   No restrictions shall be placed on the exercise of these rights other than such as are prescribed by law and are necessary in a democratic society in the interests of national security or public safety, for the prevention of disorder or crime, for the protection of health or morals or for the protection of the rights and freedoms of others. This Article shall not prevent the imposition of lawful restrictions on the exercise of these rights by members of the armed forces, of the police or of the administration of the state.

[C.1.13]
Article 12   Right to marry
Men and women of marriageable age have the right to marry and to found a family, according to the national laws governing the exercise of this right.

[C.1.14]
Article 13   Right to an effective remedy
Everyone whose rights and freedoms as set forth in this Convention are violated shall have an effective remedy before a national authority notwithstanding that the violation has been committed by persons acting in an official capacity.

[C.1.15]
Article 14   Prohibition of discrimination
The enjoyment of the rights and freedoms set forth in this Convention shall be secured without discrimination on any ground such as sex, race, colour, language, religion, political or other opinion, national or social origin, association with a national minority, property, birth or other status.

[C.1.16]
Article 15   Derogation in time of emergency
1   In time of war or other public emergency threatening the life of the nation any High contracting party may take measures derogating from its obligations under this Convention to the extent strictly required by the exigencies of the situation, provided that such measures are not inconsistent with its other obligations under international law.

2   No derogation from Article 2, except in respect of deaths resulting from lawful acts of war, or from Article 3, 4 (paragraph 1) and 7 shall be made under this provision.

3   Any High contracting party availing itself of this right of derogation shall keep the Secretary-General of the Council of Europe fully informed of the measures which it has taken and the reasons therefor. It shall also inform the Secretary-General of the Council of Europe when such measures have ceased to operate and the provisions of the Convention are again being fully executed.

[C.1.17]
Article 16   Restrictions on political activity of aliens
Nothing in Articles 10, 11 and 14 shall be regarded as preventing the High contracting parties from imposing restrictions on the political activity of aliens.

[C.1.18]
Article 17   Prohibition of abuse of rights
Nothing in this Convention may be interpreted as implying for any state, group or person any right to engage in any activity or perform any act aimed at the destruction of any of the rights and freedoms set forth herein or at their limitation to a greater extent than is provided for in the Convention.

[C.1.19]
Article 18   Limitation on use of restrictions on rights
The restrictions permitted under this Convention to the said rights and freedoms shall not be applied for any purpose other than those for which they have been prescribed.

SECTION II   EUROPEAN COURT OF HUMAN RIGHTS

[C.1.20]
Article 19   Establishment of the Court
To ensure the observance of the engagements undertaken by the High contracting parties in the Convention and the protocols thereto, there shall be set up a European Court of Human Rights, hereinafter referred to as 'the Court'. It shall function on a permanent basis.

[C.1.21]
Article 20   Number of judges
The Court shall consist of a number of judges equal to that of the High contracting parties.

[C.1.22]
Article 21   Criteria for Office
1   The judges shall be of high moral character and must either possess the qualifications required for appointment to high judicial office or be jurisconsults of recognised competence.

2   The judges shall sit on the Court in their individual capacity.

3   During their term of office the judges shall not engage in any activity which is incompatible with their independence, impartiality or with the demands of a full-time office; all questions arising from the application of this paragraph shall be decided by the Court.

[C.1.23]
Article 22   Election of judges
1   The judges shall be elected by the Parliamentary Assembly with respect to each High Contracting Party by a majority of votes cast from a list of three candidates nominated by the High Contracting Party.

2   The same procedure shall be followed to complete the Court in the event of the accession of new High Contracting Parties and in filling casual vacancies.

[C.1.24]
Article 23   Terms of office
1   The judges shall be elected for a period of six years. They may be re-elected. However, the terms of office of one-half of the judges elected at the first election shall expire at the end of three years.

2   The judges whose terms of office are to expire at the end of the initial period of three years shall be chosen by lot by the Secretary-General of the Council of Europe immediately after their election.

3   In order to ensure that, as far as possible, the terms of office of one-half of the judges are renewed every three years, the Parliamentary Assembly may decide, before proceeding to any subsequent election, that the term or terms of office of one or more judges to be elected shall be for a period other than six years but not more than nine and not less then three years.

4   In cases where more than one term of office is involved and where the Parliamentary Assembly applies the preceding paragraph, the allocation of the terms of office shall be effected by a drawing of lots by the Secretary-General of the Council of Europe immediately after the election.

5   A judge elected to replace a judge whose term of office has not expired shall hold office for the remainder of his predecessor's term.

6   The terms of office of judges shall expire when they reach the age of 70.

7   The judges shall hold office until replaced. They shall, however, continue to deal with such cases as they already have under consideration.

[C.1.25]
Article 24   Dismissal
No judge may be dismissed from his office unless the other judges decide by a majority of two-thirds that he has ceased to fulfil the required conditions.

[C.1.26]
Article 25   Registry and legal secretaries
The Court shall have a registry, the functions and organisation of which shall be laid down in the rules of the Court. The Court shall be assisted by legal secretaries.

[C.1.27]
Article 26   Plenary Court
The plenary Court shall:

(*a*) elect its President and one or two Vice-Presidents for a period of three years; they may be re-elected;

(*b*) set up Chambers, constituted for a fixed period of time;

(*c*) elect the Presidents of the Chambers of the Court; they may be re-elected;

(*d*) adopt the rules of the Court; and

(*e*) elect the Registrar and one or more Deputy Registrars.

[C.1.28]
Article 27   Committees, Chambers and Grand Chamber
1   To consider cases brought before it, the Court shall sit in committees of three judges, in Chambers of seven judges and in a Grand Chamber of seventeen judges. The Court's Chambers shall set up committees for a fixed period of time.

2   There shall sit as an *ex officio* member of the Chamber and the Grand Chamber the judge elected in respect of the State Party concerned or, if there is none or if he is unable to sit, a person of its choice who shall sit in the capacity of judge.

3   The Grand Chamber shall also include the President of the Court, the Vice-Presidents, the Presidents of the Chambers and other judges chosen in accordance with the rules of the Court. When a case is referred to the Grand Chamber under Article 43, no judge from the Chamber which rendered the judgment shall sit in the Grand Chamber, with the exception of the President of the Chamber and the judge who sat in respect of the State Party concerned.

[C.1.29]
Article 28   Declarations of inadmissibility by committees
A committee may, by a unanimous vote, declare inadmissible or strike out of its list of cases an individual application submitted under Article 34 where such a decision can be taken without further examination. The decision shall be final.

[C.1.30]
Article 29 Decisions by Chambers on admissibility and merits
1 If no decision is taken under Article 28, a Chamber shall decide on the admissibility and merits of individual applications submitted under Article 34.

2 A Chamber shall decide on the admissibility and merits of inter-State applications submitted under Article 33.

3 The decision on admissibility shall be taken separately unless the Court, in exceptional cases, decides otherwise.

[C.1.31]
Article 30 Relinquishment of jurisdiction to the Grand Chamber
Where a case pending before a Chamber raises a serious question affecting the interpretation of the Convention or the protocols thereto or where the resolution of a question before it might have a result inconsistent with a judgment previously delivered by the Court, the Chamber may, at any time before it has rendered its judgment, relinquish jurisdiction in favour of the Grand Chamber, unless one of the parties to the case objects.

[C.1.32]
Article 31 Powers of the Grand Chamber
The Grand Chamber shall:

(*a*) determine applications submitted either under Article 33 or Article 34 when a Chamber has relinquished jurisdiction under Article 30 or when the case has been referred to it under Article 43; and

(*b*) consider requests for advisory opinions submitted under Article 47.

[C.1.33]
Article 32 Jurisdiction of the Court
1 The jurisdiction of the Court shall extend to all matters concerning the interpretation and application of the Convention and the protocols thereto which are referred to it as provided in Articles 33, 34 and 47.

2 In the event of dispute as to whether the Court has jurisdiction, the Court shall decide.

[C.1.34]
Article 33 Inter-State cases
Any High contracting party may refer to the Court any alleged breach of the provisions of the Convention and the protocols thereto by another High contracting party.

[C.1.35]
Article 34 Individual applications
The Court may receive applications from any person, non-governmental organisation or group of individuals claiming to be the victim of a violation by

one of the High contracting parties of the rights set forth in the Convention or the protocols thereto. The High contracting parties undertake not to hinder in any way the effective exercise of this right.

[C.1.36]
Article 35   Admissibility criteria

1   The Court may only deal with the matter after all domestic remedies have been exhausted, according to the generally recognised rules of international law, and within a period of six months from the date on which the final decision was taken.

2   The Court shall not deal with any individual application submitted under Article 34 that:

(a)   is anonymous; or

(b)   is substantially the same as a matter that has already been examined by the Court or has already been submitted to another procedure of international investigation or settlement and contains no relevant new information.

3   The Court shall declare inadmissible any individual application submitted under Article 34 which it considers incompatible with the provisions of the Convention or the protocols thereto, manifestly ill-founded, or an abuse of the right of application.

4   The Court shall reject any application which it considers inadmissible under this Article. It may do so at any stage of the proceedings.

[C.1.37]
Article 36   Third-party intervention

1   In all cases before a Chamber or the Grand Chamber, a High contracting party one of whose nationals is an applicant shall have the right to submit written comments and to take part in hearings.

2   The President of the Court may, in the interest of the proper administration of justice, invite any High contracting party which is not a party to the proceedings or any person concerned who is not the applicant to submit written comments or take part in hearings.

[C.1.38]
Article 37   Striking out applications

1   The Court may at any stage of the proceedings decide to strike an application out of its list of cases where the circumstances lead to the conclusion that:

(a)   the applicant does not intend to pursue his application; or

(b)   the matter has been resolved; or

(c)   for any other reason established by the Court, it is no longer justified to continue the examination of the application.

However, the Court shall continue the examination of the application if respect for human rights as defined in the Convention and the protocols thereto so requires.

2   The Court may decide to restore an application to its list of cases if it considers that the circumstances justify such a course.

[C.1.39]
Article 38   Examination of the case and friendly settlement proceedings
1   If the Court declares the application admissible, it shall:

(*a*)   pursue the examination of the case, together with the representatives of the parties, and if need be, undertake an investigation, for the effective conduct of which the States concerned shall furnish all necessary facilities;

(*b*)   place itself at the disposal of the parties concerned with a view to securing a friendly settlement of the matter on the basis of respect for human rights as defined in the Convention and the protocols thereto.

2   Proceedings conducted under paragraph 1(*b*) shall be confidential.

[C.1.40]
Article 39   Finding of a friendly settlement
If a friendly settlement is effected, the Court shall strike the case out of its list by means of a decision which shall be confined to a brief statement of the facts and of the solution reached.

[C.1.41]
Article 40   Public hearings and access to documents
1   Hearings shall be public unless the Court in exceptional circumstances decides otherwise.

2   Documents deposited with the Registrar shall be accessible to the public unless the President of the Court decides otherwise.

[C.1.42]
Article 41   Just satisfaction
If the Court finds that there has been a violation of the Convention or the protocols thereto, and if the internal law of the High contracting party concerned allows only partial reparation to be made, the Court shall, if necessary, afford just satisfaction to the injured party.

[C.1.43]
Article 42   Judgments of Chambers
Judgments of Chambers shall become final in accordance with the provisions of Article 44, paragraph 2.

[C.1.44]
Article 43   Referral to the Grand Chamber
1   Within a period of three months from the date of the judgment of the Chamber, any party to the case may, in exceptional cases, request that the case be referred to the Grand Chamber.

2   A panel of five judges of the Grand Chamber shall accept the request if the case raises a serious question affecting the interpretation or application of the Convention or the protocols thereto, or a serious issue of general importance.

3   If the panel accepts the request, the Grand Chamber shall decide the case by means of a judgment.

[C.1.45]
Article 44   Final judgments
1   The judgment of the Grand Chamber shall be final.

2   the judgment of a Chamber shall become final:

(*a*)   when the parties declare that they will not request that the case be referred to the Grand Chamber; or

(*b*)   three months after the date of the judgment, if reference of the case to the Grand Chamber has not be requested; or

(*c*)   when the panel of the Grand Chamber rejects the request to refer under Article 43.

3   The final judgment shall be published.

[C.1.46]
Article 45   Reasons for judgments and decisions
1   Reasons shall be given for judgments as well as for decisions declaring applications admissible or inadmissible.

2   If a judgment does not represent, in whole or in part, the unanimous opinion of the judges, any judge shall be entitled to deliver a separate opinion.

[C.1.47]
Article 46   Binding force and execution of judgments
1   The High contracting parties undertake to abide by the final judgment of the Court in any case to which they are parties.

2   The final judgment of the Court shall be transmitted to the Committee of Ministers, which shall supervise its execution.

[C.1.48]
Article 47   Advisory opinions
1   The Court may, at the request of the Committee of Ministers, give advisory opinions on legal questions concerning the interpretation of the Convention and the protocols thereto.

2   Such opinions shall not deal with any question relating to the content or scope of the rights or freedoms defined in Section I of the Convention and the protocols thereto, or with any other question which the Court or the Committee of Ministers might have to consider in consequence of any such proceedings as could be instituted in accordance with the Convention.

3   Decisions of the Committee of Ministers to request an advisory opinion of the Court shall require a majority vote of the representatives entitled to sit on the Committee.

[C.1.49]
Article 48   Advisory jurisdiction of the Court
The Court shall decide whether a request for an advisory opinion submitted by the Committee of Ministers is within its competence as defined in Article 47.

[C.1.50]
Article 49   Reasons for advisory opinions
1   Reasons shall be given for advisory opinions of the Court.

2   If the advisory opinion does not represent, in whole or in part, the unanimous opinion of the judges, any judge shall be entitled to deliver a separate opinion.

3   Advisory opinions of the Court shall be communicated to the Committee of Ministers.

[C.1.51]
Article 50   Expenditure on the Court
The expenditure on the Court shall be borne by the Council of Europe.

[C.1.52]
Article 51   Privileges and immunities of judges
The judges shall be entitled, during the exercise of their functions, to the privileges and immunities provided for in Article 40 of the Statute of the Council of Europe and in the agreements made thereunder.

SECTION III   MISCELLANEOUS PROVISIONS

[C.1.53]
Article 52   Enquiries by the Secretary-General
On receipt of a request from the Secretary-General of the Council of Europe any High contracting party shall furnish an explanation of the manner in which its internal law ensures the effective implementation of any of the provisions of this Convention.

[C.1.54]
Article 53   Safeguard for existing human rights
Nothing in this Convention shall be construed as limiting or derogating from any of the human rights and fundamental freedoms which may be ensured under the laws of any High contracting party or under any other agreement to which it is a party.

[C.1.55]
Article 54 Powers of the Committee of Ministers
Nothing in this Convention shall prejudice the powers conferred on the Committee of Ministers by the Statute of the Council of Europe.

[C.1.56]
Article 55 Exclusion of other means of dispute settlement
The High contracting parties agree that, except by special agreement, they will not avail themselves of treaties, conventions or declarations in force between them for the purpose of submitting, by way of petition, a dispute arising out of the interpretation or application of this Convention to a means of settlement other than those provided for in this Convention.

[C.1.57]
Article 56 Territorial application
1 Any State may at the time of its ratification or at any time thereafter declare by notification addressed to the Secretary-General of the Council of Europe that the present Convention shall, subject to paragraph 4 of this Article, extend to all or any of the territories for whose international relations it is responsible.

2 The Convention shall extend to the territory or territories named in the notification as from the thirtieth day after the receipt of this notification by the Secretary-General of the Council of Europe.

3 The provisions of this Convention shall be applied in such territories with due regard, however, to local requirements.

4 Any State which has made a declaration in accordance with paragraph 1 of this Article may at any time thereafter declare on behalf of one or more of the territories to which the declaration relates that it accepts the competence of the Court to receive applications from individuals, non-governmental organisations or groups of individuals as provided in Article 34 of the Convention.

[C.1.58]
Article 57 Reservations
1 Any State may, when signing this Convention or when depositing its instrument of ratification, make a reservation in respect of any particular provision of the Convention to the extent that any law then in force in its territory is not in conformity with the provision. Reservations of a general character shall not be permitted under this Article.

2 Any reservation made under this Article shall contain a brief statement of the law concerned.

[C.1.59]
Article 58 Denunciation
1 A High Contracting Party may denounce the present Convention only after the expiry of five years from the date on which it became a Party to it and after

six months' notice contained in a notification addressed to the Secretary-General of the Council of Europe, who shall inform the other High Contracting Parties.

2   Such a denunciation shall not have the effect of releasing the High Contracting Party concerned from its obligations under this Convention in respect of any act which, being capable of constituting a violation of such obligations, may have been performed by it before the date at which the denunciation became effective.

3   Any High Contracting Party which shall cease to be a Member of the Council of Europe shall cease to be a Party to this Convention under the same conditions.

4   The Convention may be denounced in accordance with the provisions of the preceding paragraphs in respect of any territory to which it has been declared to extend under the terms of Article 56.

[C.1.60]
Article 59   Signature and ratification
1   This Convention shall be open to the signature of the members of the Council of Europe. It shall be ratified. Ratifications shall be deposited with the Secretary-General of the Council of Europe.

2   The present Convention shall come into force after the deposit of ten instruments of ratification.

3   As regards any signatory ratifying subsequently, the Convention shall come into force at the date of the deposit of its instrument of ratification.

4   The Secretary-General of the Council of Europe shall notify all the members of the Council of Europe of the entry into force of the Convention, the names of the High Contracting Parties who have ratified it, and the deposit of all instruments of ratification which may be effected subsequently.

Done at Rome this 4th day of November 1950, in English and French, both texts being equally authentic, in a single copy which shall remain deposited in the archives of the Council of Europe. The Secretary-General shall transmit certified copies to each of the signatories.

PROTOCOL No 1 TO THE EUROPEAN CONVENTION FOR THE PROTECTION OF HUMAN RIGHTS AND FUNDAMENTAL FREEDOMS

Signed in Paris on 20 March 1952

Entry into force   18 May 1954, in accordance with Article 6
Text   Council of Europe Treaty Series No 9

Note   For further analysis of the First Protocol, see *Special Bulletin* annotating the Human Rights Act 1998 (Division A Statutes).

[C.1.61]
The Governments signatory hereto, being members of the Council of Europe,

Being resolved to take steps to ensure the collective enforcement of certain rights and freedoms other than those already included in Section I of the Convention for the Protection of Human Rights and Fundamental Freedoms signed at Rome on 4th November, 1950 (hereinafter referred to as 'the Convention').

Have agreed as follows:

[C.1.62]
Article 1   Protection of property
Every natural or legal person is entitled to the peaceful enjoyment of his possessions. No one shall be deprived of his possessions except in the public interest and subject to the conditions provided for by law and by the general principles of international law.

The preceding provisions shall not, however, in any way impair the right of a State to enforce such laws as it deems necessary to control the use of property in accordance with the general interest or to secure the payment of taxes or other contributions or penalties.

[C.1.63]
Article 2   Right to education
No person shall be denied the right to education. In the exercise of any functions which it assumes in relation to education and to teaching, the State shall respect the right of parents to ensure such education and teaching in conformity with their own religious and philosophical convictions.

[C.1.64]
Article 3   Right to free elections
The High contracting parties undertake to hold free elections at reasonable intervals by secret ballot, under conditions which will ensure the free expression of the opinion of the people in the choice of the legislature.

[C.1.65]
Article 4   Territorial application
Any High contracting party may at the time of signature or ratification or at any time thereafter communicate to the Secretary-General of the Council of Europe a declaration stating the extent to which it undertakes that the provisions of the present Protocol shall apply to such of the territories for the international relations of which it is responsible as are named therein.

Any High contracting party which has communicated a declaration in virtue of the preceding paragraph may from time to time communicate a further declaration modifying the terms of any former declaration or terminating the application of the provisions of this Protocol in respect of any territory.

A declaration made in accordance with this Article shall be deemed to have been made in accordance with Paragraph (1) of Article 56 of the Convention.

[C.1.66]
Article 5   Relationship to the Convention
As between the High contracting parties the provisions of Articles 1, 2, 3 and 4 of this Protocol shall be regarded as additional Articles to the Convention and all the provisions of the Convention shall apply accordingly.

[C.1.67]
Article 6   Signature and ratification
This Protocol shall be open for signature by the members of the Council of Europe, who are the signatories of the Convention; it shall be ratified at the same time as or after the ratification of the Convention. It shall enter into force after the deposit of ten instruments of ratification. As regards any signatory ratifying subsequently, the Protocol shall enter into force at the date of the deposit of its instrument of ratification.

The instruments of ratification shall be deposited with the Secretary-General of the Council of Europe, who will notify all members of the names of those who have ratified.

Done at Paris on the 20th day of March 1952, in English and French, both texts being equally authentic, in a single copy which shall remain deposited in the archives of the Council of Europe. The Secretary-General shall transmit certified copies to each of the signatory Governments.

PROTOCOL No 4 TO THE EUROPEAN CONVENTION FOR THE PROTECTION OF HUMAN RIGHTS AND FUNDAMENTAL FREEDOMS, SECURING CERTAIN RIGHTS AND FREEDOMS OTHER THAN THOSE ALREADY INCLUDED IN THE CONVENTION AND IN THE FIRST PROTOCOL THERETO

Signed at Strasbourg on 16 September 1963

Entry into force   2 May 1968, in accordance with Article 7
Text   Council of Europe Treaty Series No 46

Note   The UK has not ratified Protocol No 4.

[C.1.68]
The Governments signatory hereto, being Members of the Council of Europe,

Being resolved to take steps to ensure the collective enforcement of certain rights and freedoms other than those already included in Section I of the Convention for the Protection of Human Rights and Fundamental Freedoms signed at Rome on 4th November 1950 (hereinafter referred to as 'the Convention') and in Articles 1 to 3 of the First Protocol to the Convention, signed at Paris on 20th March 1952,

Have agreed as follows:

[C.1.69]
Article 1   Prohibition of imprisonment for debt
No one shall be deprived of his liberty merely on the ground of inability to fulfil a contractual obligation.

[C.1.70]
Article 2   Freedom of movement
1   Everyone lawfully within the territory of a state shall, within that territory, have the right to liberty of movement and freedom to choose his residence.

2   Everyone shall be free to leave any country, including his own.

3   No restrictions shall be placed on the exercise of these rights other than such as are in accordance with law and are necessary in a democratic society in the interests of national security or public safety, for the maintenance of '*ordre public*', for the prevention of crime, for the protection of health or morals, or for the protection of the rights and freedoms of others.

4   The rights set forth in paragraph 1 may also be subject, in particular areas, to restrictions imposed in accordance with law and justified by the public interest in a democratic society.

[C.1.71]
Article 3 Prohibition of expulsion of nationals
1 No one shall be expelled, by means either of an individual or of a collective measure, from the territory of the State of which he is a national.

2 No one shall be deprived of the right to enter the territory of the State of which he is a national.

[C.1.72]
Article 4 Prohibition of collective expulsion of aliens
Collective expulsion of aliens is prohibited.

[C.1.73]
Article 5 Territorial application
1 Any High contracting party may, at the time of signature or ratification of this Protocol, or at any time thereafter, communicate to the Secretary-General of the Council of Europe a declaration stating the extent to which it undertakes that the provisions of this Protocol shall apply to such of the territories for the international relations of which it is responsible as are named therein.

2 Any High contracting party which has communicated a declaration in virtue of the preceding paragraph may, from time to time, communicate a further declaration modifying the terms of any former declaration or terminating the application of the provisions of this Protocol in respect of any territory.

3 A declaration made in accordance with this Article shall be deemed to have been made in accordance with paragraph 1 of Article 56 of the Convention.

4 The territory of any state to which this Protocol applies by virtue of ratification or acceptance by that state, and each territory to which this Protocol is applied by virtue of a declaration by that state under this Article, shall be treated as separate territories for the purpose of the references in Articles 2 and 3 to the territory of a state.

5 Any State which has made a declaration in accordance with paragraph 1 or 2 of this Article may at any time thereafter declare on behalf of one or more of the territories to which the declaration relates that it accepts the competence of the Court to receive applications from individuals, non-governmental organizations or groups of individuals as provided in Article 34 of the Convention in respect of all or any of Articles 1 to 4 of this Protocol.

[C.1.74]
Article 6 Relationship to the Convention
As between the High contracting parties the provisions of Articles 1 to 5 of this Protocol shall be regarded as additional Articles to the Convention, and all the provisions of the Convention shall apply accordingly.

[C.1.75]
Article 7 Signature and ratification
1 This Protocol shall be open for signature by the members of the Council of

Europe who are the signatories of the Convention; it shall be ratified at the same time as or after the ratification of the Convention. It shall enter into force after the deposit of five instruments of ratification. As regards any signatory ratifying subsequently, the Protocol shall enter into force at the date of the deposit of its instrument of ratification.

2 The instruments of ratification shall be deposited with the Secretary-General of the Council of Europe, who will notify all members of the names of those who have ratified.

In Witness Whereof, the undersigned, being duly authorised thereto, have signed this Protocol.

Done at Strasbourg, this 16th day of September 1963, in English and in French, both texts being equally authoritative, in a single copy which shall remain deposited in the archives of the Council of Europe. The Secretary-General shall transmit certified copies to each of the signatory States.

PROTOCOL No 6 TO THE EUROPEAN CONVENTION FOR THE PROTECTION OF HUMAN RIGHTS AND FUNDAMENTAL FREEDOMS, CONCERNING THE ABOLITION OF THE DEATH PENALTY

Note The UK has not ratified Protocol No 6.

The Sixth Protocol was not mentioned in the original Human Rights Bill, but on 20 May 1998 it was added at committee stage (on the floor of the House) in the Commons. Articles 1 and 2 only now appear as Part III of Schedule 1 Human Rights Act 1998. The United Kingdom ratified it on 27 January 1999.

[C.1.76]
The member states of the Council of Europe, signatory to this Protocol to the Convention for the Protection of Human Rights and Fundamental Freedoms, signed at Rome on 4 November 1950 (hereinafter referred to as 'the Convention'),

Considering that the evolution that has occurred in several member states of the Council of Europe expresses a general tendency in favour of abolition of the death penalty;

Have agreed as follows:

[C.1.77]
Article 1   Abolition of the death penalty
The death penalty shall be abolished. No one shall be condemned to such penalty or executed.

[C.1.78]
Article 2   Death penalty in time of war
A state may make provision in its law for the death penalty in respect of acts committed in time of war or of imminent threat of war; such penalty shall be applied only in the instances laid down in the law and in accordance with its provisions. The state shall communicate to the Secretary of the Council of Europe the relevant provisions of that law.

[C.1.79]
Article 3   Prohibition of derogations
No derogation from the provisions of this Protocol shall be made under Article 15 of the Convention.

[C.1.80]
Article 4   Prohibition of reservations
No reservation may be made under Article 57 of the Convention in respect of the provisions of this Protocol.

[C.1.81]
Article 5   Territorial application
1   Any state may at the time of signature or when depositing its instrument of ratification, acceptance or approval, specify the territory or territories to which this Protocol shall apply.

2   Any state may at any later date, by a declaration addressed to the

Secretary-General of the Council of Europe, extend the application of this Protocol to any other territory specified in the declaration. In respect of such territory the Protocol shall enter into force on the first day of the month following the date of receipt of such a declaration by the Secretary-General.

3 Any declaration made under the two preceding paragraphs may, in respect of any territory specified in such declaration, be withdrawn by a notification addressed to the Secretary-General. The withdrawal shall become effective on the first day of the month following the date of receipt of such notification by the Secretary-General.

[C.1.82]
Article 6 Relationship to the Convention
As between the states parties the provisions of Articles 1 to 5 of this Protocol shall be regarded as additional articles to the Convention and all the provisions of the Convention shall apply accordingly.

[C.1.83]
Article 7 Signature and ratification
This Protocol shall be open for signature by the member States of the Council of Europe, signatories to the Convention. It shall be subject to ratification, acceptance or approval. A member state of the Council of Europe may not ratify, accept or approve this Protocol unless it has, simultaneously or previously, ratified the Convention. Instruments of ratification, acceptance or approval shall be deposited with the Secretary-General of the Council of Europe.

[C.1.84]
Article 8 Entry into force
1 This Protocol shall enter into force on the first day of the month following the date on which five member states of the Council of Europe have expressed their consent to be bound by the Protocol in accordance with the provisions of Article 7.

2 In respect of any member state which subsequently expresses its consent to be bound by it, the Protocol shall enter into force on the first day of the month following the date of the deposit of the instrument of ratification, acceptance or approval.

[C.1.85]
Article 9 Depositary functions
The Secretary-General of the Council of Europe shall notify the member states of the Council of:
(*a*) any signature;
(*b*) the deposit of any instrument of ratification, acceptance or approval;
(*c*) any date of entry into force of this Protocol in accordance with Articles 5 and 8;
(*d*) any other act, notification or communication relating to this Protocol.

In Witness Whereof the undersigned, being duly authorised thereto, have signed this Protocol.

Done at Strasbourg, this 28th day of April 1983, in English and French, both texts being equally authentic, in a single copy which shall be deposited in the archives of the Council of Europe. The Secretary General of the Council of Europe shall transmit certified copies to each member State of the Council of Europe.

PROTOCOL No 7 TO THE EUROPEAN CONVENTION FOR THE PROTECTION OF HUMAN RIGHTS AND FUNDAMENTAL FREEDOMS, CONCERNING VARIOUS MATTERS

Note The UK has not ratified Protocol No 7.

[C.1.86]
The member states of the Council of Europe signatory hereto,

Being resolved to take further steps to ensure the collective enforcement of certain rights and freedoms by means of the Convention for the Protection of Human Rights and Fundamental Freedoms signed at Rome on 4 November 1950 (hereinafter referred to as 'the Convention'),

Have agreed as follows:

[C.1.87]
Article 1 Procedural safe-guards relating to expulsion of aliens
1 An alien lawfully resident in the territory of a state shall not be expelled therefrom except in pursuance of a decision reached in accordance with law and shall be allowed:

(*a*) to submit reasons against his expulsion,
(*b*) to have his case reviewed, and
(*c*) to be represented for these purposes before the competent authority or a person or persons designated by that authority.

2 An alien may be expelled before the exercise of his rights under paragraph 1.a, b and c of this Article, when such expulsion is necessary in the interests of public order or is grounded on reasons of national security.

[C.1.88]
Article 2 Right of appeal in criminal matters
1 Everyone convicted of a criminal offence by a tribunal shall have the right to have conviction or sentence reviewed by a higher tribunal. The exercise of this right, including the grounds on which it may be exercised, shall be governed by law.

2 This right may be subject to exceptions in regard to offences of a minor character, as prescribed by law, or in cases in which the person concerned was tried in the first instance by the highest tribunal or was convicted following an appeal against acquittal.

[C.1.89]
Article 3 Compensation for wrongful conviction
When a person has by a final decision been convicted of a criminal offence and when subsequently his conviction has been reversed, or he has been pardoned, on the ground that a new or newly discovered fact shows conclusively that there has been a miscarriage of justice, the person who has suffered punishment as a result of such conviction shall be compensated according to the law

or the practice of the state concerned, unless it is proved that the nondisclosure of the unknown fact in time is wholly or partly attributable to him.

[C.1.90]
Article 4   Right not to be tried or punished twice
1   No one shall be liable to be tried or punished again in criminal proceedings under the jurisdiction of the same state for an offence for which he has already been finally acquitted or convicted in accordance with the law and penal procedure of that state.

2   The provisions of the preceding paragraph shall not prevent the reopening of the case in accordance with the law and penal procedure of the state concerned, if there is evidence of new or newly discovered facts, or if there has been a fundamental defect in the previous proceedings, which could affect the outcome of the case.

3   No derogation from this Article shall be made under Article 15 of the Convention.

[C.1.91]
Article 5   Equality between spouses
Spouses shall enjoy equality of rights and responsibilities of a private law character between them, and in their relations with their children, as to marriage, during marriage and in the event of its dissolution. This Article shall not prevent States from taking such measures as are necessary in the interests of the children.

[C.1.92]
Article 6   Territorial applications
1   Any State may at the time of signature or when depositing its instrument of ratification, acceptance or approval, specify the territory or territories to which this Protocol shall apply and state the extent to which it undertakes that the provisions of this Protocol shall apply to this or these territories.

2   Any state may at any later date, by a declaration addressed to the Secretary-General of the Council of Europe, extend the application of this Protocol to any other territory specified in the declaration. In respect of such territory the Protocol shall enter into force on the first day of the month following the expiration of a period of two months after the date of receipt by the Secretary-General of such declaration.

3   Any declaration made under the two preceding paragraphs may, in respect of any territory specified in such declaration, be withdrawn or modified by a notification addressed to the Secretary-General. The withdrawal or modification shall become effective on the first day of the month following the expiration of a period of two months after the date of receipt of such notification by the Secretary-General.

4   A declaration made in accordance with this Article shall be deemed to have been made in accordance with paragraph 1 of Article 56 of the Convention.

5   The territory of any state to which this Protocol applies by virtue of ratification, acceptance or approval by that state, and each territory to which this

Protocol is applied by virtue of a declaration by that state under this Article, may be treated as separate territories for the purpose of the reference in Article 1 to the territory of a state.

6   Any State which has made a declaration in accordance with paragraph 1 or 2 of this Article may at any time thereafter declare on behalf of one or more of the territories to which the declaration relates that it accepts the competence of the Court to receive applications from individuals, non-governmental organizations or groups of individuals as provided in Article 34 of the Convention in respect of Articles 1 to 5 of this Protocol.

[C.1.93]
Article 7   Relationship to the Convention
1   As between the states parties, the provisions of Articles 1 to 6 of this Protocol shall be regarded as additional Articles to the Convention, and all the provisions of the Convention shall apply accordingly.

[C.1.94]
Article 8   Signature and ratification
This Protocol shall be open for signature by member states of the Council of Europe which have signed the Convention. It is subject to ratification, acceptance or approval. A member state of the Council of Europe may not ratify, accept or approve this Protocol without previously or simultaneously ratifying the Convention. Instruments of ratification, acceptance or approval shall be deposited with the Secretary-General of the Council of Europe.

[C.1.95]
Article 9   Entry into force
1   This Protocol shall enter into force on the first day of the month following the expiration of a period of two months after the date on which seven member states of the Council of Europe have expressed their consent to be bound by the Protocol in accordance with the provisions of Article 8.

2   In respect of any member state which subsequently expresses its consent to be bound by it, the Protocol shall enter into force on the first day of the month following the expiration of a period of two months after the date of the deposit of the instrument of ratification, acceptance or approval.

[C.1.96]
Article 10   Depository functions
The Secretary-General of the Council of Europe shall notify all the member states of the Council of:

(*a*) any signature;
(*b*) the deposit of any instrument of ratification, acceptance or approval;
(*c*) any date of entry into force of this Protocol in accordance with Articles 6 and 9;
(*d*) any other act, notification or declaration relating to this Protocol.

In Witness Whereof the undersigned, being duly authorised thereto, have signed this Protocol.

Done at Strasbourg, this 22nd day of November 1984, in English and French, both texts being equally authentic, in a single copy which shall be deposited in the archives of the Council of Europe. The Secretary-General of the Council of Europe shall transmit certified copies to each member state of the Council.

PROTOCOL No 11 TO THE CONVENTION FOR THE PROTECTION OF HUMAN RIGHTS AND FUNDAMENTAL FREEDOMS, RESTRUCTURING THE CONTROL MACHINERY ESTABLISHED THEREBY

[C.1.97]

The Member States of the Council of Europe signatories to this Protocol to the Convention for the Protection of Human Rights and Fundamental Freedoms, signed at Rome on 4 November 1950 (hereinafter referred to as 'the Convention').

Considering the urgent need to restructure the control machinery established by the Convention in order to maintain and improve the efficiency of its protection of human rights and fundamental freedoms, mainly in view of the increase in the number of applications and the growing membership of the Council of Europe;

Considering that it is therefore desirable to amend certain provisions of the Convention with a view, in particular, to replacing the existing European Commission and Court of Human Rights with a new permanent Court;

Having regard to Resolution No 1 adopted at the European Ministerial Conference on Human Rights, held in Vienna on 19 and 20 March 1985;

Having regard to Recommendation 1194 (1992), adopted by the Parliamentary Assembly of the Council of Europe on 6 October 1992;

Having regard to the decision taken on reform of the Convention control machinery by the Heads of State and Government of the Council of Europe member States in the Vienna Declaration on 9 October 1993.

Have agreed as follows:

[C.1.98]
Article 1
(Amends the European Convention for the Protection of Human Rights and Fundamental Freedom (Articles 19 to 56).)

[C.1.99]
Article 2
(Amends the European Convention for the Protection of Human Rights and Fundamental Freedoms (Articles 57 to 66 and Protocols).)

[C.1.100]
Article 3
1   This Protocol shall be open for signature by member States of the Council of Europe signatories to the Convention, which may express their consent to be bound by

(*a*) signature without reservation as to ratification, acceptance or approval; or (*b*) signature subject to ratification, acceptance or approval, followed by ratification, acceptance or approval.

2   The instruments of ratification, acceptance or approval shall be deposited with the Secretary General of the Council of Europe.

[C.1.101]
Article 4
This Protocol shall enter into force on the first day of the month following the expiration of a period of one year after the date on which all Parties to the Convention have expressed their consent to be bound by the Protocol in accordance with the provisions of Article 3. The election of new judges may take place, and any further necessary steps may be taken to establish the new Court, in accordance with the provisions of this Protocol from the date on which all Parties to the Convention have expressed their consent to be bound by the Protocol.

[C.1.102]
Article 5
1   Without prejudice to the provisions in paragraphs 3 and 4 below, the terms of office of the judges, members of the Commission, Registrar and Deputy Registrar shall expire at the date of entry into force of this Protocol.

2   Applications pending before the Commission which have not been declared admissible at the date of the entry into force of this Protocol shall be examined by the Court in accordance with the provisions of this Protocol.

3   Applications which have been declared admissible at the date of entry into force of this Protocol shall continue to be dealt with by members of the Commission within a period of one year thereafter. Any applications the examination of which has not been completed within the aforesaid period shall be transmitted to the Court which shall examine them as admissible cases in accordance with the provisions of this Protocol.

4   With respect to applications in which the Commission, after the entry into force of this Protocol, had adopted a report in accordance with former Article 31 of the Convention, the report shall be transmitted to the parties, who shall not be at liberty to publish it. In accordance with the provisions applicable prior to the entry into force of this Protocol, a case may be referred to the Court. The panel of the Grand Chamber shall determine whether one of the Chambers or the Grand Chamber shall decide the case. If the case is decided by a Chamber, the decision of the Chamber shall be final. Cases not referred to the Court shall be dealt with by the Committee of Ministers acting in accordance with the provisions of former Article 32 of the Convention.

5   Cases pending before the Court which have not been decided at the date of entry into force of this Protocol shall be transmitted to the Grand Chamber of the Court, which shall examine them in accordance with the provisions of this Protocol.

6   Cases pending before the Committee of Ministers which have not been decided under former Article 32 of the Convention at the date of entry into force of this Protocol shall be completed by the Committee of Ministers acting in accordance with that Article.

[C.1.103]
Article 6
Where a High Contracting Party had made a declaration recognising the competence of the Commission or the jurisdiction of the Court under former Article 25 or 46 of the Convention with respect to matters arising after or based on facts occurring subsequent to any such declaration, this limitation shall remain valid for the jurisdiction of the Court under this Protocol.

[C.1.104]
Article 7
The Secretary-General of the Council of Europe shall notify all the member states of the Council of:

(*a*) any signature;
(*b*) the deposit of any instrument of ratification, acceptance or approval;
(*c*) the date of entry into force of this Protocol or of any of its provisions in accordance with Article 4; and
(*d*) any other act, notification or communication relating to this Protocol.

In witness whereof the undersigned, being duly authorised thereto, have signed this Protocol.

Done at Strasbourg, this 11th day of May 1994 in English and French, both texts being equally authentic, in a single copy which shall be deposited in the archives of the Council of Europe. The Secretary-General of the Council of Europe shall transmit certified copies to each member State of the Council of Europe.

PROTOCOL No 12 TO THE CONVENTION FOR THE PROTECTION OF HUMAN RIGHTS AND FUNDAMENTAL FREEDOMS

[C.1.105]

The member States of the Council of Europe signatory hereto,

Having regard to the fundamental principle according to which all persons are equal before the law and are entitled to the equal protection of the law;

Being resolved to take further steps to promote the equality of all persons through the collective enforcement of a general prohibition of discrimination by means of the Convention for the Protection of Human Rights and Fundamental Freedoms signed at Rome on 4 November 1950 (hereinafter referred to as 'the Convention');

Reaffirming that the principle of non-discrimination does not prevent States Parties from taking measures in order to promote full and effective equality, provided that there is an objective and reasonable justification for those measures,

Have agreed as follows:

[C.1.106]
Article 1   General prohibition of discrimination
1   The enjoyment of any right set forth by law shall be secured without discrimination on any ground such as sex, race, colour, language, religion, political or other opinion, national or social origin, association with a
national minority, property, birth or other status.

2   No one shall be discriminated against by any public authority on any ground such as those mentioned in paragraph 1.

[C.1.107]
Article 2   Territorial application
1   Any State may, at the time of signature or when depositing its instrument of ratification, acceptance or approval, specify the territory or territories to which this Protocol shall apply.

2   Any State may at any later date, by a declaration addressed to the Secretary General of the Council of Europe, extend the application of this Protocol to any other territory specified in the declaration. In respect of such territory the Protocol shall enter into force on the first day of the month following the expiration of a period of three months after the date of receipt by the Secretary General of such declaration.

3   Any declaration made under the two preceding paragraphs may, in respect of any territory specified in such declaration, be withdrawn or modified by a notification addressed to the Secretary General of the Council of Europe. The withdrawal or modification shall become effective on the first day of the

month following the expiration of a period of three months after the date of receipt of such notification by the Secretary General.

4   A declaration made in accordance with this article shall be deemed to have been made in accordance with paragraph 1 of Article 56 of the Convention.

5   Any State which has made a declaration in accordance with paragraph 1 or 2 of this article may at any time thereafter declare on behalf of one or more of the territories to which the declaration relates that it accepts the competence of the Court to receive applications from individuals, non-governmental organisations or groups of individuals as provided by Article 34 of the Convention in respect of Article 1 of this Protocol.

[C.1.108]
Article 3   Relationship to the Convention
As between the States Parties, the provisions of Articles 1 and 2 of this Protocol shall be regarded as additional articles to the Convention, and all the provisions of the Convention shall apply accordingly.

[C.1.109]
Article 4   Signature and ratification
This Protocol shall be open for signature by member States of the Council of Europe which have signed the Convention. It is subject to ratification, acceptance or approval. A member State of the Council of Europe may not ratify, accept or approve this Protocol without previously or simultaneously ratifying the Convention. Instruments of ratification, acceptance or approval shall be deposited with the Secretary General of the Council of Europe.

[C.1.110]
Article 5   Entry into force
1   This Protocol shall enter into force on the first day of the month

following the expiration of a period of three months after the date on which ten member States of the Council of Europe have expressed their consent to be bound by the Protocol in accordance with the provisions of Article 4.

2   In respect of any member State which subsequently expresses its consent to be bound by it, the Protocol shall enter into force on the first day of the month following the expiration of a period of three months after the date of the deposit of the instrument of ratification, acceptance or approval.

[C.1.111]
Article 6   Depositary functions
The Secretary General of the Council of Europe shall notify all the member States of the Council of Europe of:

(a)   any signature;
(b)   the deposit of any instrument of ratification, acceptance or approval;
(c)   any date of entry into force of this Protocol in accordance with Articles 2 and 5;
(d)   any other act, notification or communication relating to this Protocol.

In witness whereof the undersigned, being duly authorised thereto, have signed this Protocol.

Done at Rome, this 4th day of November 2000, in English and in French, both texts being equally authentic, in a single copy which shall be deposited in the archives of the Council of Europe. The Secretary General of the Council of Europe shall transmit certified copies to each member State of the Council of Europe.

Note   The United Kingdom has yet to ratify Protocol No 12.

EUROPEAN SOCIAL CHARTER (Excerpts)

18 October 1961, Turin
Entry into force   26 February 1965, in accordance with Article 35

[C.1.112]
The governments signatory hereto, being members of the Council of Europe,

Considering that the aim of the Council of Europe is the achievement of greater unity between its members for the purpose of safeguarding and realising the ideals and principles which are their common heritage and of facilitating their economic and social progress, in particular by the maintenance and further realisation of human rights and fundamental freedoms;

Considering that in the European Convention for the Protection of Human Rights and Fundamental Freedoms signed at Rome on 4 November 1950, and the Protocol thereto signed at Paris on 20 March 1952, the member States of the Council of Europe agreed to secure to their populations the civil and political rights and freedoms therein specified;

Considering that the enjoyment of social rights should be secured without discrimination on grounds of race, colour, sex, religion, political opinion, national extraction or social origin;

Being resolved to make every effort in common to improve the standard of living and to promote the social well-being of both their urban and rural populations by means of appropriate institutions and action,

Have agreed as follows:

[C.1.113]
Article 18—The right to engage in a gainful occupation in the territory of other Contracting Parties
With a view to ensuring the effective exercise of the right to engage in a gainful occupation in the territory of any other Contracting Party, the Contracting Parties undertake:

1   to apply existing regulations in a spirit of liberality;

2   to simplify existing formalities and to reduce or abolish chancery dues and other charges payable by foreign workers or their employers;

3   to liberalise, individually or collectively, regulations governing the employment of foreign workers;

and recognise:

4   the right of their nationals to leave the country to engage in a gainful occupation in the territories of the other contracting parties.

[C.1.114]
Article 19—The right of migrant workers and their families to protection and assistance

With a view to ensuring the effective exercise of the right of migrant workers and their families to protection and assistance in the territory of any other contracting party, the contracting parties undertake:

1   to maintain or to satisfy themselves that there are maintained adequate and free services to assist such workers, particularly in obtaining accurate information, and to take all appropriate steps, so far as national laws and regulations permit, against misleading propaganda relating to emigration and immigration;

2   to adopt appropriate measures within their own jurisdiction to facilitate the departure, journey and reception of such workers and their families, and to provide, within their own jurisdiction, appropriate services for health, medical attention and good hygienic conditions during the journey;

3   to promote co-operation, as appropriate, between social services, public and private, in emigration and immigration countries;

4   to secure for such workers lawfully within their territories, in so far as such matters are regulated by law or regulations or are subject to the control of administrative authorities, treatment not less favourable than that of their own nationals in respect of the following matters:

(*a*)   remuneration and other employment and working conditions;
(*b*)   membership of trade unions and enjoyment of the benefits of collective bargaining;
(*c*)   accommodation;

5   to secure for such workers lawfully within their territories, treatment not less favourable than that of their own nationals with regard to employment taxes, dues or contributions payable in respect of employed persons;

6   to facilitate as far as possible the reunion of the family of a foreign worker permitted to establish himself in the territory;

7   to secure for such workers lawfully within their territories treatment not less favourable than that of their own nationals in respect of legal proceedings relating to matters referred to in this article;

8   to secure that such workers lawfully residing within their territories are not expelled unless they endanger national security or offend against public interest or morality;

9   to permit, within legal limits, the transfer of such parts of the earnings and savings of such workers as they may desire;

10   to extend the protection and assistance provided for in this article to self-employed migrants in so far as such measures apply.

PART III
[C.1.115]
Article 20—Undertakings
1   Each of the contracting parties undertakes:

(*a*) to consider Part I of this Charter as a declaration of the aims which it will pursue by all appropriate means, as stated in the introductory paragraph of that part;

(*b*) to consider itself bound by at least five of the following articles of Part II of this Charter: Articles, 1, 5, 6, 12, 13, 16 and 19;

(*c*) in addition to the articles selected by it in accordance with the preceding sub-paragraph, to consider itself bound by such a number of articles or numbered paragraphs of Part II of the Charter as it may select, provided that the total number of articles or numbered paragraphs by which it is bound is not less than 10 articles or 45 numbered paragraphs.

2   The articles or paragraphs selected in accordance with sub-paragraphs (*b*) and (*c*) of paragraph 1 of this article shall be notified to the Secretary General of the Council of Europe at the time when the instrument of ratification or approval of the contracting party concerned is deposited.

3   Any contracting party may, at a later date, declare by notification to the Secretary General that it considers itself bound by any articles or any numbered paragraphs of Part II of the Charter which it has not already accepted under the terms of paragraph 1 of this article. Such undertakings subsequently given shall be deemed to be an integral part of the ratification or approval, and shall have the same effect as from the thirtieth day after the date of the notification.

4   The Secretary General shall communicate to all the signatory governments and to the Director General of the International Labour Office any notification which he shall have received pursuant to this part of the Charter.

5   Each contracting party shall maintain a system of labour inspection appropriate to national conditions.

PART IV
[C.1.116]
Article 21—Reports concerning accepted provisions
The contracting parties shall send to the Secretary Central of the Council of Europe a report at two-yearly intervals, in a form to be determined by the Committee of Ministers, concerning the application of such provisions of Part II of the Charter as they have accepted.

[C.1.117]
Article 22—Reports concerning provisions which are not accepted
The contracting parties shall send to the Secretary General, at appropriate intervals as requested by the Committee of Ministers, reports relating to the provisions of Part II of the Charter which they did not accept at the time of their ratification or approval or in a subsequent notification. The Committee of Ministers shall determine from time to time in respect of which provisions such reports shall be requested and the form of the reports to be provided.

[C.1.118]
Article 23—Communication of copies
1   Each contracting party shall communicate copies of its reports referred to

in Articles 21 and 22 to such of its national organisations as are members of the international organisations of employers and trade unions to be invited under Article 27, paragraph 2, to be represented at meetings of the Sub-committee of the Governmental Social Committee.

2   The contracting parties shall forward to the Secretary General any comments on the said reports received from these national organisations, if so requested by them.

[C.1.119]
Article 24—Examination of the reports
The reports sent to the Secretary General in accordance with Articles 21 and 22 shall be examined by a committee of experts, who shall have also before them any comments forwarded to the Secretary General in accordance with paragraph 2 of Article 23.

[C.1.120]
Article 25—Committee of Experts
1   The Committee of Experts shall consist of not more than seven members appointed by the Committee of Ministers from a list of independent experts of the highest integrity and of recognised competence in international social questions, nominated by the contracting parties...

[C.1.121]
Article 31—Restrictions
1   The rights and principles set forth in Part I when effectively realised, and their effective exercise as provided for in Part II, shall not be subject to any restrictions or limitations not specified in those parts, except such as are prescribed by law and are necessary in a democratic society for the protection of the rights and freedoms of others or for the protection of public interest, national security, public health, or morals.

[C.1.122]
Article 38—Appendix
The appendix to this Charter shall form an integral part of it.

In Witness Whereof, the undersigned, being duly authorised thereto, have signed this Charter.

Done at Turin, this 18th day of October 1961, in English and French, both texts being equally authoritative, in a single copy which shall be deposited within the archives of the Council of Europe. The Secretary General shall transmit certified copies to each of the signatories.

APPENDIX TO THE SOCIAL CHARTER
[C.1.123]
Scope of the Social Charter in terms of persons protected:
1   Without prejudice to Article 12, paragraph 4, and Article 13, paragraph 4,

the persons covered by Articles 1 to 17 include foreigners only in so far as they are nationals of other contracting parties lawfully resident or working regularly within the territory of the contracting party concerned, subject to the understanding that these articles are to be interpreted in the light of the provisions of Articles 18 and 19.

This interpretation would not prejudice the extension of similar facilities to other persons by any of the contracting parties.

2   Each contracting party will grant to refugees as defined in the Convention relating to the Status of Refugees, signed at Geneva on 28 July 1951, and lawfully staying in its territory, treatment as favourable as possible, and in any case not less favourable than under the obligations accepted by the contracting party under the said Convention and under any other existing international instruments applicable to those refugees.

Part I, paragraph 18 and Part II, Article 18, paragraph 1

[C.1.124]
It is understood that these provisions are not concerned with the question of entry into the territories of the contracting parties and do not prejudice the provisions of the European Convention on Establishment, signed at Paris on 13 December 1955.

Part II

[C.1.125]
Article 19, paragraph 6
For the purpose of this provision, the term 'family of a foreign worker' is understood to mean at least his wife and dependent children under the age of 21 years.

Part III

[C.1.126]
It is understood that the Charter contains legal obligations of an international character, the application of which is submitted solely to the supervision provided for in Part IV thereof.

ADDITIONAL PROTOCOL TO THE EUROPEAN SOCIAL CHARTER

5 May 1988, Strasbourg

Preamble

The member states of the Council of Europe signatory hereto,

Resolved to take new measures to extend the protection of the social and economic rights guaranteed by the European Social Charter, opened for signature in Turin on 18 October 1961 (hereinafter referred to as 'the Charter'),

Have agreed as follows:

Part I

[C.1.127]
The Parties accept as the aim of their policy to be pursued by all appropriate means, both national and international in character, the attainment of conditions in which the following rights and principles may be effectively realised:

1   All workers have the right to equal opportunities and equal treatment in matters of employment and occupation without discrimination on the grounds of sex.

2   Workers have the right to be informed and to be consulted within the undertaking.

3   Workers have the right to take part in the determination and improvement of the working conditions and working environment in the undertaking.

4   Every elderly person has the right to social protection.

Part II

[C.1.128]
The Parties undertake, as provided for in Part III, to consider themselves bound by the obligations laid down in the following articles:

[C.1.129]
Article 1—Right to equal opportunities and equal treatment in matters of employment and occupation without discrimination on the grounds of sex
1   With a view to ensuring the effective exercise of the right to equal opportunities and equal treatment in matters of employment and occupation without discrimination on the grounds of sex, the parties undertake to recognise that right and to take appropriate measures to ensure or promote its application in the following fields:

—   access to employment, protection against dismissal and occupational resettlement;

— vocational guidance, training, retraining and rehabilitation;
— terms of employment and working conditions including remuneration;
— career development including promotion.

2   Provisions concerning the protection of women, particularly as regards pregnancy, confinement and the post-natal period, shall not be deemed to be discrimination as referred to in paragraph 1 of this article.

3   Paragraph 1 of this article shall not prevent the adoption of specific measures aimed at removing *de facto* inequalities.

4   Occupational activities which, by reason of their nature or the context in which they are carried out, can be entrusted only to persons of a particular sex may be excluded from the scope of this article or some of its provisions.

C2   UN Materials

CONVENTION RELATING TO THE STATUS OF REFUGEES

Done at Geneva on 28 July 1951

Entry into force   22 April 1954, in accordance with Article 43
Text   United Nations Treaty Series No 2545, Vol 189, p 137

PREAMBLE

[C.2.1]
The High Contracting Parties

Considering that the Charter of the United Nations and the Universal Declaration of Human Rights approved on 10 December 1948 by the General Assembly have affirmed the principle that human beings shall enjoy fundamental rights and freedoms without discrimination,

Considering that the United Nations has, on various occasions, manifested its profound concern for refugees and endeavoured to assure refugees the widest possible exercise of these fundamental rights and freedoms,

Considering that it is desirable to revise and consolidate previous international agreements relating to the status of refugees and to extend the scope of and the protection accorded by such instruments by means of a new agreement.

Considering that the grant of asylum may place unduly heavy burdens on certain countries, and that a satisfactory solution of a problem of which the United Nations has recognised the international scope and nature cannot therefore be achieved without international co-operation,

Expressing the wish that all states, recognizing the social and humanitarian nature of the problem of refugees, will do everything within their power to prevent this problem from becoming a cause of tension between states,

Noting that the United Nations High Commissioner for Refugees is charged with the task of supervising international conventions providing for the protection of refugees, and recognising that the effective co-ordination of measures taken to deal with this problem will depend upon the co-operation of states with the High Commissioner,

Have agreed as follows:

The Convention was adopted by the United Nations Conference of Plenipotentiaries on the Status of Refugees and Stateless Persons, held at Geneva from 2 to 25 July 1951. The Conference was convened pursuant to resolution 429(V), adopted by the General Assembly of the United Nations on 14 December 1950. For the text of this resolution, see Official Records of the General Assembly, Fifth Session, Supplement No 20(A/1775), p 48, The Text of the Final Act of the Conference is reproduced in the Appendix.

CHAPTER 1 GENERAL PROVISIONS

[C.2.2]
Article 1 Definition of the term 'Refugee'
A   For the purposes of the present Convention, the term 'refugee' shall apply to any person who:

(1)   Has been considered a refugee under the Arrangements of 12 May 1926 and 30 June 1928 or under the Conventions of 28 October 1933 and 10 February 1938, the Protocol of 14 September 1939 or the Constitution of the International Refugee Organization;

Decisions of non-eligibility taken by the International Refugee Organization during the period of its activities shall not prevent the status of refugee being accorded to persons who fulfil the conditions of paragraph 2 of this section;

(2)   As a result of events occurring before 1 January 1951 and owing to well-founded fear of being persecuted for reasons of race, religion, nationality, membership of a particular social group or political opinion, is outside the country of his nationality and is unable or, owing to such fear, is unwilling to avail himself of the protection of that country; or who, not having a nationality and being outside the country of his former habitual residence as a result of such events, is unable or, owing to such fear, is unwilling to return to it.

In the case of a person who has more than one nationality, the term 'the country of his nationality' shall mean each of the countries of which he is a national, and a person shall not be deemed to be lacking the protection of the country of his nationality if, without any valid reason based on well-founded fear, he has not availed himself of the protection of one of the countries of which he is a national.

B   (1)   For the purposes of this Convention, the words 'events occurring before 1 January 1951' in Article 1, Section A, shall be understood to mean either

(*a*)   'events occurring in Europe before 1 January 1951'; or
(*b*)   'events occurring in Europe or elsewhere before 1 January 1951', and each contracting state shall make a declaration at the time of signature, ratification or accession, specifying which of these meanings it applies for the purpose of its obligations under this Convention.

(2)   Any contracting state which has adopted alternative (*a*) may at any time extend its obligations by adopting alternative (*b*) by means of a notification addressed to the Secretary-General of the United Nations.

C   This Convention shall cease to apply to any person falling under the terms of section A if:

(1)   He has voluntarily re-availed himself of the protection of the country of his nationality; or

(2)   Having lost his nationality, he has voluntarily re-acquired it, or

(3)   He has acquired a new nationality, and enjoys the protection of the country of his new nationality; or

(4)   He has voluntarily re-established himself in the country which he left or outside which he remained owing to fear of persecution; or

(5)   He can no longer, because the circumstances in connection with which he has been recognized as a refugee have ceased to exist, continue to refuse to avail himself of the protection of the country of his nationality;
   Provided that this paragraph shall not apply to a refugee falling under section A(1) of this Article who is able to invoke compelling reasons arising out of previous persecution for refusing to avail himself of the protection of the country of nationality;

(6)   Being a person who has no nationality he is, because the circumstances in connection with which he has been recognized as a refugee have ceased to exist, able to return to the country of his former habitual residence;
   Provided that this paragraph shall not apply to a refugee falling under section A(1) of this Article who is able to invoke compelling reasons arising out of previous persecution for refusing to return to the country of his former habitual residence.

D   This Convention shall not apply to persons who are at present receiving from organs or agencies of the United Nations other than the United Nations High Commissioner for Refugees protection or assistance.
   When such protection or assistance has ceased for any reason, without the position of such persons being definitely settled in accordance with the relevant resolutions adopted by the General Assembly of the United Nations, these persons shall *ipso facto* be entitled to the benefits of this Convention.

E   This Convention shall not apply to a person who is recognized by the competent authorities of the country in which he has taken residence as having the rights and obligations which are attached to the possession of the nationality of that country.

F   The provisions of this Convention shall not apply to any person with respect to whom there are serious reasons for considering that:

(*a*) he has committed a crime against peace, a war crime, or a crime against humanity, as defined in the international instruments drawn up to make provision in respect of such crimes;

(*b*) he has committed a serious non-political crime outside the country of refuge prior to his admission to that country as a refugee;

(*c*) he has been guilty of acts contrary to the purposes and principles of the United Nations.

[C.2.3]
Article 2   General obligations
Every refugee has duties to the country in which he finds himself, which require in particular that he conform to its laws and regulations as well as to measures taken for the maintenance of public order.

[C.2.4]
Article 3   Non-discrimination
The contracting states shall apply the provisions of this Convention to refugees

without discrimination as to race, religion or country of origin.

[C.2.5]
Article 4   Religion
The contracting states shall accord to refugees within their territories treatment at least as favourable as that accorded to their nationals with respect to freedom to practise their religion and freedom as regards the religious education of their children.

[C.2.6]
Article 5   Rights granted apart from this Convention
Nothing in this Convention shall be deemed to impair any rights and benefits granted by a contracting state to refugees apart from this Convention.

[C.2.7]
Article 6   The term 'in the same circumstances'
For the purpose of this Convention, the term 'in the same circumstances' implies that any requirements (including requirements as to length and conditions of sojourn or residence) which the particular individual would have to fulfil for the enjoyment of the right in question, if he were not a refugee, must be fulfilled by him, with the exception of requirements which by their nature a refugee is incapable of fulfilling.

[C.2.8]
Article 7 Exemption from reciprocity
1   Except where this Convention contains more favourable provisions, a contracting state shall accord to refugees the same treatment as is accorded to aliens generally.

2   After a period of three years' residence, all refugees shall enjoy exemption from legislative reciprocity in the territory of the contracting states.

3   Each contracting state shall continue to accord to refugees the rights and benefits to which they were already entitled, in the absence of reciprocity, at the date of entry into force of this Convention for that state.

4   The contracting states shall consider favourably the possibility of according to refugees, in the absence of reciprocity, rights and benefits beyond those to which they are entitled according to paragraphs 2 and 3, and to extending exemption from reciprocity to refugees who do not fulfil the conditions provided for in paragraphs 2 and 3.

5   The provisions of paragraphs 2 and 3 apply both to the rights and benefits referred to in Articles 13, 18, 19, 21 and 22 of this Convention and to rights and benefits for which this Convention does not provide.

[C.2.9]
Article 8   Exemption from exceptional measures
With regard to exceptional measures which may be taken against the person, property or interests of nationals of a foreign state, the contracting states shall not apply such measures to a refugee who is formally a national of the said state solely on account of such nationality. Contracting states which, under

their legislation, are prevented from applying the general principle expressed in this Article, shall, in appropriate cases, grant exemptions in favour of such refugees.

[C.2.10]
Article 9   Provisional measures
Nothing in this Convention shall prevent a contracting state, in time of war or other grave and exceptional circumstances, from taking provisionally measures which it considers to be essential to the national security in the case of a particular person, pending a determination by the contracting state that that person is in fact a refugee and that the continuance of such measures is necessary in his case in the interests of national security.

[C.2.11]
Article 10   Continuity of residence
1   Where a refugee has been forcibly displaced during the Second World War and removed to the territory of a contracting state, and is resident there, the period of such enforced sojourn shall be considered to have been lawful residence within that territory.

2   Where a refugee has been forcibly displaced during the Second World War from the territory of a contracting state and has, prior to the date of entry into force of this Convention, returned there for the purpose of taking up residence, the period of residence before and after such enforced displacement shall be regarded as one uninterrupted period for any purposes for which uninterrupted residence is required.

[C.2.12]
Article 11   Refugee seamen
In the case of refugees regularly serving as crew members on board a ship flying the flag of a contracting state, that state shall give sympathetic consideration to their establishment on its territory and the issue of travel documents to them or their temporary admission to its territory particularly with a view to facilitating their establishment in another country.

CHAPTER II   JURIDICAL STATUS

[C.2.13]
Article 12   Personal status
1   The personal status of a refugee shall be governed by the law of the country of his domicile or, if he has no domicile, by the law of the country of his residence.

2   Rights previously acquired by a refugee and dependent on personal status, more particularly rights attaching to marriage, shall be respected by a contracting state, subject to compliance, if this be necessary, with the formalities required by the law of that state, provided that the right in question is one which would have been recognized by the law of that state had he not become a refugee.

[C.2.14]
Article 13   Movable and immovable property
The contracting states shall accord to a refugee treatment as favourable as possible and, in any event, not less favourable than that accorded to aliens generally in the same circumstances, as regards the acquisition of movable and immovable property and other rights pertaining thereto, and to leases and other contracts relating to movable and immovable property.

[C.2.15]
Article 14   Artistic rights and industrial property
In respect of the protection of industrial property, such as inventions, designs or models, trade marks, trade names, and of rights in literary, artistic and scientific works, a refugee shall be accorded in the country in which he has his habitual residence the same protection as is accorded to nationals of that country. In the territory of any other contracting state, he shall be accorded the same protection as is accorded in that territory to nationals of the country in which he has his habitual residence.

[C.2.16]
Article 15 Right of association
As regards non-political and non-profit-making associations and trade unions the contracting states shall accord to refugees lawfully staying in their territory the most favourable treatment accorded to nationals of a foreign country, in the same circumstances.

[C.2.17]
Article 16 Access to courts
1   A refugee shall have free access to the courts of law on the territory of all contracting states.

2   A refugee shall enjoy in the contracting state in which he has his habitual residence the same treatment as a national in matters pertaining to access to the Courts, including legal assistance and exemption from *cautio judicatum solvi*.

3   A refugee shall be accorded in the matters referred to in paragraph 2 in countries other than that in which he has his habitual residence the treatment granted to a national of the country of his habitual residence.

CHAPTER III GAINFUL EMPLOYMENT

[C.2.18]
Article 17 Wage-earning employment
1   The contracting state shall accord to refugees lawfully staying in their territory the most favourable treatment accorded to nationals of a foreign country in the same circumstances, as regards the right to engage in wage-earning employment.

2   In any case, restrictive measures imposed on aliens or the employment of aliens for the protection of the national labour market shall not be applied to a

refugee who was already exempt from them at the date of entry into force of this Convention for the contracting state concerned, or who fulfils one of the following conditions:

(*a*) He has completed three years' residence in the country,

(*b*) He has a spouse possessing the nationality of the country of residence. A refugee may not invoke the benefits of this provision if he has abandoned his spouse,

(*c*) He has one or more children possessing the nationality of the country of residence.

3 The contracting states shall give sympathetic consideration to assimilating the rights of all refugees with regard to wage-earning employment to those of nationals, and in particular of those refugees who have entered their territory pursuant to programmes of labour recruitment or under immigration schemes.

[C.2.19]
Article 18 Self-employment
The contracting states shall accord to a refugee lawfully in their territory treatment as favourable as possible and, in any event, not less favourable than that accorded to aliens generally in the same circumstances, as regards the right to engage on his own account in agriculture, industry, handicrafts and commerce and to establish commercial and industrial companies.

[C.2.20]
Article 19 Liberal professions
1 Each contracting state shall accord to refugees lawfully staying in their territory who hold diplomas recognized by the competent authorities of that state, and who are desirous of practising a liberal profession, treatment as favourable as possible and, in any event, not less favourable than that accorded to aliens generally in the same circumstances.

2 The contracting states shall use their best endeavours consistently with their laws and constitutions to secure the settlement of such refugees in the territories, other than the metropolitan territory, for whose international relations they are responsible.

CHAPTER IV WELFARE

[C.2.21]
Article 20 Rationing
Where a rationing system exists, which applies to the population at large and regulates the general distribution of products in short supply, refugees shall be accorded the same treatment as nationals.

[C.2.22]
Article 21 Housing
As regards housing, the contracting states, in so far as the matter is regulated by laws or regulations or is subject to the control of public authorities, shall

accord to refugees lawfully staying in their territory treatment as favourable as possible and, in any event, not less favourable than that accorded to aliens generally in the same circumstances.

[C.2.23]
Article 22   Public education
1   The contracting states shall accord to refugees the same treatment as is accorded to nationals with respect to elementary education.

2   The contracting states shall accord to refugees treatment as favourable as possible, and, in any event, not less favourable than that accorded to aliens generally in the same circumstances, with respect to education other than elementary education and, in particular, as regards access to studies, the recognition of foreign school certificates, diplomas and degrees, the remission of fees and charges and the award of scholarships.

[C.2.24]
Article 23   Public relief
The contracting states shall accord to refugees lawfully staying in their territory the same treatment with respect to public relief and assistance as is accorded to their nationals.

[C.2.25]
Article 24   Labour legislation and social security
1   The contracting states shall accord to refugees lawfully staying in their territory the same treatment as is accorded to nationals in respect of the following matters:

(*a*)   In so far as such matters are governed by laws or regulations or are subject to the control of administrative authorities: remuneration, including family allowances where these form part of remuneration, hours of work, overtime arrangements, holidays with pay, restrictions on home work, minimum age of employment, apprenticeship and training, women's work and the work of young persons, and the enjoyment of the benefits of collective bargaining;

(*b*)   Social security (legal provisions in respect of employment injury, occupational diseases, maternity, sickness, disability, old age, death, unemployment, family responsibilities and any other contingency which, according to national laws or regulations, is covered by a social security scheme), subject to the following limitations:

    (i)   There may be appropriate arrangements for the maintenance of acquired rights and rights in course of acquisition;

    (ii)   National laws or regulations of the country of residence may prescribe special arrangements concerning benefits or portions of benefits which are payable wholly out of public funds, and concerning allowances paid to persons who do not fulfil the contribution conditions prescribed for the award of a normal pension.

2   The right to compensation for the death of a refugee resulting from employment injury or from occupational disease shall not be affected by the

fact that the residence of the beneficiary is outside the territory of the contracting state.

3 The contracting states shall extend to refugees the benefits of agreements concluded between them, or which may be concluded between them in the future, concerning the maintenance of acquired rights and rights in the process of acquisition in regard to social security, subject only to the conditions which apply to nationals of the states signatory to the agreements in question.

4 The contracting states will give sympathetic consideration to extending to refugees so far as possible the benefits of similar agreements which may at any time be in force between such contracting states and non-contracting states.

CHAPTER V ADMINISTRATIVE MEASURES

[C.2.26]
Article 25   Administrative assistance
1 When the exercise of a right by a refugee would normally require the assistance of authorities of a foreign country to whom he cannot have recourse, the contracting states in whose territory he is residing shall arrange that such assistance be afforded to him by their own authorities or by an international authority.

2 The authority or authorities mentioned in paragraph 1 shall deliver or cause to be delivered under their supervision to refugees such documents or certifications as would normally be delivered to aliens by or through their national authorities.

3 Documents or certifications so delivered shall stand in the stead or the official instruments delivered to aliens by or through their national authorities, and shall be given credence in the absence of proof to the contrary.

4 Subject to such exceptional treatment as may be granted to indigent persons, fees may be charged for the services mentioned herein, but such fees shall be moderate and commensurate with those charged to nationals for similar services.

5 The provisions of this Article shall be without prejudice to Articles 27 and 28.

[C.2.27]
Article 26   Freedom of movement
Each contracting state shall accord to refugees lawfully in its territory the right to choose their place of residence and to move freely within its territory, subject to any regulations applicable to aliens generally in the same circumstances.

[C.2.28]
Article 27   Identity papers
The contracting states shall issue identity papers to any refugee in their territory who does not possess a valid travel document.

[C.2.29]
Article 28   Travel documents
1   The contracting states shall issue to refugees lawfully staying in their territory travel documents for the purpose of travel outside their territory unless compelling reasons of national security or public order otherwise require, and the provisions of the Schedule to this Convention shall apply with respect to such documents. The contracting states may issue such a travel document to any other refugee in their territory, they shall in particular give sympathetic consideration to the issue of such a travel document to refugees in their territory who are unable to obtain a travel document from the country of their lawful residence.

2   Travel documents issued to refugees under previous international agreements by parties thereto shall be recognized and treated by the contracting states in the same way as if they had been issued pursuant to this article.

[C.2.30]
Article 29   Fiscal charges
1   The contracting states shall not impose upon refugees duties, charges or taxes, of any description whatsoever, other or higher than those which are or may be levied on their nationals in similar situations.

2   Nothing in the above paragraph shall prevent the application to refugees of the laws and regulations concerning charges in respect of the issue to aliens of administrative documents including identity papers.

[C.2.31]
Article 30   Transfer of assets
1   A contracting state shall, in conformity with its laws and regulations, permit refugees to transfer assets which they have brought into its territory, to another country where they have been admitted for the purposes of resettlement.

2   A contracting state shall give sympathetic consideration to the application of refugees for permission to transfer assets wherever they may be and which are necessary for their resettlement in another country to which they have been admitted.

[C.2.32]
Article 31 Refugees unlawfully in the country of refuge
1   The contracting states shall not impose penalties, on account of their illegal entry or presence, on refugees who, coming directly from a territory where their life or freedom was threatened in the sense of Article 1, enter or are present in their territory without authorisation, provided they present themselves without delay to the authorities and show good cause for their illegal entry or presence.

2   The contracting states shall not apply to the movements of such refugees restrictions other than those which are necessary and such restrictions shall only be applied until their status in the country is regularised or they obtain admission into another country. The contracting states shall allow such

refugees a reasonable period and all the necessary facilities to obtain admission into another country.

[C.2.33]
Article 32   Expulsion

1   The contracting states shall not expel a refugee lawfully in their territory save on grounds of national security or public order.

2   The expulsion of such a refugee shall be only in pursuance of a decision reached in accordance with due process of law. Except where compelling reasons of national security otherwise require, the refugee shall be allowed to submit evidence to clear himself, and to appeal to and be represented for the purpose before competent authority or a person or persons specially designated by the competent authority.

3   The contracting states shall allow such a refugee a reasonable period within which to seek legal admission into another country. The contracting states reserve the right to apply during that period such internal measures as they may deem necessary.

[C.2.34]
Article 33   Prohibition of expulsion or return ('refoulement')

1   No contracting state shall expel or return ('refouler') a refugee in any manner whatsoever to the frontiers of territories where his life or freedom would be threatened on account of his race, religion, nationality, membership of a particular social group or political opinion.

2   The benefit of the present provision may not, however, be claimed by a refugee whom there are reasonable grounds for regarding as a danger to the security of the country in which he is, or who, having been convicted by a final judgment of a particularly serious crime, constitutes a danger to the community of that country.

[C.2.35]
Article 34   Naturalisation

The contracting states shall as far as possible facilitate the assimilation and naturalisation of refugees. They shall in particular make every effort to expedite naturalisation proceedings and to reduce as far as possible the charges and costs of such proceedings.

CHATER VI EXECUTORY AND TRANSITORY PROVISIONS

[C.2.36]
Article 35   Co-operation of the national authorities with the United Nations

1   The contracting states undertake to co-operate with the Office of the United Nations High Commissioner for Refugees, or any other agency of the United Nations which may succeed it, in the exercise of its functions, and shall

in particular facilitate its duty of supervising the application of the provisions of this Convention.

2   In order to enable the Office of the High Commissioner or any other agency of the United Nations which may succeed it, to make reports to the competent organs of the United Nations, the contracting states undertake to provide them in the appropriate form with information and statistical data requested concerning:

(*a*) the condition of refugees,
(*b*) the implementation of this Convention, and
(*c*) laws, regulations and decrees which are, or may hereafter be, in force relating to refugees.

[C.2.37]
Article 36   Information on national legislation
The contracting states shall communicate to the Secretary-General of the United Nations the laws and regulations which they may adopt to ensure the application of this Convention.

[C.2.38]
Article 37   Relation to previous Conventions
Without prejudice to Article 28, paragraph 2, of this Convention, this Convention replaces, as between parties to it, the Arrangements of 5 July 1922, 31 May 1924, 12 May 1926, 30 June 1928 and 30 July 1935, the Conventions of 28 October 1933 and 10 February 1938, the Protocol of 14 September 1939 and the Agreement of 15 October 1946.

CHAPTER VII FINAL CLAUSES

[C.2.39]
Article 38   Settlement of disputes
Any dispute between parties to this Convention relating to its interpretation or application, which cannot be settled by other means, shall be referred to the International Court of Justice at the request of any one of the parties to the dispute.

[C.2.40]
Article 39   Signature, ratification and accession
1   This Convention shall be opened for signature at Geneva on 28 July 1951 and shall thereafter be deposited with the Secretary-General of the United Nations. It shall be open for signature at the European Office of the United Nations from 28 July to 31 August 1951 and shall be re-opened for signature at the Headquarters of the United Nations from 17 September 1951 to 31 December 1952.

2   This Convention shall be open for signature on behalf of all states members of the United Nations, and also on behalf of any other state invited to

attend the Conference of Plenipotentiaries on the Status of Refugees and Stateless Persons or to which an invitation to sign will have been addressed by the General Assembly. It shall be ratified and the instruments of ratification shall be deposited with the Secretary-General of the United Nations.

3   This Convention shall be open from 28 July 1951 for accession by the states referred to in paragraph 2 of this Article. Accession shall be effected by the deposit of an instrument of accession with the Secretary-General of the United Nations.

[C.2.41]
Article 40   Territorial application clause
1   Any state may, at the time of signature, ratification or accession, declare that this Convention shall extend to all or any of the territories for the international relations of which it is responsible. Such a declaration shall take effect when the Convention enters into force for the state concerned.

2   At any time thereafter any such extension shall be made by notification addressed to the Secretary-General of the United Nations and shall take effect as from the ninetieth day after the day of receipt by the Secretary-General of the United Nations of this notification, or as from the date of entry into force of the Convention for the state concerned, whichever is the later.

3   With respect to those territories to which this Convention is not extended at the time of signature, ratification or accession, each state concerned shall consider the possibility of taking the necessary steps in order to extend the application of this Convention to such territories, subject, where necessary for constitutional reasons, to the consent of the governments of such territories.

[C.2.42]
Article 41   Federal clause
In the case of a federal or non-unitary state, the following provisions shall apply:

(*a*) With respect to those Articles of this Convention that come within the legislative jurisdiction of the federal legislative authority, the obligations of the Federal Government shall to this extent be the same as those of Parties which are not federal states,

(*b*) With respect to those Articles of this Convention that come within the legislative jurisdiction of constituent states, provinces or cantons which are not, under the constitutional system of the federation, bound to take legislative action, the Federal Government shall bring such Articles with a favourable recommendation to the notice of the appropriate authorities of states, provinces or cantons at the earliest possible moment.

(*c*) A federal state party to this Convention shall, at the request of any other contracting state transmitted through the Secretary-General of the United Nations, supply a statement of the law and practice of the Federation and its constituent units in regard to any particular provision of the Convention showing the extent to which effect has been given to that provision by legislative or other action.

[C.2.43]
Article 42 Reservations

1   At the time of signature, ratification or accession, any state may make reservations to articles of the Convention other than to Articles 1, 3, 4, 16(1), 33, 36–46 inclusive.

2   Any state making a reservation in accordance with paragraph 1 of this article may at any time withdraw the reservation by a communication to that effect addressed to the Secretary-General of the United Nations.

[C.2.44]
Article 43 Entry into force

1   This Convention shall come into force on the ninetieth day following the day of deposit of the sixth instrument of ratification or accession.

2   For each state ratifying or acceding to the Convention after the deposit of the sixth instrument of ratification or accession, the Convention shall enter into force on the ninetieth day following the date of deposit by such state of its instrument of ratification or accession.

[C.2.45]
Article 44 Denunciation

1   Any contracting state may denounce this Convention at any time by a notification addressed to the Secretary-General of the United Nations.

2   Such denunciation shall take effect for the contracting state concerned one year from the date upon which it is received by the Secretary-General of the United Nations.

3   Any state which has made a declaration or notification under Article 40 may, at any time thereafter, by a notification to the Secretary-General of the United Nations, declare that the Convention shall cease to extend to such territory one year after the date of receipt of the notification by the Secretary-General.

[C.2.46]
Article 45 Revision

1   Any contracting state may request revision of this Convention at any time by a notification addressed to the Secretary-General of the United Nations.
2   The General Assembly of the United Nations shall recommend the steps, if any, to be taken in respect of such request.

[C.2.47]
Article 46 Notifications by the Secretary-General of the United Nations

The Secretary-General of the United Nations shall inform all Members of the United Nations and non-member states referred to in Article 39:

(*a*) of declarations and notifications in accordance with Section B of Article 1;
(*b*) of signatures, ratifications and accessions in accordance with Article 39;
(*c*) of declarations and notifications in accordance with Article 40;

(*d*) of reservations and withdrawals in accordance with Article 42;

(*e*) of the date on which this Convention will come into force in accordance with Article 43;

(*f*) of denunciations and notifications in accordance with Article 44;

(*g*) of requests for revision in accordance with Article 45.

In Faith Whereof the undersigned, duly authorized, have signed this Convention on behalf of their respective Governments,

DONE at Geneva, this twenty-eighth day of July, one thousand nine hundred and fifty-one, in a single copy, of which the English and French texts are equally authentic and which shall remain deposited in the archives of the United Nations, and certified true copies of which shall be delivered to all Members of the United Nations and to the non-member states referred to in Article 39.

SCHEDULE

[C.2.48]
Paragraph 1
1   The travel document referred to in Article 28 of this Convention shall be similar to the specimen annexed hereto.

2   The document shall be made out in at least two languages, one of which shall be English or French.

[C.2.49]
Paragraph 2
Subject to the regulations obtaining in the country of issue, children may be included in the travel document of a parent or, in exceptional circumstances, of another adult refugee.

[C.2.50]
Paragraph 3
The fees charged for issue of the document shall not exceed the lowest scale of charges for national passports.

[C.2.51]
Paragraph 4
Save in special or exceptional cases, the document shall be made valid for the largest possible number of countries.

[C.2.52]
Paragraph 5
The document shall have a validity of either one or two years, at the discretion of the issuing authority.

[C.2.53]

Paragraph 6

1 The renewal or extension of the validity of the document is a matter for the authority which issued it, so long as the holder has not established lawful residence in another territory and resides lawfully in the territory of the said authority. The issue of a new document is, under the same conditions, a matter for the authority which issued the former document.

2 Diplomatic or consular authorities, specially authorised for the purpose, shall be empowered to extend, for a period not exceeding six months, the validity of travel documents issued by their Governments.

3 The contracting states shall give sympathetic consideration to renewing or extending the validity of travel documents or issuing new documents to refugees no longer lawfully resident in their territory who are unable to obtain a travel document from the country of their lawful residence.

[C.2.54]

Paragraph 7

The contracting states shall recognise the validity of the documents issued in accordance with the provisions of Article 28 of this Convention.

[C.2.55]

Paragraph 8

The competent authorities of the country to which the refugee desires to proceed shall, if they are prepared to admit him and if a visa is required, affix a visa on the document of which he is the holder.

[C.2.56]

Paragraph 9

1 The contracting states undertake to issue transit visas to refugees who have obtained visas for a territory of final destination.

2 The issue of such visas may be refused on grounds which would justify refusal of a visa to any alien.

[C.2.57]

Paragraph 10

The fees for the issue of exit, entry or transit visas shall not exceed the lowest scale of charges for visas on foreign passports.

[C.2.58]

Paragraph 11

When a refugee has lawfully taken up residence in the territory of another contracting state, the responsibility for the issue of a new document, under the terms and conditions of Article 28, shall be that of the competent authority of that territory, to which the refugee shall be entitled to apply.

[C.2.59]
Paragraph 12
The authority issuing a new document shall withdraw the old document and shall return it to the country of issue, if it is stated in the document that it should be so returned; otherwise it shall withdraw and cancel the document.

[C.2.60]
Paragraph 13
1   Each contracting state undertakes that the holder of a travel document issued by it in accordance with Article 28 of this Convention shall be re-admitted to its territory at any time during the period of its validity.

2   Subject to the provisions of the preceding sub-paragraph, a contracting state may require the holder of the document to comply with such formalities as may be prescribed in regard to exit from or return to its territory.

3   The contracting states reserve the right, in exceptional cases, or in cases where the refugee's stay is authorised for a specific period, when issuing the document, to limit the period during which the refugee may return to a period of not less than three months.

[C.2.61]
Paragraph 14
Subject only to the terms of paragraph 13, the provisions of this Schedule in no way affect the laws and regulations governing the conditions of admission to, transit through, residence and establishment in, and departure from, the territories of the contracting states.

[C.2.62]
Paragraph 15
Neither the issue of the document nor the entries made thereon determine or affect the status of the holder, particularly as regards nationality.

[C.2.63]
Paragraph 16
The issue of the document does not in any way entitle the holder to the protection of the diplomatic or consular authorities of the country of issue, and does not confer on these authorities a right of protection.

ANNEX

Specimen Travel Document

[C.2.64]
The document will be in booklet form (approximately 15 × 10 centimetres).

It is recommended that it be so printed that any erasure or alteration by chemical or other means can be readily detected, and that the words

'Convention of 28 July 1951' be printed in continuous repetition on each page, in the language of the issuing country.

(Cover of booklet)
TRAVEL DOCUMENT
(Convention of 28 July 1951)

No............................

(1)
TRAVEL DOCUMENT
(Convention of 28 July 1951)

This document expires on...
unless its validity is extended or renewed.
Name ....
Forename(s) ....
Accompanied by .... child (children)

1.   This document is issued solely with a view to providing the holder with a travel document which can serve in lieu of a national passport. It is without prejudice to and in no way affects the holder's nationality.

2.   The holder is authorized to return to ....
.........................[state here the country whose authorities are issuing the document] on or before .... unless   some later date is hereafter specified.
[The period during which the holder is allowed to return must not be less than three months]

3.   Should the holder take up residence in a country other than that which issued the present document, he must, if he wishes to travel again, apply to the competent authorities of his country of residence for a new document. [The old travel document shall be withdrawn by the authority issuing the new document and returned to the authority which issued it.][1]

(This document contains . . . . pages, exclusive of cover.)

---

[1]The sentence in brackets to be inserted by Governments which so desire.

---

(2)
Place and date of birth ....
Occupation ....
Present residence ....
*Maiden name and forename(s) of wife ....
....
*Name of forename(s) of husband ....
....

Description

Height ....
Hair ....
Colour of eyes ....
Nose ....
Shape of face ....
Complexion ....
Special peculiarities ....

Children accompanying holder

Name	Forename(s)	Place and date of birth	Sex

....
....
....
....

*Strike out whichever does not apply.
(This document contains . . . . . .pages, exclusive of cover.)

---

(3)

**Photograph of holder and stamp of issuing authority
Finger-prints of holder (if required)**

Signature of holder ....
(This document contains . . . . . . pages, exclusive of cover.)

---

(4)

1. This document is valid for the following countries:
....
....
....
....

2. Document or documents on the basis of which the present document is issued:
....
....
....

Issued at ....
Date ....

Signature and stamp of authority
issuing the document

Fee paid:

(This document contains . . . . . . pages, exclusive of cover.)

---

(5)

Extension or renewal of validity

Fee paid: From ....
                                       To ....
Done at ....   Date ....

Signature and stamp of authority
extending or renewing the validity
of the document:

Extension or renewal of validity

Fee paid: From ....
                                       To ....

Done at.. Date ....

Signature and stamp of authority

extending or renewing the validity

of the document:

(This document contains . . . . . . pages, exclusive of cover.)

---

(6)

Extension or renewal of validity

Fee paid: From ....

To ....

Done at .... Date ....

Signature and stamp of authority

extending or renewing the validity

of the document:

Extension or renewal of validity

Fee paid: From ....

To ....

Done at .... Date ....

Signature and stamp of authority

extending or renewing the validity

of the document:

(This document contains . . . . . . pages, exclusive of cover.)

(7–32)

Visas

The name of the holder of the document must be repeated in each visa.

(This document contains . . . . . . pages, exclusive of cover.)

APPENDIX   FINAL ACT OF THE 1951 UNITED NATIONS CONFER-
ENCE OF PLENIPOTENTIARIES ON THE STATUS OF REFUGEES AND
STATELESS PERSONS

[C.2.65]
1   The General Assembly of the United Nations, by Resolution 429(V) of 14
December 1950, decided to convene in Geneva a Conference of
Plenipotentiaries to complete the drafting of, and to sign, a Convention relat-
ing to the Status of Refugees and a Protocol relating to the Status of Stateless
Persons.

The Conference met at the European Office of the United Nations in Geneva
from 2 to 25 July 1951.

The Governments of the following twenty-six states were represented by
delegates who all submitted satisfactory credentials or other communications
of appointment authorizing them to participate in the Conference:

Australia	Italy
Austria	Luxembourg
Belgium	Monaco
Brazil	Netherlands
Canada	Norway
Colombia	Sweden
Denmark	Switzerland (the Swiss delegation
Egypt	also represented Liechtenstein)
France	Turkey
Germany, Federal Republic of	United Kingdom of Great Britain
Greece	and Northern Ireland
Holy See	United States of America
Iraq	Venezuela
Israel	Yugoslavia

The Governments of the following two states were represented by observers

Cuba
Iran

Pursuant to the request of the General Assembly, the United Nations High
Commissioner for Refugees participated, without the right to vote, in the
deliberations of the Conference.

The International Labour Organisation and the International Refugee
Organization were represented at the Conference without the right to vote.

The Conference invited a representative of the Council of Europe to be represented at the Conference without the right to vote.

Representatives of the following Non-Governmental Organizations in consultative relationship with the Economic and Social Council were also present
as observers:

Category A
International Confederation of Free Trade Unions
International Federation of Christian Trade Unions
Inter-Parliamentary Union

Category B
  Agudas Israel World Organization
  Caritas Internationalis
  Catholic International Union for Social Service
  Commission of the Churches on International Affairs
  Consultative Council of Jewish Organizations
  Co-ordinating Board of Jewish Organizations
  Friends' World Committee for Consultation
  International Association of Penal Law
  International Bureau for the Unification of Penal Law
  International Committee of the Red Cross
  International Council of Women
  International Federation of Friends of Young Women
  International League for the Rights of Man
  International Social Service
  International Union for Child Welfare
  International Union of Catholic Women's Leagues
  Pax Romana
  Women's International League for Peace and Freedom
  World Jewish Congress
  World Union for Progressive Judaism
  World Young Women's Christian Association

Register
  International Relief Committee for Intellectual Workers
  League of Red Cross Societies
  Standing Conference of Voluntary Agencies
  World Association of Girl Guides and Girl Scouts
  World University Service

Representatives of Non-Governmental Organizations which have been granted consultative status by the Economic and Social Council as well as those entered by the Secretary-General on the Register referred to in Resolution 288 B(X) of the Economic and Social Council, paragraph 17, had under the rules of procedure adopted by the Conference the right to submit written or oral statements to the Conference.

The Conference elected Mr. Knud Larsen, of Denmark, as President, and Mr A Herment, of Belgium, and Mr Talat Miras, of Turkey, as Vice-Presidents.

At its second meeting, the Conference, acting on a proposal of the representative of Egypt, unanimously decided to address an invitation to the Holy See to designate a plenipotentiary representative to participate in its work. A representative of the Holy See took his place at the Conference on 10 July 1951.

The Conference adopted as its agenda the Provisional Agenda drawn up by the Secretary-General (A/CONF 2/2/Rev 1). It also adopted the Provisional Rules of Procedure drawn up by the Secretary-General, with the addition of a provision which authorized a representative of the Council of Europe to be present at the Conference without the right to vote and to submit proposals (A/CONF 2/3/Rev 1).

[C.2.66]
In accordance with the Rules of Procedure of the Conference, the President and Vice-Presidents examined the credentials of representatives and on 17 July

1951 reported to the Conference the results of such examination, the Conference adopting the report.

The Conference used as the basis of its discussions the draft Convention relating to the Status of Refugees and the draft Protocol relating to the Status of Stateless Persons prepared by the *ad hoc* Committee on Refugees and Stateless Persons at its second session held in Geneva from 14 to 25 August 1950, with the exception of the preamble and Article 1 (Definition of the term 'refugee') of the draft Convention. The text of the preamble before the Conference was that which was adopted by the Economic and Social Council on 11 August 1950 in Resolution 319 B II(XI). The text of Article 1 before the Conference was that recommended by the General Assembly on 14 December 1950 and contained in the Annex to Resolution 429(V). The latter was a modification of the text as it had been adopted by the Economic and Social Council in Resolution 319 B II(XI)[1].

The Conference adopted the Convention relating to the Status of Refugees in two readings. Prior to its second reading it established a Style Committee composed of the President and the representatives of Belgium, France, Israel, Italy, the United Kingdom of Great Britain and Northern Ireland and the United States of America, together with the High Commissioner for Refugees, which elected as its Chairman Mr. G. Warren, of the United States of America. The Style Committee re-drafted the text which had been adopted by the Conference on first reading, particularly from the point of view of language and of concordance between the English and French texts.

The Convention was adopted on 25 July by 24 votes to none with no abstentions and opened for signature at the European Office of the United Nations from 28 July to 31 August 1951. It will be re-opened for signature at the permanent headquarters of the United Nations in New York from 17 September 1951 to 31 December 1952.

The English and French texts of the Convention, which are equally authentic, are appended to this Final Act.

---

1   The texts referred to in the paragraph above are contained in document A/CONF 2/1.

[C.2.67]
II   The Conference decided, by 17 votes to 3 with 3 abstentions, that the titles of the chapters and of the articles of the Convention are included for practical purposes and do not constitute an element of interpretation.

[C.2.68]
III   With respect to the draft Protocol relating to the Status of Stateless Persons, the Conference adopted the following resolution:

The Conference,

Having considered the draft Protocol relating to the Status of Stateless Persons,

Considering that the subject still requires more detailed study,

Decides not to take a decision on the subject at the present Conference and refers the draft Protocol back to the appropriate organs of the United Nations for further study.

[C.2.69]
IV   The Conference adopted unanimously the following recommendations:

A
(Facilitation of refugee travels)[1]

The Conference,

Considering that the issue and recognition of travel documents is necessary to facilitate the movement of refugees, and in particular their resettlement,

Urges Governments which are parties to the Inter-Governmental Agreement on Refugee Travel Documents signed in London on 15 October 1946, or which recognize travel documents issued in accordance with the Agreement, to continue to issue or to recognize such travel documents, and to extend the issue of such documents to refugees as defined in Article 1 of the Convention relating to the Status of Refugees or to recognize the travel documents so issued to such persons, until they shall have undertaken obligations under Article 28 of the said Convention.

---

1   Headline added.

B
(Principle of unity of the family)[1]

The Conference,

Considering that the unity of the family, the natural and fundamental group unit of society, is an essential right of the refugee, and that such unity is constantly threatened, and

Noting with satisfaction that, according to the official commentary of the *ad hoc* Committee on Statelessness and Related Problems (E/1618, p. 40) the rights granted to a refugee are extended to members of his family,

Recommends Governments to take the necessary measures for the protection of the refugee's family, especially with a view to:

(1) Ensuring that the unity of the refugee's family is maintained particularly in cases where the head of the family has fulfilled the necessary conditions for admission to a particular country,
(2) The protection of refugees who are minors, in particular unaccompanied children and girls, with special reference to guardianship and adoption.

---

1   Headline added.

C
(Welfare services)[1]

The Conference,
Considering that, in the moral, legal and material spheres, refugees need the help of suitable welfare services, especially that of appropriate non-governmental organizations,

Recommends Governments and inter-governmental bodies to facilitate, encourage and sustain the efforts of properly qualified organizations.

---

1   Headline added.

D
(International co-operation in the field of asylum and resettlement)[1]

The Conference,

Considering that many persons still leave their country of origin for reasons of persecution and are entitled to special protection on account of their position,

Recommends that Governments continue to receive refugees in their territories and that they act in concert in a true spirit of international co-operation in order that these refugees may find asylum and the possibility of resettlement.

E
(Extension of treatment provided by the Convention)[1]

The Conference,

Expresses the hope that the Convention relating to the Status of Refugees will have value as an example exceeding its contractual scope and that all nations will be guided by it in granting so far as possible to persons in their territory as refugees and who would not be covered by the terms of the Convention, the treatment for which it provides.

In Witness Whereof the President, Vice-Presidents and the Executive Secretary of the Conference have signed this Final Act.

Done at Geneva this twenty-eighth day of July one thousand nine hundred and fifty-one in a single copy in the English and French languages, each text being equally authentic. Translations of this Final Act into Chinese, Russian and Spanish will be prepared by the Secretary-General of the United Nations, who will, on request, send copies thereof to each of the Governments invited to attend the Conference.

The President of the Conference: Knud Larsen

The Vice-Presidents of the Conference: A Herment
                                                                                    Talat Miras

The Executive Secretary of the Conference: John P Humphrey

PROTOCOL RELATING TO THE STATUS OF REFUGEES OF 31 JANUARY 1967

Entry into force   4 October 1967, in accordance with Article VIII
Text   United Nations Treaty Series No 8791, Vol 606, p 267

[C.2.70]
The States Parties to the present Protocol,

Considering that the Convention relating to the Status of Refugees done at Geneva on 28 July 1951 (hereinafter referred to as the Convention) covers only those persons who have become refugees as a result of events occurring before 1 January, 1951,

Considering that new refugee situations have arisen since the Convention was adopted and that the refugees concerned may therefore not fall within the scope of the Convention,

Considering that it is desirable that equal status should be enjoyed by all refugees covered by the definition in the Convention irrespective of the date-line 1 January 1951,

Have agreed as follows:

[C.2.71]
Article I   General provision
1   The states parties to the present Protocol undertake to apply Articles 2 to 34 inclusive of the Convention to refugees as hereinafter defined.

2   For the purpose of the present Protocol, the term 'refugee' shall, except as regards the application of paragraph 3 of this Article, mean any person within the definition of Article 1 of the Convention as if the words 'As a result of events occurring before 1 January 1951 and ...' and the words '... as a result of such events', in Article 1 A (2) were omitted.

3   The present Protocol shall be applied by the states parties hereto without any geographic limitation, save that existing declarations made by states already Parties to the Convention in accordance with Article 1 B (1)(*a*) of the Convention, shall, unless extended under Article 1 B (2) thereof, apply also under the present Protocol.

---

1 The Protocol was signed by the President of the General Assembly and by the Secretary-General on 31 January 1967. The text of the General Assembly Resolution 2198 (XXI) of 16 December 1966 concerning the accession to the 1967 Protocol relating to the Status of Refugees is reproduced in Appendix.

[C.2.72]
Article II   Co-operation of the national authorities with the United Nations
1   The states parties to the present Protocol undertake to co-operate with the Office of the United Nations High Commissioner for Refugees, or any other

agency of the United Nations which may succeed it, in the exercise of its functions, and shall in particular facilitate its duty of supervising the application of the provisions of the present Protocol.

2   In order to enable the Office of the High Commissioner, or any other agency of the United Nations which may succeed it, to make reports to the competent organs of the United Nations, the states parties to the present Protocol undertake to provide them with the information and statistical data requested, in the appropriate form, concerning:

(*a*) The condition of refugees;
(*b*) The implementation of the present Protocol;
(*c*) Laws, regulations and decrees which are, or may hereafter be, in force relating to refugees.

[C.2.73]
Article III   Information on national legislation

The states parties to the present Protocol shall communicate to the Secretary-General of the United Nations the laws and regulations which they may adopt to ensure the application of the present Protocol.

[C.2.74]
Article IV   Settlement of disputes

Any dispute between states parties to the present Protocol which relates to its interpretation or application and which cannot be settled by other means shall be referred to the International Court of Justice at the request of any one of the parties to the dispute.

[C.2.75]
Article V   Accession

The present Protocol shall be open for accession on behalf of all states parties to the Convention and of any other State Member of the United Nations or member of any of the specialized agencies or to which an invitation to accede may have been addressed by the General Assembly of the United Nations. Accession shall be effected by the deposit of an instrument of accession with the Secretary-General of the United Nations.

[C.2.76]
Article VI   Federal clause

In the case of a federal or non-unitary state, the following provisions shall apply:

(*a*) With respect to those articles of the Convention to be applied in accordance with Article 1, paragraph 1, of the present Protocol that come within the legislative jurisdiction of the federal legislative authority, the obligations of the Federal Government shall to this extent be the same as those of states parties which are not federal states;

(*b*) With respect to those articles of the Convention to be applied in accordance with Article I, paragraph 1, of the present Protocol that come within the legislative jurisdiction of constituent states, provinces or cantons which are not, under the constitutional system of the federation, bound to take legislative action, the Federal Government shall bring such articles with a favourable recommendation to the notice of the appropriate authorities of states, provinces or cantons at the earliest possible moment;

(*c*) A Federal State Party to the present Protocol shall, at the request of any other state party hereto transmitted through the Secretary-General of the United Nations, supply a statement of the law and practice of the Federation and its constituent units in regard to any particular provision of the Convention to be applied in accordance with Article I, paragraph 1, of the present Protocol, showing the extent to which effect has been given to that provision by legislative or other action.

[C.2.77]
Article VII   Reservations and declarations
1   At the time of accession, any state may make reservations in respect of Article IV of the present Protocol and in respect of the application in accordance with Article I of the present Protocol of any provisions of the Convention other than those contained in Articles 1, 3, 4, 16(1) and 33 thereof, provided that in the case of a state party to the Convention reservations made under this Article shall not extend to refugees in respect of whom the Convention applies.

2   Reservations made by states parties to the Convention in accordance with Article 42 thereof shall, unless withdrawn, be applicable in relation to their obligations under the present Protocol.

3   Any state making a reservation in accordance with paragraph 1 of this Article may at any time withdraw such reservation by a communication to that effect addressed to the Secretary-General of the United Nations.

4   Declarations made under Article 40, paragraphs 1 and 2, of the Convention by a state party thereto which accedes to the present Protocol shall be deemed to apply in respect of the present Protocol, unless upon accession a notification to the contrary is addressed by the state party concerned to the Secretary-General of the United Nations. The provisions of Article 40, paragraphs 2 and 3, and of Article 44, paragraph 3, of the Convention shall be deemed to apply *mutatis mutandis* to the present Protocol.

[C.2.78]
Article VIII   Entry into force
1   The present Protocol shall come into force on the day of deposit of the sixth instrument of accession.

2   For each state acceding to the Protocol after the deposit of the sixth instrument of accession, the Protocol shall come into force on the date of deposit by such state of its instrument of accession.

[C.2.79]
Article IX Denunciation
1 Any state party hereto may denounce this Protocol at any time by a notification addressed to the Secretary-General of the United Nations.

2 Such denunciation shall take effect for the state party concerned one year from the date on which it is received by the Secretary-General of the United Nations.

[C.2.80]
Article X Notifications by the Secretary-General of the United Nations
The Secretary-General of the United Nations shall inform the states referred to in Article V above of the date of entry into force, accessions, reservations and withdrawals of reservations to and denunciations of the present Protocol, and of declarations and notifications relating hereto.

[C.2.81]
Article XI Deposit in the archives of the Secretariat of the United Nations
A copy of the present Protocol, of which the Chinese, English, French, Russian and Spanish texts are equally authentic, signed by the President of the General Assembly and by the Secretary-General of the United Nations, shall be deposited in the archives of the Secretariat of the United Nations. The Secretary-General will transmit certified copies thereof to all states members of the United Nations and to the other states referred to in Article V above.

APPENDIX   GENERAL ASSEMBLY RESOLUTION 2198 (XXI)

[C.2.82]
Protocol relating to the Status of Refugees
The General Assembly,

Considering that the Convention relating to the Status of Refugees, signed at Geneva on 28 July 1951[1], covers only those persons who have become refugees as a result of events occurring before 1 January 1951,

Considering that new refugee situations have arisen since the Convention was adopted and that the refugees concerned may therefore not fall within the scope of the Convention,

Considering that it is desirable that equal status should be enjoyed by all refugees covered by the definition in the Convention, irrespective of the date-line of 1 January 1951,

Taking note of the recommendation of the Executive Committee of the Programme of the United Nations High Commissioner for Refugees[2] that the draft Protocol relating to the Status of Refugees should be submitted to the General Assembly after consideration by the Economic and Social Council, in order that the Secretary-General might be authorised to open the Protocol for accession by Governments within the shortest possible time,

Considering that the Economic and Social Council, in its resolution 1186 (XLI) of 18 November 1966, took note with approval of the draft Protocol contained in the addendum to the report of the United Nations High Commissioner for Refugees and concerning measures to extend the personal scope of the Convention[3] and transmitted the addendum to the General Assembly,

1   *Takes note* of the Protocol relating to the Status of Refugees, the text of which is contained in the addendum to the report of the United Nations High Commissioner for Refugees;

2   *Requests* the Secretary-General to transmit the text of the Protocol to the States mentioned in article V thereof, with a view to enabling them to accede to the Protocol[4].

1495th plenary meeting,
16 December 1966.

---

1 United Nations, *Treaty Series*, vol 189 (1954), No 2545.
2 See A/6311/Rev 1/Add 1, part two, para 38.
3 *Ibid*, part one, para 2.
4 The Protocol was signed by the President of the General Assembly and by the Secretary-General on 31 January 1967.

Convention relating to the status of refugees, 28 July 1951 (UNTS, vol 189, p 137); entry into force: 22 April 1954.

UK GOVERNMENT RESERVATION TO THE 1951 CONVENTION RELATING TO THE STATUS OF REFUGEES

[C.2.83]

(i) The Government of the United Kingdom of Great Britain and Northern Ireland understand articles 8 and 9 as not preventing them from taking in time of war or other grave and exceptional circumstances measures in the interests of national security in the case of a refugee on the ground of his nationality. The provision of article 8 shall not prevent the Government of the United Kingdom of Great Britain and Northern Ireland from exercising any rights over property or interests which they may acquire or have acquired as an Allied or Associated Power under a Treaty of Peace or other agreement or arrangement for the restoration of peace which has been or may be completed as a result of the Second World War. Furthermore, the provision of article 8 shall not affect the treatment to be accorded to any property or interests which, at the date of entry into force of this Convention for the United Kingdom of Great Britain and Northern Ireland, are under the control of the Government of the United Kingdom of Great Britain and Northern Ireland by reason of a state of war which exists or existed between them and any other state.

(ii) The Government of the United Kingdom of Great Britain and Northern Ireland accept article 17, paragraph 2, with the substitution of 'four years' for 'three years' in subparagraph (*a*) and with the omission of subparagraph (*c*).

(iii) The Government of the United Kingdom of Great Britain and Northern Ireland cannot undertake to give effect to the obligations contained in article 25, paragraphs 1 and 2, and can only undertake to apply the provision of paragraph 3 so far as the law allows.

UK GOVERNMENT COMMENTARY:

[C.2.84]

In connection with article 24, paragraph 1, subparagraph (*b*) relating to certain matters within the scope of the National Health Service, the National Health Service (Amendment) Act, 1949, contains powers for charges to be made to persons not ordinarily resident in Great Britain (which category would include refugees) who receive treatment under the Service. While these powers have not yet been exercised it is possible that this might have to be done at some future date. In Northern Ireland the Health Services are restricted to persons ordinarily resident in the country except where regulations are made to extend the Service to others. It is for these reasons that the Government of the United Kingdom while they are prepared in the future, as in the past, to give the most sympathetic consideration to the situation of refugees, find it necessary to make a reservation to article 24, paragraph 1, subparagraph (*b*), of the Convention.

The scheme of Industrial Injuries Insurance in Great Britain does not meet the requirements of article 24, paragraph 2, of the Convention. Where an insured person has died as the result of an industrial accident or a disease due to the nature of his employment, benefit cannot generally be paid to his dependants who are abroad unless they are in any part of the British Commonwealth, in the Irish Republic or in a country with which the United Kingdom has made a reciprocal agreement concerning the payment of industrial injury benefits. There is an exception to this rule in favour of the dependants of certain seamen who die as a result of industrial accidents happening to them while they are in the service of British ships. In this matter refugees are treated in the same way as citizens of the United Kingdom and Colonies and by reason of article 24, paragraphs 3 and 4, of the Convention, the dependants of refugees will be able to take advantage of reciprocal agreements which provide for the payment of United Kingdom industrial injury benefits in other countries. By reason of article 24, paragraphs 3 and 4, refugees will enjoy under the scheme of National Insurance and Industrial Injuries Insurance certain rights which are withheld from British subjects who are not citizens of the United Kingdom and Colonies.

No arrangements exist in the United Kingdom for the administrative assistance for which provision is made in article 25 nor have any such arrangements been found necessary in the case of refugees. Any need for the documents or certifications mentioned in paragraph 2 of that article would be met by affidavits.

CONVENTION RELATING TO THE STATUS OF STATE-LESS PERSONS

Adopted on   28 September 1954
Entry into force   6 June 1960, in accordance with article 39

PREAMBLE

[C.2.85]
The High Contracting Parties,

Considering that the Charter of the United Nations and the Universal Declaration of Human Rights approved on 10 December 1948 by the General Assembly of the United Nations have affirmed the principle that human beings shall enjoy fundamental rights and freedoms without discrimination,

Considering that the United Nations has, on various occasions, manifested its profound concern for stateless persons and endeavoured to assure stateless persons the widest possible exercise of these fundamental rights and freedoms,

Considering that only those stateless persons who are also refugees are covered by the Convention relating to the Status of Refugees of 28 July 1951, and that there are many stateless persons who are not covered by that Convention,

Considering that it is desirable to regulate and improve the status of stateless persons by an international agreement,

Have agreed as follows:

CHAPTER I   GENERAL PROVISIONS

[C.2.86]
Article 1   Definition of the term 'Stateless Person'

1   For the purpose of this Convention, the term 'stateless person' means a person who is not considered as a national by any State under the operation of its law.

2   This Convention shall not apply:

(i)   To persons who are at present receiving from organs or agencies of the United Nations other than the United Nations High Commissioner for Refugees protection or assistance so long as they are receiving such protection or assistance;

(ii) To persons who are recognized by the competent authorities of the country in which they have taken residence as having the rights and obligations which are attached to the possession of the nationality of that country;

(iii) To persons with respect to whom there are serious reasons for considering that:

(a) They have committed a crime against peace, a war crime, or a crime

against humanity, as defined in the international instruments drawn up to
make provisions in respect of such crimes;

(b) They have committed a serious non-political crime outside the country of
their residence prior to their admission to that country;

(c) They have been guilty of acts contrary to the purposes and principles of
the United Nations.

[C.2.87]
Article 2   General obligations

Every stateless person has duties to the country in which he finds himself,
which require in particular that he conform to its laws and regulations as well
as to measures taken for the maintenance of public order.

[C.2.88]
Article 3   Non-discrimination

The Contracting States shall apply the provisions of this Convention to stateless persons without discrimination as to race, religion or country of origin.

[C.2.89]
Article 4   Religion

The Contracting States shall accord to stateless persons within their territories
treatment at least as favourable as that accorded to their nationals with respect
to freedom to practise their religion and freedom as regards the religious education of their children.

[C.2.90]
Article 5   Rights granted apart from this Convention

Nothing in this Convention shall be deemed to impair any rights and benefits
granted by a Contracting State to stateless persons apart from this Convention.

[C.2.91]
Article 6   The term 'in the same circumstances'

For the purpose of this Convention, the term 'in the same circumstances'
implies that any requirements (including requirements as to length and conditions of sojourn or residence) which the particular individual would have to
fulfil for the enjoyment of the right in question, if he were not a stateless person, must be fulfilled by him, with the exception of requirements which by
their nature a stateless person is incapable of fulfilling.

[C.2.92]
Article 7   Exemption from reciprocity

1   Except where this Convention contains more favourable provisions, a
Contracting State shall accord to stateless persons the same treatment as is
accorded to aliens generally.

2   After a period of three years' residence, all stateless persons shall enjoy exemption from legislative reciprocity in the territory of the Contracting States.

3   Each Contracting State shall continue to accord to stateless persons the rights and benefits to which they were already entitled, in the absence of reciprocity, at the date of entry into force of this Convention for that State.

4   The Contracting States shall consider favourably the possibility of according to stateless persons, in the absence of reciprocity, rights and benefits beyond those to which they are entitled according to paragraphs 2 and 3, and to extending exemption from reciprocity to stateless persons who do not fulfil the conditions provided for in paragraphs 2 and 3.

5   The provisions of paragraphs 2 and 3 apply both to the rights and benefits referred to in articles 13, 18, 19, 21 and 22 of this Convention and to rights and benefits for which this Convention does not provide.

[C.2.93]
Article 8   Exemption from exceptional measures

With regard to exceptional measures which may be taken against the person, property or interests of nationals or former nationals of a foreign State, the Contracting States shall not apply such measures to a stateless person solely on account of his having previously possessed the nationality of the foreign State in question. Contracting States which, under their legislation, are prevented from applying the general principle expressed in this article shall, in appropriate cases, grant exemptions in favour of such stateless persons.

[C.2.94]
Article 9   Provisional measures

Nothing in this Convention shall prevent a Contracting State, in time of war or other grave and exceptional circumstances, from taking provisionally measures which it considers to be essential to the national security in the case of a particular person, pending a determination by the Contracting State that that person is in fact a stateless person and that the continuance of such measures is necessary in his case in the interests of national security.

[C.2.95]
Article 10   Continuity of residence

1   Where a stateless person has been forcibly displaced during the Second World War and removed to the territory of a Contracting State, and is resident there, the period of such enforced sojourn shall be considered to have been lawful residence within that territory.

2   Where a stateless person has been forcibly displaced during the Second World War from the territory of a Contracting State and has, prior to the date of entry into force of this Convention, returned there for the purpose of taking up residence, the period of residence before and after such enforced displace-

ment shall be regarded as one uninterrupted period for any purposes for which uninterrupted residence is required.

[C.2.96]
Article 11   Stateless seamen

In the case of stateless persons regularly serving as crew members on board a ship flying the flag of a Contracting State, that State shall give sympathetic consideration to their establishment on its territory and the issue of travel documents to them or their temporary admission to its territory particularly with a view to facilitating their establishment in another country.

CHAPTER II   JURIDICAL STATUS

[C.2.97]
Article 12   Personal status

1   The personal status of a stateless person shall be governed by the law of the country of his domicile or, if he has no domicile, by the law of the country of his residence.

2   Rights previously acquired by a stateless person and dependent on personal status, more particularly rights attaching to marriage, shall be respected by a Contracting State, subject to compliance, if this be necessary, with the formalities required by the law of that State, provided that the right in question is one which would have been recognized by the law of that State had he not become stateless.

[C.2.98]
Article 13   Movable and immovable property

The Contracting States shall accord to a stateless person treatment as favourable as possible and, in any event, not less favourable than that accorded to aliens generally in the same circumstances, as regards the acquisition of movable and immovable property and other rights pertaining thereto, and to leases and other contracts relating to movable and immovable property.

[C.2.99]
Article 14   Artistic rights and industrial property

In respect of the protection of industrial property, such as inventions, designs or models, trade marks, trade names, and of rights in literary, artistic and scientific works, a stateless person shall be accorded in the country in which he has his habitual residence the same protection as is accorded to nationals of that country. In the territory of any other Contracting State, he shall be accorded the same protection as is accorded in that territory to nationals of the country in which he has his habitual residence.

[C.2.100]
Article 15   Right of association

As regards non-political and non-profit-making associations and trade unions the Contracting States shall accord to stateless persons lawfully staying in their territory treatment as favourable as possible, and in any event, not less favourable than that accorded to aliens generally in the same circumstances.

[C.2.101]
Article 16   Access to courts

1   A stateless person shall have free access to the courts of law on the territory of all Contracting States.

2   A stateless person shall enjoy in the Contracting State in which he has his habitual residence the same treatment as a national in matters pertaining to access to the courts, including legal assistance and exemption from cautio judicatum solvi.

3   A stateless person shall be accorded in the matters referred to in paragraph 2 in countries other than that in which he has his habitual residence the treatment granted to a national of the country of his habitual residence.

CHAPTER III   GAINFUL EMPLOYMENT

[C.2.102]
Article 17   Wage-earning employment

1   The Contracting States shall accord to stateless persons lawfully staying in their territory treatment as favourable as possible and, in any event, not less favourable that that accorded to aliens generally in the same circumstances, as regards the right to engage in wage-earning employment.

2   The Contracting States shall give sympathetic consideration to assimilating the rights of all stateless persons with regard to wage-earning employment to those of nationals, and in particular of those stateless persons who have entered their territory pursuant to programmes of labour recruitment or under immigration schemes.

[C.2.103]
Article 18   Self-employment

The Contracting States shall accord to a stateless person lawfully in their territory treatment as favourable as possible and, in any event, not less favourable than that accorded to aliens generally in the same circumstances, as regards the right to engage on his own account in agriculture, industry, handicrafts and commerce and to establish commercial and industrial companies.

[C.2.104]
Article 19   Liberal professions

Each Contracting State shall accord to stateless persons lawfully staying in their territory who hold diplomas recognized by the competent authorities of that State, and who are desirous of practising a liberal profession, treatment as favourable as possible and, in any event, not less favourable than that accorded to aliens generally in the same circumstances.

CHAPTER IV WELFARE

[C.2.105]
Article 20   Rationing

Where a rationing system exists, which applies to the population at large and regulates the general distribution of products in short supply, stateless persons shall be accorded the same treatment as nationals.

[C.2.106]
Article 21   Housing

As regards housing, the Contracting States, in so far as the matter is regulated by laws or regulations or is subject to the control of public authorities, shall accord to stateless persons lawfully staying in their territory treatment as favourable as possible and, in any event, not less favourable than that accorded to aliens generally in the same circumstances.

[C.2.107]
Article 22   Public education

1   The Contracting States shall accord to stateless persons the same treatment as is accorded to nationals with respect to elementary education.

2   The Contracting States shall accord to stateless persons treatment as favourable as possible and, in any event, not less favourable than that accorded to aliens generally in the same circumstances, with respect to education other than elementary education and, in particular, as regards access to studies, the recognition of foreign school certificates, diplomas and degrees, the remission of fees and charges and the award of scholarships.

[C.2.108]
Article 23   Public relief

The Contracting States shall accord to stateless persons lawfully staying in their territory the same treatment with respect to public relief and assistance as is accorded to their nationals.

[C.2.109]
Article 24   Labour legislation and social security

1   The Contracting States shall accord to stateless persons lawfully staying in their territory the same treatment as is accorded to nationals in respect of the following matters:

(a) In so far as such matters are governed by laws or regulations or are subject to the control of administrative authorities; remuneration, including family allowances where these form part of remuneration, hours of work, overtime arrangements, holidays with pay, restrictions on home work, minimum age of employment, apprenticeship and training, women's work and the work of young persons, and the enjoyment of the benefits of collective bargaining;

(b) Social security (legal provisions in respect of employment injury, occupational diseases, maternity, sickness, disability, old age, death, unemployment, family responsibilities and any other contingency which, according to national laws or regulations, is covered by a social security scheme), subject to the following limitations:

> (i) There may be appropriate arrangements for the maintenance of acquired rights and rights in course of acquisition;
>
> (ii) National laws or regulations of the country of residence may prescribe special arrangements concerning benefits or portions of benefits which are payable wholly out of public funds, and concerning allowances paid to persons who do not fulfil the contribution conditions prescribed for the award of a normal pension.

2   The right to compensation for the death of a stateless person resulting from employment injury or from occupational disease shall not be affected by the fact that the residence of the beneficiary is outside the territory of the Contracting State.

3   The Contracting States shall extend to stateless persons the benefits of agreements concluded between them, or which may be concluded between them in the future, concerning the maintenance of acquired rights and rights in the process of acquisition in regard to social security, subject only to the conditions which apply to nationals of the States signatory to the agreements in question.

4   The Contracting States will give sympathetic consideration to extending to stateless persons so far as possible the benefits of similar agreements which may at any time be in force between such Contracting States and non-contracting States.

CHAPTER V ADMINISTRATIVE MEASURES

[C.2.110]
Article 25   Administrative assistance

1   When the exercise of a right by a stateless person would normally require the assistance of authorities of a foreign country to whom he cannot have recourse, the Contracting State in whose territory he is residing shall arrange that such assistance be afforded to him by their own authorities.

2   The authority or authorities mentioned in paragraph I shall deliver or cause to be delivered under their supervision to stateless persons such documents or certifications as would normally be delivered to aliens by or through their national authorities.

3   Documents or certifications so delivered shall stand in the stead of the official instruments delivered to aliens by or through their national authorities and shall be given credence in the absence of proof to the contrary.

4   Subject to such exceptional treatment as may be granted to indigent persons, fees may be charged for the services mentioned herein, but such fees shall be moderate and commensurate with those charged to nationals for similar services.

5   The provisions of this article shall be without prejudice to articles 27 and 28.

[C.2.111]
Article 26   Freedom of movement

Each Contracting State shall accord to stateless persons lawfully in its territory the right to choose their place of residence and to move freely within its territory, subject to any regulations applicable to aliens generally in the same circumstances.

[C.2.112]
Article 27   Identity papers

The Contracting States shall issue identity papers to any stateless person in their territory who does not possess a valid travel document.

[C.2.113]
Article 28   Travel documents

The Contracting States shall issue to stateless persons lawfully staying in their territory travel documents for the purpose of travel outside their territory, unless compelling reasons of national security or public order otherwise require, and the provisions of the schedule to this Convention shall apply with respect to such documents. The Contracting States may issue such a travel document to any other stateless person in their territory; they shall in particular give sympathetic consideration to the issue of such a travel document to stateless persons in their territory who are unable to obtain a travel document from the country of their lawful residence.

[C.2.114]
Article 29   Fiscal charges

1   The Contracting States shall not impose upon stateless persons duties, charges or taxes, of any description whatsoever, other or higher than those which are or may be levied on their nationals in similar situations.

2   Nothing in the above paragraph shall prevent the application to stateless persons of the laws and regulations concerning charges in respect of the issue to aliens of administrative documents including identity papers.

[C.2.115]
Article 30   Transfer of assets

1   A Contracting State shall, in conformity with its laws and regulations, permit stateless persons to transfer assets which they have brought into its territory, to another country where they have been admitted for the purposes of resettlement.

2   A Contracting State shall give sympathetic consideration to the application of stateless persons for permission to transfer assets wherever they may be and which are necessary for their resettlement in another country to which they have been admitted.

[C.2.116]
Article 31   Expulsion

1   The Contracting States shall not expel a stateless person lawfully in their territory save on grounds of national security or public order.

2   The expulsion of such a stateless person shall be only in pursuance of a decision reached in accordance with due process of law. Except where compelling reasons of national security otherwise require, the stateless person shall be allowed to submit evidence to clear himself, and to appeal to and be represented for the purpose before competent authority or a person or persons specially designated by the competent authority.

3   The Contracting States shall allow such a stateless person a reasonable period within which to seek legal admission into another country. The Contracting States reserve the right to apply during that period such internal measures as they may deem necessary.

[C.2.117]
Article 32   Naturalization

The Contracting States shall as far as possible facilitate the assimilation and naturalization of stateless persons. They shall in particular make every effort to expedite naturalization proceedings and to reduce as far as possible the charges and costs of such proceedings.

CHAPTER VI FINAL CLAUSES

[C.2.118]
Article 33   Information on national legislation

The Contracting States shall communicate to the Secretary-General of the United Nations the laws and regulations which they may adopt to ensure the application of this Convention.

[C.2.119]
Article 34   Settlement of disputes

Any dispute between Parties to this Convention relating to its interpretation or application, which cannot be settled by other means, shall be referred to the International Court of Justice at the request of any one of the parties to the dispute.

[C.2.120]
Article 35 Signature, ratification and accession

1   This Convention shall be open for signature at the Headquarters of the United Nations until 31 December 1955.

2   It shall be open for signature on behalf of:

(a) Any State Member of the United Nations;

(b) Any other State invited to attend the United Nations Conference on the Status of Stateless Persons; and

(c) Any State to which an invitation to sign or to accede may be addressed by the General Assembly of the United Nations.

3   It shall be ratified and the instruments of ratification shall be deposited with the Secretary-General of the United Nations.

4   It shall be open for accession by the States referred to in paragraph 2 of this article. Accession shall be effected by the deposit of an instrument of accession with the Secretary-General of the United Nations.

[C.2.121]
Article 36 Territorial application clause

1   Any State may, at the time of signature, ratification or accession, declare that this Convention shall extend to all or any of the territories for the international relations of which it is responsible. Such a declaration shall take effect when the Convention enters into force for the State concerned.

2   At any time thereafter any such extension shall be made by notification addressed to the Secretary-General of the United Nations and shall take effect as from the ninetieth day after the day of receipt by the Secretary-General of the United Nations of this notification, or as from the date of entry into force of the Convention for the State concerned, whichever is the later.

3   With respect to those territories to which this Convention is not extended at the time of signature, ratification or accession, each State concerned shall consider the possibility of taking the necessary steps in order to extend the application of this Convention to such territories, subject, where necessary for constitutional reasons, to the consent of the Governments of such territories.

[C.2.122]
Article 37 Federal clause

In the case of a Federal or non-unitary State, the following provisions shall apply

(a) With respect to those articles of this Convention that come within the legislative jurisdiction of the federal legislative authority, the obligations of the Federal Government shall to this extent be the same as those of Parties which are not Federal States;

(b) With respect to those articles of this Convention that come within the legislative jurisdiction of constituent States, provinces or cantons which are not, under the constitutional system of the Federation, bound to take legislative action, the Federal Government shall bring such articles with a favourable recommendation to the notice of the appropriate authorities of States, provinces or cantons at the earliest possible moment;

(c) A Federal State Party to this Convention shall, at the request of any other Contracting State transmitted through the Secretary-General of the United Nations, supply a statement of the law and practice of the Federation and its constituent units in regard to any particular provision of the Convention showing the extent to which effect has been given to that provision by legislative or other action.

[C.2.123]
Article 38   Reservations

1   At the time of signature, ratification or accession, any State may make reservations to articles of the Convention other than to articles 1, 3, 4, 16 (1) and 33 to 42 inclusive.

2   Any State making a reservation in accordance with paragraph I of this article may at any time withdraw the reservation by a communication to that effect addressed to the Secretary-General of the United Nations.

[C.2.124]
Article 39   Entry into force

1   This Convention shall come into force on the ninetieth day following the day of deposit of the sixth instrument of ratification or accession.

2   For each State ratifying or acceding to the Convention after the deposit of the sixth instrument of ratification or accession, the Convention shall enter into force on the ninetieth day following the date of deposit by such State of its instrument of ratification or accession.

[C.2.125]
Article 40   Denunciation

1   Any Contracting State may denounce this Convention at any time by a notification addressed to the Secretary-General of the United Nations.

2   Such denunciation shall take effect for the Contracting State concerned one year from the date upon which it is received by the Secretary-General of the United Nations.

3   Any State which has made a declaration or notification under article 36 may, at any time thereafter, by a notification to the Secretary- General of the United Nations, declare that the Convention shall cease to extend to such territory one year after the date of receipt of the notification by the Secretary-General.

[C.2.126]
Article 41   Revision

1   Any Contracting State may request revision of this Convention at any time by a notification addressed to the Secretary-General of the United Nations.

2   The General Assembly of the United Nations shall recommend the steps, if any, to be taken in respect of such request.

[C.2.127]
Article 42   Notifications by the Secretary-General of the United Nations

The Secretary-General of the United Nations shall inform all Members of the United Nations and non-member States referred to in article 35:

(a) Of signatures, ratifications and accessions in accordance with article 35;

(b) Of declarations and notifications in accordance with article 36;

(c) Of reservations and withdrawals in accordance with article 38;

(d) Of the date on which this Convention will come into force in accordance with article 39;

(e) Of denunciations and notifications in accordance with article 40;

(f) Of request for revision in accordance with article 41.

HANDBOOK ON PROCEDURES AND CRITERIA FOR DETERMINING REFUGEE STATUS

UNDER THE 1951 CONVENTION AND THE 1967
PROTOCOL RELATING TO THE STATUS OF REFUGEES

Office of the United Nations High Commissioner for Refugees, Geneva 1979

Table of contents

References in bold are to paragraph numbers

Part One   Criteria for the Determination of Refugee Status

CHAPTER I   GENERAL PRINCIPLES

[C.2.128]
28   A person is a refugee within the meaning of the 1951 Convention as soon as he fulfils criteria contained in the definition. This would necessarily occur prior to the time at which his refugee status is formally determined. Recognition of his refugee status does not therefore make him a refugee but declares him to be one. He does not become a refugee because of recognition, but is recognized because he is a refugee.

29   Determination of refugee status is a process which takes place in two stages. Firstly, it is necessary to ascertain the relevant facts of the case. Secondly, the definitions in the 1951 Convention and the 1967 Protocol have to be applied to the facts thus ascertained.

30   The provisions of the 1951 Convention defining who is a refugee consist of three parts, which have been termed respectively 'inclusion', 'cessation' and 'exclusion' clauses.

31   The inclusion clauses define the criteria that a person must satisfy in order to be a refugee. They form the positive basis upon which the determination of refugee status is made. The so-called cessation and exclusion clauses have a negative significance; the former indicate the conditions under which a refugee ceases to be a refugee and the latter enumerate the circumstances in which a person is excluded from the application of the 1951 Convention although meeting the positive criteria of the inclusion clauses.

CHAPTER II INCLUSION CLAUSES

A Definitions

(1) Statutory Refugees

[C.2.129]
32   Article 1 A(1) of the 1951 Convention deals with statutory refugees, ie persons considered to be refugees under the provisions of international instruments preceding the Convention. This provision states that:

'For the purposes of the present Convention, the term "refugee" shall apply to any person who:
(1) Has been considered a refugee under the Arrangements of 12 May 1926 and 30 June 1928 or under the Conventions of 28 October 1933 and 10 February 1938, the Protocol of 14 September 1939 or the Constitution of the International Refugee Organisation;
Decisions of non-eligibility taken by the International Refugee Organisation during the period of its activities shall not prevent the status of refugees being accorded to persons who fulfil the conditions of paragraph 2 of this section.'

33   The above enumeration is given in order to provide a link with the past and to ensure the continuity of international protection of refugees who became the concern of the international community at various earlier periods. As already indicated (paragraph 4 above), these instruments have by now lost much of their significance, and a discussion of them here would be of little practical value. However, a person who has been considered a refugee under the terms of any of these instruments is automatically a refugee under the 1951 Convention. Thus, a holder of a so-called 'Nansen Passport'[1] or a 'Certificate of Eligibility' issued by the International Refugee Organisation must be considered a refugee under the 1951 Convention unless one of the cessation clauses has become applicable to his case or he is excluded from the application of the Convention by one of the exclusion clauses. This also applies to a surviving child of a statutory refugee.

---

1   'Nansen Passport': a certificate of identity for use as a travel document, issued to refugees under the provisions of pre-war instruments.

---

(2)   General definition in the 1951 Convention

[C.2.130]
34   According to Article 1A (2) of the 1951 Convention the term 'refugee' shall apply to any person who:

'As a result of events occurring before 1 January 1951 and owing to well-founded fear of being persecuted for reasons of race, religion, nationality, membership of a particular social group or political opinion, is outside the country of his nationality and is unable or, owing to such fear, is unwilling to avail himself of the protection of that country; or who, not having a nationality and being outside the country of his former habitual residence as a result of such events, is unable or, owing to such fear, is unwilling to return to it.'

This general definition is discussed in detail below.

B   Interpretation of terms

(1)   'Events occurring before 1 January 1951'

[C.2.131]
35   The origin of this 1951 dateline is explained in paragraph 7 of the Introduction. As a result of the 1967 Protocol this dateline has lost much of its practical significance. An interpretation of the word 'events' is therefore of interest only in the small number of States parties to the 1951 Convention that are not also party to the 1967 Protocol.

36   The word 'events' is not defined in the 1951 Convention, but was understood to mean 'happenings of major importance involving territorial or profound political changes as well as systematic programmes of persecution which are after-effects of earlier changes'[1]. The dateline refers to 'events' as a

result of which, and not to the date on which, a person becomes a refugee, nor does it apply to the date on which he left his country. A refugee may have left his country before or after the datelines, provided that his fear of persecution is due to 'events' that occurred before the dateline or to after-effects occurring at a later date as a result of such events[2].

---

1 UN Document E/1618 page 39.
2 *loc cit.*

---

(2) 'Well founded fear of being persecuted'

[C.2.132]
(a) General analysis
37 The phrase 'well-founded fear of being persecuted' is the key phrase of the definition. It reflects the views of its authors as to the main elements of refugee character. It replaces the earlier method of defining refugees by categories (ie persons of a certain origin not enjoying the protection of their country) by the general concept of 'fear' for a relevant motive. Since fear is subjective, the definition involves a subjective element in the person applying for recognition as a refugee. Determination of refugee status will therefore primarily require an evaluation of the applicant's statements rather than a judgement on the situation prevailing in his country of origin.

38 To the element of fear – a state of mind and a subjective condition – is added the qualification 'well-founded'. This implies that it is not only the frame of mind of the person concerned that determines his refugee status, but that this frame of mind must be supported by an objective situation. The term 'well-founded fear' therefore contains a subjective and an objective element, and in determining whether well-founded fear exists, both elements must be taken into consideration.

39 It may be assumed that, unless he seeks adventure or just wishes to see the world, a person would not normally abandon his home and country without some compelling reason. There may be many reasons that are compelling and understandable, but only one motive has been singled out to denote a refugee. The expression 'owing to well-founded fear of being persecuted' – for the reasons stated – by indicating a specific motive automatically makes all other reasons for escape irrelevant to the definition. It rules out such persons as victims of famine or natural disaster, unless they *also* have well-founded fear of persecution for one of the reasons stated. Such other motives may not, however, be altogether irrelevant to the process of determining refugee status, since all the circumstances need to be taken into account for a proper understanding of the applicant's case.

40 An evaluation of the *subjective element* is inseparable from an assessment of the personality of the applicant, since psychological reactions of different individuals may not be the same in identical conditions. One person may have strong political or religious convictions, the disregard of which would make his life intolerable; another may have no such strong convictions. One person may make an impulsive decision to escape; another may carefully plan his departure.

41   Due to the importance that the definition attaches to the subjective element, an assessment of credibility is indispensable where the case is not sufficiently clear from the facts on record. It will be necessary to take into account the personal and family background of the applicant, his membership of a particular racial, religious, national, social or political group, his own interpretation of his situation, and his personal experiences—in other words, everything that may serve to indicate that the predominant motive for his application is fear. Fear must be reasonable. Exaggerated fear, however, may be well-founded if, in all the circumstances of the case, such a state of mind can be regarded as justified.

42   As regards the objective element, it is necessary to evaluate the statements made by the applicant. The competent authorities that are called upon to determine refugee status are not required to pass judgement on conditions in the applicant's country of origin. The applicant's statements cannot, however, be considered in the abstract, and must be viewed in the context of the relevant background situation. A knowledge of conditions in the applicant's country of origin—while not a primary objective—is an important element in assessing the applicant's credibility. In general, the applicant's fear should be considered well-founded if he can establish, to a reasonable degree, that his continued stay in his country of origin has become intolerable to him for the reasons stated in the definition, or would for the same reasons be intolerable if he returned there.

43   These considerations need not necessarily be based on the applicant's own personal experience. What, for example, happened to his friends and relatives and other members of the same racial or social group may well show that his fear that sooner or later he also will become a victim of persecution is well-founded. The laws of the country of origin, and particularly the manner in which they are applied, will be relevant. The situation of each person must, however, be assessed on its own merits. In the case of a well-known personality, the possibility of persecution may be greater than in the case of a person in obscurity. All these factors, eg a person's character, his background, his influence, his wealth or his outspokenness, may lead to the conclusion that his fear of persecution is 'well-founded'.

44   While refugee status must normally be determined on an individual basis, situations have also arisen in which entire groups have been displaced under circumstances indicating that members of the group could be considered individually as refugees. In such situations the need to provide assistance is often extremely urgent and it may not be possible for purely practical reasons to carry out an individual determination of refugee status for each member of the group. Recourse has therefore been had to so-called 'group determination' of refugee status, whereby each member of the group is regarded prima facie (ie in the absence of evidence to the contrary) as a refugee.

45   Apart from the situations of the type referred to in the preceding paragraph, an applicant for refugee status must normally show good reason why he individually fears persecution. It may be assumed that a person has well-founded fear of being persecuted if he has already been the victim of persecution for one of the reasons enumerated in the 1951 Convention. However, the word 'fear' refers not only to persons who have actually been persecuted, but also to those who wish to avoid a situation entailing the risk of persecution.

46   The expressions 'fear of persecution' or even 'persecution' are usually foreign to a refugee's normal vocabulary. A refugee will indeed only rarely invoke 'fear of persecution' in these terms, though it will often be implicit in his story. Again, while a refugee may have very definite opinions for which he has had to suffer, he may not, for psychological reasons, be able to describe his experiences and situation in political terms.

47   A typical test of the well-foundedness of fear will arise when an applicant is in possession of a valid national passport. It has sometimes been claimed that possession of a passport signifies that the issuing authorities do not intend to persecute the holder, for otherwise they would not have issued a passport to him. Though this may be true in some cases, many persons have used a legal exit from their country as the only means of escape without ever having revealed their political opinions, a knowledge of which might place them in a dangerous situation *vis-à-vis* the authorities.

48   Possession of a passport cannot therefore always be considered as evidence of loyalty on the part of the holder, or as an indication of the absence of fear. A passport may even be issued to a person who is undesired in his country of origin, with the sole purpose of securing his departure, and there may also be cases where a passport has been obtained surreptitiously. In conclusion, therefore, the mere possession of a valid national passport is no bar to refugee status.

49   If, on the other hand, an applicant, without good reason, insists on retaining a valid passport of a country of whose protection he is allegedly unwilling to avail himself, this may cast doubt on the validity of his claim to have 'well-founded fear'. Once recognized, a refugee should not normally retain his national passport.

50   There may, however, be exceptional situations in which a person fulfilling the criteria of refugee status may retain his national passport – or be issued with a new one by the authorities of his country of origin under special arrangements. Particularly where such arrangements do not imply that the holder of the national passport is free to return to his country without prior permission, they may not be incompatible with refugee status.

[C.2.133]
(b) Persecution
51   There is no universally accepted definition of 'persecution', and various attempts to formulate such a definition have met with little success. From Article 33 of the 1951 Convention, it may be inferred that a threat to life or freedom on account of race, religion, nationality, political opinion or membership of a particular social group is always persecution. Other serious violations of human rights—for the same reasons—would also constitute persecution.

52   Whether other prejudicial actions or threats would amount to persecution will depend on the circumstances of each case, including the subjective element to which reference has been made in the preceding paragraphs. The subjective character of fear of persecution requires an evaluation of the opinions and feelings of the person concerned. It is also in the light of such opinions and feelings that any actual or anticipated measures against him must necessarily be viewed. Due to variations in the psychological make-up of individuals and

in the circumstances of each case, interpretations of what amounts to persecution are bound to vary.

53   In addition, an applicant may have been subjected to various measures not in themselves amounting to persecution (eg discrimination in different forms), in some cases combined with other adverse factors (eg general atmosphere of insecurity in the country of origin). In such situations, the various elements involved may, if taken together, produce an effect on the mind of the applicant that can reasonably justify a claim to well-founded fear of persecution on 'cumulative grounds'. Needless to say, it is not possible to lay down a general rule as to what cumulative reasons can give rise to a valid claim to refugee status. This will necessarily depend on all the circumstances, including the particular geographical, historical and ethnological context.

[C.2.134]
(c) Discrimination
54   Differences in the treatment of various groups do indeed exist to a greater or lesser extent in many societies. Persons who receive less favourable treatment as a result of such differences are not necessarily victims of persecution. It is only in certain circumstances that discrimination will amount to persecution. This would be so if measures of discrimination lead to consequences of a substantially prejudicial nature for the person concerned, eg serious restrictions on his right to earn his livelihood, his right to practise his religion, or his access to normally available educational facilities.

55   Where measures of discrimination are, in themselves, not of a serious character, they may nevertheless give rise to a reasonable fear of persecution if they produce, in the mind of the person concerned, a feeling of apprehension and insecurity as regards his future existence. Whether or not such measures of discrimination in themselves amount to persecution must be determined in the light of all the circumstances. A claim to fear of persecution will of course be stronger where a person has been the victim of a number of discriminatory measures of this type and where there is thus a cumulative element involved[1]

---

1 See also paragraph 53.

[C.2.135]
(d) Punishment
56   Persecution must be distinguished from punishment for a common law offence. Persons fleeing from prosecution or punishment for such an offence are not normally refugees. It should be recalled that a refugee is a victim – or potential victim – of injustice, not a fugitive from justice.

57   The above distinction may, however, occasionally be obscured. In the first place, a person guilty of a common law offence may be liable to excessive punishment, which may amount to persecution within the meaning of the definition. Moreover, penal prosecution for a reason mentioned in the definition (for example, in respect of 'illegal' religious instruction given to a child) may in itself amount to persecution.

58   Secondly, there may be cases in which a person, besides fearing prosecu-

tion or punishment for a common law crime, may also have 'well-founded fear of persecution'. In such cases the person concerned is a refugee. It may, however, be necessary to consider whether the crime in question is not of such a serious character as to bring the applicant within the scope of one of the exclusion clauses¹.

59   In order to determine whether prosecution amounts to persecution, it will also be necessary to refer to the laws of the country concerned, for it is possible for a law not to be in conformity with accepted human rights standards. More often, however, it may not be the law but its application that is discriminatory. Prosecution for an offence against 'public order', eg for distribution of pamphlets, could for example be a vehicle for the persecution of the individual on the grounds of the political content of the publication.

60   In such cases, due to the obvious difficulty involved in evaluating the laws of another country, national authorities may frequently have to take decisions by using their own national legislation as a yardstick. Moreover, recourse may usefully be had to the principles set out in the various international instruments relating to human rights, in particular the International Covenants on Human Rights, which contain binding commitments for the States parties and are instruments to which many States parties to the 1951 Convention have acceded.

---

1 See paragraphs 144 to 156.

[C.2.136]
(e) Consequences of unlawful departure or unauthorized stay outside country of origin
61   The legislation of certain states imposes severe penalties on nationals who depart from the country in an unlawful manner or remain abroad without authorization. Where there is reason to believe that a person, due to his illegal departure or unauthorized stay abroad is liable to such severe penalties his recognition as a refugee will be justified if it can be shown that his motives for leaving or remaining outside the country are related to the reasons enumerated in Article 1 A(2) of the 1951 Convention (see paragraph 66 below).

[C.2.137]
(f) Economic migrants distinguished from refugees
62   A migrant is a person who, for reasons other than those contained in the definition, voluntarily leaves his country in order to take up residence elsewhere. He may be moved by the desire for change or adventure, or by family or other reasons of a personal nature. If he is moved exclusively by economic considerations, he is an economic migrant and not a refugee.

63   The distinction between an economic migrant and a refugee is, however, sometimes blurred in the same way as the distinction between economic and political measures in an applicant's country of origin is not always clear. Behind economic measures affecting a person's livelihood there may be racial, religious or political aims or intentions directed against a particular group. Where economic measures destroy the economic existence of a particular section of the population (eg withdrawal of trading rights from, or discriminatory

or excessive taxation of, a specific ethnic or religious group), the victims may according to the circumstances become refugees on leaving the country.

64 Whether the same would apply to victims of general economic measures (ie those that are applied to the whole population without discrimination) would depend on the circumstances of the case. Objections to general economic measures are not by themselves good reasons for claiming refugee status. On the other hand, what appears at first sight to be primarily an economic motive for departure may in reality also involve a political element, and it may be the political opinions of the individual that expose him to serious consequences, rather than his objections to the economic measures themselves.

[C.2.138]
(g) Agents of persecution
65 Persecution is normally related to action by the authorities of a country. It may also emanate from sections of the population that do not respect the standards established by the laws of the country concerned. A case in point may be religious intolerance, amounting to persecution, in a country otherwise secular, but where sizeable fractions of the population do not respect the religious beliefs of their neighbours. Where serious discriminatory or other offensive acts are committed by the local populace, they can be considered as persecution if they are knowingly tolerated by the authorities, or if the authorities refuse, or prove unable, to offer effective protection.

(3) 'for reasons of race, religion, nationality, membership of a particular social group or political opinion'

[C.2.139]
(a) General analysis
66 In order to be considered a refugee, a person must show well-founded fear of persecution for one of the reasons stated above. It is immaterial whether the persecution arises from any single one of these reasons or from a combination of two or more of them. Often the applicant himself may not be aware of the reasons for the persecution feared. It is not, however, his duty to analyse his case to such an extent as to identify the reasons in detail.

67 It is for the examiner, when investigating the facts of the case, to ascertain the reason or reasons for the persecution feared and to decide whether the definition in the 1951 Convention is met with in this respect. It is evident that the reasons for persecution under these various headings will frequently overlap. Usually there will be more than one element combined in one person, eg a political opponent who belongs to a religious or national group, or both, and the combination of such reasons in his person may be relevant in evaluating his well-founded fear.

[C.2.140]
(b) Race
68 Race, in the present connexion, has to be understood in its widest sense

to include all kinds of ethnic groups that are referred to as 'races' in common usage. Frequently it will also entail membership of a specific social group of common descent forming a minority within a larger population. Discrimination for reasons of race has found world-wide condemnation as one of the most striking violations of human rights. Racial discrimination, therefore, represents an important element in determining the existence of persecution.

69   Discrimination on racial grounds will frequently amount to persecution in the sense of the 1951 Convention. This will be the case if, as a result of racial discrimination, a person's human dignity is affected to such an extent as to be incompatible with the most elementary and inalienable human rights, or where the disregard of racial barriers is subject to serious consequences.

70   The mere fact of belonging to a certain racial group will normally not be enough to substantiate a claim to refugee status. There may, however, be situations where, due to particular circumstances affecting the group, such membership will in itself be sufficient ground to fear persecution.

[C.2.141]
(c) Religion

71   The Universal Declaration of Human Rights and the Human Rights Covenant proclaim the right to freedom of thought, conscience and religion, which right includes the freedom of a person to change his religion and his freedom to manifest it in public or private, in teaching, practice, worship and observance.

72   Persecution for 'reasons of religion' may assume various forms, eg prohibition of membership of a religious community, of worship in private or in public, of religious instruction, or serious measures of discrimination imposed on persons because they practise their religion or belong to a particular religious community.

73   Mere membership of a particular religious community will normally not be enough to substantiate a claim to refugee status. There may, however, be special circumstances where mere membership can be a sufficient ground.

[C.2.142]
(d) Nationality

74   The term 'nationality' in this context is not to be understood only as 'citizenship'. It refers also to membership of an ethnic or linguistic group and may occasionally overlap with the term 'race'. Persecution for reasons of nationality may consist of adverse attitudes and measures directed against a national (ethnic, linguistic) minority and in certain circumstances the fact of belonging to such a minority may in itself give rise to well-founded fear of persecution.

75   The co-existence within the boundaries of a State of two or more national (ethnic, linguistic) groups may create situations of conflict and also situations of persecution or danger of persecution. It may not always be easy to distinguish between persecution for reasons of nationality and persecution for reasons of political opinion when a conflict between national groups is combined with political movements, particularly where a political movement is

identified with a specific 'nationality'.

76   Whereas in most cases persecution for reason of nationality is feared by persons belonging to a national minority, there have been many cases in various continents where a person belonging to a majority group may fear persecution by a dominant minority.

[C.2.143]
(e) Membership of a particular social group
77   A 'particular social group' normally comprises persons of similar background, habits or social status. A claim to fear of persecution under this heading may frequently overlap with a claim to fear of persecution on other grounds, ie race, religion or nationality.

78   Membership of such a particular social group may be at the root of persecution because there is no confidence in the group's loyalty to the Government or because the political outlook, antecedents or economic activity of its members, or the very existence of the social group as such, is held to be an obstacle to the Government's policies.

79   Mere membership of a particular social group will not normally be enough to substantiate a claim to refugee status. There may, however, be special circumstances where mere membership can be a sufficient ground to fear persecution.

[C.2.144]
(f) Political opinion
80   Holding political opinions different from those of the Government is not in itself a ground for claiming refugee status, and an applicant must show that he has a fear of persecution for holding such opinions. This presupposes that the applicant holds opinions not tolerated by the authorities, which are critical of their policies or methods. It also presupposes that such opinions have come to the notice of the authorities or are attributed by them to the applicant. The political opinions of a teacher or writer may be more manifest than those of a person in a less exposed position. The relative importance or tenacity of the applicant's opinions—in so far as this can be established from all the circumstances of the case—will also be relevant.

81   While the definition speaks of persecution 'for reasons of political opinion' it may not always be possible to establish a causal link between the opinion expressed and the related measures suffered or feared by the applicant. Such measures have only rarely been based expressly on 'opinion'. More frequently, such measures take the form of sanctions for alleged criminal acts against the ruling power. It will, therefore, be necessary to establish the applicant's political opinion, which is at the root of his behaviour, and the fact that it has led or may lead to the persecution that he claims to fear.

82   As indicated above, persecution 'for reasons of political opinion' implies that an applicant holds an opinion that either has been expressed or has come to the attention of the authorities. There may, however, also be situations in which the applicant has not given any expression to his opinions. Due to the strength of his convictions, however, it may be reasonable to assume that his

opinions will sooner or later find expression and that the applicant will, as a result, come into conflict with the authorities. Where this can reasonably be assumed, the applicant can be considered to have fear of persecution for reasons of political opinion.

83   An applicant claiming fear of persecution because of political opinion need not show that the authorities of his country of origin knew of his opinions before he left the country. He may have concealed his political opinion and never have suffered any discrimination or persecution. However, the mere fact of refusing to avail himself of the protection of his Government, or a refusal to return, may disclose the applicant's true state of mind and give rise to fear of persecution. In such circumstances the test of well-founded fear would be based on an assessment of the consequences that an applicant having certain political dispositions would have to face if he returned. This applies particularly to the so-called refugee 'sur place'[1].

84   Where a person is subject to prosecution or punishment for a political offence, a distinction may have to be drawn according to whether the prosecution is for political *opinion* or for politically-motivated *acts*. If the prosecution pertains to a punishable act committed out of political motives, and if the anticipated punishment is in conformity with the general law of the country concerned, fear of such prosecution will not in itself make the applicant a refugee.

85   Whether a political offender can also be considered a refugee will depend upon various other factors. Prosecution for an offence may, depending upon the circumstances, be a pretext for punishing the offender for his political opinions or the expression thereof. Again, there may be reason to believe that a political offender would be exposed to excessive or arbitrary punishment for the alleged offence. Such excessive or arbitrary punishment will amount to persecution.

86   In determining whether a political offender can be considered a refugee regard should also be had to the following elements: personality of the applicant, his political opinion, the motive behind the act, the nature of the act committed, the nature of the prosecution and its motives; finally, also, the nature of the law on which the prosecution is based. These elements may go to show that the person concerned has a fear of persecution and not merely a fear of prosecution and punishment—within the law—for an act committed by him.

---

1 See paragraphs 94 to 96.

(4) 'is outside the country of his nationality'

[C.2.145]
(a) General analysis
87   In this context, 'nationality' refers to 'citizenship'. The phrase 'is outside the country of his nationality' relates to persons who have a nationality, as distinct from stateless persons. In the majority of cases, refugees retain the nationality of their country of origin.

88 It is a general requirement for refugee status that an applicant who has a nationality be outside the country of his nationality. There are no exceptions to this rule. International protection cannot come into play as long as a person is within territorial jurisdiction of his home country[1].

89 Where, therefore, an applicant alleges fear of persecution in relation to the country of his nationality, it should be established that he does in fact possess the nationality of that country. There may, however, be uncertainty as to whether a person has a nationality. He may not know himself, or he may wrongly claim to have a particular nationality or to be stateless. Where his nationality cannot be clearly established, his refugee status should be determined in a similar manner to that of a stateless person, ie instead of the country of his nationality, the country of his former habitual residence will have to be taken into account. (See paragraphs 101 to 105 below.)

90 As mentioned above, an applicant's well-founded fear of persecution must be in relation to the country of his nationality. As long as he has no fear in relation to the country of his nationality, he can be expected to avail himself of that country's protection. He is not in need of international protection and is therefore not a refugee.

91 The fear of being persecuted need not always extend to the *whole* territory of the refugee's country of nationality. Thus in ethnic clashes or in cases of grave disturbances involving civil war conditions, persecution of a specific ethnic or national group may occur in only one part of the country. In such situations, a person will not be excluded from refugee status merely because he could have sought refuge in another part of the same country, if under all the circumstances it would not have been reasonable to expect him to do so.

92 The situation of persons having more than one nationality is dealt with in paragraphs 106 and 107 below.

93 Nationality may be proved by the possession of a national passport. Possession of such a passport creates a prima facie presumption that the holder is a national of the country of issue, unless the passport itself states otherwise. A person holding a passport showing him to be a national of the issuing country, but who claims that he does not possess that country's nationality, must substantiate his claim, for example, by showing that the passport is a so-called 'passport of convenience' (an apparently regular national passport that is sometimes issued by a national authority to non-nationals). However, a mere assertion by the holder that the passport was issued to him as a matter of convenience for travel purposes only is not sufficient to rebut the presumption of nationality. In certain cases, it might be possible to obtain information from the authority that issued the passport. If such information cannot be obtained, or cannot be obtained within reasonable time, the examiner will have to decide on the credibility of the applicant's assertion in weighing all other elements of his story.

---

1 In certain countries, particularly in Latin America, there is a custom of 'diplomatic asylum', ie granting refuge to political fugitives in foreign embassies. While a person thus sheltered may be considered to be outside his country's *jurisdiction*, he is not outside its territory and cannot therefore be considered under the terms of the 1951 Convention. The former notion of the 'extraterritoriality' of embassies has lately been

replaced by the term 'inviolability' used in the 1961 Vienna Convention on Diplomatic Relations.

[C.2.146]
(b) Refugees 'sur place'
94   The requirement that a person must be outside his country to be a refugee does not mean that he must necessarily have left that country illegally, or even that he must have left it on account of well-founded fear. He may have decided to ask for recognition of his refugee status after having already been abroad for some time. A person who was not a refugee when he left his country, but who becomes a refugee at a later date, is called a refugee 'sur place'.

95   A person becomes a refugee 'sur place' due to circumstances arising in his country of origin during his absence. Diplomats and other officials serving abroad, prisoners of war, students, migrant workers and others have applied for refugee status during their residence abroad and have been recognized as refugees.

96   A person may become a refugee 'sur place' as a result of his own actions, such as associating with refugees already recognized, or expressing his political views in his country of residence. Whether such actions are sufficient to justify a well-founded fear of persecution must be determined by a careful examination of the circumstances. Regard should be had in particular to whether such actions may have come to the notice of the authorities of the person's country of origin and how they are likely to be viewed by those authorities.

(5) 'and is unable or, owing to such fear, is unwilling to avail himself of the protection of that country'

[C.2.147]
97   Unlike the phrase dealt with under (6) below, the present phrase relates to persons who have a nationality. Whether unable or unwilling to avail himself of the protection of his Government, a refugee is always a person who does not enjoy such protection.

98   Being *unable* to avail himself of such protection implies circumstances that are beyond the will of the person concerned. There may, for example, be a state of war, civil war or other grave disturbance, which prevents the country of nationality from extending protection or makes such protection ineffective. Protection by the country of nationality may also have been denied to the applicant. Such denial of protection may confirm or strengthen the applicant's fear of persecution, and may indeed be an element of persecution.

99   What constitutes a refusal of protection must be determined according the circumstances of the case. If it appears that the applicant has been denied services (eg, refusal of a national passport or extension of its validity, or denial of admittance to the home territory) normally accorded to his co-nationals, this may constitute a refusal of protection within the definition.

100   The term *unwilling* refers to refugees who refuse to accept the protection

of the Government of the country of their nationality[1]. It is qualified by the phrase 'owing to such fear'. Where a person is willing to avail himself of the protection of his home country, such willingness would normally be incompatible with a claim that he is outside that country 'owing to well-founded fear of persecution'. Whenever the protection of the country of nationality is available, and there is no ground based on well-founded fear for refusing it, the person concerned is not in need of international protection and is not a refugee.

---

1 UN Document E/1618, page 39.

---

(6) 'or who, not having a nationality and being outside the country of his former habitual residence as a result of such events, is unable or, owing to such fear, is unwilling to return to it'

[C.2.148]

101   This phrase, which relates to stateless refugees, is parallel to the preceding phrase, which concerns refugees who have a nationality. In the case of stateless refugees, the 'country of nationality' is replaced by 'the country of his former habitual residence', and the expression 'unwilling to avail himself of the protection ...' is replaced by the words 'unwilling to return to it'. In the case of a stateless refugee, the question of 'availment of protection' of the country of his former habitual residence does not, of course, arise. Moreover, once a stateless person has abandoned the country of his former habitual residence for the reasons indicated in the definition, he is usually unable to return.

102   It will be noted that not all stateless persons are refugees. They must be outside the country of their former habitual residence for the reasons indicated in the definition. Where these reasons do not exist, the stateless person is not a refugee.

103   Such reasons must be examined in relation to the country of 'former habitual residence' in regard to which fear is alleged. This was defined by the drafters of the 1951 Convention as 'the country in which he had resided and where he had suffered or fears he would suffer persecution if he returned[1].

104   A stateless person may have more than one country of former habitual residence, and he may have a fear of persecution in relation to more than one of them. The definition does not require that he satisfies the criteria in relation to all of them.

105   Once a stateless person has been determined a refugee in relation to 'the country of his former habitual residence', any further change of country of habitual residence will not affect his refugee status.

---

1 *loc cit.*

---

(7) Dual or multiple nationality

[C.2.149]
Article 1 A (2), paragraph 2, of the 1951 Convention:

'In the case of a person who has more than one nationality, the term "the country of his nationality" shall mean each of the countries of which he is a national, and a person shall not be deemed to be lacking the protection of the country of his nationality if, without any valid reason based on well-founded fear, he has not availed himself of the protection of one of the countries of which he is a national.'

106   This clause, which is largely self-explanatory, is intended to exclude from refugee status all persons with dual or multiple nationality who can avail themselves of the protection of at least one of the countries of which they are nationals. Wherever available, national protection takes precedence over international protection.

107   In examining the case of an applicant with dual or multiple nationality, is necessary, however, to distinguish between the possession of a nationality in the legal sense and the availability of protection by the country concerned. There will be cases where the applicant has the nationality of a country in regard to which he alleges no fear, but such nationality may be deemed to be ineffective as it does not entail the protection normally granted to nationals. In such circumstances, the possession of the second nationality would not be inconsistent with refugee status. As a rule, there should have been a request for, and a refusal of, protection before it can be established that a given nationality is ineffective. If there is no explicit refusal of protection, absence of a reply within reasonable time may be considered a refusal.

(8) Geographical scope

[C.2.150]
108   At the time when the 1951 Convention was drafted, there was a desire by a number of States not to assume obligations the extent of which could not be foreseen. This desire led to the inclusion of the 1951 dateline, to which reference has already been made (paragraphs 35 and 36 above). In response to the wish of certain Governments, the 1951 Convention also gave to Contracting States the possibility of limiting their obligations under the Convention to persons who had become refugees as a result of events occurring in Europe.

109   Accordingly, Article 1 B of the 1951 Convention states that:

'(1) For the purposes of this Convention, the words "events occurring before 1 January 1951" in Article 1, Section A, shall be understood to mean either

(*a*) "events occurring in Europe before 1 January 1951"; or
(*b*) "events occurring in Europe and elsewhere before 1 January 1951";

and each Contracting State shall make a declaration at the time of signature, ratification or accession, specifying which of these meanings it applies for the purposes of its obligations under this Convention.

(2) Any Contracting State which has adopted alternative (*a*) may at any time extend its obligations by adopting alternative (*b*) by means of a notification addressed to the Secretary-General of the United Nations.'

110   Of the States parties to the 1951 Convention, at the time of writing 9 still adhere to alternative (*a*), 'events occurring in Europe'[1]. While refugees from other parts of the world frequently obtain asylum in some of these countries, they are not normally accorded refugee status under the 1951 Convention.

---

1   See Annex IV (*not reproduced*).

CHAPTER III CESSATION CLAUSES

A General

[C.2.151]
111   The so-called 'cessation clauses' (Article 1 C (1) to (6) of the 1951 Convention) spell out the conditions under which a refugee ceases to be a refugee. They are based on the consideration that international protection should not be granted where it is no longer necessary or justified.

112   Once a person's status as a refugee has been determined, it is maintained unless he comes within the terms of one of the cessation clauses[1]. This strict approach towards the determination of refugee status results from the need to provide refugees with the assurance that their status will not be subject to constant review in the light of temporary changes—not of a fundamental character—in the situation prevailing in their country of origin.

113   Article 1 C of the 1951 Convention provides that:

'This Convention shall cease to apply to any person falling under the terms of section A if:
(1) He has voluntarily re-availed himself of the protection of the country of his nationality; or
(2) Having lost his nationality, he has voluntarily re-acquired it; or
(3) He has acquired a new nationality, and enjoys the protection of the country of his new nationality; or
(4) He has voluntarily re-established himself in the country which he left or outside which he remained owing to fear of persecution; or
(5) He can no longer, because the circumstances in connexion with which he has been recognized as a refugee have ceased to exist, continue to refuse to avail himself of the protection of the country of his nationality;
Provided that this paragraph shall not apply to a refugee falling under Section A (1) of this Article who is able to invoke compelling reasons arising out of previous persecution for refusing to avail himself of the protection of the country of nationality;
(6) Being a person who has no nationality he is, because the circumstances in connexion with which he has been recognized as a refugee have ceased to exist, able to return to the country of his former habitual residence; Provided that this paragraph shall not apply to a refugee falling under section A (1) of

this Article who is able to invoke compelling reasons arising out of previous persecution for refusing to return to the country of his former habitual residence.'

114   Of the six cessation clauses, the first four reflect a change in the situation of the refugee that has been brought about by himself, namely:

(1) voluntary re-availment of national protection;
(2) voluntary re-acquisition of nationality;
(3) acquisition of a new nationality;
(4) voluntary re-establishment in the country where persecution was feared.

115   The last two cessation clauses, (5) and (6), are based on the consideration that international protection is no longer justified on account of changes in the country where persecution was feared, because the reasons for a person becoming a refugee have ceased to exist.

116   The cessation clauses are negative in character and are exhaustively enumerated. They should therefore be interpreted restrictively, and no other reasons may be adduced by way of analogy to justify the withdrawal of refugee status. Needless to say, if a refugee, for whatever reasons, no longer wishes to be considered a refugee, there will be no call for continuing to grant him refugee status and international protection.

117   Article 1 C does not deal with the cancellation of refugee status. Circumstances may, however, come to light that indicate that a person should never have been recognized as a refugee in the first place; eg if it subsequently appears that refugee status was obtained by a misrepresentation of material facts, or that the person concerned possesses another nationality, or that one of the exclusion clauses would have applied to him had all the relevant facts been known. In such cases, the decision by which he was determined to be a refugee will normally be cancelled.

---

1 In some cases refugee status may continue, even though the reasons for such status have evidently ceased to exist. Cf sub-sections (5) and (6) (paragraphs 135 to 139 below).

B Interpretation of terms

(1) Voluntary re-availment of national protection

[C.2.152]
Article 1 C (1) of the 1951 Convention:

'He has voluntarily re-availed himself of the protection of the country of his nationality;'

118   This cessation clause refers to a refugee possessing a nationality who remains outside the country of his nationality. (The situation of a refugee who has actually returned to the country of his nationality is governed by the fourth cessation clause, which speaks of a person having 're-established' himself in that country.) A refugee who has voluntarily re-availed himself of national protection is no longer in need of international protection. He has demonstrated

that he is no longer 'unable or unwilling to avail himself of the protection of the country of his nationality'.

119   This cessation clause implies three requirements:

(*a*) voluntariness: the refugee must act voluntarily;
(*b*) intention: refugee must intend by his action to re-avail himself of the protection of the country of his nationality;
(*c*) re-availment: the refugee must actually obtain such protection.

120   If the refugee does not act voluntarily, he will not cease to be a refugee. If he is instructed by an authority, eg of his country of residence, to perform against his will an act that could be interpreted as a re-availment of the protection of the country of his nationality, such as applying to his Consulate for a national passport, he will not cease to be a refugee merely because he obeys such an instruction. He may also be constrained, by circumstances beyond his control, to have recourse to a measure of protection from his country of nationality. He may, for instance, need to apply for a divorce in his home country because no other divorce may have the necessary international recognition. Such an act cannot be considered to be a 'voluntary re-availment of protection' and will not deprive a person of refugee status.

121   In determining whether refugee status is lost in these circumstances, a distinction should be drawn between actual re-availment of protection and occasional and incidental contacts with the national authorities. If a refugee applies for and obtains a national passport or its renewal, it will, in the absence of proof to the contrary, be presumed that he intends to avail himself of the protection of the country of his nationality. On the other hand, the acquisition of documents from the national authorities, for which non-nationals would likewise have to apply – such as a birth or marriage certificate – or similar services, cannot be regarded as a re-availment of protection.

122   A refugee requesting protection from the authorities of the country of his nationality has only 're-availed' himself of that protection when his request has actually been granted. The most frequent case of 're-availment of protection' will be where the refugee wishes to return to his country of nationality. He will not cease to be a refugee merely by applying for repatriation. On the other hand, obtaining an entry permit or a national passport for the purposes of returning will, in the absence of proof to the contrary, be considered as terminating refugee status[1]. This does not, however, preclude assistance being given to the repatriant – also by UNHCR – in order to facilitate his return.

123   A refugee may have voluntarily obtained a national passport, intending either to avail himself of the protection of his country of origin while staying outside that country, or to return to that country. As stated above, with the receipt of such a document he normally ceases to be a refugee. If he subsequently renounces either intention, his refugee status will need to be determined afresh. He will need to explain why he changed his mind, and to show that there has been no basic change in the conditions that originally made him a refugee.

124   Obtaining a national passport or an extension of its validity may, under certain exceptional conditions, not involve termination of refugee status (see paragraph 120 above). This could for example be the case where the holder of a national passport is not permitted to return to the country of his nationality without specific permission.

125 Where a refugee visits his former home country not with a national passport but, for example, with a travel document issued by his country of residence, he has been considered by certain States to have re-availed himself of the protection of his former home country and to have lost his refugee status under the present cessation clause. Cases of this kind should, however, be judged on their individual merits. Visiting an old or sick parent will have a different bearing on the refugee's relation to his former home country than regular visits to that country spent on holidays or for the purpose of establishing business relations.

---

1 The above applies to a refugee who is still outside his country. It will be noted that the fourth cessation clause provides that any refugee will cease to be a refugee when he has voluntarily 're-established' himself in his country of nationality or former habitual residence.

---

(2) *Voluntary re-acquisition of nationality*

[C.2.153]
Article 1 C (2) of the 1951 Convention:

'Having lost his nationality, he has voluntarily re-acquired it;'

126 This clause is similar to the preceding one. It applies to cases where a refugee, having lost the nationality of the country in respect of which he was recognized as having well-founded fear of persecution, voluntarily re-acquires such nationality.

127 While under the preceding clause (Article 1 C (1)) a person having a nationality ceases to be a refugee if he re-avails himself of the protection attaching to such nationality, under the present clause (Article 1 C (2)) he loses his refugee status by re-acquiring the nationality previously lost[1].

128 The re-acquisition of nationality must be voluntary. The granting of nationality by operation of law or by decree does not imply voluntary re-acquisition, unless the nationality has been expressly or impliedly accepted. A person does not cease to be a refugee merely because he could have re-acquired his former nationality by option, unless this option has actually been exercised. If such former nationality is granted by operation of law, subject to an option to reject, it will be regarded as a voluntary re-acquisition if the refugee, with full knowledge, has not exercised this option; unless he is able to invoke special reasons showing that it was not in fact his intention to re-acquire his former nationality.

---

1 In the majority of cases a refugee maintains the nationality of his former home country. Such nationality may be lost by individual or collective measures of deprivation of nationality. Loss of nationality (statelessness) is therefore not necessarily implicit in refugee status.

---

(3) Acquisition of a new nationality and protection

[C.2.154]
Article 1 C (3) of the 1951 Convention:

> 'He has acquired a new nationality and enjoys the protection of the country of his new nationality;'

129   As in the case of the re-acquisition of nationality, this third cessation clause derives from the principle that a person who enjoys national protection is not in need of international protection.

130   The nationality that the refugee acquires is usually that of the country of his residence. A refugee living in one country may, however, in certain cases, acquire the nationality of another country. If he does so, his refugee status will also cease, provided that the new nationality also carries the protection of the country concerned. This requirement results from the phrase 'and enjoys the protection of the country of his new nationality'.

131   If a person has ceased to be a refugee, having acquired a new nationality, and then claims well-founded fear in relation to the country of his new nationality, this creates a completely new situation and his status must be determined in relation to the country of his new nationality.

132   Where refugee status has terminated through the acquisition of a new nationality, and such new nationality has been lost, depending on the circumstances of such loss, refugee status may be revived.

(4) Voluntary re-establishment in the country where persecution was feared

[C.2.155]
Article 1 C (4) of the 1951 Convention:

> 'He was voluntarily re-established himself in the country which he left or outside which he remained owing to fear of persecution;'

133   This fourth cessation clause applies both to refugees who have a nationality and to stateless refugees. It relates to refugees who, having returned to their country of origin or previous residence, have not previously ceased to be refugees under the first or second cessation clauses while still in their country of refuge.

134   The clause refers to 'voluntary re-establishment'. This is to be understood as return to the country of nationality or former habitual residence with a view to permanently residing there. A temporary visit by a refugee to his former home country, not with a national passport but, for example, with a travel document issued by his country of residence, does not constitute 're-establishment' and will not involve loss of refugee status under the present clause[1].

---

1 See paragraph 125 above.

(5) Nationals whose reasons for becoming a refugee have ceased to exist

[C.2.156]
Article 1 C (5) of the 1951 Convention:

'He can no longer, because the circumstances in connexion with which he has been recognized as a refugee have ceased to exist, continue to refuse to avail himself of the protection of the country of his nationality; Provided that this paragraph shall not apply to a refugee falling under section A (1) of this Article who is able to invoke compelling reasons arising out of previous persecution for refusing to avail himself of the protection of the country of nationality;'

135   'Circumstances' refer to fundamental changes in the country, which can be assumed to remove the basis of the fear of persecution. A mere – possibly transitory – change in the facts surrounding the individual refugee's fear, which does not entail such major changes of circumstances, is not sufficient to make this clause applicable. A refugee's status should not in principle be subject to frequent review to the detriment of his sense of security, which international protection is intended to provide.

136   The second paragraph of this clause contains an exception to the cessation provision contained in the first paragraph. It deals with the special situation where a person may have been subjected to very serious persecution in the past and will not therefore cease to be a refugee, even if fundamental changes have occurred in his country of origin. The reference to Article 1 A (1) indicates that the exception applies to 'statutory refugees'. At the time when the 1951 Convention was elaborated, these formed the majority of refugees. The exception, however, reflects a more general humanitarian principle, which could also be applied to refugees other than statutory refugees. It is frequently recognized that a person who – or whose family – has suffered under atrocious forms of persecution should not be expected to repatriate. Even though there may have been a change of regime in his country, this may not always produce a complete change in the attitude of the population, nor, in view of his past experiences, in the mind of the refugee.

(6) Stateless persons whose reasons for becoming a refugee have ceased to exist

[C.2.157]
Article 1 C (6) of the 1951 Convention:

'Being a person who has no nationality he is, because the circumstances in connexion with which he has been recognized as a refugee have ceased to exist, able to return to the country of his former habitual residence; Provided that this paragraph shall not apply to a refugee falling under section A (1) of this Article who is able to invoke compelling reasons arising out of previous persecution for refusing to return to the country of his former habitual residence.'

137   The sixth and last cessation clause is parallel to the fifth cessation

clause, which concerns persons who have a nationality. The present clause deals exclusively with stateless persons who are able to return to the country of their former habitual residence.

138 'Circumstances' should be interpreted in the same way as under the fifth cessation clause.

139 It should be stressed that, apart from the changed circumstances in his country of former habitual residence, the person concerned must be *able* to return there. This, in the case of a stateless person, may not always be possible.

CHAPTER IV   EXCLUSION CLAUSES

A General

[C.2.158]
140 The 1951 Convention, in Sections D, E and F of Article 1, contains provisions whereby persons otherwise having the characteristics of refugees, as defined in Article 1, Section A, are excluded from refugee status. Such persons fall into three groups. The first group (Article 1D) consists of persons already receiving United Nations protection or assistance; the second group (Article 1E) deals with persons who are not considered to be in need of international protection; and the third group (Article 1F) enumerates the categories of persons who are not considered to be deserving of international protection.

141 Normally it will be during the process of determining a person's refugee status that the facts leading to exclusion under these clauses will emerge. It may, however, also happen that facts justifying exclusion will become known only after a person has been recognized as a refugee. In such cases, the exclusion clause will call for a cancellation of the decision previously taken.

B Interpretation of terms

(1) Persons already receiving United Nations protection or assistance

[C.2.159]
Article 1 D of the 1951 Convention:

'This Convention shall not apply to persons who are at present receiving from organs or agencies of the United Nations other than the United Nations High Commissioner for Refugees protection or assistance. 'When such protection or assistance has ceased for any reason, without the position of such persons being definitively settled in accordance with the relevant resolutions adopted by the General Assembly of the United Nations, these persons shall ipso facto be entitled to the benefits of this Convention.'

142 Exclusion under this clause applies to any person who is in receipt of protection or assistance from organs or agencies of the United Nations, other than the United Nations High Commissioner for Refugees. Such protection or

assistance was previously given by the former United Nations Korean Reconstruction Agency (UNKRA) and is currently given by the United Nations Relief and Works Agency for Palestine Refugees in the Near East (UNRWA). There could be other similar situations in the future.

143   With regard to refugees from Palestine, it will be noted that UNRWA operates only in certain areas of the Middle East, and it is only there that its protection or assistance are given. Thus, a refugee from Palestine who finds himself outside that area does not enjoy the assistance mentioned and may be considered for determination of his refugee status under the criteria of the 1951 Convention. It should normally be sufficient to establish that the circumstances which originally made him qualify for protection or assistance from UNRWA still persist and that he has neither ceased to be a refugee under one of the cessation clauses nor is excluded from the application of the Convention under one of the exclusion clauses.

(2) *Persons not considered to be in need of international protection*

[C.2.160]
Article 1 E of the 1951 Convention:

> 'This Convention shall not apply to a person who is recognised by the competent authorities of the country in which he has taken residence as having the rights and obligations which are attached to the possession of the nationality of that country.'

144   This provision relates to persons who might otherwise qualify for refugee status and who have been received in a country where they have been granted most of the rights normally enjoyed by nationals, but not formal citizenship. (They are frequently referred to as 'national refugees'.) The country that has received them is frequently one where the population is of the same ethnic origin as themselves[1].

145   There is no precise definition of 'rights and obligations' that would constitute a reason for exclusion under this clause. It may, however, be said that the exclusion operates if a person's status is largely assimilated to that of a national of the country. In particular he must, like a national, be fully protected against deportation or expulsion.

146   The clause refers to a person who has 'taken residence' in the country concerned. This implies continued residence and not a mere visit. A person who resides outside the country and does not enjoy the diplomatic protection of that country is not affected by the exclusion clause.

---

1 In elaborating this exclusion clause, the drafters of the Convention had principally in mind refugees of German extraction having arrived in the Federal Republic of Germany who were recognised as possessing the rights and obligations attaching to German nationality.

(3) Persons considered not to be deserving of international protection

[C.2.161]

Article 1 F of the 1951 Convention:

'The provisions of this Convention shall not apply to any person with respect to whom there are serious reasons for considering that:

(*a*) he has committed a crime against peace, a war crime, or a crime against humanity, as defined in the international instruments drawn up to make provision in respect of such crimes;

(*b*) he has committed a serious non-political crime outside the country of refuge prior to his admission to that country as a refugee;

(*c*) he has been guilty of acts contrary to the purposes and principles of the United Nations.'

147   The pre-war international instruments that defined various categories of refugees contained no provisions for the exclusion of criminals. It was immediately after the Second World War that for the first time special provisions were drawn up to exclude from the large group of then assisted refugees certain persons who were deemed unworthy of international protection.

148   At the time when the Convention was drafted, the memory of the trials of major war criminals was still very much alive, and there was agreement on the part of States that war criminals should not be protected. There was also a desire on the part of States to deny admission to their territories of criminals who would present a danger to security and public order.

149   The competence to decide whether any of these exclusion clauses are applicable is incumbent upon the Contracting State in whose territory the applicant seeks recognition of his refugee status. For these clauses to apply, it is sufficient to establish that there are 'serious reasons for considering' that one of the acts described has been committed. Formal proof of previous penal prosecution is not required. Considering the serious consequences of exclusion for the person concerned, however, the interpretation of these exclusion clauses must be restrictive.

[C.2.162]
(a) War crimes, etc

'(*a*) he has committed a crime against peace, a war crime against humanity, as defined in the international instruments drawn up to make provision in respect of such crimes.'

150   In mentioning crimes against peace, war crimes or crimes against humanity, the Convention refers generally to 'international instruments drawn up to make provision in respect of such crimes'. There are a considerable number of such instruments dating from the end of the Second World War up to the present time. All of them contain definitions of what constitute 'crimes against peace, war crimes and crimes against humanity'. The most comprehensive definition will be found in the 1945 London Agreement and Charter of the International Military Tribunal. The definitions contained in the above-mentioned London Agreement and a list of other pertinent instruments are given in Annexes V and VI (*not reproduced*).

[C.2.163]
(b) Common crimes

'(*b*) he has committed a serious non-political crime outside the country of refuge prior to his admission to that country as a refugee.'

151   The aim of this exclusion clause is to protect the community of a receiving country from the danger of admitting a refugee who has committed a serious common crime. It also seeks to render due justice to a refugee who has committed a common crime (or crimes) of a less serious nature or has committed a political offence.

152   In determining whether an offence is 'non-political' or is, on the contrary, a 'political' crime, regard should be given in the first place to its nature and purpose ie whether it has been committed out of genuine political motives and riot merely for personal reasons or gain. There should also be a close and direct causal link between the crime committed and its alleged political purpose and object. The political element of the offence should also outweigh its common-law character. This would not be the case if the acts committed are grossly out of proportion to the alleged objective. The political nature of the offence is also more difficult to accept if it involves acts of an atrocious nature.

153   Only a crime committed or presumed to have been committed by an applicant 'outside the country of refuge prior to his admission to that country as a refugee' is a ground for exclusion. The country outside would normally be the country of origin, but it could also be another country, except the country of refuge where the applicant seeks recognition of his refugee status.

154   A refugee committing a serious crime in the country of refuge is subject to due process of law in that country. In extreme cases, Article 33 paragraph 2 of the Convention permits a refugee's expulsion or return to his former home country if, having been convicted by a final judgement of a 'particularly serious' common crime, he constitutes a danger to the community of his country of refuge.

155   What constitutes a 'serious' non-political crime for the purposes of this exclusion clause is difficult to define, especially since the term 'crime' has different connotations in different legal systems. In some countries the word 'crime' denotes only offences of a serious character. In other countries it may comprise anything from petty larceny to murder. In the present context, however, a 'serious' crime must be a capital crime or a very grave punishable act. Minor offences punishable by moderate sentences are not grounds for exclusion under Article 1 F (*b*) even if technically referred to as 'crimes' in the penal law of the country concerned.

156   In applying this exclusion clause, it is also necessary to strike a balance between the nature of the offence presumed to have been committed by the applicant and the degree of persecution feared. If a person has well-founded fear of very severe persecution, eg persecution endangering his life or freedom, a crime must be very grave in order to exclude him. If the persecution feared is less serious, it will be necessary to have regard to the nature of the crime or crimes presumed to have been committed in order to establish whether the applicant is not in reality a fugitive from justice or whether his criminal character does not outweigh his character as a bona fide refugee.

157   In evaluating the nature of the crime presumed to have been committed,

all the relevant factors – including any mitigating circumstances – must be taken into account. It is also necessary to have regard to any aggravating circumstances as, for example, the fact that the applicant may already have a criminal record. The fact that an applicant convicted of a serious non-political crime has already served his sentence or has been granted a pardon or has benefited from an amnesty is also relevant. In the latter case, there is a presumption that the exclusion clause is no longer applicable, unless it can be shown that, despite the pardon or amnesty, the applicant's criminal character still predominates.

158   Considerations similar to those mentioned in the preceding paragraphs will apply when a crime – in the widest sense – has been committed as a means of, or concomitant with, escape from the country where persecution was feared. Such crimes may range from the theft of a means of locomotion to endangering or taking the lives of innocent people. While for the purposes of the present exclusion clause it may be possible to overlook the fact that a refugee, not finding any other means of escape, may have crashed the border in a stolen car, decisions will be more difficult where he has hijacked an aircraft, ie forced its crew, under threat of arms or with actual violence, to change destination in order to bring him to a country of refuge.

159   As regards hijacking, the question has arisen as to whether, if committed in order to escape from persecution, it constitutes a serious non-political crime within the meaning of the present exclusion clause. Governments have considered the unlawful seizure of aircraft on several occasions within the framework of the United Nations, and a number of international conventions have been adopted dealing with the subject. None of these instruments mentions refugees. However, one of the reports leading to the adoption of a resolution on the subject states that 'the adoption of the draft Resolution cannot prejudice any international legal rights or duties of States under instruments relating to the status of refugees and stateless persons'. Another report states that 'the adoption of the draft Resolution cannot prejudice any international legal rights or duties of States with respect to asylum'[1].

160   The various conventions adopted in this connexion[2] deal mainly with the manner in which the perpetrators of such acts have to be treated. They invariably give Contracting States the alternative of extraditing such persons or instituting penal proceedings for the act on their own territory, which implies the right to grant asylum.

161   While there is thus a possibility of granting asylum, the gravity of the persecution of which the offender may have been in fear, and the extent to which such fear is well-founded, will have to be duly considered in determining his possible refugee status under the 1951 Convention. The question of the exclusion under Article 1F(*b*) of an applicant who has committed an unlawful seizure of an aircraft will also have to be carefully examined in each individual case.

---

1 Reports of the Sixth Committee on General Assembly resolutions 2645(XXV) United Nations document A/8716, and 2551 (XXIV), United Nations document A/7845.

2 Convention on Offences and Certain Other Acts Committed on Board Aircraft, Tokyo, 14 September 1963; Convention for the Suppression of Unlawful Seizure of

Aircraft, the Hague, 16 December 1970; Convention for the Suppression of Unlawful Acts against the Safety of Civil Aviation, Montreal, 23 September 1971.

[C.2.164]
(c) Acts contrary to the purposes and principles of the United Nations

'(c) he has been guilty of acts contrary to the purposes and principles of the United Nations.'

162   It will be seen that this very generally-worded exclusion clause overlaps with the exclusion clause in Article 1 F (*a*); for it is evident that a crime against peace, a war crime or a crime against humanity is also an act contrary to the purposes and principles of the United Nations. While Article 1 F (*c*) does not introduce any specific new element, it is intended to cover in a general way such acts against the purposes and principles of the United Nations that might not be fully covered by the two preceding exclusion clauses. Taken in conjunction with the latter, it has to be assumed, although this is not specifically stated, that the acts covered by the present clause must also be of a criminal nature.

163   The purposes and principles of the United Nations are set out in the Preamble and Articles 1 and 2 of the Charter of the United Nations. They enumerate fundamental principles that should govern the conduct of their members in relation to each other and in relation to the international community as a whole. From this it could be inferred that an individual, in order to have committed an act contrary to these principles, must have been in a position of power in a member State and instrumental to his State's infringing these principles. However, there are hardly any precedents on record for the application of this clause, which, due to its very general character, should be applied with caution.

CHAPTER V   SPECIAL CASES

A War refugees

[C.2.165]
164   Persons compelled to leave their country of origin as a result of international or national armed conflicts are not normally considered refugees under the 1951 Convention or 1967 Protocol[1]. They do, however, have the protection provided for in other international instruments, eg the Geneva Conventions of 1949 on the Protection of War Victims and the 1977 Protocol additional to the Geneva Conventions of 1949 relating to the protection of Victims of International Armed Conflicts[2].

165   However, foreign invasion or occupation of all or part of a country can result – and occasionally has resulted – in persecution for one or more of the reasons enumerated in the 1951 Convention. In such cases, refugee status will depend upon whether the applicant is able to show that he has a 'well-founded fear of being persecuted' in the occupied territory and, in addition, upon whether or not he is able to avail himself of the protection of his government, or of a protecting power whose duty it is to safeguard the interests of his coun-

try during the armed conflict, and whether such protection can be considered to be effective.

166   Protection may not be available if there are no diplomatic relations between the applicant's host country and his country of origin. If the applicant's government is itself in exile, the effectiveness of the protection that it is able to extend may be open to question. Thus, every case has to be judged on its merits, both in respect of well-founded fear of persecution and of the availability of effective protection on the part of the government of the country of origin.

---

1 In respect of Africa, however, see the definition, in Article 1(2) of the OAU Convention concerning the Specific Aspects of Refugee Problems in Africa, quoted in paragraph 27 above.
2 See Annex VI, items (6) and (7) (*not reproduced*).

B   Deserters and persons avoiding military service

[C.2.166]
167   In countries where military service is compulsory, failure to perform this duty is frequently punishable by law. Moreover, whether military service is compulsory or not, desertion is invariably considered a criminal offence. The penalties may vary from country to country, and are not normally regarded as persecution. Fear of prosecution and punishment for desertion or draft-evasion does not in itself constitute well-founded fear of persecution under the definition. Desertion or draft-evasion does not, on the other hand, exclude a person from being a refugee, and a person may be a refugee in addition to being a deserter or draft-evader.

168   A person is clearly not a refugee if his only reason for desertion or draft-evasion is his dislike of military service or fear of combat. He may, however, be a refugee if his desertion or evasion of military service is concomitant with other relevant motives for leaving or remaining outside his country, or if he otherwise has reasons, within the meaning of the definition, to fear persecution.

169   A deserter or draft-evader may also be considered a refugee if it can be shown that he would suffer disproportionately severe punishment for the military offence on account of his race, religion, nationality, membership of a particular social group or political opinion. The same would apply if it can be shown that he has well-founded fear of persecution on these grounds above and beyond the punishment for desertion.

170   There are, however, also cases where the necessity to perform military service may be the sole ground for a claim to refugee status, ie when a person can show that the performance of military service would have required his participation in military action contrary to his genuine political, religious or moral convictions, or to valid reasons of conscience.

171   Not every conviction, genuine though it may be, will constitute a sufficient reason for claiming refugee status after desertion or draft-evasion. It is

not enough for a person to be in disagreement with his government regarding the political justification for a particular military action. Where, however, the type of military action, with which an individual does not wish to be associated, is condemned by the international community as contrary to basic rules of human conduct, punishment for desertion or draft-evasion could, in the light of all other requirements of the definition, in itself be regarded as persecution.

172   Refusal to perform military service may also be based on religious convictions. If an applicant is able to show that his religious convictions are genuine, and that such convictions are not taken into account by the authorities of his country in requiring him to perform military service, he may be able to establish a claim to refugee status. Such a claim would, of course, be supported by any additional indications that the applicant or his family may have encountered difficulties due to their religious convictions.

173   The question as to whether objection to performing military service for reasons of conscience can give rise to a valid claim to refugee status should also be considered in the light of more recent developments in this field. An increasing number of States have introduced legislation or administrative regulations whereby persons who can invoke genuine reasons of conscience are exempted from military service, either entirely or subject to their performing alternative (ie civilian) service. The introduction of such legislation or administrative regulations has also been the subject of recommendations by international agencies[1]. In the light of these developments, it would be open to Contracting States, to grant refugee status to persons who object to performing military service for genuine reasons of conscience.

174   The genuineness of a person's political, religious or moral convictions, or of his reasons of conscience for objecting to performing military service, will of course need to be established by a thorough investigation of his personality and background. The fact that he may have manifested his views prior to being called to arms, or that he may already have encountered difficulties with the authorities because of his convictions, are relevant considerations. Whether he has been drafted into compulsory service or joined the army as a volunteer may also be indicative of the genuineness of his convictions.

---

1 Cf recommendation 816 (1977) on the Right of Conscientious Objection to Military Service, adopted at the Parliamentary Assembly of the Council of Europe at its Twenty-ninth Ordinary Session (5–13 October 1977).

C   Persons having resorted to force or committed acts of violence

175   Applications for refugee status are frequently made by persons who used force or committed acts of violence. Such conduct is frequently associated with, or claimed to be associated with, political activities or political opinions. They may be the result of individual initiatives, or may have been committed within the framework of organized groups. The latter may either be clandestine groupings or political cum military organizations that are officially recog-

nized or whose activities are widely acknowledged[1]. Account should also be taken of the fact that the use of force is an aspect of the maintenance of law and order and may—by definition—be lawfully resorted to by the police and armed forces in the exercise of their functions.

176   An application for refugee status by a person having (or presumed to have) used force, or to have committed acts of violence of whatever nature and within whatever context, must in the first place—like any other application—be examined from the standpoint of the inclusion clauses in the 1951 Convention (paragraphs 32–110 above).

177   Where it has been determined that an applicant fulfils the inclusion criteria, the question may arise as to whether, in view of the acts involving the use of force or violence committed by him, he may not be covered by the terms of one or more of the exclusion clauses. These exclusion clauses, which figure in Article 1 F (*a*) to (*c*) of the 1951 Convention, have already been examined (paragraphs 147 to 163 above).

178   The exclusion clause in Article 1 F (*a*) was originally intended to exclude from refugee status any person in respect of whom there were serious reasons for considering that he has 'committed a crime against peace, a war crime, or a crime against humanity' in an official capacity. This exclusion clause is, however, also applicable to persons who have committed such crimes within the framework of various non-governmental groupings, whether officially recognized, clandestine or self-styled.

179   The exclusion clause in Article 1 F (*b*), which refers to 'a serious non-political crime', is normally not relevant to the use of force or to acts of violence committed in an official capacity. The interpretation of this exclusion clause has already been discussed. The exclusion clause in Article 1 F (*c*) has also been considered. As previously indicated, because of its vague character, it should be applied with caution.

180   It will also be recalled that, due to their nature and the serious consequences of their application to a person in fear of persecution, the exclusion clauses should be applied in a restrictive manner.

---

1 A number of liberation movements, which often include an armed wing, have officially been recognised by the General Assembly of the United Nations. Other liberation movements have only been recognised by a limited number of governments. Others again have no official recognition.

CHAPTER VI   THE PRINCIPLE OF FAMILY UNITY

[C.2.168]
181   Beginning with the Universal Declaration of Human Rights, which states that 'the family is the natural and fundamental group unit of society and is entitled to protection by society and the State', most international instruments dealing with human rights contain similar provisions for the protection of the unit of a family.

182   The Final Act of the Conference that adopted the 1951 Convention:

'Recommends Governments to take the necessary measures for the protection of the refugee's family, especially with a view to:
(1) Ensuring that the unity of the refugee's family is maintained particularly in cases where the head of the family has fulfilled the necessary conditions for admission to a particular country.
(2) The protection of refugees who are minors, in particular unaccompanied children and girls, with special reference to guardianship and adoption.'

183   The 1951 Convention does not incorporate the principle of family unity in the definition of the term refugee. The above-mentioned Recommendation in the Final Act of the Conference is, however, observed by the majority of States, whether or not parties to the 1951 Convention or to the 1967 Protocol.

184   If the head of a family meets the criteria of the definition, his dependants are normally granted refugee status according to the principle of family unity. It is obvious, however, that formal refugee status should not be granted to a dependant if this is incompatible with his personal legal status. Thus, a dependant member of a refugee family may be a national of the country of asylum or of another country, and may enjoy that country's protection. To grant him refugee status in such circumstances would not be called for.

185   As to which family members may benefit from the principle of family unity, the minimum requirement is the inclusion of the spouse and minor children. In practice, other dependants, such as aged parents of refugees, are normally considered if they are living in the same household. On the other hand, if the head of the family is not a refugee, there is nothing to prevent any one of his dependants, if they can invoke reasons on their own account, from applying for recognition as refugees under the 1951 Convention or the 1967 Protocol. In other words, the principle of family unity operates in favour of dependants, and not against them.

186   The principle of the unity of the family does not only operate where all family members become refugees at the same time. It applies equally to cases where a family unit has been temporarily disrupted through the flight of one or more of its members.

187   Where the unity of a refugee's family is destroyed by divorce, separation or death, dependants who have been granted refugee status on the basis of family unity will retain such refugee status unless they fall within the terms of a cessation clause; or if they do not have reasons other than those of personal convenience for wishing to retain refugee status; or if they themselves no longer wish to be considered as refugees.

188   If the dependant of a refugee falls within the terms of one of the exclusion clauses, refugee status should be denied to him.

Part Two   Procedures for the Determination of Refugee Status

A General

[C.2.169]
189   It has been seen that the 1951 Convention and the 1967 Protocol define who is a refugee for the purposes of these instruments. It is obvious that, to enable states parties to the Convention and to the Protocol to implement their provisions, refugees have to be identified. Such identification, ie the determination of refugee status, although mentioned in the 1951 Convention (cf Article 9), is not specifically regulated. In particular, the Convention does not indicate what type of procedures are to be adopted for the determination of refugee status. It is therefore left to each Contracting State to establish the procedure that it considers most appropriate, having regard to its particular constitutional and administrative structure.

190   It should be recalled that an applicant for refugee status is normally in a particularly vulnerable situation. He finds himself in an alien environment and may experience serious difficulties, technical and psychological, in submitting his case to the authorities of a foreign country, often in a language not his own. His application should therefore be examined within the framework of specially established procedures by qualified personnel having the necessary knowledge and experience, and an understanding of an applicant's particular difficulties and needs.

191   Due to the fact that the matter is not specifically regulated by the 1951 Convention, procedures adopted by states parties to the 1951 Convention and to the 1967 Protocol vary considerably. In a number of countries, refugee status is determined under formal procedures specifically established for this purpose. In other countries, the question of refugee status is considered within the framework of general procedures for the admission of aliens. In yet other countries, refugee status is determined under informal arrangements, or ad hoc for specific purposes, such as the issuance of travel documents.

192   In view of this situation and of the unlikelihood that all States bound by the 1951 Convention and the 1967 Protocol could establish identical procedures, the Executive Committee of the High Commissioner's Programme, at its twenty-eighth session in October 1977, recommended that procedures should satisfy certain basic requirements. These *basic requirements*, which reflect the special situation of the applicant for refugee status, to which reference has been made above, and which would ensure that the applicant is provided with certain essential guarantees, are the following:

'(i)   The competent official (eg immigration officer or border police officer) to whom the applicant addresses himself at the border or in the territory of a contracting state should have clear instructions for dealing with cases which might come within the purview of the relevant international instruments. He should be required to act in accordance with the principle of non-refoulement and to refer such cases to a higher authority.

(ii)   The applicant should receive the necessary guidance as to the procedure to be followed.

(iii) There should be a clearly identified authority — wherever possible a single central authority — With responsibility for examining requests for refugee status and taking a decision in the first instance.

(iv) The applicant should be given the necessary facilities, including the services of a competent interpreter, for submitting his case to the authorities concerned. Applicants should also be given the opportunity, of which they should be duly informed, to contact a representative of UNHCR.

(v) If the applicant is recognized as a refugee, he should be informed accordingly and issued with documentation certifying his refugee status.

(vi) If the applicant is not recognized, he should be given a reasonable time to appeal for a formal reconsideration of the decision, either to the same or to a different authority, whether administrative or judicial, according to the prevailing system.

(vii) The applicant should be permitted to remain in the country pending a decision on his initial request by the competent authority referred to in paragraph (iii) above, unless it has been established by that authority that his request is clearly abusive. He should also be permitted to remain in the country while an appeal to a higher administrative authority or to the courts is pending.'

193   The Executive Committee also expressed the hope that all States parties to the 1951 Convention and the 1967 Protocol that had not yet done so would take appropriate steps to establish such procedures in the near future and give favourable consideration to UNHCR participation in such procedures in appropriate form.

194   Determination of refugee status, which is closely related to questions of asylum and admission, is of concern to the High Commissioner in the exercise of his function to provide international protection for refugees. In a number of countries, the Office of the High Commissioner participates in various forms, in procedures for the determination of refugee status. Such participation is based on Article 35 of the 1951 Convention and the corresponding Article 11 of the 1967 Protocol, which provide for co-operation by the Contracting States with the High Commissioner's Office.

---

1 *Official Records of the General Assembly, Thirty-second Session, Supplement No 12* (A/32/12/Add 1), paragraph 53 (6) (*e*).

B Establishing the facts

(1) Principles and methods

[C.2.170]
195   The relevant facts of the individual case will have to be furnished in the first place by the applicant himself. It will then be up to the person charged with determining his status (the examiner) to assess the validity of any evidence and the credibility of the applicant's statements.

196   It is a general legal principle that the burden of proof lies on the person submitting a claim. Often, however, an applicant may not be able to support his statements by documentary or other proof, and cases in which an applicant can provide evidence of all his statements will be the exception rather than the rule. In most cases a person fleeing from persecution will have arrived with the barest necessities and very frequently even without personal documents. Thus, while the burden of proof in principle rests on the applicant, the duty to ascertain and evaluate all the relevant facts is shared between the applicant and the examiner. Indeed, in some cases, it may be for the examiner to use all the means at his disposal to produce the necessary evidence in support of the application. Even such independent research may not, however, always be successful and there may also be statements that are not susceptible of proof. In such cases, if the applicant's account appears credible, he should, unless there are good reasons to the contrary, be given the benefit of the doubt.

197   The requirement of evidence should thus not be too strictly applied in view of the difficulty of proof inherent in the special situation in which an applicant for refugee status finds himself. Allowance for such possible lack of evidence does not, however, mean that unsupported statements must necessarily be accepted as true if they are inconsistent with the general account put forward by the applicant.

198   A person who, because of his experiences, was in fear of the authorities in his own country may still feel apprehensive vis-à-vis any authority. He may therefore be afraid to speak freely and give a full and accurate account of his case.

199   While an initial interview should normally suffice to bring an applicant's story to light, it may be necessary for the examiner to clarify any apparent inconsistencies and to resolve any contradictions in a further interview, and to find an explanation for any misrepresentation or concealment of material facts. Untrue statements by themselves are not a reason for refusal of refugee status and it is the examiner's responsibility to evaluate such statements in the light of all the circumstances of the case.

200   An examination in depth of the different methods of fact-finding is outside the scope of the present Handbook. It may be mentioned, however, that basic information is frequently given, in the first instance, by completing a standard questionnaire. Such basic information will normally not be sufficient to enable the examiner to reach a decision, and one or more personal interviews will be required. It will be necessary for the examiner to gain the confidence of the applicant in order to assist the latter in putting forward his case and in fully explaining his opinions and feelings. In creating such a climate of confidence it is, of course, of the utmost importance that the applicant's statements will be treated as confidential and that he be so informed.

201   Very frequently the fact-finding process will not be complete until a wide range of circumstances has been ascertained. Taking isolated incidents out of context may be misleading. The cumulative effect of the applicant's experience must be taken into account. Where no single incident stands out above the others, sometimes a small incident may be 'the last straw'; and although no single incident may be sufficient, all the incidents related by the applicant taken together, could make his fear 'well-founded' (see paragraph 53 above).

202   Since the examiner's conclusion on the facts of the case and his person-al impression of the applicant will lead to a decision that affects human lives, he must apply the criteria in a spirit of justice and understanding and his judge-ment should not, of course, be influenced by the personal consideration that the applicant may be an 'undeserving case'.

(2) Benefit of the doubt

[C.2.171]
203   After the applicant has made a genuine effort to substantiate his story there may still be a lack of evidence for some of his statements. As explained above (paragraph 196), it is hardly possible for a refugee to 'prove' every part of his case and, indeed, if this were a requirement the majority of refugees would not be recognized. It is therefore frequently necessary to give the appli-cant the benefit of the doubt.

204   The benefit of the doubt should, however, only be given when all avail-able evidence has been obtained and checked and when the examiner is satis-fied as to the applicant's general credibility. The applicant's statements must be coherent and plausible, and must not run counter to generally known facts.

(3) Summary

[C.2.172]
205   The process of ascertaining and evaluating the facts can therefore be summarized as follows:

(*a*) The *applicant* should:
  (i)   Tell the truth and assist the examiner to the full in establishing the facts of his case.
  (ii)   Make an effort to support his statements by any available evidence and give a satisfactory explanation for any lack of evidence. If neces-sary he must make an effort to procure additional evidence.
  (iii) Supply all pertinent information concerning himself and his past experience in as much detail as is necessary to enable the examiner to establish the relevant facts. He should be asked to give a coherent explanation of all the reasons invoked in support of his application for refugee status and he should answer any questions put to him.
(*b*) The *examiner* should:
  (i)   Ensure that the applicant presents his case as fully as possible and with all available evidence.
  (ii)   Assess the applicant's credibility and evaluate the evidence (if neces-sary giving the applicant the benefit of the doubt), in order to estab-lish the objective and the subjective elements of the case.
  (iii) Relate these elements to the relevant criteria of the 1951 Convention, in order to arrive at a correct conclusion as to the applicant's refugee status.

C Cases giving rise to special problems in establishing the facts

(1) Mentally disturbed persons

[C.2.173]

206   It has been seen that in determining refugee status the subjective element of fear and the objective element of its well-foundedness need to be established.

207   It frequently happens that an examiner is confronted with an applicant having mental or emotional disturbances that impede a normal examination of his case. A mentally disturbed person may, however, be a refugee, and while his claim cannot therefore be disregarded, it will call for different techniques of examination.

208   The examiner should, in such cases, whenever possible, obtain expert medical advice. The medical report should provide information on the nature and degree of mental illness and should assess the applicant's ability to fulfil the requirements normally expected of an applicant in presenting his case (see paragraph 205 (*a*) above). The conclusions of the medical report will determine the examiner's further approach.

209   This approach has to vary according to the degree of the applicant's affliction and no rigid rules can be laid down. The nature and degree of the applicant's 'fear' must also be taken into consideration, since some degree of mental disturbance is frequently found in persons who have been exposed to severe persecution. Where there are indications that the fear expressed by the applicant may not be based on actual experience or may be an exaggerated fear, it may be necessary, in arriving at a decision, to lay greater emphasis on the objective circumstances, rather than on the statements made by the applicant.

210   It will, in any event, be necessary to lighten the burden of proof normally incumbent upon the applicant, and information that cannot easily be obtained from the applicant may have to be sought elsewhere, eg from friends, relatives and other persons closely acquainted with the applicant, or from his guardian, if one has been appointed. It may also be necessary to draw certain conclusions from the surrounding circumstances. If, for instance, the applicant belongs to and is in the company of a group of refugees, there is a presumption that he shares their fate and qualifies in the same manner as they do.

211   In examining his application, therefore, it may not be possible to attach the same importance as is normally attached to the subjective element of 'fear', which may be less reliable, and it may be necessary to place greater emphasis on the objective situation.

212   In view of the above considerations, investigation into the refugee status of a mentally disturbed person will, as a rule, have to be more searching than in a 'normal' case and will call for a close examination of the applicant's past history and background, using whatever outside sources of information may be available.

(2) Unaccompanied minors

[C.2.174]

213 There is no special provision in the 1951 Convention regarding the refugee status of persons under age. The same definition of a refugee applies to all individuals, regardless of their age. When it is necessary to determine the refugee status of a minor, problems may arise due to the difficulty of applying the criteria of 'well-founded fear' in his case. If a minor is accompanied by one (or both) of his parents, or another family member on whom he is dependent, who requests refugee status, the minor's own refugee status will be determined according to the principle of family unity (paragraphs 181 to 188 above).

214 The question of whether an unaccompanied minor may qualify for refugee status must be determined in the first instance according to the degree of his mental development and maturity. In the case of children, it will generally be necessary to enrol the services of experts conversant with child mentality. A child — and for that matter, an adolescent — not being legally independent should, if appropriate, have a guardian appointed whose task it would be to promote a decision that will be in the minor's best interests. In the absence of parents or of a legally appointed guardian, it is for the authorities to ensure that the interests of an applicant for refugee status who is a minor are fully safeguarded.

215 Where a minor is no longer a child but an adolescent, it will be easier to determine refugee status as in the case of an adult, although this again will depend upon the actual degree of the adolescent's maturity. It can be assumed that—in the absence of indications to the contrary — a person of 16 or over may be regarded as sufficiently mature to have a well-founded fear of persecution. Minors under 16 years of age may normally be assumed not to be sufficiently mature. They may have fear and a will of their own, but these may not have the same significance as in the case of an adult.

216 It should, however, be stressed that these are only general guidelines and that a minor's mental maturity must normally be determined in the light of his personal, family and cultural background.

217 Where the minor has not reached a sufficient degree of maturity to make it possible to establish well-founded fear in the same way as for an adult, it may be necessary to have greater regard to certain objective factors. Thus, if an unaccompanied minor finds himself in the company of a group of refugees, this may—depending on the circumstances—indicate that the minor is also a refugee.

218 The circumstances of the parents and other family members, including their situation in the minor's country of origin, will have to be taken into account. If there is reason to believe that the parents wish their child to be outside the country of origin on grounds of well-founded fear of persecution, the child himself may be presumed to have such fear.

219 If the will of the parents cannot be ascertained or if such will is in doubt or in conflict with the will of the child, then the examiner, in co-operation with the experts assisting him, will have to come to a decision as to the well-foundedness of the minor's fear on the basis of all the known circumstances, which may call for a liberal application of the benefit of the doubt.

D Conclusion

[C.2.175]

220   In the present Handbook an attempt has been made to define certain guidelines that, in the experience of UNHCR, have proved useful in determining refugee status for the purposes of the 1951 Convention and the 1967 Protocol relating to the Status of Refugees. In so doing, particular attention has been paid to the definitions of the term 'refugee' in these two instruments, and to various problems of interpretation arising out of these definitions. It has also been sought to show how these definitions may be applied in concrete cases and to focus attention on various procedural problems arising in regard to the determination of refugee status.

221   The Office of the High Commissioner is fully aware of the shortcomings inherent in a Handbook of this nature, bearing in mind that it is not possible to encompass every situation in which a person may apply for refugee status. Such situations are manifold and depend upon the infinitely varied conditions prevailing in countries of origin and on the special personal factors relating to the individual applicant.

222   The explanations given have shown that the determination of refugee status is by no means a mechanical and routine process. On the contrary, it calls for specialised knowledge, training and experience and—what is more important—an understanding of the particular situation of the applicant and of the human factors involved.

223   Within the above limits it is hoped that the present Handbook may provide some guidance to those who in their daily work are called upon to determine refugee status.

E Annexes

[C.2.176]

Note   The UNHCR edition of the 1979 Handbook has 6 Annexes:

— *Annex I: (Excerpt from the Final Act of the United Nations Conference of Plenipotentiaries on the Status of Refugees and Stateless Persons* (Article IV)

— *Annex II: 1951 Convention relating to the Status of Refugees*

— *Annex III: 1967 Protocol relating to the Status of Refugees*

Thus the Annexes that follow are:

— *Annex IV: List of State Parties to the 1951 Convention and to the 1967 Protocol*

— *Annex V: Excerpt from the Charter of the International Military Tribunal,* (Article 6), and

— *Annex VI: International instruments relating to Article 1.F(a) of the 1951 Convention (crimes against peace, war crimes, crimes against humanity)*

[C.2.177]

Annex IV

Convention Relating to the Status of Refugees of 28 July 1951

(Entry into force — 22 April 1954)

Protocol Relating to the Status of Refugees of 31 January 1967

(Entry into force — 4 October 1967)

List of States Parties

States Party to the 1951 UN Convention
States Party to the 1967 Protocol
States Party to both the 1951 Convention and the 1967 Protocol
States Party to either one or both of these instruments

I   Africa

Algeria	Ethiopia	Nigeria
Angola	Gabon	Rwanda
Benin	Gambia	Sao Tome and Principe
Botswana	Ghana	Senegal
Burkina Faso	Guinea	Seychelles
Burundi	Guinea-Bissau	Sierra Leone
Cameroon	Kenya	Somalia
Cape Verde (P)	Lesotho	Sudan
Central African	Liberia	Swaziland (P)
Republic	Madagascar (C)*	Togo
Chad	Malawi	Tunisia
Congo	Mali	Uganda
Côte d'Ivoire	Mauritania	United Rep of
Djibouti	Morocco	Tanzania
Egypt	Mozambique (C)	Zaire
Equatorial Guinea	Niger	Zambia

II   Americas

Guinea-Bissau	Niger	Togo
Kenya	Nigeria	Tunisia
Lesotho	Rwanda	Uganda
Liberia	Sao Tome and Principe	United Rep of
Madagascar (C)*	Senegal	Tanzania
Malawi	Seychelles	Zaire
Mali	Sierra Leone	Zambia
Mauritania	Somalia	Zimbabwe
Morocco	Sudan	
Mozambique (C)	Swaziland (P)	

III Asia

China	Israel	Philippines
Iran (Islamic Rep of)	Japan	Yemen

IV Europe

Austria	Iceland	Norway
Belgium	Ireland	Portugal
Cyprus	Italy*	Spain
Denmark²	Liechtenstein	Sweden
Finland	Luxembourg	Switzerland
France³	Malta*	Turkey*
Germany, Fed Rep of⁴	Monaco (C)*	United Kingdom*
Greece	Netherlands⁵	Yugoslavia
Holy See		

V Oceania

Australia¹	New Zealand	Tuvalu
Fiji	Papua New Guinea	

Notes

The above list and the following notes are reproduced in the same form as found in the text of the 1979 UNHCR Handbook. As at 1 January 2000 the number of states which have ratified the 1951 Convention and its 1967 Protocol had risen to 134.

* The seven States marked with an asterisk: Brazil, Italy, Madagascar, Malta, Monaco, Paraguay and Turkey have made a declaration in accordance with Article 1(B) 1 of the 1951 Convention to the effect that the words 'events occurring before 1 January 1951' in Article 1, Section A, should be understood to mean 'events occuring in *Europe* before 1 January 1951'. All other States Parties apply the Convention without geographical limitation. The following five States have expressly maintained their declarations of geographical limitation with regard to the 1951 Convention upon acceding to the 1967 Protocol: Brazil, Italy, Malta, Paraguay and Turkey. Madagascar and Monaco have not yet adhered to the 1967 Protocol.

'(C)'   the three States marked with a 'C' are Party to the 1951 Convention only.

'(P)'   the four States marked with a 'P' are Party to the 1967 Protocol only.

1 *Australia* extended application of the Convention to Norfolk Island.
2 *Denmark* declared that the Convention was also applicable to Greenland.
3 *France* declared that the Convention applied to all territories for the international relations of which France was responsible.
4 The *Federal Republic of Germany* made a separate declaration stating that the Convention and the Protocol also applied to Land Berlin.
5 The *Netherlands* extended application of the Protocol to Aruba.
6 The *United Kingdom* extended application of the Convention to the following territories for the conduct of whose international relations the Government of the United Kingdom is responsible;

Channel Islands, Falkland Islands (Malvinas), Isle of Man, St Helena.
The United Kingdom declared that its accession to the Protocol did not apply to Jersey, but extended its application to Montserrat.

Annex V

Excerpt from the Charter of the International Military Tribunal*

[C.2.178]
Article 6
'The Tribunal established by the Agreement referred to in Article 1 hereof for the trial and punishment of the major war criminals of the European Axis countries shall have the power to try and punish persons who, acting in the interests of the European Axis countries, whether as individuals or as members of organisations, committed any of the following crimes.

'The following acts, or any of them, are crimes coming within the jurisdiction of the Tribunal for which there shall be individual responsibility:

(a) *Crimes against peace*   namely, planning, preparation, initiation or waging of a war of aggression, or a war in violation of international treaties, agreements or assurances, or participation in a common plan or conspiracy for the accomplishment of any of the foregoing;

(b) *War crimes*   namely, violations of the laws or customs of war. Such violations shall include, but not be limited to, murder, ill-treatment or deportation to slave labour or for any other purpose, of civilian population of or in occupied territory, murder or ill-treatment of prisoners of war or persons on the seas, killing of hostages, plunder of public or private property, wanton destruction of cities, towns or villages, or devastation not justified by military necessity;

(c) *Crimes against humanity*   namely, murder, extermination, enslavement, deportation and other inhumane acts committed against any civilian population, before or during the war; or persecutions on political, racial or religious grounds in execution of or in connection with any crime within the jurisdiction of the Tribunal, whether or not in violation of the domestic law of the country where perpetrated.

'Leaders, organisers, instigators and accomplices participating in the formulation or execution of a common plan or conspiracy to commit any of the foregoing crimes are responsible for all acts performed by any persons in execution of such plan.'

Note
See '*The Charter and Judgement of the Nürenberg Tribunal: History and Analysis*' Appendix II — United Nations General Assembly-International Law Commission 1949 (A/CN 4/5 of 3 March 1949).

Annex VI

International Instruments Relating to Article 1F(*a*) of the 1951 Convention

[C.2.179]
The main international instruments which pertain to Article 1F(*a*) of the 1951 Convention are as follows:

(1) the London Agreement of 8 August 1945 and Charter of the International Military Tribunal;

(2) Law No 10 of the Control Council for Germany of 20 December 1945 for the Punishment of Persons Guilty of War Crimes, Crimes Against Peace and Crimes against Humanity;

(3) United Nations General Assembly Resolution 3(1) of 13 February 1946 and 95(1) of 11 December 1946 which confirm war crimes and crimes against humanity as they are defined in the Charter of the International Military Tribunal of 8 August 1945;

(4) Convention on the Prevention and Punishment of the Crime of Genocide of 1948 (Article III); (entered into force 12 January 1951);

(5) Convention of the Non-Applicability of Statutory Limitations of War Crimes and Crimes Against Humanity of 1968 (entered into force 11 November 1970);

(8) Geneva Conventions for the protection of victims of war of August 12, 1949 (Convention for the protection of the wounded, and sick, Article 50; Convention for the protection of wounded, sick and shipwrecked, Article 51; Convention relative to the treatment of prisoners of war, Article 130; Convention relative to the protection of civilian persons, Article 147);

(7) Additional Protocol to the Geneva Conventions of 12 August 1949 Relating to the Protection of Victims of International Armed Conflicts (Article 85 on the repression of breaches of this Protocol).

UNIVERSAL DECLARATION OF HUMAN RIGHTS 1948

(Adopted and proclaimed by General Assembly resolution 217 A(III) of 10 December 1948.)

PREAMBLE

[C.2.180]

Whereas recognition of the inherent dignity and of the equal and inalienable rights of all members of the human family is the foundation of freedom, justice and peace in the world,

Whereas disregard and contempt for human rights have resulted in barbarous acts which have outraged the conscience of mankind, and the advent of a world in which human beings shall enjoy freedom of speech and belief and freedom from fear and want has been proclaimed as the highest aspiration of the common people,

Whereas it is essential, if man is not to be compelled to have recourse, as a last resort, to rebellion against tyranny and oppression, that human rights should be protected by the rule of law,

Whereas it is essential to promote the development of friendly relations between nations,

Whereas the peoples of the United Nations have in the Charter reaffirmed their faith in fundamental human rights, in the dignity and worth of the human persons and in the equal rights of men and women and have determined to promote social progress and better standards of life in larger freedom,

Whereas Member States have pledged themselves to achieve, in co-operation with the United Nations, the promotion of universal respect for and observance of human rights and fundamental freedoms,

Whereas a common understanding of these rights and freedoms is one of the greatest importance for the full realisation of this pledge,

Now, therefore, THE GENERAL ASSEMBLY *proclaims*

This Universal Declaration of Human Rights as a common standard of achievement for all peoples and all nations, to the end that every individual and every organ of society, keeping this Declaration constantly in mind, shall strive by teaching and education to promote respect for these rights and freedoms and by progressive measures, national and international; to secure their universal and effective recognition and observance, both among the peoples of Member States themselves and among the peoples of territories under their jurisdiction.

[C.2.181]
Article 1

All human beings are born free and equal in dignity and rights. They are endowed with reason and conscience and should act towards one another in a spirit of brotherhood.

[C.2.182]
Article 2
Everyone is entitled to all the rights and freedoms set forth in this Declaration, without distinction of any kind, such as race, colour, sex, language, religion, political or other opinion, national or social origin, property, birth or other status.

Furthermore, no distinction shall be made on the basis of the political, jurisdictional or international status of the country or territory to which a person belongs, whether it be independent trust, non self-governing or under any other limitation of sovereignty.

[C.2.183]
Article 3
Everyone has the right to life, liberty and the security of person.

[C.2.184]
Article 4
No one shall be held in slavery or servitude; slavery and the slave trade shall be prohibited in all their forms.

[C.2.185]
Article 5
No one shall be subjected to torture or to cruel, inhuman or degrading treatment or punishment.

[C.2.186]
Article 6
Everyone has the right to recognition everywhere as a person before the law.

[C.2.187]
Article 7
All are equal before the law and are entitled without any discrimination to equal protection of the law. All are entitled to equal protection against any discrimination in violation of this Declaration and against any incitement to such discrimination.

[C.2.188]
Article 8
Everyone has the right to an effective remedy by the competent national tribunals for acts violating the fundamental rights granted him by the constitution or by law.

[C.2.189]
Article 9
No one shall be subjected to arbitrary arrest, detention or exile.

[C.2.190]
Article 10
Everyone is entitled to full equality to a fair and public hearing by an independent and impartial tribunal, in the determination of his rights and obligations and of any criminal charge against him.

[C.2.191]
Article 11
1   Everyone charged with a penal offence has the right to be presumed innocent until proved guilty according to law in a public trial at which he has had all the guarantees necessary for his defence.
2   No one shall be held guilty of any penal offence on account of any act or omission which did not constitute a penal offence, under national or international law, at the time when it was committed. Nor shall a heavier penalty be imposed than the one that was applicable at the time the penal offence was committed.

[C.2.192]
Article 12
No one shall be subjected to arbitrary interference with his privacy, family, home or correspondence, nor to attacks upon his honour and reputation. Everyone has the right to the protection of the law against such interference or attacks.

[C.2.193]
Article 13
1   Everyone has the right to freedom of movement and residence within the borders of each State.
2   Everyone has the right to leave any country, including his own, and to return to his country.

[C.2.194]
Article 14
1   Everyone has the right to seek and to enjoy in other countries asylum from persecution.
2   This right may not be invoked in the case of prosecutions genuinely arising from non-political crimes or from acts contrary to the purposes and principles of the United Nations.

[C.2.195]
Article 15
1   Everyone has the right to a nationality.
2   No one shall be arbitrarily deprived of his nationality nor denied the right to change his nationality.

[C.2.196]
Article 16
1   Men and women of full age, without any limitation due to race, nationality or religion, have the right to marry and to found a family. They are entitled to equal rights as to marriage, during marriage and at its dissolution.
2   Marriage shall be entered into only with the free and full consent of the intending spouses.
3   The family is the natural and fundamental group unit of society and is entitled to protection by society and the State.

[C.2.197]
Article 17
1   Everyone has the right to own property alone as well as in association with others.
2   No one shall be arbitrarily deprived of his property.

[C.2.198]
Article 18
Everyone has the right to freedom of thought, conscience and religion; this right includes freedom to change his religion or belief, and freedom, either alone or in community with others and in public or private, to manifest his religion or belief in teaching, practice, worship and observance.

[C.2.199]
Article 19
Everyone has the right to freedom of opinion and expression; this right includes freedom to hold opinions without interference and to seek, receive and impart information and ideas through any media and regardless of frontiers.

[C.2.200]
Article 20
1   Everyone has the right to freedom of peaceful assembly and association.
2   No one may be compelled to belong to an association.

[C.2.201]
Article 21
1   Everyone has the right to take part in the government of his country, directly or through freely chosen representatives.
2   Everyone has the right of equal access to public service in his country.
3   The will of the people shall be the basis of the authority of government; this will shall be expressed in periodic and genuine elections which shall be by universal and equal suffrage and shall be held by secret vote or by equivalent free voting procedures.

[C.2.202]
Article 22
Everyone, as a member of society, has the right to social security and is entitled to realisation, through national effort and international co-operation and in accordance with the organisation and resources of each State, of the economic, social and cultural rights indispensable for his dignity and the free development of his personality.

[C.2.203]
Article 23
1 Everyone has the right to work, to free choice of employment, to just and favourable conditions of work and to protection against unemployment.
2 Everyone, without any discrimination, has the right to equal pay for equal work.
3 Everyone who works has the right to just and favourable remuneration ensuring for himself and his family an existence worthy of human dignity, and supplemented, if necessary, by other means of social protection.
4 Everyone has the right to form and to join trade unions for the protection of his interests.

[C.2.204]
Article 24
Everyone has the right to rest and leisure, including reasonable limitation of working hours and periodic holidays with pay.

[C.2.205]
Article 25
1 Everyone has the right to a standard of living adequate for the health and well-being of himself and of his family, including food, clothing, housing and medical care and necessary social services, and the right to security in the event of unemployment, sickness, disability, widowhood, old age or other lack of livelihood in circumstances beyond his control.
2 Motherhood and childhood are entitled to special care and assistance. All children, whether born in or out of wedlock, shall enjoy the same social protection.

[C.2.206]
Article 26
1 Everyone has the right to education. Education shall be free, at least in the elementary and fundamental stages. Elementary education shall be compulsory. Technical and professional education shall be made generally available and higher education shall be equally accessible to all on the basis of merit.
2 Education shall be directed to the full development of the human personality and to the strengthening of respect for human rights and fundamental freedoms. It shall promote understanding, tolerance and friendship among all nations, racial or religious groups, and shall further the activities of the United Nations for the maintenance of peace.
3 Parents have a prior right to choose the kind of education that shall be given to their children.

[C.2.207]
Article 27
1   Everyone has the right freely to participate in the cultural life of the community, to enjoy the arts and to share in scientific advancement and its benefits.
2   Everyone has the right to the protection of the moral and material interests resulting from any scientific, literary or artistic production of which he is the author.

[C.2.208]
Article 28
Everyone is entitled to a social and international order in which the rights and freedoms set forth in this Declaration can be fully realised.

[C.2.209]
Article 29
1   Everyone has duties to the community in which alone the free and full development of his personality is possible.
2   In the exercise of his rights and freedoms, everyone shall be subject only to such limitations as are determined by law solely for the purpose of securing due recognition and respect for the rights and freedoms of others and of meeting the just requirements of morality, public order and the general welfare in a democratic society.
3   These rights and freedoms may in no case be exercised contrary to the purposes and principles of the United Nations.

[C.2.210]
Article 30
Nothing in this Declaration may be interpreted as implying for any State, group or person any right to engage in any activity or to perform any act aimed at the destruction of any of the rights and freedoms set forth herein.

INTERNATIONAL COVENANT ON CIVIL AND POLITICAL RIGHTS

16 December 1966
UNTS Vol 999, p 171
Entry into force   23 March 1976

Note   The UK has ratified this Covenant, but not its optional Protocol, which confers on individuals the right to communicate complaints.

PREAMBLE
[C.2.211]
The states parties to the present Covenant,
Considering that, in accordance with the principles proclaimed in the Charter of the United Nations, recognition of the inherent dignity and of the equal and inalienable rights of all members of the human family is the foundation of freedom, justice and peace in the world,

Recognising that these rights derive from the inherent dignity of the human person,

Recognising that, in accordance with the Universal Declaration of Human Rights, the ideal of free human beings enjoying civil and political freedom and freedom from fear and want can only be achieved if conditions are created whereby everyone may enjoy his civil and political rights, as well as his economic, social and cultural rights,

Considering the obligation of states under the Charter of the United Nations to promote universal respect for, and observance of, human rights and freedoms,

Realising that the individual, having duties to other individuals and to the community to which he belongs, is under a responsibility to strive for the promotion and observance of the rights recognised in the present Covenant,

Agree upon the following articles:

PART I
[C.2.212]
Article 1
1   All peoples have the right of self-determination. By virtue of that right they freely determine their political status and freely pursue their economic, social and cultural development.
2   All peoples may, for their own ends, freely dispose of their natural wealth and resources without prejudice to any obligations arising out of international economic co-operation, based upon the principle of mutual benefit, and international law. In no case may a people be deprived of its own means of subsistence.
3   The states parties to the present Covenant, including those having responsibility for the administration of Non-Self-Governing and Trust Territories, shall promote the realization of the right of self-determination, and shall respect that right, in conformity with the provisions of the Charter of the United Nations.

PART II
[C.2.213]
Article 2
1   Each state party to the present Covenant undertakes to respect and to ensure to all individuals within its territory and subject to its jurisdiction the rights recognized in the present Covenant, without distinction of any kind, such as race, colour, sex, language, religion, political or other opinion, national or social origin, property, birth or other status.
2   Where not already provided for by existing legislative or other measures, each state party to the present Covenant undertakes to take the necessary steps, in accordance with its constitutional processes and with the provisions of the present Covenant, to adopt such legislative or other measures as may be necessary to give effect to the rights recognized in the present Covenant.
3   Each state party to the present Covenant undertakes:

(*a*)   to ensure that any person whose rights or freedoms as herein recognised are violated shall have an effective remedy, notwithstanding that the violation has been committed by persons acting in an official capacity;
(*b*)   to ensure that any person claiming such a remedy shall have his right thereto determined by competent judicial, administrative or legislative authorities, or by any other competent authority provided for by the legal system of the state, and to develop the possibilities of judicial remedy;
(*c*)   to ensure that the competent authorities shall enforce such remedies when granted.

[C.2.214]
Article 3
The states parties to the present Covenant undertake to ensure the equal right of men and women to the enjoyment of all civil and political rights set forth in the present Covenant.

[C.2.215]
Article 4
1   In time of public emergency which threatens the life of the nation and the existence of which is officially proclaimed, the states parties to the present Covenant may take measures derogating from their obligations under the present Covenant to the extent strictly required by the exigencies of the situation, provided that such measures are not inconsistent with their other obligations under international law and do not involve discrimination solely on the ground of race, colour, sex, language, religion or social origin.
2   No derogation from articles 6, 7, 8 (paragraphs 1 and 2), 11, 15, 16 and 18 may be made under this provision.
3   Any state party to the present Covenant availing itself of the right of derogation shall immediately inform the other states parties to the present Covenant, through the intermediary of the Secretary-General of the United Nations, of the provisions from which it has derogated and of the reasons by which it was actuated. A further communication shall be made, through the same intermediary, on the date on which it terminates such derogation.

[C.2.216]
Article 5
1   Nothing in the present Covenant may be interpreted as implying for any state, group or person any right to engage in any activity or perform any act aimed at the destruction of any of the rights and freedoms recognized herein or at their limitation to a greater extent than is provided for in the present Covenant.
2   There shall be no restriction upon or derogation from any of the fundamental human rights recognized or existing in any state party to the present Covenant pursuant to law, conventions, regulations or custom on the pretext that the present Covenant does not recognize such rights or that it recognizes them to a lesser extent.

PART III
[C.2.217]
Article 6
1   Every human being has the inherent right to life. This right shall be protected by law. No one shall be arbitrarily deprived of his life.
2   In countries which have not abolished the death penalty, sentence of death may be imposed only for the most serious crimes in accordance with the law in force at the time of the commission of the crime and not contrary to the provisions of the present Covenant and to the Convention on the Prevention and Punishment of the Crime of Genocide. This penalty can only be carried out pursuant to a final judgement rendered by a competent court.
3   When deprivation of life constitutes the crime of genocide, it is understood that nothing in this article shall authorize any state party to the present Covenant to derogate in any way from any obligation assumed under the provisions of the Convention on the Prevention and Punishment of the Crime of Genocide.
4   Anyone sentenced to death shall have the right to seek pardon or commutation of the sentence. Amnesty, pardon or commutation of the sentence of death may be granted in all cases.
5   Sentence of death shall not be imposed for crimes committed by persons below eighteen years of age and shall not be carried out on pregnant women.
6   Nothing in this article shall be invoked to delay or to prevent the abolition of capital punishment by any state party to the present Covenant.

[C.2.218]
Article 7
No one shall be subjected to torture or to cruel, inhuman or degrading treatment or punishment. In particular, no one shall be subjected without his free consent to medical or scientific experimentation.

[C.2.219]
Article 8
1   No one shall be held in slavery; slavery and the slave-trade in all their forms shall be prohibited.
2   No one shall be held in servitude.
3   (*a*) No one shall be required to perform forced or compulsory labour;
     (*b*) paragraph 3 (*a*) shall not be held to preclude, in countries where

imprisonment with hard labour may be imposed as a punishment for a crime, the performance of hard labour in pursuance of a sentence to such punishment by a competent court;

(*c*) for the purpose of this paragraph the term 'forced or compulsory labour' shall not include:

(i) any work or service, not referred to in subparagraph (*b*), normally required of a person who is under detention in consequence of a lawful order of a court, or of a person during conditional release from such detention;

(ii) any service of a military character and, in countries where conscientious objection is recognised, any national service required by law of conscientious objectors;

(iii) any service exacted in cases of emergency or calamity threatening the life or well-being of the community;

(iv) any work or service which forms part of normal civil obligations.

[C.2.220]
Article 9
1 Everyone has the right to liberty and security of person. No one shall be subjected to arbitrary arrest or detention. No one shall be deprived of his liberty except on such grounds and in accordance with such procedure as are established by law.
2 Anyone who is arrested shall be informed, at the time of arrest, of the reasons for his arrest and shall be promptly informed of any charges against him.
3 Anyone arrested or detained on a criminal charge shall be brought promptly before a judge or other officer authorized by law to exercise judicial power and shall be entitled to trial within a reasonable time or to release. It shall not be the general rule that persons awaiting trial shall be detained in custody, but release may be subject to guarantees to appear for trial, at any other stage of the judicial proceedings, and, should occasion arise, for execution of the judgement.
4 Anyone who is deprived of his liberty by arrest or detention shall be entitled to take proceedings before a court, in order that that court may decide without delay on the lawfulness of his detention and order his release if the detention is not lawful.
5 Anyone who has been the victim of unlawful arrest or detention shall have an enforceable right to compensation.

[C.2.221]
Article 10
1 All persons deprived of their liberty shall be treated with humanity and with respect for the inherent dignity of the human person.
2 (*a*) Accused persons shall, save in exceptional circumstances, be segregated from convicted persons and shall be subject to separate treatment appropriate to their status as unconvicted persons;

(*b*) Accused juvenile persons shall be separated from adults and brought as speedily as possible for adjudication.

3 The penitentiary system shall comprise treatment of prisoners the essential aim of which shall be their reformation and social rehabilitation. Juvenile

offenders shall be segregated from adults and be accorded treatment appropriate to their age and legal status.

[C.2.222]
Article 11
No one shall be imprisoned merely on the ground of inability to fulfil a contractual obligation.

[C.2.223]
Article 12
1   Everyone lawfully within the territory of a state shall, within that territory, have the right to liberty of movement and freedom to choose his residence.
2   Everyone shall be free to leave any country, including his own.
3   The above-mentioned rights shall not be subject to any restrictions except those which are provided by law, are necessary to protect national security, public order (*ordre public*), public health or morals or the rights and freedoms of others, and are consistent with the other rights recognized in the present Covenant.
4   No one shall be arbitrarily deprived of the right to enter his own country.

[C.2.224]
Article 13
An alien lawfully in the territory of a state party to the present Covenant may be expelled therefrom only in pursuance of a decision reached in accordance with law and shall, except where compelling reasons of national security otherwise require, be allowed to submit the reasons against his expulsion and to have his case reviewed by, and be represented for the purpose before, the competent authority or a person or persons especially designated by the competent authority.

[C.2.225]
Article 14
1   All persons shall be equal before the courts and tribunals. In the determination of any criminal charge against him, or of his rights and obligations in a suit at law, everyone shall be entitled to a fair and public hearing by a competent, independent and impartial tribunal established by law. The Press and the public may be excluded from all or part of a trial for reasons of morals, public order (*ordre public*) or national security in a democratic society, or when the interest of the private lives of the parties so requires, or to the extent strictly necessary in the opinion of the court in special circumstances where publicity would prejudice the interests of justice; but any judgement rendered in a criminal case or in a suit at law shall be made public except where the interest of juvenile persons otherwise requires or the proceedings concern matrimonial disputes or the guardianship of children.
2   Everyone charged with a criminal offence shall have the right to be presumed innocent until proved guilty according to law.
3   In the determination of any criminal charge against him, everyone shall be entitled to the following minimum guarantees, in full equality:

(*a*) to be informed promptly and in detail in a language which he understands of the nature and cause of the charge against him;

(*b*) to have adequate time and facilities for the preparation of his defence and to communicate with counsel of his own choosing;

(*c*) to be tried without undue delay;

(*d*) to be tried in his presence, and to defend himself in person or through legal assistance of his own choosing; to be informed, if he does not have legal assistance, of this right; and to have legal assistance assigned to him, in any case where the interests of justice so require, and without payment by him in any such case if he does not have sufficient means to pay for it;

(*e*) to examine, or have examined, the witnesses against him and to obtain the attendance and examination of witnesses on his behalf under the same conditions as witnesses against him;

(*f*) to have the free assistance of an interpreter if he cannot understand or speak the language used in court;

(*g*) not to be compelled to testify against himself or to confess guilt.

4   In the case of juvenile persons, the procedure shall be such as will take account of their age and the desirability of promoting their rehabilitation.

5   Everyone convicted of a crime shall have the right to his conviction and sentence being reviewed by a higher tribunal according to law.

6   When a person has by a final decision been convicted of a criminal offence and when subsequently his conviction has been reversed or he has been pardoned on the ground that a new or newly discovered fact shows conclusively that there has been a miscarriage of justice, the person who has suffered punishment as a result of such conviction shall be compensated according to law, unless it is proved that the non-disclosure of the unknown fact in time is wholly or partly attributable to him.

7   No one shall be liable to be tried or punished again for an offence for which he has already been finally convicted or acquitted in accordance with the law and penal procedure of each country.

[C.2.226]
Article 15

1   No one shall be held guilty of any criminal offence on account of any act or omission which did not constitute a criminal offence, under national or international law, at the time when it was committed. Nor shall a heavier penalty be imposed than the one that was applicable at the time when the criminal offence was committed. If, subsequent to the commission of the offence, provision is made by law for the imposition of a lighter penalty, the offender shall benefit thereby.

2   Nothing in this article shall prejudice the trial and punishment of any person for any act or omission which, at the time when it was committed, was criminal according to the general principles of law recognized by the community of nations.

[C.2.227]
Article 16

Everyone shall have the right to recognition everywhere as a person before the law.

[C.2.228]
Article 17
1   No one shall be subjected to arbitrary or unlawful interference with his privacy, family, home or correspondence, nor to unlawful attacks on his honour and reputation.
2   Everyone has the right to the protection of the law against such interference or attacks.

[C.2.229]
Article 18
1   Everyone shall have the right to freedom of thought, conscience and religion. This right shall include freedom to have or to adopt a religion or belief of his choice, and freedom, either individually or in community with others and in public or private, to manifest his religion or belief in worship, observance, practice and teaching.
2   No one shall be subject to coercion which would impair his freedom to have or to adopt a religion or belief of his choice.
3   Freedom to manifest one's religion or beliefs may be subject only to such limitations as are prescribed by law and are necessary to protect public safety, order, health, or morals or the fundamental rights and freedoms of others.
4   The states parties to the present Covenant undertake to have respect for the liberty of parents and, when applicable, legal guardians to ensure the religious and moral education of their children in conformity with their own convictions.

[C.2.230]
Article 19
1   Everyone shall have the right to hold opinions without interference.
2   Everyone shall have the right to freedom of expression; this right shall include freedom to seek, receive and impart information and ideas of all kinds, regardless of frontiers, either orally, in writing or in print, in the form of art, or through any other media of his choice.
3   The exercise of the rights provided for in paragraph 2 of this article carries with it special duties and responsibilities. It may therefore be subject to certain restrictions, but these shall only be such as are provided by law and are necessary:

(*a*) for respect of the rights or reputations of others;
(*b*) for the protection of national security or of public order (*ordre public*), or of public health or morals.

[C.2.231]
Article 20
1   Any propaganda for war shall be prohibited by law.
2   Any advocacy of national, racial or religious hatred that constitutes incitement to discrimination, hostility or violence shall be prohibited by law.

[C.2.232]
Article 21
The right of peaceful assembly shall be recognized. No restrictions may be placed on the exercise of this right other than those imposed in conformity with the law and which are necessary in a democratic society in the interests of national security or public safety, public order (*ordre public*), the protection of public health or morals or the protection of the rights and freedoms of others.

[C.2.233]
Article 22
1   Everyone shall have the right to freedom of association with others, including the right to form and join trade unions for the protection of his interests.
2   No restrictions may be placed on the exercise of this right other than those which are prescribed by law and which are necessary in a democratic society in the interests of national security or public safety, public order (*ordre public*), the protection of public health or morals or the protection of the rights and freedoms of others. This article shall not prevent the imposition of lawful restrictions on members of the armed forces and of the police in their exercise of this right.
3   Nothing in this article shall authorize States Parties to the International Labour Organisation Convention of 1948 concerning Freedom of Association and Protection of the Right to Organise to take legislative measures which would prejudice, or to apply the law in such a manner as to prejudice, the guarantees provided for in that Convention.

[C.2.234]
Article 23
1   The family is the natural and fundamental group unit of society and is entitled to protection by society and the state.
2   The right of men and women of marriageable age to marry and to found a family shall be recognized.
3   No marriage shall be entered into without the free and full consent of the intending spouses.
4   States parties to the present Covenant shall take appropriate steps to ensure equality of rights and responsibilities of spouses as to marriage, during marriage and at its dissolution. In the case of dissolution, provision shall be made for the necessary protection of any children.

[C.2.235]
Article 24
1   Every child shall have, without any discrimination as to race, colour, sex, language, religion, national or social origin, property or birth, the right to such measures of protection as are required by his status as a minor, on the part of his family, society and the state.
2   Every child shall be registered immediately after birth and shall have a name.
3   Every child has the right to acquire a nationality.

[C.2.236]
Article 25
Every citizen shall have the right and the opportunity, without any of the distinctions mentioned in article 2 and without unreasonable restrictions:

(*a*) to take part in the conduct of public affairs, directly or through freely chosen representatives;
(*b*) to vote and to be elected at genuine periodic elections which shall be by universal and equal suffrage and shall be held by secret ballot, guaranteeing the free expression of the will of the electors;
(*c*) to have access, on general terms of equality, to public service in his country.

[C.2.237]
Article 26
All persons are equal before the law and are entitled without any discrimination to the equal protection of the law. In this respect, the law shall prohibit any discrimination and guarantee to all persons equal and effective protection against discrimination on any ground such as race, colour, sex, language, religion, political or other opinion, national or social origin, property, birth or other status.

[C.2.238]
Article 27
In those states in which ethnic, religious or linguistic minorities exist, persons belonging to such minorities shall not be denied the right, in community with the other members of their group, to enjoy their own culture, to profess and practise their own religion, or to use their own language.

PART IV
[C.2.239]
Article 28
1   There shall be established a Human Rights Committee (hereafter referred to in the present Covenant as the Committee). It shall consist of eighteen members and shall carry out the functions hereinafter provided.
2   The Committee shall be composed of nationals of the states parties to the present Covenant who shall be persons of high moral character and recognised competence in the field of human rights, consideration being given to the usefulness of the participation of some persons having legal experience.
3   The members of the Committee shall be elected and shall serve in their personal capacity.

[C.2.240]
Article 29
1   The members of the Committee shall be elected by secret ballot from a list of persons possessing the qualifications prescribed in article 28 and nominated for the purpose by the states parties to the present Covenant.
2   Each state party to the present Covenant may nominate not more than two

persons. These persons shall be nationals of the nominating state.

3   A person shall be eligible for renomination.

[C.2.241]
Article 30

1   The initial election shall be held no later than six months after the date of the entry into force of the present Covenant.

2   At least four months before the date of each election to the Committee, other than an election to fill a vacancy declared in accordance with article 34, the Secretary-General of the United Nations shall address a written invitation to the states parties to the present Covenant to submit their nominations for membership of the Committee within three months.

3   The Secretary-General of the United Nations shall prepare a list in alphabetical order of all the persons thus nominated, with an indication of the states parties which have nominated them, and shall submit it to the states parties to the present Covenant no later than one month before the date of each election.

4   Elections of the members of the Committee shall be held at a meeting of the states parties to the present Covenant convened by the Secretary-General of the United Nations at the Headquarters of the United Nations. At that meeting, for which two thirds of the states parties to the present Covenant shall constitute a quorum, the persons elected to the Committee shall be those nominees who obtain the largest number of votes and an absolute majority of the votes of the representatives of states parties present and voting.

[C.2.242]
Article 31

1   The Committee may not include more than one national of the same state.

2   In the election of the Committee, consideration shall be given to equitable geographical distribution of membership and to the representation of the different forms of civilization and of the principal legal systems.

[C.2.243]
Article 32

1   The members of the Committee shall be elected for a term of four years. They shall be eligible for re-election if renominated. However, the terms of nine of the members elected at the first election shall expire at the end of two years; immediately after the first election, the names of these nine members shall be chosen by lot by the Chairman of the meeting referred to in article 30, paragraph 4.

2   Elections at the expiry of office shall be held in accordance with the preceding articles of this part of the present Covenant.

[C.2.244]
Article 33

1   If, in the unanimous opinion of the other members, a member of the Committee has ceased to carry out his functions for any cause other than absence of a temporary character, the Chairman of the Committee shall notify the Secretary-General of the United Nations, who shall then declare the seat of

that member to be vacant.

2   In the event of the death or the resignation of a member of the Committee, the Chairman shall immediately notify the Secretary-General of the United Nations, who shall declare the seat vacant from the date of death or the date on which the resignation takes effect.

[C.2.245]
Article 34

1   When a vacancy is declared in accordance with article 33 and if the term of office of the member to be replaced does not expire within six months of the declaration of the vacancy, the Secretary-General of the United Nations shall notify each of the states parties to the present Covenant, which may within two months submit nominations in accordance with article 29 for the purpose of filling the vacancy.

2   The Secretary-General of the United Nations shall prepare a list in alphabetical order of the persons thus nominated and shall submit it to the states parties to the present Covenant. The election to fill the vacancy shall then take place in accordance with the relevant provisions of this part of the present Covenant.

3   A member of the Committee elected to fill a vacancy declared in accordance with article 33 shall hold office for the remainder of the term of the member who vacated the seat on the Committee under the provisions of that article.

[C.2.246]
Article 35

The members of the Committee shall, with the approval of the General Assembly of the United Nations, receive emoluments from United Nations resources on such terms and conditions as the General Assembly may decide, having regard to the importance of the Committee's responsibilities.

[C.2.247]
Article 36

The Secretary-General of the United Nations shall provide the necessary staff and facilities for the effective performance of the functions of the Committee under the present Covenant.

[C.2.248]
Article 37

1   The Secretary-General of the United Nations shall convene the initial meeting of the Committee at the Headquarters of the United Nations.

2   After its initial meeting, the Committee shall meet at such times as shall be provided in its rules of procedure.

3   The Committee shall normally meet at the Headquarters of the United Nations or at the United Nations Office at Geneva.

[C.2.249]
Article 38
Every member of the Committee shall, before taking up his duties, make a solemn declaration in open committee that he will perform his functions impartially and conscientiously.

[C.2.250]
Article 39
1 The Committee shall elect its officers for a term of two years. They may be re-elected.
2 The Committee shall establish its own rules of procedure, but these rules shall provide, *inter alia*, that:

(*a*) twelve members shall constitute a quorum;
(*b*) decisions of the Committee shall be made by a majority vote of the members present.

[C.2.251]
Article 40
1 The states parties to the present Covenant undertake to submit reports on the measures they have adopted which give effect to the rights recognized herein and on the progress made in the enjoyment of those rights:

(*a*) within one year of the entry into force of the present Covenant for the states parties concerned;
(*b*) thereafter whenever the Committee so requests.

2 All reports shall be submitted to the Secretary-General of the United Nations, who shall transmit them to the Committee for consideration. Reports shall indicate the factors and difficulties, if any affecting the implementation of the present Covenant.
3 The Secretary-General of the United Nations may, after consultation with the Committee, transmit to the specialized agencies concerned copies of such parts of the reports as may fall within their field of competence.
4 The Committee shall study the reports submitted by the states parties to the present Covenant. It shall transmit its reports, and such general comments as it may consider appropriate, to the states parties. The Committee may also transmit to the Economic and Social Council these comments along with the copies of the reports it has received from states parties to the present Convenant.
5 The states parties to the present Covenant may submit to the Committee observations on any comments that may be made in accordance with paragraph 4 of this article.

[C.2.252]
Article 41
1 A state party to the present Covenant may at any time declare under this article that it recognizes the competence of the Committee to receive and consider communications to the effect that a state party claims that another state party is not fulfilling its obligations under the present Covenant.

Communications under this article may be received and considered only if submitted by a state party which has made a declaration recognizing in regard to itself the competence of the Committee. No communication shall be received by the Committee if it concerns a state party which has not made such a declaration. Communications received under this article shall be dealt with in accordance with the following procedure:

(*a*) If a state party to the present Covenant considers that another state party is not giving effect to the provisions of the present Covenant, it may, by written communication, bring the matter to the attention of that state party. Within three months after the receipt of the communication, the receiving state shall afford the state which sent the communication an explanation or any other statement in writing clarifying the matter, which should include, to the extent possible and pertinent, reference to domestic procedures and remedies taken, pending, or available in the matter.

(*b*) If the matter is not adjusted to the satisfaction of both states parties concerned within six months after the receipt by the receiving state of the initial communication, either state shall have the right to refer the matter to the Committee, by notice given to the Committee and to the other state.

(*c*) The Committee shall deal with a matter referred to it only after it has ascertained that all available domestic remedies have been invoked and exhausted in the matter, in conformity with the generally recognized principles of international law. This shall not be the rule where the application of the remedies is unreasonably prolonged.

(*d*) The Committee shall hold closed meetings when examining communications under this article.

(*e*) Subject to the provisions of subparagraph (*c*), the Committee shall make available its good offices to the states parties concerned with a view to a friendly solution of the matter on the basis of respect for human rights and fundamental freedoms as recognized in the present Covenant.

(*f*) In any matter referred to it, the Committee may call upon the states parties concerned, referred to in subparagraph (*b*), to supply any relevant information.

(*g*) The states parties concerned, referred to in subparagraph (*b*), shall have the right to be represented when the matter is being considered in the Committee and to make submissions orally and/or in writing.

(*h*) The Committee shall, within twelve months after the date of receipt of notice under subparagraph (*b*), submit a report:

   (i) if a solution within the terms of subparagraph (*e*) is reached, the Committee shall confine its report to a brief statement of the facts and of the solution reached;

   (ii) if a solution within the terms of subparagraph (*e*) is not reached, the Committee shall confine its report to a brief statement of the facts; the written submissions and record of the oral submissions made by the states parties concerned shall be attached to the report.

In every matter, the report shall be communicated to the states parties concerned.

2   The provisions of this article shall come into force when ten states parties to the present Covenant have made declarations under paragraph 1 of this article. Such declarations shall be deposited by the states parties with the

Secretary-General of the United Nations, who shall transmit copies thereof to the other states parties. A declaration may be withdrawn at any time by notification to the Secretary-General. Such a withdrawal shall not prejudice the consideration of any matter which is the subject of a communication already transmitted under this article; no further communication by any state party shall be received after the notification of withdrawal of the declaration has been received by the Secretary-General, unless the state party concerned has made a new declaration.

[C.2.253]
Article 42
1 (*a*) If a matter referred to the Committee in accordance with article 41 is not resolved to the satisfaction of the states parties concerned, the Committee may, with the prior consent of the states parties concerned, appoint an *ad hoc* Conciliation Commission (hereinafter referred to as the Commission). The good offices of the Commission shall be made available to the states parties concerned with a view to an amicable solution of the matter on the basis of respect for the present Covenant;

   (*b*) the Commission shall consist of five persons acceptable to the states parties concerned. If the states parties concerned fail to reach agreement within three months on all or part of the composition of the Commission, the members of the Commission concerning whom no agreement has been reached shall be elected by secret ballot by a two-thirds majority vote of the Committee from among its members.

2 The members of the Commission shall serve in their personal capacity. They shall not be nationals of the states parties concerned, or of a state not party to the present Covenant, or of a state party which has not made a declaration under article 41.

3 The Commission shall elect its own Chairman and adopt its own rules of procedure.

4 The meetings of the Commission shall normally be held at the Headquarters of the United Nations or at the United Nations Office at Geneva. However, they may be held at such other convenient places as the Commission may determine in consultation with the Secretary-General of the United Nations and the states parties concerned.

5 The secretariat provided in accordance with article 36 shall also service the commissions appointed under this article.

6 The information received and collated by the Committee shall be made available to the Commission and the Commission may call upon the states parties concerned to supply any other relevant information.

7 When the Commission has fully considered the matter, but in any event not later than twelve months after having been seized of the matter, it shall submit to the Chairman of the Committee a report for communication to the states parties concerned:

(*a*) if the Commission is unable to complete its consideration of the matter within twelve months, it shall confine its report to a brief statement of the status of its consideration of the matter;

(*b*) if an amicable solution to the matter on the basis of respect for human rights as recognized in the present Covenant is reached, the Commission shall confine its report to a brief statement of the facts and of the solution reached;

(c) if a solution within the terms of subparagraph (b) is not reached, the Commission's report shall embody its findings on all questions of fact relevant to the issues between the states parties concerned, and its views on the possibilities of an amicable solution of the matter. This report shall also contain the written submissions and a record of the oral submissions made by the states parties concerned;

(d) if the Commission's report is submitted under subparagraph (c), the states parties concerned shall, within three months of the receipt of the report, notify the Chairman of the Committee whether or not they accept the contents of the report of the Commission.

8   The provisions of this article are without prejudice to the responsibilities of the Committee under article 41.

9   The states parties concerned shall share equally all the expenses of the members of the Commission in accordance with estimates to be provided by the Secretary-General of the United Nations.

10   The Secretary-General of the United Nations shall be empowered to pay the expenses of the members of the Commission, if necessary, before reimbursement by the states parties concerned, in accordance with paragraph 9 of this article.

[C.2.254]
Article 43

The members of the Committee, and of the *ad hoc* conciliation commissions which may be appointed under article 42, shall be entitled to the facilities, privileges and immunities of experts on mission for the United Nations as laid down in the relevant sections of the Convention on the Privileges and Immunities of the United Nations.

[C.2.255]
Article 44

The provisions for the implementation of the present Covenant shall apply without prejudice to the procedures prescribed in the field of human rights by or under the constituent instruments and the conventions of the United Nations and of the specialised agencies and shall not prevent the states parties to the present Covenant from having recourse to other procedures for settling a dispute in accordance with general or special international agreements in force between them.

[C.2.256]
Article 45

The Committee shall submit to the General Assembly of the United Nations, through the Economic and Social Council, an annual report on its activities.

PART V
[C.2.257]
Article 46
Nothing in the present Covenant shall be interpreted as impairing the provisions of the Charter of the United Nations and of the constitutions of the specialised agencies which define the respective responsibilities of the various organs of the United Nations and of the specialised agencies in regard to the matters dealt with in the present Covenant.

[C.2.258]
Article 47
Nothing in the present Covenant shall be interpreted as impairing the inherent right of all peoples to enjoy and utilise fully and freely their natural wealth and resources.

PART VI
[C.2.259]
Article 48
1　The present Covenant is open for signature by any state member of the United Nations or member of any of its specialised agencies, by any state party to the Statute of the International Court of Justice, and by any other state which has been invited by the General Assembly of the United Nations to become a party to the present Covenant.
2　The present Covenant is subject to ratification. Instruments of ratification shall be deposited with the Secretary-General of the United Nations.
3　The present Covenant shall be open to accession by any state referred to in paragraph 1 of this article.
4　Accession shall be effected by the deposit of an instrument of accession with the Secretary-General of the United Nations.
5　The Secretary-General of the United Nations shall inform all states which have signed this Covenant or acceded to it of the deposit of each instrument of ratification or accession.

[C.2.260]
Article 49
1　The present Covenant shall enter into force three months after the date of the deposit with the Secretary-General of the United Nations of the thirty-fifth instrument of ratification or instrument of accession.
2　For each state ratifying the present Covenant or acceding to it after the deposit of the thirty-fifth instrument of ratification or instrument of accession, the present Covenant shall enter into force three months after the date of the deposit of its own instrument of ratification or instrument of accession.

[C.2.261]
Article 50
The provisions of the present Covenant shall extend to all parts of federal states without any limitations or exceptions.

[C.2.262]
Article 51

1   Any state party to the present Covenant may propose an amendment and file it with the Secretary-General of the United Nations. The Secretary-General of the United Nations shall thereupon communicate any proposed amendments to the states parties to the present Covenant with a request that they notify him whether they favour a conference of states parties for the purpose of consider-ing and voting upon the proposals. In the event that at least one third of the states parties favours such a conference, the Secretary-General shall convene the conference under the auspices of the United Nations. Any amendment adopted by a majority of the states parties present and voting at the conference shall be submitted to the General Assembly of the United Nations for approval.

2   Amendments shall come into force when they have been approved by the General Assembly of the United Nations and accepted by a two-thirds majori-ty of the states parties to the present Covenant in accordance with their respec-tive constitutional processes.

3   When amendments come into force, they shall be binding on those states parties which have accepted them, other states parties still being bound by the provisions of the present Covenant and any earlier amendment which they have accepted.

[C.2.263]
Article 52

Irrespective of the notifications made under article 48, paragraph 5, the Secretary-General of the United Nations shall inform all states referred to in paragraph 1 of the same article of the following particulars:

(*a*) signatures, ratifications and accessions under article 48;
(*b*) the date of the entry into force of the present Covenant under article 49 and the date of the entry into force of any amendments under article 51.

[C.2.264]
Article 53

1   The present Covenant, of which the Chinese, English, French, Russian and Spanish texts are equally authentic, shall be deposited in the archives of the United Nations.

2   The Secretary-General of the United Nations shall transmit certified copies of the present Covenant to all states referred to in article 48.

UK GOVERNMENT RESERVATION TO THE INTERNATIONAL COVENANT ON CIVIL AND POLITICAL RIGHTS

[C.2.265]

The Government of the United Kingdom reserve the right to continue to apply such immigration legislation governing entry into, stay in and departure from, the United Kingdom as they may deem necessary from time to time and, accordingly, their acceptance of article 12(4) and of the other provisions of the Covenant is subject to the provisions of any such legislation as regards persons not at the time having the right under the law of the United Kingdom to enter and remain in the United Kingdom. The United Kingdom also reserves a similar right in regard to each of its dependent territories.

The Government of the United Kingdom reserve the right not to apply article 13 in Hong Kong in so far as it confers a right of review of a decision to deport an alien and a right to be represented for this purpose before the competent authority.

The Government of the United Kingdom reserve the right to enact such nationality legislation as they may deem necessary from time to time to reserve the acquisition and possession of citizenship under such legislation to those having sufficient connection with the United Kingdom or any of its dependent territories and accordingly their acceptance of article 24(3) and of the other provisions of the Covenant is subject to the provisions of any such legislation.

INTERNATIONAL COVENANT ON ECONOMIC, SOCIAL AND CULTURAL RIGHTS

16 December 1966
Entry into force   3 January 1976

PREAMBLE

[C.2.266]
The States Parties to the present Covenant,

Considering that, in accordance with the principles proclaimed in the Charter of the United Nations, recognition of the inherent dignity and of the equal and inalienable rights of all members of the human family is the foundation of freedom, justice and peace in the world,
Recognizing that these rights derive from the inherent dignity of the human person,
Recognizing that, in accordance with the Universal Declaration of Human Rights, the ideal of free human beings enjoying freedom from fear and want can only be achieved if conditions are created whereby everyone may enjoy his economic, social and cultural rights, as well as his civil and political rights,
Considering the obligation of States under the Charter of the United Nations to promote universal respect for, and observance of, human rights and freedoms,
Realizing that the individual, having duties to other individuals and to the community to which he belongs, is under a responsibility to strive for the promotion and observance of the rights recognized in the present Covenant,

Agree upon the following articles:

PART I

[C.2.267]
Article 1
1   All peoples have the right of self-determination. By virtue of that right they freely determine their political status and freely pursue their economic, social and cultural development.
2   All peoples may, for their own ends, freely dispose of their natural wealth and resources without prejudice to any obligations arising out of international economic co-operation, based upon the principle of mutual benefit, and international law. In no case may a people be deprived of its own means of subsistence.
3   The States Parties to the present Covenant, including those having responsibility for the administration of Non-Self-Governing and Trust Territories, shall promote the realization of the right of self-determination, and shall respect that right, in conformity with the provisions of the Charter of the United Nations.

PART II

[C.2.268]
Article 2
1   Each State Party to the present Covenant undertakes to take steps, individually and through international assistance and co-operation, especially economic and technical, to the maximum of its available resources, with a view to achieving progressively the full realization of the rights recognized in the present Covenant by all appropriate means, including particularly the adoption of legislative measures.
2   The States Parties to the present Covenant undertake to guarantee that the rights enunciated in the present Covenant will be exercised without discrimination of any kind as to race, colour, sex, language, religion, political or other opinion, national or social origin, property, birth or other status.
3   Developing countries, with due regard to human rights and their national economy, may determine to what extent they would guarantee the economic rights recognized in the present Covenant to non-nationals.

[C.2.269]
Article 3
The States Parties to the present Covenant undertake to ensure the equal right of men and women to the enjoyment of all economic, social and cultural rights set forth in the present Covenant.

[C.2.270]
Article 4
The States Parties to the present Covenant recognize that, in the enjoyment of those rights provided by the State in conformity with the present Covenant, the State may subject such rights only to such limitations as are determined by law only in so far as this may be compatible with the nature of these rights and solely for the purpose of promoting the general welfare in a democratic society.

[C.2.271]
Article 5
1   Nothing in the present Covenant may be interpreted as implying for any State, group or person any right to engage in any activity or to perform any act aimed at the destruction of any of the rights or freedoms recognized herein, or at their limitation to a greater extent than is provided for in the present Covenant.
2   No restriction upon or derogation from any of the fundamental human rights recognized or existing in any country in virtue of law, conventions, regulations or custom shall be admitted on the pretext that the present Covenant does not recognize such rights or that it recognizes them to a lesser extent.

PART III

[C.2.272]
Article 6
1   The States Parties to the present Covenant recognize the right to work,

which includes the right of everyone to the opportunity to gain his living by work which he freely chooses or accepts, and will take appropriate steps to safeguard this right.

2 The steps to be taken by a State Party to the present Covenant to achieve the full realization of this right shall include technical and vocational guidance and training programmes, policies and techniques to achieve steady economic, social and cultural development and full and productive employment under conditions safeguarding fundamental political and economic freedoms to the individual.

[C.2.273]
Article 7
The States Parties to the present Covenant recognize the right of everyone to the enjoyment of just and favourable conditions of work which ensure, in particular:

(a) Remuneration which provides all workers, as a minimum, with:

  (i) Fair wages and equal remuneration for work of equal value without distinction of any kind, in particular women being guaranteed conditions of work not inferior to those enjoyed by men, with equal pay for equal work;

  (ii) A decent living for themselves and their families in accordance with the provisions of the present Covenant;

(b) Safe and healthy working conditions;

(c) Equal opportunity for everyone to be promoted in his employment to an appropriate higher level, subject to no considerations other than those of seniority and competence;

(d) Rest, leisure and reasonable limitation of working hours and periodic holidays with pay, as well as remuneration for public holidays

[C.2.274]
Article 8
1 The States Parties to the present Covenant undertake to ensure:

(a) The right of everyone to form trade unions and join the trade union of his choice, subject only to the rules of the organization concerned, for the promotion and protection of his economic and social interests. No restrictions may be placed on the exercise of this right other than those prescribed by law and which are necessary in a democratic society in the interests of national security or public order or for the protection of the rights and freedoms of others;

(b) The right of trade unions to establish national federations or confederations and the right of the latter to form or join international trade-union organizations;

(c) The right of trade unions to function freely subject to no limitations other than those prescribed by law and which are necessary in a democratic society in the interests of national security or public order or for the protection of the rights and freedoms of others;

(d) The right to strike, provided that it is exercised in conformity with the laws of the particular country.

2   This article shall not prevent the imposition of lawful restrictions on the exercise of these rights by members of the armed forces or of the police or of the administration of the State.

3   Nothing in this article shall authorize States Parties to the International Labour Organisation Convention of 1948 concerning Freedom of Association and Protection of the Right to Organize to take legislative measures which would prejudice, or apply the law in such a manner as would prejudice, the guarantees provided for in that Convention.

[C.2.275]
Article 9
The States Parties to the present Covenant recognize the right of everyone to social security, including social insurance.

[C.2.276]
Article 10
The States Parties to the present Covenant recognize that:

1   The widest possible protection and assistance should be accorded to the family, which is the natural and fundamental group unit of society, particularly for its establishment and while it is responsible for the care and education of dependent children. Marriage must be entered into with the free consent of the intending spouses.

2   Special protection should be accorded to mothers during a reasonable period before and after childbirth. During such period working mothers should be accorded paid leave or leave with adequate social security benefits.

3   Special measures of protection and assistance should be taken on behalf of all children and young persons without any discrimination for reasons of parentage or other conditions. Children and young persons should be protected from economic and social exploitation. Their employment in work harmful to their morals or health or dangerous to life or likely to hamper their normal development should be punishable by law. States should also set age limits below which the paid employment of child labour should be prohibited and punishable by law.

[C.2.277]
Article 11
1   The States Parties to the present Covenant recognize the right of everyone to an adequate standard of living for himself and his family, including adequate food, clothing and housing, and to the continuous improvement of living conditions. The States Parties will take appropriate steps to ensure the realization of this right, recognizing to this effect the essential importance of international co-operation based on free consent.

2   The States Parties to the present Covenant, recognizing the fundamental right of everyone to be free from hunger, shall take, individually and through

international co-operation, the measures, including specific programmes, which are needed:

(a) To improve methods of production, conservation and distribution of food by making full use of technical and scientific knowledge, by disseminating knowledge of the principles of nutrition and by developing or reforming agrarian systems in such a way as to achieve the most efficient development and utilization of natural resources;

(b) Taking into account the problems of both food-importing and food-exporting countries, to ensure an equitable distribution of world food supplies in relation to need.

[C.2.278]
Article 12
1   The States Parties to the present Covenant recognize the right of everyone to the enjoyment of the highest attainable standard of physical and mental health.
2   The steps to be taken by the States Parties to the present Covenant to achieve the full realization of this right shall include those necessary for:

(a) The provision for the reduction of the stillbirth-rate and of infant mortality and for the healthy development of the child;

(b) The improvement of all aspects of environmental and industrial hygiene;

(c) The prevention, treatment and control of epidemic, endemic, occupational and other diseases;

(d) The creation of conditions which would assure to all medical service and medical attention in the event of sickness.

[C.2.279]
Article 13
1   The States Parties to the present Covenant recognize the right of everyone to education. They agree that education shall be directed to the full development of the human personality and the sense of its dignity, and shall strengthen the respect for human rights and fundamental freedoms. They further agree that education shall enable all persons to participate effectively in a free society, promote understanding, tolerance and friendship among all nations and all racial, ethnic or religious groups, and further the activities of the United Nations for the maintenance of peace.
2   The States Parties to the present Covenant recognize that, with a view to achieving the full realization of this right:

(a) Primary education shall be compulsory and available free to all;

(b) Secondary education in its different forms, including technical and vocational secondary education, shall be made generally available and accessible to all by every appropriate means, and in particular by the progressive introduction of free education;

(c) Higher education shall be made equally accessible to all, on the basis of capacity, by every appropriate means, and in particular by the progressive introduction of free education;

(d) Fundamental education shall be encouraged or intensified as far as possible for those persons who have not received or completed the whole period of their primary education;

(e) The development of a system of schools at all levels shall be actively pursued, an adequate fellowship system shall be established, and the material conditions of teaching staff shall be continuously improved.

3   The States Parties to the present Covenant undertake to have respect for the liberty of parents and, when applicable, legal guardians to choose for their children schools, other than those established by the public authorities, which conform to such minimum educational standards as may be laid down or approved by the State and to ensure the religious and moral education of their children in conformity with their own convictions.

4   No part of this article shall be construed so as to interfere with the liberty of individuals and bodies to establish and direct educational institutions, subject always to the observance of the principles set forth in paragraph I of this article and to the requirement that the education given in such institutions shall conform to such minimum standards as may be laid down by the State.

[C.2.280]
Article 14
Each State Party to the present Covenant which, at the time of becoming a Party, has not been able to secure in its metropolitan territory or other territories under its jurisdiction compulsory primary education, free of charge, undertakes, within two years, to work out and adopt a detailed plan of action for the progressive implementation, within a reasonable number of years, to be fixed in the plan, of the principle of compulsory education free of charge for all.

[C.2.281]
Article 15
1   The States Parties to the present Covenant recognize the right of everyone:

(a) To take part in cultural life;

(b) To enjoy the benefits of scientific progress and its applications;

(c) To benefit from the protection of the moral and material interests resulting from any scientific, literary or artistic production of which he is the author.

2   The steps to be taken by the States Parties to the present Covenant to achieve the full realization of this right shall include those necessary for the conservation, the development and the diffusion of science and culture.

3   The States Parties to the present Covenant undertake to respect the freedom indispensable for scientific research and creative activity.

4   The States Parties to the present Covenant recognize the benefits to be derived from the encouragement and development of international contacts and co-operation in the scientific and cultural fields.

PART IV

[C.2.282]
Article 16
1   The States Parties to the present Covenant undertake to submit in conformity with this part of the Covenant reports on the measures which they have adopted and the progress made in achieving the observance of the rights recognized herein.
2   (a) All reports shall be submitted to the Secretary-General of the United Nations, who shall transmit copies to the Economic and Social Council for consideration in accordance with the provisions of the present Covenant;

(b) The Secretary-General of the United Nations shall also transmit to the specialized agencies copies of the reports, or any relevant parts therefrom, from States Parties to the present Covenant which are also members of these specialized agencies in so far as these reports, or parts therefrom, relate to any matters which fall within the responsibilities of the said agencies in accordance with their constitutional instruments.

[C.2.283]
Article 17
1   The States Parties to the present Covenant shall furnish their reports in stages, in accordance with a programme to be established by the Economic and Social Council within one year of the entry into force of the present Covenant after consultation with the States Parties and the specialized agencies concerned.
2   Reports may indicate factors and difficulties affecting the degree of fulfilment of obligations under the present Covenant.
3   Where relevant information has previously been furnished to the United Nations or to any specialized agency by any State Party to the present Covenant, it will not be necessary to reproduce that information, but a precise reference to the information so furnished will suffice.

[C.2.284]
Article 18
Pursuant to its responsibilities under the Charter of the United Nations in the field of human rights and fundamental freedoms, the Economic and Social Council may make arrangements with the specialized agencies in respect of their reporting to it on the progress made in achieving the observance of the provisions of the present Covenant falling within the scope of their activities. These reports may include particulars of decisions and recommendations on such implementation adopted by their competent organs.

[C.2.285]
Article 19
The Economic and Social Council may transmit to the Commission on Human Rights for study and general recommendation or, as appropriate, for information the reports concerning human rights submitted by States in accordance

with articles 16 and 17, and those concerning human rights submitted by the specialized agencies in accordance with article 18.

[C.2.286]
Article 20
The States Parties to the present Covenant and the specialized agencies concerned may submit comments to the Economic and Social Council on any general recommendation under article 19 or reference to such general recommendation in any report of the Commission on Human Rights or any documentation referred to therein.

[C.2.287]
Article 21
The Economic and Social Council may submit from time to time to the General Assembly reports with recommendations of a general nature and a summary of the information received from the States Parties to the present Covenant and the specialized agencies on the measures taken and the progress made in achieving general observance of the rights recognized in the present Covenant.

[C.2.288]
Article 22
The Economic and Social Council may bring to the attention of other organs of the United Nations, their subsidiary organs and specialized agencies concerned with furnishing technical assistance any matters arising out of the reports referred to in this part of the present Covenant which may assist such bodies in deciding, each within its field of competence, on the advisability of international measures likely to contribute to the effective progressive implementation of the present Covenant.

[C.2.289]
Article 23
The States Parties to the present Covenant agree that international action for the achievement of the rights recognized in the present Covenant includes such methods as the conclusion of conventions, the adoption of recommendations, the furnishing of technical assistance and the holding of regional meetings and technical meetings for the purpose of consultation and study organized in conjunction with the Governments concerned.

[C.2.290]
Article 24
Nothing in the present Covenant shall be interpreted as impairing the provisions of the Charter of the United Nations and of the constitutions of the specialized agencies which define the respective responsibilities of the various organs of the United Nations and of the specialized agencies in regard to the matters dealt with in the present Covenant.

[C.2.291]
Article 25
Nothing in the present Covenant shall be interpreted as impairing the inherent right of all peoples to enjoy and utilize fully and freely their natural wealth and resources.

PART V

[C.2.292]
Article 26
1   The present Covenant is open for signature by any State Member of the United Nations or member of any of its specialized agencies, by any State Party to the Statute of the International Court of Justice, and by any other State which has been invited by the General Assembly of the United Nations to become a party to the present Covenant.
2   The present Covenant is subject to ratification. Instruments of ratification shall be deposited with the Secretary-General of the United Nations.
3   The present Covenant shall be open to accession by any State referred to in paragraph 1 of this article.
4   Accession shall be effected by the deposit of an instrument of accession with the Secretary-General of the United Nations.
5   The Secretary-General of the United Nations shall inform all States which have signed the present Covenant or acceded to it of the deposit of each instrument of ratification or accession.

[C.2.293]
Article 27
1   The present Covenant shall enter into force three months after the date of the deposit with the Secretary-General of the United Nations of the thirty-fifth instrument of ratification or instrument of accession.
2   For each State ratifying the present Covenant or acceding to it after the deposit of the thirty-fifth instrument of ratification or instrument of accession, the present Covenant shall enter into force three months after the date of the deposit of its own instrument of ratification or instrument of accession.

[C.2.294]
Article 28
The provisions of the present Covenant shall extend to all parts of federal States without any limitations or exceptions.

[C.2.295]
Article 29
1   Any State Party to the present Covenant may propose an amendment and file it with the Secretary-General of the United Nations. The Secretary-General shall thereupon communicate any proposed amendments to the States Parties to the present Covenant with a request that they notify him whether they

favour a conference of States Parties for the purpose of considering and voting upon the proposals. In the event that at least one third of the States Parties favours such a conference, the Secretary-General shall convene the conference under the auspices of the United Nations. Any amendment adopted by a majority of the States Parties present and voting at the conference shall be submitted to the General Assembly of the United Nations for approval.

2   Amendments shall come into force when they have been approved by the General Assembly of the United Nations and accepted by a two-thirds majority of the States Parties to the present Covenant in accordance with their respective constitutional processes.

3   When amendments come into force they shall be binding on those States Parties which have accepted them, other States Parties still being bound by the provisions of the present Covenant and any earlier amendment which they have accepted.

[C.2.296]
Article 30
Irrespective of the notifications made under article 26, paragraph 5, the Secretary-General of the United Nations shall inform all States referred to in paragraph I of the same article of the following particulars:

(a) Signatures, ratifications and accessions under article 26;

(b) The date of the entry into force of the present Covenant under article 27 and the date of the entry into force of any amendments under article 29.

[C.2.297]
Article 31
1   The present Covenant, of which the Chinese, English, French, Russian and Spanish texts are equally authentic, shall be deposited in the archives of the United Nations.

2   The Secretary-General of the United Nations shall transmit certified copies of the present Covenant to all States referred to in article 26.

CONVENTION ON THE RIGHTS OF THE CHILD, 1989 (Excerpts)

20 November 1989
UN DOC A/44/25
Entry into force   2 September 1990

TEXT
Convention on the Rights of the Child

PREAMBLE
[C.2.298]
The states parties to the present Convention
Considering that, in accordance with the principles proclaimed in the Charter of the United Nations, recognition of the inherent dignity and of the equal and inalienable rights of all members of the human family is the foundation of freedom, justice and peace in the world,
Bearing in mind that the peoples of the United Nations have, in the Charter, reaffirmed their faith in fundamental human rights and in the dignity and worth of the human person, and have determined to promote social progress and better standards of life in larger freedom,
Recognising that the United Nations has, in the Universal Declaration of Human Rights and in the International Covenants on Human Rights, proclaimed and agreed that everyone is entitled to all the rights and freedoms set forth therein, without distinction of any kind, such as race, colour, sex, language, religion, political or other opinion, national or social origin, property, birth or other status,
Recalling that, in the Universal Declaration of Human Rights, the United Nations has proclaimed that childhood is entitled to special care and assistance,
Convinced that the family, as the fundamental group of society and the natural environment for the growth and well-being of all its members and particularly children, should be afforded the necessary protection and assistance so that it can fully assume its responsibilities within the community,
Recognising that the child, for the full and harmonious development of his or her personality, should grow up in a family environment, in an atmosphere of happiness, love and understanding,
Considering that the child should be fully prepared to live an individual life in society, and brought up in the spirit of the ideals proclaimed in the Charter of the United Nations, and in particular in the spirit of peace, dignity, tolerance, freedom, equality and solidarity,
Bearing in mind that the need to extend particular care to the child has been stated in the Geneva Declaration of the Rights of the Child of 1924 and in the Declaration of the Rights of the Child adopted by the General Assembly on 20 November 1959 and recognised in the Universal Declaration of Human Rights, in the International Covenant on Civil and Political Rights (in particular in Articles 23 and 24), in the International Covenant on Economic, Social and Cultural Rights (in particular in Article 10) and in the statutes and relevant

instruments of specialised agencies and international organisations concerned with the welfare of children,

Bearing in mind that, as indicated in the Declaration of the Rights of the Child, 'the child, by reason of his physical and mental immaturity, needs special safeguards and care, including appropriate legal protection, before as well as after birth',

Recalling the provisions of the Declaration on Social and Legal Principles relating to the Protection and Welfare of Children, with Special Reference to Foster Placement and Adoption Nationally and Internationally; the United Nations Standard Minimum Rules for the Administration of Juvenile Justice (The Beijing Rules); and the Declaration on the Protection of Women and Children in Emergency and Armed Conflict,

Recognising that, in all countries in the world, there are children living in exceptionally difficult conditions, and that such children need special consideration,

Taking due account of the importance of the traditions and cultural values of each people for the protection and harmonious development of the child,

Recognising the importance of international co-operation for improving the living conditions of children in every country, in particular in the developing countries,

Have agreed as follows:

PART I
[C.2.299]
Article 1
For the purposes of the present Convention, a child means every human being below the age of eighteen years unless, under the law applicable to the child, majority is attained earlier.

[C.2.300]
Article 2
1   States parties shall respect and ensure the rights set forth in the present Convention to each child within their jurisdiction without discrimination of any kind, irrespective of the child's or his or her parent's or legal guardian's race, colour, sex, language, religion, political or other opinion, national, ethnic or social origin, property, disability, birth or other status.
2   States parties shall take all appropriate measures to ensure that the child is protected against all forms of discrimination or punishment on the basis of the status, activities, expressed opinions, or beliefs of the child's parents, legal guardians, or family members.

[C.2.301]
Article 3
1   In all actions concerning children, whether undertaken by public or private social welfare institutions, courts of law, administrative authorities or legislative bodies, the best interests of the child shall be a primary consideration.
2   States parties undertake to ensure the child such protection and care as is necessary for his or her well-being, taking into account the rights and duties of

his or her parents, legal guardians, or other individuals legally responsible for him or her, and, to this end, shall take all appropriate legislative and administrative measures.

3 States parties shall ensure that the institutions, services and facilities responsible for the care or protection of children shall conform with the standards established by competent authorities, particularly in the areas of safety, health, in the number and suitability of their staff, as well as competent supervision.

[C.2.302]
Article 4

States parties shall undertake all appropriate legislative, administrative, and other measures for the implementation of the rights recognised in the present Convention. With regard to economic, social and cultural rights, states parties shall undertake such measures to the maximum extent of their available resources and, where needed, within the framework of international co-operation.

[C.2.303]
Article 5

States parties shall respect the responsibilities, rights and duties of parents or, where applicable, the members of the extended family or community as provided for by local custom, legal guardians or other persons legally responsible for the child, to provide, in a manner consistent with the evolving capacities of the child, appropriate direction and guidance in the exercise by the child of the rights recognised in the present Convention.

[C.2.304]
Article 6

1 States parties recognize that every child has the inherent right to life.
2 States parties shall ensure to the maximum extent possible the survival and development of the child.

[C.2.305]
Article 7

1 The child shall be registered immediately after birth and shall have the right from birth to a name, the right to acquire a nationality and, as far as possible, the right to know and be cared for by his or her parents.
2 States parties shall ensure the implementation of these rights in accordance with their national law and their obligations under the relevant international instruments in this field, in particular where the child would otherwise be stateless.

[C.2.306]
Article 8

1 States parties undertake to respect the right of the child to preserve his or her identity, including nationality, name and family relations as recognised by

law without unlawful interference.

2   Where a child is illegally deprived of some or all of the elements of his or her identity, states parties shall provide appropriate assistance and protection, with a view to speedily re-establishing his or her identity.

[C.2.307]
Article 9

1   States parties shall ensure that a child shall not be separated from his or her parents against their will, except when competent authorities subject to judicial review determine, in accordance with applicable law and procedures, that such separation is necessary for the best interests of the child. Such determination may be necessary in a particular case such as one involving abuse or neglect of the child by the parents, or one where the parents are living separately and a decision must be made as to the child's place of residence.

2   In any proceedings pursuant to paragraph 1 of the present Article, all interested parties shall be given an opportunity to participate in the proceedings and make their views known.

3   States parties shall respect the right of the child who is separated from one or both parents to maintain personal relations and direct contact with both parents on a regular basis, except if it is contrary to the child's best interests.

4   Where such separation results from any action initiated by a state party, such as the detention, imprisonment exile, deportation or death (including death arising from any cause while the person is in the custody of the State) of one or both parents or of the child, that state party shall, upon request, provide the parents, the child or, if appropriate, another member of the family with the essential information concerning the whereabouts of the absent member(s) of the family unless the provision of the information would be detrimental to the well-being of the child. States parties shall further ensure that the submission of such a request shall of itself entail no adverse consequences for the person(s) concerned.

[C.2.308]
Article 10

1   In accordance with the obligation of states parties under Article 9, paragraph 1, applications by a child or his or her parents to enter or leave a state party for the purpose of family reunification shall be dealt with by states parties in a positive, humane and expeditious manner. States parties shall further ensure that the submission of such a request shall entail no adverse consequences for the applicants and for the members of their family.

2   A child whose parents reside in different states shall have the right to maintain on a regular basis, save in exceptional circumstances personal relations and direct contacts with both parents. Towards that end and in accordance with the obligation of states parties under Article 9, paragraph 2, states parties shall respect the right of the child and his or her parents to leave any country, including their own, and to enter their own country. The right to leave any country shall be subject only to such restrictions as are prescribed by law and which are necessary to protect the national security, public order (*ordre public*), public health or morals or the rights and freedoms of others and are consistent with the other rights recognised in the present Convention.

[C.2.309]
Article 11
1   States parties shall take measures to combat the illicit transfer and non-return of children abroad.

2   To this end, states parties shall promote the conclusion of bilateral or multilateral agreements or accession to existing agreements.

[C.2.310]
Article 12
1   States parties shall assure to the child who is capable of forming his or her own views the right to express those views freely in all matters affecting the child, the views of the child being given due weight in accordance with the age and maturity of the child.

2   For this purpose, the child shall in particular be provided the opportunity to be heard in any judicial and administrative proceedings affecting the child, either directly, or through a representative or an appropriate body, in a manner consistent with the procedural rules of national law.

[C.2.311]
Article 16
1   No child shall be subjected to arbitrary or unlawful interference with his or her privacy, family, home or correspondence, nor to unlawful attacks on his or her honour and reputation.

2   The child has the right to the protection of the law against such interference or attacks.

[C.2.312]
Article 18
1   States parties shall use their best efforts to ensure recognition of the principle that both parents have common responsibilities for the upbringing and development of the child. Parents or, as the case may be, legal guardians, have the primary responsibility for the upbringing and development of the child. The best interests of the child will be their basic concern.

2   For the purpose of guaranteeing and promoting the rights set forth in the present Convention, states parties shall render appropriate assistance to parents and legal guardians in the performance of their child-rearing responsibilities and shall ensure the development of institutions, facilities and services for the care of children.

3   States parties shall take all appropriate measures to ensure that children of working parents have the right to benefit from child-care services and facilities for which they are eligible.

[C.2.313]
Article 19
1   States parties shall take all appropriate legislative, administrative, social and educational measures to protect the child from all forms of physical or mental violence, injury or abuse, neglect or negligent treatment, maltreatment or exploitation, including sexual abuse, while in the care of parent(s), legal

guardian(s) or any other person who has the care of the child.

2   Such protective measures should, as appropriate, include effective procedures for the establishment of social programmes to provide necessary support for the child and for those who have the care of the child, as well as for other forms of prevention and for identification, reporting, referral, investigation, treatment and follow-up of instances of child maltreatment described heretofore, and, as appropriate, for judicial involvement.

[C.2.314]
Article 20

1   A child temporarily or permanently deprived of his or her family environment, or in whose own best interests cannot be allowed to remain in that environment, shall be entitled to special protection and assistance provided by the State.

2   States Parties shall in accordance with their national laws ensure alternative care for such a child.

3   Such care could include, *inter alia*, foster placement, *kafalah* of Islamic law, adoption or if necessary placement in suitable institutions for the care of children. When considering solutions, due regard shall be paid to the desirability of continuity in a child's upbringing and to the child's ethnic, religious, cultural and linguistic background.

[C.2.315]
Article 21

States parties that recognise and/or permit the system of adoption shall ensure that the best interests of the child shall be the paramount consideration and they shall:

(*a*) ensure that the adoption of a child is authorised only by competent authorities who determine, in accordance with applicable law and procedures and on the basis of all pertinent and reliable information, that the adoption is permissible in view of the child's status concerning parents, relatives and legal guardians and that, if required, the persons concerned have given their informed consent to the adoption on the basis of such counselling as may be necessary;

(*b*) recognise that inter-country adoption may be considered as an alternative means of child's care, if the child cannot be placed in a foster or an adoptive family or cannot in any suitable manner be cared for in the child's country of origin;

(*c*) ensure that the child concerned by inter-country adoption enjoys safeguards and standards equivalent to those existing in the case of national adoption;

(*d*) take all appropriate measures to ensure that, in inter-country adoption, the placement does not result in improper financial gain for those involved in it;

(*e*) promote, where appropriate, the objectives of the present article by concluding bilateral or multilateral arrangements or agreements, and endeavour, within this framework, to ensure that the placement of the child in another country is carried out by competent authorities or organs.

[C.2.316]
Article 22

1   States parties shall take appropriate measures to ensure that a child who is seeking refugee status or who is considered a refuge in accordance with applicable international or domestic law and procedures shall, whether unaccompanied or accompanied by his or her parents or by any other person, receive appropriate protection and humanitarian assistance in the enjoyment of applicable rights set forth in the present convention and in other international human rights or humanitarian instruments to which the said States are Parties.

2   For this purpose, states parties shall provide, as they consider appropriate, co-operation in any efforts by the United Nations and other competent inter-governmental organisations or non-governmental organisations co-operating with the United Nations to protect and assist such a child and to trace the parents or other members of the family of any refugee child in order to obtain information necessary for reunification with his or her family. In cases where no parents or other members of the family can be found the child shall be accorded the same protection as any other child permanently or temporarily deprived of his or her family environment for any reason, as set forth in the present Convention.

[C.2.317]
Article 37

States parties shall ensure that:

(*a*) no child shall be subjected to torture or other cruel, inhuman or degrading treatment or punishment. Neither capital punishment nor life imprisonment without possibility of release shall be imposed for offences committed by persons below eighteen years of age;

(*b*) no child shall be deprived of his or her liberty unlawfully or arbitrarily. The arrest, detention or imprisonment of a child shall be in conformity with the law and shall be used only as a measure of last resort and for the shortest appropriate period of time;

(*c*) every child deprived of liberty shall be treated with humanity and respect for the inherent dignity of the human person, and in a manner which takes into account the needs of persons of his or her age. In particular, every child deprived of liberty shall be separated from adults unless it is considered in the child's best interest not to do so and shall have the right to maintain contact with his or her family through correspondence and visits, save in exceptional circumstances;

(*d*) every child deprived of his or her liberty shall have the right to prompt access to legal and other appropriate assistance, as well as the right to challenge the legality of the deprivation of his or her liberty before a court or other competent, independent and impartial authority, and to a prompt decision on any such action.

[C.2.318]
Article 38

1   States parties undertake to respect and to ensure respect for rules of international humanitarian law applicable to them in armed conflicts which are relevant to the child.

2   States parties shall take all feasible measures to ensure that persons who have not attained the age of fifteen years do not take a direct part in hostilities.

3   States parties shall refrain from recruiting any person who has not attained the age of fifteen years into their armed forces. In recruiting among those persons who have attained the age of fifteen years but who have not attained the age of eighteen years, states parties shall endeavour to give priority to those who are oldest.

4   In accordance with their obligations under international humanitarian law to protect the civilian population in armed conflicts, states parties shall take all feasible measures to ensure protection and care of children who are affected by an armed conflict.

[C.2.319]
Article 39
States parties shall take all appropriate measures to promote physical and psychological recovery and social reintegration of a child victim of: any form of neglect, exploitation, or abuse; torture or any other form of cruel, inhuman or degrading treatment or punishment; or armed conflicts. Such recovery and reintegration shall take place in an environment which fosters the health, self-respect and dignity of the child.

UK GOVERNMENT RESERVATION TO THE CONVENTION ON THE RIGHTS OF THE CHILD

[C.2.320]
The United Kingdom reserves the right to apply such legislation, in so far as it relates to the entry into, stay in and departure from the United Kingdom of those who do not have the right under the law of the United Kingdom to enter and remain in the United Kingdom, and to the acquisition and possession of citizenship, as it may deem necessary from time to time.

CONVENTION AGAINST TORTURE AND OTHER CRUEL, INHUMAN OR DEGRADING TREATMENT OR PUNISHMENT, 1984 (Excerpts)

UN Doc A/RES/39/46
Adopted on   10 December 1984
Entry into force   26 July 1987

TEXT
[C.2.321]
The States Parties to this Convention,

Considering that, in accordance with the principles proclaimed in the Charter of the United Nations, recognition of the equal and inalienable rights of all members of the human family is the foundation of freedom, justice and peace in the world,

Recognising that those rights derive from the inherent dignity of the human person,

Considering the obligation of States under the Charter, in particular Article 55, to promote universal respect for, and observance of, human rights and fundamental freedoms,

Having regard to article 5 of the Universal Declaration of Human Rights and article 7 of the International Covenant on Civil and Political Rights, both of which provide that no one shall be subjected to torture or to cruel, inhuman or degrading treatment or punishment,

Having regard also to the Declaration on the Protection of All Persons from Being Subjected to Torture and Other Cruel, Inhuman or Degrading Treatment or Punishment, adopted by the General Assembly on 9 December 1975,

Desiring to make more effective the struggle against torture and other cruel, inhuman or degrading treatment or punishment throughout the world,

Have agreed as follows:

PART I

[C.2.322]
Article 1

1   For the purposes of this Convention, the term 'torture' means any act by which severe pain or suffering, whether physical or mental, is intentionally inflicted on a person for such purposes as obtaining from him or a third person information or a confession, punishing him for an act he or a third person has committed or is suspected of having committed, or intimidating or coercing him or a third person, or for any reason based on discrimination of any kind, when such pain or suffering is inflicted by or at the instigation of or with the consent or acquiescence of a public official or other person acting in an official capacity. It does not include pain or suffering arising only from, inherent in or incidental to lawful sanctions.

2   This article is without prejudice to any international instrument or national legislation which does or may contain provisions of wider application.

[C.2.323]
Article 2
1   Each state party shall take effective legislative, administrative, judicial or other measures to prevent acts of torture in any territory under its jurisdiction.

2   No exceptional circumstances whatsoever, whether a state of war or a threat of war, internal political instability or any other public emergency, may be invoked as a justification of torture.

3   An order from a superior officer or a public authority may not be invoked as a justification of torture.

[C.2.324]
Article 3
1   No state party shall expel, return (*'refouler'*) or extradite a person to another State where there are substantial grounds for believing that he would be in danger of being subjected to torture.

2   For the purpose of determining whether there are such grounds, the competent authorities shall take into account all relevant considerations including, where applicable, the existence in the state concerned of a consistent pattern of gross, flagrant or mass violations of human rights.

[C.2.325]
Article 4
1   Each state party shall ensure that all acts of torture are offences under its criminal law. The same shall apply to an attempt to commit torture and to commit an act by any person which constitutes complicity or participation in torture.

2   Each state party shall make these offences punishable by appropriate penalties which take into account their grave nature.

[C.2.326]
Article 5
1   Each state party shall take such measures as may be necessary to establish its jurisdiction over the offences referred to in article 4 in the following cases:

(*a*) When the offences are committed in any territory under its jurisdiction or on board a ship or aircraft registered in that state;
(*b*) When the alleged offender is a national of that state;
(*c*) When the victim is a national of that state if that state considers it appropriate.

2   Each state party shall likewise take such measures as may be necessary to establish its jurisdiction over such offences in cases where the alleged offender is present in any territory under its jurisdiction and it does not extradite him pursuant to article 8 to any of the states mentioned in paragraph 1 of this article.

1053

3   This Convention does not exclude any criminal jurisdiction exercised in accordance with internal law.

[C.2.327]
Article 6
1   Upon being satisfied, after an examination of information available to it, that the circumstances so warrant, any state party in whose territory a person alleged to have committed any offence referred to in article 4 is present shall take him into custody or take other legal measures to ensure his presence. The custody and other legal measures shall be as provided in the law of that state but may be continued only for such time as is necessary to enable any criminal or extradition proceedings to be instituted.

2   Such State shall immediately make a preliminary inquiry into the facts.

3   Any person in custody pursuant to paragraph 1 of this article shall be assisted in communicating immediately with the nearest appropriate representative of the state of which he is a national, or, if he is a stateless person, with the representative of the state where he usually resides.

4   When a state, pursuant to this article, has taken a person into custody, it shall immediately notify the states referred to in article 5, paragraph 1, of the fact that such person is in custody and of the circumstances which warrant his detention. The state which makes the preliminary inquiry contemplated in paragraph 2 of this article shall promptly report its findings to the said states and shall indicate whether it intends to exercise jurisdiction.

[C.2.328]
Article 7
1   The state party in the territory under whose jurisdiction a person alleged to have committed any offence referred to in article 4 is found shall in the cases contemplated in article 5, if it does not extradite him, submit the case to its competent authorities for the purpose of prosecution.

2   These authorities shall take their decision in the same manner as in the case of any ordinary offence of a serious nature under the law of that state. In the cases referred to in article 5, paragraph 2, the standards of evidence required for prosecution and shall in no way be less stringent than those which apply in the cases referred to in article 5, paragraph 1.

3   Any person regarding whom proceedings are brought in connection with any of the offences referred to in article 4 shall be guaranteed fair treatment at all stages of the proceedings.

[C.2.329]
Article 8
1   The offences referred to in article 4 shall be deemed to be included as extraditable offences in any extradition treaty existing between states parties. States parties undertake to include such offences as extraditable offences in every extradition treaty to be concluded between them.

2   If a state party which makes extradition conditional on the existence of a

treaty receives a request for extradition from another state party with which it has no extradition treaty, it may consider this Convention as the legal basis for extradition in respect of such offences. Extradition shall be subject to the other conditions provided by the law of the requested state.

3 States parties which do not make extradition conditional on the existence of a treaty shall recognise such offences as extraditable offences between themselves subject to the conditions provided by the law of the requested state.

4 Such offences shall be treated, for the purpose of extradition between states parties, as if they had been committed not only in the place in which they occurred but also in the territories of the states required to establish their jurisdiction in accordance with article 5, paragraph 1.

[C.2.330]
Article 9
1 States parties shall afford one another the greatest measure of assistance in connection with criminal proceedings brought in respect of any of the offences referred to in article 4, including the supply of all evidence at their disposal necessary for the proceedings.

2 States parties shall carry out their obligations under paragraph 1 of this article in conformity with any treaties on mutual judicial assistance that may exist between them.

[C.2.331]
Article 10
1 Each state party shall ensure that education and information regarding the prohibition against torture are fully included in the training of law enforcement personnel, civil or military, medical personnel, public officials and other persons who may be involved in the custody, interrogation or treatment of any individual subjected to any form of arrest, detention or imprisonment.

2 Each state party shall include this prohibition in the rules or instructions issued in regard to the duties and functions of any such persons.

[C.2.332]
Article 16
1 The provisions of this Convention are without prejudice to the provisions of any other international instrument or national law which prohibits cruel, inhuman or degrading treatment or punishment or which relates to extradition or expulsion.

PART II

[C.2.333]
Article 17
1 There shall be established a Committee against Torture (hereinafter referred to as the Committee) which shall carry out the functions hereinafter provided.

[C.2.334]
Article 19

1   The states parties shall submit to the Committee, through the Secretary-General of the United Nations, reports on the measures they have taken to give effect to their undertakings under this Convention, within one year after the entry into force of the Convention for the state party concerned. Thereafter the states parties shall submit supplementary reports every four years on any new measures taken and such other reports as the Committee may request.

2   The Secretary-General of the United Nations shall transmit the reports to all states parties.

3   Each report shall be considered by the Committee which may make such general comments on the report as it may consider appropriate and shall forward these to the state party concerned. That state party may respond with any observations it chooses to the Committee.

4   The Committee may, at its discretion, decide to include any comments made by it in accordance with paragraph 3 of this article, together with the observations thereon received from the state party concerned, in its annual report made in accordance with article 24. If so requested by the state party concerned, the Committee may also include a copy of the report submitted under paragraph 1 of this article.

[C.2.335]
Article 20

1   If the Committee receives reliable information which appears to it to contain well-founded indications that torture is being systematically practised in the territory of a state party, the Committee shall invite that state party to co-operate in the examination of the information and to this end to submit observations with regard to the information concerned.

2   Taking into account any observations which may have been submitted by the state party concerned, as well as any other relevant information available to it, the Committee may, if it decides that this is warranted, designate one or more of its members to make a confidential inquiry and to report to the Committee urgently.

3   If an inquiry is made in accordance with paragraph 2 of this article, the Committee shall seek the co-operation of the state party concerned. In agreement with that state party, such an inquiry may include a visit to its territory.

4   After examining the findings of its member or members submitted in accordance with paragraph 2 of this article, the Committee shall transmit these findings to the state party concerned together with any comments or suggestions which seem appropriate in view of the situation.

5   All the proceedings of the Committee referred to in paragraphs 1 to 4 of this article shall be confidential, and at all stages of the proceedings the co-operation of the state party shall be sought. After such proceedings have been completed with regard to an inquiry made in accordance with paragraph 2, the Committee may, after consultations with the state party concerned, decide to include a summary account of the results of the proceedings in its annual report made in accordance with article 24.

[C.2.336]
Article 22[1]

1   A state party to this Convention may at any time declare under this article that it recognizes the competence of the Committee to receive and consider communications from or on behalf of individuals subject to its jurisdiction who claim to be victims of a violation by a state party of the provisions of the Convention. No communication shall be received by the Committee if it concerns a state party which has not made such a declaration.

2   The Committee shall consider inadmissible any communication under this article which is anonymous or which it considers to be an abuse of the right of submission of such communications or to be incompatible with the provisions of this Convention.

3   Subject to the provisions of paragraph 2, the Committee shall bring any communications submitted to it under this article to the attention of the state party to this Convention which has made a declaration under paragraph 1 and is alleged to be violating any provisions of the Convention. Within six months, the receiving state shall submit to the Committee written explanations or statements clarifying the matter and the remedy, if any, that may have been taken by that state.

4   The Committee shall consider communications received under this article in the light of all information made available to it by or on behalf of the individual and by the state party concerned.

5   The Committee shall not consider any communications from an individual under this article unless it has ascertained that:

(*a*)   The same matter has not been, and is not being, examined under another procedure of international investigation or settlement;
(*b*)   The individual has exhausted all available domestic remedies; this shall not be the rule where the application of the remedies is unreasonably prolonged or is unlikely to bring effective relief to the person who is the victim of the violation of this Convention.

6   The Committee shall hold closed meetings when examining communications under this article.

7   The Committee shall forward its views to the state party concerned and to the individual.

8   The provisions of this article shall come into force when five states parties to this Convention have made declarations under paragraph 1 of this article. Such declarations shall be deposited by the states parties with the Secretary-General of the United Nations, who shall transmit copies thereof to the other states parties. A declaration may be withdrawn at any time by notification to the Secretary-General. Such a withdrawal shall not prejudice the consideration of any matter which is the subject of a communication already transmitted under this article; no further communication by or on behalf of an individual shall be received under this article after the notification of withdrawal of the declaration has been received by the Secretary-General, unless the state party has made a new declaration.

---

1   The UK has not made a declaration under Article 22.

[C.2.337]
Article 24
The Committee shall submit an annual report on its activities under this Convention to the states parties and to the General Assembly of the United Nations.

Index

All references are to paragraph numbers.

A.1.102
marriage, by virtue of, **A.1.101**

British Dependent Territories citizenship—*cont*
registration, right to—*cont*
replacing right to resume citizenship of UK and Colonies, **A.1.103**
residence in territory, by virtue of, **A.1.100**
renunciation and resumption, **A.1.105**
territories whose citizens qualify for, **A.1.139**

British National (Overseas), A.2.12

British Nationality Act 1981
decisions involving exercise of discretion, **A.1.125**
evidence, **A.1.126**
extent, **A.1.134**
interpretation, **A.1.131**
meaning of certain expressions relating to nationality in other Acts/instruments, **A.1.132**
offences/proceedings, **A.1.127**
repeals, **A.1.141**
text, **A.1.82** *ff*
transitional provisions, **A.1.140**

British Overseas citizenship
admission to UK and, **A.2.12**
citizens of UK and Colonies acquiring at commencement of 1981 Act, **A.1.107**
oath of allegiance, **A.1.138**
registration for—
marriage, by virtue of, **A.1.109**
minors, **A.1.108**
renunciation of, **A.1.110**
special vouchers for settlement in UK for holders of. *See* Special vouchers

British protected persons, A.1.119; A.2.12

British subjects
British subjects continuing to be at commencement of 1981 Act, **A.1.111**
Eire, former citizens of, continuance as British subjects, **A.1.112**
losing status of, **A.1.116**
oath of allegiance, **A.1.138**
registration as—
minors, **A.1.113**
women, certain alien, **A.1.114**
renunciation of status, **A.1.115**

British visitor's passport
leave to enter, **A.4.9**

Broadcasting organisations, overseas
representatives of—
children of, **A.2.199–201**
extension of stay, **A.2.142–144**
indefinite leave to remain, **A.2.145, 146**
leave to enter, **A.2.139–141**
settlement, **A.2.145, 146**
spouses of, **A.2.196–198**

Brothers, dependent, A.2.330–332

Bulgaria
businessmen and women, **A.2.210–217**

Businessmen and women
accounts, provision of, **A.2.202**
Bulgaria, from, **A.2.210–217**
capital to be invested, **A.2.202**
children of, **A.2.237–239**
Czech Republic, from, **A.2.210–217**
Estonia, from, **A.2.210–217**
EU association agreements and—
Immigration Rules, **A.2.210–217**
existing business, joining/taking over, **A.2.202**
extension of stay—
EU association agreements, **A.2.213–215**
generally, **A.2.205–207**
full-time employment, to create, **A.2.202**
Hungary, from, **A.2.210–217**
indefinite leave to remain—
EU association agreements, **A.2.216, 217**
generally, **A.2.208, 209**
Latvia, from, **A.2.210–217**
leave to enter—
EU association agreements, **A.2.210–212**
generally, **A.2.202–204**
Lithuania, from, **A.2.210–217**
meaning of business, **A.2.202**
new business, establishing, **A.2.202**
Poland, from, **A.2.210–217**
police, registration with, **A.2.343**
Romania, from, **A.2.210–217**
settlement—
EU association agreements, **A.2.216, 217**
generally, **A.2.208, 209**
Slovakia, from, **A.2.210–217**
spouses of, **A.2.234–236**

Carriers
code of practice for system for
preventing carriage of clandestine
entrants, **A.1.266**
information about passengers, provision
by, **A.1.47; A.4.36–38**
interpretation of Part II of 1999 Act,
A.1.276
liability for passengers without proper
documents—
detention of vehicles etc, **A.1.275**
prescribed sum, **A.1.273**
sale of transporters, **A.1.275, 404**
notification of non-EEA arrivals,
A.1.47
penalty for carrying clandestine
entrants—
defences, **A.1.267**
detention of vehicles etc, **A.1.269,
270**
generally, **A.1.265**
meaning of clandestine entrant,
A.1.265
notice of objection, **A.1.268**
prescribed control zone, **A.1.265**
prescribed period for payment,
A.1.265
prescribed sum, **A.1.265**
procedure, **A.1.268**
rail freight wagon, concealment in,
A.1.272
sale of transporters, **A.1.270, 404**

Channel Islands. *See* Common travel
area; Islands

Channel Tunnel
requirements for persons arriving in
UK/seeking entry through, **A.2.9**

Children
access to—
leave to enter etc for persons
exercising rights of, **A.2.240–248**
adoption. *See* Adoption of children
artists, of, **A.2.237–239**
asylum seekers, as, **A.2.352**
born in UK who are not British
citizens—
leave to enter/remain, **A.2.316–319**
registration as British citizens, **A.1.82**
businessmen and women, of,
A.2.237–239
composers, of, **A.2.237–239**

Children—*cont*
Convention on the Rights of the
Child—
text, **C.2.298–319**
UK government reservation, **C.2.320**
deportation of, **A.1.3, 8; A.2.355, 356**
EU nationals, of. *See* European Union
fiancé(e)s, of, **A.2.310–315**
Immigration Rules, **A.2.302–329**
indefinite leave to enter, **A.2.303, 305,
306**
indefinite leave to remain, **A.2.304–306**
investors, of, **A.2.237–239**
language assistants, of, **A.2.128–130**
legitimated, BNA 1981 and, **A.1.128**
limited leave to enter/remain,
A.2.307–309
polygamous marriages, of, **A.2.302**
posthumous, BNA 1981 and, **A.1.129**
retired persons of independent means,
of, **A.2.268–270**
special voucher holders, of,
A.2.252–254
students, of, **A.2.76–78**
teachers, of, **A.2.128–130**
trainees, of, **A.2.128–130**
work experience, persons seeking, of,
A.2.128–130
working holidaymakers, of,
A.2.104–106
writers, of, **A.2.237–239**

Citizenship. *See* British etc citizenship;
Commonwealth citizenship

**Civil and Political Rights,
International Covenant on**
text, **C.2.211–264**
UK government reservation, **C.2.265**

Collective passport
exemption from control, **A.4.9**

Common travel area
see also Ireland, Republic of; Islands
definition, **A.1.1**
exclusion from control, **A.1.1**
leave to enter and, **A.1.1, 14, 50;
A.2.11, 13; A.4.51**
leave to remain, cancellation, **A.2.13**
local journey, meaning, **A.1.16**
provisions, **A.1.14, 50; A.2.11; A.4.51**

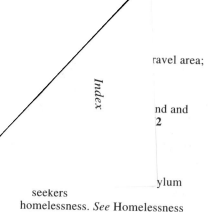

Immigration advice. *See* Immigration
services/advice providers

Immigration and Asylum Act 1999
commencement, **A.1.403**
commencement etc orders—
No 6, **A.4.137–142**
No 8, **A.4.143–146**
consequential amendments, **A.1.417**
extent, **A.1.403**
interpretation, **A.1.400**
regulations and orders, **A.1.399**
repeals, **A.1.419**
text, **A.1.234** *ff*
transitional provisions and savings,
A.1.418

Immigration Appeal Tribunal
appeals from, **A.1.407; A.3.54, 55**
appeals to—
abandoned appeals, **A.3.60**
absence of a party, hearing in, **A.3.69**
adjournment of hearings, **A.3.59**
adjudicator's decision, from,
A.1.407; A.3.45–53, 56–79
appeals remitted by Tribunal to
adjudicator, **A.3.51**
burden of proof, **A.3.67**
combined hearings, **A.3.70**
conduct of, **A.3.58**
correction of accidental errors,
A.3.78
determination, **A.3.52, 53**
summary, **A.3.72**
without hearing, **A.3.71**
documentary evidence, inspection,
A.3.66
evidence, **A.3.50, 64–66**
failure to comply with Rules, **A.3.61**
forms, **A.3.79**
irregularities in proceedings, **A.3.77**
leave to appeal, **A.3.46, 47**
notice of appeal, **A.3.48, 49**
parties, **A.3.57**
public, exclusion of, **A.3.68**
representation, **A.3.63**
service of notices etc, **A.3.74–76**
transfer of proceedings, **A.3.73**
witnesses, **A.3.64**
Immigration and Asylum Act 1999
provisions, **A.1.289**
members, **A.1.405**
proceedings, **A.1.405**

Immigration officers
appointment, **A.1.47**
arrest etc powers. *See* Criminal
proceedings
definition, **A.2.4**

Immigration officers—*cont*
examination of passengers, **A.1.47**
exercise of functions, **A.1.47**
force, use of, **A.1.1013**
generally, **A.1.47**
leave to enter, power to give/refuse,
A.1.7, 47
non-discriminatory, to be, **A.2.1**
PACE codes of practices and, **A.1.378**
search powers—
criminal proceedings, in relation to.
See Criminal proceedings
examination of passengers, in relation
to, **A.1.47**

Immigration Rules
application, **A.2.3**
EEA nationals and, **A.2.3**
generally, **A.1.3**
implementation, **A.2.2**
interpretation, **A.2.4**
text, **A.2.1** *ff*
transitional provisions, **A.2.2**

**Immigration services/advice
providers**
code of standards, **A.1.408**
designated professional bodies,
A.1.319, 323
disciplinary charges, **A.1.322**
disclosure of information by, **A.1.326**
disqualifications, **A.1.409**
enforcement of provisions, **A.1.325**
fees, **A.1.322**
injunctions against, **A.1.325**
interim directions
restricting/prohibiting provision of
immigration advice/services, **A.4.123**
interpretation, **A.1.315**
offences, **A.1.324**
orders by disciplinary bodies, **A.1.323**
qualification requirement, **A.1.317, 409**
registration—
appeals, **A.1.320, 321**
applications, **A.1.409**
exemption, **A.1.318, 322**
fees, **A.1.409; A.4.104–108**
generally, **A.1.317, 409**
inspection of register, **A.1.409**
restraining orders, **A.1.322, 323, 324**

Immigration Services Commissioner
annual report, **A.1.408**
code of standards, **A.1.408**
compensation, **A.1.408**